Feminist Theory

FEMINIST THEORY

A Reader

Third Edition

Wendy K. Kolmar

Drew University

Frances Bartkowski

Rutgers University

 **Higher Education**

Boston   Burr Ridge, IL   Dubuque, IA   New York   San Francisco   St. Louis
Bangkok   Bogotá   Caracas   Kuala Lumpur   Lisbon   London   Madrid   Mexico City
Milan   Montreal   New Delhi   Santiago   Seoul   Singapore   Sydney   Taipei   Toronto

Higher Education

Published by McGraw-Hill, an imprint of The McGraw-Hill Companies, Inc., 1221 Avenue of the Americas, New York, NY 10020. Copyright © 2010, 2005, 2000. All rights reserved. No part of this publication may be reproduced or distributed in any form or by any means, or stored in a database or retrieval system, without the prior written consent of The McGraw-Hill Companies, Inc., including, but not limited to, in any network or other electronic storage or transmission, or broadcast for distance learning.

This book is printed on acid-free paper.

1   2   3   4   5   6   7   8   9   0   DOC/DOC   0 9

ISBN: 978-0-07-351226-6
MHID: 0-07-351226-5

Editor in Chief: *Michael Ryan*
Editorial Director: *Beth Mejia*
Publisher: *David Patterson*
Sponsoring Editor: *Gina Boedeker*
Managing Editor: *Nicole Bridge and Suzie Flores*
Developmental Editor: *Phillip Butcher*
Marketing Manager: *Pamela Cooper*
Production Editor: *Rachel J. Castillo*
Project Management: *Jill Traut, Macmillan Publishing Solutions*
Cover Designer: *Margarite Reynolds*
Production Supervisor: *Tandra Jorgensen*
Composition: *Macmillan Publishing Solutions*
Printing: *45# New Era Matte Plus, R.R. Donnelley*

Library of Congress Cataloging-in-Publication Data

Feminist theory : a reader / [edited by] Wendy K. Kolmar, Frances Bartkowski. —3rd ed.
     p. cm.
   Includes bibliographical references and index.
   ISBN-13: 978-0-07-351226-6 (pbk.)
   ISBN-10: 0-07-351226-5 (pbk.)
   1. Feminist theory.   2. Women—Social conditions.   I. Kolmar, Wendy K., 1950–
II. Bartkowski, Frances, 1948–
HQ1190.F4633 2010
305.4201—dc22   2009017848

The Internet addresses listed in the text were accurate at the time of publication. The inclusion of a Web site does not indicate an endorsement by the authors or McGraw-Hill, and McGraw-Hill does not guarantee the accuracy of the information presented at these sites.

www.mhhe.com

Contents

PART II: 1792–1920   57

PART III: 1920–1963   123

PART VII: 1995–2008

1995–2008: Introduction

Preface to the Third Edition

Like the previous editions of *Feminist Theory*, this third edition is informed by conversations with the many women's studies faculty and students who use this book and have been willing to share their thoughts about it with us. Your suggestions for readings, shared course syllabi, and comments about how you've been using the book have been vital to us as we've worked on this edition, which is also informed by comments from our students and our own experiences of teaching with the two previous editions. While the basic structure of the reader remains the same in this edition, we have shifted the emphasis toward late 20th- and 21st-century theory in response to the recommendations of many of the faculty who use the book. Later sections of the text have been expanded with the addition or substitution of pieces on militarism, transgender, sexuality, Islamic feminism, and the body, among other issues.

As feminist theory continues to develop and the threads of its thought become increasingly entwined with theorizing in the disciplines and in other interdisciplinary fields, we are ever more aware of the difficulties of drawing anything but a highly permeable boundary around a field called "feminist theory." Our selections attempt to represent some of the vast variety of debate and conversation in this field—and some of the additions to the reader attempt to expand the perspectives on those debates— but the very stringent constraints of space in a book such as this one have meant that again, we have had to leave out more than we have been able to put in. We have tried to make strategic choices that will give students a sense of the range of the debates in the field. But we strongly encourage faculty to supplement these readings, as we do ourselves, with whatever additional readings you find essential to mapping the ever-changing landscape of feminist theory. We urge all readers of this book to be aware that, again because of the constraints of space and price, many of the pieces in this book are edited versions of a longer original, which should be consulted by any student working closely with this material.

CHANGES IN THE THIRD EDITION

The basic structure of the reader remains as it was in the previous two editions. The reader is organized into historical periods with brief introductions; the "Lexicon of the Debates" has been updated to reflect new readings but remains largely unchanged. More than in the previous two editions, we have been pressed to limit the length of this edition, so pieces have been edited for length and many are excerpts from full-length works. In both cases, we try to provide a substantial enough portion of the work that students can get a sense of the argument from their own reading of it. In editing, we have done our best to preserve the main thread of an argument (in the case of essays) or to provide an essential component of the argument (in the case of books). While such editing is never ideal, it is the only way to provide students with access to a broad range of materials within a volume of manageable size. Some 19th-century readings have also been further cut, and several early 20th-century pieces have been dropped because readers told us that they used them less than other material or because permission for their inclusion in this edition was denied. We, like some of you who have made frequent use of the readings we've eliminated, will feel the loss of those key voices.

Coverage

The time span of the book has been extended with the expansion of the most recent period through 2005 and of the bibliographies through 2008. In all of the sections, some deletions, additions, and substitutions have been made, partly on the basis of readers' suggestions and partly on the basis of our own sense of what was missing, more or less useful, or newly visible or available. We have added some new pieces and restored some pieces that were in the first edition to the sections after 1965, mainly on the basis of faculty suggestions about what they need or have used to supplement the material in the second edition. In choosing a very limited number of more recent readings, we have selected readings that either represent a new thread of conversation or new voices and, at the same time, have tried to find versions of certain arguments that would be more accessible to undergraduates at various levels.

Bibliographies

The bibliographies have been updated to include work published after the last edition, but, in the interest of limiting length, we have also made several modifications to the structure of the bibliographies included in the volume. Lexicon entries are now followed by two bibliographies: one of relevant readings inside the text and one of relevant readings outside the text; no bibliographies by topic are provided at the back of the book. No text is listed in more than one bibliography. For example, if a text is mentioned in a headnote, it will no longer appear in the chronological bibliographies at the back; likewise with texts that are mentioned in the lexicon bibliographies. By imposing these limits on the bibliographies, we have tried to save some more room for additional readings.

ACKNOWLEDGMENTS

First, as always, we'd like to thank our students in feminist theory seminars at Drew University and Rutgers University, who remain the reason for and inspiration for this book. The fall 2008 WMST 112 at Drew has been especially zealous in hunting for second-edition typos and making other suggestions. Our students' suggestions and comments, and our classroom conversations with them, have made crucial contributions to the revision of this reader.

We thank our institutions—Drew University and Rutgers University-Newark—for their continued support of this project, and the library staffs at both institutions, particularly Jody Caldwell (Drew) and Ann Watkins and Lynn Mullins (Rutgers).

Also indispensable in this process were our indefatigable research assistants, Robin Mako and Anna Muldoon; the readers whose comments on the second edition directed our revisions, Christina Weber, North Dakota State University; Cynthia Deitch, George Washington State University; Brian J. Jara, Pennsylvania State University; Diana York Blaine, University of California; Kathy Holland, Pierce College; Denise Witzig, Saint Mary's College; Claire L. Sahlin, Texas Woman's University; the many colleagues who suggested readings for inclusion, helped us track down information, and offered support, particularly Gail Cohee and Judy Gerson; the editors and staff at McGraw-Hill, particularly Phil

Butcher and Anne Wallingford, with their patience, support and good advice; and the copyeditor, Susan McClung.

And finally our children, Jules and Anna Rachel, who have grown up with this book. This book is also for them.

SECOND EDITION ACKNOWLEDGMENTS

Our thanks to those whose contribution to the previous edition continues to shape this new one: our research assistants, Madhuparna Sanyal (Drew University) and Alexis Stoumbelis (Smith College); the readers whose comments on the first edition directed our revisions: Cynthia H. Deitch, George Washington University; Brian R. Jara, The Pennsylvania State University; Marie Laberge, University of Delaware; Claire L. Sahlin, Texas Women's University; and Kathleen Slobin, North Dakota University; the many colleagues who suggested readings for inclusion and helped us track down information: Martha Ackelsberg, Lisa Armstrong, Gail Cohee, Paula Giddings, Marilyn Schuster, Rosemarie Garland Thomson, and Susan van Dyne; editors and staff at McGraw-Hill, Sherith Pankratz, Amy Shaffer, Diane Folliard, and Marty Granahan; and copyeditor Judith Gallagher.

Feminist Theory

PART I

What Is Feminist Theory?
What Is Feminism?

Reading Feminist Theory

"I came to theory desperate, wanting to comprehend—to grasp what was happening around and within me."—bell hooks

This book is a collection of readings loosely grouped under the rubric "feminist theory." As you begin to read, you may be nervous, unsure of what you will find here, and perhaps a little put off, because of both the "feminist" part of its title and the "theory" part. Unfortunately, for many students the word "feminist" conjures up scary man-haters, and the word "theory" suggests equally scary and totally unintelligible texts written in unfamiliar language. We trust you will come to realize that neither of those preconceived notions adequately describes the variety of views, voices, and writings included in this book.

Put most simply, feminist theory is a body of writing that attempts to describe, explain, and analyze the conditions of women's lives. According to Charlotte Bunch, feminist theory is "a way of viewing the world"; it "provides a basis for understanding every area of our lives" (Bunch, "Not by Degrees: Feminist Theory and Education," 250). According to bell hooks, it is a way "to grasp what is happening around and within" us (hooks, "Theory as Liberatory Practice," 59). Feminist theory also proposes strategies for activism and action to ameliorate the conditions in which women live and work.

The basic issue that has concerned feminist theory is, depending on the terms one prefers, women's inequality, subordination, or domination by men. At the root of these is the issue of gender asymmetry—the designation of women and things associated with women as different from, inferior to, of lesser value than men and things associated with men. Feminist theories examine and try to explain the causes and conditions in which men are more powerful and men's production, ideas, and activities are seen as having greater value and higher status than women's. For many feminist theorists this comes to mean examining and explaining all structures of domination, whether based on gender, race, class, age, sexuality, nation, or some other difference.

How any feminist theory explains and proposes to address gender asymmetry depends on the assumptions forming the basis of that theory. For example, psychoanalytic feminist theories locate the sources of gender asymmetry in the familial and psychosexual processes that form individual psyches. Materialist feminist theories pay more attention to the ways that concrete economic and social conditions contribute to gender inequality. Feminist theorists of color ground their theory in the assumption that one cannot understand women's lives without also understanding the role of race/ethnicity in shaping their experience. As a reader of feminist theory, you will learn to tease out the assumptions that underpin each theory and to understand how they affect the theory's explanation of women's situation and of the construction of gender and the solutions proposed to ameliorate the conditions of human lives.

Through the choices we made in putting this book together, we want to suggest several things about feminist theory. First, theorizing has been done by many women in many different situations and from many perspectives. Second, feminist theories have a history but not one that is unilinear or monocausal. Third, our reading of contemporary theory needs to be grounded in this history of debates and conversations.

Over its history, feminist theorizing has been an activity engaged in by many women and some men in many different situations. We have tried to suggest this variety by including a range of writing, from manifestos to scholarly essays. Among these are readings by political and social activists, scholars and academics, poor women, working-class women, and privileged women. Women of different sexual orientations and racial and ethnic backgrounds are included, as well as women writing out of different national backgrounds and religious traditions. For example, in the 1792–1920 section, an excerpt from Mary Wollstonecraft's *Vindication of the Rights of Woman* immediately follows an early Navajo origin myth in order to suggest that feminist theory has many points of origin and lines of development. Wollstonecraft's liberal humanist argument for the rights of women is one origin point often cited in the history of feminist thought; we suggest that the Navajo myth's attempt to understand the place of woman in creation is another among many possible points of origin. The writers we include here have not always named their writing "feminist," nor have they always named it "theory." They are included because their writing engages in the activities and thought we describe as feminist theorizing; that is, they attempt to explain women's situation, to understand gender asymmetry, or to understand unequal distributions of privilege and power using gender as one element of their analysis.

Although thinking that meets our definition of feminist theory has probably been done in most cultures and nations, we do not attempt to represent that kind of breadth here. This reader centers on U.S. feminist theory produced since the end of the 18th century. It includes some British, French, and Third World theorists who have been particularly important to the development of feminist theory in the United States, but the history it represents is largely that which grounds contemporary feminist theory in the United States.

However, in the choices we have made here, we are not trying to delineate, even for the United States, what Rosalind Delmar calls "a progressive and cumulative history of feminism." Rather we want to provide a body of material that allows us to study, as Delmar suggests we should, the "dynamics of persistence and change within feminism" (Delmar, "What Is Feminism?" 18). In other words, we want to suggest that certain ideas, issues, and themes have been discussed and debated throughout the history of feminism and feminist theory, although approaches to those issues depend on each writer's perspective and historical and social location. For example, you will find writings in every time period discussing the sexual division of labor and power in one way or another, although how those divisions between the sexes are understood may vary. On the other hand, new insights and perspectives do emerge within feminism. Some of these are triggered by dialogue with other intellectual and social movements, some by the evolution of thinking within women's movements, and still others as a result of historical, political, and social developments and crises.

CONTENTS AND ORGANIZATION OF THE READER

We believe that the organization of this reader, with the majority of the readings in chronological order, allows you best to explore this multifaceted history of persistence and change within feminist theory. This organization is flexible, so that the readings can be approached in a variety of ways. At the same time, the reader provides various tools for contextualizing the selections and grappling with the sometimes difficult language and thought you will encounter while reading these examples of feminist theory.

The readings in the first section give you some preliminary definitions of feminism and of feminist theory. To work effectively with feminist theory, you will need to pay close attention to the language and terminology used by different theorists and to notice when theorists share terms, redefine terms, or use terms in very different ways. We have tried to suggest the importance of close attention to words and definitions by beginning our first section with multiple definitions of "feminist" and "feminism" taken from *The Feminist Dictionary* and by creating the "Lexicon" entries, which will help you associate some of the major debates in feminist theory with keywords and terms.

The "Lexicon of Debates," which follows the introductory section of readings, identifies 10 debates that are central to contemporary feminist theory. Most, but not all, of these debates surface in some way in the feminist theorizing done in earlier periods. Each lexicon entry attempts to trace both the persistence of and the changes in each thread of debate, using as examples selections from this reader. It would be possible to organize your reading of most, if not all, of the material by following the multiple threads of thought identified in the lexicon. In addition, the lexicon entries will familiarize you with important words and terms associated with each debate.

After these initial sections, the readings are organized into six chronological periods:

    II   1792–1920
    III 1920–1963
    IV   1963–1975
    V   1975–1985
    VI   1985–1995
    VII 1995–2008

The boundaries of these periods are to some extent arbitrary, but the dates seem to us to mark, in broad terms, significant historical and epistemological shifts in women's movements and thought over the past three centuries. Our understanding of those shifts is sketched briefly here; each section introduction provides further historical context.

The reader begins in 1792 when Mary Wollstonecraft's *Vindication of the Rights of Woman* was published in England. We begin at this point because Wollstonecraft's text is arguably one of the first in the Anglo-American tradition that attempts overtly to theorize the position of women within the dominant political and social discourses of its moment. Although issues of concern to later feminist theory are certainly raised by earlier writers (for example, Christine de Pisan, Sor Juana, Julian of Norwich), we chose Wollstonecraft's text as our starting point for its attempt at comprehensive analysis and because later feminist theorists have viewed it as a significant origin text.

Part II of the book ends with 1920, the year in which women in the United States were granted the right to vote. We chose the date of suffrage as our first division because, before its achievement, the demand for women's enfranchisement in politics and other areas dominated much of the thinking about women, even by those who felt that centering suffrage as *the* issue for women was a mistake. The achievement of suffrage, a crucial moment of democratic, political victory for women, brought feminist concerns into public culture and discourse. After that moment, however, conversations about women and feminism were necessarily redirected and refocused.

Part III begins with 1920 and ends with 1963, the date of the publication of *The Feminine Mystique*, the text most historians identify as giving birth to the second wave of the U.S. women's movement. This period between the achievement of the vote and the 1960s is often viewed as an era of diminished feminist activity. The only text from this second period usually included in feminist theory anthologies and courses is Simone de Beauvoir's *The Second Sex*. However, writing and thinking about women continued throughout this period and across a variety of disciplines and areas, as the material we have included here demonstrates.

Unlike Parts II and III of the reader, the latter parts are defined not so much by specific historical events or publication dates as they are by shifts in the prevailing discourse and concerns of feminist theory. These shifts are gradual and evolve over a number of years through the impact of a variety of conversations and challenges, but they seem to us to bear fruit in changes that are roughly marked by the years 1975 and 1985.

The period 1963 through 1975, covered in Part IV of the reader, is defined largely by theorizing done as a part of the activism of the women's movement. In contrast, the period 1975 through 1985, comprising Part V, is characterized by theory produced primarily and for the first time by academic women associated with the new field of women's studies. This latter period is characterized by institution building within women's studies (founding of women's studies programs, campus women's centers, curriculum transformation projects, and the formation of the National Women's Studies Association); feminist canon formation and the continuing rediscovery of women's lives, texts, and practices; and efforts to disseminate this expanding body of knowledge and methods across the disciplines.

Part VI takes us through 1995, the year in which 40,000 women gathered in Beijing and Huairou for the fourth United Nations Conference on Women to attempt to articulate a common global agenda for change in women's lives. Part VII selects readings which suggest key directions in feminist theory since 1995. Together, Parts VI and VII trace the development of feminist theory since 1985 as it shifts in response to multiple challenges from within and to intellectual and global change outside its borders. Internal critiques come from groups who have felt excluded from feminism as an academic discourse, among them women of color, Third World women, poor and working-class women, grassroots activists, older women, and women with disabilities. External intellectual influences on feminist inquiry have come from postmodernism, cultural studies, queer theory, gay, lesbian, bisexual and transgender studies, postcolonial theory, ethnic studies, and biological and information sciences, as well as from massive shifts in global power relations, social arrangements, reproductive technologies, and the global rise of fundamentalism. At their best, feminist theorists have responded with creativity, openness and invention to these changing landscapes.

Throughout much of the history we have traced here, the phrases "women's thinking" and "feminist theory" were considered oxymorons. For most of the history of Western culture, and certainly since the 17th-century philosopher Descartes theorized a split between the mind and the body, women have been associated with nature, the body, and the concrete conditions of life, whereas men have been associated with culture, the mind and intellect, and abstract philosophizing. Throughout much of this period, women have had little access to higher education and intellectual culture. Women today still have differential access to educational, intellectual, and cultural resources. Yet, as the selections in this reader profoundly demonstrate, women have thought in thorough and complex ways about their own condition, their bodies and their lives, social, political, and cultural institutions, creativity and science, justice and liberty. Like bell hooks, they have found in the activity of theorizing many ways "to grasp what was happening around and within" them, to comprehend it and to change it.

1

Feminism

PAULA TREICHLER and
CHERIS KRAMARAE

PAULA TREICHLER United States. ND. Feminist scholar in communications and medicine. *For Alma Mater: Theory and Practice in Feminist Scholarship* (1985), *The Visible Woman: Imaging Technologies, Gender, and Science* (1998), *How to Have Theory in an Epidemic: Cultural Chronicles of AIDS* (1999).

CHERIS KRAMARAE United States. ND. Feminist scholar in communications. *Women and Men Speaking* (1981), *For Alma Mater: Theory and Practice in Feminist Scholarship* (1985), *Women, Information Technology, and Scholarship* (1993).

FEMINISM

(See all entries above and below)

A movement with a long history. Three basic positions of feminism during 1400–1789: (1) a conscious stand in opposition to male defamation and mistreatment of women; a dialectical opposition to misogyny. (2) a belief that the sexes are culturally, and not just biologically, formed; a belief that women were a social group shaped to fit male notions about a defective sex. (3) an outlook that transcended the accepted value systems of the time by exposing and opposing the prejudice and narrowness; a desire for a truly general conception of humanity. (Joan Kelly 1982, 6–7)

Has as its goal to give every woman "the opportunity of becoming the best that her natural faculties make her capable of." (Millicent Garrett Fawcett 1878, 357)

Has as a goal: The liberation of women for women. "We don't have to have anything to do with men at all. They've taken excellent care of themselves." (Jill Johnston 1973, 91)

"May be defined as a movement seeking the reorganization of the world upon a basis of sex-equality in all human relations; a movement which would reject every differentiation between individuals upon the ground of sex, would abolish all sex privileges and sex burdens, and would strive to set up the recognition of the common humanity of woman and man as the foundation of law and custom." (Teresa Billington-Greig 1911, 694, 703)

". . . has as yet no defined creed. . . . [Is] the articulate consciousness of mind in women . . . in its different forms of expression." ("The Freewoman" 1911, *Votes for Women,* 17 November, 103)

Is that part of the progress of democratic freedom which applies to women. (Beatrice Forbes-Robertson Hale 1914, 3)

"A many-headed monster which cannot be destroyed by singular decapitation. We spread and grow in ways that are incomprehensible to a hierarchical mentality." (Peggy Kornegger 1979, 243)

"Feminism at heart is a massive complaint. Lesbianism is the solution. . . . Until all women are lesbians there will be no true political revolution. No feminist per se has advanced a solution outside of accommodation to the man." (Jill Johnston 1973, 166)

"An integration of various here-to-fore incompatible elements built on a collective base of thought–action–feeling. Feminism integrates the subjective and objective, the rational and the intuitive, the mystical and the scientific, the abstract and concrete aspects of the universe and considers them harmonious parts of a whole rather than in opposition to one another." (Anne Kent Rush and Anica Vesel Mander 1974, 14–15)

"Begins but cannot end with the discovery by an individual of her self-consciousness as a woman. It is not, finally, even the recognition of her reasons for anger, or the decision to change her life, to go back to school, to leave a marriage. . . . Feminism means finally that we renounce our obedience to the fathers and recognize that the world they have described is not the whole world. . . . Feminism implies that we recognize fully the inadequacy for us, the distortion, of male-created ideologies, and that we proceed to think, and act, out of that recognition." (Adrienne Rich 1976; rpt. 1979, 207)

"A method of analysis as well as a discovery of new material. It asks new questions as well as coming up with new answers. Its central concern is with the social distinction between men and women, with the fact of this distinction, with its meanings, and with its causes and consequences." (Juliet Mitchell and Ann Oakley 1976, 14)

"We are actively committed to struggling against racial, sexual, heterosexual, and class oppression and see as our particular task the development of integrated analysis and practice based upon the fact that the major systems of oppression are interlocking. The synthesis of these oppressions creates the conditions of our lives. As Black women we see Black feminism as the logical political movement to combat the manifold and simultaneous oppressions that all women of color face." (Combahee River Collective 1977; rpt. in Cherríe Moraga and Gloria Anzaldúa eds 1981, 210)

Women uniting as women to generate "a force which presses society to accept and accommodate femaleness as equal, even if different, in its attributes." (Devaki Jain 1978, 9)

"Potentially the most threatening of movements to Black and other Third World people because it makes it absolutely essential that we examine the way we live, how we treat each other, and what we believe. It calls into question the most basic assumptions about our existence and this is the idea that biological, i.e., sexual identity, determines all, that it is the rationale for power relationships as well as for all levels of human identity and action." (Barbara Smith 1983, xxv–xxvi)

"Is a mode of analysis, a method of approaching life and politics, a way of asking questions and searching for answers, rather than a set of political conclusions about the oppression of women." (Nancy Hartsock 1979, 58–59)

"Feminism is the political theory and practice to free all women: women of color, working-class women, poor women, physically challenged women, lesbians, old women, as well as white economically privileged heterosexual women. Anything less than this is not feminism, but merely female self-aggrandizement." (Barbara Smith 1979; quoted in Cherríe Moraga and Gloria Anzaldúa eds 1981, 61)

(See BLACK FEMINISM)

Woman responding to question, "As an Asian-American woman, do you consider yourself a feminist?": "There is feminism where all the problems of women in society are seen as caused by men. I don't believe in that. I don't believe men are the creators of the problems in society. . . . I do believe that men and women have to work together to solve the problems in society." (In Susie Ling's dissertation; quoted by Lucie Cheng 1984, 11)

"Feminism means you have to read a lot, to understand a lot, to feel a lot, and to be honest." "To me, real feminism means being revolutionary. To be revolutionary means that one examines the problems of women from all aspects: historically, sociologically, economically, and psychologically. . . . And as a radical feminist, I think you should oppose imperialism, Zionism, feudalism, and inequality between nations, sexes, and classes." (Nawal el Saadawi 1980, 3)

A philosophy "based on the recognition that we live in a male-dominated culture in which women remain unacknowledged, and where women are forced into sex roles which demand that they be dependent, passive, nurturant, etc. Men too must assume sex roles [but these] are not nearly as crippling as women's." (*Banshee: Journal of Irishwomen United* 1981, 8:10)

"Is a commitment to eradicating the ideology of domination that permeates Western culture on various levels—sex, race, and class, to name a few—and a commitment to reorganizing U.S. society, so that the self-development of people can take precedence over imperialism, economic expansion, and material desires." (bell hooks 1981, 194–195)

"Means to me the movement towards creating a society where women can live a full, self-determined life. This may seem a bland statement but in terms of the changes we need to achieve this, it is revolutionary." (Mary MacNamara c. 1982, 6)

Is "the desire and struggle for freedom," which is the same for each of us—Black, Latina, Native American, etc.—"even though our methods may differ." (Deborah Aslan Jamieson 1982, 6)

"Is an entire worldview or *gestalt*, not just a laundry list of 'women's issues.' Feminist theory provides a basis for understanding every area of our lives, and a feminist perspective can affect the world politically, culturally, economically, and spiritually." (Charlotte Bunch 1983, 250)

"Two elements constitute the discipline of feminism: political, ideological, and strategic confrontation with the sex–class system—with sex hierarchy and sex segregation—and a single standard of human dignity. Abandon either element and the sex–class system is unbreachable, indestructible; feminism loses its rigor, the toughness of its visionary heart. . . . One other discipline is essential both to the practice of feminism and to its theoretical integrity: the firm, unsentimental, continuous recognition that women are a class having a common condition." (Andrea Dworkin 1983, 200)

"Is a theory that calls for women's attainment of social, economic, and political rights and opportunities equal to those possessed by men. Feminism is also a model for a social state—an ideal, or a desired standard of perfection not yet attained in the world." (Rebecca Lewin 1983, 17)

Is the fairy godmother. "Do you remember the story of Cinderella? She is sitting at home rather pissed off, wanting to go to the ball, and not having a thing to wear, when the fairy godmother whizzes in and puts it all right. One of the most important things about the fairy godmother is that she transforms all the old stuff around Cinderella into new and useful equipment: the rags, the pumpkin, the rats, and so forth. This little girl's fairy godmother turned out to be called Feminism. As well as cheering the little girl up no end, Feminism also transformed all the old things around her." (Sara Maitland 1983, 18)

"Third World feminism is about feeding people in all their hungers." (Cherríe Moraga 1983, 132) "[It] is bringing the strains together." (Barbara Smith; quoted in Cherríe Moraga 1983, 133)

Is a powerful homeopathic remedy which goes beyond the symptoms to the deeper causes of our troubles: the imbalance between masculine and feminine energies, manifested in the ills of patriarchy. (Jill Raymond and Janice Wilson 1983, 59)

Is neither original nor radical; women's ideas about the relationship of women and men are either co-opted or lost by men and have to be recreated every 50 years or so. (Dale Spender 1982)

A set of beliefs and "theoretical constructions about the nature of women's oppression and the part that this oppression plays within social reality more generally." (Liz Stanley and Sue Wise 1983, 55)

With a capital 'F' it is a theory, a position. With small 'f' it is an organic conviction based on experience. (Osha Davidson 1984, 11A)

· · ·

FEMINIST

"I myself have never been able to find out precisely what feminism is: I only know that people call me a feminist whenever I express sentiments that differentiate me from a doormat . . ." (Rebecca West 1913, *The Clarion,* Nov. 14)

"Mother, what is a Feminist?"
  "A Feminist, my daughter,
Is any woman now who cares
To think about her own affairs
  As men don't think she oughter"
  (Alice Duer Miller 1915; in Redstockings eds 1975, 52)

"Feminist is formed with the word 'femme,' 'woman,' and means: someone who fights for women. For many of us this means someone who fights for women as a class and for the disappearance of this class. For many others it means someone who fights for woman and her defense—for the myth, then, and its reinforcement." (Monique Wittig 1981, 50)

A person who knows that we hold up half the sky and who is going to make everyone else notice it. (Dawn Russell 1979, 75)

What is unique about the feminist mode of analysis: "(1) The focus on everyday life and experience makes action a necessity, not a moral choice or an option. We are not fighting other people's battles but our own. (2) The nature of our understanding of theory is altered and theory is brought into an integral and everyday relation with practice. (3) Theory leads directly to a transformation of social relations both in consciousness and in reality because of its close connection to real needs." (Nancy Hartsock 1979, 64)

A word that frightens some people. "For the feminist [literary] critic, however, it is less a bogey or a bugaboo than a badge of honor. . . . It refers to the conviction that our production of culture and meaning, like our consumption of culture and meaning, influences our sex/gender systems. In turn, our sex/gender systems influence our production and consumption of culture and meaning." (Catharine Stimpson 1981, 59)

"From the early generalizations about 'all women,' feminists are recognizing the need to understand the specific nature and conditions of women's oppression in differing cultures, societies, and economies." (Jill Lewis 1981; in Gloria I. Joseph and Jill Lewis 1981, 67)

"To be a feminist means recognizing that one is associated with all women not as an act of choice but as a matter of fact. . . . Feminists do not create this common condition by making alliances; feminists recognize this common condition because it exists as an intrinsic part of sex oppression. . . . What is that common condition? Subordination to men, sexually colonized in a sexual system of dominance and submission, denied rights on the basis of sex, historically chattel, generally considered biologically inferior, confined to sex and reproduction; this is the general description of the social environment in which all women live." (Andrea Dworkin 1983, 221)

"Well, I'm convinced that many frustrated and crabby women are merely feminists in restraints." (Diane F. Germain 1983, 154)

"A person, female or male, whose worldview places the female in the center of life and society, and/or who is not prejudiced based on gender or sexual preference. Also, anyone in a male-dominated or patriarchal society who works toward the political, economic, spiritual, sexual, and social equality of women." (*The Wise Woman* 1982, 4:2 [June 21], 7)

When used by a man to refer to himself it is a "male appropriation of language no less stupidly defensive than a white man imagining myself a black radical." Profeminist is a term used to describe the male who works towards feminist goals. (Irving Weinman 1983, 133–134)

(See WOMANIST)

FEMINIST DICTIONARY

A word book which calls into question the androcentric nature of much "standard language usage" and problematizes many words and phrases in the light of feminist perspectives and commentary. *This* feminist dictionary (1) recognizes women as linguistically creative speakers, (2) explicitly acknowledges the sociopolitical aspects of dictionary-making, (3) draws heavily on excerpted material from feminist publications, (4) does not generally specify "parts of speech" (noun, verb, etc.) or linguistic status (coinage, obsolete, etc.) but rather provides commentary on the general cultural knowledge that the reader brings to this book, (5) assumes that a book about words is inevitably a book about the world as well, (6) emphasizes definitions by feminists without making continual reference to male authorities, (7) sometimes offers "contradictions" without resolving them. That this book is incomplete goes without saying. It is not intended to be the last word. We urge readers to make their own contributions using the blank pages at the back of the book and send them to us for the next edition.

[1985]

REFERENCES

Banshee: Journal of Irishwomen United 1981 8:10.

Billington-Greig, Teresa. 1911. "Feminism and Politics." *The Contemporary Review*, November, 693–703.

Bunch, Charlotte. 1983. "Not by Degrees: Feminist Theory and Education." In *Learning Our Way*. Ed. Charlotte Bunch and Sandra Pollack. Trumansburg, NY: The Crossing Press, 248–260.

Cheng, Lucie. 1984. "Asian American Women and Feminism." *Sojourner*, October, 11.

Combahee River Collective. 1977. "A Black Feminist Statement." Rpt. In *This Bridge Called My Back: Writings by Radical Women of Color*. Ed. Cherríe Moraga and Gloria Anzaldúa. Watertown, MA: Persephone Press, 1981, 210–218.

Davidson, Osha. 1984. "How Feminism Rescued Desperate Single Father." *Des Moines Register*, 16 November, 11A.

Dworkin, Andrea. 1983. *Right-wing Women*. New York: Perigree Books.

Fawcett, Millicent Garrett. 1878. "The Future of Englishwomen: A Reply." *Nineteenth Century*, 4, 347–357.

"The Freewoman" 1911, *Votes for Women*, 17 November, 103.

Germain, Diane F. 1983. "Feminist Art and Education at Califia: My Personal Experience." *In Learning Our Way*. Ed. Charlotte Bunch and Sandra Pollack. Trumansburg, New York: The Crossing Press, 154–159.

Hale, Beatrice Forbes-Robertson. 1914. *What Women Want: An Interpretation of the Feminist Movement*. New York: Frederick A. Stokes.

Hartsock, Nancy. 1979. "Feminist Theory and the Development of Revolutionary Strategy." In *Capitalist Patriarchy and the Case for Socialist Feminism*. Ed. Zillah Eisenstein. New York and London: Monthly Review Press, 56–82.

hooks, bell. 1981. *Ain't I a Woman: Black Women and Feminism*. Boston: South End Press.

Jain, Devaki. 1978. "Can Feminism Be a Global Ideology?" *Quest: A Feminist Quarterly*, 4:2 (Winter), 9–15.

Jamieson, Deborah Aslan. 1982. Review of *This Bridge Called My Back: Writings by Radical Women of Color*, ed. Cherrié Moraga and Gloria Anzaldúa. *off our backs*, April, 6, 11.

Johnston, Jill. 1973. *Lesbian Nation: The Feminist Solution*. New York: Simon & Schuster.

Joseph, Gloria I. and Jill Lewis. 1981. *Common Differences: Conflicts in Black and White Feminist Perspectives*. Garden City, NY: Anchor/Doubleday.

Kelly, Joan. 1982. "Early Feminist Theory and the *Querelle des Femmes*, 1400–1789." *Signs*, 8:1 (Autumn), 4–28.

Kornegger, Peggy. 1979. "Anarchism: The Feminist Connection." In *Reinventing Anarchy*. Ed. Howard J. Ehrlich, Carol Ehrlich, David DeLeon, and Glenda Morris. London: Routledge & Kegan Paul, 237–249.

Lewin, Rebecca. 1983. "Truth-Telling Through Feminist Fiction." *Womanews*, 4:9 (October), 17.

MacNamara, Mary, c. 1982. "What Is Feminism? Another View . . ." *Wicca: 'Wise Woman' Irish Feminist Magazine*, 12, 6–7.

Maitland, Sara. 1983. "A Feminist Writer's Progress." In *On Gender and Writing*. Ed. Michelene Wandor. London: Pandora Press, 17–23.

Mitchell, Juliet and Ann Oakley, eds. 1976. *The Rights and Wrongs of Women*. Harmondsworth, Middlesex: Penguin Books.

Moraga, Cherríe. 1983. *Loving in the War Years*. Boston: South End Press.

Moraga, Cherríe and Gloria Anzaldúa, eds. 1981. *This Bridge Called My Back: Writings by Radical Women of Color*. Watertown, MA: Persephone Press.

Raymond, Jill and Janice Wilson. 1983. "Feminism— Healing the Patriarchal Disease." In *Reclaim the Earth: Women Speak Out for Life on Earth*. Ed. Léonie Caldecott and Stephanie Leland. London: The Women's Press, 59–65.

Redstockings of the Women's Liberation Movement, eds. 1975. *Feminist Revolution*. New York: Random House.

Rich, Adrienne. 1976. *Of Woman Born: Motherhood as Experience and Institution*. New York: W. W. Norton.

Rush, Anne Kent and Anica Vesel Mander. 1974. *Feminism as Therapy*. New York: Random House.

Russell, Dawn. 1979. "Black Women and Work: My Experiences." *Heresies*, 2:4 (Issue 8), 72–75.

Saadawi, Nawal el. 1980. Interview. *Newsfront International*, October. Excerpted in *Connexions*, 1 May, 1981, 3.

Smith, Barbara. 1979. "Notes for Yet Another Paper on Black Feminism, Or Will the Real Enemy Please Stand Up?" *Conditions: 5 The Black Women's Issue*, 2:2 (Autumn), 123–132.

Smith, Barbara. 1983. Introduction to *Home Girls: A Black Feminist Anthology*. Ed. Barbara Smith. New York: Kitchen Table: Women of Color Press, xix–lvi.

Spender, Dale. 1982. *Women of Ideas and What Men Have Done to Them: From Aphra Behn to Adrienne Rich*. London: Routledge & Kegan Paul.

Stanley, Liz and Sue Wise. 1983. *Breaking Out: Feminist Consciousness and Feminist Research*. London: Routledge & Kegan Paul.

Stimpson, Catharine. 1981. "Feminist Criticism and Feminist Critics." In *Feminist Literary Criticism*. Research Triangle Park, North Carolina: National Humanities Center, 57–63.

Weinman, Irving. 1983. "On the Edge." In *On Gender and Writing*. Ed. Michelene Wandor. London: Pandora Press, 133–140.

West, Rebecca. 1911–17. Selections of Rebecca West's Writings. In *The Young Rebecca*. Ed. Jane Marcus. London: Macmillan, 1982.

Wittig, Monique. 1981. "One Is Not Born a Woman." *Feminist Issues*, 1:2 (Winter), 47–54.

 2

Womanist

ALICE WALKER

ALICE WALKER United States. 1944–   .Novelist. Poet. Essayist. Activist. *Meridian* (1976), *The Color Purple* (1982), *The Temple of My Familiar* (1989), *In Search of Our Mothers' Gardens: Womanist Prose* (1983), *Possessing the Secret of Joy* (1992).

1.   From *womanish*. (Opp. of "girlish," i.e., frivolous, irresponsible, not serious.) A black feminist or feminist of color. From the black folk expression of mothers to female children, "You acting womanish," i.e., like a woman. Usually referring to outrageous, audacious, courageous or *willful* behavior. Wanting to know more and in greater depth than is considered "good" for one. Interested in grown-up doings. Acting grown up. Being grown up. Interchangeable with another black folk expression: "You trying to be grown." Responsible. In charge. *Serious*.

2.   *Also:* A woman who loves other women, sexually and/or nonsexually. Appreciates and prefers women's culture, women's emotional flexibility (values tears as natural counterbalance of laughter), and women's strength. Sometimes loves individual men, sexually and/or nonsexually. Committed to survival and wholeness of entire people, male *and* female. Not a separatist, except periodically, for health. Traditionally universalist, as in: "Mama, why are we brown, pink, and yellow, and our cousins are white, beige, and black?" Ans.: "Well, you know the colored race is just like a flower garden, with every color flower represented." Traditionally capable, as in: "Mama, I'm walking to Canada and I'm taking you and a bunch of other slaves with me." Reply: "It wouldn't be the first time."

3.   Loves music. Loves dance. Loves the moon. *Loves* the Spirit. Loves love and food and roundness. Loves struggle. *Loves* the Folk. Loves herself. *Regardless*.

4.   Womanist is to feminist as purple to lavender.

[1983]

3

Not by Degrees: Feminist Theory and Education

CHARLOTTE BUNCH

CHARLOTTE BUNCH United States. 1944–   . International feminist and human rights activist. Organizer. Educator. In 1970s, founder of The Furies, a lesbian-feminist collective, and *Quest: A Feminist Quarterly*. Founding director of the Center for Women's Global Leadership. *Passionate Politics: Feminist Theory in Action: Essays, 1968–1986* (1987), *Demanding Accountability: The Global Campaign and Vienna Tribunal for Women's Human Rights* (1994).

The development of feminist theory and rigorous analysis of society are more important for us today than ever before. Feminists need to understand the forces working against us, as well as to analyze our experiences as a movement, if we are to survive the anti-woman backlash and keep our visions alive. When feminists despair, burn out, or give up, it is often because the forces against us are strong and because our theoretical framework does not give us a sense of how individual activities contribute to significant victories in the future. A solid feminist theory would help us understand present events in a way that would enable us to develop the visions and plans for change that sustain people engaged in day-to-day political activity.

When I left the university to do full-time work in "the movement" in the 1960s, it didn't occur to me that I would return one day to teach or write feminist theory. Like many others who chose to become movement activists then, I felt that I was leaving behind not only the academic world, but also what I saw as irrelevant theorizing. However, as I experienced the problems of movement organizing when an overall analysis was lacking, felt the frustration of conflicts where issues were not clear, and observed people dropping out of political activity, I became aware of the critical role of theory in the movement. I began to see feminist theory not as academic, but as a process based on understanding and advancing the activist movement.

While my growing sense of the importance of theory applied to all my feminist work, the urgency that I felt about it became clearest during my involvement with lesbian-feminism. When the lesbian issue became a major controversy in the women's movement in the early 1970s, I realized that in order for lesbians to function openly, we would have to understand *why* there was so much resistance to this issue. It was not enough to document discrimination against homosexuals or to appeal to fairness. We had to figure out why lesbianism was taboo, why it was a threat to feminists, and then devise strategies accordingly. I saw that my life as a lesbian in the movement depended on, among other things, the development of a theory that would explain our immediate conflicts in the context of a long-term view of feminism. This theoretical perspective developed along with our activism, but it required us to consciously ask certain questions, to look at our experiences in and out of the movement, and to consider existing feminist theory in new ways. Through this process, new interpretations of the relationship between lesbianism and feminism, and new strategies for ending lesbian oppression, emerged.

For example, as we examined feminists' fear of being called lesbians, we were able to confront directly the role that such name calling played in the oppression of all women. Having a theory about lesbian oppression did not tell us what to do tactically, but it did provide a framework for understanding situations, for placing them in a broader context, and for evaluating possible courses of action. This experience showed me that theory was not simply intellectually interesting, but was crucial to the survival of feminism.

THE FUNCTIONS OF FEMINIST THEORY

Theory enables us to see immediate needs in terms of long-range goals and an overall perspective on the world.[1] It thus gives us a framework for evaluating various strategies in both the long and the short run, and for seeing the types of changes that they are likely to produce. Theory is not just a body of facts or a set of personal opinions. It involves explanations and hypotheses that are based on available knowledge and experience. It is also dependent on conjecture and insight about how to interpret those facts and experiences and their significance.

No theory is totally "objective," since it reflects the interests, values, and assumptions of those who created it. Feminist theory relies on the underlying assumption that it will aid the liberation of women. Feminist theory, therefore, is not an unengaged study of women. It is an effort to bring insights from the movement and from various female experiences together with research and data gathering to produce new approaches to understanding and ending female oppression.

While feminist theory begins with the immediate need to end women's oppression, it is also a way of viewing the world. Feminism is an entire worldview or *gestalt,* not just a laundry list of "women's issues." Feminist theory provides a basis for understanding every area of our lives, and a feminist perspective can affect the world politically, culturally, economically, and spiritually. The initial tenets of feminism have already been established—the idea that power is based on gender differences and that men's illegitimate power over women taints all aspects of society, for instance. But now we face the arduous task of systematically working through these ideas, fleshing them out and discovering new ones.

When the development of feminist theory seems too slow for the changes that we seek, feminists are tempted to submerge our insights into one of the century's two dominant progressive theories of reality and change: democratic liberalism or Marxist socialism.[2] However, the limitations of both of these systems are increasingly obvious. While feminism can learn from both of them, it must not be tied to either because its greatest strength lies in providing an alternative view of the world.

The full implications of feminism will evolve over time, as we organize, experiment, think, analyze, and revise our ideas and strategies in light of our experiences. No theory emerges in full detail overnight; the dominant theories of our day have expanded and changed over many decades. That it will take time should not discourage us. That we might fail to pursue our ideas—given the enormous need for them in society today—is unconscionable.

Because feminist theory is still emerging and does not have agreed-upon answers (or even approaches to many questions), it is difficult to work out strategies based on that theory. This difficulty can lead feminists to rely on the other theories

of change or to fall into the "any action/no action" bind. When caught in this bind, one may go ahead with action—any action—for its own sake, or be paralyzed, taking no action for lack of a sense of what is "right." To escape this bind, we must remember that we do not need, and indeed never will have, all the answers before we act, and that it is often only through taking action that we can discover some of them. The purpose of theory, then, is not to provide a pat set of answers about what to do, but to guide us in sorting out options, and to keep us out of the "any action/no action" bind. Theory also keeps us aware of the questions that need to be asked, so that what we learn in each activity will lead to more effective strategies in the future. Theory thus both grows out of and guides activism in a continuous, spiraling process.

In pursuing feminist theory as an activist, I have become increasingly aware of the need to demystify it. Theory is not something set apart from our lives. Our assumptions about reality and change influence our actions constantly. The question is not whether we have a theory, but how aware we are of the assumptions behind our actions, and how conscious we are of the choices we make—daily—among different theories. For example, when we decide whether to put our energies into a rape crisis center or into efforts to change rape laws, we are acting according to certain theories about how service projects and legislation affect change. These theories may be implicit or explicit, but they are always there.

A MODEL FOR THEORY

Theory doesn't necessarily progress in a linear fashion, but examining its components is useful in understanding existing political theory as well as in developing new insights. In the model I have developed, I divide theory into four interrelated parts: description, analysis, vision, and strategy.

1. Description: *Describing what exists* may sound simple, but the choices that we make about interpreting and naming reality provide the basis for the rest of our theory. Changing people's perceptions of the world through new descriptions of reality is usually a prerequisite for altering that reality. For example, fifteen years ago, few people would say

that women in the U.S. were oppressed. Today, the oppression of women is acknowledged by a large number of people, primarily because of feminist work which described that oppression in a number of ways. This work has involved consciousness raising, as well as gathering and interpreting facts about women in order to substantiate our assertions. Description is necessary for all theory; unfortunately for feminism, much of our work has not yet gone beyond this point.

2.   Analysis: *Analyzing why that reality exists* involves determining its origins and the reasons for its perpetuation. This is perhaps the most complex task of theory and is often seen as its entire function. In seeking to understand the sources of women's oppression and why it is perpetuated, we have to examine biology, economics, psychology, sexuality, and so on. We must also look at what groups and institutions benefit from oppression, and why they will, therefore, strive to maintain it. Analyzing why women are oppressed involves such things as sorting out how the forms of oppression change over time while the basic fact of oppression remains, or probing how the forms of oppression vary in different cultures while there are cross-cultural similarities.

Analysis of why something happens sometimes gets short-circuited by the temptation to ascribe everything to one single factor, such as capitalism or motherhood. In developing an analysis, I find that it is useful to focus initially on a phenomenon in a limited context and consider a wide range of factors that may affect it. Then, as that context is understood, the analysis can be expanded. Above all, we need not feel that we must answer the "why" of everything all at once with a single explanation.

3.   Vision: *Determining what should exist* requires establishing principles (or values) and setting goals. In taking action to bring about change, we operate consciously or unconsciously out of certain assumptions about what is right or what we value (principles), and out of our sense of what society ought to be (goals). This aspect of theory involves making a conscious choice about those principles in order to make our visions and goals concrete. We must look at our basic assumptions about such things as "human nature" and how it

can be changed, about the relationships of individuals to groups, about whether men and women are essentially different, for example. We may choose not to address some of these issues yet, but since every action carries implicit assumptions, we must be conscious of them so that we do not operate out of old theoretical frameworks by default. The clearer we are about our principles—for example, whether we think that women should gain as much power as possible in every area, or believe, instead, that power itself should be eliminated—the more easily we can set our long-term goals. Immediate goals can then be based on an assessment of what can be accomplished that may be short of our long-term vision but moves toward, not away, from it. Visions, principles, and goals will change with experience, but the more explicit we make them, the more our actions can be directed toward creating the society we want, as well as reacting to what we don't like.

4.   Strategy: *Hypothesizing how to change what is to what should be* moves directly into questions of changing reality. Some people see strategy not as part of theory, but rather as a planning process based on theory. But I include strategy here in its broadest sense—the overall approach one takes to how to accomplish one's goals. The descriptive and analytic processes of theory help develop a more systematic understanding of the way things work, but they usually do not make obvious what one should do. Developing a strategy requires that we draw out the consequences of our theory and suggest general directions for change.

Like the other aspects of theory, this involves a combination of information gathering and creative speculation. It entails making judgments about what will lead to change—judgments that are based both on description and analysis of reality, and on visions, principles, and goals. Developing a strategy also involves examining various tools for change— legislative, military, spiritual—and determining which are most effective in what situations. There are many questions to consider, such as what sectors of society can best be mobilized to carry out which types of action. And in working out which strategies will be most effective, the interaction between developing theory and actively experimenting with it becomes most clear. For in all aspects of theory development, theory and activism continually inform and alter each other.

[1979]

NOTES

1. There are many approaches to theory, and those interested in exploring more about how theory is constructed should look at the literature of political philosophy. A model for feminist theory similar to the one that I discuss in this paper was developed by Judy Smith of the Women's Resource Center, in Missoula, Montana.
2. For more discussion of this problem and of nonaligned feminism as a response to it, see Charlotte Bunch, "Beyond Either/Or: Feminist Options," *Quest: A Feminist Quarterly,* vol. 3, no. 1 (Summer 1976), pp. 2–17.

 4

The Master's Tools Will Never Dismantle the Master's House*

AUDRE LORDE

AUDRE LORDE United States. 1934–1992. Poet. Activist. Theorist. Self-described "Black Lesbian Feminist Warrior Poet." Founder of Kitchen Table: Women of Color Press. *The Black Unicorn* (1978), *Zami: A New Spelling of My Name* (1982), *Cancer Journals* (1980), *A Burst of Light* (1988).

I AGREED TO TAKE PART in a New York University Institute for the Humanities conference a year ago, with the understanding that I would be commenting upon papers dealing with the role of difference within the lives of american women: difference of race, sexuality, class, and age. The absence of these considerations weakens any feminist discussion of the personal and the political.

It is a particular academic arrogance to assume any discussion of feminist theory without examining our many differences, and without a significant input from poor women, Black and Third World women, and lesbians. And yet, I stand here as a Black lesbian feminist, having been invited to comment within the only panel at this conference where the input of Black feminists and lesbians is represented. What this says about the vision of this conference is sad, in a country where racism, sexism, and homophobia are inseparable. To read this program is to assume that lesbian and Black women have nothing to say about existentialism, the erotic, women's culture and silence, developing feminist theory, or heterosexuality and power. And what does it mean in personal and political terms when even the two Black women who did present here were literally found at the last hour? What does it mean when the tools of a racist patriarchy are used to examine the fruits of that same patriarchy? It means that only the most narrow perimeters of change are possible and allowable.

The absence of any consideration of lesbian consciousness or the consciousness of Third World women leaves a serious gap within this conference and within the papers presented here. For example, in a paper on material relationships between women, I was conscious of an either/or model of nurturing which totally dismissed my knowledge as a Black lesbian. In this paper there was no examination of mutuality between women, no systems of shared support, no interdependence as exists between lesbians and women-identified women. Yet it is only in the patriarchal model of nurturance that women "who attempt to emancipate themselves pay perhaps too high a price for the results," as this paper states.

For women, the need and desire to nurture each other is not pathological but redemptive, and it is within that knowledge that our real power is rediscovered. It is this real connection which is so feared by a patriarchal world. Only within a patriarchal structure is maternity the only social power open to women.

Interdependency between women is the way to a freedom which allows the *I* to *be*, not in order to be used, but in order to be creative. This is a difference between the passive *be* and the active *being*.

Advocating the mere tolerance of difference between women is the grossest reformism. It is a total denial of the creative function of difference in our lives. Difference must be not merely tolerated, but seen as a fund of necessary polarities between which our creativity can spark like a dialectic. Only then does the necessity for interdependency

---

*Comments at "The Personal and the Political Panel," Second Sex Conference, New York, September 29, 1979.

become unthreatening. Only within that interdependency of different strengths, acknowledged and equal, can the power to seek new ways of being in the world generate, as well as the courage and sustenance to act where there are no charters.

Within the interdependence of mutual (nondominant) differences lies that security which enables us to descend into the chaos of knowledge and return with true visions of our future, along with the concomitant power to effect those changes which can bring that future into being. Difference is that raw and powerful connection from which our personal power is forged.

As women, we have been taught either to ignore our differences, or to view them as causes for separation and suspicion rather than as forces for change. Without community there is no liberation, only the most vulnerable and temporary armistice between an individual and her oppression. But community must not mean a shedding of our differences, nor the pathetic pretense that these differences do not exist.

Those of us who stand outside the circle of this society's definition of acceptable women; those of us who have been forged in the crucibles of difference—those of us who are poor, who are lesbians, who are Black, who are older—know that *survival is not an academic skill*. It is learning how to stand alone, unpopular and sometimes reviled, and how to make common cause with those others identified as outside the structures in order to define and seek a world in which we can all flourish. It is learning how to take our differences and make them strengths. *For the master's tools will never dismantle the master's house*. They may allow us temporarily to beat him at his own game, but they will never enable us to bring about genuine change. And this fact is only threatening to those women who still define the master's house as their only source of support.

Poor women and women of Color know there is a difference between the daily manifestations of marital slavery and prostitution because it is our daughters who line 42nd Street. If white american feminist theory need not deal with the differences between us, and the resulting difference in our oppressions, then how do you deal with the fact that the women who clean your houses and tend your children while you attend conferences on feminist theory are, for the most part, poor women and women of Color? What is the theory behind racist feminism?

In a world of possibility for us all, our personal visions help lay the groundwork for political action. The failure of academic feminists to recognize difference as a crucial strength is a failure to reach beyond the first patriarchal lesson. In our world, divide and conquer must become define and empower.

Why weren't other women of Color found to participate in this conference? Why were two phone calls to me considered a consultation? Am I the only possible source of names of Black feminists? And although the Black panelist's paper ends on an important and powerful connection of love between women, what about interracial cooperation between feminists who don't love each other?

In academic feminist circles, the answer to these questions is often, "We did not know who to ask." But that is the same evasion of responsibility, the same cop-out, that keeps Black women's art out of women's exhibitions, Black women's work out of most feminist publications except for the occasional "Special Third World Women's Issue," and Black women's texts off your reading lists. But as Adrienne Rich pointed out in a recent talk, white feminists have educated themselves about such an enormous amount over the past ten years, how come you haven't also educated yourselves about Black women and the differences between us—white and Black—when it is key to our survival as a movement?

Women of today are still being called upon to stretch across the gap of male ignorance and to educate men as to our existence and our needs. This is an old and primary tool of all oppressors to keep the oppressed occupied with the master's concerns. Now we hear that it is the task of women of Color to educate white women—in the face of tremendous resistance—as to our existence, our differences, our relative roles in our joint survival. This is a diversion of energies and a tragic repetition of racist patriarchal thought.

Simone de Beauvoir once said: "It is in the knowledge of the genuine conditions of our lives that we must draw our strength to live and our reasons for acting."

Racism and homophobia are real conditions of all our lives in this place and time. *I urge each one of us here to reach down into that deep place of knowledge inside herself and touch that terror and loathing of any difference that lives there. See whose face it wears.* Then the personal as the political can begin to illuminate all our choices.

 5

Have We Got a Theory for You! Feminist Theory, Cultural Imperialism and the Demand for "The Woman's Voice"

MARIA C. LUGONES and ELIZABETH V. SPELMAN

MARIA LUGONES Argentina. 1944– . Feminist philosopher. Activist. Grassroots educator. Lives and works in the United States. "Playfulness, 'World Traveling' and Loving Perception." (1987), "Structure/Antistructure and Agency under Oppression" (1990).

ELIZABETH V. SPELMAN United States. 1945– . Philosopher. *Inessential Woman: Problems of Exclusion in Feminist Thought* (1988), *Fruits of Suffering: Framing Our Attention to Suffering* (1997), *Repair: The Impulse to Restore in a Fragile World* (2002).

PROLOGUE

(*In a Hispana voice*) A veces quisiera mezclar en una voz el sonido canyenge, tristón y urbano del porteñismo que llevo adentro con la cadencia apacible, serrana y llena de corage de la hispana nuevo mejicana. Contrastar y unir

el piolín y la cuerda
el traé y el pepéname
el camion y la troca
la lluvia y el llanto

Pero este querer se me va cuando veo que he confundido la solidaridad con la falta de diferencia. La solidaridad requiere el reconocer, comprender, respetar y amar lo que nos lleva a llorar en distintas cadencias. El imperialismo cultural desea lo contrario, por eso necesitamos muchas voces. Porque una sola voz nos mata a las dos.

No quiero hablar por ti sino contigo. Pero si no aprendo tus modos y tu los mios la conversación es sólo aparente. Y la apariencia se levanta como una barrera sin sentido entre las dos. Sin sentido y sin sentimiento. Por eso no me debes dejar que te dicte tu ser y no me dictes el mio. Porque entonces ya no dialogamos. El diálogo entre nosotras requiere dos voces y no una.

Tal vez un día jugaremos juntas y nos hablaremos no en una lengua universal sino que vos me hablarás mi voz y yo la tuya.

PREFACE

This paper is the result of our dialogue, of our thinking together about differences among women and how these differences are silenced. (Think, for example, of all the silences there are connected with the fact that this paper is in English—for that is a borrowed tongue for one of us.) In the process of our talking and writing together, we saw that the differences between us did not permit our speaking in one voice. For example, when we agreed we expressed the thought differently; there were some things that both of us thought were true but could not express as true of each of us; sometimes we could not say "we"; and sometimes one of us could not express the thought in the first person singular, and to express it in the third person would be to present an outsider's and not an insider's perspective. Thus the use of two voices is central both to the process of constructing this paper and to the substance of it. We are both the authors of this paper and not just sections of it but we write together without presupposing unity of expression or of experience. So when we speak in unison it means just that—there are two voices and not just one.

INTRODUCTION

(*In the voice of a white/Anglo woman who has been teaching and writing about feminist theory*) Feminism is, among other things, a response to the fact that women either have been left out of or included in demeaning and disfiguring ways in what has been an almost exclusively male account of the world. And so while part of what feminists want and demand for women is the right to move and to act in accordance with our own wills and not against them, another part is the desire and insistence that we give our *own* accounts of these movements and actions. For it matters to us what is said about us, who says it, and to whom it is said: having the opportunity to talk about one's life, to give an account of it, to interpret it, is integral to leading that life rather than being led through it; hence our distrust of the male monopoly over accounts of women's lives. To put the same point slightly differently, part of human life, human living, is talking about it, and we can be sure that being silenced in one's own account of one's life is a kind of amputation that signals oppression. Another reason for not divorcing life from the telling of it or talking about it is that as humans our experiences are deeply influenced by what is said about them, by ourselves or powerful (as opposed to significant) others. Indeed, the phenomenon of internalized oppression is only possible because this is so: one experiences her life in terms of the impoverished and degrading concepts others have found it convenient to use to describe her. We can't separate lives from the accounts given of them; the articulation of our experience is part of our experience.

Sometimes feminists have made even stronger claims about the importance of speaking about our own lives and the destructiveness of others presuming to speak about us or for us. First of all, the claim has been made that on the whole men's accounts of women's lives have been at best false, a function of ignorance, and at worst malicious lies, a function of a knowledgeable desire to exploit and oppress. Since it matters to us that falsehood and lies not be told about us, we demand, of those who have been responsible for those falsehoods and lies, or those who continue to transmit them, not just that we speak but that they learn to be able to hear us. It has also been claimed that talking about one's life, telling one's story, in the company of those doing the same (as in consciousness-raising sessions), is constitutive of feminist method.[1]

And so the demand that the woman's voice be heard and attended to has been made for a variety of reasons: not just so as to greatly increase the chances that true accounts of women's lives will be given, but also because the articulation of experience (in myriad ways) is among the hallmarks of a self-determining individual or community. There are not just epistemological but moral and political reasons for demanding that the woman's voice be heard, after centuries of androcentric din.

But what more exactly is the feminist demand that the woman's voice be heard? There are several crucial notes to make about it. First of all, the demand grows out of a complaint, and in order to understand the scope and focus of the demand we have to look at the scope and focus of the complaint. The complaint does not specify *which* women have been silenced, and in one way this is appropriate to the conditions it is a complaint about: virtually no women have had a voice, whatever their race, class, ethnicity, religion, sexual alliance, whatever place and period in history they lived. And if it is as women that women have been silenced, then of course the demand must be that women as women have a voice. But in another way the complaint is very misleading, insofar as it suggests that it is women as women who have been silenced, and that whether a woman is rich or poor, Black, brown or white, etc., is irrelevant to what it means for her to be a woman. For the demand thus simply made ignores at least two related points: (1) it is only possible for a woman who does not feel highly vulnerable with respect to other parts of her identity, e.g., race, class, ethnicity, religion, sexual alliance, etc., to conceive of her voice simply or essentially as a "woman's voice"; (2) just because not all women are equally vulnerable with respect to race, class, etc., some women's voices are more likely to be heard than others by those who have heretofore been giving—or silencing—the accounts of women's lives. For all these reasons, the women's voices most likely to come forth and the women's voices most likely to be heard are, in the United States anyway, those of white, middle-class, heterosexual Christian (or anyway not self-identified non-Christian) women. Indeed, many Hispanas, Black women, Jewish women—to name a few groups—have felt it an invitation to silence rather than speech to be requested—if they are requested at all—to speak about being "women" (with the plain wrapper—as if there were one) in distinction from speaking about being Hispana, Black, Jewish, working-class, etc., women.

The demand that the "woman's voice" be heard, and the search for the "woman's voice" as central to feminist methodology, reflects nascent feminist theory. It reflects nascent empirical theory insofar as it presupposes that the silencing of women is systematic, shows up in regular, patterned ways, and that there are discoverable causes of this widespread observable phenomenon; the demand reflects nascent political theory insofar as it presupposes that the silencing of women reveals a systematic pattern of power and authority; and it reflects nascent moral theory insofar as it presupposes that the silencing is unjust and that there are particular ways of remedying this injustice. Indeed, whatever else we know feminism to include—e.g., concrete direct political action—theorizing is integral to it: theories about the nature of oppression, the causes of it, the relation of the oppression of women to other forms of oppression. And certainly the concept of the woman's voice is itself a theoretical concept, in the sense that it presupposes a theory according to which our identities as human beings are actually compound identities, a kind of fusion or confusion of our otherwise separate identities as women or men, as Black or brown or white, etc. That is no less a theoretical stance than Plato's division of the person into soul and body or Aristotle's parceling of the soul into various functions.

The demand that the "woman's voice" be heard also invites some further directions in the exploration of women's lives and discourages or excludes others. For reasons mentioned above, systematic, sustained reflection on being a woman—the kind of contemplation that "doing theory" requires—is most likely to be done by women who vis-à-vis other women enjoy a certain amount of political, social and economic privilege because of their skin color, class membership, ethnic identity. There is a relationship between the content of our contemplation and the fact that we have the time to engage in it at some length—otherwise we shall have to say that it is a mere accident of history that white middle-class women in the United States have in the main developed "feminist theory" (as opposed to "Black feminist theory," "Chicana feminist theory," etc.) and that so much of the theory has failed to be relevant to the lives of women who are not white or middle class. Feminist theory—of all kinds—is to be based on, or anyway touch base with, the variety of real-life stories women provide about themselves. But in fact, because, among other things, of the structural political and social and economic inequalities among women, the tail has been wagging the dog: feminist theory has not for the most part arisen out of a medley of women's voices; instead, the theory has arisen out of the voices, the experiences, of a fairly small handful of women, and if other women's voices do not sing in harmony with the theory, they aren't counted as women's voices—rather, they are the voices of the woman as Hispana, Black, Jew, etc. There is another sense in which the tail is wagging the dog, too: it is presumed to be the case that those who do the theory know more about those who are theorized than vice versa; hence it ought to be the case that if it is white/Anglo women who write for and about all other women, the white/Anglo women must know more about all other women than other women know about them. But in fact just in order to survive, brown and Black women have to know a lot more about white/Anglo women—not through the sustained contemplation theory requires, but through the sharp observation stark exigency demands.

(In an Hispana voice) I think it necessary to explain why in so many cases when women of color appear in front of white/Anglo women to talk about feminism and women of color, we mainly raise a complaint: the complaint of exclusion, of silencing, of being included in a universe we have not chosen. We usually raise the complaint with a certain amount of disguised or undisguised anger. I can only attempt to explain this phenomenon from a Hispanic viewpoint and a fairly narrow one at that: the viewpoint of an Argentinian woman who has lived in the U.S. for 16 years, who has attempted to come to terms with the devaluation of things Hispanic and Hispanic people in "America" and who is most familiar with Hispano life in the Southwest of the U.S. I am quite unfamiliar with daily Hispano life in the urban centers, though not with some of the themes and some of the salient experiences of urban Hispano life.

When I say "we,"[2] I am referring to Hispanas. I am accustomed to use the "we" in this way. I am also pained by the tenuousness of this "we" given that I am not a native of the United States. Through the years I have come to be recognized and I have come to recognize myself more and more firmly as part of this "we." I also have a profound yearning for this firmness since I am a displaced person and I am conscious of not being of and I am unwilling to make myself of—even if this were possible—the white/Anglo community.

When I say "you" I mean not the non-Hispanic but the white/Anglo women that I address. "We" and "you" do not capture my relation to other non-white women. The complexity of that relation is not addressed here, but it is vivid to me as I write down my thoughts on the subject at hand.

I see two related reasons for our complaint-full discourse with white/Anglo women. Both of these reasons plague our world, they contaminate it through and through. It takes some hardening of oneself, some self-acceptance of our own anger to face them, for to face them is to decide that maybe we can change our situation in self-constructive ways and we know fully well that the possibilities are minimal. We know that we cannot rest from facing these reasons, that the tenderness towards others in us undermines our possibilities, that we have to fight our own niceness because it clouds our minds and hearts. Yet we know that a thoroughgoing hardening would dehumanize us. So, we have to walk through our days in a peculiarly fragile psychic state, one that we have to struggle to maintain, one that we do not often succeed in maintaining.

We and you do not talk the same language. When we talk to you we use your language: the language of your experience and of your theories. We try to use it to communicate our world of experience. But since your language and your theories are inadequate in expressing our experiences, we only succeed in communicating our experience of exclusion. We cannot talk to you in our language because you do not understand it. So the brute facts that we understand your language and that the place where most theorizing about women is taking place is your place both combine to require that we either use your language and distort our experience not just in the speaking about it, but in the living of it, or that we remain silent. Complaining about exclusion is a way of remaining silent.

You are ill at ease in our world. You are ill at ease in our world in a very different way than we are ill at ease in yours. You are not of our world and again, you are not of our world in a very different way than we are not of yours. In the intimacy of a personal relationship we appear to you many times to be wholly there, to have broken through or to have dissipated the barriers that separate us because you are Anglo and we are raza. When we let go of the psychic state that I referred to above in the direction of sympathy, we appear to ourselves equally whole in your presence but our intimacy is thoroughly incomplete. When we are in your world many times you remake us in your own image, although sometimes you clearly and explicitly acknowledge that we are not wholly there in our being with you. When we are in your world we ourselves feel the discomfort of having our own being Hispanas disfigured or not understood. And yet, we have had to be in your world and learn its ways. We have to participate in it, make a living in it, live in it, be mistreated in it, be ignored in it, and, rarely, be appreciated in it. In learning to do these things or in learning to suffer them or in learning to enjoy what is to be enjoyed or in learning to understand your conception of us, we have had to learn your culture and thus your language and self-conceptions. But there is nothing that necessitates that you understand our world: understand, that is, not as an observer understands things, but as a participant, as someone who has a stake in them understands them. So your being ill at ease in our world lacks the features of our being ill at ease in yours precisely because you can leave and you can always tell yourselves that you will be soon out of there and because the wholeness of your selves is never touched by us, we have no tendency to remake you in our image.

But you theorize about women and we are women, so you understand yourselves to be theorizing about us, and we understand you to be theorizing about us. Yet none of the feminist theories developed so far seems to me to help Hispanas in the articulation of our experience. We have a sense that in using them we are distorting our experiences. Most Hispanas cannot even understand the language used in these theories—and only in some cases the reason is that the Hispana cannot understand English. We do not recognize ourselves in these theories. They create in us a schizophrenic split between our concern for ourselves as women and ourselves as Hispanas, one that we do not feel otherwise. Thus they seem to us to force us to assimilate to some version of Anglo culture, however revised that version may be. They seem to ask that we leave our communities or that we become alienated so completely in them that we feel hollow. When we see that you feel alienated in your own communities, this confuses us because we think that maybe every feminist has to suffer this alienation. But we see that recognition of your alienation leads many of you to be empowered into the remaking of your culture, while we are paralyzed into a state of displacement with no place to go.

So I think that we need to think carefully about the relation between the articulation of our own experience, the interpretation of our own experience, and theory making by us and other non-Hispanic women about themselves and other "women."

The only motive that makes sense to me for your joining us in this investigation is the motive of friendship, out of friendship. A non-imperialist feminism requires that you make a real space for our articulating, interpreting, theorizing and reflecting about the connections among them—a real space must be a non-coerced space—and/or that you follow us into our world out of friendship. I see the "out of friendship" as the only sensical motivation for this following because the task at hand for you is one of extraordinary difficulty. It requires that you be willing to devote a great part of your life to it and that you be willing to suffer alientation and self-disruption. Self-interest has been proposed as a possible motive for entering this task. But self-interest does not seem to me to be a realistic motive, since whatever the benefits you may accrue from such a journey, they cannot be concrete enough for you at this time and they may not be worth your while. I do not think that you have any obligation to understand us. You do have an obligation to abandon your imperialism, your universal claims, your reduction of us to your selves, simply because they seriously harm us.

I think that the fact that we are so ill at ease with your theorizing in the ways indicated above does indicate that there is something wrong with these theories. But what is it that is wrong? Is it simply that the theories are flawed if meant to be universal but accurate so long as they are confined to your particular group(s)? Is it that the theories are not really flawed but need to be translated? Can they be translated? Is it something about the process of theorizing that is flawed? How do the two reasons for our complaint-full discourse affect the validity of your theories? Where do *we* begin? To what extent are our experience and its articulation affected by our being a colonized people, and thus by your culture, theories, and conceptions? Should we theorize in community and thus as part of community life and outside the academy and other intellectual circles? What is the point of making theory? Is theory making a good thing for us to do at this time? When are we making theory and when are we just articulating and/or interpreting our experiences?

SOME QUESTIONABLE ASSUMPTIONS ABOUT FEMINIST THEORIZING

(Unproblematically in Vicky's and Maria's voice)
Feminist theories aren't just about what happens to the female population in any given society or across all societies; they are about the meaning of those experiences in the lives of women. They are about beings who give their own accounts of what is happening to them or of what they are doing, who have culturally constructed ways of reflecting on their lives. But how can the theorizer get at the meaning of those experiences? What should the relation be between a woman's own account of her experiences and the theorizer's account of it?

Let us describe two different ways of arriving at an account of another woman's experience. It is one thing for both me and you to observe you and come up with our different accounts of what you are doing; it is quite another for me to observe myself and others much like me culturally and in other ways and to develop an account of myself and then use that account to give an account of you. In the first case you are the "insider" and I am the "outsider." When the outsider makes clear that she is an outsider and that this is an outsider's account of your behavior, there is a touch of honesty about what she is doing. Most of the time the "interpretation by an outsider" is left understood and most of the time the distance of outsidedness is understood to mark objectivity in the interpretation. But why is the outsider as an outsider interpreting your behavior? Is she doing it so that you can understand how she sees you? Is she doing it so that other outsiders will understand how you *are*? Is she doing it so that *you* will understand how you are? It would seem that if the outsider wants you to understand how she sees you and you have given your account of how you see yourself to her, there is a possibility of genuine dialogue between the two. It also seems that the lack of reciprocity could bar genuine dialogue. For why should you engage in such a one-sided dialogue? As soon as we ask this question, a host of other conditions for the possibility of a genuine dialogue between us arise: conditions having to do with your position relative to me in the various social, political, and economic structures in which we might come across each other or in which you may run face to face with my account of you and my use of your account of yourself. Is this kind of dialogue necessary for me to get at the meaning of your experiences? That is, is this kind of dialogue necessary for feminist theorizing that is not seriously flawed?

Obviously the most dangerous of the understanding of what I—an outsider—am doing in giving an account of your experience is the one that describes what I'm doing as giving an account of who and how you are, whether it be given to you or to other outsiders. Why should you or anyone else believe me; that is, why should you or anyone else believe that you are as I say you are? Could I be right? What conditions would have to obtain for my being right? That many women are put in the position of not knowing whether or not to believe outsiders' accounts of their experiences is clear. The pressures to believe these accounts are enormous even when the woman in question does not see herself in the account. She is thus led to doubt her own judgment and to doubt all interpretation of her experience. This leads her to experience her life differently. Since the consequences of outsiders' accounts can be so significant, it is crucial that we reflect on whether or not this type of account can ever be right and if so, under what conditions.

The last point leads us to the second way of arriving at an account of another woman's experience, viz., the case in which I observe myself and others like me culturally and in other ways and use that account to give an account of you. In doing this, I remake you in my own image. Feminist theorizing approaches this remaking insofar as it depends on the concept of women as women. For it has not arrived at this concept as a consequence of dialogue with many women who are culturally different, or by any other kind of investigation of cultural differences which may include different conceptions of what it is to be a woman: it has simply presupposed this concept.

Our suggestion in this paper, and at this time it is no more than a suggestion, is that only when genuine and reciprocal dialogue takes place between "outsiders" and "insiders" can we trust the outsider's account. At first sight it may appear that the insider/outsider distinction disappears in the dialogue, but it is important to notice that all that happens is that we are now both outsider and insider with respect to each other. The dialogue puts us both in position to give a better account of each other's and our own experience. Here we should again note that white/Anglo women are much less prepared for this dialogue with women of color than women of color are for dialogue with them in that women of color have had to learn white/Anglo ways, self-conceptions, and conceptions of them.

But both the possibility and the desirability of this dialogue are very much in question. We need to think about the possible motivations for engaging in this dialogue, whether doing theory jointly would be a good thing, in what ways and for whom, and whether doing theory is in itself a good thing at this time for women of color or white/Anglo women. In motivating the last question let us remember the hierarchical distinctions between theorizers and those theorized about and between theorizers and doers. These distinctions are endorsed by the same views and institutions which endorse and support hierarchical distinctions between men/women, master race/inferior race, intellectuals/manual workers. Of what use is the activity of theorizing to those of us who are women of color engaged day in and day out in the task of empowering women and men of color face to face with them? Should we be articulating and interpreting their experience for them with the aid of theories? Whose theories?

WAYS OF TALKING OR BEING TALKED ABOUT THAT ARE HELPFUL, ILLUMINATING, EMPOWERING, RESPECTFUL

(Unproblematically in Maria's and Vicky's voice) Feminists have been quite diligent about pointing out ways in which empirical, philosophical, and moral theories have been androcentric. They have thought it crucial to ask, with respect to such theories: who makes them? for whom do they make them? about what or whom are the theories? why? how are theories tested? what are the criteria for such tests and where did the criteria come from? Without posing such questions and trying to answer them, we'd never have been able to begin to mount evidence for our claims that particular theories are androcentric, sexist, biased, paternalistic, etc. Certain philosophers have become fond of—indeed, have made their careers on—pointing out that characterizing a statement as true or false is only one of many ways possible of characterizing it; it might also be, oh, rude, funny, disarming, etc.; it may be intended to soothe or to hurt; or it may have the effect, intended or not, of soothing or hurting. Similarly, theories appear to be the kinds of things that are true or false; but they also are the kinds of things that can be, e.g., useless, arrogant, disrespectful, ignorant, ethnocentric, imperialistic. The immediate point is that feminist theory is no less immune to such characterizations than, say, Plato's political theory, or Freud's theory of female psychosexual development. Of course this is not to say that if feminist theory manages to be respectful or helpful it will follow that it must be true. But if, say, an empirical theory is purported to be about "women" and in fact is only about certain women, it is certainly false, probably ethnocentric, and of dubious usefulness except to those whose position in the world it strengthens (and theories, as we know, don't have to be true in order to be used to strengthen people's positions in the world).

Many reasons can be and have been given for the production of accounts of people's lives that plainly have nothing to do with illuminating those lives for the benefit of those living them. It is likely that both the method of investigation and the content of many accounts would be different if illuminating the lives of the people the accounts are about were the aim of the studies. Though we cannot say ahead of time how feminist theory making would be different if all (or many more) of those people it is meant to be about were more intimately part of the theory-making process, we do suggest some specific ways being talked about can be helpful:

1. The theory or account can be helpful if it enables one to see how parts of one's life fit together, for example, to see connections among parts of one's life one hasn't seen before. No account can do this if it doesn't get the parts right to begin with, and this cannot happen if the concepts used to described a life are utterly foreign.

2. A useful theory will help one locate oneself concretely in the world, rather than add to the mystification of the world and one's location in it. New concepts may be of significance here, but they will not be useful if there is no way they can be translated into already existing concepts. Suppose a theory locates you in the home, because you are a woman, but you know full well that is not where you spend most of your time? Or suppose you can't locate yourself easily in any particular class as defined by some version of Marxist theory?

3. A theory or account not only ought to accurately locate one in the world but also enable one to think about the extent to which one is responsible or not for being in that location. Otherwise, for those whose location is as oppressed peoples, it usually occurs that the oppressed have no way to see themselves as in any way self-determining, as having any sense of being worthwhile or having grounds for pride, and paradoxically at the same time feeling at fault for the position they are in. A useful theory will help people work out just what is and is not due to themselves and their own activities as opposed to those who have power over them.

It may seem odd to make these criteria of a useful theory, if the usefulness is not to be at odds with the issue of the truth of the theory; for the focus on feeling worthwhile or having pride seems to rule out the possibility that the truth might just be that such-and-such a group of people has been under the control of others for centuries and that the only explanation of that is that they are worthless and weak people, and will never be able to change that. Feminist theorizing seems implicity if not explicitly committed to the moral view that women *are* worthwhile beings, and the metaphysical theory that we are beings capable of bringing about a change in our situations. Does this mean feminist theory is "biased"? Not any more than any other theory, e.g., psychoanalytic theory. What is odd here is not the feminist presupposition that women are worthwhile but rather that feminist theory (and other theory) often has the effect of empowering one group and demoralizing another.

Aspects of feminist theory are as unabashedly value-laden as other political and moral theories. It is not just an examination of women's positions, for it includes, indeed begins with, moral and political judgments about the injustice (or, where relevant, justice) of them. This means that there are implicit or explicit judgments also about what kinds of changes constitute a better or worse situation for women.

4.　In this connection a theory that is useful will provide criteria for change and make suggestions for modes of resistance that don't merely reflect the situation and values of the theorizer. A theory that is respectful of those about whom it is a theory will not assume that changes that are perceived as making life better for some women are changes that will make, and will be perceived as making, life better for other women. This is *not* to say that if some women do not find a situation oppressive, other women ought never to suggest to the contrary that there might be very good reasons to think that the situation nevertheless *is* oppressive. But it is to say that, e.g., the prescription that life for women will be better when we're in the workforce rather than at home, when we are completely free of religious beliefs with patriarchal origins, when we live in complete separation from men, etc., are seen as slaps in the face to women whose life would be better if they could spend more time at home, whose identity is inseparable from their religious beliefs and cultural practices (which is not to say those beliefs and practices are to remain completely uncriticized and unchanged), who have ties to

men—whether erotic or not—such that to have them severed in the name of some vision of what is "better" is, at that time and for those women, absurd. Our visions of what is better are always informed by our perception of what is bad about our present situation. Surely we've learned enough from the history of clumsy missionaries, and the white suffragists of the 19th century (who couldn't imagine why Black women "couldn't see" how crucial getting the vote for "women" was) to know that we can clobber people to destruction with our visions, our versions, of what is better. *But:* this does not mean women are not to offer supportive and tentative criticism of one another. But there is a very important difference between (a) developing ideas together, in a "pre-theoretical" stage, engaged as equals in joint enquiry, and (b) one group developing, on the basis of their own experience, a set of criteria for good change for women—and then reluctantly making revisions in the criteria at the insistence of women to whom such criteria seem ethnocentric and arrogant. The deck is stacked when one group takes it upon itself to develop the theory and then have others criticize it. Categories are quick to congeal, and the experiences of women whose lives do not fit the categories will appear as anomalous when in fact the theory should have grown out of them as much as others from the beginning. This, of course, is why any organization or conference having to do with "women"—with no qualification—that seriously does not want to be "solipsistic" will from the beginning be multicultural or state the appropriate qualifications. How we think and what we think about does depend in large part on who is there—not to mention who is expected or encouraged to speak. (Recall the boys in the *Symposium* sending the flute girls out.) Conversations and criticism take place in particular circumstances. Turf matters. So does the fact of who if anyone already has set up the terms of the conversations.

5.　Theory cannot be useful to anyone interested in resistance and change unless there is reason to believe that knowing what a theory means and believing it to be true have some connection to resistance and change. As we make theory and offer it up to others, what do we assume is the connection between theory and consciousness? Do we expect others to read theory, understand it, believe it, and have their consciousnesses and lives thereby transformed? If we really want theory to make a difference to people's lives, how ought we to present it? Do we think people come to consciousness by reading? only by reading? Speaking to people through theory (orally or in writing) is a *very* specific context-dependent activity. That is, theory makers and their methods and concepts constitute a community of people and of shared meanings. Their language can be just as opaque and foreign to those not in the community as a foreign tongue or dialect.[3] Why do we engage in *this* activity and what effect do we think it ought to have? As Helen Longino has asked: "Is 'doing theory' just a bonding ritual for academic or educationally privileged feminist women?" Again, whom does our theory making serve?

SOME SUGGESTIONS ABOUT HOW TO DO THEORY THAT IS NOT IMPERIALISTIC, ETHNOCENTRIC, DISRESPECTFUL

(Problematically in the voice of a woman of color)
What are the things we need to know about others, and about ourselves, in order to speak intelligently, intelligibly, sensitively, and helpfully about their lives? We can show respect, or lack of it, in writing theoretically about others no less than in talking directly with them. This is not to say that here we have a well-worked-out concept of respect, but only to suggest that together all of us consider what it would mean to theorize in a respectful way.

When we speak, write, and publish our theories, to whom do we think we are accountable? Are the concerns we have in being accountable to "the profession" at odds with the concerns we have in being accountable to those about whom we theorize? Do commitments to "the profession," method, getting something published, getting tenure, lead us to talk and act in ways at odds with what we ourselves (let alone others) would regard as ordinary, decent behavior? To what extent do we presuppose that really understanding another person or culture requires our behaving in ways that are disrespectful, even violent? That is, to what extent do we presuppose that getting and/or publishing the requisite information requires or may require disregarding the wishes of others, lying to them, wresting

information from them against their wills? Why and how do we think theorizing about others provides *understanding* of them? Is there any sense in which theorizing about others is a short-cut to understanding them?

Finally, if we think doing theory is an important activity, and we think that some conditions lead to better theorizing than others, what are we going to do about creating those conditions? If we think it not just desirable but necessary for women of different racial and ethnic identities to create feminist theory jointly, how shall that be arranged for? It may be the case that at this particular point we ought not even try to do that—that feminist theory by and for Hispanas needs to be done separately from feminist theory by and for Black women, white women, etc. But it must be recognized that white/Anglo women have more power and privilege than Hispanas, Black women, etc., and at the very least they can use such advantage to provide space and time for other women to speak (with the above caveats about implicit restrictions on what counts as "the woman's voice"). And once again it is important to remember that the power of white/Anglo women vis-à-vis Hispanas and Black women is in inverse proportion to their working knowledge of each other.

This asymmetry is a crucial fact about the background of possible relationships between white women and women of color, whether as political co-workers, professional colleagues, or friends.

If white/Anglo women and women of color are to do theory jointly, in helpful, respectful, illuminating and empowering ways, the task ahead of white/Anglo women, because of this asymmetry, is a very hard task. The task is a very complex one. In part, to make an analogy, the task can be compared to learning a text without the aid of teachers. We all know the lack of contact felt when we want to discuss a particular issue that requires knowledge of a text with someone who does not know the text at all. Or the discomfort and impatience that arise in us when we are discussing an issue that presupposes a text and someone walks into the conversation who does not know the text. That person is either left out or will impose herself on us and either try to engage in the discussion or try to change the subject. Women of color are put in these situations by white/Anglo women and men constantly. Now imagine yourself simply left out but wanting to do theory with us. The first thing to recognize and accept is that you disturb our own dialogues by putting yourself in the left-out position and not leaving us in some meaningful sense to ourselves.

You must also recognize and accept that you must learn the text. But the text is an extraordinarily complex one: viz., our many different cultures. You are asking us to make ourselves more vulnerable to you than we already are before we have any reason to trust that you will not take advantage of this vulnerability. So you need to learn to become unintrusive, unimportant, patient to the point of tears, while at the same time open to learning any possible lessons. You will also have to come to terms with the sense of alienation, of not belonging, of having your world thoroughly disrupted, having it criticized and scrutinized from the point of view of those who have been harmed by it, having important concepts central to it dismissed, being viewed with mistrust, being seen as of no consequence except as an object of mistrust.

Why would any white/Anglo woman engage in this task? Out of self-interest? What in engaging in this task would be, not just in her interest, but perceived as such by her before the task is completed or well under way? Why should we want you to come into our world out of self-interest? Two points need to be made here. The task as described could be entered into with the intention of finding out as much as possible about us so as to better dominate us. The person engaged in this task would act as a spy. The motivation is not unfamiliar to us. We have heard it said that now that Third World countries are more powerful as a bloc, westerners need to learn more about them, that it is in their self-interest to do so. Obviously there is no reason why people of color should welcome white/Anglo women into their world for the carrying out of this intention. It is also obvious that white/Anglo feminists should not engage in this task under this description since the task under this description would not lead to joint theorizing of the desired sort: respectful, illuminating, helpful, and empowering. It would be helpful and empowering only in a one-sided way.

Self-interest is also mentioned as a possible motive in another way. White/Anglo women sometimes say that the task of understanding women of color would entail self-growth or self-expansion. If the task is conceived as described here, then one should doubt that growth or expansion will be the result. The severe self-disruption that the task entails should place a doubt in anyone who takes the task seriously about her possibilities of coming out of the task whole, with a self that is not as fragile as the selves of those who have been the victims of racism. But also, why should women of color embrace white/Anglo women's self-betterment without reciprocity? At this time women of color cannot afford this generous affirmation of white/Anglo women.

Another possible motive for engaging in this task is the motive of duty, "out of obligation," because white/Anglos have done people of color wrong. Here again two considerations: coming into Hispano, Black, Native American worlds out of obligation puts white/Anglos in a morally self-righteous position that is inappropriate. You are active, we are passive. We become the vehicles of your own redemption. Secondly, we couldn't want you to come into our worlds "out of obligation." That is like wanting someone to make love to you out of obligation. So, whether or not you have an obligation to do this (and we would deny that you do), or whether this task could even be done out of obligation, this is an inappropriate motive.

Out of obligation you should stay out of our way, respect us and our distance, and forgo the use of whatever power you have over us—for example, the power to use your language in our meetings, the power to overwhelm us with your education, the power to intrude in our communities in order to research us and to record the supposed dying of our cultures, the power to engrain in us a sense that we are members of dying cultures and are doomed to assimilate, the power to keep us in a defensive posture with respect to our own cultures.

So the motive of friendship remains as both the only appropriate and understandable motive for white/Anglo feminists engaging in the task as described above. If you enter the task out of friendship with us, then you will be moved to attain the appropriate reciprocity of care for your and our well-being as whole beings, you will have a stake in us and in our world, you will be moved to satisfy the need for reciprocity of understanding that will enable you to follow us in our experiences as we are able to follow you in yours.

We are not suggesting that if the learning of the text is to be done out of friendship, you must enter into a friendship with a whole community and for the purpose of making theory. In order to understand what it is that we are suggesting, it is important to remember that during the description of her experience of exclusion, the Hispana voice said that Hispanas experience the intimacy of friendship with white/Anglo women friends as thoroughly incomplete. It is not until this fact is acknowledged by our white/Anglo women friends and felt as a profound lack in our experience of each other that white/Anglo women can begin to see us. Seeing us in our communities will make clear and concrete to you how incomplete we really are in our relationships with you. It is this beginning that forms the proper background for the yearning to understand the text of our cultures that can lead to joint theory making.

Thus, the suggestion made here is that if white/Anglo women are to understand our voices, they must understand our communities and us in them. Again, this is not to suggest that you set out to make friends with our communities, though you may become friends with some of the members, nor is it to suggest that you should try to befriend us for the purpose of making theory with us. The latter would be a perversion of friendship. Rather, from within friendship you may be moved by friendship to undergo the very difficult task of understanding the text of our cultures by understanding our lives in our communities. This learning calls for circumspection, for questioning of yourselves and your roles in your own culture. It necessitates a striving to understand while in the comfortable position of not having an official calling card (as "scientific" observers of our communities have); it demands recognition that you do not have the authority of knowledge; it requires coming to the task without ready-made theories to frame our lives. This learning is then extremely hard because it requires openness (including openness to severe criticism of the white/Anglo world), sensitivity, concentration, self-questioning, circumspection.

It should be clear that it does not consist in a passive immersion in our cultures, but in a striving to understand what it is that our voices are saying. Only then can we engage in a mutual dialogue that does not reduce each one of us to an instance of the abstraction called "woman."

[1983]

NOTES

1. For a recent example, see MacKinnon, Catharine, 1982. Feminism, Marxism, Method and the State: An Agenda for Theory. *Signs* 7 (3): 515–544.
2. I must note that when I think this "we," I think it in Spanish—and in Spanish this "we" is gendered, "nosotras." I also use "nosotros" lovingly and with ease and in it I include all members of "La raza cosmica" (Spanish-speaking people of the Americas, la gente de colores: people of many colors). In the U.S., I use "we" contextually with varying degrees of discomfort: "we" in the house, "we" in the department, "we" in the classroom, "we" in the meeting. The discomfort springs from the sense of community in the "we" and the varying degrees of lack of community in the context in which the "we" is used.
3. See Bernstein, Basil. 1972. "Social Class, Language, and Socialization." In Giglioli, Pier Paolo, ed., *Language and Social Context*, pp. 157–178. Penguin, Harmondsworth, Middlesex. Bernstein would probably, and we think wrongly, insist that theoretical terms and statements have meanings *not* "tied to a local relationship and to a local social structure," unlike the vocabulary of, e.g., working-class children.

 6

Theory as Liberatory Practice

bell hooks

bell hooks United States. 1952–   . Feminist scholar. Writer. *Ain't I a Woman* (1981), *Feminist Theory: From Margin to Center* (1984), *Black Looks: Race and Representation* (1992), *Killing Rage: Ending Racism* (1995), *Bone Black: Memories of Girlhood* (1996).

I came to theory because I was hurting—the pain within me was so intense that I could not go on living. I came to theory desperate, wanting to comprehend—to grasp what was happening around and within me. Most importantly, I wanted to make the hurt go away. I saw in theory then a location for healing.

I came to theory young, when I was still a child. In *The Significance of Theory* Terry Eagleton says:

Children make the best theorists, since they have not yet been educated into accepting our routine social practices as "natural," and so insist on posing to those practices the most embarrassingly general and fundamental questions, regarding them with a wondering estrangement which we adults have long forgotten. Since they do not yet grasp our social practices as inevitable, they do not see why we might not do things differently.

Whenever I tried in childhood to compel folks around me to do things differently, to look at the world differently, using theory as intervention, as a way to challenge the status quo, I was punished. I remember trying to explain at a very young age to Mama why I thought it was highly inappropriate for Daddy, this man who hardly spoke to me, to have the right to discipline me, to punish me physically with whippings. Her response was to suggest I was losing my mind and in need of more frequent punishment.

Imagine if you will this young black couple struggling first and foremost to realize the patriarchal norm (that is of the woman staying home, taking care of the household and children while the man worked) even though such an arrangement meant that economically, they would always be living with less. Try to imagine what it must have been like for them, each of them working hard all day, struggling to maintain a family of seven children, then having to cope with one bright-eyed child relentlessly questioning, daring to challenge male authority, rebelling against the very patriarchal norm they were trying so hard to institutionalize.

It must have seemed to them that some monster had appeared in their midst in the shape and body of a child—a demonic little figure who threatened to subvert and undermine all that they were seeking to build. No wonder then that their response was to repress, contain, punish. No wonder that Mama would say to me, now and then, exasperated, frustrated, "I don't know where I got you from, but I sure wish I could give you back."

Imagine then, if you will, my childhood pain. I did not feel truly connected to these strange people, to these familial folks who could not only fail to grasp my worldview but who just simply did not want to hear it. As a child, I didn't know where I had come from. And when I was not desperately seeking to belong to this family community that never seemed to accept or want me, I was desperately trying to discover the place of my belonging. I was desperately trying to find my way home. How I envied Dorothy her journey in *The Wizard of Oz*, that she could travel to her worst fears and nightmares only to find at the end that "there is no place like home." Living in childhood without a sense of home, I found a place of sanctuary in "theorizing," in making sense out of what was happening. I found a place where I could imagine possible futures, a place where life could be lived differently. This "lived" experience of critical thinking, of reflection and analysis, became a place where I worked at explaining the hurt and making it go away. Fundamentally, I learned from this experience that theory could be a healing place.

Psychoanalyst Alice Miller lets you know in her introduction to the book *Prisoners of Childhood* that it was her own personal struggle to recover from the wounds of childhood that led her to rethink and theorize anew prevailing social and critical thought about the meaning of childhood pain, of child abuse. In her adult life, through her practice, she experienced theory as a healing place. Significantly, she had to imagine herself in the space of childhood, to look again from that perspective, to remember "crucial information, answers to questions which had gone unanswered throughout [her] study of philosophy and psychoanalysis." When our lived experience of theorizing is fundamentally linked to processes of self-recovery, of collective liberation, no gap exists between theory and practice. Indeed, what such experience makes more evident is the bond between the two—that ultimately reciprocal process wherein one enables the other.

Theory is not inherently healing, liberatory, or revolutionary. It fulfills this function only when we ask that it do so and direct our theorizing towards this end. When I was a child, I certainly did not describe the processes of thought and critique I engaged in as "theorizing." Yet, as I suggested in *Feminist Theory: From Margin to Center,* the possession of a term does not bring a process or practice into being; concurrently one may practice theorizing without ever knowing/possessing the term, just as we can live and act in feminist resistance without ever using the word "feminism."

Often individuals who employ certain terms freely—terms like "theory" or "feminism"—are not necessarily practitioners whose habits of being and living most embody the action, the practice of theorizing or engaging in feminist struggle. Indeed, the privileged act of naming often affords those in power access to modes of communication and enables them to project an interpretation, a definition, a description of their work and actions, that may not be accurate, that may obscure what is really taking place. Katie King's essay "Producing Sex, Theory, and Culture: Gay/Straight Re-Mappings in Contemporary Feminism" (in *Conflicts in Feminism*) offers a very useful discussion of the way in which academic production of feminist theory formulated in hierarchical settings often enables women, particularly white women, with high status and visibility to draw upon the works of feminist scholars who may have less or no status, less or no visibility, without giving recognition to these sources. King discusses the way work is appropriated and the way readers will often attribute ideas to a well-known scholar/feminist thinker, even if that individual has cited in her work that she is building on ideas gleaned from less well-known sources. Focusing particularly on the work of Chicana theorist Chela Sandoval, King states, "Sandoval has been published only sporadically and eccentrically, yet her circulating unpublished manuscripts are much more cited and often appropriated, even while the range of her influence is rarely understood." Though King risks positioning herself in a caretaker role as she rhetorically assumes the posture of feminist authority, determining the range and scope of Sandoval's influence, the critical point she works to emphasize is that the production of feminist theory is complex, that it is an individual practice less often than we think and usually emerges from engagement with collective sources. Echoing feminist theorists, especially women of color who have worked consistently to resist the construction of restrictive critical boundaries within feminist thought, King encourages us to have an expansive perspective on the theorizing process.

Critical reflection on contemporary production of feminist theory makes it apparent that the shift from early conceptualizations of feminist theory (which insisted that it was most vital when it encouraged and enabled feminist practice) begins to occur or at least becomes most obvious with the segregation and institutionalization of the feminist theorizing process in the academy, with the privileging of written feminist thought/theory over oral narratives. Concurrently, the efforts of black women and women of color to challenge and deconstruct the category "woman"—the insistence on recognition that gender is not the sole factor determining constructions of femaleness—was a critical intervention, one which led to a profound revolution in feminist thought and truly interrogated and disrupted the hegemonic feminist theory produced primarily by academic women, most of whom were white.

In the wake of this disruption, the assault on white supremacy made manifest in alliances between white women academics and white male peers seems to have been formed and nurtured around common efforts to formulate and impose standards of critical evaluation that would be used to define what is theoretical and what is not. These standards often led to appropriation and/or devaluation of work that did not "fit," that was suddenly deemed not theoretical—or not theoretical enough. In some circles, there seems to be a direct connection between white feminist scholars turning towards critical work and theory by white men, and the turning away of white feminist scholars from fully respecting and valuing the critical insights and theoretical offerings of black women or women of color.

Work by women of color and marginalized groups of white women (for example, lesbians, sex radicals), especially if written in a manner that renders it accessible to a broad reading public, is often de-legitimized in academic settings, even if that work enables and promotes feminist practice. Though such work is often appropriated by the very individuals setting restrictive critical standards, it is this work that they most often claim is not really theory. Clearly, one of the uses these individuals make of theory is instrumental. They use it to set up unnecessary and competing hierarchies of thought which reinscribe the politics of domination by designating work as either inferior, superior, or more or less worthy of attention. King emphasizes that "theory finds different uses in different locations." It is evident that one of the many uses of theory in academic locations is in the production of an intellectual class hierarchy where the only work deemed truly theoretical is work that is highly abstract, jargonistic, difficult to read, and containing obscure references. In Childers and hooks's "A Conversation about Race and Class" (also in *Conflicts in Feminism*) literary critic Mary Childers declares that it is highly ironic that "a certain kind of theoretical performance which only a small cadre of people can possibly understand" has come to be seen as representative of any production of critical thought that will be given recognition within many academic circles as "theory." It is especially ironic when this is the case with feminist theory. And, it is easy to imagine different locations, spaces outside academic exchange, where such theory would not only be seen as useless, but as politically nonprogressive, a kind of narcissistic, self-indulgent practice that most seeks to create a gap between theory and practice so as to perpetuate class elitism. There are so many settings in this country where the written word has only slight visual meaning, where individuals who cannot read or write can find no use for a published theory however lucid or opaque. Hence, any theory that cannot be shared in everyday conversation cannot be used to educate the public.

Imagine what a change has come about within feminist movements when students, most of whom are female, come to Women's Studies classes and read what they are told is feminist theory only to feel that what they are reading has no meaning, cannot be understood, or when understood in no way connects to "lived" realities beyond the classroom. As feminist activists we might ask ourselves, of what use is feminist theory that assaults the fragile psyches of women struggling to throw off patriarchy's oppressive yoke? We might ask ourselves, of what use is feminist theory that literally beats them down, leaves them stumbling bleary-eyed from classroom settings feeling humiliated, feeling as though they could easily be standing in a living room or bedroom somewhere naked with someone who has seduced them or is going to, who also subjects them to a process of interaction that humiliates, that strips them of their sense of value? Clearly, a feminist theory that can do this may function to legitimize Women's Studies and feminist scholarship in the eyes of the ruling patriarchy, but it undermines and subverts feminist movements. Perhaps it is the existence of this most highly visible feminist theory that compels us to talk about the gap between theory and practice. For it is indeed the purpose of such theory to divide, separate, exclude, keep at a distance. And because this theory continues to be used to silence, censor, and devalue various feminist theoretical voices, we cannot simply ignore it. Yet, despite its uses as an instrument of domination, it may also contain important ideas, thoughts, visions, that could, if used differently, serve a healing, liberatory function. However, we cannot ignore the dangers it poses to feminist struggle which must be rooted in a theory that informs, shapes, and makes feminist practice possible.

Within feminist circles, many women have responded to hegemonic feminist theory that does not speak clearly to us by trashing theory, and, as a consequence, further promoting the false dichotomy between theory and practice. Hence, they collude with those whom they would oppose. By internalizing the false assumption that theory is not a social practice, they promote the formation within feminist circles of a potentially oppressive hierarchy where all concrete action is viewed as more important than any theory written or spoken. Recently, I went to a gathering of predominantly black women where we discussed whether or not black male leaders, such as Martin Luther King and Malcolm X, should be subjected to feminist critiques that pose hard questions about their stance on gender issues. The entire discussion was less than two hours. As it drew to a close, a black woman who had been particularly silent said that she was not interested in all this theory and rhetoric, all this talk, that she was more interested in action, in doing something, that she was "tired" of all the talk.

This woman's response disturbed me: it is a familiar reaction. Perhaps in her daily life she inhabits a world different from mine. In the world

I live in daily, there are few occasions when black women or women-of-color thinkers come together to debate rigorously issues of race, gender, class, and sexuality. Therefore, I did not know where she was coming from when she suggested that the discussion we were having was common, so common as to be something we could dispense with or do without. I felt that we were engaged in a process of critical dialogue and theorizing that has long been taboo. Hence, from my perspective we were charting new journeys, claiming for ourselves as black women an intellectual terrain where we could begin the collective construction of feminist theory.

In many black settings, I have witnessed the dismissal of intellectuals, the putting down of theory, and remained silent. I have come to see that silence is an act of complicity, one that helps perpetuate the idea that we can engage in revolutionary black liberation and feminist struggle without theory. Like many insurgent black intellectuals, whose intellectual work and teaching is often done in predominantly white settings, I am often so pleased to be engaged with a collective group of black folks that I do not want to make waves, or make myself an outsider by disagreeing with the group. In such settings, when the work of intellectuals is devalued, I have in the past rarely contested prevailing assumptions or have spoken affirmatively or ecstatically about intellectual process. I was afraid that if I took a stance that insisted on the importance of intellectual work, particularly theorizing, or if I just simply stated that I thought it was important to read widely, I would risk being seen as uppity, or as lording it over. I have often remained silent.

These risks to one's sense of self now seem trite when considered in relation to the crises we are facing as African Americans, to our desperate need to rekindle and sustain the flame of black liberation struggle. At the gathering I mentioned, I dared to speak, saying in response to the suggestion that we were just wasting our time talking, that I saw our words as an action, that our collective struggle to discuss issues of gender and blackness without censorship was subversive practice. Many of the issues that we continue to confront as black people—low self-esteem, intensified nihilism and despair, repressed rage and violence that destroys

our physical and psychological well-being—cannot be addressed by survival strategies that have worked in the past. I insisted that we needed new theories rooted in an attempt to understand both the nature of our contemporary predicament and the means by which we might collectively engage in resistance that would transform our current reality. I was, however, not as rigorous and relentless as I would have been in a different setting in my efforts to emphasize the importance of intellectual work, the production of theory as a social practice that can be liberatory. Though not afraid to speak, I did not want to be seen as the one who "spoiled" the good time, the collective sense of sweet solidarity in blackness. This fear reminded me of what it was like more than ten years ago to be in feminist settings, posing questions about theory and practice, particularly about issues of race and racism that were seen as potentially disruptive of sisterhood and solidarity.

It seemed ironic that at a gathering called to honor Martin Luther King, Jr., who had often dared to speak and act in resistance to the status quo, black women were still negating our right to engage in oppositional political dialogue and debate, especially since this is not a common occurrence in black communities. Why did the black women there feel the need to police one another, to deny one another a space within blackness where we could talk theory without being self-conscious? Why, when we could celebrate together the power of a black male critical thinker who dared to stand apart, was there this eagerness to repress any viewpoint that would suggest we might collectively learn from the ideas and visions of insurgent black female intellectuals/theorists, who by the nature of the work they do are necessarily breaking with the stereotype that would have us believe the "real" black woman is always the one who speaks from the gut, who righteously praises the concrete over the abstract, the material over the theoretical?

Again and again, black women find our efforts to speak, to break silence and engage in radical progressive political debates, opposed. There is a link between the silencing we experience, the censoring, the anti-intellectualism in predominantly black settings that are supposedly supportive (like all-black woman space), and that silencing that takes place in institutions wherein black women and women of color are told that we cannot be fully heard or listened to because our work is not theoretical enough. In "Travelling Theory: Cultural Politics of Race and Representation," cultural critic Kobena Mercer reminds us that blackness is complex and multifaceted and that black people can be interpolated into reactionary and antidemocratic politics. Just as some elite academics who construct theories of "blackness" in ways that make it a critical terrain which only the chosen few can enter—using theoretical work on race to assert their authority over black experience, denying democratic access to the process of theory making—threaten collective black liberation struggle, so do those among us who react to this by promoting anti-intellectualism by declaring all theory as worthless. By reinforcing the idea that there is a split between theory and practice or by creating such a split, both groups deny the power of liberatory education for critical consciousness, thereby perpetuating conditions that reinforce our collective exploitation and repression.

I was reminded recently of this dangerous anti-intellectualism when I agreed to appear on a radio show with a group of black women and men to discuss Shahrazad Ali's *The Blackman's Guide to Understanding the Blackwoman.* I listened to speaker after speaker express contempt for intellectual work and speak against any call for the production of theory. One black woman was vehement in her insistence that "we don't need no theory." Ali's book, though written in plain language, in a style that makes use of engaging black vernacular, has a theoretical foundation. It is rooted in theories of patriarchy (for example, the sexist, essentialist belief that male domination of females is "natural"), that misogyny is the only possible response black men can have to any attempt by women to be fully self-actualized. Many black nationalists will eagerly embrace critical theory and thought as a necessary weapon in the struggle against white supremacy, but suddenly lose the insight that theory is important when it comes to questions of gender, of analyzing sexism and sexist oppression in the particular and specific ways it is manifest in black experience. The discussion of Ali's book is one of many possible examples illustrating the way contempt and disregard for theory undermines collective struggle to resist oppression and exploitation.

Within revolutionary feminist movements, within revolutionary black liberation struggles, we must continually claim theory as necessary practice within a holistic framework of liberatory activism. We must do more than call attention to ways theory is misused. We must do more than critique the conservative and at times reactionary uses some academic women make of feminist theory. We must actively work to call attention to the importance of creating a theory that can advance renewed feminist movements, particularly highlighting that theory which seeks to further feminist opposition to sexism and sexist oppression. Doing this, we necessarily celebrate and value theory that can be and is shared in oral as well as written narrative.

. . .

I am grateful to the many women and men who dare to create theory from the location of pain and struggle, who courageously expose wounds to give us their experience to teach and guide, as a means to chart new theoretical journeys. Their work is liberatory. It not only enables us to remember and recover ourselves, it charges and challenges us to renew our commitment to an active, inclusive feminist struggle. We have still to collectively make feminist revolution. I am grateful that we are collectively searching as feminist thinkers/theorists for ways to make this movement happen. Our search leads us back to where it all began, to that moment when an individual woman or child, who may have thought she was all alone, began a feminist uprising, began to name her practice, indeed began to formulate theory from lived experience. Let us imagine that this woman or child was suffering the pain of sexism and sexist oppression, that she wanted to make the hurt go away. I am grateful that I can be a witness, testifying that we can create a feminist theory, a feminist practice, a revolutionary feminist movement that can speak directly to the pain that is within folks, and offer them healing words, healing strategies, healing theory. There is no one among us who has not felt the pain of sexism and sexist oppression, the anguish that male domination can create in daily life, the profound and unrelenting misery and sorrow.

Mari Matsuda has told us that "we are fed a lie that there is no pain in war," and that patriarchy makes this pain possible. Catharine MacKinnon reminds us that "we know things with our lives and we live that knowledge, beyond what any theory has yet theorized." Making this theory is the challenge before us. For in its production lies the hope of our liberation, in its production lies the possibility of naming all our pain—of making all our hurt go away. If we create feminist theory, feminist movements that address this pain, we will have no difficulty building a mass-based feminist resistance struggle. There will be no gap between feminist theory and feminist practice.

[1994]

Lexicon of the Debates

INTRODUCTION

This lexicon has two purposes. Its first purpose is to familiarize you with some of the keywords of feminist theory and to put that vocabulary in context. The terms with which we have named these short essays come, for the most part, from the language of contemporary feminist theory. Nevertheless, they point to debates that have, in one way or another, contributed to shaping feminist theories throughout their history. Although Sojourner Truth and Simone de Beauvoir did not cast their arguments specifically in terms of "intersections of race, class, and gender" or "essentialism," for example, the understanding and issues that these terms bring into focus were very much a part of their thinking about women. A few of the terms, most particularly "psychoanalysis" and "Third World feminism," emerged from specific historical moments along with new questions for theory and the need for new frameworks.

The second purpose of the lexicon is to define some threads of debate that run through the readings collected here. Clearly these debates are not the only ones that a reader might identify. Nevertheless, those we have named do seem to us to raise major questions that have been of concern to feminist theory throughout the 200-year history covered by this volume. The 10 debates identified by the lexicon entries are, of course, interconnected and intersecting. Short bibliographies at the end of the lexicon entries suggest readings inside and outside the reader that elaborate the debates and arguments we have briefly outlined in each short essay.

These essays are meant to be starting places for thinking and reading. They attempt to raise very briefly some of the variety of perspectives that have, in different periods, shaped these debates in feminist theory and to help students connect these debates with the words and terms most frequently used to articulate them. We recommend that students pursue a thorough understanding of the debates through the articles and books in the bibliographies. In addition, we suggest using some of the excellent references available on the language of feminist theory for more specific definitions of terms you encounter here and throughout the readings in this volume:

Kramarae, Cheris, and Paula Treichler. (1985). *A Feminist Dictionary.* Boston: Pandora.
Humm, Maggie. (1995). *A Dictionary of Feminist Theory,* 2nd ed. Columbus, OH: Ohio State University Press.
Boles, Janet. (1996). *Historical Dictionary of Feminism.* Lanham, MD: Scarecrow.
Andermahr, Sonya, Terry Lovell, and Carol Walkowitz. (1997). *A Glossary of Feminist Theory.* London: Edward Arnold.
Code, Loraine. (2000). *Encylopedia of Feminist Theories.* New York: Taylor & Francis.
Gamble, Sarah. (2008). *The Routledge Companion to Feminism and Postmodernism.* New York: Routledge.

BODIES

In Western thought (Euro/North American), bodies have historically been distinct from minds; the **mind** is privileged ("**I think, therefore I am**") and the province of men/rational beings, whereas bodies are denigrated and associated with women. Because women have been linked with the **material** world through their bodies, they have become objects, property, and valuable for their exchangeability among men. Because they have been identified through their bodies with nature, they have become in Judeo-Christian discourse part of that over which "man" has dominion (Ortner, Plaskow). Because of the construction of their genitalia, their lack of a penis or phallus, psychology after Freud viewed women as inferior to men in their mental and moral development. Because of their reproductive capacities, their pregnant bodies and monthly cycles, culture marks women as mysterious, taboo, or dangerous (Douglas). Thus societies assign them to the **private sphere**, denying them access to employment, education, and civic life. Such assumptions about unambiguous anatomical and physiological distinctions—of **sexual difference**—have grounded both historical and contemporary discussions of "men" and "women."

Women's bodies are continually reshaped, covered, and uncovered according to prevailing ideology through fashion, corsets, diets, exercise programs, foot binding, cosmetic surgery, or veiling, among other things. As material objects, women's bodies are **"to be looked at"** (Mulvey). They are displayed in art, film, advertising, and pornography. Bodily intactness, women's virginity, is protected to ensure marriageability and determination of paternity and inheritance. **Race** and **class** also determine the use of women's bodies: one body for leisure, decoration, and protection (the middle or upper-class woman's body); another body for labor and exploitation (the working-class/woman of color's body).

Varied conceptions of women's bodies were central to many 19th-century feminist campaigns. In the 1848 "Declaration of Sentiments," U.S. suffragists sought to end husbands' absolute power over their wives and their right of "chastisement" of their wives' bodies. Campaigns against the **trafficking in women** and the Contagious Diseases Acts condemned the sexual double standard, which ignored men's sexual promiscuity but permitted the sale and sexual exploitation of women's bodies in prostitution (Josephine Butler; Goldman). Advocates of birth control and reproductive choice see a woman's ability "to determine whether she will be a mother" (Sanger) as the basis of all other freedoms.

The focus on of women's difference, particularly based on their capacity for motherhood, also divided feminists in the 19th and early 20th centuries. Labor advocates often used women's bodily differences and their role as childbearers to argue for **protective** measures that would shorten their hours and improve their working conditions (Jones). Others, like Alice Paul and the Women's Party campaigners for an Equal Rights Amendment, saw such arguments for protection based on bodily difference as dooming women to continued second-class status.

The struggle for women's right to control their bodies underlies much of second-wave feminist activism in the movement for reproductive rights and choice, the women's health movement, and the lesbian and gay liberation movement. Second-wave feminists analyzed the exploitation of women's bodies in advertising, pornography, film, art, and other visual media (Millett, Susan Griffin, *Pornography and Silence*), and protested the violation of women's bodies through battering, rape, and forced sterilization. In the United States, such efforts are rooted for the most part in **radical and cultural feminism,** which take women's differences (motherhood in particular) to be resources for feminism that they must wrest from **patriarchal** control. So, for example, Adrienne Rich in *Of Woman Born* analyzed the history of male control of childbirth and argued that women must see motherhood as a resource and a power and take back control of that process. Influenced by French feminists Hélène Cixous and Luce Irigaray, who upended Lacan's consignment of women to prelinguistic immanence, feminist writers and critics have seen the body as a creative resource and speak of "**writing the body**" and of writing in the "white ink" of mother's milk.

More recently, feminist activists have analyzed the impact of cultural ideology on the bodies of girls by examining the pervasiveness of anorexia nervosa, bulimia, and negative body image. They have continued to struggle for reproductive rights in the United States, looking now also at the proliferation of new reproductive technologies and joining the international struggle of women against coercive family planning policies and female genital mutilation, against the continued use of rape as a tool of war, and against environmental degradation and its particular impact on women's and children's health. Feminist scholars of disability have theorized the links between the subjugated bodies of women and the **disabled** and their similar disciplining by medicine and fashion (Garland-Thomson). Feminists, in this and other generations, have also recognized in myriad ways that just as the body is the basis for subjection and oppression, it is also where resistance is first enacted— through speaking out, marching, and fighting back.

Contemporary feminists also theorize the body not as the **essential** ground of women's difference, but as the site on which gender is constructed, inscribed, reinscribed, and through which gender is performed (Judith Butler). Donna Haraway's "A Cyborg Manifesto" explores the body as a contested site overdetermined by science, technology, and culture. Haraway proposes the **cyborg,** "a hybrid of machine and organism," as a way out of the dilemmas of the Western construction of the body, "a way out of the maze of dualisms in which we have explained our bodies and our tools to ourselves" (Haraway), while other theorists urge that we embrace the cyber and the technological with caution, always attentive to the potential for erasure of the body and of women in the multiple unfolding fields of technological possibility.

FURTHER READING

In the Reader:

Truth, Sojourner. (1851). "Ain't I a Woman?"
Butler, Josephine. (1871). "Petition to Parliament against the Contagious Diseases Acts."
Goldman, Emma. (1910). *The Traffic in Women.*
Sanger, Margaret. (1920). From *Women and the New Race.*
Douglas, Mary. (1966). "The System at War with Itself" from *Purity and Danger.*
Millett, Kate. (1969). From *Sexual Politics.*
Ortner, Sherry B. (1974). "Is Female to Male as Nature Is to Culture?"
Cixous, Hélène. (1975). "The Laugh of the Medusa."
Irigaray, Luce. (1977). From *This Sex Which Is Not One.*
Haraway, Donna. (1985). "A Cyborg Manifesto: Science, Technology and Socialist-Feminism in the Late Twentieth Century."
Butler, Judith. (1990). From *Gender Trouble: Feminism and the Subversion of Identity.*

Davis, Angela Y. (1991). "Outcast Mothers and Surrogates: Racism and Reproductive Politics in the Nineties."

Bordo, Susan. (1993). "The Body and the Reproduction of Feminity."

Fausto-Sterling, Anne. (2000). "Should there Be Only, Two Sexes."

Garland-Thomson, Rosemarie. (2001). "Integrating Disability, Transforming Feminist Theory."

Outside the Reader: Bodies

Boston Women's Health Collective. (1971). *Our Bodies, Our Selves.* New York: Simon and Schuster.

Rich, Adrienne. (1976). *Of Woman Born: Motherhood as Institution and Experience.* New York: Norton.

Lacan, Jacques. (1977). "The Signification of the Phallus." *Ecrits: A Selection.* Alan Sheridan, trans. New York: Norton. (Originally published 1966)

Griffin, Susan. (1978). *Woman and Nature: The Roaring Inside Her.* New York: Harper.

Lorde, Audre. (1984). "The Uses of the Erotic" *Sister/Outsider.* Trumansburg, NY: Crossing.

Suleiman, Susan. (1986). *The Female Body in Western Culture.* Cambridge, MA: Harvard.

Hubbard, Ruth. (1990). *The Politics of Women's Biology.* New York: Routledge.

Young, Iris Marion. (1990). *Throwing Like a Girl and Other Essays.* Princeton, NJ: Princeton.

Martin, Emily. (1991). *The Woman in the Body: A Cultural Analysis of Reproduction.* Boston: Beacon.

Grosz, Elizabeth. (1994). *Volatile Bodies: Toward a Corporeal Feminism.* Bloomington: Indiana University Press.

Roberts, Dorothy. (1998). *Killing the Black Body: Race, Reproduction, and the Meaning of Liberty.* New York: Vintage.

Hayles, N. Katherine. (1999). *How We Became Posthuman: Virtual Bodies in Cybernetics, Literature and Informatics.* Chicago: University of Chicago Press.

Braidotti, Rosi. (2002). *Metamorphoses: Towards a Materialist Theory of Becoming.* Cambridge, U.K.: Polity Press.

Wilson, Elizabeth. (2004). *Psychosomatic: Feminism and the Neurological Body.* Durham, NC: Duke University Press.

Haraway, Donna. (2007). *When Species Meet (Posthumanities).* Minneapolis, MN: University of Minnesota Press.

EPISTEMOLOGIES

Since "knowledge is power," it is not surprising that epistemologies, theories of **knowledge** and **knowledge production,** have been and are central to feminist theory. Knowledge is that body of information, facts, and theories through which a society or culture defines what is true and important, what constitutes its past, and how it understands the complexities of the natural and social worlds. To be excluded from these bodies of knowledge and the sites and processes of knowledge production, as women and other marginalized groups have been, is to live in a "reality" not of one's own making.

One project of feminist epistemology is therefore to critique this "partial knowledge" (Minnich) and to understand how it perpetuates hierarchy and domination. Creating an inclusive curriculum in all disciplines, expanding the canon in literature, music, art, and philosophy, as well as women's studies and feminist theory themselves—all represent such strategies. Another project of feminist epistemology is to ask how **social location**—gender, as well as race, class, sexuality, age, and ability—affects knowing and the processes of knowledge production. Are there "**women's ways of knowing**"? How does the knowledge women produce about themselves differ from that produced by patriarchy and the dominant culture? Is the margin occupied by women and people of color a better location for knowledge production than the center? Do they, in other words, occupy a site of **epistemological privilege?**

In 19th-century and early 20th-century feminist thought, the first of these feminist projects is most evident in the analysis of the exclusion of women from sites of knowledge production (education, government, the church, arts and letters, and the professions), the omission of women from the knowledge produced and the denial to women, no matter their race or class, of authority as knowers. Thus Virginia Woolf found in the British Library catalog only a distorted history of women written by men and Elizabeth Cady Stanton grappled with equally skewed interpretations of women in the Bible. Stanton's *Women's Bible* also engaged in the second project of feminist epistemology in that it attempted to replace patriarchal readings of biblical texts with feminist readings.

Nineteenth-century women's public telling of their own experiences of sexuality (Josephine Butler), marriage, and racism and sexism (Cooper) were all attempts to produce new knowledge—women's knowledge—about women's lives. Many 19th-century arguments for women's political and professional enfranchisement assumed that women would bring to public life special kinds of knowledge acquired through lives of nurturance and care. Such arguments are not unlike the arguments made by **cultural feminists** in the 1970s and early 1980s.

Second-wave feminism developed its own epistemology in the process of **consciousness raising,** a model for generating knowledge from the **authority** of individual women's **experience.** At the same time, academic women's studies and feminist scholarship in the disciplines began to transform both the knowledge base and the theoretical and critical methodologies of academic research. In the 1980s, work by Carol Gilligan in *In a Different Voice* and by Blanche Clinchy and colleagues in *Women's Ways of Knowing* suggested that women employ alternative processes of thought, moral decision making, and theorizing. Simultaneously, French feminists and others influenced by postmodernism critiqued the **dualisms** inherent in **hegemonic** Western thought and sought to disrupt them, as well as to reclaim sources of knowledge that would rupture, subvert, and free them from the control of being the devalued term "woman" in the equation (Cixous, Wittig).

At the same time, and sometimes in response to these theories, feminists of color (hooks, Collins) and Third World feminists (Minh Ha, Chow) argued that the marginal positions they occupy confer a certain **epistemological privilege** as locations for knowledge production and from which to analyze the structure of oppression and domination that constitute patriarchal Western thought. Gloria Anzaldúa, for example, suggested that a **mestiza consciousness,** a consciousness that comes from inhabiting contradictory locations simultaneously, can be a particularly productive location for knowledge production because it challenges dualism and is flexible and tolerant of ambiguity.

Feminist debates about epistemology have also focused particularly on what Sandra Harding called "the science question in feminism." Theorists have closely scrutinized Western enlightenment models of knowledge seeking, specifically **objectivity, empiricism,** and **positivism,** methods that supposedly guarantee neutrality and prevent the knower from "biasing," the knowledge "he" produces. These models, characterized as "the Archimedean perspective" (Jehlen), "the view from nowhere" (Harding, Minnich), and the "God's eye trick" (Haraway), deny the relevance of the identity and social location of knowers; they perpetuate the worldview of privileged, included groups and they exclude the knowledge, experience, and questions of women and other marginalized groups.

With Audre Lorde, who asserts that "the master's tools will never dismantle the master's house," some feminists have entirely rejected positivism and empiricism and the methodologies they have produced, and have argued instead that knowledge must always be produced out of women's **experience** and tested against it. Others have argued that empiricism, the scientific method, and quantitative analysis are neutral tools that have been deployed in biased research but that can, with care and close scrutiny, be used to advance feminist research as well.

In either case, articulation of the position or social location of the researchers thus becomes a crucial component of research. Feminist theorists have proposed concepts such as **feminist standpoint** (Harding, Hartsock, Smith) and **situated knowledge** (Haraway) as models of knowing that can replace "the view from nowhere" with the "view from women's lives" (Harding, "Reinventing" 269). They may also provide feminism with epistemologies and methodologies that can be used in the cause of liberation rather than of domination.

FURTHER READING

In the Reader:

Wollstonecraft, Mary. (1792). From *A Vindication of the Rights of Woman.*
Wittig, Monique. (1978). "The Straight Mind."
Lorde, Audre. (1979). "The Master's Tools Will Never Dismantle the Master's House."
Lugones, Maria C. and Elizabeth V. Spelman, (1983). "Have We Got a Theory for You! Feminist Theory, Cultural Imperialism and the Demand for 'The Woman's Voice.' "
Haraway, Donna. (1985). "A Cyborg Manifesto: Science, Technology, and Socialist-Feminism in the Late Twentieth Century."
Harding, Sandra. (1986). From *The Science Question in Feminism.*
Anzaldúa, Gloria. (1987). "La Consciencia de la Mestiza: Towards a New Consciousness."
Collins, Patricia Hill. (1990). From *Black Feminist Thought: Knowledge, Consciousness and the Politics of Empowerment.*
Keller, Evelyn Fox. (1993). "Making Gender Visible in the Pursuit of Nature's Secrets."
Narayan, Uma. (1997). "Contesting Cultures: 'Westernization,' Respect for Cultures, and Third World Feminists' from *Dislocating Cultures: Identities, Traditions and Third World Feminisms.*
Mahmood, Saba. (2005). "The Subject of Freedom."

Outside the Reader:

Smith, Dorothy. (1974). "Women's Perspective as a Radical Critique of Sociology." *Sociological Inquiry.* Vol. 4. 1, pp. 7–13.
Harding, Sandra, and Merrill B. Hintikka (eds.). (1983). *Discovering Reality: Feminist Perspectives on Epistemology, Metaphysics, Methodology and Philosophy of Science.* Boston: Reidel.
Hartsock, Nancy. (1983). "The Feminist Standpoint: Developing the Ground of a Specifically Feminist Historical Materialism." *Money, Sex and Power: Toward a Feminist Historical Materialism.*
Jaggar, Alison. (ed.). (1983). *Feminist Politics and Human Nature.* Totowa, NJ: Roman and Allenheld.
hooks, bell. (1984). *Feminist Theory: From Margin to Center.* Boston: South End.
Belenky, Mary Field, et al., (eds.). (1986). *Women's Ways of Knowing: The Development of Self, Voice, and Mind.* New York: Basic Books.
Chow, Rey. (1989). "It's You and Not Me: Domination and 'Othering' in Theorizing the 'Third World.' " In Elizabeth Weed (ed.). *Coming to Terms.* New York: Routledge.
Jaggar, Alison M., and Susan Bordo (eds.). (1989). *Gender/Body/Knowledge: Feminist Reconstructions of Being and Knowing.* New Brunswick: Rutgers University Press.
Minnich, Elizabeth. (1990). *Transforming Knowledge.* Philadelphia, PA: Temple University Press.
Haraway, Donna. (1991). "Situated Knowledge: The Science Question in Feminism and the Privilege of Partial Perspective." *Simians, Cyborgs and Women.* New York: Routledge.
Sandoval, Chela. (2002). *Methodology of the Oppressed.* Minneapolis, MN: University of Minnesota Press.
Duran, Jane. (2001). *Worlds of Knowing: Global Feminist Epistemologies.* New York: Routledge.
Code, Lorraine. (2006). *Ecological Thinking: The Politics of Epistemic Location.* Oxford: Oxford University Press.

ESSENTIALISM/SOCIAL CONSTRUCTION/DIFFERENCE

One of the defining conversations in feminist theory has been that between an essentialist position—the belief that there is an immutable, eternal, and transhistorical essence of femaleness and maleness—and a social constructionist position, in which women and men are seen as produced through a "complex system of cultural, social, psychical, and historical differences" (Fuss, xii). For the essentialist, sexual **difference** is innate, natural, inborn, and persistent, whereas the social constructionist would argue, with Simone de Beauvoir, Monique Wittig, and others, that "one is not born a woman" but becomes one through social and cultural processes.

Essentialism is exemplified by arguments invoking **sisterhood** or a unitary female culture or voice (Gilligan), by radical feminist assertions of the universal oppression/subordination of women (Daly), by psychological theories that assume that female genitalia or a single developmental pattern adequately explain all women (Freud), and by the assertion that "the" women's movement could speak with one voice for all women (NOW).

Social constructionists, on the other hand, root their arguments in understandings of differences between and among women. Following on Margaret Mead's work in *Sex and Temperament*, they argue that there is a socially produced distinction between biological **sex and gender.** Therefore, to study women and sexual difference, the social constructionist would argue, one must specify and particularize the different social, cultural, and historical situations by which they are produced.

Though "essentialism" and "**social construction**" are 20th-century terms, the issues to which they point were also concerns of earlier feminists. For example, both Mary Wollstonecraft in the 18th century and Florence Nightingale in the 19th century saw the socially prescribed frivolity and aimlessness of middle-class women's lives, rather than any innate inferiority, as the roots of sexual difference. Women's contributions to public life and thought have been limited not because they have different capacities or natures but because they live in different social circumstances. Sojourner Truth's question, "Ain't I a Woman?" challenged any concept of an essential "woman's nature" that is generalized from a white, middle-class idea of femininity.

However, many 19th-century feminists based their arguments in an essentialist view of women. John Stuart Mill argued for women's right to exercise their talents in all facets of public and private life, yet he believed that they might naturally prefer motherhood and child rearing to public life. Some suffrage campaigners and social reformers made distinctly essentialist arguments, which, like the arguments of 20th-century cultural feminists, valorized women's difference. They believed that women should have the vote and be involved in the formation of public and social policy because their moral natures were inherently different from and superior to those of men.

Pointing out that the **essential woman** who became the subject of **second-wave feminism** was in fact white, middle-class, and heterosexual, 20th-century feminists of color, lesbian feminists, and postcolonial feminists have called for anti-essentialist feminist theory based on confronting and examining differences of race, class, gender, sexual orientation, age, ability, and nationality. "Women," said bell hooks in *Feminist Theory: From Margin to Center,* "do not need to eradicate difference to feel solidarity. We do not need to share common oppression to fight equally to end oppression" (65).

As hooks' comment suggests, questions of essentialism have been central to recent discussions of **identity** and **identity politics.** Is a sense of gender, race, or sexual orientation as innate and inborn, or at least unitary and persistent, the only possible basis for resisting domination and oppression? Or can such a politics be rooted in an identity defined as "an active construction and a discursively mediated interpretation of one's history" (de Lauretis, 263)? Some, like Gayatri Spivak, have argued that a feminist politics can be rooted in a "**strategic essentialism,**" constructed by a subordinate group as a ground for organizing and resistance.

Since the 1990s, feminist theorists, among them Ruth Hubbard, Diana Fuss, Teresa de Lauretis, Linda Alcoff, and Rosi Braidotti have resisted the rigid opposition of the essentialist and social constructionist positions and have come to see them as unhelpful and reductionist ways to characterize feminist thought. Hubbard, for example, argued that biological and social determinants of gender are continually interacting and mutually constituting effects rather than opposing forces. Others articulated theoretical understandings that reconcile the two positions (Alcoff) or see how fully implicated in each other they are (Fuss); they argue like de Lauretis and Braidotti that the subject of feminism is not "Woman" but rather the "female-embodied social **subject**" (267).

FURTHER READING

In the Reader:

Wollstonecraft, Mary. (1792). From *A Vindication of the Rights of Woman.*
Truth, Sojourner. (1851). "Ain't I a Woman?."
Mill, John Stuart. (1870). From *The Subjection of Women.*
Browne, Stella. (1923). "Studies in Feminine Inversion."
Mead, Margaret. (1935). From *Sex and Temperament in Three Primitive Societies.*
Beauvoir, Simone de. (1949). From *The Second Sex.*
Ortner, Sherry, B. (1974). "Is Female to Male as Nature Is to Culture?."
Alcoff, Linda. (1988). "Cultural Feminism versus Post-Structuralism: The Identity Crisis in Feminist Theory."
Scott, Joan W. (1988). "Deconstructing Equality versus Difference."
Alarcon, Norma. (1990). "The Theoretical Subjects of *This Bridge Called My Back* and Anglo-American Feminism."

Outside the Reader:

Firestone, Shulamith. (1970). *The Dialectic of Sex.* New York: Bantam Books.
hooks, bell. (1984). *Feminist Theory: From Margin to Center.* Boston: South End.
Spelman, Elizabeth V. (1988). *Inessential Woman: Problems of Exclusion in Feminist Thought.* Boston: Beacon.
Braidotti, Rosi. (1989). "The Politics of Ontological Difference." In Teresa Brennan (ed.). *Between Psychoanalysis and Feminism.* New York: Routledge.
Hubbard, Ruth. (1990). *The Politics of Women's Biology.* New York: Routledge.
Lauretis, Teresa de. (1991). "Upping the Anti (sic) in Feminist Theory." In Evelyn Fox Keller and Marianne Hirsch (eds.). *Conflicts in Feminism.* New York: Routledge.
Spivak, Gayatri. (1993). Interview with Sara Danius and Stefan Jonsson. *Boundary 2 (1987). In Other Worlds: Essays in Cultural Politics.* London: Methuen.
Schor, Naomi, and Elizabeth Weed (eds.). (1994). *The Essential Difference.* New York: Routledge.
Fuss, Diana. (1996). *Essentially Speaking: Feminism, Nature & Difference.* New York: Routledge.
Dowd, Nancy, and Michelle S. Jacobs (eds.). (2003). *Feminist Legal Theory: An Anti-Essentialist Reader.* New York: New York University Press.

INTERSECTIONS OF RACE, CLASS, AND GENDER

The "**intersections of race, class, and gender**," or **intersectionality**, is one contemporary naming of the understanding that our lives are not shaped by gender alone. Rather, individuals are multiply constituted by gender, race, class, sexuality, nationality, age, ability, and other social experiences, identities, and phenomena that we live simultaneously rather than separately. Other phrases like bell hooks' "**interlocking systems of domination**" and Deborah King's "**multiple jeopardy**" also express this understanding. An intersectional analysis allows us to understand "our capacity as women and men to be either dominated or dominating [as] a point of connection, or commonality" (hooks).

This paradigm is posed against a **hierarchy of oppression** in which one oppressive structure—**racism, classism, sexism,** or **heterosexism**—is seen as the first, deepest, or most pervasive oppression. Examples of such thinking are found in the oppositions posed at some points in the 19th century between the cause of the **abolition** of slavery and the cause of women's **suffrage** or, in the 1960s, between civil rights and women's rights. Women working in labor and leftist movements have been urged to work for a revolution that will overthrow capitalist class oppression and allegedly, in the process, end gender oppression (Hartmann). Women of color and poor and working-class women have been urged by the women's movement to join in sisterhood with white women to struggle against sexism, and to give that work priority over struggling with men of color against racism or with poor and working-class men against class oppression. Black women "are made to feel disloyal to racial interests if they insist on women's rights" (Murray). An intersectional analysis would propose that we understand all of these causes as interlocking pieces of a structure of domination that must be dismantled in toto.

Nineteenth-century women in the United States, black and white, did attempt to analyze the relationship between race and gender. Angelina Grimké spoke of the particularities of the sexual exploitation of female slaves and of the complicity and degradation of white women who witnessed this exploitation and did nothing. Anna Julia Cooper, Mary Church Terrell, and others saw "the colored woman" as confronting both a "woman question" and a "race problem" (Cooper), and Ida B. Wells saw the ways in which black and white women's sexuality were interlocked in the issue of lynching.

For the most part, however, the white women's movement in the first and second waves failed to incorporate such understandings and was critiqued by women of color, beginning with Sojourner Truth. The work of feminist scholars of color, along with lesbian and socialist/working-class scholars, in the 1970s and 1980s (Audre Lorde, Gloria Anzaldúa, Barbara Smith, bell hooks, Charlotte Bunch, Marilyn Frye) in particular, extended this critique and attempted to insist on difference as a resource for feminist thinking and organizing. "It is not those differences between us that are separating us," writes Audre Lorde. "It is rather our refusal to recognize those differences and to examine the distortions that result from our misnaming them and their effects upon human behavior and expectation" ("Age, Race, Sex, and Class"). More recently, Kimberlé Crenshaw has argued that intersectionality "mediates the tension between assertions of multiple identities and the ongoing necessity of group politics," while at the same time intersectionality provides a "basis for reconceptualizing" a single identity as coalition, for example "race as a coalition between men and women of color."

FURTHER READING

In the Reader:

Truth, Sojourner. (1851). "Ain't I a Woman?"
Cooper, Anna Julia. (1892). From *A Voice from the South: By a Black Woman of the South*.
Murray, Pauli. (1970). "The Liberation of Black Women."
Combahee River Collective. (1977). "A Black Feminist Statement."
Lorde, Audre. (1978). "Age, Race, Class, and Sex: Women Redefining Difference."
Hartmann, Heidi. (1981). "The Unhappy Marriage of Marxism and Feminism: Towards a More Progressive Union."
Yamada, Mitsuye. (1981). "Asian American Women and Feminism."
Lugones, Maria C., and Elizabeth V. Spelman. (1983). "Have We Got a Theory for You! Feminist Theory, Cultural Imperialism and the Demand for 'The Woman's Voice.' "
hooks, bell. (1989). "Feminism: A Transformational Politic."
Alarcón, Norma. (1990). "The Theoretical Subject(s) of *This Bridge Called My Back* and Anglo-American Feminism."
Crenshaw, Kimberlé. (1997). "Intersectionality and Identity Politics: Learning from Violence against Women of Color."

Outside the Reader:

Smith, Barbara. (Oct. 1977). "Toward a Black Feminist Criticism." *Conditions: Two, 1*, no. 2.
Hull, Gloria, Patricia Bell Scott, and Barbara Smith. (1982). *All the Women Are White, All the Blacks Are Men, but Some of Us Are Brave*. Old Westbury, NY: Feminist Press.
Dill, Bonnie Thornton. (Spring 1983). "Race, Class and Gender: Prospects for an All-Inclusive Sisterhood." *Feminist Studies*. Vol. 9, 131–150.
hooks, bell. (1984). *Feminist Theory: From Margin to Center*. Boston: South End.
King, Deborah. (Autumn 1988). "Multiple Jeopardy, Multiple Consciousness: The Context of Black Feminist Ideology." *Signs: Journal of Women in Culture and Society*. Vol. 14, no. 1, 42–72.
Geok-lin Lim, Shirley. (1993). "Feminist and Ethnic Theories in Asian American Literature," *Feminist Studies*.
Eisenstein, Zillah. (1994). *The Color of Gender: Reimagining Democracy*. Berkeley: University of California Press.
Guy-Sheftall, Beverly. (1995). *Words of Fire*. New York: New Press.
Hurtado, Aida. (1997). *The Color of Privilege: Three Blasphemies on Race and Feminism*. Ann Arbor; University of Michigan Press.
Wing, Adrien Katherine. (1997). *Critical Race Feminism: A Reader*. New York: New York University Press.
Ella, Shohat. (ed.) (2002). *Talking Visions: Multicultural Feminism in a Transnational Age*. Cambridge, MA: MIT Press.
Collins, Patricia Hill. (2006). *From Black Power to Hip Hop: Racism, Nationalism, and Feminism*. Philadelphia: Temple University Press.

LANGUAGE

"The words we use daily reflect our cultural understandings and at the same time transmit them to the next generation through an agency that subserves the culture's needs" (Casey Miller and Kate Swift). Language constructs assumptions about gender along with other cultural understandings. Therefore, critiques of language use have been central to feminist analysis: the most basic objections about forms of address, formal ("Miss," "Mrs.," "Ms.") and informal ("baby," "chick," "bitch," "honey"); the use of the generic "man"; and challenges to religious systems in which "God the Father" is the primary way of designating the sacred. Women writers have questioned the possibility of writing in language, forms, or genres so burdened with patriarchal cultural assumptions that they may be unusable to express women's knowledge or experience.

"Finding one's **voice**," "**naming** oneself," reclaiming, reconstructing, and "stealing" the language are therefore essential activities and metaphors for feminist work and feminist theory. For some feminists, this means trying to rewrite the lexicon at the most basic level: by changing the titles of women who do certain jobs (as in actor not actress, flight attendant not stewardess); by reclaiming and redefining derogatory words like "dyke," "crone," and "bitch"; and by dictionary making, as in Treichler and Kramarae's *Feminist Dictionary*, Mary Daly's *Intergalactic Wickedary*, and this lexicon itself. For others, this means recovering or transforming literary forms and genres or looking for sites of expression outside of language, in the nonverbal, in **silence**, and in the body.

Nineteenth-century feminists grappled first with the assumption of women's public silence; their culture told them that the very acts of speaking and writing were unwomanly. In order to write novels or poetry or to speak or write publicly about politics, suffrage, or birth control, women had first to assert their right of access to language and then to claim for themselves the name of "**author**" or "citizen." The 1848 Seneca Falls Declaration of Sentiments, appropriating the language of the founding documents of the United States, simultaneously asserted women's right to **citizenship** and women's right to the language of citizenship (Anthony). Early in the 20th century, Virginia Woolf attempted to imagine in *A Room of One's Own* how women may claim language and authorship for themselves and what their work and their words would look like undistorted by patriarchal culture.

Feminists of the second wave continued this project of giving public language to women's work and experience. The title that Betty Friedan gave to the first section of *The Feminine Mystique*—"The Problem That Has No Name"—pointed directly to the problem of language: women did not have the words to name their experiences. Among the activities of second-wave feminism was this activity of giving name and voice to women's experience through **consciousness raising**, through the recovery of women's writing, through attempts to reform the discourse of the church, the academy, the household and the workplace, and through cracking open generic concepts like "man" and "masculine" to reveal their asymmetry and women's invisibility in them.

French feminist theorists such as Cixous and Irigaray approached these questions through Lacan's understanding of psychological development as the entry into language or the symbolic order, which he named the Law of the Father. Women, according to Lacan, are outside of language. They belong to **immanence,** the prelinguistic moment when the child is not separate from the mother and therefore has no need of language. Cixous and Irigaray have suggested that this **immanence,** this association with the body and a location outside phallogocentric discourse, can be made a resource for speech and language; women must **write the body** in their own language (**l'écriture féminine**), they suggest, rather than in the father's words.

Throughout the 19th and 20th centuries, women writers wrestled with these language questions. They asked with Virginia Woolf whether there is a "female sentence," whether language is distinctly marked by gender. They both transformed traditional forms and sought out the literary forms (letters, diaries, autobiographies, novels, memoirs) that seemed most apt for the expression of their lived experience. In seeking expression for their experience, Latina, Asian, and Native American women writers and scholars (Anzaldúa, Lugones and Spelman) produced bilingual texts that raise questions about translation and cultural identity and that explore in their form and language the experience of the borderlands.

FURTHER READING

In the Reader:

Anthony, Susan B. (1872). Speech after Arrest for Illegal Voting.

Woolf, Virginia. (1929). *A Room of One's Own.*

Cixous, Hélène. (1975). "The Laugh of the Medusa."

Irigaray, Luce. (1977). From *This Sex Which Is Not One.*

Daly, Mary. (1978). "The Metaphysical Journey of Exorcism and Ecstasy" from *Gyn/Ecology: A Metaethics of Radical Feminism.*

Lugones, Maria, and Elizabeth Spelman. (1983). "Have We Got a Theory for you: Feminist Theory, Cultural Imperialism, and the Demand for the Woman's Voice."

Kramarae, Cheris, and Paula Treichler. (1985). From *The Feminist Dictionary.*

Anzaldúa, Gloria. (1987). "La Consciencia de la Mestiza: Towards a New Consciousness."

Outside the Reader:

Henley, Nancy, and Barrie Thorne. (1975). *Language and Sex: Difference and Dominance.* Rowley, MA: Newbury House.

Lakoff, Robin. (1975). *Language and Woman's Place.* New York: Harper & Row.

Miller, Casey, and Kate Swift. (1976). *Words and Women.* New York: Harper Collins.

Olsen, Tillie. (1978). *Silences.* New York: Delacorte.

Kolodny, Annette. (1980, Spring), "Dancing Through the Minefield: Some Observations on the Theory, Practice, and Politics of a Feminist Literary Criticism." *Feminist Studies.* Vol. 6, no. 1, 1–25.

Kristeva, Julia. (1980). *Desire in Language.* Leon S. Roudiez, ed. Thomas Gora, Alice Jardine, and Leon S. Roudiez, trans. New York: Columbia, (Originally published 1969)

Spender, Dale. (1980). *Man Made Language,* New York: Pergamon.

Ruether, Rosemary Radford. (1983). *Sexism and God-Talk: Toward a Feminist Theology,* Boston: Beacon.

Cameron, Deborah. (1985). *Feminism and Linguistic Theory.* London: Macmillan.

Daly, Mary. (1987). *Webster's First New Intergalactic Wickedary of the English Language.* Boston: Beacon.

Cameron, Deborah. (1990). *The Feminist Critique of Language.* New York: Routledge.

Butler, Judith. (1997). *Excitable Speech: A Politics of the Performative.* New York: Routledge.

POWER

Power is one of the two primary divisions in social and economic life decided on the basis of gender; the division of labor is the other. Any analysis of women's situations and conditions is grounded in the assumption of power's **asymmetrical** division, that "woman [is] always and everywhere subject to male man" (Beard). Power has been and remains a complex and vexing question for feminist theory. Power as force exerted through **domination** and **exploitation** has been condemned and repudiated by most feminist theorists, whereas power embodied as equality in political, legal, and economic rights has been sought by many. As feminist theorists have critiqued abuses of public power in militarism, economic exploitation, and colonialism, and private power in rape, battering, harassment, and incest, they have also asked how power can be redefined and whether women have any special or distinctive contribution to make to that redefinition. Feminists have fruitfully disentangled the concept of **power over,** as opposed to the **power to** act, think, speak, and demand change (Starhawk). This principle of empowerment underlies feminist activism and theory.

Power operates in all aspects of the public and private realm. Nineteenth-century feminists examined the effects of women's exclusion from public power as it emanates through laws, governments, and other social institutions. They sought women's enfranchisement in these institutions, primarily through political suffrage but also through campaigns for women's admission to full professional participation in law, education, medicine, and politics. But they also understood, as John Stuart Mill asserted, that "the family is a school for despotism," that the private sphere was as much a site for the exercise and abuse of power as the public sphere. And they realized that women always have the power of even the most abject subjects—the power to resist their conditions and situations.

Like their 19th-century sisters, 20th-century liberal feminists attempted to address the unequal distribution of power through reform of public legal and political institutions. On the other hand, second-wave radical feminists made central the theoretical insight that the "**personal is political,**" that power relations operate in personal as in public life. This is one of the many things meant by Kate Millett's notion of "**sexual politics**"—that male dominance suffuses our most local and intimate lives. Hence the focus in radical feminist analysis on rape, battering, pornography, and all forms of violence against women. However, the emergence of lesbian writings on sadomasochism (also in the 1980s) opened up discussions of women's own relations to power in the realm of sexuality, and certainly helped to demystify the assumption that women wanted nothing to do with power.

A suspicion of power led to feminist organizing that attempted to make decisions on the basis of consensus, by assuming that this was a more "feminist" approach to forms of governance: "**sisterhood is powerful.**" Cultural feminism theorizes women's more benign use of power as an inherent inclination to peace rather than to war and domination. Such a notion of women's rejection of paradigms of domination and exploitation in relation to the earth has been particularly crucial to **ecofeminism** (King). Similarly, a suspicion of institutional power has led to close feminist scrutiny of militarism and of the distinct and particular ways in which women's lives are militarized (Enloe).

Since the 1980s, feminist theorists have rethought power primarily through several mutually informing perspectives: materialist analyses of technologies of production and **commodification,** post-colonial critiques of imperialism and **globalization,** and Foucault's notion of power as exercised not through monolithic state institutions but through pervasive regulatory mechanisms of self-surveillance and **self-discipline.**

FURTHER READING

In the Reader:

Truth, Sojourner. (1867). "Keeping the Thing Going While Things Are Stirring."
Cooper, Anna Julia. (1892). From *A Voice of the South.*
Cixous, Hélène. (1975). "The Laugh of the Medusa."
Frye, Marilyn. (1978). "Some Reflections on Separatism and Power."
King, Ynestra. (1989). "The Ecology of Feminism and the Feminism of Ecology."
Mohanty, Chandra Talpade. (1984/1991). "Under Western Eyes: Feminist Scholarship and Colonial Discourses."

MacKinnon, Catharine A. (1989). "Sexuality, Pornography, and Method: 'Pleasure under Patriarchy'."
Enloe, Cynthia. (2000). "When Soldeiers Rape" from *Maneuvers: The International Politics of Militarizing Women's Lives.*

Outside the Reader:

Pankhurst, Emmeline. (1913). "When Civil War Is Waged by Women."
Beard, Mary. (1946). *Woman as a Force in History.* New York: Macmillan.
Morgan, Robin (ed.). (1970). *Sisterhood is Powerful.* New York: Vintage.
Foucault, Michel. (1977). *Discipline and Punish: The Birth of the Prison.* New York: Pantheon.
Sanday, Peggy. (1981). *Female Power and Male Dominance.* Cambridge: Cambridge University Press.
SAMOIS (ed.). (1982). *Coming to Power: Writing and Graphics on Lesbian S/M.*
Starhawk. (1982). *Dreaming the Dark.* Boston: Beacon.
Enloe, Cynthia. (1983). *Does Khaki Become You?: The Militarization of Women's Lives.* Boston: South End Press.
Hartsock, Nancy. (1983). *Money, Sex and Power: Toward a Feminist Historical Materialism.* New York: Longman.
Stansell, Christine (ed.). (1983). *Powers of Desire.* New York: Monthly Review Press.
MacKinnon, Catharine. (1989). *Toward a Feminist Theory of the State.* Cambridge, MA: Harvard University Press.
Butler, Judith, and Joan Scott (eds.). (1992). *Feminists Theorize the Political.* New York: Routledge.
Inderpal, Grewal, and Caren Kaplan (eds.). (1994). *Scattered Hegemonies: Postmodernity and Transnational Feminist Practices.* Minneapolis: University of Minnesota Press.
Alexander, Jacqui, and Chandra Mohanty (eds) (1997). *Feminist Genealogies, Colonial Legacies, Democratic Futures.* New York: Routledge.
Berlant. Lauren. (1997). *The Queen of America Goes to Washington City: Essays on Sex and Citizenship.* Durham, NC: Duke University Press.

PSYCHOANALYSIS IN/AND FEMINISM

Psychoanalysis has been both a productive and a problematic framework for feminism and feminist theory. Psychoanalytic theory as developed by Sigmund Freud in the late 19th and early 20th centuries locates the roots of adult identity and male/female difference in sexuality and psychosexual development. Feminists throughout the past century have critiqued the **biological determinism** of Freud's assertion that women are inferior and that their development is troubled because of their deficient genitalia, their **lack of and envy of the penis.** However, feminists have also found useful analytical tools in such key Freudian concepts as the **unconscious** and such methods as the talking cure.

Women were important in the very early decades of the establishment of psychoanalysis as practitioners and as some of Freud's most written-about patients (Dora, Anna O.), whose analysis led to some of the grounding insights of this new field. Karen Horney, an early disciple of psychoanalysis and one of the early feminist critics of Freud, argued that social process and social relations rather than differences in genitalia are the source of differences between the sexes. Horney asserted that it is men's greater social power, not their penises, that women envy and desire. Joan Riviére, the first translator of Freud, also took up women's ambivalent relationship to power.

In *The Second Sex* (1949), Simone de Beauvoir continued this critique. Although de Beauvoir saw some of the methods and insights of psychoanalysis as an advance over earlier wholly biological explanations of difference, she saw as problematic for women Freud's construction of the male as the human norm and the female as "mutilated male." Freud's description of women as deviations from the male was, for de Beauvoir, one example of the ways that culture constructs woman as man's other, rather than as an autonomous being.

Freud's work was attacked by such second-wave feminists as Betty Friedan, Shulamith Firestone, and Kate Millett as hostile to women and a contributing factor in their continued subordination. However, some of Freud's concepts were eagerly assimilated in the United States and Great Britain in what would come to be characterized as object relations theory, a school of thought most closely associated with Melanie Klein and her followers, such as D. W. Winnicott in Great Britain or Nancy Chodorow and Jessica Benjamin in the United States.

In Paris, psychoanalysis underwent a transformation through the work of Jacques Lacan, who meticulously reread Freud and reinterpreted his ideas. In Lacan's work, sexual difference is marked not by different genitalia but by different relationships with language. Males break away from prelinguistic connection with the mother to enter into language, **subjectivity,** and the **symbolic order;** females never do make this transition but remain tied to the mother and outside of language.

Despite its continued reinforcement of a concept of sexual difference, Lacan's work has been of tremendous use to feminist theory. Feminist film theorists have deployed Lacanian psychoanalysis to discuss relations established between filmgoers and cinematic representations. French feminist theorists, Cixous and Irigaray in particular, have borrowed from Lacanian discussions their critique of what they named **phallogocentrism**—the rule of language, the law, and the phallus as "**transcendental signifier.**" However, they have also found ways to reimagine Lacan's relegation of women to a place outside of language as a resource for a new and subversive feminist thinking and writing, **l'écriture féminine.**

By the mid-1970s in the United States, with the publication of Juliet Mitchell's *Psychoanalysis and Feminism,* a reconsideration of psychoanalysis began that has continued to produce rich and complex questions about both the intersubjective (relations between people) and the intrapsychic (our understanding of our selves). Mitchell argued that psychoanalysis provides feminism with important tools for understanding the history of the **subject** and that Freud's work is not misogynistic, prescribing what woman is or should be, but rather an attempt, valuable to feminism, to "set about enquiring how she comes into being" (Mitchell, 252).

In the past two decades, psychoanalysis as practiced and theorized by feminists in Europe and the United States—Jane Flax, Jane Gallop, Teresa de Lauretis, Diana Fuss, and Judith Butler among them—has remained an important tool for understanding the interrelationships of gender, sexuality, and subjectivity. Although feminism's engagements with psychoanalysis have been among the most politically charged and epistemologically troubled dialectics, many would still argue that a thoroughgoing analysis of gender and sexuality cannot be achieved without a psychology or an operative sense of the unconscious.

FURTHER READING

In the Reader:

Browne, Stella. (1923). "Studies in Feminine Inversion."
Riviére, Joan. (1929). "Womanliness as Masquerade."
Horney, Karen. (1932). "The Dread of Woman."

Beauvoir, Simone de. (1949). From *The Second Sex.*

Millett, Kate. (1969). From *Sexual Politics.*

Rubin, Gayle. (1975). "The Traffic in Women: Notes on the 'Political Economy' of Sex."

Chodorow, Nancy. (1978). From *The Reproduction of Mothering: Psychoanalysis and the Sociology of Gender.*

Wittig, Monique. (1978). "The Straight Mind."

Gilligan, Carol. (1982). From *In a Different Voice.*

Outside the Reader:

Klein, Melanie. (1937). *The Psychoanalysis of Children.* Alix Strachey, trans. London: Hogath P.

Breuer, Josef, and Sigmund Freud. (1953). *Studies on Hysteria.* London: Hogarth Press. (Originally published 1895).

Freud, Sigmund. (1953) [orig. pub. 1905]. *Dora: An Analysis of a Case of Hysteria.* London: Hogarth Press.

Chesler, Phyllis. (1972). *Women and Madness.* New York: Doubleday.

Macoby, Eleanor, and Carol Jacklin. (1974). *The Psychology of Sex Differences.* Stanford: Stanford University Press.

Mitchell, Juliet. (1974). *Psychoanalysis and Feminism.* Harmondsworth, U.K.: Penguin.

Miller, Jean Baker. (1976). *Toward a New Psychology of Women.* Boston: Beacon.

Gallop, Jane. (1982). *The Daughter's Seduction: Psychoanalysis and Feminism.* Ithaca, NY: Cornell.

Lauretis, Teresa de. (1984). *Alice Doesn't: Feminism, Semiotics, Cinema.* Bloomington: Indiana University Press.

Elaine, Showalter. (1985). *The Female Malady: Women, Madness and English Culture, 1830–1980.* New York: Pantheon.

Belenky, Mary Field. et al. (1986). *Women's Ways of Knowing.* Verso. New York: Basic Books.

Benjamin, Jessica. (1988). *The Bonds of Love: Psychoanalysis, Feminism, and the Problems of Domination.* New York: Pantheon.

Flax, Jane. (1992). *Thinking Fragments: Psychoanalysis, Feminism, and Postmodernism in the Contemporary West.* Berkeley: University of California.

Abel, Elizabeth, Beth Christian, and Helene Moglen (eds.). (1997). *Female Subjects in Black and White: Race, Psychoanalysis and Feminism.* Berkeley: University of California Press.

SEXUAL DIVISION OF LABOR

The sexual division of labor, the arrangement of work into clearly gendered **public** and **private** spheres or spheres of **production** and **reproduction,** has been theorized particularly by **Marxist, materialist,** and **socialist feminists** in the 19th and 20th centuries. Their analysis is rooted in Friedrich Engels' *The Origin of the Family, Private Property and the State* (1884), which added an understanding of the sphere of reproduction and women's work to Marx's largely gender-blind division of labor analysis. Recent work of feminist ethnographers has also suggested that virtually every known society exhibits such a gendered division of labor, although specifics vary from culture to culture. "Women's work" is always devalued, although the nature of the work itself may vary.

In *The Origin of the Family,* Engels argued that "the worldwide defeat of the female sex" occurred at the moment at which early societies were able to produce surplus value (i.e., more wealth than the community or family needed to subsist) consolidated as private property. The need to pass private property on through inheritance, then, necessitated the control of women's sexuality and thus the confinement of women in the family, the private sphere of reproduction. This division of labor serves the goals of industrial capitalism well, as women's unpaid labor in the private sphere is exploited by capital to reproduce and sustain the workforce.

Feminists in the 19th and 20th centuries extended this division of labor analysis as a primary tool for understanding the gendered division of the work of child rearing as well as occupational segregation of the paid workforce and the division of psychological and emotional labor in the family and society. Alexandra Kollontai noted the class bias of this ideology, which valorizes middle-class women's motherhood while not protecting pregnant working-class women from drudgery as household servants. Later, Shulamith Firestone argued that the division of reproductive labor is the cornerstone of the **sex/gender system.** Other **radical feminists** and **cultural feminists** have suggested that women's separate sphere can be a retreat, a resource, a place of safety for women, an entirely separate culture.

Engels' solution to women's oppression under capitalist patriarchy was both to bring women into the public sphere of labor and to abolish the family as primary economic unit. Socialist feminists in the 20th century have offered similar solutions. Charlotte Perkins Gilman, for example, proposed turning all of women's **unwaged labor** into **paid labor** through communal nurseries, laundries, and kitchens; other socialist feminists have proposed that women be paid "wages for housework." Psychologists Nancy Chodorow and Dorothy Dinnerstein, who saw the roots of inequality in the sexual division of child-rearing labor, argued that moving men into the private sphere to share the work of parenting equally with women would ultimately end inequality.

Women of color and Third World women have also found the division of labor analysis a powerful tool for understanding their own situations in so-called developing economies. More recently, they have used it to understand the situation of Third World workers, particularly women workers, on the global assembly line.

FURTHER READING

In the Reader:

Wollstonecraft, Mary. (1792). From *A Vindication of the Rights of Woman*.
Engels, Friedrich. (1884). From *The Origin of the Family, Private Property and the State*.
Gilman, Charlotte Perkins. (1898). From *Women and Economics*.
Kollontai, Alexandra. (1914). From *Working Woman and Mother*.
Hartmann, Heidi. (1981). "The Unhappy Marriage of Marxism and Feminism: Towards a More Progressive Union."

Outside the Reader:

Firestone, Shulamith. (1970). *The Dialectic of Sex*. New York: Bantam Books.
Mitchell, Juliet. (1971). *Woman's Estate*. Harmondsworth, U.K.: Penguin.
Rowbowthan, Sheila. (1973). *Women's Consciousness, Man's World*. Harmondsworth, U.K.: Penguin.
Delphy, Christine. (1975). *Close to Home: A Materialist Analysis of Women's Oppression*. London: Hutchinson.
Dinnerstein, Dorothy. (1977). *The Mermaid and the Minotaur: Sexual Arrangements and Human Malaise*. New York: Harper.
Eisenstein, Zillah. (1979). *Capitalist Patriarchy and the Case for Socialist Feminism* Monthly Review Press.
Barrett, Michelle. (1980). *Women's Oppression Today*. London: Verso.
Beneria, Lourdes. (1982). *Women and Development*. New York: Praeger.
Fuentes, Annette, and Barbara Ehrenreich. (1983). *Women in the Global Factory*. Boston: South End Press.
Mies, Maria. (1986). *Patriarchy and Accumulation on a World Scale*. London: Zed Books.
Humphries, Jane. (1987). "Origins of the Family, Born Out of Scarcity Not Wealth." In Janet Sayers et al. (eds.). *Engels Revisited. New Feminist Essays*. London: Routledge.
Folbre, Nancy. (1994). *Who Pays for the Kids?: Gender and the Structure of Constraint (Economics As Social Theory)*. New York: Routlege.
Hennessy, Rosemary, and Chris Ingraham (eds). (1997). *Materialist Feminism: A Reader in Class, Difference, and Women's Lives*. New York: Routledge.

SEXUALITIES

"Because sexuality is," according to Gayle Rubin, "the nexus of relationship between the genders, much of the oppression of women is borne by, mediated through, and constituted within, sexuality" ("Thinking Sex," 35). Our use of the plural "sexualities" suggests that contemporary feminists theorized multiple possibilities for **sexual identity, sexual orientation,** and **sexual expression,** which have been defined through feminist theory as well as through **gay** and **lesbian** theory and **queer** theory. Feminists have theorized sexuality as both a site of women's domination and a potential resource for resistance, self-definition, and subjectivity.

Nineteenth-century feminists' first project was to claim sexuality for women, because prevailing ideologies defined women's "virtue" traditionally as the absence of sexual expression and experience. Women's sexlessness was simply assumed so that even physical intimacies between women were not for the most part considered to be sex. Feminists organized to resist government, legal, and medical attempts to define and regulate women's sexuality, particularly such legislation as the Contagious Disease Acts, which attempted to regulate prostitution, and the Comstock Act, which regulated "obscene" material and thus prevented the distribution of information on birth control. In response to these acts, Josephine Butler, Margaret Sanger, Victoria Woodhull, and others argued and organized for women's right to control their own bodies and sexuality and to be free from male sexual exploitation. Their analyses offered the first comprehensive feminist challenge to the **sexual double standard**—a standard that demanded female chastity while permitting and even admiring male promiscuity.

Freud and his followers introduced into Western theory the notion that sexuality is the key determinant of identity, declaring the superiority of the penis over the inferior clitoris and defining for women "normal" sexuality as vaginally oriented and determined by penetration with the objective of producing a male child. All other forms of sexual expression, lesbianism in particular, were viewed as regressive and immature.

Loosening the grip of Freudian theory in defining female sexuality was a major project of 1960s and 1970s feminists. Though they shared a common critique of the biological determinism of Freudian theory and of the "myth of the vaginal orgasm" (Koedt) at its center, they proposed many alternative views and theories of women's sexuality. American second-wave feminists like Friedan and Millett rejected Freud and argued that the social circumstances of middle-class women's lives within patriarchy, not their genitalia, are the origins of their inequality and suppression. Some feminists proposed **sexual liberation,** a rejection of the sexual double standard and a sexual freedom for women equivalent to that of men. Others proposed **androgyny,** a breaking of the rigid **dualism** of male and female and an acceptance of mingling male and female characteristics in each individual.

Radical feminists like Shulamith Firestone foregrounded the link between women's sexuality and reproduction. Firestone proposed in *The Dialectic of Sex* (1970) that women's liberation would be accomplished only when the link between sexuality and reproduction was severed through the use of technologies. French feminists Luce Irigaray and Hélène Cixous also critiqued the phallocentrism of Western thought, particularly as expressed by neo-Freudian theorist Jacques Lacan. They defined a female sexual economy that is multiple and fluid as opposed to monofocal, unitary, and linear (defined by relation to the singular phallus).

The work of lesbian theorists Charlotte Bunch, Marilyn Frye, Ti-Grace Atkinson, Andrea Dworkin, and Monique Wittig was central to shaping feminist understandings of sexuality. They argued from a variety of perspectives that lesbianism is the only sexual and political choice that can free women from the domination of patriarchal **heterosexuality.** Adrienne Rich's essay "Compulsory Heterosexuality and Lesbian Existence" redirected this debate by arguing that heterosexuality is a political institution that deploys a vast ideological apparatus to enforce it as normative. The essay proposes the concept of a **lesbian continuum,** "a range through each woman's life and throughout history, of woman-identified experience, not simply the fact that a woman has had or consciously desired genital sexual experience with another woman."

In the 1980s, feminists were bitterly divided over issues of sexuality, particularly pornography, prostitution, and the status of such sexual identities and practices as sadomasochism. Organizing against pornography and the commercial sex industry, so-called **anti–sex** feminists saw the commercial sex industry and all graphic representations of sexuality as the source of women's oppression. At the same time, so-called **pro–sex** feminists argued for women's sexual autonomy, sexual liberation, sexual pleasure, and sexual pluralism.

Recently, feminist discussion of sexuality expanded in a variety of directions. Arguing that sexual desire is not innate or natural but constituted through specific social and historical processes, Foucault's *History of Sexuality* continues to be an important influence on feminist and queer discussions of sexuality. Queer theorists have pushed these arguments further by suggesting that neither sex nor gender exists except as fluid performances of arbitrary categories (Judith Butler), while the transgendered and transsexual have reintroduced questions of the essential nature of the sexual self (Halberstam). Global/Third world feminisms have focused attention on the impact of Western sexual values on the commercial sex trade, AIDS, and international health and family planning policies, as well as on the conceptualization of sexuality itself (Grewal and Kaplan).

FURTHER READING

In the Reader:

Woodhull, Victoria. (1873). "The Elixir of Life; or, Why Do We Die?"
Sanger, Margaret. (1920). From *Woman and the New Race.*
Browne, Stella. (1923). "Studies in Feminine Inversion."
Mead, Margaret. (1935). From *Sex and Temperament in Three Primitive Societies.*
Millett, Kate. (1969). From *Sexual Politics.*
Radicalesbians. (1970). "The Woman-Identified Woman."
Cixous, Hélène. (1975). "The Laugh of the Medusa."
Bunch, Charlotte. (1975). "Not for Lesbians Only."
Rich, Adrienne. (1980). "Compulsory Heterosexuality and Lesbian Existence."
Vance, Carol. (1984). "Pleasure and Danger: Toward a Politics of Sexuality."
MacKinnon, Catharine A. (1989). "Sexuality, Pornography and Method: 'Pleasure under Patriarchy.'"

Butler, Judith. (1990). From *Gender Trouble: Feminism and the Subversion of Identity.*

Halberstam, Judith. (1998). "The Bathroom Problem" from *Female Masculinity.*

Grewal, Inderpal, and Caren Kaplan. (2001). "Global Identities: Theorizing Transnational Studies of Sexuality."

Outside the Reader:

Firestone, Shulamith. (1970). *The Dialectic of Sex.* New York: Bantam Books.

Snitow, Ann. *et al.* (1983). *Powers of Desire: The Politics of Sexuality.* New York: Monthly Review Press.

Atkinson, Ti-Grace. (1984). *Amazon Odyssey.* New York: Links.

Rubin, Gayle. (1984). "Thinking Sex: Notes for a Radical Theory of Sexuality." *Pleasure and Danger: Exploring Female Sexuality.* Ed. Carol Vance. New York: Routledge.

Bunch, Charlotte. (1987). *Passionate Politics.* New York: St. Martin's.

Dworkin, Andrea. (1987). *Intercourse.* New York: Free Press.

Sedgwick, Eve. (1991). *Epistemology of the Closet.* Berkeley: University of California Press.

Foucault, Michel. (1989). *History of Sexuality.* Robert Hurley, trans. New York: Vintage.

Feinberg, Leslie. (1993). *Stone Butch Blues.* Ithaca, NY: Firebrand Books.

Hausman, Bernice L. (1995). *Changing Sex: Transsexualism, Technology, and the Idea of Gender.* Durham, NC: Duke University Press.

Weed, Elizabeth, and Naomi Schor. (1995). *Feminism Meets Queer Theory.* Bloomington, IN: Indiana University Press.

Martin, Biddy. (1997). *Femininity Played Straight: The Significance of Being Lesbian.* New York: Routledge.

Phelan, Shane. (2001). *Sexual Strangers: Gays, Lesbians and the Dilemmas of Citizenship.* Philadelphia: Temple University Press.

Koyama, Emi. (2001). "The Transfeminist Manifesto."

Hemmings, Clare. (2002). *Bisexual Spaces: Geography of Sexuality and Gender.* New York: Routledge.

Halberstam, Judith. (2005). *In a Queer Time and Place: Transgender Bodies, Subcultural Lives.* New York: NYU Press.

"THIRD WORLD"/GLOBAL/TRANSNATIONAL FEMINISM

The term **"Third World women"** is used variously to designate the majority of the world's women, who live outside the industrialized West, and sometimes also to include women of color within Western countries. The quotation marks indicate the need to problematize this term in several ways. First, the term lumps together in a single category a vast number of women whose experiences vary widely according to class, nation, culture, and sexuality. Whatever coherence "Third World women" as a group might claim is political, coming not from an identity of experience but, as Chandra Mohanty suggested, from a common context of struggle. Second, the term "Third World" itself must be handled critically, as it suggests a hierarchy between First and Third Worlds that is the legacy of **colonialism** and **imperialism.** Some have suggested that the term **Two-Thirds World** might more appropriately be used, as it indicates the reality that the majority of the world's people live outside Europe and the United States. According to Mohanty in her introduction to *Third World Women and the Politics of Feminism,* "histories of third world women's engagement with feminism are in short supply." Certainly, 19th-century colonialism left Third World women largely invisible or represented them as the "exotic other."

Discussion of "Third World women" entered Anglo-American scholarship in the 20th century through the work of anthropologists, who began to describe and particularize the lives of women in their ethnographic work, and through sociologists and economists, who discussed **women and/in development.** While these discourses have been and must be extensively critiqued for the persistence of Eurocentrism and imperialism, they also bring into Western feminism some awareness of the lives of women who had previously been invisible. Feminists working in ethnography have also been at the forefront of discussions about feminist methods; through grappling with problems of gender and cultural bias in the research of Western anthropologists studying Third World peoples, they have articulated the importance of researchers taking account in their work of their social and institutional locations, standpoints, and metaphysical and political commitments.

With the 1975–1985 U.N. Decade on Women meetings in Mexico City, Copenhagen, and Nairobi, attempts began to forge a **global feminism**, which means, as Charlotte Bunch put it, "recognizing that the oppression of women in one part of the world is often affected by what happens in another, and that no woman is free until the conditions of oppression of women are eliminated everywhere." Global feminism, for Bunch and others, necessitates making the global local and the local global, understanding the different experiences of women in different parts of the world, and working in coalitions with other women without imposing Western agendas on them.

Some of the efforts of Western women to begin to talk about the situation of Third World women were heavily critiqued by Third World women for their attempts to export a Western feminist agenda around the world and the failure to recognize the resistance and liberation struggles already being undertaken by Third World women or even to name them as feminist. The complexities of the debate over female genital mutilation are most emblematic of the difficulties of forging such global alliances. Yet the development of a global economy and workforce, the international trafficking in women, and other refugee and human rights issues for women, have made it increasingly clear how necessary it is to forge global feminist alliances. The 1995 U.N. Conference on Women in Beijing Platform for Action is one clear statement of these basic needs.

Along with the work of U.S. women of color, theory produced by Third World feminist scholars, among them Rey Chow, Chandra Mohanty, and Trinh T. Minh Ha, has made crucial methodological and epistemological contributions to Anglo-American feminism. They have challenged its Eurocentrism, "uprooting dualistic thinking," as Anzaldúa suggested in her essay on a mestiza consciousness, and have demanded "a plural consciousness" . . . that "requires understanding multiple, often opposing, ideas and knowledges, and negotiating these knowledges" (Mohanty, 36).

Much of this recent theory intersects with **postcolonial theory.** This work, produced by Third World and Western scholars, is closely allied with postmodernism in its attack on the hegemonic discourses of the West, in this case particularly that of colonialism/imperialism. Postcolonial feminist theory thus seeks a space and discourse in which the knowledge, activism, and subjectivity of Third World women can be articulated (Narayan).

FURTHER READING

In the Reader:

Mead, Margaret. (1935). From *Sex and Temperament in Three Primitive Societies.*
Mernissi, Fatima. (1975). From *Beyond the Veil: Male–Female Dynamics in Modern Muslim Society.*
Mohanty, Chandra Talpade. (1984/1991). "Under Western Eyes: Feminist Scholarship and Colonial Discourses."
Anzaldúa, Gloria. (1987). "La Consciencia de la Mestiza: Towards a New Consciousness."
The Beijing Declaration and Platform for Action (1995).

Narayan, Uma. (1997). "Contesting Cultures: 'Westernization,' Respect for Cultures, and Third World Feminists" from *Dislocating Cultures: Identities, Traditions and Third World Feminism.*

Grewal, Inderpal, and Caren Kaplan. (2001). "Global Identities: Theorizing Transnational Studies of Sexuality."

Mahmood, Saha. (2005). "The Subject of Freedom."

Outside the Reader:

Morgan, Robin. (ed.) (1984). *Sisterhood Is Global: the International Women's Movement Anthology.* Garden City: Doubleday.

Bunch, Charlotte. (1987). "Bringing the Global Home," "Prospects for Global Feminism," "Reflections on Global Feminism after Nairobi." *Passionate Politics.* New York. St. Martin's.

Spivak, Gayatri. (1987). *In Other Worlds: Essays in Cultural Politics.* London: Methuen.

Enloe, Cynthia. (1989). *Bananas, Beaches and Bases: Making Feminist Sense of International Politics.* Berkeley: University of California Press

Minh Ha, Trinh T. (1989). *Woman/Native/Other: Writing Postcoloniality and Feminism.* Bloomington, IN: Indiana University Press.

Chow, Rey. (1993). *Writing Diaspora.* Bloomington, IN: Indiana University Press.

Ahmed, Leila. (1993). *Women and Gender in Islam: Historical Roots of a Modern Debate.* New Haven. Yale University Press.

McClintock, Ann. (1995). *Imperial Leather: Race. Gender and Sexuality in the Imperial Context.* New York: Routledge.

Yuval-Davis, Nira. (1997). *Gender and Nation.* London: Sage.

Ong, Aihwa. (1998). *Flexible Citizenship: The Cultural Logics of Transnationality.* Durham, NC: Duke University Press.

Perez, Emma. (1999). *The Decolonial Imagination: Writing Chicanas into History.* Bloomington, IN: Indiana University Press.

Mohanty, Chandra. (2003). *Feminism without Borders: Decolonizing Theory, Practicing Solidarity.* Durham, NC: Duke University Press.

Moghadam, Valentine M. (2005). *Globalizing Women: Transnational Feminist Networks.* Baltimore: Johns Hopkins University Press.

PART II

1792–1920

1792–1920: Introduction

At the end of the 18th century, most women in the United States and Great Britain had no public legal existence. They were either daughters identified by their fathers' status or wives identified by their husbands'. During this period, feminist theory (though this term would not have been used) for the most part attempted to analyze the legal and social disabilities women faced and to argue for the most basic rights for women. The principles of enlightenment and liberal humanism—arguments for the "rights of man," which had supported the French and American revolutions of the end of the 18th century—provided a theoretical basis for much 19th-century feminist writing. Mary Wollstonecraft's *Vindication of the Rights of Woman* (1792) and the Seneca Falls "Declaration of Sentiments" (1848) attempted to bring the language of "rights" to bear on the situations of women and to include women among the "humans" and "citizens" on behalf of whom rights had been won.

The major women's rights struggle of the 19th century was the campaign for women's suffrage, which began in the United States with the 1848 Seneca Falls meeting and continued through 1920, when the ratification of the 19th Amendment gave U.S. women the vote. Such liberal arguments for basic rights were used by women's advocates in other areas as well. They supported middle-class women's struggles for the right to own property, to have custody of their children, to sue for divorce, and to gain admission to higher education, professional training, and the professions themselves. They also supported working-class women's struggles for access to employment, decent housing, and adequate wages.

Many of the women who became involved in the suffrage struggle were already involved in progressive or radical politics, mainly in the abolition movement. One of the debates that divided the suffrage movement through much of its history was how much the cause of suffrage could or should be linked to radical movements for reform, the movement to abolish slavery in particular, or even other women's campaigns, such as those for sexual integrity, birth control, or protective legislation for women workers. These political disputes were grounded in a fundamental theoretical disagreement about women's sameness to or difference from men and from each other. The proponents of liberal feminism argued for women's admission to the same legal rights as men. Others—looking at women's work, productive and reproductive, their sexuality, and their social and cultural assignments and trying to understand the nature of their subordination—examined women's difference and argued that women's special roles and duties resulted in unique contributions but also required special protections.

Much of the writing about women's situation in the 19th century focuses on the ways in which it was shaped by urbanization and industrialization. The development of a sizable urban middle class, beginning in the late 18th century, had some advantages for women in the increased prosperity of their households and the availability of more household services. However, the concomitant ideology of separate spheres, which assigned middle-class women ever more determinedly to the private world of mothering and domesticity, also imposed severe limitations on women's access to the public world. John Stuart Mill, Harriet Taylor, and Friedrich Engels attempted to analyze the "subjection of women" that resulted from this middle-class ideology. Late in the century, Charlotte Perkins Gilman, deploying the tools of socialist analysis, proposed moving women's work out of the household to end entirely the tyranny of separate spheres.

For working-class women, urbanization meant factory or service work at low wages and in poor conditions, as well as the need to feed and care for a family under these circumstances. Many working-class girls found employment, not just in mills and factories, but also in the growing service sector with jobs as household servants and later as clerks, waitresses, and hospital aides. Mother Jones was one of many women who became active in labor organizing and in writing and thinking about industrial working conditions and their particular effects on women.

Many working-class women newly arrived in the cities found that the only work they could get was as prostitutes, a situation that precipitated much concern and debate in both the United States and Great Britain. During the 1860s, attempts in Great Britain to regulate prostitution through the Contagious Diseases Acts provoked feminists like Josephine Butler to critique publicly the sexual double standard that demanded sexual restraint from women but condoned promiscuity in men. Arguments that developed in these struggles were deployed later by activists fighting for women's access to birth control and their right to make decisions about their own sexuality.

Although much 19th-century writing and thinking was directed at the lives of women in the new urban middle and working classes, through most of this period the majority of U.S. women—European American, Native American, African American, Asian American, and Latina—lived in rural settings and spent their lives in agricultural and household labor without wages. The circumstances of their lives varied greatly, from the relatively privileged lives of wives and daughters on long-established farms in the East and Midwest, to those women in poor white southern sharecropping families and in families who moved west during the westward expansion, to the lives of Native American women driven with their tribes from traditional homelands to reservations, to the lives of African American women living as slaves in the South.

By 1920, suffrage had been achieved, as well as many other rights for women. Some women were better educated and had achieved more legal rights and professional access than women ever had before. Those who had worked so hard to gain the franchise for women saw its achievement as an acknowledgment of women's status as full social and political participants in U.S. democracy. Whether, finally, this vision would be realized and whether, in fact, it was the vision most likely to change the lives of most women remained questions for the next decades.

7

The Changing Woman

(NAVAJO ORIGIN MYTH)
ANONYMOUS. N.D.

In the great desert of multicolored sand stood the Mountain - Around -Which - Moving -Was - Done, and at the foot of this great mountain was found a baby girl.

First Man and First Woman found the child when the earth was still unformed and incomplete. They took her home with them and raised her carefully, and the gods smiled on her and loved her. As she grew into womanhood, the world itself reached maturity as the mountains and valleys were all put into the proper places.

At last she was grown and the world was complete, and to celebrate her becoming a woman, the gods gave her a Blessing Way, Walking-into-Beauty. Songs and chants were sung to her, and her body was shaped with a sacred stick so that it would grow strong and beautiful. Each morning of the ceremony, she ran to greet the sun as it arose. The sacred ceremony was preserved and it is now given to all Navajo girls when they reach adulthood.

But the young girl did not stay the same. Each winter she became withered and white-haired, just as the earth became bare and snow-covered. But each spring as the colors of life grew back on the land, the colors of youth and beauty appeared in her cheeks and in her hair. So she is called Changing Woman, or "A Woman She Becomes Time and Again."

The sun fell in love with Changing Woman, but she did not know what to do with him. So she went to First Woman for advice. On the advice of First Woman, she met the sun and he made love to her. Nine months later, twin sons were born to her and she raised them with love and care. For monsters had now appeared in the world, and the people were being destroyed. Changing Woman hoped her sons could save the world from the monsters.

When the twin boys were grown, Changing Woman sent them to the sun, their father, to get power from him so that they could fight the monsters. After undergoing severe tests by their father, the boys returned and destroyed all the monsters.

Now the world was complete and the monsters were dead. It was a perfect place for people, but there were very few left. Changing Woman pondered over this problem, and at last she took two baskets of corn. One was of white corn and one was of yellow corn. From the white cornmeal she shaped a man and from the yellow cornmeal she shaped a woman.

And so the earth was populated again, a changing world and a beautiful world—the world of Changing Woman.

 8

From A Vindication of the Rights of Woman

MARY WOLLSTONECRAFT

MARY WOLLSTONECRAFT England. 1759–1797. Writer, editor, social and educational reformer. *Thoughts on the Education of Daughters* (1787), *A Vindication of the Rights of Man* (1790), *Mary: A Fiction* (1788).

CHAPTER II: THE PREVAILING OPINION OF A SEXUAL CHARACTER DISCUSSED

To account for, and excuse the tyranny of man, many ingenious arguments have been brought forward to prove, that the two sexes, in the acquirement of virtue, ought to aim at attaining a very different character: or, to speak explicitly, women are not allowed to have sufficient strength of mind to acquire what really deserves the name of virtue. Yet it should seem, allowing them to have souls, that there is but one way appointed by Providence to lead *mankind* to either virtue or happiness.

If then women are not a swarm of ephemeron triflers, why should they be kept in ignorance under the specious name of innocence? Men complain, and with reason, of the follies and caprices of our sex, when they do not keenly satirize our head-strong passions and groveling vices. —Behold, I should answer, the natural effect of ignorance! The mind will ever be unstable that has only prejudices to rest on, and the current will run with destructive fury when there are no barriers to break its force. Women are told from their infancy, and taught by the example of their mothers, that a little knowledge of human weakness, justly termed cunning, softness of temper, *outward* obedience, and a scrupulous attention to a puerile kind of propriety, will obtain for them the protection of man; and should they be beautiful, everything else is needless, for, at least, twenty years of their lives.

Thus Milton describes our first frail mother; though when he tells us that women are formed for softness and sweet attractive grace, I cannot comprehend his meaning, unless in the true Mahometan strain, he meant to deprive us of souls, and insinuate that we were beings only designed by sweet attractive grace, and docile blind obedience, to gratify the senses of man when he can no longer soar on the wing of contemplation.

How grossly do they insult us who thus advise us only to render ourselves gentle, domestic brutes! For instance, the winning softness so warmly, and frequently, recommended, that governs by obeying. What childish expressions, and how insignificant is the being—can it be an immortal one? who will condescend to govern by such sinister methods! 'Certainly,' says Lord Bacon, 'man is of kin to the beasts by his body; and if he be not of kin to God by his spirit, he is a base and ignoble creature!' Men, indeed, appear to me to act in a very unphilosophical manner when they try to secure the good conduct of women by attempting to keep them always in a state of childhood. Rousseau was more consistent when he wished to stop the progress of reason in both sexes, for if men eat of the tree of knowledge, women will come in for a taste; but, from the imperfect cultivation which their understandings now receive, they only attain a knowledge of evil. . . .

In treating, therefore, of the manners of women, let us, disregarding sensual arguments, trace what we should endeavour to make them in order to cooperate, if the expression be not too bold, with the supreme Being.

. . . Men and women must be educated, in a great degree, by the opinions and manners of the society they live in. In every age there has been a stream of popular opinion that has carried all before it, and given a family character, as it were, to

the century. It may then fairly be inferred, that, till society be differently constituted, much cannot be expected from education. It is, however, sufficient for my present purpose to assert, that, whatever effect circumstances have on the abilities, every being may become virtuous by the exercise of its own reason; for if but one being was created with vicious inclinations, that is positively bad, what can save us from atheism? or if we worship a God, is not that God a devil?

Consequently, the most perfect education, in my opinion, is such an exercise of the understanding as is best calculated to strengthen the body and form the heart. Or, in other words, to enable the individual to attain such habits of virtue as will render it independent. In fact, it is a farce to call any being virtuous whose virtues do not result from the exercise of its own reason. This was Rousseau's opinion respecting men: I extend it to women, and confidently assert that they have been drawn out of their sphere by false refinement, and not by an endeavour to acquire masculine qualities. Still the regal homage which they receive is so intoxicating, that till the manners of the times are changed, and formed on more reasonable principles, it may be impossible to convince them that the illegitimate power, which they obtain, by degrading themselves, is a curse, and that they must return to nature and equality, if they wish to secure the placid satisfaction that unsophisticated affections impart. But for this epoch we must wait—wait, perhaps, till kings and nobles, enlightened by reason, and, preferring the real dignity of man to childish state, throw off their gaudy hereditary trappings: and if then women do not resign the arbitrary power of beauty—they will prove that they have *less* mind than man.

. . . [I]n the education of women, the cultivation of the understanding is always subordinate to the acquirement of some corporeal accomplishment; even while enervated by confinement and false notions of modesty, the body is prevented from attaining that grace and beauty which relaxed half-formed limbs never exhibit. Besides, in youth their faculties are not brought forward by emulation; and having no serious scientific study, if they have natural sagacity it is turned too soon on life and manners. They dwell on effects, and modifications, without tracing them back to causes; and complicated rules to adjust behaviour are a weak substitute for simple principles.

As a proof that education gives this appearance of weakness to females, we may instance the example of military men, who are, like them, sent into the world before their minds have been stored with knowledge or fortified by principles. The consequences are similar; soldiers acquire a little superficial knowledge, snatched from the muddy current of conversation, and, from continually mixing with society, they gain, what is termed a knowledge of the world; and this acquaintance with manners and customs has frequently been confounded with a knowledge of the human heart. But can the crude fruit of casual observation, never brought to the test of judgment, formed by comparing speculation and experience, deserve such a distinction? Soldiers, as well as women, practice the minor virtues with punctilious politeness. Where is then the sexual difference, when the education has been the same? All the difference that I can discern, arises from the superior advantage of liberty, which enables the former to see more of life. . . .

CHAPTER VII: OF THE PERNICIOUS EFFECTS WHICH ARISE FROM THE UNNATURAL DISTINCTIONS ESTABLISHED IN SOCIETY

From the respect paid to property flow, as from a poisoned fountain, most of the evils and vices which render this world such a dreary scene to the contemplative mind. For it is in the most polished society that noisome reptiles and venomous serpents lurk under the rank herbage; and there is voluptuousness pampered by the still sultry air, which relaxes every good disposition before it ripens into virtue.

One class presses on another, for all are aiming to procure respect on account of their property; and property once gained will procure the respect due only to talents and virtue. Men neglect the duties incumbent on man, yet are treated like demigods. Religion is also separated from morality by a ceremonial veil, yet men wonder that the world is almost, literally speaking, a den of sharpers or oppressors.

There is a homely proverb, which speaks a shrewd truth, that whoever the devil finds idle he will employ.

And what but habitual idleness can hereditary wealth and titles produce? For man is so constituted that he can only attain a proper use of his faculties by exercising them, and will not exercise them unless necessity of some kind first set the wheels in motion. Virtue likewise can only be acquired by the discharge of relative duties; but the importance of these sacred duties will scarcely be felt by the being who is cajoled out of his humanity by the flattery of sycophants. There must be more equality established in society, or morality will never gain ground, and this virtuous equality will not rest firmly even when founded on a rock, if one-half of mankind be chained to its bottom by fate, for they will be continually undermining it through ignorance or pride.

It is vain to expect virtue from women till they are in some degree independent of men; nay, it is vain to expect that strength of natural affection which would make them good wives and mothers. Whilst they are absolutely dependent on their husbands they will be cunning, mean, and selfish; and the men who can be gratified by the fawning fondness of spaniel-like affection have not much delicacy, for love is not to be bought; in any sense of the words, its silken wings are instantly shrivelled up when anything beside a return in kind is sought. Yet whilst wealth enervates men, and women live, as it were, by their personal charms, how can we expect them to discharge those ennobling duties which equally require exertion and self-denial?

· · ·

The preposterous distinctions of rank, which render civilization a curse, by dividing the world between voluptuous tyrants and cunning envious dependents, corrupt, almost equally, every class of people, because respectability is not attached to the discharge of the relative duties of life, but to the station, and when the duties are not fulfilled the affections cannot gain sufficient strength to fortify the virtue of which they are the natural reward. Still there are some loop-holes out of which a man may creep, and dare to think and act for himself; but for a woman it is an herculean task, because she has difficulties peculiar to her sex to overcome, which require almost superhuman powers.

A truly benevolent legislator always endeavours to make it the interest of each individual to be virtuous; and thus private virtue becoming the cement of public happiness, an orderly whole is consolidated by the tendency of all the parts towards a common centre. But the private or public virtue of woman is very problematical, for Rousseau, and a numerous list of male writers, insist that she should all her life be subjected to a severe restraint, that of propriety. Why subject her to propriety—blind propriety—if she be capable of acting from a nobler spring, if she be an heir of immortality? Is sugar always to be produced by vital blood? Is one half of the human species, like the poor African slaves, to be subjected to prejudices that brutalize them, when principles would be a surer guard, only to sweeten the cup of man? Is not this indirectly to deny woman reason? For a gift is a mockery, if it be unfit for use.

Women are, in common with men, rendered weak and luxurious by the relaxing pleasures which wealth procures; but added to this they are made slaves to their persons, and must render them alluring that man may lend them his reason to guide their tottering steps aright. Or should they be ambitious, they must govern their tyrants by sinister tricks, for without rights there cannot be any incumbent duties. The laws respecting woman, which I mean to discuss in a future part, make an absurd unit of a man and his wife; and then, by the easy transition of only considering him as responsible, she is reduced to a mere cipher.

The being who discharges the duties of its station is independent; and, speaking of women at large, their first duty is to themselves as rational creatures, and the next, in point of importance, as citizens, is that, which includes so many, of a mother. The rank in life which dispenses with their fulfilling this duty, necessarily degrades them by making them mere dolls. Or should they turn to something more important than merely fitting drapery upon a smooth block, their minds are only occupied by some soft platonic attachment; or the actual management of an intrigue may keep their thoughts in motion; for when they neglect domestic duties, they have it not in their power to take the field and march and counter-march like soldiers, or wrangle in the senate to keep their faculties from rusting.

CHAPTER XIII: SOME INSTANCES OF THE FOLLY WHICH THE IGNORANCE OF WOMEN GENERATES, WITH CONCLUDING REFLECTIONS ON THE MORAL IMPROVEMENT THAT A REVOLUTION IN FEMALE MANNERS MIGHT NATURALLY BE EXPECTED TO PRODUCE

Sect. VI
· · ·

To render women truly useful members of society, I argue that they should be led, by having their understandings cultivated on a large scale, to acquire a rational affection for their country, founded on knowledge, because it is obvious that we are little interested about what we do not understand. And to render this general knowledge of due importance, I have endeavoured to shew that private duties are never properly fulfilled unless the understanding enlarges the heart; and that public virtue is only an aggregate of private. But, the distinctions established in society undermine both, by beating out the sold gold of virtue, till it becomes only the tinsel-covering of vice; for whilst wealth renders a man more respectable than virtue, wealth will be sought before virtue; and, whilst women's persons are caressed, when a childish simper shews an absence of mind—the mind will lie fallow. Yet, true voluptuousness must proceed from the mind—for what can equal the sensations produced by mutual affection, supported by mutual respect? What are the cold, or feverish caresses of appetite, but sin embracing death, compared with the modest over-flowings of a pure heart and exalted imagination? Yes, let me tell the libertine of fancy when he despises understanding in woman—that the mind, which he disregards, gives life to the enthusiastic affection from which rapture, short-lived as it is, alone can flow! And, that, without virtue, a sexual attachment must expire, like a tallow candle in the socket, creating intolerable disgust. To prove this, I need only observe, that men who have wasted great part of their lives with women, and with whom they have sought for pleasure with eager thirst, entertain the meanest opinion of the sex.—Virtue, true refiner of joy!—if foolish men were to fright thee from earth, in order to give loose to all their appetites without a check—some sensual weight of taste would scale the heavens to invite thee back, to give a zest to pleasure!

That women at present are by ignorance rendered foolish or vicious, is, I think, not to be disputed; and, that the most salutary effects tending to improve mankind might be expected from a REVOLUTION in female manners, appears, at least, with a face of probability, to rise out of the observation. For as marriage has been termed the parent of those endearing charities which draw man from the brutal herd, the corrupting intercourse that wealth, idleness, and folly, produce between the sexes, is more universally injurious to morality than all the other vices of mankind collectively considered. To adulterous lust the most sacred duties are sacrificed, because before marriage, men, by a promiscuous intimacy with women, learned to consider love as a selfish gratification—learned to separate it not only from esteem, but from the affection merely built on habit, which mixes a little humanity with it. Justice and friendship are also set at defiance, and that purity of taste is vitiated which would naturally lead a man to relish an artless display of affection rather than affected airs. But that noble simplicity of affection, which dares to appear unadorned, has few attractions for the libertine, though it be the charm, which by cementing the matrimonial tie, secures to the pledges of a warmer passion the necessary parental attention; for children will never be properly educated till friendship subsists between parents. Virtue flies from a house divided against itself—and a whole legion of devils take up their residence there.

The affection of husbands and wives cannot be pure when they have so few sentiments in common, and when so little confidence is established at home, as must be the case when their pursuits are so different. That intimacy from which tenderness should flow, will not, cannot subsist between the vicious.

Contending, therefore, that the sexual distinction which men have so warmly insisted upon, is arbitrary, I have dwelt on an observation, that several sensible men, with whom I have conversed on the subject, allowed to be well founded; and it is

simply this, that the little chastity to be found amongst men, and consequent disregard of modesty, tend to degrade both sexes; and further, that the modesty of women, characterized as such, will often be only the artful veil of wantonness instead of being the natural reflection of purity, till modesty be universally respected.

From the tyranny of man, I firmly believe, the greater number of female follies proceed; and the cunning, which I allow makes at present a part of their character, I likewise have repeatedly endeavoured to prove, is produced by oppression. . . .

Asserting the rights which women in common with men ought to contend for, I have not attempted to extenuate their faults; but to prove them to be the natural consequence of their education and station in society. If so, it is reasonable to suppose that they will change their character, and correct their vices and follies, when they are allowed to be free in a physical, moral, and civil sense.

Let woman share the rights and she will emulate the virtues of man; for she must grow more perfect when emancipated, or justify the authority that chains such a weak being to her duty.—If the latter, it will be expedient to open a fresh trade with Russia for whips; a present which a father should always make to his son-in-law on his wedding day, that a husband may keep his whole family in order by the same means; and without any violation of justice reign, wielding this sceptre, sole master of his house, because he is the only being in it who has reason:—the divine, indefeasible earthly sovereignty breathed into man by the Master of the universe. Allowing this position, women have not any inherent rights to claim; and, by the same rule, their duties vanish, for rights and duties are inseparable.

Be just then, O ye men of understanding! and mark not more severely what women do amiss, than the vicious tricks of the horse or the ass for whom ye provide provender—and allow her the privileges of ignorance, to whom ye deny the rights of reason, or ye will be worse than Egyptian taskmasters, expecting virtue where nature has not given understanding!

[1792]

9

From Letters on the Equality of the Sexes and the Condition of Women

SARAH M. GRIMKÉ

SARAH M. GRIMKÉ United States. 1792–1873. Teacher. Lecturer. Cofounder of several progressive schools. A Southern woman, who moved North with her sister Angelina to become active in both abolition and suffrage campaigns. First woman to speak in public at antislavery meetings. Antislavery pamphlet, *An Epistle to the Clergy of the Southern States* (1835).

LETTER VIII: ON THE CONDITION OF WOMEN IN THE UNITED STATES

Brookline, 1837.

My dear sister,

I have now taken a brief survey of the condition of woman in various parts of the world. I regret that my time has been so much occupied by other things, that I have been unable to bestow that attention upon the subject which it merits, and that my constant change of place has prevented me from having access to books, which might probably have assisted me in this part of my work. I hope that the principles I have asserted will claim the attention of some of my sex, who may be able to bring into view, more thoroughly than I have done, the situation and degradation of woman. I shall now proceed to make a few remarks on the condition of women in my own country.

During the early part of my life, my lot was cast among the butterflies of the *fashionable* world; and of this class of women, I am constrained to say, both from experience and observation, that their education is miserably deficient; that they are taught to regard marriage as the one thing needful, the only avenue to distinction; hence to attract the notice and win the attentions of men, by their external charms, is the chief business of fashionable girls. They seldom think that men will be allured by intellectual acquirements, because they find, that where any mental superiority exists, a woman is generally shunned and regarded as stepping out of

her 'appropriate sphere,' which, in their view, is to dress, to dance, to set out to the best possible advantage her person, to read the novels which inundate the press, and which do more to destroy her character as a rational creature, than anything else. Fashionable women regard themselves, and are regarded by men, as pretty toys or as mere instruments of pleasure; and the vacuity of mind, heartlessness, the frivolity which is the necessary result of this false and debasing estimate of women, can only be fully understood by those who have mingled in the folly and wickedness of fashionable life; and who have been called from such pursuits by the voice of the Lord Jesus, inviting their weary and heavy-laden souls to come unto Him and learn of Him, that they may find something worthy of their immortal spirit, and their intellectual powers; that they may learn the high and holy purposes of their creation, and consecrate themselves unto the service of God; and not, as is now the case, to the pleasure of man.

There is another and much more numerous class in this country, who are withdrawn by education or circumstances from the circle of fashionable amusements, but who are brought up with the dangerous and absurd idea, that *marriage* is a kind of preferment; and that to be able to keep their husband's house, and render his situation comfortable, is the end of her being. Much that she does and says and thinks is done in reference to this situation; and to be married is too often held up to the view of girls as the sine qua non of human happiness and human existence. For this purpose more than for any other, I verily believe the majority of girls are trained. This is demonstrated by the imperfect education which is bestowed upon them, and the little pains taken to cultivate their minds, after they leave school, by the little time allowed them for reading, and by the idea being constantly inculcated, that although all household concerns should be attended to with scrupulous punctuality at particular seasons, the improvement of their intellectual capacities is only a secondary consideration, and may serve as an occupation to fill up the odds and ends of time. In most families, it is considered a matter of far more consequence to call a girl off from making a pie, or a pudding, than to interrupt her whilst engaged in her studies. This mode of training necessarily exalts, in their view, the animal above the intellectual and spiritual nature, and teaches women to regard themselves as a kind of machinery, necessary to keep the domestic engine in order, but of little value as the *intelligent* companions of men.

. . .

There is another way in which the general opinion, that women are inferior to men, is manifested, that bears with tremendous effect on the laboring class, and indeed on almost all who are obliged to earn a subsistence, whether it be by mental or physical exertion—I allude to the disproportionate value set on the time and labor of men and of women. A man who is engaged in teaching, can always, I believe, command a higher price for tuition than a woman—even when he teaches the same branches, and is not in any respect superior to the woman. This I know is the case in boarding and other schools with which I have been acquainted, and it is so in every occupation in which the sexes engage indiscriminately. As for example, in tailoring, a man has twice, or three times as much for making a waistcoat or pantaloons as a woman, although the work done by each may be equally good. In those employments which are peculiar to women, their time is estimated at only half the value of that of men. A woman who goes out to wash, works as hard in proportion as a wood sawyer, or a coal heaver, but she is not generally able to make more than half as much by a day's work. The low remuneration which women receive for their work, has claimed the attention of a few philanthropists, and I hope it will continue to do so until some remedy is applied for this enormous evil. I have known a widow, left with four or five children, to provide for, unable to leave home because her helpless babes demand her attention, compelled to earn a scanty subsistence, by making coarse shirts at 12½ cents apiece, or by taking in washing, for which she was paid by some wealthy persons 12½ cents per dozen. All these things evince the low estimation in which woman is held. There is yet another and more disastrous consequence arising from this unscriptural notion—women being educated, from earliest childhood, to regard themselves as inferior creatures, have not that self-respect which conscious equality would engender, and hence when their virtue is assailed, they yield to temptation with facility, under the idea that it rather exalts than debases them, to be connected with a superior being.

There is another class of women in this country, to whom I cannot refer, without feelings of the deepest shame and sorrow. I allude to our female slaves. Our southern cities are whelmed beneath a tide of pollution; the virtue of female slaves is wholly at the mercy of irresponsible tyrants, and women are bought and sold in our slave markets, to gratify the brutal lust of those who bear the name of Christians. In our slave States, if amid all her degradation and ignorance, a woman desires to preserve her virtue unsullied, she is either bribed or whipped into compliance, or if she dares resist her seducer, her life by the laws of some of the slave States may be, and has actually been sacrificed to the fury of disappointed passion. Where such laws do not exist, the power which is necessarily vested in the master over his property, leaves the defenceless slave entirely at his mercy, and the sufferings of some females on this account, both physical and mental, are intense. Mr. Gholson, in the House of Delegates of Virginia, in 1832, said, 'He really had been under the impression that he owned his slaves. He had lately purchased four women and ten children, in whom he thought he had obtained a great bargain; for he supposed they were his own property, *as were his brood mares.*' But even if any laws existed in the United States, as in Athens formerly, for the protection of female slaves, they would be null and void, because the evidence of a colored person is not admitted against a white, in any of our Courts of Justice in the slave States. 'In Athens, if a female slave had cause to complain of any want of respect to the laws of modesty, she could seek the protection of the temple, and demand a change of owners; and such appeals were never discountenanced, or neglected by the magistrate.' In Christian America, the slave has no refuge from unbridled cruelty and lust.

. . .

Nor does the colored woman suffer alone: the moral purity of the white woman is deeply contaminated. In the daily habit of seeing the virtue of her enslaved sister sacrificed without hesitancy or remorse, she looks upon the crimes of seduction and illicit intercourse without horror, and although not personally involved in the guilt, she loses that value for innocence in her own, as well as the other sex, which is one of the strongest safeguards to virtue. She lives in habitual intercourse with men, whom she knows to be polluted by licentiousness, and often is she compelled to witness in her own domestic circle, those disgusting and heart-sickening jealousies and strifes which disgraced and distracted the family of Abraham. In addition to all this, the female slaves suffer every species of degradation and cruelty, which the most wanton barbarity can inflict; they are indecently divested of their clothing, sometimes tied up and severely whipped, sometimes prostrated on the earth, while their naked bodies are torn by the scorpion lash.

'The whip on WOMAN's shrinking flesh!
Our soil yet reddening with the stains
Caught from her scourging warm and fresh.'

Can any American woman look at these scenes of shocking licentiousness and cruelty, and fold her hands in apathy, and say, 'I have nothing to do with slavery'? *She cannot and be guiltless.*

I cannot close this letter, without saying a few words on the benefits to be derived by men, as well as women, from the opinions I advocate relative to the equality of the sexes. Many women are now supported, in idleness and extravagance, by the industry of their husbands, fathers, or brothers, who are compelled to toil out their existence, at the counting house, or in the printing office, or some other laborious occupation, while the wife and daughters and sisters take no part in the support of the family, and appear to think that their sole business is to spend the hard-bought earnings of their male friends. I deeply regret such a state of things, because I believe that if women felt their responsibility, for the support of themselves, or their families it would add strength and dignity to their characters, and teach them more true sympathy for their husbands, than is now generally manifested,—a sympathy which would be exhibited by actions as well as words. Our brethren may reject my doctrine, because it runs counter to common opinions, and because it wounds their pride; but I believe they would be 'partakers of the benefit' resulting from the Equality of the Sexes, and would find that

woman, as their equal, was unspeakably more valuable than woman as their inferior, both as a moral and an intellectual being.

Thine in the bonds of womanhood,

Sarah M. Grimké
[1838]

 10

"Declaration of Sentiments" from The History of Women's Suffrage

ELIZABETH CADY STANTON

SENECA FALLS WOMEN'S RIGHTS CONVENTION Convened by Elizabeth Cady Stanton, Lucretia Mott, and several other Quaker abolitionist women, the First Women's Rights Convention in the United States took place in a chapel in Seneca Falls, New York, July 19–20, 1848. This document, drafted by Elizabeth Cady Stanton, was debated at and adopted by the convention.

When, in the course of human events, it becomes necessary for one portion of the family of man to assume among the people of the earth a position different from that which they have hitherto occupied, but one to which the laws of nature and of nature's God entitle them, a decent respect to the opinions of mankind requires that they should declare the causes that impel them to such a course.

We hold these truths to be self-evident: that all men and women are created equal; that they are endowed by their Creator with certain inalienable rights; that among these are life, liberty, and the pursuit of happiness; that to secure these rights governments are instituted, deriving their just powers from the consent of the governed. Whenever any form of government becomes destructive of these ends, it is the right of those who suffer from it to refuse allegiance to it, and to insist upon the institution of a new government, laying its foundation on such principles, and organizing its powers in such form, as to them shall seem most likely to effect their safety and happiness. Prudence, indeed, will dictate that governments long established should not be changed for light and transient causes; and accordingly all experience hath shown that mankind are more disposed to suffer, while evils are sufferable, than to right themselves by abolishing the forms to which they were accustomed. But when a long train of abuses and usurpations, pursuing invariably the same object evinces a design to reduce them under absolute despotism, it is their duty to throw off such government, and to provide new guards for their future security. Such has been the patient sufferance of the women under this government, and such is now the necessity which constrains them to demand the equal station to which they are entitled.

The history of mankind is a history of repeated injuries and usurpations on the part of man toward woman, having in direct object the establishment of an absolute tyranny over her. To prove this, let facts be submitted to a candid world.

He has never permitted her to exercise her inalienable right to the elective franchise.

He has compelled her to submit to laws, in the formation of which she had no voice.

He has withheld from her rights which are given to the most ignorant and degraded men—both natives and foreigners.

Having deprived her of this first right of a citizen, the elective franchise, thereby leaving her without representation in the halls of legislation, he has oppressed her on all sides.

He has made her, if married, in the eye of the law, civilly dead.

He has taken from her all right in property, even to the wages she earns.

He has made her, morally, an irresponsible being, as she can commit many crimes with impunity, provided they be done in the presence of her husband. In the covenant of marriage, she is compelled to promise obedience to her husband, he becoming, to all intents and purposes, her master—the law giving him power to deprive her of her liberty, and to administer chastisement.

He has so framed the laws of divorce, as to what shall be the proper causes, and in case of separation, to whom the guardianship of the children shall be given, as to be wholly regardless of the happiness of women—the law, in all cases, going upon a false supposition of the supremacy of man, and giving all power into his hands.

After depriving her of all rights as a married woman, if single and the owner of property, he has taxed her to support a government which recognizes her only when her property can be made profitable to it.

He has monopolized nearly all the profitable employments, and from those she is permitted to follow, she receives but a scanty remuneration. He closes against her all the avenues to wealth and distinction which he considers most honorable to himself. As a teacher of theology, medicine, or law, she is not known.

He has denied her the facilities for obtaining a thorough education, all colleges being closed against her.

He allows her in Church, as well as State, but a subordinate position, claiming Apostolic authority for her exclusion from the ministry, and, with some exceptions, from any public participation in the affairs of the Church.

He has created a false public sentiment by giving to the world a different code of morals for men and women, by which moral delinquencies which exclude women from society are not only tolerated, but deemed of little account in man.

He has usurped the prerogative of Jehovah himself, claiming it as his right to assign for her a sphere of action, when that belongs to her conscience and to her God.

He has endeavored, in every way that he could, to destroy her confidence in her own powers, to lessen her self-respect, and to make her willing to lead a dependent and abject life.

Now, in view of this entire disfranchisement of one-half the people of this country, their social and religious degradation—in view of the unjust laws above mentioned, and because women do feel themselves aggrieved, oppressed, and fraudulently deprived of their most sacred rights, we insist that they have immediate admission to all the rights and privileges which belong to them as citizens of the United States.

In entering upon the great work before us, we anticipate no small amount of misconception, misrepresentation, and ridicule; but we shall use every instrumentality within our power to effect our object. We shall employ agents, circulate tracts, petition the State and National legislatures, and endeavor to enlist the pulpit and the press in our behalf. We hope this Convention will be followed by a series of Conventions embracing every part of the country.

. . .

Whereas, the great precept of nature is conceded to be, that "man shall pursue his own true and substantial happiness." Blackstone in his Commentaries remarks, that this law of Nature being coeval with mankind, and dictated by God himself, is of course superior in obligation to any other. It is binding over all the globe, in all countries and at all times; no human laws are of any validity if contrary to this, and such of them as are valid, derive all their force, and all their validity, and all their authority, mediately and immediately, from this original; therefore,

Resolved, That such laws as conflict, in any way, with the true and substantial happiness of woman, are contrary to the great precept of nature and of no validity, for this is "superior in obligation to any other."

Resolved, That all laws which prevent woman from occupying such a station in society as her conscience shall dictate, or which place her in a position inferior to that of man, are contrary to the great precept of nature, and therefore of no force or authority.

Resolved, That woman is man's equal—was intended to be so by the Creator, and the highest good of the race demands that she should be recognized as such.

Resolved, That the women of this country ought to be enlightened in regard to the laws under which they live, that they may no longer publish their degradation by declaring themselves satisfied with their present position, nor their ignorance, by asserting that they have all the rights they want.

Resolved, That inasmuch as man, while claiming for himself intellectual superiority, does accord to woman moral superiority, it is pre-eminently his duty to encourage her to speak and teach, as she has an opportunity, in all religious assemblies.

Resolved, That the same amount of virtue, delicacy, and refinement of behavior that is required of woman in the social state, should also be required of man, and the same transgressions should be visited with equal severity on both man and woman.

Resolved, That the objection of indelicacy and impropriety, which is so often brought against woman when she addresses a public audience, comes with a very ill-grace from those who encourage, by their attendance, her appearance on the stage, in the concert, or in feats of the circus.

Resolved, That woman has too long rested satisfied in the circumscribed limits which corrupt customs and a perverted application of the Scriptures have marked out for her, and that it is time she should move in the enlarged sphere which her great Creator has assigned her.

Resolved, That it is the duty of the women of this country to secure to themselves their sacred right to the elective franchise.

Resolved, That the equality of human rights results necessarily from the fact of the identity of the race in capabilities and responsibilities.

Resolved, therefore, That, being invested by the Creator with the same capabilities, and the same consciousness of responsibility for their exercise, it is demonstrably the right and duty of woman, equally with man, to promote every righteous cause by every righteous means; and especially in regard to the great subjects of morals and religion, it is self-evidently her right to participate with her brother in teaching them, both in private and in public, by writing and by speaking, by any instrumentalities proper to be used, and in any assemblies proper to be held; and this being a self-evident truth growing out of the divinely implanted principles of human nature, any custom or authority adverse to it, whether modern or wearing the hoary sanction of antiquity, is to be regarded as a self-evident falsehood, and at war with mankind.

. . .

Resolved, That the speedy success of our cause depends upon the zealous and untiring efforts of both men and women, for the overthrow of the monopoly of the pulpit, and for the securing to woman an equal participation with men in the various trades, professions, and commerce.

. . .

[1848]

11

Enfranchisement of Women

HARRIET TAYLOR

HARRIET TAYLOR England. 1807–1858. Suffragist. Essayist. Though she published little in her lifetime, John Stuart Mill credits her as a major contributor to all of his work of the late 1840s and 1850s, particularly *The Subjection of Women* (1869), published after her death. She became the subject of scandal when she chose to live separately from her husband, devoting herself to her work with Mill, whom she married two years after her husband's death in 1849. *Enfranchisement* was published originally in *The Westminster Review* under J. S. Mill's name.

Most of our readers will probably learn from these pages for the first time that there has arisen in the United States, and in the most civilized and enlightened portion of them, an organized agitation on a new question—new, not to thinkers, nor to any one by whom the principles of free and popular government are felt as well as acknowledged, but new, and even unheard-of, as a subject for public meetings and practical political action. This question is the enfranchisement of women; their admission, in law and in fact, to equality in all rights, political, civil, and social, with the male citizens of the community.

It will add to the surprise with which many will receive this intelligence, that the agitation which has commenced is not a pleading by male writers and orators for women, those who are professedly to be benefited remaining either indifferent or ostensibly hostile. It is a political movement, practical in its objects, carried on in a form which denotes an intention to persevere. And it is a movement not merely *for* women, but *by* them. . . .

That the promoters of this new agitation take their stand on principles, and do not fear to declare these in their widest extent, without time-serving or compromise, will be seen from the resolutions adopted by the Convention,[1] part of which we transcribe.

Resolved—That every human being, of full age, and resident for a proper length of time on the soil of the nation, who is required to obey the law, is entitled to a voice in its enactment; that every such person, whose property or labour is taxed for the support of the government, is entitled to a direct share in such government; therefore,

Resolved—That women are entitled to the right of suffrage, and to be considered eligible to office, . . . and that every party which claims to represent the humanity, the civilization, and the progress of the age is bound to inscribe on its banners equality before the law, without distinction of sex or colour.

Resolved—That civil and political rights acknowledge no sex, and therefore the word "male" should be struck from every State Constitution.

Resolved—That, since the prospect of honourable and useful employment in after-life is the best stimulus to the use of educational advantages, and since the best education is that we give ourselves, in the struggles, employments, and discipline of life; therefore it is impossible that women should make full use of the instruction already accorded to them, or that their career should do justice to their faculties, until the avenues to the various civil and professional employments are thrown open to them.

Resolved—That every effort to educate women, without according to them their rights, and arousing their conscience by the weight of their responsibilities, is futile and a waste of labour.

Resolved—That the laws of property, as affecting married persons, demand a thorough revisal, so that all rights be equal between them; that the wife have, during life, an equal control over the property gained by their mutual toil and sacrifices, and be heir to her husband precisely to that extent that he is heir to her, and entitled at her death to dispose by will of the same share of the joint property as he is.

The following is a brief summary of the principal demands.

1. *Education* in primary and high schools, universities, medical, legal, and theological institutions.

2. *Partnership* in the labours and gains, risks and remunerations, of productive industry.

3. *A coequal share* in the formation and administration of laws—municipal, state, and national—through legislative assemblies, courts, and executive offices.

· · ·

That women have as good a claim as men have, in point of personal right, to the suffrage, or to a place in the jurybox, it would be difficult for any one to deny. It cannot certainly be denied by the United States of America, as a people or as a community. Their democratic institutions rest avowedly on the inherent right of everyone to a voice in the government. Their Declaration of Independence, framed by the men who are still their great constitutional authorities—that document which has been from the first, and is now, the acknowledged basis of their polity, commences with this express statement:

> We hold these truths to be self-evident: that all men are created equal; that they are endowed by their Creator with certain inalienable rights; that among these are life, liberty, and the pursuit of happiness; that to secure these rights, governments are instituted among men, deriving their just powers from the consent of the governed. . . .

After a struggle which, by many of its incidents, deserves the name of heroic, the abolitionists are now so strong in numbers and in influence that they hold the balance of parties in the United States. It was fitting that the men whose names will remain associated with the extirpation, from the democratic soil of America, of the aristocracy of colour, should be among the originators, for America and for the rest of the world, of the first collective protest against the aristocracy of sex; a distinction as accidental as that of colour, and fully as irrelevant to all questions of government.

Not only to the democracy of America, the claim of women to civil and political equality makes an irresistible appeal, but also to those Radicals and Chartists in the British islands, and democrats on the Continent, who claim what is called universal suffrage as an inherent right, unjustly and oppressively withheld from them. For with what truth or rationality could the suffrage be termed universal, while half the human species remained excluded from it? To declare that a voice in the government is the right of all, and demand it only for a part— the part, namely, to which the claimant himself belongs—is to renounce even the appearance of principle. The Chartist who denies the suffrage to women is a Chartist only because he is not a lord: he is one of those levelers who would level only down to themselves.

Even those who do not look upon a voice in the government as a matter of personal right, nor profess principles which require that it should be extended to all, have usually traditional maxims of political justice with which it is impossible to reconcile the exclusion of all women from the common rights of citizenship. It is an axiom of English freedom that taxation and representation should be co-extensive. Even under the laws which give the wife's property to the husband, there are many unmarried women who pay taxes. It is one of the fundamental doctrines of the British Constitution that all persons should be tried by their peers: yet women, whenever tried, are tried by male judges and a male jury. To foreigners the law accords the privilege of claiming that half the jury should be composed of themselves; not so to women. Apart from maxims of detail, which represent local and national rather than universal ideas; it is an acknowledged dictate of justice to make no degrading distinctions without necessity. In all things the presumption ought to be on the side of equality. A reason must be given why anything should be permitted to one person and interdicted to another. But when that which is interdicted includes nearly everything which those to whom it is permitted most prize, and to be deprived of which they feel to be most insulting; when not only political liberty but personal freedom of action is the prerogative of a caste; when even in the exercise of industry, almost all employments which task the higher faculties in an important field, which lead to distinction, riches, or even pecuniary independence, are fenced round as the exclusive domain of the predominant section, scarcely any doors being left open to the dependent class, except such as all who can enter elsewhere disdainfully pass by; the miserable expediencies which are advanced as excuses for so grossly partial a dispensation would not be sufficient, even if they were real, to render it other than a flagrant injustice. While, far from being expedient, we are firmly convinced that the division of mankind into two castes, one born to rule over the other, is in this case, as in all cases, an unqualified mischief; a source of perversion and demoralization, both to the favoured class and to those at whose expense they are favoured[.] . . .

These propositions it is now our purpose to maintain. But before entering on them, we would endeavour to dispel the preliminary objections which, in the minds of persons to whom the subject is new, are apt to prevent a real and conscientious examination of it. The chief of these obstacles is that most formidable one, custom. Women never have had equal rights with men. The claim in their behalf, of the common rights of mankind, is looked upon as barred by universal practice. This strongest of prejudices, the prejudice against what is new and unknown, has, indeed, in an age of changes like the present, lost much of its force; if it had not, there would be little hope of prevailing against it. . . .

That an institution or a practice is customary is no presumption of its goodness, when any other sufficient cause can be assigned for its existence. There is no difficulty in understanding why the subjection of women has been a custom. No other explanation is needed than physical force.

That those who were physically weaker should have been made legally inferior is quite conformable to the mode in which the world has been governed. Until very lately, the rule of physical strength was the general law of human affairs. . . . The world is very young and has but just begun to cast off injustice. It is only now getting rid of negro slavery. It is only now getting rid of monarchical despotism. It is only now getting rid of hereditary feudal nobility. It is only now getting rid of disabilities on the ground of religion. It is only beginning to treat any *men* as citizens, except the rich and a favoured portion of the middle class. Can we wonder that it has not yet done as much for women? As society was constituted until the last few generations, inequality was its very basis; association grounded on equal rights scarcely existed; to be equals was to be enemies; two persons could hardly co-operate in anything, or meet in any amicable relation, without the law's appointing that one of them should be the superior of the other. Mankind have outgrown this state, and all things now tend to substitute as the general principle of human relations, a just equality, instead of the dominion of the strongest. But of all relations, that between men and women being the nearest and most intimate, and connected with the greatest number of strong emotions, was sure to be the last to throw off the old rule and receive the new: for in proportion to the strength of a feeling is

the tenacity with which it clings to the forms and circumstances with which it has even accidentally become associated. . . .

Thus, many persons think they have sufficiently justified the restrictions on women's field of action when they have said that the pursuits from which women are excluded are *unfeminine*, and that the *proper sphere* of women is not politics or publicity, but private and domestic life.

We deny the right of any portion of the species to decide for another portion, or any individual for another individual, what is and what is not their "proper sphere." The proper sphere for all human beings is the largest and highest which they are able to attain to. What this is, cannot be ascertained, without complete liberty of choice. The speakers at the Convention in America have therefore done wisely and right in refusing to entertain the question of the peculiar aptitudes either of women or of men, or the limits within this or that occupation may be supposed to be more adapted to the one or to the other. They justly maintain that these questions can only be satisfactorily answered by perfect freedom. Let every occupation be open to all, without favour or discouragement to any, and employments will fall into the hands of those men or women who are found by experience to be most capable of worthily exercising them. There need be no fear that women will take out of the hands of men any occupation which men perform better than they. Each individual will prove his or her capacities, in the only way in which capacities can be proved—by trial; and the world will have the benefit of the best faculties of all its inhabitants. But to interfere beforehand by an arbitrary limit, and declare that whatever be the genius, talent, energy, or force of mind of an individual of a certain sex or class, those faculties shall not be exerted, or shall be exerted only in some few of the many modes in which others are permitted to use theirs, is not only an injustice to the individual, and a detriment to society, which loses what it can ill spare, but is also the most effectual mode of providing that, in the sex or class so fettered, the qualities which are not permitted to be exercised shall not exist.

We shall follow the very proper example of the Convention in not entering into the question of the alleged differences in physical or mental qualities between the sexes; not because we have nothing to say, but because we have too much[.] . . .

The real question is whether it is right and expedient that one-half of the human race should pass through life in a state of forced subordination to the other half. If the best state of human society is that of being divided into two parts, one consisting of persons with a will and a substantive existence, the other of humble companions to these persons, attached, each of them to one, for the purpose of bringing up *his* children, and making *his* home pleasant to him; if this is the place assigned to women, it is but kindness to educate them for this; to make them believe that the greatest good fortune which can befall them is to be chosen by some man for this purpose; and that every other career which the world deems happy or honourable is closed to them by the law, not of social institutions, but of nature and destiny.

When, however, we ask why the existence of one-half the species should be merely ancillary to that of the other—why each woman should be a mere appendage to a man, allowed to have no interests of her own, that there may be nothing to compete in her mind with his interests and his pleasure; the only reason which can be given is that men like it. It is agreeable to them that men should live for their own sake, women for the sake of men: and the qualities and conduct in subjects which are agreeable to rulers, they succeed for a long time in making the subjects themselves consider as their appropriate virtues. . . .

Under a nominal recognition of a moral code common to both [men and women], in practice self-will and self-assertion form the type of what are designated as manly virtues, while abnegation of self, patience, resignation, and submission to power, unless when resistance is commanded by other interests than their own, have been stamped by general consent as pre-eminently the duties and graces required of women. The meaning being merely that power makes itself the centre of moral obligation, and that a man likes to have his own will, but does not like that his domestic companion should have a will different from his.

We are far from pretending that in modern and civilized times, no reciprocity of obligation is acknowledged on the part of the stronger. Such an assertion would be very wide of the truth. But even this reciprocity, which has disarmed tyranny, at least in the higher and middle classes, of its most revolting features, yet when combined with the original evil of the dependent condition of women has introduced in its turn serious evils.

No man now thinks that his wife has no claim upon his actions but such as he may accord to her. All men of any conscience believe that their duty to their wives is one of the most binding of their obligations. Nor is it supposed to consist solely in protection, which, in the present state of civilization, women have almost ceased to need: it involves care for their happiness and consideration of their wishes, with a not unfrequent sacrifice of their own to them. The power of husbands has reached the stage which the power of kings had arrived at when opinion did not yet question the rightfulness of arbitrary power, but in theory, and to a certain extent in practice, condemned the selfish use of it. This improvement in the moral sentiments of mankind, and increased sense of the consideration due by every man to those who have no one but himself to look to, has tended to make home more and more the centre of interest, and domestic circumstances and society a larger and larger part of life, and of its pursuits and pleasures. The tendency has been strengthened by the changes of tastes and manners which have so remarkably distinguished the last two or three generations. In days not far distant, men found their excitement and filled up their time in violent bodily exercises, noisy merriment, and intemperance. They have now, in all but the very poorest classes, lost their inclination for these things, and for the coarser pleasures generally; they have now scarcely any tastes but those which they have in common with women, and, for the first time in the world, men and women are really companions. A most beneficial change, if the companionship were between equals; but being between unequals, it produces, what good observers have noticed, though without perceiving its cause, a progressive deterioration among men in what had hitherto been considered the masculine excellences. Those who are so careful that women should not become men do not see that men are becoming what they have decided that women should be—are falling into the feebleness which they have so long cultivated in their companions. Those who are associated in their lives tend to become assimilated in character. In the present closeness of association between the sexes, men cannot retain manliness unless women acquire it.

There is hardly any situation more unfavourable to the maintenance of elevation of character or force of intellect, than to live in the society, and seek by preference the sympathy, of inferiors in mental endowments. . . .

It is from having intellectual communion only with those to whom they can lay down the law that so few men continue to advance in wisdom beyond the first stages. The most eminent men cease to improve if they associate only with disciples. When they have overtopped those who immediately surround them, if they wish for further growth, they must seek for others of their own stature to consort with. The mental companionship which is improving is communion between active minds, not mere contact between an active mind and a passive. This inestimable advantage is even now enjoyed, when a strong-minded man and a strong-minded woman are, by a rare chance, united: and would be had far oftener, if education took the same pains to form strong-minded women which it takes to prevent them from being formed. . . . What makes intelligent beings is the power of thought: the stimuli which call forth that power are the interest and dignity of thought itself, and a field for its practical application. Both motives are cut off from those who are told from infancy that thought, and all its greater applications, are other people's business, while theirs is to make themselves agreeable to other people. High mental powers in women will be but an exceptional accident until every career is open to them, and until they, as well as men, are educated for themselves and for the world—not one sex for the other. . . .

The common opinion is, that whatever may be the case with the intellectual, the moral influence of women over men is almost salutary. It is, we are often told, the great counteractive of selfishness. However the case may be as to personal influence, the influence of the position tends eminently to promote selfishness. The most insignificant of men, the man who can obtain influence or consideration nowhere else, finds one place where he is chief and head. There is one person, often greatly his superior in understanding, who is obliged to consult him, and whom he is not obliged to consult. He is judge, magistrate, ruler, over their joint concerns; arbiter of all differences between them. The justice or conscience to which her appeal must be made is his justice and conscience: it is his to hold the balance and adjust the scales between his own claims or wishes and those of another. His is now the only tribunal, in civilized life, in which the same person is judge and party. A generous mind, in such a situation, makes the balance incline against its own side, and gives the other not less, but more, than a fair equality; and thus the weaker side may be enabled to turn the very fact of dependence into an instrument of power, and in default of justice, take an ungenerous advantage of generosity; rendering the unjust power, to those who make an unselfish use of it, a torment and a burthen. But how is it when average men are invested with this power, without reciprocity and without responsibility? . . . If there is any self-will in the man, he becomes either the conscious or unconscious despot of his household. The wife, indeed, often succeeds in gaining her objects, but it is by some of the many various forms of indirectness and management.

Thus the position is corrupting equally to both; in the one it produces the vices of power, in the other those of artifice. Women, in their present physical and moral state, having stronger impulses, would naturally be franker and more direct than men; yet all the old saws and traditions represent them as artful and dissembling. Why? Because their only way to their objects is by indirect paths. In all countries where women have strong wishes and active minds, this consequence is inevitable: and if it is less conspicuous in England than in some other places, it is because Englishwomen, saving occasional exceptions, have ceased to have either strong wishes or active minds.

We are not now speaking of cases in which there is anything deserving the name of strong affection on both sides. That, where it exists, is too powerful a principle not to modify greatly the bad influences of the situation; it seldom, however, destroys them entirely. Much oftener the bad influences are too strong for the affection, and destroy it. The highest order of durable and happy attachments would be a hundred times more frequent than they are if the affection which the two sexes sought from one another were that genuine friendship which only exists between equals in privileges as in faculties. But with regard to what is commonly called affection in married life—the habitual and almost mechanical feeling of kindliness, and pleasure in each other's society, which generally grows up between persons who constantly live together, unless there is actual dislike—there is nothing in this to contradict or qualify the mischievous influence of the unequal relation.

. . .

[1851]

NOTE

1. Worcester, MA, Oct. 23–24, 1850.

 12

Ain't I a Woman?

SOJOURNER TRUTH

SOJOURNER TRUTH (ISABELLA BAUMFREE) United States. 1797–1883. Born a slave in New York State. A traveling preacher and powerful lecturer on abolition and suffrage. Spoke before Congress and two presidents. Dictated autobiography, *The Narrative of Sojourner Truth: A Northern Slave* (1850). Her "Ain't I a Woman?" speech was delivered at the Women's Rights Convention in Akron, Ohio, in 1851.

Well, children, where there is so much racket there must be something out of kilter. I think that 'twixt the negroes of the South and the women at the North, all talking about rights, the white men will be in a fix pretty soon. But what's all this here talking about?

That man over there says that women need to be helped into carriages, and lifted over ditches, and to have the best place everywhere. Nobody ever helps me into carriages, or over mud-puddles, or gives me any best place! And ain't I a woman? Look at me! Look at my arm! I have ploughed and planted, and gathered into barns, and no man could head me! And ain't I a woman? I could work as much and eat as much as a man—when I could get it—and bear the lash as well! And ain't I a woman? I have borne thirteen children, and seen them most all sold off to slavery, and when I cried out with my mother's grief, none but Jesus heard me! And ain't I a woman?

Then they talk about this thing in the head; what's this they call it? [Intellect, someone whispers.] That's it, honey. What's that got to do with women's rights or negro's rights? If my cup won't hold but a pint, and yours holds a quart, wouldn't you be mean not to let me have my little half-measure full?

Then that little man in black there, he says women can't have as much rights as men, 'cause Christ wasn't a woman! Where did your Christ come from? From God and a woman! Man had nothing to do with Him.

If the first woman God ever made was strong enough to turn the world upside down all alone, these women together ought to be able to turn it back, and get it right side up again! And now they is asking to do it, the men better let them.

Obliged to you for hearing me, and now old Sojourner ain't got nothing more to say.

[1851]

 13

Keeping the Thing Going While Things Are Stirring

SOJOURNER TRUTH

SOJOURNER TRUTH (ISABELLA BAUMFREE) United States. 1797–1883. Born a slave in New York State. A traveling preacher and powerful lecturer on abolition and suffrage. Spoke before Congress and two presidents. Dictated autobiography, *The Narrative of Sojourner Truth: A Northern Slave* (1850). Her "Ain't I a Woman?" speech was delivered at the Women's Rights Convention in Akron, Ohio, in 1851.

My friends, I am rejoiced that you are glad, but I don't know how you will feel when I get through. I come from another field—the country of the slave.

They have got their liberty—so much good luck to have slavery partly destroyed; not entirely. I want it root and branch destroyed. Then we will all be free indeed. I feel that if I have to answer for the deeds done in my body just as much as a man, I have a right to have just as much as a man. There is a great stir about colored men getting their rights, but not a word about the colored women; and if colored men get their rights, and not colored women theirs, you see the colored men will be masters over the women, and it will be just as bad as it was before. So I am for keeping the thing going while things are stirring; because if we wait till it is still, it will take a great while to get it going again. White women are a great deal smarter, and know more than colored women, while colored women do not know scarcely anything. They go out washing, which is about as high as a colored woman gets, and their men go about idle, strutting up and down; and when the women come home, they ask for their money and take it all, and then scold because there is no food. I want you to consider on that, chil'n. I call you chil'n; you are somebody's chil'n, and I am old enough to be mother of all that is here. I want women to have their rights. In the courts women have no right, no voice; nobody speaks for them. I wish woman to have her voice there among the pettifoggers. If it is not a fit place for women, it is unfit for men to be there.

I am above eighty years old; it is about time for me to be going. I have been forty years a slave and forty years free, and would be here forty years more to have equal rights for all. I suppose I am kept here because something remains for me to do; I suppose I am yet to help to break the chain. I have done a great deal of work; as much as a man, but did not get so much pay. I used to work in the field and bind grain, keeping up with the cradler, but men doing no more got twice as much pay; so with the German women. They work in the field and do as much work, but do not get the pay. We do as much, we eat as much, we want as much. I suppose I am about the only colored woman that goes about to speak for the rights of the colored women. I want to keep the thing stirring, now that the ice is cracked. What we want is a little money. You men know that you get as much again as women when you write, or for what you do. When we get our rights we shall

not have to come to you for money, for then we shall have money enough in our own pockets; and maybe you will ask us for money. But help us now until we get it. It is a good consolation to know that when we have got this battle once fought we shall not be coming to you any more. You have been having our rights so long, that you think, like a slaveholder, that you own us. I know that it is hard for one who has held the reins for so long to give up; it cuts like a knife. It will feel all the better when it closes up again. I have been in Washington about three years, seeing about these colored people. Now colored men have the right to vote. There ought to be equal rights now more than ever, since colored people have got their freedom. I am going to talk several times while I am here; so now I will do a little singing. I have not heard any singing since I came here.

[1867]

 14

From The Subjection of Women

JOHN STUART MILL

JOHN STUART MILL England. 1806–1873. Essayist. Politician. Social Reformer. As a member of the House of Commons, advocated women's rights and workers' rights. *Principles of Political Economy* (1848); *On Liberty* (1851); *Utilitarianism* (1861); *Autobiography* (1873). Mill credits Harriet Taylor as a significant contributor to this text, though it was published after her death.

CHAPTER 2

It will be well to commence the detailed discussion of the subject by the particular branch of it to which the course of our observations has led us: the conditions which the laws of this and all other countries annex to the marriage contract. Marriage being the destination appointed by society for women, the prospect they are brought up to, and the object which it is intended should be sought by all of them, except those who are too little attractive to be chosen by any man as his companion, one might have supposed that everything would have been done to make this condition as eligible to them as possible, that they might have no cause to regret being denied the option of any other. Society, however, both in this, and, at first, in all other cases, has preferred to attain its object by foul rather than fair means: but this is the only case in which it has substantially persisted in them even to the present day. Originally women were taken by force, or regularly sold by their father to the husband. Until a late period in European history, the father had the power to dispose of his daughter in marriage at his own will and pleasure, without any regard to hers. The Church, indeed, was so far faithful to a better morality as to require a formal "yes" from the woman at the marriage ceremony; but there was nothing to shew that the consent was other than compulsory; and it was practically impossible for the girl to refuse compliance if the father persevered, except perhaps when she might obtain the protection of religion by a determined resolution to take monastic vows. After marriage, the man had anciently (but this was anterior to Christianity) the power of life and death over his wife. She could invoke no law against him; he was her sole tribunal and law. For a long time he could repudiate her, but she had no corresponding power in regard to him. By the old laws of England, the husband was called the *lord* of the wife; he was literally regarded as her sovereign, inasmuch that the murder of a man by his wife was called treason (*petty* as distinguished from *high* treason), and was more cruelly avenged than was usually the case with high treason, for the penalty was burning to death. Because the various enormities have fallen into disuse (for most of them were never formally abolished, or not until they had long ceased to be practised) men suppose that all is now as it should be in regard to the marriage contract; and we are continually told that civilization and Christianity have restored to the woman her just rights. Meanwhile the wife is the actual bond-servant of her husband: no less so, as far as legal obligation goes, than slaves commonly so called. She vows a lifelong obedience to him at the altar, and is held to it all through her life by law. Casuists may say that the obligation of obedience stops short of participation

in crime, but it certainly extends to everything else. She can do no act whatever but by his permission, at least tacit. She can acquire no property but for him; the instant it becomes hers, even if by inheritance, it becomes *ipso facto* his. In this respect the wife's position under the common law of England is worse than that of slaves in the laws of many countries: by the Roman law, for example, a slave might have his peculium, which to a certain extent the law guaranteed to him for his exclusive use. The higher classes in this country have given an analogous advantage to their women, through special contracts setting aside the law, by conditions of pin-money, etc.: since parental feeling being stronger with fathers than the class feeling of their own sex, a father generally prefers his own daughter to a son-in-law who is a stranger to him. By means of settlements, the rich usually contrive to withdraw the whole or part of the inherited property of the wife from the absolute control of the husband: but they do not succeed in keeping it under her own control; the utmost they can do only prevents the husband from squandering it, at the same time debarring the rightful owner from its use. The property itself is out of the reach of both; and as to the income derived from it, the form of settlement most favourable to the wife (that called "to her separate use") only precludes the husband from receiving it instead of her: it must pass through her hands, but if he takes it from her by personal violence as soon as she receives it, he can neither be punished, nor compelled to restitution. This is the amount of the protection which, under the laws of this country, the most powerful nobleman can give to his own daughter as respects her husband. In the immense majority of cases there is no settlement: and the absorption of all rights, all property, as well as all freedom of action, is complete. The two are called "one person in law," for the purpose of inferring that whatever is hers is his, but the parallel inference is never drawn that whatever is his is hers; the maxim is not applied against the man, except to make him responsible to third parties for her acts, as a master is for the acts of his slaves or of his cattle. I am far from pretending that wives are in general no better treated than slaves; but no slave is a slave to the same lengths, and in so full a sense of the word, as a wife is. Hardly any slave, except one immediately attached to the master's person, is a slave at all hours and all minutes; in general he has, like a soldier, his fixed task, and when it is done, or when he is off duty, he disposes, within certain limits, of his own time, and has a family life into which the master rarely intrudes. "Uncle Tom" under his first master had his own life in his "cabin," almost as much as any man whose work takes him away from home, is able to have in his own family. But it cannot be so with the wife. Above all, a female slave has (in Christian countries) an admitted right, and is considered under a moral obligation, to refuse to her master the last familiarity. Not so the wife: however brutal a tyrant she may unfortunately be chained to—though she may know that he hates her, though it may be his daily pleasure to torture her, and though she may feel it impossible not to loathe him—he can claim from her and enforce the lowest degradation of a human being, that of being made the instrument of an animal function contrary to her inclinations. While she is held in this worst description of slavery as to her own person, what is her position in regard to the children in whom she and her master have a joint interest? They are by law *his* children. He alone has any legal rights over them. Not one act can she do towards or in relation to them, except by delegation from him. Even after he is dead she is not their legal guardian, unless he by will has made her so. He could even send them away from her, and deprive her of the means of seeing or corresponding with them, until this power was in some degree restricted by Serjeant Talfourd's Act. This is her legal state. And from this state she has no means of withdrawing herself. If she leaves her husband, she can take nothing with her, neither her children nor anything which is rightfully her own. If he chooses, he can compel her to return, by law, or by physical force; or he may content himself with seizing for his own use anything which she may earn, or which may be given to her by her relations. It is only legal separation by a decree of a court of justice, which entitles her to live apart, without being forced back into the custody of an exasperated jailer—or which empowers her to apply any earnings to her own use, without fear that a man whom perhaps she has not seen for twenty years will pounce upon her some day and carry all off. This legal separation, until lately,

the courts of justice would only give at an expense which made it inaccessible to any one out of the higher ranks. Even now it is only given in cases of desertion, or of the extreme of cruelty; and yet complaints are made every day that it is granted too easily. Surely, if a woman is denied any lot in life but that of being the personal body-servant of a despot, and is dependent for everything upon the chance of finding one who may be disposed to make a favourite of her instead of merely a drudge, it is a very cruel aggravation of her fate that she should be allowed to try this chance only once. The natural sequel and corollary from this state of things would be, that since her all in life depends upon obtaining a good master, she should be allowed to change again and again until she finds one. I am not saying that she ought to be allowed this privilege. That is a totally different consideration. The question of divorce, in the sense involving liberty of remarriage, is one into which it is foreign to my purpose to enter. All I now say is that to those to whom nothing but servitude is allowed, the free choice of servitude is the only, though a most insufficient, alleviation. Its refusal completes the assimilation of the wife to the slave—and the slave under not the mildest form of slavery: for in some slave codes the slave could, under certain circumstances of ill usage, legally compel the master to sell him. But no amount of ill usage, without adultery superadded, will in England free a wife from her tormentor.

· · ·

The equality of married persons before the law is not only the sole mode in which that particular relation can be made consistent with justice to both sides, and conducive to the happiness of both, but it is the only means of rendering the daily life of mankind, in any high sense, a school of moral cultivation. Though the truth may not be felt or generally acknowledged for generations to come, the only school of genuine moral sentiment is society between equals. The moral education of mankind has hitherto emanated chiefly from the law of force, and is adapted almost solely to the relations which force creates. In the less advanced states of society, people hardly recognise any relation with their equals. To be an equal is to be an enemy. Society, from its highest place to its lowest, is one long chain, or rather ladder, where every individual is either above or below his nearest neighbour, and wherever he does not command he must obey. Existing moralities, accordingly, are mainly fitted to a relation of command and obedience. Yet command and obedience are but unfortunate necessities of human life: society in equality is its normal state. Already in modern life, and more and more as it progressively improves, command and obedience become exceptional facts in life, equal association its general rule. The morality of the first ages rested on the obligation to submit to power; that of the ages next following, on the right of the weak to the forbearance and protection of the strong. How much longer is one form of society and life to content itself with the morality made for another? We have had the morality of submission, and the morality of chivalry and generosity; the time is now come for the morality of justice. Whenever, in former ages, any approach has been made to society in equality, Justice has asserted its claims as the foundation of virtue. It was thus in the free republics of antiquity. But even in the best of these, the equals were limited to the free male citizens; slaves, women, and the unenfranchised residents were under the law of force. . . .

But the true virtue of human beings is fitness to live together as equals; claiming nothing for themselves but what they as freely concede to every one else; regarding command of any kind as an exceptional necessity, and in all cases a temporary one; and preferring, whenever possible, the society of those with whom leading and following can be alternate and reciprocal. To these virtues, nothing in life as at present constituted gives cultivation by exercise. The family is a school of despotism, in which the virtues of despotism, but also its vices, are largely nourished. Citizenship, in free countries, is partly a school of society in equality; but citizenship fills only a small place in modern life, and does not come near the daily habits or inmost sentiments. The family, justly constituted, would be the real school of the virtues of freedom. It is sure to be a sufficient one of everything else. It will always be a school of obedience for the children, of command for the parents. What is needed is that it should be a school of sympathy in equality, of living together in love, without power on one side or obedience on the other. . . . The moral training of mankind will

never be adapted to the conditions of the life for which all other human progress is a preparation until they practise in the family the same moral rule which is adapted to the normal constitution of human society.

. . .

CHAPTER 4

There remains a question, not of less importance than those already discussed, and which will be asked the most importunately by those opponents whose conviction is somewhat shaken on the main point. What good are we to expect from the changes proposed in our customs and institutions? Would mankind be at all better off if women were free? If not, why disturb their minds and attempt to make a social revolution in the name of an abstract right?

It is hardly to be expected that this question will be asked in respect to the change proposed in the condition of women in marriage. The sufferings, immoralities, evils of all sorts, produced in innumerable cases by the subjection of individual women to individual men, are far too terrible to be overlooked. Unthinking or uncandid persons, counting those cases alone which are extreme, or which attain publicity, may say that the evils are exceptional; but no one can be blind to their existence, nor, in many cases, to their intensity. And it is perfectly obvious that the abuse of the power cannot be very much checked while the power remains. It is a power given, or offered, not to good men, or to decently respectable men, but to all men; the most brutal, and the most criminal. There is no check but that of opinion, and such men are in general within the reach of no opinion but that of men like themselves. If such men did not brutally tyrannize over the one human being whom the law compels to bear everything from them, society must already have reached a paradisiacal state. There could be no need any longer to curb men's vicious propensities. Astræa must not only have returned to earth, but the heart of the worst man must have become her temple. The law of servitude in marriage is a monstrous contradiction to all the principles of the modern world, and to all the experience through which those principles have been slowly and painfully worked out. It is the sole case, now that negro slavery has been abolished, in which a human being in the plenitude of every faculty is delivered up to the tender mercies of another human being, in the hope forsooth that this other will use the power solely for the good of the person subjected to it. Marriage is the only actual bondage known to our law. There remain no legal slaves, except the mistress of every house.

. . .

Think what it is to a boy, to grow up to manhood in the belief that without any merit or any exertion of his own, though he may be the most frivolous and empty or the most ignorant and stolid of mankind, by the mere fact of being born a male he is by right the superior of all and every one of an entire half of the human race: including probably some whose real superiority to himself he has daily or hourly occasion to feel; but even if in his whole conduct he habitually follows a woman's guidance, still, if he is a fool, she thinks that of course she is not, and cannot be, equal in ability and judgment to himself; and if he is not a fool, he does worse—he sees that she is superior to him, and believes that, notwithstanding her superiority, he is entitled to command and she is bound to obey. What must be the effect on his character of this lesson? And men of the cultivated classes are often not aware how deeply it sinks into the immense majority of male minds. For, among right-feeling and well-bred people, the inequality is kept as much as possible out of sight; above all, out of sight of the children. As much obedience is required from boys to their mother as to their father: they are not permitted to domineer over their sisters, nor are they accustomed to see these postponed to them, but the contrary; the compensations of the chivalrous feeling being made prominent, while the servitude which requires them is kept in the background. Well-brought-up youths in the higher classes thus often escape the bad influences of the situation in their early years, and only experience them when, arrived at manhood, they fall under the dominion of facts as they really exist. Such people are little aware, when a boy is differently brought up, how early the notion of his inherent superiority to a girl arises in his mind; how it grows with his growth and strengthens with his strength; how it is inoculated by one schoolboy upon another; how early the youth thinks himself

superior to his mother, owing her perhaps forbearance, but no real respect; and how sublime and sultan-like a sense of superiority he feels, above all, over the woman whom he hon-ours by admitting her to a partnership of his life. Is it imagined that all this does not pervert the whole manner of existence of the man, both as an individual and as a social being? . . .

The example afforded, and the education given to the sentiments, by laying the foundation of domestic existence upon a relation contradictory to the first principles of social justice, must, from the very nature of man, have a perverting influence of such magnitude that it is hardly possible with our present experience to raise our imaginations to the conception of so great a change for the better as would be made by its removal. All that education and civilization are doing to efface the influences on character of the law of force, and replace them by those of justice, remains merely on the surface, as long as the citadel of the enemy is not attacked. The principle of the modern movement in morals and politics is that conduct, and conduct alone, entitles to respect: that not what men are, but what they do, constitutes their claim to deference; that, above all, merit, and not birth, is the only rightful claim to power and authority. If no authority, not in its nature temporary, were allowed to one human being over another, society would not be employed in building up propensities with one hand which it has to curb with the other. The child would really, for the first time in man's existence on earth, be trained in the way he should go, and when he was old there would be a chance that he would not depart from it. But so long as the right of the strong to power over the weak rules in the very heart of society, the attempt to make the equal right of the weak the principle of its outward actions will always be an uphill struggle; for the law of justice, which is also that of Christianity, will never get possession of men's inmost sentiments; they will be working against it, even when bending to it.

The second benefit to be expected from giving to women the free use of their faculties, by leaving them the free choice of their employments, and opening to them the same field of occupation and the same prizes and encouragements as to other human beings, would be that of doubling the mass of mental faculties available for the higher service of humanity. Where there is now one person qualified to benefit mankind and promote the general improvement, as a public teacher, or an administrator of some branch of public or social affairs, there would then be a chance of two. . . .

This great accession to the intellectual power of the species, and to the amount of intellect available for the good management of its affairs, would be obtained, partly, through the better and more complete intellectual education of women, which would then improve *pari passu* with that of men. Women in general would be brought up equally capable of understanding business, public affairs, and the higher matters of speculation, with men in the same class of society; and the select few of the one as well as of the other sex who were qualified not only to comprehend what is done or thought by others, but to think or do something considerable themselves, would meet with the same facilities for improving and training their capacities in the one sex as in the other. In this way, the widening of the sphere of action for women would operate for good, by raising their education to the level of that of men, and making the one participate in all improvements made in the other. But independently of this, the mere breaking down of the barrier would of itself have an educational virtue of the highest worth. The mere getting rid of the idea that all the wider subjects of thought and action, all the things which are of general and not solely of private interest, are men's business, from which women are to be warned off—positively interdicted from most of it, coldly tolerated in the little which is allowed them—the mere consciousness a woman would then have of being a human being like any other, entitled to choose her pursuits, urged or invited by the same inducements as any one else to interest herself in whatever is interesting to human beings, entitled to exert the share of influence on all human concerns which belongs to an individual opinion, whether she attempted actual participation in them or not—this alone would effect an immense expansion of the faculties of women, as well as enlargement of the range of their moral sentiments.

· · ·

[1870]

 15

Petition to Parliament against the Contagious Diseases Acts

JOSEPHINE BUTLER

JOSEPHINE BUTLER England. 1828–1906. Lecturer. Social reformer. Advocate for higher education for women. An outstanding orator, best known for campaigns against the Contagious Diseases Acts and against child prostitution. *The Education and Employment of Women* (1868), *Women's Work and Women's Culture* (1869), *Personal Reminiscences of a Great Crusade* (1896).

PETITION TO PARLIAMENT

Protest

We, the undersigned, enter our solemn protest against the Contagious Diseases Acts.

First, because involving as they do such a momentous change in the legal safeguards enjoyed by women in common with men, they have been passed, not only without the knowledge of the country, but unknown to Parliament itself; and we hold that neither the representatives of the people, nor the press, fulfill the duties which are expected of them, when they allow such legislation to take place without the fullest discussion.

Second, because so far as women are concerned, they remove every guarantee of personal security which the law has established and held sacred, and put their reputation, their freedom, and their persons absolutely in the power of the police.

Third, because the law is bound in any country, professing to give civil liberty to its subjects, to define clearly an offence which it punishes.

Fourth, because it is unjust to punish the sex who are the victims of a vice, and leave unpunished the sex who are the main cause both of the vice and its dreaded consequences; and we consider that liability to arrest, forced surgical examination, or (where this is resisted) imprisonment with hard labour, to which these Acts subject women, are punishments of the most degrading kind.

Fifth, because, by such a system, the path of evil is made more easy to our sons and to the whole of the youth of England; inasmuch as a moral restraint is withdrawn the moment the State recognises, and provides convenience for the practice of a vice which it thereby declares to be necessary and venial.

Sixth, because these measures are cruel to the women who come under their action—violating the feelings of those whose sense of shame is not wholly lost, and further brutalising even the most abandoned.

Seventh, because the disease which these Acts seek to remove has never been removed by any such legislation. The advocates of the system have utterly failed to show, by statistics or otherwise, that these regulations have in any case, after several years' trial, and when applied to one sex only, diminished disease, reclaimed the fallen, or improved the general morality of the country. We have, on the contrary, the strongest evidence to show that in Paris and other continental cities where women have long been outraged by this forced inspection, the public health and morals are worse than at home.

Eighth, because the conditions of this disease, in the first instance, are moral, not physical. The moral evil through which the disease makes it way separates the case entirely from that of the plague, or other scourges which have been placed under police control or sanitary care. We hold that we are bound, before rushing into the experiment of legalising a revolting vice, to try to deal with the *causes* of the evil and we dare to believe that with wiser teaching and more capable legislation, those causes would not be beyond control.

. . .

[1871]

 16

Speech after Arrest for Illegal Voting

SUSAN B. ANTHONY

SUSAN B. ANTHONY United States. 1820–1906. A leader of the U.S. suffrage movement. Teacher and educational reformer. Began organizing in the temperance movement. Traveled extensively across the United States making speeches and rallying support for women's suffrage. Cofounder with Stanton of the National American Women's Suffrage Association and publisher of *The Revolution*, a suffrage newspaper. *The History of Women's Suffrage* (1881–1886). This speech was given on the occasion of her trial for voting illegally, along with 15 other women, in the 1872 presidential election.

Friends and Fellow-Citizens:—I stand before you under indictment for the alleged crime of having voted at the last presidential election, without having a lawful right to vote. It shall be my work this evening to prove to you that in thus doing, I not only committed no crime, but instead simply exercised my citizen's right, guaranteed to me and all United States citizens by the National Constitution beyond the power of any State to deny.

Our democratic-republican government is based on the idea of the natural right of every individual member thereof to a voice and a vote in making and executing the laws. We assert the province of government to be to secure the people in the enjoyment of their inalienable rights. We throw to the winds the old dogma that government can give rights. No one denies that before governments were organized each individual possessed the right to protect his own life, liberty and property. When 100 to 1,000,000 people enter into a free government, they do not barter away their natural rights; they simply pledge themselves to protect each other in the enjoyment of them through prescribed judicial and legislative tribunals. They agree to abandon the methods of brute force in the adjustment of their differences and adopt those of civilization. . . . The Declaration of Independence, the United States Constitution, the constitutions of the several States and the organic laws of the Territories, all alike propose to *protect* the people in the exercise of their God-given rights. Not one of them pretends to bestow rights.

All men are created equal, and endowed by their Creator with certain inalienable rights. Among these are life, liberty and the pursuit of happiness. To secure these, governments are instituted among men, deriving their just powers from the consent of the governed.

Here is no shadow of government authority over rights, or exclusion of any class from their full and equal enjoyment. Here is pronounced the right of all men, and "consequently," as the Quaker preacher said, "of all women," to a voice in the government. And here, in this first paragraph of the Declaration, is the assertion of the natural right of all to the ballot; for how can "the consent of the governed" be given, if the right to vote be denied? . . . The women, dissatisfied as they are with this form of government, that enforces taxation without representation—that compels them to obey laws to which they never have given their consent—that imprisons and hangs them without a trial by a jury of their peers—that robs them, in marriage, of the custody of their own persons, wages and children—are this half of the people who are left wholly at the mercy of the other half, in direct violation of the spirit and letter of the declarations of the framers of this government, every one of which was based on the immutable principle of equal rights to all. By these declarations, kings, popes, priests, aristocrats, all were alike dethroned and placed on a common level, politically, with the lowliest born subject or serf. By them, too, men, as such, were deprived of their divine right to rule and placed on a political level with women. By the practice of these declarations all class and caste distinctions would be abolished, and slave, serf, plebeian, wife, woman, all alike rise from their subject position to the broader platform of equality.

The preamble of the Federal Constitution says:

We, the people of the United States, in order to form a more perfect union, establish justice, insure domestic tranquility, provide for the common defence, promote the general welfare and secure the blessings of liberty to ourselves and our posterity, do ordain and establish this Constitution for the United States of America.

It was we, the people, not we, the white male citizens, nor we, the male citizens; but we, the whole people, who formed this Union. We formed it not to give the blessings of liberty but to secure them; not to the half of ourselves and the half of our posterity, but to the whole people—women as well as men. It is downright mockery to talk to women of their enjoyment of the blessings of liberty while they are denied the only means of securing them provided by this democratic-republican government— the ballot. . . .

The preamble of the constitution of the State of New York declares the same purpose. It says: "We, the people of the State of New York, grateful to Almighty God for our freedom, in order to secure its blessings, do establish this constitution." Here is not the slightest intimation either of receiving freedom from the United States Constitution, or of the State's conferring the blessings of liberty upon the people; and the same is true of every other State constitution. Each and all declare rights God-given, and that to secure the people in the enjoyment of their inalienable rights is their one and only object in ordaining and establishing government. All of the State constitutions are equally emphatic in their recognition of the ballot as the means of securing the people in the enjoyment of these rights. . . .

I submit that in view of the explicit assertions of the equal right of the whole people, both in the preamble and previous article of the constitution, this omission of the adjective "female" should not be construed into a denial; but instead should be considered as of no effect. . . . No barriers whatever stand today between women and the exercise of their right to vote save those of precedent and prejudice, which refuse to expunge the word "male" from the constitution.

· · ·

For any State to make sex a qualification, which must ever result in the disfranchisement of one entire half of the people, is to pass a bill of attainder, an ex post facto law, and is therefore a violation of the supreme law of the land. By it the blessings of liberty are forever withheld from women and their female posterity. For them, this government has no just powers derived from the consent of the governed. For them this government is not a democracy; it is not a republic. It is the most odious aristocracy ever established on the face of the globe. An oligarchy of wealth, where the rich govern the poor; an oligarchy of learning, where the educated govern the ignorant; or even an oligarchy of race, where the Saxon rules the African, might be endured; but this oligarchy of sex which makes father, brothers, husband, sons, the oligarchs over the mother and sisters, the wife and daughters of every household; which ordains all men sovereigns, all women subjects—carries discord and rebellion into every home of the nation. This most odious aristocracy exists, too, in the face of Section 4, Article IV, which says: "The United States shall guarantee to every State in the Union a republican form of government." . . .

It is urged that the use of the masculine pronouns *he, his* and *him* in all the constitutions and laws is proof that only men were meant to be included in their provisions. If you insist on this version of the letter of the law, we shall insist that you be consistent and accept the other horn of the dilemma, which would compel you to exempt women from taxation for the support of the government and from penalties for the violation of laws. There is no *she* or *her* or *hers* in the tax laws, and this is equally true of all the criminal laws.

Take for example the civil rights law which I am charged with having violated; not only are all the pronouns in it masculine, but everybody knows that it was intended expressly to hinder the rebel men from voting. It reads, "If any person shall knowingly vote without *his* having a lawful right." . . . I insist if government officials may thus manipulate the pronouns to tax, fine, imprison and hang women, it is their duty to thus change them in order to protect us in our right to vote. . . .

Though the words *persons, people, inhabitants, electors, citizens*, are all used indiscriminately in the national and State constitutions, there was always a conflict of opinion, prior to the war, as to whether they were synonymous terms, but whatever room there was for doubt, under the old regime, the adoption of the Fourteenth Amendment settled that question forever in its first sentence:

> All persons born or naturalized in the United States, and subject to the jurisdiction thereof, are citizens of the United States, and of the State wherein they reside.

The second settles the equal status of all citizens:

> No State shall make or enforce any law which shall abridge the privileges or immunities of citizens of the United States; nor shall any State deprive any person of life, liberty or property without due process of law, or deny to any person within its jurisdiction the equal protection of the laws.

The only question left to be settled now is: Are women persons? I scarcely believe any of our opponents will have the hardihood to say they are not.

Being persons, then, women are citizens, and no State has a right to make any new law, or to enforce any old law, which shall abridge their privileges or immunities. Hence, every discrimination against women in the constitutions and laws of the several States is today null and void, precisely as is every one against negroes. . . .

If once we establish the false principle that United States citizenship does not carry with it the right to vote in every State in this Union, there is no end to the petty tricks and cunning devices which will be attempted to exclude one and another class of citizens from the right of suffrage. It will not always be the men combining to disfranchise all women; native born men combining to abridge the rights of all naturalized citizens, as in Rhode Island. It will not always be the rich and educated who may combine to cut off the poor and ignorant; but we may live to see the hard-working, uncultivated day laborers, foreign and native born, learning the power of the ballot and their vast majority of numbers, combine and amend State constitutions so as to disfranchise the Vanderbilts, the Stewarts, the Conklings and the Fentons. It is a poor rule that won't work more ways than one. Establish this precedent, admit the State's right to deny suffrage, and there is no limit to the confusion, discord and disruption that may await us. There is and can be but one safe principle of government—equal rights to all. Discrimination against any class on account of color, race, nativity, sex, property, culture, can but embitter and disaffect that class, and thereby endanger the safety of the whole people. Clearly, then, the national government not only must define the rights of citizens, but must stretch out its powerful hand and protect them in every State in this Union.

If, however, you will insist that the Fifteenth Amendment's emphatic interdiction against robbing United States citizens of their suffrage "on account of race, color or previous condition of servitude," is a recognition of the right of either the United States or any State to deprive them of the ballot for any or all other reasons, I will prove to you that the class of citizens for whom I now plead are, by all the principles of our government and many of the laws of the States, included under the term "previous conditions of servitude."

Consider first married women and their legal status. What is servitude? "The condition of a slave." What is a slave? "A person who is robbed of the proceeds of his labor; a person who is subject to the will of another." By the laws of Georgia, South Carolina and all the States of the South, the negro had no right to the custody and control of his person. He belonged to his master. If he were disobedient, the master had the right to use correction. If the negro did not like the correction and ran away, the master had the right to use coercion to bring him back. By the laws of almost every State in this Union today, North as well as South, the married woman has no right to the custody and control of her person. The wife belongs to the husband; and if she refuse obedience he may use moderate correction, and if she do not like his moderate correction and leave his "bed and board," the husband may use moderate coercion to bring her back. The little word "moderate," you see, is the saving clause for the wife, and would doubtless be overstepped should her offended husband administer his correction with the "cat-o'-nine-tails," or accomplish his coercion with blood-hounds.

Again the slave had no right to the earnings of his hands, they belonged to his master; no right to the custody of his children, they belonged to his master; no right to sue or be sued, or to testify in the courts. If he committed a crime, it was the master who must sue or be sued. In many of the States there has been special legislation giving married women the right to property inherited or received by bequest, or earned by the pursuit of any avocation outside the home; also giving them the right to sue and be sued in matters pertaining to such separate property; but not a single State of this Union has ever secured the wife in the enjoyment of her right to equal ownership of the joint earnings of the marriage copartnership. And since, in the nature of things, the vast majority of married women never earn a dollar by work outside their families, or inherit a dollar from their fathers, it follows that from the day of their marriage to the day of the death of their husbands not one of them ever has a dollar, except it shall please her husband to let her have it. . . .

A good farmer's wife in Illinois, who had all the rights she wanted, had made for herself a full set of false teeth. The dentist pronounced them an admirable fit, and the wife declared it gave her fits to wear them. The dentist sued the husband for his bill; his counsel brought the wife as witness; the judge ruled her off the stand, saying, "A married woman can not be a witness in matters of joint interest between herself and her husband." Think of it, ye good wives, the false teeth in your mouth are a joint interest with your husbands, about which you are legally incompetent to speak! If a married woman is injured by accident, in nearly all of the States it is her husband who must sue, and it is to him that the damages will be awarded. . . . Isn't such a position humiliating enough to be called "servitude"? That husband sued and obtained damages for the loss of the services of his wife, precisely as he would have done had it been his ox, cow, or horse; and exactly as the master, under the old regime, would have recovered for the services of his slave.

I submit the question, if the deprivation by law of the ownership of one's own person, wages, property, children, the denial of the right as an individual to sue and be sued and testify in the courts, is not a condition of servitude most bitter and absolute, even though under the sacred name of marriage? . . . The facts also prove that, by all the great fundamental principles of our free government, not only married women but the entire womanhood of the nation are in a "condition of servitude" as surely as were our Revolutionary fathers when they rebelled against King George. Women are taxed without representation, governed without their consent, tried, convicted and punished without a jury of their peers. Is all this tyranny any less humiliating and degrading to women under our democratic-republican government today than it was to men under their aristocratic, monarchial government one hundred years ago? . . .

Is anything further needed to prove woman's condition of servitude sufficient to entitle her to the guarantees of the Fifteenth Amendment? Is there a man who will not agree with me that to talk of freedom without the ballot is mockery to the women of this republic, precisely as New England's orator, Wendell Phillips, at the close of the late war declared it to be to the newly emancipated black man? I admit that, prior to the rebellion, by common consent, the right to enslave, as well as to disfranchise, both native and foreign born persons, was conceded to the States. But the one grand principle settled by the war and the reconstruction legislation, is the supremacy of the national government to protect the citizens of the United States in their right to freedom and the elective franchise, against any and every interference on the part of the several States.

· · ·

[1872]

 17

The Elixir of Life: or, Why Do We Die?

VICTORIA WOODHULL

VICTORIA WOODHULL United States. 1838–1927. Free-love advocate. Suffragist. First woman stockbroker on Wall Street. First woman to run for president. Spiritualist. Editor with her sister, Tennessee Claflin, of *Woodhull and Claflin's Weekly* (1870–1876).

What are and what are not proper sexual relations? In endeavoring to answer this, I must be permitted to speak so as to be properly understood. And why should I not? Are we not endowed by nature with the sexual passion; and is it not given us for a purpose—one that should be a blessing, instead of a curse as it mostly is, to humanity? Nobody will pretend to answer, No! Then why should we not discuss it as freely as we do any other subject? Is it because our thoughts and desires about it have become so abominable, so perverted and so impure, obscene and vulgar, that any, even needed reference to the subject, brings the blush of shame to the face and a sense of degradation to the soul? Are we indeed so impure that to us all sexual things are impure? I lay it down as an axiom that he or she who blushes and is ashamed at any mention of sexual intercourse has, at some time or other, done something sexually of which to be ashamed. I hold

that everything connected with the manner and method in which human life has its fountain, is a proper and a modest subject for either public or private discussion, and I simply pit all who say Nay! to this.

Sexual intercourse that is in accordance with nature, and therefore proper, is that which is based upon mutual love and desire, and that ultimates in reciprocal benefit. Sexual intercourse that is improper is that which is not based upon mutual love and desire, and that does not ultimate in reciprocal benefit. Of the former there is but one class of cases, since in this class, all the conditions of perfectness are present. First, Love; Second, desire based upon love; and, Third, mutual happiness as the result. Who is there that shall dare to interfere with such sexual relations? Let it be whoever it may, he is an impious wretch, and an enemy to human happiness, and consequently to humanity.

Of the latter there are several classes, which deserve to be enumerated, so that they may be understood wherever any of them may be met. First, that class where it is claimed by legal right; second, that class where the female, to please the male, submits without the proper self desire; third, that class where, for money, or any motive other than love, the female sells the use of her body to the male for his gratification; fourth, that class where mutual love and desire exist, but where there is such want of adaptation as to make mutual consummation impossible.

Now, under either of these conditions, if sexual intercourse be maintained for any considerable length of time, disease and sexual demoralization will surely follow; but the most destructive to health, as well as the most numerous, are the first and the last classes, which occur almost against her wishes or desires, [she] virtually commits suicide; while the husband who compels it, commits murder, and ought just as much to be punished for it, as though he strangled her to death for refusing him.

But this even is not so destructive to health as is that intercourse, carried on habitually, without regard to perfect and reciprocal consummation. And when it is known that three-fourths of all married women, who otherwise might be happily mated, suffer from this cause, the terrible and widespread results may be readily understood. I need not explain to any woman the effects of unconsummated intercourse, though she may attempt to deceive herself about it; but every man needs to have it thundered in his ears until he wakes to the fact that he is not the only party to the act, and that the other party demands a return for all that he receives; demands that he shall not be enriched at her expense; demands that he shall not, either from ignorance or selfish desire, carry her impulse forward on its mission only to cast it backward with the mission unfulfilled, to prostrate the impelling power and to breed nervous debility or irritability and sexual demoralization, and to sow the seeds of disease broadcast among humanity. What is merely hinted at here involves a whole science and a fine art, incomparably the most important of all the sciences and of all the arts, hardly yet broached to the human thought, and now criminally repressed and defeated in their effort at birth by the prejudices of mankind—by your prejudices, and even, perhaps, by mine.

It is a fact terrible to contemplate, yet it is nevertheless true, and ought to be pressed upon the world for its recognition: that fully one-half of all women seldom or never experience any pleasure whatever in the sexual act. Now this is an impeachment of nature, a disgrace to our civilization—an eternal blotch upon the otherwise chivalrous conduct of men toward women. It is a standing reproach upon physiological science that this ignorance has existed so long; and upon medical science, that its dire effects have been so long concealed. I have recently had repeated interviews with a member, in high standing, of the New York College of Physicians; and he does no hesitate to acknowledge that, more than all I have yet said is true, about the sexual demoralization of the race; but the age of hypocrisy reigns as supremely in this as in the clerical profession. Its members are waiting for the world to get ready to hear the truth, and have thus made it necessary that an authority, competent to enforce her statements, is almost crucified, because she feels it her duty to do what they should have done, whose business it is to guard the health of humanity.

Now it is as impossible for a woman to remain in health under unnatural sexual conditions, as it is for a person to take poison and not suffer from its effects; and every woman who hears me knows this is true. They know that the demoralized and degenerate condition of female humanity is to be attributed to false sexual relations; but who among them have the courage to declare it? I have had hundreds of wives say to me, "I would not endure these conditions a single moment, were I not dependent upon my husband, for a home," or "if society would not ostracize me for leaving him;" or some other equally lamentable excuses. To these my reply has been, "You have the face to tell me this, and almost in the same moment you shrug your shoulders at a passing prostitute whose features beam with health, and whose rounded form speaks of unmistakable strength and beauty, while your face and form are a living condemnation of your life, let it be what it may."

Out upon such damned hypocrisy. I hold that the poor woman who cast out by society, because, in ignorance, she admitted her love, without procuring a license to the sacred relations of love, is compelled to sell her body to some demanding man, for the pitiful means to keep life in her body, and perhaps in that of her unrecognized child, is as high as heaven above her who, in silks and satins and with a long retinue of friends, and the sanction of the priest and the law, marries a home for life, with a repugnance in her soul for the man who furnishes it.

I can have a deep sympathy and respect for the modest prostitute who feels the degradation in which she is almost compelled by the ostracism of society; but for her who goes through the gorgeous pageantry of a modern marriage, to proclaim to the world that she is now going to enter into sexual relations with the man, with whom she has consorted, every other way, for an indefinite time, according to the recognized standard of sexual things, I can regard only as brazen and immodest. To me this farce of marriage is a public placarding, merely, to this effect: that I, the bearer, am this day sold, to be the sexual slave of the person to whom the law, holding that I do not know enough and am unable to protect myself, has committed the care of my person. Wives may not think they are slaves, and yet be open to this charge. Some may not be; but let the large majority attempt to assert their sexual freedom, and they will quickly come to the realization.

To what does modern marriage amount, if it be not to hold sexual slaves, who otherwise would be free? I ask the married: Do you live together because the law compels you? And they scout the idea; but in the same breath they condemn me for saying that the law only binds people who ought to be set free, and who, without the law, would be free: that those whom God—Love—has bound together no man, or woman, can put asunder.

Besides the evils of improper sexual relations resulting from legalized prostitution, there are the still more terrific conditions to which they are condemned, who languish in the single cursedness. To this very considerable portion of female humanity the right to the exercise and enjoyment of their sexual instincts is absolutely denied, under the penalty of social death. They are condemned to a life of degradation and misery, from which there is no escape. Add to this class who are sexually starved, those who are compelled to undesired relations with the legal owners of their sexual organs, and a sum total of misery is formed which altogether beggars description.

. . .

To sum up what I have to say on this most important of questions, and to generalize what I have said upon the subject of sexuality, I would repeat that the conditions under which progressive rejuvenation or immortality in the form may be attained can only be secured under the auspices of absolute and entire freedom—a freedom not incompatible with perfect law, but its certain consequent and proper consummation. Let us hope that it may soon be established, notwithstanding the fact that it has taken ages to evolve the yet imperfect law which obtains among us. To the credit of our country, in our Revolutionary War we placed the keystone in the arch of man's spiritual freedom when we decreed in our Constitution, if not civil, at least religious liberty, and guaranteed it to our people by law. We must now advance upon that position and ordain Social Freedom, which is its natural ally, and its necessary aid and support.

And of all freedom that the spirit of man or woman can conceive, or the heart of woman or man can desire, the highest—Social Freedom—culminating in personal liberty, is the most valuable. It is the natural foundation, the true basis of all

other liberties. We must affirm, and, as far as we are able, must secure for all human beings this most sacred of all rights—a right which belongs to every man and every woman (unconvicted of crime) at all times, in all places, and under all circumstances; and of all functions in the body of a man or woman to which this greatest of liberties most especially pertains, the sexual function is the most important: it must not and ought not to be disturbed in its offices by arbitrary laws, unless it unwarrantedly invades another's liberties; and the effort to reduce it to legal or religious bondage has resulted, and ever must result, in introducing into society misery, bestiality, anarchy and destruction. If we would change the present rotten state of the world with regard to our sexual horrors, all that we have to do is to acknowledge and inaugurate this grandest of all liberties; to recognize the right of woman to rule in the domain of the affections; to aid the full development of the natural love that yet exists between the sexes; and to guard our children from that ignorance in sexual matters which has decimated and is decimating the present generation of mankind.

Then, and not till then, when we have performed all the above-mentioned duties, may we look for our reward in that progressive and progressing life, which I believe is even now at our doors. . . .

[1873]

 18

Why I Became a 'Woman's-Rights Man' from The Life and Times of Frederick Douglass, Written by Himself

FREDERICK DOUGLASS

FREDERICK DOUGLASS United States. 1818–1895. Abolitionist. Lecturer. Publisher. Born a slave. One of the leaders of the U.S. abolition movement. Known for his powerful oratory. Suffrage supporter and friend of Stanton and Anthony, attended the Seneca Falls Women's Rights Convention in 1848. Edited and published the *North Star,* an antislavery paper. *Narrative of the Life of Frederick Douglass* (1845).

When the true history of the antislavery cause shall be written, women will occupy a large space in its pages; for the cause of the slave has been peculiarly woman's cause. Her heart and her conscience have supplied in large degree its motive and mainspring. Her skill, industry, patience, and perseverance have been wonderfully manifest in every trial hour. Not only did her feet run on "willing errands," and her fingers do the work which in large degree supplied the sinews of war, but her deep moral convictions, and her tender human sensibilities, found convincing and persuasive expression by her pen and her voice.

. . .

Observing woman's agency, devotion, and efficiency in pleading the cause of the slave, gratitude for this high service early moved me to give favorable attention to the subject of what is called "woman's-rights" and caused me to be denominated a woman's-rights man. I am glad to say that I have never been ashamed to be thus designated. Recognizing not sex nor physical strength, but moral intelligence and the ability to discern right from wrong, good from evil, and the power to choose between them, as the true basis of republican government, to which all are alike subject and all bound alike to obey, I was not long in reaching the conclusion that there was no foundation in reason or justice for woman's exclusion from the right choice in the selection of the persons who should frame the laws, and thus shape the destiny of all the people, irrespective of sex.

In a conversation with Mrs. Elizabeth Cady Stanton when she was yet a young lady and an earnest abolitionist, she was at the pains of setting before me in a very strong light the wrong and injustice of this exclusion. I could not meet her arguments except with the shallow plea of "custom," "natural division of duties," "indelicacy of woman's taking part in politics," the common talk of "woman's sphere," and the like, all of which that able woman, who was then no less logical than now, brushed away by those arguments which she

has so often and effectively used since, and which no man has yet successfully refuted. If intelligence is the only true and rational basis of government, it follows that that is the best government which draws its life and power from the largest sources of wisdom, energy, and goodness at its command. The force of this reasoning would be easily comprehended and readily assented to in any case involving the employment of physical strength. We should all see the folly and madness of attempting to accomplish with a part what could only be done with the united strength of the whole. Though his folly may be less apparent, it is just as real when one-half of the moral and intellectual power of the world is excluded from any voice or vote in civil government. In this denial of the right to participate in government, not merely the degradation of woman and the perpetuation of a great injustice happens, but the maiming and repudiation of one-half of the moral and intellectual power of the government of the world. Thus far all human governments have been failures, for none have secured, except in a partial degree, the ends for which governments are instituted.

War, slavery, injustice and oppression, and the idea that might makes right have been uppermost in all such governments, and the weak, for whose protection governments are ostensibly created, have had practically no rights which the strong have felt bound to respect. The slayers of thousands have been exalted into heroes, and the worship of mere physical force has been considered glorious. Nations have been and still are but armed camps, expending their wealth and strength and ingenuity in forging weapons of destruction against each other; and while it may not be contended that the introduction of the feminine element in government would entirely cure this tendency to exalt might over right, many reasons can be given to show that woman's influence would greatly tend to check and modify this barbarous and destructive tendency. At any rate, seeing that the male governments of the world have failed, it can do no harm to try the experiment of a government by man and woman united. But it is not my purpose to argue the question here, but simply to state in a brief way the ground of my espousal of the cause of woman's suffrage. I believed that the exclusion of my race from participation in government was not only wrong, but a great mistake, because it took from that race motives for high thought and endeavor and degraded them in the eyes of the world around them. Man derives a sense of his consequences in the world not merely subjectively, but objectively. If from the cradle through life the outside world brands a class as unfit for this or that work, the character of the class will come to resemble and conform to the character described. To find valuable qualities in our fellows, such qualities must be presumed and expected. I would give woman a vote, give her a motive to qualify herself to vote, precisely as I insisted upon giving the colored man the right to vote: in order that she shall have the same motives for making herself a useful citizen as those in force in the case of other citizens. In a word, I have never yet been able to find one consideration, one argument, or suggestion in favor of man's right to participate in civil government which did not equally apply to the right of woman.

[1882]

 19

From The Origin of the Family, Private Property and the State

FRIEDRICH ENGELS

FRIEDRICH ENGELS Germany. 1829–1895. Lived and worked in Belgium, England, and France. Socialist. Political and economic theorist. Writer. Close friend and collaborator of Karl Marx, and editor and translator of his work, *Condition of the Working Class in England* (1845), *The Communist Manifesto* (1848).

The family [says Morgan][1] represents an active principle. It is never stationary, but advances from a lower to a higher form as society advances from a lower to a higher condition. . . . Systems of consanguinity, on the contrary, are passive; recording the progress made by the family at long intervals apart, and only changing radically when the family has radically changed.

"And," adds Marx, "the same is true of the political, juridicial, religious, and philosophical systems in general." While the family undergoes living changes, the system of consanguinity ossifies; while the system survives by force of custom, the family outgrows it. . . . [W]e can deduce from the historical survival of a system of consanguinity that an extinct form of family once existed which corresponded to it.

The systems of consanguinity and the forms of the family we have just mentioned differ from those of today in the fact that every child has more than one father and mother. In the American system of consanguinity, to which the Hawaiian family corresponds, brother and sister cannot be the father and mother of the same child; but the Hawaiian system of consanguinity, on the contrary, presupposes a family in which this was the rule. Here we find ourselves among forms of family which directly contradict those hitherto generally assumed to be alone valid. The traditional view recognizes only monogamy, with, in addition, polygamy on the part of individual men, and at the very most polyandry on the part of individual women; being the view of moralizing philistines, it conceals the fact that in practice these barriers raised by official society are quietly and calmly ignored. The study of primitive history, however, reveals conditions where the men live in polygamy and their wives in polyandry at the same time, and their common children are therefore considered common to them all—and these conditions in their turn undergo a long series of changes before they finally end in monogamy.

. . .

Thus the history of the family in primitive times consists in the progressive narrowing of the circle, originally embracing the whole tribe, within which the two sexes have a common conjugal relation. The continuous exclusion, first of nearer, then of more and more remote relatives, and at last even of relatives by marriage, ends by making any kind of group marriage practically impossible. Finally, there remains only the single, still loosely linked pair, the molecule with whose dissolution marriage itself ceases. This in itself shows what a small part individual sex love, in the modern sense of the word, played in the rise of monogamy. Yet stronger proof is afforded by the practice of all peoples at this stage of development. Whereas in the earlier forms of the family, men never lacked women but on the contrary, had too many rather than too few, women had now become scarce and highly sought after. Hence it is with the pairing marriage that there begins the capture and purchase of women—widespread *symptoms,* but no more than symptoms, of the much deeper change that had occurred. . . .

The pairing family, itself too weak and unstable to make an independent household necessary or even desirable, in no wise destroys the communistic household inherited from earlier times. Communistic housekeeping, however, means the supremacy of women in the house; just as the exclusive recognition of the female parent, owing to the impossibility of recognizing the male parent with certainty, means that the women—the mothers—are held in high respect. One of the most absurd notions taken over from 18th-century enlightenment is that in the beginning of society woman was the slave of man. Among all savages and all barbarians of the lower and middle stages, and to a certain extent of the upper stage also, the position of women is not only free, but honorable. . . .

The communistic household, in which most or all of the women belong to one and the same gens, while the men come from various gentes, is the material foundation of that supremacy of the women which was general in primitive times.

· · ·

The first beginnings of the pairing family appear on the dividing line between savagery and barbarism; they are generally to be found already at the upper stage of savagery, but occasionally not until the lower stage of barbarism. The pairing family is the form characteristic of barbarism, as group marriage is characteristic of savagery and monogamy of civilization. To develop it further, to strict monogamy, other causes were required than those we have found active hitherto. In the single pair the group was already reduced to its final unit, its two-atom molecule: one man and one woman. Natural selection, with its progressive exclusions from the marriage community, had accomplished its task; there was nothing more for it to do in this direction. Unless new, *social* forces came into play, there was no reason why a new form of family should arise

from the single pair. But these new forces did come into play.

· · ·

[T]he domestication of animals and the breeding of herds had developed a hitherto unsuspected source of wealth and created entirely new social relations. Up to the lower stage of barbarism, permanent wealth had consisted almost solely of house, clothing, crude ornaments and the tools for obtaining and preparing food—boat, weapons, and domestic utensils of the simplest kind. Food had to be won afresh day by day. Now, with their herds of horses, camels, asses, cattle, sheep, goats, and pigs, the advancing pastoral peoples—the Semites on the Euphrates and the Tigris, and the Aryans in the Indian country of the Five Streams (Punjab), in the Ganges region, and in the steppes then much more abundantly watered by the Oxus and the Jaxartes—had acquired property which only needed supervision and the rudest care to reproduce itself in steadily increasing quantities and to supply the most abundant food in the form of milk and meat. All former means of procuring food now receded into the background; hunting, formerly a necessity, now became a luxury.

But to whom did this new wealth belong? Originally to the gens, without a doubt. Private property in herds must have already started at an early period, however. It is difficult to say whether the author of the so-called first book of Moses regarded the patriarch Abraham as the owner of his herds in his own right as head of a family community or by right of his position as actual hereditary head of a gens. What is certain is that we must not think of him as a property owner in the modern sense of the word. And it is also certain that at the threshold of authentic history we already find the herds everywhere separately owned by heads of families, as are the artistic products of barbarism (metal implements, luxury articles and, finally, the human cattle—the slaves).

For now slavery had also been invented. To the barbarian of the lower stage, a slave was valueless. Hence the treatment of defeated enemies by the American Indians was quite different from that at a higher stage. The men were killed or adopted as brothers into the tribe of the victors; the women were taken as wives or otherwise adopted with their surviving children. At this stage human labor power still does not produce any considerable surplus over and above its maintenance costs. That was no longer the case after the introduction of cattle breeding, metalworking, weaving and, lastly, agriculture. Just as the wives whom it had formerly been so easy to obtain had now acquired an exchange value and were bought, so also with labor power, particularly since the herds had definitely become family possessions. The family did not multiply so rapidly as the cattle. More people were needed to look after them; for this purpose use could be made of the enemies captured in war, who could also be bred just as easily as the cattle themselves.

Once it had passed into the private possession of families and there rapidly begun to augment, this wealth dealt a severe blow to the society founded on pairing marriage and the matriarchal gens. Pairing marriage had brought a new element into the family. By the side of the natural mother of the child it placed its natural and attested father with a better warrant of paternity, probably, than that of many a "father" today. According to the division of labor within the family at that time, it was the man's part to obtain food and the instruments of labor necessary for the purpose. He therefore also owned the instruments of labor, and in the event of husband and wife separating, he took them with him, just as she retained her household goods. Therefore, according to the social custom of the time, the man was also the owner of the new source of subsistence, the cattle, and later of the new instruments of labor, the slaves. But according to the custom of the same society, his children could not inherit from him. For as regards inheritance, the position was as follows:

At first, according to mother right—so long, therefore, as descent was reckoned only in the female line—and according to the original custom of inheritance within the gens, the gentile relatives inherited from a deceased fellow member of their gens. His property had to remain within the gens. His effects being insignificant, they probably always passed in practice to his nearest gentile relations— that is, to his blood relations on the mother's side. The children of the dead man, however, did not belong to his gens, but to that of their mother; it was from her that they inherited, at first conjointly with her other blood-relations, later perhaps with rights of priority; they could not inherit from their father because they did not belong to his gens within which his property had to remain. When the owner of the herds died, therefore, his herds would go first to his brothers and sisters and to his sister's children, or to the issue of his mother's sisters. But his own children were disinherited.

Thus on the one hand, in proportion as wealth increased it made the man's position in the family more important than the woman's, and on the other hand it created an impulse to exploit this strengthened position in order to overthrow, in favor of his children, the traditional order of inheritance. This, however, was impossible so long as descent was reckoned according to mother right. Mother right, therefore, had to be overthrown, and overthrown it was. This was by no means so difficult as it looks to us today. For this revolution—one of the most decisive ever experienced by humanity—could take place without disturbing a single one of the living members of a gens. All could remain as they were. A simple decree sufficed that in the future the offspring of the male members should remain within the gens, but that of the female should be excluded by being transferred to the gens of their father. The reckoning of descent in the female line and the matriarchal law of inheritance were thereby overthrown, and the male line of descent and the paternal law of inheritance were substituted for them. As to how and when this revolution took place among civilized peoples, we have no knowledge. It falls entirely within prehistoric times. But that it *did* take place is more than sufficiently proved by the abundant traces of mother right which have been collected.

· · ·

The overthrow of mother right was the *world historical defeat of the female sex*. The man took command in the home also; the woman was degraded and reduced to servitude; she became the slave of his lust and a mere instrument for the production of children. This degraded position of the woman, especially conspicuous among the Greeks of the heroic and still more of the classical age, has gradually been palliated and glossed over, and sometimes clothed in a milder form; in no sense has it been abolished.

[1884]

NOTE

1. Lewis H. Morgan, 19th-century anthropologist.

20

The Status of Woman in America from A Voice of the South: By a Black Woman of the South

ANNA JULIA COOPER

ANNA JULIA COOPER United States. 1858–1964. Teacher. School principal. Essayist. Lecturer. Organizer for women's and civil rights and educational reform. Born a slave. Earned a Ph.D. from the Sorbonne at the age of 65. Helped found the Colored Women's YWCA.

To-day America counts her millionaires by the thousand; questions of tariff and questions of currency are the most vital ones agitating the public mind. In this period, when material prosperity and well-earned ease and luxury are assured facts from a national standpoint, woman's work and woman's influence are needed as never before; needed to bring a heart power into this money-getting, dollar-worshipping civilization; needed to bring a moral force into the utilitarian motives and interests of the time needed to stand for God and Home and Native Land *versus gain and greed and grasping selfishness.*

There can be no doubt that this fourth centenary of America's discovery which we celebrate at Chicago strikes the keynote of another important transition in the history of this nation; and the prominence of woman in the management of its celebration is a fitting tribute to the part she is destined to play among the forces of the future. This is the first congressional recognition of woman in this country, and this Board of Lady Managers constitute the first women legally appointed by any government to act in a national capacity. This of itself marks the dawn of a new day.

Now the periods of discovery, of settlement, of developing resources and accumulating wealth have passed in rapid succession. Wealth in the nation as in the individual brings leisure, repose, reflection. The struggle with nature is over, the struggle with ideas begins. We stand then, it seems to me, in this last decade of the nineteenth century, just in the portals of a new and untried movement on a higher plain and in a grander strain than any the past has called forth. It does not require a prophet's eye to divine its trend and image its possibilities from the forces we see already at work around us; nor is it hard to guess what must be the status of woman's work under the new regime.

In the pioneer days her role was that of a camp-follower, an additional something to fight for and be burdened with, only repaying the anxiety and labor she called forth by her own incomparable gifts of sympathy and appreciative love; unable herself ordinarily to contend with the bear and the Indian, or to take active part in clearing the wilderness and constructing the home.

In the second or wealth producing period her work is abreast of man's, complementing and supplementing; counteracting excessive tendencies, and mollifying over rigorous proclivities.

In the era now about to dawn, her sentiments must strike the keynote and give the dominant tone. And this because of the nature of her contribution to the world.

Her kingdom is not over physical forces. Not by might, nor by power can she prevail. Her position must ever be inferior where strength of muscle creates leadership. If she follows the instincts of her nature, however, she must always stand for the conservation of those deeper moral forces which make for the happiness of homes and the righteousness of the country. In a reign of moral ideas she is easily queen.

There is to my mind no grander and surer prophecy of the new era and of woman's place in it than the work already begun in the waning years of the nineteenth century by the WCTU [Women's Christian Temperance Union] in America, an organization which has even now reached not only national but international importance, and seems destined to permeate and purify the whole civilized world. It is the living embodiment of woman's activities and woman's ideas, and its extent and strength rightly prefigure her increasing power as a moral factor.

The colored woman of to-day occupies, one may say, a unique position in this country. In a period itself transitional and unsettled, her status seems one of the least ascertainable and definitive of all the forces which make for our civilization. She is confronted by both a woman question and a race problem, and is as yet an unknown or an unacknowledged factor in both. While the women of the white race can with calm assurance enter upon the work they feel by nature appointed to do, while their men give loyal support and appreciative countenance to their efforts, recognizing in most avenues of usefulness the propriety and the need of woman's distinctive cooperation, the colored woman too often finds herself hampered and shamed by a less liberal sentiment and a more conservative attitude on the part of those for whose opinion she cares most. That this is not universally true I am glad to admit. There are to be found both intensely conservative white men and exceedingly liberal colored men. But as far as my experience goes the average man of our race is less frequently ready to admit the actual need among the sturdier forces of the world for woman's help or influence. That great social and economic questions await her interference, that she could throw any light on problems of national import, that her intermeddling could improve the management of school systems, or elevate the tone of public institutions, or humanize and sanctify the far-reaching influence of prisons and reformatories and improve the treatment of lunatics and imbeciles—that she has a word worth hearing on mooted questions in political economy, that she could contribute a suggestion on the relations of labor and capital, or offer a thought on honest money and honorable trade, I fear the majority of "Americans of the colored variety" are not yet prepared to concede. It may be that they do not yet see these questions in their right perspective, being absorbed in the immediate needs of their own political complications. A good deal depends on where we put the emphasis in this world; and our men are not perhaps to blame if they see everything colored by the light of those agitations in the midst of which they live and move and have their being. The part they have had to play in American history during the last twenty-five or thirty years has tended rather to exaggerate the importance of mere political advantage, as well as to set a fictitious valuation on those able to secure

such advantage. It is the astute politician, the manager who can gain preferment for himself and his favorites, the demagogue known to stand in with the powers at the White House and consulted on the bestowal of government plums, whom we set in high places and denominate great. It is they who receive the hosannas of the multitude and are regarded as leaders of the people. The thinker and the doer, the man who solves the problem by enriching his country with an invention worth thousands or by a thought inestimable and precious, is given neither bread nor a stone. He is too often left to die in obscurity and neglect even if spared in his life the bitterness of fanatical jealousies and detraction.

And yet politics, and surely American politics, is hardly a school for great minds. Sharpening rather than deepening, it develops the faculty of taking advantage of present emergencies rather than the insight to distinguish between the true and the false, the lasting and the ephemeral advantage. Highly cultivated selfishness rather than consecrated benevolence is its passport to success. Its votaries are never seers. At best they are but manipulators—often only jugglers. It is conducive neither to profound statesmanship nor to the higher type of manhood. Altruism is its *mauvais succès* and naturally enough it is indifferent to any factor which cannot be worked into its own immediate aims and purposes. As woman's influence as a political element is as yet nil in most of the commonwealths of our republic, it is not surprising that with those who place the emphasis on mere political capital she may yet seem almost a nonentity so far as it concerns the solution of great national or even racial perplexities.

There are those, however, who value the calm elevation of the thoughtful spectator who stands aloof from the heated scramble; and, above the turmoil and din of corruption and selfishness, can listen to the teachings of eternal truth and righteousness. There are even those who feel that the black man's unjust and unlawful exclusion temporarily from participation in the elective franchise in certain states is after all but a lesson "in the desert" fitted to develop in him insight and discrimination against the day of his own appointed time. One needs occasionally to stand aside from the hum and rush of human interests and passions to hear the voices of God. And it not unfrequently happens that the All-loving gives a great push to certain souls to thrust them out, as it were, from the distracting current for awhile to promote their discipline and growth, or to enrich them by communion and reflection. And similarly it may be woman's privilege from her peculiar coigne of vantage as a quiet observer, to whisper just the needed suggestion or the almost forgotten truth. The colored woman, then, should not be ignored because her bark is resting in the silent waters of the sheltered cove. She is watching the movements of the contestants none the less and is all the better qualified, perhaps, to weigh and judge and advise because not herself in the excitement of the race. Her voice, too, has always been heard in clear, unfaltering tones, ringing the changes on those deeper interests which make for permanent good. She is always sound and orthodox on questions affecting the well-being of her race. You do not find the colored woman selling her birthright for a mess of pottage. Nay, even after reason has retired from the contest, she has been known to cling blindly with the instinct of a turtle dove to those principles and policies which to her mind promise hope and safety for children yet unborn. It is notorious that ignorant black women in the South have actually left their husbands' homes and repudiated their support for what was understood by the wife to be race disloyalty, or "voting away," as she expresses it, the privileges of herself and little ones.

It is largely our women in the South to-day who keep the black men solid in the Republican party. The latter as they increase in intelligence and power of discrimination would be more apt to divide on local issues at any rate. They begin to see that the Grand Old Party regards the Negro's cause as an outgrown issue, and on Southern soil at least finds a too intimate acquaintanceship with him a somewhat unsavory recommendation. Then, too, their political wits have been sharpened to appreciate the fact that it is good policy to cultivate one's neighbors and not depend too much on a distant friend to fight one's home battles. But the black woman can never forget—however lukewarm the party may to-day appear—that it was a Republican president who struck the manacles from her own wrists

and gave the possibilities of manhood to her helpless little ones; and to her mind a Democratic Negro is a traitor and a time-server. Talk as much as you like of venality and manipulation in the South, there are not many men, I can tell you, who would dare face a wife quivering in every fiber with the consciousness that her husband is a coward who could be paid to desert her deepest and dearest interests.

Not unfelt, then, if unproclaimed have been the work and influence of the colored women of America. Our list of chieftains in the service, though not long, is not inferior in strength and excellence, I dare believe, to any similar list which this country can produce.[1]

. . .

These women represent all shades of belief and as many departments of activity; but they have one thing in common—their sympathy with the oppressed race in America and the consecration of their several talents in whatever line to the work of its deliverance and development.

Fifty years ago woman's activity according to orthodox definitions was on a pretty clearly cut "sphere," including primarily the kitchen and the nursery, and rescued from the barrenness of prison bars by the womanly mania for adorning every discoverable bit of china or canvas with forlorn looking cranes balanced idiotically on one foot. The woman of to-day finds herself in the presence of responsibilities which ramify through the profoundest and most varied interests of her country and race. Not one of the issues of this plodding, toiling, sinning, repenting, falling, aspiring humanity can afford to shut her out, or can deny the reality of her influence. No plan for renovating society, no scheme for purifying politics, no reform in church or in state, no moral, social, or economic question, no movement upward or downward in the human plane is lost on her. A man once said when told his house was afire: "Go tell my wife; I never meddle with household affairs." But no woman can possibly put herself or her sex outside any of the interests that affect humanity. All departments in the new era are to be hers, in the sense that her interests are in all and through all; and it is incumbent on her to keep intelligently and sympathetically *en rapport* with all the great movements of her time, that she may know on which side to throw the weight of her influence. She stands now at the gateway of this new era of American civilization. In her hands must be moulded the strength, the wit, the statesmanship, the morality, all the psychic force, the social and economic intercourse of that era. To be alive at such an epoch is a privilege, to be a woman then is sublime.

In this last decade of our century, changes of such moment are in progress, such new and alluring vistas are opening out before us, such original and radical suggestions for the adjustment of labor and capital, of government and the governed, of the family, the church, and the state, that to be a possible factor though an infinitesimal one in such a movement is pregnant with hope and weighty with responsibility. To be a woman in such an age carries with it a privilege and an opportunity never implied before. But to be a woman of the Negro race in America, and to be able to grasp the deep significance of the possibilities of the crisis, is to have a heritage, it seems to me, unique in the ages. . . .

[1892]

NOTE

1. She lists Frances Watkins Harper, Sojourner Truth, Sarah Woodson, Martha Biggs, Charlotte Forten Grimké, Fannie Jackson Coppin, and Hallie Quinn Brown.

 21

Solitude of Self

ELIZABETH CADY STANTON

ELIZABETH CADY STANTON United States. 1815–1902. One of the organizers of the 1848 Seneca Falls Women's Rights Convention and a leader and key thinker in the U.S. suffrage movement. In 1851, cofounded with Anthony the National American Women's Suffrage Association and began publishing *The Revolution,* a suffrage newspaper. In addition to speeches and pamphlets, *The Women's Bible* (1895), *The History of Women's Suffrage* (1881–1886) Volumes 1–3 with Susan B. Anthony and Matilda Jocelyn Gage.

· · ·

The point I wish plainly to bring before you on this occasion is the individuality of each human soul;

our Protestant idea, the right of individual conscience and judgment—our republican idea, individual citizenship. In discussing the rights of woman, we are to consider, first, what belongs to her as an individual, in a world of her own, the arbiter of her own destiny, an imaginary Robinson Crusoe with her woman Friday on a solitary island. Her rights under such circumstances are to use all her faculties for her own safety and happiness.

Secondly, if we consider her as a citizen, as a member of a great nation, she must have the same rights as all other members, according to the fundamental principles of our Government.

Thirdly, viewed as a woman, an equal factor in civilization, her rights and duties are still the same—individual happiness and development. Fourthly, it is only the incidental relations of life, such as mother, wife, sister, daughter, that may involve some special duties and training. . . .

In discussing the sphere of man, we do not decide his rights as an individual, as a citizen, as a man by his duties as a father, a husband, a brother, or a son, relations some of which he may never fill. Moreover, he would be better fitted for these very relations and whatever special work he might choose to do to earn his bread by the complete development of all his faculties as an individual.

Just so with woman. The education that will fit her to discharge the duties in the largest sphere of human usefulness will best fit her for whatever special work she may be compelled to do.

The isolation of every human soul and the necessity of self-dependence must give each individual the right to choose his own surroundings. The strongest reason for giving woman all the opportunities for higher education, for the full development of her faculties, forces of mind and body; for giving her the most enlarged freedom of thought and action; a complete emancipation from all forms of bondage, of custom, dependence, superstition; from all the crippling influences of fear, is the solitude and personal responsibility of her own individual life. The strongest reason why we ask for woman a voice in the government under which she lives; in the religion she is asked to believe; equality in social life, where she is the chief factor; a place in the trades and professions, where she may earn her bread, is because of her birthright to self-sovereignty; because, as an individual, she must rely on herself. No matter how much women prefer to lean, to be protected and supported, nor how much men desire to have them do so, they must make the voyage of life alone, and for safety in an emergency they must know something of the laws of navigation. To guide our own craft, we must be captain, pilot, engineer; with chart and compass to stand at the wheel; to match the wind and waves and know when to take in the sail, and to read the signs in the firmament over all. It matters not whether the solitary voyager is man or woman.

Nature, having endowed them equally, leaves them to their own skill and judgment in the hour of danger, and, if not equal to the occasion, alike they perish. To appreciate the importance of fitting every human soul for independent action, think for a moment of the immeasurable solitude of self. We come into the world alone, unlike all who have gone before us; we leave it alone under circumstances peculiar to ourselves. No mortal ever has been, no mortal ever will be like the soul just launched on the sea of life. There can never again be just such environments as make up the infancy, youth and manhood of this one. Nature never repeats herself, and the possibilities of one human soul will never be found in another. No one has ever found two blades of ribbon grass alike, and no one will ever find two human beings alike. Seeing, then, what must be the infinite diversity in human character, we can in a measure appreciate the loss to a nation when any large class of the people are uneducated and unrepresented in the government. We ask for the complete development of every individual, first, for his own benefit and happiness. In fitting out an army we give each soldier his own knapsack, arms, powder, his blanket, cup, knife, fork and spoon. We provide alike for all their individual necessities, then each man bears his own burden.

Again we ask complete individual development for the general good; for the consensus of the competent on the whole round of human interest; on all questions of national life, and here each man must bear his share of the general burden. It is sad to see how soon friendless children are left to bear their own burdens before they can analyze their feelings; before they can even tell their joys and sorrows, they are thrown on their own resources. The great

lesson that nature seems to teach us at all ages is self-dependence, self-protection, self-support. . . . In youth our most bitter disappointments, our brightest hopes and ambitions are known only to otherwise, even our friendship and love we never fully share with another; there is something of every passion in every situation we conceal. Even so in our triumphs and our defeats.

The successful candidate for Presidency and his opponent each have a solitude peculiarly his own, and good form forbids either to speak of his pleasure or regret. The solitude of the king on his throne and the prisoner in his cell differs in character and degree, but it is solitude nevertheless. We ask no sympathy from others in the anxiety and agony of a broken friendship or shattered love. When death sunders our nearest ties, alone we sit in the shadows of our affliction. Alike mid the greatest triumphs and darkest tragedies of life we walk alone. On the divine heights of human attainments, eulogized and worshiped as a hero or saint, we stand alone. In ignorance, poverty, and vice, as a pauper or criminal, alone we starve or steal; alone we suffer the sneers and rebuffs of our fellows; alone we are hunted and hounded thro dark courts and alleys, in by-ways and highways; alone we stand in the judgment seat; alone in the prison cell we lament our crimes and misfortunes; alone we expiate them on the gallows. In hours like these we realize the awful solitude of individual life, its pains, its penalties, its responsibilities; hours in which the youngest and most helpless are thrown on their own resources for guidance and consolation. Seeing then that life must ever be a march and a battle, that each soldier must be equipped for his own protection, it is the height of cruelty to rob the individual of a single natural right.

To throw obstacles in the way of a complete education is like putting out the eyes; to deny the rights of property, like cutting off the hands. To deny political equality is to rob the ostracized of all self-respect; of credit in the market place; of recompense in the world of work; of a voice among those who make and administer the law; a choice in the jury before whom they are tried, and in the judge who decides their punishment. Shakespeare's play of Titus and Andronicus contains a terrible satire on woman's position in the nineteenth century.

"Rude men" (the play tells us) "seized the king's daughter, cut out her tongue, cut off her hands, and then bade her go call for water and wash her hands." What a picture of woman's position. Robbed of her natural rights, handicapped by law and custom at every turn, yet compelled to fight her own battles, and in the emergencies of life to fall back on herself for protection.

The girl of sixteen, thrown on the world to support herself, to make her own place in society, to resist the temptations that surround her and maintain a spotless integrity, must do all this by native force or superior education. She does not acquire this power by being trained to trust others and distrust herself. If she wearies of the struggle, finding it hard work to swim upstream, and allows herself to drift with the current, she will find plenty of company, but not one to share her misery in the hour of her deepest humiliation. If she tried to retrieve her position, to conceal the past, her life is hedged about with fears lest willing hands should tear the veil from what she fain would hide. Young and friendless, she knows the bitter solitude of self. How the little courtesies of life on the surface of society, deemed so important from man towards woman, fade into utter insignificance in view of the deeper tragedies in which she must play her part alone, where no human aid is possible.

The young wife and mother, at the head of some establishment with a kind husband to shield her from the adverse winds of life, with wealth, fortune, and position, has a certain harbor of safety, secure against the ordinary ills of life. But to manage a household, have a desirable influence in society, keep her friends and the affections of her husband, train her children and servants well, she must have rare common sense, wisdom, diplomacy, and a knowledge of human nature. To do all this she needs the cardinal virtues and the strong points of character that the most successful statesman possesses.

An uneducated woman, trained to dependence, with no resources in herself must make a failure of any position in life. But society says women do not need a knowledge of the world, the liberal training that experience in public life must give, all the advantages of collegiate education; but when for the lack of all this, the woman's happiness is wrecked, alone she bears her humiliation; and the attitude of the weak and the ignorant is indeed pitiable. In the wild chase for the price of life they are ground to powder.

In age, when the pleasures of youth are past, children grown up, married and gone, the hurry and hustle of life in a measure over, when the hands are weary of active service, when the old armchair and the fireside are the chosen resorts, then men and women alike must fall back on their own resources. If they cannot find companionship in books, if they have no interest in the vital questions of the hour, no interest in watching the consummation of reforms, with which they might have been identified, they soon pass into their dotage. The more fully the faculties of the mind are developed and kept in use, the longer the period of vigor and active interest in all around us continues. If from a lifelong participation in public affairs a woman feels responsible for the laws regulating our system of education, the discipline of our jails and prisons, the sanitary conditions of our private homes, public buildings, and thoroughfares, an interest in commerce, finance, our foreign relations, in any or all of these questions, here solitude will at least be respectable, and she will not be driven to gossip or scandal for entertainment.

The chief reason for opening to every soul the doors to the whole round of human duties and pleasures is the individual development thus attained, the resources thus provided under all circumstances to mitigate the solitude that at times must come to everyone. . . .

As women of times share a similar fate, should they not have all the consolation that the most liberal education can give? Their suffering in the prisons of St. Petersburg; in the long, weary marches to Siberia, and in the mines, working side by side with men, surely call for all the self-support that the most exalted sentiments of heroism can give. When suddenly roused at midnight, with the startling cry of "Fire! fire!" to find the house over their heads in flames, do women wait for men to point the way to safety? And are the men, equally bewildered and half suffocated with smoke, in a position to more than try to save themselves?

At such times the most timid women have shown a courage and heroism in saving their husbands and children that has surprised everybody. Inasmuch, then, as woman shares equally the joys and sorrows of time and eternity, is it not the height of presumption in man to propose to represent her at the ballot box and the throne of grace, do her voting in the state, her praying in the church, and to assume the position of priest at the family altar.

Nothing strengthens the judgment and quickens the conscience like individual responsibility. Nothing adds such dignity to character as the recognition of one's self-sovereignty; the right to an equal place, everywhere conceded; a place earned by personal merit, not an artificial attainment by inheritance, wealth, family, and position. Seeing, then that the responsibilities of life rest equally on man and woman, that their destiny is the same, they need the same preparation for time and eternity. The talk of sheltering woman from the fierce storms of life is the sheerest mockery, for they beat on her from every point of the compass, just as they do on man, and with more fatal results, for he has been trained to protect himself, to resist, to conquer. Such are the facts in human experience, the responsibilities of individual sovereignty. Rich and poor, intelligent and ignorant, wise and foolish, virtuous and vicious, man and woman, it is ever the same, each soul must depend wholly on itself.

Whatever the theories may be of woman's dependence on man, in the supreme moments of her life he cannot bear her burdens. Alone she goes to the gates of death to give life to every man that is born into the world. No one can share her fears, no one mitigate her pangs; and if her sorrow is greater than she can bear, alone she passes beyond the gates into the vast unknown.

From the mountaintops of Judea, long ago, a heavenly voice bade His disciples, "Bear ye one another's burdens," but humanity has not yet risen to that point of self-sacrifice, and if ever so willing, how few the burdens are that one soul can bear for another. In the highways of Palestine; in prayer and fasting on the solitary mountain top; in the Garden of Gethsemane; before the judgment seat of Pilate; betrayed by one of His trusted disciples at His last supper; in His agonies on the cross, even Jesus of Nazareth, in these last sad days on earth, felt the awful solitude of self. Deserted by man, in agony he cried, "My God! My God! why hast Thou forsaken me?" And so it ever must be in the conflicting scenes of life. On the long weary march, each one walks alone. We may have many friends, love, kindness, sympathy and charity to smooth our pathway in everyday life, but in the tragedies and triumphs of human experience each mortal stands alone.

But when all artificial trammels are removed, and women are recognized as individuals, responsible for their own environments, thoroughly educated for all the positions in life they may be called to fill; with all the resources in themselves that liberal thought and broad culture can give; guided by their own conscience and judgment; trained to self-protection by a healthy development of the muscular system and skill in the use of weapons of defense, and stimulated to self-support by the knowledge of the business world and the pleasure that pecuniary independence must ever give; when women are trained in this way they will, in a measure, be fitted for those hours of solitude that come alike to all, whether prepared or otherwise. As in our extremity we must depend on ourselves, the dictates of wisdom point to complete individual development.

In talking of education how shallow the argument that each class must be educated for the special work it proposes to do, and all those faculties not needed in this special work must lie dormant and utterly wither for want of use, when, perhaps, these will be the very faculties needed in life's greatest emergencies. Some say, Where is the use of drilling girls in the languages, the Sciences, in law, medicine, theology? As wives, mothers, housekeepers, cooks, they need a different curriculum from boys, who are to fill all positions. The chief cooks in our great hotels and ocean steamers are men. In large cities men run the bakeries; they make our bread, cake, and pies. They manage the laundries; they are now considered our best milliners and dressmakers. Because some men fill these departments of usefulness, shall we regulate the curriculum in Harvard and Yale to their present necessities?

If not, why this talk in our best colleges of a curriculum for girls who are crowding into the trades and professions; teachers in all our public schools rapidly filling many lucrative and honorable positions in life? . . .

Women are already the equals of men in the whole realm of thought, in art, science, literature, and government. With telescope vision they explore the starry firmament, and bring back the history of the planetary world. With chart and compass they pilot ships across the mighty deep, and with skillful finger send electric messages around the globe. In galleries of art the beauties of nature and the virtues of humanity are immortalized by them on their canvas and by their inspired touch dull blocks of marble are transformed into angels of light. . . .

Is it, then, consistent to hold the developed woman of this day within the same narrow political limits as the dame with the spinning wheel and knitting needle occupied in the past? No! no! Machinery has taken the labors of woman as well as man on its tireless shoulders; the loom and the spinning wheel are but dreams of the past; the pen, the brush, the easel, the chisel, have taken their places, while the hopes and ambitions of women are essentially changed. We see reason sufficient in the outer conditions of human being for individual liberty and development, but when we consider the self dependence of every human soul we see the need of courage, judgment, and the exercise of every faculty of mind and body, strengthened and developed by use, in woman as well as man.

. . .

[T]here is a solitude, which each and every one of us has always carried with him, more inaccessible than the ice-cold mountains, more profound than the midnight sea; the solitude of self. Our inner being, which we call ourself, no eye nor touch of man or angel has ever pierced. It is more hidden than the caves of the gnome; the sacred adytum of the oracle; the hidden chamber of Eleusinian mystery, for to it only omniscience is permitted to enter. Such is individual life. Who, I ask you, can take, dare take, on himself the rights, the duties, the responsibilities of another human soul?

[1892]

 22

From Women and Economics: A Study of the Economic Relation between Men and Women as a Factor in Social Evolution

CHARLOTTE PERKINS GILMAN

CHARLOTTE PERKINS GILMAN United States. 1860–1935. Author. Social critic. Lecturer. Editor of *The Forerunner* (1909–1916). Cofounder of the Women's Peace Party. She published more than 180 short stories, the best known of which is "The Yellow Wallpaper." *Women and Economics* (1898), *The Man-Made World; or, Our Androcentric Culture* (1911), *Herland* (1915), *The Living of Charlotte Perkins Gilman: An Autobiography* (1935).

CHAPTER VII

. . .

The economic status of the human race in any nation, at any time, is governed mainly by the activities of the male: the female obtains her share in the racial advance only through him.

Studied individually, the facts are even more plainly visible, more open and familiar. From the day laborer to the millionaire, the wife's worn dress or Flashing jewels, her low roof or her lordly one, her weary feet or her rich equipage,—these speak of the economic ability of the husband. The comfort, the luxury, the necessities of life itself, which the woman receives, are obtained by the husband, and given her by him. And, when the woman, left alone with no man to "support" her, tries to meet her own economic necessities, the difficulties which confront her prove conclusively what the general economic status of the woman is. None can deny these patent facts,—that the economic status of women generally depends upon that of men generally, and that the economic status of women individually depends upon that of men individually, those men to whom they are related. But we are instantly confronted by the commonly received opinion that, although it must be admitted that men make and distribute the wealth of the world, yet women earn their share of it as wives. This assumes either that the husband is in the position of employer and the wife of employee, or that marriage is a "partnership," and the wife an equal factor with the husband in producing wealth.

Economic independence is a relative condition at best. In the broadest sense, all living things are economically dependent upon others,—the animals upon the vegetables, and man upon both. In a narrower sense, all social life is economically interdependent, man producing collectively what he could by no possibility produce separately. But, in the closest interpretation, individual economic independence among human beings means that the individual pays for what he gets, works for what he gets, gives to the other an equivalent for what the other gives him. I depend on the shoemaker for shoes, and the tailor for coats; but, if I give the shoemaker and the tailor enough of my own labor as a house-builder to pay for the shoes and coats they give me, I retain my personal independence. I have not taken of their product, and given nothing of mine. As long as what I get is obtained by what I give, I am economically independent.

Women consume economic goods. What economic product do they give in exchange for what they consume? The claim that marriage is a partnership, in which the two persons married produce wealth which neither of them, separately, could produce, will not bear examination. A man happy and comfortable can produce more than one unhappy and uncomfortable, but this is as true of a father or son as of a husband. To take from a man any of the conditions which make him happy and strong is to cripple his industry, generally speaking. But those relatives who make him happy are not therefore his business partners, and entitled to share his income.

Grateful return for happiness conferred is not the method of exchange in a partnership. The comfort a man takes with his wife is not in the nature of a business partnership, nor are her frugality and industry. A housekeeper, in her place, might be as frugal, as industrious, but would not therefore be a partner. Man and wife are partners truly in their mutual obligation to their children,—their common

love, duty, and service. But a manufacturer who marries, or a doctor, or a lawyer, does not take a partner in his business, when he takes a partner in parenthood, unless his wife is also a manufacturer, a doctor, or a lawyer. In his business, she cannot even advise wisely without training and experience. To love her husband, the composer, does not enable her to compose; and the loss of a man's wife, though it may break his heart, does not cripple his business, unless his mind is affected by grief. She is in no sense a business partner, unless she contributes capital or experience or labor, as a man would in like relation. Most men would hesitate very seriously before entering a business partnership with any woman, wife or not.

If the wife is not, then, truly a business partner, in what way does she earn from her husband the food, clothing, and shelter she receives at his hands? By house service, it will be instantly replied. This is the general misty idea upon the subject,— that women earn all they get, and more, by house service. Here we come to a very practical and definite economic ground. Although not producers of wealth, women serve in the final processes of preparation and distribution. Their labor in the household has a genuine economic value.

For a certain percentage of persons to serve other persons, in order that the ones so served may produce more, is a contribution not to be overlooked. The labor of women in the house, certainly, enables men to produce more wealth than they otherwise could; and in this way women are economic factors in society. But so are horses. The labor of horses enables men to produce more wealth than they otherwise could. The horse is an economic factor in society. But the horse is not economically independent, nor is the woman. If a man plus a valet can perform more useful service than he could minus a valet, then the valet is performing useful service. But, if the valet is the property of the man, is obliged to perform this service, and is not paid for it, he is not economically independent.

The labor which the wife performs in the household is given as part of her functional duty, not as employment. The wife of the poor man, who works hard in a small house, doing all the work for the family, or the wife of the rich man, who wisely and gracefully manages a large house and administers its functions, each is entitled to fair pay for services rendered.

To take this ground and hold it honestly, wives, as earners through domestic service, are entitled to the wages of cooks, housemaids, nursemaids, seamstresses, or housekeepers, and to no more. This would of course reduce the spending money of the wives of the rich, and put it out of the power of the poor man to "support" a wife at all, unless, indeed, the poor man faced the situation fully, paid his wife her wages as house servant, and then she and he combined their funds in the support of their children. He would be keeping a servant: she would be helping keep the family. But nowhere on earth would there be "a rich woman" by these means. Even the highest class of private housekeeper, useful as her services are, does not accumulate a fortune. She does not buy diamonds and sables and keep a carriage. Things like these are not earned by house service.

But the salient fact in this discussion is that, whatever the economic value of the domestic industry of women is, they do not get it. The women who do the most work get the least money, and the women who have the most money do the least work. Their labor is neither given nor taken as a factor in economic exchange. It is held to be their duty as women to do this work; and their economic status bears no relation to their domestic labors, unless an inverse one. Moreover, if they were thus fairly paid,—given what they earned, and no more,—all women working in this way would be reduced to the economic status of the house servant. Few women—or men either—care to face this condition. The ground that women earn their living by domestic labor is instantly forsaken, and we are told that they obtain their livelihood as mothers. This is a peculiar position. We speak of it commonly enough, and often with deep feeling, but without due analysis.

In treating of an economic exchange, asking what return in goods or labor women make for the goods and labor given them,—either to the race collectively or to their husbands individually,—what payment women make for their clothes and shoes and furniture and food and shelter, we are told that the duties and services of the mother entitle her to support.

If this is so, if motherhood is an exchangeable commodity given by women in payment for clothes and food, then we must of course find some relation between the quantity or quality of the motherhood and the quantity and quality of the pay. This being true, then the women who are not mothers have no economic status at all; and the economic status of those who are must be shown to be relative to their motherhood. This is obviously absurd. The childless wife has as much money as the mother of many,—more; for the children of the latter consume what would otherwise be hers; and the inefficient mother is no less provided for than the efficient one. Visibly, and upon the face of it, women are not maintained in economic prosperity proportioned to their motherhood. Motherhood bears no relation to their economic status. Among primitive races, it is true,—in the patriarchal period, for instance,—there was some truth in this position. Women being of no value whatever save as bearers of children, their favor and indulgence did bear direct relation to maternity; and they had reason to exult on more grounds than one when they could boast a son. To-day, however, the maintenance of the woman is not conditioned upon this. A man is not allowed to discard his wife because she is barren. The claim of motherhood as a factor in economic exchange is false to-day. But suppose it were true. Are we willing to hold this ground, even in theory? Are we willing to consider motherhood as a business, a form of commercial exchange? Are the cares and duties of the mother, her travail and her love, commodities to be exchanged for bread? . . .

CHAPTER XIV

The changes in our conception and expression of home life, so rapidly and steadily going on about us, involve many far-reaching effects, all helpful to human advancement. Not the least of these is the improvement in our machinery of social intercourse.

This necessity of civilization was unknown in those primitive ages when family intercourse was sufficient for all, and when any further contact between individuals meant war. Trade and its travel, the specialization of labor and the distribution of its products, with their ensuing development, have produced a wider, freer, and more frequent movement and interchange among the innumerable individuals whose interaction makes society. Only recently, and as yet but partially, have women as individuals come to their share of this fluent social intercourse which is the essential condition of civilization. It is not merely a pleasure or an indulgence: it is the human necessity.

For women as individuals to meet men and other women as individuals, with no regard whatever to the family relation, is a growing demand of our time. As a social necessity, it is perforce being met in some fashion; but its right development is greatly impeded by the clinging folds of domestic and social customs derived from the sexuo-economic relation. The demand for a wider and freer social intercourse between the sexes rests, primarily, on the needs of their respective natures, but is developed in modern life to a far subtler and higher range of emotion than existed in the primitive state, where they had but one need and but one way of meeting it; and this demand, too, calls for a better arrangement of our machinery of living.

· · ·

What the human race requires is permanent provision for the needs of individuals, disconnected from the sex-relation. Our assumption that only married people and their immediate relatives have any right to live in comfort and health is erroneous. Every human being needs a home,—bachelor, husband, or widower, girl, wife, or widow, young or old. They need it from the cradle to the grave, and without regard to sex-connections. We should so build and arrange for the shelter and comfort of humanity as not to interfere with marriage, and yet not to make that comfort dependent upon marriage. With the industries of home life managed professionally, with rooms and suites of rooms and houses obtainable by any person or persons desiring them, we could live singly without losing home comfort and general companionship, we could meet bereavement without being robbed of the common conveniences of living as well as of the heart's love, and we could marry in ease and freedom without involving any change in the economic base of either party concerned.

Married people will always prefer a home together, and can have it; but groups of women

or groups of men can also have a home together if they like, or contiguous rooms. And individuals even could have a house to themselves, without having, also, the business of a home upon their shoulders.

Take the kitchens out of the houses, and you leave rooms which are open to any form of arrangement and extension; and the occupancy of them does not mean "housekeeping." In such living, personal character and taste would flower as never before; the home of each individual would be at last a true personal expression; and the union of individuals in marriage would not compel the jumbling together of all the external machinery of their lives,—a process in which much of the delicacy and freshness of love, to say nothing of the power of mutual rest and refreshment, is constantly lost. The sense of lifelong freedom and self-respect and of the peace and permanence of one's own home will do much to purify and uplift the personal relations of life, and more to strengthen and extend the social relations. The individual will learn to feel himself an integral part of the social structure, in close, direct, permanent connection with the needs and uses of society.

This is especially needed for women, who are generally considered, and who consider themselves, mere fractions of families, and incapable of any wholesome life of their own. The knowledge that peace and comfort may be theirs for life, even if they do not marry,—and may be still theirs for life, even if they do,—will develope a serenity and strength in women most beneficial to them and to the world. It is a glaring proof of the insufficient and irritating character of our existing form of marriage that women must be forced to it by the need of food and clothes, and men by the need of cooks and housekeepers. We are absurdly afraid that, if men or women can meet these needs of life by other means, they will cheerfully renounce the marriage relation.

· · ·

The economic independence of woman will change all these conditions as naturally and inevitably as her dependence has introduced them. In her specialization in industry, she will develope more personality and less sexuality; and this will lower the pressure on this one relation in both women and men. And, in our social intercourse, the new character and new method of living will allow of broad and beautiful developments in human association. As the private home becomes a private home indeed, and no longer the woman's social and industrial horizon; as the workshops of the world—woman's sphere as well as man's—become home-like and beautiful under her influence; and as men and women move freely together in the exercise of common racial functions,—we shall have new channels for the flow of human life.

We shall not move from the isolated home to the sordid shop and back again, in a world torn and dissevered by the selfish production of one sex and the selfish consumption of the other; but we shall live in a world of men and women humanly related, as well as sexually related, working together, as they were meant to do, for the common good of all. The home will be no longer an economic entity, with its cumbrous industrial machinery huddled vulgarly behind it, but a peaceful and permanent expression of personal life[.]

[1898]

 23

From The Progress of Colored Women

MARY CHURCH TERRELL

MARY CHURCH TERRELL United States. 1863–1954. Educator. Writer and lecturer on women's rights and civil rights. Born to parents who were former slaves. First Black woman appointed to the District of Columbia Board of Education. First president of the National Association of Colored Women. *A Colored Woman in a White World* (1940).

"I expected to see a dozen clever colored women, but instead of twelve I saw two hundred. It was simply an eye opener." This is the way one white woman expressed herself, after she had attended a convention of colored women held in Chicago about four years ago. This sentiment was echoed by many other white women who assisted at the delib-

erations of the colored women on that occasion. These Chicagoans were no more surprised at the intelligence, culture, and taste in dress which the colored women displayed than white people of other cities. When the National Association of Colored Women held its biennial two years ago in Buffalo, New York, the logic, earnestness and common sense of the delegates were quite as much a nine days' wonder as it was in Chicago. "I hold myself above the pettiness of race prejudice, of course," said one of the best women journalists in the country, "but for all my liberal mindedness the four days session of this federation of colored women's clubs has been a revelation. It has been my lot, first and last, to attend a good many conventions of women—'Mothers, Daughters,' and what not, and of them all, the sanest, the liveliest, the most practical was that of the colored women." And so quotation after quotation might be cited to prove that even the white people who think they know all about colored people and are perfectly just in their estimate of them are surprised when they have an ocular demonstration of the rapidity with which a large number of colored women has advanced. When one considers the obstacles encountered by colored women in their effort to educate and cultivate themselves, since they became free, the work they have accomplished and the progress they have made will bear favorable comparisons at least with that of their more fortunate sisters, from whom the opportunity of acquiring knowledge and the means of self culture have never been entirely withheld. Not only are colored women with ambition and aspiration handicapped on account of their sex, but they are almost everywhere baffled and mocked because of their race. Not only because they are women, but because they are colored women, are discouragement and disappointment meeting them at every turn. But in spite of the obstacles encountered, the progress made by colored women along many lines appears like a veritable miracle of modern times. Forty years ago for the great masses of colored women there was no such thing as home. To-day in each and every section of the country there are hundreds of homes among colored people, the mental and moral tone of which is as high and as pure as can be found among the best people of any land. To the women of the race may be attributed in large measure the refinement and purity of the colored home. The immorality of colored women is a theme upon which those who know little about them or those who maliciously misrepresent them love to descant. Foul aspersions upon the character of colored women are assiduously circulated by the press of certain sections and especially by the direct descendants of those who in years past were responsible for the moral degradation of their female slaves. And yet, in spite of the fateful heritage of slavery, even though the safe guards usually thrown around maidenly youth and innocence are in some sections entirely withheld from colored girls, statistics compiled by men not inclined to falsify in favor of my race show that immorality among the colored women of the United States is not so great as among women with similar environment and temptations in Italy, Germany, Sweden, and France.

Scandals in the best colored society are exceedingly rare, while the progressive game of divorce and remarriage is practically unknown.

The intellectual progress of colored women has been marvelous. So great has been their thirst for knowledge and so herculean their efforts to acquire it that there are few colleges, universities, high, and normal schools in the North, East, and West from which colored girls have not graduated with honor. In Wellesley, Vassar, Ann Arbor, Cornell, and in Oberlin, my dear alma mater, whose name will always be loved and whose praise will always be sung as the first college in the country broad, just, and generous enough to extend a cordial welcome to the Negro and to open its doors to women on an equal footing with the men, colored girls by their splendid records have forever settled the question of their capacity and worth. The instructors in these and other institutions cheerfully bear testimony to their intelligence, their diligence, and their success. As the brains of colored women expanded, their hearts began to grow. No sooner had the heads of a favored few been filled with knowledge than their hearts yearned to dispense blessings to the less fortunate of their race. With tireless energy and eager zeal colored women have worked in every conceivable way to elevate their race. Of the colored teachers engaged in instructing our youth it is probably no exaggeration to say that fully eighty percent

are women. In the backwoods, remote from the civilization and comforts of the city and town, colored women may be found courageously battling with those evils which such conditions always entail. Many a heroine of whom the world will never hear has thus sacrificed her life to her race amid surroundings and in the face of privations which only martyrs can bear.

Through the medium of their societies in the church, beneficial organizations out of it, and clubs of various kinds, colored women are doing a vast amount of good. It is almost impossible to ascertain exactly what the Negro is doing in any field, for the records are so poorly kept. This is particularly true in the case of the women of the race. During the past forty years there is no doubt that colored women in their poverty have contributed large sums of money to charitable and educational institutions as well as to the foreign and home missionary work. Within the twenty-five years in which the educational work of the African Methodist Episcopal church has been systematized, the women of that organization have contributed at least five hundred thousand dollars to the cause of education. Dotted all over the country are charitable institutions for the aged, orphaned, and poor which have been established by colored women, just how many it is difficult to state, owing to the lack of statistics bearing on the progress, possessions, and prowess of colored women. Among the charitable institutions either founded, conducted, or supported by colored women, may be mentioned the Hale Infirmary of Montgomery, Alabama, the Carrie Steele Orphanage of Atlanta, the Reed Orphan Home of Covington, and the Haines Industrial School of Augusta, all three in the state of Georgia; a home for the aged of both races in New Bedford and St. Monica's home of Boston, in Massachusetts; Old Folks Home of Memphis, Tennessee, and the Colored Orphan's Home of Lexington, Kentucky, together with others which lack of space forbids me to mention. Mt. Meigs Institute is an excellent example of a work originated and carried into successful execution by a colored woman. The school was established for the benefit of colored people on the plantations in the black belt of Alabama. In the township of Mt. Meigs the population is practically all colored.

Instruction given in this school is of the kind best suited to the needs of the people for whom it was established. Along with some scholastic training, girls are taught everything pertaining to the management of the home, while boys are taught practical farming, wheelwrighting, blacksmithing, and have some military training. Having started with almost nothing, at the end of eight years the trustees of the school owned nine acres of land and five buildings in which several thousand pupils had received instructions, all through the energy, the courage, and the sacrifice of one little woman.

Up to date, politics have been religiously eschewed by colored women, although questions affecting our legal status as a race are sometimes agitated by the most progressive class. In Louisiana and Tennessee colored women have several times petitioned the legislatures of their respective states to repel the obnoxious Jim Crow Car Laws. Against the Convict Lease System, whose atrocities have been so frequently exposed of late, colored women here and there in the South are waging a ceaseless war. So long as hundreds of their brothers and sisters, many of whom have committed no crime or misdemeanor whatever, are thrown into cells, whose cubic contents are less than those of a good size grave, to be overworked, underfed, and only partially covered with vermin-infested rags, and so long as children are born to the women in these camps who breathe the polluted atmosphere of these dens of horror and vice from the time they utter their first cry in the world till they are released from their suffering by death, colored women who are working for the emancipation and elevation of their race know where their duty lies. By constant agitation of this painful and hideous subject, they hope to touch the conscience of the country, so that this stain upon its escutcheon shall be forever wiped away.

Alarmed at the rapidity with which the Negro is losing ground in the world of trade, some of the far-sighted women are trying to solve the labor question, so far as it concerns the women at least, by urging the establishment of Schools of Domestic Science wherever means therefor can be secured. Those who are interested in this particular work hope and believe that if colored women and girls are thoroughly trained in domestic service, the boycott which has undoubtedly been placed upon them in many sections of the country will be removed. With so few vocations open to the Negro and with the labor organizations increasingly hostile to him, the future of the boys and girls of the race appears to some of our women very foreboding and dark.

The cause of temperance has been eloquently espoused by two women, each of whom has been appointed National Superintendent of work among colored people by the Woman's Christian Temperance Union. In business, colored women have had signal success. There is in Alabama a large milling and cotton business belonging to and controlled by a colored woman who has sometimes as many as seventy-five men in her employ. Until a few years ago the principal ice plant of Nova Scotia was owned and managed by a colored woman, who sold it for a large amount. In the professions there are dentists and doctors, whose practice is lucrative and large. Ever since a book was published in 1773 entitled "Poems on Various Subjects, Religious and Moral by Phyllis Wheatley, Negro Servant of Mr. John Wheatley," of Boston, colored women have given abundant evidence of literary ability. In sculpture we are represented by a woman upon whose chisel Italy has set her seal of approval; in painting by one of Bouguereau's pupils; and in music by young women holding diplomas from the best conservatories in the land.

In short, to use a thought of the illustrious Frederick Douglass, if judged by the depths from which they have come, rather than by the heights to which those blessed with centuries of opportunities have attained, colored women need not hang their heads in shame. They are slowly but surely making their way up to the heights, wherever they can be scaled. In spite of handicaps and discouragements they are not losing heart. In a variety of ways they are rendering valiant service to their race. Lifting as they climb, onward and upward they go, struggling and striving and hoping that the buds and blossoms of their desires may burst into glorious fruition ere long. Seeking no favors because of their color nor charity because of their needs, they knock at the door of Justice and ask for an equal chance.

[1898]

24

Lynching and the Excuse for It

IDA B. WELLS-BARNETT

IDA B. WELLS-BARNETT United States. 1862–1931. Teacher. Journalist. Newspaper editor. Born in slavery. Civil rights and women's rights speaker and advocate. Leader in antilynching campaigns. Participated in founding the NAACP. *Southern Horrors: Lynch Law in All Its Phases* (1892), *A Red Record* (1895), *Crusade for Justice: The Autobiography of Ida B. Wells* (1970).

It was eminently befitting that *The Independent*'s[1] first number in the new century should contain a strong protest against lynching. The deepest-dyed infamy of the nineteenth century was that which, in its supreme contempt for law, defied all constitutional guarantees of citizenship, and during the last fifteen years of the century put to death two thousand men, women and children, by shooting, hanging and burning alive. Well would it have been if every preacher in every pulpit in the land had made so earnest a plea as that which came from Miss Addams's forceful pen.

Appreciating the helpful influences of such a dispassionate and logical argument as that made by the writer referred to, I earnestly desire to say nothing to lessen the force of the appeal. At the same time an unfortunate presumption used as a basis for her argument works so serious, tho doubtless unintentional, an injury to the memory of thousands of victims of mob law that it is only fair to call attention to this phase of the writer's plea. It is unspeakably infamous to put thousands of people to death without a trial by jury; it adds to that infamy to charge that these victims were moral monsters, when, in fact, four-fifths of them were not so accused even by the fiends who murdered them.

Almost at the beginning of her discussion, the distinguished writer says:

> "Let us assume that the Southern citizens who take part in and abet the lynching of negroes honestly believe that that is the only successful method of dealing with a certain class of crimes."

It is this assumption, this absolutely unwarrantable assumption, that vitiates every suggestion which it inspires Miss Addams to make. It is the same baseless assumption which influences ninety-nine out of every one hundred persons who discuss this question. Among many thousand editorial clippings I have received in the past five years, ninety-nine percent discuss the question upon the presumption that lynchings are the desperate effort of the Southern people to protect their women from black monsters, and while the large majority condemn lynching, the condemnation is tempered with a plea for the lyncher—that human nature gives way under such awful provocation and that the mob, insane for the moment, must be pitied as well as condemned. It is strange that an intelligent, law-abiding and fair-minded people should so persistently shut their eyes to the facts in the discussion of what the civilized world now concedes to be America's national crime.

This almost universal tendency to accept as true the slander which the lynchers offer to civilization as an excuse for their crime might be explained if the true facts were difficult to obtain. But not the slightest difficulty intervenes. The Associated Press dispatches, the press clipping bureau, frequent book publications and the annual summary of a number of influential journals give the lynching record every year. This record, easily within the reach of everyone who wants it, makes inexcusable the statement and cruelly unwarranted the assumption that negroes are lynched only because of their assaults upon womanhood.

For an example in point: For fifteen years past, on the first day of each year, the *Chicago Tribune* has given to the public a carefully compiled record of all the lynchings of the previous year. Space will not permit a *résumé* of these fifteen years, but as fairly representing the entire time. I desire to briefly tabulate here the record of the five years last past. The statistics of the ten years preceding do not vary, they simply emphasize the record here presented.

The record gives the name and nationality of the man or woman lynched, the alleged crime, the time and place of the lynching. With this is given a *résumé* of the offenses charged, with the number of persons lynched for the offenses named. That enables the reader to see at a glance the causes assigned for the lynchings, and leaves nothing to be assumed. The lynchers, at the time and place of the lynching, are the best authority for the causes which actuate them. Every presumption is in favor of this record, especially as it remains absolutely unimpeached. This record gives the following state-ment of the colored persons lynched and the causes of the lynchings for the years named:

1896

Murder 24	Arson 2
Attempted murder 4	Assault 3
Rape 31	Unknown cause 1
Incendiarism 2	Slapping a child 1
No cause 2	Shooting at officer 1
Alleged rape 2	Alleged murder. 2
Cattle stealing 1	Threats 1
Miscegenation 2	Passing counterfeit
Attempted rape 4	money. 1
Murderous assault 1	Theft 1

1897

Murder 55	Writing insulting letter . . . 1
Attempted rape 8	Cattle thief 1
Mistaken identity 1	Felony. 1
Arson 3	Train wrecking 1
Murderous assault 2	Rape. 22
Running quarantine 1	Race prejudice 1
Burglary 1	Alleged arson 1
Bad reputation 1	Robbery 6
Unknown offense 3	Assault 2
Killing white cap 1	Disobeying Fed. regula-
Attempted murder 1	tions 1
Insulting white woman . . . 1	Theft 2
Suspected arson 1	Elopement 1
Giving evidence 2	Concealing murderer 1
Refusing to give evidence . 1	

1898

Murder 42	Theft 6
Rape 14	Miscegenation 1
Attempted rape 7	Unknown offense 2
Complicity in rape 1	Violation of contract. 1
Highway robbery 1	Insults. 2
Burglary 1	Race prejudice 3
Mistaken identity 1	Resisting arrest 1
Arson 1	Suspected murder 13
Murderous assault 1	Assaults upon whites 4

1899

Murder 24	Arson 8
Robbery 6	Unknown offense 4
Inflammatory language . . 1	Resisting arrest 1
Desperado 1	Mistaken identity 1
Complicity in murder 3	Aiding escape of
Rape 11	murderer. 3
Attempted rape 8	

1900

Murder 30	No offense 1
Rape 16	Arson 2
Attempted assault 12	Suspicion of arson 1
Race prejudice 9	Aiding escape of
Plot to kill whites 2	murderer. 1
Suspected robbery 1	Unpopularity 1
Giving testimony 1	Making threats 1
Attacking white men 3	Informer 1
Attempted murder 4	Robbery 2
Threats to kill 1	Burglary 4
Suspected murder 2	Assault 2
Unknown offense 2	

With this record in view there should be no dif-ficulty in ascertaining the alleged offenses given as justification for lynchings during the last five years. If the Southern citizens lynch negroes because "that is the only successful method of dealing with a certain class of crimes," then that class of crimes should be shown unmistakably by this record. Now consider the record.

It would be supposed that the record would show that all, or nearly all, lynchings were caused by outrageous assaults upon women; certainly that this particular offense would outnumber all other causes for putting human beings to death without a trial by jury and the other safeguards of our Consti-tution and laws.

But the record makes no such disclosure. Instead, it shows that five women have been lynched, put to death with unspeakable savagery, during the past five years. They certainly were not under the ban of the outlawing crime. It shows that men, not a few, but hundreds, have been lynched for misde-meanors, while others have suffered death for no offense known to the law, the causes assigned being "mistaken identity," "insult," "bad reputation," "unpopularity," "violating contract," "running quarantine," "giving evidence," "frightening child by shooting at rabbits," etc. Then, strangest of all, the record shows that the sum total of lynchings for these offenses—not crimes—and for the alleged offenses which are only misdemeanors, greatly exceeds the lynchings for the very crime universally declared to be the cause of lynching.

A careful classification of the offenses which have caused lynchings during the past five years shows that contempt for law and race prejudice constitute the real cause of all lynchings. During the past five years 147 white persons were lynched. It may be argued that fear of the "law's delays" was the cause of their being lynched. But this is not true. Not a single white victim of the mob was wealthy or had friends or influence to cause a miscarriage of justice. There was no such possibility—it was contempt for law which incited the mob to put so many white men to death without a complaint under oath, much less a trial.

In the case of the negroes lynched, the mobs' incentive was race prejudice. Few white men were lynched for any such trivial offenses as are detailed in the causes for lynching colored men. Negroes are lynched for "violating contracts," "unpopularity," "testifying in court" and "shooting at rabbits." As only negroes are lynched for "no offense," "unknown offenses," offenses not criminal, misdemeanors and crimes not capital, it must be admitted that the real cause of lynching in all such cases is race prejudice, and should be so classified. Grouping these lynchings under that classification and excluding rape, which in some States is made a capital offense, the record for the five years, so far as the negro is concerned, reads as follows:

Year	Race prejudice	Murder	Rape	Total lynchings
1896	31	24	31	86
1897	46	55	22	123
1898	39	47	16	102
1899	56	23	11	90
1900	57	30	16	103
Total	229	179	96	504

This table tells its own story, and shows how false is the excuse which lynchers offer to justify their fiendishness. Instead of being the sole cause of lynching, the crime upon which lynchers build their defense furnishes the least victims for the mob. In 1896 less than thirty-nine percent of the negroes lynched were charged with this crime; in 1897, less than eighteen per cent; in 1898, less than sixteen per cent; in 1899, less than fourteen per cent, and in 1900, less than fifteen per cent were so charged.

No good result can come from any investigation which refuses to consider the facts. A conclusion that is based upon a presumption, instead of the best evidence, is unworthy of a moment's consideration.

The lynching record, as it is compiled from day to day by unbiased, reliable and responsible public journals, should be the basis of every investigation which seeks to discover the cause and suggest the remedy for lynching. The excuses of lynchers and the specious pleas of their apologists should be considered in the light of the record, which they invariably misrepresent or ignore. The Christian and moral forces of the nation should insist that misrepresentation should have no place in the discussion of this all-important question, that the figures of the lynching record should be allowed to plead, trumpet tongued, in defense of the slandered dead, that the silence of concession be broken, and that truth, swift-winged and courageous, summon this nation to do its duty to exalt justice and preserve inviolate the sacredness of human life.

CHICAGO, ILL.

[1901]

NOTE

1. Published in *The Independent,* a progressive weekly newspaper, May 16, 1901, with an article by Jane Addams to which Wells-Barnett's article is a response.

 25

The Traffic in Women from Anarchism and Other Essays

EMMA GOLDMAN

EMMA GOLDMAN Russia. 1869–1940. Anarchist. Wrote and lectured extensively on free speech, birth control, women's rights, and union organizing. Lived and worked in United States until jailed and deported in 1919 for antidraft organizing during World War I. *Anarchism and Other Essays* (1910), *Philosophy of Atheism and the Failure of Christianity* (1916), *Living My Life* (1931).

Our reformers have suddenly made a great discovery—the white slave traffic. The papers are full of these "unheard-of conditions," and lawmakers are already planning a new set of laws to check the horror.

It is significant that whenever the public mind is to be diverted from a great social wrong, a crusade is inaugurated against indecency, gambling, saloons, etc. And what is the result of such crusades? Gambling is increasing, saloons are doing a lively business through back entrances, prostitution is at its height, and the system of pimps and cadets is but aggravated.

How is it that an institution, known almost to every child, should have been discovered so suddenly? How is it that this evil, known to all sociologists, should now be made such an important issue?

To assume that the recent investigation of the white slave traffic (and, by the way, a very superficial investigation) has discovered anything new, is, to say the least, very foolish. Prostitution has been, and is, a widespread evil, yet mankind goes on its business, perfectly indifferent to the sufferings and distress of the victims of prostitution. As indifferent, indeed, as mankind has remained to our industrial system, or to economic prostitution.

· · ·

What is really the cause of the trade in women? Not merely white women, but yellow and black women as well. Exploitation, of course; the merciless Moloch of capitalism that fattens on underpaid labor, thus driving thousands of women and girls into prostitution. With Mrs. Warren these girls feel, "Why waste your life working for a few shillings a week in a scullery, eighteen hours a day?"

Naturally our reformers say nothing about this cause. They know it well enough, but it doesn't pay to say anything about it. It as much more profitable to play the Pharisee, to pretend an outraged morality, than to go to the bottom of things.

· · ·

Nowhere is woman treated according to the merit of her work, but rather as a sex. It is therefore almost inevitable that she should pay for her right to exist, to keep a position in whatever line, with sex favors. Thus it is merely a question of degree whether she sells herself to one man, in or out of marriage, or to many men. Whether our reformers admit it or not, the economic and social inferiority of woman is responsible for prostitution.

Just at present our good people are shocked by the disclosures that in New York City alone one out of every ten women works in a factory, that the average wage received by women is six dollars per week for forty-eight to sixty hours of work, and that the majority of female wage workers face many months of idleness which leaves the average wage about $280 a year. In view of these economic horrors, is it to be wondered at that prostitution and the white slave trade have become such dominant factors?

Lest the preceding figures be considered an exaggeration, it is well to examine what some authorities on prostitution have to say:

"A prolific cause of female depravity can be found in the several tables, showing the description of the employment pursued, and the wages received, by the women previous to their fall, and it will be a question for the political economist to decide how far mere business consideration should be an apology on the part of employers for a reduction in their rates of remuneration, and whether the savings of a small percentage on wages is not more than counterbalanced by the enormous amount of taxation enforced on the public at large to defray the expenses incurred on account of a system of vice, *which is the direct result, in many cases, of insufficient compensation of honest labor.*"[1]

Our present-day reformers would do well to look into Dr. Sanger's book. There they will find that out of 2,000 cases under his observation, but few came from the middle classes, from well-ordered conditions, or pleasant homes. By far the largest majority were working girls and working women; some driven into prostitution through sheer want, others because of a cruel, wretched life at home, others again because of thwarted and crippled physical natures (of which I shall speak later on). Also it will do the maintainers of purity and morality good to learn that out of two thousand cases, 490 were married women, women who lived with their husbands. Evidently there was not much of a guaranty for their "safety and purity" in the sanctity of marriage.[2]

Dr. Alfred Blaschko, in *Prostitution in the Nineteenth Century,* is even more emphatic in characterizing economic conditions as one of the most vital factors of prostitution.

"Although prostitution has existed in all ages, it was left to the nineteenth century to develop it into a gigantic social institution. The development of industry with vast masses of people in the competitive market, the growth and congestion of large cities, the insecurity and uncertainty of employment, has given prostitution an impetus never dreamed of at any period in human history."

And again Havelock Ellis, while not so absolute in dealing with the economic cause, is nevertheless compelled to admit that it is indirectly and directly the main cause. Thus he finds that a large percentage of prostitutes is recruited from the servant class, although the latter have less care and greater security. On the other hand, Mr. Ellis does not deny that the daily routine, the drudgery, the monotony of the servant girl's lot, and especially the fact that she may never partake of the companionship and joy of a home, is no mean factor in forcing her to seek recreation and forgetfulness in the gaiety and glimmer of prostitution. In other words, the servant girl, being treated as a drudge, never having the right to herself, and worn out by the caprices of her mistress, can find an outlet, like the factory or shop-girl, only in prostitution.

The most amusing side of the question now before the public is the indignation of our "good, respectable people," especially the various Christian gentlemen, who are always to be found in the front ranks of every crusade. Is it that they are absolutely ignorant of the history of religion, and especially of the Christian religion? Or is it that they hope to blind the present generation to the part played in the past by the Church in relation to prostitution? Whatever their reason, they should be the last to cry out against the unfortunate victims of today, since it is known to every intelligent student that prostitution is of religious origin, maintained and fostered for many centuries, not as a shame, but as a virtue, hailed as such by the Gods themselves.

"It would seem that the origin of prostitution is to be found primarily in a religious custom, religion, the great conserver of social tradition, preserving in a transformed shape a primitive freedom that was passing out of the general social life. The typical example is that recorded by Herodotus, in the fifth century before Christ, at the Temple of Mylitta, the Babylonian Venus, where every woman, once in her life, had to come and give herself to the first stranger, who threw a coin in her lap,

to worship the goddess. Very similar customs existed in other parts of western Asia, in North Africa, in Cyprus, and other islands of the eastern Mediterranean, and also in Greece, where the temple of Aphrodite on the fort at Corinth possessed over a thousand hierodules, dedicated to the service of the goddess.

"The theory that religious prostitution developed, as a general rule, out of the belief that the generative activity of human beings possessed a mysterious and sacred influence in promoting the fertility of Nature, is maintained by all authoritative writers on the subject. Gradually, however, and when prostitution became an organized institution under priestly influence, religious prostitution developed utilitarian sides, thus helping to increase public revenue.

"The rise of Christianity to political power produced little change in policy. The leading fathers of the Church tolerated prostitution. Brothels under municipal protection are found in the thirteenth century. They constituted a sort of public service, the directors of them being considered almost as public servants."[3]

To this must be added the following from Dr. Sanger's work:

"Pope Clement II issued a bull that prostitutes would be tolerated if they pay a certain amount of their earnings to the Church."

"Pope Sixtus IV was more practical; from one single brothel, which he himself had built, he received an income of 20,000 ducats."

In modern times the Church is a little more careful in that direction. At least she does not openly demand tribute from prostitutes. She finds it much more profitable to go in for real estate, like Trinity Church, for instance, to rent out death traps at an exorbitant price to those who live off and by prostitution.

· · ·

It would be one-sided and extremely superficial to maintain that the economic factor is the only cause of prostitution. There are others no less important and vital. That, too, our reformers know, but dare discuss even less than the institution that saps the very life out of both men and women. I refer to the sex question, the very mention of which causes most people moral spasms.

It is a conceded fact that woman is being reared as a sex commodity, and yet she is kept in absolute ignorance of the meaning and importance of sex. Everything dealing with that subject is suppressed, and persons who attempt to bring light into this terrible darkness are persecuted and thrown into prison. Yet it is nevertheless true that so long as a girl is not to know how to take care of herself, not to know the function of the most important part of her life, we need not be surprised if she becomes an easy prey to prostitution, or to any other form of a relationship which degrades her to the position of an object for mere sex gratification.

It is due to this ignorance that the entire life and nature of the girl is thwarted and crippled. We have long ago taken it as a self-evident fact that the boy may follow the call of the wild; that is to say, that the boy may, as soon as his sex nature asserts itself, satisfy that nature; but our moralists are scandalized at the very thought that the nature of a girl should assert itself. To the moralist prostitution does not consist so much in the fact that the woman sells her body, but rather that she sells it out of wedlock. That this is no mere statement is proved by the fact that marriage for monetary considerations is perfectly legitimate, sanctified by law and public opinion, while any other union is condemned and repudiated. Yet a prostitute, if properly defined, means nothing else than "any person for whom sexual relationships are subordinated to gain."[4]

. . .

Of course, marriage is the goal of every girl, but as thousands of girls cannot marry, our stupid social customs condemn them either to a life of celibacy or prostitution. Human nature asserts itself regardless of all laws, nor is there any plausible reason why nature should adapt itself to a perverted conception of morality.

Society considers the sex experiences of a man as attributes of his general development, while similar experiences in the life of a woman are looked upon as a terrible calamity, a loss of honor and of all that is good and noble in a human being. This double standard of morality has played no little part in the creation and perpetuation of prostitution. It involves the keeping of the young in absolute ignorance on sex matters, which alleged "innocence," together with an overwrought and stifled sex nature, helps to bring about a state of affairs that our Puritans are so anxious to avoid or prevent.

Not that the gratification of sex must needs lead to prostitution; it is the cruel, heartless, criminal persecution of those who dare divert from the beaten track, which is responsible for it.

Girls, mere children, work in crowded, over-heated rooms ten to twelve hours daily at a machine, which tends to keep them in a constant over-excited sex state. Many of these girls have no home or comforts of any kind; therefore the street or some place of cheap amusement is the only means of forgetting their daily routine. This naturally brings them into close proximity with the other sex. It is hard to say which of the two factors brings the girl's oversexed condition to a climax, but it is certainly the most natural thing that a climax should result. That is the first step toward prostitution. Nor is the girl to be held responsible for it. On the contrary, it is altogether the fault of society, the fault of our lack of understanding, of our lack of appreciation of life in the making; especially is it the criminal fault of our moralists, who condemn a girl for all eternity, because she has gone from the "path of virtue"; that is, because her first sex experience has taken place without the sanction of the Church.

The girl feels herself a complete outcast, with the doors of home and society closed in her face. Her entire training and tradition is such that the girl herself feels depraved and fallen, and therefore has no ground to stand upon, or any hold that will lift her up, instead of dragging her down. Thus society creates the victims that it afterwards vainly attempts to get rid of. The meanest, most depraved and decrepit man still considers himself too good to take as his wife the woman whose grace he was quite willing to buy, even though he might thereby save her from a life of horror. Nor can she turn to her own sister for help. In her stupidity the latter deems herself too pure and chaste, not realizing that her own position is in many respects even more deplorable than her sister's of the street.

. . .

Moralists are ever ready to sacrifice one-half of the human race for the sake of some miserable institution which they cannot outgrow. As a matter of fact, prostitution is no more a safeguard for the purity of the home than rigid laws are a safeguard against prostitution. Fully fifty percent of married men are patrons of brothels. It is through this virtuous element that the married women—nay, even the children—are infected with venereal diseases. Yet society has not a word of condemnation for the man, while no law is too monstrous to be set in motion against the helpless victim. She is not only preyed upon by those who use her, but she is also absolutely at the mercy of every policeman and miserable detective on the beat, the officials at the station house, the authorities in every prison.

· · ·

Much stress is laid on white slaves being imported into America. How would America ever retain her virtue if Europe did not help her out? I will not deny that this may be the case in some instances, any more than I will deny that there are emissaries of Germany and other countries luring economic slaves into America; but I absolutely deny that prostitution is recruited to any appreciable extent from Europe. It may be true that the majority of prostitutes of New York City are foreigners, but that is because the majority of the population is foreign. The moment we go to any other American city, to Chicago or the Middle West, we shall find that the number of foreign prostitutes is by far a minority.

Equally exaggerated is the belief that the majority of street girls in this city were engaged in this business before they came to America. Most of the girls speak excellent English, are Americanized in habits and appearance,—a thing absolutely impossible unless they had lived in this country many years. That is, they were driven into prostitution by American conditions, by the thoroughly American custom for excessive display of finery and clothes, which, of course, necessitates money,—money that cannot be earned in shops or factories.

In other words, there is no reason to believe that any set of men would go to the risk and expense of getting foreign products, when American conditions are overflooding the market with thousands of girls. On the other hand, there is sufficient evidence to prove that the export of American girls for the purpose of prostitution is by no means a small factor.

· · ·

In view of the above facts it is rather absurd to point to Europe as the swamp whence come all the social diseases of America. Just as absurd is it to proclaim the myth that the Jews furnish the largest contingent of willing prey. I am sure that no one will accuse me of nationalistic tendencies. I am glad to say that I have developed out of them, as out of many other prejudices. If, therefore, I resent the statement that Jewish prostitutes are imported, it is not because of any Judaistic sympathies, but because of the facts inherent in the lives of these people. No one but the most superficial will claim that Jewish girls migrate to strange lands, unless they have some tie or relation that brings them there. The Jewish girl is not adventurous. Until recent years she had never left home, not even so far as the next village or town, except it were to visit some relative. Is it then credible that Jewish girls would leave their parents or families, travel thousands of miles to strange lands, through the influence and promises of strange forces? Go to any of the large incoming steamers and see for yourself if these girls do not come either with their parents, brothers, aunts, or other kinsfolk. There may be exceptions, of course, but to state that large numbers of Jewish girls are imported for prostitution, or any other purpose, is simply not to know Jewish psychology.

Those who sit in a glass house do wrong to throw stones about them; besides, the American glass house is rather thin, it will break easily, and the interior is anything but a gainly sight.

· · ·

An educated public opinion, freed from the legal and moral hounding of the prostitute, can alone help to ameliorate present conditions. Wilful shutting of eyes and ignoring of the evil as a social factor of modern life can but aggravate matters. We must rise above our foolish notions of "better than thou," and learn to recognize in the prostitute a product of social conditions. Such a realization will sweep away the attitude of hypocrisy, and insure a greater understanding and more humane treatment. As to a thorough eradication of prostitution, nothing can accomplish that save a complete transvaluation of all accepted values—especially the moral ones—coupled with the abolition of industrial slavery.

[1910]

NOTES

1. Dr. Sanger, *The History of Prostitution.*
2. It is a significant fact that Dr. Sanger's book has been excluded from the U.S. mails. Evidently the authorities are not anxious that the public be informed as to the true cause of prostitution.
3. Havelock Ellis, *Sex and Society.*
4. Guyot, *La Prostitution.*

 26

Girl Slaves of the Milwaukee Breweries

MOTHER (MARY) JONES

MOTHER (MARY) JONES Ireland. 1830[1837]–1930. U.S. labor union organizer, particularly for the United Mine Workers and in the textile industry. A founder of the Industrial Workers of the World. *Autobiography* (1925).

It is the same old story, as pitiful as old, as true as pitiful.

When the whistle blows in the morning it calls the girl slaves of the bottle-washing department of the breweries to don their wet shoes and rags and hustle to the bastile to serve out their sentences. It is indeed true, they are *sentenced* to hard, brutal labor—labor that gives no cheer, brings no recompense. Condemned for life, to slave daily in the washroom in wet shoes and wet clothes, surrounded with foul-mouthed, brutal foremen, whose orders and language would not look well in print and would surely shock over-sensitive ears or delicate nerves! And their crime? Involuntary poverty. It is hereditary. They are no more to blame for it than is a horse for having the glanders. It is the accident of birth. This accident that throws them into the surging, seething mass known as the working class is what forces them out of the cradle into servitude, to be willing(?) slaves of the mill, factory, department store, hell, or bottling shop in Milwaukee's colossal breweries; to create wealth for the brewery barons, that they may own palaces, theaters, automobiles, blooded stock, farms, banks, and Heaven knows what all, while the poor girls slave on all day in the vile smell of sour beer, lifting cases of empty and full bottles weighing from 100 to 150 pounds, in their wet shoes and rags, for God knows they cannot buy clothes on the miserable pittance doled out to them by their soulless master class. The conscienceless rich see no reason why the slave should not be content on the crust of bread for its share of all the wealth created. That these slaves of the dampness should contract rheumatism is a foregone conclusion. Rheumatism is one of the chronic ailments, and is closely followed by consumption. Consumption is well known to be only a disease of poverty. The Milwaukee lawmakers, of course, enacted an antispit ordinance to protect the public health, and the brewers contributed to the Red Cross Society to make war on the shadow of tuberculosis, and all the while the big capitalists are setting out incubators to hatch out germs enough among the poor workers to destroy the nation. Should one of these poor girl slaves spit on the sidewalk, it would cost her more than she can make in two weeks' work. Such is the *fine* system of the present-day affairs. The foreman even regulates the time that they may stay in the toilet room, and in the event of overstaying it gives the foreman an opportunity he seems to be looking for to indulge in indecent and foul language. Should the patient slave forget herself and take offense, it will cost her the job in that prison. And after all, bad as it is, it is all that she knows how to do. To deprive her of the job means less crusts and worse rags in "the land of the free and the home of the brave." Many of the girls have no home nor parents and are forced to feed and clothe and shelter themselves, and all this on an average of $3.00 per week. Ye Gods! What a horrible nightmare! What hope is there for decency when unscrupulous wealth may exploit its producers so shamelessly?

No matter how cold, how stormy, how inclement the weather, many of these poor girl slaves must walk from their shacks to their work, for their miserable stipend precludes any possibility of squeezing a street car ride out of it. And to this is due our much-vaunted greatness. Is this civilization? If so, what, please, is barbarism?

As an illustration of what these poor girls must submit to, one about to become a mother told me with tears in her eyes that every other day a depraved specimen of mankind took delight in measuring her girth and passing such comments as befits such humorous(?) occasion.

While the wage paid is 75 to 85 cents a day, the poor slaves are not permitted to work more than three or four days a week, and the continual threat of idle days makes the slave much more tractable and submissive than would otherwise obtain. Often when their day's work is done they are put to washing off the tables and lunch room floors and the other odd jobs, for which there is not even the suggestion of compensation. Of course, abuse always follows power, and nowhere is it more in evidence than in this miserable treatment the brewers and their hirelings accord their girl slaves.

The foreman also uses his influence, through certain living mediums near at hand, to neutralize any effort having in view the organization of these poor helpless victims of an unholy and brutal profit system, and threats of discharge were made, should these girls attend my meetings.

One of these foremen actually carried a union card, but the writer of this article reported him to the union and had him deprived of it for using such foul language to the girls under him. I learned of him venting his spite by discharging several girls, and I went to the superintendent and told him the character of the foreman. On the strength of my charges, he was called to the office and when he was informed of the nature of the visit, he patted the superintendent familiarly on the back and whined out how loyal he was to the superintendent, the whole performance taking on the character of servile lickspittle. As he fawns on his superior, so he expects to play autocrat with his menials and exact the same cringing from them under him. Such is the petty boss who holds the living of the working-class girls in his hands.

The brewers themselves were always courteous when I called on them, but their underlings were not so tactful, evidently working under instructions. The only brewer who treated me rudely or denied me admittance was Mr. Blatz, who brusquely told me his feelings in the following words: "The Brewers' Association of Milwaukee met when you first came to town and decided not to permit these girls to organize." This Brewers' Association is a strong union of all the brewery plutocrats, composed of Schlitz, Pabst, Miller, and Blatz breweries, who are the principal employers of women. And this union met and decided as above stated, that these women should not be permitted to organize! I then told Mr. Blatz that he could not shut me out of the halls of legislation, that as soon as the legislature assembles I shall appear there and put these conditions on record and demand an investigation and the drafting of suitable laws to protect the womanhood of the state.

Organized labor and humanity demand protection for these helpless victims of insatiable greed, in the interest of motherhood of our future state.

Will the people of this country at large, and the organized wage-workers in particular, tolerate and stand any longer for such conditions as existing in the bottling establishments of these Milwaukee breweries? I hope not! Therefore, I ask all fair-minded people to refrain from purchasing the product of these baron brewers until they will change things for the better for these poor girls working in their bottling establishments.

Exploited by the brewers! Insulted by the petty bosses! Deserted by the press, which completely ignored me and gave no helping hand to these poor girls' cause. Had they had a vote, however, their case would likely have attracted more attention from all sides. Poor peons of the brewers! Neglected by all the Gods! Deserted by all mankind. The present shorn of all that makes life worth living, the future hopeless, without a comforting star or glimmer. What avails our boasted greatness built upon such human wreckage? What is civilization and progress to them? What "message" bears the holy brotherhood in the gorgeous temples of modern worship? What terrors has the over-investigated white-slave traffic for her? What a prolific recruiting station for the red-light district! For after all, the white slave *eats, drinks,* and wears good clothing, and to the hopeless this means living, if it only lasts a minute. What has the beer slave to look forward to—the petty boss will make her job cost her virtue anyhow. This has come to be a price of a job everywhere nowadays. Is it any wonder the white-slave traffic abounds on all sides? No wonder the working class has lost all faith in Gods. Hell itself has no terrors worse than a term in industrial slavery. I will give these brewery lords of Milwaukee notice that my two months' investigation and efforts to organize, in spite of all obstacles placed in my way, will bear fruit, and the sooner they realize their duty the better it will be for themselves. Will they do it?

Think of it, fathers and mothers. Think of it, men and women. When it is asked of thee, "What hast thou done for the economic redemption of the sisters of thy brother Abel?" what will thy answer be?

[1910]

 ## 27

Working Woman and Mother

ALEXANDRA KOLLONTAI

ALEXANDRA KOLLONTAI Russia. 1872–1952. Socialist. Spoke and wrote on sexual emancipation and workers' rights. Diplomat. Participated in Russian Revolution and was made a member of the Central Committee by Lenin. Active in the international socialist women's movement. *The Social Basis of the Woman Question* (1909), *Communism and the Family* (1920), *The Autobiography of a Sexually Emancipated Communist Woman* (1926), *Love of Worker Bees* (1923).

MASHENKA THE FACTORY DIRECTOR'S WIFE

Mashenka is the factory director's wife. Mashenka is expecting a baby. Although everyone in the factory director's house is a little bit anxious, there is a festive atmosphere. This is not surprising, for Mashenka is going to present her husband with an heir. There will be someone to whom he can leave all his wealth—the wealth created by the hands of working men and women. The doctor has ordered them to look after Mashenka very carefully. Don't let her get tired, don't let her lift anything heavy. Let her eat just what she fancies. Fruit? Give her some fruit. Caviare? Give her caviare.

The important thing is that Mashenka should not feel worried or distressed in any way. Then the baby will be born strong and healthy; the birth will be easy and Mashenka will keep her bloom. That is how they talk in the factory director's family. That

is the accepted way of handling an expectant mother, in families where the purses are stuffed with gold and credit notes. They take good care of Mashenka the lady.

Do not tire yourself, Mashenka, do not try and move the armchair. That is what they say to Mashenka the lady.

The humbugs and hypocrites of the bourgeoisie maintain that the expectant mother is sacred to them. But is that really in fact the case?

MASHENKA THE LAUNDRESS

In the same house as the factory director's wife, but in the back part in a corner behind a printed calico curtain, huddles another Mashenka. She does the laundry and the housework. Mashenka is eight months pregnant. But she would open her eyes wide in surprise if they said to her, "Mashenka, you must not carry heavy things, you must look after yourself, for your own sake, for the child's sake, and for the sake of humanity. You are expecting a baby and that means your condition is, in the eyes of society, 'sacred'." Masha would take this either as uncalled-for interference or as a cruel joke. Where have you seen a woman of the working class given special treatment because she is pregnant? Masha and the hundreds of thousands of other women of the propertyless classes who are forced to sell their working hands know that the owners have no mercy when they see women in need; and they have no other alternative, however exhausted they may be, but to go out to work.

"An expectant mother must have, above all, undisturbed sleep, good food, fresh air, and not too much physical strain." That is what the doctor says. Masha the laundress and the hundreds and thousands of women workers, the slaves of capital, would laugh in his face. A minimum of physical strain? Fresh air? Wholesome food and enough of it? Undisturbed sleep? What working woman knows these blessings? They are only for Mashenka the lady, and for the wives of the factory owners.

Early in the morning before the darkness has given way to dawn and while Mashenka the lady is still having sweet dreams, Mashenka the laundress gets up from her narrow bed and goes into the damp, dark laundry. She is greeted by the fusty smell of dirty linen; she slips around on the wet floor; yesterday's puddles still have not dried. It is not of her own free will that Masha slaves away in the laundry. She is driven by that tireless overseer—need. Masha's husband is a worker, and his pay packet is so small two people could not possibly keep alive on it. And so in silence, gritting her teeth, she stands over the tub until the very last possible day, right up until the birth. Do not be mistaken into thinking that Masha the laundress has "iron health" as the ladies like to say when they are talking about working women. Masha's legs are heavy with swollen veins, through standing at the tub for such long periods. She can walk only slowly and with difficulty. There are bags under her eyes, her arms are puffed up and she has had no proper sleep for a long time.

The baskets of wet linen are often so heavy that Masha has to lean against the wall to prevent herself from falling. Her head swims and everything becomes dark in front of her eyes. It often feels as if there is a huge rotten tooth lodged at the back of her spine, and that her legs are made of lead. If only she could lie down for an hour . . . have some rest . . . but working women are not allowed to do such things. Such pamperings are not for them. For, after all, they are not ladies. Masha puts up with her hard lot in silence. The only "sacred" women are those expectant mothers who are not driven by that relentless taskmaster, need.

MASHA THE MAID

Mashenka the lady needs another servant. The master and mistress take in a lass from the country. Mashenka the lady likes the girl's ringing laughter and the plait that reaches down below her knee, and the way the girl flies around the house like a bird on the wing and tries to please everyone. A gem of a girl. They pay her three rubles a month and she does enough work for three people. The lady is full of praise.

Then the factory director begins to glance at the girl. His attentions grow. The girl does not see the danger; she is inexperienced, unsophisticated. The master gets very kind and loving. The doctor has advised him not to make any demands on his lady-wife. Quiet, he says, is the best medicine. The factory director is willing to let her give birth in peace, as long as he does not have to suffer. The maid is also called Masha. Things can easily be arranged; the girl is ignorant, stupid. It is not difficult to frighten her. She can be scared into anything. And so Masha gets pregnant. She stops laughing and begins to look haggard. Anxiety gnaws at her heart day and night.

Masha the lady finds out. She throws a scene. The girl is given twenty-four hours to pack her bags. Masha wanders the streets. She has no friends, nowhere to go. Who is going to employ "that kind of a girl" in any "honest" house? Masha wanders without work, without bread, without help. She passes a river. She looks at the dark waves and turns away shivering. The cold and gloomy river terrifies her, but at the same time seems to beckon.

MASHA THE DYE-WORKER

There is confusion in the factory's dye department; a woman worker has been carried out looking as if she is dead. What has happened to her? Was she poisoned by the steam? Could she no longer bear the fumes? She is no newcomer. It is high time she got used to the factory poison.

"It is absolutely nothing," says the doctor. "Can't you see? She is pregnant. Pregnant women are likely to behave in all sorts of strange ways. There is no need to give in to them."

So they send the woman back to work. She stumbles like a drunkard through the workshop back to her place. Her legs are numb and refuse to obey her. It is no joke working ten hours a day, day after day, amidst the toxic stench, the steam and the damaging fumes. And there is no rest for the working mother, even when the ten hours are over. At home there is her old blind mother waiting for her dinner, and her husband returns from his factory tired and hungry. She has to feed them all and look after them all. She is the first to get up in the morning, she's on her legs from sunrise, and she is the last to get to sleep. And then to crown it they have introduced overtime. Things are going well at the factory; the owner is raking in the profits with both hands. He only gives a few extra kopeks for overtime, but if you object, you know the way to the gates. There are, heaven be praised, enough unemployed in the world. Masha tries to get leave, by applying to the director himself.

"I am having my baby soon. I must get everything ready. My children are tiny and there is the housework; and then I have my old mother to look after."

But he will not listen. He is rude to her and humiliates her in front of the other workers. "If I started giving every pregnant woman time off, it would be simpler to close the factory. If you didn't sleep with men you wouldn't get pregnant."

So Masha the dye-worker has to labour on until the last minute. That is how much bourgeois society esteems motherhood.

CHILDBIRTH

For the household of Masha the lady the birth is a big event. It is almost a holiday. The house is a flurry of doctors, midwives, and nurses. The mother lies in a clean, soft bed. There are flowers on the tables. Her husband is by her side; letters and telegrams are delivered. A priest gives thanksgiving prayers. The baby is born healthy and strong. That is not surprising. They have taken such care and made such a fuss of Masha.

Masha the laundress is also in labour. Behind the calico curtain, in the corner of a room full of other people. Masha is in pain. She tries to stifle her moaning, burying her head in the pillow. The neighbours are all working people and it would not do to deprive them of their sleep. Towards morning the midwife arrives. She washes and tucks up the baby and then hurries off to another birth. Mashenka is now alone in the room. She looks at the baby. What a thin little mite. Skinny and wrinkled. Its eyes seem to reproach the mother for having given birth at all. Mashenka looks at him and cries silently so as not to disturb the others.

Masha the maid gives birth to her child under a fence in a suburban backstreet. She enquired at a maternity home, but it was full. She knocked at another but they would not accept her, saying she needed various bits of paper with signatures. She gives birth; she walks on. She walks and staggers. She wraps the baby in a scarf. Where can she go? There is nowhere to go. She remembers the dark river, terrifying and yet fascinating. In the morning the policeman drags a body out of the river. That is how bourgeois society respects motherhood.

The baby of Masha the dye-worker is stillborn. It has not managed to survive the nine months. The steam the mother inhales at the factory has poisoned the child while it was in the womb. The birth was difficult. Masha herself was lucky to come through alive. But by the evening of the following day she is already up and about, getting things straight, washing and doing the cooking. How can it be otherwise? Who else will look after Masha's home and organise the household? Who would see that the children were fed? Masha the lady can lie in bed for nine days on doctor's orders, for she has a whole establishment of servants to dance round her. If Masha the dye-worker develops a serious illness from going to work so soon after the birth and cripples herself as a result, that is just too bad.

There is no one to look after the working mother. No one to lift the heavy burdens from the shoulders of these tired women. Motherhood, they say, is sacred. But that is only true in the case of Masha the lady.

THE CROSS OF MOTHERHOOD

For Masha the lady, motherhood is a joyful occasion. In a bright, tidy nursery the factory owner's heir grows up under the eye of various nannies and the supervision of a doctor. If Masha the lady has too little milk of her own or does not want to spoil her figure, a wet-nurse can be found. Masha the lady amuses herself with the baby and then goes out visiting, goes shopping, or to the theatre, or to a ball. There is someone at hand to look after the baby. Motherhood is amusing, it is entertainment for Masha the lady.

For the other Mashas, the working women—the dyers, weavers, laundresses and the other hundreds and thousands of working-class women—motherhood is a cross. The factory siren calls the woman to work but her child is fretting and crying. How can she leave it? Who will look after it? She pours the milk into a bottle and gives the child to the old woman next door or leaves her young daughter in charge. She goes off to work, but she never stops worrying about the child. The little girl, well-intentioned but ignorant, might try feeding her brother porridge or bits of bread.

Masha the lady's baby looks better every day. Like white sugar or a firm rosy apple; so strong and healthy. The children of the factory worker, the laundress and the craft-worker grow thinner with every day. At nights the baby curls up small and cries. The doctor comes and scolds the mother for not breast-feeding the child or for not feeding it properly. "And you call yourself a mother. Now you have only yourself to blame if the baby dies." The hundreds and thousands of working mothers do not try to explain themselves. They stand with bent heads, furtively wiping away the tears. Could they tell the doctor of the difficulties they face? Would he believe them? Would he understand?

. . .

WORK AND MATERNITY

There was a time not so long ago, a time that our grandmothers remember, when women were only involved in work at home: in housework and domestic crafts. The women of the non-property-owning classes were not idle, of course, The work around the house was hard. They had to cook, sew, wash, weave, keep the linen white and work in the kitchen garden and in the fields. But this work did not tear the women away from the cradle; there were no factory walls separating her from her children. However poor the woman was, her child was in her arms. Times have changed. Factories have been set up; workshops have been opened. Poverty has driven women out of the home; the factory has pulled them in with its iron claws. When the factory gates slam behind her, a woman has to say farewell to maternity, for the factory has no mercy on the pregnant woman or the young mother.

When a woman works day in day out over a sewing machine, she develops a disease of the ovaries. When she works at a weaving or spinning factory, a rubber or china works or a lead or chemical plant, she and her baby are in danger of being poisoned by noxious fumes and by contact with harmful substances. When a woman works with lead or mercury, she becomes infertile or her children are stillborn. When she works at a cigarette or tobacco factory, the nicotine in her milk may poison her child. Pregnant women can also maim or kill their children by carrying heavy loads, standing for long hours at a bench or counter, or hurrying up and downstairs at the whim of the lady of the house. There is no dangerous and harmful work from which working women are barred. There is no type of industry which does not employ pregnant women or nursing mothers. Given the conditions in which working women live, their work in production is the grave of maternity.

. . .

WHAT IS THE ALTERNATIVE?

Imagine a society, a people, a community, where there are no longer Mashenka ladies and Mashenka laundresses. Where there are no parasites and no hired workers. Where all people do the same amount of work and society in return looks after them and helps them in life. Just as now the Mashenka ladies are taken care of by their relatives, those who need more attention—the woman and children—will be taken care of by society, which is like one large, friendly family. When Mashenka, who is now neither a lady nor a servant but simply a citizen, becomes pregnant, she does not have to worry about what will happen to her or her child. Society, that big happy family, will look after everything.

A special home with a garden and flowers will be ready to welcome her. It will be so designed that every pregnant woman and every woman who has just given birth can live there joyfully in health and comfort. The doctors in this society-family are concerned not just about preserving the health of the mother and child but about relieving the woman of the pain of childbirth. Science is making progress in this field, and can help the doctor here. When the child is strong enough, the mother returns to her normal life and takes up again the work that she does for the benefit of the large family-society. She does not have to worry about her child. Society is there to help her. Children will grow up in the kindergarten, the children's colony, the creche and the school under the care of experienced nurses. When the mother wants to be with her children, she only has to say the word; and when she has no time, she knows they are in good hands. Maternity is no longer a cross. Only its joyful aspects remain; only the great happiness of being a mother, which at the moment only the Mashenka ladies enjoy.

But such a society, surely, is only to be found in fairy tales? Could such a society ever exist? The science of economics and the history of society and the state show that such a society must and will come into being. However hard the rich capitalists, factory-owners, landowners and men of property fight, the fairy-tale will come true. The working class all over the world is fighting to make this dream come true. And although society is as yet far from being one happy family, although there are still many struggles and sacrifices ahead, it is at the same time true that the working class in other countries has made great gains. Working men and women are trying to lighten the cross of motherhood by getting laws passed and by taking other measures.

. . .

WHAT MUST EVERY WORKING WOMAN DO?

How are all these demands to be won?[1] What action must be taken? Every working-class woman, every woman who reads this pamphlet must throw off her indifference and begin to support the working-class movement, which is fighting for these demands and is shaping the old world into a better future where mothers will no longer weep bitter tears and where the cross of maternity will become a great joy and a great pride. We must say to ourselves, "There is strength in unity"; the more of us working women join the working-class movement, the greater will be our strength and the quicker we will get what we want. Our happiness and the life and future of our children are at stake.

[1914]

NOTE

1. E.g., maternal protection laws, maternity insurance, maternity homes, child care and kindergartens, plans for which are detailed in omitted passages.

 28

Now We Can Begin

CRYSTAL EASTMAN

CRYSTAL EASTMAN United States. 1881–1928. Labor lawyer. Socialist. Suffragist. Journalist. One of the four authors of the Equal Rights Amendment.

Cofounder of the Women's Peace Party (1915), later the Women's International League for Peace and Freedom, and the American Civil Liberties Union (1920). Wrote for socialist newspapers *The Masses* and *The Liberator*.

Most women will agree that August 23, the day when the Tennessee legislature finally enacted the Federal suffrage amendment, is a day to begin with, not a day to end with. Men are saying perhaps "Thank God, this everlasting woman's fight is over!" But women, if I know them, are saying, "Now at last we can begin." In fighting for the right to vote, most women have tried to be either noncommittal or thoroughly respectable on every other subject. Now they can say what they are really after; and what they are after, in common with all the rest of the struggling world, is *freedom*.

Freedom is a large word.

Many feminists are socialists, many are communists, not a few are active leaders in these movements. But the true feminist, no matter how far to the left she may be in the revolutionary movement, sees the woman's battle as distinct in its objects and different in its methods from the workers' battle for industrial freedom. She knows, of course, that the vast majority of women as well as men are without property, and are of necessity bread and butter slaves under a system of society which allows the very sources of life to be privately owned by a few, and she counts herself a loyal soldier in the working-class army that is marching to overthrow that system. But as a feminist she also knows that the whole of woman's slavery is not summed up in the profit system, nor her complete emancipation assured by the downfall of capitalism.

Woman's freedom, in the feminist sense, can be fought for and conceivably won before the gates open into industrial democracy. On the other hand, woman's freedom, in the feminist sense, is not inherent in the communist ideal. All feminists are familiar with the revolutionary leader who "can't see" the woman's movement. "What's the matter with the women? My wife's all right," he says. And his wife, one usually finds, is raising his children in a Bronx flat or a dreary suburb, to which he returns occasionally for food and sleep when all possible excitement and stimulus have been wrung from the fight. If we should graduate into communism to-morrow this man's attitude to his wife would not be changed. The proletarian dictatorship may or may not free women. We must begin now to enlighten the future dictators.

What, then, is "the matter with women"? What is the problem of women's freedom? It seems to me to be this: how to arrange the world so that women can be human beings, with a chance to exercise their infinitely varied gifts in infinitely varied ways, instead of being destined by the accident of their sex to one field of activity—housework and child-raising. And second, if and when they choose housework and child-raising to have that occupation recognized by the world as work, requiring a definite economic reward and not merely entitling the performer to be dependent on some man.

This is not the whole of feminism, of course, but it is enough to begin with. "Oh! don't begin with economics," my friends often protest, "Woman does not live by bread alone. What she needs first of all is a free soul." And I can agree that women will never be great until they achieve a certain emotional freedom, a strong healthy egotism, and some unpersonal sources of joy—that in this inner sense we cannot make woman free by changing her economic status. What we can do, however, is to create conditions of outward freedom in which a free woman's soul can be born and grow. It is these outward conditions with which an organized feminist movement must concern itself.

Freedom of choice in occupation and individual economic independence for women: How shall we approach this next feminist objective? First, by breaking down all remaining barriers, actual as well as legal, which make it difficult for women to enter or succeed in the various professions, to go into and get on in business, to learn trades and practice them, to join trades unions. Chief among these remaining barriers is inequality in pay. Here the ground is already broken. This is the easiest part of our program.

Second, we must institute a revolution in the early training and education of both boys and girls. It must be womanly as well as manly to earn your own living, to stand on your own feet. And it must be manly as well as womanly to know how to cook and sew and clean and take care of yourself in the ordinary exigencies of life. I need not add that the second part of this revolution will be more passionately resisted than the first. Men will not give up their privilege of helplessness without a struggle. The average man has a carefully cultivated ignorance about household matters—from what to do with the crumbs to the grocer's telephone number—a sort of cheerful inefficiency which protects him better than the reputation for having a violent temper. It was his mother's fault in the beginning, but even as a boy he was quick to see how a general reputation for being "no good around the house" would serve him throughout life, and half-consciously he began to cultivate that helplessness until to-day it is the despair of feminist wives.

A growing number of men admire the woman who has a job, and, especially since the cost of living doubled, rather like the idea of their own wives contributing to the family income by outside work. And of course for generations there have been whole towns full of wives who are forced by the bitterest necessity to spend the same hours at the factory that their husbands spend. But these bread-winning wives have not yet developed home-making husbands. When the two come home from the factory the man sits down while his wife gets supper, and he does so with exactly the same sense of fore-ordained right as if he were "supporting her." Higher up in the economic scale the same thing is true. The business or professional woman who is married perhaps engages a cook, but the responsibility is not shifted, it is still hers. She "hires and fires," she orders meals, she does the buying, she meets and resolves all domestic crises, she takes charge of moving, furnishing, settling. She may be, like her husband, a busy executive at her office all day, but unlike him, she is also an executive in a small way every night and morning at home. Her noon hour is spent in planning, and too often her Sundays and holidays are spent in "catching up."

Two business women can "make a home" together without either one being over-burdened or over-bored. It is because they both know how and both feel responsible. But it is a rare man who can marry one of them and continue the home-making partnership. Yet if there are no children, there is nothing essentially different in the combination.

Two self-supporting adults decide to make a home together: if both are women it is a pleasant partnership, more fun than work; if one is a man, it is almost never a partnership—the woman simply adds running the home to her regular outside job. Unless she is very strong, it is too much for her, she gets tired and bitter over it, and finally perhaps gives up her outside work and condemns herself to the tiresome half-job of housekeeping for two.

Cooperative schemes and electrical devices will simplify the business of home-making, but they will not get rid of it entirely. As far as we can see ahead people will always want homes, and a happy home cannot be had without a certain amount of rather monotonous work and responsibility. How can we change the nature of man so that he will honorably share the work and responsibility and thus make the home-making enterprise a song instead of a burden? Most assuredly not by laws or revolutionary decrees. Perhaps we must cultivate or simulate a little of that highly prized helplessness ourselves. But fundamentally it is a problem of education, of early training—we must bring up feminist sons.

Sons? Daughters? They are born of women—how can women be free to choose their occupation, at all times cherishing their economic independence, unless they stop having children? This is a further question for feminism. If the feminist program goes to pieces on the arrival of the first baby, it is false and useless. For ninety-nine out of every hundred women want children, and seventy-five out of every hundred want to take care of their own children, or at any rate so closely superintend their care as to make any other full-time occupation impossible for at least ten or fifteen years. Is there any such thing then as freedom of choice in occupation for women? And is not the family the inevitable economic unit and woman's individual economic independence, at least during that period, out of the question?

The feminist must have an answer to these questions, and she has. The immediate feminist program must include voluntary motherhood. Freedom of any kind for women is hardly worth considering unless it is assumed that they will know how to control the size of their families. "Birth control" is just as elementary an essential in our propaganda as "equal pay." Women are to have children when they want them, that's the first thing. That ensures some freedom of occupational choice; those who do not wish to be mothers will not have an undesired occupation thrust upon them by accident, and those who do wish to be mothers may choose in a general way how many years of their lives they will devote to the occupation of child-raising.

But is there any way of insuring a woman's economic independence while child-raising is her chosen occupation? Or must she sink into the dependent state from which, as we all know, it is so hard to rise again? That brings us to the fourth feature of our program—motherhood endowment. It seems that the only way we can keep mothers free, at least in a capitalist society, is by the establishment of a principle that the occupation of raising children is peculiarly and directly a service to society, and that the mother upon whom the necessity and privilege of performing this service naturally falls is entitled to an adequate economic reward from the political government. It is idle to talk of real economic independence for women unless this principle is accepted. But with a generous endowment of motherhood provided by legislation, with all laws against voluntary motherhood and education in its methods repealed, with the feminist ideal of education accepted in home and school, and with all special barriers removed in every field of human activity, there is no reason why woman should not become almost a human thing.

It will be time enough then to consider whether she has a soul.

[1919]

PART III

1920–1963

1920–1963: Introduction

It has become a truism of American women's history that the decades immediately after 1920 represented the "doldrums" of American feminism. That might appear to be the case, if one identifies the campaign for suffrage as the exclusive site of feminist thinking and activity. During this period, proponents of suffrage were disappointed to discover that the women's vote did not radically alter the outcome of elections, that women voted in relatively small numbers and, for the most part, with their husbands, fathers, and brothers. At the same time, suffrage organizations were disbanding and their members dispersing into a variety of organizations. The image of the "flapper" suggests a 1920s woman who is socially and sexually freer but is not a political activist in the way her suffragist foremothers might have hoped.

However, as Leila Rupp and Verta Taylor have documented in *Survival in the Doldrums,* feminist thinking and activity did continue. Women's political activity moved into organizations like the moderate League of Women Voters and the more radical Women's Party with its campaign to pass an Equal Rights Amendment to address forms of discrimination not ameliorated by achieving the vote. Black and white women and women from new immigrant populations were active in labor organizing, confronting both workplace discrimination (exacerbated by postwar and Depression female unemployment) and sexism within labor organizations themselves.

Following World War I and throughout this period, women also became active in internationalist and peace movements through organizations like the Women's International League for Peace and Freedom (WILPF) and, during the 1950s, in opposition to nuclear testing. After World War II, working with such leaders as Eleanor Roosevelt, these women also worked to help found the United Nations. African-American women in this period also found outlets for social activism through the club movement and for creative and intellectual energy through the ferment of the Harlem Renaissance. And in the 1950s, African-American women and a few white women became involved in the beginning of civil rights activism.

The readings in this section clearly express the persistence of many 19th-century discussions into this period. The selections by Margaret Sanger, Stella Browne, and Joan Riviére continue the discussion about women's right to sexual autonomy and sexual self-definition. *A Room of One's Own* by Virginia Woolf attempts to understand women's erasure from literary and historical knowledge as well as from public intellectual and political life. Karen Horney's "The Dread of Woman" asks similar questions in the context of psychology.

In this period, with women entering higher education and the professions in unprecedented numbers, academically trained women working in specific fields were beginning to produce substantial writing about women and feminism. The essays by Simone de Beauvoir and Margaret Mead, both fall into this category.

Interestingly, these essays are related too in the perspectives they try to explore. Both of them, in attempting to understand women's subordination, examine it from the perspective of difference. Margaret Mead examines sex difference in three non-Western societies. Simone de Beauvoir expresses woman's difference—her otherness where man is the one, the subject, the norm—as a cultural construct layered onto the biological difference of the female body, observing that "one is not born but rather becomes a woman" (de Beauvoir).

Certainly, this middle period of the 20th century demonstrates that culture and ideology make women what they are. When the United States needed women's labor in war industries during the early 1940s, Rosie the Riveter became the model of good womanhood. By the late 1940s, however, when men returning from the war needed jobs, the ideological representation of women placed the highest value on the homemaker and full-time mother. Though women of all classes continued to seek training and to enter the workforce during this period, many of them did so with the kinds of conflicts about roles and identity that Betty Friedan documents, at least among middle-class women. Friedan's *The Feminine Mystique* (1963) is often credited with launching the second wave of the women's movement.

◆ 29

Birth Control—A Parents' Problem or Woman's? from Woman and the New Race

MARGARET SANGER

MARGARET SANGER United States. 1879–1966. Nurse. Socialist. Activist. Established first birth-control clinic in America. Founder of organization that became planned parenthood. Jailed for distributing birth-control information pamphlet, "Family Limitation" (1915). Published *The Woman Rebel*, a feminist monthly. *The Pivot of Civilization* (1922), *Motherhood in Bondage* (1928), *Autobiography* (1938).

The problem of birth control has arisen directly from the effort of the feminine spirit to free itself from bondage. Woman herself has wrought that bondage through her reproductive powers and while enslaving herself has enslaved the world. The physical suffering to be relieved is chiefly woman's. Hers, too, is the love life that dies first under the blight of too prolific breeding. Within her is wrapped up the future of the race—it is hers to make or mar. All of these considerations point unmistakably to one fact—it is woman's duty as well as her privilege to lay hold of the means of freedom. Whatever men may do, she cannot escape the responsibility. For ages she has been deprived of the opportunity to meet this obligation. She is now emerging from her helplessness. Even as no one can share the suffering of the overburdened mother, so no one can do this work for her. Others may help, but she and she alone can free herself.

The basic freedom of the world is woman's freedom. A free race cannot be born out of slave mothers. A woman enchained cannot choose but give a measure of that bondage to her sons and daughters. No woman can call herself free who does not own and control her body. No woman can call herself free until she can choose consciously whether she will or will not be a mother.

It does not greatly alter the case that some women call themselves free because they earn their own livings, while others profess freedom because they defy the conventions of sex relationship. She who earns her own living gains a sort of freedom that is not to be undervalued, but in quality and in quantity it is of little account beside the untrammeled choice of mating or not mating, of being a mother or not being a mother. She gains food and clothing and shelter, at least, without submitting to the charity of her companion, but the earning of her own living does not give her the development of her inner sex urge, far deeper and more powerful in its outworkings than any of these externals. In order to have that development, she must still meet and solve the problem of motherhood.

With the so-called "free" woman, who chooses a mate in defiance of convention, freedom is largely a question of character and audacity. If she does attain to an unrestricted choice of a mate, she is still in a position to be enslaved through her reproductive powers. Indeed, the pressure of law and custom upon the woman not legally married is likely to make her more of a slave than the woman fortunate enough to marry the man of her choice.

Look at it from any standpoint you will, suggest any solution you will, conventional or unconventional, sanctioned by law or in defiance of law, woman is in the same position, fundamentally, until she is able to determine for herself whether she will be a mother and to fix the number of her offspring. This unavoidable situation is alone enough to make birth control, first of all, a woman's problem. On the very face of the matter, voluntary motherhood is chiefly the concern of the woman.

It is persistently urged, however, that since sex expression is the act of two, the responsibility of controlling the results should not be placed upon woman alone. Is it fair, it is asked, to give her, instead of the man, the task of protecting herself when she is, perhaps, less rugged in physique than her mate, and has, at all events, the normal, periodic inconveniences of her sex?

We must examine this phase of her problem in two lights—that of the ideal, and of the conditions working toward the ideal. In an ideal society, no doubt, birth control would become the concern of the man as well as the woman. The hard, inescapable fact which we encounter to-day is that man has not only refused any such responsibility, but has individually and collectively sought to prevent woman from obtaining knowledge by which she could assume this responsibility for herself. She is still in the position of a dependent to-day because her mate has refused to consider her as an individual apart from his needs. She is still bound because she has in the past left the solution of the problem to him. Having left it to him, she finds that instead of rights, she has only such privileges as she has gained by petitioning, coaxing and cozening. Having left it to him, she is exploited, driven and enslaved to his desires.

While it is true that he suffers many evils as the consequence of this situation, she suffers vastly more. While it is true that he should be awakened to the cause of these evils, we know that they come home to her with crushing force every day. It is she who has the long burden of carrying, bearing and rearing the unwanted children. . . . It is her heart that the sight of the deformed, the subnormal, the undernourished, the overworked child smites first and oftenest and hardest. It is *her* love life that dies first in the fear of undesired pregnancy. It is her opportunity for self expression that perishes first and most hopelessly because of it.

Conditions, rather than theories, facts, rather than dreams, govern the problem. They place it squarely upon the shoulders of woman. She has learned that whatever the moral responsibility of the man in this direction may be, he does not discharge it. She has learned that, lovable and considerate as the individual husband may be, she has nothing to expect from men in the mass, when they make laws and decree customs. She knows that regardless of what ought to be, the brutal, unavoidable fact is that she will never receive her freedom until she takes it for herself.

Having learned this much, she has yet something more to learn. Women are too much inclined to follow in the footsteps of men, to try to think as men think, to try to solve the general problems of life as men solve them. If after attaining their freedom, women accept conditions in the spheres of government, industry, art, morals and religion as they find them, they will be but taking a leaf out of man's book. The woman is not needed to do man's work. She is not needed to think man's thoughts. She need not fear that the masculine mind, almost universally dominant, will fail to take care of its own. Her mission is not to enhance the masculine spirit, but to express the feminine; hers is not to preserve a man-made world, but to create a human world by the infusion of the feminine element into all of its activities.

Woman must not accept; she must challenge. She must not be awed by that which has been built up around her; she must reverence that within her which struggles for expression. Her eyes must be less upon what is and more clearly upon what should be. She must listen only with a frankly questioning attitude to the dogmatized opinions of man-made society. When she chooses her new, free course of action, it must be in the light of her own opinion—of her own intuition. Only so can she give play to the feminine spirit. Only thus can she free her mate from the bondage which he wrought for himself when he wrought hers. Only thus can she restore to him that of which he robbed himself in restricting her. Only thus can she remake the world. . . .

Woman must have her freedom—the fundamental freedom of choosing whether or not she shall be a mother and how many children she will have. Regardless of what man's attitude may be, that problem is hers—and before it can be his, it is hers alone.

She goes through the vale of death alone, each time a babe is born. As it is the right neither of man nor the state to coerce her into this ordeal, so it is her right to decide whether she will endure it. That right to decide imposes upon her the duty of clearing the way to knowledge by which she may make and carry out the decision.

Birth control is woman's problem. The quicker she accepts it as hers and hers alone, the quicker will society respect motherhood. The quicker, too, will the world be made a fit place for her children to live.

[1920]

30

Studies in Feminine Inversion

STELLA BROWNE

STELLA BROWNE Britain. 1880–1955. Socialist. Sex radical. Writer. Campaigner for women's rights to reproductive control. *The Sexual Variety and Variability of Women* (1915/1917), *The Work of Margaret Sanger: Birth Control in America* (1917), *The 'Women's Question'* (1922).

I must apologise for what I feel to be a misleading title chosen for reasons of brevity and economy of effort in the framing of notices; for, what I have to put before you today are only very fragmentary data, and suggestions of a peculiarly obscure subject. They have, however, this validity: that they are the result of close and careful observation, conducted, so far as I am consciously aware, without any prejudice, though they would probably be much more illuminating had they been recorded by an observer who was herself entirely or predominantly homosexual. . . .

My material would have been both less limited and much more definite and intimate had I been able to include cases which have been told me in confidence. Those, of course, I have omitted.

The cases which I will now briefly describe to you are all well-known to me; they are all innate, and very pronounced and deeply rooted, not episodical. At the same time though I am sure there has been, in some of them at least, no definite and conscious physical expression, they are absolutely distinguishable from affectionate friendship. They have all of them, in varying degrees, the element of passion; and here I should like to quote a definition of passion by Desmond McCarthy, which seems to me very apt and very true:

> It differs from lust in the intensity with which the personality of the object is apprehended, and in being also an excitement of the whole being, and, therefore, not satisfied so simply: from other kinds of love, in that it is intensely sexual and not accompanied, necessarily, by any contemplation of the object as good, or any strong desire for his or her welfare apart from the satisfaction of itself.

Now for my cases, and then a few comments and conclusions.

Case A. Member of a small family, but numerous cousins on both sides. The mother's family is nervous, with a decided streak of eccentricity of varying kinds, and some of its members much above the average in intelligence. The father's family much more commonplace, but robust. She is of small-boned frame, but childish rather than feminine in appearance, the liberating and illuminating effect of some definite and direct physical sex-expression, have had, and still have, a disastrous effect on a nature which has much inherent force and many fine qualities. Her whole outlook on life is subtly distorted and dislocated, moral values are confused, and a false standard of values is set up. The hardening and narrowing effect of her way of life is shown in a tremendous array of prejudices on every conceivable topic: caste prejudices, race prejudices, down to prejudices founded on the slightest eccentricity of dress or unconventionality of behaviour; also in an immense intolerance of normal passion, even in its most legally sanctioned and certificated forms. As to unlegalised sex-relationships, they are of course considered the very depth alike of depravity and of crass folly. And all the while, her life revolves round a deep and ardent sex-passion, frustrated and exasperated through functional repression, but entirely justified in her own opinion as pure family affection and duty! Though the orthodox and conventional point of view she takes on sex questions, generally, would logically condemn just *that* form of sex-passion, as peculiarly reprehensible.

Case B. Also the member of a small family, though with numerous cousins, paternal and maternal. Family of marked ability—on both sides, especially the mother's. Of very graceful and attractive appearance, entirely feminine, beautiful eyes and classical features, but indifferent to her looks and abnormally lacking in vanity, self-confidence and animal vitality generally, though no one is quicker to appreciate any beauty or charm in other women. I think she is a pronounced psychic invert whose intuitive faculties and bent towards mysticism have never been cultivated. Keen instinctive delicacy and emotional depth, enthusiastically devoted and generous to friends; much personal pride (though no vanity) and reserve. Too amenable to group suggestions and the influences of tradition. Artistic and musical tastes and a faculty for literary criticism which has lain fallow for want of systematic exercise. Rather fond of animals and devoted to children, especially to young relatives and the children of friends. Has done good philanthropic work for children, but is essentially interested in *persons* rather than in theories, or institutions. Is a devout Christian and I think gets much support and comfort from her religious beliefs. A distaste, even positive disgust, for the physical side of sex, which is tending more and more to manifest itself in conventional moral attitudes and judgements. General social attitude towards men less definitely *hostile* than that of Case A, but absolutely aloof. Devoted to women friends and relatives, yet has had no full and satisfying expression of this devotion. This inhibition of a whole infinitely important set of feelings and activities has weakened her naturally very sound judgement, and also had a bad permanent effect on her bodily health.

Case C. The sixth, and second youngest of a large and very able and vigorous family. Tall, and of the typical Diana build; long limbs, broad shoulders, slight bust, narrow hips. Decidedly athletic. Voice agreeable in tone and quite deep, can whistle well. Extremely energetic and capable, any amount of initiative and enthusiasm, never afraid to assume responsibility; very dominating and managing, something of a tyrant in practice, though an extreme democrat in theory, and most intolerant towards different emotional temperaments. Scientific training, interested in politics and public affairs; logical and rationalistic bent of mind. Emotionally reserved, intense, jealous and monopolistic. Will always try to express all emotion in terms of reason and moral theory, and is thus capable of much mental dishonesty, while making a fetish of complete and meticulous truthfulness. An agnostic and quite militant and aggressive. The episode in her life which I observed fairly closely was a long and intimate friendship with a young girl—ten years her junior—of a very attractive and vivacious type, who roused the interest of both men and women keenly. Cleverness and physical charm in girls appealed to her, but she instinctively resented any independent divergent views or standard of values. For years she practically formed this girl's

mental life, and they spent their holidays together. When the girl fell in love with and impulsively married a very masculine and brilliantly gifted man, who has since won great distinction in his special profession, C's agony of rage and desolation was terrible and pitiable, though here again, she tried to hide the real nature of her loss by misgivings as to the young man's 'type of ethical theory'—her own phrase! I cannot for a moment believe that she was ignorant of her own sex-nature, and I hope she has by now found free and full personal realisation with some beloved woman—though, unless the beloved woman is exceptionally understanding or exceptionally docile, it will be a stormy relationship. She is a very strong personality, and a born ruler. Her attitude towards men was one of perfectly unembarrassed and equal comradeship.

Case D. Is on a less evolved plane than the three aforementioned, being conspicuously lacking in refinement of feeling and, to some extent, of habit. But it is well above the average in vigor, energy and efficiency. A decided turn for carpentry, mechanics and executive manual work. Not tall; slim, boyish figure; very hard, strong muscles, singularly impassive face, with big magnetic eyes. The dominating tendency is very strong here, and is not held in leash by a high standard of either delicacy or principle. Is professionally associated with children and young girls, and shows her innate homosexual tendency by excess of petting and spoiling, and intense jealousy of any other person's contact with, or interest in the children. I do not definitely know if there is any physical expression of her feelings, beyond the kissing and embracing which is normal, and even in some cases conventional, between women or between women and children. But the *emotional tone* is quite unmistakable; will rave for hours over some 'lovely kiddy', and injure the children's own best interests, as well as the working of the establishment, by reasonable and unfair indulgence.

Her sexual idiosyncrasy in the post which she occupies is extremely harmful, and together with her jealous and domineering nature, leads to a general atmosphere of slackness and intrigue, and the children under her care, of course, take advantage of it. As she has had medical training, I cannot suppose she is ignorant on the subject of her own sex nature. Member of a large family, mostly brothers.

Case E. This was a case which at one time was fairly well-known to me, and is very well-marked. Two assistant mistresses at a girl's boarding-school were completely inseparable. They took all their walks together, and spent all their time when they were 'off-duty' and not walking, in one another's rooms—they occupied adjoining rooms.

One of them was a slim, graceful, restless, neurotic girl with a distinct consumptive tendency; quick in perception and easy in manner, but it seemed to me then, and it seems still, decidedly superficial and shallow. The other partner was an invert of the most pronounced physical type. Her tall, stiff, rather heavily muscular figure, her voice, and her chubby, fresh-coloured face, which was curiously eighteenth-century in outline and expression, were so like those of a very young and very well-groomed youth, that all the staff of the school nicknamed her 'Boy', though I do not believe any of them clearly realised what this epithet—and her intimacy with a woman of such strongly contrasted type, implied. 'Boy' was extremely self-conscious and curiously inarticulate; she had musical tastes and played rather well—not in the colourless and amateurish style of the musical hack. I think music was an outlet for her. She was also fond of taking long walks, and of driving, and of dogs and horses. Beyond these matters I don't think I ever heard her express an opinion about anything. The intimacy with her restless, tricky adored one ran its course, unhindered either by circumstances, or by unconscious public opinion. There was some idealism in the relationship, at least on 'Boy's' side.

There was no community of intellectual interests—or rather there was community in the mutual absence of intellectual interests. I lost sight of them completely, but heard later that the friend had taken a post in South Africa, and 'Boy' was planning to join her there, but I do not know whether this plan materialised.

I have omitted from consideration that episodical homosexuality on the part of women who are normally much more attracted to men, of which every experienced observer must know instances.

I have also left out of consideration here, various instances known to me of passionate but unconscious inversion in girls whose sex-life is just beginning. All of these are important, and may throw helpful light not only on the problem [of] inversion, but on the sexual impulse of women generally.

There exists no document in modern English literature comparable in authenticity or artistic merit, as a study of the female homosexual or bisexual temperaments, with the hauntingly beautiful verse of Renee Vivien (Pauline Tarn) or the vivid autobiographical novels of Colette Willy (Gabrielle Gauthier Villars).

I know of two modern English novels in which the subject is touched on with a good deal of subtlety, and in both cases in association with school life. *Regiment of Women* by Clemence Dane—a brilliant piece of psychology, and a novel by an Australian writer, cruder and shorter, but unmistakably powerful, *The Getting of Wisdom* by Henry Handel Richardson. There is frank and brilliant description of the feminine intermediate and homosexual temperaments in *I, Mary MacLane* (New York, Stokes & Co).

I would draw your attention to one quality which two of my cases have in common, and to a very marked degree: the maternal instinct. Two of the most intensely maternal women I know are cases A and B, both congenital inverts.

A friend has suggested to me that in such cases in the future, the resources of developed chemistry and biology will be made use of, in artificial fertilisation. And I now see in reading Dr Marie Stopes's interesting essay 'Married Love', that she makes a similar suggestion, though not with reference to inversion.

This problem of feminine inversion is very pressing and immediate, taking into consideration the fact that in the near future, for at least a generation, the circumstances of women's lives and work will tend, even more than at present, to favour the frigid, and next to the frigid, the inverted types. Even at present, the social and affectional side of the invert's nature has often fuller opportunity of satisfaction than the heterosexual woman's, but often at the cost of adequate and definite physical expression. And how decisive for vigour, sanity and serenity of body and mind, for efficiency, for happiness, for the mastery of life, and the understanding of one's fellow-creatures—just this definite physical expression is! The lack of it, 'normal' and 'abnormal', is at the root of most of what is most trivial and unsatisfactory in women's intellectual output, as well as of their besetting vice of cruelty. How can anyone be finely or greatly creative, if one's supreme moral law is negation! Not to *live*, not to *do*, not even to try to understand.

In the cases which I have called A and B, sexual experience along the lines of their own psychic idiosyncracy would have revealed to them definitely where they stood, and as both are well above the average in intelligence, would have been a key to many mysteries of human conduct which are now judged with dainty shrinking from incomprehensible folly and perversity.

I am sure that much of the towering spiritual arrogance which is found, e.g., in many high places in the Suffrage movement . . . is really unconscious inversion.

I think it is perhaps not wholly uncalled-for, to underline very strongly my opinion that the homosexual impulse *is not in any way superior* to the normal; it has a fully equal right to existence and expression, it is no worse, no lower; *but no better*.

By all means let the invert—let all of us—have as many and varied 'channels of sublimation' as possible; and far more than are at present available. But, to be honest, are we not too inclined to make 'sublimation' an excuse for refusing to tackle fundamentals? The tragedy of the repressed invert is apt to be not only one of emotional frustration, but complete dislocation of mental values.

Moreover, our present social arrangements, founded as they are on the repression and degradation of the normal erotic impulse, artificially stimulate inversion and have thus forfeited all right to condemn it. There is a huge, persistent, indirect pressure on women of strong passions and fine brains to find an emotional outlet with other women. A woman who is unwilling to accept either marriage—under present laws—or prostitution, and at the same time refuses to limit her sexual life to auto-erotic manifestations, will find she has to struggle against the whole social order for what is nevertheless her most precious personal right. The right sort of woman faces the struggle and counts the cost well worth while; but it is impossible to avoid seeing that she risks the most painful experiences, and spends an incalculable amount of time and energy on things that should be matters of course. Under these conditions, some women who

are not innately or predominantly homosexual do form more or less explicitly erotic relations with other women, yet these are makeshifts and essentially substitutes, which cannot replace the vital contact, mental and bodily, with congenial men.

No one who has observed the repressed inverted impulse flaring into sex-antagonism, or masked as the devotion of daughter or cousin or the solicitude of teacher or nurse, or perverted into the cheap, malignant cant of conventional moral indignation, can deny its force. Let us recognise this force, as frankly as we recognise and reverence the love between men and women. When Paris was devouring and disputing over Willy and Colette Willy's wonderful Claudine stories, another gifted woman-writer, who had also touched on the subject of inversion, defended not only the artistic conception and treatment of the stories (they need no defence, and remain one of the joys and achievements of modern French writing), but also their ethical content: Mme Rachilde wrote *'une amoureuse d'amour n'est pas une vicieuse'*.

After all: every strong passion, every deep affection, has its own endless possibilities, of pain, change, loss, incompatibility, satiety, jealousy, incompleteness: why add wholly extraneous difficulties and burdens? Harmony may be incompatible with freedom; we do not yet know, for few of us know either. But both truth and the most essential human dignity are incompatible with things as they are.

[1923]

 31

Womanliness as a Masquerade

JOAN RIVIÉRE

JOAN RIVIÉRE Britain. 1883–1962. Psychoanalyst. Translator of Freud into English. Collaborated with Melanie Klein. *The Inner World and Joan Riviére: Collected Papers, 1920–1958* (1991).

Every direction in which psycho-analytic research has pointed seems in its turn to have attracted the interest of Ernest Jones, and now that of recent years investigation has slowly spread to the development of the sexual life of women, we find as a matter of course one by him among the most important contributions to the subject. As always, he throws great light on his material, with his peculiar gift both clarifying the knowledge we had already and also adding to it fresh observations of his own.

In his paper on 'The early development of female sexuality' (Jones, 1927) he sketches out a rough scheme of types of female development, which he first divides into heterosexual and homosexual, subsequently subdividing the latter homosexual group into two types. He acknowledges the roughly schematic nature of his classification and postulates a number of intermediate types. It is with one of these intermediate types that I am to-day concerned. In daily life types of men and women are constantly met with who, while mainly heterosexual in their development, plainly display strong features of the other sex. This has been judged to be an expression of the bisexuality inherent in us all; and analysis has shown that what appear as homosexual or heterosexual character traits, or sexual manifestation, are the end-result of the interplay of conflicts and not necessarily evidence of a radical or fundamental tendency. The difference between homosexual and heterosexual development results from differences in the degree of anxiety, with the corresponding effect this has on development. Ferenczi (1916) pointed out a similar reaction in behaviour, namely, that homosexual men exaggerate their heterosexuality as a 'defence' against their homosexuality. I shall attempt to show that women who wish for masculinity may put on a mask of womanliness to avert anxiety and retribution feared from men.

It is with a particular type of intellectual woman that I have to deal. Not long ago intellectual pursuits for women were associated almost exclusively with an overtly masculine type of woman, who in pronounced cases made no secret of her wish or claim to be a man. This has now changed. Of all the women engaged in professional work to-day, it would be hard to say whether the greater number are more feminine than masculine in their mode of life and character. In University life, in scientific professions and in business, one constantly meets

women who seem to fulfil every criterion of complete feminine development. They are excellent wives and mothers, capable housewives; they maintain social life and assist culture; they have no lack of feminine interests, e.g. in their personal appearance, and when called upon they can still find time to play the part of devoted and disinterested mother-substitutes among a wide circle of relatives and friends. At the same time they fulfil the duties of their profession at least as well as the average man. It is really a puzzle to know how to classify this type psychologically.

Some time ago, in the course of an analysis of a woman of this kind, I came upon some interesting discoveries. She conformed in almost every particular to the description just given; her excellent relations with her husband included a very intimate affectionate attachment between them and full and frequent sexual enjoyment; she prided herself on her proficiency as a housewife. She had followed her profession with marked success all her life. She had a high degree of adaptation to reality, and managed to sustain good and appropriate relations with almost everyone with whom she came in contact.

Certain reactions in her life showed, however, that her stability was not as flawless as it appeared; one of these will illustrate my theme. She was an American woman engaged in work of a propagandist nature, which consisted principally in speaking and writing. All her life a certain degree of anxiety, sometimes very severe, was experienced after every public performance, such as speaking to an audience. In spite of her unquestionable success and ability, both intellectual and practical, and her capacity for managing an audience and dealing with discussions, etc., she would be excited and apprehensive all night after, with misgivings whether she had done anything inappropriate, and obsessed by a need for reassurance. This need for reassurance led her compulsively on any such occasion to seek some attention or complimentary notice from a man or men at the close of the proceedings in which she had taken part or been the principal figure; and it soon became evident that the men chosen for the purpose were always unmistakeable father-figures, although often not persons whose judgement on her performance would in reality carry much weight. There were clearly two types of reassurance sought from these father-figures: first, direct reassurance of the nature of compliments about her performance; secondly, and more important, indirect reassurance of the nature of sexual attentions from these men. To speak broadly, analysis of her behaviour after her performance showed that she was attempting to obtain sexual advances from the particular type of men by means of flirting and coquetting with them in a more or less veiled manner. The extraordinary incongruity of this attitude with her highly impersonal and objective attitude during her intellectual performance, which it succeeded so rapidly in time, was a problem. . . .

Womanliness therefore could be assumed and worn as a mask, both to hide the possession of masculinity and to avert the reprisals expected if she was found to possess it—much as a thief will turn out his pockets and ask to be searched to prove that he has not the stolen goods. The reader may now ask how I define womanliness or where I draw the line between genuine womanliness and the 'masquerade'. My suggestion is not, however, that there is any such difference; whether radical or superficial, they are the same thing. The capacity for womanliness was there in this woman—and one might even say it exists in the most completely homosexual woman—but owing to her conflicts it did not represent her main development and was used far more as a device for avoiding anxiety than as a primary mode of sexual enjoyment. . . .

In every-day life one may observe the mask of femininity taking curious forms. One capable housewife of my acquaintance is a woman of great ability and can herself attend to typically masculine matters. But when, e.g., any builder or upholsterer is called in, she has a compulsion to hide all her technical knowledge from him and show deference to the workman, making her suggestions in an innocent and artless manner, as if they were 'lucky guesses'. She has confessed to me that even with the butcher and baker, whom she rules in reality with a rod of iron, she cannot openly take up a firm straightforward stand; she feels herself as it were 'acting a part', she puts on the semblance of a rather uneducated, foolish and bewildered woman, yet in the end always making her point. In all other relations in life this woman is a gracious, cultured lady,

competent and well informed, and can manage her affairs by sensible rational behaviour without any subterfuges. This woman is now aged fifty, but she tells me that as a young woman she had great anxiety in dealings with men such as porters, waiters, cabmen, tradesmen, or any other potentially hostile father-figures, such as doctors, builders and lawyers; moreover, she often quarreled with such men and had altercations with them, accusing them of defrauding her, and so forth.

Another case from every-day observation is that of a clever woman, wife and mother, a University lecturer in an abstruse subject which seldom attracts women. When lecturing, not to students but to colleagues, she chooses particularly feminine clothes. Her behaviour on these occasions is also marked by an inappropriate feature: she becomes flippant and joking, so much that it has caused comment and rebuke. She has to treat the situation of displaying her masculinity to men as a 'game', as something *not real*, as a 'joke'. She cannot treat herself and her subject seriously, cannot seriously contemplate herself as on equal terms with men; moreover, the flippant attitude enables some of her sadism to escape, hence the offence it causes. . . .

To return to the case I first described: Underneath her apparently satisfactory heterosexuality it is clear that this woman displayed well-known manifestations of the castration complex. Horney was the first among others to point out the sources of that complex in the Oedipus situation; my belief is that the fact that womanliness may be assumed as a mask may contribute further in this direction to the analysis of female development. With that in view I will now sketch the early libido-development in this case.

But before this I must give some account of her relations with women. She was conscious of rivalry with almost any woman who had either good looks or intellectual pretensions. She was conscious of flashes of hatred against almost any woman with whom she had much to do, but where permanent or close relations with women were concerned she was none the less able to establish a very satisfactory footing. Unconsciously she did this almost entirely by means of feeling herself superior in some way to them (her relations with her inferiors were uniformly excellent). Her proficiency as a housewife largely had its root in this. By it she surpassed her mother, won her approval and proved her superiority among rival 'feminine' women. Her intellectual attainments undoubtedly had in part the same object. They too proved her superiority to her mother; it seemed probable that since she reached womanhood her rivalry with women had been more acute in regard to intellectual things than in regard to beauty, since she could usually take refuge in her superior brains where beauty was concerned.

. . . [S]he identifies herself with the father; and then she uses the masculinity she thus obtains by *putting it at the service of the mother*. She becomes the father and takes his place, so she can 'restore' him to the mother. This position was very clear in many typical situations in my patient's life. She delighted in using her great practical ability to aid or assist weaker and more helpless women and could maintain this attitude successfully so long as rivalry did not emerge too strongly. But this restitution could be made on one condition only; it must procure her a lavish return in the form of gratitude and 'recognition'. . . .

In regard to the father, resentment against him arose in two ways: (1) during the primal scene he took from the mother the milk, etc., which the child missed; (2) at the same time he gave to the mother the penis or children instead of to her. Therefore all that he had or took should be taken from him by her; he was castrated and reduced to nothingness, like the mother. Fear of him, though never so acute as of the mother, remained; partly, too, because his vengeance for the death and destruction of the mother was expected. So he too must be placated and appeased. This was done by masquerading in a feminine guise for him, thus showing him her 'love' and guiltlessness towards him. It is significant that this woman's mask, though transparent to other women, was successful with men and served its purpose very well. Many men were attracted in this way and gave her reassurance by showing her favour. Closer examination showed that these men were of the type who themselves fear the ultra-womanly woman. They prefer a woman who herself has male attributes, for to them her claims on them are less.

. . .

It appeared, therefore, that this woman had saved herself from the intolerable anxiety resulting from her sadistic fury against both parents by creating in phantasy a situation in which she became supreme and no harm could be done to her. The essence of the phantasy was her *supremacy* over the parent-objects; by it her sadism was gratified, she triumphed over them. By this same supremacy she also succeeded in averting their revenges: the means she adopted for this were reaction-formations and concealment of her hostility. Thus she could gratify her id-impulses, her narcissistic ego and her super-ego at one and the same time. The phantasy was the main-spring of her whole life and character, and she came within a narrow margin of carrying it through to complete perfection. But its weak point was the megalomanic character, under all the disguises, of the necessity for supremacy. When this supremacy was seriously disturbed during analysis, she fell into an abyss of anxiety, rage, and abject depression; before the analysis, into illness.

. . .

These conclusions compel one once more to face the question: what is the essential nature of fully developed femininity? What is *das ewig Weibliche*? The conception of womanliness as a mask, behind which man suspects some hidden danger, throws a little light on the enigma. Fully developed heterosexual womanhood is founded, as Helene Deutsch and Ernest Jones have stated, on the oral-sucking stage. The sole gratification of a primary order in it is that of receiving the (nipple, milk) penis, semen, child from the father. For the rest it depends upon reaction-formations. The acceptance of 'castration', the humility, the admiration of men, come partly from the over-estimation of the object on the oral-sucking plane; but chiefly from the renunciation (lesser intensity) of sadistic castration-wishes deriving from the later oral-biting level. 'I must not take, I must not even ask; it must be *given* me'. The capacity for self-sacrifice, devotion, self-abnegation expresses efforts to restore and make good, whether to mother or to father figures, what has been taken from them. It is also what Radó has called a 'narcissistic insurance' of the highest value.

It becomes clear how the attainment of full heterosexuality coincides with that of genitality. And once more we see, as Abraham first stated, that genitality implies attainment of a *post-ambivalent* state. Both the 'normal' woman and the homosexual desire the father's penis and rebel against frustration (or castration); but one of the differences between them lies in the difference in the degree of sadism and of the power of dealing both with it and with the anxiety it gives rise to in the two types of women.

[1929]

NOTES

1. Jones, Ernest. (1927). "The Early Development of Female Sexuality." *International Journal of Psycho-Analysis, 8:* 459–472.
2. Ferenczi, S. (1916). "The Nosology of Male Homosexuality." *First Contributions to Psycho-Analysis.* London: Hogarth Press and the Institute of Psychoanalysis (1952).

 32

From A Room of One's Own

VIRGINIA WOOLF

VIRGINIA WOOLF Britain. 1882–1941. Novelist. Essayist. Founder and publisher with Leonard Woolf of Hogarth Press. Central Figure of Bloomsbury Group. *Mrs. Dalloway* (1925), *To the Lighthouse* (1927), *Orlando: A Biography* (1928), *Three Guineas* (1938).

CHAPTER 2

. . .

But while I pondered I had unconsciously, in my listlessness, in my desperation, been drawing a picture where I should, like my neighbour, have been writing a conclusion. I had been drawing a face, a figure. It was the face and the figure of Professor von X engaged in writing his monumental work entitled *The Mental, Moral, and Physical Inferiority of the Female Sex.* He was not in my picture a man attractive to women. He was heavily built; he had a great jowl; to balance that he had very small eyes; he was very red in the face. His expression suggested that he was labouring under some emotion that made him jab his pen on the paper as if he were killing some noxious insect as he wrote, but even when he had killed it that did not satisfy him; he must go on killing it; and even so, some cause for anger and irritation remained. Could it be his wife, I asked, looking at my picture. Was she in love with a cavalry officer? Was the cavalry officer slim and elegant and dressed in astrachan? Had he been laughed at, to adopt the Freudian theory, in his cradle by a pretty girl? For even in his cradle the professor, I thought, could not have been an attractive child. Whatever the reason, the professor was made to look very angry and very ugly in my sketch, as he wrote his great book upon the mental, moral and physical inferiority of women. Drawing pictures was an idle way of finishing an unprofitable morning's work. Yet it is in our idleness, in our dreams, that the submerged truth sometimes comes to the top. A very elementary exercise in psychology, not to be dignified by the name of psycho-analysis, showed me, on looking at my notebook, that the sketch of the angry professor had been made in anger. Anger had snatched my pencil while I dreamt. But what was anger doing there? Interest, confusion, amusement, boredom—all these emotions I could trace and name as they succeeded each other throughout the morning. Had anger, the black snake, been lurking among them? Yes, said the sketch, anger had. It referred me unmistakably to the one book, to the one phrase, which had roused the demon; it was the professor's statement about the mental, moral and physical inferiority of women. My heart had leapt. My cheeks had burnt. I had flushed with anger. There was nothing specially remarkable, however foolish, in that. One does not like to be told that one is naturally the inferior of a little man—I looked at the student next me—who breathes hard, wears a ready-made tie, and has not shaved this fortnight. One has certain foolish vanities. It is only human nature, I reflected, and began drawing cart-wheels and circles over the angry professor's face till he looked like a burning bush or a flaming comet—anyhow, an apparition without human semblance or significance. The professor was nothing now but a faggot burning on the top of Hampstead Heath. Soon my own anger was explained and done with; but curiosity remained. How explain the anger of the professors? Why were they angry? For when it came to analysing the impression left by these books there was always an element of heat. This heat took many forms; it showed itself in satire, in sentiment, in curiosity, in reprobation. But there was another element which was often present and could not immediately be identified. Anger, I called it. But it was anger that had gone underground and mixed itself with all kinds of other emotions. To judge from its odd effects, it was anger disguised and complex, not anger simple and open.

Whatever the reason, all these books, I thought, surveying the pile on the desk, are worthless for my purposes. They were worthless scientifically, that is to say, though humanly they were full of instruction, interest, boredom, and very queer facts about the habits of the Fiji Islanders. They had been written in the red light of emotion and not in the white light of truth. Therefore they must be returned to the central desk and restored each to his own cell in the enormous honeycomb. All that I had retrieved from that morning's work had been the one fact of anger. The professors—I lumped them together thus—were angry. But why, I asked myself, having returned the books, why, I repeated, standing under the colonnade among the pigeons and the prehistoric canoes, why are they angry? And, asking myself this question, I strolled off to find a place for luncheon. What is the real nature of what I call for the moment their anger? I asked. Here was a puzzle that would last all the time that it takes to be served with food in a small restaurant somewhere near the British Museum. Some previous luncher had left the lunch edition of the evening paper on a chair, and, waiting to be served, I began idly reading the headlines. A ribbon of very large letters ran across the page. Somebody had made a big score in South Africa. Lesser ribbons announced that Sir Austen Chamberlain was at Geneva. A meat axe with human hair on it had been found in a cellar. Mr. Justice_____ commented in the Divorce Courts upon the Shamelessness of Women. Sprinkled about the paper were other pieces of news. A film actress had been lowered from a peak in California and hung suspended in mid-air. The weather was going to be foggy. The most transient visitor to this planet, I thought, who picked up this paper could not fail to be aware, even from this scattered testimony, that England is under the rule of a patriarchy. Nobody in their senses could fail to detect the dominance of the professor. His was the power and the money and the influence. He was the proprietor of the paper and its editor and sub-editor. He was the Foreign Secretary and the Judge. He was the cricketer; he owned the racehorses and the yachts. He was the director of the company that pays two hundred per cent to its shareholders. He left millions to charities and colleges that were ruled by himself. He suspended the film actress in mid-air. He will decide if the hair on the meat axe is human; he it is who will acquit or convict the murderer, and hang him or let him go free. With the exception of the fog he seemed to control everything. Yet he was angry. I knew that he was angry by this token. When I read what he wrote about women I thought, not of what he was saying, but of himself. When an arguer argues dispassionately he thinks only of the argument; and the reader cannot help thinking of the argument too. If he had written dispassionately about women, had used indisputable proofs to establish his argument and had shown no trace of wishing that the result should be one thing rather than another, one would not have been angry either. One would have accepted the fact, as one accepts the fact that a pea is green or a canary yellow. So be it, I should have said. But I had been angry because he was angry. Yet it seemed absurd, I thought, turning over the evening paper, that a man with all this power should be angry. Or is anger, I wondered, somehow, the familiar, the attendant sprite on power? Rich people, for example, are often angry because they suspect that the poor want to seize their wealth. The professors, or patriarchs, as it might be more accurate to call them, might be angry for that reason partly, but partly for one that lies a little less obviously on the surface. Possibly they were not "angry" at all; often, indeed, they were admiring, devoted, exemplary in the relations of private life. Possibly when the professor insisted a little too emphatically upon the inferiority of women, he was concerned not with their inferiority, but with his own superiority. That was what he was protecting rather hot-headedly and with too much emphasis, because it was a jewel to him of the rarest price. Life for both sexes—and I looked at them, shouldering their way along the pavement—is arduous, difficult, a perpetual struggle. It calls for gigantic courage and strength. More than anything, perhaps, creatures of illusion as we are, it calls for confidence in oneself. Without self-confidence we are as babes in the cradle. And how can we generate this imponderable quality, which is yet so invaluable, most quickly? By thinking that other people are inferior to oneself. By feeling that one has some innate superiority—it may be wealth, or rank, a straight nose, or the portrait of a grandfather by Romney—for there is no end to the pathetic devices of the human imagination—over other people. Hence the enormous importance to a patriarch who has to conquer, who has to rule, of feeling that great numbers of people, half the human race indeed, are by nature inferior to himself. It must indeed be one of the chief sources of his power.

· · ·

CHAPTER 5

I had come at last, in the course of this rambling, to the shelves which hold books by the living; by women and by men; for there are almost as many books written by women now as by men. . . .

I took down one of them at random. It stood at the very end of the shelf, was called *Life's Adventure,* or some such title, by Mary Carmichael, and was published in this very month of October. It seems to be her first book, I said to myself, but one must read it as if it were the last volume in a fairly long series, continuing all those other books that I have been glancing at—Lady Winchilsea's poems and Aphra Behn's plays and the novels of the four great novelists. For books continue each other, in spite of our habit of judging them separately. And I must also consider her—this unknown woman—as the descendant of all those other women whose circumstances I have been glancing at and see what she inherits of their characteristics and restrictions. So, with a sigh, because novels so often provide an anodyne and not an antidote, glide one into torpid slumbers instead of rousing one with a burning brand, I settled down with a notebook and a pencil to make what I could of Mary Carmichael's first novel, *Life's Adventure.*

To begin with, I ran my eye up and down the page. I am going to get the hang of her sentences first, I said, before I load my memory with blue eyes and brown and the relationship that there may be between Chloe and Roger. There will be time for that when I have decided whether she has a pen in her hand or a pickaxe. So I tried a sentence or two on my tongue. Soon it was obvious that something was not quite in order. The smooth gliding of sentence after sentence was interrupted. Something tore, something scratched; a single word here and there flashed its torch in my eyes. She was "unhanding" herself as they say in the old plays. She is like a person striking a match that will not light, I thought. But why, I asked her as if she were present, are Jane Austen's sentences not of the right shape for you? Must they all be scrapped because Emma and Mr. Woodhouse are dead? Alas, I sighed, that it should be so. For while Jane Austen breaks from melody to melody as Mozart from song to song, to read this writing was like being out at sea in an open boat. Up one went, down one sank. This terseness, this short-windedness, might mean that she was afraid of something; afraid of being called "sentimental" perhaps; or she remembers that women's writing has been called flowery and so provides a superfluity of thorns; but until I have read a scene with some care, I cannot be sure whether she is being herself or someone else. At any rate, she does not lower one's vitality, I thought, reading more carefully. But she is heaping up too many facts. She will not be able to use half of them in a book of this size. (It was about half the length of *Jane Eyre.*) However, by some means or other she succeeded in getting us all—Roger, Chloe, Olivia, Tony and Mr. Bigham—in a canoe up the river. Wait a moment, I said, leaning back in my chair, I must consider the whole thing more carefully before I go any further.

I am almost sure, I said to myself, that Mary Carmichael is playing a trick on us. For I feel as one feels on a switchback railway when the car, instead of sinking, as one has been led to expect, swerves up again. Mary is tampering with the expected sequence. First she broke the sentence; now she has broken·the sequence. Very well, she has every right to do both these things if she does them not for the sake of breaking, but for the sake of creating. Which of the two it is I cannot be sure until she has faced herself with a situation. I will give her every liberty, I said, to choose what that situation shall be; she shall make it of tin cans and old kettles if she likes;

but she must convince me that she believes it to be a situation; and then when she has made it she must face it. She must jump. And, determined to do my duty by her as reader if she would do her duty by me as writer, I turned the page and read . . . I am sorry to break off so abruptly. Are there no men present? Do you promise me that behind that red curtain over there the figure of Sir Chartres Biron is not concealed? We are all women, you assure me? Then I may tell you that the very next words I read were these—"Chloe liked Olivia . . ." Do not start. Do not blush. Let us admit in the privacy of our own society that these things sometimes happen. Sometimes women do like women.

"Chloe liked Olivia," I read. And then it struck me how immense a change was there. Chloe liked Olivia perhaps for the first time in literature. . . . And I tried to remember any case in the course of my reading where two women are represented as friends. There is an attempt at it in *Diana of the Crossways*. They are confidantes, of course, in Racine and the Greek tragedies. They are now and then mothers and daughters. But almost without exception they are shown in their relation to men. It was strange to think that all the great women of fiction were, until Jane Austen's day, not only seen by the other sex, but seen only in relation to the other sex. And how small a part of a woman's life is that; and how little can a man know even of that when he observes it through the black or rosy spectacles which sex puts upon his nose. Hence, perhaps, the peculiar nature of woman in fiction; the astonishing extremes of her beauty and horror; her alternations between heavenly goodness and hellish depravity—for so a lover would see her as his love rose or sank, was prosperous or unhappy. This is not so true of the nineteenth-century novelists, of course. Woman becomes much more various and complicated there. Indeed it was the desire to write about women perhaps that led men by degrees to abandon the poetic drama which, with its violence, could make so little use of them, and to devise the novel as a more fitting receptacle. Even so it remains obvious, even in the writing of Proust, that a man is terribly hampered and partial in his knowledge of women, as a woman in her knowledge of men.

Also, I continued, looking down at the page again, it is becoming evident that women, like men, have other interests besides the perennial interests of domesticity. "Chloe liked Olivia. They shared a laboratory together. . . ." I read on and discovered that these two young women were engaged in mincing liver, which is, it seems, a cure for pernicious anaemia: although one of them was married and had—I think I am right in stating—two small children. Now all that, of course, has had to be left out, and thus the splendid portrait of the fictitious woman is much too simple and much too monotonous. Suppose, for instance, that men were only represented in literature as the lovers of women, and were never the friends of men, soldiers, thinkers, dreamers; how few parts in the plays of Shakespeare could be allotted to them; how literature would suffer! We might perhaps have most of *Othello*; and a good deal of *Antony*; but no Caesar, no Brutus, no Hamlet, no Lear, no Jaques—literature would be incredibly impoverished, as indeed literature is impoverished beyond our counting by the doors that have been shut upon women. Married against their will, kept in one room, and to one occupation, how could a dramatist give a full or interesting or truthful account of them? Love was the only possible interpreter. The poet was forced to be passionate or bitter, unless indeed he chose to "hate women," which meant more often than not that he was unattractive to them.

Now if Chloe likes Olivia and they share a laboratory, which of itself will make their friendship more varied and lasting because it will be less personal; if Mary Carmichael knows how to write, and I was beginning to enjoy some quality in her style; if she has a room to herself, of which I am not quite sure; if she has five hundred a year of her own—but that remains to be proved—then I think that something of great importance has happened.

· · ·

CHAPTER 6

· · ·

Here I would stop, but the pressure of convention decrees that every speech must end with a peroration. And a peroration addressed to women should have something, you will agree, particularly exalting and ennobling about it. I should implore you to remember your responsibilities, to be higher, more spiritual; I should remind you how much depends upon you, and what an influence you can exert upon the future. But those exhortations can safely, I think, be left to the other sex, who will put them, and indeed have put them, with far greater eloquence than I can compass. When I rummage in my own mind I find no noble sentiments about being companions and equals and influencing the world to higher ends. I find myself saying briefly and prosaically that it is much more important to be oneself than anything else. Do not dream of influencing other people, I would say, if I knew how to make it sound exalted. Think of things in themselves.

· · ·

How can I further encourage you to go about the business of life? Young women, I would say, and please attend, for the peroration is beginning, you are, in my opinion, disgracefully ignorant. You have never made a discovery of any sort of importance. You have never shaken an empire or led an army into battle. The plays of Shakespeare are not by you, and you have never introduced a barbarous race to the blessings of civilisation. What is your excuse? It is all very well for you to say, pointing to the streets and squares and forests of the globe swarming with black and white and coffee-coloured inhabitants, all busily engaged in traffic and enterprise and lovemaking, we have had other work on our hands. Without our doing, those seas would be unsailed and those fertile lands a desert. We have borne and bred and washed and taught, perhaps to the age of six or seven years, the one thousand six hundred and twenty-three million human beings who are, according to statistics, at present in existence, and that, allowing that some had help, takes time.

There is truth in what you say—I will not deny it. But at the same time may I remind you that there have been at least two colleges for women in existence in England since the year 1866; that after the year 1880 a married woman was allowed by law to possess her own property; and that in 1919—which is a whole nine years ago—she was given a vote? May I also remind you that the most of the professions have been open to you for close on ten years now? When you reflect upon these immense privileges and the length of time during which they have been enjoyed, and the fact that there must be at this moment some two thousand women capable of earning over five hundred a year in one way or another, you will agree that the excuse of lack of opportunity, training, encouragement, leisure and money no longer holds good. Moreover, the economists are telling us that Mrs. Seton has had too many children. You must, of course, go on bearing children, but, so they say, in twos and threes, not in tens and twelves.

Thus, with some time on your hands and with some book learning in your brains—you have had enough of the other kind, and are sent to college partly, I suspect, to be uneducated—surely you should embark upon another stage of your very long, very laborious and highly obscure career. A thousand pens are ready to suggest what you should do and what effect you will have. My own suggestion is a little fantastic, I admit; I prefer, therefore, to put it in the form of fiction.

I told you in the course of this paper that Shakespeare had a sister; but do not look for her in Sir Sidney Lee's life of the poet. She died young— alas, she never wrote a word. She lies buried where the omnibuses now stop, opposite the Elephant and Castle. Now my belief is that this poet who never wrote a word and was buried at the crossroads still lives. She lives in you and in me, and in many other women who are not here tonight, for they are washing up the dishes and putting the children to bed. But she lives; for great poets do not die; they are continuing presences; they need only the opportunity to walk among us in the flesh. This opportunity, as I think, it is now coming within your power to give her. For my belief is that if we live another century or so—I am talking of the common life which is the real life and not of the little separate lives which we live as individuals—and have five hundred a year each of us and rooms of our own; if we have the habit of freedom and the courage to write exactly what we think; if we escape a little from the common sitting-room and see human beings not always in their relation to each other but in relation to reality; and the sky, too, and the trees or whatever it may be in themselves; if we look past Milton's bogey, for no human being should shut out the view; if we face the fact, for it is a fact, that there is no arm to cling to, but that we go alone and that our relation is to the world of reality and not only to the world of men and women, then the opportunity will come and the dead poet who was Shakespeare's sister will put on the body which she has so often laid down. Drawing her life from the lives of the unknown who were her fore-runners, as her brother did before her, she will be born. As for her coming without that preparation, without that effort on our part, without that determination that when she is born again she shall find it possible to live and write her poetry, that we cannot expect, for that would be impossible. But I maintain that she would come if we worked for her, and that so to work, even in poverty and obscurity, is worth while.

[1929]

 33

The Dread of Woman: Observations on a Specific Difference in the Dread Felt by Men and by Women Respectively for the Opposite Sex

KAREN HORNEY

KAREN HORNEY Germany. 1885–1952. Psychiatrist and psychoanalyst trained in Berlin. Early critic of Freud. Worked in the United States from the 1930s on. Helped found the American Institute for Psychoanalysis. *New Ways in Psychoanalysis* (1939), *Self-Analysis* (1942), *Our Inner Conflicts* (1945), *Neurosis and Human Growth* (1950), *Feminine Psychology* (1967).

· · ·

Is it not really remarkable . . . that so little recognition and attention are paid to the fact of men's secret dread of women? It is almost more remarkable that women themselves have so long been able to overlook it; I will discuss in detail elsewhere the reasons for their attitude in this connection (i.e., their own anxiety and the impairment of their self-respect). The man on his side has in the first place very obvious strategic reasons for keeping his dread quiet. But he also tries by every means to deny it

even to himself. This is the purpose of the efforts to which we have alluded, to "objectify" it in artistic and scientific creative work. We may conjecture that even his glorification of women has its source not only in his cravings for love, but also in his desire to conceal his dread. A similar relief, however, is also sought and found in the disparagement of women that men often display ostentatiously in their attitudes. The attitude of love and adoration signifies: "There is no need for me to dread a being so wonderful, so beautiful, nay, so saintly." That of disparagement implies: "It would be too ridiculous to dread a creature who, if you take her all around, is such a poor thing."[1] This last way of allaying his anxiety has a special advantage for the man: It helps to support his masculine self-respect. The latter seems to feel itself far more threatened at its very core by the admission of a dread of women than by the admission of dread of a man (the father). The reason why the self-feeling of men is so peculiarly sensitive just in relation to women can only be understood by reference to their early development, to which I will return later.

In analysis this dread of women is revealed quite clearly. Male homosexuality has for its basis, in common indeed with all the other perversions, the desire to escape from the female genital, or to deny its very existence. Freud has shown that this is a fundamental trait in fetishism,[2] in particular; he believes it to be based, however, not on anxiety, but on a feeling of abhorrence due to the absence of the penis in women. I think, however, that even from his account we are absolutely forced to the conclusion that there is anxiety at work as well. What we actually see is dread of the vagina, thinly disguised under the abhorrence. Only *anxiety* is a strong enough motive to hold back from his goal a man whose libido is assuredly urging him on to union with the woman. But Freud's account fails to explain this anxiety. A boy's castration anxiety in relation to his father is not an adequate reason for his dread of a being to whom this punishment has already happened. Besides the dread of the father, there must be a further dread, the object of which is the woman or the female genital. Now this dread of the vagina itself appears unmistakably not only in homosexuals and perverts, but also in the dreams of male analysands. All analysts are familiar with dreams of this sort and I need only give the merest outline of them: e.g., a motorcar is rushing along and suddenly falls into a pit and is dashed to pieces; a boat is sailing in a narrow channel and is suddenly sucked into a whirlpool; there is a cellar with uncanny, blood-stained plants and animals; one is climbing a chimney and is in danger of falling and being killed.

. . .

From all this I think it probable that the masculine dread of the woman (the mother) or of the female genital is more deep-seated, weighs more heavily, and is usually more energetically repressed than the dread of the man (father), and that the endeavor to find the penis in women represents first and foremost a convulsive attempt to deny the existence of the sinister female genital.

. . .

When we endeavor to understand this anxiety in psychological and ontogenetic terms, we find ourselves rather at a loss if we take our stand on Freud's notion that what distinguishes infantile from adult sexuality is precisely that the vagina remains "undiscovered" for the child. According to that view, we cannot properly speak of a genital primacy; we must rather term it a primacy of the phallus. Hence it would be better to describe the period of infantile genital organization as the "phallic phase."[3] The many recorded remarks of boys at that period of life leave no doubt of the correctness of the observations on which Freud's theory is based. But if we look more closely at the essential characteristics of this phase, we cannot help asking whether his description really sums up infantile genitality as such, in its specific manifestation, or applies only to a relatively later phase of it. Freud states that it is characteristic that the boy's interest is concentrated in a markedly narcissistic manner on his own penis: "The driving force which this male portion of his body will generate later at puberty expresses itself in childhood essentially as an impulsion to inquire into things—as sexual curiosity." A very important part is played by questions as to the existence and size of the phallus in other living beings.

But surely the essence of the phallic impulses proper, starting as they do from organ sensations, is a desire to *penetrate*. That these impulses do exist can hardly be doubted; they manifest themselves too

plainly in children's games and in the analysis of little children. Again, it would be difficult to say what the boy's sexual wishes in relation to his mother really consisted in if not in these very impulses; or why the object of his masturbation anxiety should be the father as the castrator, were it not that masturbation was largely the autoerotic expression of heterosexual phallic impulses.

In the phallic phase the boy's psychic orientation is predominantly narcissistic; hence the period in which his genital impulses are directed toward an object must be an earlier one. The possibility that they are not directed toward a female genital, of which he instinctively divines the existence, must certainly be considered. In dreams, both of earlier and later life, as well as in symptoms and particular modes of behavior, we find, it is true, representations of coitus that are oral, anal, or sadistic without specific localization. But we cannot take this as a proof of the primacy of corresponding impulses, for we are uncertain whether, or how far, these phenomena already express a displacement from the genital goal proper. At bottom, all that they amount to is to show that a given individual is influenced by specific oral, anal, or sadistic trends. Their evidential value is the less because these representations are always associated with certain affects directed against women, so that we cannot tell whether they may not be essentially the product or the expression of these affects. For instance, the tendency to debase women may express itself in anal representations of the female genital, while oral representations may express anxiety.

But besides all this, there are various reasons why it seems to me improbable that the existence of a specific female opening should remain "undiscovered." On the one hand, of course, a boy will automatically conclude that everyone else is made like himself; but on the other hand his phallic impulses surely bid him instinctively to search for the appropriate opening in the female body—an opening, moreover, that he himself lacks, for the one sex always seeks in the other that which is complementary to it or of a nature different from its own. If we seriously accept Freud's dictum that the sexual theories formed by children are modeled on their own sexual constitution, it must surely mean in the present connection that the boy, urged on by his impulses to penetrate, pictures in fantasy a complementary female organ. And this is just what we should infer from all the material I quoted at the outset in connection with the masculine dread of the female genital.

It is not at all probable that this anxiety dates only from puberty. At the beginning of that period the anxiety manifests itself quite clearly, if we look behind the often very exiguous façade of boyish pride that conceals it. At puberty a boy's task is obviously not merely to free himself from his incestuous attachment to his mother, but more generally, to master his dread of the whole female sex. His success is as a rule only gradual; first of all he turns his back on girls altogether, and only when his masculinity is fully awakened does it drive him over the threshold of anxiety. But we know that as a rule the conflicts of puberty do but revive, *mutatis mutandis,* conflicts belonging to the early ripening of infantile sexuality and that the course they take is often essentially a faithful copy of a series of earlier experiences. Moreover, the grotesque character of the anxiety, as we meet with it in the symbolism of dreams and literary productions, points unmistakably to the period of early infantile fantasy.

At puberty a normal boy has already acquired a conscious knowledge of the vagina, but what he fears in women is something uncanny, unfamiliar, and mysterious. If the grown man continues to regard women as the great mystery, in whom is a secret he cannot divine, this feeling of his can only relate ultimately to one thing in her: the mystery of motherhood. Everything else is merely the residue of his dread of this.

What is the origin of this anxiety? What are its characteristics? And what are the factors that cloud the boy's early relations with his mother?

In an article on female sexuality[4] Freud has pointed out the most obvious of these factors: It is the mother who first forbids instinctual activities, because it is she who tends the child in its babyhood. Secondly, the child evidently experiences sadistic impulses against its mother's body,[5] presumably connected with the rage evoked by her prohibitions, and according to the talion principle, this anger has left behind a residue of anxiety. Finally—and this is perhaps the principal point—

the specific fate of the genital impulses itself constitutes another such factor. The anatomical differences between the sexes lead to a totally different situation in girls and in boys, and really to understand both their anxiety and the diversity of their anxiety we must take into account first of all *the children's real situation* in the period of their early sexuality. The girl's nature as biologically conditioned gives her the desire to receive, to take into herself;[6] she feels or knows that her genital is too small for her father's penis and this makes her react to her own genital wishes with direct anxiety; she dreads that if her wishes were fulfilled, she herself or her genital would be destroyed.[7]

The boy, on the other hand, feels or instinctively judges that his penis is much too small for his mother's genital and reacts with the dread of his own inadequacy, of being rejected and derided. Thus his anxiety is located in quite a different quarter from the girl's; his original dread of women is not castration anxiety at all, but a reaction to the menace to his self-respect.[8]

In order that there may be no misunderstanding, let me emphasize that I believe these processes take place purely instinctively on the basis of organ sensations and the tensions of organic needs; in other words, I hold that these reactions would occur even if the girl had never seen her father's penis or the boy his mother's genital, and neither had any sort of intellectual knowledge of the existence of these genitalia.

Because of this reaction on the part of the boy, he is affected in another way and more severely by his frustration at the hands of his mother than is the girl by her experience with her father. A blow is struck at the libidinal impulses in either case. But the girl has a certain consolation in her frustration—she preserves her physical integrity. But the boy is hit in a second sensitive spot—his sense of genital inadequacy, which has presumably accompanied his libidinal desires from the beginning. If we assume that the most general reason for violent anger is the foiling of impulses that at the moment are of vital importance, it follows that the boy's frustration by his mother must arouse a twofold fury in him: first through the thrusting back of his libido upon itself, and secondly, through the wounding of his masculine self-regard.

· · ·

[1932]

NOTES

1. I well remember how surprised I was myself the first time I heard the above ideas asserted—by a man—in the shape of a universal proposition. The speaker was Groddeck, who obviously felt that he was stating something quite self-evident when he remarked in conversation, "Of course men are afraid of women." In his writings Groddeck has repeatedly emphasized this fear.
2. Freud, "Fetishism," *Int. J. Psycho-Anal.*, Vol. IX (1928).
3. Freud, "The Infantile Genital Organization of the Libido" (1923), *Collected Papers,* Vol. II.
4. *Int. J. Psycho-Anal.*, Vol. XI (1930), p. 281.
5. Cf. the work of Melanie Klein, to which I think insufficient attention has been paid.
6. This is not to be equated with passivity.
7. In another paper I will discuss the girl's situation more fully.
8. I would refer here also to the points I raised in a paper entitled "Das Misstrauen zwischen den Geschlechtern," *Die psychoanalytische Bewegung* (1930).

 34

Sex and Temperament from Sex and Temperament in Three Primitive Societies

MARGARET MEAD

MARGARET MEAD United States. 1901–1978. Anthropologist. Activist. Lecturer. Advocate on issues related to women, children, and aging. *Coming of Age in Samoa* (1928), *Male and Female: A Study of the Sexes in a Changing World* (1949), *Blackberry Winter: My Earlier Years* (1972).

This study is not concerned with whether there are or are not actual and universal differences between the sexes, either quantitative or qualitative. It is not concerned with whether women are more variable than men, which was claimed before the doctrine of evolution exalted variability, or less variable, which was claimed afterwards. It is not a treatise on the rights of women, nor an inquiry into the basis of feminism. It is, very simply, an account of how three primitive societies have grouped their social attitudes towards temperament about the very obvious facts of sex-difference. I studied this problem in simple societies because here we have the drama of civilization writ small, a social microcosm alike in kind, but different in size and magnitude, from the complex social structures of peoples who, like our own, depend upon a written tradition and upon the integration of a great number of conflicting historical traditions. Among the gentle mountain-dwelling Arapesh, the fierce cannibalistic Mundugumor, and the graceful head-hunters of Tchambuli, I studied this question. Each of these tribes had, as has every human society, the point of sex-difference to use as one theme in the plot of social life, and each of these three peoples has developed that theme differently. In comparing the way in which they have dramatized sex-difference, it is possible to gain a greater insight into what elements are social constructs, originally irrelevant to the biological facts of sex-gender.

. . .

We know that human cultures do not all fall into one side or the other of a single scale and that it is possible for one society to ignore completely an issue which two other societies have solved in contrasting ways. Because a people honour the old may mean that they hold children in slight esteem, but a people may also, like the Ba Thonga of South Africa, honour neither old people nor children; or, like the Plains Indians, dignify the little child and the grandfather; or, again, like the Manus and parts of modern America, regard children as the most important group in society. In expecting simple reversals—that if an aspect of social life is not specifically sacred, it must be specifically secular; that if men are strong, women must be weak—we ignore the fact that cultures exercise far greater license than this in selecting the possible aspects of human life which they will minimize, overemphasize, or ignore. And while every culture has in some way institutionalized the roles of men and women, it has not necessarily been in terms of contrast between the prescribed personalities of the two sexes, nor in terms of dominance or submission. With the paucity of material for elaboration, no culture has failed to seize upon the conspicuous facts of age and sex in some way, whether it be the convention of one Philippine tribe that no man can keep a secret, the Manus assumption that only men enjoy playing with babies, the Toda prescription of almost all domestic work as too sacred for women, or the Arapesh insistence that women's heads are stronger than men's. In the division of labour, in dress, in manners, in social and religious functioning—sometimes in only a few of these respects, sometimes in all—men and women are socially differentiated, and each sex, as a sex, forced to conform to the role assigned to it. In some societies, these socially defined roles are mainly expressed in dress or occupation, with no insistence upon innate temperamental differences. Women wear long hair and men wear short hair, or men wear curls and women shave their heads; women wear skirts and men wear trousers, or women wear trousers, and men wear skirts. Women weave and men do not, or men weave and women do not. Such simple tie-ups as these between dress and occupation and sex are easily taught to every child and make no assumptions to which a given child cannot easily conform.

It is otherwise in societies that sharply differentiate the behaviour of men and of women in terms which assume a genuine difference in temperament. Among the Dakota Indians of the Plains, the importance of an ability to stand any degree of danger or hardship was frantically insisted upon as a masculine characteristic. From the time that a boy was five or six, all the conscious educational effort of the household was bent towards shaping him into an indubitable male. Every tear, every timidity, every clinging to a protective hand or desire to continue to play with younger children or with girls, was obsessively interpreted as proof that he was not going to develop into a real man. In such a society it is not surprising to find the *berdache*, the man who had voluntarily given up the struggle to conform to the masculine role and who wore female attire and followed the occupations of a women. The institution of the *berdache* in turn served as a warning to every father; the fear that the son might become a *berdache* informed the parental efforts with a extra desperation, and the very pressure which helped to drive a boy to that choice was redoubled. The invert who lacks any discernable physical basis for his inversion has long puzzled students of sex, who when they can find no observable glandular abnormality turn to theories of early conditioning or identification with a parent of opposite sex. In the course of this investigation, we shall have occasion to examine the "masculine" woman and the

"feminine" man as they occur in these different tribes, to inquire whether it is always a woman of dominating nature who is conceived as masculine, or a man who is gentle, submissive, or fond of children or embroidery who is conceived as feminine.

. . . [W]e shall be concerned with the patterning of sex-behaviour from the standpoint of temperament, with the cultural assumptions that certain temperamental attitudes are "naturally" masculine and others "naturally" feminine. In this matter, primitive people seem to be, on the surface, more sophisticated than we are. Just as they know that the gods, the food habits, and the marriage customs of the next tribe differ from those of their own people, and do not insist that one form is true or natural while the other is false or unnatural, so they often know that the temperamental proclivities which they regard as natural for men or for women differ from the natural temperaments of the men and women among their neighbours. Nevertheless, within a narrower range and with less of a claim for the biological or divine validity of their social forms than we often advance, each tribe has certain definite attitudes towards temperament, a theory of what human beings, either men or women or both, are naturally like, a norm in terms of which to judge and condemn those individuals who deviate from it.

· · ·

The knowledge that the personalities of the two sexes are socially produced is congenial to every programme that looks forward towards a planned order of society. It is a two-edged sword that can be used to hew a more flexible, more varied society than the human race has ever built, or merely to cut a narrow path down which one sex or both sexes will be forced to march, regimented, looking neither to the right nor to the left. . . .

There are at least three courses open to a society that has realized the extent to which male and female personality are socially produced. Two of these courses have been tried before, over and over again, at different times in the long, irregular, repetitious history of the race. The first is to standardize the personality of men and women as clearly contrasting, complementary, and antithetical, and to make every institution in the society congruent with this standardization. If the society declared that women's sole function was motherhood and the teaching and care of young children, it could so arrange matters that every woman who was not physiologically debarred should become a mother and be supported in the exercise of this function. It could abolish the discrepancy between the doctrine that women's place is the home and the number of homes that were offered to them. It could abolish the discrepancy between training women for marriage and then forcing them to become the spinster supports of their parents.

Such a system would be wasteful of the gifts of many women who could exercise other functions far better than their ability to bear children in an already overpopulated world. It would be wasteful of the gifts of many men who could exercise their special personality gifts far better in the home than in the market-place. It would be wasteful, but it would be clear. It could attempt to guarantee to each individual the role for which society insisted upon training him or her, and such a system would penalize only those individuals who, in spite of all the training, did not display the approved personalities. There are millions of persons who would gladly return to such a standardized method of treating the relationship between the sexes, and we must bear in mind the possibility that the greater opportunities open in the twentieth century to women may be quite withdrawn, and that we may return to a strict regimentation of women.

The waste, if this occurs, will be not only of many women, but also of as many men, because regimentation of one sex carries with it, to a greater or less degree, the regimentation of the other also. Every parental behest that defines a way of sitting, a response to a rebuke or a threat, a game, or an attempt to draw or sing or dance or paint, as feminine, is moulding the personality of each little girl's brother as well as moulding the personality of the sister. There can be no society which insists that women follow one special personality-pattern, defined as feminine, which does not do violence also to the individuality of many men.

Alternatively, society can take the course that has become especially associated with the plans of most radical groups: admit that men and women are capable of being moulded to a single pattern as easily as to a diverse one, and cease to make any distinction in the approved personality of both sexes. Girls can be trained exactly as boys are trained, taught the same code, the same forms of expression, the same occupations. This course might seem to be the logic which follows from the conviction that the potentialities which different societies label as either masculine or feminine are really potentialities of some members of each sex, and not sex-linked at all. If this is accepted, is it not reasonable to abandon the kind of artificial standardizations of sex-differences that have been so long characteristic of European society, and admit that they are social fictions for which we have no longer any use? In the world today, contraceptives make it possible for women not to bear children against their will. The most conspicuous actual difference between the sexes, the difference in strength, is progressively less significant. Just as the difference in height between males is no longer a realistic issue, now that lawsuits have been substituted for hand-to-hand encounters, so the difference in strength between men and women is no longer worth elaboration in cultural institutions.

· · ·

To insist that there are no sex-differences in a society that has always believed in them and depended upon them may be as subtle a form of standardizing personality as to insist that there are many sex-differences. This is particularly so in a changing tradition, when a group in control is attempting to develop a new social personality, as is the case today in many European countries. Take, for instance, the current assumption that women are more opposed to war than men, that any outspoken approval of war is more horrible, more revolting, in women than in men. Behind this assumption women can work for peace without encountering social criticism in communities that would immediately criticize their brothers or husbands if they took a similarly active part in peace propaganda. This belief that women are naturally more interested in peace is undoubtedly artificial, part of the whole mythology that considers women to be gentler than men. But in contrast let us consider the possibility of a powerful minority that wished to turn a whole society whole-heartedly towards war. One way of doing this would be to insist that women's motives, women's interests, were identical with men's, that women should take as bloodthirsty a delight in preparing for war as ever men do. The insistence upon the opposite point of view, that the woman as a mother prevails over the woman as a citizen, at least puts a slight drag upon agitation for war, prevents a blanket enthusiasm for war from being thrust upon the entire younger generation. The same kind of result follows if the clergy are professionally committed to a belief in peace. The relative bellicosity of different individual clerics may be either offended or gratified by the prescribed pacific role, but a certain protest, a certain dissenting note, will be sounded in society. The dangerous standardization of attitudes that disallows every type of deviation is greatly reinforced if neither age nor sex nor religious belief is regarded as automatically predisposing certain individuals to hold minority attitudes. The removal of all legal and economic barriers against women's participating in the world on an equal footing with men may be in itself a standardizing move towards the wholesale stamping-out of the diversity of attitudes that is such a dearly bought product of civilization.

· · ·

Let us suppose that, instead of the classification laid down on the "natural" bases of sex and race, a society had classified personality on the basis of eye-colour. It had decreed that all blue-eyed people were gentle, submissive, and responsive to the needs of others, and all brown-eyed people were arrogant, dominating, self-centred, and purposive. In this case two complementary social themes would be woven together—the culture, in its art, its religion, its formal personal relations, would have two threads instead on one. There would be blue-eyed men, and blue-eyed women, which would mean that there were gentle, "maternal" women, and gentle, "maternal" men. A blue-eyed man might marry a woman who had been bred to the same personality as himself, or a brown-eyed woman who had been bred to the contrasting personality. One of the strong tendencies that makes for homosexuality, the tendency to love the similar rather than the antithetical persons, would be eliminated. Hostility between the two sexes as groups would be minimized, since the individual interests of members of each sex could be woven together in different ways, and marriages of similarity and

friendships of contrast need carry no necessary handicap of possible psycho-sexual maladjustment. The individual would still suffer a mutilation of his temperamental preferences, for it would be the unrelated fact of eye-colour that would determine the attitudes which he was educated to show. Every blue-eyed person would be forced into submissiveness and declared maladjusted if he or she showed any traits that it had been decided were only appropriate to the brown-eyed. The greatest social loss, however, in the classification of personality on the basis of sex would not be present in this society which based its classification on eye-colour. Human relations, and especially those which involve sex, would not be artificially distorted.

But such a course, the substitution of eye-colour for sex as a basis upon which to educate children into groups showing contrasting personalities, while it would be a definite advance upon a classification by sex, remains a parody of all the attempts that society has made through history to define an individual's role in terms of sex, or colour, or date of birth, or shape of head.

However, the only solution of the problem does not lie between an acceptance of standardization of sex-differences with the resulting cost in individual happiness and adjustment, and the abolition of these differences with the consequent loss in social values. A civilization might take its cues not from such categories as age or sex, race or hereditary position in a family line, but instead of specializing personality along such simple lines recognize, train, and make a place for many and divergent temperamental endowments. It might build upon the different potentialities that it now attempts to extirpate artificially in some children and create artificially in others.

· · ·

To break down one line of division, that between the sexes, and substitute another, that between classes, is no real advance. It merely shifts the irrelevancy to a different point. And meanwhile, individuals born in the upper classes are shaped inexorably to one type of personality, to an arrogance that is again uncongenial to at least some of them, while the arrogant among the poor fret and fume beneath their training for submissiveness. At one end of the scale is the mild, unaggressive young son of wealthy parents who is forced to lead, at the other the aggressive, enterprising child of the slums who is condemned to a place in the ranks. If our aim is greater expression for each individual temperament, rather than any partisan interest in one sex or its fate, we must see these historical developments which have aided in freeing some women as nevertheless a kind of development that also involved major social losses.

The second way in which categories of sex-differences have become less rigid is through a recognition of genuine individual gifts as they occurred in either sex. Here a real distinction has been substituted for an artificial one, and the gains are tremendous for society and for the individual. Where writing is accepted as a profession that may be pursued by either sex with perfect suitability, individuals who have the ability to write need not be debarred from it by their sex, nor need they, if they do write, doubt their essential masculinity or femininity. An occupation that has no basis in sex-determined gifts can now recruit its ranks from twice as many potential artists. And it is here that we can find a ground-plan for building a society that would substitute real differences for arbitrary ones. We must recognize that beneath the superficial classifications of sex and race the same potentialities exist, recurring generation after generation, only to perish because society has no place for them. Just as society now permits the practice of an art to members of either sex, so it might also permit the development of many contrasting temperamental gifts in each sex. It might abandon its various attempts to make boys fight and to make girls remain passive, or to make all children fight, and instead shape our educational institutions to develop to the full the boy who shows a capacity for maternal behaviour, the girl who shows an opposite capacity that is stimulated by fighting against obstacles. No skill, no special aptitude, no vividness of imagination or precision of thinking would go unrecognized because the child who possessed it was of one sex rather than the other. No child would be relentlessly shaped to one pattern of behaviour, but instead there should be many patterns, in a world that had learned to allow to each individual the pattern which was most congenial to his gifts.

Such a civilization would not sacrifice the gains of thousands of years during which society has built up standards of diversity. The social gains would be conserved, and each child would be encouraged on the basis of his actual temperament. Where we now have patterns of behaviour for women and patterns of behaviour for men, we would then have patterns of behaviour that expressed the interests of individuals with many kinds of endowment. There would be ethical codes and social symbolisms, an art and a way of life, congenial to each endowment.

Historically our own culture has relied for the creation of rich and contrasting values upon many artificial distinctions, the most striking of which is sex. It will not be by the mere abolition of these distinctions that society will develop patterns in which individual gifts are given place instead of being forced into an ill-fitting mould. If we are to achieve a richer culture, rich in contrasting values, we must recognize the whole gamut of human potentialities, and so weave a less arbitrary social fabric, one in which each diverse human gift will find a fitting place.

[1935]

 ## 35

From The Second Sex

SIMONE DE BEAUVOIR

SIMONE DE BEAUVOIR France. 1908–1986. Philosopher. Novelist. Social critic. Memoirist. Political activist. Signed a statement by 343 French women saying they had had illegal abortions (1970). Cofounder with Jean-Paul Sartre of the journal *Les Temps Moderne* (1945). Cofounder with Monique Wittig and Christine Delphy of *Questions feministes* (1979). *Memoirs of a Dutiful Daughter* (1958), *The Prime of Life* (1960).

INTRODUCTION

For a long time I have hesitated to write a book on woman. The subject is irritating, especially to women; and it is not new. Enough ink has been spilled in the quarreling over feminism, now practically over, and perhaps we should say no more about it. It is still talked about, however, for the voluminous nonsense uttered during the last century seems to have done little to illuminate the problem. After all, is there a problem? And if so, what is it? Are there women, really? Most assuredly the theory of the eternal feminine still has its adherents who will whisper in your ear: "Even in Russia women still are *women*"; and other erudite persons—sometimes the very same—say with a sigh: "Woman is losing her way, woman is lost." One wonders if women still exist, if they will always exist, whether or not it is desirable that they should, what place they occupy in this world, what their place should be. "What has become of women?" was asked recently in an ephemeral magazine.[1]

But first we must ask: what is a woman? *"Tota mulier in utero,"* says one, "woman is a womb." But in speaking of certain women, connoisseurs declare that they are not women, although they are equipped with a uterus like the rest. All agree in recognizing the fact that females exist in the human species; today as always they make up about one-half of humanity. And yet we are told that femininity is in danger; we are exhorted to be women, remain women, become women. It would appear, then, that every female human being is not necessarily a woman; to be so considered she must share in that mysterious and threatened reality known as femininity. Is this attribute something secreted by the ovaries? Or is it a Platonic essence, a product of the philosophic imagination? Is a rustling petticoat enough to bring it down to earth? Although some women try zealously to incarnate this essence, it is hardly patentable. It is frequently described in vague and dazzling terms that seem to have been borrowed from the vocabulary of the seers, and indeed in the times of St. Thomas it was considered an essence as certainly defined as the somniferous virtue of the poppy.

But conceptualism has lost ground. The biological and social sciences no longer admit the existence of unchangeably fixed entities that determine given characteristics, such as those ascribed to woman, the Jew, or the Negro. Science regards any characteristic as a reaction dependent in part upon a *situation*. If today femininity no longer exists, then it never existed. But does the word *woman*, then, have no specific content? This is stoutly affirmed by those who hold to the philosophy of the enlightenment, of rationalism, of nominalism; women, to them, are merely the human beings arbitrarily designated by the word *woman*. Many American women particularly are prepared to think that there is no longer any place for woman as such; if a backward individual still takes herself for a woman, her friends advise her to be psychoanalyzed and thus get rid of this obsession. In regard to a work, *Modern Woman: The Lost Sex*, which in other respects has its irritating features, Dorothy Parker has written: "I cannot be just to books which treat of woman as woman. . . . My idea is that all of us, men as well as women, should be regarded as human beings." But nominalism is a rather inadequate doctrine, and the antifeminists have had no trouble in showing that women simply *are not* men. Surely woman is, like man, a human being; but such a declaration is abstract. The fact is that every concrete human being is always a singular, separate individual. To decline to accept such notions as the eternal feminine, the black soul, the Jewish character, is not to deny that Jews, Negroes, women exist today—this denial does not represent a liberation for those concerned, but rather a flight from reality. Some years ago a well-known woman writer refused to permit her portrait to appear in a series of photographs especially devoted to women writers; she wished to be counted among the men. But in order to gain this privilege she made use of her husband's influence! Women who assert that they are men lay claim nonetheless to masculine consideration and respect. I recall also a young Trotskyite standing on a platform at a boisterous meeting and getting ready to use her fists, in spite of her evident fragility. She was denying her feminine weakness; but it was for love of a militant male whose equal she wished to be. The attitude of defiance of many American women proves that they are haunted by a sense of their femininity. In truth, to go for a walk with one's eyes open is enough to demonstrate that humanity is divided into two classes of individuals whose clothes, faces, bodies, smiles, gaits, interests, and occupations are manifestly different. Perhaps these differences are superficial, perhaps they are destined to disappear. What is certain is that right now they do most obviously exist.

If her functioning as a female is not enough to define woman, if we decline also to explain her through "the eternal feminine," and if nevertheless we admit, provisionally, that women do exist, then we must face the question: what is a woman?

To state the question is, to me, to suggest, at once, a preliminary answer. The fact that I ask it is in itself significant. A man would never get the notion of writing a book on the peculiar situation of the human male.[2] But if I wish to define myself, I must first of all say: "I am a woman"; on this truth must be based all further discussion. A man never begins by presenting himself as an individual of a certain sex; it goes without saying that he is a man. The terms *masculine* and *feminine* are used symmetrically only as a matter of form, as on legal papers. In actuality the relation of the two sexes is not quite like that of two electrical poles, for man represents both the positive and the neutral, as is indicated by the common use of *man* to designate human beings in general; whereas woman represents only the negative, defined by limiting criteria, without reciprocity. In the midst of an abstract discussion it is vexing to hear a man say: "You think thus and so because you are a woman"; but I know that my only defense is to reply: "I think thus and so because it is true," thereby removing my subjective self from the argument. It would be out of the question to reply: "And you think the contrary because you are a man," for it is understood that the fact of being a man is no peculiarity. A man is in the right in being a man; it is the woman who is in the wrong. It amounts to this: just as for the ancients there was an absolute vertical with reference to which the oblique was defined, so there is an absolute human type, the masculine. Woman has ovaries, a uterus; these peculiarities imprison her in her subjectivity, circumscribe her within the limits of her own nature. It is often said that she thinks with her glands. Man superbly ignores the fact that his anatomy also includes glands, such as the testicles, and that they secrete hormones. He thinks of his body as a direct and normal connection with the world, which he believes he apprehends objectively, whereas he regards the body of woman as a hindrance, a prison, weighed down by everything peculiar to it. "The female is a female by virtue of a certain *lack* of qualities," said Aristotle; "we should regard the female nature as afflicted with a natural defectiveness." And St. Thomas for his part pronounced woman to be an "imperfect man," an "incidental" being. This is symbolized in Genesis, where Eve is depicted as made from what Bossuet called "a supernumerary bone" of Adam.

Thus humanity is male and man defines woman not in herself but as relative to him; she is not regarded as an autonomous being. Michelet writes: "Woman, the relative being. . . ." And Benda is most positive in his *Rapport d' Uriel:* "The body of man makes sense in itself quite apart from that of woman, whereas the latter seems wanting in significance by itself. . . . Man can think of himself without woman. She cannot think of herself without man." And she is simply what man decrees; thus she is called "the sex," by which is meant that she appears essentially to the male as a sexual being. For him she is sex—absolute sex, no less. She is defined and differentiated with reference to man and not he with reference to her; she is the incidental, the inessential as opposed to the essential. He is the Subject, he is the Absolute—she is the Other.[3]

The category of the *Other* is as primordial as consciousness itself. In the most primitive societies, in the most ancient mythologies, one finds the expression of a duality—that of the Self and the Other. This duality was not originally attached to the division of the sexes; it was not dependent upon any empirical facts. It is revealed in such works as that of Granet on Chinese thought and those of Dumézil on the East Indies and Rome. The feminine element was at first no more involved in such pairs as Varuna-Mitra, Uranus-Zeus, Sun-Moon, and Day-Night than it was in the contrasts between Good and Evil, lucky and unlucky auspices, right and left, God and Lucifer. Otherness is a fundamental category of human thought.

Thus it is that no group ever sets itself up as the One without at once setting up the Other over against itself. If three travelers chance to occupy the same compartment, that is enough to make vaguely hostile "others" out of all the rest of the passengers on the train. In small-town eyes all persons not belonging to the village are "strangers" and suspect; to the native of a country all who inhabit other countries are "foreigners"; Jews are "different" for the anti-Semite, Negroes are "inferior" for American racists, aborigines are "natives" for colonists, proletarians are the "lower class" for the privileged.

Lévi-Strauss, at the end of a profound work on the various forms of primitive societies, reaches the following conclusion: "Passage from the state of Nature to the state of Culture is marked by man's ability to view biological relations as a series of contrasts; duality, alternation, opposition, and symmetry, whether under definite or vague forms, constitute not so much phenomena to be explained as fundamental and immediately given data of social reality."[4] These phenomena would be incomprehensible if in fact human society were simply a *Mitsein* or fellowship based on solidarity and friendliness. Things become clear, on the contrary, if, following Hegel, we find in consciousness itself a fundamental hostility toward every other consciousness; the subject can be posed only in being opposed—he sets himself up as the essential, as opposed to the other, the inessential, the object.

But the other consciousness, the other ego, sets up a reciprocal claim. The native traveling abroad is shocked to find himself in turn regarded as a "stranger" by the natives of neighboring countries. As a matter of fact, wars, festivals, trading, treaties, and contests among tribes, nations, and classes tend to deprive the concept *Other* of its absolute sense and to make manifest its relativity; willy-nilly, individuals and groups are forced to realize the reciprocity of their relations. How is it, then, that this reciprocity has not been recognized between the sexes, that one of the contrasting terms is set up as the sole essential, denying any relativity in regard to its correlative and defining the latter as pure otherness? Why is it that women do not dispute male sovereignty? No subject will readily volunteer to become the object, the inessential; it is not the Other who, in defining himself as the Other, establishes the One. The Other is posed as such by the One in defining himself as the One. But if the Other is not to regain the status of being the One, he must be submissive enough to accept this alien point of view. Whence comes this submission in the case of woman?

There are, to be sure, other cases in which a certain category has been able to dominate another completely for a time. Very often this privilege depends upon inequality of numbers—the majority imposes its rule upon the minority or persecutes it. But women are not a minority, like the American

Negroes or the Jews; there are as many women as men on earth. Again, the two groups concerned have often been originally independent; they may have been formerly unaware of each other's existence, or perhaps they recognized each other's autonomy. But a historical event has resulted in the subjugation of the weaker by the stronger. The scattering of the Jews, the introduction of slavery into America, the conquests of imperialism are examples in point. In these cases the oppressed retained at least the memory of former days; they possessed in common a past, a tradition, sometimes a religion or a culture.

The parallel drawn by Bebel between women and the proletariat is valid in that neither ever formed a minority or a separate collective unit of mankind. And instead of a single historical event it is in both cases a historical development that explains their status as a class and accounts for the membership of *particular individuals* in that class. But proletarians have not always existed, whereas there have always been women. They are women in virtue of their anatomy and physiology. Throughout history they have always been subordinated to men,[5] and hence their dependency is not the result of a historical event or a social change—it was not something that *occurred*. The reason why otherness in this case seems to be an absolute is in part that it lacks the contingent or incidental nature of historical facts. A condition brought about at a certain time can be abolished at some other time, as the Negroes of Haiti and others have proved; but it might seem that a natural condition is beyond the possibility of change. In truth, however, the nature of things is no more immutably given, once for all, than is historical reality. If woman seems to be the inessential which never becomes the essential, it is because she herself fails to bring about this change. Proletarians say "We"; Negroes also. Regarding themselves as subjects, they transform the bourgeois, the whites, into "others." But women do not say "We," except at some congress of feminists or similar formal demonstration; men say "women," and women use the same word in referring to themselves. They do not authentically assume a subjective attitude. The proletarians have accomplished the revolution in Russia, the Negroes in Haiti, the Indo-Chinese are battling for it in

Indo-China; but the women's effort has never been anything more than a symbolic agitation. They have gained only what men have been willing to grant; they have taken nothing, they have only received.[6]

The reason for this is that women lack concrete means for organizing themselves into a unit which can stand face to face with the correlative unit. They have no past, no history, no religion of their own; and they have no such solidarity of work and interest as that of the proletariat. They are not even promiscuously herded together in the way that creates community feeling among the American Negroes, the ghetto Jews, the workers of Saint-Denis, or the factory hands of Renault. They live dispersed among the males, attached through residence, housework, economic condition, and social standing to certain men—fathers or husbands—more firmly than they are to other women. If they belong to the bourgeoisie, they feel solidarity with men of that class, not with proletarian women; if they are white, their allegiance is to white men, not to Negro women. The proletariat can propose to massacre the ruling class, and a sufficiently fanatical Jew or Negro might dream of getting sole possession of the atomic bomb and making humanity wholly Jewish or black; but woman cannot even dream of exterminating the males. The bond that unites her to her oppressors is not comparable to any other. The division of the sexes is a biological fact, not an event in human history. Male and female stand opposed within a primordial *Mitsein,* and woman has not broken it. The couple is a fundamental unity with its two halves riveted together, and the cleavage of society along the line of sex is impossible. Here is to be found the basic trait of woman: she is the Other in a totality of which the two components are necessary to one another.

One could suppose that this reciprocity might have facilitated the liberation of woman. When Hercules sat at the feet of Omphale and helped with her spinning, his desire for her held him captive; but why did she fail to gain a lasting power? To revenge herself on Jason, Medea killed their children; and this grim legend would seem to suggest that she might have obtained a formidable influence over him through his love for his offspring. In *Lysistrata* Aristophanes gaily depicts a band of women who joined forces to gain social ends through the sexual

needs of their men; but this is only a play. In the legend of the Sabine women, the latter soon abandoned their plan of remaining sterile to punish their ravishers. In truth woman has not been socially emancipated through man's need—sexual desire and the desire for offspring—which makes the male dependent for satisfaction upon the female.

Master and slave, also, are united by a reciprocal need, in this case economic, which does not liberate the slave. In the relation of master to slave the master does not make a point of the need that he has for the other; he has in his grasp the power of satisfying this need through his own action; whereas the slave, in his dependent condition, his hope and fear, is quite conscious of the need he has for his master. Even if the need is at bottom equally urgent for both, it always works in favor of the oppressor and against the oppressed. That is why the liberation of the working class, for example, has been slow.

Now, woman has always been man's dependent, if not his slave; the two sexes have never shared the world in equality. And even today woman is heavily handicapped, though her situation is beginning to change. Almost nowhere is her legal status the same as man's,[7] and frequently it is much to her disadvantage. Even when her rights are legally recognized in the abstract, long-standing custom prevents their full expression in the mores. In the economic sphere men and women can almost be said to make up two castes; other things being equal, the former hold the better jobs, get higher wages, and have more opportunity for success than their new competitors. In industry and politics men have a great many more positions and they monopolize the most important posts. In addition to all this, they enjoy a traditional prestige that the education of children tends in every way to support, for the present enshrines the past—and in the past all history has been made by men. At the present time, when women are beginning to take part in the affairs of the world, it is still a world that belongs to men—they have no doubt of it at all and women have scarcely any. To decline to be the Other, to refuse to be a party to the deal—this would be for women to renounce all the advantages conferred upon them by their alliance with the superior caste. Man-the-sovereign will provide woman-the-liege with material protection and will undertake the moral justification of her existence; thus she can evade at once both economic risk and the metaphysical risk of a liberty in which ends and aims must be contrived without assistance. Indeed, along with the ethical urge of each individual to affirm his subjective existence, there is also the temptation to forgo liberty and become a thing. This is an inauspicious road, for he who takes it—passive, lost, ruined—becomes henceforth the creature of another's will, frustrated in his transcendence and deprived of every value. But it is an easy road; on it one avoids the strain involved in undertaking an authentic existence. When man makes of woman the Other, he may, then, expect her to manifest deep-seated tendencies toward complicity. Thus, woman may fail to lay claim to the status of subject because she lacks definite resources, because she feels the necessary bond that ties her to man regardless of reciprocity, and because she is often very well pleased with her role as the Other.

But it will be asked at once: how did all this begin? It is easy to see that the duality of the sexes, like any duality, gives rise to conflict. And doubtless the winner will assume the status of absolute. But why should man have won from the start? It seems possible that women could have won the victory; or that the outcome of the conflict might never have been decided. How is it that this world has always belonged to the men and that things have begun to change only recently? Is this change a good thing? Will it bring about an equal sharing of the world between men and women?

These questions are not new, and they have often been answered. But the very fact that woman *is the Other* tends to cast suspicion upon all the justifications that men have ever been able to provide for it. These have all too evidently been dictated by men's interest. A little-known feminist of the seventeenth century, Poulain de la Barre, put it this way: "All that has been written about women by men should be suspect, for the men are at once judge and party to the lawsuit." Everywhere, at all times, the males have displayed their satisfaction in feeling that they are the lords of creation. "Blessed be God . . . that He did not make me a woman," say the Jews in their morning prayers, while their wives pray a note of resignation: "Blessed be the Lord, who created me according to His will." The first among the blessings

for which Plato thanked the gods was that he had been created free, not enslaved; the second, a man, not a woman. But the males could not enjoy this privilege fully unless they believed it to be founded on the absolute and the eternal; they sought to make the fact of their supremacy into a right. "Being men, those who have made and compiled the laws have favored their own sex, and jurists have elevated these laws into principles," to quote Poulain de la Barre once more.

Legislators, priests, philosophers, writers, and scientists have striven to show that the subordinate position of woman is willed in heaven and advantageous on earth. The religions invented by men reflect this wish for domination. In the legends of Eve and Pandora men have taken up arms against women. They have made use of philosophy and theology, as the quotations from Aristotle and St. Thomas have shown. Since ancient times satirists and moralists have delighted in showing up the weaknesses of women. We are familiar with the savage indictments hurled against women throughout French literature. Montherlant, for example, follows the tradition of Jean de Meung, though with less gusto. This hostility may at times be well founded, often it is gratuitous; but in truth it more or less successfully conceals a desire for self-justification. As Montaigne says, "It is easier to accuse one sex than to excuse the other." Sometimes what is going on is clear enough. For instance, the Roman law limiting the rights of woman cited "the imbecility, the instability of the sex" just when the weakening of family ties seemed to threaten the interests of male heirs. And in the effort to keep the married woman under guardianship, appeal was made in the sixteenth century to the authority of St. Augustine, who declared that "woman is a creature neither decisive nor constant," at a time when the single woman was thought capable of managing her property. Montaigne understood clearly how arbitrary and unjust was woman's appointed lot: "Women are not in the wrong when they decline to accept the rules laid down for them, since the men make these rules without consulting them. No wonder intrigue and strife abound." But he did not go so far as to champion their cause.

It was only later, in the eighteenth century, that genuinely democratic men began to view the matter objectively. Diderot, among others, strove to show that woman is, like man, a human being. Later John Stuart Mill came fervently to her defense. But these philosophers displayed unusual impartiality. In the nineteenth century the feminist quarrel became again a quarrel of partisans. One of the consequences of the industrial revolution was the entrance of women into productive labor, and it was just here that the claims of the feminists emerged from the realm of theory and acquired an economic basis, while their opponents became the more aggressive. Although landed property lost power to some extent, the bourgeoisie clung to the old morality that found the guarantee of private property in the solidity of the family. Woman was ordered back into the home the more harshly as her emancipation became a real menace. Even within the working class the men endeavored to restrain woman's liberation, because they began to see the women as dangerous competitors—the more so because they were accustomed to work for lower wages.[8]

In proving woman's inferiority, the antifeminists then began to draw not only upon religion, philosophy, and theology, as before, but also upon science—biology, experimental psychology, etc. At most they were willing to grant "equality in difference" to the *other* sex. That profitable formula is most significant; it is precisely like the "equal but separate" formula of the Jim Crow laws aimed at the North American Negroes. As is well known, this so-called egalitarian segregation has resulted only in the most extreme discrimination. The similarity just noted is in no way due to chance, for whether it is a race, a caste, a class, or a sex that is reduced to a position of inferiority, the methods of justification are the same. "The eternal feminine" corresponds to "the black soul" and to "the Jewish character." True, the Jewish problem is on the whole very different from the other two—to the anti-Semite the Jew is not so much an inferior as he is an enemy for whom there is to be granted no place on earth, for whom annihilation is the fate desired. But there are deep similarities between the situation of woman and that of the Negro. Both are being emancipated today from a like paternalism, and the former master class wishes to "keep them in their place"—that is, the place chosen for them. In both cases the former masters lavish more or less sincere eulogies, either on the virtues of "the good Negro" with his dormant, childish, merry soul—the submissive Negro—or on the merits of the woman who is "truly feminine"—that is, frivolous, infantile, irresponsible—the submissive woman. In both cases the dominant class bases its argument on a state of affairs that it has itself created. As George Bernard Shaw puts it, in substance, "The American white relegates the black to the rank of shoeshine boy; and he concludes from this that the black is good for nothing but shining shoes." This vicious circle is met with in all analogous circumstances; when an individual (or a group of individuals) is kept in a situation of inferiority, the fact is that he *is* inferior. But the significance of the verb *to be* must be rightly understood here; it is in bad faith to give it a static value when it really has the dynamic Hegelian sense of "to have become." Yes, women on the whole *are* today inferior to men; that is, their situation affords them fewer possibilities. The question is: should that state of affairs continue?

Many men hope that it will continue; not all have given up the battle. The conservative bourgeoisie still see in the emancipation of women a menace to their morality and their interests. Some men dread feminine competition. Recently a male student wrote in the *Hebdo-Latin:* "Every woman student who goes into medicine or law robs us of a job." He never questioned his rights in this world. And economic interests are not the only ones concerned. One of the benefits that oppression confers upon the oppressors is that the most humble among them is made to *feel* superior; thus, a "poor white" in the South can console himself with the thought that he is not a "dirty nigger"—and the more prosperous whites cleverly exploit this pride.

Similarly, the most mediocre of males feels himself a demigod as compared with women. It was much easier for M. de Montherlant to think himself a hero when he faced women (and women chosen for his purpose) than when he was obliged to act the man among men—something many women have done better than he, for that matter. And in September 1948, in one of his articles in the *Figaro littéraire,* Claude Mauriac—whose great originality is admired by all—could[9] write regarding women: "*We* listen on a tone [*sic!*] of polite indifference . . .

to the most brilliant among them, well knowing that her wit reflects more or less luminously ideas that come from *us*." Evidently the speaker referred to is not reflecting the ideas of Mauriac himself, for no one knows of his having any. It may be that she reflects ideas originating with men, but then, even among men there are those who have been known to appropriate ideas not their own; and one can well ask whether Claude Mauriac might not find more interesting a conversation reflecting Descartes, Marx, or Gide rather than himself. What is really remarkable is that by using the questionable *we* he identifies himself with St. Paul, Hegel, Lenin, and Nietzsche, and from the lofty eminence of their grandeur looks down disdainfully upon the bevy of women who make bold to converse with him on a footing of equality. In truth, I know of more than one woman who would refuse to suffer with patience Mauriac's "tone of polite indifference."

I have lingered on this example because the masculine attitude is here displayed with disarming ingenuousness. But men profit in many more subtle ways from the otherness, the alterity of woman. Here is miraculous balm for those afflicted with an inferiority complex, and indeed no one is more arrogant toward women, more aggressive or scornful, than the man who is anxious about his virility. Those who are not fear-ridden in the presence of their fellow men are much more disposed to recognize a fellow creature in woman; but even to these the myth of woman, the Other, is precious for many reasons.[10] They cannot be blamed for not cheerfully relinquishing all the benefits they derive from the myth, for they realize what they would lose in relinquishing woman as they fancy her to be, while they fail to realize what they have to gain from the woman of tomorrow. Refusal to pose oneself as the Subject, unique and absolute, requires great self-denial. Furthermore, the vast majority of men make no such claim explicitly. They do not *postulate* woman as inferior, for today they are too thoroughly imbued with the ideal of democracy not to recognize all human beings as equals.

In the bosom of the family, woman seems in the eyes of childhood and youth to be clothed in the same social dignity as the adult males. Later on, the young man, desiring and loving, experiences the resistance, the independence of the woman desired and loved; in marriage, he respects woman as wife and mother, and in the concrete events of conjugal life she stands there before him as a free being. He can therefore feel that social subordination as between the sexes no longer exists and that on the whole, in spite of differences, woman is an equal. As, however, he observes some points of inferiority—the most important being unfitness for the professions—he attributes these to natural causes. When he is in a cooperative and benevolent relation with woman, his theme is the principle of abstract equality, and he does not base his attitude upon such inequality as may exist. But when he is in conflict with her, the situation is reversed: his theme will be the existing inequality, and he will even take it as justification for denying abstract equality.[11]

So it is that many men will affirm as if in good faith that women *are* the equals of man and that they have nothing to clamor for, while *at the same time* they will say that women can never be the equals of man and that their demands are in vain. It is, in point of fact, a difficult matter for man to realize the extreme importance of social discriminations which seem outwardly insignificant but which produce in woman moral and intellectual effects so profound that they appear to spring from her original nature.[12] The most sympathetic of men never fully comprehend woman's concrete situation. And there is no reason to put much trust in the men when they rush to the defense of privileges whose full extent they can hardly measure. We shall not, then, permit ourselves to be intimidated by the number and violence of the attacks launched against women, nor to be entrapped by the self-seeking eulogies bestowed on the "true woman," nor to profit by the enthusiasm for woman's destiny manifested by men who would not for the world have any part of it.

We should consider the arguments of the feminists with no less suspicion, however, for very often their controversial aim deprives them of all real value. If the "woman question" seems trivial, it is because masculine arrogance has made of it a "quarrel"; and when quarreling, one no longer reasons well. People have tirelessly sought to prove that woman is superior, inferior, or equal to man. Some say that, having been created after Adam, she is evidently a secondary being; others say on the contrary that Adam was only a rough draft and that God succeeded in producing the human being in perfection when He created Eve. Woman's brain is smaller; yes, but it is relatively large. Christ was made a man; yes, but perhaps for his greater humility. Each argument at once suggests its opposite, and both are often fallacious. If we are to gain understanding, we must get out of these ruts; we must discard the vague notions of superiority, inferiority, equality which have hitherto corrupted every discussion of the subject and start afresh.

Very well, but just how shall we pose the question? And, to begin with, who are we to propound it at all? Man is at once judge and party to the case; but so is woman. What we need is an angel—neither man nor woman—but where shall we find one? Still, the angel would be poorly qualified to speak, for an angel is ignorant of all the basic facts involved in the problem. With a hermaphrodite we should be no better off, for here the situation is most peculiar; the hermaphrodite is not really the combination of a whole man and a whole woman, but consists of parts of each and thus is neither. It looks to me as if there are, after all, certain women who are best qualified to elucidate the situation of woman. Let us not be misled by the sophism that because Epimenides was a Cretan he was necessarily a liar; it is not a mysterious essence that compels men and women to act in good or in bad faith, it is their situation that inclines them more or less toward the search for truth. Many of today's women, fortunate in the restoration of all the privileges pertaining to the estate of the human being, can afford the luxury of impartiality—we even recognize its necessity. We are no longer like our partisan elders; by and large we have won the game. In recent debates on the status of women the United Nations has persistently maintained that the equality of the sexes is now becoming a reality, and already some of us have never had to sense in our femininity an inconvenience or an obstacle. Many problems appear to us to be more pressing than those which concern us in particular, and this detachment even allows us to hope that our attitude will be objective. Still, we know the feminine world more intimately than do the men because we have our roots in it, we grasp more immediately than do

men what it means to a human being to be feminine; and we are more concerned with such knowledge. I have said that there are more pressing problems, but this does not prevent us from seeing some importance in asking how the fact of being women will affect our lives. What opportunities precisely have been given us and what withheld? What fate awaits our younger sisters, and what directions should they take? It is significant that books by women on women are in general animated in our day less by a wish to demand our rights than by an effort toward clarity and understanding. As we emerge from an era of excessive controversy, this book is offered as one attempt among others to confirm that statement.

But it is doubtless impossible to approach any human problem with a mind free from bias. The way in which questions are put, the points of view assumed, presuppose a relativity of interest; all characteristics imply values, and every objective description, so called, implies an ethical background. Rather than attempt to conceal principles more or less definitely implied, it is better to state them openly at the beginning. This will make it unnecessary to specify on every page in just what sense one uses such words as *superior, inferior, better, worse, progress, reaction,* and the like. If we survey some of the works on woman, we note that one of the points of view most frequently adopted is that of the public good, the general interest; and one always means by this the benefit of society as one wishes it to be maintained or established. For our part, we hold that the only public good is that which assures the private good of the citizens; we shall pass judgment on institutions according to their effectiveness in giving concrete opportunities to individuals. But we do not confuse the idea of private interest with that of happiness, although that is another common point of view. Are not women of the harem more happy than women voters? Is not the housekeeper happier than the working woman? It is not too clear just what the word *happy* really means and still less what true values it may mask. There is no possibility of measuring the happiness of others, and it is always easy to describe as happy the situation in which one wishes to place them.

In particular those who are condemned to stagnation are often pronounced happy on the pretext that happiness consists in being at rest. This notion we reject, for our perspective is that of existentialist ethics. Every subject plays his part as such specifically through exploits or projects that serve as a mode of transcendence; he achieves liberty only through a continual reaching out toward other liberties. There is no justification for present existence other than its expansion into an indefinitely open future. Every time transcendence falls back into immanence, stagnation, there is a degradation of existence into the *"en-soi"*—the brutish life of subjection to given conditions—and of liberty into constraint and contingence. This downfall represents a moral fault if the subject consents to it; if it is inflicted upon him, it spells frustration and oppression. In both cases it is an absolute evil. Every individual concerned to justify his existence feels that his existence involves an undefined need to transcend himself, to engage in freely chosen projects.

Now, what peculiarly signalizes the situation of woman is that she—a free and autonomous being like all human creatures—nevertheless finds herself living in a world where men compel her to assume the status of the Other. They propose to stabilize her as object and to doom her to immanence since her transcendence is to be overshadowed and forever transcended by another ego *(conscience)* which is essential and sovereign. The drama of woman lies in this conflict between the fundamental aspirations of every subject (ego)—who always regards the self as the essential—and the compulsions of a situation in which she is the inessential. How can a human being in woman's situation attain fulfillment? What roads are open to her? Which are blocked? How can independence be recovered in a state of dependency? What circumstances limit woman's liberty and how can they be overcome? These are the fundamental questions on which I would fain throw some light. This means that I am interested in the fortunes of the individual as defined not in terms of happiness but in terms of liberty.

Quite evidently this problem would be without significance if we were to believe that woman's destiny is inevitably determined by physiological, psychological, or economic forces. Hence I shall discuss first of all the light in which woman is viewed by biology, psychoanalysis, and historical materialism. Next I shall try to show exactly how the concept of the "truly feminine" has been fashioned—why woman has been defined as the Other—and what have been the consequences from man's point of view. Then from woman's point of view I shall describe the world in which women must live; and thus we shall be able to envisage the difficulties in their way as, endeavoring to make their escape from the sphere hitherto assigned them, they aspire to full membership in the human race.

CHAPTER 12: CHILDHOOD

One is not born, but rather becomes, a woman. No biological, psychological, or economic fate determines the figure that the human female presents in society; it is civilization as a whole that produces this creature, intermediate between male and eunuch, which is described as feminine. Only the intervention of someone else can establish an individual as an *Other*. Insofar as he exists in and for himself, the child would hardly be able to think of himself as sexually differentiated. In girls as in boys the body is first of all the radiation of a subjectivity, the instrument that makes possible the comprehension of the world: it is through the eyes, the hands, that children apprehend the universe, and not through the sexual parts. The dramas of birth and of weaning unfold after the same fashion for nurslings of both sexes; these have the same interests and the same pleasures; sucking is at first the source of their most agreeable sensations; then they go through an anal phase in which they get their greatest satisfaction from the excretory functions, which they have in common. Their genital development is analogous; they explore their bodies with the same curiosity and the same indifference; from clitoris and penis they derive the same vague pleasure. As their sensibility comes to require an object, it is turned toward the mother: the soft, smooth, resilient feminine flesh is what arouses sexual desires, and these desires are prehensile; the girl, like the boy, kisses, handles, and caresses her mother in an aggressive way; they feel the same jealousy if a new child is born, and they show it in similar behavior patterns: rage, sulkiness, urinary difficulties; and they resort to the same coquettish tricks to gain the love of adults. Up to the age of twelve the little girl is as strong as her brothers, and she shows the same mental powers; there is no field where she is debarred from engaging in rivalry with them. If, well before puberty and sometimes even from early infancy, she seems to us to be already sexually determined, this is not because mysterious instincts directly doom her to passivity, coquetry, maternity; it is because the influence of others upon the child is a factor almost from the start, and thus she is indoctrinated with her vocation from her earliest years.

· · ·

At ten or twelve years of age most little girls are truly *"garçons manqués"*—that is to say, children who lack something of being boys. Not only do they feel it as a deprivation and an injustice, but they find that the regime to which they are condemned is unwholesome. In girls the exuberance of life is restrained, their idle vigor turns into nervousness; their too prissy occupations do not use up their superabundant energy; they become bored, and, through boredom and to compensate for their position of inferiority, they give themselves up to gloomy and romantic daydreams; they get a taste for these easy escape mechanisms and lose their sense of reality; they yield to their emotions with uncontrolled excitement; instead of acting, they talk, often commingling serious phrases and senseless words in hodge-podge fashion. Neglected, "misunderstood," they seek consolation in narcissistic fancies: they view themselves as romantic heroines of fiction, with self-admiration and self-pity. Quite naturally they become coquettish and stagy, these defects becoming more conspicuous at puberty. Their malaise shows itself in impatience, tantrums, tears; they enjoy crying—a taste that many women retain in later years—largely because they like to play the part of victims: at once a protest against their hard lot and a way to make themselves appealing. Little girls sometimes watch themselves cry in a mirror, to double the pleasure.

Most young girls' dramas concern their family relationships; they seek to break their ties with mother: now they show hostility toward her, now they retain a keen need for her protection; they would like to monopolize father's love; they are jealous, sensitive, demanding. They often make up stories, imagining that their parents are not really their parents, that they are adopted children. They attribute to their parents a secret life; they muse on their relationships; they often imagine that father is misunderstood, unhappy, that he does not find in his wife an ideal companion such as his daughter could be for him; or, on the contrary, that mother regards him rightly as coarse and brutal, that she is horrified at all physical relations with him. Fantasies, histrionics, childish tragedies, false enthusiasms, odd behavior—the reason for all these must be sought not in a mysterious feminine soul but in the child's environment, her situation.

It is a strange experience for an individual who feels himself to be an autonomous and transcendent subject, an absolute, to discover inferiority in himself as a fixed and preordained essence: it is a strange experience for whoever regards himself as the One to be revealed to himself as otherness, alterity. This is what happens to the little girl when, doing her apprenticeship for life in the world, she grasps what it means to be a woman therein. The sphere to which she belongs is everywhere enclosed, limited, dominated, by the male universe: high as she may raise herself, far as she may venture, there will always be a ceiling over her head, walls that will block her way. The gods of man are in a sky so distant that in truth, for him, there are no gods: the little girl lives among gods in human guise.

This situation is not unique. The American Negroes know it, being partially integrated in a civilization that nevertheless regards them as constituting an inferior caste; what Bigger Thomas, in Richard Wright's *Native Son*,[13] feels with bitterness at the dawn of his life is this definitive inferiority, this accursed alterity, which is written in the color of his skin: he sees airplanes flying by and he knows that because he is black the sky is forbidden to him. Because she is a woman, the little girl knows that she is forbidden the sea and the polar regions, a thousand adventures, a thousand joys: she was born on the wrong side of the line. There is this great difference: the Negroes submit with a feeling of revolt, no privileges compensating for their hard lot, whereas woman is offered inducements to complicity. I have previously called to mind the fact that along with the authentic demand of the subject who wants sovereign freedom, there is in the existent an inauthentic longing for resignation and escape; the delights of passivity are made to seem desirable to the young girl by parents and educators, books and myths, women and men; she is taught to enjoy them from earliest childhood; the temptation becomes more and more insidious; and she is the more fatally bound to yield to those delights as the flight of her transcendence is dashed against harsher obstacles.

But in thus accepting her passive role, the girl also agrees to submit unresistingly to a destiny that is going to be imposed upon her from without, and this calamity frightens her. The young boy, be he ambitious, thoughtless, or timid, looks toward an open future; he will be a seaman or an engineer, he will stay on the farm or go away to the city, he will see the world, he will get rich; he feels free, confronting a future in which the unexpected awaits him. The young girl will be wife, mother, grandmother; she will keep house just as her mother did, she will give her children the same care she herself received when young—she is twelve years old and already her story is written in the heavens. She will discover it day after day without ever making it; she is curious but frightened when she contemplates this life, every stage of which is foreseen and toward which each day moves irresistibly.

[1952]

NOTES

1. *Franchise,* dead today.
2. The Kinsey Report [Alfred C. Kinsey and others: *Sexual Behavior in the Human Male* (W. B. Saunders Co., 1948)] is no exception, for it is limited to describing the sexual characteristics of American men, which is quite a different matter.
3. E. Lévinas expresses this idea most explicitly in his essay *Temps et l'Autre.* "Is there not a case in which otherness, alterity [*altérité*], unquestionably marks the nature of a being, as its essence, an instance of otherness not consisting purely and simply in the opposition of two species of the same genus? I think that the feminine represents the contrary in its absolute sense, this contrariness being in no wise affected by any relation between it and its correlative and thus remaining absolutely other. Sex is not a certain specific difference . . . no more is the sexual difference a mere contradiction. . . . Nor does this difference lie in the duality of two complementary terms, for two complementary terms imply a pre-existing whole. . . . Otherness reaches its full flowering in the feminine, a term of the same rank as consciousness but of opposite meaning."

   I suppose that Lévinas does not forget that woman, too, is aware of her own consciousness, or ego. But it is striking that he deliberately takes a man's point of view, disregarding the reciprocity of subject and object. When he writes that woman is mystery, he implies that she is mystery for man. Thus his description, which is intended to be objective, is in fact an assertion of masculine privilege.
4. See C. Lévi-Strauss: *Les Structures élémentaires de la parenté.* My thanks are due to C. Lévi-Strauss for his kindness in furnishing me with the proofs of his work, which, among others, I have used liberally in Part II.
5. With rare exceptions, perhaps, like certain matriarchal rulers, queens, and the like—Tʀ.
6. See Part II, ch. viii.
7. At the moment an "equal rights" amendment to the Constitution of the United States is before Congress.—Tʀ.
8. See Part II, pp. 129–131.
9. Or at least he thought he could.
10. A significant article on this theme by Michel Carrouges appeared in No. 292 of the *Cahiers du Sud.* He writes indignantly: "Would that there were no woman-myth at all but only a cohort of cooks, matrons, prostitutes, and bluestockings serving functions of pleasure or usefulness!" That is to say, in his view woman has no existence in and for herself; he thinks only of her *function* in the male world. Her reason for existence lies in man. But then, in fact, her poetic "function" as a myth might be more valued than any other. The real problem is precisely to find out why woman should be defined with relation to man.
11. For example, a man will say that he considers his wife in no wise degraded because she has no gainful occupation. The profession of housewife is just as lofty, and so on. But when the first quarrel comes he will exclaim: "Why, you couldn't make your living without me!"
12. The specific purpose of Book II of this study is to describe this process.
13. New York: Harper & Brothers; 1940.

PART IV

1963–1975

1963–1975: Introduction

The 1960s were a decade of social upheaval in the United States marked by the assassinations of President John Kennedy in 1963 and of Martin Luther King, Jr., and Robert Kennedy in 1968. Movements for civil rights and gay rights and against the United States' escalating military involvement in Vietnam strengthened as the decade progressed. The anger and unrest of the period were epitomized by the riots and urban uprisings that foregrounded the poverty and racism of large Northern cities (Detroit, Newark, and Los Angeles); by the 1968 Stonewall Rebellion, which founded the gay/lesbian rights movement; as well as by the bus boycotts, freedom rides, and sit-ins that were a direct response to Southern segregation. Many of the women who became active in the women's movement in this decade learned political activism in these other social justice movements, where they also experienced sexism firsthand.

The so-called second wave of the women's movement was catalyzed by the 1963 publication of Betty Friedan's *The Feminine Mystique*. Her book captured in its analysis of "the problem that has no name" the restlessness and discontent that predominated in the lives of many middle-class white college-educated women, trapped in domesticity by the conservative social values of the 1950s. Some of those women helped to found the National Organization for Women. Many of their college-age daughters became involved in groups like Redstockings or a variety of feminist collectives. Many other women across the spectrum of middle-class American life joined consciousness-raising groups, where they began to share their experiences of life as women. Much feminist activism in the period, influenced by NOW's basically liberal position, continued to focus on issues of access and equal opportunity for women in education, employment, athletics, and politics. Some successes in these areas prompted NOW to revive the campaign for the Equal Rights Amendment, which continued through the 1970s and finally ended in failure in 1982 with the amendment ratified by only 32 of the required 36 states.

For women of color (a designation that no one had yet learned), identification with feminist issues cut across and into their alliances with and allegiances to their racial and ethnic origins and struggles. Despite those strains and crosscurrents, women of color, trained in radical politics and organizing in the civil rights movement, wrote feminist theory and worked in the feminist movement, both in separate organizations like the National Black Feminist Organization and in organizations with white women.

The work and activism of radical feminists and lesbian feminists was essential to development of feminist thought in this period. With their analysis of the sex/gender system, and particularly of sexuality and reproduction as the root causes of women's oppression, key texts like Shulamith Firestone's *The Dialectic of Sex* (1970) and Kate Millett's *Sexual Politics* (1970) as well as lesbian theory by Charlotte Bunch and

Ti-Grace Atkinson, crystallized the notion that "the personal is political." These women articulated the necessity of radical transformations in sexuality and the patriarchal family and the value of separatism as a strategy of survival and resistance in women's lives, spaces, institutions, and organizations.

In the early 1970s, although U.S. national politics were in disarray with the end of the Vietnam War and the resignation of President Nixon, feminists were able to consolidate some gains and establish some institutions. The first women's studies programs were created in these years, as were rape crisis centers and hotlines, battered women's shelters, women's centers, and women's bookstores. Feminist activism in this period achieved perhaps its greatest victory in the 1973 Supreme Court decision of *Roe v. Wade,* which legalized women's access to abortion. This campaign for reproductive choice pulled together many of the strands of argument about birth control and women's sexuality that had run through the century. However, the climate in which this success occurred was heated from the start, and the scope of women's reproductive choice and freedom remains a flashpoint in national politics.

In the years between 1963 and 1975, one might say that a U.S. women's movement re-emerged as a force for change in national politics, and thousands of women learned that "sisterhood is powerful" through work in liberal and radical organizations. The work of the next decade was to re-examine this sisterhood from the perspective and through the critiques of the women it excluded: women of color, poor and working-class women, Third World women. The 1975 World Conference on Women in Mexico City and the 1976 founding conference of the U.N. Decade for Women can perhaps be seen as preliminary markers of a feminism that thinks both locally and globally.

36

The Problem That Has No Name from The Feminine Mystique

BETTY FRIEDAN

BETTY FRIEDAN United States. 1921– .Writer. Social reformer. Cofounder and first president of National Organization for Women. Led campaign to ratify Equal Rights Amendment. Founding member of National Women's Political Caucus. *The Second Stage* (1981).

The problem lay buried, unspoken, for many years in the minds of American women. It was a strange stirring, a sense of dissatisfaction, a yearning that women suffered in the middle of the twentieth century in the United States. Each suburban wife struggled with it alone. As she made the beds, shopped for groceries, matched slipcover material, ate peanut-butter sandwiches with her children, chauffeured Cub Scouts and Brownies, lay beside her husband at night—she was afraid to ask even of herself the silent question—"Is this all?"

For over fifteen years there was no word of this yearning in the millions of words written about women, for women, in all the columns, books and articles by experts telling women their role was to seek fulfillment as wives and mothers. Over and over women heard in voices of tradition and of Freudian sophistication that they could desire no greater destiny than to glory in their own femininity. Experts told them how to catch a man and keep him, how to breastfeed children and handle their toilet training, how to cope with sibling rivalry and adolescent rebellion; how to buy a dishwasher, bake bread, cook gourmet snails, and build a swimming pool with their own hands; how to dress, look, and act more feminine and make marriage more exciting; how to keep their husbands from dying young and their sons from growing into delinquents. They were taught to pity the neurotic, unfeminine, unhappy women who wanted to be poets or physicists or presidents. They learned that truly feminine women do not want careers, higher education,

political rights—the independence and the opportunities that the old-fashioned feminists fought for. Some women, in their forties and fifties, still remembered painfully giving up those dreams, but most of the younger women no longer even thought about them. A thousand expert voices applauded their femininity, their adjustment, their new maturity. All they had to do was devote their lives from earliest girlhood to finding a husband and bearing children.

By the end of the nineteen-fifties, the average marriage age of women in American dropped to 20, and was still dropping, into the teens. Fourteen million girls were engaged by 17. The proportion of women attending college in comparison with men dropped from 47 percent in 1920 to 35 percent in 1958. A century earlier, women had fought for higher education; now girls went to college to get a husband. By the mid-fifties, 60 percent dropped out of college to marry, or because they were afraid too much education would be a marriage bar. Colleges built dormitories for "married students," but the students were almost always the husbands. A new degree was instituted for the wives—"Ph.T." (Putting Husband Through).

Then American girls began getting married in high school. And the women's magazines, deploring the unhappy statistics about these young marriages, urged that courses on marriage, and marriage counselors, be installed in the high schools. Girls started going steady at twelve and thirteen, in junior high. Manufacturers put out brassieres with false bosoms of foam rubber for little girls of ten. And an advertisement for a child's dress, sizes 3–6x, in the *New York Times* in the fall of 1960, said: "She Too Can Join the Man-Trap Set."

By the end of the fifties, the United States birthrate was overtaking India's. The birth-control movement, renamed Planned Parenthood, was asked to find a method whereby women who had been advised that a third or fourth baby would be born dead or defective might have it anyhow. Statisticians were especially astounded at the fantastic increase in the number of babies among college women. Where once they had two children, now they had four, five, six. Women who had once wanted careers were now making careers out of having babies. So rejoiced *Life* magazine in a 1956 paean to the movement of American women back to the home.

In a New York hospital, a woman had a nervous breakdown when she found she could not breast-feed her baby. In other hospitals, women dying of cancer refused a drug which research had proved might save their lives: its side effects were said to be unfeminine: "If I have only one life, let me live it as a blonde," a larger-than-life-sized picture of a pretty, vacuous woman proclaimed from news-paper, magazine, and drugstore ads. And across America, three out of every ten women dyed their hair blonde. They ate a chalk called Metrecal, instead of food, to shrink to the size of the thin young models. Department-store buyers reported that American women, since 1939, had become three and four sizes smaller. "Women are out to fit the clothes, instead of vice-versa," one buyer said.

Interior decorators were designing kitchens with mosaic murals and original paintings, for kitchens were once again the center of women's lives. Home sewing became a million-dollar industry. Many women no longer left their homes, except to shop, chauffeur their children, or attend a social engage-ment with their husbands. Girls were growing up in America without ever having jobs outside the home. In the late fifties, a sociological phenomenon was suddenly remarked: a third of American women now worked, but most were no longer young and very few were pursuing careers. They were married women who held part-time jobs, selling or secretar-ial, to put their husbands through school, their sons through college, or to help pay the mortgage. Or they were widows supporting families. Fewer and fewer women were entering professional work. The shortages in the nursing, social work, and teaching professions caused crises in almost every American city. Concerned over the Soviet Union's lead in the space race, scientists noted that America's greatest source of unused brain-power was women. But girls would not study physics: it was "unfeminine." A girl refused a science fellowship at Johns Hopkins to take a job in a real-estate office. All she wanted, she said, was what every other American girl wanted—to get married, have four children and live in a nice house in a nice suburb.

The suburban housewife—she was the dream image of the young American women and the envy, it was said, of women all over the world. The Amer-ican housewife—freed by science and labor-saving appliances from the drudgery, the dangers of child-birth and the illnesses of her grandmother. She was healthy, beautiful, educated, concerned only about her husband, her children, her home. She had found true feminine fulfillment. As a housewife and mother, she was respected as a full and equal part-ner to man in his world. She was free to choose automobiles, clothes, appliances, supermarkets; she had everything that women ever dreamed of.

In the fifteen years after World War II, this mys-tique of feminine fulfillment became the cherished and self-perpetuating core of contemporary Amer-ican culture. Millions of women lived their lives in the image of those pretty pictures of the American suburban housewife, kissing their husbands good-bye in front of the picture window, depositing their stationwagonsful of children at school, and smiling as they ran the new electric waxer over the spotless kitchen floor. They baked their own bread, sewed their own and their children's clothes, kept their new washing machines and dryers running all day. They changed the sheets on the beds twice a week instead of once, took the rug-hooking class in adult education, and pitied their poor frustrated mothers, who had dreamed of having a career. Their only dream was to be perfect wives and mothers; their highest ambition to have five children and a beauti-ful house, their only fight to get and keep their hus-bands. They had no thought for the unfeminine problems of the world outside the home; they wanted the men to make the major decisions. They gloried in their role as women, and wrote proudly on the census blank: "Occupation: housewife."

For over fifteen years, the words written for women, and the words women used when they talked to each other, while their husbands sat on the other side of the room and talked shop or politics or septic tanks, were about problems with their chil-dren, or how to keep their husbands happy, or improve their children's school, or cook chicken, or make slipcovers. Nobody argued whether women were inferior or superior to men; they were simply different. Words like "emancipation" and "career" sounded strange and embarrassing; no one had used them for years. When a Frenchwoman named Simone de Beauvoir wrote a book called *The Second*

Sex, an American critic commented that she obviously "didn't know what life was all about," and besides, she was talking about French women. The "woman problem" in America no longer existed.

If a woman had a problem in the 1950s and 1960s, she knew that something must be wrong with her marriage, or with herself. Other women were satisfied with their lives, she thought. What kind of a woman was she if she did not feel this mysterious fulfillment waxing the kitchen floor? She was so ashamed to admit her dissatisfaction that she never knew how many other women shared it. If she tried to tell her husband, he didn't understand what she was talking about. She did not really understand it herself. For over fifteen years women in America found it harder to talk about this problem than about sex. Even the psychoanalysts had no name for it. When a woman went to a psychiatrist for help, as many women did, she would say, "I'm so ashamed," or "I must be hopelessly neurotic." "I don't know what's wrong with women today," a suburban psychiatrist said uneasily. "I only know something is wrong because most of my patients happen to be women. And their problem isn't sexual." Most women with this problem did not go to see a psychoanalyst, however. "There's nothing wrong really," they kept telling themselves. "There isn't any problem."

But on an April morning in 1959, I heard a mother of four, having coffee with four other mothers in a suburban development fifteen miles from New York, say in a tone of quiet desperation, "the problem." And the others knew, without words, that she was not talking about a problem with her husband, or her children, or her home. Suddenly they realized they all shared the same problem, the problem that has no name. They began, hesitantly, to talk about it. Later, after they had picked up their children at nursery school and taken them home to nap, two of the women cried, in sheer relief, just to know they were not alone.

Gradually I came to realize that the problem that has no name was shared by countless women in America. As a magazine writer I often interviewed women about problems with their children, or their marriages, or their houses, or their communities. But after a while I began to recognize the telltale signs of this other problem. I saw the same signs in suburban ranch houses and split-levels on Long Island and in New Jersey and Westchester County; in colonial houses in a small Massachusetts town; on patios in Memphis; in suburban and city apartments; in living rooms in the Midwest. Sometimes I sensed the problem, not as a reporter, but as a suburban housewife, for during this time I was also bringing up my own three children in Rockland County, New York. I heard echoes of the problem in college dormitories and semi-private maternity wards, at PTA meetings and luncheons of the League of Women Voters, at suburban cocktail parties, in station wagons waiting for trains, and in snatches of conversation overheard at Schrafft's. The groping words I heard from other women, on quiet afternoons when children were at school or on quiet evenings when husbands worked late, I think I understood first as a woman long before I understood their larger social and psychological implications.

Just what was this problem that has no name? What were the words a woman used when they tried to express it? Sometimes women would say "I feel empty somehow . . . incomplete." Or she would say, "I feel as if I don't exist." Sometimes she blotted out the feeling with a tranquilizer. Sometimes she thought the problem was with her husband, or her children, or that what she really needed was to redecorate her house, or move to a better neighborhood, or have an affair, or another baby. Sometimes, she went to a doctor with symptoms she could hardly describe: "A tired feeling . . . I get so angry with the children it scares me . . . I feel like crying without any reason." (A Cleveland doctor called it "the housewife's syndrome.") A number of women told me about great bleeding blisters that break out on their hands and arms. "I call it the housewife's blight," said a family doctor in Pennsylvania. "I see it so often lately in these young women with four, five and six children who bury themselves in their dishpans. But it isn't caused by detergent and it isn't cured by cortisone."

Sometimes a woman would tell me that the feeling gets so strong she runs out of the house and walks through the streets. Or she stays inside her house and cries. Or her children tell her a joke, and she doesn't laugh because she doesn't hear it. I talked to women who had spent years on the analyst's couch, working out their "adjustment to the feminine role," their blocks to "fulfillment as a wife and mother." But the desperate tone in these women's voices, and the look in their eyes, was the same as the tone and the look of other women, who were sure they had no problem, even though they did have a strange feeling of desperation.

. . .

And so she must accept the fact that "American women's unhappiness is merely the most recently won of women's rights," and adjust and say with the happy housewife found by *Newsweek:* "We ought to salute the wonderful freedom we all have and be proud of our lives today. I have had college and I've worked, but being a housewife is the most rewarding and satisfying role. . . . My mother was never included in my father's business affairs . . . she couldn't get out of the house and away from us children. But I am an equal to my husband; I can go along with him on business trips and to social business affairs."

The alternative offered was a choice that few women would contemplate. In the sympathetic words of the *New York Times:* "All admit to being deeply frustrated at times by the lack of privacy, the physical burden, the routine of family life, the confinement of it. However, none would give up her home and family if she had the choice to make again." *Redbook* commented: "Few women would want to thumb their noses at husbands, children and community and go off on their own. Those who do may be talented individuals, but they rarely are successful women."

The year American women's discontent boiled over, it was also reported (*Look*) that the more than 21,000,000 American women who are single, widowed, or divorced do not cease even after fifty their frenzied, desperate search for a man. And the search begins early—for seventy percent of all American women now marry before they are twenty-four. A pretty twenty-five-year-old secretary took thirty-five different jobs in six months in the futile hope of finding a husband. Women were moving from one political club to another, taking evening courses in accounting or sailing, learning to play golf or ski, joining a number of churches in succession, going to bars alone, in their ceaseless search for a man.

Of the growing thousands of women currently getting private psychiatric help in the United States, the married ones were reported dissatisfied with their marriages, the unmarried ones suffering from anxiety and, finally, depression. Strangely, a number of psychiatrists stated that, in their experience, unmarried women patients were happier than married ones. So the doors of all those pretty suburban houses opened a crack to permit a glimpse of uncounted thousands of American housewives who suffered alone from a problem that suddenly everyone was talking about, and beginning to take for granted, as one of those unreal problems in American life that can never be solved—like the hydrogen bomb. By 1962 the plight of the trapped American housewife had become a national parlor game. Whole issues of magazines, newspaper columns, books learned and frivolous, educational conferences and television panels were devoted to the problem.

Even so, most men, and some women, still did not know that this problem was real. But those who had faced it honestly knew that all the superficial remedies, the sympathetic advice, the scolding words and the cheering words were somehow drowning the problem in unreality. A bitter laugh was beginning to be heard from American women. They were admired, envied, pitied, theorized over until they were sick of it, offered drastic solutions or silly choices that no one could take seriously. They got all kinds of advice from the growing armies of marriage and child-guidance counselors, psychotherapists, and armchair psychologists, on how to adjust to their role as housewives. No other road to fulfillment was offered to American women in the middle of the twentieth century. Most adjusted to their role and suffered or ignored the problem that has no name. It can be less painful for a woman not to hear the strange, dissatisfied voice stirring within her.

It is no longer possible to ignore that voice, to dismiss the desperation of so many American women. This is not what being a woman means, no matter what the experts say. For human suffering there is a reason; perhaps the reason has not been found because the right questions have not been asked, or pressed far enough. I do not accept the answer that there is no problem because American women have luxuries that women in other times and lands never dreamed of; part of the strange newness of the problem is that it cannot be understood in terms of the age-old material problems of man: poverty, sickness, hunger, cold. The women who suffer this problem have a hunger that food cannot fill. It persists in women whose husbands are struggling interns and law clerks, or prosperous doctors and lawyers; in wives of workers and executives who make $5,000 a year or $50,000. It is not caused by lack of material advantages; it may not even be felt by women preoccupied with desperate problems of hunger, poverty or illness. And women who think it will be solved by more money, a bigger house, a second car, moving to a better suburb, often discover it gets worse.

It is no longer possible today to blame the problem on loss of femininity: to say that education and independence and equality with men have made American women unfeminine. I have heard so many women try to deny this dissatisfied voice within themselves because it does not fit the pretty picture of femininity the experts have given them. I think, in fact, that this is the first clue to the mystery: the problem cannot be understood in the generally accepted terms by which scientists have studied women, doctors have treated them, counselors have advised them, and writers have written about them. Women who suffer this problem, in whom this voice is stirring, have lived their whole lives in the pursuit of feminine fulfillment. They are not career women (although career women may have other problems); they are women whose greatest ambition has been marriage and children. For the oldest of these women, these daughters of the American middle class, no other dream was possible. The ones in their forties and fifties who once had other dreams gave them up and threw themselves joyously into life as housewives. For the youngest, the new wives and mothers, this was the only dream. They are the ones who quit high school and college to marry, or marked time in some job in which they had no real interest until they married. These women are very "feminine" in the usual sense, and yet they still suffer the problem.

. . .

The fact is that no one today is muttering angrily about "women's rights," even though more and more women have gone to college. In a recent study of all the classes that have graduated from Barnard College,[1] a significant minority of earlier graduates blamed their education for making them want "rights," later classes blamed their education for giving them career dreams, but recent graduates blamed the college for making them feel it was not enough simply to be a housewife and mother; they did not want to feel guilty if they did not read books or take part in community activities. But if education is not the cause of the problem, the fact that education somehow festers in these women may be a clue.

. . .

Can the problem that has no name be somehow related to the domestic routine of the housewife? When a woman tries to put the problem into words, she often merely describes the daily life she leads. What is there in this recital of comfortable domestic detail that could possibly cause such a feeling of desperation? Is she trapped simply by the enormous demands of her role as modern housewife: wife, mistress, mother, nurse, consumer, cook, chauffeur; expert on interior decoration, child care, appliance repair, furniture refinishing, nutrition, and education? Her day is fragmented as she rushes from dishwasher to washing machine to telephone to dryer to station wagon to supermarket, and delivers Johnny to the Little League field, takes Janey to dancing class, gets the lawnmower fixed and meets the 6:45. She can never spend more than 15 minutes on any one thing; she has no time to read books, only magazines; even if she had time, she has lost the power to concentrate. At the end of the day, she is so terribly tired that sometimes her husband has to take over and put the children to bed.

This terrible tiredness took so many women to doctors in the 1950s that one decided to investigate it. He found, surprisingly, that his patients suffering from "housewife's fatigue" slept more than an adult needed to sleep—as much as ten hours a day—and that the actual energy they expended on housework did not tax their capacity. The real problem must be something else, he decided—perhaps boredom. Some doctors told their women patients they must get out of the house for a day, treat themselves to a movie in town. Others prescribed tranquilizers.

Many suburban housewives were taking tranquilizers like cough drops. "You wake up in the morning, and you feel as if there's no point in going on another day like this. So you take a tranquilizer because it makes you not care so much that it's pointless."

It is easy to see the concrete details that trap the suburban housewife, the continual demands on her time. But the chains that bind her in her trap are chains in her own mind and spirit. They are chains made up of mistaken ideas and misinterpreted facts, of incomplete truths and unreal choices. They are not easily seen and not easily shaken off.

How can any woman see the whole truth within the bounds of her own life? How can she believe that voice inside herself, when it denies the conventional, accepted truths by which she has been living? And yet the women I have talked to, who are finally listening to that inner voice, seem in some incredible way to be groping through to a truth that has defied the experts.

I think the experts in a great many fields have been holding pieces of that truth under their microscopes for a long time without realizing it. I found pieces of it in certain new research and theoretical developments in psychological, social and biological science whose implications for women seem never to have been examined. I found many clues by talking to suburban doctors, gynecologists, obstetricians, child-guidance clinicians, college professors, marriage counselors, psychiatrists and ministers—questioning them not on their theories, but on their actual experience in treating American women. I became aware of a growing body of evidence, much of which has not been reported publicly because it does not fit current modes of thought about women—evidence which throws into question the standards of feminine normality, feminine adjustment, feminine fulfillment, and feminine maturity by which most women are still trying to live.

I began to see in a strange new light the American return to early marriage and the large families that are causing the population explosion; the recent movement to natural childbirth and breastfeeding; suburban conformity, and the new neuroses, character pathologies and sexual problems being reported by the doctors. I began to see new dimensions to old problems that have long been taken for granted among women: menstrual difficulties, sexual frigidity, promiscuity, pregnancy fears, childbirth depression, the high incidence of emotional breakdown and suicide among women in their twenties and thirties, the menopause crises, the so-called passivity and immaturity of American men, the discrepancy between women's tested intellectual abilities in childhood and their adult achievement, the changing incidence of adult sexual orgasm in American women, and persistent problems in psychotherapy and in women's education.

If I am right, the problem that has no name stirring in the minds of so many American women today is not a matter of loss of femininity or too much education, or the demands of domesticity. It is far more important than anyone recognizes. It is the key to these other new and old problems which have been torturing women and their husbands and children, and puzzling their doctors and educators for years. It may well be the key to our future as a nation and a culture. We can no longer ignore that voice within women that says: "I want something more than my husband and my children and my home."

[1963]

NOTE

1. Marian Freda Poverman, "Alumnae on Parade," *Barnard Alumnae Magazine,* July 1957.

 37

The System at War with Itself from Purity and Danger

M A R Y   D O U G L A S

MARY DOUGLAS Italy. 1921–   . Anthropologist. Theorist of ritual. Lives and works primarily in England. *Natural Symbols* (1970), *Leviticus as Literature* (1999), *Implicit Meanings: Selected Essays in Anthropology* (1999).

Perhaps all social systems are built on contradiction, in some sense at war with themselves. But in some cases the various ends which individuals are encouraged to pursue are more harmoniously related than in others.

Sexual collaboration is by nature fertile, constructive, the common basis of social life. But sometimes we find that instead of dependence and harmony, sexual institutions express rigid separation and violent antagonism.

· · ·

In primitive cultures, almost by definition, the distinction of the sexes is the primary social distinction. This means that some important institutions always rest on the difference of sex. If the social structure were weakly organised, then men and women might still hope to follow their own fancies in choosing and discarding sexual partners, with no grievous consequences for society at large. But if the primitive social structure is strictly articulated, it is almost bound to impinge heavily on the relation between men and women. Then we find pollution ideas enlisted to bind men and women to their allotted roles.

There is one exception we should note at once. Sex is likely to be pollution-free in a society where sexual roles are enforced directly. In such a case anyone who threatened to deviate would be promptly punished with physical force. This supposes an administrative efficiency and consensus which are rare anywhere and specially in primitive societies. As an example we can consider the Walbiri of Central Australia, a people who unhesitatingly apply force to ensure that the sexual behaviour of individuals shall not undermine that part of the social structure which rests upon marital relations (Meggitt). As in the rest of Australia, a great part of the social system depends upon rules governing marriage. The Walbiri live in a hard desert environment. They are aware of the difficulty of community survival and their culture accepts as one of its objectives that all members of the community shall work and be cared for according to their ability and needs. This means that responsibility for the infirm and old falls upon the hale. A strict discipline is asserted throughout the community, young are subject to their seniors, and above all, women are subject to men. A married woman usually lives at a distance from her father and brothers. This means that though she has a theoretical claim

to their protection, in practice it is null. She is in the control of her husband. As a general rule if the female sex were completely subject to the male, no problem would be posed by the principle of male dominance. It could be enforced ruthlessly and directly wherever it applied. This seems to be what happens among the Walbiri. For the least complaint or neglect of duty Walbiri women are beaten or speared. No blood compensation can be claimed for a wife killed by her husband, and no one has the right to intervene between husband and wife. Public opinion never reproaches the man who has violently, or even lethally, asserted his authority over his wife. Thus it is impossible for a woman to play off one man against another. However energetically they may try to seduce one another's wives the men are in perfect accord on one point. They are agreed that they should never allow their sexual desires to give an individual woman bargaining power or scope for intrigue.

These people have no beliefs concerning sex pollution. Even menstrual blood is not avoided, and there are no beliefs that contact with it brings danger. Although the definition of married status is important in their society it is protected by overt means. Here there is nothing precarious or contradictory about male dominance.

No constraints are imposed on individual Walbiri men. They seduce one another's women if they get a chance, without showing any special concern for the social structure based on marriage. The latter is preserved by the thoroughgoing subordination of women to men and by the recognised system of self-help. When a man poaches on another's sexual preserve he knows what he risks, a fight and possible death. The system is perfectly simple. There are conflicts between men, but not between principles. No moral judgment is evoked in one situation which is likely to be contradicted in another. People are held to these particular roles by the threat of physical violence. . . .

It is important to recognise that male dominance does not always flourish with such ruthless simplicity. [W]hen moral rules are obscure or contradictory, there is a tendency for pollution beliefs to simplify or clarify the point at issue. The Walbiri case suggests a correlation. When male dominance is accepted as a central principle of social organisation and applied without inhibition and with full rights of physical coercion, beliefs in sex pollution are not likely to be highly developed. On the other hand, when the principle of male dominance is applied to the ordering of social life but is contradicted by other principles such as that of female independence, or the inherent right of women as the weaker sex to be more protected from violence than men, then sex pollution is likely to flourish. Before we take up this case there is another kind of exception to consider.

We find many societies in which individuals are not coerced or otherwise held strictly to their allotted sexual roles and yet the social structure is based upon the association of the sexes. In these cases a subtle, legalistic development of special institutions provides relief. Individuals can to some extent follow their personal whims, because the social structure is cushioned by fictions of one kind or another.

The political organisation of the Nuer is totally unformulated. They have no explicit institutions of government or administration. Such fluid and intangible political structure as they exhibit is a spontaneous, shifting expression of their conflicting loyalties. The only principle of any firmness which gives form to their tribal life is the principle of genealogy. By thinking of their territorial units as if they represented segments of a single genealogical structure, they impose some order on their political groupings. The Nuer afford a natural illustration of how people can create and maintain a social structure in the realm of ideas and not primarily, or at all, in the external, physical realm of ceremonial palaces or courts of justice (Evans-Pritchard, 1940).

The genealogical principle which they apply to the political relations of a whole tribe is important to them in another context, at the intimate personal level of claims to cattle and wives. Thus, not only his place in the larger political scheme, but his personal inheritance is determined for a Nuer man by the allegiances defined through marriage. On rights of paternity their lineage structure and their whole political structure depend. Yet the Nuer do not take adultery and desertion so tragically as some other peoples with agnatic lineage systems in which paternity is established by marriage. True, a Nuer husband can spear his wife's seducer if he catches him red-handed. But otherwise, if he learns of her infidelity, he can only demand two head of cattle, one for compensation and one for sacrifice—hardly a severe penalty compared with other peoples of whom we read that they used to banish adulterers (Meek, pp. 218–9) or enslave them. Or compared with a Bedouin who would not be allowed to raise his head in society again until a dishonoured kinswoman had been killed (Salim, p. 61). The difference is that Nuer legal marriage is relatively invulnerable to the whims of individual partners. Husbands and wives can be allowed to separate and live apart without altering the legal status of their marriage, or of the wife's children (Evans-Pritchard, Chapter III, 1951). Nuer women enjoy a strikingly free and independent status. If one is widowed her husband's brothers have the right to take her in leviratic marriage, to raise seed to the dead man's name. But if she does not choose to accept this arrangement, they cannot force her. She is left free to choose her own lovers. The one security that is guaranteed to the dead man's lineage is that any offspring, begotten by whomsoever they may have been, count as affiliated to that lineage from which the original marriage cattle were paid. The rule that whoever paid cattle has the right to the children is the rule which distinguishes legal marriage, practically indefeasible, from conjugal relations. The social structure rests on the series of legal marriages, established by the transfer of cattle. Thus it is protected by practical institutional means from any uncertainty which may threaten from the free behaviour of men and women. By contrast with the stark, unstated simplicity of their political organisation, Nuer display astonishing legal subtlety in the definition of marriage, concubinage, divorce and conjugal separation.

It is this development, I suggest, which enables them to organise their social institutions without burdensome beliefs in sex pollution. It is true that they protect their cattle from menstruating women, but a man does not have to purify himself if he touches one. He should merely avoid sexual intercourse with his wife during her menstrual periods, a rule of respect which is said to express concern for his unborn children. This is a very much milder regulation than some rules of avoidance we shall mention later.

Another example of a legal fiction which lifts the weight of the social structure from sexual relations . . . is Nur Yalman's discussion of female purity in South India and Ceylon (1963). Here the purity of women is protected as the gate of entry to the castes. The mother is the decisive parent for establishing caste membership. Through women the blood and purity of the caste is perpetuated. Therefore their sexual purity is all-important, and every possible whisper of threat to it is anticipated and barred against. This should lead us to expect an intolerable life of restriction for women. Indeed, this is what we find for the highest and purest caste of all.

The Nambudiri Brahmins of Malabar are a small, rich, exclusive caste of priestly land-owners. They have remained so by observing a rule forbidding the division of their estates. In each family only the eldest son marries. The others can keep lower-caste concubines, but never enter into marriage. As for their unfortunate womenfolk, strict seclusion is their lot. Few of them ever marry at all until on their deathbed a rite of marriage affirms their freedom from the control of their guardians. If they go out of their houses, their bodies are completely enveloped in clothing and umbrellas hide their faces. When one of their brothers is married they can watch the celebration through chinks in the walls. Even at her own wedding a Nambudiri woman has to be replaced in the usual public appearance of the bride by a Nayar girl. Only a very rich group could afford to commit its women to a life sentence of barrenness for most and of seclusion for all. This kind of ruthlessness corresponds in its own way to the ruthlessness with which Walbiri men apply their principles.

· · ·

So much for the exceptions.

We should now look at some examples of social structures which rest on grave paradox or contradiction. In these cases where no softening legal fictions intervene to protect the freedom of the sexes exaggerated avoidances develop around sexual relations.

New Guinea is an area where fear of sexual pollution is a cultural characteristic (Read, 1954). But within the same cultural idiom a great contrast separates the way the Arapesh of Sepik River and the Mae Enga of the Central Highlands handle the theme of sexual difference. The former, it seems, try to create a total symmetry between the sexes. All power is thought of on the model of sexual energy. Femininity is only dangerous to men as masculinity is to women. Females are life-giving and in pregnancy they nourish their children with their own blood; once the children are born males nourish them with life-giving blood drawn for the purpose from the penis. Margaret Mead emphasises that equal watchfulness is necessary from both sexes on their own dangerous powers. Each sex approaches the other with deliberate control (1940).

The Mae Enga, on the other hand, do not look for any symmetry. They fear female pollution for their males and for all male enterprises, and there is no question of a balance between two kinds of sexual danger and powers (Meggitt, 1964). For such differences we can tentatively look for sociological correlations.

The Mae Enga live in an area of dense population. Their local organisation is based on the clan, a compact, well-defined military and political unit. The men of the clan choose their wives from other clans. Thus they marry foreigners. The rule of clan exogamy is common enough. Whether it imports strain and difficulty into the marriage situation depends on how exclusive, localised and rivalrous are the intermarrying clans. In the Enga case they are not only foreigners but traditional enemies. The Mae Enga men are individually involved in an intense competition for prestige. They fiercely compete to exchange pigs and valuables. Their wives are chosen from the very outsiders with whom they habitually exchange pigs and shells and with whom they habitually fight. So for each man his male affines are also likely to be his ceremonial exchange partners (a competitive relationship) and their clan is the military enemy of his own clan. Thus the marital relation has to bear the tensions of the strongly competitive social system. The Enga belief about sex pollution suggests that sexual relations take on the character of a conflict between enemies in which the man sees himself as endangered by his sexual partner, the intrusive member of the enemy clan. There is a strongly held belief that contacts with women weaken male strength. So preoccupied are they with avoiding female contact that the fear of sexual contamination effectively reduces the amount of commerce between the sexes.

· · ·

[T]he Mae Enga fear of female pollution contrasts with the belief in the balanced power and danger from both sexes that appears in the culture of the Mountain Arapesh. It is very interesting to note further that the Arapesh disapprove of local exogamy. If a man should marry a woman of the plains Arapesh he observes elaborate precautions to cool off her more dangerous sexuality.

> 'If he marries one, he should not marry her hastily but permit her to remain about the house for several months growing accustomed to him, cooling down the possible passion of slight acquaintance and strangeness. Then he may copulate with her, and watch. Do his yams prosper? Does he find game when he goes hunting? If so, all is well. If not, let him abstain from relationship with this dangerous, oversexed woman still many more moons, lest the part of his potency, his own physical strength, the ability to feed others, which he most cherishes, should be permanently injured.' (Mead, 1940, p. 345)

This example would seem to support Meggitt's view that local exogamy in the strained and competitive conditions of Enga life imports a heavy load of strain into their marriage. If this is so then the Enga could presumably be free of their very inconvenient beliefs if they could relieve their anxieties at source. But this is an utterly impractical suggestion. It would mean either giving up their violently competitive exchanges with rival clans, or their exogamous marriages—either stop fighting or stop marrying the sisters of the men they fight. Either choice would mean a major readjustment to their social system. In practice and in historical fact, when such an adjustment came from outside, with the coming of missionary preaching on sex and of the Australian administration's pax on fighting, the Enga gave up their beliefs in the danger of female sex quite easily.

The contradiction which the Enga strive to overcome by avoidance is the attempt to build marriage on enmity. But another difficulty perhaps more common in primitive societies arises from a contradiction in the phrasing of male and female roles.

If the principle of male domination is elaborated absolutely consistently it need not necessarily contradict any other basic principles. We have mentioned two very different instances in which male dominance is applied with ruthless simplicity. But the principle runs into trouble if there is any other principle which protects women from physical control. For this gives women scope to play off one man against another, and so to confound the principle of male dominance.

The whole society is especially likely to be founded on a contradiction if the system is one in which men define their status in terms of rights over women. If there is free competition between the men, this gives scope for a discontented woman to turn to her husband's or her guardian's rivals, gain new protectors and new allegiance, and so to dissolve into nothing the structure of rights and duties which had formerly been built around her. This sort of contradiction in the social system arises only if there is no *de facto* possibility of coercing women. For example, it does not appear if there is a centralised political system which throws the weight of its authority against women. Where the legal system can be exerted against women, they cannot make havoc of the system. But a centralised political system is not one in which male status is mainly phrased in terms of rights over women.

The Lele are an example of a social system which is continually liable to founder on the contradiction that female manoeuvring gives to male dominance. All male rivalries are expressed in the competition for wives. A man with no wife is below the bottom rung of the status ladder. With one wife he can get a start, by begetting and thus qualifying for entry to remunerative cult associations. With a daughter born to him he can start claiming the services of a son-in-law. With several daughters, as many betrothed sons-in-law and above all with granddaughters, he is high up on the ladder of privilege and esteem. This is because women whom he has engendered are women he can offer in marriage to other men. And so he builds up a following of men. Every mature man could hope to acquire two or three wives, and in the meanwhile young men had to wait in bachelorhood. Polygyny in itself made the competition for wives intense. But the various other ways in which male success in the men's sphere was hitched to the control of women would be complicated to relate here (see Douglas, 1963). Their whole social life was dominated by an institution for paying compensation by transferring rights over women. The net effect was that women were treated, from one aspect, as a kind of currency in which men claimed and settled debts against one another. Men's mutual indebtedness piled up so that they had staked out claims to unborn girls for generations ahead. A man with no rights over women to transfer was in as parlous a case as a modern businessman with no bank account. From a man's point of view women were the most desirable objects their culture had to offer. Since all insults and obligations could be settled by the transfer of rights over women, it was perfectly true to say, as they did, that the only reason they ever went to war was about women.

A little Lele girl would grow up a coquette. From infancy she was the centre of affectionate, teasing, flirting attention. Her affianced husband never gained more than a very limited control over her. He had the right to chastise, certainly, but if he exerted it too violently, and above all if he lost her affection, she could find some pretext for persuading her brothers that her husband neglected her. Infant mortality was high and the miscarriage or death of a child brought the wife's kinsmen sternly to the husband's door asking for an explanation. Since men competed with one another for women there was scope for women to manoeuvre and intrigue. Hopeful seducers were never lacking and no woman doubted that she could get another husband if it suited her. The husband whose wives were faithful until middle age had to be very attentive, both to the wife and to her mother. Quite an elaborate etiquette governed marital relations, with many occasions on which big or small gifts were due from the husband. When the wife was pregnant or sick or newly delivered, he had to be assiduous in arranging proper medical care. A woman who was known to be dissatisfied with her life would soon be courted—and there were various ways open to her by which she could take initiative for ending her marriage.

I have said enough to show why Lele men should be anxious about their relations with women. Although in some contexts they thought of women

as desirable treasures, they spoke of them also as worthless, worse than dogs, unmannerly, ignorant, fickle, unreliable. Socially, women were indeed all these things. They were not in the least interested in the men's world in which they and their daughters were swapped as pawns in men's games of prestige. They were cunning in exploiting the opportunities that came their way. If they connived, mother and daughter together could wreck any plans that they disliked. So ultimately men had to assert their vaunted dominance by charming, coaxing and flattering. There was a special wheed-ling tone of voice they used for women.

The Lele attitude to sex was compounded of enjoyment, desire for fertility and recognition of danger. They had every reason for desiring fertility, as I have shown, and their religious cults were directed towards this end. Sexual activity was held to be in itself dangerous, not for the partners to it, but dangerous for the weak and the sick. Anyone coming fresh from sexual intercourse should avoid the sick, lest by the indirect contact their fever should increase. New-born babies would be killed by such a contact. Consequently yellow raffia fronds were hung at the entrance of a compound to warn all responsible persons that a sick person or new born baby was within. This was a general danger. But there were special dangers for men. A wife had the duty of cleaning her husband after sexual intercourse and then of washing herself before she touched the cooking. Each married woman kept a little pot of water hidden in the grass outside the village where she could wash in secret. It should be well hidden and out of the way, for if a man were to trip on that pot by chance, his sexual vigour would be weakened. If she neglected her ablution and he were to eat food cooked by her, he would lose his virility. These are just the dangers following legitimate sexual intercourse. But a menstruating woman could not cook for her husband or poke the fire, lest he fall ill. She could prepare the food, but when it came to approaching the fire she had to call a friend in to help. These dangers were only risked by men, not by other women or children. Finally, a menstruating woman was a danger to the whole community if she entered the forest. Not only was her menstruation certain to wreck any enterprise in the forest that she might undertake, but it was thought to produce unfavourable conditions for men. Hunting would be difficult for a long time after, and rituals based on forest plants would have no efficacy. Women found these rules extremely irksome, specially as they were regularly short-handed and late in their planting, weeding, harvesting and fishing.

The danger of sex was also controlled by rules which protected male enterprises from female pollution and female enterprises from male pollution. All ritual had to be protected from female pollution, the male officiants (women were generally excluded from cult affairs) abstaining from sexual intercourse the night before. The same for warfare, hunting, tapping palms for wine. Similarly women should abstain from sexual intercourse before planting ground nuts or maize, fishing, making salt or pottery. These fears were symmetrical for men and for women. The generally stipulated condition for handling any great ritual crisis was to call for sexual abstinence from the whole village. . . .

The Lele anxiety about the ritual dangers of sex I attribute to the real disruptive role allotted to sex in their social system. Their men created a status ladder whose successive stages they mounted as they acquired control over more and more women. But they threw the whole system open to competition and so allowed women a double role, as passive pawns and again as active intriguers. Individual men were right to fear that individual women would spoil their plans, and fears of the dangers of sex only too accurately reflect its working in their social structure.

Female pollution in a society of this type is largely related to the attempt to treat women simultaneously as persons and as the currency of male transactions. Males and females are set off as belonging to distinct, mutually hostile spheres. Sexual antagonism inevitably results and this is reflected in the idea that each sex constitutes a danger to the other. The particular dangers which female contact threatens to males express the contradictions of trying to use women as currency without reducing them to slavery. If ever it was felt in a commercial culture that money is the root of all evil, the feeling that women are the root of all evils to Lele men is more justified. Indeed the story of the Garden of Eden touched a deep chord of

sympathy in Lele male breasts. Once told by the missionaries, it was told and retold round pagan hearths with smug relish.

The Yurok of Northern California have more than once interested anthropologists and psychologists by the radical nature of their ideas of purity and impurity as we have said. Theirs is a dying culture. When Professor Robins studied the Yurok language in 1951 there were only about six Yurok-speaking adults left alive. This seems to have been another example of a highly competitive, acquisitive culture. Men's minds were preoccupied with acquiring wealth in the form of prestige-carrying shell-money, rare feathers and pelts and imported obsidian blades. . . . Adulteries of wives and marriages of daughters were important sources of wealth. A man who pursued other men's wives would pour out his fortune in adultery compensation.

The Yurok so much believed that contact with women would destroy their powers of acquiring wealth that they held that women and money should never be brought into contact. Above all it was felt to be fatal to future prosperity for a man to have sexual intercourse in the house where he kept his strings of shell money. In the winter, when it was too cold to be out of doors, they seem to have abstained altogether. . . . It is significant for understanding their idea of female pollution that for the Yurok men there was a real sense in which pursuit of wealth and of women were contradictory.

We have traced this Delilah complex, the belief that women weaken or betray, in various extreme forms among the New Guinea Mae Enga and among the Lele of the Congo and the Yurok Indians of California. Where it occurs we find that men's anxieties about women's behaviour are justified and that the situation of male/female relations is so biased that women are cast as betrayers from the start.

It is not always the men who are afraid of sex pollution. For the sake of symmetry we should look at one example where it is the women who behave as if sexual activity were highly dangerous. Audrey Richards says that the Bemba of Northern Rhodesia behave as if they were obsessed by fear of sexual impurity. But she notes that this is culturally standardised behaviour, and in fact no fears seem to check their individual freedom. At the cultural level the fear of sexual intercourse seems dominant to an extent 'which cannot be exaggerated.' At the personal level there is 'the open pleasure in sex relations which the Bemba express' (1956, p. 154).

In other places sexual pollution is incurred by direct contact, but here it is held to be mediated by contact with fire. There is no danger in seeing or touching a sexually active, unpurified person, someone hot with sex, as the Bemba say. But let such a person come near a fire and any food cooked on those flames is dangerously contaminated.

It takes two to have sexual intercourse, but only one to cook a meal. By supposing the pollution to be transmitted through cooked food responsibility is firmly fixed on the Bemba women. A Bemba woman has to be continually alert to protect her cooking hearth from the contact of any adult who may have had sexual intercourse without ritual purification. The danger is lethal. Any child who eats food cooked on a contaminated fire may die. A Bemba mother is kept busy putting out suspect fires and lighting new, pure ones.

Although the Bemba believe that all sexual activity is dangerous, the bias of their beliefs points to adultery as the real, practical danger. A married couple are able to administer ritual purification, each for the other, after every sexual act. But an adulterer cannot be purified unless he can ask his wife to help, as it is not a solo rite.

Notice that in this society the women are more anxious than the men about sexual pollution. If their children die (and the infant mortality rate is very high) they can be blamed for carelessness by the men. In Nyasaland among the Yao and Cewa a similar complex of beliefs is expressed concerning pollution of salt. All three tribes reckon descent in the female line, and in all three tribes the men are supposed to leave their natal village and join each the village of his wife. This gives a pattern of village structure by which a core of lineally related females attracts men from other villages to settle as their husbands. The future of the village as a political unit depends on keeping these male outsiders living there. But we would expect the men to have much less interest in building a stable marriage. The same rule of matrilineal succession turns their interest to their sisters' children. Though the village is built on the conjugal tie, the matrilineal lineage is not. The men are brought to the village by marriage, the women are born in it.

Throughout Central Africa the idea of the good village which grows and endures is a value strongly held by men and women. But the women have a double interest in keeping their husbands. A Bemba woman fulfils her most satisfying role when, in middle life, as a matriarch in her own village she can expect to grow old surrounded by her daughters and her daughters' daughters. But if a Bemba man finds the early years of marriage irksome, he will simply leave his wife and go home (Richards, p. 41). Moreover, if all the men go, or even half of them, the village is no longer viable as an economic unit. The division of labour puts Bemba women in a particularly dependent position. Indeed, in a region where it is now common for fifty percent of the adult males to be absent on labour migration, Bemba villages suffered more disintegration than villages of other tribes in Northern Rhodesia (Watson).

The teaching of Bemba girls in their puberty ceremonies helps us to relate these aspects of social structure and of women's ambitions to their fears of sex pollution. Dr. Richards records that the girls are strictly indoctrinated with the need to behave submissively to their husbands; interesting since they are reputed to be particularly overbearing and difficult to manage. The candidates are humiliated while their husbands' virility is extolled. This makes good sense if we consider the Bemba husband's role as analogous, in a contrary way, to that of the Mae Enga wife. He is alone and an outsider in his wife's village. But he is a man and not a woman. If he is not happy he goes away and there is an end to it. He cannot be chastised like a runaway wife. There are no legal adjustments by which the fiction of a legal marriage can be preserved without insisting on the reality. His physical presence in his wife's village is more important to that village than the rights he gains in marriage are to himself, and he cannot be browbeaten into staying there. If the Enga wife is a Delilah, he is Samson in the camp of the Philistines. If he feels humiliated he can bring the pillars of society tumbling down, for if all the husbands were to rise up and go the village would be ruined. No wonder that the women are anxious to flatter and cajole him. No wonder they would like to protect against the effects of adultery. The husband appears not to be dangerous or sinister, but shy, liable to be frightened off, needing to be convinced of his own masculinity and of the dangers thereof. He needs to be assured that his wife is looking after him, standing by to purify him, watching over the fire. He can do nothing without her, not even approach his own ancestral spirits. In her self-imposed anxieties about sex pollution the Bemba wife appears as the opposite number of the Mae Enga husband. Both find in the marriage situation anxieties concerning the structure of the wider society. If the Bemba woman did not want to stay at home and become an influential matron there, if she were prepared to follow her husband meekly to his village, she could relieve her anxiety about sexual pollution.

In all the examples quoted of this kind of pollution, the basic problem is a case of wanting to have your cake and eat it. The Enga want to fight their enemy clans but yet to marry with their clanswomen. The Lele want to use women as the pawns of men, and yet will take sides with individual women against other men. The Bemba women want to be free and independent and to behave in ways which threaten to wreck their marriages, and yet they want their husbands to stay with them. In each case the dangerous situation which has to be handled with washings and avoidances has in common with the others that the norms of behaviour are contradictory. The left hand is fighting the right hand, as in the Trickster myth of the Winnebago.

Is there any reason why all these examples of the social system at war with itself are drawn from sexual relations? There are many other contexts in which we are led into contradictory behaviour by the normal canons of our culture. National income policy is one modern field in which this sort of analysis could easily be applied. Yet pollution fears do not seem to cluster round contradictions which do not involve sex. The answer may be that no other social pressures are potentially so explosive as those which constrain sexual relations. We can come to sympathise with St. Paul's extraordinary demand that in the new Christian society there should be neither male nor female.

[1966]

REFERENCES

Douglas, M. *The Lele of the Kasai*, London, 1963.
Evans-Pritchard, E. E. *The Nuer*, Oxford, 1940.
Mead, M. "The Mountain Arapesh." *Anthropological Papers*, American Museum of Natural History, vol. 37, 1940.
Meek, C. K. *Law and Authority in a Nigerian Tribe*. Oxford, 1937.
Meggitt, M. "Male-Female Relationships in the Highlands of Australian New Guinea." *American Anthropologist*, 66 (2): 204–224.
Read, K. E. "Cultures of the Central Highlands." *South Western Journal of Anthropology*, 10, 1–43.
Robins, R. H. *The Yurok Language*, Berkeley, CA, 1958.
Richards, A. I. *Chisungu*. New York, 1956.
Salim, S. M. *Marshdwellers of the Euphrates Delta*. London, 1962.
Watson, W. *Tribal Cohesion in a Money Economy*. Manchester, 1958.
Yalman, N. "The Purity of Women in Ceylon and Southern India." *Journal of the Royal Anthropological Institute*, 1963.

 38

Statement of Purpose (1966)

NATIONAL ORGANIZATION FOR WOMEN

NATIONAL ORGANIZATION FOR WOMEN (NOW) Founded in 1966, NOW is the largest U.S. feminist organization. Betty Friedan was its first president. Among its major long-term objectives has been passage of an Equal Rights Amendment.

We, men and women who hereby constitute ourselves as the National Organization for Women, believe that the time has come for a new movement toward true equality for all women in America, and toward a fully equal partnership of the sexes, as part of the world-wide revolution of human rights now taking place within and beyond our national borders.

The purpose of NOW is to take action to bring women into full participation in the mainstream of American society now, exercising all the privileges and responsibilities thereof in truly equal partnership with men.

We believe the time has come to move beyond the abstract argument, discussion and symposia over the status and special nature of women which has raged in America in recent years; the time has come to confront, with concrete action, the conditions that now prevent women from enjoying the equality of opportunity and freedom of choice which is their right, as individual Americans, and as human beings.

NOW is dedicated to the proposition that women, first and foremost, are human beings, who, like all other people in our society, must have the chance to develop their fullest human potential. We believe that women can achieve such equality only by accepting to the full the challenges and responsibilities they share with all other people in our society, as part of the decision-making mainstream of American political, economic and social life.

We organize to initiate or support action, nationally, or in part of this nation, by individuals or organizations, to break through the silken curtain of prejudice and discrimination against women in government, industry, the professions, the churches, the political parties, the judiciary, the labor unions, in education, science, medicine, law, religion and every other field of importance in American society.

Enormous changes taking place in our society make it both possible and urgently necessary to advance the unfinished revolution of women toward true equality, now. With a life span lengthened to nearly 75 years it is no longer either necessary or possible for women to devote the greater part of their lives to child-rearing; yet childbearing and rearing—which continues to be a most important part of most women's lives—still is used to justify barring women from equal professional and economic participation and advance.

· · ·

There is no civil rights movement to speak for women, as there has been for Negroes and other victims of discrimination. The National Organization for Women must therefore begin to speak.

WE BELIEVE that the power of American law, and the protection guaranteed by the U.S. Constitution to the civil rights of all individuals, must be effectively applied and enforced to isolate and remove patterns of sex discrimination, to ensure quality of opportunity in employment and education, and equality of civil and political rights and responsibilities on behalf of women, as well as for Negroes and other deprived groups.

We realize that women's problems are linked to many broader questions of social justice; their solution will require concerted action by many groups. Therefore, convinced that human rights for all are indivisible, we expect to give active support to the common cause of equal rights for all those who suffer discrimination and deprivation, and we call upon other organizations committed to such goals to support our efforts toward quality for women.

WE DO NOT ACCEPT the token appointment of a few women to high-level positions in government and industry as a substitute for a serious continuing effort to recruit and advance women according to their individual abilities. To this end, we urge American government and industry to mobilize the same resources of ingenuity and command with which they have solved problems of far greater difficulty than those now impeding the progress of women.

WE BELIEVE that this nation has a capacity at least as great as other nations to innovate new social institutions which will enable women to enjoy true equality of opportunity and responsibility in society, without conflict with their responsibilities as mothers and homemakers. In such innovations, America does not lead the Western world, but lags by decades behind many European countries. We do not accept the traditional assumption that a woman has to choose between marriage and motherhood, on the one hand, and serious participation in industry or the professions on the other. We question the present expectation that all normal women will retire from job or profession for 10 or 15 years, to devote their full time to raising children, only to reenter the job market at a relatively minor level. This, in itself, is a deterrent to the aspirations of women, to their acceptance into management or professional training courses, and to the very possibility of equality of opportunity or real choice, for all but a few women. Above all, we reject the assumption that these problems are the unique responsibility of each individual woman, rather than a basic social dilemma which society must solve. True equality of opportunity and freedom of choice for women require such practical and possible innovations as a nationwide network of childcare centers, which will make it unnecessary for women to retire completely from society until their children are grown, and national programs to provide retraining for women who have chosen to care for their own children full-time.

WE BELIEVE that it is as essential for every girl to be educated to her full potential of human ability as it is for every boy—with the knowledge that such education is the key to effective participation in today's economy and that, for a girl as for a boy, education can only be serious where there is expectation that it will be used in society. We believe that American educators are capable of devising means of imparting such expectations to girl students. Moreover, we consider the decline in the proportion of women receiving higher and professional education to be evidence of discrimination. This discrimination may take the form of quotas against the admission of women to colleges and professional schools; lack of encouragement by parents, counsellors and educators; denial of loans or fellowships; or the traditional or arbitrary procedures in graduate and professional training geared in terms of men, which inadvertently discriminate against women. We believe that the same serious attention must be given to high school dropouts who are girls as to boys.

WE REJECT the current assumptions that a man must carry the sole burden of supporting himself, his wife, and family, and that a woman is automatically entitled to lifelong support by a man upon her marriage, or that marriage, home and family are primarily woman's world and responsibility—hers to dominate—his to support. We believe that a true partnership between the sexes demands a different concept of marriage, an equitable sharing of the responsibilities of home and children and of the economic burdens of their support. We believe that proper recognition should be given to the economic and social value of homemaking and child-care. To these ends, we will seek to open a reexamination of laws and mores governing marriage and divorce, for we believe that the current state of "half-equality" between the sexes discriminates against both men and women, and is the cause of much unnecessary hostility between the sexes.

WE BELIEVE that women must now exercise their political rights and responsibilities as American citizens. They must refuse to be segregated on the basis of sex into separate-and-not-equal ladies' auxiliaries in the political parties, and they must demand representation according to their numbers in the regularly constituted party committees—at local, state, and national levels—and in the informal power structure, participating fully in the selection of candidates and political decision-making, and running for office themselves.

IN THE INTERESTS OF THE HUMAN DIGNITY OF WOMEN, we will protest, and endeavor to change, the false image of women now prevalent in the mass media, and in the texts, ceremonies, laws, and practices of our major social institutions. Such images perpetuate contempt for women by society and by women for themselves. We are similarly opposed to all policies and practices—in church, state, college, factory, or office—which, in the guise of protectiveness, not only deny opportunities but also foster in women self-denigration, dependence, and evasion of responsibility, undermine their confidence in their own abilities and foster contempt for women.

NOW WILL HOLD ITSELF INDEPENDENT OF ANY POLITICAL PARTY in order to mobilize the political power of all women and men intent on our goals. We will strive to ensure that no party, candidate, president, senator, governor, congressman, or any public official who betrays or ignores the principle of full equality between the sexes is elected or appointed to office. If it is necessary to mobilize the votes of men and women who believe in our cause, in order to win for women the final right to be fully free and equal human beings, we so commit ourselves.

WE BELIEVE THAT women will do most to create a new image of women by *acting* now, and by speaking out in behalf of their own equality, freedom, and human dignity—not in pleas for special privilege, nor in enmity toward men, who are also victims of the current, half-equality between the sexes—but in an active, self-respecting partnership with men. By so doing, women will develop confidence in their own ability to determine actively, in partnership with men, the conditions of their life, their choices, their future and their society.

[1966]

39

From SCUM Manifesto

VALERIE SOLANAS

VALERIE SOLANAS United States. 1936–1988. Radical feminist writer called by Ti-Grace Atkinson "the first outstanding champion of women's rights." Best known for shooting Andy Warhol. Wrote several unpublished plays and manuscripts; one play was produced posthumously.

Life in this society being, at best, an utter bore and no aspect of society being at all relevant to women, there remains to civic-minded, responsible, thrill-seeking females only to overthrow the government, eliminate the money system, institute complete automation, and destroy the male sex.

It is now technically possible to reproduce without the aid of males (or, for that matter, females) and to produce only females. We must begin immediately to do so. Retaining the male has not even the dubious purpose of reproduction. The male is a biological accident: the Y (male) gene is an incomplete X (female) gene, that is, has an incomplete set of chromosomes. In other words, the male is an incomplete female, a walking abortion, aborted at the gene stage. To be male is to be deficient, emotionally limited; maleness is a deficiency disease and males are emotional cripples.

· · ·

But SCUM is impatient; SCUM is not consoled by the thought that future generations will thrive; SCUM wants to grab some thrilling living for itself. And, if a large majority of women were SCUM, they could acquire complete control of this country within a few weeks simply by withdrawing from the labor force, thereby paralyzing the entire nation. Additional measures, any one of which would be sufficient to completely disrupt the economy and everything else, would be for women to declare themselves off the money system, stop buying, just loot and simply refuse to obey all laws they don't care to obey. The police force, National Guard, Army, Navy, and Marines combined couldn't squelch a rebellion of over half the population, particularly when it's made up of people they are utterly helpless without.

If all women simply left men, refused to have anything to do with any of them—ever, all men, the government, and the national economy would collapse completely. Even without leaving men, women who are aware of the extent of their superiority to and power over men, could acquire complete control over everything within a few weeks, could effect a total submission of males to females. In a sane society the male would trot along obediently after the female. The male is docile and easily led, easily subjected to the domination of any female who cares to dominate him. The male, in fact, wants desperately to be led by females, wants Mama in charge, wants to abandon himself to her care. But this is not a sane society, and most women are not even dimly aware of where they're at in relation to men.

The conflict, therefore, is not between females and males, but between SCUM—dominant, secure, self-confident, nasty, violent, selfish, independent, proud, thrill-seeking, free-wheeling, arrogant females, who consider themselves fit to rule the universe, who have freewheeled to the limits of this "society," and are ready to wheel on to something far beyond what it has to offer—and nice, passive, accepting, "cultivated," polite, dignified, subdued, dependent, scared, mindless, insecure, approval-seeking Daddy's Girls, who can't cope with the unknown; who want to continue to wallow in the sewer that is, at least, familiar, who want to hang back with the apes; who feel secure only with Big Daddy standing by, with a big, strong man to lean on and with a fat, hairy face in the White House; who are too cowardly to face up to the hideous reality of what a man is, what Daddy is; who have cast their lot with the swine, who have adapted themselves to animalism, feel superficially comfortable with it and know no other way of "life;" who have reduced their minds, thoughts and sights to the male level; who, lacking sense, imagination, and wit can have value only in a male "society;" who can have a place in the sun, or, rather, in the slime, only as soothers, ego-boosters, relaxers, and breeders; who are dismissed as inconsequents by other females, who project their deficiencies, their maleness, onto all females and see the female as a worm.

But SCUM is too impatient to hope and wait for the debrainwashing of millions of assholes. Why should the swinging females continue to plod dismally along with the dull male ones? Why should the fates of the groovy and the creepy be intertwined? Why should the active and imaginative consult the passive and dull on social policy? Why should the independent be confined to the sewer along with the dependent who need Daddy to cling to?

A small handful of SCUM can take over the country within a year by systematically fucking up the system, selectively destroying property, and murder:

• SCUM will become members of the unwork force, the fuck-up force; they will get jobs of various kinds and unwork. For example, SCUM sales-girls will not charge for merchandise; SCUM telephone operators will not charge for calls; SCUM office and factory workers, in addition to fucking up their work, will secretly destroy equipment.

• SCUM will unwork at a job until fired, then get a new job to unwork at.

• SCUM will forcibly relieve bus drivers, cab drivers, and subway-token sellers of their jobs and run buses and cabs and dispense free tokens to the public.

• SCUM will destroy all useless and harmful objects—cars, store windows, "Great Art," etc.

• Eventually SCUM will take over the airwaves—radio and TV networks—by forcibly relieving of their jobs all radio and TV employees who would impede SCUM's entry into the broadcasting studios.

• SCUM will couple-bust—barge into mixed (male-female) couples, wherever they are, and bust them up.

SCUM will kill all men who are not in the Men's Auxiliary of SCUM. Men in the Men's Auxiliary are those men who are working diligently to eliminate themselves, men who, regardless of their motives, do good, men who are playing ball with SCUM. A few examples of the men in the Men's Auxiliary are: men who kill men; biological scientists who are working on constructive programs, as opposed to biological warfare; journalists, writers, editors, publishers, and producers who disseminate and promote ideas that will lead to the achievement of SCUM's goals; faggots who, by their shimmering, flaming example, encourage other men to de-man themselves and thereby make themselves relatively inoffensive; men who consistently give

things away—money, things, services; men who tell it like it is (so far not one ever has), who put women straight, who reveal the truth about themselves, who give the mindless male females correct sentences to parrot, who tell them a woman's primary goal in life should be to squash the male sex (to aid men in this endeavor SCUM will conduct Turd Sessions, at which every male present will give a speech beginning with the sentence: "I am a turd, a lowly, abject turd," then proceed to list all the ways in which he is. His reward for so doing will be the opportunity to fraternize after the session for a whole, solid hour with the SCUM who will be present. Nice, clean-living male women will be invited to the sessions to help clarify any doubts and misunderstandings they may have about the male sex); makers and promoters of sex books and movies, etc., who are hastening the day when all that will be shown on the screen will be Suck and Fuck (males, like the rats following the Pied Piper, will be lured by Pussy to their doom, will be overcome and submerged by and will eventually drown in the passive flesh that they are); drug pushers and advocates, who are hastening the dropping out of men.

· · ·

It is most tempting to pick off the female "Great Artists," liars and phonies, etc., along with the men, but that would be inexpedient, as it would not be clear to most of the public that the female killed was a male. All women have a fink streak in them, to a greater or lesser degree, but it stems from a lifetime of living among men. Eliminate men and women will shape up. Women are improvable; men are not, although their behavior is. When SCUM gets hot on their asses, it'll shape up fast.

Simultaneously with the fucking-up, looting, couple-busting, destroying, and killing, SCUM will recruit. SCUM, then, will consist of recruiters; the elite corps—the hard-core activists (the fuck-ups, looters and destroyers) and the elite of the elite—the killers.

Dropping out is not the answer; fucking-up is. Most women are already dropped out; they were never in. Dropping out gives control to those few who don't drop out; dropping out is exactly what the establishment leaders want; it plays into the hands of the enemy; it strengthens the system instead of undermining it, since it is based entirely on the nonparticipation, passivity, apathy, and noninvolvement of the mass of women. Dropping out, however, is an excellent policy for men, and SCUM will enthusiastically encourage it.

. . .

SCUM will keep on destroying, looting, fucking-up, and killing until the money-work system no longer exists and automation is completely instituted or until enough women cooperate with SCUM to make violence unnecessary to achieve these goals, that is, until enough women either un-work or quit work, start looting, leave men, and refuse to obey all laws inappropriate to a truly civilized society. Many women will fall into line; but many others, who surrendered long ago to the enemy, who are so adapted to animalism, to maleness, that they like restrictions and restraints, don't know what to do with freedom, will continue to be toadies and doormats, just as peasants in rice paddies remain peasants in rice paddies as one regime topples another. A few of the more volatile will whimper and sulk and throw their toys and dishrags on the floor, but SCUM will continue to steam-roller over them.

A completely automated society can be accomplished very simply and quickly once there is a public demand for it. The blueprints for it are already in existence, and its construction will only take a few weeks with millions of people working at it. Even though off the money system, everyone will be most happy to pitch in and get the automated society built; it will mark the beginning of a fantastic new era, and there will be a celebration atmosphere accompanying the construction. The elimination of money and the complete institution of automation are basic to all other SCUM reforms; without these two the others can't take place; with them the others will take place very rapidly. The government will automatically collapse. With complete automation it will be possible for every woman to vote directly on every issue by means of an electronic voting machine in her house. Since the government is occupied almost entirely with regulating economic affairs and legislating against purely private matters, the elimination of money and with it the elimination of males who wish to legislate "morality" will mean that there will be practically no issues to vote on.

After the elimination of money there will be no further need to kill men; they will be stripped of the only power they have over psychologically independent females. They will be able to impose themselves only on the doormats, who like to be imposed on. The rest of the women will be busy solving the few remaining unsolved problems before planning their agenda for eternity and Utopia—completely revamping educational programs so that millions of women can be trained within a few months for high-level intellectual work that now requires years of training (this can be done very easily once our educational goal is to educate and not to perpetuate an academic and intellectual elite); solving the problems of disease and old age and death and completely redesigning our cities and living quarters. Many women will for awhile continue to think they dig men, but as they become accustomed to female society and as they become absorbed in their projects, they will eventually come to see the utter uselessness and banality of the male.

. . .

[1967]

 40

Theory of Sexual Politics
from Sexual Politics

KATE MILLETT

KATE MILLETT United States. 1934– . Writer. Sculptor. Photographer. Painter. Leader of women's liberation movement; founder of Women's Art Colony. *The Loony-Bin Trip* (1990), *The Politics of Cruelty* (1994), *A.D.: A Memoir* (1995).

The three instances of sexual description we have examined so far were remarkable for the large part which notions of ascendancy and power played within them. Coitus can scarcely be said to take place in a vacuum; although of itself it appears a biological and physical activity, it is set so deeply within the larger context of human affairs that it serves as a charged microcosm of the variety of attitudes and values to which culture subscribes. Among other things, it may serve as a model of sexual politics on an individual or personal plane.

But of course the transition from such scenes of intimacy to a wider context of political reference is a great step indeed. In introducing the term "sexual politics," one must first answer the inevitable question "Can the relationship between the sexes be viewed in a political light at all?" The answer depends on how one defines politics.[1] This essay does not define the political as that relatively narrow and exclusive world of meetings, chairmen, and parties. The term "politics" shall refer to power-structured relationships, arrangements whereby one group of persons is controlled by another. By way of parenthesis one might add that although an ideal politics might simply be conceived of as the arrangement of human life on agreeable and rational principles from whence the entire notion of power *over* others should be banished, one must confess that this is not what constitutes the political as we know it, and it is to this that we must address ourselves.

The following sketch, which might be described as "notes toward a theory of patriarchy," will attempt to prove that sex is a status category with political implications. Something of a pioneering effort, it must perforce be both tentative and imperfect. Because the intention is to provide an overall description, statements must be generalized, exceptions neglected, and subheadings overlapping and, to some degree, arbitrary as well.

The word "politics" is enlisted here when speaking of the sexes primarily because such a word is eminently useful in outlining the real nature of their relative status, historically and at the present. It is opportune, perhaps today even mandatory, that we develop a more relevant psychology and philosophy of power relationships beyond the simple conceptual framework provided by our traditional formal politics. Indeed, it may be imperative that we give some attention to defining a theory of politics which treats of power relationships on grounds less conventional than those to which we are accustomed.[2] I have therefore found it pertinent to define them on grounds of personal contact and interaction between members of well-defined and coherent groups: races, castes, classes, and sexes. For it is precisely because certain groups have no representation in a number of recognized political structures that their position tends to be so stable, their oppression so continuous.

In America, recent events have forced us to acknowledge at last that the relationship between the races is indeed a political one which involves the general control of one collectivity, defined by birth, over another collectivity, also defined by birth. Groups who rule by birthright are fast disappearing, yet there remains one ancient and universal scheme for the domination of one birth group by another—the scheme that prevails in the area of sex. The study of racism has convinced us that a truly political state of affairs operates between the races to perpetuate a series of oppressive circumstances. The subordinated group has inadequate redress through existing political institutions, and is deterred thereby from organizing into conventional political struggle and opposition.

Quite in the same manner, a disinterested examination of our system of sexual relationship must point out that the situation between the sexes now, and throughout history, is a case of that phenomenon Max Weber defined as *herrschaft,* a relationship of dominance and subordinance.[3] What goes largely unexamined, often even unacknowledged (yet is institutionalized nonetheless) in our social order, is the birthright priority whereby males rule females. Through this system a most ingenious form of "interior colonization" has been achieved. It is one which tends moreover to be sturdier than any form of segregation, and more rigorous than class stratification, more uniform, certainly more enduring. However muted its present appearance may be, sexual dominion obtains nevertheless as perhaps the most pervasive ideology of our culture and provides its most fundamental concept of power.

This is so because our society, like all other historical civilizations, is a patriarchy.[4] The fact is evident at once if one recalls that the military, industry, technology, universities, science, political office, and finance—in short, every avenue of power within the society, including the coercive force of the police—is entirely in male hands. As the essence of politics is power, such realization cannot fail to carry impact. What lingers of supernatural authority, the Deity, "His" ministry, together with the ethics and values, the philosophy and art of our culture—its very civilization—as T. S. Eliot once observed, is of male manufacture.

If one takes patriarchal government to be the institution whereby that half of the populace which is female is controlled by that half which is male, the principles of patriarchy appear to be twofold: male shall dominate female, elder male shall dominate younger. However, just as with any human institution, there is frequently a distance between the real and the ideal; contradictions and exceptions do exist within the system. While patriarchy as an institution is a social constant so deeply entrenched as to run through all other political, social, or economic forms, whether of caste or class, feudality or bureaucracy, just as it pervades all major religions, it also exhibits great variety in history and locale. In democracies,[5] for example, females have often held no office or do so (as now) in such minuscule numbers as to be below even token representation. Aristocracy, on the other hand, with its emphasis upon the magic and dynastic properties of blood, may at times permit women to hold power. The principle of rule by elder males is violated even more frequently. Bearing in mind the variation in degree in patriarchy—as say between Saudi Arabia and Sweden, Indonesia and Red China—we also recognize our own form in the United States and Europe to be much altered and attenuated by the reforms described in the next chapter.

[1969]

NOTES

1. The American Heritage Dictionary's fourth definition is fairly approximate: "methods or tactics involved in managing a state or government." *American Heritage Dictionary* (New York: American Heritage and Houghton Mifflin, 1969). One might expand this to a set of stratagems designed to maintain a system. If one understands patriarchy to be an institution perpetuated by such techniques of control, one has a working definition of how politics is conceived in this essay.
2. I am indebted here to Ronald V. Samson's *The Psychology of Power* (New York: Random House, 1968) for his intelligent investigation of the connection between formal power structures and the family and for his analysis of how power corrupts basic human relationships.
3. "Domination in the quite general sense of power, i.e., the possibility of imposing one's will upon the behavior of other persons, can emerge in the most diverse forms." In this central passage of *Wirtschaft und Gesellschaft* Weber is particularly interested in two such forms: control through social authority ("patriarchal, magisterial, or princely") and control through economic force. In patriarchy as in other forms of domination "that control over economic goods, i.e., economic power, is a frequent, often purposively willed, consequence of domination as

well as one of its most important instruments." Quoted from Max Rheinstein's and Edward Shil's translation of portions of *Wirtschaft und Gesellschaft* entitled *Max Weber on Law in Economy and Society* (New York: Simon and Schuster, 1967), pp. 323–24.
4. No matriarchal societies are known to exist at present. Matrilineality, which may be, as some anthropologists have held, a residue or a transitional stage of matriarchy, does not constitute an exception to patriarchal rule, it simply channels the power held by males through female descent—e.g., the Avunculate.
5. Radical democracy would, of course, preclude patriarchy. One might find evidence of a general satisfaction with a less than perfect democracy in the fact that women have so rarely held power within modern "democracies."

 41

Redstockings Manifesto

REDSTOCKINGS

REDSTOCKINGS Founded in 1969, Redstockings was a short-lived radical feminist organization. The name combines "bluestockings," a pejorative word used in the 18th and 19th centuries for educated women, with "red" for the group's radical and socialist roots.

I. After centuries of individual and preliminary political struggle, women are uniting to achieve their final liberation from male supremacy. Redstockings is dedicated to building this unity and winning our freedom.

II.   Women are an oppressed class. Our oppression is total, affecting every facet of our lives. We are exploited as sex objects, breeders, domestic servants, and cheap labor. We are considered inferior beings, whose only purpose is to enhance men's lives. Our humanity is denied. Our prescribed behavior is enforced by the threat of physical violence.

Because we have lived so intimately with our oppressors, in isolation from each other, we have been kept from seeing our personal suffering as a political condition. This creates the illusion that a woman's relationship with her man is a matter of interplay between two unique personalities, and can be worked out individually. In reality, every such relationship is a *class* relationship, and the conflicts between individual men and women are *political* conflicts that can only be solved collectively.

III.   We identify the agents of our oppression as men. Male supremacy is the oldest, most basic form of domination. All other forms of exploitation and oppression (racism, capitalism, imperialism, etc.) are extensions of male supremacy: men dominate women, a few men dominate the rest. All power structures throughout history have been male-dominated and male-oriented. Men have controlled all political, economic and cultural institutions and backed up this control with physical force. They have used their power to keep women in an inferior position. *All men* receive economic, sexual, and psychological benefits from male supremacy. *All men* have oppressed women.

IV.   Attempts have been made to shift the burden of responsibility from men to institutions or to women themselves. We condemn these arguments as evasions. Institutions alone do not oppress; they are merely tools of the oppressor. To blame institutions implies that men and women are equally victimized, obscures the fact that men benefit from the subordination of women, and gives men the excuse that they are forced to be oppressors. On the contrary, any man is free to renounce his superior position provided that he is willing to be treated like a woman by other men.

We also reject the idea that women consent to or are to blame for their own oppression. Women's submission is not the result of brainwashing, stupidity, or mental illness but of continual, daily pressure from men. We do not need to change ourselves, but to change men.

The most slanderous evasion of all is that women can oppress men. The basis for this illusion is the isolation of individual relationships from their political context and the tendency of men to see any legitimate challenge to their privileges as persecution.

V.   We regard our personal experience, and our feelings about that experience, as the basis for an analysis of our common situation. We cannot rely on existing ideologies as they are all products of male supremacist culture. We question every generalization and accept none that are not confirmed by our experience.

Our chief task at present is to develop female class consciousness through sharing experience and publicly exposing the sexist foundation of all our institutions. Consciousness-raising is not "therapy," which implies the existence of individual solutions

and falsely assumes that the male–female relationship is purely personal, but the only method by which we can ensure that our program for liberation is based on the concrete realities of our lives.

The first requirement for raising class consciousness is honesty, in private and in public, with ourselves and other women.

VI.   We identify with all women. We define our best interest as that of the poorest, most brutally exploited woman.

We repudiate all economic, racial, educational or status privileges that divide us from other women. We are determined to recognize and eliminate any prejudices we may hold against other women.

We are committed to achieving internal democracy. We will do whatever is necessary to ensure that every woman in our movement has an equal chance to participate, assume responsibility, and develop her political potential.

VII.   We call on all our sisters to unite with us in struggle.

We call on all men to give up their male privileges and support women's liberation in the interest of our humanity and their own.

In fighting for our liberation we will always take the side of women against their oppressors. We will not ask what is "revolutionary" or "reformist," only what is good for women.

The time for individual skirmishes has passed. This time we are going all the way.

July 7, 1969
[1969]

 42

An Argument for Black Women's Liberation as a Revolutionary Force

MARY ANN WEATHERS

MARY ANN WEATHERS United States. ND. Activist. Came to work in Black feminism from work in the civil rights movement of the 1960s.

"Nobody can fight your battles for you; you have to do it yourself." This will be the premise used for the time being for stating the case for Black women's liberation, although certainly it is the least significant. Black women, at least the Black women I have come in contact with in the movement, have been expending all their energies in "liberating" Black men (if you yourself are not free, how can you "liberate" someone else?). Consequently, the movement has practically come to a standstill. Not entirely due however to wasted energies, but adhering to basic false concepts rather than revolutionary principles, and at this stage of the game, we should understand that if it is not revolutionary, it is false.

We have found that Women's Liberation is an extremely emotional issue, as well as an explosive one. Black men are still parroting the master's prattle about male superiority. This now brings us to a very pertinent question: How can we seriously discuss reclaiming our African Heritage—cultural living modes which clearly refute not only patriarchy and matriarchy, but our entire family structure as we know it? African tribes live communally where households, let alone heads of households, are non-existent.

It is really disgusting to hear Black women talk about giving Black men their manhood—or allowing them to get it. This is degrading to other Black women and thoroughly insulting to Black men (or at least it should be). How can someone "give" one something as personal as one's adulthood? That's precisely like asking the beast for your freedom. We also chew the fat about standing behind our men. This forces me to the question: Are we women or leaning posts and props? It sounds as if we are saying if we come out from behind him, he'll fall down. To me, these are clearly maternal statements and should be closely examined.

Women's Liberation should be considered as a strategy for an eventual tie-up with the entire revolutionary movement consisting of women, men, and children. We are now speaking of real revolution (armed). If you cannot accept this fact purely and without problems, examine your reactions closely. We are playing to win and so are they. Viet Nam is simply a matter of time and geography.

Another matter to be discussed is the liberation of children from a sick slave culture. Although we don't like to see it, we are still operating within the confines of the slave culture. Black women use their children for their own selfish needs of worth and love. We try to live our lives, which are too oppressing to bear, through our children and thereby destroy them in the process. Obviously the much acclaimed plaudits of the love of the Black mother have some discrepancies. If we allow ourselves to run from the truth we run the risk of spending another 400 years in self-destruction. Assuming of course the beast would tolerate us that long, and we know he wouldn't.

Women have fought with men and we have died with men in every revolution, more timely in Cuba, Algeria, China, and now in Viet Nam. If you notice, it is a woman heading the "Peace Talks" in Paris for the NLF. What is wrong with Black women? We are clearly the most oppressed and degraded minority in the world, let alone the country. Why can't we rightfully claim our place in the world?

Realizing fully what is being said, you should be warned that the opposition for liberation will come from everyplace, particularly from other women and from Black men. Don't allow yourselves to be intimidated any longer with this nonsense about the "Matriarchy" of Black women. Black women are not matriarchs but we have been forced to live in abandonment and been used and abused. The myth of the matriarchy must stop and we must not allow ourselves to be sledgehammered by it any longer—not if we are serious about change and ridding ourselves of the wickedness of this alien culture. Let it be clearly understood that Black women's liberation is not anti-male; any such sentiment or interpretation as such cannot be tolerated. It must be taken clearly for what it is—pro-human for all peoples.

The potential for such a movement is boundless. Whereas in the past only certain types of Black people have been attracted to the movement—younger people, radicals, and militants. The very poor, the middle class, older people and women have not become aware or have not been able to translate their awareness into action. Women's liberation offers such a channel for these energies.

Even though middle-class Black women may not have suffered the brutal suppression of poor Black people, they most certainly have felt the scourge of the male-superiority-oriented society as women, and would be more prone to help in alleviating some of the conditions of our more oppressed sisters by teaching, raising awareness and consciousness, verbalizing the ills of women and this society, helping to establish communes.

Older women have a wealth of information and experience to offer and would be instrumental in closing the communications gap between the generations. To be Black and to tolerate this jive about discounting people over 30 is madness.

Poor women have knowledge to teach us all. Who else in this society see more and are more realistic about ourselves and this society and about the faults that lie within our own people than our poor women? Who else could profit and benefit from a communal setting that could be established than these sisters? We must let the sisters know that we are capable and some of us already do love them. We women must begin to unabashedly learn to use the word "love" for one another. We must stop the petty jealousies, the violence that we Black women have for so long perpetrated on one another about fighting over this man or the other. (Black men should have better sense than to encourage this kind of destructive behavior.) We must turn to ourselves and one another for strength and solace. Just think for a moment what it would be like if we got together and organized our own 24-hour-a-day communal centers, knowing our children would be safe and loved constantly. Not to mention what it would do for everyone's egos, especially the children. Women should not have to be enslaved by this society's concept of motherhood through their children; and then the kids suffer through a mother's resentment of it by beatings, punishment, and rigid discipline. All one has to do is look at the statistics of Black women who are rapidly filling the beast's mental institutions to know that the time for innovation and change and creative thinking is here. We cannot sit on our behinds waiting for someone else to do it for us. We must save ourselves.

We do not have to look at ourselves as someone's personal sex objects, maids, baby sitters, domestics and the like in exchange for a man's attention. Men hold this power, along with that of the breadwinner, over our heads for these services and that's all it is—servitude. In return we torture him, and fill him with insecurities about his manhood, and literally force him to "cat" and "mess around," bringing in all sorts of conflicts. This is not the way really human people live. This is whitey's thing. And we play the game with as much proficiency as he does.

If we are going to bring about a better world, where best to begin than with our selves? We must rid ourselves of our own hang-ups before we can begin to talk about the rest of the world and we mean the world and nothing short of just that. (Let's not kid ourselves.) We will be in a position soon of having to hook up with the rest of the oppressed peoples of the world who are involved in liberation just as we are, and we had better be ready to act.

All women suffer oppression, even white women, particularly poor white women, and especially Indian, Mexican, Puerto Rican, Oriental and Black American women, whose oppression is tripled by any of the above mentioned. But we do have females' oppression in common. This means that we can begin to talk to other women with this common factor and start building links with them and thereby build and transform the revolutionary force we are now beginning to amass. This is what Dr. King was doing. We can no longer allow ourselves to be duped by the guise of racism. Any time the White man admits to something you know he is trying to cover something else up. We are all being exploited, even the white middle class, by the few people in control of this entire world. And to keep the real issue clouded, he keeps us at one another's throats with this racism jive. Although Whites are most certainly racist, we must understand that they have been programmed to think in these patterns to divert their attention. If they are busy fighting us, then they have no time to question the policies of the war being run by this government. With the way the elections went down it is clear that they are as powerless as the rest of us. Make no question about it, folks, this fool knows what he is doing. This man is playing the death game for money and power, not because he doesn't like us. He couldn't care less one way or the other. But think for a moment if we all got together and just walked on out. Who would fight his wars, who would run his police state, who would work his factories, who would buy his products?

We women must start this thing rolling.

[1969]

43

The Myth of the Vaginal Orgasm

ANNE KOEDT

ANNE KOEDT United States. ND. Activist. Cofounder of New York Radical Women and New York Radical Feminists. Co-editor of *Notes from the Second Year* (1970) and *Notes from the Third Year* (1971). "Lesbianism and Feminism" (1971).

Whenever female orgasm and frigidity are discussed, a false distinction is made between the vaginal and the clitoral orgasm. Frigidity has generally been defined by men as the failure of women to have vaginal orgasms. Actually the vagina is not a highly sensitive area and is not constructed to achieve orgasm. It is the clitoris which is the center of sexual sensitivity and which is the female equivalent of the penis.

I think this explains a great many things: first of all, the fact that the so-called frigidity rate among women is phenomenally high. Rather than tracing female frigidity to the false assumptions about female anatomy, our "experts" have declared frigidity a psychological problem of women. Those women who complained about it were recommended psychiatrists, so that they might discover their "problem"—diagnosed generally as a failure to adjust to their role as women.

The facts of female anatomy and sexual response tell a different story. There is only one area for sexual climax, although there are many areas for sexual arousal; that area is the clitoris. All orgasms are extensions of sensation from this area. Since the clitoris is not necessarily stimulated sufficiently in the conventional sexual positions, we are left "frigid."

Aside from physical stimulation, which is the common cause of orgasm for most people, there is also stimulation through primarily mental processes. Some women, for example, may achieve orgasm through sexual fantasies or through fetishes. However, while the stimulation may be psychological, the orgasm manifests itself physically. Thus, while

the cause is psychological, the *effect* is still physical, and the orgasm necessarily takes place in the sexual organ equipped for sexual climax—the clitoris. The orgasm experience may also differ in degree of intensity—some more localized, and some more diffuse and sensitive. But they are all clitoral orgasms.

All this leads to some interesting questions about conventional sex and our role in it. Men have orgasms essentially by friction with the vagina, not the clitoral area, which is external and not able to cause friction the way penetration does. Women have thus been defined sexually in terms of what pleases men; our own biology has not been properly analyzed. Instead, we are fed the myth of the liberated woman and her vaginal orgasm—an orgasm which in fact does not exist.

What we must do is redefine our sexuality. We must discard the "normal" concepts of sex and create new guidelines which take into account mutual sexual enjoyment. While the idea of mutual enjoyment is liberally applauded in marriage manuals, it is not followed to its logical conclusion. We must begin to demand that if certain sexual positions now defined as "standard" are not mutually conducive to orgasm, they no longer be defined as standard. New techniques must be used or devised which transform this particular aspect of our current sexual exploitation.

FREUD—A FATHER OF THE VAGINAL ORGASM

Freud contended that the clitoral orgasm was adolescent, and that upon puberty, when women began having intercourse with men, women should transfer the center of orgasm to the vagina. The vagina, it was assumed, was able to produce a parallel, but more mature, orgasm than the clitoris. Much work was done to elaborate on this theory, but little was done to challenge the basic assumptions. . . .

Once having laid down the law about the nature of our sexuality, Freud not so strangely discovered a tremendous problem of frigidity in women. His recommended cure for a woman who was frigid was psychiatric care. She was suffering from failure to mentally adjust to her "natural" role as a woman. Frank S. Caprio, a contemporary follower of these ideas, states: ". . . Whenever a woman is incapable of achieving an orgasm via coitus, provided her husband is an adequate partner, and prefers clitoral stimulation to any other form of sexual activity, she can be regarded as suffering from frigidity and requires psychiatric assistance" (*The Sexually Adequate Female,* p. 64). The explanation given was that women were envious of men—"renunciation of womanhood." Thus it was diagnosed as an anti-male phenomenon.

It is important to emphasize that Freud did not base his theory upon a study of woman's anatomy, but rather upon his assumptions of woman as an inferior appendage to man, and her consequent social and psychological role. In their attempts to deal with the ensuing problem of mass frigidity, Freudians created elaborate mental gymnastics. Marie Bonaparte, in *Female Sexuality,* goes so far as to suggest surgery to help women back on their rightful path. Having discovered a strange connection between the nonfrigid woman and the location of the clitoris near the vagina,

> it then occurred to me that where, in certain women, this gap was excessive, and clitoridal fixation obdurate, a clitoridal-vaginal reconciliation might be effected by surgical means, which would then benefit the normal erotic function. Professor Halban, of Vienna, as much a biologist as surgeon, became interested in the problem and worked out a simple operative technique. In this, the suspensory ligament of the clitoris was severed and the clitoris secured to the underlying structures, thus fixing it in a lower position, with eventual reduction of the labia minora. [p. 148]

But the severest damage was not in the area of surgery, where Freudians ran around absurdly trying to change female anatomy to fit their basic assumptions. The worse damage was done to the mental health of women, who either suffered silently with self-blame or flocked to the psychiatrists looking desperately for the hidden and terrible repression that kept from them their vaginal destiny.

LACK OF EVIDENCE?

One may perhaps at first claim that these are unknown and unexplored areas, but upon closer examination this is certainly not true today, nor was it true even in the past. For example, men have known that women suffered from frigidity often during intercourse. So the problem was there. Also, there is much specific evidence. Men knew that the clitoris was and is the essential organ for masturbation, whether in children or adult women. So obviously women made it clear where *they* thought their sexuality was located. Men also seem suspiciously aware of the clitoral powers during "foreplay," when they want to arouse women and produce the necessary lubrication for penetration. Foreplay is a concept created for male purposes, but works to the disadvantage of many women, since as soon as the woman is aroused the man changes to vaginal stimulation, leaving her both aroused and unsatisfied.

It has also been known that women need no anesthesia inside the vagina during surgery, thus pointing to the fact that the vagina is in fact not a highly sensitive area.

Today, with extensive knowledge of anatomy, with Kinsey, and Masters and Johnson, to mention just a few sources, there is no ignorance on the subject. There are, however, social reasons why this knowledge has not been popularized. We are living in a male society which has not sought change in women's role.

ANATOMICAL EVIDENCE

Rather than starting with what women *ought* to feel, it would seem logical to start out with the anatomical facts regarding the clitoris and vagina.

The Clitoris is a small equivalent of the penis, except for the fact that the urethra does not go through it as in the man's penis. Its erection is similar to the male erection, and the head of the clitoris has the same type of structure and function as the head of the penis. G. Lombard Kelly, in *Sexual Feelings in Married Men and Women,* says:

> The head of the clitoris is also composed of erectile tissue, and it possesses a very sensitive epithelium or surface covering, supplied with special nerve endings called genital corpuscles, which are peculiarly adapted for sensory stimulation that under proper mental conditions terminates in the sexual orgasm. No other part of the female generative tract has such corpuscles. [Pocketbooks; p. 35]

The clitoris has no other function than that of sexual pleasure.

The Vagina—Its functions are related to the reproductive function. Principally, (1) menstruation, (2) receive penis, (3) hold semen, and (4) birth passage. The interior of the vagina, which according to the defenders of the vaginally caused orgasm is the center and producer of the orgasm, is "like nearly all other internal body structures, poorly supplied with end organs of touch. The internal endodermal origin of the lining of the vagina makes it similar in this respect to the rectum and other parts of the digestive tract" (Kinsey, *Sexual Behavior in the Human Female,* p. 580). The degree of insensitivity inside the vagina is so high that "among the women who were tested in our gynecologic sample, less than 14 percent were at all conscious that they had been touched" (Kinsey, p. 580).

Even the importance of the vagina as an *erotic* center (as opposed to an orgasmic center) has been found to be minor.

Other Areas—Labia minora and the vestibule of the vagina. These two sensitive areas may trigger off a clitoral orgasm. Because they can be effectively stimulated during "normal" coitus, though infrequent, this kind of stimulation is incorrectly thought to be vaginal orgasm. However, it is important to distinguish between areas which can stimulate the clitoris, incapable of producing the orgasm themselves, and the clitoris: "Regardless of what means of excitation is used to bring the individual to the state of sexual climax, the sensation is perceived by the genital corpuscles and is localized where they are situated: in the head of the clitoris or penis" (Kelly, p. 49).

Psychologically Stimulated Orgasm—Aside from the above-mentioned direct and indirect stimulations of the clitoris, there is a third way an orgasm may be triggered. This is through mental (cortical) stimulation, where the imagination stimulates the brain, which in turn stimulates the genital corpuscles of the glans to set off an orgasm.

WOMEN WHO SAY THEY HAVE VAGINAL ORGASMS

Confusion—Because of the lack of knowledge of their own anatomy, some women accept the idea that an orgasm felt during "normal" intercourse was vaginally caused. This confusion is caused by a combination of two factors. One, failing to locate the center of the orgasm, and two, by a desire to fit her experience to the male-defined idea of sexual normalcy. Considering that women know little about their anatomy, it is easy to be confused.

Deception—The vast majority of women who pretend vaginal orgasm to their men are faking it to, as Ti-Grace Atkinson says, "get the job." In a new best-selling Danish book, *I Accuse* (my own translation), Mette Ejlersen specifically deals with this common problem, which she calls the "sex comedy." This comedy has many causes. First of all, the man brings a great deal of pressure to bear on the woman, because he considers his ability as a lover at stake. So as not to offend his ego, the woman will comply with the prescribed role and go through simulated ecstasy. In some of the other Danish women mentioned, women who were left frigid were turned off to sex, and pretended vaginal orgasm to hurry up the sex act. Others admitted that they had faked vaginal orgasm to catch a man. In one case, the woman pretended vaginal orgasm to get him to leave his first wife, who admitted being vaginally frigid. Later she was forced to continue the deception, since obviously she couldn't tell him to stimulate her clitorally.

Many more women were simply afraid to establish their right to equal enjoyment, seeing the sexual act as being primarily for the man's benefit, and any pleasure that the woman got as an added extra.

Other women, with just enough ego to reject the man's idea that they needed psychiatric care, refused to admit their frigidity. They wouldn't accept self-blame, but they didn't know how to solve the problem, not knowing the physiological facts about themselves. So they were left in a peculiar limbo.

Again, perhaps one of the most infuriating and damaging results of this whole charade has been that women who were perfectly healthy sexually were taught that they were not. So in addition to being sexually deprived, these women were told to blame themselves when they deserved no blame. Looking for a cure to a problem that has none can lead a woman on an endless path of self-hatred and insecurity. For she is told by her analyst that not even in her one role allowed in a male society—the role of a woman—is she successful. She is put on the defensive, with phony data as evidence that she'd better try to be even more feminine, think more feminine, and reject her envy of men. That is, shuffle even harder, baby.

WHY MEN MAINTAIN THE MYTH

1. *Sexual Penetration Is Preferred*—the best stimulant for the penis is the woman's vagina. It supplies the necessary friction and lubrication. From a strictly technical point of view this position offers the best physical conditions, even though the man may try other positions for variation.

2. *The Invisible Woman*—One of the elements of male chauvinism is the refusal or inability to see women as total, separate human beings. Rather, men have chosen to define women only in terms of how they benefited men's lives. Sexually, a woman was not seen as an individual wanting to share equally in the sexual act, any more than she was seen as a person with independent desires when she did anything else in society. Thus, it was easy to make up what was convenient about women; for on top of that, society has been a function of male interests, and women were not organized to form even a vocal opposition to the male experts.

3. *The Penis as Epitome of Masculinity*—Men define their lives greatly in terms of masculinity. It is a *universal,* as opposed to racial, ego boosting, which is localized by the geography of racial mixtures.

The essence of male chauvinism is not the practical, economic services women supply. It is the psychological superiority. This kind of negative definition of self, rather than positive definition based upon one's own achievements and development, has of course chained the victim and the oppressor both. But by far the more brutalized of the two is the victim.

An analogy is racism, where the white racist compensates his feelings of unworthiness by creating an image of the black man (it is primarily a male struggle) as biologically inferior to him. Because of his power in a white male power structure, the white man can socially enforce this mythical division.

To the extent that men try to rationalize and justify male superiority through physical differentiation, masculinity may be symbolized by being the *most* muscular, the most hairy, the deepest voice, and the biggest penis. Women, on the other hand, are approved of (i.e., called feminine) if they are weak, petite, shave their legs, have high soft voices, and no penis.

Since the clitoris is almost identical to the penis, one finds a great deal of evidence of men in various societies trying to either ignore the clitoris and emphasize the vagina (as did Freud), or, as in some places in the Mideast, actually performing clitoridectomy. Freud saw this ancient and still practiced custom as a way of further "feminizing" the female by removing this cardinal vestige of her masculinity. It should be noted also that a big clitoris is considered ugly and masculine. Some cultures engage in the practice of pouring a chemical on the clitoris to make it shrivel up into proper size.

It seems clear to me that men in fact fear the clitoris as a threat to their masculinity.

4. *Sexually Expendable Male*—Men fear that they will become sexually expendable if the clitoris is substituted for the vagina as the center of pleasure for women. Actually this has a great deal of validity if one considers *only* the anatomy. The position of the penis inside the vagina, while perfect for reproduction, does not necessarily stimulate an orgasm in women because the clitoris is located externally and higher up. Women must rely upon indirect stimulation in the "normal" position.

Lesbian sexuality could make an excellent case, based upon anatomical data, for the extinction of the male organ. Albert Ellis says something to the effect that a man without a penis can make a woman an excellent lover.

Considering that the vagina is very desirable from a man's point of view, purely on physical grounds, one begins to see the dilemma for men. And it forces us as well to discard many "physical" arguments explaining why women go to bed with men. What is left, it seems to me, are primarily psychological reasons why women select men at the exclusion of women as sexual partners.

5. *Control of Women*—One reason given to explain the Mideastern practice of clitoridectomy is that it will keep the women from straying. By

removing the sexual organ capable of orgasm, it must be assumed that her sexual drive will diminish. Considering how men look upon their women as property, particularly in very backward nations, we should begin to consider a great deal more why it is not in the men's interest to have women totally free sexually. The double standard, as practiced for example in Latin America, is set up to keep the woman as total property of the husband, while he is free to have affairs as he wishes.

6. *Lesbianism and Bisexuality*—Aside from the strictly anatomical reasons why women might equally seek other women as lovers, there is a fear on men's part that women will seek the company of other women on a full, human basis. The establishment of clitoral orgasm as fact would threaten the heterosexual *institution*. For it would indicate that sexual pleasure was obtainable from either men *or* women, thus making heterosexuality not an absolute, but an option. It would thus open up the whole question of *human* sexual relationships beyond the confines of the present male–female role system.

BOOKS MENTIONED IN THIS ESSAY

Sexual Behavior in the Human Female, Alfred C. Kinsey; Pocket Books.
Female Sexuality, Marie Bonaparte; Grove Press.
Sex Without Guilt, Albert Ellis; Grove Press.
Sexual Feelings in Married Men and Women, G. Lombard Kelly; Pocket Books.
I Accuse (Jeg Anklager), Mette Ejlersen; Award Books.
The Sexually Adequate Female, Frank S. Caprio; Fawcett Gold Medal Books.

[1970]

 44

The Liberation of Black Women

PAULI MURRAY

PAULI MURRAY United States. 1910–1985. Writer. Poet. Lawyer. Priest. Civil rights and women's rights activist. Cofounder of National Organization for Women. First Black woman ordained in the Episcopal Church. *Proud Shoes: The Story of an American Family* (1956), *Song in a Weary Throat: An American Pilgrimage* (1987).

Black women, historically, have been doubly victimized by the twin immoralities of Jim Crow and Jane Crow. Jane Crow refers to the entire range of assumptions, attitudes, stereotypes, customs, and arrangements which have robbed women of a positive self-concept and prevented them from participating fully in society as equals with men. Traditionally, racism and sexism in the United States have shared some common origins, displayed similar manifestations, reinforced one another, and are so deeply intertwined in the country's institutions that the successful outcome of the struggle against racism will depend in large part upon the simultaneous elimination of all discrimination based upon sex. Black women, faced with these dual barriers, have often found that sex bias is more formidable than racial bias. If anyone should ask a Negro woman in America what has been her greatest achievement, her honest answer should be, "I survived!"

Negro women have endured their double burden with remarkable strength and fortitude. With dignity they have shared with black men a partnership as members of an embattled group excluded from the normal protections of the society and engaged in a struggle for survival during nearly four centuries of a barbarous slave trade, two centuries of chattel slavery, and a century or more of illusive citizenship. Throughout this struggle, into which have been poured most of the resources and much of the genius of successive generations of American Negroes, these women have often carried a disproportionate share of responsibility for the black family as they strove to keep its integrity intact against a host of indignities to which it has been subjected. Black women have not only stood shoulder to shoulder with black men in every phase of the struggle, but they have often continued to stand firmly when their men were destroyed by it. Few Blacks are unfamiliar with that heroic, if formidable, figure exhorting her children and grandchildren to overcome every obstacle and humiliation and to "Be somebody!"

In the battle for survival, Negro women developed a tradition of independence and self-reliance, characteristics which according to the late Dr. E. Franklin Frazier, Negro sociologist, have "provided generally a pattern of equalitarian relationship between men and women in America." The historical factors which have fostered the black women's feeling of independence have been the economic necessity to earn a living to help support their families—if indeed they were not the sole breadwinners—and the need for the black community to draw heavily upon the resources of all of its members in order to survive.

Yet these survival values have often been distorted, and the qualities of strength and independence observable in many Negro women have been stereotyped as "female dominance" attributed to the "matriarchal" character of the Negro family developed during slavery and its aftermath. The popular conception is that because society has emasculated the black male, he has been unable to assume his economic role as head of the household and the black woman's earning power has placed her in a dominant position. The black militant's cry for the retrieval of black manhood suggests an acceptance of this stereotype, an association of masculinity with male dominance and a tendency to treat the values of self-reliance and independence as purely masculine traits. Thus, while Blacks generally have recognized the fusion of white supremacy and male dominance (note the popular expressions "The Man" and "Mr. Charlie"), male spokesmen for Negro rights have sometimes pandered to sexism in their fight against racism. When nationally known civil rights leader James Farmer ran for Congress against Mrs. Shirley Chisholm in 1968, his campaign literature stressed the need for a "strong male image" and a "man's voice" in Washington.

If idealized values of masculinity and femininity are used as criteria, it would be hard to say whether the experience of slavery subjected the black male to any greater loss of his manhood than the black female of her womanhood. The chasm between the slave woman and her white counterpart (whose own enslavement was masked by her position as a symbol of high virtue and an object of chivalry) was as impassable as the gulf between the male slave and his arrogant white master. If black males suffered from real and psychological castration, black females bore the burden of real or psychological rape. Both situations involved the negation of the individual's personal integrity and attacked the foundations of one's sense of personal worth.

The history of slavery suggests that black men and women shared a rough equality of hardship and degradation. While the black woman's position as sex object and breeder may have given her temporarily greater leverage in dealing with her white master than the black male enjoyed, in the long run it denied her a positive image of herself. On the other hand, the very nature of slavery foreclosed certain conditions experienced by white women. The black women had few expectations of economic dependence upon the male or of derivative status through marriage. She emerged from slavery without the illusions of a specially protected position as a woman or the possibilities of a parasitic existence as a woman. As Dr. Frazier observed, "Neither economic necessity nor tradition has instilled in her the spirit of subordination to masculine authority. Emancipation only tended to confirm in many cases the spirit of self-sufficiency which slavery had taught."

Throughout the history of Black America, its women have been in the forefront of the struggle for human rights. A century ago Harriet Tubman and Sojourner Truth were titans of the Abolitionist movement. In the 1890s Ida B. Wells-Barnett carried on a one-woman crusade against lynching. Mary McLeod Bethune and Mary Church Terrell symbolize the stalwart woman leaders of the first half of the twentieth century. At the age of ninety, Mrs. Terrell successfully challenged segregation in public places in the nation's capital through a Supreme Court decision in 1953.

In contemporary times we have Rosa Parks setting off the mass struggle for civil rights in the South by refusing to move to the back of the bus in Montgomery in 1955; Daisy Bates guiding the Little Rock Nine through a series of school desegregation crises in 1957–59; Gloria Richardson facing down the National Guard in Cambridge, Maryland, in the early sixties; or Coretta Scott King picking up the fallen standard of her slain husband to continue the fight. Not only these and many other women whose names are well known have given this great human effort its peculiar vitality, but also women in many communities whose name will never be known have revealed the courage and strength of the black woman in America. They are the mothers who stood in schoolyards of the South with their children, many times alone. One cannot help asking: "Would the black struggle have come this far without the indomitable determination of its women?"

Now that some attention is finally given to the place of the Negro in American history, how much do we hear of the role of the Negro woman? Of the many books published on the Negro experience and the Black Revolution in recent times, to date not one has concerned itself with the struggles of black women and their contributions to history. Of approximately 800 full-length articles published in the *Journal of Negro History* since its inception in 1916, only six have dealt directly with the Negro woman. Only two have considered Negro women as a group: Carter G. Woodson's "The Negro Washerwoman: A Vanishing Figure" (14 *JNH*, 1930) and Jessie W. Pankhurst's "The Role of the Black Mammy in the Plantation Household" (28 *JNH*, 1938).

This historical neglect continues into the present. A significant feature of the civil rights revolution of the 1950s and 1960s was its inclusiveness born of the broad participation of men, women, and children without regard to age and sex. As indicated, schoolchildren, often led by their mothers, in the 1950s won world-wide acclaim for their courage in desegregating the schools. A black child can have no finer heritage to give a sense of "somebodiness" than the knowledge of having personally been part of the great sweep of history. (An older generation, for example, takes pride in the use of the term "Negro," having been part of a seventy-five-year effort to dignify the term by capitalizing it. Now some black militants with a woeful lack of historical perspective have allied themselves symbolically with white racists by downgrading the term to lower case again.) Yet, despite the crucial role which Negro women have played in the struggle, in the great mass of magazine and newspaper print expended on the racial crisis, the aspirations of the black community have been articulated almost exclusively by black males. There has been very little public discussion of the problems, objectives, or concerns of black women.

Reading through much of the current literature on the Black Revolution, one is left with the impression that for all the rhetoric about self-determination, the main thrust of black militancy is a bid of black males to share power with white males in a continuing patriarchal society in which both black and white females are relegated to a secondary status. For example, *Ebony* magazine published a special issue on the Negro woman in 1966. Some of the articles attempted to delineate the contributions of Negro women as heroines in the civil rights battle in Dixie, in the building of the New South, in the arts and professions, and as intellectuals. The editors, however, felt it necessary to include a full-page editorial to counter the possible effect of the articles by women contributors. After paying tribute to the Negro woman's contributions in the past, the editorial reminded *Ebony*'s readers that "the past is behind us," that "the immediate goal of the Negro woman today should be the establishment of a strong family unit in which the father is the dominant person," and that the Negro woman would do well to follow the example of the Jewish mother "who pushed her husband to success, educated her male children first and engineered good marriages for her daughters." The editors also declared that the career woman "should be willing to postpone her aspirations until her children, too, are old enough to be on their own," and, as if the point had not been made clear enough, suggested that if "the woman should, by any chance, make more money than her husband, the marriage could be in real trouble."

While not as blatantly Victorian as *Ebony,* other writers on black militancy have shown only slightly less myopia. In *Black Power and Urban Crisis,* Dr. Nathan Wright, Chairman of the 1967 National Black Power Conference, made only three brief references to women: "the employment of female skills," "the beauty of black women," and housewives. His constant reference to Black Power was in terms of black males and black manhood. He appeared to be wholly unaware of the parallel struggles of women and youth for inclusion in decision-making, for when he dealt with the reallocation of power, he noted that "the churches and housewives of America" are the most readily influential groups which can aid in this process.

In *Black Rage,* psychiatrists Greer and Cobbs devote a chapter to achieving womanhood. While they sympathetically describe the traumatic experience of self-deprecation which a black woman undergoes in a society in which the dominant standard of beauty is "the blond, blue-eyed, white-skinned girl with regular features," and make a telling point about the burden of the stereotype that Negro women are available to white men, they do not get beyond a framework in which the Negro woman is seen as a sex object. Emphasizing her concern with "feminine narcissism" and the need to be "lovable" and "attractive," they conclude: "Under the sign of discouragement and rejection which governs so much of her physical operation, she is inclined to organize her personal ambitions in terms of her achievements serving to compensate for other losses and hurts." Nowhere do the authors suggest that Negro women, like women generally, might be motivated to achieve as *persons*. Implied throughout the discussion is the sexuality of Negro females.

The ultimate expression of this bias is the statement attributed to a black militant male leader: "The position of the black woman should be prone." Thus, there appears to be a distinctly conservative and backward-looking view in much of what black males write today about black women, and many black women have been led to believe that the restoration of the black male to his lost manhood must take precedence over the claims of black women to egalitarian status. Consequently, there has been a tendency to acquiesce without vigorous protest to policies which emphasize the "underemployment" of the black male in relation to the black female and which encourage the upgrading and education of black male youth while all but ignoring the educational and training needs of black female youth, although the highest rates of unemployment today are among black female teenagers. A parallel tendency to concentrate on career and training opportunities primarily for black males is evident in government and industry.

As this article goes to press, further confirmation of a patriarchal view on the part of organizations dominated by black males is found in the BLACK DECLARATION OF INDEPENDENCE published as a full-page advertisement in *The New York Times* on July 3, 1970. Signed by members of the National Committee of Black Churchmen and presuming to speak "By Order and on Behalf of Black People," this document ignores both the personhood and the contributions of black women to the cause of human rights. The drafters show a shocking insensitivity to the revitalized women's rights/women's liberation movement which is beginning to capture the front pages of national newspapers and the mass media. It evidences a parochialism which has hardly moved beyond the eighteenth century in its thinking about women. Not only does it paraphrase the 1776 Declaration about the equality of "all Men" with a noticeable lack of imagination, but it also declares itself "in the Name of our good People and our own Black Heroes." Then follows a list of black males prominent in the historical struggle for liberation. The names of Harriet Tubman, Sojourner Truth, Mary McLeod Bethune, or Daisy Bates, or any other black women are conspicuous by their absence. If black male leaders of the Christian faith—who concededly have suffered much through denigration of their personhood and who are committed to the equality of all in the eyes of God—are callous to the indivisibility of human rights, who is to remember?

In the larger society, of course, black and white women share the common burden of discrimination based upon sex. The parallels between racism and sexism have been distinctive features of American society, and the movements to eliminate these two evils have often been allied and sometimes had interchangeable leadership. The beginnings of a women's rights movement in this country is linked with the Abolitionist movement. In 1840, William Lloyd Garrison and Charles Remond, the latter a Negro, refused to be seated as delegates to the World Anti-Slavery Convention in London when they learned that women members of the American delegation had been excluded because of their sex and could sit only in the balcony and observe the proceedings. The seed of the Seneca Falls Convention of 1848, which marked the formal beginning of the women's rights struggle in the United States, was planted at that London conference. Frederick Douglass attended the Seneca Falls Convention and rigorously supported Elizabeth Cady Stanton's daring resolution on woman's suffrage. Except for a temporary defection during the controversy over adding "sex" to the Fifteenth Amendment,

Douglass remained a staunch advocate of women's rights until his death in 1895. Sojourner Truth and other black women were also active in the movement for women's rights, as indicated earlier.

Despite the common interests of black and white women, however, the dichotomy of a racially segregated society which has become increasingly polarized has prevented them from cementing a natural alliance. Communication and cooperation have been hesitant, limited, and formal. In the past Negro women have tended to identify discrimination against them as primarily racial and have accorded high priority to the struggle for Negro rights. They have had little time or energy for consideration of women's rights. And, until recent years, their egalitarian position in the struggle seemed to justify such preoccupation.

As the drive for black empowerment continues, however, black women are becoming increasingly aware of a new development which creates for them a dilemma of competing identities and priorities. On the one hand, as Dr. Jeanne Noble has observed, "establishing 'black manhood' became a prime goal of black revolution," and black women began to realize "that black men wanted to determine the policy and progress of black people without female participation in decisionmaking and leadership positions." On the other hand, a rising movement for women's liberation is challenging the concept of male dominance which the Black Revolution appears to have embraced. Confronted with the multiple barriers of poverty, race, and sex, the quandary of black women is how best to distribute their energies among these issues and what strategies to pursue which will minimize conflicting interests and objectives.

Cognizant of the similarities between paternalism and racial arrogance, black women are nevertheless handicapped by the continuing stereotype of the black "matriarchy" and the demand that black women now step back and push black men into positions of leadership. They are made to feel disloyal to racial interests if they insist upon women's rights. Moreover, to the extent that racial polarization often accompanies the thrust for Black Power, black women find it increasingly difficult to make common cause with white women. These developments raise several questions. Are black women gaining or losing in the drive toward human rights? As the movement for women's liberation becomes increasingly a force to be reckoned with, are black women to take a backward step and sacrifice their egalitarian tradition? What are the alternatives to matriarchal dominance on the one hand or male supremacy on the other?

Much has been written in the past about the matriarchal character of Negro family life, the relatively favored position of Negro women, and the tensions and difficulties growing out of the assumptions that they are better educated and more able to obtain employment than Negro males. These assumptions require closer examination. It is true that according to reports of the Bureau of the Census, in March 1968 an estimated 278,000 nonwhite women had completed four or more years of college—86,000 more than male college graduates in the nonwhite population (Negro women constitute 93 percent of all nonwhite women), and that in March 1966 the median years of school completed by Negro females (10.1) was slightly higher than that for Negro males (9.4). It should be borne in mind that this is not unique to the black community. In the white population as well, females exceed males in median years of school completed (12.2 to 12.0) and do not begin to lag behind males until the college years. The significant fact is that the percentage of both sexes in the Negro population eighteen years of age and over in 1966 who had completed four years of college was roughly equivalent (males: 2.2 percent; females: 2.3 percent). When graduate training is taken into account, the proportion of Negro males with five or more years of college training (3.3 percent) moved ahead of the Negro females (3.2 percent). Moreover, 1966 figures show that a larger proportion of Negro males (63 percent) than Negro females (57 percent) was enrolled in school and that this superiority continued into college enrollments (males: 5 percent; females: 4 percent). These 1966 figures reflect a concerted effort to broaden educational opportunities for Negro males manifested in recruitment policies and scholarship programs made available primarily to Negro male students. Though later statistics are not now available, this trend appears to have accelerated each year.

The assumption that Negro women have more education than Negro men also overlooks the possibility that the greater number of college-trained Negro women may correspond to the larger number of Negro women in the population. Of enormous importance to a consideration of Negro family life and the relation between the sexes is the startling fact of the excess of females over males. The Bureau of the Census estimated that in July 1968 there were 688,000 more Negro females than Negro males. Although census officials attribute this disparity to errors in counting a "floating" Negro male population, this excess has appeared in steadily increasing numbers in every census since 1860, but has received little analysis beyond periodic comment. Over the past century the reported ratio of black males to black females has decreased. In 1966, there were less than 94 black males to every 100 females.

The numerical imbalance between the sexes in the black population is more dramatic than in any other group in the United States. Within the white population the excess of women shows up in the middle or later years. In the black population, however, the sex imbalance is present in every age group over fourteen and is greatest during the age when most marriages occur. In the twenty-five to forty-four age group, the percentage of males within the black population drops to 86.9 as compared to 96.9 for white males.

It is now generally known that females tend to be constitutionally stronger than males, that male babies are more fragile than female babies, that boys are harder to rear than girls, that the male death rate is slightly higher and life expectancy for males is shorter than that of females. Add to these general factors the special hardships to which the Negro minority is exposed—poverty, crowded living conditions, poor health, marginal jobs, and minimum protection against hazards of accident and illness—and it becomes apparent that there is much in the American environment that is particularly hostile to the survival of the black male. But even if we discount these factors and accept the theory that the sex ratio is the result of errors in census counting, it is difficult to avoid the conclusion that a large number of black males have so few stable ties that they are not included as functioning units of the society. In either case formidable pressures are created for black women.

The explosive social implications of an excess of more than half a million black girls and women over fourteen years of age are obvious in a society in which the mass media intensify notions of glamour and expectations of romantic love and marriage, while at the same time there are many barriers against interracial marriages. When such marriages do take place they are more likely to involve black males and white females, which tends to aggravate the issue. (No value judgment about interracial marriages is implied here. I am merely trying to describe a social dilemma.) The problem of an excess female population is a familiar one in countries which have experienced heavy male casualties during wars, but an excess female ethnic minority as an enclave within a larger population raises important social issues. To what extent are the tensions and conflicts traditionally associated with the matriarchal framework of Negro family life in reality due to this imbalance and the pressures it generates? Does this excess explain the active competition between Negro professional men and women seeking employment in markets which have limited or excluded Negroes? And does this competition intensify the stereotype of the matriarchal society and female dominance? What relationship is there between the high rate of illegitimacy among black women and the population figures we have described?

These figures suggest that the Negro woman's fate in the United States, while inextricably bound with that of the Negro male in one sense, transcends the issue of Negro rights. Equal opportunity for her must mean equal opportunity to compete for jobs and to find a mate in the total society. For as long as she is confined to an area in which she must compete fiercely for a mate, she will remain the object of sexual exploitation and the victim of all the social evils which such exploitation involves.

When we compare the position of the black woman to that of the white woman, we find that she remains single more often, bears more children, is in the labor market longer and in greater proportion, has less education, earns less, is widowed earlier, and carries a relatively heavier economic responsibility as family head than her white counterpart.

In 1966, black women represented one of every seven women workers, although Negroes generally constitute only 11 percent of the total population in the United States. Of the 3,105,000 black women eighteen years of age and over who were in the labor force, however, nearly half (48.2 percent) were either single, widowed, divorced, separated from their husbands, or their husbands were absent for other reasons, as compared with 31.8 percent of white women in similar circumstances. Moreover, six of every ten black women were in household employment or other service jobs. Conversely, while 58.8 percent of all women workers held white collar positions, only 23.2 percent of black women held such jobs.

As working wives, black women contribute a higher proportion to family income than do white women. Along nonwhite wives in 1965, 58 percent contributed 20 percent or more of the total family income, 43 percent contributed 30 percent or more and 27 percent contributed 40 percent or more. The comparable percentages for white wives were 56 percent, 40 percent, and 24 percent respectively.

Black working mothers are more heavily represented in the labor force than white mothers. In March 1966, nonwhite working mothers with children under eighteen years of age represented 48 percent of all nonwhite mothers with children this age as compared with 35 percent of white working mothers. Nonwhite working mothers also represented four of every ten of all nonwhite mothers of children under six years of age. Of the 12,300,000 children under fourteen years of age in February 1965 whose mothers worked, only 2 percent were provided group care in day-care centers. Adequate child care is an urgent need for working mothers generally, but it has particular significance for the high proportion of black working mothers of young children.

Black women also carry heavy responsibilities as family heads. In 1966, one-fourth of all black families were headed by a woman as compared with less than one-tenth of all white families. The economic disabilities of women generally are aggravated in the case of black women. Moreover, while all families headed by women are more vulnerable to poverty than husband–wife families, the black woman family head is doubly victimized. For example, the median wage or salary income of all

women workers who were employed full time the year round in 1967 was only 58 percent of that of all male workers, and the median earnings of white females was less than that of black males. The median wage of nonwhite women workers, however, was $3,268, or only 71 percent of the median income of white women workers. In 1965, one-third of all families headed by women lived in poverty, but 62 percent of the 1,132,000 nonwhite families with a female head were poor.

A significant factor in the low economic and social status of black women is their concentration at the bottom rung of the employment ladder. More than one-third of all nonwhite working women are employed as private household workers. The median wages of women private household workers who were employed full time the year round in 1968 was only $1,701. Furthermore, these workers are not covered by the Federal minimum wage and hours law and are generally excluded from state wage and hours laws, unemployment compensation, and workmen's compensation.

The black woman is triply handicapped. She is heavily represented in nonunion employment and thus has few of the benefits to be derived from labor organization or social legislation. She is further victimized by discrimination because of race and sex. Although she has made great strides in recent decades in closing the educational gap, she still suffers from inadequate education and training. In 1966, only 71.1 percent of all Negro women had completed eight grades of elementary school compared to 88 percent of all white women. Only one-third (33.2 percent) of all Negro women had completed high school as compared with more than one-half of all white women (56.3). More than twice as many white women, proportionally, have completed college (7.2 percent) as black women (3.2 percent).

The notion of the favored economic position of the black female in relation to the black male is a myth. The 1966, median earnings of full-time year-round nonwhite female workers was only 65 percent of that of nonwhite males. The unemployment rate for adult nonwhite women (6.6) was higher than for their male counterparts (4.9). Among nonwhite teenagers, the unemployment rate for girls was 31.1 as compared with 21.2 for boys.

In the face of their multiple disadvantages, it seems clear that black women can neither postpone nor subordinate the fight against sex discrimination to the Black Revolution. Many of them must expect to be self-supporting and perhaps to support others for a considerable period or for life. In these circumstances, while efforts to raise educational and employment levels for black males will ease some of the economic and social burdens now carried by many black women, for a large and apparently growing minority these burdens will continue. As a matter of sheer survival black women have no alternative but to insist upon equal opportunities without regard to sex in training, education, and employment. Given their heavy family responsibilities, the outlook for their children will be bleak indeed unless they are encouraged in every way to develop their potential skills and earning power.

Because black women have an equal stake in women's liberation and black liberation, they are key figures at the juncture of these two movements. White women feminists are their natural allies in both causes. Their own liberation is linked with the issues which are stirring women today: adequate income maintenance and the elimination of poverty, repeal or reform of abortion laws, a national system of child-care centers, extension of labor standards to workers now excluded, cash maternity benefits as part of a system of social insurance, and the removal of all sex barriers to educational and employment opportunities at all levels. Black women have a special stake in the revolt against the treatment of women primarily as sex objects, for their own history has left them with the scars of the most brutal and degrading aspects of sexual exploitation.

The middle-class Negro woman is strategically placed by virtue of her tradition of independence and her long experience in civil rights and can play a creative role in strengthening the alliance between the Black Revolution and Women's Liberation. Her advantages of training and her values make it possible for her to communicate with her white counterparts, interpret the deepest feelings within the black community, and cooperate with white women on the basis of mutual concerns as women. The possibility of productive interchange between black and white women is greatly facilitated by the absence of power relationships which separate black and white males as antagonists. By asserting a leadership role in the growing feminist movement, the black woman can help to keep it allied to the objectives of black liberation while simultaneously advancing the interests of all women.

The lesson of history that all human rights are indivisible and that the failure to adhere to this principle jeopardizes the rights of all is particularly applicable here. A built-in hazard of an aggressive ethnocentric movement which disregards the interests of other disadvantaged groups is that it will become parochial and ultimately self-defeating in the face of hostile reactions, dwindling allies, and mounting frustrations. As Dr. Caroline F. Ware has pointed out, perhaps the most essential instrument for combating the divisive effects of a black-only movement is the voice of black women insisting upon the unity of civil rights of women and Negroes as well as other minorities and excluded groups. Only a broad movement for human rights can prevent the Black Revolution from becoming isolated and can insure its ultimate success.

Beyond all the present conflict lies the important task of reconciliation of the races in America on the basis of genuine equality and human dignity. A powerful force in bringing about this result can be generated through the process of black and white women working together to achieve their common humanity.

[1970]

 45

The Woman-Identified Woman

RADICALESBIANS

RADICALESBIANS Grew out of the group that staged a "Lavender Menace" protest at the 1970 New York Congress to Unite Women, objecting to the invisibility of lesbians in the women's movement and in NOW in particular.

Our awareness is due to all women who have struggled and learned in consciousness-raising groups, but particularly to gay women, whose path has delineated and focused the women's movement on the nature and underlying causes of our oppression.

What is a lesbian? A lesbian is the rage of all women condensed to the point of explosion. She is the woman who, often beginning at an extremely early age, acts in accordance with her inner compulsion to be a more complete and freer human being than her society—perhaps then, but certainly later—cares to allow her. These needs and actions, over a period of years, bring her into painful conflict with people, situations, the accepted ways of thinking, feeling and behaving, until she is in a state of continual war with everything around her, and usually with her self. She may not be fully conscious of the political implications of what for her began as personal necessity, but on some level she has not been able to accept the limitations and oppression laid on her by the most basic role of her society—the female role. The turmoil she experiences tends to induce guilt proportional to the degree to which she feels she is not meeting social expectations and/or eventually drives her to question and analyze what the rest of her society more or less accepts. She is forced to evolve her own life pattern, often living much of her life alone, learning usually much earlier than her "straight" (heterosexual) sisters about the essential aloneness of life (which the myth of marriage obscures) and about the reality of illusions. To the extent that she cannot expel the heavy socialization that goes with being female, she can never truly find peace with herself. For she is caught somewhere between accepting society's view of her—in which case she cannot accept herself—and coming to understand what this sexist society has done to her and why it is functional and necessary for it to do so. Those of us who work that through find ourselves on the other side of a tortuous journey through a night that may have been decades long. The perspective gained from that journey, the liberation of self, the inner peace, the real love of self and of all women, is something to be shared with all women—because we are all women.

It should first be understood that lesbianism, like male homosexuality, is a category of behavior possible only in a sexist society characterized by rigid sex roles and dominated by male supremacy. Those sex roles dehumanize women by defining us as a supportive/serving caste *in relation to* the master caste of men, and emotionally cripple men by demanding that they be alienated from their own bodies and emotions in order to perform their economic/political/military functions effectively. Homosexuality is a by-product of a particular way of setting up roles (or approved patterns of behavior) on the basis of sex; as such it is an inauthentic (not consonant with "reality") category. In a society in which men do not oppress women, and sexual expression is allowed to follow feelings, the categories of homosexuality and heterosexuality would disappear.

But lesbianism is also different from male homosexuality, and serves a different function in the society. "Dyke" is a different kind of put-down from "faggot," although both imply you are not playing your socially assigned sex role . . . are not therefore a "real woman" or a "real man." The grudging admiration felt for the tomboy and the queasiness felt around a sissy boy point to the same thing: the contempt in which women—or those who play a female role—are held. And the investment in keeping women in that contemptuous role is very great. Lesbian is the word, the label, the condition that holds women in line. When a woman hears this word tossed her way, she knows she is stepping out of line. She knows that she has crossed the terrible boundary of her sex role. She recoils, she protests, she reshapes her actions to gain approval. Lesbian is a label invented by the Men to throw at any woman who dares to be his equal, who dares to challenge his prerogatives (including that of all women as part of the exchange medium among men), who dares to assert the primacy of her own needs. To have the label applied to people active in women's liberation is just the most recent instance of a long history; older women will recall that not so long ago, any woman who was successful, independent, not orienting her whole life about a man, would hear this word. For in this sexist society, for a woman to be independent means she *can't be* a woman—she must be a dyke. That in itself should tell us where women are at. It says as clearly as can be said: women and person are contradictory terms. For a lesbian is not considered a "real woman." And yet, in popular thinking, there is really only one essential difference between a lesbian and other women: that of sexual orientation—which is to say, when you strip off all the packaging, you must finally realize that the essence of being a "woman" is to get fucked by men.

"Lesbian" is one of the sexual categories by which men have divided up humanity. While all women are dehumanized as sex objects, as the objects of men they are given certain compensations: identification with his power, his ego, his status, his protection (from other males), feeling like a "real woman," finding social acceptance by adhering to her role, etc. Should a woman confront herself by confronting another woman, there are fewer rationalizations, fewer buffers by which to avoid the stark horror of her dehumanized condition. Herein we find the overriding fear of many women toward being used as a sexual object by a woman, which not only will bring her no male-connected compensations, but also will reveal the void which is woman's real situation. This dehumanization is expressed when a straight woman learns that a sister is a lesbian; she begins to relate to her lesbian sister as her potential sex object, laying a surrogate male role on the lesbian. This reveals her heterosexual conditioning to make herself into an object when sex is potentially involved in a relationship, and it denies the lesbian her full humanity. For women, especially those in the movement, to perceive their lesbian sisters through this male grid of role definitions is to accept this male cultural conditioning and to oppress their sisters much as they themselves have been oppressed by men. Are we going to continue the male classification system of defining all females in sexual relation to some other category of people? Affixing the label *lesbian* not only to a woman who aspires to be a person, but also to any situation of real love, real solidarity, real primacy among women, is a primary form of divisiveness among women: it is the condition which keeps women within the confines of the feminine role, and it is the debunking/scare term that keeps women from forming any primary attachments, groups, or associations among ourselves.

Women in the movement have in most cases gone to great lengths to avoid discussion and confrontation with the issue of lesbianism. It puts people up-tight. They are hostile, evasive, or try to incorporate it into some "broader issue." They would rather not talk about it. If they have to, they try to dismiss it as a "lavender herring." But it is no side issue. It is absolutely essential to the success and fulfillment of the women's liberation movement that this issue be dealt with. As long as the label "dyke" can be used to frighten a woman into a less militant stand, keep her separate from her sisters, keep her from giving primacy to anything other than men and family—then to that extent she is controlled by the male culture. Until women see in each other the possibility of a primal commitment which includes sexual love, they will be denying themselves the love and value they readily accord to men, thus affirming their second class status. As long as male acceptability is primary—both to individual women and to the movement as a whole—the term *lesbian* will be used effectively against women. Insofar as women want only more privileges within the system, they do not want to antagonize male power. They instead seek acceptability for women's liberation, and the most crucial aspect of the acceptability is to deny lesbianism—i.e., to deny any fundamental challenge to the basis of the female. It should also be said that some younger, more radical women have honestly begun to discuss lesbianism, but so far it has been primarily as a sexual "alternative" to men. This, however, is still giving primacy to men, both because the idea of relating more completely to women occurs as a negative reaction to men, and because the lesbian relationship is being characterized simply by sex, which is divisive and sexist. On one level, which is both personal and political, women may withdraw emotional and sexual energies from men, and work out various alternatives for those energies in their own lives. On a different political/psychological level, it must be understood that what is crucial is that women begin disengaging from male-defined response patterns. In the privacy of our own psyches, we must cut those cords to the core. For irrespective of where our love and sexual energies flow, if we are male-identified in our heads, we cannot realize our autonomy as human beings.

But why is it that women have related to and through men? By virtue of having been brought up in a male society, we have internalized the male culture's definition of ourselves. That definition consigns us to sexual and family functions, and excludes us from defining and shaping the terms of our lives. In exchange for our psychic servicing and for performing society's non-profitmaking functions, the man confers on us just one thing: the slave status which makes us legitimate in the eyes of the society in which we live. This is called "femininity" or "being a real woman" in our cultural lingo. We are authentic, legitimate, real to the extent that we are the property of some man whose name we bear. To be a woman who belongs to no man is to be invisible, pathetic, inauthentic, unreal. He confirms his image of us—of what we have to be in order to be acceptable by him—but not our real selves; he confirms our womanhood—as he defines it, in relation to him—but cannot confirm our personhood, our own selves as absolutes. As long as we are dependent on the male culture for this definition, for this approval, we cannot be free.

The consequence of internalizing this role is an enormous reservoir of self-hate. This is not to say the self-hate is recognized or accepted as such; indeed most women would deny it. It may be experienced as discomfort with her role, as feeling empty, as numbness, as restlessness, as a paralyzing anxiety at the center. Alternatively, it may be expressed in shrill defensiveness of the glory and destiny of her role. But it does exist, often beneath the edge of her consciousness, poisoning her existence, keeping her alienated from herself, her own needs, and rendering her a stranger to other women. They try to escape by identifying with the oppressor, living through him, gaining status and identity from his ego, his power, his accomplishments. And by not identifying with other "empty vessels" like themselves. Women resist relating on all levels to other women who will reflect their own oppression, their own secondary status, their own self-hate. For to confront another woman is finally to confront oneself—the self we have gone to such lengths to avoid. And in the mirror we know we cannot really respect and love that which we have been made to be.

As the source of self-hate and the lack of real self are rooted in our male-given identity, we must create a new sense of self. As long as we cling to the idea of "being a woman," we will sense some conflict with that incipient self, that sense of I, that sense of a whole person. It is very difficult to realize and accept that being "feminine" and being a whole person are irreconcilable. Only women can give to each other a new sense of self. That identity we have to develop with reference to ourselves, and not in relation to men. This consciousness is the revolutionary force from which all else will follow, for ours is an organic revolution. For this we must be available and supportive to one another, give our commitment and our love, give the emotional support necessary to sustain this movement. Our energies must flow toward our sisters, not backward toward our oppressors. As long as women's liberation tries to free women without facing the basic heterosexual structure that binds us in one-to-one-relationship with our oppressors, tremendous energies will continue to flow into trying to straighten up each particular relationship with a man, into finding how to get better sex, how to turn his head around—into trying to make the "new man" out of him, in the delusion that this will allow us to be the "new woman." This obviously splits our energies and commitments, leaving us unable to be committed to the construction of the new patterns which will liberate us.

It is the primacy of women relating to women, of women creating a new consciousness of and with each other, which is at the heart of women's liberation, and the basis for the cultural revolution. Together we must find, reinforce, and validate our authentic selves. As we do this, we confirm in each other that struggling, incipient sense of pride and strength, the divisive barriers begin to melt, we feel this growing solidarity with our sisters. We see ourselves as prime, find our centers inside of ourselves. We find receding the sense of alienation, of being cut off, of being behind a locked window, of being unable to get out what we know is inside. We feel a real-ness, feel at last we are coinciding with ourselves. With that real self, with that consciousness, we begin a revolution to end the imposition of all coercive identifications, and to achieve maximum autonomy in human expression.

[1970]

46

Why OWL (Older Women's Liberation)?

OLDER WOMEN'S LEAGUE

OLDER WOMEN'S LEAGUE (OWL) Founded in 1970 (as the Older Women's League) after a White House mini-conference on aging in Des Moines, Iowa, OWL is an activist chapter organization.

In general, the Women's Liberation Movement is a young movement. Statistics on age are not available but observation indicates the average age of women participating in the movement to be around 25. Older women in the movement are exceedingly rare. OWL (women 30 and above), unlike the younger women's liberation groups, was consciously created by women who:

1. felt different from the main body of the movement because of age, life experiences, family commitments and goal orientations.
2. felt that we had experienced long years of personal oppression and participated in the events of life (child birth, child rearing, marriage, divorce, homemaking and careers) that many of the younger groups theorized about.
3. felt that our special skills and knowledge could be utilized for the benefit of the movement.

OWL addresses itself to problems that do not often arise at other meetings. *Problems* like:

1. How does one live equitably with a husband when the relationship is not egalitarian?
2. How does one bring up children in an oppressive society?
3. How does a mother relate to adolescent sons who are attempting to reach male maturity by emulating male stereotyped role models?
4. How does one raise a daughter?
5. Problems of rearing children when there is one parent.
6. Problems of alimony.
7. How to cope with aging and dependent parents.

8. How to pursue a job, career or *anything* while raising a family.
9. How to participate in the movement if one's husband objects.
10. How to change from 20 to 40 years of behavioral response.

We of OWL believe that we can speak to a broad segment of Amerikan women. Having shared the problems of housewives, of the poor, of the dependent, OWL is developing programs that will speak to all our needs. Programs like:

1. Pay for housewives, the housewives' bill of rights.
2. Divorce referral service.
3. Transitional communes.
4. Job training, employment services.
5. Child care, total health care.

Sisters, join with us to create a new society.

[1970]

47

Is Female to Male as Nature Is to Culture?

SHERRY B. ORTNER

SHERRY B. ORTNER United States. 1941– . Cultural anthropologist. *High Religion: A Cultural and Political History of Sherpa Buddhism* (1989), *Making Gender: Politics and Erotics of Culture* (1996). *Anthropology and Social Theory: Culture, Power, and the Acting Subject* (2006)

Much of the creativity of anthropology derives from the tension between two sets of demands: that we explain human universals, and that we explain cultural particulars. By this canon, woman provides us with one of the more challenging problems to be dealt with. The secondary status of woman in society is one of the true universals, a pan-cultural fact. Yet within that universal fact, the specific cultural conceptions and symbolizations of woman are extraordinarily diverse and even mutually contradictory. Further, the actual treatment of women and their relative power and contribution vary enormously from culture to culture, and over different periods in the history of particular cultural traditions. Both of these points—the universal fact and the cultural variation—constitute problems to be explained.

My interest in the problem is of course more than academic: I wish to see genuine change come about, the emergence of a social and cultural order in which as much of the range of human potential is open to women as is open to men. The universality of female subordination, the fact that it exists within every type of social and economic arrangement and in societies of every degree of complexity, indicates to me that we are up against something very profound, very stubborn, something we cannot rout out simply by rearranging a few tasks and roles in the social system, or even by reordering the whole economic structure. In this paper I try to expose the underlying logic of cultural thinking that assumes the inferiority of women; I try to show the highly persuasive nature of the logic, for if it were not so persuasive, people would not keep subscribing to it. But I also try to show the social and cultural sources of that logic, to indicate wherein lies the potential for change.

· · ·

We may differentiate three levels of the problem:

1. The universal fact of culturally attributed second-class status of woman in every society. Two questions are important here. First, what do we mean by this; what is our evidence that this is a universal fact? And second, how are we to explain this fact, once having established it?

2. Specific ideologies, symbolizations, and socio-structural arrangements pertaining to women that vary widely from culture to culture. The problem at this level is to account for any particular cultural complex in terms of factors specific to that group—the standard level of anthropological analysis.

3. Observable on-the-ground details of women's activities, contributions, powers, influence, etc., often at variance with cultural ideology (although always constrained within the assumption that women may never be officially preeminent in the total system). This is the level of direct observation, often adopted now by feminist-oriented anthropologists.

This paper is primarily concerned with the first of these levels, the problem of the universal devaluation of women. The analysis thus depends not upon specific cultural data but rather upon an analysis of "culture" taken generically as a special sort of process in the world. A discussion of the second level, the problem of cross-cultural variation in conceptions and relative valuations of women, will entail a great deal of cross-cultural research and must be postponed to another time. As for the third level, it will be obvious from my approach that I would consider it a misguided endeavor to focus only upon women's actual though culturally unrecognized and unvalued powers in any given society, without first understanding the overarching ideology and deeper assumptions of the culture that render such powers trivial.

THE UNIVERSALITY OF FEMALE SUBORDINATION

· · ·

On any or all of these counts, then, I would flatly assert that we find women subordinated to men in every known society. The search for a genuinely egalitarian, let alone matriarchal, culture has proved fruitless. An example from one society that has traditionally been on the credit side of this ledger will suffice. Among the matrilineal Crow, as Lowie (1956) points out, "Women . . . had highly honorific offices in the Sun Dance; they could become directors of the Tobacco Ceremony and played, if anything, a more conspicuous part in it than the men; they sometimes played the hostess in the Cooked Meat Festival; they were not debarred from sweating or doctoring or from seeking a vision" (p. 61). Nonetheless, "Women [during menstruation] formerly rode inferior horses and evidently this loomed as a source of contamination, for they were not allowed to approach either a wounded man or men starting on a war party. A taboo still lingers against their coming near sacred objects at these times" (p. 44). Further, just before enumerating women's rights of participation in the various rituals noted above, Lowie mentions one particular

Sun Dance Doll bundle that was not supposed to be unwrapped by a woman (p. 60). Pursuing this trail we find: "According to all Lodge Grass inform- ants and most others, the doll owned by Wrinkled- face took precedence not only of other dolls but of all other Crow medicines whatsoever. . . . This par- ticular doll was not supposed to be handled by a woman" (p. 229).[1]

In sum, the Crow are probably a fairly typical case. Yes, women have certain powers and rights, in this case some that place them in fairly high posi- tions. Yet ultimately the line is drawn: menstruation is a threat to warfare, one of the most valued insti- tutions of the tribe, one that is central to their self- definition; and the most sacred object of the tribe is taboo to the direct sight and touch of women.

Similar examples could be multiplied ad infini- tum, but I think the onus is no longer upon us to demonstrate that female subordination is a cultural universal; it is up to those who would argue against the point to bring forth counterexamples. I shall take the universal secondary status of women as a given, and proceed from there.

NATURE AND CULTURE

. . .

I translate the problem, in other words, into the following simple question. What could there be in the generalized structure and conditions of exis- tence, common to every culture, that would lead every culture to place a lower value upon women? Specifically, my thesis is that woman is being identi- fied with—or, if you will, seems to be a symbol of— something that every culture devalues, something that every culture defines as being of a lower order of existence than itself. Now it seems that there is only one thing that would fit that description, and that is "nature" in the most generalized sense. Every culture, or, generically, "culture," is engaged in the process of generating and sustaining systems of meaningful forms (symbols, artifacts, etc.) by means of which humanity transcends the givens of natural existence, bends them to its purposes, controls them in its interest. We may thus broadly equate culture with the notion of human consciousness, or with the products of human consciousness (i.e., systems of thought and technology), by means of which human- ity attempts to assert control over nature.

Now the categories of "nature" and "culture" are of course conceptual categories—one can find no boundary out in the actual world between the two states or realms of being. And there is no question that some cultures articulate a much stronger oppo- sition between the two categories than others—it has even been argued that primitive peoples (some or all) do not see or intuit any distinction between the human cultural state and the state of nature at all. Yet I would maintain that the universality of rit- ual betokens an assertion in all human cultures of the specifically human ability to act upon and regu- late, rather than passively move with and be moved by, the givens of natural existence. In ritual, the purposive manipulation of given forms toward reg- ulating and sustaining order, every culture asserts that proper relations between human existence and natural forces depend upon culture's employing its special powers to regulate the overall processes of the world and life.

One realm of cultural thought in which these points are often articulated is that of concepts of purity and pollution. Virtually every culture has some such beliefs, which seem in large part (though not, of course, entirely) to be concerned with the relationship between culture and nature (see Ortner, 1973, n.d.). A well-known aspect of purity/pollution beliefs cross-culturally is that of the natural "conta- gion" of pollution; left to its own devices, pollution (for these purposes grossly equated with the unreg- ulated operation of natural energies) spreads and overpowers all that it comes in contact with. Thus a puzzle—if pollution is so strong, how can anything be purified? Why is the purifying agent not itself polluted? The answer, in keeping with the present line of argument, is that purification is effected in a ritual context; purification ritual, as a purposive activity that pits self-conscious (symbolic) action against natural energies, is more powerful than those energies.

In any case, my point is simply that every cul- ture implicitly recognizes and asserts a distinction between the operation of nature and the operation of culture (human consciousness and its products); and further, that the distinctiveness of culture rests precisely on the fact that it can under most circum- stances transcend natural conditions and turn them to its purposes. Thus culture (i.e., every culture) at some level of awareness asserts itself to be not only distinct from but superior to nature, and that sense of distinctiveness and superiority rests precisely on the ability to transform—to "socialize" and "culturalize"—nature.

Returning now to the issue of women, their pancultural second-class status could be accounted for, quite simply, by postulating that women are being identified or symbolically associated with nature, as opposed to men, who are identified with culture. Since it is always culture's project to subsume and transcend nature, if women were considered part of nature, then culture would find it "natural" to subordinate, not to say oppress, them. Yet although this argument can be shown to have considerable force, it seems to oversimplify the case. The formulation I would like to defend and elaborate on in the following section, then, is that women are seen "merely" as being *closer* to nature than men. That is, culture (still equated relatively unambiguously with men) recognizes that women are active participants in its special processes, but at the same time sees them as being more rooted in, or having more direct affinity with, nature.

· · ·

WHY IS WOMAN SEEN AS CLOSER TO NATURE?

It all begins of course with the body and the natural procreative functions specific to women alone. We can sort out for discussion three levels at which this absolute physiological fact has significance: (1) woman's *body and its functions,* more involved more of the time with "species life," seem to place her closer to nature, in contrast to man's physiology, which frees him more completely to take up the projects of culture; (2) woman's body and its functions place her in *social roles* that in turn are considered to be at a lower order of the cultural process than man's; and (3) woman's traditional social roles, imposed because of her body and its functions, in turn give her a different *psychic structure,* which, like her physiological nature and her social roles, is seen as being closer to nature. I shall discuss each of these points in turn, showing first how in each instance certain factors strongly tend to align woman with nature, then indicating other factors that demonstrate her full alignment with

culture, the combined factors thus placing her in a problematic intermediate position. It will become clear in the course of the discussion why men seem by contrast less intermediate, more purely "cultural" than women. And I reiterate that I am dealing only at the level of cultural and human universals. These arguments are intended to apply to generalized humanity; they grow out of the human condition, as humanity has experienced and confronted it up to the present day.

1. *Woman's physiology seen as closer to nature.* This part of my argument has been anticipated, with subtlety, cogency, and a great deal of hard data, by de Beauvoir (1953). De Beauvoir reviews the physiological structure, development, and functions of the human female and concludes that "the female, to a greater extent than the male, is the prey of the species" (p. 60). She points out that many major areas and processes of the woman's body serve no apparent function for the health and stability of the individual; on the contrary, as they perform their specific organic functions, they are often sources of discomfort, pain, and danger. The breasts are irrelevant to personal health; they may be excised at any time of a woman's life. "Many of the ovarian secretions function for the benefit of the egg, promoting its maturation and adapting the uterus to its requirements; in respect to the organism as a whole, they make for disequilibrium rather than for regulation—the woman is adapted to the needs of the egg rather than to her own requirements" (p. 24). Menstruation is often uncomfortable, sometimes painful; it frequently has negative emotional correlates and in any case involves bothersome tasks of cleansing and waste disposal; and—a point that de Beauvoir does not mention—in many cultures it interrupts a woman's routine, putting her in a stigmatized state involving various restrictions on her activities and social contacts. In pregnancy many of the woman's vitamin and mineral resources are channeled into nourishing the fetus, depleting her own strength and energies. And finally, childbirth itself is painful and dangerous (pp. 24–27 *passim*). In sum, de Beauvoir concludes that the female "is more enslaved to the species than the male, her animality is more manifest" (p. 239).

· · ·

Thus if male is, as I am suggesting, everywhere (unconsciously) associated with culture and female seems closer to nature, the rationale for these associations is not very difficult to grasp, merely from considering the implications of the physiological contrast between male and female. At the same time, however, woman cannot be consigned fully to the category of nature, for it is perfectly obvious that she is a full-fledged human being endowed with human consciousness just as a man is; she is half of the human race, without whose cooperation the whole enterprise would collapse. She may seem more in the possession of nature than man, but having consciousness, she thinks and speaks; she generates, communicates, and manipulates symbols, categories, and values. She participates in human dialogues not only with other women but also with men. As Lévi-Strauss says, "Woman could never become just a sign and nothing more, since even in a man's world she is still a person, and since insofar as she is defined as a sign she must [still] be recognized as a generator of signs" (1969a: 496).

Indeed, the fact of woman's full human consciousness, her full involvement in and commitment to culture's project of transcendence over nature, may ironically explain another of the great puzzles of "the woman problem"—woman's nearly universal unquestioning acceptance of her own devaluation. For it would seem that, as a conscious human and member of culture, she has followed out the logic of culture's arguments and has reached culture's conclusions along with the men. As de Beauvoir puts it (p. 59):

> For she, too, is an existent, she feels the urge to surpass, and her project is not mere repetition but transcendence towards a different future—in her heart of hearts she finds confirmation of the masculine pretensions. She joins the men in the festivals that celebrate the successes and victories of the males. Her misfortune is to have been biologically destined for the repetition of Life, when even in her own view Life does not carry within itself its reasons for being, reasons that are more important than life itself.

In other words, woman's consciousness—her membership, as it were, in culture—is evidenced in part by the very fact that she accepts her own devaluation and takes culture's point of view.

I have tried here to show one part of the logic of that view, the part that grows directly from the physiological differences between men and women. Because of woman's greater bodily involvement with the natural functions surrounding reproduction, she is seen as more a part of nature than man is. Yet in part because of her consciousness and participation in human social dialogue, she is recognized as a participant in culture. Thus she appears as something intermediate between culture and nature, lower on the scale of transcendence than man.

2. *Woman's social role seen as closer to nature.* Woman's physiological functions, I have just argued, may tend in themselves to motivate[2] a view of woman as closer to nature, a view she herself, as an observer of herself and the world, would tend to agree with. Woman creates naturally from within her own being, whereas man is free to, or forced to, create artificially, that is, through cultural means, and in such a way as to sustain culture. In addition, I now wish to show how woman's physiological functions have tended universally to limit her social movement, and to confine her universally to certain social contexts which *in turn* are seen as closer to nature. That is, not only her bodily processes but the social situation in which her bodily processes locate her may carry this significance. And insofar as she is permanently associated (in the eyes of culture) with these social milieux, they add weight (perhaps the decisive part of the burden) to the view of woman as closer to nature. I refer here of course to woman's confinement to the domestic family context, a confinement motivated, no doubt, by her lactation processes.

. . .

Woman's association with the domestic circle would contribute to the view of her as closer to nature in several ways. In the first place, the sheer fact of constant association with children plays a role in the issue; one can easily see how infants and children might themselves be considered part of nature. Infants are barely human and utterly unsocialized; like animals they are unable to walk upright, they excrete without control, they do not speak. Even slightly older children are clearly not yet fully under the sway of culture. They do not yet understand social duties, responsibilities, and morals; their vocabulary and their range of learned skills are small. One finds implicit recognition of an association between children and nature in many cultural practices. For example, most cultures have initiation rites for adolescents (primarily for boys; I shall return to this point below), the point of which is to move the child ritually from a less than fully human state into full participation in society and culture; many cultures do not hold funeral rites for children who die at early ages, explicitly because they are not yet fully social beings. Thus children are likely to be categorized with nature, and woman's close association with children may compound her potential for being seen as closer to nature herself. It is ironic that the rationale for boys' initiation rites in many cultures is that the boys must be purged of the defilement accrued from being around mother and other women so much of the time, when in fact much of the woman's defilement may derive from her being around children so much of the time.

· · ·

Now, since women are associated with, and indeed are more or less confined to, the domestic context, they are identified with this lower order of social/cultural organization. What are the implications of this for the way they are viewed? First, if the specifically biological (reproductive) function of the family is stressed, as in Lévi-Strauss's formulation, then the family (and hence woman) is identified with nature pure and simple, as opposed to culture. But this is obviously too simple; the point seems more adequately formulated as follows: the family (and hence woman) represents lower-level, socially fragmenting, particularistic sort of concerns, as opposed to interfamilial relations representing higher-level, integrative, universalistic sorts of concerns. Since men lack a "natural" basis (nursing, generalized to child care) for a familial orientation, their sphere of activity is defined at the level of interfamilial relations. And hence, so the cultural reasoning seems to go, men are the "natural" proprietors of religion, ritual, politics, and other realms of cultural thought and action in which universalistic statements of spiritual and social synthesis are made. Thus men are identified not only with culture, in the sense of all human creativity, as opposed to nature; they are identified in

particular with culture in the old-fashioned sense of the finer and higher aspects of human thought—art, religion, law, etc.

Here again, the logic of cultural reasoning aligning woman with a lower order of culture than man is clear and, on the surface, quite compelling. At the same time, woman cannot be fully consigned to nature, for there are aspects of her situation, even within the domestic context, that undeniably demonstrate her participation in the cultural process. It goes without saying, of course, that except for nursing newborn infants (and artificial nursing devices can cut even this biological tie), there is no reason why it has to be mother—as opposed to father, or anyone else—who remains identified with child care. But even assuming that other practical and emotional reasons conspire to keep woman in this sphere, it is possible to show that her activities in the domestic context could as logically put her squarely in the category of culture.

In the first place, one must point out that woman not only feeds and cleans up after children in a simple caretaker operation; she in fact is the primary agent of their early socialization. It is she who transforms newborn infants from mere organisms into cultured humans, teaching them manners and the proper ways to behave in order to become full-fledged members of the culture. On the basis of her socializing functions alone, she could not be more a representative of culture. Yet in virtually every society there is a point at which the socialization of boys is transferred to the hands of men. The boys are considered, in one set of terms or another, not yet "really" socialized; their entrée into the realm of fully human (social, cultural) status can be accomplished only by men. We still see this in our own schools, where there is a gradual inversion in the proportion of female to male teachers up through the grades: most kindergarten teachers are female; most university professors are male.[3]

Or again, take cooking. In the overwhelming majority of societies cooking is the woman's work. No doubt this stems from practical considerations—since the woman has to stay home with the baby, it is convenient for her to perform the chores centered in the home. But if it is true, as Lévi-Strauss has argued (1969b), that transforming the raw into the cooked may represent, in many systems of thought, the transition from nature to culture, then here we have woman aligned with this important culturalizing process, which could easily place her in the category of culture, triumphing over nature. Yet it is also interesting to note that when a culture (e.g., France or China) develops a tradition of *haute cuisine*—"real" cooking, as opposed to trivial ordinary domestic cooking—the high chefs are almost always men. Thus the pattern replicates that in the area of socialization—women perform lower-level conversions from nature to culture, but when the culture distinguishes a higher level of the same functions, the higher level is restricted to men.

. . .

3. *Woman's psyche seen as closer to nature.* The suggestion that woman has not only a different body and a different social locus from man but also a different psychic structure is most controversial. I will argue that she probably *does* have a different psychic structure, but I will draw heavily on Chodorow's paper to establish first that her psychic structure need not be assumed to be innate; it can be accounted for, as Chodorow convincingly shows, by the facts of the probably universal female socialization experience. Nonetheless, if we grant the empirical near universality of a "feminine psyche" with certain specific characteristics, these characteristics would add weight to the cultural view of woman as closer to nature.

It is important to specify what we see as the dominant and universal aspects of the feminine psyche. If we postulate emotionality or irrationality, we are confronted with those traditions in various parts of the world in which women functionally are, and are seen as, more practical, pragmatic, and this-worldly than men. One relevant dimension that does seem pan-culturally applicable is that of relative concreteness versus relative abstractness: the feminine personality tends to be involved with concrete feelings, things, and people, rather than with abstract entities; it tends toward personalism and particularism. A second, closely related dimension seems to be that of relative subjectivity versus relative objectivity: Chodorow cites Carlson's study (1971), which concludes that "males represent experiences of self, others, space, and time in individualistic, objective, and distant ways, while

females represent experiences in relatively interpersonal, subjective, immediate ways" (quoting Carlson, p. 270). Although this and other studies were done in Western societies, Chodorow sees their findings on the differences between male and female personality—roughly, that men are more objective and inclined to relate in terms of relatively abstract categories, women more subjective and inclined to relate in terms of relatively concrete phenomena—as "general and nearly universal differences" (p. 43).

. . .

It is thus not difficult to see how the feminine personality would lend weight to a view of women as being "closer to nature." Yet at the same time, the modes of relating characteristic of women undeniably play a powerful and important role in the cultural process. For just as relatively unmediated relating is in some sense at the lower end of the spectrum of human spiritual functions, embedded and particularizing rather than transcending and synthesizing, yet that mode of relating also stands at the upper end of that spectrum. Consider the mother–child relationship. Mothers tend to be committed to their children as individuals, regardless of sex, age, beauty, clan affiliation, or other categories in which the child might participate. Now any relationship with this quality—not just mother and child but any sort of highly personal, relatively unmediated commitment—may be seen as a challenge to culture and society "from below," insofar as it represents the fragmentary potential of individual loyalties vis-à-vis the solidarity of the group. But it may also be seen as embodying the synthesizing agent for culture and society "from above," in that it represents generalized human values above and beyond loyalties to particular social categories. Every society must have social categories that transcend personal loyalties, but every society must also generate a sense of ultimate moral unity for all its members above and beyond those social categories. Thus that psychic mode seemingly typical of women, which tends to disregard categories and to seek "communion" (Chodorow, p. 55, following Bakan, 1966) directly and personally with others, although it may appear infracultural from one point of view, is at the same time associated with the highest levels of the cultural process.

THE IMPLICATIONS OF INTERMEDIACY

My primary purpose in this paper has been to attempt to explain the universal secondary status of women. Intellectually and personally, I felt strongly challenged by this problem; I felt compelled to deal with it before undertaking an analysis of woman's position in any particular society. Local variables of economy, ecology, history, political and social structure, values, and world view—these could explain variations within this universal, but they could not explain the universal itself. And if we were not to accept the ideology of biological determinism, then explanation, it seemed to me, could only proceed by reference to other universals of the human cultural situation. Thus the general outlines of the approach—although not of course the particular solution offered—were determined by the problem itself, and not by any predilection on my part for global abstract structural analysis.

I argued that the universal devaluation of women could be explained by postulating that women are seen as closer to nature than men, men being seen as more unequivocally occupying the high ground of culture. The culture/nature distinction is itself a product of culture, culture being minimally defined as the transcendence, by means of systems of thought and technology, of the natural givens of existence. This of course is an analytic definition, but I argued that at some level every culture incorporates this notion in one form or other, if only through the performance of ritual as an assertion of the human ability to manipulate those givens. In any case, the core of the paper was concerned with showing why women might tend to be assumed, over and over, in the most diverse sorts of worldviews and in cultures of every degree of complexity, to be closer to nature than men. Woman's physiology, more involved more of the time with "species life"; woman's association with the structurally subordinate domestic context, charged with the crucial function of transforming animal-like infants into cultured beings; "woman's psyche," appropriately molded to mothering functions by her own socialization and tending toward greater personalism and less mediated modes of relating—all these factors make woman appear to be rooted more directly and deeply in nature. At the same time, however, her "membership" and fully necessary participation in culture are recognized by culture and cannot be denied. Thus she is seen to occupy an intermediate position between culture and nature.

This intermediacy has several implications for analysis, depending upon how it is interpreted. First, of course, it answers my primary question of why woman is everywhere seen as lower than man, for even if she is not seen as nature pure and simple, she is still seen as achieving less transcendence of nature than man. Here intermediate simply means "middle status" on a hierarchy of being from culture to nature.

Second, intermediate may have the significance of "mediating," i.e., performing some sort of synthesizing or converting function between nature and culture, here seen (by culture) not as two ends of a continuum but as two radically different sorts of processes in the world. The domestic unit—and hence woman, who in virtually every case appears as its primary representative—is one of culture's crucial agencies for the conversion of nature into culture, especially with reference to the socialization of children. Any culture's continued viability depends upon properly socialized individuals who will see the world in that culture's terms and adhere more or less unquestioningly to its moral precepts. The functions of the domestic unit must be closely controlled in order to ensure this outcome; the stability of the domestic unit as an institution must be placed as far as possible beyond question. (We see some aspects of the protection of the integrity and stability of the domestic group in the powerful taboos against incest, matricide, patricide, and fratricide.[4]) Insofar as woman is universally the primary agent of early socialization and is seen as virtually the embodiment of the functions of the domestic group, she will tend to come under the heavier restrictions and circumscriptions surrounding that unit. Her (culturally defined) intermediate position between nature and culture, here having the significance of her *mediation* (i.e., performing conversion functions) between nature and culture, would thus account not only for her lower status but for the greater restrictions placed upon her activities. In virtually every culture her permissible sexual activities are more closely circumscribed than man's, she is offered a much smaller range of role choices, and she is afforded direct access to a far more limited range of its social institutions. Further, she is almost universally socialized to have a narrower and generally more conservative set of attitudes and views than man, and the limited social contexts of her adult life reinforce this situation. This socially engendered conservatism and traditionalism of woman's thinking is another—perhaps the worst, certainly the most insidious—mode of social restriction, and would clearly be related to her traditional function of producing well-socialized members of the group.

Finally, woman's intermediate position may have the implication of greater symbolic ambiguity (see also Rosaldo). Shifting our image of the culture/nature relationship once again, we may envision culture in this case as a small clearing within the forest of the larger natural system. From this point of view, that which is intermediate between culture and nature is located on the continuous periphery of culture's clearing; and though it may thus appear to stand both above and below (and beside) culture, it is simply outside and around it. We can begin to understand then how a single system of cultural thought can often assign to woman completely polarized and apparently contradictory meanings, since extremes, as we say, meet. That she often represents both life and death is only the simplest example one could mention.

For another perspective on the same point, it will be recalled that the psychic mode associated with women seems to stand at both the bottom and the top of the scale of human modes of relating. The tendency in that mode is to get involved more directly with people as individuals and not as representatives of one social category or another; this mode can be seen as either "ignoring" (and thus subverting) or "transcending" (and thus achieving a higher synthesis of) those social categories, depending upon the cultural view for any given purpose. Thus we can account easily for both the subversive feminine symbols (witches, evil eye, menstrual pollution, castrating mothers) and the feminine symbols of transcendence (mother goddesses, merciful dispensers of salvation, female symbols of justice, and the strong presence of feminine symbolism in the realms of art, religion, ritual, and law). Feminine symbolism, far more often than masculine symbolism, manifests this propensity

toward polarized ambiguity—sometimes utterly exalted, sometimes utterly debased, rarely within the normal range of human possibilities.

If woman's (culturally viewed) intermediacy between culture and nature has this implication of generalized ambiguity of meaning characteristic of marginal phenomena, then we are also in a better position to account for those cultural and historical "inversions" in which women are in some way or other symbolically aligned with culture and men with nature. A number of cases come to mind: the Sirionó of Brazil, among whom, according to Ingham (1971: 1098), "nature, the raw, and maleness" are opposed to "culture, the cooked, and femaleness";[5] Nazi Germany, in which women were said to be the guardians of culture and morals; European courtly love, in which man considered himself the beast and woman the pristine exalted object—a pattern of thinking that persists, for example, among modern Spanish peasants (see Pitt-Rivers, 1961; Rosaldo). And there are no doubt other cases of this sort, including some aspects of our own culture's view of women. Each such instance of an alignment of women with culture rather than nature requires detailed analysis of specific historical and ethnographic data. But in indicating how nature in general, and the feminine mode of interpersonal relations in particular, can appear from certain points of view to stand both under and over (but really simply outside of) the sphere of culture's hegemony, we have at least laid the groundwork for such analyses.

In short, the postulate that woman is viewed as closer to nature than man has several implications for further analysis, and can be interpreted in several different ways. If it is viewed simply as a *middle* position on a scale from culture down to nature, then it is still seen as lower than culture and thus accounts for the pan-cultural assumption that woman is lower than man in the order of things. If it is read as a *mediating* element in the culture–nature relationship, then it may account in part for the cultural tendency not merely to devalue woman but to circumscribe and restrict her functions, since culture must maintain control over its (pragmatic and symbolic) mechanisms for the conversion of nature into culture. And if it is read as an *ambiguous* status between culture and nature, it may help account for the fact that, in specific cultural ideologies and symbolizations, woman can occasionally be aligned with culture, and in any event is often assigned polarized and contradictory meanings within a single symbolic system. Middle status, mediating functions, ambiguous meaning—all are different readings, for different contextual purposes, of woman's being seen as intermediate between nature and culture.

CONCLUSIONS

Ultimately, it must be stressed again that the whole scheme is a construct of culture rather than a fact of nature. Woman is not "in reality" any closer to (or further from) nature than man—both have consciousness, both are mortal. But there are certainly reasons why she appears that way, which is what I have tried to show in this paper. The result is a (sadly) efficient feedback system: various aspects of woman's situation (physical, social, psychological) contribute to her being seen as closer to nature, while the view of her as closer to nature is in turn embodied in institutional forms that reproduce her situation. The implications for social change are similarly circular: a different cultural view can only grow out of a different social actuality; a different social actuality can only grow out of a different cultural view.

It is clear, then, that the situation must be attacked from both sides. Efforts directed solely at changing the social institutions—through setting quotas on hiring, for example, or through passing equal-pay-for-equal-work laws—cannot have far-reaching effects if cultural language and imagery continue to purvey a relatively devalued view of women. But at the same time efforts directed solely at changing cultural assumptions—through male and female consciousness-raising groups, for example, or through revision of educational materials and mass-media imagery—cannot be successful unless the institutional base of the society is changed to support and reinforce the changed cultural view. Ultimately, both men and women can and must be equally involved in projects of creativity and transcendence. Only then will women be seen as aligned with culture, in culture's ongoing dialectic with nature.

[1974]

REFERENCES

Bakan, David, 1966. *The Duality of Human Existence*. Boston.
Carlson, Rae. 1971. "Sex Differences in Ego Functioning: Exploratory Studies of Agency and Communion," *Journal of Consulting and Clinical Psychology,* 37: 267–77.
De Beauvoir, Simone. 1953. *The Second Sex*. New York. Originally published in French in 1949.
Ingham, John M. 1971. "Are the Sirionó Raw or Cooked?" *American Anthropologist,* 73: 1092–99.
Lévi-Strauss, Claude. 1969a. *The Elementary Structures of Kinship*. Trans. J. H. Bell and J. R. von Strumer; ed. R. Needham. Boston.
_____ 1969b. *The Raw and the Cooked*. Trans. J. and D. Weightman. New York.
Lowie, Robert. 1956. *The Crow Indians*. New York. Originally published in 1935.
Ortner, Sherry B. 1973. "Sherpa Purity," *American Anthropologist,* 75: 49–63.
_____ n. d. "Purification Beliefs and Practices," *Encyclopaedia Britannica,* forthcoming.
Pitt-Rivers, Julian. 1961. *People of the Sierra*. Chicago.
Ullman, Stephen. 1963. "Semantic Universals," in Joseph H. Greenberg, ed., *Universals of Language*. Cambridge, MA.

NOTES

1. While we are on the subject of injustices of various kinds, we might note that Lowie secretly bought this doll, the most sacred object in the tribal repertoire, from its custodian, the widow of Wrinkled-face. She asked $400 for it, but this price was "far beyond [Lowie's] means," and he finally got it for $80 (p. 300).
2. Semantic theory uses the concept of motivation of meaning, which encompasses various ways in which a meaning may be assigned to a symbol because of certain objective properties of that symbol, rather than by arbitrary association. In a sense, this entire paper is an inquiry into the motivation of the meaning of woman as a symbol, asking why woman may be unconsciously assigned the significance of being closer to nature. For a concise statement on the various types of motivation of meaning, see Ullman (1963).
3. I remember having my first male teacher in the fifth grade, and I remember being excited about that—it was somehow more grown-up.
4. Nobody seems to care much about sororicide—a point that ought to be investigated.
5. Ingham's discussion is rather ambiguous itself, since women are also associated with animals: "The contrasts man/animal and man/woman are evidently similar . . . hunting is the means of acquiring women as well as animals" (p. 1095). A careful reading of the data suggests that both women and animals are mediators between nature and culture in this tradition.

48

Not for Lesbians Only

CHARLOTTE BUNCH

CHARLOTTE BUNCH United States. 1944–   . International feminist and human rights activist. Organizer. Educator. In 1970s, founder of The Furies, a lesbian-feminist collective, and of *Quest: A Feminist Quarterly.* Founding director of the Center for Women's Global Leadership. *Passionate Politics: Feminist Theory in Action: Essays, 1968–1986* (1987), *Demanding Accountability: The Global Campaign and Vienna Tribunal for Women's Human Rights* (1994).

The following is an expanded and revised version of a speech given at the Socialist-Feminist Conference, Antioch College, Yellow Springs, Ohio, July 5, 1975. Many of the ideas expressed here about lesbian-feminist politics were first developed several years ago in The Furies. Nevertheless, I am continually discovering that most feminists, including many lesbians, have little idea what lesbian-feminist politics is. This speech takes those basic political ideas and develops them further, particularly as they relate to socialist-feminism.

I am listed in your program as Charlotte Bunch-Weeks—a rather ominous slip-of-the-tongue (or slip in historical timing), which reflects a subject so far avoided at this conference that I, for one, want to talk about.

Five years ago, when I *was* Charlotte Bunch-Weeks, and straight, and married to a man, I was also a socialist-feminist. When I left the man and the marriage, I also left the newly developing socialist-feminist movement—because, for one reason, my politics then, as now, were inextricably joined with the way I lived my personal, my daily life. With men, with male politics, I was a socialist; with women, engaged in the articulation of women's politics, I became a lesbian-feminist—and, in the gay–straight split, a lesbian-feminist separatist.

It's that gay–straight split that no one here seems to want to remember—and I bring it up now, not because I want to relive a past painful to all concerned, but because it is an essential part of our political history which, if ignored, will eventually force lesbians to withdraw again from other political women. There were important political reasons for that split, reasons explicitly related to the survival of

lesbians—and those reasons and the problems causing them are still with us. It is important—especially for political groups who wish to give credence and priority to lesbian issues—to remember why separatism happened, why it is not a historical relic but still vital to the ongoing debate over lesbianism and feminism.

In my own personal experience, I, and the other women of The Furies collective, left the women's movement because it had been made clear to us that there was no space to develop a lesbian-feminist politics and life-style without constant and nonproductive conflict with heterosexual fear, antagonism, and insensitivity. This was essentially the same experience shared by many other lesbian-feminists at about the same time around the country. What the women's movement could not accept then—and still finds it difficult to accept—is that lesbianism is political: which is the essence of lesbian-feminist politics. Sounds simple. Yet most feminists still view lesbianism as a personal decision or, at best, as a civil rights concern or a cultural phenomenon. Lesbianism is more than a question of civil rights and culture, although the daily discrimination against lesbians is real and its alleviation through civil-libertarian reforms is important. Similarly, although lesbianism is a primary force in the emergence of a dynamic women's culture, it is much more. Lesbian-feminist politics is a political critique of the institution and ideology of heterosexuality as a cornerstone of male supremacy. It is an extension of the analysis of sexual politics to an analysis of sexuality itself as an institution. It is a commitment to women as a political group, which is the basis of a political/economic strategy leading to power for women, not just an "alternative community."

There are many lesbians still who feel that there is no place in socialist-feminist organizations in particular, or the women's movement in general, for them to develop that politics or live that life. Because of this, I am still, in part, a separatist; but I don't want to be a total separatist again: few who have experienced that kind of isolation believe it is the ultimate goal of liberation. Since unity and coalition seem necessary, the question for me is unity on what terms? with whom? and around what politics? For instance, to unify the lesbian-feminist politics developed within the past four years with socialist-feminism requires more than token reference to queers. It requires an acknowledgment of lesbian-feminist analysis as central to understanding and ending woman's oppression.

The heart of lesbian-feminist politics, let me repeat, is a recognition that heterosexuality as an institution and an ideology is a cornerstone of male supremacy. Therefore, women interested in destroying male supremacy, patriarchy, and capitalism must, equally with lesbians, fight heterosexual domination—or we will never end female oppression. This is what I call "the heterosexual question"—it is *not* the lesbian question.

Although lesbians have been the quickest to see the challenge to heterosexuality as a necessity for feminists' survival, straight feminists are not precluded from examining and fighting against heterosexuality. The problem is that few have done so. This perpetuates lesbian fears that women remaining tied to men prevents them from seeing the function of heterosexuality and acting to end it. It is not lesbianism (women's ties to women), but heterosexuality (women's ties to men), and thus men themselves, which divides women politically and personally. This is the "divisiveness" of the lesbian issue to the women's movement. We won't get beyond it by demanding that lesbians retreat, politics in hand, back into the closet. We will only get beyond it by struggling over the institutional and ideological analysis of lesbian-feminism. We need to discover what lesbian consciousness means for any woman, just as we struggle to understand what class or race consciousness means for women of any race or class. And we must develop strategies that will destroy the political institutions that oppress us.

It is particularly important for those at this conference to understand that heterosexuality—as an ideology and as an institution—upholds all those aspects of female oppression which have been discussed here. For example, heterosexuality is basic to our oppression in the workplace. When we look at how women are defined and exploited as secondary, marginal workers, we recognize that this definition assumes that all women are tied to men. I mention the workplace because it upset me yesterday at the economics panel that no one made that

connection; and further, no one recognized that a high percentage of women workers are lesbian and therefore their relationship to, and attitudes toward, work are fundamentally different from those assumed by straight workers. It is obvious that heterosexuality upholds the home, housework, the family as both a personal and economic unit. It is apparently not so obvious that the whole framework of heterosexuality defines our lives, that it is fundamental to the negative self-image and self-hatred of women in this society. Lesbian-feminism is based on a rejection of male definitions of our lives and is therefore crucial to the development of a positive woman-identified identity, of redefining who we are supposed to be in every situation, including the workplace.

What is that definition? Basically, heterosexuality means men first. That's what it's all about. It assumes that every woman is heterosexual; that every woman is defined by and is the property of men. Her body, her services, her children belong to men. If you don't accept that definition, you're a queer—no matter who you sleep with; if you do not accept that definition in this society, you're queer. The original imperialist assumption of the right of men to the bodies and services of women has been translated into a whole variety of forms of domination throughout this society. And as long as people accept that initial assumption—and question everything *but* that assumption—it is impossible to challenge the other forms of domination.

What makes heterosexuality work is heterosexual privilege—and if you don't have a sense of what that privilege is, I suggest that you go home and announce to everybody that you know—a roommate, your family, the people you work with—everywhere you go—that you're a queer. Try being a queer for a week. Do not walk out on the street with men; walk only with women, especially at night. For a whole week, experience life as if you were a lesbian, and I think you will know what heterosexual privilege is very quickly. And, hopefully, you will also learn that heterosexual privilege is the method by which women are given a stake in male supremacy—and that it is therefore the method by which women are given a stake in their own oppression. Simply stated, a woman who stays in line—by staying straight or by refusing to resist straight privileges—receives some of the benefits of male privilege indirectly and is thus given a stake in continuing those privileges and maintaining their source—male supremacy.

Heterosexual women must realize—no matter what their personal connection to men—that the benefits that they receive from men will always be in diluted form and will ultimately result in their own self-destruction. When a woman's individual survival is tied to men, she is at some intrinsic place separated from other women and from the survival needs of those other women. The question arises not because of rhetorical necessity—whether a woman is personally loyal to other women—but because we must examine what stake each of us has in the continuation of male supremacy. For example, if you are receiving heterosexual benefits through a man (or through his social, cultural, or political systems), are you clear about what those benefits are doing to you, both personally, and in terms of other women? I have known women who are very strong in fighting against female job discrimination, but when the battle closes in on their man's job, they desert that position. In universities, specifically, when a husband's job is threatened by feminist hiring demands, I have seen feminists abandon their political positions in order to keep the privileges they receive from their man's job.

This analysis of the function of heterosexuality in women's oppression is available to any woman, lesbian or straight. Lesbian-feminism is not a political analysis "for lesbians only." It is a political perspective and fight against one of the major institutions of our oppression—a fight which heterosexual women can engage in. The problem is that few do. Since lesbians are materially oppressed by heterosexuality daily, it is not surprising that we have seen and understood its impact first—not because we are more moral, but because our reality is different—and it is a *materially* different reality. We are trying to convey this fact of our oppression to you because, whether you feel it directly or not, it also oppresses you; and because if we are going to change society and survive, we must all attack heterosexual domination.

CLASS AND LESBIANISM

There is another important aspect of lesbian-feminism which should be of interest to a socialist-feminist conference: the connection between lesbianism and class. One of the ways that lesbianism has affected the movement is in changing women's individual lives. Those of us who are out of the closet have, in particular, learned that we must create our own world—we haven't any choice in the matter, because there is no institution in this society that is created for us. Once we are out, there is no place that wholeheartedly accepts us. Coming out is important, partly because it puts us in a materially different reality in terms of what we have to do. And it is the impact of reality that moves anyone to understand and change. I don't believe that idealism is the primary force that moves people; necessity moves people. And lesbians who are out are moved by necessity—not by choice—to create our own world. Frequently (and mistakenly), that task has been characterized as cultural. While the culture gives us strength, the impetus is economic: the expression of necessity is always material. For middle-class women this is especially true—lesbianism means discovering that we have to support ourselves for the rest of our lives, something that lower- and working-class women have always known. This discovery makes us begin to understand what lower- and working-class women have been trying to tell us all along: "What do you know about survival?"

I heard a lot about class analysis when I was in the Left, and some of it was helpful. But it wasn't until I came out as a lesbian and had to face my own survival on that basis—as an outlaw, as a woman alone—that I learned about class in my own life. Then I learned what the Left had never taught me—what my middle-class assumptions were and the way in which my background crippled me as a woman. I began to understand how my own middle-class background was holding me back personally and the ways in which middle-class assumptions were holding back the growth of our movement. Class affects the way we operate every day—as has been obvious in much of what has happened in this conference. And theories of class should help us understand that. The only way to understand the function of class in society, as far as

I'm concerned, is to understand how it functions right here, on the spot, day to day, in our lives.

Another way in which class consciousness has occurred in the lesbian community—and I want to acknowledge it because it is frequently one of the things kept locked in the bedroom closet—is the cross-class intimacy that occurs among lesbians. This intimacy usually leads to an on-the-spot analysis of class oppression and conflict based on the experience of being hit over the head with it. Understand that I am not advising every middle-class woman to go out and get herself a lower-class lesbian to teach her about class-in-the-raw; but also understand that I am saying that there's no faster way to learn how class functions in our world.

Cross-class contact occurs all the time in the lesbian community, frequently without any self-conscious politics attached to it. For example, in lesbian bars, a political process that is often misinterpreted as a purely social process is going on in women's lives. Because there are no men in that environment, the conflicts around class and race—those issues basic to women's survival—become crystal clear, if you understand them not in rhetorical or theoretical terms, but in the ways that women's lives are interacting with each other's. This is one reason why a lot of class analysis, particularly the practical kind, has come out of the lesbian-feminist movement—analysis based on our experience of class contact and conflict, our recognition of it, and our integration of its meanings in the way we live our lives. This material experience of class realities produces real commitment to struggle and to the class question not out of idealism but as integral to our survival. Idealism can be abandoned at any time. Survival cannot.

I want to be clear about what it is that I am *not* saying. I am not saying that all lesbians are feminists; all lesbians are not politically conscious. I *am* saying that the particular material reality of lesbian life makes political consciousness more likely; we can build on the fact that it is not in the interests of lesbians to maintain and defend the system as it is.

I am also *not* saying that the only way to have this political analysis is to be a lesbian. But I *am* saying that so far most of the people with lesbian-feminist politics who have challenged heterosexuality are lesbians. But ours is not the only way, and we've got to make it not the only way. We, as lesbians, are a minority. We cannot survive alone. We will not survive alone, but if we do not survive the entire women's movement will be defeated and female oppression will be reenacted in other forms. As we all understand survival more clearly, we see that the politics and analysis of women's oppression coming out of the lesbian's life experience have got to be integrated into the politics of socialist-feminism and the rest of the women's movement.

It is not okay to be queer under patriarchy—and the last thing we should be aiming to do is to make it okay. Nothing in capitalist-patriarchal America works to our benefit and I do not want to see us working in any way to integrate ourselves into that order. I'm not saying that we should neglect work on reforms—we must have our jobs, our housing, and so on. But in so doing we must not lose sight of our ultimate goal. Our very strength as lesbians lies in the fact that we are outside of patriarchy; our existence challenges its life. To work for "acceptance" is to work for our own disintegration and an end to the clarity and energy we bring to the women's movement.

It is not okay, and I do not want it ever to be okay, to be queer in patriarchy. The entire system of capitalism and patriarchy must be changed. And essential to that change is an end to heterosexual domination. Lesbians cannot work in movements that do not recognize that heterosexuality is central to all women's oppression: that would be to work for our own self-destruction. But we can coalesce with groups which share the lesbian-feminist analysis and are committed to the changes essential to our survival. This is the basis upon which we can begin to build greater unity and a stronger, more powerful feminist movement.

[1975]

NOTE

1. "Not for Lesbians Only" first appeared in *Quest: A Feminist Quarterly,* vol. II, no. 2 (Fall 1975).

49

The Laugh of the Medusa

HÉLÈNE CIXOUS

HÉLÈNE CIXOUS Algeria. 1937– . Novelist. Essayist. Playwright. Lives and works in France. Key voice in French feminism, which is concerned with women's use of language, or *l'écriture féminine*. Helped establish first center for women's studies in France. *The Newly Born Woman* (1986), *Coming to Writing and Other Essays* (1991).

I shall speak about women's writing: about *what it will do*. Woman must write her self: must write about women and bring women to writing, from which they have been driven away as violently as from their bodies—for the same reasons, by the same law, with the same fatal goal. Woman must put herself into the text—as into the world and into history—by her own movement.

The future must no longer be determined by the past. I do not deny that the effects of the past are still with us. But I refuse to strengthen them by repeating them, to confer upon them an irremovability the equivalent of destiny, to confuse the biological and the cultural. Anticipation is imperative.

Since these reflections are taking shape in an area just on the point of being discovered, they necessarily bear the mark of our time—a time during which the new breaks away from the old, and, more precisely, the (feminine) new from the old (*la nouvelle de l'ancien*). Thus, as there are no grounds for establishing a discourse, but rather an arid millennial ground to break, what I say has at least two sides and two aims: to break up, to destroy; and to foresee the unforeseeable, to project.

I write this as a woman, toward women. When I say "woman," I'm speaking of woman in her inevitable struggle against conventional man; and of a universal woman subject who must bring women to their senses and to their meaning in history. But first it must be said that in spite of the enormity of the repression that has kept them in the "dark"—that dark which people have been trying to make them accept as their attribute—there is, at this time, no general woman, no one typical woman. What they have *in common* I will say. But what strikes me is the infinite richness of their individual constitutions: you can't talk about *a* female sexuality, uniform, homogeneous, classifiable into codes—any more than you can talk about one unconscious resembling another. Women's imaginary is inexhaustible, like music, painting, writing: their stream of phantasms is incredible.

I have been amazed more than once by a description a woman gave me of a world all her own which she had been secretly haunting since early childhood. A world of searching, the elaboration of a knowledge, on the basis of a systematic experimentation with the bodily functions, a passionate and precise interrogation of her erotogeneity. This practice, extraordinarily rich and inventive, in particular as concerns masturbation, is prolonged or accompanied by a production of forms, a veritable aesthetic activity, each stage of rapture inscribing a resonant vision, a composition, something beautiful. Beauty will no longer be forbidden.

I wished that that woman would write and proclaim this unique empire so that other women, other unacknowledged sovereigns, might exclaim: I, too, overflow; my desires have invented new desires, my body knows unheard-of songs. Time and again I, too, have felt so full of luminous torrents that I could burst—burst with forms much more beautiful than those which are put up in frames and sold for a stinking fortune. And I, too, said nothing, showed nothing; I didn't open my mouth, I didn't repaint my half of the world. I was ashamed. I was afraid, and I swallowed my shame and my fear. I said to myself: You are mad! What's the meaning of these waves, these floods, these outbursts? Where is the ebullient, infinite woman who, immersed as she was in her naiveté, kept in the dark about herself, led into self-disdain by the great arm of parental-conjugal phallocentrism, hasn't been ashamed of her strength? Who, surprised and horrified by the fantastic tumult of her drives (for she was made to believe that a well-adjusted normal woman has a . . . divine composure), hasn't accused herself of being a monster? Who, feeling a funny desire stirring inside her (to sing, to write, to dare to speak, in short, to bring out something new), hasn't thought she was sick? Well, her shameful sickness is that she resists death, that she makes trouble.

And why don't you write? Write! Writing is for you, you are for you; your body is yours, take it. I know why you haven't written. (And why I didn't write before the age of twenty-seven.) Because writing is at once too high, too great for you, it's reserved for the great—that is for "great men"; and it's "silly." Besides, you've written a little, but in secret. And it wasn't good, because it was in secret, and because you punished yourself for writing, because you didn't go all the way, or because you wrote, irresistibly, as when we would masturbate in secret, not to go further, but to attenuate the tension a bit, just enough to take the edge off. And then as soon as we come, we go and make ourselves feel guilty—so as to be forgiven; or to forget, to bury it until the next time.

Write, let no one hold you back, let nothing stop you: not man; not the imbecilic capitalist machinery, in which publishing houses are the crafty, obsequious relayers of imperatives handed down by an economy that works against us and off our backs; and not *yourself*. Smug-faced readers, managing editors, and big bosses don't like the true texts of women—female-sexed texts. That kind scares them.

I write woman: woman must write woman. And man, man. So only an oblique consideration will be found here of man; it's up to him to say where his masculinity and femininity are at: this will concern us once men have opened their eyes and seen themselves clearly.[1]

Now women return from afar, from always: from "without," from the heath where witches are kept alive; from below, from beyond "culture"; from their childhood which men have been trying desperately to make them forget, condemning it to "eternal rest." The little girls and their "ill-mannered" bodies immured, well-preserved, intact unto themselves, in the mirror. Frigidified. But are they ever seething underneath! What an effort it takes—there's no end to it—for the sex cops to bar their threatening return. Such a display of forces on both sides that the struggle has for centuries been immobilized in the trembling equilibrium of a deadlock.

Here they are, returning, arriving over and again, because the unconscious is impregnable. They have wandered around in circles, confined to the narrow room in which they've been given a deadly brainwashing. You can incarcerate them, slow them down, get away with the old Apartheid routine, but for a time only. As soon as they begin to speak, at the same time as they're taught their name, they can be taught that their territory is black: because you are Africa, you are black. Your continent is dark. Dark is dangerous. You can't see anything in the dark, you're afraid. Don't move, you might fall. Most of all, don't go into the forest. And so we have internalized this horror of the dark.

Men have committed the greatest crime against women. Insidiously, violently, they have led them to hate women, to be their own enemies, to mobilize their immense strength against themselves, to be the executants of their virile needs. They have made for women an antinarcissism! A narcissism which loves itself only to be loved for what women haven't got! They have constructed the infamous logic of antilove.

We the precocious, we the repressed of culture, our lovely mouths gagged with pollen, our wind knocked out of us, we the labyrinths, the ladders, the trampled spaces, the bevies—we are black and we are beautiful.

We're stormy, and that which is ours breaks loose from us without our fearing any debilitation. Our glances, our smiles, are spent; laughs exude from all our mouths; our blood flows and we extend ourselves without ever reaching an end; we never hold back our thoughts, our signs, our writing; and we're not afraid of lacking.

What happiness for us who are omitted, brushed aside at the scene of inheritances; we inspire ourselves and we expire without running out of breath, we are everywhere!

· · ·

She must write her self, because this is the invention of a *new insurgent* writing which, when the moment of her liberation has come, will allow her to carry out the indispensable ruptures and transformations in her history, first at two levels that cannot be separated.

(a) Individually. By writing her self, woman will return to the body which has been more than confiscated from her, which has been turned into the uncanny stranger on display—the ailing or dead figure, which so often turns out to be the nasty companion, the cause and location of inhibitions. Censor the body and you censor breath and speech at the same time.

Write your self. Your body must be heard. Only then will the immense resources of the unconscious spring forth. Our naphtha will spread, throughout the world, without dollars—black or gold—nonassessed values that will change the rules of the old game.

To write. An act which will not only "realize" the decensored relation of woman to her sexuality, to her womanly being, giving her access to her native strength; it will give her back her goods, her pleasures, her organs, her immense bodily territories which have been kept under seal; it will tear her away from the superegoized structure in which she has always occupied the place reserved for the guilty (guilty of everything, guilty at every turn: for having desires, for not having any; for being frigid, for being "too hot"; for not being both at once; for being too motherly and not enough; for having children and for not having any; for nursing and for not nursing . . .)—tear her away by means of this research, this job of analysis and illumination, this emancipation of the marvelous text of her self that she must urgently learn to speak. A woman without a body, dumb, blind, can't possibly be a good fighter. She is reduced to being the servant of the militant male, his shadow. We must kill the false woman who is preventing the live one from breathing. Inscribe the breath of the whole woman.

(b) An act that will also be marked by woman's *seizing* the occasion to *speak,* hence her shattering entry into history, which has always been based *on her suppression.* To write and thus to forge for herself the antilogos weapon. To become *at will* the taker and initiator, for her own right, in every symbolic system, in every political process.

. . .

Because the "economy" of her drives is prodigious, she cannot fail, in seizing the occasion to speak, to transform directly and indirectly *all* systems of exchange based on masculine thrift. Her libido will produce far more radical effects of political and social change than some might like to think.

Because she arrives, vibrant, over and again, we are at the beginning of a new history, or rather of a process of becoming in which several histories intersect with one another. As subject for history, woman always occurs simultaneously in several places. Woman un-thinks[2] the unifying, regulating history that homogenizes and channels forces, herding contradictions into a single battlefield. In woman, personal history blends together with the history of all women, as well as national and world history. As a militant, she is an integral part of all liberations. She must be farsighted, not limited to a blow-by-blow interaction. She foresees that her liberation will do more than modify power relations or toss the ball over to the other camp; she will bring about a mutation in human relations, in thought, in all praxis: hers is not simply a class struggle, which she carries forward into a much vaster movement. Not that in order to be a woman-in-struggle(s) you have to leave the class struggle or repudiate it; but you have to split it open, spread it out, push it forward, fill it with the fundamental struggle so as to prevent the class struggle, or any other struggle for the liberation of a class or people, from operating as a form of repression, pretext for postponing the inevitable, the staggering alteration in power relations and in the production of individualities. This alteration is already upon us—in the United States, for example, where millions of night crawlers are in the process of undermining the family and disintegrating the whole of American sociality.

The new history is coming; it's not a dream, though it does extend beyond men's imagination, and for good reason. It's going to deprive them of their conceptual orthopedics, beginning with the destruction of their enticement machine.

It is impossible to *define* a feminine practice of writing, and this is an impossibility that will remain, for this practice can never be theorized, enclosed, coded—which doesn't mean that it doesn't exist. But it will always surpass the discourse that regulates the phallocentric system; it does and will take place in areas other than those subordinated to philosophico-theoretical domination. It will be conceived of only by subjects who are breakers of automatisms, by peripheral figures that no authority can ever subjugate.

Hence the necessity to affirm the flourishes of this writing, to give form to its movement, its near and distant byways. Bear in mind to begin with (1) that sexual opposition, which has always worked for man's profit to the point of reducing writing, too, to his laws, is only a historico-cultural limit. There is, there will be more and more rapidly pervasive now, a fiction that produces irreducible effects of femininity. (2) That it is through ignorance that most readers, critics, and writers of both sexes hesitate to admit or deny outright the possibility or the pertinence of a distinction between feminine and masculine writing. It will usually be said, thus disposing of sexual difference: either that all writing, to the extent that it materializes, is feminine; or, inversely—but it comes to the same thing—that the act of writing is equivalent to masculine masturbation (and so the woman who writes cuts herself out a paper penis); or that writing is bisexual, hence neuter, which again does away with differentiation. To admit that writing is precisely working (in) the in-between, inspecting the process of the same and of the other without which nothing can live, undoing the work of death—to admit this is first to want the two, as well as both, the ensemble of the one and the other, not fixed in sequences of struggle and expulsion or some other form of death but infinitely dynamized by an incessant process of exchange from one subject to another. A process of different subjects knowing one another and beginning one another anew only from the living boundaries of the other: a multiple and inexhaustible course with millions of encounters and transformations of the same into the other and into the in-between, from which woman takes her forms (and man, in his turn; but that's his other history).

In saying "bisexual, hence neuter," I am referring to the classic conception of bisexuality, which, squashed under the emblem of castration fear and along with the fantasy of a "total" being (though composed of two halves), would do away with the difference experienced as an operation incurring loss, as the mark of dreaded sectility.

To this self-effacing, merger-type bisexuality, which would conjure away castration (the writer who puts up his sign: "bisexual written here, come and see," when the odds are good that it's neither one nor the other), I oppose the *other bisexuality* on which every subject not enclosed in the false theater of phallocentric representationalism has founded his/her erotic universe. Bisexuality: that is, each one's location in self (*répérage en soi*) of the

presence—variously manifest and insistent according to each person, male or female—of both sexes, nonexclusion either of the difference or of one sex, and, from this "self-permission," multiplication of the effects of the inscription of desire, over all parts of my body and the other body.

Now it happens that at present, for historico-cultural reasons, it is women who are opening up to and benefiting from this vatic bisexuality which doesn't annul differences but stirs them up, pursues them, increases their number. In a certain way, "woman is bisexual"; man—it's a secret to no one—being poised to keep glorious phallic monosexuality in view. By virtue of affirming the primacy of the phallus and of bringing it into play, phallocratic ideology has claimed more than one victim. As a woman, I've been clouded over by the great shadow of the scepter and been told: idolize it, that which you cannot brandish. But at the same time, man has been handed that grotesque and scarcely enviable destiny (just imagine) of being reduced to a single idol with clay balls. And consumed, as Freud and his followers note, by a fear of being a woman! For, if psychoanalysis was constituted from woman, to repress femininity (and not so successful a repression at that—men have made it clear), its account of masculine sexuality is now hardly refutable; as with all the "human" sciences, it reproduces the masculine view, of which it is one of the effects.

Here we encounter the inevitable man-with-rock, standing erect in his old Freudian realm, in the way that, to take the figure back to the point where linguistics is conceptualizing it "anew," Lacan preserves it in the sanctuary of the phallos (φ) "sheltered" from *castration's lack!* Their "symbolic" exists, it holds power—we, the sowers of disorder, know it only too well. But we are in no way obliged to deposit our lives in their banks of lack, to consider the constitution of the subject in terms of a drama manglingly restaged, to reinstate again and again the religion of the father. Because we don't want that. We don't fawn around the supreme hole. We have no womanly reason to pledge allegiance to the negative. The feminine (as the poets suspected) affirms: ". . . And yes," says Molly, carrying *Ulysses* off beyond any book and toward the new writing, "I said yes, I will Yes."

The Dark Continent is neither dark nor unexplorable.—It is still unexplored only because we've been made to believe that it was too dark to be explorable. And because they want to make us believe that what interests us is the white continent, with its monuments to Lack. And we believed. They riveted us between two horrifying myths: between the Medusa and the abyss. That would be enough to set half the world laughing, except that it's still going on. For the phallologocentric sublation[3] is with us, and it's militant, regenerating the old patterns, anchored in the dogma of castration. They haven't changed a thing: they've theorized their desire for reality! Let the priests tremble, we're going to show them our sexts!

Too bad for them if they fall apart upon discovering that women aren't men, or that the mother doesn't have one. But isn't this fear convenient for them? Wouldn't the worst be, isn't the worst, in truth, that women aren't castrated, that they have only to stop listening to the Sirens (for the Sirens were men) for history to change its meaning? You only have to look at the Medusa straight on to see her. And she's not deadly. She's beautiful and she's laughing.

. . .

. . . Her libido is cosmic, just as her unconscious is worldwide. Her writing can only keep going, without ever inscribing or discerning contours, daring to make these vertiginous crossings of the other(s) ephemeral and passionate sojourns in him, her, them, whom she inhabits long enough to look at from the point closest to their unconscious from the moment they awaken, to love them at the point closest to their drives; and then further, impregnated through and through with these brief, identificatory embraces, she goes and passes into infinity. She alone dares and wishes to know from within, where she, the outcast, has never ceased to hear the resonance of fore-language. She lets the other language speak—the language of 1,000 tongues which knows neither enclosure nor death. To life she refuses nothing. Her language does not contain, it carries; it does not hold back, it makes possible. When id is ambiguously uttered—the wonder of being several—she doesn't defend herself against these unknown women whom she's surprised at becoming, but derives pleasure from this gift of

alterability. I am spacious, singing flesh, on which is grafted no one knows which I, more or less human, but alive because of transformation.

Write! and your self-seeking text will know itself better than flesh and blood, rising, insurrectionary dough kneading itself, with sonorous, perfumed ingredients, a lively combination of flying colors, leaves, and rivers plunging into the sea we feed. "Ah, there's her sea," he will say as he holds out to me a basin full of water from the little phallic mother from whom he's inseparable. But look, our seas are what we make of them, full of fish or not, opaque or transparent, red or black, high or smooth, narrow or bankless; and we are ourselves sea, sand, coral, seaweed, beaches, tides, swimmers, children, waves. . . . More or less wavily sea, earth, sky—what matter would rebuff us? We know how to speak them all.

Heterogeneous, yes. For her joyous benefits she is erogenous; she is the erotogeneity of the heterogeneous: airborne swimmer, in flight, she does not cling to herself; she is dispersible, prodigious, stunning, desirous and capable of others, of the other woman that she will be, of the other woman she isn't, of him, of you.

. . .

The woman who still allows herself to be threatened by the big dick, who's still impressed by the commotion of the phallic stance, who still leads a loyal master to the beat of the drum: that's the woman of yesterday. They still exist, easy and numerous victims of the oldest of farces: either they're cast in the original silent versions in which, as titanesses lying under the mountains they make with their quivering, they never see erected that theoretic monument to the golden phallus looming, in the old manner, over their bodies. Or, coming today out of their *infans* period and into the second, "enlightened" version of their virtuous debasement, they see themselves suddenly assaulted by the builders of the analytic empire and, as soon as they've begun to formulate the new desire, naked, nameless, so happy at making an appearance, they're taken in their bath by the new old men, and then, whoops! Luring them with flashy signifiers, the demon of interpretation—oblique, decked out in modernity—sells them the same old handcuffs, baubles, and chains. Which castration do you prefer? Whose degrading do you like better, the father's or the mother's? Oh, what pwetty eyes, you pwetty little girl. Here, buy my glasses and you'll see the Truth-Me-Myself tell you everything you should know. Put them on your nose and take a fetishist's look (you are me, the other analyst—that's what I'm telling you) at your body and the body of the other. You see? No? Wait, you'll have everything explained to you, and you'll know at last which sort of neurosis you're related to. Hold still, we're going to do your portrait, so that you can begin looking like it right away.

Yes, the naives to the first and second degree are still legion. If the New Women, arriving now, dare to create outside the theoretical, they're called in by the cops of the signifier, fingerprinted, remonstrated, and brought into the line of order that they are supposed to know; assigned by force of trickery to a precise place in the chain that's always formed for the benefit of a privileged signifier. We are pieced back to the string which leads back, if not to the Name-of-the-Father, then, for a new twist, to the place of the phallic-mother.

Beware, my friend, of the signifier that would take you back to the authority of a signified! Beware of diagnoses that would reduce your generative powers. "Common" nouns are also proper nouns that disparage your singularity by classifying it into species. Break out of the circles; don't remain within the psychoanalytic closure. Take a look around, then cut through!

And if we are legion, it's because the war of liberation has only made as yet a tiny breakthrough. But women are thronging to it. I've seen them, those who will be neither dupe nor domestic, those who will not fear the risk of being a woman; will not fear any risk, any desire, any space still unexplored in themselves, among themselves and others or anywhere else. They do not fetishize, they do not deny, they do not hate. They observe, they approach, they try to see the other woman, the child, the lover—not to strengthen their own narcissism or verify the solidity or weakness of the master, but to make love better, to invent.

Other love.—In the beginning are our differences. The new love dares for the other, wants the other, makes dizzying, precipitous flights between knowledge and invention. The woman arriving over

and over again does not stand still; she's everywhere, she exchanges, she is the desire-that-gives. (Not enclosed in the paradox of the gift that takes nor under the illusion of unitary fusion. We're past that.) She comes in, comes-in-between herself me and you, between the other me where one is always infinitely more than one and more than me, without the fear of ever reaching a limit; she thrills in our becoming. And we'll keep on becoming! She cuts through defensive loves, motherages, and devourations: beyond selfish narcissism, in the moving, open, transitional space, she runs her risks. Beyond the struggle-to-the-death that's been removed to the bed, beyond the love-battle that claims to represent exchange, she scorns an Eros dynamic that would be fed by hatred. Hatred: a heritage, again, a reminder, a duping subservience to the phallus. To love, to watch-think-seek the other in the other, to despecularize, to unhoard. Does this seem difficult? It's not impossible, and this is what nourishes life—a love that has no commerce with the apprehensive desire that provides against the lack and stultifies the strange; a love that rejoices in the exchange that multiplies. Wherever history still unfolds as the history of death, she does not tread. Opposition, hierarchizing exchange, the struggle for mastery which can end only in at least one death (one master = one slave, or two nonmasters ≠ two dead)—all that comes from a period in time governed by phallocentric values. The fact that this period extends into the present doesn't prevent woman from starting the history of life somewhere else. Elsewhere, she gives. She doesn't "know" what she's giving, she doesn't measure it; she gives, though, neither a counterfeit impression nor something she hasn't got. She gives more, with no assurance that she'll get back even some unexpected profit from what she puts out. She gives that there may be life, thought, transformation. This is an "economy" that can no longer be put in economic terms. Wherever she loves, all the old concepts of management are left behind. At the end of a more or less conscious computation, she finds not her sum but her differences. I am for you what you want me to be at the moment you look at me in a way you've never seen me before: at every instant. When I write, it's everything that we don't know we can be that is written out of me, without exclusions, with stipulation, and everything we will be calls us to the unflagging, intoxicating, unappeasable search for love. In one another we will never be lacking.

Translated by Keith Cohen and Paula Cohen

[1975]

NOTES

1. Men still have everything to say about their sexuality, and everything to write. For what they have said so far, for the most part, stems from the opposition activity/passivity from the power relation between a fantasized obligatory virility meant to invade, to colonize, and the consequential phantasm of woman as a "dark continent" to penetrate and to "pacify." (We know what "pacify" means in terms of scotomizing the other and misrecognizing the self.) Conquering her, they've made haste to depart from her borders, to get out of sight, out of body. The way man has of getting out of himself and into her whom he takes not for the other but for his own, deprives him, he knows, of his own bodily territory. One can understand how man, confusing himself with his penis and rushing in for the attack, might feel resentment and fear of being "taken" by the woman, of being lost in her, absorbed or alone.
2. *Dé•pense,* a neologism formed on the verb *penser,* hence "unthinks" but also "spends" (from *dépenser*).—Tr.
3. Standard English term for the Hegelian *Aufhebung,* the French *la relève.*

 50

Conclusion: Women's Liberation in Muslim Countries from Beyond the Veil: Male-Female Dynamics in Modern Muslim Society

FATIMA MERNISSI

FATIMA MERNISSI Morocco. 1940– . Writer. Sociologist. *Dreams of Trespass: Tales of a Harem Girlhood* (1994), *Women's Rebellion and Islamic Memory* (1996), *Scheherazade Goes West: Different Cultures, Different Harems* (2001), *Women and Islam: An Historical and Theological Inquiry* (2004), *Harem* (2005).

People tend to perceive women's liberation as a spiritual and not a material problem. We have seen this to be true in the case of Islam, where changes in conditions for women were perceived by Muslim male literature as involving solely religious problems. Muslims argued that changes in women's conditions were a direct attack on Allah's realm and order. But changes in the twentieth century, mainly in socialist societies, have showed that the liberation of women is predominantly an economic issue. Liberation is a costly affair for any society, and women's liberation is primarily a question of the allocation of resources. A society that decides to liberate women not only has to provide them with jobs, but also has to take upon itself the responsibility for providing child care and food for all workers regardless of sex. A system of kindergartens and canteens is an indispensable investment promoting the liberation of women from traditional domestic chains.

The capacity to invest in women's liberation is not a function of a society's wealth, but of its goals and objectives. A society whose ultimate goal is profit rather than the development of human potential proves reluctant and finally unable to afford a state system of child-care centres and canteens. Mariarosa Della Costa explains how capitalism maintains, in the midst of its modern management of human resources and services, a pre-capitalist army of wageless workers—housewives—who provide unpaid child-care and domestic services.[1] Hence the paradox: the 'richest' nation in the world (the nation that controls most of the world's resources), the United States, is unable in spite of its much publicized abundance to afford a system of free kindergartens and canteens to promote women's humanhood.

Have Arab societies taken a stand on the question? Until now, they have had no effective systematic and coherent programme. In the absence of such programmes, and because it is too soon to judge the emerging trends concerning the liberation of women in independent Arab-Muslim states, I will limit myself to a few speculative remarks on the likely future of women in the Arab world. Before going any further, I want to draw attention to the inadequacy of the only two models for 'women's liberation' presently available in the Arab-Muslim world.

The scarcity of effective models for 'liberated women' might explain the particularly strong reaction that 'women's liberation' evokes from most

Muslims. (By effective models I mean models which evoke images specific enough to stir people's emotions.) One of these is an intrinsic Arab model, that of pre-Islamic family and sexuality patterns, the other is exogenous, the Western Model. The socialist models of sexuality and family patterns are hardly known and enjoy a carefully cultivated indifference, based more often on ignorance than on knowledgeable analysis. Both the pre-Islamic and Western models provoke traumatizing images of sexuality, although for different reasons.

Pre-Islamic sexuality is described in Arab literature as a chaotic, all-embracing, rampant promiscuity whose essence is women's self-determination, freedom to choose and dismiss their sexual partner, or partners, and the utter unimportance of the biological father and paternal legitimacy. The idea of female sexual self-determination which is suggested by the term 'women's liberation' is likely to stir ancestral fears of this mythical (pre-civilized) *jahiliya* woman before whom the male is deprived of all his initiative, control, and privilege. The way to win over a 'liberated woman' is to please her and make her love you, not to coerce and threaten her. But Muslim society does not socialize men to win women through love; they are badly equipped to deal with a self-determined woman; hence the repulsion and fear that accompany the idea of women's liberation.

Confusing sexual self-determination of women with chaotic, lawless animalistic promiscuity is not exclusive to Muslim societies facing drastic changes in their family structure. This confusion existed and still exists in any society whose family system is based on the enslavement of the woman. Marx and Engels had to attack repeatedly the confusion of bourgeois writers which distorted their thinking about any family in which the woman was not reduced to an acquiescent slave.[2] They had to show again and again that a non-bourgeois sexuality based on equality of the sexes does not necessarily lead to promiscuity, and that the bourgeois family pattern was an unjustified dehumanization of half of society. The same argument holds for Muslim societies. Muslim marriage is based on the premises that social order can be maintained only if women's dangerous potential for chaos is restrained by a dominating non-loving husband who has, besides his wife, other females (concubines, co-wives, and prostitutes) available for his sexual pleasure under equally degrading conditions.[3] A new sexual order based on the absence of dehumanizing limitations of women's potential means the destruction of the traditional Muslim family. In this respect, fears associated with changes in the family and the condition of women are justified. These fears, embedded in the culture through centuries of women's oppression, are echoed and nourished by the vivid, equally degrading images of Western sexuality and its disintegrating family patterns portrayed on every imported television set.

It is understandable that Muslim fathers and husbands feel horrified at the idea of their own family and sexuality patterns being transformed into Western patterns. The striking characteristic of Western sexuality is the mutilation of the woman's integrity, her reduction to a few inches of nude flesh whose shades and forms are photographed *ad infinitum* with no goal other than profit. While Muslim exploitation of the female is cloaked under veils and hidden behind walls, Western exploitation has the bad taste of being bare and over-exposed.

It is worth noting that the fears of Muslim fathers and husbands are not totally unfounded; the nascent 'liberation' of Muslim women has indeed borrowed many characteristics of Western women's way of life. The first gesture of 'liberated' Arab women was to discard the veil for Western dress, which in the thirties, forties, and fifties was that of the wife of the colonizer. Speaking a foreign language was often a corollary to discarding the veil, the first 'liberated' women usually being members of the upper and middle classes. And here we touch upon another aspect of the difficulty Muslim societies have in adjusting to female self-determination. The Westernization of the first 'liberated' women was and still is part and parcel of the Westernization of the Arab-Muslim ruling classes. The fears awakened by the Westernization of women can be interpreted as simply another instance of Muslim society believing that males are able to select what is good in Western civilization and discard bad elements, while women are unable to choose correctly. This is concordant with the classical Muslim view of women as being unable to judge what is good and what is bad.

Another factor that helps in understanding men's fears of the changes now taking place is that Westernization of women has enhanced their seductive powers. We have seen that the Muslim ethic is against women's ornamenting themselves and exposing their charms; veil and walls were particularly effective anti-seduction devices. Westernization allowed ornamented and seductively clad female bodies to appear on the streets. It is interesting that while Western women's liberation movements had to repudiate the body in pornographic mass media, Muslim women are likely to claim the right to their bodies as part of their liberation movement. Previously a Muslim woman's body belonged to the man who possessed her, father or husband. The mushrooming of beauty salons and ready-to-wear boutiques in Moroccan towns can be interpreted as a forerunner of women's urge to claim their own bodies, which will culminate in more radical claims, such as the claim to birth control and abortion.

Having described the available models and their negative reception, let me hazard a few speculations on the future of women's liberation in Muslim societies, based on a projection from the current situation.

It is hardly contestable that there have been substantial changes in Muslim women's condition. Women have gained many rights that were denied them before, such as the right to education, the right to vote and be elected, and the right to use nondomestic spaces. But an important characteristic of this nascent 'liberation' is that it is not the outcome of a careful plan of controlled nation-wide development. Neither is it the outcome of the massive involvement of women in labour markets, coupled with organized women's movements. The partial, fragmented acquisition of rights by women in Arab-Muslim countries is a random, non-planned, non-systematic phenomenon, due mainly to the disintegration of the traditional system under pressures from within and without. Muslim women's liberation is therefore likely to follow a *sui generis* pattern.

To the dismay of rigid conservatives desperately preoccupied with static tradition, change is shaking the foundations of the Muslim world. Change is multidimensional and hard to control, especially for those who deny it. Whether accepted or rejected, change gnaws continuously at the intricate mechanisms of social life, and the more it is thwarted, the deeper and more surprising are its implications. The heterosexual unit is not yet officially admitted by Muslim rulers to be a crucial focus of the process of national development. Development plans devote hundreds of pages to the mechanization of agriculture, mining, and banking, and only a few pages to the family and women's condition. I want to emphasize on the one hand the deep and far-reaching processes of change at work in the Muslim family, and on the other hand the decisive role of women and the family in any serious development plan in the Third World economy.

THE FAMILY AND WOMEN

As shown earlier, one of the distinctive characteristics of Muslim sexuality is its territoriality, which reflects a specific division of labour and a specific conception of society and power. The territoriality of Muslim sexuality sets patterns of ranks, tasks, and authority. Spatially confined, women were taken care of materially by the men who possessed them, in exchange for total obedience and sexual and reproductive services. The whole system was organized so that the Muslim *umma* was actually a society of male citizens who possessed, among other things, the female half of the population. In his introduction to *Women and Socialism,* George Tarabishi remarks that people generally say that there are one hundred million Arabs, but in fact there are only fifty million, the female population being prevented from taking part in social responsibilities.[4] Muslim men have always had many more rights and privileges than Muslim women, including even the right to kill their women. (The Moroccan penal code still shows a trace of this power in Article 418, which grants extenuating circumstances to a man who kills his adulterous wife.[5]) Men imposed on women an artificially narrow existence both physically and spiritually.

· · ·

One of the results of the break-up of traditional family life is that, for the first time in the history of modern Morocco, the husband is facing his wife directly. Men and women live more closely and interact more than they ever did before, partly because of the decline of anti-heterosexual factors such as the mother-in-law's presence and sexual segregation. This direct confrontation between men and women brought up in sexually antagonistic traditions is likely to be laden with tensions and fears on both sides.

The future of male-female dynamics greatly depends on the way modern states handle the readjustment of sexual rights and the reassessment of sexual status. In Morocco the legislature has retained the traditional concept of marriage. The ancient definition of sex statuses based on division of labour according to sex was reenacted as the basis of family law: Article 35 defines the man as the sole provider for the family. He is responsible not only for himself but also for his able-bodied wife, who is consequently defined as economically dependent, her participation being limited to sexual services, reproduction, and housework.

To define masculinity as the capacity to earn a salary is to condemn those men suffering from unemployment (or the threat of it) to perceive economic problems as castration threats. Moreover, since the *Code* defines earning a salary as a man's role, a woman who earns a salary will be perceived as either masculine or castrating. If the privileges of men become more easily accessible to women, then men will be perceived as becoming more feminine.

· · ·

THE STATE AS THE MAIN THREAT TO TRADITIONAL MALE SUPREMACY

In spite of its continuous support for traditional male rights, the state constitutes a threat and a mighty rival to the male as both father and husband. The state is taking over the traditional functions of the male head of the family, such as education and the provision of economic security for members of the household. By providing a nation-wide state school system and an individual salary for working wives, daughters, and sons, the state has destroyed two pillars of the father's authority. The increasingly preeminent role of the state has stripped the traditionally powerful family head of his privileges and placed him in a subordinate position with respect to the state not very different from the position of women in the traditional family. The head of the family is dependent on the

state (the main employer) to provide for him just as women are dependent on their husbands in traditional settings. Economic support is given in exchange for obedience, and this tends to augment male-female solidarity as a defence against the state and its daily frustrations.

The word 'sexist' as it is currently employed in English has the connotation that males are favoured at the expense of females. It is my belief that, in spite of appearances, the Muslim system does not favour men; the self-fulfillment of men is just as impaired and limited as that of women. Though this equality of oppression is concealed by the world-renowned 'privileges' of the Muslim male, I have tried to illustrate it by showing how polygamy and repudiation are oppressive devices for both sexes. The Muslim theory of sexuality views women as fatally attractive and the source of many delights. Any restrictions on the man's right to such delights, even if they take the form of restrictions on women alone (seclusion, for example), are really attacks on the male's potential for sexual fulfillment.

It might well be argued that the Muslim system makes men pay a higher psychological price for the satisfaction of sexual needs than women, precisely because women are conditioned to accept sexual restrictions as 'natural', while men are encouraged to expect a thorough satisfaction of their sexual needs. Men and women are socialized to deal with sexual frustration differently. We know that an individual's discontent grows as his expectations rise. From the age of four or earlier, a woman in Moroccan society is made aware of the sexual restrictions she has to face. The difficulties a Moroccan male experiences in dealing with sexual frustration are almost unknown to the Moroccan woman, who is traumatized early enough to build adequate defences. In this sense also the Muslim order is not 'sexist'.

· · ·

FUTURE TRENDS

· · ·

Islam's basically positive attitude toward sexuality is more conducive to healthy perspectives of a self-realizing sexuality, harmoniously integrated in social life, than the West's basically negative attitude towards sexuality. Serious changes in male-female conditioning in Western countries imply revolutionary changes in society which these reformist countries are determined to avoid at any cost. Muslim societies *cannot* afford to be reformist; they do not have sufficient resources to be able to offer palliatives. A superficial replastering of the system is not a possible solution for them.

At a deeper level than laws and official policy, the Muslim social order views the female as a potent aggressive individual whose power can, if not tamed and curbed, corrode the social order. It is very likely that in the long run such a view will facilitate women's integration into the networks of decision-making and power. One of the main obstacles Western women have been dealing with is their society's view of women as passive inferior beings. The fact that generations of university-educated women in both Europe and America failed to win access to decision-making posts is due in part to this deeply ingrained image of women as inferior. The Muslim image of women as a source of power is likely to make Muslim women set higher and broader goals than just equality with men. The most recent studies on the aspirations of both men and women seem to come to the same conclusion: the goal is not to achieve equality with men. Women have seen that what men have is not worth getting. Women's goals are already being phrased in terms of a global rejection of established sexual patterns, frustrating for males and degrading for females. This implies a revolutionary reorganization of the entire society, starting from its economic structure and ending with its grammar. Jalal al-Azm excuses himself at the beginning of the book for using the term 'he' throughout the book while in fact he should be using a neutral term, because his findings are valid for both men and women.[6] As a social scientist he resents being a prisoner of Arabic grammar, which imposes a sex-defined pronoun.[7] But not many Arab males yet feel ill-at-ease with sex-biased Arabic grammar, though a majority already feel indisposed by the economic situation.

The holders of power in Arab countries, regardless of their political make-up, are condemned to promote change, and they are aware of this, no matter how loud their claim to uphold the 'prestigious past' as the path to modernity. Historians have interpreted the somewhat cyclical resurgence of traditional rhetoric as a reflex of ruling groups threatened by acute and deep processes of change.[8] The problem Arab societies face is not whether or not to change, but how fast to change. The link between women's liberation and economic development is shown by the similarities in the conditions of the two sexes in the Third World; both sexes suffer from exploitation and deprivation. Men do not have, as in the so-called abundant Western societies, glaring advantages over women. Illiteracy and unemployment are suffered by males as well as females. This similarity of men and women as equally deprived and exploited individuals assumes enormous importance in the likely evolution of Third World family structure. George Tarabishi has pointed out the absurdity of men who argue that women should not be encouraged to get jobs in Arab society, where men suffer from unemployment.[9] He argues that society should not waste human resources in unemployment, but systematically channel the wealth of resources into productive tasks. The female half of human resources is more than welcome in the Arab future.

One may speculate that women's liberation in an Arab context is likely to take a faster and more radical path than in Western countries. Women in Western liberal democracies are organizing themselves to claim their rights, but their oppressors are strong, wealthy, and reformist regimes. The dialogue takes place within the reformist framework characteristic of bourgeois democracies. In such situations, serious changes are likely to take a long time. American women will get the right to abortion but it will be a long time before they can prevent the female's body from being exploited as a marketable product. Muslim women, on the contrary, engage in a silent but explosive dialogue with a fragile ruling class whose major task is to secure economic growth and plan a future without exploitation and deprivation. The Arab ruling classes are beginning to realize that they are charged with building a sovereign future, which necessarily revolves around the location and adequate utilization of all human and natural resources for the benefit of the entire populations. The Arab woman is a central element in any sovereign future. Those who have not realized this fact are misleading themselves and their countries.

[1975]

NOTES

1. Mariarosa Della Costa, *Women and the Subversion of the Community*, Bristol 1972.
2. 'Communism in Marriage', article by David Riazanov, published in Moscow in 1926, reproduced in *al-Mar'a wa al-Ishtiraqiya* (Women and Socialism), translated and edited by George Tarabishi, Beirut 1974 (2nd edition), pp. 33–70.
3. Dr. Salwa Khammash, *al-Mar'a al-Arabiya wa'l-Mujtama al-Taqlidiya* (Arab Women and Traditional Society), Beirut 1973, particularly chapter V (the relation between the sexes) and chapter VII (the position of the wife).
4. George Tarabishi, in his introduction to *Women and Socialism*, p. 13.
5. The article states: 'Killing, wounding, and beating are excusable if they are committed by a husband against his wife and/or her accomplice at the moment that he surprises them *in flagrante delicto* committing adultery.'
6. Sadiq al-Azm, pp. 110–111.
7. Ibid., p. 28.
8. Abdallah Laroui, 'La Crise des Intellectuels Arabes', paper read at colloquium in Louvain, 1970, published in *La Crise des Intellectuels Arabes*, Paris 1974.
9. George Tarabishi, introduction to *Women and Socialism*, p. 13.

PART V

1975–1985

1975–1985: Introduction

The period from 1975 through 1985 is marked by conflicting political, social, and intellectual currents. In national politics, the war in Vietnam had ended in defeat for the United States. The Nixon presidency also ended, after the Watergate hearings, with Nixon's resignation, leaving a general sense of political disillusionment. At the same time, for women inside and outside of the academia, this was a period of excitement, of some fulfillment of earlier struggles, and of hope for future transformation. In colleges and universities, new women's studies programs were being founded every year, and a large-scale effort, supported by prestigious funders like the Ford Foundation and FIPSE (the Fund for the Improvement of Post-Secondary Education), was mounted to transform the entrenched masculinist curriculum in every field. The campaign to ratify the Equal Rights Amendment was in full swing and the creation of women's organizations, businesses, and institutions continued. In 1975, the United Nations declared 1976–1985 the Decade for Women, and many women in the United States and around the world thought it could be. By 1982, however, Ronald Reagan had been elected and ratification of the ERA had failed. With hindsight we see that organizing in opposition to the ERA laid the groundwork intellectually and organizationally for full-scale backlash against feminist and other social activism in the latter part of the 1980s.

In terms of feminist theory, 1975 stands out as a year of significant publication. In 1975, Gayle Rubin published her landmark essay "The Traffic in Women" and, across the Atlantic, Hélène Cixous published "The Laugh of the Medusa." We could almost without exaggeration use these two essays to define the span of feminist thinking over the next decade—the one materialist and social, the other heavily invested in discourse and the symbolic. In this period, the breadth of disciplines in which the work of feminist theory is being done becomes apparent, including philosophers (Frye), theologians (Pagels), poets (Lorde, Rich), anthropologists (Ortner), historians (Scott), and psychoanalysts (Chodorow, Irigaray), all of whom attempt to understand from different perspectives the divisions of labor and power that undergird sexism and women's oppression.

Arguments for female difference, articulated in radical and cultural feminism, also shaped the development (or further development) in this period of ecofeminism, feminist spirituality, and a feminist peace politics. The work of ecofeminists, among them Susan Griffin and Ynestra King, suggested an analogy between man's domination of woman and his domination of nature, and the possibility of a different relationship between women and nature. Feminist spirituality found expression both in the critiques of such established religions as Christianity, Judaism, and Islam, and in explorations of goddess religion and pre-Christian practice to develop feminist and womanist theologies and liturgical practices. Feminist peace politics is perhaps best embodied in the Greenham Women's Peace Camp established in 1981 outside the gates of the U.S. missile base at Greenham Common in the United Kingdom. Analyses like Sara Ruddick's of "maternal thinking" and women's "preservative love" provide the theoretical grounding for this kind of peace activism.

Various rifts within feminism—focused around race, sexuality, and activism, and probably always there under the surface—became apparent in the latter part of this period. The publication of *This Bridge Called My Back* (1981) and *All the Women Are White, All the Blacks Are Men, But Some of Us Are Brave: Black Women's Studies* (1982) articulated a critique by women of color of the domination of both women's studies and women's movement by white women. These volumes also claimed attention for the growing body of creative and intellectual work being produced by women of color that should become a part of the knowledge base of feminist thought. Conflicts between lesbians and straight women over separatism, heterosexism, and the role of men in the feminist movement tore organizations apart. At the same time, a perhaps artificial divide between those still doing grassroots work and those now working primarily within academic institutions was perceived and described as a split between theory and practice.

The U.N. Decade for Women closed in 1985 with a conference in Nairobi, Kenya, which was for many women the beginning of attempts to understand what a truly global feminism might be. Published in 1984, Chandra Mohanty's essay on "Third World Women and the Politics of Feminism" is one attempt to provide a theoretical frame for this project.

◆ 51

The Traffic in Women: Notes on the "Political Economy" of Sex

GAYLE RUBIN

GAYLE RUBIN United States. 1949– . Anthropologist. Activist. A key voice on the "pro-sex" side of the pornography debate. "Thinking Sex" (1984), "Of Catamites and Kings: Reflections on Butch, Gender, and Boundaries" (1992), "Misguided, Dangerous, and Wrong: an Analysis of Antipornography Politics" (1993).

The literature on women—both feminist and antifeminist—is a long rumination on the question of the nature and genesis of women's oppression and social subordination. The question is not a trivial one, since the answers given it determine our visions of the future, and our evaluation of whether or not it is realistic to hope for a sexually egalitarian society. More importantly, the analysis of the causes of women's oppression forms the basis for any assessment of just what would have to be changed in order to achieve a society without gender hierarchy. Thus, if innate male aggression and dominance are at the root of female oppression, then the feminist program would logically require either the extermination of the offending sex, or else a eugenics project to modify its character. If sexism is a by-product of capitalism's relentless appetite for profit, then sexism would wither away in the advent of a successful socialist revolution. . . .

· · ·

The purpose of this essay is to arrive at a more fully developed definition of the sex/gender system, by way of a somewhat idiosyncratic and exegetical reading of Lévi-Strauss and Freud. I use the word "exegetical" deliberately. The dictionary defines "exegesis" as a "critical explanation or analysis; especially, interpretation of the Scriptures." At times, my reading of Lévi-Strauss and Freud is freely interpretive, moving from the explicit content of a text to its presuppositions and implications. My reading of certain psychoanalytic texts is filtered through a lens provided by Jacques Lacan, whose own interpretation of the Freudian scripture has been heavily influenced by Lévi-Strauss.

I will return later to a refinement of the definition of a sex/gender system. First, however, I will try to demonstrate the need for such a concept by discussing the failure of classical Marxism to fully express or conceptualize sex oppression. This failure results from the fact that Marxism, as a theory of social life, is relatively unconcerned with sex. In Marx's map of the social world, human beings are workers, peasants, or capitalists; that they are also men and women is not seen as very significant. By contrast, in the maps of social reality drawn by Freud and Lévi-Strauss, there is a deep recognition of the place of sexuality in society, and of the profound differences between the social experience of men and women.

MARX

There is no theory which accounts for the oppression of women—in its endless variety and monotonous similarity, cross-culturally and throughout history—with anything like the explanatory power of the Marxist theory of class oppression. Therefore, it is not surprising that there have been numerous attempts to apply Marxist analysis to the question of women. There are many ways of doing this. It has been argued that women are a reserve labor force for capitalism, that women's generally lower wages provide extra surplus to a capitalist employer, that women serve the ends of capitalist consumerism in their roles as administrators of family consumption, and so forth.

· · ·

Briefly, Marx argued that capitalism is distinguished from all other modes of production by its unique aim: the creation and expansion of capital. Whereas other modes of production might find their purpose in making useful things to satisfy human needs, or in producing a surplus for a ruling nobility, or in producing to insure sufficient sacrifice for the edification of the gods, capitalism produces capital. Capitalism is a set of social relations—forms of property, and so forth—in which production takes the form of turning money, things, and people into capital. And capital is a quantity of goods or money which, when exchanged for labor, reproduces and augments itself by extracting unpaid labor, or surplus value, from labor and into itself.

> The result of the capitalist production process is neither a mere produce (use-value) nor a *commodity*, that is, a use-value which has exchange value. Its result, its product, is the creation of *surplus-value* for capital, and consequently the actual *transformation* of money or commodity into capital. . . . (Marx, 1969:399; italics in the original)

The exchange between capital and labor which produces surplus value, and hence capital, is highly specific. The worker gets a wage; the capitalist gets the things the worker has made during his or her time of employment. If the total value of the things the worker has made exceeds the value of his or her wage, the aim of capitalism has been achieved. The capitalist gets back the cost of the wage, plus an increment—surplus value. This can occur because the wage is determined not by the value of what the laborer makes, but by the value of what it takes to keep him or her going—to reproduce him or her from day to day, and to reproduce the entire work force from one generation to the next. Thus, surplus value is the difference between what the laboring class produces as a whole, and the amount of that total which is recycled into maintaining the laboring class.

· · ·

The amount of the difference between the reproduction of labor power and its products depends, therefore, on the determination of what it takes to reproduce that labor power. Marx tends to make that determination on the basis of the quantity of commodities—food, clothing, housing, fuel—which would be necessary to maintain the health, life, and strength of a worker. But these commodities must be consumed before they can be sustenance, and they are not immediately in consumable form when they are purchased by the wage. Additional labor must be performed upon these things before they can be turned into people. Food must be cooked, clothes cleaned, beds made, wood chopped, etc. Housework is therefore a key element in the process of the reproduction of the laborer from whom surplus value is taken. Since it is usually women who do housework, it has been observed that it is through the reproduction of

labor power that women are articulated into the surplus value nexus which is the *sine qua non* of capitalism. . . .

· · ·

ENGELS

In *The Origin of the Family, Private Property, and the State*, Engels sees sex oppression as part of capitalism's heritage from prior social forms. Moreover, Engels integrates sex and sexuality into his theory of society. . . . Nevertheless, it is a book whose considerable insight should not be overshadowed by its limitations. The idea that the "relations of sexuality" can and should be distinguished from the "relations of production" . . . indicates an important recognition—that a human group must do more than apply its activity to reshaping the natural world in order to clothe, feed, and warm itself. We usually call the system by which elements of the natural world are transformed into objects of human consumption the "economy." But the needs which are satisfied by economic activity even in the richest, Marxian sense, do not exhaust fundamental human requirements. A human group must also reproduce itself from generation to generation. The needs of sexuality and procreation must be satisfied as much as the need to eat. . . . Sex is sex, but what counts as sex is equally culturally determined and obtained. Every society also has a sex/gender system—a set of arrangements by which the biological raw material of human sex and procreation is shaped by human, social intervention and satisfied in a conventional manner, no matter how bizarre some of the conventions may be.

The realm of human sex, gender, and procreation has been subjected to, and changed by, relentless social activity for millennia. Sex as we know it—gender identity, sexual desire and fantasy, concepts of childhood—is itself a social product. We need to understand the relations of its production, and forget, for awhile, about food, clothing, automobiles, and transistor radios. In most Marxist tradition, and even in Engels' book, the concept of the "second aspect of material life" has tended to fade into the background, or to be incorporated into the usual notions of "material life." Engels' suggestion has never been followed up and subjected to the refinement which it needs.

But he does indicate the existence and importance of the domain of social life which I want to call the sex/gender system.

. . .

KINSHIP
(ON THE PART PLAYED BY SEXUALITY IN THE TRANSITION FROM APE TO "MAN")

To an anthropologist, a kinship system is not a list of biological relatives. It is a system of categories and statuses which often contradict actual genetic relationships. There are dozens of examples in which socially defined kinship statuses take precedence over biology. The Nuer custom of "woman marriage" is a case in point. The Nuer define the status of fatherhood as belonging to the person in whose name cattle bridewealth is given for the mother. Thus, a woman can be married to another woman, and be husband to the wife and father of her children, despite the fact that she is not the inseminator (Evans-Pritchard, 1951:107–109).

In pre-state societies, kinship is the idiom of social interaction, organizing economic, political, and ceremonial, as well as sexual, activity. One's duties, responsibilities, and privileges vis-à-vis others are defined in terms of mutual kinship or lack thereof. The exchange of goods and services, production and distribution, hostility and solidarity, ritual and ceremony, all take place within the organizational structure of kinship. The ubiquity and adaptive effectiveness of kinship has led many anthropologists to consider its invention, along with the invention of language, to have been the developments which decisively marked the discontinuity between semihuman hominids and human beings (Sahlins, 1960a; Livingstone, 1969; Lévi-Strauss, 1969).

While the idea of the importance of kinship enjoys the status of a first principle in anthropology, the internal workings of kinship systems have long been a focus for intense controversy. Kinship systems vary wildly from one culture to the next. They contain all sorts of bewildering rules which govern whom one may or may not marry. Their internal complexity is dazzling. Kinship systems have for decades provoked the anthropological imagination into trying to explain incest taboos, cross-cousin marriage, terms of descent, relationships of avoidance or forced intimacy, clans and sections, taboos

on names—the diverse array of items found in descriptions of actual kinship systems. In the nineteenth century, several thinkers attempted to write comprehensive accounts of the nature and history of human sexual systems (see Fee, 1973). One of these was *Ancient Society,* by Lewis Henry Morgan. It was this book which inspired Engels to write *The Origin of the Family, Private Property, and the State.* Engels' theory is based upon Morgan's account of kinship and marriage.

In taking up Engels' project of extracting a theory of sex oppression from the study of kinship, we have the advantage of the maturation of ethnology since the nineteenth century. We also have the advantage of a peculiar and particularly appropriate book, Lévi-Strauss' *The Elementary Structures of Kinship.* This is the boldest twentieth-century version of the nineteenth-century project to understand human marriage. It is a book in which kinship is explicitly conceived of as an imposition of cultural organization upon the facts of biological procreation. It is permeated with an awareness of the importance of sexuality in human society. It is a description of society which does not assume an abstract, genderless human subject. On the contrary, the human subject in Lévi-Strauss' work is always either male or female, and the divergent social destinies of the two sexes can therefore be traced. Since Lévi-Strauss sees the essence of kinship systems to lie in an exchange of women between men, he constructs an implicit theory of sex oppression. Aptly, the book is dedicated to the memory of Lewis Henry Morgan.

"VILE AND PRECIOUS MERCHANDISE"
—MONIQUE WITTIG

The Elementary Structures of Kinship is a grand statement on the origin and nature of human society. It is a treatise on the kinship systems of approximately one-third of the ethnographic globe. Most fundamentally, it is an attempt to discern the structural principles of kinship. Lévi-Strauss argues that the application of these principles (summarized in the last chapter of *Elementary Structures*) to kinship data reveals an intelligible logic to the taboos and marriage rules which have perplexed and mystified Western anthropologists. He constructs a chess game of such complexity that it cannot be recapitulated here. But two of his chess pieces are particularly relevant to women—the "gift" and the incest taboo, whose dual articulation adds up to his concept of the exchange of women.

The Elementary Structures is in part a radical gloss on another famous theory of primitive social organization, Mauss' *Essay on the Gift* (See also Sahlins, 1972:Chap. 4). It was Mauss who first theorized as to the significance of one of the most striking features of primitive societies: the extent to which giving, receiving, and reciprocating gifts dominates social intercourse. In such societies, all sorts of things circulate in exchange—food, spells, rituals, words, names, ornaments, tools, and powers.

· · ·

Although both Mauss and Lévi-Strauss emphasize the solidary aspects of gift exchange, the other purposes served by gift giving only strengthen the point that it is an ubiquitous means of social commerce. Mauss proposed that gifts were the threads of social discourse, the means by which such societies were held together in the absence of specialized governmental institutions. "The gift is the primitive way of achieving the peace that in civil society is secured by the state. . . . Composing society, the gift was the liberation of culture" (Sahlins, 1972: 169, 175).

Lévi-Strauss adds to the theory of primitive reciprocity the idea that marriages are a most basic form of gift exchange, in which it is women who are the most precious of gifts. He argues that the incest taboo should best be understood as a mechanism to insure that such exchanges take place between families and between groups. Since the existence of incest taboos is universal, but the content of their prohibitions variable, they cannot be explained as having the aim of preventing the occurrence of genetically close matings. Rather, the incest taboo imposes the social aim of exogamy and alliance upon the biological events of sex and procreation. The incest taboo divides the universe of sexual choice into categories of permitted and prohibited sexual partners. Specifically, by forbidding unions within a group it enjoins marital exchange between groups.

The prohibition on the sexual use of a daughter or a sister compels them to be given in marriage to another man, and at the same time it establishes a right to the daughter or sister of this other man. . . . The woman whom one does not take is, for that very reason, offered up. (Lévi-Strauss, 1969:51)

The prohibition of incest is less a rule prohibiting marriage with the mother, sister, or daughter, than a rule obliging the mother, sister, or daughter to be given to others. It is the supreme rule of the gift. . . . (Ibid.:481)

The result of a gift of women is more profound than the result of other gift transactions, because the relationship thus established is not just one of reciprocity, but one of kinship. The exchange partners have become affines, and their descendents will be related by blood: "Two people may meet in friendship and exchange gifts and yet quarrel and fight in later times, but intermarriage connects them in a permanent manner" (Best, cited in Lévi-Strauss, 1969: 481). As is the case with other gift giving, marriages are not always so simply activities to make peace. Marriages may be highly competitive, and there are plenty of affines who fight each other. Nevertheless, in a general sense the argument is that the taboo on incest results in a wide network of relations, a set of people whose connections with one another are a kinship structure. All other levels, amounts, and directions of exchange—including hostile ones—are ordered by this structure. The marriage ceremonies recorded in the ethnographic literature are moments in a ceaseless and ordered procession in which women, children, shells, words, cattle names, fish, ancestors, whale's teeth, pigs, yams, spells, dances, mats, etc., pass from hand to hand, leaving as their tracks the ties that bind. Kinship is organization, and organization gives power. But who is organized?

If it is women who are being transacted, then it is the men who give and take them who are linked, the woman being a conduit of a relationship rather than a partner to it. The exchange of women does not necessarily imply that women are objectified, in the modern sense, since objects in the primitive world are imbued with highly personal qualities. But it does imply a distinction between gift and giver. If women are the gifts, then it is men who are the exchange partners. And it is the partners, not the presents, upon whom reciprocal exchange confers its quasimystical power of social linkage. The relations of such a system are such that women are in no position to realize the benefits of their own circulation. As long as the relations specify that men exchange women, it is men who are the beneficiaries of the product of such exchanges—social organization.

> The total relationship of exchange which constitutes marriage is not established between a man and a woman, but between two groups of men, and the woman figures only as one of the objects in the exchange, not as one of the partners. . . . This remains true even when the girl's feelings are taken into consideration, as, moreover, is usually the case. In acquiescing to the proposed union, she precipitates or allows the exchange to take place, she cannot alter its nature. . . . (Lévi-Strauss in ibid.:115)

To enter into a gift exchange as a partner, one must have something to give. If women are for men to dispose of, they are in no position to give themselves away.

> "What woman," mused a young Northern Melpa man, "is ever strong enough to get up and say, 'Let us make *moka*, let us find wives and pigs, let us give our daughters to men, let us wage war, let us kill our enemies!' No indeed not! . . . they are little rubbish things who stay at home simply, don't you see?" (Strathern, 1972:161)

What women indeed! The Melpa women of whom the young man spoke can't get wives, they *are* wives, and what they get are husbands, an entirely different matter. The Melpa women can't give their daughters to men, because they do not have the same rights in their daughters that their male kin have, rights of bestowal (although *not* of ownership).

The "exchange of women" is a seductive and powerful concept. It is attractive in that it places the oppression of women within social systems, rather than in biology. Moreover, it suggests that we look for the ultimate locus of women's oppression within the traffic in women, rather than within the traffic in merchandise. It is certainly not difficult to find ethnographic and historical examples of trafficking in women. Women are given in marriage, taken in battle, exchanged for favors, sent as tribute, traded, bought, and sold. Far from being confined to the "primitive" world, these practices seem only to become more pronounced and commercialized in more "civilized" societies. Men are of course also trafficked—but as slaves, hustlers, athletic stars,

serfs, or as some other catastrophic social status, rather than as men. Women are transacted as slaves, serfs, and prostitutes, but also simply as women. And if men have been sexual subjects—exchangers—and women sexual semi-objects—gifts—for much of human history, then many customs, clichés, and personality traits seem to make a great deal of sense (among others, the curious custom by which a father gives away the bride).

The "exchange of women" is also a problematic concept. Since Lévi-Strauss argues that the incest taboo and the results of its application constitute the origin of culture, it can be deduced that the world historical defeat of women occurred with the origin of culture, and is a prerequisite of culture. If his analysis is adopted in its pure form, the feminist program must include a task even more onerous than the extermination of men; it must attempt to get rid of culture and substitute some entirely new phenomena on the face of the earth. However, it would be a dubious proposition at best to argue that if there were no exchange of women there would be no culture, if for no other reason than that culture is, by definition, inventive. It is even debatable that "exchange of women" adequately describes all of the empirical evidence of kinship systems. Some cultures, such as the Lele and the Luma, exchange women explicitly and overtly. In other cultures, the exchange of women can be inferred. In some—particularly those hunters and gatherers excluded from Lévi-Strauss' sample—the efficacy of the concept becomes altogether questionable. What are we to make of a concept which seems so useful and yet so difficult?

The "exchange of women" is neither a definition of culture nor a system in and of itself. The concept is an acute, but condensed, apprehension of certain aspects of the social relations of sex and gender. A kinship system is an imposition of social ends upon a part of the natural world. It is therefore "production" in the most general sense of the term: a molding, a transformation of objects (in this case, people) to and by a subjective purpose (for this sense of production, see Marx, 1971:80–99). It has its own relations of production, distribution, and exchange, which include certain "property" forms in people. These forms are not exclusive, private property rights, but rather different sorts of rights that various people have in other people. Marriage transactions—the gifts and material which circulate in the ceremonies marking a marriage—are a rich source of data for determining exactly who has which rights in whom. It is not difficult to deduce from such transactions that in most cases women's rights are considerably more residual than those of men.

Kinship systems do not merely exchange women. They exchange sexual access, genealogical statuses, lineage names and ancestors, rights and *people*—men, women, and children—in concrete systems of social relationships. These relationships always include certain rights for men, others for women. "Exchange of women" is a shorthand for expressing that the social relations of a kinship system specify that men have certain rights in their female kin, and that women do not have the same rights either to themselves or to their male kin. In this sense, the exchange of women is a profound perception of a system in which women do not have full rights to themselves. The exchange of women becomes an obfuscation if it is seen as a cultural necessity, and when it is used as the single tool with which an analysis of a particular kinship system is approached.

If Lévi-Strauss is correct in seeing the exchange of women as a fundamental principle of kinship, the subordination of women can be seen as a product of the relationships by which sex and gender are organized and produced. The economic oppression of women is derivative and secondary. But there is an "economics" of sex and gender, and what we need is a political economy of sexual systems. We need to study each society to determine the exact mechanisms by which particular conventions of sexuality are produced and maintained. The "exchange of women" is an initial step toward building an arsenal of concepts with which sexual systems can be described.

DEEPER INTO THE LABYRINTH

More concepts can be derived from an essay by Lévi-Strauss, "The Family," in which he introduces other considerations into his analysis of kinship. In *The Elementary Structures of Kinship*, he describes rules and systems of sexual combination. In "The Family," he raises the issue of the preconditions

necessary for marriage systems to operate. He asks what sort of "people" are required by kinship systems, by way of an analysis of the sexual division of labor.

Although every society has some sort of division of tasks by sex, the assignment of any particular task to one sex or the other varies enormously. In some groups, agriculture is the work of women, in others, the work of men. Women carry the heavy burdens in some societies, men in others. There are even examples of female hunters and warriors, and of men performing child-care tasks. Lévi-Strauss concludes from a survey of the division of labor by sex that it is not a biological specialization, but must have some other purpose. This purpose, he argues, is to insure the union of men and women by making the smallest viable economic unit contain at least one man and one woman.

> The very fact that it [the sexual division of labor] varies endlessly according to the society selected for consideration shows that . . . it is the mere fact of its existence which is mysteriously required, the form under which it comes to exist being utterly irrelevant, at least from the point of view of any natural necessity . . . the sexual division of labor is nothing else than a device to institute a reciprocal state of dependency between the sexes. (Lévi-Strauss, 1971:347–348)

The division of labor by sex can therefore be seen as a "taboo": a taboo against the sameness of men and women, a taboo dividing the sexes into two mutually exclusive categories, a taboo which exacerbates the biological differences between the sexes and thereby *creates* gender. The division of labor can also be seen as a taboo against sexual arrangements other than those containing at least one man and one woman, thereby enjoining heterosexual marriage.

The argument in "The Family" displays a radical questioning of all human sexual arrangements, in which no aspect of sexuality is taken for granted as "natural" (Hertz, 1960, constructs a similar argument for a thoroughly cultural explanation of the denigration of left-handedness). Rather, all manifest forms of sex and gender are seen as being constituted by the imperatives of social systems. From such a perspective, even *The Elementary Structures of Kinship* can be seen to assume certain preconditions. In purely logical terms, a rule for-bidding some marriages and commanding others presupposes a rule enjoining marriage. And marriage presupposes individuals who are disposed to marry.

It is of interest to carry this kind of deductive enterprise even further than Lévi-Strauss does, and to explicate the logical structure which underlies his entire analysis of kinship. At the most general level, the social organization of sex rests upon gender, obligatory heterosexuality, and the constraint of female sexuality.

Gender is a socially imposed division of the sexes. It is a product of the social relations of sexuality. Kinship systems rest upon marriage. They therefore transform males and females into "men" and "women," each an incomplete half which can only find wholeness when united with the other. Men and women are, of course, different. But they are not as different as day and night, earth and sky, yin and yang, life and death. In fact, from the standpoint of nature, men and women are closer to each other than either is to anything else—for instance, mountains, kangaroos, or coconut palms. The idea that men and women are more different from one another than either is from anything else must come from somewhere other than nature. Furthermore, although there is an average difference between males and females on a variety of traits, the range of variation of those traits shows considerable overlap. There will always be some women who are taller than some men, for instance, even though men are on the average taller than women. But the idea that men and women are two mutually exclusive categories must arise out of something other than a nonexistent "natural" opposition. Far from being an expression of natural differences, exclusive gender identity is the suppression of natural similarities. It requires repression: in men, of whatever is the local version of "feminine" traits; in women, of the local definition of "masculine" traits. The division of the sexes has the effect of repressing some of the personality characteristics of virtually everyone, men and women. The same social system which oppresses women in its relations of exchange, oppresses everyone in its insistence upon a rigid division of personality.

Furthermore, individuals are engendered in order that marriage be guaranteed. Lévi-Strauss comes dangerously close to saying that heterosexuality is an instituted process. If biological and hormonal imperatives were as overwhelming as popular mythology would have them, it would hardly be necessary to insure heterosexual unions by means of economic interdependency. Moreover, the incest taboo presupposes a prior, less articulate taboo on homosexuality. A prohibition against *some* heterosexual unions assumes a taboo against *non*-heterosexual unions. Gender is not only an identification with one sex; it also entails that sexual desire be directed toward the other sex. The sexual division of labor is implicated in both aspects of gender—male and female it creates them, and its creates them heterosexual. The suppression of the homosexual component of human sexuality, and by corollary, the oppression of homosexuals, is therefore a product of the same system whose rules and relations oppress women.

In fact, the situation is not so simple, as is obvious when we move from the level of generalities to the analysis of specific sexual systems. Kinship systems do not merely encourage heterosexuality to the detriment of homosexuality. In the first place, specific forms of heterosexuality may be required. For instance, some marriage systems have a rule of obligatory cross-cousin marriage. A person in such a system is not only heterosexual, but "cross-cousin-sexual." If the rule of marriage further specifies matrilateral cross-cousin marriage, then a man will be "mother's-brother's-daughter-sexual" and a woman will be "father's-sister's-son-sexual."

· · ·

[T]he rules of gender division and obligatory heterosexuality are present even in their transformations. These two rules apply equally to the constraint of both male and female behavior and personality. Kinship systems dictate some sculpting of the sexuality of both sexes. But it can be deduced from *The Elementary Structures of Kinship* that more constraint is applied to females when they are pressed into the service of kinship than to males. If women are exchanged, in whatever sense we take the term, marital debts are reckoned in female flesh. A woman must become the sexual partner of some man to whom she is owed as return on a previous marriage. If a girl is promised in infancy, her refusal to participate as an adult would disrupt the flow of debts and promises. It would be in the interests of the smooth and continuous operation of such a system if the woman in question did not have too many ideas of her own about whom she might want to sleep with. From the standpoint of the system, the preferred female sexuality would be one which responded to the desire of others, rather than one which actively desired and sought a response.

· · ·

One last generality could be predicted as a consequence of the exchange of women under a system in which rights to women are held by men. What would happen if our hypothetical woman not only refused the man to whom she was promised, but asked for a woman instead? If a single refusal were disruptive, a double refusal would be insurrectionary. If each woman is promised to some man, neither has a right to dispose of herself. If two women managed to extricate themselves from the debt nexus, two other women would have to be found to replace them. As long as men have rights in women which women do not have in themselves, it would be sensible to expect that homosexuality in women would be subject to more suppression than in men.

In summary, some basic generalities about the organization of human sexuality can be derived from an exegesis of Lévi-Strauss' theories of kinship. These are the incest taboo, obligatory heterosexuality, and an asymmetric division of the sexes. The asymmetry of gender—the difference between exchanger and exchanged—entails the constraint of female sexuality. Concrete kinship systems will have more specific conventions, and these conventions vary a great deal. While particular sociosexual systems vary, each one is specific, and individuals within it will have to conform to a finite set of possibilities. Each new generation must learn and become its sexual destiny, each person must be encoded with its appropriate status within the system. It would be extraordinary for one of us to calmly assume that we would conventionally marry a mother's brother's daughter, or a father's sister's son. Yet there are groups in which such a marital future is taken for granted.

Anthropology, and descriptions of kinship systems, do not explain the mechanisms by which children are engraved with the conventions of sex and gender. Psychoanalysis, on the other hand, is a theory about the reproduction of kinship. Psychoanalysis describes the residue left within individuals by their confrontation with the rules and regulations of sexuality of the societies to which they are born.

· · ·

THE OEDIPUS HEX

· · ·

Freud was never as much of a biological determinist as some would have him. He repeatedly stressed that all adult sexuality resulted from psychic, not biologic, development. But his writing is often ambiguous, and his wording leaves plenty of room for the biological interpretations which have been so popular in American psychoanalysis. In France, on the other hand, the trend in psychoanalytic theory has been to de-biologize Freud, and to conceive of psychoanalysis as a theory of information rather than organs. Jacques Lacan, the instigator of this line of thinking, insists that Freud never meant to say anything about anatomy, and that Freud's theory was instead about language and the cultural meanings imposed upon anatomy. The debate over the "real" Freud is extremely interesting, but it is not my purpose here to contribute to it. Rather, I want to rephrase the classic theory of femininity in Lacan's terminology, after introducing some of the pieces on Lacan's conceptual chessboard.

KINSHIP, LACAN, AND THE PHALLUS

Lacan suggests that psychoanalysis is the study of the traces left in the psyches of individuals as a result of their conscription into systems of kinship.

> Isn't it striking that Lévi-Strauss, in suggesting that implication of the structures of language with that part of the social laws which regulate marriage ties and kinship, is already conquering the very terrain in which Freud situates the unconscious? (Lacan, 1968:48)

For where on earth would one situate the determinations of the unconsciousness if it is not in those nominal cadres in which marriage ties and kin-ship are always grounded.... And how would one apprehend the analytical conflicts and their Oedipean prototype outside the engagements which have fixed, long before the subject came into the world, not only his destiny, but his identity itself? (Ibid.: 126)

This is precisely where the Oedipus complex ... may be said, in this connection, to mark the limits which our discipline assigns to subjectivity: that is to say, what the subject can know of his uncon-scious participation in the movement of the com-plex structures of marriage ties, by verifying the symbolic effects in his individual existence of the tangential movement towards incest.... (Ibid.:40)

Kinship is the culturalization of biological sexuality on the societal level; psychoanalysis describes the transformation of the biological sexuality of indi-viduals as they are enculturated.

Kinship terminology contains information about the system. Kin terms demarcate statuses, and indi-cate some of the attributes of those statuses. For instance, in the Trobriand Islands a man calls the women of his clan by the term for "sister." He calls the women of clans into which he can marry by a term indicating their marriageability. When the young Trobrian male learns these terms, he learns which women he can safely desire. In Lacan's scheme, the Oedipal crisis occurs when a child learns of the sexual rules embedded in the terms for family and relatives. The crisis begins when the child comprehends the system and his or her place in it; the crisis is resolved when the child accepts that place and accedes to it. Even if the child refuses its place, he or she cannot escape knowledge of it. Before the Oedipal phase, the sexuality of the child is labile and relatively unstructured. Each child contains all of the sexual possibilities available to human expression. But in any given society, only some of these possibilities will be expressed, while others will be constrained. When the child leaves the Oedipal phase, its libido and gender identity have been organized in conformity with the rules of the culture which is domesticating it.

The Oedipal complex is an apparatus for the production of sexual personality. It is a truism to say that societies will inculcate in their young the character traits appropriate to carrying on the business of society. For instance, E. P. Thompson (1963) speaks of the transformation of the person-ality structure of the English working class, as arti-sans were changed into good industrial workers. Just as the social forms of labor demand certain kinds of personality, the social forms of sex and gender demand certain kinds of people. In the most general terms, the Oedipal complex is a machine which fashions the appropriate forms of sexual individuals (see also the discussion of different forms of "historical individuality" in Althusser and Balibar, 1970: 112, 251–253).

In the Lacanian theory of psychoanalysis, it is the kin terms that indicate a structure of relationships which will determine the role of any individual or object within the Oedipal drama. For instance, Lacan makes a distinction between the "function of the father" and a particular father who embodies this function. In the same way, he makes a radical distinc-tion between the penis and the "phallus," between organ and information. The phallus is a set of mean-ings conferred upon the penis. The differentiation between phallus and penis in contemporary French psychoanalytic terminology emphasizes the idea that the penis could not and does not play the role attrib-uted to it in the classical terminology of the castra-tion complex.[1]

In Freud's terminology, the Oedipal complex presents two alternatives to a child: to have a penis or to be castrated. In contrast, the Lacanian theory of the castration complex leaves behind all refer-ence to anatomical reality:

The theory of the castration complex amounts to having the male organ play a dominant role—this time as a symbol—*to the extent that its absence or presence transforms an anatomical difference into a major classification of humans, and to the extent that, for each subject, this presence or absence is not taken for granted, is not reduced purely and simply to a given, but is the problematical result of an intra- and inter-subjective process* (the subject's assumption of his own sex). (Laplanche and Pontalis, in Mehlman, 1972: 198–199; my italics)

The alternative presented to the child may be rephrased as an alternative between having, or not having, the phallus. Castration is not having the (symbolic) phallus. Castration is not a real "lack," but a meaning conferred upon the genitals of a woman:

Castration may derive support from . . . the apprehension in the Real of the absence of the penis in women—but even this supposes a symbolization of the object, since the Real is full, and "lacks" nothing. Insofar as one finds castration in the genesis of neurosis, it is never real but symbolic. . . . (Lacan, 1968:271)

The phallus is, as it were, a distinctive feature differentiating "castrated" and "noncastrated." The presence or absence of the phallus carries the differences between two sexual statuses, "man" and "woman" (see Jakobson and Halle, 1971, on distinctive features). Since these are not equal, the phallus also carries a meaning of the dominance of men over women, and it may be inferred that "penis envy" is a recognition thereof. Moreover, as long as men have rights in women which women do not have in themselves, the phallus also carries the meaning of the difference between "exchanger" and "exchanged," gift and giver. Ultimately, neither the classical Freudian nor the rephrased Lacanian theories of the Oedipal process make sense unless at least this much of the paleolithic relations of sexuality are still with us. We still live in a "phallic" culture.

Lacan also speaks of the phallus as a symbolic object which is exchanged within and between families (see also Wilden, 1968:303–305). It is interesting to think about this observation in terms of primitive marriage transactions and exchange networks. In those transactions, the exchange of women is usually one of many cycles of exchange. Usually, there are other objects circulating as well as women. Women move in one direction, cattle, shells, or mats in the other. In one sense, the Oedipal complex is an expression of the circulation of the phallus in intrafamily exchange, an inversion of the circulation of women in interfamily exchange. In the cycle of exchange manifested by the Oedipal complex, the phallus passes through the medium of women from one man to another—from father to son, from mother's brother to sister's son, and so forth. In this family *Kula* ring, women go one way, the phallus the other. It is where we aren't. In this sense, the phallus is more than a feature which distinguishes the sexes: it is the embodiment of the male status, to which men accede, and in which certain rights inhere—among them, the right to a woman. It is an expression of the transmission of

male dominance. It passes through women and settles upon men. The tracks which it leaves include gender identity, the division of the sexes. But it leaves more than this. It leaves "penis envy," which acquires a rich meaning of the disquietude of women in a phallic culture.

OEDIPUS REVISITED

We return now to the two pre-Oedipal androgynes, sitting on the border between biology and culture. Lévi-Strauss places the incest taboo on that border, arguing that its initiation of the exchange of women constitutes the origin of society. In this sense, the incest taboo and the exchange of women are the content of the original social contract (see Sahlins, 1972: Chap. 4). For individuals, the Oedipal crisis occurs at the same divide, when the incest taboo initiates the exchange of the phallus.

The Oedipal crisis is precipitated by certain items of information. The children discover the differences between the sexes, and that each child must become one or the other gender. They also discover the incest taboo, and that some sexuality is prohibited—in this case, the mother is unavailable to either child because she "belongs" to the father. Lastly, they discover that the two genders do not have the same sexual "rights" or futures.

In the normal course of events, the boy renounces his mother for fear that otherwise his father would castrate him (refuse to give him the phallus and make him a girl). But by this act of renunciation, the boy affirms the relationships which have given mother to father and which will give him, if he becomes a man, a woman of his own. In exchange for the boy's affirmation of his father's right to his mother, the father affirms the phallus in his son (does not castrate him). The boy exchanges his mother for the phallus, the symbolic token which can later be exchanged for a woman. The only thing required of him is a little patience. He retains his initial libidinal organization and the sex of his original love object. The social contract to which he has agreed will eventually recognize his own rights and provide him with a woman of his own.

What happens to the girl is more complex. She, like the boy, discovers the taboo against incest and the division of the sexes. She also discovers some unpleasant information about the gender to which she is being assigned. For the boy, the taboo on incest is a taboo on certain women. For the girl, it is a taboo on all women. Since she is in a homosexual position vis-à-vis the mother, the rule of heterosexuality which dominates the scenario makes her position excruciatingly untenable. The mother, and all women by extension, can only be properly beloved by someone "with a penis" (phallus). Since the girl has no "phallus," she has no "right" to love her mother or another woman, since she is herself destined to some man. She does not have the symbolic token which can be exchanged for a woman.

If Freud's wording of this moment of the female Oedipal crisis is ambiguous, Lampl de Groot's formulation makes the context which confers meaning upon the genitals explicit:

> . . . *if the little girl comes to the conclusion that such an organ is really indispensable to the possession of the mother, she experiences* in addition to the narcissistic insults common to both sexes still another blow, namely *a feeling of inferiority about her genitals.* (Lampl de Groot, 1933:497; my italics)

The girl concludes that the "penis" is indispensable for the possession of the mother because only those who possess the phallus have a "right" to a woman, and the token of exchange. She does not come to her conclusion because of the natural superiority of the penis either in and of itself, or as an instrument for making love. The hierarchical arrangement of the male and female genitals is a result of the definitions of the situation—the rule of obligatory heterosexuality and the relegation of women (those without the phallus, castrated) to men (those with the phallus).

The girl then begins to turn away from the mother, and to the father.

> To the girl, it [castration] is an accomplished fact, which is irrevocable, but the recognition of which compels her finally to renounce her first love object and to taste to the full the bitterness of its loss . . . the father is chosen as a love-object, the enemy becomes the beloved. . . . (Lampl de Groot, 1948:213)

This recognition of "castration" forces the girl to redefine her relationship to herself, her mother, and her father.

She turns from the mother because she does not have the phallus to give her. She turns from the mother also in anger and disappointment, because the mother did not give her a "penis" (phallus). But the mother, a woman in a phallic culture, does not have the phallus to give away (having gone through the Oedipal crisis herself a generation earlier). The girl then turns to the father because only he can "give her the phallus," and it is only through him that she can enter into the symbolic exchange system in which the phallus circulates. But the father does not give her the phallus in the same way that he gives it to the boy. The phallus is affirmed in the boy, who then has it to give away. The girl never gets the phallus. It passes through her, and in its passage is transformed into a child. When she "recognizes her castration," she accedes to the place of a woman in a phallic exchange network. She can "get" the phallus—in intercourse, or as a child—but only as a gift from a man. She never gets to give it away.

When she turns to the father, she also represses the "active" portions of her libido:

> The turning away from her mother is an extremely important step in the course of a little girl's development. It is more than a mere change of object . . . hand in hand with it there is to be observed a marked lowering of the active sexual impulses and a rise of the passive ones. . . . The transition to the father object is accomplished with the help of the passive trends in so far as they have escaped the catastrophe. The path to the development of femininity now lies open to the girl. (Freud, 1961:239)

The ascendance of passivity in the girl is due to her recognition of the futility of realizing her active desire, and of the unequal terms of the struggle. Freud locates active desire in the clitoris and passive desire in the vagina, and thus describes the repression of active desire as the repression of clitoral eroticism in favor of passive vaginal eroticism. In this scheme, cultural stereotypes have been mapped onto the genitals. Since the work of Masters and Johnson, it is evident that this genital division is a false one. Any organ—penis, clitoris, vagina—can be the locus of either active or passive eroticism. What is important in Freud's scheme, however, is not the geography of desire, but its self-confidence. It is not an organ which is repressed, but a segment of erotic possibility. Freud notes that "more constraint has been applied to the libido when it is pressed into the service of the feminine function . . ." (Freud, 1965:131). The girl has been robbed.

If the Oedipal phase proceeds normally and the girl "accepts her castration," her libidinal structure and object choice are now congruent with the female gender role. She has become a little woman—feminine, passive, heterosexual. Actually, Freud suggests that there are three alternate routes out of the Oedipal catastrophe. The girl may simply freak out, repress sexuality altogether, and become asexual. She may protest, cling to her narcissism and desire, and become either "masculine" or homosexual. Or she may accept the situation, sign the social contract, and attain "normality."

Karen Horney is critical of the entire Freud/ Lampl de Groot scheme. But in the course of her critique she articulates its implications:

> . . . when she [the girl] first turns to a man (the father), it is in the main only by way of the narrow bridge of resentment . . . we should feel it a contradiction if the relation of woman to man did not retain throughout life some tinge of this enforced substitute for that which was really desired. . . . The same character of something remote from instinct, secondary and substitutive, would, even in normal women, adhere to the wish for motherhood. . . . The special point about Freud's viewpoint is rather that it sees the wish for motherhood not as an innate formation, but as something that can be reduced psychologically to its ontogenetic elements and draws its energy originally from homosexual or phallic instinctual elements. . . . It would follow, finally, that women's whole reaction to life would be based on a strong subterranean resentment. (Horney, 1973:148–149)

Horney considers these implications to be so far-fetched that they challenge the validity of Freud's entire scheme. But it is certainly plausible to argue instead that the creation of "femininity" in women in the course of socialization is an act of psychic brutality, and that it leaves in women an immense resentment of the suppression to which they were subjected. It is also possible to argue that women have few means for realizing and expressing their residual anger. One can read Freud's essays on femininity as descriptions of how a group is prepared psychologically, at a tender age, to live with its oppression.

There is an additional element in the classic discussions of the attainment of womanhood. The girl first turns to the father because she must, because she is "castrated" (a woman, helpless, etc.). She then discovers that "castration" is a prerequisite to the father's love, that she must be a woman for him to love her. She therefore begins to desire "castration," and what had previously been a disaster becomes a wish.

> Analytic experience leaves no room for doubt that the little girl's first libidinal relation to her father is masochistic, and the masochistic wish in its earliest distinctively feminine phase is: "I want to be castrated by my father." (Deutsch, 1948a:228)

Deutsch argues that such masochism may conflict with the ego, causing some women to flee the entire situation in defense of their self-regard. Those women to whom the choice is "between finding bliss in suffering or peace in renunciation" (Ibid.:231) will have difficulty in attaining a healthy attitude to intercourse and motherhood. Why Deutsch appears to consider such women to be special cases, rather than the norm, is not clear from her discussion.

The psychoanalytic theory of femininity is one that sees female development based largely on pain and humiliation, and it takes some fancy footwork to explain why anyone ought to enjoy being a woman. At this point in the classic discussions biology makes a triumphant return. The fancy footwork consists in arguing that finding joy in pain is adaptive to the role of women in reproduction, since childbirth and defloration are "painful." Would it not make more sense to question the entire procedure? If women, in finding their place in a sexual system, are robbed of libido and forced into a masochistic eroticism, why did the analysts not argue for novel arrangements, instead of rationalizing the old ones?

Freud's theory of femininity has been subjected to feminist critique since it was first published. To the extent that it is a rationalization of female subordination, this critique has been justified. To the extent that it is a description of a process which subordinates women, this critique is a mistake. As a description of how phallic culture domesticates women, and the effects in women of their domestication, psychoanalytic theory has no parallel (see also Mitchell, 1971 and 1974; Lasch, 1974). And since psychoanalysis is a theory of gender, dismissing it would be suicidal for a political movement dedicated to eradicating gender hierarchy (or gender itself). We cannot dismantle something that we underestimate or do not understand. The oppression of women is deep; equal pay, equal work, and all of the female politicians in the world will not extirpate the roots of sexism. Lévi-Strauss and Freud elucidate what would otherwise be poorly perceived parts of the deep structures of sex oppression. They serve as reminders of the intractability and magnitude of what we fight, and their analyses provide preliminary charts of the social machinery we must rearrange.

WOMEN UNITE TO OFF THE OEDIPAL RESIDUE OF CULTURE

· · ·

The organization of sex and gender once had functions other than itself—it organized society. Now, it only organizes and reproduces itself. The kinds of relationships of sexuality established in the dim human past still dominate our sexual lives, our ideas about men and women, and the ways we raise our children. But they lack the functional load they once carried. One of the most conspicuous features of kinship is that it has been systematically stripped of its functions—political, economic, educational, and organizational. It has been reduced to its barest bones—*sex and gender.*

Human sexual life will always be subject to convention and human intervention. It will never be completely "natural," if only because our species is social, cultural, and articulate. The wild profusion of infantile sexuality will always be tamed. The confrontation between immature and helpless infants and the developed social life of their elders will probably always leave some residue of disturbance. But the mechanisms and aims of this process need not be largely independent of conscious choice. Cultural evolution provides us with the opportunity to seize control of the means of sexuality, reproduction, and socialization, and to make conscious decisions to liberate human sexual life from the archaic relationships which deform it. Ultimately, a thoroughgoing feminist revolution would liberate more than women. It would liberate forms of sexual expression, and it would liberate human personality from the straightjacket of gender.

"DADDY, DADDY, YOU BASTARD, I'M THROUGH."   —SYLVIA PLATH

In the course of this essay I have tried to construct a theory of women's oppression by borrowing concepts from anthropology and psychoanalysis. But Lévi-Strauss and Freud write within an intellectual tradition produced by a culture in which women are oppressed. The danger in my enterprise is that the sexism in the tradition of which they are a part tends to be dragged in with each borrowing. "We cannot utter a single destructive proposition which has not already slipped into the form, the logic, and the implicit postulations of precisely what it seeks to contest" (Derrida, 1972:250). And what slips in is formidable. Both psychoanalysis and structural anthropology are, in one sense, the most sophisticated ideologies of sexism around.[2]

For instance, Lévi-Strauss sees women as being like words, which are misused when they are not "communicated" and exchanged. On the last page of a very long book, he observes that this creates something of a contradiction in women, since women are at the same time "speakers" and "spoken." His only comment on this contradiction is this:

> But woman could never become just a sign and nothing more, since even in a man's world she is still a person, and since insofar as she is defined as a sign she must be recognized as a generator of signs. In the matrimonial dialogue of men, woman is never purely what is spoken about; for if women in general represent a certain category of signs, destined to a certain kind of communication, each woman preserves a particular value arising from her talent, before and after marriage, for taking her part in a duet. In contrast to words, which have wholly become signs, woman has remained at once a sign and a value. *This explains why the relations between the sexes have preserved that affective richness, ardour and mystery which doubtless originally permeated the entire universe of human communications.* (Lévi-Strauss, 1969:496; my italics)

This is an extraordinary statement. Why is he not, at this point, denouncing what kinship systems do to women, instead of presenting one of the greatest rip-offs of all time as the root of romance?

A similar insensitivity is revealed within psychoanalysis by the inconsistency with which it assimilates the critical implications of its own theory. For instance, Freud did not hesitate to recognize that his findings posed a challenge to conventional morality:

> We cannot avoid observing with critical eyes, and we have found that it is impossible to give our support to conventional sexual morality or to approve highly of the means by which society attempts to arrange the practical problems of sexuality in life. *We can demonstrate with ease that what the world calls its code of morals demands more sacrifices than it is worth*, and that its behavior is neither dictated by honesty nor instituted with wisdom. (Freud, 1943: 376–377; my emphasis)

Nevertheless, when psychoanalysis demonstrates with equal facility that the ordinary components of feminine personality are masochism, self-hatred, and passivity,[3] a similar judgment is *not* made. Instead, a double standard of interpretation is employed. Masochism is bad for men, essential to women. Adequate narcissism is necessary for men, impossible for women. Passivity is tragic in man, while lack of passivity is tragic in a woman.

It is this double standard which enables clinicians to try to accommodate women to a role whose destructiveness is so lucidly detailed in their own theories. It is the same inconsistent attitude which permits therapists to consider lesbianism as a problem to be cured, rather than as the resistance to a bad situation that their own theory suggests.

There are points within the analytic discussions of femininity where one might say, "This is oppression of women," or "We can demonstrate with ease that what the world calls femininity demands more sacrifices than it is worth." It is precisely at such points that the implications of the theory are ignored, and are replaced with formulations whose purpose is to keep those implications firmly lodged in the theoretical unconscious. It is at these points that all sorts of mysterious chemical substances, joys in pain, and biological aims are substituted for a critical assessment of the costs of femininity.

These substitutions are the symptoms of theoretical repression, in that they are not consistent with the usual canons of psychoanalytic argument. The extent to which these rationalizations of femininity go against the grain of psychoanalytic logic is strong evidence for the extent of the need to suppress the radical and feminist implications of the theory of femininity (Deutsch's discussions are excellent examples of this process of substitution and repression).

The argument which must be woven in order to assimilate Lévi-Strauss and Freud into feminist theory is somewhat tortuous. I have engaged it for several reasons. First, while neither Lévi-Strauss nor Freud questions the undoubted sexism endemic to the systems they describe, the questions which ought to be posed are blindingly obvious. Secondly, their work enables us to isolate sex and gender from "mode of production," and to counter a certain tendency to explain sex oppression as a reflex of economic forces. Their work provides a framework in which the full weight of sexuality and marriage can be incorporated into an analysis of sex oppression. It suggests a conception of the women's movement as analogous to, rather than isomorphic with, the working-class movement, each addressing a different source of human discontent. In Marx's vision, the working-class movement would do more than throw off the burden of its own exploitation. It also had the potential to change society, to liberate humanity, to create a classless society. Perhaps the women's movement has the task of effecting the same kind of social change for a system of which Marx had only an imperfect apperception. Something of this sort is implicit in Wittig (1973)—the dictatorship of the Amazon *guérillères* is a temporary means for achieving a genderless society.

The sex/gender system is not immutably oppressive and has lost much of its traditional function. Nevertheless, it will not wither away in the absence of opposition. It still carries the social burden of sex and gender, of socializing the young, and of providing ultimate propositions about the nature of human beings themselves. And it serves economic and political ends other than those it was originally designed to further (cf. Scott, 1965). The sex/gender system must be reorganized through political action.

Finally, the exegesis of Lévi-Strauss and Freud suggests a certain vision of feminist politics and the feminist utopia. It suggests that we should not aim for the elimination of men, but for the elimination of the social system which creates sexism and gender. I personally find a vision of an Amazon matriarchate, in which men are reduced to servitude or oblivion (depending on the possibilities for parthenogenetic reproduction), distasteful and inadequate. Such a vision maintains gender and the division of the sexes. It is a vision which simply inverts the arguments of those who base their case for inevitable male dominance or ineradicable and *significant* biological differences between the sexes. But we are not only oppressed *as* women, we are oprressed by having to *be* women, or men as the case may be. I personally feel that the feminist movement must dream of even more than the elimination of the oppression of women. It must dream of the elimination of obligatory sexualities and sex roles. The dream I find most compelling is one of an androgynous and genderless (though not sexless) society, in which one's sexual anatomy is irrelevant to who one is, what one does, and with whom one makes love.

. . .

[1975]

REFERENCES

Althusser, Louis and Balibar, Etienne. 1970. *Reading Capital.* London: New Left Books.

Derrida, Jacques. 1972. "Structure, Sign, and Play in the Discourse of the Human Sciences." In *The Structuralist Controversy,* edited by R. Macksey and E. Donato. Baltimore: Johns Hopkins Press.

Deutsch, Helene. 1948. "The Significance of Masochism in the Mental Life of Women." In *The Psychoanalytic Reader,* edited by R. Fleiss. New York: International Universities Press.

Engels, Frederick. 1891. *The Origins of the Family, Private Property, and the State.* 4th ed. Moscow: Foreign Languages Publishing House.

Evans-Pritchard, E. E. 1951. *Kinship and Marriage among the Nuer.* London: Oxford University Press.

Fee, Elizabeth. 1973. "The Sexual Politics of Victorian Social Anthropology." *Feminist Studies* (Winter/Spring): 23–29.

Freud, Sigmund. 1943. *A General Introduction to Psychoanalysis.* Garden City, N.Y.: Garden City Publishing Company.

_____. 1961. "Female Sexuality." In *The Complete Works of Sigmund Freud,* vol. 21, edited by J. Strachey. London: Hogarth.

_____. 1965. "Femininity." In *New Introductory Lectures in Psychoanalysis,* edited by J. Strachey. New York: W. W. Norton.

Hertz, Robert. 1960. *Death and the Right Hand.* Glencoe: Free Press.

Horney, Karen. 1973. "The Denial of the Vagina." In Karen Horney, *Feminine Psychology,* edited by Harold Kelman. New York: W. W. Norton.

Jakobson, Roman, and Halle, Morris. 1971. *Fundamentals of Language.* The Hague: Mouton.

Lacan, Jacques. 1968. "The Function of Language in Psychoanalysis." In Anthony Wilden, *The Language of Self.*

Lampl de Groot, Jeanne. 1933. "Problems of Femininity." *Psychoanalytic Quarterly* 2: 489–518.

_____. 1948. "The Evolution of the Oedipus Complex in Women." In *The Psychoanalytic Reader,* edited by R. Fleiss. New York: International Universities Press.

Lasch, Christopher. 1974. "Freud and Women." *New York Review of Books* 21, no. 15: 12–17.

Lévi-Strauss, Claude. 1969. *The Elementary Structures of Kinship.* Boston: Beacon Press.

_____. 1971. "The Family." In *Man, Culture, and Society,* edited by H. Shapiro. London: Oxford University Press.

Livingstone, Frank. 1969. "Genetics, Ecology, and the Origins of Incest and Exogamy." *Current Anthropology* 10, no. 1: 45–49.

Marx, Karl. 1969. *Theories of Surplus Value,* Part I. Moscow: Progress Publishers.

_____. 1971. *Pre-Capitalist Economic Formations.* New York: International Publishers.

Mehlman, Jeffrey. 1972. *French Freud: Structural Studies in Psychoanalysis.* New Haven: Yale French Studies #48.

Mitchell, Juliet. 1971. *Women's Estate.* New York: Vintage.

_____. 1974. *Psychoanalysis and Feminism.* New York: Pantheon.

Sahlins, Marshall. 1960*a*. "The Origin of Society." *Scientific American* 203, no. 3: 76–86.

_____. 1960*b*. "Political Power and the Economy in Primitive Society." In *Essays in the Science of Culture,* edited by Robert Dole and Robert Carneiro. New York: Crowell.

_____. 1972. *Stone Age Economics.* Chicago: Aldine-Atherton.

Scott, John Finley. 1965. "The Role of Collegiate Sororities in Maintaining Class and Ethnic Endogamy." *American Sociological Review* 30, no. 4: 415–26.

Strathern, Marilyn. 1972. *Women in Between.* New York: Seminar.

Thompson, E. P. 1963. *The Making of the English Working Class.* New York: Vintage.

Wilden, Anthony. 1968. *The Language of the Self.* Baltimore: Johns Hopkins Press.

Wittig, Monique. 1973. *Les Guérillères.* New York: Avon.

NOTES

1. This analysis of society as based on bonds between men by means of women makes the separatist responses of the women's movement thoroughly intelligible. Separatism can be seen as a mutation in social structure, as an attempt to form social groups based on unmediated bonds between women. It can also be seen as a radical denial of men's "rights" in women, and as a claim by women of rights in themselves.

2. I have taken my position on Freud somewhere between the French structuralist interpretations and American biologistic ones, because I think that Freud's wording is similarly somewhere in the middle. He does talk about

penises, about the "inferiority" of the clitoris, about the psychic consequences of anatomy. The Lacanians, on the other hand, argue from Freud's text that he is unintelligible if his words are taken literally, and that a thoroughly nonanatomical theory can be deduced as Freud's intention (see Althusser, 1969). I think that they are right; the penis is walking around too much for its role to be taken literally. The detachability of the penis, and its transformation in fantasy (e.g., penis = feces = child = gift), argue strongly for a symbolic interpretation. Nevertheless, I don't think that Freud was as consistent as either I or Lacan would like him to have been, and some gesture must be made to what he said, even as we play with what he must have meant.

3. The pre-Oedipal mother is the "phallic mother," e.g., she is believed to possess the phallus. The Oedipal-inducing information is that the mother does not possess the phallus. In other words, the crisis is precipitated by the "castration" of the mother, by the recognition that the phallus only passes through her, but does not settle on her. The "phallus" must pass through her, since the relationship of a male to every other male is defined through a woman. A man is linked to a son by a mother, to his nephew by virtue of a sister, etc. Every relationship between male kin is defined by the woman between them. If power is a male prerogative, and must be passed on, it must go through the woman-in-between. Marshall Sahlins (personal communication) once suggested that the reason women are so often defined as stupid, polluting, disorderly, silly, profane, or whatever, is that such categorizations define women as "incapable" of possessing the power which must be transferred through them.

 52

Chicana Feminism

ANNA NIETOGOMEZ

ANNA NIETOGOMEZ ND. Activist. Lives and works in the United States. Edited *Encuentro Femenil: The First Feminist Chicana Journal,* begun in 1973. "La Chicana: Legacy of Suffering and Self Denial" (1995); "Sexism in the Moviemiento" (1976); "Chicanas and the Labor Force" (1974).

I want to address myself to the common questions that come up in regard to Chicana feminism. What is Chicana feminism? I am a Chicana feminist. I make that statement very proudly, although there is a lot of intimidation in our community and in the society in general, against people who define themselves as Chicana feminists. It sounds like a contradictory statement, a *"Malinche"* statement—

if you're a Chicana you're on one side, if you're a feminist, you must be on the other side. They say you can't stand on both sides—which is a bunch of bull. Why? Because when you say you're Chicana, you mean you come from a particular community, one that is subject to racism and the exploitation of centuries. When you say you are a feminist you mean you're a woman who opposes the oppression of not only the group in general, but of women in particular. In fact, the statement is not contradictory at all, it is a very unified statement: I support my community and I do not ignore the women in my community (who have been long forgotten). The feminist movement is a unified front made up of both men and women—a feminist can be a man as well as a woman—it is a group of people that advocates the end of women's oppression.

People—reactionaries I call them—sometimes define a feminist as someone who hates men. Maybe this is not totally erroneous, but the label is a tactic used to keep people from listening to the issues. If somebody attacks you for being a Chicana feminist, he's diverting attention from some of the important issues at hand. What are these issues? The movement is one that supports social, economic and political issues in regard to the position of women—bettering the position of the Chicana. The Chicana is a woman and she cannot separate herself from that. One of the primary social issues is the double standard. It says that there is such a thing as male privilege and such a thing as female submission. Another issue is education—women have the right to education. When the woman was conceived it was not automatically determined that she was going to be barefoot, pregnant and tied to the stove. A third issue is child care—it's not a female duty, it is a community responsibility. Economically, the woman should have equal employment regardless of race—equal pay, equal training and an economic position which is not dependent on fathers, husbands and sons. As long as she is economically dependent she will have to allow male privilege, to compromise herself. She will always have to accept the secondary position. Politically, it means equal participation, equal representation, and inclusion of issues which address her as a woman, as a Chicana in the Raza community.

IS FEMINISM FOR ANGLOS?

Marta Cotera wrote an article several years ago saying that feminism is not an Anglo idea. I resent the usual remark that if you're a feminist you have somehow become an Anglo or been influenced by Anglos. That's a sexist remark, whether it comes from hermanos or hermanas. Why? Because of what it is saying—that you, as a Chicana, a Chicana woman, don't have the mentality to think for yourself! Somehow we are only supposed to be repositories—everything we say is either his idea, or the white anglo "her" idea, but not our idea. When we're confronted with these remarks about Chicana feminism, we can say, "Just a minute. Chicanas can think, too. You'd better sit down and listen to what we're thinking, because we're not only thinking it, we're doing it."

. . .

FEMINISM IN TEJAS

Here in the United States we have women who are very involved in the labor movement. I'm sure you know that most of the outstanding, internationally known women recognized for their efforts in the labor movement are Tejanas. Louisa González was a Tejana associated with the Haymarket Massacre. She was involved in organizing an international workers' alliance, and she advocated women's workers rights to pressure unions, to remind unions that women were working in the factories and should have their needs addressed, and that women should support the issues of the union. You have Emma Tenayuca, who was a farmworker organizer, who at the age of 18 had to support the majority of farmworkers in the pecan-shellers strike of 1938. And in El Paso you have the strike against Farah [1972], which was primarily an issue of women. Most of the workers in the factory were women, and 85 percent of them were Chicanas. The women who went around the nation to ask people to strike Farah Pants for Chicanas did a fantastic thing—the quiet, non-obtrusive, submissive women were coming to say, "You'd better strike Farah Pants."— Because we are workers. Because we demand workers' rights. Because as women, we demand maternity leave, because we ask for free birth control (and not false birth control), and because we

ask for better working conditions for everybody. All these things are part of the history of the *Tejana*, and they are things that Chicanas all over the nation admire and identify with.

TODAY, WHAT IS CHICANA FEMINISM DOING?

Today, Chicana feminism is trying to rally enough women and get them to come out from behind the doors so that everybody can hear us say, "We're a legitimate body. No one can deny that any more. Ask us about our political stance, not our validity, as women fighting for women's rights within the Chicano community." Right now, we're in the process of making the Chicano movement responsible to Chicana issues, making it support issues that involve race, welfare rights, forced sterilization— making the Chicano movement address itself to the double standard about male and female workers, and making it live up to its cry of *Carnalisimo* and community responsibility. We're saying, "Prove it! Let's carry it out! Let's support child care. Children are not our individual responsibility but the responsibility of our community." We are working to get women together to build up a base, and working to get the Chicano movement to support and advocate our issues as women.

IS THE CHICANA FEMINIST MOVEMENT DIFFERENT FROM THE ANGLO WOMEN'S MOVEMENT?

I myself feel that some of the distinctions made are irrelevant, but it's still very much like asking how the Chicano movement is different from the Black movement. These questions indicate that you're still fighting for recognition of your own identity, and at times I just think, "Well, I'm not here to talk about the Anglo women's movement. If you want to find out about the Anglo movement, you go and find out, and then go and find out about the Chicana movement, and compare them for yourself." Besides, the answers are obvious. The Chicana movement has to address itself to racism, and it is obvious from what Marta Cotera has written, what Evey Chapa has written, in terms of the Texas Women's Caucus (which is primarily Anglo), what you have to deal with. The issue of racism and the issue of class interest. And that class interest is not our interest. However, at the same time, I believe that not all Anglo women are middle class. It's the media that leads you to believe that, and you swallow it. What is the Anglo women's movement? First, you have to understand that it is not a unified movement. There are at least three positions. There are the liberal feminists, who say, "I want access to power. I want access to whatever men have access to. I want women's oppression to end insofar as they do not have these things." Then there are radical feminists, who say that men have the power, and that men are responsible for the oppression of women. A third position is that of women's liberationists, which says that women's oppression is one of the many oppressions in the economic system of this country, that we must understand and support that system as well as correct it and unify people to end all oppressions. Where does the Chicana women's movement stand in relation to these three positions? I do not have the authority to represent anyone in answering that, and the Chicana feminist is in the making from one place to another. But from my point of view, in my own private Los Angeles experience, the general feeling is that men do not have the power. Certainly Chicanos do not have the power, otherwise there would not be a Chicano movement. We recognize that obvious fact. At the same time, we recognize and criticize the fact that the Chicano seems to try to compensate for that lack of power with the use of "male privilege"—coming down with the double standard.

WHAT IS MALE PRIVILEGE?

Here's the double standard: "If I have a meeting, you stay at the house and take care of the kids. If you have a meeting, have it at the house and take care of the kids at the same time." Male privilege is, "Let's fight for equal pay for me, and maybe later on for you." Male privilege sometimes makes the Chicano movement just like a male liberation movement. The implication is this: "Our problem is that women have to work because we are not given our economic position as men." So once the men are paid what they're due, have an economic base as workers, then women won't have to be out in the public world. When liberation comes along, everything will be hunky-dory and the women can stay at home. That says to me, "Whose liberation are you fighting for, anyway? I'm fighting for people's liberation." If the answer is, "I am fighting for people's liberation," I say, "Okay, then if you are, it means there is no 'proper place' for the Chicana except the world as a whole. There is no one place for the Chicana—just the world as a whole."

· · ·

RAZA POWER MEANS AN END TO COLONIZATION

These are some of the issues in Chicana feminism. We are saying something very positive. Raza power! Men, women, and children. Everybody. When we say jobs, we mean jobs for all. But something I haven't mentioned is that a lot of the things that are going to change are those things that maybe we revere and sanction and call a part of our culture. If something in our culture that is advocating oppression is unable to be criticized, evaluated and changed, this is wrong. In our culture we happen to say *"la mujer buena"* [the Good Woman] and *"la mujer mala"* [the bad woman]. And if you're active in *Raza Unida*, you're suspected of being *la mujer mala*, and in order to prove that you're not, you have to live the life of a nun. Well, I say the life of a nun is oppressive. *"La mujer buena"* and *"la mujer mala"* are historical ideas that came from the colonization of the people in Mexico. In order to assimilate and acculturate the Indians, they used to control the women by setting up two models. First, they imported poor Spanish women to marry the Spaniards. Their oppressed role was that of the woman who stays home, and the only place she goes is to church or to visit her in-laws. That was the model of the Spanish woman. The model of the Indian woman was very different, a very active one. She was the business person; she was the one who controlled the market place, did the crafts, worked in the fields, participated in child care. She was the priestess of religious functions. This was a total role. Don't get me wrong, I'm not saying she wasn't oppressed; I'm not saying that at all. I'm saying it was different, and comparatively speaking, it was a freer role. In order for the colonization to affect everybody, they put up these two roles. They used the concepts of the church, *Marianismo* on the one hand, Mary Magdalene on the other. The Spanish woman and the Indian woman. *La mujer buena* and *la mujer mala*. Clear who's on the top and who's on the bottom! So we perpetuate those two roles and we perpetuate our own colonized situation. We have to recognize what change will bring to this colonization, which we have unintentionally continued.

[1976]

 ## 53

What Became of God the Mother? Conflicting Images of God in Early Christianity

ELAINE H. PAGELS

ELAINE H. PAGELS United States. 1943– . Scholar of religion. *The Gnostic Gospels* (1988), *Adam, Eve, and the Serpent* (1988), *The Origin of Satan* (1996).

Unlike many of his contemporaries among the deities of the ancient Near East, the God of Israel shares his power with no female divinity, nor is he the divine Husband or Lover of any.[1] He scarcely can be characterized in any but masculine epithets: King, Lord, Master, Judge, and Father.[2] Indeed, the absence of feminine symbolism of God marks Judaism, Christianity, and Islam in striking contrast to the world's other religious traditions, whether in Egypt, Babylonia, Greece, and Rome or Africa, Polynesia, India, and North America. Jewish, Christian, and Islamic theologians, however, are quick to point out that God is not to be considered in sexual terms at all. Yet the actual language they use daily in worship and prayer conveys a different message and gives the distinct impression that God is thought of in exclusively *masculine* terms. And while it is true that Catholics revere Mary as the mother of Jesus, she cannot be identified as divine in her own right: if she is "mother of God," she is not "God the Mother" on an equal footing with God the Father.

Christianity, of course, added the trinitarian terms to the Jewish description of God. And yet of the three divine "Persons," two—the Father and Son—are described in masculine terms, and the third—the Spirit—suggests the sexlessness of the Greek neuter term *pneuma*. This is not merely a subjective impression. Whoever investigates the early development of Christianity—the field called "patristics," that is, study of "the fathers of the church"—may not be surprised by the passage that concludes the recently discovered, secret *Gospel of Thomas*: "Simon Peter said to them [the disciples]: Let Mary be excluded from among us, for she is a woman, and not worthy of Life. Jesus said: Behold I will take Mary, and make her a male, so that she may become a living spirit, resembling you males. For I tell you truly, that every female who makes herself male will enter the Kingdom of Heaven."[3] Strange as it sounds, this only states explicitly what religious rhetoric often assumes: that the men form the legitimate body of the community, while women will be allowed to participate only insofar as their own identity is denied and assimilated to that of the men.

Further exploration of the texts which include this *Gospel*—written on papyrus, hidden in large clay jars nearly 1,600 years ago—has identified them as Jewish and Christian gnostic works which were attacked and condemned as "heretical" as early as A.D. 100–150. What distinguishes these "heterodox" texts from those that are called "orthodox" is at least partially clear: they abound in feminine symbolism that is applied, in particular, to God. Although one might expect, then, that they would recall the archaic pagan traditions of the Mother Goddess, their language is to the contrary specifically Christian, unmistakably related to a Jewish heritage. Thus we can see that certain gnostic Christians diverged even more radically from the Jewish tradition than the early Christians who described God as the "three Persons" or the Trinity. For instead of a monistic and masculine God, certain of these texts describe God as a dyadic being, who consists of *both* masculine and feminine elements. One such group of texts, for example, claims to have received a secret tradition from Jesus through James, and significantly, through Mary Magdalene.[4] Members of this group offer prayer to *both* the divine Father and Mother: "From Thee, Father, and through Thee, Mother, the two immortal names, Parents of the divine being, and thou, dweller in heaven, mankind of the mighty name. . . ."[5] Other texts indicate that their authors had pondered the nature of the beings to whom a single, masculine God proposed, "Let us make mankind in our image, after our likeness" (Gen. 1:26). Since the Genesis account goes on to say that mankind was created "male and female" (1:27), some concluded, apparently, that the God in whose image we are created likewise must be both masculine and feminine—both Father and Mother.

The characterization of the divine Mother in these sources is not simple since the texts themselves are extraordinarily diverse. Nevertheless, three primary characterizations merge. First, a certain poet and teacher, Valentinus, begins with the premise that God is essentially indescribable. And yet he suggests that the divine can be imagined as a Dyad consisting of two elements: one he calls the Ineffable, the Source, the Primal Father; the other, the Silence, the Mother of all things.[6] Although we might question Valentinus's reasoning that Silence is the appropriate complement of what is Ineffable, his equation of the former with the feminine and the latter with the masculine may be traced to the grammatical gender of the Greek words. Followers of Valentinus invoke this feminine power, whom they also call "Grace" (in Greek, the feminine term *charis*), in their own private celebration of the Christian eucharist: they call her "divine, eternal Grace, She who is before all things."[7] At other times they pray to her for protection as the Mother, "Thou enthroned with God, eternal, mystical Silence."[8] Marcus, a disciple of Valentinus, contends that "when Moses began his account of creation, he mentioned the Mother of all things at the very beginning, when he said, 'In the beginning God created the heavens and the earth,'"[9] for the word "beginning" (in Greek, the feminine *arche*) refers to the divine Mother, the source of the cosmic elements. When they describe God in this way different gnostic writers have different interpretations. Some maintain that the divine is to be considered masculo-feminine—the "great male-female power." Others insist that the terms are meant only as metaphors—for, in reality, the divine is *neither* masculine nor feminine. A third group suggests that one can describe the Source of all things in *either* masculine nor feminine terms, depending on which aspect one intends to stress.[10] Proponents of these diverse views agree, however, that the divine is to be understood as consisting of a harmonious, dynamic relationship of opposites—a concept that may be akin to the eastern view of *yin* and *yang* but remains antithetical to orthodox Judaism and Christianity.

A second characterization of the divine Mother describes her as Holy Spirit. One source, the *Secret Book of John*, for example, relates how John, the brother of James, went out after the crucifixion with "great grief," and had a mystical vision of the Trinity: "As I was grieving . . . the heavens were opened, and the whole creation shone with an unearthly light, and the universe was shaken. I was afraid . . . and behold . . . a unity in three forms appeared to me, and I marvelled: how can a unity have three forms?" To John's question the vision answers: "It said to me, 'John, John, why do you doubt, or why do you fear? . . . I am the One who is with you always: I am the Father; I am the Mother; I am the Son.'"[11] John's interpretation of the Trinity—as Father, Mother, and Son—may not at first seem shocking but is perhaps the more natural and spontaneous interpretation. Where the Greek terminology for the Trinity, which includes the neuter term for spirit (*pneuma*), virtually requires that the third "Person" of the Trinity be asexual, the author of the *Secret Book* looks to the Hebrew term for spirit, *ruah*—a feminine word. He thus concludes, logically enough, that the feminine "Person" conjoined with Father and Son must be the Mother! Indeed, the text goes on to describe the Spirit as Mother: ". . . the image of the invisible virginal perfect spirit. . . . She became the mother of the all, for she existed before them all, the mother-father [matropater]."[12] This same author, therefore, alters Genesis 1:2 ("the Spirit of God moved upon the face of the deep"). To say "the Mother then was moved. . . ."[13] The secret *Gospel to the Hebrews* likewise has Jesus speak of "my Mother, the Spirit."[14] And in the *Gospel of Thomas*, Jesus contrasts his earthly parents, Mary and Joseph, with his divine Father—the Father of Truth—and his divine Mother, the Holy Spirit. The author interprets a puzzling saying of Jesus in the New Testament ("whoever does not hate his father and mother is not worthy of me") by adding: "Whoever does not love his father and mother in my way cannot be my disciple; for my [earthly] mother gave me death but my true Mother gave me the Life."[15]

Another secret gnostic gospel, the *Gospel of Phillip*, declares that whoever becomes a Christian "gains both a father and a mother."[16] The author refers explicitly to the feminine Hebrew term to describe the Spirit as "Mother of many."[17]

In these sources suggest that the Spirit constitutes the maternal element of the Trinity, the *Gospel of Phillip* makes an equally radical suggestion concerning the doctrine that later developed as the virgin birth. Here again the Spirit is praised as both Mother and Virgin, the counterpart—and consort—of the Heavenly Father: "If I may utter a mystery, the Father and the all united with the Virgin who came down,"[18] that is, with the Holy Spirit. Yet because this process is to be understood symbolically, and not literally, the Spirit remains a virgin! The author explains that "for this reason, Christ was 'born of a virgin'"—that is, of the Spirit, his divine Mother. But the author ridicules those "literal-minded" Christians who mistakenly refer the virgin birth to Mary, Jesus' earthly mother, as if she conceived apart from Joseph: "Such persons do not know what they are saying; for when did a female ever impregnate a female?"[19] Instead, he argues, virgin birth refers to the mysterious union of the two divine powers, the Father of the All with the Holy Spirit.

Besides the eternal, mystical Silence, and besides the Holy Spirit, certain gnostics suggest a third characterization of the divine Mother as Wisdom. Here again the Greek feminine term for wisdom, *sophia*, like the term for spirit, *ruah*, translates a Hebrew feminine term, *hokhmah*. Early interpreters had pondered the meaning of certain biblical passages, for example, Proverbs: "God made the world in Wisdom." And they wondered if Wisdom could be the feminine power in which God's creation is "conceived"? In such passages, at any rate, Wisdom bears two connotations: first, she bestows the Spirit that makes mankind wise; second, she is a creative power. One gnostic source calls her the first universal creator";[20] another says that God the Father was speaking to her when he proposed to "make mankind in our image."[21] The *Great Announcement*, a mystical writing, explains the Genesis account in the following terms: ". . . One Power that is above and below, self-generating, self-discovering, its own mother; its own father; its own sister; its own son: Father, Mother, unity, Root of all things."[22] The

same author explains the mystical meaning of the Garden of Eden as a symbol of the womb: "Scripture teaches us that this is what is meant when Isaiah says, 'I am he that formed thee in thy mother's womb' [Isaiah 44:2]. The Garden of Eden, then, is Moses' symbolic term for the womb, and Eden the placenta, and the river which comes out of Eden the navel, which nourishes the fetus. . . ."[23] This teacher claims that the Exodus, consequently, symbolizes the exodus from the womb, "and the crossing of the Red Sea, they say, refers to the blood." Evidence for this view, he adds, comes directly from "the cry of the newborn," a spontaneous cry of praise for "the glory of the primal being, in which all the powers above are in harmonious embrace."[24]

The introduction of such symbolism in gnostic texts clearly bears implications for the understanding of human nature. The *Great Announcement* for example, having described the Source as a masculo-feminine being, a "bisexual Power," goes on to say that "what came into being from the Power, that is, humanity, being one, is found to be two: a male-female being that bears the female within it."[25] This refers to the story of Eve's "birth" out of Adam's side (so that Adam, being one, is "discovered to be two," an androgyne who "bears the female within him"). Yet this reference to the creation story of Genesis 2—an account which inverts the biological birth process, and so effectively denies the creative function of the female—proves to be unusual in gnostic sources. More often, such sources refer instead to the first creation account in Genesis 1:26–27. ("And God said, let us make mankind in Our image, after Our image and likeness . . . in the image of God he created him: male and female he created them"). Rabbis in Talmudic times knew a Greek version of the passage, one that suggested to Rabbi Samuel bar Nahman that "when the Holy One . . . first created mankind, he created him with two faces, two sets of genitals, four arms, and legs, back to back: Then he split Adam in two, and made two backs, one on each side."[26] Some Jewish teachers (perhaps influenced by the story in Plato's *Symposium*) had suggested that Genesis 1:26–27 narrates an androgynous creation—an idea that gnostics adopted and developed. Marcus (whose prayer to the Mother is given above) not only concludes from this account that God is dyadic ("Let *us* make mankind"), but also that "mankind, which was formed according to the image and likeness of God [Father and Mother] was masculofeminine."[27] And his contemporary, Theodotus, explains, "the saying that Adam was created 'male and female' means that the male and female elements together constitute the finest production of the Mother, Wisdom."[28] We can see, then, that the gnostic sources which describe God in both masculine and feminine terms often give a similar description of human nature as a dyadic entity, consisting of two equal male and female components.

All the texts cited above—secret "gospels," revelations, mystical teachings—are among those rejected from the select list of twenty-six that comprise the "New Testament" collection. As these and other writings were sorted and judged by various Christian communities, every one of these texts which gnostic groups revered and shared was rejected from the canonical collection as "heterodox" by those who called themselves "orthodox" (literally, straight-thinking) Christians. By the time this process was concluded, probably as late as the year A.D. 200, virtually all the feminine imagery for God (along with any suggestion of an androgynous human creation) had disappeared from "orthodox" Christian tradition.

What is the reason for this wholesale rejection? The gnostics themselves asked this question of their "orthodox" attackers and pondered it among themselves. Some concluded that the God of Israel himself initiated the polemics against gnostic teaching which his followers carried out in his name. They argued that he was a derivative, merely instrumental power, whom the divine Mother had created to administer the universe, but who remained ignorant of the power of Wisdom, his own Mother: "They say that the creator believed that he created everything by himself, but that, in reality, he had made them because his Mother, Wisdom, infused him with energy, and had given him her ideas. But he was unaware that the ideas he used came from her: He was even ignorant of his own Mother."[29] Followers of Valentinus suggested that the Mother herself encouraged the God of Israel to think that he was acting autonomously in creating the world; but, as one teacher adds, "It was

because he was foolish and ignorant of his Mother that he said, 'I am God; there is none beside me.'"[30] Others attribute to him the more sinister motive of jealousy, among them the *Secret Book of John,* "He said, 'I am a jealous God, and you shall have no other God before me,' already indicating that another god does exist. For if there were no other god, of whom would he be jealous? Then the Mother began to be distressed. . . ."[31] A third gnostic teacher describes the Lord's shock, terror, and anxiety "when he discovered that he was not the God of the universe." Gradually his shock and fear gave way to wonder, and finally he came to welcome the teaching of Wisdom. The gnostic teacher concluded: "This is the meaning of the saying, 'The fear of the Lord is the beginning of wisdom.'"[32]

All of these are, of course, mythical explanations. To look for the actual, historical reasons why these gnostic writings were suppressed is an extremely difficult proposition, for it raises the much larger question of how (i.e., by what means and what criteria) certain ideas, including those expressed in the texts cited above, came to be classified as heretical and others as orthodox by the beginning of the third century. Although the research is still in its early stages, and this question is far from being solved, we may find one clue if we ask whether these secret groups derived any practical, social consequences from their conception of God—and of mankind—that included the feminine element? Here again, the answer is yes and can be found in the orthodox texts themselves. Irenaeus, an orthodox bishop, for example, notes with dismay that women in particular are attracted to heretical groups—especially to Marcus's circle, in which prayers are offered to the Mother in her aspects as Silence, Grace, and Wisdom; women priests serve the eucharist together with men; and women also speak as prophets, uttering to the whole community what "the Spirit" reveals to them.[33] Professing himself to be at a loss to understand the attraction that Marcus's group holds, he offers only one explanation: that Marcus himself is a diabolically successful seducer, a magician who compounds special aphrodisiacs to "deceive, victimize, and defile" these "many foolish women!" Whether his accusation has any factual basis is difficult, probably impossible, to ascertain. Nevertheless, the historian notes that accusations of sexual license are a stock-in-trade of polemical arguments.[34] The bishop refuses to admit the possibility that the group might attract Christians—especially women—for sound and comprehensible reasons. While expressing his own moral outrage, Tertullian, another "father of the church," reveals his fundamental desire to keep women out of religion: "These heretical women—how audacious they are! They have no modesty: they are bold enough to teach, to engage in argument, to enact exorcisms, to undertake cures, and, it may be, even to baptize!"[35] Tertullian directs yet another attack against "that viper"—a woman teacher who led a congregation in North Africa.[36] Marcion had, in fact, scandalized his "orthodox" contemporaries by appointing women on an equal basis with men as priests and bishops among his congregations.[37] The teacher Marcillina also traveled to Rome to represent the Carpocratian group, an esoteric circle that claimed to have received secret teaching from Mary, Salome, and Martha.[38] And among the Montanists, a radical prophetic circle, the prophet Philumene was reputed to have hired a male secretary to transcribe her inspired oracles.[39]

Other secret texts, such as the *Gospel of Mary Magdalene* and the *Wisdom of Faith,* suggest that the activity of such women leaders challenged and therefore was challenged by the orthodox communities who regarded Peter as their spokesman. The *Gospel of Mary* relates that Mary tried to encourage the disciples after the crucifixion and to tell them what the Lord had told her privately. Peter, furious at the suggestion, asks, "Did he then talk secretly with a woman, instead of to us? Are we to go and learn from *her* now? Did he love her more than us?" Distressed at his rage, Mary then asks Peter: "What do you think? Do you think I made this up in my heart? Do you think I am lying about the Lord?" Levi breaks in at this point to mediate the dispute: "Peter, you are always irascible. You object to the woman as our enemies do. Surely the Lord knew her very well, and indeed, he loved her more than us. . . ." Then he and the others invite Mary to teach them what she knows.[40] Another argument between Peter and Mary occurs in *Wisdom of Faith.* Peter complains that Mary is dominating the conversation, even to the point of displacing the rightful priority of Peter himself and his brethren; he urges Jesus to silence her—and is quickly rebuked. Later, however, Mary admits to Jesus that she hardly dares to speak freely with him, because "Peter makes me hesitate: I am afraid of him, because he hates the female race." Jesus replies, that whoever receives inspiration from the Spirit is divinely ordained to speak, whether man or woman.[41]

As these texts suggest, then, women were considered equal to men, they were revered as prophets, and they acted as teachers, traveling evangelists, healers, priests, and even bishops. In some of these groups they played leading roles and were *excluded* from them in the orthodox churches, at least by A.D. 150–200. Is it possible, then, that the recognition of the feminine element in God and the recognition of mankind as a male and female entity bore within it the explosive social possibility of women acting on an equal basis with men in positions of authority and leadership? If this were true it might lead to the conclusion that these gnostic groups, together with their conception of God and human nature, were suppressed only because of their positive attitude toward women. But such a conclusion would be a mistake—a hasty and simplistic reading of the evidence. In the first place, orthodox Christian doctrine is far from wholly negative in its attitude toward women. Second, many other elements of the gnostic sources diverge in fundamental ways from what came to be accepted as orthodox Christian teaching. To examine this process in detail would require a much more extensive discussion than is possible here. Nevertheless the evidence does indicate that two very different patterns of sexual attitudes emerged in orthodox and gnostic circles. In simplest form, gnostic theologians correlate their description of God in both masculine and feminine terms with a complementary description of human nature. Most often they refer to the creation account of Genesis 1, which suggests an equal (or even androgynous) creation of mankind. This conception carries the principle of equality between men and women into the practical social and political structures of gnostic communities. The orthodox pattern is strikingly different: it describes God in exclusively masculine terms, and often uses Genesis 2 to describe how Eve was created from Adam and for his fulfillment.

Like the gnostic view, the orthodox also translates into sociological practice: by the late second century, orthodox Christians came to accept the domination of men over women as the proper, God-given order—not only for the human race, but also for the Christian churches. This correlation between theology, anthropology, and sociology is not lost on the apostle Paul. In his letter to the disorderly Corinthian community, he reminds them of a divinely ordained chain of authority: as God has authority over Christ, so the man has authority over the woman, argues Paul, citing Genesis 2: "The man is the image and glory of God, but the woman is the glory of man. For man is not from woman, but woman from man; and besides, the man was not created for the woman's sake, but the woman for the sake of the man."[42] Here the three elements of the orthodox pattern are welded into one simple argument: the description of God corresponds to a description of human nature which authorizes the social pattern of male domination.

A striking exception to this orthodox pattern occurs in the writings of one revered "father of the church," Clement of Alexandria. Clement identifies himself as orthodox, although he knows members of gnostic groups and their writings well; some scholars suggest that he was himself a gnostic initiate. Yet his own works demonstrate how all three elements of what we have called the "gnostic pattern" could be worked into fully "orthodox" teaching. First, Clement characterizes God not only in masculine but also in feminine terms: "The Word is everything to the child, both father and mother, teacher and nurse. . . . The nutriment is the milk of the Father . . . and the Word alone supplies us children with the milk of love, and only those who suck at this breast are truly happy. . . . For this reason seeking is called sucking; to those infants who seek the Word, the Father's loving breasts supply milk."[43] Second, in describing human nature, he insists that "men and women share equally in perfection, and are to receive the same instruction and discipline. For the name 'humanity' is common to both men and women; and for us 'in Christ there is neither male nor female.'"[44] Even in considering the active participation of women with men in the Christian community Clement offers a list—unique in orthodox tradition—of women whose achievements he

admires. They range from ancient examples, like Judith, the assassin who destroyed Israel's enemy, to Queen Esther, who rescued her people from genocide, as well as others who took radical political stands. He speaks of Arignole the historian, of Themisto the Epicurean philosopher, and of many other women philosophers including two who studied with Plato and one trained by Socrates. Indeed, he cannot contain his praise: "What shall I say? Did not Theano the Pythagoran make such progress in philosophy than when a man, staring at her, said, 'Your arm is beautiful,' she replied, 'Yes, but it is not on public display.'"[45] Clement concludes his list with famous women poets and painters.

If the work of Clement, who taught in Egypt before the lines of orthodoxy and heresy were rigidly drawn (ca. A.D. 160–180) demonstrates how gnostic principles could be incorporated even into orthodox Christian teaching, the majority of communities in the western empire headed by Rome did not follow his example. By the year A.D. 200, Roman Christians endorsed as "canonical" the pseudo-Pauline letter to Timothy, which interpreted Paul's views: "Let a woman learn in silence with full submissiveness. I do not allow any woman to teach or to exercise authority over a man; she is to remain silent, *for* [note Gen. 2!] Adam was formed first, then Eve and furthermore, Adam was not deceived, but the woman was utterly seduced and came into sin. . . ."[46] How are we to account for this irreversible development? The question deserves investigation which this discussion can only initiate. For example, one would need to examine how (and for what reasons) the zealously patriarchal traditions of Israel were adopted by the Roman (and other) Christian communities. Further research might disclose how social and cultural forces converged to suppress feminine symbolism—and women's participation—from western Christian tradition. Given such research, the history of Christianity never could be told in the same way again.

[1976]

NOTES

1. Where the God of Israel is characterized as husband and lover in the Old Testament (OT), his spouse is described as the community of Israel (i.e., Isa. 50:1, 54:1–8; Jer. 2: 2–3, 20–25, 3:1–20; Hos. 1–4, 14) or as the land of Israel (cf. Isa. 62:1–5).

2. One may note several exceptions to this rule: Deut. 32:11; Hos. 11:1; Isa. 66:12 ff; Num. 11:12.

3. *The Gospel according to Thomas* (hereafter cited as *ET*), ed. A. Guillaumount, H. Ch. Puech, G. Quispel, W. Till, Yassah 'Abd-al-Masih (London: Collins, 1959), logion 113–114.

4. Hippolytus, *Refutationis Omnium Haeresium* (hereafter cited as *Ref*), ed. L. Dunker, F. Schneidewin (Göttingen, 1859), 5. 7.

5. *Ref*, 5.6.

6. Irenaeus, *Adversus Haereses* (hereafter cited as *AH*), ed. W. W. Harvey (Cambridge, 1857), 1.11.1.

7. Ibid., 1.13.2.

8. Ibid., 1.13.6.

9. Ibid., 1.18.2.

10. Ibid., 1.11.5. –21.1, 3; *Ref*, 6.29.

11. *Apocryphon Johannis* (hereafter cited as *AJ*), ed. S. Giversen (Copenhagen: Prostant Apud Munksgaard, 1963), 47.20–48.14.

12. *AJ*, 52.34–53.6.

13. Ibid., 61.13–14.

14. Origen, *Commentary on John*, 2.12; *Hom. On Jeremiah*, 15.4.

15. *ET*, 101. The text of this passage is badly damaged; I follow here the reconstruction of G. MacRae of the Harvard Divinity School.

16. *L'Evangile selon Phillipe* (hereafter cited as *EP*), ed. J. E. Ménard (Leiden: Brill, 1967) logion 6.

17. *EP*, logion 36.

18. Ibid., logion 82.

19. Ibid., logion 17.

20. *Extraits de Théodote* (hereafter cited as Exc), ed. F. Sagnard, Sources chrétiennes 23 (Paris: Sources chrétiennes, 1948).

21. *AH*, 1.30.6.

22. *Ref*, 6.17.

23. Ibid., 6.14.

24. *AH*, 1.14.7–8.

25. *Ref*, 6.18.

26. Genesis Rabba 8.1, also 17.6; cf. Levitius Rabba 14. For an excellent discussion of androgyny, see W. Meeks, "The Image of the Androgyne: Some Uses of a Symbol in Earliest Christianity," *History of Religions* 13 (1974): 165–208.

27. *AH*, 1.18.2.

28. *Exc*, 21.1.

29. *Ref*, 6.33.

30. *AH*, 1.5.4; *Ref*, 6.33.

31. *AJ*, 61.8–14.

32. *Ref*, 7.26.

33. *AH*, 1.13.7.

34. Ibid., 1.13.2–5.

35. Tertullian, *De Praescriptione Haereticorum* (hereafter cited as *DP*), ed. E. Oehler (Lipsius, 1853–54), p. 41.

36. *De Baptismo* 1. I am grateful to Cyril Richardson for calling my attention to this passage and to the three subsequent ones.

37. Epiphanes *De Baptismo*, 42.5.

38. *AH*, 1.25.6.

39. *DP*, 6.30.

40. *The Gospel According to Mary*, Codex Berolinensis, *BG*, 8502, 1.7.1–1.19.5, ed., intro., and trans. G. MacRae, unpublished manuscript.

41. *Pistis Sophia*, ed. Carl Schmidt (Berlin: Academie-Verlag, 1925), 36 (57), 71 (161).

42. 1 Cor. 11:7–9. For discussion, see R. Scroggs, "Paul and the Eschatological Woman," *Journal of the American Academy of Religion* 40 (1972): 283–303; R. Scroggs, "Paul and the Eschatological Woman: Revisted," *Journal of the American Academy of Religion* 42 (1974): 532–537; and E. Pagels, "Paul and Women: A Response to Recent Discussion," *Journal of the American Academy of Religion* 42 (1974): 538–549.

43. Clement Alexandrinus, *Paidegogos*, ed. O. Stählin (Leipzig, 1905), 1.6.

44. Ibid., 1.4.

45. Ibid., 1.19.

46. 2 Tim. 2:11–14.

 54

A Black Feminist Statement

COMBAHEE RIVER COLLECTIVE

COMBAHEE RIVER COLLECTIVE Founded in 1974. Evolved out of the Boston chapter of the National Black Feminist Organization, founded in 1973. The statement was written by three members of the collective, Barbara Smith, Beverly Smith, and Demita Frazier.

We are a collective of Black feminists who have been meeting together since 1974.[1] During that time we have been involved in the process of defining and clarifying our politics, while at the same time doing political work within our own group and in coalition with other progressive organizations and movements. The most general statement of our politics at the present time would be that we are actively committed to struggling against racial, sexual, heterosexual, and class oppression and see as our particular task the development of integrated analysis and practice based upon the fact that the major systems of oppression are interlocking. The synthesis of these oppressions creates the conditions of our lives. As Black women we see Black feminism as the logical political movement to combat the manifold and simultaneous oppressions that all women of color face.

We will discuss four major topics in the paper that follows: (1) the genesis of contemporary Black feminism; (2) what we believe, i.e., the specific province of our politics; (3) the problems in organizing Black feminists, including a brief herstory of our collective; and (4) Black feminist issues and practice.

1. THE GENESIS OF CONTEMPORARY BLACK FEMINISM

Before looking at the recent development of Black feminism we would like to affirm that we find our origins in the historical reality of Afro-American women's continuous life-and-death struggle for survival and liberation. Black women's extremely negative relationship to the American political system (a system of white male rule) has always been determined by our membership in two oppressed racial and sexual castes. As Angela Davis points out in "Reflections on the Black Women's Role in the Community of Slaves," Black women have always embodied, if only in their physical manifestation, an adversary stance to white male rule and have actively resisted its inroads upon them and their communities in both dramatic and subtle ways. There have always been Black women activists—some known, like Sojourner Truth, Harriet Tubman, Frances E. W. Harper, Ida B. Wells Barnett, and Mary Church Terrell, and thousands upon thousands unknown—who had a shared awareness of how their sexual identity combined with their racial identity to make their whole life situation and the focus of their political struggles unique. Contemporary Black feminism is the outgrowth of countless generations of personal sacrifice, militancy, and work by our mothers and sisters.

A Black feminist presence has evolved most obviously in connection with the second wave of the American women's movement beginning in the late 1960s. Black, other Third World, and working women have been involved in the feminist movement from its start, but both outside reactionary forces and racism and elitism within the movement itself have served to obscure our participation. In 1973 Black feminists, primarily located in New York, felt the necessity of forming a separate Black feminist group. This became the National Black Feminist Organization (NBFO).

Black feminist politics also have an obvious connection to movements for Black liberation, particularly those of the 1960s and 1970s. Many of us were active in those movements (civil rights, Black nationalism, the Black Panthers), and all of our lives were greatly affected and changed by their ideology, their goals, and the tactics used to achieve their goals. It was our experience and disillusionment within these liberation movements, as well as experience on the periphery of the white male left, that led to the need to develop a politics that was antiracist, unlike those of white women, and antisexist, unlike those of Black and white men.

There is also undeniably a personal genesis for Black feminism, that is, the political realization that comes from the seemingly personal experiences of individual Black women's lives. Black feminists and many more Black women who do not define themselves as feminists have all experienced sexual oppression as a constant factor in our day-to-day existence. As children we realized that we were different from boys and that we were treated differently. For example, we were told in the same breath to be quiet both for the sake of being "ladylike" and to make us less objectionable in the eyes of white people. As we grew older we became aware of the threat of physical and sexual abuse by men. However, we had no way of conceptualizing what was so apparent to us, what we *knew* was really happening.

Black feminists often talk about their feelings of craziness before becoming conscious of the concepts of sexual politics, patriarchal rule, and most importantly, feminism, the political analysis and practice that we women use to struggle against our oppression. The fact that racial politics and indeed racism are pervasive factors in our lives did not allow us, and still does not allow most Black women, to look more deeply into our experiences and, from that sharing and growing consciousness, to build a politics that will change our lives and inevitably end our oppression. Our development must also be tied to the contemporary economic and political position of Black people. The post World War II generation of Black youth was the first to be able to minimally partake of certain educational and employment options, previously closed completely to Black people. Although our economic position is still at the very bottom of the American capitalistic economy, a handful of us have been able to gain certain tools as a result of tokenism in education and employment which potentially enable us to more effectively fight our oppression.

A combined antiracist and antisexist position drew us together initially, and as we developed politically we addressed ourselves to hetero-sexism and economic oppression under capitalism.

2. WHAT WE BELIEVE

Above all else, our politics initially sprang from the shared belief that Black women are inherently valuable, that our liberation is a necessity not as an adjunct to somebody else's but because of our need as human persons for autonomy. This may seem so obvious as to sound simplistic, but it is apparent that no other ostensibly progressive movement has ever considered our specific oppression as a priority or worked seriously for the ending of that oppression. Merely naming the pejorative stereotypes attributed to Black women (e.g. mammy, matriarch, Sapphire, whore, bulldagger), let alone cataloguing the cruel, often murderous, treatment we receive, indicates how little value has been placed upon our lives during four centuries of bondage in the Western hemisphere. We realize that the only people who care enough about us to work consistently for our liberation is us. Our politics evolve from a healthy love for ourselves, our sisters and our community which allows us to continue our struggle and work.

This focusing upon our own oppression is embodied in the concept of identity politics. We believe that the most profound and potentially the most radical politics come directly out of our own identity, as opposed to working to end somebody else's oppression. In the case of Black women this is a particularly repugnant, dangerous, threatening, and therefore revolutionary concept because it is obvious from looking at all the political movements that have preceded us that anyone is more worthy of liberation than ourselves. We reject pedestals, queenhood, and walking ten paces behind. To be recognized as human, levelly human, is enough.

We believe that sexual politics under patriarchy is as pervasive in Black women's lives as are the politics of class and race. We also often find it difficult to separate race from class from sex oppression because in our lives they are most often experienced simultaneously. We know that there is such a thing as racial-sexual oppression which is neither solely racial nor solely sexual, e.g., the history of rape of Black women by white men as a weapon of political repression.

Although we are feminists and lesbians, we feel solidarity with progressive Black men and do not advocate the fractionalization that white women who are separatists demand. Our situation as Black people necessitates that we have solidarity around the fact of race, which white women of course do not need to have with white men, unless it is their negative solidarity as racial oppressors. We struggle together with Black men against racism, while we also struggle with Black men about sexism.

We realize that the liberation of all oppressed peoples necessitates the destruction of the political-economic systems of capitalism and imperialism as well as patriarchy. We are socialists because we believe the work must be organized for the collective benefit of those who do the work and create the products, and not for the profit of the bosses. Material resources must be equally distributed among those who create those resources. We are not convinced, however, that a socialist revolution that is not also a feminist and antiracist revolution will guarantee our liberation. We have arrived at the necessity for developing an understanding of class relationships that takes into account the specific class position of Black women, who are generally marginal in the labor force, while at this particular time some of us are temporarily viewed as doubly desirable tokens at white-collar and professional levels. We need to articulate the real class situation of persons who are not merely raceless, sexless workers, but for whom racial and sexual oppression are significant determinants in their working/economic lives. Although we are in essential agreement with Marx's theory as it applied to the very specific economic relationships he analyzed, we know that his analysis must be extended further in order for us to understand our specific economic situation as Black women.

A political contribution which we feel we have already made is the expansion of the feminist principle that the personal is political. In our consciousness-raising sessions, for example, we have in many ways gone beyond white women's revelations because we are dealing with the implications of race and class as well as sex. Even our Black women's style of talking/testifying in Black language about what we have experienced has a resonance that is both cultural and political. We have spent a great deal of energy delving into the cultural and experiential nature of our oppression out of necessity because none of these matters has ever been looked at before. No one before has ever examined the multilayered texture of Black women's lives. An example of this kind of revelation/ conceptualization occurred at a meeting as we discussed the ways in which our early intellectual interests had been attacked by our peers, particularly Black males. We discovered that all of us, because we were "smart" had been considered "ugly," *i.e.,* "smart-ugly." "Smart-ugly" crystallized the way in which most of us had been forced to develop our intellects at great cost to our "social" lives. The sanction in the Black and white communities against Black women thinkers is comparatively much higher than for white women, particularly ones from the educated middle and upper classes.

As we have already stated, we reject the stance of lesbian separatism because it is not a viable political analysis or strategy for us. It leaves out far too much and far too many people, particularly Black men, women, and children. We have a great deal of criticism and loathing for what men have been socialized to be in this society: what they support, how they act, and how they oppress. But we do not have the misguided notion that it is their maleness, per se—i.e., their biological maleness—that makes them what they are. As Black women we find any type of biological determinism a particularly dangerous and reactionary basis upon which to build a politic. We must also question whether lesbian separatism is an adequate and progressive political analysis and strategy, even for those who practice it, since it so completely denies any but the sexual sources of women's oppression, negating the facts of class and race.

3. PROBLEMS IN ORGANIZING BLACK FEMINISTS

During our years together as a Black feminist collective we have experienced success and defeat, joy and pain, victory and failure. We have found that it is very difficult to organize around Black feminist issues,

difficult even to announce in certain contexts that we *are* Black feminists. We have tried to think about the reasons for our difficulties, particularly since the white women's movement continues to be strong and to grow in many directions. In this section we will discuss some of the general reasons for the organizing problems we face and also talk specifically about the stages in organizing our own collective.

The major source of difficulty in our political work is that we are not just trying to fight oppression on one front or even two, but instead to address a whole range of oppressions. We do not have racial, sexual, heterosexual, or class privilege to rely upon, nor do we have even the minimal access to resources and power that groups who possess any one of these types of privilege have.

The psychological toll of being a Black woman and the difficulties this presents in reaching political consciousness and doing political work can never be underestimated. There is a very low value placed upon Black women's psyches in this society, which is both racist and sexist. As an early group member once said, "We are all damaged people merely by virtue of being Black women." We are dispossessed psychologically and on every other level, and yet we feel the necessity to struggle to change the condition of all Black women. In "A Black Feminist's Search for Sisterhood," Michele Wallace arrives at this conclusion:

> "We exist as women who are Black who are feminists, each stranded for the moment, working independently because there is not yet an environment in this society remotely congenial to our struggle—because, being on the bottom, we would have to do what no one else has done: we would have to fight the world."[2]

Wallace is pessimistic but realistic in her assessment of Black feminists' position, particularly in her allusion to the nearly classic isolation most of us face. We might use our position at the bottom, however, to make a clear leap into revolutionary action. If Black women were free, it would mean that everyone else would have to be free since our freedom would necessitate the destruction of all the systems of oppression.

Feminism is, nevertheless, very threatening to the majority of Black people because it calls into question some of the most basic assumptions about our existence, i.e., that sex should be a determinant of power relationships. Here is the way male and female voices were defined in a Black nationalist pamphlet from the early 1970's.

"We understand that it is and has been traditional that the man is the head of the house. He is the leader of the house/nation because his knowledge of the world is broader, his awareness is greater, his understanding is fuller and his application of this information is wiser . . . After all, it is only reasonable that the man be the head of the house because he is able to defend and protect the development of his home . . . Women cannot do the same things as men—they are made by nature to function differently. Equality of men and women is something that cannot happen even in the abstract world. Men are not equal to other men, i.e. ability, experience or even understanding. The value of men and women can be seen as in the value of gold and silver—they are not equal but both have great value. We must realize that men and women are a complement to each other because there is no house/family without a man and his wife. Both are essential to the development of any life."[3]

The material conditions of most Black women would hardly lead them to upset both economic and sexual arrangements that seem to represent some stability in their lives. Many Black women have a good understanding of both sexism and racism, but because of the everyday constrictions of their lives cannot risk struggling against them both.

The reaction of Black men to feminism has been notoriously negative. They are, of course, even more threatened than Black women by the possibility that Black feminists might organize around our own needs. They realize that they might not only lose valuable and hardworking allies in their struggles but that they might also be forced to change their habitually sexist ways of interacting with and oppressing Black women. Accusations that Black feminism divides the Black struggle are powerful deterrents to the growth of an autonomous Black women's movement.

Still, hundreds of women have been active at different times during the three-year existence of our group. And every Black woman who came, came out of a strongly felt need for some level of possibility that did not previously exist in her life.

When we first started meeting early in 1974 after the NBFO first eastern regional conference, we did not have a strategy for organizing, or even a focus. We just wanted to see what we had. After a period of months of not meeting, we began to meet again late in the year and started doing an intense variety of consciousness-raising. The overwhelming feeling that we had is that after years and years we had finally found each other. Although we were not doing political work as a group, individuals continued their involvement in Lesbian politics, sterilization abuse and abortion rights work, Third World Women's International Women's Day activities, and support activity for the trials of Dr. Kenneth Edelin, Joan Little, and Inéz Garcia. During our first summer, when membership had dropped off considerably, those of us remaining devoted serious discussion to the possibility of opening a refuge for battered women in a Black community. (There was no refuge in Boston at the time.) We also decided around that time to become an independent collective since we had serious disagreements with NBFO's bourgeois-feminist stance and their lack of a clear political focus.

We also were contacted at that time by socialist feminists, with whom we had worked on abortion rights activities, who wanted to encourage us to attend the National Socialist Feminist Conference in Yellow Springs. One of our members did attend and despite the narrowness of the ideology that was promoted at that particular conference, we became more aware of the need for us to understand our own economic situation and to make our own economic analysis.

In the fall, when some members returned, we experienced several months of comparative inactivity and internal disagreements which were first conceptualized as a Lesbian-straight split but which were also the result of class and political differences. During the summer those of us who were still meeting had determined the need to do political work and to move beyond consciousness-raising and serving exclusively as an emotional support group. At the beginning of 1976, when some of the women who had not wanted to do political work and who also had voiced disagreements stopped attending of their own accord, we again looked for a focus. We decided at that time, with the addition of new members, to become a study group. We had always shared our reading with each other, and some of us had written papers on Black feminism for group discussion a few months before this decision was made. We began functioning as a study group and also began discussing the possibility of starting a Black feminist publication. We had a retreat in the late spring which provided a time for both political discussion and working out interpersonal issues. Currently we are planning to gather together a collection of Black feminist writing. We feel that it is absolutely essential to demonstrate the reality of our politics to other Black women and believe that we can do this through writing and distributing our work. The fact that individual Black feminists are living in isolation all over the country, that our own numbers are small, and that we have some skills in writing, printing, and publishing makes us want to carry out these kinds of projects as a means of organizing Black feminists as we continue to do political work in coalition with other groups.

4. BLACK FEMINIST ISSUES AND PROJECTS

During our time together we have identified and worked on many issues of particular relevance to Black women. The inclusiveness of our politics makes us concerned with any situation that impinges upon the lives of women, Third World and working people. We are of course particularly committed to working on those struggles in which race, sex and class are simultaneous factors in oppression. We might, for example, become involved in workplace organizing at a factory that employs Third World women or picket a hospital that is cutting back on already inadequate health care to a Third World community, or set up a rape crisis center in a Black neighborhood. Organizing around welfare and daycare concerns might also be a focus. The work to be done and the countless issues that this work represents merely reflect the pervasiveness of our oppression.

Issues and projects that collective members have actually worked on are sterilization abuse, abortion rights, battered women, rape and health care. We have also done many workshops and educationals on Black feminism on college campuses, at

women's conferences, and most recently for high school women.

One issue that is of major concern to us and that we have begun to publicly address is racism in the white women's movement. As Black feminists we are made constantly and painfully aware of how little effort white women have made to understand and combat their racism, which requires among other things that they have a more than superficial comprehension of race, color, and Black history and culture. Eliminating racism in the white women's movement is by definition work for white women to do, but we will continue to speak to and demand accountability on this issue.

In the practice of our politics we do not believe that the end always justifies the means. Many reactionary and destructive acts have been done in the name of achieving "correct" political goals. As feminists we do not want to mess over people in the name of politics. We believe in collective process and a nonhierarchical distribution of power within our own group and in our vision of a revolutionary society. We are committed to a continual examination of our politics as they develop through criticism and self-criticism as an essential aspect of our practice. In her introduction to *Sisterhood Is Powerful* Robin Morgan writes:

> "I haven't the faintest notion what possible revolutionary role white heterosexual men could fulfill, since they are the very embodiment of reactionary-vested-interest-power."

As Black feminists and Lesbians we know that we have a very definite revolutionary task to perform and we are ready for the lifetime of work and struggle before us.

[1977]

NOTES

The Combahee River Collective is a Black feminist group in Boston whose name comes from the guerrilla action conceptualized and led by Harriet Tubman on June 2, 1863, in the Port Royal region of South Carolina. This action freed more than 750 slaves and is the only military campaign American history planned and led by a woman.

1. This statement is dated April 1977.
2. Michele Wallace, "A Black Feminist's Search for Sisterhood," *Village Voice*, 28 July 1975, pp. 6–7.
3. Mumininas of Committee for Unified Newark, *Mwanamke Mwananchi (The Nationalist Woman)*, Newark, N.J., 1971, pp. 4–5.

55

From This Sex Which Is Not One

LUCE IRIGARAY

LUCE IRIGARAY Belgium. 1930– . Psycho-linguist. Philosopher. Lives and works primarily in France. Central voice in French feminism. Feminist critic of Lacan. *Speculum of the Other Woman* (1985), *Thinking the Difference: For a Peaceful Revolution* (1989), *An Ethics of Sexual Difference* (1993), *Speech Is Never Neuter* (1995), *Sharing the World* (2008).

Female sexuality has always been conceptualized on the basis of masculine parameters. Thus the opposition between "masculine" clitoral activity and "feminine" vaginal passivity, an opposition which Freud—and many others—saw as stages, or alternatives, in the development of a sexually "normal" woman, seems rather too clearly required by the practice of male sexuality. For the clitoris is conceived as a little penis pleasant to masturbate so long as castration anxiety does not exist (for the boy child), and the vagina is valued for the "lodging" it offers the male organ when the forbidden hand has to find a replacement for pleasure-giving.

In these terms, woman's erogenous zones never amount to anything but a clitoris-sex that is not comparable to the noble phallic organ, or a hole-envelope that serves to sheathe and massage the penis in intercourse: a non-sex, or a masculine organ turned back upon itself, self-embracing.

About woman and her pleasure, this view of the sexual relation has nothing to say. Her lot is that of "lack," "atrophy" (of the sexual organ), and "penis envy," the penis being the only sexual organ of recognized value. Thus she attempts by every means available to appropriate that organ for herself: through her somewhat servile love of the father-husband capable of giving her one, through her desire for a child-penis, preferably a boy, through access to the cultural values still reserved by right to males alone and therefore always masculine, and so on. Woman lives her own desire only as the expectation that she may at last come to possess an equivalent of the male organ.

Yet all this appears quite foreign to her own pleasure, unless it remains within the dominant phallic economy. Thus, for example, woman's auto-eroticism is very different from man's. In order to touch himself, man needs an instrument: his hand, a woman's body, language . . . And this self-caressing requires at least a minimum of activity. As for woman, she touches herself in and of herself without any need for mediation, and before there is any way to distinguish activity from passivity. Woman "touches herself" all the time, and moreover no one can forbid her to do so, for her genitals are formed of two lips in continuous contact. Thus, within herself, she is already two—but not divisible into one(s)—that caress each other.

This autoeroticism is disrupted by a violent break-in: the brutal separation of the two lips by a violating penis, an intrusion that distracts and deflects the woman from this "self-caressing" she needs if she is not to incur the disappearance of her own pleasure in sexual relations. If the vagina is to serve *also*, but *not only*, to take over for the little boy's hand in order to assure an articulation between autoeroticism and hetero-eroticism in intercourse (the encounter with the totally other always signifying death), how, in the classic representation of sexuality, can the perpetuation of auto-eroticism for woman be managed? Will woman not be left with the impossible alternative between a defensive virginity, fiercely turned in upon itself, and a body open to penetration that no longer knows, in this "hole" that constitutes its sex, the pleasure of its own touch? The more or less exclusive—and highly anxious—attention paid to erection in Western sexuality proves to what extent the imaginary that governs it is foreign to the feminine. For the most part, this sexuality offers nothing but imperatives dictated by male rivalry: the "strongest" being the one who has the best "hard-on," the longest, the biggest, the stiffest penis, or even the one who "pees the farthest" (as in little boys' contests). Or else one finds imperatives dictated by the enactment of sadomasochistic fantasies, these in turn governed by man's relation to his mother: the desire to force entry, to penetrate, to appropriate for himself the mystery of this womb where he has been conceived, the secret of his begetting, of his "origin." Desire/need, also to make blood flow again in order to revive a very old relationship—intrauterine, to be sure, but also prehistoric—to the maternal.

Woman, in this sexual imaginary, is only a more or less obliging prop for the enactment of man's fantasies. That she may find pleasure there in that role, by proxy, is possible, even certain. But such pleasure is above all a masochistic prostitution of her body to a desire that is not her own, and it leaves her in a familiar state of dependency upon man. Not knowing what she wants, ready for anything, even asking for more, so long as he will "take" her as his "object" when he seeks his own pleasure. Thus she will not say what she herself wants; moreover, she does not know, or no longer knows, what she wants. As Freud admits, the beginnings of the sexual life of a girl child are so "obscure," so "faded with time," that one would have to dig down very deep indeed to discover beneath the traces of this civilization, of this history, the vestiges of a more archaic civilization that might give some clue to woman's sexuality. That extremely ancient civilization would undoubtedly have a different alphabet, a different language . . . Woman's desire would not be expected to speak the same language as man's; woman's desire has doubtless been submerged by the logic that has dominated the West since the time of the Greeks.

Within this logic, the predominance of the visual, and of the discrimination and individualization of form, is particularly foreign to female eroticism. Woman takes pleasure more from touching than from looking, and her entry into a dominant scopic economy signifies, again, her consignment to passivity: she is to be the beautiful object of contemplation. While her body finds itself thus eroticized, and called to a double movement of exhibition and of chaste retreat in order to stimulate the drives of the "subject," her sexual organ represents *the horror of nothing to see*. A defect in this systematics of representation and desire. A "hole" in its scopophilic lens. It is already evident in

Greek statuary that this nothing-to-see has to be excluded, rejected, from such a scene of representation. Woman's genitals are simply absent, masked, sewn back up inside their "crack."

This organ which has nothing to show for itself also lacks a form of its own. And if woman takes pleasure precisely from this incompleteness of form which allows her organ to touch itself over and over again, indefinitely, by itself, that pleasure is denied by a civilization that privileges phallomorphism. The value granted to the only definable form excludes the one that is in play in female autoeroticism. The *one* of form, of the individual, of the (male) sexual organ, of the proper name, of the proper meaning . . . supplants, while separating and dividing, that contact of *at least two* (lips) which keeps woman in touch with herself, but without any possibility of distinguishing what is touching from what is touched.

Whence the mystery that woman represents in a culture claiming to count everything, to number everything by units, to inventory everything as individualities. *She is neither one nor two.* Rigorously speaking, she cannot be identified either as one person, or as two. She resists all adequate definition. Further, she has no "proper" name. And her sexual organ, which is not *one* organ, is counted as *none*. The negative, the underside, the reverse of the only visible and morphologically designatable organ (even if the passage from erection to detumescence does pose some problems): the penis.

But the "thickness" of that "form," the layering of its volume, its expansions and contractions and even the spacing of the moments in which it produces itself as form—all this the feminine keeps secret. Without knowing it. And if woman is asked to sustain, to revive, man's desire, the request neglects to spell out what it implies as to the value of her own desire. A desire of which she is not aware, moreover, at least not explicitly. But one whose force and continuity are capable of nurturing repeatedly and at length all the masquerades of "femininity" that are expected of her.

It is true that she still has the child, in relation to whom her appetite for touch, for contact, has free rein, unless it is already lost, alienated by the taboo against touching of a highly obsessive civilization. Otherwise her pleasure will find, in the child, compensations for and diversions from the frustrations that she too often encounters in sexual relations per se. Thus maternity fills the gaps in a repressed female sexuality. Perhaps man and woman no longer caress each other except through that mediation between them that the child—preferably a boy—represents? Man, identified with his son, rediscovers the pleasure of maternal fondling; woman touches herself again by caressing that part of her body: her baby-penis-clitoris.

What this entails for the amorous trio is well known. But the Oedipal interdiction seems to be a somewhat categorical and factitious law—although it does provide the means for perpetuating the authoritarian discourse of fathers—when it is promulgated in a culture in which sexual relations are impracticable because man's desire and woman's are strangers to each other. And in which the two desires have to try to meet through indirect means, whether the archaic one of a sense-relation to the mother's body, or the present one of active or passive extension of the law of the father. These are regressive emotional behaviors, exchanges of words too detached from the sexual arena not to constitute an exile with respect to it: "mother" and "father" dominate the interactions of the couple, but as social roles. The division of labor prevents them from making love. They produce or reproduce. Without quite knowing how to use their leisure. Such little as they have, such little indeed as they wish to have. For what are they to do with leisure? What substitute for amorous resource are they to invent? Still . . .

Perhaps it is time to return to that repressed entity, the female imaginary. So woman does not have a sex organ? She has at least two of them, but they are not identifiable as ones. Indeed, she has many more. Her sexuality, always at least double, goes even further: it is *plural*. Is this the way culture is seeking to characterize itself now? Is this the way texts write themselve / are written now? Without quite knowing what censorship they are evading? Indeed, woman's pleasure does not have to choose between clitoral activity and vaginal passivity, for example. The pleasure of the vaginal caress does not have to be substituted for that of the clitoral caress. They each contribute, irreplaceably, to woman's pleasure. Among other caresses . . . Fondling the breasts, touching the vulva, spreading the lips, stroking the posterior wall of the vagina, brushing against the mouth of the uterus, and so on. To evoke only a few of the most specifically female pleasures. Pleasures which are somewhat misunderstood in sexual difference as it is imagined—or not imagined, the other sex being only the indispensable complement to the only sex.

But *woman has sex organs more or less everywhere*. She finds pleasure almost anywhere. Even if we refrain from invoking the hystericization of her entire body, the geography of her pleasure is far more diversified, more multiple in its differences, more complex, more subtle, than is commonly imagined—in an imaginary rather too narrowly focused on sameness.

"She" is indefinitely other in herself. This is doubtless why she is said to be whimsical, incomprehensible, agitated, capricious . . . not to mention her language, in which "she" sets off in all directions, leaving "him" unable to discern the coherence of any meaning. Hers are contradictory words, somewhat mad from the standpoint of reason, inaudible for whoever listens to them with ready-made grids, with a fully elaborated code in hand. For in what she says, too, at least when she dares, woman is constantly touching herself. She steps ever so slightly aside from herself with a murmur, an exclamation, a whisper, a sentence left unfinished. . . . When she returns, it is to set off again from elsewhere. From another point of pleasure, or of pain. One would have to listen with another ear, as if hearing an *"other meaning" always in the process of weaving itself, of embracing itself with words, but also of getting rid of words in order not to become fixed, congealed in them*. For if "she" says something, it is not, it is already no longer, identical with what she means. What she says is never identical with anything, moreover; rather, it is contiguous. *It touches (upon)*. And when it strays too far from that proximity, she breaks off and starts over at "zero": her body-sex.

It is useless, then, to trap women in the exact definition of what they mean, to make them repeat (themselves) so that it will be clear; they are already elsewhere in that discursive machinery where you expected to surprise them. They have returned within themselves. Which must not be understood in the same way as within yourself. They do not have the interiority that you have, the one you perhaps suppose they have. Within themselves means *within the intimacy of that silent, multiple, diffuse touch.* And if you ask them insistently what they are thinking about, they can only reply: Nothing. Everything.

Thus what they desire is precisely nothing, and at the same time everything. Always something more and something else besides that *one*—sexual organ, for example,—that you give them, attribute to them. Their desire is often interpreted, and feared, as a sort of insatiable hunger, a voracity that will swallow you whole. Whereas it really involves a different economy more than anything else, one that upsets the linearity of a project, undermines the goal-object of a desire, diffuses the polarization toward a single pleasure, disconcerts fidelity to a single discourse. . . .

Must this multiplicity of female desire and female language be understood as shards, scattered remnants of a violated sexuality? A sexuality denied? The question has no simple answer. The rejection, the exclusion of a female imaginary certainly puts woman in the position of experiencing herself only fragmentarily, in the little-structured margins of a dominant ideology, as waste, or excess, what is left of a mirror invested by the (masculine) "subject" to reflect himself, to copy himself. Moreover, the role of "femininity" is prescribed by this masculine specula(riza)tion and corresponds scarcely at all to woman's desire, which may be recovered only in secret, in hiding, with anxiety and guilt.

But if the female imaginary were to deploy itself, if it could bring itself into play otherwise than as scraps, uncollected debris, would it represent itself, even so, in the form of *one* universe? Would it even be volume instead of surface? No. Not unless it were understood, yet again, as a privileging of the maternal over the feminine. Of a phallic maternal,

at that. Closed in upon the jealous possession of its valued product. Rivaling man in his esteem for productive excess. In such a race for power, woman loses the uniqueness of her pleasure. By closing herself off as volume, she renounces the pleasure that she gets from the *nonsuture of her lips:* she is undoubtedly a mother, but a virgin mother; the role was assigned to her by mythologies long ago. Granting her a certain social power to the extent that she is reduced, with her own complicity, to sexual impotence.

(Re-)discovering herself, for a woman, thus could only signify the possibility of sacrificing no one of her pleasures to another, of identifying herself with none of them in particular, *of never being simply one*. A sort of expanding universe to which no limits could be fixed and which would not be incoherence nonetheless—nor that polymorphous perversion of the child in which the erogenous zones would lie waiting to be regrouped under the primacy of the phallus.

Woman always remains several, but she is kept from dispersion because the other is already within her and is autoerotically familiar to her. Which is not to say that she appropriates the other for herself, that she reduces it to her own property. Ownership and property are doubtless quite foreign to the feminine. At least sexually. But not *nearness*. Nearness so pronounced that it makes all discrimination of identity, and thus all forms of property, impossible. Woman derives pleasure from what is *so near that she cannot have it, nor have herself*. She herself enters into a ceaseless exchange of herself with the other without any possibility of identifying either. This puts into question all prevailing economies: their calculations are irremediably stymied by woman's pleasure, as it increases indefinitely from its passage in and through the other.

However, in order for woman to reach the place where she takes pleasure as woman, a long detour by way of the analysis of the various systems of oppression brought to bear upon her is assuredly necessary. And claiming to fall back on the single solution of pleasure risks making her miss the process of going back through a social practice that *her* enjoyment requires.

For woman is traditionally a use-value for man, an exchange value among men; in other words, a commodity. As such, she remains the guardian of material substance, whose price will be established, in terms of the standard of their work and of their need/desire, by "subjects": workers, merchants, consumers. Women are marked phallically by their fathers, husbands, procurers. And this branding determines their value in sexual commerce. Woman is never anything but the locus of a more or less competitive exchange between two men, including the competition for the possession of mother earth.

How can this object of transaction claim a right to pleasure without removing her/itself from established commerce? With respect to other merchandise in the marketplace, how could this commodity maintain a relationship other than one of aggressive jealousy? How could material substance enjoy her/itself without provoking the consumer's anxiety over the disappearance of his nurturing ground? How could that exchange—which can in no way be defined in terms "proper" to woman's desire—appear as anything but a pure mirage, mere foolishness, all too readily obscured by a more sensible discourse and by a system of apparently more tangible values?

A woman's development, however radical it may seek to be, would thus not suffice to liberate woman's desire. And to date no political theory or political practice has resolved, or sufficiently taken into consideration, this historical problem, even though Marxism has proclaimed its importance. But women do not constitute, strictly speaking, a class, and their dispersion among several classes makes their political struggle complex, their demands sometimes contradictory.

There remains, however, the condition of underdevelopment arising from women's submission by and to a culture that oppresses them, uses them, makes of them a medium of exchange, with very little profit to them. Except in the quasi monopolies of masochistic pleasure, the domestic labor force, and reproduction. The powers of slaves? Which are not negligible powers, moreover. For where pleasure is concerned, the master is not necessarily well served. Thus to reverse the relation, especially in the economy of sexuality, does not seem a desirable objective.

But if women are to preserve and expand their autoeroticism, their homo-sexuality, might not the renunciation of heterosexual pleasure correspond once again to that disconnection from power that is traditionally theirs? Would it not involve a new prison, a new cloister, built of their own accord? For women to undertake tactical strikes, to keep themselves apart from men long enough to learn to defend their desire, especially through speech, to discover the love of other women while sheltered from men's imperious choices that put them in the position of rival commodities, to forge for themselves a social status that compels recognition, to earn their living in order to escape from the condition of prostitute . . . these are certainly indispensable stages in the escape from their proletarization on the exchange market. But if their aim were simply to reverse the order of things, even supposing this to be possible, history would repeat itself in the long run, would revert to sameness: to phallocratism. It would leave room neither for women's sexuality, nor for women's imaginary, nor for women's language to take (their) place.

[1977]

 56

The Sexual Sociology of Adult Life from The Reproduction of Mothering: Psychoanalysis and the Sociology of Gender

NANCY CHODOROW

NANCY CHODOROW United States. 1944– . Sociologist. Psychoanalyst. Key feminist critic of Freudian model of female development; advances an alternative based in object relations theory. *Feminism and Psychoanalytic Theory* (1989), *Femininities, Masculinities, Sexualities: Freud and Beyond* (1994), *The Power of Feelings: Personal Meaning in Psychoanalysis, Gender, and Culture* (1999).

Hence, there is a typically asymmetrical relation of the marriage pair to the occupational structure.

This asymmetrical relation apparently both has exceedingly important positive functional significance and is at the same time an important source of strain in relation to the patterning of sex roles.

—Talcott Parsons,
"The Kinship System of the
Contemporary United States"

Girls and boys develop different relational capacities and senses of self as a result of growing up in a family in which women mother. These gender personalities are reinforced by differences in the identification processes of boys and girls that also result from women's mothering. Differing relational capacities and forms of identification prepare women and men to assume the adult gender roles which situate women primarily within the sphere of reproduction in a sexually unequal society.

GENDER IDENTIFICATION AND GENDER ROLE LEARNING

All social scientists who have examined processes of gender role learning and the development of a sense of identification in boys and girls have argued that the asymmetrical organization of parenting in which women mother is the basic cause of significant contrasts between feminine and masculine identification processes.[1] Their discussions range from concern with the learning of appropriate gender role behavior—through imitation, explicit training and admonitions, and cognitive learning processes—to concern with the development of basic gender identity. The processes these people discuss seem to be universal, to the extent that all societies are constituted around a structural split, growing out of women's mothering, between the private, domestic world of women and the public, social world of men.[2] Because the first identification for children of both genders has always been with their mother, they argue, and because children are first around women, women's family roles and being feminine are more available and often more intelligible to growing children than masculine roles and being masculine. Hence, male development is more complicated than female because of the difficult shifts of identification which a boy

must make to attain his expected gender identification and gender role assumption. Their view contrasts sharply to the psychoanalytic stress on the difficulties inherent in feminine development as girls make their convoluted way to heterosexual object choice.[3]

Because all children identify first with their mother, a girl's gender and gender role identification processes are continuous with her earliest identifications and a boy's are not. A girl's oedipal identification with her mother, for instance, is continuous with her earliest primary identification (and also in the context of her early dependence and attachment). The boy's oedipal crisis, however, is supposed to enable him to shift in favor of an identification with his father. He gives up, in addition to his oedipal and preoedipal attachment to his mother, his primary identification with her.

What is true specifically for oedipal identification is equally true for more general gender identification and gender role learning. A boy, in order to feel himself adequately masculine, must distinguish and differentiate himself from others in a way that a girl need not—must categorize himself as someone apart. Moreover, he defines masculinity negatively as that which is not feminine and/or connected to women, rather than positively.[4] This is another way boys come to deny and repress relation and connection in the process of growing up.

These distinctions remain even where much of a girl's and boy's socialization is the same, and where both go to school and can participate in adulthood in the labor force and other nonfamilial institutions. Because girls at the same time grow up in a family where mothers are the salient parent and caretaker, they also can begin to identify more directly and immediately with their mothers and their mothers' familial roles than can boys with their fathers and men. Insofar as a woman's identity remains primarily as a wife/mother, moreover, there is greater generational continuity in role and life-activity from mother to daughter than there can be from father to son. This identity may be less than totally appropriate, as girls must realistically expect to spend much of their life in the labor force, whereas their mothers were less likely to do so. Nevertheless, family organization and ideology still produce these gender differences, and generate expectations that women much more than men will find a primary identity in the family.

Permanent father-absence, and the "father absence" that is normal in our society, do not mean that boys do not learn masculine roles or proper masculine behavior, just as there is no evidence that homosexuality in women correlates with father absence.[5] What matters is the extent to which a child of either gender can form a personal relationship with their object of identification, and the differences in modes of identification that result from this. Mitscherlich, Slater, Winch, and Lynn all speak to these differences.[6] They suggest that girls in contemporary society develop a personal identification with their mother, and that a tie between affective processes and role learning—between libidinal and ego development—characterizes feminine development. By contrast, boys develop a positional identification with aspects of the masculine role. For them, the tie between affective processes and role learning is broken.

Personal identification, according to Slater and Winch, consists in diffuse identification with someone else's general personality, behavioral traits, values, and attitudes. Positional identification consists, by contrast, in identification with specific aspects of another's role and does not necessarily lead to the internalization of the values or attitudes of the person identified with. According to Slater, children preferentially choose personal identification because this grows out of a positive affective relationship to a person who is there. They resort to positional identification residually and reactively, and identify with the perceived role or situation of another when possibilities for personal identification are not available.

In our society, a girl's mother is present in a way that a boy's father, and other adult men, are not. A girl, then, can develop a personal identification with her mother, because she has a real relationship with her that grows out of their early primary tie. She learns what it is to be womanlike in the context of this personal identification with her mother and often with other female models (kin, teachers, mother's friends, mothers of friends). Feminine identification, then, can be based on the gradual learning of a way of being familiar in everyday life, exemplified by the relationship with the person with whom a girl has been most involved.

A boy must attempt to develop a masculine gender identification and learn the masculine role in the absence of a continuous and ongoing personal relationship to his father (and in the absence of a continuously available masculine role model). This positional identification occurs both psychologically and sociologically. Psychologically, as is clear from descriptions of the masculine oedipus complex, boys appropriate those specific components of the masculinity of their father that they fear will be otherwise used against them, but do not as much identify diffusely with him as a person. Sociologically, boys in father-absent and normally father-remote families develop a sense of what it is to be masculine through identification with cultural images of masculinity and men chosen as masculine models.

Boys are taught to be masculine more consciously than girls are taught to be feminine. When fathers or men are not present much, girls are taught the heterosexual components of their role, whereas boys are assumed to learn their heterosexual role without teaching, through interaction with their mothers.[7] By contrast, other components of masculinity must be more consciously imposed. Masculine identification, then, is predominantly a gender role identification. By contrast, feminine identification is predominantly *parental*: "Males tend to identify with a cultural stereotype of the masculine role; whereas females tend to identify with aspects of their own mother's role specifically."[8]

Girls' identification processes, then, are more continuously embedded in and mediated by their ongoing relationship with their mother. They develop through and stress particularistic and affective relationships to others. A boy's identification processes are not likely to be so embedded in or mediated by a real affective relation to his father. At the same time, he tends to deny identification with and relationship to his mother and reject what he takes to be the feminine world; masculinity is defined as much negatively as positively. Masculine identification processes stress differentiation from others, the denial of affective relation, and categorical universalistic components of the masculine role. Feminine identification processes are relational, whereas masculine identification processes tend to deny relationship.

These distinctions do not mean that the development of femininity is all sugar and spice for a girl, but that it poses different *kinds* of problems for her than the development of masculinity does for a boy. The feminine identification that a girl attains and the masculine identification about which a boy remains uncertain are valued differently. In their unattainability, masculinity and the masculine role are fantasized and idealized by boys (and often by girls), whereas femininity and the feminine role remain for a girl all too real and concrete. The demands on women are often contradictory—for instance, to be passive and dependent in relation to men, and active and independently initiating toward children. In the context of the ego and object-relational issues . . . , moreover, it is clear that mother-identification presents difficulties. A girl identifies with and is expected to identify with her mother in order to attain her adult feminine identification and learn her adult gender role. At the same time she must be sufficiently differentiated to grow up and experience herself as a separate individual—must overcome primary identification while maintaining and building a secondary identification.

Studies suggest that daughters in American society have problems with differentiation from and identification with their mothers.[9] Slater reports that all forms of personal parental identification (cross-gender and same-gender) correlate with freedom from psychosis or neurosis except personal identification of a daughter with her mother. Johnson reports that a boy's identification with his father relates to psychological adjustment, whereas a girl's with her mother does not. The implication in both accounts is that for a girl, just as for a boy, there can be too much of mother. It may be easy, but possibly too easy, for a girl to attain a feminine gender identification.

. . .

Even when men and women cross into the other's sphere, their roles remain different. Within the family, being a husband and father is different from being a wife and mother; as women have become more involved in the family, men have become less so. Parson's characterization of men's instrumental role in the family may be too extreme, but points us in the right direction. A father's first responsibility is to "provide" for his family monetarily. His emotional contribution is rarely seen as of equal importance. Men's work in the home, in all but a few households, is defined in gender-stereotyped ways. When men do "women's" chores—the dishes, shopping, putting children to bed—this activity is often organized and delegated by the wife/mother, who retains residual responsibility (men "babysit" their own children; women do not). Fathers, though they relate to their children, do so in order to create "independence."[10] This is facilitated by a father's own previous socialization for repression and denial of relation, and his current participation in the public nonrelational world. Just as children know their fathers "under the sway of the reality principle,"[11] so also do fathers know their children more as separate people than mothers do.

. . .

MOTHERING, MASCULINITY, AND CAPITALISM

. . .

Masculinity is presented to a boy as less available and accessible than femininity, as represented by his mother. A boy's mother is his primary caretaker. At the same time, masculinity is idealized or accorded superiority, and thereby becomes even more desirable. Although fathers are not as salient as mothers in daily interaction, mothers and children often idealize them and give them ideological primacy, precisely because of their absence and seeming inaccessibility, and because of the organization and ideology of male dominance in the larger society.

Masculinity becomes an issue in a way that femininity does not. Masculinity does not become an issue because of some intrinsic male biology, nor because masculine roles are inherently more difficult than feminine roles, however. Masculinity becomes an issue as a direct result of a boy's experience of himself in his family—as a result of his being parented by a woman. For children of both genders, mothers represent regression and lack of autonomy. A boy associates these issues with his gender identification as well. Dependence on his mother, attachment to her, and identification with her represent that which is not masculine; a boy must reject dependence and deny attachment and identification. Masculine gender role training becomes much more rigid than feminine. A boy represses those qualities he takes to be feminine inside himself, and rejects and devalues women and whatever he considers to be feminine in the social world.

Thus, boys define and attempt to construct their sense of masculinity largely in negative terms. Given that masculinity is so elusive, it becomes important for masculine identity that certain social activities are defined as masculine and superior, and that women are believed unable to do many of the things defined as socially important. It becomes important to think that women's economic and social contribution cannot equal men's. The secure possession of certain realms, and the insistence that these realms are superior to the maternal world of youth, become crucial both to the definition of masculinity and to a particular boy's own masculine gender identification.[12]

Freud describes the genesis of this stance in the masculine oedipal crisis. A boy's struggle to free himself from his mother and become masculine generates "the contempt felt by men for a sex which is the lesser"[13]—"What we have come to consider the normal male contempt for women."[14]

Both sexes learn to feel negatively toward their mother during the oedipal period. A girl's negative feelings, however, are not so much contempt and devaluation as fear and hostility: "The little girl, incapable of such contempt because of her own identical nature, frees herself from the mother with a degree of hostility far greater than any comparable hostility in the boy."[15] A boy's contempt serves to free him not only from his mother but also from the femininity within himself. It therefore becomes entangled with the issue of masculinity and is generalized to all women. A girl's hostility remains tied more to her relationship to her mother (and/or becomes involved in self-depreciation).

A boy's oedipus complex is directly tied to issues of masculinity, and the devaluation of women is its "normal" outcome. A girl's devaluation of or hostility toward her mother may be a part of the process, but its "normal" outcome, by contrast, entails acceptance of her own femininity and identification with her mother. Whatever the individual resolution of the feminine Oedipus complex, however, it does not become institutionalized in the same way.

· · ·

Women's mothering produces a psychological and ideological complex in men concerning women's secondary valuation and sexual inequality. Because women are responsible for early child care and for most later socialization as well, because fathers are more absent from the home, and because men's activities generally have been removed from the home while women's have remained within it, boys have difficulty in attaining a stable masculine gender role identification. Boys fantasize about and idealize the masculine role and their fathers, and society defines it as desirable.

Given that men control not only major social institutions but the very definition and constitution of society and culture, they have the power and ideological means to enforce these perceptions as more general norms, and to hold each other accountable for their enforcement. (This is not solely a matter of force. Since these norms define men as superior, men gain something by maintaining them.[16]) The structure of parenting creates ideological and psychological modes which reproduce orientations to and structures of male dominance in individual men, and builds an assertion of male superiority into the definition of masculinity itself.

The same repressions, denials of affect and attachment, rejection of the world of women and things feminine, appropriation of the world of men and identification with the father that create a psychology of masculine superiority also condition men for participation in the capitalist work world. Both capitalist accumulation and proper work habits in workers have never been purely a matter of economics. Particular personality characteristics and behavioral codes facilitated the transition to capitalism. Capitalists developed inner direction, rational planning, and organization, and workers developed a willingness to come to work at certain hours and work steadily, whether or not they needed money that day.

Psychological qualities become perhaps even more important with the expansion of bureaucracy and hierarchy: In modern capitalism different personality traits are required at different levels of the bureaucratic hierarchy.[17] Lower level jobs are often directly and continuously supervised, and are best performed by someone willing to obey rules and conform to external authority. Moving up the hierarchy, jobs require greater dependability and predictability, the ability to act without direct and continuous supervision. In technical, professional, and managerial positions, workers must on their own initiative carry out the goals and values of the organization for which they work, making those goals and values their own. Often they must be able to draw on their interpersonal capacities as a skill. Parental child-rearing values and practices (insofar as these latter reflect parental values) reflect these differences: Working class parents are more likely to value obedience, conformity to external authority, neatness, and other "behavioral" characteristics in their children; middle-class parents emphasize more "internal" and interpersonal characteristics like responsibility, curiosity, self-motivation, self-control, and consideration.[18]

. . .

In American families, Parsons argues, where mothers tend not to have other primary affective figures around, a mutual erotic investment between son[19] and mother develops—an investment the mother can then manipulate. She can love, reward, and frustrate him at appropriate moments in order to get him to delay gratification and sublimate or repress erotic needs. This close, exclusive, pre-oedipal mother-child relationship first develops dependency in a son, creating a motivational basis for early learning and a foundation for dependency on others. When a mother "rejects" her son or pushes him to be more independent, the son carries his still powerful dependence with him, creating in him both a general need to please and conform outside of the relationship to the mother herself and a strong assertion of independence. The isolated, husband-absent mother thus helps to create in her son a pseudo-independence masking real dependence, and a generalized sense that he ought to "do well" rather than an orientation to specific goals. This generalized sense can then be used to serve a variety of specific goals—goals not set by these men themselves. The oedipus complex in the contemporary family creates a "'dialectical' relationship between dependency, on the one hand, independence and achievement on the other."[20]

In an earlier period of capitalist development, individual goals were important for more men, and entrepreneurial achievement as well as worker discipline had to be based more on inner moral direction and repression. Earlier family arrangements, where dependency was not so salient nor the mother-child bond so exclusive, produced this greater inner direction. Today, with the exception of a very few, individual goals have become increasingly superseded by the goals of complex organizations: "Goals can no longer be directly the individual's responsibility and cannot be directly specified to him as a preparation for his role."[21] The contemporary family, with its manipulation of dependency in the mother-child relationship, and its production of generalized achievement orientation rather than inner goals and standards, produces personalities "that have become a fully fluid resource for societal functions."[22]

Slater extends Parsons's discussion. People who start life with only one or two emotional objects, he argues, develop a "willingness to put all [their] emotional eggs in one symbolic basket."[23] Boys who grow up in American middle-class nuclear families have this experience.[24] Because they received such a great amount of gratification from their mother relative to what they got from anyone else, and because their relationship to her was so exclusive, it is unlikely that they can repeat such a relationship. They relinquish their mother as an object of dependent attachment and deny their dependence on her, but, because she was so uniquely important, they retain her as an oedipally motivated object to win in fantasy—they retain an unconscious sense that there is one finally satisfying prize to be won. They turn their lives into a search for a success that will both prove their independence and win their mother. But because they have no inner sense of goals or real autonomy apart from this unconscious, unattainable goal from the past, and because success in the external world does not for the most part bring real satisfactions or real independence, their search is likely to be never-ending. They are likely to continue to work and to continue to accept the standards of the situation that confronts them.

This situation contrasts to that of people who have had a larger number of pleasurable relationships in early infancy. Such people are more likely to expect gratification in immediate relationships and maintain commitments to more people, and are less likely to deny themselves now on behalf of the future. They would not be the same kind of good worker, given that work is defined in individualist, noncooperative, outcome-oriented ways, as it is in our society.

. . .

Contemporary family structure produces not only malleability and lack of internalized standards, but often a search for manipulation. These character traits lend themselves to the manipulations of modern capitalism—to media and product consumerism, to the attempt to legitimate a polity that serves people unequally, and finally to work performance. The decline of the oedipal father creates an orientation to external authority and behavioral obedience. Exclusive maternal involvement and the extension of dependence create a generalized need to please and to "succeed," and a seeming independence. This need to succeed can help to make someone dependable and reliable. Because it is divorced from specific goals and real inner standards but has involved the maintenance of an internal dependent relationship, it can also facilitate the taking of others' goals as one's own, producing the pseudo-independent organization man.

An increasingly father-absent mother-involved family produces in men a personality that both corresponds to masculinity and male dominance as these are currently constituted in the sex-gender system, and fits appropriately with participation in capitalist relations of production. Men continue to enforce the sexual division of spheres as a defense against powerlessness in the labor market. Male denial of dependence and of attachment to women helps to guarantee both masculinity and performance in the world of work. The relative unavailability of the father and overavailability of the mother create negative definitions of masculinity and men's fear and resentment of women, as well as the lack of inner autonomy in men that enables, depending on particular family constellation and class origin, either rule-following or the easy internalization of the values of the organization.

Thus, women's and men's personality traits and orientations mesh with the sexual and familial division of labor and unequal ideology of gender and shape their asymmetric location in a structure of production and reproduction in which women are in the first instance mothers and wives and men are workers. This structure of production and reproduction requires and presupposes those specific relational modes, between husband and wife, and

mother and children, which form the center of the family in contemporary society. An examination of the way that gender personality is expressed in adulthood reveals how women and men create, and are often committed to creating, the interpersonal relationships which underlie and reproduce the family structure that produced them.

[1978]

NOTES

1. For a review of the literature which argues this, see Biller, 1971, *Father, Child.* See also Stoller, 1965, "The Sense of Maleness." For a useful recent formulation, see Johnson, 1975, "Fathers, Mothers."

2. See Mead, 1949, *Male and Female;* Michelle Z. Rosaldo, 1974, "Woman, Culture, and Society"; Nancy Chodorow, 1971, "Being and Doing," and 1974, "Family Structure and Feminine Personality," in Rosaldo and Lamphere, eds., *Woman, Culture and Society,* pp. 43–66; Beatrice Whiting, ed., 1963, *Six Cultures;* Beatrice B. Whiting and John W. M. Whiting, 1975, *Children of Six Cultures;* John Whiting, 1959, "Sorcery, Sin"; Burton and Whiting, 1961, "The Absent Father."

3. The extent of masculine difficulty varies, as does the extent to which identification processes for boys and girls differ. This variance depends on the extent of the public-domestic split in a subculture or society—the extent to which men, men's work, and masculine activities are removed from the home, and therefore masculinity and personal relations with adult men are hard to come by for a child.

4. See Richard T. Roessler, 1971, "Masculine Differentiation and Feminine Constancy," *Adolescence,* 6, #22, pp. 187–196; E. M. Bennett and L. R. Cohen, 1959, "Men and Women, Personality Patterns and Contrasts," *Genetic Psychology Monographs,* 59, pp. 101–155; Johnson, 1963, "Sex Role Learning," and 1975, "Fathers, Mothers"; Stoller, 1964, "A Contribution to the Study," 1965, "The Sense of Maleness," and 1968, "The Sense of Femaleness," *Psychoanalytic Quarterly,* 37, #1, pp. 42–55.

5. See Biller, 1971, *Father, Child.*

6. Mitscherlich, 1963, *Society Without the Father;* Philip E. Slater, 1961, "Toward a Dualistic Theory of Identification," *Merrill-Palmer Quarterly of Behavior and Development,* 7, #2, pp. 113–126; Robert F. Winch, 1962, *Identification and Its Familial Determinants;* David B. Lynn, 1959, "A Note on Sex Differences," and 1962, "Sex Role and Parent."

7. Johnson, 1975, "Fathers, Mothers," and Maccoby and Jacklin, 1974, *The Psychology of Sex Differences,* point this out.

8. D. B. Lynn, 1959, "A Note on Sex Differences," p. 130.

9. See Slater, 1961, "Toward a Dualistic Theory," and Johnson, 1975, "Fathers, Mothers."

10. See, for example, Johnson, 1975, "Fathers, Mothers"; Parsons and Bales, 1955, *Family, Socialization;* Deutsch, 1944, *Psychology of Women.*

11. Alice Balint, 1939, "Love for the Mother."

12. On these issues, see Lynn, 1959, "A Note on Sex Differences," and 1962, "Sex Role and Parent"; Parsons,

1942, "Age and Sex"; Mitscherlich, 1963, *Society Without the Father;* Slater, 1968, *The Glory of Hera;* Mead, 1949, *Male and Female.*

13. Freud, 1925, "Some Psychical Consequences," p. 253.
14. Brunswick, 1940, "The Preoedipal Phase," p. 246.
15. Ibid.
16. But for discussions of ways that this accountability is actively maintained, see Joseph H. Plock and Jack Sawyer, 1974. *Men and Masculinity,* and Marc F. Fasteau, 1974, *The Male Machine.*
17. It is certainly possible that these same characteristics apply in all extensively bureaucratic and hierarchical settings (in the U.S.S.R. and Eastern Europe, for instance); however, the work I am drawing on has investigated only the capitalist West, and especially the United States. My formulation of the personality requirements of the hierarchical firm follows Edwards, 1975, "The Social Relations of Production."
18. See Melvin L. Kohn, 1969, *Class and Conformity.*
19. Parsons and his colleagues talk of the "mother-child" relationship. However, they focus on erotic, oedipal attachment as motivating, and on the development of character traits which are appropriate to masculine work capacity and not to feminine expressive roles. It is safe to conclude, therefore, that the child they have in mind is male.
20. Talcott Parsons with Winston White, 1961, "The Link between Character and Society," in *Social Structure and Personality,* p. 218.
21. Ibid., p. 203.
22. Ibid., p. 233.
23. Slater, 1974. *Earthwalk.* See also Slater, 1970. *The Pursuit of Loneliness.*
24. Again, girls do as well, and both genders transfer it to monogamic, jealous tendencies. But Slater is talking about the sexually toned oedipal/preoedipal relationship that is more specific to boys.

 57

The Metapatriarchal Journey of Exorcism and Ecstasy from Gyn/Ecology: The Metaethics of Radical Feminism

MARY DALY

MARY DALY United States. 1928–   . Theologian and philosopher. Key voice in the development of a feminist critique of Christianity, particularly Catholicism. *The Church and the Second Sex* (1968), *Beyond God the Father* (1975), *Pure Lust* (1984), *Websters' First Intergalactic Wickedary of the English Language* (1987), *Amazon Grace* (2006).

All mother goddesses spin and weave. . . . Everything that is comes out of them: They weave the world tapestry out of genesis and demise, "threads appearing and disappearing rhythmically."

Helen Diner,
Mothers and Amazons

This book is about the journey of women becoming, that is, radical feminism. The voyage is described and roughly charted here. I say "roughly" by way of understatement and pun. We do not know exactly what is on the Other Side until we arrive there—and the journey *is rough.* The charting done here is based on some knowledge from the past, upon present experience, and upon hopes for the future. These three sources are inseparable, intertwined. Radical feminist consciousness spirals in all directions, dis-covering the past, creating/dis-closing the present/future.

The radical be-ing of women is very much an Otherworld Journey. It is both discovery and creation of a world other than patriarchy. Patriarchy appears to be "everywhere." Even outer space and the future have been colonized. As a rule, even the more imaginative science-fiction writers (allegedly the most foretelling futurists) cannot/will not create a space and time in which women get far beyond the role of space stewardess. Nor does this colonization exist simply "outside" women's minds, securely fastened into institutions we can physically leave behind. Rather, it is also internalized, festering inside women's heads, even feminist heads.

The Journey, then, involves exorcism of the internalized Godfather in his various manifestations (his name is legion). It involves dangerous encounters with these demons. Within the christian tradition, particularly in medieval times, evil spirits have sometimes been associated with the "Seven Deadly Sins," both as personifications and as causes.[1] A standard listing of the Sins is the following: pride, avarice, anger, lust, gluttony, envy, and sloth.[2] The feminist voyage discloses that these have all been radically misnamed, that is, inadequately and perversely "understood." They are particularized expressions of the overall use of "evil" to victimize women. Our journey involves confrontations with the demonic manifestations of evil.

Why has it seemed "appropriate" in this culture that the plot of a popular book and film (*The Exorcist*) centers around a Jesuit who "exorcises" a girl who is "possessed"? Why is there no book or film about a woman who exorcises a Jesuit?[3] From a radical feminist perspective it is clear that "Father" is precisely the one who cannot exorcise, for he is allied with and identified with The Possessor. The fact that he is himself possessed should not be women's essential concern. It is a mistake to see men as pitiable victims or vessels to be "saved" through female self-sacrifice. However possessed males may be within patriarchy, it is *their* order; it is they who feed on women's stolen energy. It is a trap to imagine that women should "save" men from the dynamics of demonic possession; and to attempt this is to fall deeper into the pit of patriarchal possession. It is women ourselves who will have to expel the Father from ourselves, becoming our own exorcists.

Within a culture possessed by the myth of feminine evil, the naming, describing, and theorizing about good and evil has constituted a maze/haze of deception. The journey of women becoming is breaking through this maze—springing into free space, which is an a-mazing process.

Breaking through the Male Maze is both exorcism and ecstasy. It is spinning through and beyond the fathers' foreground, which is the arena of games. This spinning involves encountering the demons who block the various thresholds as we move through gateway after gateway into the deepest chambers of our homeland, which is the Background of our Selves. As Denise Connors has pointed out, the Background is the realm of the wild reality of women's Selves. Objectification and alienation take place when we are locked into the male-centered, monodimensional foreground.[4] Thus the monitors of the foreground, the male myth-masters, fashion prominent and eminently forgettable images of women in their art, literature, and mass media—images intended to mold women for male purposes.

The Background into which feminist journeying spins is the wild realm of Hags and Crones. It is Hag-ocracy. The demons who attempt to block the gateways to the deep spaces of this realm often take ghostly/ghastly forms, comparable to noxious gases not noticeable by ordinary sense perception.[5] Each time we move into deeper space, these numbing ghostly gases work to paralyze us, to trap us, so that we will be unable to move further. Each time we succeed in overcoming their numbing effect, more dormant senses come alive. Our inner eyes open, our inner ears become unblocked. We are strengthened to move through the next gateway and the next. This movement inward/outward is be-ing. It is spinning cosmic tapestries. It is spinning and whirling into the Background.

The spinning process requires seeking out the sources of the ghostly gases that have seeped into the deep chambers of our minds. "The way back to reality is to destroy our perceptions of it," said Bergson. Yes, but these deceptive perceptions were/are implanted through language—the all-pervasive language of myth, conveyed overtly and subliminally through religion, "great art," literature, the dogmas of professionalism, the media, grammar. Indeed, deception is embedded in the very texture of the words we use, and here is where our exorcism can begin. Thus, for example, the word *spinster* is commonly used as a deprecating term, but it can only function this way when apprehended exclusively on a superficial (foreground) level. Its deep meaning, which has receded into the Background so far that we have to spin deeply in order to retrieve it, is clear and strong: "a woman whose occupation is to spin." There is no reason to limit the meaning of this rich and cosmic verb. A woman whose occupation is to spin participates in the whirling movement of creation. She who has chosen her Self, who defines her Self, by choice, neither in relation to children nor to men, who is Self-identified, is a Spinster, a whirling dervish, spinning in a new time/space. Another example is the term *glamour,* whose first definition as given in Merriam-Webster is "a magic spell." Originally it was believed that witches possessed the power of glamour, and according to the authors of the *Malleus Maleficarum,* witches by their glamour could cause the male "member" to disappear. In modern usage, this meaning has almost disappeared into the Background, and the power of the term is masked and suffocated by such foreground images as those associated with *Glamour* magazine.

Journeying is multidimensional. The various meanings and images conjured up by the word are not sharply distinguishable. We can think of mystical journeys, quests, adventurous travel, advancement in skills, in physical and intellectual prowess. So also the barriers are multiple and intertwined. These barriers are not mere immobile blocks, but are more like deceptive tongues that prevent us from hearing our Selves, as they babble incessantly in the Tower of Babel which is the erection of phallocracy.[6] The voices and the silences of Babel pierce all of our senses. They are the invasive extensions of the enemy of women's hearing, dreaming, creating. *Babel* is said to be derived from an Assyrian-Babylonian word meaning "gate of god." When women break through this multiple barrier composed of deceptions ejaculated by "god" we can begin to glimpse the true gateways to our depths, which are the Gates of the Goddess.

Spinsters can find our way back to reality by destroying the false perceptions of it inflicted upon us by the language and myths of Babel. We must learn to dis-spell the language of phallocracy, which keeps us under the spell of brokenness. This spell splits our perceptions of our Selves and of the cosmos, overtly and subliminally. Journeying into our Background will mean recognizing that both the "spirit" and the "matter" presented to us in the father's foreground are reifications, condensations. They are not really "opposites," for they have much in common: both are dead, inert. This is unmasked when we begin to see through patriarchal language. Thus, the Latin term *texere*, meaning to weave, is the origin and root both for *textile* and for *text*. It is important for women to note the irony in this split of meanings. For our process of cosmic weaving has been stunted and minimized to the level of the manufacture and maintenance of textiles. While there is nothing demeaning about this occupation in itself, the limitation of women to the realm of "distaff" has mutilated and condensed our Divine Right of creative weaving to the darning of socks. If we look at the term *text* in contrast to *textile*, we see that this represents the other side of the schizoid condensation of weaving/spinning. "Texts" are the kingdom of males; they are the realm of the reified word, of condensed spirit. In patriarchal tradition, sewing and spinning are for girls; books are for boys.

Small wonder that many women feel repugnance for the realm of the distaff, which has literally been the sweatshop and prison of female bodies and spirits. Small wonder that many women have seen the male kingdom of texts as an appealing escape from the tomb-town of textiles which has symbolized the confinement/reduction of female energy.★ The kingdom of male-authored texts has appeared to be the ideal realm to be reached/entered, for we have been educated to forget that professional "knowledge" is our stolen process. As Andrée Collard remarked, in the society of cops and robbers, we learn to forget that the cops are the robbers, that they rob us of everything: our myths, our energy, our divinity, our Selves.[7]

Women's minds have been mutilated and muted to such a state that "Free Spirit" has been branded into them as a brand name for girdles and bras rather than as the name of our verb-ing, be-ing Selves. Such brand names brand women "Morons." Moronized, women believe that male-written texts (biblical, literary, medical, legal, scientific) are "true." Thus manipulated, women become eager for acceptance as docile tokens mouthing male texts, employing technology for male ends, accepting male fabrications as the true texture of reality. Patriarchy has stolen our cosmos and returned it in the form of *Cosmopolitan* magazine and cosmetics. They have made up our cosmos, our Selves. Spinning deeper into the Background is courageous sinning against the Sins of the Fathers. As our senses become more alive we can see/hear/feel how we have been tricked by their texts. We begin unweaving our winding sheets. The process of exorcism, of peeling off the layers of mindbindings and cosmetics, is movement past the patriarchally imposed sense of reality and identity. This demystification process, a-mazing The Lies, *is* ecstasy.

Journeying centerward is Self-centering movement in all directions. It erases implanted psuedodichotomies between the Self and "other" reality, while it unmasks the unreality of both "self" and "world" as these are portrayed, betrayed, in the

---

★ We should not forget that countless women's lives have been consumed in the sweatshops of textile manufacturers and garment makers as well as in the everyday tedium of sewing, mending, laundering, and ironing.

language of the fathers' foreground. Adrienne Rich has written:

> In bringing the light of critical thinking to bear on her subject, in the very act of *becoming more conscious* of her situation in the world, a woman may feel herself coming deeper than ever into touch with her unconscious and with her body.[8]

Moving into the Background/Center is not navel-gazing. It is be-ing in the world. The foreground fathers offer dual decoys labeled "thought" and "action," which distract from the reality both of deep knowing and of external action. There is no authentic separation possible.

The Journey is itself participation in Paradise. This word, which is said to be from the Iranian *pairi* (meaning around) and *daēza* (meaning wall), is commonly used to conjure an image of a walled-in pleasure garden. Patriarchal Paradise, as projected in Western and Eastern religious mythology, is imaged as a place or a state in which the souls of the righteous after death enjoy eternal bliss, that is, heaven. Despite theological attempts to make this seem lively, the image is one of stagnation (in a stag-nation) as suggested in the expression, "the Afterlife." In contrast to this, the Paradise which is cosmic spinning is not containment within walls. Rather, it is movement that is not containable, weaving around and past walls, leaving them in the past. It moves into the Background, which is the moving center of the Self, enabling the Self to act "outwardly" in the cosmos as she comes alive. This metapatriarchal movement is not Afterlife, but Living now, dis-covering Life.

A primary definition of *paradise* is "pleasure park." The walls of the Patriarchal Pleasure Park represent the condition of being perpetually parked, locked into the parking lot of the past. A basic meaning of *park* is a "game preserve." The fathers' foreground is precisely this: an arena where the wildness of nature and of women's Selves is domesticated, preserved. It is the place for the preservation of females who are the "fair game" of the fathers, that they may be served to these predatory Park Owners, and service them at their pleasure. Patriarchal Paradise is the arena of games, the place where the pleas of women are silenced, where the law is: Please the Patrons. Women who break through the imprisoning walls of the Playboys' Playground are entering the process which is our happening/happiness. This is

Paradise beyond the boundaries of "paradise." Since our passage into this process requires making breaks in the walls, it means setting free the fair game, breaking the rules of the games, breaking the names of the games. Breaking through the foreground which is the Playboys' Playground means letting out the bunnies, the bitches, the beavers, the squirrels, the chicks, the pussycats, the cows, the nags, the foxy ladies, the old bats and biddies, so that they can at last begin naming themselves.

I have coined the term *metapatriarchal* to describe the journey, because the prefix *meta* has multiple meanings. It incorporates the idea of "post-patriarchal," for it means occurring later. It puts patriarchy in the past without denying that its walls/ruins and demons are still around. Since *meta* also means "situated behind," it suggests that the direction of the journey is into the Background. Another meaning of this prefix is "change in, transformation of." This, of course, suggests the transforming power of the journey. By this I do not mean that women's movement "reforms" patriarchy, but that it transforms our Selves. Since *meta* means "beyond, transcending," it contains a built-in corrective to reductive notions of mere reformism.

This metapatriarchal process of encountering the unknown involves also a continual conversion of the previously unknown into the familiar.[9] Since the "unknown" is stolen/hidden know-ing, frozen and stored by the Abominable Snowmen of Androcratic Academia, Spinsters must melt these masses of "knowledge" with the fire of Female Fury.

Amazon expeditions into the male-controlled "fields" are necessary in order to leave the fathers' caves and live in the sun. A crucial problem for us has been to learn how to re-possess righteously while avoiding being caught too long in the caves. In universities, and in all of the professions, the omnipresent poisonous gases gradually stifle women's minds and spirits. Those who carry out the necessary expeditions run the risk of shrinking into the mold of the mystified Athena, the twice-born, who forgets and denies her Mother and Sisters, because she has forgotten her original Self. "Re-born" from Zeus, she becomes Daddy's Girl, the mutant who serves the master's purposes. The token woman, who in reality is enchained, possessed, "knows" that she is free. She is a useful tool of the patriarchs, particularly against her sister Artemis, who knows better, respects her Self, bonds with her Sisters, and refuses to sell her freedom, her original birthright, for a mess of respectability.

A-mazing Amazons must be aware of the male methods of mystification. Elsewhere I have discussed four methods which are essential to the games of the fathers.[10] First, there is *erasure* of women. (The massacre of millions of women as witches is erased in patriarchal scholarship.) Second, there is *reversal.* (Adam gives birth to Eve, Zeus to Athena, in patriarchal myth.) Third, there is *false polarization.* (Male-defined "feminism" is set up against male-defined "sexism" in the patriarchal media.) Fourth, there is *divide and conquer.* (Token women are trained to kill off feminists in patriarchal professions.) As we move further on the metapatriarchal journey, we find deeper and deeper layers of these demonic patterns embedded in the culture, implanted in our souls. These constitute mindbindings comparable to the footbindings which mutilated millions of Chinese women for a thousand years. Stripping away layer after layer of these mindbinding societal/mental embeds is the a-mazing essential to the journey.

Spinsters are not only A-mazing Amazons cutting away layers of deceptions. Spinsters are also Survivors. We must survive, not merely in the sense of "living on," but in the sense of living beyond. Surviving (from the Latin *super* plus *vivere*) I take to mean living above, through, around the obstacles thrown in our paths. This is hardly the dead "living on" of possessed tokens. The process of Survivors is meta-living, be-ing.

[1978]

NOTES

1. See Morton W. Bloomfield, *The Seven Deadly Sins: An Introduction to the History of a Religious Concept, with Special Reference to Medieval English Literature* (Michigan State University Press, 1967), especially pp. 7–27.
2. This listing became common in catholic doctrine. The number seven came to be favored for the cardinal sins, although there have been many different lists of the sins. See Bloomfield, *The Seven Deadly Sins.*
3. See Dolores Bargowski, "Moving Media: The Exorcist," *Quest: A Feminist Quarterly,* Vol. 1, No. 1 (summer 1974), pp. 53–57.
4. Conversation, Boston, October 1976.
5. See Mary Daly, "The Qualitative Leap beyond Patriarchal Religion," *Quest: A Feminist Quarterly,* Vol. 1, No. 4 (spring 1975), pp. 20–40.
6. Françoise d'Eaubonne uses the term *phallocratisme* in her book, *Le Féminisme ou la mort* (Paris: Pierre Horay, 1974), especially pp. 113–24.
7. Conversation, Boston, September 1976.
8. Adrienne Rich, *Of Woman Born: Motherhood as Experience and Institution* (New York: W. W. Norton, 1976), p. 95.
9. See Daly, "The Qualitative Leap."
10. See Mary Daly, *Beyond God the Father: Toward a Philosophy of Women's Liberation,* (Boston: Beacon Press, 1973), *passim.*

 58

Some Reflections on Separatism and Power

MARILYN FRYE

MARILYN FRYE United States 1941– . Philosopher. Theorist. Important voice in lesbian feminist theory. *Willful Virgin: Essays in Feminism, 1976–1992* (1992), "The Necessity of Differences: Constructing a Positive Category of Women" (1996).

I have been trying to write something about separatism almost since my first dawning of feminist consciousness, but it has always been for me somehow a mercurial topic which, when I tried to grasp it, would softly shatter into many other topics like sexuality, man-hating, so-called reverse discrimination, apocalyptic utopianism, and so on. What I have to share with you today is my latest attempt to get to the heart of the matter.

In my life, and within feminism as I understand it, separatism is not a theory or a doctrine, nor a demand for certain specific behaviors on the part of feminists, though it is undeniably connected with lesbianism. Feminism seems to me to be kaleidoscopic—something whose shapes, structures and patterns alter with every turn of feminist creativity; and one element which is present through all the changes is an element of separation. This element has different roles and relations in different turns of the glass—it assumes different meanings, is variously conspicuous, variously determined or determining, depending on how the pieces fall and who is the beholder. The theme of separation, in its multitude variations, is there in everything from divorce to exclusive lesbian separatist communities, from shelters for battered women to witch covens, from women's studies programs to women's bars, from expansion of daycare to abortion on demand. The presence of this theme is vigorously obscured, trivialized, mystified and outright denied by many feminist apologists, who seem to find it embarrassing, while it is embraced, explored, expanded and ramified by most of the more inspiring theorists and activists. The theme of separation is noticeably absent or heavily qualified in most of the things I take to be personal solutions and Band-Aid projects, like legalization of prostitution, liberal marriage contracts, improvement of the treatment of rape victims and affirmative action. It is clear to me, in my own case at least, that the contrariety of assimilation and separation is one of the main things that guides or determines assessments of various theories, actions and practices as reformist or radical, as going to the root of the thing or being relatively superficial. So my topical question comes to this: What is it about separation, in any or all of its many forms and degrees, that makes it so basic and so sinister, so exciting and so repellent?

Feminist separation is, of course, separation of various sorts or modes from men and from institutions, relationships, roles and activities which are male-defined, male-dominated and operating for the benefit of males and the maintenance of male privilege—this separation being initiated or maintained, at will, *by women*. (Masculist separatism is the partial segregation of women from men and male domains *at the will of men*. This difference is crucial.) The feminist separation can take many forms. Breaking up or avoiding close relationships or working relationships; forbidding someone to enter your house; excluding someone from your company, or from your meeting; withdrawal from participation in some activity or institution, or avoidance of participation; avoidance of communications and influence from certain quarters (not listening to music with sexist lyrics, not watching tv); withholding commitment or support; rejection of or rudeness toward obnoxious individuals. Some separations are subtle realignments of identification, priorities and commitments, or working with agendas which only incidently coincide with the agendas of the institution one works in. Ceasing to be loyal to

something or someone is a separation; and ceasing to love. The feminist's separations are rarely if ever sought or maintained directly as ultimate personal or political ends. The closest we come to that, I think, is the separation which is the instinctive and self-preserving recoil from the systematic misogyny that surrounds us. Generally, the separations are brought about and maintained for the sake of something else like independence, liberty, growth, invention, sisterhood, safety, health, or the practice of novel or heretical customs. Often the separations in question evolve, unpremeditated, as one goes one's way and finds various persons, institutions or relationships useless, obstructive or noisome and leaves them aside or behind. Sometimes the separations are consciously planned and cultivated as necessary prerequisites or conditions for getting on with one's business. Sometimes the separations are accomplished or maintained easily, or with a sense of relief, or even joy; sometimes they are accomplished or maintained with difficulty, by dint of constant vigilance, or with anxiety, pain or grief.

Most feminists, probably all, practice some separation from males and male-dominated institutions. A separatist practices separation consciously, systematically, and probably more generally than the others, and advocates thorough and "broadspectrum" separation as part of the conscious strategy of liberation. And, contrary to the image of the separatist as a cowardly escapist, hers is the life and program which inspires the greatest hostility, disparagement, insult and confrontation and generally she is the one against whom economic sanctions operate most conclusively. The penalty for refusing to work with or for men is usually starvation (or, at the very least, doing without medical insurance); and if one's policy of noncooperation is more subtle, one's livelihood is still constantly on the line, since one is not a loyal partisan, a proper member of the team, or what have you. The penalties for being a lesbian are ostracism, harassment and job insecurity or joblessness. The penalty for rejecting men's sexual advances is often rape and, perhaps even more often, forfeit of such things as professional or job opportunities. And the separatist lives with the added burden of being assumed by many to be a morally depraved man-hating bigot. But there is a clue here: if you are doing something that is so strictly forbidden by the patriarchs, you must be doing something right.

There is an idea floating around in both feminist and antifeminist literature to the effect that females and males generally live in a relation of parasitism, a parasitism of the male on the female . . . that it is, generally speaking, the strength, energy, inspiration and nurturance of women that keeps men going, and not the strength, aggression, spirituality and hunting of men that keeps women going.

It is sometimes said that the parasitism goes the other way around, that the female is the parasite. But one can conjure the appearance of the female as parasite only if one takes a very narrow view of human living—historically parochial, narrow with respect to class and race, and limited in conception of what are the necessary goods. Generally, the female's contribution to her material support is and always has been substantial; in many times and places it has been independently sufficient. One can and should distinguish between a partial and contingent material dependence created by a certain sort of money economy and class structure, and the nearly ubiquitous spiritual, emotional and material dependence of males on females. Males presently provide, off and on, a portion of the material support of women, within circumstances apparently designed to make it difficult for women to provide it for themselves. But females provide and generally have provided for males the energy and spirit for living; the males are nurtured by the females. And this the males apparently cannot do for themselves, even partially.

The parasitism of males on females is, as I see it, demonstrated by the panic, rage and hysteria generated in so many of them by the thought of being abandoned by women. But it is demonstrated in a way that is perhaps more generally persuasive by both literary and sociological evidence. Evidence cited in Jesse Bernard's work in *The Future of Marriage* and in George Gilder's *Sexual Suicide* and *Men Alone* convincingly shows that males tend in shockingly significant numbers and in alarming degree to fall into mental illness, petty crime, alcoholism, physical infirmity, chronic unemployment, drug addiction and neurosis when deprived of the care and companionship of a female mate, or keeper. (While on the other hand, women without male mates are significantly healthier and happier than women with male mates.) And masculist literature is abundant with indications of male cannibalism, of males deriving essential sustenance from females. Cannibalistic imagery, visual and verbal, is common in pornography: images likening women to food, and sex to eating. And, as documented in Millett's *Sexual Politics* and many other feminist analyses of masculist literature, the theme of men getting high off beating, raping or killing women (or merely bullying them) is common. These interactions with women, or rather, these actions upon women, make men feel good, walk tall, feel refreshed, in*vigor*ated. Men are drained and depleted by their living by themselves and with and among other men, and are revived and refreshed, re-created, by going home and being served dinner, changing to clean clothes, having sex with the wife; or by dropping by the apartment of a woman friend to be served coffee or a drink and stroked in one way or another; or by picking up a prostitute for a quicky or for a dip in favorite sexual escape fantasies; or by raping refugees from their wars (foreign and domestic). The ministrations of women, be they willing or unwilling, free or paid for, are what restore in men the strength, will and confidence to go on with what they call living.

If it is true that a fundamental aspect of the relations between the sexes is male parasitism, it might help to explain why certain issues are particularly exciting to patriarchal loyalists. For instance, in view of the obvious advantages of easy abortion to population control, to control of welfare rolls, and to ensuring sexual availability of women to men, it is a little surprising that the loyalists are so adamant and riled up in their objection to it. But look . . .

The fetus lives parasitically. It is a distinct animal surviving off the life (the blood) of another animal creature. It is incapable of surviving on its own resources, of independent nutrition; incapable even of symbiosis. If it is true that males live parasitically upon females, it seems reasonable to suppose that many of them and those loyal to them are in some way sensitive to the parallelism between their situation and that of the fetus. They could easily identify with the fetus. The woman who is free to see the fetus as a parasite might be free to see the man as a parasite. The woman's willingness to cut off the life line to one parasite suggests a willingness to cut off the life line to another parasite. The woman who is capable (legally, psychologically, physically) of decisively, self-interestedly, independently rejecting the one parasite is capable of rejecting, with the same decisiveness and independence, the like burden of the other parasite. In the eyes of the other parasite, the image of the wholly self-determined abortion, involving not even a ritual submission to male veto power, is the mirror image of death.

Another clue here is that one line of argument against free and easy abortion is the slippery slope argument that if fetuses are to be freely dispensed with, old people will be next. Old people? Why are old people next? And why the great concern for them? Most old people are women, indeed, and patriarchal loyalists are not generally so solicitous of the welfare of any women. Why old people? Because, I think, in the modern patriarchal divisions of labor, old people too are parasites on women. The anti-abortion folks seem not to worry about wife beating and wife murder—there is no broad or emotional popular support for stopping these violences. They do not worry about murder and involuntary sterilization in prisons, nor murder in war, nor murder by pollution and industrial accidents. Either these are not real to them or they cannot identify with the victims; but anyway, killing in general is not what they oppose. They worry about the rejection *by women, at women's discretion*, of something which lives parasitically on women. I suspect that they fret not because old people are next, but because men are next.

There are other reasons, of course, why patriarchal loyalists should be disturbed about abortion on demand; a major one being that it would be a significant form of female control of reproduction, and at least from certain angles it looks like the progress of patriarchy *is* the progress toward male control of reproduction, starting with possession of wives and continuing through the invention of obstetrics and the technology of extrauterine gestation. Giving up that control would be giving up patriarchy. But such an objection to abortion is too abstract, and requires too historical a vision, to generate the hysteria there is now in the reaction against abortion. The hysteria is, I think, to be accounted for more in terms of a much more immediate and personal presentiment of ejection by the woman-womb.

I discuss abortion here because it seems to me to be the most publicly emotional and most physically dramatic ground on which the theme of separation and male parasitism is presently being played out. But there are other locales for this play. For instance, women with newly raised consciousnesses tend to leave marriages and families, either completely through divorce, or partially, through unavailability of their cooking, housekeeping and sexual services. And women academics tend to become alienated from their colleagues and male mentors and no longer serve as sounding board, ego booster, editor, mistress or proofreader. Many awakening women become celibate or lesbian, and the others become a very great deal more choosy about when, where and in what relationships they will have sex with men. And the men affected by these separations generally react with defensive hostility, anxiety and guilt-tripping, not to mention descents into illogical argument which match and exceed their own most fanciful images of female irrationality. My claim is that they are very afraid because they depend very heavily upon the goods they receive from women, and these separations cut them off from those goods.

Male parasitism means that males *must have access* to women; it is the Patriarchal Imperative. But feminist no-saying is more than a substantial removal (redirection, reallocation) of goods and services because Access is one of the faces of Power. Female denial of male access to females substantially cuts off a flow of benefits, but it has also the form and full portent of assumption of power.

Differences of power are always manifested in asymmetrical access. The President of the United States has access to almost everybody for almost anything he might want of them, and almost nobody has access to him. The super-rich have access to almost everybody; almost nobody has access to them. The resources of the employee are available to the boss as the resources of the boss are not to the employee. The parent has unconditional access to the child's room; the child does not have similar access to the parent's room. Students adjust to professor's office hours;

professors do not adjust to student's conference hours. The child is required not to lie; the parent is free to close out the child with lies at her discretion. The slave is unconditionally accessible to the master. Total power is unconditional access; total powerlessness is being unconditionally accessible. The creation and manipulation of power is constituted of the manipulation and control of access.

All-woman groups, meetings, projects seem to be great things for causing controversy and confrontation. Many women are offended by them; many are afraid to be the one to announce the exclusion of men; it is seen as a device whose use needs much elaborate justification. I think this is because conscious and deliberate exclusion of men by women, from anything, is blatant insubordination, and generates in women fear of punishment and reprisal (fear which is often well-justified). Our own timidity and desire to avoid confrontations generally keep us from doing very much in the way of all-woman groups and meetings. But when we do, we invariably run into the male champion who challenges our right to do it. Only a small minority of men go crazy when an event is advertised to be for women only—just one man tried to crash our women-only Rape Speak-Out, and only a few hid under the auditorium seats to try to spy on a women-only meeting at a NOW convention in Philadelphia. But these few are onto something their less rabid com-patriots are missing. The woman-only meeting is a fundamental challenge to the structure of power. It is always the privilege of the master to enter the slave's hut. The slave who decides to exclude the master from her hut is declaring herself not a slave. The exclusion of men from the meeting not only deprives them of certain benefits (which they might survive without); it is a controlling of access, hence an assumption of power. It is not only mean, it is arrogant.

It becomes clearer now why there is always an off-putting aura of negativity about separatism—one which offends the feminine pollyanna in us and smacks of the purely defensive to the political theorist in us. It is this: First: When those who control access have made you totally accessible, your first act of taking control must be denying access, or must have denial of access as one of its aspects. This is not because you are charged up with (unfeminine

or politically incorrect) negativity; it is because of the logic of the situation. When we start from a position of total accessibility there *must* be an aspect of no-saying (which is the beginning of control) in *every effective* act and strategy, the effective ones being precisely those which *shift power*, i.e., ones which involve manipulation and control of access. Second: Whether or not one says "no," or withholds or closes out or rejects, on this occasion or that, the capacity and ability to say "no" (with effect) is logically necessary to control. When we are in control of access to ourselves there will be some no-saying, and when we are more accustomed to it, when it is more common, an ordinary part of living, it will not seem so prominent, obvious, or strained . . . we will not strike ourselves or others as being particularly negative. In this aspect of ourselves and our lives, we will strike ourselves pleasingly as active beings with momentum of our own, with sufficient shape and structure—with sufficient integrity—to generate friction. Our experience of our no-saying will be an aspect of our experience of our definition.

When our feminist acts or practices have an aspect of separation, we are assuming power by controlling access and simultaneously by undertaking definition. The slave who excludes the master from her hut thereby declares herself *not a slave*. And *definition* is another face of power.

The powerful normally determine what is said and sayable. When the powerful label something or dub it or baptize it, the thing becomes what they call it. When the Secretary of Defense calls something a peace negotiation, for instance, then whatever it is that he called a peace negotiation is an instance of negotiating peace. If the activity in question is the working out of terms of a trade-off of nuclear reactors and territorial redistributions, complete with arrangements for the resulting refugees, that is peacemaking. People laud it, and the negotiators get Noble Piece Prizes for it. On the other hand, when I call a certain speech act a rape, my "calling" it does not make it so. At best, I have to explain and justify and make it clear exactly what it is about this speech act which is assaultive in just what way, and then the others acquiesce in saying the act was *like* rape or could figuratively be called a rape. My counterassault will not be counted a simple case of self-defense.

And what I called rejection of parasitism, they call the loss of the womanly virtues of compassion and "caring." And generally, when renegade women call something one thing and patriarchal loyalists call it another, the loyalists get their way.

Women generally are not the people who do the defining, and we cannot from our isolation and powerlessness simply commence saying different things than others say and make it stick. There is a humpty-dumpty problem in that. But we are able to arrogate definition to ourselves when we repattern access. Assuming control of access, we draw new boundaries and create new roles and relationships. This, though it causes some strain, puzzlement and hostility, is to a fair extent within the scope of individuals and small gangs, as outright verbal redefinition is not, at least in the first instance.

One may see access as coming in two sorts, "natural" and humanly arranged. A grizzly bear has what you might call natural access to the picnic basket of the unarmed human. The access of the boss to the personal services of the secretary is humanly arranged access; the boss exercises institutional power. It looks to me, looking from a certain angle, like institutions *are* humanly designed patterns of access—access to persons and their services. But institutions are artifacts of definition. In the case of intentionally and formally designed institutions, this is very clear, for the relevant definitions are explicitly set forth in by-laws and constitutions, regulations and rules. When one defines the term "president," one defines presidents in terms of what they can do and what is owed them by other offices, and "what they can do" is a matter of their access to the services of others. Similarly, definitions of *dean, student, judge,* and *cop* set forth patterns of access, and definitions of *writer, child, owner,* and of course, *husband, wife,* and *man* and *girl.* When one changes the pattern of access, one forces new uses of words on those affected. The term 'man' has to shift in meaning when rape is no longer possible. When we take control of sexual access to us, of access to our nurturance and to our reproductive function, access to mothering and sistering, we redefine the word 'woman.' The shift of usage is pressed on others by a change in social reality; it does not await their recognition of our definitional authority.

When women separate (withdraw, break out, regroup, transcend, shove aside, step outside, migrate, say *no*), we are simultaneously controlling access and defining. We are doubly insubordinate, since neither of these is permitted. And access and definition are fundamental ingredients in the alchemy of power, so we are doubly, and radically insubordinate.

If these, then, are some of the ways in which separation is at the heart of our struggle, it helps to explain why separation is such a hot topic. If there is one thing women are queasy about it is *actually taking power.* As long as one stops just short of that, the patriarchs will for the most part take an indulgent attitude. We are afraid of what will happen to us when we really frighten them. This is not an irrational fear. It is our experience in the movement generally that the defensiveness, nastiness, violence, hostility and irrationality of the reaction to feminism tend to correlate with the blatancy of the element of separation in the strategy or project which triggers the reaction. The separations involved in women leaving homes, marriages and boyfriends, separations from fetuses, and the separation of lesbianism are all pretty dramatic. That is, they are dramatic and blatant when perceived from within the framework provided by the patriarchal world view and male parasitism. Matters pertaining to marriage and divorce, lesbianism and abortion touch individual men (and their sympathizers) because they can feel the relevance of these to themselves—they can feel the threat that they might be the next. Hence, heterosexuality, marriage and motherhood, which are the institutions which most obviously and individually maintain female accessibility to males, form the core triad of antifeminist ideology; and all-woman spaces, all-woman organizations, all-woman meetings, all-woman classes, are outlawed, suppressed, harassed, ridiculed and punished—in the name of that other fine and enduring patriarchal institution, Sex Equality.

To some of us these issues can seem almost foreign . . . strange ones to be occupying center stage. We are busily engaged in what seem to *us* our blatant insubordinations: living our own lives, taking care of ourselves and one another, doing our work, and in particular, telling it as we see it. Still, the original sin is the separation which these presuppose, and it is that, not our art or philosophy, not our speechmaking, nor our "sexual acts" (or abstinences), for which we will be persecuted, when worse comes to worst.

[1978]

◆ 59

Age, Race, Class, and Sex: Women Redefining Difference

AUDRE LORDE

AUDRE LORDE United States. 1934–1992. Poet. Activist. Self-described "Black Lesbian Feminist Warrior Poet." Founder of Kitchen Table: Women of Color Press. *The Black Unicorn* (1978), *Zami: A New Spelling of My Name* (1982), *Cancer Journals* (1980), *A Burst of Light* (1988).

Much of Western European history conditions us to see human differences in simplistic opposition to each other: dominant/subordinate, good/bad, up/down, superior/inferior. In a society where the good is defined in terms of profit rather than in terms of human need, there must always be some group of people who, through systematized oppression, can be made to feel surplus, to occupy the place of the dehumanized inferior. Within this society, that group is made up of Black and Third World people, working-class people, older people, and women.

As a forty-nine-year-old Black lesbian feminist socialist mother of two, including one boy, and a member of an interracial couple, I usually find myself a part of some group defined as other, deviant, inferior, or just plain wrong. Traditionally, in american society, it is the members of oppressed, objectified groups who are expected to stretch out and bridge the gap between the actualities of our lives and the consciousness of our oppressor. For in order to survive, those of us for whom oppression is as american as apple pie have always had to be watchers, to become familiar with the language and manners of the oppressor, even sometimes adopting

them for some illusion of protection. Whenever the need for some pretense of communication arises, those who profit from our oppression call upon us to share our knowledge with them. In other words, it is the responsibility of the oppressed to teach the oppressors their mistakes. I am responsible for educating teachers who dismiss my children's culture in school. Black and Third World people are expected to educate white people as to our humanity. Women are expected to educate men. Lesbians and gay men are expected to educate the heterosexual world. The oppressors maintain their position and evade responsibility for their own actions. There is a constant drain of energy which might be better used in redefining ourselves and devising realistic scenarios for altering the present and constructing the future.

Institutionalized rejection of difference is an absolute necessity in a profit economy which needs outsiders as surplus people. As members of such an economy, we have *all* been programmed to respond to the human differences between us with fear and loathing and to handle that difference in one of three ways: ignore it, and if that is not possible, copy it if we think it is dominant, or destroy it if we think it is subordinate. But we have no patterns for relating across our human differences as equals. As a result, those differences have been misnamed and misused in the service of separation and confusion.

Certainly there are very real differences between us of race, age, and sex. But it is not those differences between us that are separating us. It is rather our refusal to recognize those differences, and to examine the distortions which result from our misnaming them and their effects upon human behavior and expectation.

Racism, the belief in the inherent superiority of one race over all others and thereby the right to dominance. Sexism, the belief in the inherent superiority of one sex over the other and thereby the right to dominance. Ageism. Heterosexism. Elitism. Classism.

It is a lifetime pursuit for each one of us to extract these distortions from our living at the same time as we recognize, reclaim, and define those differences upon which they are imposed. For we have all been raised in a society where those distortions were endemic within our living. Too often, we pour the energy needed for recognizing and exploring difference into pretending those differences are insurmountable barriers, or that they do not exist at all. This results in a voluntary isolation, or false and treacherous connections. Either way, we do not develop tools for using human difference as a springboard for creative change within our lives. We speak not of human difference, but of human deviance.

Somewhere, on the edge of consciousness, there is what I call a *mythical norm,* which each one of us within our hearts knows "that is not me." In america, this norm is usually defined as white, thin, male, young, heterosexual, christian, and financially secure. It is with this mythical norm that the trappings of power reside within this society. Those of us who stand outside that power often identify one way in which we are different, and we assume that to be the primary cause of all oppression, forgetting other distortions around difference, some of which we ourselves may be practising. By and large within the women's movement today, white women focus upon their oppression as women and ignore differences of race, sexual preference, class, and age. There is a pretense to a homogeneity of experience covered by the word *sisterhood* that does not in fact exist.

Unacknowledged class differences rob women of each others' energy and creative insight. Recently a women's magazine collective made the decision for one issue to print only prose, saying poetry was a less "rigorous" or "serious" art form. Yet even the form our creativity takes is often a class issue. Of all the art forms, poetry is the most economical. It is the one which is the most secret, which requires the least physical labor, the least material, and the one which can be done between shifts, in the hospital pantry, on the subway, and on scraps of surplus paper. Over the last few years, writing a novel on tight finances, I came to appreciate the enormous differences in the material demands between poetry and prose. As we reclaim our literature, poetry has been the major voice of poor, working-class, and Colored women. A room of one's own may be a necessity for writing prose, but so are reams of paper, a typewriter, and plenty of time. The actual requirements to produce the visual arts also help determine, along class lines, whose art is whose. In this day of inflated prices for material, who are our sculptors, our painters, our photographers? When we speak of a broadly based women's culture, we need to be aware of the effect of class and economic differences on the supplies available for producing art.

As we move toward creating a society within which we can each flourish, ageism is another distortion of relationship which interferes with our vision. By ignoring the past, we are encouraged to repeat its mistakes. The "generation gap" is an important social tool for any repressive society. If the younger members of a community view the older members as contemptible or suspect or excess, they will never be able to join hands and examine the living memories of the community, nor ask the all important question, "Why?" This gives rise to a historical amnesia that keeps us working to invent the wheel every time we have to go to the store for bread.

We find ourselves having to repeat and relearn the same old lessons over and over that our mothers did because we do not pass on what we have learned, or because we are unable to listen. For instance, how many times has this all been said before? For another, who would have believed that once again, our daughters are allowing their bodies to be hampered and purgatoried by girdles and high heels and hobble skirts?

Ignoring the differences of race between women and the implications of those differences presents the most serious threat to the mobilization of women's joint power.

As white women ignore their built-in privilege of whiteness and define *woman* in terms of their own experience alone, then women of Color become "other," the outsider whose experience and tradition are too "alien" to comprehend. An example of this is the signal absence of the experience of women of Color as a resource for women's studies courses. The literature of women of Color is seldom included in women's literature courses and almost never in other literature courses nor in women's studies as a whole. All too often, the excuse given is that the literatures of women of Color can only be taught by Colored women, or that they are too difficult to understand, or that classes cannot "get into" them because they come out of experiences that are "too different." I have heard this argument presented by white women of otherwise quite clear intelligence, women who seem to have no trouble at all teaching and reviewing work that comes out of the vastly different experiences of Shakespeare, Molière, Dostoyevski, and Aristophanes. Surely there must be some other explanation.

This is a very complex question, but I believe one of the reasons white women have such difficulty reading Black women's work is because of their reluctance to see Black women as women and different from themselves. To examine Black women's literature effectively requires that we be seen as whole people in our actual complexities—as individuals, as women, as human—rather than as one of those problematic but familiar stereotypes provided in this society in place of genuine images of Black women. And I believe this holds true for the literatures of other women of Color who are not Black.

The literatures of all women of Color recreate the textures of our lives, and many white women are heavily invested in ignoring the real differences. For as long as any difference between us means one of us must be inferior, then the recognition of any difference must be fraught with guilt. To allow women of Color to step out of stereotypes is too guilt provoking, for its threatens the complacency of those women who view oppression only in terms of sex.

Refusing to recognize difference makes it impossible to see the different problems and pitfalls facing us as women.

Thus, in a patriarchal power system where white-skin privilege is a major prop, the entrapments used to neutralize Black women and white women are not the same. For example, it is easy for Black women to be used by the power structure against Black men, not because they are men, but because they are Black. Therefore, for Black women, it is necessary at all times to separate the needs of the oppressor from our own legitimate conflicts within our communities. This same problem does not exist for white women. Black women and men have shared racist oppression and still share it, although in different ways. Out of that shared oppression we have developed joint defenses and joint vulnerabilities to each other that are not duplicated in the white community, with the exception of the relationship between Jewish women and Jewish men.

On the other hand, white women face the pitfall of being seduced into joining the oppressor under the pretense of sharing power. This possibility does not exist in the same way for women of Color. The tokenism that is sometimes extended to us is not an invitation to join power; our racial "otherness" is a visible reality that makes that quite clear. For white women there is a wider range of pretended choices and rewards for identifying with patriarchal power and its tools.

Today, with the defeat of ERA, the tightening economy, and increased conservatism, it is easier once again for white women to believe the dangerous fantasy that if you are good enough, pretty enough, sweet enough, quiet enough, teach the children to behave, hate the right people, and marry the right men, then you will be allowed to co-exist with patriarchy in relative peace, at least until a man needs your job or the neighborhood rapist happens along. And true, unless one lives and loves in the trenches it is difficult to remember that the war against dehumanization is ceaseless.

But Black women and our children know the fabric of our lives is stitched with violence and with hatred, that there is no rest. We do not deal with it only on the picket lines, or in dark midnight alleys, or in the places where we dare to verbalize our resistance. For us, increasingly, violence weaves through the daily tissues of our living—in the supermarket, in the classroom, in the elevator, in the clinic and the schoolyard, from the plumber, the baker, the saleswoman, the bus driver, the bank teller, the waitress who does not serve us.

Some problems we share as women, some we do not. You fear your children will grow up to join the patriarchy and testify against you, we fear our children will be dragged from a car and shot down in the street, and you will turn your backs upon the reasons they are dying.

The threat of difference has been no less blinding to people of Color. Those of us who are Black must see that the reality of our lives and our struggle does not make us immune to the errors of ignoring and misnaming difference. Within Black communities where racism is a living reality, differences among us often seem dangerous and suspect. The need for unity is often misnamed as a need for homogeneity, and a Black feminist vision mistaken for betrayal of our common interests as a people. Because of a continuous battle against racial erasure that Black women and Black men share, some

Black women still refuse to recognize that we are also oppressed as women, and that sexual hostility against Black women is practiced not only by the white racist society, but implemented within our Black communities as well. It is a disease striking the heart of Black nationhood, and silence will not make it disappear. Exacerbated by racism and the pressures of powerlessness, violence against Black women and children often becomes a standard within our communities, one by which manliness can be measured. But these woman-hating acts are rarely discussed as crimes against Black women.

As a group, women of Color are the lowest paid wage earners in america. We are the primary targets of abortion and sterilization abuse, here and abroad. In certain parts of Africa, small girls are still being sewed shut between their legs to keep them docile and for men's pleasure. This is known as female circumcision, and it is not a cultural affair as the late Jomo Kenyatta insisted, it is a crime against Black women.

Black women's literature is full of the pain of frequent assault, not only by a racist patriarchy, but also by Black men. Yet the necessity for and history of shared battle have made us, Black women, particularly vulnerable to the false accusation that anti-sexist is anti-Black. Meanwhile, womanhating as a recourse of the powerless is sapping the strength from Black communities, and our very lives. Rape is on the increase, reported and unreported, and rape is not aggressive sexuality, it is sexualized aggression. As Kalamu ya Salaam, a Black male writer, points out, "As long as male domination exists, rape will exist. Only women revolting and men made conscious of their responsibility to fight sexism can collectively stop rape."[1]

Differences between ourselves as Black women are also being misnamed and used to separate us from one another. As a Black lesbian feminist comfortable with the many different ingredients of my identity, and a woman committed to racial and sexual freedom from oppression, I find I am constantly being encouraged to pluck out some one aspect of myself and present this as the meaningful whole, eclipsing or denying the other parts of self. But this is a destructive and fragmenting way to live. My fullest concentration of energy is available to me only when I integrate all the parts of who I am, openly, allowing power from particular sources of my living to flow back and forth freely through all my different selves, without the restrictions of externally imposed definition. Only then can I bring myself and my energies as a whole to the service of those struggles which I embrace as part of my living.

A fear of lesbians, or of being accused of being a lesbian, has led many Black women into testifying against themselves. It has led some of us into destructive alliances, and others into despair and isolation. In the white women's communities, heterosexism is sometimes a result of identifying with the white patriarchy, a rejection of that interdependence between women-identified women which allows the self to be, rather than to be used in the service of men. Sometimes it reflects a die-hard belief in the protective coloration of heterosexual relationships, sometimes a self-hate which all women have to fight against, taught us from birth.

Although elements of these attitudes exist for all women, there are particular resonances of heterosexism and homophobia among Black women. Despite the fact that woman-bonding has a long and honorable history in the African and African-american communities, and despite the knowledge and accomplishments of many strong and creative women-identified Black women in the political, social and cultural fields, heterosexual Black women often tend to ignore or discount the existence and work of Black lesbians. Part of this attitude has come from an understandable terror of Black male attack within the close confines of Black society, where the punishment for any female self-assertion is still to be accused of being a lesbian and therefore unworthy of the attention or support of the scarce Black male. But part of this need to misname and ignore Black lesbians comes from a very real fear that openly women-identified Black women who are no longer dependent upon men for their self-definition may well reorder our whole concept of social relationships.

Black women who once insisted that lesbianism was a white woman's problem now insist that Black lesbians are a threat to Black nationhood, are consorting with the enemy, are basically un-Black. These accusations, coming from the very women to whom we look for deep and real understanding, have served to keep many Black lesbians in hiding, caught between the racism of white women and the homophobia of their sisters. Often, their work has been ignored, trivialized, or misnamed, as with the work of Angelina Grimké, Alice Dunbar-Nelson, Lorraine Hansberry. Yet women-bonded women have always been some part of the power of Black communities, from our unmarried aunts to the amazons of Dahomey.

And it is certainly not Black lesbians who are assaulting women and raping children and grand-mothers on the streets of our communities.

Across this country, as in Boston during the spring of 1979 following the unsolved mur-ders of twelve Black women, Black lesbians are spearheading movements against violence against Black women.

What are the particular details within each of our lives that can be scrutinized and altered to help bring about change? How do we redefine differ-ence for all women? It is not our differences which separate women, but our reluctance to recognize those differences and to deal effectively with the distortions which have resulted from the ignoring and misnaming of those differences.

As a tool of social control, women have been encouraged to recognize only one area of human difference as legitimate, those differences which exist between women and men. And we have learned to deal across those differences with the urgency of all oppressed subordinates. All of us have had to learn to live or work or co-exist with men, from our fathers on. We have recognized and negotiated these differences, even when this recog-nition only continued the old dominant/subordinate mode of human relationship, where the oppressed must recognize the masters' difference in order to survive.

But our future survival is predicated upon our ability to relate within equality. As women, we must root out internalized patterns of oppression within ourselves if we are to move beyond the most super-ficial aspects of social change. Now we must recog-nize differences among women who are our equals, neither inferior nor superior, and devise ways to use each others' differences to enrich our visions and our joint struggles.

The future of our earth may depend upon the ability of all women to identify and develop new definitions of power and new patterns of relating across difference. The old definitions have not served us, nor the earth that supports us. The old patterns, no matter how cleverly rearranged to imi-tate progress, still condemn us to cosmetically altered repetitions, of the same old exchanges, the same old guilt, hatred, recrimination, lamentation, and suspicion.

For we have, built into all of us, old blueprints of expectation and response, old structures of oppres-sion, and these must be altered at the same time as we alter the living conditions which are a result of those structures. For the master's tools will never dismantle the master's house.

As Paulo Freire shows so well in *The Pedagogy of the Oppressed*,[2] the true focus of revolutionary change is never merely the oppressive situations which we seek to escape, but that piece of the oppressor which is planted deep within each of us, and which knows only the oppressors' tactics, the oppressors' relationships.

Change means growth, and growth can be painful. But we sharpen self-definition by exposing the self in work and struggle together with those whom we define as different from ourselves, although sharing the same goals. For Black and white, old and young, lesbian and heterosexual women alike, this can mean new paths to our survival.

We have chosen each other
and the edge of each others battles
the war is the same
if we lose
someday women's blood will congeal
upon a dead planet
if we win
there is no telling
we seek beyond history
for a new and more possible meeting.[3]

[1984]

NOTES

1. From "Rape: A Radical Analysis, An African-American Perspective" by Kalamu ya Salaam in *Black Books Bulletin*, vol. 6, no. 4 (1980).
2. Seabury Press, New York, 1970.
3. From "Outlines," unpublished poem.

◈ 60

The Straight Mind

MONIQUE WITTIG

MONIQUE WITTIG France. 1935–2003. Writer. Theorist. Leader of French women's liberation movement. Avant-garde experimental novelist. Lived and worked in United States from 1980s on. *Les Guérillères* (1971), *The Lesbian Body* (1973), *Lesbian Peoples: Material for a Dictionary* (1979).

In recent years in Paris, language as a phenomenon has dominated modern theoretical systems and the social sciences and has entered the political discussions of the lesbian and women's liberation movements. This is because it relates to an important political field where what it is at play is power, or more than that, a network of powers, since there is a multiplicity of languages that constantly act upon the social reality. The importance of language as such as a political stake has only recently been perceived.[1] But the gigantic development of linguistics, the multiplication of schools of linguistics, and the advent of the sciences of communication, and the technicality of the metalanguages that these sciences utilize, represent the symptoms of the importance of what is politically at stake. The science of language has invaded other sciences, such as anthropology through Lévi-Strauss, psychoanalysis through Lacan, and all the disciplines which have developed from the basis of structuralism.

The early semiology of Roland Barthes nearly escaped from linguistic domination to become a political analysis of the different systems of signs, to establish a relationship between this or that system of signs—for example, the myths of the petit bourgeois class—and the class struggle within capitalism that this system tends to conceal. We were almost saved, for political semiology is a weapon (a method) that we need to analyze what is called ideology. But the miracle did not last. Rather than introducing into semiology concepts which are foreign to it—in this case Marxist concepts— Barthes quickly stated that semiology was only a branch of linguistics and that language was its only object.

Thus, the entire world is only a great register where the most diverse languages come to have themselves recorded such as the language of the Unconscious,[2] the language of fashion, the language of the exchange of women where human beings are literally the signs which are used to communicate. These languages, or rather these discourses, fit into one another, interpenetrate one another, support one another, reinforce one another, auto-engender, and engender one another. Linguistics engenders semiology and structural linguistics, structural linguistics engenders structuralism, which engenders the Structural Unconscious. The ensemble of these discourses produces a confusing static for the oppressed, which makes them lose sight of the material cause of their oppression and plunges them into a kind of ahistoric vacuum.

For they produce a scientific reading of the social reality in which human beings are given as invariants, untouched by history and unworked by class conflicts, with identical psyches because genetically programmed. This psyche, equally untouched by history and unworked by class conflicts, provides the specialists, from the beginning of the twentieth century, with a whole arsenal of invariants: the symbolic language which very advantageously functions with very few elements, since, like digits (0–9), the symbols "unconsciously" produced by the psyche are not very numerous. Therefore, these symbols are very easy to impose, through therapy and theorization, upon the collective and individual unconscious. . . .

. . .

The discourses which particularly oppress all of us, lesbians, women, and homosexual men, are those which take for granted that what founds society, any society, is heterosexuality.[3] These discourses speak about us and claim to say the truth in an apolitical field, as if anything of that which signifies could escape the political in this moment of history, and as if, in what concerns us, politically insignificant signs could exist. These discourses of heterosexuality oppress us in the sense that they prevent us from speaking unless we speak in their terms. Everything which puts them into question is at once disregarded as elementary. Our refusal of the totalizing interpretation of psychoanalysis makes the theoreticians say that we neglect the symbolic dimension. These discourses deny us every possibility of creating our own categories. But their most ferocious action is the unrelenting tyranny that they exert upon physical and mental selves.

When we use the overgeneralizing term "ideology" to designate all the discourses of the dominating group, we relegate these discourses to the domain of Irreal Ideas; we forget the material (physical) violence that they directly do to the oppressed people, a violence produced by the abstract and "scientific" discourses as well as by the discourses of the mass media. I would like to insist on the material oppression of individuals by discourses, and I would like to underline its immediate effects through the example of pornography.

Pornographic images, films, magazine photos, publicity posters on the walls of the cities, constitute a discourse, and this discourse covers our world with its signs, and this discourse has a meaning: it signifies that women are dominated. Semioticians can interpret the system of this discourse, describe its disposition. What they read in that discourse are signs whose function is not to signify and which have no *raison d'être* except to be elements of a certain system or disposition. But for us this discourse is not divorced from the real as it is for semioticians. Not only does it maintain very close relations with the social reality which is our oppression (economically and politically), but also it is in itself real since it is one of the aspects of oppression, since it exerts a precise power over us. The pornographic discourse is one of the strategies of violence which are exercised upon us: it humiliates, it degrades, it is a crime against our "humanity." As a harassing tactic it has another function, that of a warning. It orders us to stay in line, and it keeps those who would tend to forget who they are in step; it calls upon fear. These same experts in semiotics, referred to earlier, reproach us for confusing, when we demonstrate against pornography, the discourses with the reality. They do not see that this discourse *is* reality for us, one of the facets of the reality of our oppression. They believe that we are mistaken in our level of analysis.

I have chosen pornography as an example because its discourse is the most symptomatic and the most demonstrative of the violence which is done to us through discourses, as well as in the society at large. There is nothing abstract about the power that sciences and theories have to act materially and actually upon our bodies and our minds, even if the discourse that produces it is abstract. It is one of the forms of domination, its very expression. I would say, rather, one of its exercises. All of the oppressed know this power and have had to deal with it. It is the one which says: you do not have the right to speech because your discourse is not scientific and not theoretical, you are on the wrong level of analysis, you are confusing discourse and reality, your discourse is naive, you misunderstand this or that science.

If the discourse of modern theoretical systems and social science exerts a power upon us, it is because it works with concepts which closely touch us. In spite of the historic advent of the lesbian, feminist, and gay liberation movements, whose proceedings have already upset the philosophical and political categories of the discourses of the social sciences, their categories (thus brutally put into question) are nevertheless utilized without examination by contemporary science. They function like primitive concepts in a conglomerate of all kinds of disciplines, theories, and current ideas that I will call the straight mind. (See *The Savage Mind* by Claude Lévi-Strauss.) They concern "woman," "man," "sex," "difference," and all of the series of concepts which bear this mark, including such concepts as "history," "culture," and the "real." And although it has been accepted in recent years that there is no such thing as nature, that everything is culture, there remains within that culture a core of nature which resists examination, a relationship excluded from the social in the analysis—a relationship whose characteristic is ineluctably in culture, as well as in nature, and which is the heterosexual relationship. I will call it the obligatory social relationship between "man" and "woman." (Here I refer to Ti-Grace Atkinson and her analysis of sexual intercourse as an institution.[4]) With its ineluctability as knowledge, as an obvious principle, as a given prior to any science, the straight mind develops a totalizing interpretation of history, social reality, culture, language, and all the subjective phenomena at the same time. I can only underline the oppressive character that the straight mind is clothed in in its tendency to immediately universalize its production of concepts into general laws which claim to hold true for all societies, all epochs, all individuals. Thus one speaks of *the* exchange of women, *the* difference between the sexes, *the* symbolic order, *the* Unconscious, Desire, *Jouissance,* Culture, History, giving an absolute meaning to these concepts when they are only categories founded upon heterosexuality, or thought which produces the difference between the sexes as a political and philosophical dogma.

The consequence of this tendency toward universality is that the straight mind cannot conceive of a culture, a society where heterosexuality would not order not only all human relationships but also its very production of concepts and all the processes which escape consciousness, as well. Additionally, these unconscious processes are historically more and more imperative in what they teach us about ourselves through the instrumentality of specialists. The rhetoric which expresses them (and whose seduction I do not underestimate) envelops itself in myths, resorts to enigma, proceeds by accumulating metaphors, and its function is to poeticize the obligatory character of the "you-will-be-straight-or-you-will-not-be."

In this thought, to reject the obligation of coitus and the institutions that this obligation has produced as necessary for the constitution of a society, is simply an impossibility, since to do this would mean to reject the possibility of the constitution of the other and to reject the "symbolic order," to make the constitution of meaning impossible, without which no one can maintain an internal coherence. Thus lesbianism, homosexuality, and the societies that we form cannot be thought of or spoken of, even though they have always existed. Thus, the straight mind continues to affirm that incest, and not homosexuality, represents its major interdiction. Thus, when thought by the straight mind, homosexuality is nothing but heterosexuality.

Yes, straight society is based on the necessity of the different/other at every level. It cannot work economically, symbolically, linguistically, or politically without this concept. This necessity of the different/other is an ontological one for the whole conglomerate of sciences and disciplines that I call the straight mind. But what is the different/other if not the dominated? For heterosexual society is the society which not only oppresses lesbians and

gay men, it oppresses many different/others, it oppresses all women and many categories of men, all those who are in the position of the dominated. To constitute a difference and to control it is an "act of power, since it is essentially a normative act. Everybody tries to show the other as different. But not everybody succeeds in doing so. One has to be socially dominant to succeed in it."[5]

For example, the concept of differences between the sexes ontologically constitutes women into different/others. Men are not different, whites are not different, nor are the masters. But the blacks, as well as the slaves, are. This ontological characteristic of the difference between the sexes affects all the concepts which are part of the same conglomerate. But for us there is no such thing as being-woman or being-man. "Man" and "woman" are political concepts of opposition, and the copula which dialectically unites them is, at the same time, the one which abolishes them.[6] It is the class struggle between women and men which will abolish men and women.[7] The concept of difference has nothing ontological about it. It is only the way that the masters interpret a historical situation of domination. The function of difference is to mask at every level the conflicts of interest, including ideological ones.

In other words, for us, this means there cannot any longer be women and men, and that as classes and categories of thought or language they have to disappear, politically, economically, ideologically. If we, as lesbians and gay men, continue to speak of ourselves and to conceive of ourselves as women and as men, we are instrumental in maintaining heterosexuality. I am sure that an economic and political transformation will not dedramatize these categories of language. Can we redeem *slave?* Can we redeem *nigger, negress?* How is *woman* different? Will we continue to write *white, master, man?* The transformation of economic relationships will not suffice. We must produce a political transformation of the key concepts, that is, of the concepts which are strategic for us. For there is another order of materiality, that of language, and language is worked upon from within by these strategic concepts. It is at the same time tightly connected to the political field, where everything that concerns language, science and thought refers to the person as subjectivity and to her/his relationship to society.

And we cannot leave this within the power of the straight mind or the thought of domination.

If among all the productions of the straight mind I especially challenge the models of the Structural Unconscious, it is because: at the moment in history when the domination of social groups can no longer appear as a logical necessity to the dominated, because they revolt, because they question the differences, Lévi-Strauss, Lacan, and their epigones call upon necessities which escape the control of consciousness and therefore the responsibility of individuals.

They call upon unconscious processes, for example, which require the exchange of women as a necessary condition for every society. According to them, that is what the unconscious tells us with authority, and the symbolic order, without which there is no meaning, no language, no society, depends on it. But what does women being exchanged mean if not that they are dominated? No wonder then that there is only one Unconscious, and that it is heterosexual. It is an Unconscious which looks too consciously after the interests of the masters[8] in whom it lives for them to be dispossessed of their concepts so easily. Besides, domination is denied; there is no slavery of women, there is difference. To which I will answer with this statement made by a Rumanian peasant at a public meeting in 1848: "Why do the gentlemen say it was not slavery, for we know it to have been slavery, this sorrow that we have sorrowed." Yes, we know it, and this science of oppression cannot be taken away from us.

It is from this science that we must track down the "what-goes-without-saying" heterosexual, and (I paraphrase the early Roland Barthes) we must not bear "seeing Nature and History confused at every turn."[9] We must make it brutally apparent that psychoanalysis after Freud and particularly Lacan have rigidly turned their concepts into myths—Difference, Desire, the-Name-of-the-father, etc. They have even "over-mythified" the myths, an operation that was necessary for them in order to systematically heterosexualize that personal dimension which suddenly emerged through the dominated individuals into the historical field, particularly through women, who started their struggle almost two centuries ago. And it has been done

systematically, in a concert of interdisciplinarity, never more harmonious than since the heterosexual myths started to circulate with ease from one formal system to another, like sure values that can be invested in anthropology as well as in psychoanalysis and in all the social sciences.

This ensemble of heterosexual myths is a system of signs which uses figures of speech, and thus it can be politically studied from within the science of our oppression; "for-we-know-it-to-have-been-slavery" is the dynamic which introduces the diachronism of history into the fixed discourse of eternal essences. This undertaking should somehow be a political seminology, although with "this sorrow that we have sorrowed" we work also at the level of language/manifesto, of language/action, that which transforms, that which makes history.

In the meantime, in the systems that seemed so eternal and universal that laws could be extracted from them, laws that could be stuffed into computers, and in any case for the moment stuffed into the unconscious machinery, in these systems, thanks to our action and our language, shifts are happening. Such a model, as for example, the exchange of women, reengulfs history in so violent and brutal a way that the whole system, which was believed to be formal, topples over into another dimension of knowledge. This dimension of history belongs to us, since somehow we have been designated, and since, as Lévi-Strauss said, we talk, let us say that we break off the heterosexual contract.

So, this is what lesbians say everywhere in this country and in some others, if not with theories at least through their social practice, whose repercussions upon straight culture and society are still unenvisionable. An anthropologist might say that we have to wait for fifty years. Yes, if one wants to universalize the functioning of these societies and make their invariants appear. Meanwhile the straight concepts are undermined. What is woman? Panic, general alarm for an active defense. Frankly, it is a problem that the lesbians do not have because of a change in perspective, and it would be incorrect to say that lesbians associate, make love, live with women, for "woman" has meaning only in heterosexual systems of thought and heterosexual economic systems. Lesbians are not women.

[1978]

NOTES

1. However, the classical Greeks knew that there was no political power without mastery of the art of rhetoric, especially in a democracy.

2. Throughout this paper, when Lacan's use of the term "the Unconscious" is referred to it is capitalized, following his style.

3. Heterosexuality: a word which first appears in the French language in 1911.

4. Ti-Grace Atkinson, *Amazon Odyssey* (New York: Links Books, 1974), pp. 13–23.

5. Claude Faugeron and Philippe Robert, *La Justice et son public et les représentations sociales du système pénal* (Paris: Masson, 1978).

6. See, for her definition of "social sex," Nicole-Claude Mathieu, "Notes pour une définition sociologique des catégories de sexe," *Epistémologie Sociologique* 11 (1971). Translated as *Ignored by Some, Denied by Others: The Social Sex Category in Sociology* (pamphlet), Explorations in Feminism 2 (London: Women's Research and Resources Centre Publications, 1977), pp. 16–37.

7. In the same way that in every other class struggle the categories of opposition are "reconciled" by the struggle whose goal is to make them disappear.

8. Are the millions of dollars a year made by the psychoanalysts symbolic?

9. Roland Barthes, *Mythologies* (New York: Hill and Wang, 1972), p. 11.

 61

Compulsory Heterosexuality and Lesbian Existence

ADRIENNE RICH

ADRIENNE RICH United States. 1929– . Poet. Essayist. Activist. Theorist. *Of Woman Born: Motherhood as an Experience and Institution* (1976), *On Lies, Secrets, and Silence: Selected Prose 1966–1978* (1979), *What Is Found There: Notebooks on Poetry and Politics* (1993), *Arts of the Possible: Essays and Conversations* (2001).

· · ·

II

If women are the earliest sources of emotional caring and physical nurture for both female and male children, it would seem logical, from a feminist perspective at least, to pose the following questions: whether the search for love and tenderness in both sexes does not originally lead toward women; *why in fact women would ever redirect that search;* why species survival, the means of impregnation, and emotional/erotic relationships should ever have become so rigidly identified with each other; and why such violent strictures should be found necessary to enforce women's total emotional, erotic loyalty and subservience to men. I doubt that enough feminist scholars and theorists have taken the pains to acknowledge the societal forces which wrench women's emotional and erotic energies away from themselves and other women and from woman-identified values. These forces, as I shall try to show, range from literal physical enslavement to the disguising and distorting of possible options.

I do not assume the mothering by women is a "sufficient cause" of lesbian existence. But the issue of mothering by women has been much in the air of late, usually accompanied by the view that increased parenting by men would minimize antagonism between the sexes and equalize the sexual imbalance of power of males over females. These discussions are carried on without reference to compulsory heterosexuality as a phenomenon, let alone as an ideology. I do not wish to psychologize here, but rather to identify sources of male power. I believe large numbers of men could, in fact, undertake child care on a large scale without radically altering the balance of male power in a male-identified society.

In her essay "The Origin of the Family," Kathleen Gough lists eight characteristics of male power in archaic and contemporary societies which I would like to use as a framework: "men's ability to deny women sexuality or to force it upon them; to command or exploit their labor to control their produce; to control or rob them of their children; to confine them physically and prevent their movement; to use them as objects in male transactions; to cramp their creativeness; or to withhold from them large areas of the society's knowledge and cultural attainments."[1] (Gough does not perceive these power characteristics as specifically enforcing heterosexuality, only as producing sexual inequality.) Below, Gough's words appear in italics; the elaboration of each of her categories, in brackets, is my own.

Characteristics of male power include *the power of men*

1. *to deny women* [their own] *sexuality*—[by means of clitoridectomy and infibulation; chastity belts; punishment, including death, for female adultery; punishment, including death, for lesbian sexuality; psychoanalytic denial of the clitoris; strictures against masturbation; denial of maternal and post-menopausal sensuality; unnecessary hysterectomy; pseudolesbian images in the media and literature; closing of archives and destruction of documents relating to lesbian existence]

2. *or to force it* [male sexuality] *upon them*—[by means of rape (including marital rape) and wife beating; father-daughter, brother-sister incest; the socialization of women to feel that male sexual "drive" amounts to a right,[2] idealization of heterosexual romance in art, literature, the media, advertising, etc.; child marriage; arranged marriage; prostitution; the harem; psychoanalytic doctrines of frigidity and vaginal orgasm; pornographic depictions of women responding pleasurably to sexual violence and humiliation (a subliminal message being that sadistic heterosexuality is more "normal" than sensuality between women)]

3. *to command or exploit their labor to control their produce*—[by means of the institutions of marriage and motherhood as unpaid production; horizontal segregation of women in paid employment; the decoy of the upwardly mobile token woman; male control of abortion, contraception, sterilization, and childbirth; pimping; female infanticide, which robs mothers of daughters and contributes to generalized devaluation of women]

4. *to control or rob them of their children*—[by means of father right and "legal kidnapping";[3] enforced sterilization; systematized infanticide; seizure of children from lesbian mothers by the courts; the malpractice of male obstetrics; use of the mothers as "token torturer"[4] in genital mutilation or in binding the daughter's feet (or mind) to fit her for marriage]

5. *to confine them physically and prevent their movement*—[by means of rape as terrorism, keeping women off the streets; purdah; foot binding; atrophying of women's athletic capabilities; high heels and "feminine" dress codes in fashion; the veil; sexual harassment on the streets; horizontal segregation of women in employment; prescriptions for "full-time" mothering at home; enforced economic dependence of wives]

6. *to use them as objects in male transactions*—[use of women as "gifts"; bride price; pimping; arranged marriage; use of women as entertainers to facilitate male deals—e.g., wife-hostess, cocktail waitress required to dress for male sexual titillation, call girls, "bunnies," geisha, *kisaeng* prostitutes, secretaries]

7. *to cramp their creativeness*—[witch persecutions as campaigns against midwives and female healers, and as pogrom against independent, "unassimilated" women;[5] definition of male pursuits as more valuable than female within any culture, so that cultural values become the embodiment of male subjectivity; restriction of female self-fulfillment to marriage and motherhood; sexual exploitation of women by male artists and teachers; the social and economic disruption of women's creative aspirations;[6] erasure of female tradition][7]

8. *to withhold from them large areas of the society's knowledge and cultural attainments*—[by means of noneducation of females; the "Great Silence" regarding women and particularly lesbian existence in history and culture;[8] sex-role tracking which deflects women from science, technology, and other "masculine" pursuits; male social/professional bonding which excludes women; discrimination against women in the professions]

These are some of the methods by which male power is manifested and maintained. Looking at the schema, what surely impresses itself is the fact that we are confronting not simple maintenance of inequality and property possession, but a pervasive cluster of forces, ranging from physical brutality to control of consciousness, which suggests that an enormous potential counterforce is having to be restrained.

· · ·

III

I have chosen to use the terms *lesbian existence* and *lesbian continuum* because the word *lesbianism* has a clinical and limiting ring. *Lesbian existence* suggests both the fact of the historical presence of lesbians and our continuing creation of the meaning of that existence. I mean the term *lesbian continuum* to include a range—through each woman's life and throughout history—of woman-identified experience, not simply the fact a woman has had or consciously desired genital sexual experience with another woman. If we expand it to embrace many more forms of primary intensity between and among women, including the sharing of a rich inner life, the bonding against male tyranny, the giving and receiving of practical and political support, if we can also hear it in such associations as *marriage resistance* and the "haggard" behavior identified by Mary Daly (obsolete meanings: "intractable," "willful," "wanton," and "unchaste," "a woman reluctant to yield to wooing"),[9] we begin to grasp breadths of female history and psychology which have lain out of reach as a consequence of limited, mostly clinical, definitions of *lesbianism.*

Lesbian existence comprises both the breaking of a taboo and the rejection of a compulsory way of life. It is also a direct or indirect attack on male right of access to women. But it is more than these, although we may first begin to perceive it as form of naysaying to patriarchy, an act of resistance. It has of course, included isolation, self-hatred, breakdown, alcoholism, suicide, and intrawoman violence; we romanticize at our peril what it means to love and act against the grain, and under heavy penalties; and lesbian existence has been lived (unlike, say, Jewish or Catholic existence) without access to any knowledge of a tradition, a continuity, a social underpinning. The destruction of records and memorabilia and letters documenting the realities of lesbian existence must be taken very seriously as a means of keeping heterosexuality compulsory for women, since what has been kept from our knowledge is joy, sensuality, courage, and community, as well as guilt, self-betrayal, and pain.[10]

Lesbians have historically been deprived of a political existence through "inclusion" as female versions of male homosexuality. To equate lesbian existence with male homosexuality because each is stigmatized is to erase female reality once again. Part of the history of lesbian existence is, obviously, to be found where lesbians, lacking a coherent female community, have shared a kind of social life

and common cause with homosexual men. But there are differences: women's lack of economic and cultural privilege relative to men; qualitative differences in female and male relationships—for example, the patterns of anonymous sex among male homosexuals, and the pronounced ageism in male homosexual standards of sexual attractiveness. I perceive the lesbian experience as being, like motherhood, a profoundly *female* experience, with particular oppressions, meanings, and potentialities we cannot comprehend as long as we simply bracket it with other sexually stigmatized existences. Just as the term *parenting* serves to conceal the particular and significant reality of being a parent who is actually a mother, the term *gay* may serve the purpose of blurring the very outlines we need to discern, which are of crucial value for feminism and for the freedom of women as a group.[11]

As the term *lesbian* has been held to limiting, clinical associations in its patriarchal definition, female friendship and comradeship have been set apart from the erotic, thus limiting the erotic itself. But as we deepen and broaden the range of what we define as lesbian existence, as we delineate a lesbian continuum, we begin to discover the erotic in female terms: as that which is unconfined to any single part of the body or solely to the body itself; as an energy not only diffuse but, as Audre Lorde has described it, omnipresent in "the sharing of joy, whether physical, emotional, psychic," and in the sharing of work; as the empowering joy which "makes us less willing to accept powerlessness, or those other supplied states of being which are not native to me, such as resignation, despair, self-effacement, depression, self-denial."[12] In another context, writing of women and work, I quoted the autobiographical passage in which the poet H. D. described how her friend Bryher supported her in persisting with the visionary experience which was to shape her mature work:

> I knew that this experience, this writing-on-the-wall before me, could not be shared with anyone except the girl who stood so bravely there beside me. This girl said without hesitation, "Go on." It was she really who had the detachment and integrity of the Pythoness of Delphi. But it was I, battered and dissociated . . . who was seeing the

pictures, and who was reading the writing or granted the inner vision. Or perhaps, in some sense, we were "seeing" it together, for without her, admittedly, I could not have gone on.[13]

If we consider the possibility that all women—from the infant suckling at her mother's breast, to the grown woman experiencing orgasmic sensations while suckling her own child, perhaps recalling her mother's milk smell in her own, to two women, like Virginia Woolf's Chloe and Olivia, who share a laboratory,[14] to the woman dying at ninety, touched and handled by women—exist on a lesbian continuum, we can see ourselves as moving in and out of this continuum, whether we identify ourselves as lesbian or not.

We can then connect aspects of woman identification as diverse as the impudent, intimate girl friendships of eight or nine year olds and the banding together of those women of the twelfth and fifteenth centuries known as Beguines who "shared houses, rented to one another, bequeathed houses to their room-mates . . . in cheap subdivided houses in the artisans' area of town," who "practiced Christian virtue on their own, dressing and living simply and not associating with men," who earned their livings as spinsters, bakers, nurses, or ran schools for young girls, and who managed—until the Church forced them to disperse—to live independent both of marriage and of conventual restrictions.[15] It allows us to connect these women with the more celebrated "Lesbians" of the women's school around Sappho of the seventh century B.C., with the secret sororities and economic networks reported among African women, and with the Chinese marriage-resistance sisterhoods—communities of women who refused marriage or who, if married, often refused to consummate their marriages and soon left their husbands, the only women in China who were not footbound and who, Agnes Smedley tells us, welcomed the births of daughters and organized successful women's strikes in the silk mills.[16] It allows us to connect and compare disparate individual instances of marriage resistance: for example, the strategies available to Emily Dickinson, a nineteenth-century white woman genius, with the strategies available to Zora Neale Hurston, a twentieth-century Black woman genius.

Dickinson never married, had tenuous intellectual friendships with men, lived self-convented in her genteel father's house in Amherst, and wrote a lifetime of passionate letters to her sister-in-law Sue Gilbert and a smaller group of such letters to her friend Kate Scott Anthon. Hurston married twice but soon left each husband, scrambled her way from Florida to Harlem to Columbia University to Haiti and finally back to Florida, moved in and out of white patronage and poverty, professional success and failure; her survival relationships were all with women, beginning with her mother. Both of these women in their vastly different circumstances were marriage resisters, committed to their own work and self-hood, and were later characterized as "apolitical." Both were drawn to men of intellectual quality; for both of them women provided the ongoing fascination and sustenance of life.

If we think of heterosexuality as *the* natural emotional and sensual inclination for women, lives such as these are seen as deviant, as pathological, or as emotionally and sensually deprived. Or, in more recent and permissive jargon, they are banalized as "life styles." And the work of such women, whether merely the daily work of individual or collective survival and resistance or the work of the writer, the activist, the reformer, the anthropologist, or the artist—the work of self-creation—is undervalued, or seen as the bitter fruit of "penis envy" or the sublimation of repressed eroticism or the meaningless rant of a "man-hater." But when we turn the lens of vision and consider the degree to which and the methods whereby heterosexual "preference" has actually been imposed on women, not only can we understand differently the meaning of individual lives and work, but we can begin to recognize a central fact of women's history: that women have always resisted male tyranny. A feminism of action, often though not always without a theory, has constantly re-emerged in every culture and in every period. We can then begin to study women's struggle against powerlessness, women's radical rebellion, not just in male-defined "concrete revolutionary situations"[17] but in all the situations male ideologies have not perceived as revolutionary—for example, the refusal of some women to produce children, aided at great risk by other women;[18] the refusal to produce a higher standard of living and leisure for men (Leghorn and Parker show how both are part of women's unacknowledged, unpaid, and ununionized economic contribution). We can no longer have patience with Dinnerstein's view that women have simply collaborated with men in the "sexual arrangements" of history. We begin to observe behavior, both in history and in individual biography, that has hitherto been invisible or misnamed, behavior which often constitutes, given the limits of the counterforce exerted in a given time and place, radical rebellion. And we can connect these rebellions and the necessity for them with the physical passion of woman for woman which is central to lesbian existence: the erotic sensuality which has been, precisely, the most violently erased fact of female experience.

Heterosexuality has been both forcibly and subliminally imposed on women. Yet everywhere women have resisted it, often at the cost of physical torture, imprisonment, psychosurgery, social ostracism, and extreme poverty. "Compulsory heterosexuality" was named as one of the "crimes against women" by the Brussels International Tribunal on Crimes against Women in 1976. Two pieces of testimony from two very different cultures reflect the degree to which persecution of lesbians is a global practice here and now. A report from Norway relates:

> A lesbian in Oslo was in a heterosexual marriage that didn't work, so she started taking tranquilizers and ended up at the health sanatorium for treatment and rehabilitation. . . . The moment she said in family group therapy that she believed she was a lesbian, the doctor told her she was not. He knew from "looking into her eyes," he said. She had the eyes of a woman who wanted sexual intercourse with her husband. So she was subjected to so-called "couch therapy." She was put into a comfortably heated room, naked, on a bed, and for an hour her husband was to . . . try to excite her sexually. . . . The idea was that the touching was always to end with sexual intercourse. She felt stronger and stronger aversion. She threw up and sometimes ran out of the room to avoid this "treatment." The more strongly she asserted that she was a lesbian, the more violent the forced heterosexual intercourse became. This treatment went on for about six months. She escaped from the hospital, but she was brought back. Again she escaped. She has not been

there since. In the end she realized that she had been subjected to forcible rape for six months.

And from Mozambique:

> I am condemned to a life of exile because I will not deny that I am a lesbian, that my primary commitments are, and will always be to other women. In the new Mozambique, lesbianism is considered a leftover from colonialism and decadent Western civilization. Lesbians are sent to rehabilitation camps to learn through self-criticism the correct line about themselves. . . . If I am forced to denounce my own love for women, if I therefore denounce myself, I could go back to Mozambique and join forces in the exciting and hard struggle of rebuilding a nation, including the struggle for the emancipation of Mozambiquan women. As it is, I either risk the rehabilitation camps, or remain in exile.[19]

Nor can it be assumed that women like those in Carroll Smith-Rosenberg's study, who married, stayed married, yet dwelt in a profoundly female emotional and passional world, "preferred" or "chose" heterosexuality. Women have married because it was necessary, in order to survive economically, in order to have children who would not suffer economic deprivation or social ostracism, in order to remain respectable, in order to do what was expected of women, because coming out of "abnormal" childhoods they wanted to feel "normal" and because heterosexual romance has been represented as the great female adventure, duty, and fulfillment. We may faithfully or ambivalently have obeyed the institution, but our feelings—and our sensuality—have not been tamed or contained within it. There is no statistical documentation of the numbers of lesbians who have remained in heterosexual marriages for most of their lives. But in a letter to the early lesbian publication *The Ladder,* the playwright Lorraine Hansberry had this to say:

> I suspect that the problem of the married woman who would prefer emotional-physical relationships with other women is proportionally much higher than a similar statistic for men. (A statistic surely no one will ever really have.) This because the estate of woman being what it is, how could we ever begin to guess the numbers of women who are not prepared to risk a life alien to what they have been taught all their lives to believe was their "natural" destiny—AND—their only expectation for ECONOMIC

security. It seems to be that this is why the question has an immensity that it does not have for male homosexuals. . . . A woman of strength and honesty may, if she chooses, sever her marriage and marry a new male mate and society will be upset that the divorce rate is rising so—but there are few places in the United States, in any event, where she will be anything remotely akin to an "outcast." Obviously this is not true for a woman who would end her marriage to take up life with another woman.[20]

This *double life*—this apparent acquiescence to an institution founded on male interest and prerogative—has been characteristic of female experience: in motherhood and in many kinds of heterosexual behavior, including the rituals of courtship; the pretense of asexuality by the nineteenth-century wife; the simulation of orgasm by the prostitute, the courtesan, the twentieth-century "sexually liberated" woman.

Meridel LeSueur's documentary novel of the depression, *The Girl,* is arresting as a study of female double life. The protagonist, a waitress in a St. Paul working-class speakeasy, feels herself passionately attracted to the young man Butch, but her survival relationships are with Clara, an older waitress and prostitute, with Belle, whose husband owns the bar, and with Amelia, a union activist. For Clara and Belle and the unnamed protagonist, sex with men is in one sense an escape from the bedrock misery of daily life, a flare of intensity in the gray, relentless, often brutal web of day-to-day existence:

It was like he was a magnet pulling me. It was exciting and powerful and frightening. He was after me too and when he found me I would run, or be petrified, just standing in front of him like a zany. And he told me not to be wandering with Clara to the Marigold where we danced with strangers. He said he would knock the shit out of me. Which made me shake and tremble, but it was better than being a husk full of suffering and not knowing why.[21]

Throughout the novel the theme of double life emerges; Belle reminisces about her marriage to the bootlegger Hoinck:

You know, when I had that black eye and said I hit it on the cupboard, well he did it the bastard, and then he says don't tell anybody. . . . He's nuts, that's what he is, nuts, and I don't see why I live with him,

why I put up with him a minute on this earth. But listen kid, she said, I'm telling you something. She looked at me and her face was wonderful. She said, Jesus Christ, Goddam him I love him that's why I'm hooked like this all my life, Goddam him I love him.[22]

After the protagonist has her first sex with Butch, her women friends care for her bleeding, give her whiskey and compare notes.

My luck, the first time and I got into trouble. He gave me a little money and I come to St. Paul where for ten bucks they'd stick a huge vet's needle into you and you start it and then you were on your own. . . . I never had no child. I've just had Hoinck to mother, and a hell of a child he is.[23]

Later they made me go back to Clara's room to lie down. . . . Clara lay down beside me and put her arms around me and wanted me to tell her about it but she wanted to tell about herself. She said she started it when she was twelve with a bunch of boys in an old shed. She said nobody had paid any attention to her before and she became very popular. . . . They like it so much, she said, why shouldn't you give it to them and get presents and attention? I never cared anything for it and neither did my mama. But it's the only thing you got that's valuable.[24]

Sex is thus equated with attention from the male, who is charismatic though brutal, infantile, or unreliable. Yet it is the women who make life endurable for each other, give physical affection without causing pain, share, advise, and stick by each other. *(I am trying to find my strength through women— without my friends, I could not survive.)* LeSueur's *The Girl* parallels Toni Morrison's remarkable *Sula,* another revelation of female double life:

Nel was the one person who had wanted nothing from her, who had accepted all aspects of her. . . . Nel was one of the reasons Sula had drifted back to Medallion. . . . The men . . . had merged into one large personality: the same language of love, the same entertainments of love, the same cooling of love. Whenever she introduced her private thoughts into their rubbings and goings, they hooded their eyes. They taught her nothing but love tricks, shared nothing but worry, gave nothing but money. She had been looking all along for a friend, and it took her awhile to discover that a lover was not a comrade and could never be—for a woman.

But Sula's last thought at the second of her death is "Wait'll I tell Nel." And after Sula's death, Nel looks back at her own life:

> "All that time, all that time, I thought I was missing Jude." And the loss pressed down on her chest and came up into her throat. "We was girls together," she said as though explaining something. "O Lord, Sula," she cried, "Girl, girl, girlgirlgirl!" It was a fine cry—loud and long—but it had no bottom and it had no top, just circles and circles of sorrow.[25]

The Girl and *Sula* are both novels which examine what I am calling the lesbian continuum, in contrast to the shallow or sensational "lesbian scenes" in recent commercial fiction.[26] Each shows us woman identification untarnished (till the end of LeSueur's novel) by romanticism; each depicts the competition of heterosexual compulsion for women's attention, the diffusion and frustration of female bonding that might, in a more conscious form, reintegrate love and power.

IV

Woman identification is a source of energy, a potential springhead of female power, curtailed and contained under the institution of heterosexuality. The denial of reality and visibility to women's passion for women, women's choice of women as allies, life companions, and community, the forcing of such relationships into dissimulation and their disintegration under intense pressure have meant an incalculable loss to the power of all women *to change the social relations of the sexes, to liberate ourselves and each other.* The lie of compulsory female heterosexuality today afflicts not just feminist scholarship, but every profession, every reference work, every curriculum, every organizing attempt, every relationship or conversation over which it hovers. It creates, specifically, a profound falseness, hypocrisy, and hysteria in the heterosexual dialogue, for every heterosexual relationship is lived in the queasy strobe light of that lie. However we choose to identify ourselves, however we find ourselves labeled, it flickers across and distorts our lives.[27]

The lie keeps numberless women psychologically trapped, trying to fit mind, spirit, and sexuality into a prescribed script because they cannot look beyond the parameters of the acceptable. It pulls on the energy of such women even as it drains the energy of "closeted" lesbians—the energy exhausted in the double life. The lesbian trapped in the "closet," the woman imprisoned in prescriptive ideas of the "normal" share the pain of blocked options, broken connections, lost access to self-definition freely and powerfully assumed.

The lie is many-layered. In Western tradition, one layer—the romantic—asserts that women are inevitably, even if rashly and tragically, drawn to men; that even when that attraction is suicidal (e.g., *Tristan and Isolde,* Kate Chopin's *The Awakening*), it is still an organic imperative. In the tradition of the social sciences it asserts that primary love between the sexes is "normal"; that women *need* men as social and economic protectors, for adult sexuality, and for psychological completion; that the heterosexually constituted family is the basic social unit; that women who do not attach their primary intensity to men must be, in functional terms, condemned to an even more devastating outsiderhood than their outsiderhood as women. Small wonder that lesbians are reported to be a more hidden population than male homosexuals. The Black lesbian-feminist critic Lorraine Bethel, writing on Zora Neale Hurston, remarks that for a Black woman—already twice an outsider—to choose to assume still another "hated identity" is problematic indeed. Yet the lesbian continuum has been a life line for Black women both in Africa and the United States.

> Black women have a long tradition of bonding together . . . in a Black/women's community that has been a source of vital survival information, psychic and emotional support for us. We have a distinct Black woman-identified folk culture based on our experiences as Black women in this society; symbols, language and modes of expression that are specific to the realities of our lives. . . . Because Black women were rarely among those Blacks and females who gained access to literary and other acknowledged forms of artistic expression, this Black female bonding and Black woman-identification has often been hidden and unrecorded except in the individual lives of Black women through our own memories of our particular Black female tradition.[28]

Another layer of the lie is the frequently encountered implication that women turn to women out of hatred for men. Profound skepticism, caution, and righteous paranoia about men may indeed be part of any healthy woman's response to the misogyny of male-dominated culture, to the forms assumed by "normal" male sexuality, and to *the failure even of "sensitive" or "political" men to perceive or find these troubling.* Lesbian existence is also represented as mere refuge from male abuses, rather than as an electric and empowering charge between women. One of the most frequently quoted literary passages on lesbian relationship is that in which Colette's Renée, in *The Vagabond,* describes "the melancholy and touching image of two weak creatures who have perhaps found shelter in each other's arms, there to sleep and weep, safe from man who is often cruel, and there to taste *better than any pleasure, the bitter happiness of feeling themselves akin, frail and forgotten* [emphasis added]."[29] Colette is often considered a lesbian writer. Her popular reputation has I think, much to do with the fact the she writes about lesbian existence as if for a male audience; her earliest "lesbian" novels, the Claudine series, were written under compulsion for her husband and published under both their names. At all events, except for her writings on her mother, Colette is a less reliable source on the lesbian continuum than, I would think, Charlotte Brontë, who understood that while women may, indeed must, be one another's allies, mentors, and comforters in the female struggle for survival, there is quite extraneous delight in each other's company and attraction to each others' minds and character, which attend a recognition of each other's strengths.

By the same token, we can say that there is a *nascent* feminist political content in the act of choosing a woman lover or life partner in the face of institutionalized heterosexuality.[30] But for lesbian existence to realize this political content in an ultimately liberating form, the erotic choice must deepen and expand into conscious woman identification—into lesbian feminism.

The work that lies ahead, of unearthing and describing what I call here "lesbian existence," is potentially liberating for all women. It is work that must assuredly move beyond the limits of white and middle-class Western Women's Studies to examine women's lives, work, and groupings within every racial, ethnic, and political structure. There are differences, moreover, between "lesbian existence" and the "lesbian continuum," differences we can discern even in the movement of our own lives. The lesbian continuum, I suggest, needs delineation in light of the "double life" of women, not only women self-described as heterosexual but also of self-described lesbians. We need a far more exhaustive account of the forms the double life has assumed. Historians need to ask at every point how heterosexuality as institution has been organized and maintained through the female wage scale, the enforcement of middle-class women's "leisure," the glamorization of so-called sexual liberation, the withholding of education from women, the imagery of "high art" and popular culture, the mystification of the "personal" sphere, and much else. We need an economics which comprehends the institution of heterosexuality, with its doubled workload for women and its sexual divisions of labor, as the most idealized of economic relations.

The question inevitably will arise: Are we then to condemn all heterosexual relationships, including those which are least oppressive? I believe this question, though often heartfelt, is the wrong question here. We have been stalled in a maze of false dichotomies which prevents our apprehending the institution as a whole: "good" versus "bad" marriages; "marriage for love" versus arranged marriage; "liberated" sex versus prostitution; heterosexual intercourse versus rape; *Liebeschmerz* versus humiliation and dependency. Within the institution exist, of course, qualitative differences of experience; but the absence of choice remains the great unacknowledged reality, and in the absence of choice, women will remain dependent upon the chance or luck of particular relationships and will have no collective power to determine the meaning and place of sexuality in their lives. As we address the institution itself, moreover, we begin to perceive a history of female resistance which has never fully understood itself because it has been so fragmented, miscalled, erased. It will require a courageous grasp of the politics and economics, as well as the cultural propaganda, of heterosexuality to carry us beyond individual cases or diversified group situations into the complex kind of overview needed to undo the power men everywhere wield over women, power which has become a model for every other form of exploitation and illegitimate control.

[1980]

NOTES

1. Kathleen Gough, "The Origin of the Family," in *Toward and Anthropology of Women,* ed. Rayna [Rapp] Reiter (New York: Monthly Review Press, 1975), pp. 69–70.

2. Kathleen Barry, *Female Sexual Slavery* (Englewood Cliffs, N.J.: Prentice-Hall, 1979), pp. 216–219.

3. Anna Demeter, *Legal Kidnapping* (Boston: Beacon, 1977), pp. xx, 126–128.

4. Mary Daly, *Gyn/Ecology: The Metaethics of Radical Feminism* (Boston: Beacon, 1978), pp. 139–141, 163–165.

5. Barbara Ehrenreich and Deirdre English, *Witches, Midwives and Nurses: A History of Women Healers* (Old Westbury, N.Y.: Feminist Press, 1973); Andrea Dworkin, *Woman Hating* (New York: Dutton, 1974), pp. 118–154; Daly, pp. 178–222.

6. See Virginia Woolf, *A Room of One's Own* (London: Hogarth, 1929), and *id., Three Guineas* (New York: Harcourt Brace, [1938] 1966); Tillie Olsen, *Silences* (Boston: Delacorte, 1978); Michelle Cliff, "The Resonance of Interruption," *Chrysalis: A Magazine of Women's Culture* 8 (1979): 29–37.

7. Mary Daly, *Beyond God the Father* (Boston: Beacon, 1973), pp. 347–351; Olsen, pp. 22–46.

8. Daly, *Beyond God the Father,* p. 93.

9. Daly, *Gyn/Ecology,* p. 15.

10. "In a hostile world in which women are not supposed to survive except in relation with and in service to men, entire communities of women were simply erased. History tends to bury what it seeks to reject" (Blanche W. Cook, "'Women Alone Stir My Imagination': Lesbianism and the Cultural Tradition," *Signs: Journal of Women in Culture and Society* 4, no. 4 [Summer 1979]: 719–720. The Lesbian Herstory Archives in New York City is one attempt to preserve contemporary documents on lesbian existence—a project of enormous value and meaning, working against the continuing censorship and obliteration of relationships, networks, communities in other archives and elsewhere in the culture.

11. [A.R., 1986: The shared historical and spiritual "crossover" functions of lesbians and gay men in cultures past and present are traced by Judy Grahn in *Another Mother Tongue: Gay Words, Gay Worlds* (Boston: Beacon, 1984). I now think we have much to learn both from the uniquely female aspects of lesbian existence and from the complex "gay" identity we share with gay men.]

12. Audre Lorde, "Uses of the Erotic: The Erotic as Power," in *Sister Outsider* (Trumansburg, N. Y.: Crossing Press, 1984).

13. Adrienne Rich, "Conditions for Work: The Common World of Women," in *On Lies, Secrets, and Silence,* p. 209; H. D., *Tribute to Freud* (Oxford: Carcanet, 1971), pp. 50–54.

14. Woolf, *A Room of One's Own,* p. 126.

15. Gracia Clark, "The Beguines: A Mediaeval Women's Community," *Quest: A Feminist Quarterly* 1, no. 4 (1975): 73–80.

16. See Denise Paulmé, ed., *Women of Tropical Africa* (Berkeley: University of California Press, 1963), pp. 7, 266–267. Some of these sororities are described as "a kind of defensive syndicate against the male element," their aims being "to offer concerted resistance to an oppressive patriarchate," "independence in relation to one's husband and with regard to motherhood,

mutual aid, satisfaction of personal revenge." See also Audre Lorde, "Scratching the Surface: Some Notes on Barriers to Women and Loving," in *Sister Outsider,* pp. 45–52; Marjorie Topley, "Marriage Resistance in Rural Kwangtung," in *Women in Chinese Society,* ed. M. Wolf and R. Witke (Stanford, Calif.: Stanford University Press, 1978), pp. 67–89; Agnes Smedley, *Portraits of Chinese Women in Revolution,* ed. J. MacKinnon and S. MacKinnon (Old Westbury, N.Y.: Feminist Press, 1976), pp. 103–110.

17. See Rosalind Petchesky, "Dissolving the Hyphen: A Report on Marxist-Feminist Groups 1–5," in *Capitalist Patriarchy and the Case for Socialist Feminism,* ed. Zillah Eisenstein (New York: Monthly Review Press, 1979), p. 387.

18. [A.R., 1986: See Angela Davis, *Women, Race and Class* (New York: Random House, 1981), p. 102; Orlando Patterson, *Slavery and Social Death: A Comparative Study* (Cambridge: Harvard University Press, 1982), p. 133.]

19. Diana Russell and Nichole van de Ven, eds., *Proceedings of the International Tribunal of Crimes against Women* (Millbrae, Calif.: Les Femmes, 1976), pp. 42–43, 56–57.

20. I am indebted to Jonathan Katz's *Gay American History (op. cit.)* for bringing to my attention Hansberry's letters to *The Ladder* and to Barbara Grier for supplying me with copies of relevant pages from *The Ladder,* quoted here by permission of Barbara Grier. See also the reprinted series of *The Ladder,* ed. Jonathan Katz *et al.* (New York: Arno, 1975), and Deirdre Carmody, "Letters by Eleanor Roosevelt Detail Friendship with Lorena Hickok," *New York Times* (October 21, 1979).

21. Meridel LeSueur, *The Girl* (Cambridge, Mass.: West End Press, 1978), pp. 10–11. LeSueur describes, in an afterword, how this book was drawn from the writings and oral narrations of women in the Workers Alliance who met as a writers' group during the Depression.

22. *Ibid.,* p. 20.

23. *Ibid.,* pp. 53–54.

24. *Ibid.,* p. 55.

25. Toni Morrison, *Sula* (New York: Bantam, 1973), pp. 103–104, 149. I am indebted to Lorraine Bethel's essay "'This Infinity of Conscious Pain': Zora Neale Hurston and the Black Female Literary Tradition," in *All the Women Are White, All the Blacks Are Men, but Some of Us Are Brave: Black Women's Studies,* ed. Gloria T. Hull, Patricia Bell Scott, and Barbara Smith (Old Westbury, N.Y.: Feminist Press, 1982).

26. See Maureen Brady and Judith McDaniel, "Lesbians in the Mainstream: The Image of Lesbians in Recent Commercial Fiction," *Conditions* 6 (1979): 82–105.

27. See Russell and van de Ven, p. 40: "Few heterosexual women realize their lack of free choice about their sexuality, and few realize how and why compulsory heterosexuality is also a crime against them."

28. Bethel, "'This Infinity of Conscious Pain,'" *op. cit.*

29. Dinnerstein, the most recent writer to quote this passages, adds ominously: "But what has to be added to her account is that these 'women enlaced' are sheltering each other not just from what men want to do to them, but also from what they want to do to each other" (Dorothy Dinnerstein, *The Mermaid and the Minotaur: Sexual Arrangements and Human Malaise* (New York: Harper & Row, 1976), p. 103). The fact is, however, that

woman-to-woman violence is a minute grain in the universe of male-against-female violence perpetuated and rationalized in every social institution.

30. Conversations with Blanche W. Cook, New York City, March 1979.

 62

The Unhappy Marriage of Marxism and Feminism: Towards a More Progressive Union

HEIDI I. HARTMANN

HEIDI I. HARTMANN United States 1945– . Economist. Founding Director of the Institute for Women's Policy Research (1987). *Capitalism and Women's Work in the Home, 1900–1930* (1976), *Women's Work, Men's Work: Sex Segregation on the Job* (1981), *Comparable Worth: New Directions for Research* (1985).

The "marriage" of marxism and feminism has been like the marriage of husband and wife depicted in English common law: marxism and feminism are one, and that one is marxism.[1] Recent attempts to integrate marxism and feminism are unsatisfactory to us as feminists because they subsume the feminist struggle into the "larger" struggle against capital. To continue our simile further, either we need a healthier marriage or we need a divorce.

The inequalities in this marriage, like most social phenomena, are no accident. Many marxists typically argue that feminism is at best less important than class conflict and at worst divisive of the working class. This political stance produces an analysis that absorbs feminism into the class struggle. Moreover, the analytic power of marxism with respect to capital has obscured its limitations with respect to sexism. We will argue here that while marxist analysis provides essential insight into the laws of historical development, and those of capital in particular, the categories of marxism are sex-blind. Only a specifically feminist analysis reveals the systemic character of relations between men and women.

Yet feminist analysis by itself is inadequate because it has been blind to history and insufficiently materialist. Both marxist analysis, particularly its historical and materialist method, and feminist analysis, especially the identification of patriarchy as a social and historical structure, must be drawn upon if we are to understand the development of western capitalist societies and the predicament of women within them. In this essay we suggest a new direction for marxist feminist analysis.

. . .

I. MARXISM AND THE WOMAN QUESTION

The woman question has never been the "feminist question." The feminist question is directed at the causes of sexual inequality between women and men, of male dominance over women. Most marxist analyses of women's position take as their question the relationship of women to the economic system, rather than that of women to men, apparently assuming the latter will be explained in their discussion of the former. Marxist analysis of the woman question has taken three main forms. All see women's oppression in our connection (or lack of it) to production. Defining women as part of the working class, these analyses consistently subsume women's relation to men under worker's relation to capital. First, early marxists, including Marx, Engels, Kautsky, and Lenin, saw capitalism drawing all women into the wage labor force, and saw this process destroying the sexual division of labor. Second, contemporary marxists have incorporated women into an analysis of everyday life in capitalism. In this view, all aspects of our lives are seen to reproduce the capitalist system and we are all workers in the system. And third, marxist feminists have focussed on housework and its relation to capital, some arguing that housework produces surplus value and that houseworkers work directly for capitalists. . . .

. . .

While the approach of the early marxists ignored housework and stressed women's labor force participation, the two more recent approaches emphasize housework to such an extent they ignore women's current role in the labor market. Nevertheless, all three attempt to include women in the category working class and to understand women's oppression as another aspect of class oppression. In doing so all give short shrift to the object of feminist analysis, the relations between women and men. While our "problems" have been elegantly analyzed, they have been misunderstood. The focus of marxist analysis has been class relations; the object of marxist analysis has been understanding the laws of motion of capitalist society. While we believe marxist methodology *can* be used to formulate feminist strategy, these marxist feminist approaches discussed above clearly do not do so; their marxism clearly dominates their feminism.

· · ·

Marxism enables us to understand many aspects of capitalist societies: the structure of production, the generation of a particular occupational structure, and the nature of the dominant ideology. Marx's theory of the development of capitalism is a theory of the development of "empty places." Marx predicted, for example, the growth of the proletariat and the demise of the petit bourgeoisie. More precisely and in more detail, Braverman among others has explained the creation of the "places" clerical worker and service worker in advanced capitalist societies.[2] Just as capital creates these places indifferent to the individuals who fill them, the categories of marxist analysis, class, reserve army of labor, wage-laborer, do not explain why particular people fill particular places. They give no clues about why *women* are subordinate to *men* inside and outside the family and why it is not the other way around. *Marxist categories, like capital itself, are sex-blind.* The categories of marxism cannot tell us who will fill the empty places. Marxist analysis of the woman question has suffered from this basic problem.

· · ·

II. RADICAL FEMINISM AND PATRIARCHY

The great thrust of radical feminist writing has been directed to the documentation of the slogan "the personal is political." Women's discontent, radical feminists argued, is not the neurotic lament of the maladjusted, but a response to a social structure in which women are systematically dominated, exploited, and oppressed. Women's inferior position in the labor market, the male-centered emotional structure of middle class marriage, the use of

women in advertising, the so-called understanding of women's psyche as neurotic—popularized by academic and clinical psychology—aspect after aspect of women's lives in advanced capitalist society was researched and analyzed. . . .

· · ·

Radical feminist analysis has greatest strength in its insights into the present. Its greatest weakness is a focus on the psychological, which blinds it to history. The reason for this lies not only in radical feminist method, but also in the nature of patriarchy itself, for patriarchy is a strikingly resilient form of social organization. Radical feminists use patriarchy to refer to a social system characterized by male domination over women. Kate Millett's definition is classic:

> our society . . . is a patriarchy. The fact is evident at once if one recalls that the military, industry, technology, universities, science, political offices, finances—in short, every avenue of power within the society, including the coercive force of the police, is entirely in male hands.[3]

This radical feminist definition of patriarchy applies to most societies we know of and cannot distinguish among them. The use of history by radical feminists is typically limited to providing examples of the existence of patriarchy in all times and places.[4] For both marxist and mainstream social scientists before the women's movement, patriarchy referred to a system of relations between men, which formed the political and economic outlines of feudal and some pre-feudal societies, in which hierarchy followed ascribed characteristics. Capitalist societies are understood as meritocratic, bureaucratic, and impersonal by bourgeois social scientists; marxists see capitalist societies as systems of class domination. For both kinds of social scientists neither the historical patriarchal societies nor today's western capitalist societies are understood as systems of relations between men that enable them to dominate women.

Towards a Definition of Patriarchy

We can usually define patriarchy as a set of social relations between men, which have a material base, and which, though hierarchical, establish or create interdependence and solidarity among men that enable them to dominate women. Though patri-archy is hierarchical and men of different classes, races, or ethnic groups have different places in the patriarchy, they also are united in their shared rela-tionship of dominance over their women; they are dependent on each other to maintain that domina-tion. Hierarchies "work" at least in part because they create vested interests in the status quo. Those at the higher levels can "buy off" those at the lower levels by offering them power over those still lower. In the hierarchy of patriarchy, all men, whatever their rank in the patriarchy, are bought off by being able to control at least some women. There is some evidence to suggest that when patriarchy was first institutionalized in state societies, the ascending rulers literally made men the heads of their families (enforcing their control over their wives and chil-dren) in exchange for the men's ceding some of their tribal resources to the new rulers.[5] Men are dependent on one another (despite their hierarchi-cal ordering) to maintain their control over women.

The material base upon which patriarchy rests lies most fundamentally in men's control over women's labor power. Men maintain this control by excluding women from access to some essential productive resources (in capitalist societies, for example, jobs that pay living wages) and by restrict-ing women's sexuality. Monogamous heterosexual marriage is one relatively recent and efficient form that seems to allow men to control both these areas. Controlling women's access to resources and their sexuality, in turn, allows men to control women's labor power, both for the purpose of serving men in many personal and sexual ways and for the purpose of rearing children. The services women render men, and which exonerate men from having to per-form many unpleasant tasks (like cleaning toilets) occur outside as well as inside the family setting. Examples outside the family include the harassment of women workers and students by male bosses and professors as well as the common use of secretaries to run personal errands, make coffee, and provide "sexy" surroundings. Rearing children, whether or not the children's labor power is of immediate bene-fit to their fathers, is nevertheless a crucial task in perpetuating patriarchy as a system. Just as class society must be reproduced by schools, work places, consumption norms, etc., so must patriarchal social

relations. In our society children are generally reared by women at home, women socially defined and recognized as inferior to men, while men appear in the domestic picture only rarely. Children raised in this way generally learn their places in the gender hierarchy well. Central to this process, however, are the areas outside the home where patriarchal behav-iors are taught and the inferior position of women enforced and reinforced: churches, schools, sports, clubs, unions, armies, factories, offices, health cen-ters, the media, etc.

The material base of patriarchy, then, does not rest solely on childrearing in the family, but on all the social structures that enable men to control women's labor. The aspects of social structures that perpetuate patriarchy are theoretically identifiable, hence separable from their other aspects. Gayle Rubin has increased our ability to identify the patriarchal element of these social structures enor-mously by identifying "sex/gender systems":

> a "sex/gender system" is the set of arrangements by which a society transforms biological sexuality into products of human activity, and in which these transformed sexual needs are satisfied.[6]

We are born female and male, biological sexes, but we are created woman and man, socially recognized genders. *How* we are so created is that second aspect of the *mode* of production of which Engels spoke, "the production of human beings them-selves, the propagation of the species."

How people propagate the species is socially determined. If, biologically, people are sexually polymorphous, and society were organized in such a way that all forms of sexual expression were equally permissible, production would result only from some sexual encounters, the heterosexual ones. The strict division of labor by sex, a social invention common to all known societies, creates two very separate genders and a need for men and women to get together for economic reasons. It thus helps to direct their sexual needs toward het-erosexual fulfillment, and helps to ensure biological reproduction. In more imaginative societies, biolog-ical reproduction might be ensured by other tech-niques, but the division of labor by sex appears to be the universal solution to date. Although it is the-oretically possible that a sexual division of labor not imply inequality between the sexes, in most known societies, the socially acceptable division of labor by sex is one which accords lower status to women's work. The sexual division of labor is also the underpinning of sexual subcultures in which men and women experience life differently; it is the material base of male power which is exercised (in our society) not just in not doing housework and in securing superior employment, but psychologically as well.

How people meet their sexual needs, how they reproduce, how they inculcate social norms in new generations, how they learn gender, how it feels to be a man or a woman—all occur in the realm Rubin labels the sex/gender system. Rubin emphasizes the influence of kinship (which tells you with whom you can satisfy sexual needs) and the development of gender specific personalities via childrearing and the "oedipal machine." In addition, however, we can use the concept of the sex/gender system to examine all other social institutions for the roles they play in defining and reinforcing gender hierarchies. Rubin notes that theoretically a sex/gender system could be female dominant, male dominant, or egalitarian, but declines to label various known sex/gender systems or to periodize history accordingly. We choose to label our present sex/gender system patriarchy, because it appropriately captures the notion of hierarchy and male dominance which we see as central to the present system.

Economic production (what marxists are used to referring to as *the* mode of production) and the production of people in the sex/gender sphere both determine "the social organization under which the people of a particular historical epoch and a particular country live," according to Engels. The whole of society, then, can be understood by looking at both these types of production and reproduction, people and things.[7] There is no such thing as "pure capitalism," nor does "pure patriarchy" exist, for they must of necessity coexist. What exists is patriarchal capitalism, or patriarchal feudalism, or egalitarian hunting/gathering societies, or matriarchal horticultural societies, or patriarchal horticultural societies, and so on. There appears to be no necessary connection between *changes* in the one aspect of production and changes in the other. A society could undergo transition from capitalism to socialism,

for example, and remain patriarchal. Common sense, history, and our experience tell us, however, that these two aspects of production are so closely intertwined that change in one ordinarily creates movement, tension, or contradiction in the other.

Racial hierarchies can also be understood in this context. Further elaboration may be possible along the lines of defining color/race systems, arenas of social life that take biological color and turn it into a social category, race. Racial hierarchies, like gender hierarchies, are aspects of our social organization, of how people are produced and reproduced. They are not fundamentally ideological; they constitute that second aspect of our mode of production, the production and reproduction of people. It might be most accurate then to refer to our societies not as, for example, simply capitalist, but as patriarchal capitalist white supremacist. In Part III below, we illustrate one case of capitalism adapting to and making use of racial orders and several examples of the interrelations between capitalism and patriarchy.

Capitalist development creates the places for a hierarchy of workers, but traditional marxist categories cannot tell us who will fill which places. Gender and racial hierarchies determine who fills the empty places. *Patriarchy is not simply hierarchical organization*, but hierarchy in which *particular* people fill *particular* places. It is in studying patriarchy that we learn why it is women who are dominated and how. While we believe that most known societies have been patriarchal, we do not view patriarchy as a universal, unchanging phenomenon. Rather patriarchy, the set of interrelations among men that allow men to dominate women, has changed in form and intensity over time. It is crucial that the hierarchy among men, and their differential access to patriarchal benefits, be examined. Surely, class, race, nationality, and even marital status and sexual orientation, as well as the obvious age, come into play here. And women of different class, race, national, marital status, or sexual orientation groups are subjected to different degrees of patriarchal power. Women may themselves exercise class, race, or national power, or even patriarchal power (through their family connections) over men lower in the patriarchal hierarchy than their own male kin.

To recapitulate, we define patriarchy as a set of social relations which has a material base and in which there are hierarchical relations between men and solidarity among them which enable them in turn to dominate women. The material base of patriarchy is men's control over women's labor power. That control is maintained by excluding women from access to necessary economically productive resources and by restricting women's sexuality. Men exercise their control in receiving personal service work from women, in not having to do housework or rear children, in having access to women's bodies for sex, and in feeling powerful and being powerful. The crucial elements of patriarchy as we *currently* experience them are: heterosexual marriage (and consequent homophobia), female childrearing and housework, women's economic dependence on men (enforced by arrangements in the labor market), the state, and numerous institutions based on social relations among men—clubs, sports, unions, professions, universities, churches, corporations and armies. All of these elements need to be examined if we are to understand patriarchal capitalism.

Both hierarchy and interdependence among men and the subordination of women are *integral* to the functioning of our society; that is, these relationships are *systemic*. We leave aside the question of the creation of these relations and ask, can we recognize patriarchal relations in capitalist societies? Within capitalist societies we must discover those same bonds between men which both bourgeois and marxist social scientists claim no longer exist or are, at the most, unimportant leftovers. Can we understand how these relations among men are perpetuated in capitalist societies? Can we identify ways in which patriarchy has shaped the course of capitalist development?

III. THE PARTNERSHIP OF PATRIARCHY AND CAPITAL

How are we to recognize patriarchal social relations in capitalist societies? It appears as if each woman is oppressed by her own man alone; her oppression seems a private affair. Relationships among men and among families seem equally fragmented. It is hard to recognize relationships among men, and between men and women, as *systematically* patriarchal.

We argue, however, that patriarchy as a system of relations between men and women exists in capitalism, and that in capitalist societies a healthy and strong partnership exists between patriarchy and capital. Yet if one begins with the concept of patriarchy and an understanding of the capitalist mode of production, one recognizes immediately that the partnership of patriarchy and capital was not inevitable; men and capitalists often have conflicting interests, particularly over the use of women's labor power. Here is one way in which this conflict might manifest itself: the vast majority of men might want their women at home to personally service them. A smaller number of men, who are capitalists, might want most women (not their own) to work in the wage labor market. In examining the tensions of this conflict over women's labor power historically, we will be able to identify the material base of patriarchal relations in capitalist societies, as well as the basis for the partnership between capital and patriarchy.

Industrialization and the Development of Family Wages

Marxists made quite logical inferences from a selection of the social phenomena they witnessed in the nineteenth century. But marxists ultimately underestimated the strength of preexisting patriarchal social forces with which fledgling capital had to contend and the need for capital to adjust to these forces. The industrial revolution was drawing all people into the labor force, including women and children; in fact, the first factories used child and female labor almost exclusively. That women and children could earn wages separately from men both undermined authority relations (as discussed in Part I above) and kept wages low for everyone. . . .

. . .

Male workers resisted the wholesale entrance of women and children into the labor force, and sought to exclude them from union membership and the labor force as well. In 1846 the *Ten-Hours' Advocate* stated:

> It is needless for us to say, that all attempts to improve the morals and physical condition of female factory workers will be abortive, unless their hours are materially reduced. Indeed we may go so far as to say, that married females would be much

better occupied in performing the domestic duties of the household, than following the never-tiring motion of machinery. We therefore hope the day is not distant, when the husband will be able to provide for his wife and family, without sending the former to endure the drudgery of a cotton mill.[8]

In the United States in 1854 the National Typographical Union resolved not to "encourage by its act the employment of female compositors." Male unionists did not want to afford union protection to women workers; they tried to exclude them instead. In 1879 Adolph Strasser, president of the Cigarmakers International Union, said: "We cannot drive the females out of the trade, but we can restrict their daily quota of labor through factory laws."[9]

While the problem of cheap competition could have been solved by organizing the wage earning of women and youths, the problem of disrupted family life could not be. Men reserved union protection for men and argued for protective labor laws for women and children. Protective labor laws, while they may have ameliorated some of the worst abuses of female and child labor, also limited the participation of adult women in many "male" jobs. Men sought to keep high wage jobs for themselves and to raise male wages generally. They argued for wages sufficient for their wage labor alone to support their families. This "family wage" system gradually came to be the norm for stable working-class families at the end of the nineteenth century and the beginning of the twentieth. Several observers have declared the non-wage-working wife to be part of the standard of living of male workers. Instead of fighting for equal wages for men and women, male workers sought the family wage, wanting to retain their wives' services at home. In the absence of patriarchy a unified working class might have confronted capitalism, but patriarchal social relations divided the working class, allowing one part (men) to be bought off at the expense of the other (women). Both the hierarchy between men and the solidarity among them were crucial in this process of resolution. Family wages may be understood as a resolution of the conflict over women's labor power which was occurring between patriarchal and capitalist interests at that time.

. . .

While the family wage shows that capitalism adjusts to patriarchy, the changing status of children shows that patriarchy adjusts to capital. Children, like women, came to be excluded from wage labor. As children's ability to earn money declined, their legal relationship to their parents changed. At the beginning of the industrial era in the United States, fulfilling children's need for their fathers was thought to be crucial, even primary, to their happy development; fathers had legal priority in cases of contested custody. As children's ability to contribute to the economic well-being of the family declined, mothers came increasingly to be viewed as crucial to the happy development of their children, and gained legal priority in cases of contested custody.[10] Here, patriarchy adapted to the changing economic role of children: when children were productive, men claimed them; as children became unproductive, they were given to women.

. . .

The Family and the Family Wage Today

We argued above that with respect to capitalism and patriarchy, the adaptation, or mutual accommodation, took the form of the development of the family wage in the early twentieth century. The family wage cemented the partnership between patriarchy and capital. Despite women's increased labor force participation, particularly rapid since World War II, the family wage is still, we argue, the cornerstone of the present sexual division of labor—in which women are primarily responsible for housework and men primarily for wage work. Women's lower wages in the labor market (combined with the need for children to be reared by someone) assure the continued existence of the family as a necessary income pooling unit. The family, supported by the family wage, thus allows the control of women's labor by men both within and without the family.

Though women's increased wage work may cause stress for the family (similar to the stress Kautsky and Engels noted in the nineteenth century), it would be wrong to think that as a consequence, the concepts and the realities of the family and of the sexual division of labor will soon disappear. The sexual division of labor reappears in the labor market, where women work at women's jobs, often the very jobs they used to do only at home—food preparation and service, cleaning of all kinds, caring for people, and so on. As these jobs are low-status and low-paying, patriarchal relations remain intact, though their material base shifts somewhat from the family to the wage differential, from family-based to industrially-based patriarchy.[11]

Industrially based patriarchal relations are enforced in a variety of ways. Union contracts which specify lower wages, lesser benefits, and fewer advancement opportunities for women are not just atavistic hangovers—a case of sexist attitudes or male supremacist ideology—they maintain the material base of the patriarchal system. While some would go so far as to argue that patriarchy is already absent from the family (see, for example, Stewart Ewen, *Captains of Consciousness*)[12] we would not. Although the terms of the compromise between capital and patriarchy are changing as additional tasks formerly located in the family are capitalized, and the location of the deployment of women's labor power shifts, it is nevertheless true, as we have argued above, that the wage differential caused by extreme job segregation in the labor market reinforces the family, and, with it, the domestic division of labor, by encouraging women to marry. The "ideal" of the family wage—that a man can earn enough to support an entire family—may be giving way to a new ideal that both men and women contribute through wage earning to the cash income of the family. The wage differential, then, will become increasingly necessary in perpetuating patriarchy, the male control of women's labor power. The wage differential will aid in *defining* women's work as secondary to men's at the same time it necessitates women's actual continued economic dependence on men. The sexual division of labor in the labor market and elsewhere should be understood as a manifestation of patriarchy which serves to perpetuate it.

Many people have argued that though the partnership between capital and patriarchy exists now, it may *in the long run* prove intolerable to capitalism; capital may eventually destroy both familial relations and patriarchy. The argument proceeds logically that capitalist social relations (of which the family is not an example) tend to become universalized, that women will become increasingly able to earn money and will increasingly refuse to submit to subordination in the family, and that since the family is oppressive particularly to women and children, it will collapse as soon as people can support themselves outside it.

We do not think that the patriarchal relations embodied in the family can be destroyed so easily by capital, and we see little evidence that the family system is presently disintegrating. Although the increasing labor force participation of women has made divorce more feasible, the incentives to divorce are not overwhelming for women. Women's wages allow very few women to support themselves and their children independently and adequately. . . .

The argument that capital destroys the family also overlooks the social forces which make family life appealing. Despite critiques of nuclear families as psychologically destructive, in a competitive society the family still meets real needs for many people. This is true not only of long-term monogamy, but even more so for raising children. Single parents bear both financial and psychic burdens. For working class women, in particular, these burdens make the "independence" of labor force participation illusory. Single parent families have recently been seen by policy analysts as transitional family formations which become two-parent families upon remarriage.[13]

It could be that the effects of women's increasing labor force participation are found in a declining sexual division of labor within the family, rather than in more frequent divorce, but evidence for this is also lacking. Statistics on who does housework, even in families with wage-earning wives, show little change in recent years; women still do most of it.[14] The double day is a reality for wage-working women. This is hardly surprising since the sexual division of labor outside the family, in the labor market, keeps women financially dependent on men—even when they earn a wage themselves. The future of patriarchy does not, however, rest solely on the future of familial relations. For patriarchy, like capital, can be surprisingly flexible and adaptable.

Whether or not the patriarchal division of labor, inside the family and elsewhere, is "ultimately" intolerable to capital, it is shaping capitalism now. . . . [P]atriarchy both legitimates capitalist control and delegitimates certain forms of struggle against capital.

. . .

IV. TOWARDS A MORE PROGRESSIVE UNION

Many problems remain for us to explore. Patriarchy as we have used it here remains more a descriptive term than an analytical one. If we think marxism alone inadequate, and radical feminism itself insufficient, then we need to develop new categories. What makes our task a difficult one is that the same features, such as the division of labor, often reinforce both patriarchy and capitalism, and in a thoroughly patriarchal capitalist society, it is hard to isolate the mechanisms of patriarchy. Nevertheless, this is what we must do. We have pointed to some starting places: looking at who benefits from women's labor power, uncovering the material base of patriarchy, investigating the mechanisms of hierarchy and solidarity among men. The questions we must ask are endless.

Can we speak of the laws of motion of a patriarchal system? How does patriarchy generate feminist struggle? What kinds of sexual politics and struggle between the sexes can we see in societies other than advanced capitalist ones? What are the contradictions of the patriarchal system and what is their relation to the contradictions of capitalism? We know that patriarchal relations gave rise to the feminist movement, and that capital generates class struggle—but how has the relation of feminism to class struggle been played out in historical contexts? In this section we attempt to provide an answer to this last question.

Feminism and the Class Struggle

Historically and in the present, the relation of feminism and class struggle has been either that of fully separate paths ("bourgeois" feminism on one hand, class struggle on the other), or, within the left, the dominance of feminism by marxism. With respect to the latter, this has been a consequence both of the analytic power of marxism, and of the power of men within the left. These have produced both open struggles on the left, and a contradictory position for marxist feminists.

Most feminists who also see themselves as radicals (antisystem, anti-capitalist, anti-imperialist, socialist, communist, marxist, whatever) agree that the radical wing of the women's movement has lost momentum while the liberal sector seems to have

seized the time and forged ahead. Our movement is no longer in that exciting, energetic period when no matter what we did, it worked—to raise consciousness, to bring more women (more even than could be easily incorporated) into the movement, to increase the visibility of women's issues in the society, often in ways fundamentally challenging to both the capitalist and patriarchal relations in society. Now we sense parts of the movement are being coopted and "feminism" is being used against women—for example, in court cases when judges argue that women coming out of long-term marriages in which they were housewives don't need alimony because we all know women are liberated now. The failure to date to secure the passage of the Equal Rights Amendment in the United States indicates the presence of legitimate fears among many women that feminism will continue to be used against women, and it indicates a real need for us to reassess our movement, to analyze why it has been coopted in this way. It is logical for us to turn to marxism for help in that reassessment because it is a developed theory of social change. Marxist theory is well developed compared to feminist theory, and in our attempt to use it, we have sometimes been sidetracked from feminist objectives.

The left has always been ambivalent about the women's movement, often viewing it as dangerous to the cause of socialist revolution. When left women espouse feminism, it may be personally threatening to left men. And of course many left organizations benefit from the labor of women. Therefore, many left analyses (both in progressive and traditional forms) are self-serving, both theoretically and politically. They seek to influence women to abandon attempts to develop an independent understanding of women's situation and to adopt the "left's" analyses of the situation. As for our response to this pressure, it is natural that, as we ourselves have turned to marxist analysis, we would try to join the "fraternity" using this paradigm, and we may end up trying to justify our struggle to the fraternity rather than trying to analyze the situation of women to improve our political practice. Finally, many marxists are satisfied with the traditional marxist analysis of the woman question. They see class as the correct framework with which to understand women's position. Women should be understood as part of the working class; the working class's struggle against capitalism should take precedence over any conflict between men and women. Sex conflict must not be allowed to interfere with class solidarity.

· · ·

The struggle against capital and patriarchy cannot be successful if the study and practice of the issues of feminism are abandoned. A struggle aimed only at capitalist relations of oppression will fail, since their underlying supports in patriarchal relations of oppression will be overlooked. And the analysis of patriarchy is essential to a definition of the kind of socialism useful to women. While men and women share a need to overthrow capitalism, they retain interests particular to their gender group. It is not clear—from our sketch, from history, or from male socialists—that the socialism being struggled for is the same for both men and women. For a humane socialism would require not only consensus on what the new society should look like and what a healthy person should look like, but more concretely, it would require that men relinquish their privilege.

As women we must not allow ourselves to be talked out of the urgency and importance of our tasks, as we have so many times in the past. We must fight the attempted coercion, both subtle and not so subtle, to abandon feminist objectives.

This suggests two strategic considerations. First, a struggle to establish socialism must be a struggle in which groups with different interests form an alliance. Women should not trust men to liberate them after the revolution, in part, because there is no reason to think they would know how; in part, because there is no necessity for them to do so. In fact their immediate self-interest lies in our continued oppression. Instead we must have our own organizations and our own power base. Second, we think the sexual division of labor within capitalism has given women a practice in which we have learned to understand what human interdependence and needs are. While men have long struggled *against* capital, women know what to struggle *for*.[15] As a general rule, men's position in patriarchy and capitalism prevents them from recognizing both human needs for nurturance, sharing, and growth, and the potential for meeting those needs in a nonhierarchical, nonpatriarchal society. But even if we raise their consciousness, they might assess the potential gains against the potential losses and choose the status quo. Men have more to lose than their chains.

As feminist socialists, we must organize a practice which addresses both the struggle against patriarchy and the struggle against capitalism. We must insist that the society we want to create is a society in which recognition of interdependence is liberation rather than shame, nurturance is a universal, not an oppressive practice, and in which women do not continue to support the false as well as the concrete freedoms of men.

[1981]

NOTES

1. Often paraphrased as "the husband and wife are one and that one is the husband," English law held that "by marriage, the husband and wife are one person in law; that is, the very being or legal existence of the woman is suspended during the marriage, or at least is incorporated and consolidated into that of the Husband," I. Blackstone, *Commentaries*, 1965, pp. 442–445, cited in Kenneth M. Davidson, Ruth B. Ginsburg, and Herma H. Kay, *Sex Based Discrimination* (St. Paul, Minn.: West Publishing Co., 1974), p. 117.

2. Harry Braverman, *Labor and Monopoly Capital* (New York: Monthly Review Press, 1975).

3. Kate Millet, *Sexual Politics* (New York: Avon Books, 1971), p. 25.

4. One example of this type of radical feminist history is Susan Brownmiller's *Against Our Will: Men, Women, and Rape* (New York: Simon & Schuster, 1975).

5. See Viana Muller, "The Formation of the State and the Oppression of Women: Some Theoretical Considerations and a Case Study in England and Wales," *Review of Radical Political Economy*, Vol. 9, no. 3 (Fall 1977), pp. 7–21.

6. Gayle Rubin, "The Traffic in Women," in *Anthropology of Women*, ed. Reiter, p. 159.

7. Himmelweit and Mohun point out that both aspects of production (people and things) are logically necessary to describe a mode of production because by definition a mode of production must be capable of reproducing itself. Either aspect alone is not self-sufficient. To put it simply, the production of things requires people, and the production of people requires things. Marx, though recognizing capitalism's need for people, did not concern himself with how they were produced or what the connections between the two aspects of production were. See Himmelweit and Mohun, "Domestic Labour and Capital." *Cambridge Journal of Economics*, Vol. 1, no. 1 (March 1977), pp. 15–31.

8. Cited in Neil Smelser, *Social Change and the Industrial Revolution* (Chicago: University of Chicago Press, 1959), p. 301.

9. These examples are from Heidi I. Hartmann, "Capitalism, Patriarchy, and Job Segregation by Sex," *Signs:*

Journal of Women in Culture and Society, Vol. 1, no. 3, pt. 2 (Spring 1976), pp. 162–163.

10. Carol Brown, "Patriarchal Capitalism and the Female-Headed Family," *Social Scientist* (India); no. 40–41 (November/December 1975), pp. 28–39.

11. Carol Brown, in "Patriarchal Capitalism," argues, for example, that we are moving from a "family-based" to "industrially-based" patriarchy within capitalism.

12. Stewart Ewen, *Captains of Consciousness* (New York: Random House, 1976).

13. Heather L. Ross and Isabel B. Sawhill, *Time of Transition: The Growth of Families Headed by Women* (Washington, D.C.: The Urban Institute, 1975).

14. See Kathryn E. Walker and Margaret E. Woods, *Time Use: A Measure of Household Production of Family Goods and Services* (Washington, D.C.: American Home Economics Association, 1976; and Heidi I. Hartmann, "The Family as the Locus of Gender, Class, and Political Struggle: The Example of Housework," *Signs: Journal of Women in Culture and Society*, Vol. 6, no. 3 (Spring 1981).

15. Lise Vogel, "The Earthly Family." *Radical America*, Vol. 7, no. 4–5 (July/October 1973), pp. 9–50.

 63

Asian Pacific American Women and Feminism

MITSUYE YAMADA

MITSUYE YAMADA Japan. 1923– . Writer. Poet. Academic. Lecturer. Lives and works in the United States. *Camp Notes and Other Poems* (1976), *Desert Run: Poems and Stories* (1988).

Most of the Asian Pacific American women I know agree that we need to make ourselves more visible by speaking out on the condition of our sex and race and on certain political issues which concern us. Some of us feel that visibility through the feminist perspective is the only logical step for us. However, this path is fraught with problems which we are unable to solve among us, because in order to do so, we need the help and cooperation of the white feminist leaders, the women who coordinate programs, direct women's buildings, and edit women's publications throughout the country. Women's organizations tell us they would like to have us "join" them and give them "input." These are the better ones; at least they know we exist and feel we might possibly have something to say of interest to them, but every time I read or speak to a group of people about the condition of my life as an Asian Pacific woman, it is as if I had never spoken before, as if I were speaking to a brand new audience of people who had never known an Asian Pacific woman who is other than the passive, sweet, etc., stereotype of the "Oriental" woman.

When Third World women are asked to speak representing our racial or ethnic group, we are expected to move, charm or entertain, but not to educate in ways that are threatening to our audiences. We speak to audiences that sift out those parts of our speech (if what we say does not fit the image they have of us), come up to shake our hands with "That was lovely my dear, just lovely," and go home with the same mind set they came in with. No matter what we say or do, the stereotype still hangs on. I am weary of starting from scratch each time I speak or write, as if there were no history behind us, of hearing that among the women of color, Asian women are the least political, or the least oppressed, or the most polite. It is too bad not many people remember that one of the two persons in Seattle who stood up to contest the constitutionality of the Evacuation Order in 1942 was a young Japanese American woman. As individuals and in groups, we Asian Pacific women have been (more intensively than ever in the past few years) active in community affairs and speaking and writing about our activities. From the highly political writings published in *Asian Women* in 1971 (incisive and trenchant articles, poems and articles), to more recent voices from the Basement Workshop in New York to Unbound Feet in San Francisco, as well as those Asian Pacific women showcased at the Asian Pacific Women's Conferences in New York, Hawaii and California this year, these all tell us we *have* been active and vocal. And yet, we continue to hear, "Asian women are of course traditionally not attuned to being political," as if most other women are; or that Asian women are too happily bound to their traditional roles as mothers and wives, as if the same cannot be said of a great number of white American women among us.

When I read in *Plexus* recently that at a workshop for Third World women in San Francisco, Cherríe Moraga exploded with "What each of us needs to do about what we don't know is to go look for it," I felt like standing up and cheering her. She was speaking at the Women's Building to a group of white sisters who were saying, in essence, "it is *your* responsibility as Third World women to teach *us*." If the majority culture knows so little about us, it must be *our* problem, they seem to be telling us; the burden of teaching is on us. I do not want to be unfair; I know individual women and some women's groups that have taken on the responsibility of teaching themselves through reaching out to women of color, but such gestures by the majority of women's groups are still tentatively made because of the sometimes touchy reaction of women who are always being asked to be "tokens" at readings and workshops.

Earlier this year, when a group of Asian Pacific American women gathered together in San Francisco poet Nellie Wong's home to talk about feminism, I was struck by our general agreement on the subject of feminism *as an ideal*. We all believed in equality for women. We agreed that it is important for each of us to know what it means to be a woman in our society, to know the historical and psychological forces that have shaped and are shaping our thoughts, which in turn determine the directions of our lives. We agreed that feminism means a commitment to making changes in our own lives and a conviction that as women we have the equipment to do so. One by one, as we sat around the table and talked (we women of all ages ranging from our early twenties to the mid-fifties, single and married, mothers and lovers, straight women and lesbians), we knew what it was we wanted out of feminism, and what it was supposed to mean to us. For women to achieve equality in our society, we agreed, we must continue to work for a common goal.

But there was a feeling of disappointment in that living room toward the women's movement as it stands today. One young woman said she had made an effort to join some women's groups with high expectations but came away disillusioned because these groups were not receptive to the issues that were important to her as an Asian woman. Women in these groups, were, she said "into pushing their own issues" and were no different from the other organizations that imposed opinions and goals on their members rather than having them shaped by the needs of the members in the organizations. Some of the other women present said that they felt the women's organizations with feminist goals are still "a middle-class women's thing." This pervasive feeling of mistrust toward the women in the movement is fairly representative of a large group of women who live in the psychological place we now call Asian Pacific America. A movement that fights sexism in the social structure must deal with racism, and we had hoped the leaders in the women's movement would be able to see the parallels in the lives of the women of color and themselves, and would "join" *us* in our struggle and give *us* "input."

It should not be difficult to see that Asian Pacific women need to affirm our own culture while working within it to change it. Many of the leaders in the women's organizations today had moved naturally from the civil rights politics of the 60's to sexual politics, while very few of the Asian Pacific women who were involved in radical politics during the same period have emerged as leaders in these same women's organizations. Instead they have become active in groups promoting ethnic identity, most notably ethnic studies in universities, ethnic theater groups or ethnic community agencies. This doesn't mean that we have placed our loyalties on the side of ethnicity over womanhood. The two are not at war with one another; we shouldn't have to sign a "loyalty oath" favoring one over the other. However, women of color are often made to feel that we must make a choice between the two.

If I have more recently put my energies into the Pacific Asian American Center (a job center for Asians established in 1975, the only one of its kind in Orange County, California) and the Asian Pacific Women's Conference (the first of its kind in our history), it is because the needs in these areas are so great. I have thought of myself as a feminist first, but my ethnicity cannot be separated from my feminism.

Through the women's movement, I have come to truly appreciate the meaning of my mother's life and the lives of immigrant women like her. My mother, at nineteen years of age, uprooted from her large extended family, was brought to this country to bear and raise four children alone. Once here, she found that her new husband, who had been here as a student for several years prior to their marriage, was a bachelor-at-heart and had no intention of changing his lifestyle. Stripped of the protection and support of her family, she found the responsibilities of raising us alone in a strange country almost intolerable during those early years. I thought for many years that my mother did not love us because she often spoke of suicide as an easy way out of her miseries. I know now that for her to have survived "just for the sake" of her children took great strength and determination.

If I digress it is because I, a second generation Asian American woman who grew up believing in the American Dream, have come to know who I am through understanding the nature of my mother's experience; I have come to see connections in our lives as well as the lives of many women like us, and through her I have become more sensitive to the needs of Third World women throughout the world. We need not repeat our past histories; my daughters and I need not merely survive with strength and determination. We can, through collective struggle, live fuller and richer lives. My politics as a woman are deeply rooted in my immigrant parents' and my own past.

Not long ago at one of my readings a woman in the audience said she was deeply moved by my "beautifully tragic but not bitter camp poems which were apparently written long ago,"[1] but she was distressed to hear my poem "To A Lady." "Why are you, at this late date, so angry, and why are you taking it so personally?" she said. "We need to look to the future and stop wallowing in the past so much." I responded that this poem *is not* at all about the past. I am talking about what is happening to us right now, about our nonsupport of each other, about our noncaring about each other, about not seeing connections between racism and sexism in our lives. As a child of immigrant parents, as a woman of color in a white society and as a woman in a patriarchal society, what is personal to me *is* political.

These are the connections we expected our white sisters to see. It should not be too difficult, we feel, for them to see why being a feminist activist is more dangerous for women of color. They should be able to see that political views held by women of color are often misconstrued as being personal rather than ideological. Views critical of the system held by a person in an "out group" are often seen as expressions of personal angers against the dominant society. (If they hate it so much here, why don't they go back?) Many lesbians I know have felt the same kind of frustration when they supported

unpopular causes regarded by their critics as vindictive expressions to "get back" at the patriarchal system. They too know the disappointments of having their intentions misinterpreted.

In the 1960's when my family and I belonged to a neighborhood church, I became active in promoting the Fair Housing Bill, and one of my church friends said to me, "Why are you doing this to us? Haven't you and your family been happy with us in our church? Haven't we treated you well?" I knew then that I was not really part of the church at all in the eyes of this person, but only a guest who was being told I should have the good manners to behave like one.

Remembering the blatant acts of selective racism in the past three decades in our country, our white sisters should be able to see how tenuous our position in this country is. Many of us are now third and fourth generation Americans, but this makes no difference; periodic conflicts involving Third World peoples can abruptly change white Americans' attitudes towards us. This was clearly demonstrated in 1941 to the Japanese Americans who were in hot pursuit of the great American Dream, who went around saying, "Of course I don't eat Japanese food, I'm an American." We found our status as true-blooded Americans was only an illusion in 1942 when we were singled out to be imprisoned for the duration of the war by our own government. The recent outcry against Iranians because of the holding of American hostages tells me that the situation has not changed since 1941. When I hear my students say "We're not against the Iranians here who are minding their own business. We're just against those ungrateful ones who overstep our hospitality by demonstrating and badmouthing our government," I know they speak about me.

Asian Pacific American women will not speak out to say what we have on our minds until we feel secure within ourselves that this is our home too; and until our white sisters indicate by their actions that they want to join us in our struggle because it is theirs also. This means a commitment to a truly communal education where we learn from each other because we want to learn from each other, the kind of commitment we do not seem to have at the present time. I am still hopeful that the women of color in our country will be the link to Third World women throughout the world, and that we can help each other broaden our visions.

[1981]

NOTE

1. *Camp Notes and Other Poems* by Mitsuye Yamada (San Francisco: Shameless Hussy Press, 1976).

 64

Foreword *from* This Bridge Called My Back: Writings by Radical Women of Color

TONI CADE BAMBARA

TONI CADE BAMBARA 1939–1995. United States. Activist. Novelist. Short Story Writer. *Gorilla, My Love* (1972). *The Sea Birds Are Still Alive* (1977), *The Salt Eaters* (1980), *Deep Sightings and Rescue Missions* (1996), *Those Bones Are Not My Child* (1999).

. . .

How I cherish this collection of cables, esoesses, conjurations and fusile missles. Its motive force. Its gathering-us-in-ness. Its midwifery of mutually wise understandings. Its promise of autonomy and community. And its pledge of an abundant life for us all. On time. That is to say—overdue, given the times. ("Arrogance rising, moon in oppression, sun in destruction"—*Cameron.*)

Blackfoot amiga Nisei hermana Down Home Up Souf Sistuh sister El Barrio suburbia Korean The Bronx Lakota Menominee Cubana Chinese Puertoriqueña reservation Chicana campañera and letters testimonials poems interviews essays journal entries sharing Sisters of the yam Sisters of the rice Sisters of the corn Sisters of the plantain putting in telecalls to each other. And we're all on the line.

Now that we've begun to break the silence and begun to break through the diabolically erected barriers and can hear each other and see each other, we can sit down with trust and break bread together. Rise up and break our chains as well. For though the

initial motive of several siter/riters here may have been to protest, complain or explain to white feminist would-be allies that there are other ties and visions that bind, prior allegiances and priorities that supercede their invitations to coalesce on their terms ("Assimilation within a solely western-european herstory is not acceptable"—*Lorde*), the process of examining that would-be alliance awakens us to new tasks ("We have a lot more to concentrate on beside the pathology of white wimmin"—davenport)

and a new connection:	US
a new set of recognitions:	US
a new site of accountability:	US
a new source of power:	US

And the possibilities intuited here or alluded to there or called forth in various pieces in flat out talking in tongues—the possibility of several million women refuting the numbers game inherent in "minority," the possibility of denouncing the insulated/orchestrated conflict game of divide and conquer—through the fashioning of potent networks of all the daughters of the ancient mother cultures is awesome, mighty, a glorious life work. This Bridge lays down the planks to cross over on to a new place where stooped labor cramped quartered down pressed and caged up combatants can straighten the spine and expand the lungs and make the vision manifest ("The dream is real, my friends. The failure to realize it is the only unreality."—Street Preacher in *The Salt Eaters*).

This Bridge documents particular rites of passage. Coming of age and coming to terms with community—race, group, class, gender, self—its expectations, supports, and lessons. And coming to grips with its perversions—racism, prejudice, elitism, misogyny, homophobia, and murder. And coming to terms with the incorporation of disease, struggling to overthrow the internal colonial/pro-racist loyalties—color/hue/hair caste within the household, power perversities engaged in under the guise of "personal relationships," accommodation to and collaboration with self-ambush and amnesia and murder. And coming to grips with those false awakenings too that give us ease as we substitute a militant mouth for a radical politic, delaying our true coming of age as committed, competent, principled combatants.

There is more than a hint in these pages that too many of us still equate tone with substance, a hot eye with clear vision, and congratulate ourselves for our political maturity. For of course it takes more than pique to unite our wrath ("the capacity of heat to change the shape of things"—*Moraga*) and to wrest power from those who have it and abuse it, to reclaim our ancient powers lying dormant with neglect ("i wanna ask billie to teach us how to use our voices like she used hers on that old 78 record"—*gossett*), and create new powers in arenas where they never before existed. And of course it takes more than the self-disclosure and the bold glimpse of each others' life documents to make the grand resolve to fearlessly work toward potent meshings. Takes more than a rinsed lens to face unblinkingly the particular twists of the divide and conquer tactics of this moment: the practice of withdrawing small business loans from the Puerto Rican grocer in favor of the South Korean wig shop, of stripping from Black students the Martin Luther King scholarship fund fought for and delivering those funds up to South Vietnamese or white Cubans or any other group the government has made a commitment to in its greedy grab for empire. We have got to know each other better and teach each other our ways, our views, if we're to remove the scales ("seeing radical differences where they don't exist and not seeing them when they are critical"—*Quintanales*) and get the work done.

This Bridge can get us there. Can coax us into the habit of listening to each other and learning each other's ways of seeing and being. Of hearing each other as we heard each other in Pat Lee's *Freshtones*, as we heard each other in Pat Jones and Faye Chiang, et. al.'s *Ordinary Women*, as we heard each other in Fran Beale's *Third World Women's Alliance* newspaper. As we heard each other over the years in snatched time moments in hallways and conference corridors, caucusing between sets. As we heard each other in those split second interfacings of yours and mine and hers student union meetings. As we heard each other in that rainbow attempt under the auspices of IFCO years ago. And way before that when Chinese, Mexican, and African women in this country saluted each other's attempts to form protective leagues. And before that when New Orleans African women and Yamassee and Yamacrow women went into the swamps to meet with Filipino wives of "draftees" and "defectors" during the so called French and Indian War. And when members of the maroon communities and women of the long lodge held council together while the Seminole Wars raged. And way way before that, before the breaking of the land mass when we mothers of the yam, of the rice, of the maize, of the plantain sat together in a circle, staring into the camp fire, the answers in our laps, knowing how to focus. . . .

Quite frankly, This Bridge needs no Foreword. It is the Afterward that'll count. The coalitions of women determined to be a danger to our enemies, as June Jordan would put it. The will to be dangerous ("ask billie so we can learn how to have those bigtime bigdaddies jumping outta windows and otherwise offing theyselves in droves"—*gossett*). And the contracts we creative combatants will make to mutually care and cure each other into wholesomeness. And the blueprints we will draw up of the new order we will make manifest. And the personal unction we will discover in the mirror, in the dreams, or on the path across This Bridge. The work: To make revolution irresistible.

 65

Images of Relationship from In a Different Voice: Psychological Theory and Women's Development

C A R O L   G I L L I G A N

CAROL GILLIGAN United States 1936–   . Social psychologist. Educational theorist. *Mapping the Moral Domain: A Contribution of Women's Thinking to Psychological Theory and Education* (1989), *Meeting at the Crossroads: Women's Psychology and Girl's Development* (1992), *The Birth of Pleasure* (2002), *The Deepening Darkness: Patriarchy, Resistance and Democracies Future* (2008).

. . .

In 1914, with his essay "On Narcissism," Freud swallows his distaste at the thought of "abandoning observation for barren theoretical controversy" and extends his map of the psychological domain. Tracing the development of the capacity to love, which he equates with maturity and psychic health, he locates its origins in the contrast between love for the mother and love for the self. But in thus dividing the world of love into narcissism and "object" relationships, he finds that while men's development becomes clearer, women's becomes increasingly opaque. The problem arises because the contrast between mother and self yields two different images of relationships. Relying on the imagery of men's lives in charting the course of human growth, Freud is unable to trace in women the development of relationships, morality, or a clear sense of self. This difficulty in fitting the logic of his theory to women's experience leads him in the end to set women apart, marking their relationships, like their sexual life, as "a 'dark continent' for psychology" (1926, p. 212).

Thus the problem of interpretation that shadows the understanding of women's development arises from the differences observed in their experience of relationships. To Freud, though living surrounded by women and otherwise seeing so much and so well, women's relationships seemed increasingly mysterious, difficult to discern, and hard to describe. While this mystery indicates how theory can blind observation, it also suggests that development in women is masked by a particular conception of human relationships. Since the imagery of relationships shapes the narrative of human development, the inclusion of women, by changing that imagery, implies a change in the entire account.

The shift in imagery that creates the problem in interpreting women's development is elucidated by the moral judgments of two eleven-year-old children, a boy and a girl, who see, in the same dilemma, two very different moral problems. While current theory brightly illuminates the line and the logic of the boy's thought, it casts scant light on that of the girl. The choice of a girl whose moral judgments elude existing categories of developmental assessment is meant to highlight the issue of interpretation rather than to exemplify sex differences per se. Adding a new line of interpretation, based on the imagery of the girl's thought, makes it possible not only to see development where previously development was not discerned but also to consider differ-

ences in the understanding of relationships without scaling these differences from better to worse.

The two children were in the same sixth-grade class at school and were participants in the rights and responsibilities study, designed to explore different conceptions of morality and self. The sample selected for this study was chosen to focus the variables of gender and age while maximizing developmental potential by holding constant, at a high level, the factors of intelligence, education, and social class that have been associated with moral development, at least as measured by existing scales. The two children in question, Amy and Jake, were both bright and articulate and, at least in their eleven-year-old aspirations, resisted easy categories of sex-role stereotyping, since Amy aspired to become a scientist while Jake preferred English to math. Yet their moral judgments seem initially to confirm familiar notions about differences between the sexes, suggesting that the edge girls have on moral development during the early school years gives way at puberty with the ascendance of formal logical thought in boys.

The dilemma that these eleven-year-olds were asked to resolve was one in the series devised by Kohlberg to measure moral development in adolescence by presenting a conflict between moral norms and exploring the logic of its resolution. In this particular dilemma, a man named Heinz considers whether or not to steal a drug which he cannot afford to buy in order to save the life of his wife. In the standard format of Kohlberg's interviewing procedure, the description of the dilemma itself—Heinz's predicament, the wife's disease, the druggist's refusal to lower his price—is followed by the question, "Should Heinz steal the drug?" The reasons for and against stealing are then explored through a series of questions that vary and extend the parameters of the dilemma in a way designed to reveal the underlying structure of moral thought.

Jake, at eleven, is clear from the outset that Heinz should steal the drug. Constructing the dilemma, as Kohlberg did, as a conflict between the values of property and life, he discerns the logical priority of life and uses that logic to justify his choice:

> For one thing, a human life is worth more than money, and if the druggist only makes $1,000, he is still going to live, but if Heinz doesn't steal the drug, his wife is going to die. (*Why is life worth more*

than money?) Because the druggist can get a thousand dollars later from rich people with cancer, but Heinz can't get his wife again. (*Why not?*) Because people are all different and so you couldn't get Heinz's wife again.

Asked whether Heinz should steal the drug if he does not love his wife, Jake replies that he should, saying that not only is there "a difference between hating and killing," but also, if Heinz were caught, "the judge would probably think it was the right thing to do." Asked about the fact that, in stealing, Heinz would be breaking the law, he says that "the laws have mistakes, and you can't go writing up a law for everything that you can imagine."

Thus, while taking the law into account and recognizing its function in maintaining social order (the judge, Jake says, "should give Heinz the lightest possible sentence"), he also sees the law as man-made and therefore subject to error and change. Yet his judgment that Heinz should steal the drug, like his view of the law as having mistakes, rests on the assumption of agreement, a societal consensus around moral values that allows one to know and expect others to recognize what is "the right thing to do."

Fascinated by the power of logic, this eleven-year-old boy locates truth in math, which, he says, is "the only thing that is totally logical." Considering the moral dilemma to be "sort of like a math problem with humans," he sets it up as an equation and proceeds to work out the solution. Since his solution is rationally derived, he assumes that anyone following reason would arrive at the same conclusion and thus that a judge would also consider stealing to be the right thing for Heinz to do. Yet he is also aware of the limits of logic. Asked whether there is a right answer to moral problems, Jake replies that "there can only be right and wrong in judgment," since the parameters of action are variable and complex. Illustrating how actions undertaken with the best of intentions can eventuate in the most disastrous of consequences, he says, "like if you give an old lady your seat on the trolley, if you are in a trolley crash and that seat goes through the window, it might be that reason that the old lady dies."

Theories of developmental psychology illuminate well the position of this child, standing at the juncture of childhood and adolescence, at what Piaget describes as the pinnacle of childhood intelligence, and beginning through thought to discover a wider universe of possibility. The moment of preadolescence is caught by the conjunction of formal operational thought with a description of self still anchored in the factual parameters of his childhood world—his age, his town, his father's occupation, the substance of his likes, dislikes, and beliefs. Yet as his self-description radiates the self-confidence of a child who has arrived, in Erikson's terms, at a favorable balance of industry over inferiority—competent, sure of himself, and knowing well the rules of the game—so his emergent capacity for formal thought, his ability to think about thinking and to reason things out in a logical way, frees him from dependence on authority and allows him to find solutions to problems by himself.

This emergent autonomy follows the trajectory that Kohlberg's six stages of moral development trace, a three-level progression from an egocentric understanding of fairness based on individual need (stages one and two), to a conception of fairness anchored in the shared conventions of societal agreement (stages three and four), and finally to a principled understanding of fairness that rests on the free-standing logic of equality and reciprocity (stages five and six). While this boy's judgments at eleven are scored as conventional on Kohlberg's scale, a mixture of stages three and four, his ability to bring deductive logic to bear on the solution of moral dilemmas, to differentiate morality from law, and to see how laws can be considered to have mistakes points toward the principled conception of justice that Kohlberg equates with moral maturity.

In contrast, Amy's response to the dilemma conveys a very different impression, an image of development stunted by a failure of logic, an inability to think for herself. Asked if Heinz should steal the drug, she replies in a way that seems evasive and unsure:

> Well, I don't think so. I think there might be other ways besides stealing it, like if he could borrow the money or make a loan or something, but he really shouldn't steal the drug—but his wife shouldn't die either.

Asked why he should not steal the drug, she considers neither property nor law but rather the effect that theft could have on the relationship between Heinz and his wife:

> If he stole the drug, he might save his wife then, but if he did, he might have to go to jail, and then his wife might get sicker again, and he couldn't get more of the drug, and it might not be good. So, they should really just talk it out and find some other way to make the money.

Seeing in the dilemma not a math problem with humans but a narrative of relationships that extends over time, Amy envisions the wife's continuing need for her husband and the husband's continuing concern for his wife and seeks to respond to the druggist's need in a way that would sustain rather than sever connection. Just as she ties the wife's survival to the preservation of relationships, so she considers the value of the wife's life in a context of relationships, saying that it would be wrong to let her die because, "if she died, it hurts a lot of people and it hurts her." Since Amy's moral judgment is grounded in the belief that, "if somebody has something that would keep somebody alive, then it's not right not to give it to them," she considers the problem in the dilemma to arise not from the druggist's assertion of rights but from his failure of response.

As the interviewer proceeds with the series of questions that follow from Kohlberg's construction of the dilemma, Amy's answers remain essentially unchanged, the various probes serving neither to elucidate nor to modify her initial response. Whether or not Heinz loves his wife, he still shouldn't steal or let her die; if it were a stranger dying instead, Amy says that "if the stranger didn't have anybody near or anyone she knew," then Heinz should try to save her life, but he should not steal the drug. But as the interviewer conveys through the repetition of questions that the answers she gave were not heard or not right, Amy's confidence begins to diminish, and her replies become more constrained and unsure. Asked again why Heinz should not steal the drug, she simply repeats, "Because it's not right." Asked again to explain why, she states again that theft would not be a good solution, adding lamely, "if he took it, he might not know how to give it to his wife, and so his wife might still die." Failing to see the dilemma as a self-contained problem in moral logic, she does not discern the internal structure of its resolution; as she constructs the problem differently herself, Kohlberg's conception completely evades her.

Instead, seeing a world comprised of relationships rather than of people standing alone, a world that coheres through human connection rather than through systems of rules, she finds the puzzle in the dilemma to lie in the failure of the druggist to respond to the wife. Saying that "it is not right for someone to die when their life could be saved," she assumes that if the druggist were to see the consequences of his refusal to lower his price, he would realize that "he should just give it to the wife and then have the husband pay back the money later." Thus she considers the solution to the dilemma to lie in making the wife's condition more salient to the druggist or, that failing, in appealing to others who are in a position to help.

Just as Jake is confident the judge would agree that stealing is the right thing for Heinz to do, so Amy is confident that, "if Heinz and the druggist had talked it out long enough, they could reach something besides stealing." As he considers the law to "have mistakes," so she sees this drama as a mistake, believing that "the world should just share things more and then people wouldn't have to steal." Both children thus recognize the need for agreement but see it as mediated in different ways— he impersonally through systems of logic and law, she personally through communication in relationship. Just as he relies on the conventions of logic to deduce the solution to this dilemma, assuming these conventions to be shared, so she relies on a process of communication, assuming connection and believing that her voice will be heard. Yet while his assumptions about agreement are confirmed by the convergence in logic between his answers and the questions posed, her assumptions are belied by the failure of communication, the interviewer's inability to understand her response.

Although the frustration of the interview with Amy is apparent in the repetition of questions and its ultimate circularity, the problem of interpretation is focused by the assessment of her response. When considered in the light of Kohlberg's definition of the stages and sequence of moral development, her moral judgments appear to be a full stage lower in maturity than those of the boy. Scored as a mixture of stages two and three, her responses seem to reveal a feeling of powerlessness in the world, an inability to think systematically about the concepts of morality or law, a reluctance to challenge authority or to examine the logic of received moral truths, a failure even to conceive of acting directly to save a life or to consider that such action, if taken, could possibly have an effect. As her reliance on relationships seems to reveal a continuing dependence and vulnerability, so her belief in communication as the mode through which to resolve moral dilemmas appears naive and cognitively immature.

Yet Amy's description of herself conveys a markedly different impression. Once again, the hallmarks of the preadolescent child depict a child secure in her sense of herself, confident in the substance of her beliefs, and sure of her ability to do something of value in the world. Describing herself at eleven as "growing and changing," she says that she "sees some things differently now, just because I know myself really well now, and I know a lot more about the world." Yet the world she knows is a different world from that refracted by Kohlberg's construction of Heinz's dilemma. Her world is a world of relationships and psychological truths where an awareness of the connection between people gives rise to a recognition of responsibility for one another, a perception of the need for response. Seen in this light, her understanding of morality as arising from the recognition of relationship, her belief in communication as the mode of conflict resolution, and her conviction that the solution to the dilemma will follow from its compelling representation seem far from naive or cognitively immature. Instead, Amy's judgments contain the insights central to an ethic of care, just as Jake's judgments reflect the logic of the justice approach. Her incipient awareness of the "method of truth," the central tenet of nonviolent conflict resolution, and her belief in the restorative activity of care, lead her to see the actors in the dilemma arrayed not as opponents in a contest of rights but as members of a network of relationships on whose continuation they all depend. Consequently her solution to the dilemma lies in activating the network by communication, securing the inclusion of the wife by strengthening rather than severing connections.

But the different logic of Amy's response calls attention to the interpretation of the interview itself. Conceived as an interrogation, it appears instead as a dialogue, which takes on moral dimensions of its own, pertaining to the interviewer's uses of power and to the manifestations of respect. With this shift in the conception of the interview, it immediately becomes clear that the interviewer's problem in understanding Amy's response stems from the fact that Amy is answering a different question from the one the interviewer thought had been posed. Amy is considering not *whether* Heinz should act in this situation ("*should* Heinz steal the drug?") but rather *how* Heinz should act in response to his awareness of his wife's need ("Should Heinz *steal* the drug?"). The interviewer takes the mode of action for granted, presuming it to be a matter of fact; Amy assumes the necessity for action and considers what form it should take. In the interviewer's failure to imagine a response not dreamt of in Kohlberg's moral philosophy lies the failure to hear Amy's question and to see the logic in her response, to discern that what appears, from one perspective, to be an evasion of the dilemma signifies in other terms a recognition of the problem and a search for a more adequate solution.

Thus in Heinz's dilemma these two children see two very different moral problems—Jake a conflict between life and property that can be resolved by logical deduction, Amy a fracture of human relationship that must be mended with its own thread. Asking different questions that arise from different conceptions of the moral domain, the children arrive at answers that fundamentally diverge, and the arrangement of these answers as successive stages on a scale of increasing moral maturity calibrated by the logic of the boy's response misses the different truth revealed in the judgment of the girl. To the question, "What does he see that she does not?" Kohlberg's theory provides a ready response, manifest in the scoring of Jake's judgments a full stage higher than Amy's in moral maturity; to the question, "What does she see that he does not?" Kohlberg's theory has nothing to say. Since most of her responses fall through the sieve of Kohlberg's scoring system, her responses appear from his perspective to lie outside the moral domain.

Yet just as Jake reveals a sophisticated understanding of the logic of justification, so Amy is equally sophisticated in her understanding of the nature of choice. Recognizing that "if both the roads went in totally separate ways, if you pick one, you'll never know what would happen if you went the other way," she explains that "that's the chance you have to take, and like I said, it's just really a guess." . . .

In this way, these two eleven-year-old children, both highly intelligent and perceptive about life, though in different ways, display different modes of moral understanding, different ways of thinking about conflict and choice. In resolving Heinz's dilemma, Jake relies on theft to avoid confrontation and turns to the law to mediate the dispute. Transposing a hierarchy of power into a hierarchy of values, he defuses a potentially explosive conflict between people by casting it as an impersonal conflict of claims. In this way, he abstracts the moral problem from the interpersonal situation, finding in the logic of fairness an objective way to decide who will win the dispute. But this hierarchical ordering, with its imagery of winning and losing and the potential for violence which it contains, gives way in Amy's construction of the dilemma to a network of connection, a web of relationships that is sustained by a process of communication. With this shift, the moral problem changes from one of unfair domination, the imposition of property over life, to one of unnecessary exclusion, the failure of the druggist to respond to the wife.

· · ·

If the trajectory of development were drawn through either of these children's responses, it would trace a correspondingly different path. For Jake, development would entail coming to see the other as equal to the self and the discovery that equality provides a way of making connection safe. For Amy, development would follow the inclusion of herself in an expanding network of connection and the discovery that separation can be protective and need not entail isolation. In view of these different paths of development and particularly of the different ways in which the experiences of separation and connection are aligned with the voice of the self, the representation of the boy's development as the single line of adolescent growth for both sexes creates a continual problem when it comes to interpreting the development of the girl.

Since development has been premised on separation and told as a narrative of failed relationships—of pre-Oedipal attachments, Oedipal fantasies, preadolescent chumships, and adolescent loves—relationships that stand out against a background of separation, only successively to erupt and give way to an increasingly emphatic individuation, the development of girls appears problematic because of the continuity of relationships in their lives. Freud attributes the turning inward of girls at puberty to an intensification of primary narcissism, signifying a failure of love or "object" relationships. But if this turning inward is construed against a background of continuing connection, it signals a new responsiveness to the self, an expansion of care rather than a failure of relationship. In this way girls, seen not to fit the categories of relationships derived from male experience, call attention to the assumptions about relationships that have informed the account of human development by replacing the imagery of explosive connection with images of dangerous separation.

· · ·

Claire, a participant in the college student study, was interviewed first as a senior in college and then again at the age of twenty-seven.

· · ·

Bringing [her] perspective to Heinz's dilemma, Claire identifies the same moral problem as the eleven-year-old Amy, focusing not on the conflict of rights but on the failure of response. Claire believes that Heinz should steal the drug ("His wife's life was much more important than anything. He should have done anything to save her life"), but she counters the rights construction with her own interpretation. Although the druggist "had a right, I mean he had the legal right, I also think he had the moral obligation to show compassion in this case. I don't think he had the right to refuse." In tying the necessity for Heinz's action to the fact that "the wife needed him at this point to do it; she couldn't have done it, and it's up to him to do for her what she needs," Claire elaborates the same concept of responsibility that was articulated by Amy. They both equate responsibility with the need for response that arises from the recognition that others are counting on you and that you are in a position to help.

Whether Heinz loves his wife or not is irrelevant to Claire's decision, not because life has priority over affection, but because his wife "is another human being who needs help." Thus the moral injunction to act stems not from Heinz's feelings about his wife but from his awareness of her need, an awareness mediated not by identification but by a process of communication. Just as Claire considers the druggist morally responsible for his refusal, so she ties morality to the awareness of connection, defining the moral person as one who, in acting, "seriously considers the consequences to everybody involved." Therefore, she criticizes her mother for "neglecting her responsibility to herself" at the same time that she criticizes herself for neglecting her responsibility to others.

Although Claire's judgments of Heinz's dilemma for the most part do not fit the categories of Kohlberg's scale, her understanding of the law and her ability to articulate its function in a systematic way earn her a moral maturity score of stage four. Five years later, when she is interviewed at the age of twenty-seven, this score is called into question because she subsumes the law to the considerations of responsibility that informed her thinking about the druggist, Heinz, and his wife. Judging the law now in terms of whom it protects, she extends her ethic of responsibility to a broader vision of societal connection. But the disparity between this vision and the justice conception causes her score on Kohlberg's scale to regress.

· · ·

Impatient now with Heinz's dilemma, she structures it starkly as a contrast between the wife's life and the druggist's greed, seeing in the druggist's preoccupation with profit a failure of understanding as well as of response. Life is worth more than money because "everybody has the right to live." But then she shifts her perspective, saying, "I'm not sure I should phrase it that way." In her rephrasing, she replaces the hierarchy of rights with a web of relationships. Through this replacement, she challenges the premise of separation underlying the notion of rights and articulates a "guiding principle of connection." Perceiving relationships as primary rather than as derived from separation, considering the interdependence of people's lives, she envisions

"the way things are" and "the way things should be" as a web of interconnection where "everybody belongs to it and you all come from it." Against this conception of social reality, the druggist's claim stands in fundamental contradiction. Seeing life as dependent on connection, as sustained by activities of care, as based on a bond of attachment rather than a contract of agreement, she believes that Heinz should steal the drug, whether or not he loves his wife, "by virtue of the fact that they are both there." Although a person may not like someone else, "you have to love someone else, because you are inseparable from them. In a way it's like loving your right hand; it is part of you. That other person is part of that giant collection of everybody." Thus she articulates an ethic of responsibility that stems from an awareness of interconnection: "The stranger is still another person belonging to that group, people you are connected to by virtue of being another person."

Claire describes morality as "the constant tension between being part of something larger and a sort of self-contained entity," and she sees the ability to live with that tension as the source of moral character and strength.

· · ·

Describing the people whom she admires—her mother for being "as giving as she is," her husband who "lives by what he believes"—Claire envisions for herself a life of integrity centered on activities of care. This vision is illuminated by the actions of a woman physician who, seeing the loneliness of an old woman in the hospital, "would go out and her a root beer float and sit at her bedside just so there would be somebody there for her." The ideal of care is thus an activity of relationship, of seeing and responding to need, taking care of the world by sustaining the web of connection so that no one is left alone.

While the truths of psychological theory have blinded psychologists to the truth of women's experience, that experience illuminates a world which psychologists have found hard to trace, a territory where violence is rare and relationships appear safe. The reason women's experience has been so difficult to decipher or even discern is that a shift in the imagery of relationships gives rise to a problem of interpretation. The images of hierarchy and web, drawn from the texts of men's and women's fantasies and thoughts, convey different ways of structuring relationships and are associated with different views of morality and self. But these images create a problem in understanding because each distorts the other's representation. As the top of the hierarchy becomes the edge of the web and as the center of a network of connection becomes the middle of a hierarchical progression, each image marks as dangerous the place which the other defines as safe. Thus the images of hierarchy and web inform different modes of assertion and response: the wish to be alone at the top and the consequent fear that others will get too close; the wish to be at the center of connection and the consequent fear of being too far out on the edge. These disparate fears of being stranded and being caught give rise to different portrayals of achievement and affiliation, leading to different modes of action and different ways of assessing the consequences of choice.

The reinterpretation of women's experience in terms of their own imagery of relationships thus clarifies that experience and also provides a non-hierarchical vision of human connection. Since relationships, when cast in the image of hierarchy, appear inherently unstable and morally problematic, their transposition into the image of web changes an order of inequality into a structure of interconnection. But the power of the images of hierarchy and web, their evocation of feelings and their recurrence in thought, signifies the embeddedness of both of these images in the cycle of human life. The experiences of inequality and interconnection, inherent in the relation of parent and child, then give rise to the ethics of justice and care, the ideals of human relationship—the vision that self and other will be treated as of equal worth, that despite differences in power, things will be fair; the vision that everyone will be responded to and included, that no one will be left alone or hurt. These disparate visions in their tension reflect the paradoxical truths of human experience—that we know ourselves as separate only insofar as we live in connection with others, and that we experience relationship only insofar as we differentiate other from self.

66

Under Western Eyes: Feminist Scholarship and Colonial Discourses

CHANDRA TALPADE MOHANTY

CHANDRA TALPADE MOHANTY 1955– Scholar of transnational feminism and cultural studies. *Third World Women and the Politics of Feminism* (1990), *Feminist Genealogies, Colonial Legacies, Democratic Futures* (1996), *Feminism without Borders: Decolonizing Theory, Practicing Solidarity* (2003).

Any discussion of the intellectual and political construction of "third world feminisms" must address itself to two simultaneous projects: the internal critique of hegemonic "Western" feminisms, and the formulation of autonomous, geographically, historically, and culturally grounded feminist concerns and strategies. The first project is one of deconstructing and dismantling; the second, one of building and constructing. While these projects appear to be contradictory, the one working negatively and the other positively, unless these two tasks are addressed simultaneously, "third world" feminisms run the risk of marginalization or ghettoization from both mainstream (right and left) and Western feminist discourses.

It is to the first project that I address myself. What I wish to analyze is specifically the production of the "third world woman" as a singular monolithic subject in some recent (Western) feminist texts. The definition of colonization I wish to invoke here is a predominantly *discursive* one, focusing on a certain mode of appropriation and codification of "scholarship" and "knowledge" about women in the third world by particular analytic categories employed in specific writings on the subject which take as their referent feminist interests as they have been articulated in the U.S. and Western Europe. If one of the tasks of formulating and understanding the locus of "third world feminisms" is delineating the way in which it resists and *works against* what I am referring to as "Western feminist discourse," an analysis of the discursive construction of "third world women" in Western feminism is an important first step.

Clearly Western feminist discourse and political practice is neither singular nor homogeneous in its goals, interests, or analyses. However, it is possible to trace a coherence of *effects* resulting from the implicit assumption of "the West" (in all its complexities and contradictions) as the primary referent in theory and praxis. My reference to "Western feminism" is by no means intended to imply that it is a monolith. Rather, I am attempting to draw attention to the similar effects of various textual strategies used by writers which codify Others as non-Western and hence themselves as (implicitly) Western. It is in this sense that I use the term *Western feminist.* Similar arguments can be made in terms of middle-class urban African or Asian scholars producing scholarship on or about their rural or working-class sisters which assumes their own middle-class cultures as the norm, and codifies working-class histories and cultures as Other. Thus, while this essay focuses specifically on what I refer to as "Western feminist" discourse on women in the third world, the critiques I offer also pertain to third world scholars writing about their own cultures, who employ identical analytic strategies.

It ought to be of some political significance, at least, that the term *colonization* has come to denote a variety of phenomena in recent feminist and left writings in general. From its analytic value as a category of exploitative economic exchange in both traditional and contemporary Marxisms (cf. particularly contemporary theorists such as Baran 1962 , Amin 1977, and Gunder-Frank 1967) to its use by feminist women of color in the U.S. to describe the appropriation of their experiences and struggles by hegemonic white women's movements (cf. especially Moraga and Anzaldúa 1983, Smith 1983, Joseph and Lewis 1981, and Moraga 1984), colonization has been used to characterize everything from the most evident economic and political hierarchies to the production of a particular cultural discourse abut what is called the "third world."[1] However sophisticated or problematical its use as an explanatory construct, colonization almost invariably implies a relation of structural domination and a suppression—often violent—of the heterogeneity of the subject(s) in question.

My concern about such writings derives from my own implication and investment in contemporary debates in feminist theory, and the urgent political necessity (especially in the age of Reagan/Bush) of forming strategic coalitions across class, race, and national boundaries. The analytic principles discussed below serve to distort Western feminist political practices, and limit the possibility of coalitions among (usually white) Western feminists and working-class feminists and feminists of color around the world. These limitations are evident in the construction of the (implicitly consensual) priority of issues around which apparently *all* women are expected to organize. The necessary and integral connection between feminist scholarship and feminist political practice and organizing determines the significance and status of Western feminist writings on women in the third world, for feminist scholarship, like most other kinds of scholarship, is not the mere production of knowledge about a certain subject. It is a directly political and discursive *practice* in that it is purposeful and ideological. It is best seen as a mode of intervention into particular hegemonic discourses (for example, traditional anthropology, sociology, literary criticism, etc.); it is a political praxis which counters and resists the totalizing imperative of age-old "legitimate" and "scientific" bodies of knowledge. Thus, feminist scholarly practices (whether reading, writing, critical, or textual) are inscribed in relations of power—relations which they counter, resist, or even perhaps implicitly support. There can, of course, be no apolitical scholarship.

The relationship between "Woman"—a cultural and ideological composite Other constructed through diverse representational discourses (scientific literary juridical, linguistic, cinematic, etc.)—and "women"—real, material subjects of their collective histories—is one of the central questions the practice of feminist scholarship seeks to address. This connection between women as historical subjects and the representation of Woman produced by hegemonic discourses is not a relation of direct identity, or a relation of correspondence or simple implication.[2] It is an arbitrary relation set up by particular cultures. I would like to suggest that the feminist writings I analyze here discursively colonize the material and historical heterogeneities of the lives of women in the third world, thereby producing/ re-presenting a composite, singular "third world woman"—an image which appears arbitrarily constructed, but nevertheless carries with it the authorizing signature of Western humanist discourse.[3]

I argue that assumption of privilege and ethnocentric universality, on the one hand, and inadequate self-consciousness about the effect of Western scholarship on the "third world" in the context of a world system dominated by the West, on the other, characterize a sizeable extent of Western feminist work on women in the third world. An analysis of "sexual difference" in the form of a cross-culturally singular, monolithic, notion of patriarchy or male dominance leads to the construction of a similarly reductive and homogeneous notion of what I call the "third world difference"—that stable, ahistorical something that apparently oppresses most if not all the women in these countries. And it is in the production of this "third world difference" that Western feminisms appropriate and "colonize" the constitutive complexities which characterize the lives of women in these countries. It is in this process of discursive homogenization and systematization of the oppression of women in the third world that power is exercised in much of recent Western feminist discourse, and this power needs to be defined and named.

· · ·

The first analytic presupposition I focus on is involved in the strategic location of the category "women" vis-à-vis the context of analysis. The assumption of women as an already constituted, coherent group with identical interests and desires, regardless of class, ethnic or racial location, or contradictions, implies a notion of gender or sexual difference or even patriarchy which can be applied universally and cross-culturally. (The context of analysis can be anything from kinship structures and the organization of labor to media representations.) The second analytical presupposition is evident on the methodological level, in the uncritical way "proof" of universality and cross-cultural validity are provided. The third is a more specifically political presupposition underlying the methodologies and the analytic strategies, i.e., the model of power and struggle they imply and suggest. I argue that as a result of the two modes—or, rather, frames—of

analysis described above, a homogeneous notion of the oppression of women as a group is assumed, which, in turn, produces the image of an "average third world woman." This average third world woman leads an essentially truncated life based on her feminine gender (read: sexually constrained) and her being "third world" (read: ignorant, poor, uneducated, tradition-bound, domestic, family-oriented, victimized, etc.). This, I suggest, is in contrast to the (implicit) self-representation of Western women as educated, as modern, as having control over their own bodies and sexualities and the freedom to make their own decisions.

The distinction between Western feminist representation of women in the third world and Western feminist self-presentation is a distinction of the same order as that made by some Marxists between the "maintenance" function of the housewife and real "productive" role of wage labor, or the characterization by developmentalists of the third world as being engaged in the lesser production of "raw materials" in contrast to the "real" productive activity of the first world. These distinctions are made on the basis of the privileging of a particular group as the norm or referent. Men involved in wage labor, first world producers, and, I suggest, Western feminists who sometimes cast third world women in terms of "ourselves undressed" (Michelle Rosaldo's [1980] term), all construct themselves as the normative referent in such a binary analytic.

"WOMEN" AS CATEGORY OF ANALYSIS, OR: WE ARE ALL SISTERS IN STRUGGLE

By women as a category of analysis, I am referring to the crucial assumption that all of us of the same gender, across classes and cultures, are somehow socially constituted as a homogeneous group identified prior to the process of analysis. This is an assumption which characterizes much feminist discourse. The homogeneity of women as a group is produced not on the basis of biological essentials but rather on the basis of secondary sociological and anthropological universals. Thus, for instance, in any given piece of feminist analysis, women are characterized as a singular group on the basis of a shared oppression. What binds women together is a sociological notion of the "sameness" of their oppression. It is at this point that an elision takes place between "women" as a discursively constructed group and "women" as material subjects of their own history. Thus, the discursively consensual homogeneity of "women" as a group is mistaken for the historically specific material reality of groups of women. This results in an assumption of women as an always already constituted group, one which has been labeled "powerless," "exploited," "sexually harassed," etc., by feminist scientific, economic, legal, and sociological discourses. (Notice that this is quite similar to sexual discourse labeling women weak, emotional, having math anxiety, etc.) This focus is not on uncovering the material and ideological specificities that constitute a particular group of women as "powerless" in a particular context. It is, rather, on finding a variety of cases of "powerless" groups of women to prove the general point that women as a group are powerless.

· · ·

WOMEN & RELIGIOUS IDEOLOGIES

· · ·

What is problematical about this kind of use of "women" as a group, as a stable category of analysis, is that it assumes an ahistorical, universal unity between women based on a generalized notion of their subordination. Instead of analytically *demonstrating* the production of women as socioeconomic political groups within particular local contexts, this analytical move limits the definition of the female subject to gender identity, completely bypassing social class and ethnic identities. What characterizes women as a group is their gender (sociologically, not necessarily biologically, defined) over and above everything else, indicating a monolithic notion of sexual difference. Because women are thus constituted as a coherent group, sexual difference becomes coterminous with female subordination, and power is automatically defined in binary terms: people who have it (read: men), and people who do not (read: women). Men exploit, women are exploited. Such simplistic formulations are historically reductive; they are also ineffectual in designing strategies to combat oppressions. All they do is reinforce binary divisions between men and women.

What would an analysis which did not do this look like? Maria Mies's work illustrates the strength of Western feminist work on women in the third world which does not fall into the traps discussed above. Mies's study of the lace makers of Narsapur, India (1982), attempts to carefully analyze a substantial household industry in which "housewives" produce lace doilies for consumption in the world market. Through a detailed analysis of the structure of the lace industry, production and reproduction relations, the sexual division of labor, profits and exploitation, and the overall consequences of defining women as "non-working housewives" and their work as "leisure-time activity," Mies demonstrates the levels of exploitation in this industry and the impact of this production system on the work and living conditions of the women involved in it. In addition, she is able to analyze the "ideology of the housewife," the notion of a woman sitting in the house, as providing the necessary subjective and sociocultural element for the creation and maintenance of a production system that contributes to the increasing pauperization of women, and keeps them totally atomized and disorganized as workers. Mies's analysis shows the effect of a certain historically and culturally specific mode of patriarchal organization, an organization constructed on the basis of the definition of the lace makers as "non-working housewives" at familial, local, regional, statewide, and international levels. The intricacies and the effects of particular power networks not only are emphasized, but they form the basis of Mies's analysis of how this particular group of women is situated at the center of a hegemonic, exploitative world market.

This is a good example of what careful, politically focused, local analyses can accomplish. It illustrates how the category of women is constructed in a variety of political contexts that often exist simultaneously and overlaid on top of one another. There is no easy generalization in the direction of "women" in India, or "women in the third world"; nor is there a reduction of the political construction of the exploitation of the lace makers to cultural explanations about the passivity or obedience that might characterize these women and their situation. Finally, this mode of local, political analysis, which generates theoretical categories from within the situation and context being analyzed, also suggests corresponding effective strategies for organizing against the exploitation faced by the lace makers. Narsapur women are not mere victims of the production process, because they resist, challenge, and subvert the process at various junctures. Here is one instance of how Mies delineates the connections between the housewife ideology, the self-consciousness of the lace makers, and their interrelationships as contributing to the latent resistances she perceives among the women:

> The persistence of the housewife ideology, the self-perception of the lace makers as petty commodity producers rather than as workers, is not only upheld by the structure of the industry as such but also by the deliberate propagation and reinforcement of reactionary patriarchal norms and institutions. Thus, most of the lace makers voiced the same opinion about the rules of *purdah* and seclusion in their communities which were also propagated by the lace exporters. In particular, the *Kapu* women said that they had never gone out of their houses, that women of their community could not do any other work than housework and lace work etc. but in spite of the fact that most of them still subscribed fully to the patriarchal norms of the *gosha* women, there were also contradictory elements in their consciousness. Thus, although they looked down with contempt upon women who were able to work outside the house—like the untouchable *Mala* and *Madiga* women or women of other lower castes, they could not ignore the fact that these women were earning more money precisely because they were *not* respectable housewives but workers. At one discussion, they even admitted that it would be better if they could also go out and do coolie work. And when they were asked whether they would be ready to come out of their houses and work in one place in some sort of factory, they said they would do that. This shows that the *purdah* and housewife ideology, although still fully internalized, already had some cracks, because it has been confronted with several contradictory realities. (157)

It is only by understanding the *contradictions* inherent in women's location within various structures that effective political action and challenges can be devised. Mies's study goes a long way toward offering such analysis. While there are now an increasing number of Western feminist writings in this tradition, there is also, unfortunately, a large block of writing which succumbs to the cultural reductionism discussed earlier.

METHODOLOGICAL UNIVERSALISMS, OR: WOMEN'S OPPRESSION IS A GLOBAL PHENOMENON

Western feminist writings on women in the third world subscribe to a variety of methodologies to demonstrate the universal cross-cultural operation of male dominance and female exploitation. I summarize and critique three such methods below, moving from the simplest to the most complex.

First, proof of universalism is provided through the use of an arithmetic method. The argument goes like this: the greater the number of women who wear the veil, the more universal is the sexual segregation and control of women (Deardon 1975, 4–5). Similarly, a large number of different, fragmented examples from a variety of countries also apparently add up to a universal fact. For instance, Muslim women in Saudi Arabia, Iran, Pakistan, India, and Egypt all wear some sort of a veil. Hence, this indicates that the sexual control of women is a universal fact in those countries in which the women are veiled (Deardon 1975, 7, 10). Fran Hosken writes, "Rape, forced prostitution, polygamy, genital mutilation, pornography, the beating of girls and women, purdah (segregation of women) are all violations of basic human rights" (1981, 15). By equating purdah with rape, domestic violence, and forced prostitution, Hosken asserts its "sexual control" function as the primary explanation for purdah, whatever the context. Institutions of purdah are thus denied any cultural and historical specificity, and contradictions and potentially subversive aspects are totally ruled out.

In both these examples, the problem is not in asserting that the practice of wearing a veil is widespread. This assertion can be made on the basis of numbers. It is a descriptive generalization. However, it is the analytic leap from the practice of veiling to an assertion of its general significance in controlling women that must be questioned. While there may be a physical similarity in the veils worn by women in Saudi Arabia and Iran, the specific meaning attached to this practice varies according to the cultural and ideological context. In addition, the symbolic space occupied by the practice of purdah may be similar in certain contexts, but this does not automatically indicate that the practices themselves have identical significance in the social realm. For example, as is well known, Iranian middle-class women veiled themselves during the 1979 revolution to indicate solidarity with their veiled working-class sisters, while in contemporary Iran, mandatory Islamic laws dictate that all Iranian women wear veils. While in both these instances, similar reasons might be offered for the veil (opposition to the Shah and Western cultural colonization the first case, and the true Islamicization of Iran in the second), the concrete *meanings* attached to Iranian women wearing the veil are clearly different in both historical contexts. In the first case, wearing the veil is both an oppositional and a revolutionary gesture on the part of Iranian middle-class women; in the second case, it is a coercive, institutional mandate (see Tabari 1980 for detailed discussion). It is on the basis of such context-specific differentiated analysis that effective political strategies can be generated. To assume that the mere practice of veiling women in a number of Muslim countries indicates the universal oppression of women through sexual segregation not only is analytically reductive, but also proves quite useless when it comes to the elaboration of oppositional political strategy.

Second, concepts such as reproduction, the sexual division of labor, the family, marriage, household, patriarchy, etc., are often used without their specification in local cultural and historical contexts. Feminists use these concepts in providing explanations for women's subordination, apparently assuming their universal applicability. For instance, how is it possible to refer to "the" sexual division of labor when the *content* of this division changes radically from one environment to the next, and from one historical juncture to another? At its most abstract level, it is the fact of the differential assignation of tasks according to sex that is significant; however, this is quite different from the *meaning* or *value* that the content of this sexual division of labor assumes in different contexts. In most cases the assigning of tasks on the basis of sex has an ideological origin. There is no question that a claim such as "women are concentrated in service-oriented occupations in a large number of countries around the world" is descriptively valid. Descriptively, then, perhaps the existence of a similar sexual division of labor (where women work in

service occupations such as nursing, social work, etc., and men in other kinds of occupations) in a variety of different countries can be asserted. However, the concept of the "sexual division of labor" is more than just a descriptive category. It indicates the differential *value* placed on men's work versus "women's work."

Finally, some writers confuse the use of gender as a superordinate category of analysis with the universalistic proof and instantiation of this category. In other words, empirical studies of gender differences are confused with the analytical organization of cross-cultural work. Beverly Brown's (1983) review of the book *Nature, Culture and Gender* (Strathern and McCormack 1980) best illustrates this point. Brown suggests that nature:culture and female:male are superordinate categories that organize and locate lesser categories (such as wild:domestic and biology:technology) within their logic. These categories are universal in the sense that they organize the universe of a system of representations. This relation is totally independent of the universal substantiation of any particular category. Brown's critique hinges on the fact that rather than clarify the generalizability of nature:culture :: female:male as superordinate organization categories, *Nature, Culture and Gender* construes the universality of this equation to lie at the level of empirical truth, which can be investigated through fieldwork. Thus, the usefulness of the nature:culture :: female:male paradigm as a universal mode of the organization of representation within any particular sociohistorical system is lost. Here, methodological universalism is assumed on the basis of the reduction of the nature:culture :: female:male analytic categories to a demand for empirical proof of its existence in different cultures. Discourses of representation are confused with material realities, and the distinction made earlier between "Woman" and "women" is lost. Feminist work that blurs this distinction (which is, interestingly enough, often present in certain Western feminists' self-representation) eventually ends up constructing monolithic images of "Third World women" by ignoring the complex and mobile relationships between their historical materiality on the level of specific oppressions and political choices, on the one hand, and their general discursive representations, on the other.

To summarize: I have discussed three methodological moves identifiable in feminist (and other academic) cross-cultural work which seeks to uncover a universality in women's subordinate position in society. The next and final section pulls together the previous sections, attempting to outline the political effects on the analytical strategies in the context of Western feminist writing on women in the third world. These arguments are not against generalization as much as they are for careful, historically specific generalizations responsive to complex realities. Nor do these arguments deny the necessity of forming strategic political identities and affinities. Thus, while Indian women of different religions, castes, and classes might forge a political unity on the basis of organizing against police brutality toward women (see Kishwar and Vanita 1984), an *analysis* of police brutality must be contextual. Strategic coalitions which construct oppositional political identities for themselves are based on generalization and provisional unities, but the analysis of these group identities can be based on universalistic, ahistorical categories.

· · ·

THE SUBJECT(S) OF POWER

· · ·

What happens when this assumption of "women as an oppressed group" is situated in the context of Western feminist writing about third world women? It is here that I locate the colonialist move. By contrasting the representation of women in the third world with what I referred to earlier as Western feminisms' self-presentation in the same context, we see how Western feminists alone become the true "subjects" of this counterhistory. Third world women, on the other hand, never rise above the debilitating generality of their "object" status.

While radical and liberal feminist assumptions of women as a sex class might elucidate (however inadequately) the autonomy of particular women's struggles in the West, the application of the notion of women as a homogeneous category to women in the third world colonizes and appropriates the pluralities of the simultaneous location of different groups of women in social class and ethnic frameworks; in doing so it ultimately robs them of their historical and political *agency*. Similarly, many Zed Press authors who ground themselves in the basic analytical strategies of traditional Marxism also implicitly create a "unity" of women by substituting "women's activity" for "labor" as the primary theoretical determinant of women's situation. Here again, women are constituted as a coherent group not on the basis of "natural" qualities or needs but on the basis of the sociological "unity" of their role in domestic production and wage labor (see Haraway 1985, esp. p. 76). In other words, Western feminist discourse, by assuming women as a coherent, already constituted group which is placed in kinship, legal, and other structures, defines third world women as subjects *outside* social relations, instead of looking at the way women are constituted *through* these very structures.

Legal, economic, religious, and familial structures are treated as phenomena to be judged by Western standards. It is here that ethnocentric universality comes into play. When these structures are defined as "underdeveloped" or "developing" and women are placed within them, an implicit image of the "average third world woman" is produced. This is the transformation of the (implicitly Western) "oppressed woman" into the "oppressed third world woman." While the category of "oppressed woman" is generated through an exclusive focus on gender difference, "the oppressed third world woman" category has an additional attribute—the "third world difference!" The "third world difference" includes a paternalistic attitude toward women in the third world. Since discussions of the various themes I identified earlier (kinship, education, religion, etc.) are conducted in the context of the relative "underdevelopment" of the third world (which is nothing less than unjustifiably confusing development with the separate path taken by the West in its development, as well as ignoring the directionality of the first-third world power relationship), third world women as a group or category are automatically and necessarily defined as religious (read "not progressive"), family-oriented (read "traditional"), legal minors (read "they-are-still-not-conscious-of-their-rights"), illiterate (read "ignorant"), domestic (read "backward"), and sometimes revolutionary (read "their-country-is-in-a-state-of-war; they-must-fight!"). This is how the "third world difference" is produced.

When the category of "sexually oppressed women" is located within particular systems in the third world which are defined on a scale which is normed through Eurocentric assumptions, not only are third world women defined in a particular way prior to their entry into social relations, but since no connections are made between first and third world power shifts, the assumption is reinforced that the third world has just not evolved to the extent that the West has. This mode of feminist analysis, by homogenizing and systematizing the experiences of different groups of women in these countries, erases all marginal and resistant modes and experiences. It is significant that none of the texts I reviewed in the Zed Press series focuses on lesbian politics or the politics of ethnic and religious marginal organizations in third world women's groups. Resistance can thus be defined only as cumulative reactive, not as something inherent in the operation of power. If power, as Michel Foucault has argued recently, can really be understood only in the context of resistance,[4] this misconceptualization is both analytically and strategically problematical. It limits theoretical analysis as well as reinforces Western cultural imperialism. For in the context of a first/third world balance of power, feminist analyses which perpetrate and sustain the hegemony of the idea of the superiority of the West produce a corresponding set of universal images of the "third world woman," images such as the veiled woman, the powerful mother, the chaste virgin, the obedient wife, etc. These images exist in universal, ahistorical splendor, setting in motion a colonialist discourse which exercises a very specific power in defining, coding, and maintaining existing first/third world connections.

To conclude, then, let me suggest some disconcerting similarities between the typically authorizing signature of such Western feminist writings on women in the third world, and the authorizing signature of the project of humanism in general—humanism as a Western ideological and political project which involves the necessary recuperation of the "East" and "Woman" as Others.

· · ·

As discussed earlier, a comparison between Western feminist self-presentation and Western feminist re-presentation of women in the third world yields significant results. Universal images of "the third world woman" (the veiled woman, chaste virgin, etc.), images constructed from adding the "third world difference" to "sexual difference," are predicated upon (and hence obviously bring into sharper focus) assumptions about Western women as secular, liberated, and having control over their own lives. This is not to suggest that Western women *are* secular, liberated, and in control over their own lives. I am referring to a *discursive* self-presentation, not necessarily to material reality. If this were a material reality, there would be no need for political movements in the West. Similarly, only from the vantage point of the West is it possible to define the "third world" as underdeveloped and economically dependent. Without the overdetermined discourse that creates the *third* world, there would be no (singular and privileged) first world. Without the "third world woman," the particular self-presentation of Western women mentioned above would be problematical. I am suggesting, then, that the one enables and sustains the other. This is not to say that the signature of Western feminist writings on the third world has the same authority as the project of Western humanism. However, in the context of the hegemony of the Western scholarly establishment in the production and dissemination of texts, and in the context of the legitimating imperative of humanistic and scientific discourse, the definition of "the third world woman" as a monolith might well tie into the larger economic and ideological praxis of "disinterested" scientific inquiry and pluralism which are the surface manifestations of a latent economic and cultural colonization of the "non-Western" world. It is time to move beyond the Marx who found it possible to say: They cannot represent themselves; they must be represented.

[1984/1991]

NOTES

1. Terms such as *third* and *first world* are very problematical, both in suggesting oversimplified similarities between and among countries labeled thus, and in implicitly reinforcing existing economic, cultural, and ideological hierarchies which are conjured up in using such terminology. I use the term *"third world"* with full awareness of its problems, only because this is the terminology available to us at the moment. The use of quotation marks is meant to suggest a continuous questioning of the designation. Even when I do not use quotation marks, I mean to use the term critically.

2. I am indebted to Teresa de Lauretis for this particular formulation of the project of feminist theorizing. See especially her introduction in de Lauretis, *Alice Doesn't: Feminism, Semiotics, Cinema* (Bloomington: Indiana University Press, 1984); see also Sylvia Wynter, "The Politics of Domination," unpublished manuscript.

3. This argument is similar to Homi Bhabha's definition of colonial discourse as strategically creating a space for a subject people through the production of knowledges and the exercise of power. The full quote reads: "[colonial discourse is] an apparatus of power. . . . an apparatus that turns on the recognition and disavowal of racial/cultural/historical differences. Its predominant strategic function is the creation of a space for a subject people through the production of knowledges in terms of which surveillance is exercised and a complex form of pleasure/unpleasure is incited. It (i.e., colonial discourse) seeks authorization for its strategies by the production of knowledges by coloniser and colonised which are stereotypical but antithetically evaluated" (1983, 23).

4. This is one of M. Foucault's (1978, 1980) central points in his reconceptualization of the strategies and workings of power networks.

REFERENCES

Amin, Samir. 1977. *Imperialism and Unequal Development*, New York: Monthly Review Press.

Baran, Paul A. 1962. *The Political Economy of Growth*, New York: Monthly Review Press.

Brown, Beverly. 1983. "Displacing the Difference: Review of *Nature, Culture Gender*." *m/f*: 8:79–89.

Deardon, Ann, ed. 1975. *Arab Women*. London: Minority Rights Group Report No. 27.

Foucalt, Michel. 1978. *History of Sexuality:Volume One*, New York: Random House.

———. 1980. *Power/Knowledge*. New York: Pantheon.

Gunder-Frank, Audre, 1967. *Capitalism and Underdevelopment in Latin America*. New York: Monthly Review Press.

Haraway, Donna. 1985. "A Manifesto for Cyborgs: Science Technology and Socialist Feminism in the 1980s." *Socialist Review* 80 (March/April): 65–108.

Hosken, Fran. 1981. "Female Genital Mutilation and Human Rights." *Feminist Issues* 1, no. 3.

Joseph, Gloria, and Jill Lewis. 1981. *Common Differences: Conflicts in Black and White Feminist Perspectives*. Boston: Beacon Press.

Kishwar, Madhu, and Ruth Vanita. 1984. *In Search of Answers: Indian Women's Voices from Manushi*. London: Zed Press.

Mies, Maria. 1982. *The Lace Makers of Naraspur: Indian Housewives Produce for the World Market*. London: Zed Press.

Moraga, Cherríe. 1984. *Loving in the War Years*. Boston: South End Press.

Moraga, Cherríe, and Gloria Anzaldúa, eds. 1983. *This Bridge Called My Back: Writings by Radical Women of Color*. New York: Kitchen Table Press.

Rosaldo, M.A. 1980. "The Use and Abuse of Anthropology: Reflections on Feminism and Cross-Cultural Understanding." *Signs* 53:389–417.

Smith, Barbara, ed. 1983. *Home Girls: A Black Feminist Anthology*. New York: Kitchen Table Press.

Tabari, Azar. 1980. "The Enigma of the Veiled Iranian Women." *Feminist Review* 5:19–32.

 67

Pleasure and Danger: Toward a Politics of Sexuality

CAROLE S. VANCE

CAROLE S. VANCE United States. ND. Anthropologist, specializes in sexuality, human rights, health. A key feminist voice in sexuality studies. "Negotiating Sex and Gender in the Attorney General's Commission on Pornography" (1990), "Sexuality, Human Rights, and Health" with A.M. Miller (2004).

The tension between sexual danger and sexual pleasure is a powerful one in women's lives. Sexuality is simultaneously a domain of restriction, repression, and danger as well as a domain of exploration, pleasure, and agency. To focus only on pleasure and gratification ignores the patriarchal structure in which women act, yet to speak only of sexual violence and oppression ignores women's experience with sexual agency and choice and unwittingly increases the sexual terror and despair in which women live.

The juxtaposition of pleasure and danger has engaged the attention of feminist theorists and activists in both the nineteenth and twentieth centuries, just as it has been an ongoing subject in the lives of individual women who must weigh the pleasures of sexuality against its cost in their daily calculations, choices, and acts. For some, the dangers of sexuality—violence, brutality, and coercion, in the form of rape, forcible incest, and exploitation, as well as everyday cruelty and humiliation—make the pleasures pale by comparison. For others, the positive possibilities of sexuality—explorations of the body, curiosity, intimacy, sensuality, adventure, excitement, human connection, basking in the infantile and non-rational—are not only worthwhile but provide sustaining energy. Nor are these positions fixed, since a woman might chose one perspective or the other at different points in her life in response to external and internal events.

Since the nineteenth century, feminist theorists have disagreed on how to improve women's sexual situation and, even more basically, on what women want sexually. Some have been broadly protectionist, attempting to secure some measure of safety from male lust and aggression, assuming either that women's sexuality is intrinsically muted or at least that it cannot flower until greater safety is established. Others, more often in the twentieth century than the nineteenth, have been expansionist and exploratory, believing that women could venture to be sexual in more visible and daring ways, especially as material changes which favored women's autonomy in general (wage labor, urbanization, contraception, and abortion) also supported sexual autonomy.[1] Throughout one hundred years of intermittent but intense dialogue among theorists, organizers, and activists run a host of questions to which we do not fully know the answers, despite the progress we have made:

- Are male and female sexual natures essentially different, or the product of specific historical and cultural conditions?
- Has women's sexuality been muted by repression, or is it wholly different from men's?
- Does the source of sexual danger to women lie in an intrinsically aggressive or violent male nature, or in the patriarchal conditions that socialize male sexuality to aggression and female sexuality to compliance and submission?
- How can male sexual violence be reduced or eliminated?
- How does the procreative possibility of sex enter into women's experience of sexuality?
- Should feminism be promoting maximum or minimum differentiation in the sexual sphere, and what shape should either vision take?

· · ·

The second wave of feminism mounted a major critique of male sexual violence, indicting the complicity of state institutions and the cultural ideologies that justify it. However, feminism is newly beginning to appreciate the intra-psychic effects of a gender system that places pleasure and safety in opposition for women. Sexual constriction, invisibility, timidity, and uncuriosity are less the signs of an intrinsic and specific female sexual nature and more the signs of thoroughgoing damage. The resulting polarization of male and female sexuality is a likely product of the prevailing gender system, which is used to justify women's need for a restricted, but supposedly safe space and highly controlled sexual expression. The horrific effects of gender inequality may include not only brute violence, but the internalized control of women's impulses, poisoning desire at its very root with self-doubt and anxiety. The subtle connection between how patriarchy interferes with female desire and how women experience their own passion as dangerous is emerging as a critical issue to be explored.

· · ·

The hallmark of sexuality is its complexity: its multiple meanings, sensations, and connections. It is all too easy to cast sexual experience as either wholly pleasurable or dangerous; our culture encourages us to do so. Women are encouraged to assent that all male sexuality done to them is pleasurable and liberatory: women really enjoy being raped but can't admit it, and the often horrid cartoons in *Hustler* are just a lighthearted joke. In a counter-move, the feminist critique emphasized the ubiquity of sexual danger and humiliation in a patriarchal surround. Initially useful as an ideological interruption, this critique now shares the same undialectical and simplistic focus as its opposition. Women's actual sexual experience is more complicated, more difficult to grasp, more unsettling. Just as agreeing not to mention danger requires that one's sexual autobiography be recast, agreeing not to speak about pleasure requires a similar dishonest alchemy, the transmutation of sexuality into unmitigated danger and unremitting victimization.

· · ·

Women are vulnerable to being shamed about sex, and the anti-pornography ideology makes new forms of shaming possible. Traditional objections that women's concern with sex is unimportant are restated in suggestions that sexuality is trivial, diversionary, or not political. If sexual desire is coded as male, women begin to wonder if they are really ever sexual. Do we distrust our passion, thinking it perhaps not our own, but the construction of patriarchal culture? Can women be sexual actors? Can we act on our own behalf? Or are we purely victims, whose efforts must be directed at resisting male depredations in a patriarchal culture? Must our passion await expression for a safer time? When will that time come? Will any of us remember what her passion was? Does exceeding the bounds of femininity—passivity, helplessness, and victimization—make us deeply uncomfortable? Do we fear that if we act on our most deeply felt sexual passion that we will no longer be women? Do we wish, instead, to bind ourselves together into a sisterhood which seeks to curb male lust but does little to promote female pleasure? Sex is always guilty before proven innocent, an expensive undertaking considering the negative sanctions it easily evokes.

The overemphasis on danger runs the risk of making speech about sexual pleasure taboo. Feminists are easily intimidated by the charge that their own pleasure is selfish, as in political rhetoric which suggests that no woman is entitled to talk about sexual pleasure while any woman remains in danger—that is—never. Some also believe that sexuality is a privileged topic, important only to affluent groups, so to talk of it betrays bad manners and bad politics on the part of sexual betters toward the deprived, who reputedly are only interested in issues that are concrete, material, and life-saving, as if sexuality were not all of these. The result is that sexual pleasure in whatever form has become a great guilty secret among feminists.

Hiding pleasure and its sources in feminist discussion does not make the world safe for women, any more than women's acceding to the system of male protection made the world safe for them. When pleasure occupies a smaller and smaller public space and a more guilty private space, individuals do not become empowered; they are merely cut off from the source of their own strength and energy. If women increasingly view themselves entirely as victims through the lens of the oppressor and allow themselves to be viewed that way by others, they become enfeebled and miserable. The taboo on investigating pleasure led to an abstract sexual theory which bears little relationship to daily life. If theory is to have any valid relationship to experience, we need to acknowledge that sexuality is worth talking about seriously. We cannot create a body of knowledge that is true to women's lives, if sexual pleasure cannot be spoken about safely, honestly, and completely.

· · ·

The parallels between social constructionist approaches to gender (the cultural marking of biological sex) and sexuality (desire and erotic pleasure) make it possible to see that although both may be socially constructed, sexuality and gender are separate but overlapping domains or, as Gayle Rubin calls them, "vectors of oppression." Of particular interest is the articulation between specific features of each system, namely how the configurations of the sexual system bear on the experience of being female and, conversely, how the definitions of gender resonate with and are reflected in sexuality. Despite the many interrelationships of sexuality and gender, sexuality is not a residual category, a subcategory of gender; nor are theories of gender fully adequate to account for sexuality.[2] The task is to describe and analyze how cultural connections are made between female bodies and what comes to be understood as "women" and "female sexuality."

· · ·

The information we have—social science surveys, literary analyses, fiction, poetry, visual art, biomedical observations, biographies and autobiographies—raises serious questions of interpretation. None is the straightforward report about women's sexual reality that we wish, and sometimes imagine, we had. If sex is a cultural product, all the representations, descriptions, and depictions of that sexuality are too. Just as our own bodily experience is mediated through culture, so reports or descriptions of others' experience are mediated through cultural forms, conventions, and codes of meaning.[3] . . . Even the most empirically oriented form requires a cultural frame of organization, a code of meaning, a language that classifies feelings and the body. Since the 1890s, for example, sex researchers' attempts to define female pleasure and sexual gratification have undergone dramatic shifts, from vague euphemisms about marital harmony to Masters and Johnson's measurement of the strength and number of vaginal contractions during orgasm. For the viewer or reader, the question remains the same: what is the relationship between what is written in the text or shown in the image, and what *is*? We are most aware of embedded assumptions when reading material from another time or place, which may appear incongruous or disjunctive. Yet we must admit that contemporary work by both men and women has embedded meanings too. These embedded assumptions are especially significant, because so much of the literature on female sexuality has been written by men, suggesting the need for critical reading.

Whether scientific, religious, or political, prescriptive texts that aim to tell people what to do or what is normal pose a number of questions. Are they a self-assured restatement of prevailing norms, safely read as literal indicators of behavior? Or are they anxious attempts to resocialize renegade readers to norms they are flouting? To what degree do prescriptive texts reach a mass audience, and did they in the past, and with what effect?

· · ·

It is no accident that recent feminist sexual controversies about pornography, S/M and butch/femme all demonstrate a need for a more developed analysis of symbolic context and transformation, especially difficult in regard to visual material where our education, vocabulary, and sophistication are far less developed than in regard to literary texts. Our visual illiteracy renders the image overpowering. The emotion aroused by an image is easily attached to rhetorical arguments, overwhelming more subtle analysis and response, and the audience as well, by manipulative imagery, as in polemical slide shows mounted by Right to Life groups or some feminist anti-pornography groups. In each case, the shock induced by the image of a fetus in a bottle or a woman in chains is effectively used to propel the viewer to the desired conclusion.

Sexuality poses a challenge to feminist inquiry, since it is an intersection of the political, social, economic, historical, personal, and experiential, linking behavior and thought, fantasy and action. That these domains intersect does not mean that they are identical. Feminists need sophisticated methodologies and analyses that permit the recognition of each discrete domain as well as their multiple intersections. Recognizing these layers of sexual information, we form and adopt generalizations about even one apparently homogeneous group, white middle-class women, for example, more cautiously. Popular sex manuals, content analysis of women's fiction magazines, vibrator sales, number of contraceptive prescriptions registered, clothing styles—each provides a clue, but even for well-studied groups there are many lacunae. We recognize these lacunae only if we stop extrapolating from one domain to the other. This recognition spurs inquiry into missing areas, and ultimately makes possible the comparison of one domain to another.

A sophisticated analysis of sexual symbols requires that we look beyond easy generalization. Feminist scholarship has delivered a scathing critique of an androcentric and falsely universalizing history in which the historical Everyman, like his authors, was male, white, heterosexual, and affluent. Such accounts omitted women as both subjects of inquiry and as self-conscious historical actors. Corrective research indicates that social characteristics modify the perception and experience of historical events, with gender a significant social marker. Despite its critique of false universals, feminist scholarship and inquiry has not escaped the same sin. . . . Self-criticism of feminist parochialism has proliferated in recent years[4] and has been persuasive in showing why feminist analysis must attempt to include the experience of diverse groups of women, with conclusions specific to particular groups identified as such.

This development, when applied to female sexuality, suggests that sexuality may be thought about, experienced, and acted on differently according to age, class, ethnicity, physical ability, sexual orientation and preference, religion, and region. Confrontation with the complex intersection of social identities leads us away from simple dichotomies (black/white, lesbian/heterosexual working-class/middle-class) toward recognizing the multiple intersection of categories and the resulting complexity of women's lived experience.[5]

· · ·

Although a portion of feminist reluctance to acknowledge differences among women derives from arrogance on the part of mainstream feminists, a significant part derives from another source: the fear of difference among women. If women organize around their oppression by and through differentiation from men, should they not maintain a united front, stressing their shared and unifying characteristic, femaleness? . . . Exploration of differences has, in fact, been a painful experience, beginning with lesbian and heterosexual differences in the early stages of the women's movement and continuing in recent years to differences involving class, religion, ethnicity, and race. Although some have retreated to doctrines which emphasize women's commonality on the one hand, or women's total separation by factors of race and class on the other, many feminists see the importance of dealing with difference, while they remain wary and uncertain of how to do so.

Our discomfort with difference is especially evident around questions of sexual variation, which have expanded beyond the topic of lesbian and heterosexual difference to include all the ways women can obtain pleasure. Sexual orientation is not the only, and may not be the most significant, sexual difference among women. Our ability to think about sexual difference is limited, however, by a cultural system that organizes sexual differences in a hierarchy in which some acts and partners are privileged and others are punished. Privileged forms of sexuality, for example heterosexuality, marriage, and procreation, are protected and rewarded by the state and subsidized through social and economic incentives. . . . Less privileged forms of sexuality are regulated and interdicted by the state, religion, medicine, and public opinion. Those practicing less privileged forms of sexuality . . . suffer from stigma and invisibility, although they also resist.

· · ·

The quest for politically appropriate sexual behavior has led to what Alice Echols calls pre-scriptivism, the tendency to transform broad, general principles like equality, autonomy, and self-determination into fairly specific and rigid standards to which all feminists are expected to conform. There is a very fine line between talking about sex and setting norms; we err very easily given our ignorance of diversity, our fear of difference, and our naive expectation that all like the same sexual food as we. Although we need open discussion to expand theory, we are especially vulnerable to transforming statements of personal preference that inevitably appear in honest discussion ("I like oral sex") into statements that may be probabalistically true ("Women like clitoral stimulation more than penetration") into statements that are truly prescriptive ("Women should avoid penetration"). Certainly, there are intentional efforts at chauvinism. But even mere statements of individual, personal preference are often heard as statements of superiority, criticisms of the listener's practice, or an exhortation to try something new. Women's insecurity, deprivation, and guilt make it difficult to hear a description of personal practice as anything but a prescription.

All political movements, feminism included, espouse social and ethical ideals as they articulate their vision of the good life of more just society. Such movements attempt to analyze and change current behavior, as well as the prevailing social institutions that shape such behavior. Beginning as radical renegades, visionaries, and outsiders, their political success exposes them to the danger of becoming the orthodoxy, if only to their own members, with their own structure of deadening conformity. The dangers of political analysis transmuted from illuminating vision to stale dogma loom especially large in regard to sexuality. Our vast ignorance, our reliance on overgeneralization, and the invisibility of so many groups suggest that we are in a particularly resourceless position to determine which sexual paths will lead to heaven. Although declaring opposition to patriarchal culture, some recent feminist pronouncements about politically desirable and undesirable forms of sexuality bear a striking resemblance to those of the dominant culture, with one possible exception: the repositioning of certain varieties of lesbianism. Within feminism, lesbianism has been rehabilitated, undergoing a transition from the realm of bad sex to the realm of good sex, and within some sectors of the movement, given a privileged position as the most egalitarian and feminist sexual identity. With this exception, new feminist punishments are still meted out to the denizens of the same old sexual lower orders.

Quite apart from our ignorance and prejudice, sexuality may be a particularly unpromising domain for regulation. As Muriel Dimen argues, sexuality remains fluid and everchanging, evolving through adult life in response to internal and external vicissitudes: flexible, anarchic, ambiguous, layered with multiple meanings, offering doors that open to unexpected experience. The connection of both sexual behavior and fantasy to infancy, the irrational, the unconscious is a source of both surprise and pleasure. We impose simplistic and literal standards congruent with political goals at our own peril, ultimately undermining the search for pleasure and expansiveness that motivates visions of political change and human connection.[6]

· · ·

What directions might a feminist politics on sex take in the future? Above all, feminism must be a movement that speaks to sexuality, that does not forfeit the field to reactionary groups who are more than willing to speak. We cannot be cowardly, pretending that feminism is not sexually radical. Being a sex radical at this time, as at most, is less a matter of what you do, and more a matter of what you are willing to think, entertain, and question.

Feminism must, of course, continue to work for material changes that support women's autonomy, including social justice, economic equality, and reproductive choice. At the same time, feminism must speak to sexuality as a site of oppression, not only the oppression of male violence, brutality, and coercion which it has already spoken about eloquently and effectively, but also the repression of female desire that comes from ignorance, invisibility, and fear. Feminism must put forward a politics that resists deprivation and supports pleasure. It must understand pleasure as life-affirming, empowering, desirous of human connection and the future, and not fear it as destructive, enfeebling, or corrupt. Feminism must speak to sexual pleasure as a fundamental right, which cannot be put off to a better or easier time. It must understand that the women to whom it speaks, and those it hopes to reach, care deeply about sexual pleasure and displeasure in their daily lives; that sexuality is a site of struggle—visceral, engaging, riveting—and not a domain of interest only to a narrow, small, and privileged group.

Feminism should encourage women to resist not only coercion and victimization, but also sexual ignorance, deprivation and fear of difference. Feminism should support women's experiments and analyses, encouraging the acquisition of knowledge. We can begin by examining our own experience, sharing it with each other, knowing that in sexuality as in the rest of social life, our adventures, risks, impulses, and terrors provide clues to the future. Feminism must insist that women are sexual subjects, sexual actors, sexual agents; that our histories are complex and instructive; that our experience is not a blank, nor a mere repetition of what has been said about us, and that the pleasure we have experienced is as much a guide to future action as the brutality.

In doing so, we admit that it is not safe to be a woman, and it never has been. Female attempts to claim pleasure are especially dangerous, attacked not only by men, but by women as well. But to wait until a zone of safety is established to begin to explore and organize for pleasure is to cede it as an arena, to give it up, and to admit that we are weaker and more frightened than our enemies ever imagined.

Social movements, feminism included, move toward a vision; they cannot operate solely on fear. It is not enough to move women away from danger and oppression; it is necessary to move toward something: toward pleasure, agency, self-definition. Feminism must increase women's pleasure and joy not just decrease our misery. It is difficult for political movements to speak for any extended time to the ambiguities, ambivalences, and complexities that underscore human experience. Yet movements remain vital and vigorous to the extent that they are able to tap this wellspring of human experience. Without it, they become dogmatic, dry, compulsive, and ineffective. To persist amid frustrations and obstacles, feminism must reach deeply into women's pleasure and draw on this energy.

[1984]

NOTES

1. Ellen Carol DuBois and Linda Gordon, "Seeking Ecstasy on the Battlefield: Danger and Pleasure in Nineteenth-century Feminist Sexual Thought", in *Pleasure & Danger: Exploring Female Sexuality*, Carol S. Vance, ed., 1984.
2. See Gayle Rubin, "Thinking Sex", for a fuller development of this argument.
3. For varied approaches to the question of representation, see: Meryl Altman, "Everything They Always Wanted You to Know: The Ideology of Popular Sex Literature"; Bette Gordon, "*Variety:* The Pleasure in Looking"; Barbara Kruger, "No Progress in Pleasure"; and Kaja Silverman, "*Histoire d'O:* The Construction of a Female Subject", in *Pleasure and Danger*.
4. See, for example, Margaret Cruikshank (ed.), *Lesbian Studies*, op. cit.; Lorraine Bethel and Barbara Smith (eds), *Conditions Five:* "The Black Women's Issue", 1979; Cherríe Moraga and Gloria Anzaldúa (eds), *This Bridge Called My Back*, Massachusetts, Persephone Press, 1981; Gloria T. Hull, Patricia Bell Scott, and Barbara Smith (eds), *But Some of Us Are Brave*, New York, Feminist Press, 1982.
5. Frances Doughty, "Introduction: The Daily Life of Lesbian Sexuality", unpublished paper, National Women's Studies Association, Columbus, Ohio, June 1983; and Oliva M. Espín, "Cultural and Historical Influences on Sexuality in Hispanic/Latin Women: Implications for Psychotherapy"; Roberta Galler, "The Myth of the Perfect Body"; Carol Munter, "Fat and the Fantasy of Perfection", in *Pleasure and Danger*.
6. Muriel Dimen. "Politically Correct? Politically Incorrect?" in *Pleasure and Danger*.

PART VI

1985–1995

1985–1995: Introduction

By the end of the 1980s, feminism and women's studies could reasonably be said to have made a substantial impact inside and outside the academy. Women could mark real increases in their access to most areas of education and employment. A large percentage of colleges and universities had women's studies programs and some had begun to establish graduate degrees in the field. Most disciplines showed the significant impact of feminist thought. In addition, work in women's studies and other ethnic studies had helped to catalyze a serious conversation about interdisciplinary knowledge across the academy.

On the other hand, the latter part of the 1980s, after more than a decade of Republican presidencies and Reaganomics, was a time of confronting backlash and dealing with an organized academic and political right. The academic right used the rhetoric of "political correctness" and the funding of right-wing political organizations to attack women's studies programs; curriculum transformation projects; and feminist, gay, and lesbian scholars and scholarship; as well as funding agencies that supported such activities. At the same time, this was the height of antichoice politics, expressed in clinic blockades, bombings, and assaults on and killing of doctors and other medical personnel providing reproductive services.

The shift in feminist theory in this period may be charted by reference to the 1985 publication of Donna Haraway's "Cyborg Manifesto." It argues for epistemologies that resist such dualisms as nature/culture and are more interested in boundaries, partiality, and coalition than in hierarchies, organic wholes, and coherent identities. The trajectories that Haraway's argument suggests are played out both in Teresa de Lauretis' concept of positionality, as Linda Alcoff explores it, and in the epistemologies proposed by Gloria Anzaldúa and Patricia Hill Collins. Feminist theory's other major engagements in this period are with postmodernism, represented here in essays by Linda Alcoff and Joan Scott; with science and its assumption of objectivity, seen in the essays by Sandra Harding and Evelyn Fox Keller; and with queer theory, engaged by Judith Butler.

The globalization of economies, markets, technologies, and the workforce made feminists increasingly aware of the need for a theory and practice appropriate to this "new world order." The war in the Persian Gulf, the conflict in the former Yugoslavia, the disintegration of the U.S.S.R. and communist Eastern Europe, and the integration of Europe all signaled global realignments of power. These developments challenged U.S. feminists to work in coalition with women throughout the world and to think from multiple perspectives. The 1995 U.N. Conference in Beijing and NGO Forum in Huairou were perhaps the most productive of these conferences, due both to the synergy between technologies of dissemination of knowledge and to a renewed emphasis on women's rights as human rights.

In the latter part of this period, "Third Wave" feminism and self-described "girls" or "grrls" began to challenge the articulations of their feminist predecessors. The new technologies and practices of networks, webs, online services, chat rooms, and listservs offered new possibilities and yet also seemed to be forms of commodification of information and knowledge. Even as these new areas opened, we continued to debate questions that have been with us for more than a hundred years. Though new voices continued to enter its multilayered conversation, feminist theory and scholarship had clearly, by the end of this period, traced out a field of inquiry that has quite thoroughly permeated both *what* we know and *how* we know it.

68

A Cyborg Manifesto: Science, Technology, and Socialist-Feminism in the Late Twentieth Century

D O N N A   H A R A W A Y

DONNA HARAWAY United States. 1944–   .
Historian of science and technology. *Primate Visions:
Gender, Race, and Nature in the World of Modern
Science* (1989), *Simians, Cyborgs and Women: The
Reinvention of Nature* (1991), *Modest-Witness@
Second-Millennium. FemaleMan-Meets-OncoMouse:
Feminism and Technoscience* (1997), *When Species Meet
(Posthumanities)* (2007).

AN IRONIC DREAM OF A COMMON LANGUAGE FOR WOMEN IN THE INTEGRATED CIRCUIT

This chapter is an effort to build an ironic political
myth faithful to feminism, socialism, and materialism. Perhaps more faithful as blasphemy is faithful than as reverent worship and identification.
Blasphemy has always seemed to require taking
things very seriously. I know no better stance to
adopt from within the secular-religious, evangelical
traditions of United States politics, including the
politics of socialist-feminism. Blasphemy protects
one from the moral majority within, while still
insisting on the need for community. Blasphemy is
not apostasy. Irony is about contradictions that do
not resolve into larger wholes, even dialectically,
about the tension of holding incompatible things
together because both or all are necessary and true.
Irony is about humour and serious play. It is also a
rhetorical strategy and a political method, one I
would like to see more honoured within socialist-
feminism. At the centre of my ironic faith, my blasphemy, is the image of the cyborg.

A cyborg is a cybernetic organism, a hybrid of
machine and organism, a creature of social reality
as well as a creature of fiction. Social reality is lived
social relations, our most important political construction, a world-changing fiction. The international

women's movements have constructed 'women's
experience', as well as uncovered or discovered this
crucial collective object. This experience is a fiction
and fact of the most crucial, political kind. Liberation rests on the construction of the consciousness,
the imaginative apprehension of oppression, and
so of possibility. The cyborg is a matter of fiction
and lived experience that changes what counts as
women's experience in the late twentieth century.
This is a struggle over life and death, but the
boundary between science fiction and social reality
is an optical illusion.

Contemporary science fiction is full of cyborgs—
creatures simultaneously animal and machine, who
populate worlds ambiguously natural and crafted.
Modern medicine is also full of cyborgs, of couplings between organism and machine, each conceived as coded devices, in an intimacy and with a
power that was not generated in the history of sexuality. Cyborg 'sex' restores some of the lovely replica-
tive baroque of ferns and invertebrates (such nice
organic prophylactics against heterosexism). Cyborg
replication is uncoupled from organic reproduction.
Modern production seems like a dream of cyborg
colonization work, a dream that makes the night-
mare of Taylorism seem idyllic. And modern war is
a cyborg orgy, coded by C^3I, command-control-
communication-intelligence, an $84 billion item in
1984's US defence budget. I am making an argument for the cyborg as a fiction mapping our social
and bodily reality and as an imaginative resource
suggesting some very fruitful couplings. Michel
Foucault's biopolitics is a flaccid premonition of
cyborg politics, a very open field.

By the late twentieth century, our time, a mythic
time, we are all chimeras, theorized and fabricated
hybrids of machine and organism; in short, we are
cyborgs. The cyborg is our ontology; it gives us our
politics. The cyborg is a condensed image of both
imagination and material reality, the two joined
centres structuring any possibility of historical
transformation. In the traditions of 'Western' science and politics—the tradition of racist, male-
dominant capitalism; the tradition of progress; the
tradition of the appropriation of nature as resource
for the productions of culture; the tradition of
reproduction of the self from the reflections of the
other—the relation between organism and machine

has been a border war. The stakes in the border war have been the territories of production, reproduction, and imagination. This chapter is an argument for *pleasure* in the confusion of boundaries and for *responsibility* in their construction. It is also an effort to contribute to socialist-feminist culture and theory in a post-modernist, non-naturalist mode and in the utopian tradition of imagining a world without gender, which is perhaps a world without genesis, but maybe also a world without end. The cyborg incarnation is outside salvation history. Nor does it mark time on an oedipal calendar, attempting to heal the terrible cleavages of gender in an oral symbiotic utopia or post-oedipal apocalypse. As Zoe Sofoulis argues in her unpublished manuscript on Jacques Lacan, Melanie Klein, and nuclear culture, *Lacklein,* the most terrible and perhaps the most promising monsters in cyborg worlds are embodied in non-oedipal narratives with a different logic of repression, which we need to understand for our survival.

The cyborg is a creature in a post-gender world; it has no truck with bisexuality, pre-oedipal symbiosis, unalienated labour, or other seductions to organic wholeness through a final appropriation of all the powers of the parts into a higher unity. In a sense, the cyborg has no origin story in the Western sense—a 'final' irony since the cyborg is also the awful apocalyptic *telos* of the 'West's' escalating dominations of abstract individuation, an ultimate self untied at last from all dependency, a man in space. An origin story in the 'Western', humanist sense depends on the myth of original unity, fullness, bliss and terror, represented by the phallic mother from whom all humans must separate, the task of individual development and of history, the twin potent myths inscribed most powerfully for us in psychoanalysis and Marxism. Hilary Klein has argued that both Marxism and psychoanalysis, in their concepts of labour and of individuation and gender formation, depend on the plot of original unity out of which difference must be produced and enlisted in a drama of escalating domination of woman/nature. The cyborg skips the step of original unity, of identification with nature in the Western sense. This is its illegitimate promise that might lead to subversion of its teleology as star wars.

The cyborg is resolutely committed to partiality, irony, intimacy, and perversity. It is oppositional, utopian, and completely without innocence. No longer structured by the polarity of public and private, the cyborg defines a technological polis based partly on a revolution of social relations in the *oikos,* the household. Nature and culture are reworked; the one can no longer be the resource for appropriation or incorporation by the other. The relationships for forming wholes from parts, including those of polarity and hierarchical domination, are at issue in the cyborg world. Unlike the hopes of Frankenstein's monster, the cyborg does not expect its father to save it through a restoration of the garden; that is, through the fabrication of a heterosexual mate, through its completion in a finished whole, a city and cosmos. The cyborg does not dream of community on the model of the organic family, this time without the oedipal project. The cyborg would not recognize the Garden of Eden; it is not made of mud and cannot dream of returning to dust. Perhaps that is why I want to see if cyborgs can subvert the apocalypse of returning to nuclear dust in the manic compulsion to name the Enemy. Cyborgs are not reverent; they do not remember the cosmos. They are wary of holism, but needy for connection—they seem to have a natural feel for united front politics, but without the vanguard party. The main trouble with cyborgs, of course, is that they are the illegitimate offspring of militarism and patriarchal capitalism, not to mention state socialism. But illegitimate offspring are often exceedingly unfaithful to their origins. Their fathers, after all, are inessential.

· · ·

So my cyborg myth is about transgressed boundaries, potent fusions, and dangerous possibilities which progressive people might explore as one part of needed political work. One of my premises is that most Americans socialists and feminists see deepened dualisms of mind and body, animal and machine, idealism and materialism in the social practices, symbolic formulations, and physical artefacts associated with 'high technology' and scientific culture. From *One-Dimensional Man* (Marcuse, 1964) to *The Death of Nature* (Merchant, 1980), the analytic resources developed by progressives have insisted on the necessary domination of technics and recalled us to an imagined organic body to integrate our resistance. Another of my premises is that the need for unity of people trying to resist worldwide intensification of domination has never been more acute. But a slightly perverse shift of perspective might better enable us to contest for meanings, as well as for other forms of power and pleasure in technologically mediated societies.

From one perspective, a cyborg world is about the final imposition of a grid of control on the planet, about the final abstraction embodied in a Star Wars apocalypse waged in the name of defence, about the final appropriation of women's bodies in a masculinist orgy of war (Sofia, 1984). From another perspective, a cyborg world might be about lived social and bodily realities in which people are not afraid of their joint kinship with animals and machines, not afraid of permanently partial identities and contradictory standpoints. The political struggle is to see from both perspectives at once because each reveals both dominations and possibilities unimaginable from the other vantage point. Single vision produces worse illusions than double vision or many-headed monsters. Cyborg unities are monstrous and illegitimate; in our present political circumstances, we could hardly hope for more potent myths for resistance and recoupling. I like to imagine LAG, the Livermore Action Group, as a kind of cyborg society, dedicated to realistically converting the laboratories that most fiercely embody and spew out the tools of technological apocalypse, and committed to building a political form that actually manages to hold together witches, engineers, elders, perverts, Christians, mothers, and Leninists long enough to disarm the state. Fission Impossible is the name of the affinity group in my town. (Affinity: related not by blood but by choice, the appeal of one chemical nuclear group for another, avidity.)

· · ·

THE INFORMATICS OF DOMINATION

In this attempt at an epistemological and political position, I would like to sketch a picture of possible unity, a picture indebted to socialist and feminist principles of design. The frame for my sketch is set by the extent and importance of rearrangements in worldwide social relations tied to science and technology. I argue for a politics rooted in claims about fundamental changes in the nature of class, race, and gender in an emerging system of world order analogous in its novelty and scope to that created by industrial capitalism; we are living through a movement from an organic, industrial society to a polymorphous, information system—from all work to all play, a deadly game. Simultaneously material and ideological, the dichotomies may be expressed in the following chart of transitions from the comfortable old hierarchal dominations to the scary new networks I have called the informatics of domination:

Representation	Simulation
Bourgeois novel, realism	Science fiction, postmodernism
Organism	Biotic component
Depth, integrity	Surface, boundary
Heat	Noise
Biology as clinical practice	Biology as inscription
Physiology	Communications engineering
Small group	Subsystem
Perfection	Optimization
Eugenics	Population control
Decadence, *Magic Mountain*	Obsolescence, *Future Shock*
Hygiene	Stress management
Microbiology, tuberculosis	Immunology, AIDS
Organic division of labour	Ergonomics/ Cybernetics of labour
Functional specialization	Modular construction
Reproduction	Replication
Organic sex role specialization	Optimal genetic strategies
Biological determinism	Evolutionary inertia, constraints
Community ecology	Ecosystem
Racial chain of being	Neo-imperialism, United Nations humanism
Scientific management in home/factory	Global factory/ Electronic cottage
Family/Market/Factory	Women in the Integrated Circuit

Family wage	Comparable worth
Public/Private	Cyborg citizenship
Nature/Culture	Fields of difference
Co-operation	Communications enhancement
Freud	Lacan
Sex	Genetic engineering
Labour	Robotics
Mind	Artificial Intelligence
Second World War	Star Wars
White Capitalist Patriarchy	Informatics of Domination

This list suggests several interesting things. First, the objects on the right-hand side cannot be coded as 'natural', a realization that subverts naturalistic coding for the left-hand side as well. We cannot go back ideologically or materially. It's not just that 'god' is dead; so is the 'goddess'. Or both are revivified in the worlds charged with microelectronic and biotechnological politics. In relation to objects like biotic components, one must think not in terms of essential properties, but in terms of design, boundary constraints, rates of flows, systems logics, costs of lowering constraints. Sexual reproduction is one kind of reproductive strategy among many, with costs and benefits as a function of the system environment. Ideologies of sexual reproduction can no longer reasonably call on notions of sex and sex role as organic aspects in natural objects like organisms and families. Such reasoning will be unmasked as irrational, and ironically corporate executives reading *Playboy* and antiporn radical feminists will make strange bedfellows in jointly unmasking the irrationalism.

Likewise for race, ideologies about human diversity have to be formulated in terms of frequencies of parameters, like blood groups or intelligence scores. It is 'irrational' to invoke concepts like primitive and civilized. For liberals and radicals, the search for integrated social systems gives way to a new practice called 'experimental ethnography' in which an organic object dissipates in attention to the play of writing. At the level of ideology, we see translations of racism and colonialism into languages of development and under-development, rates and constraints of modernization. Any objects or persons can be reasonably thought of in terms of disassembly and reassembly; no 'natural' architectures constrain

system design. The financial districts in all the world's cities, as well as the export-processing and free-trade zones, proclaim this elementary fact of 'late capitalism'. The entire universe of objects that can be known scientifically must be formulated as problems in communications engineering (for the managers) or theories of the text (for those who would resist). Both are cyborg semiologies.

One should expect control strategies to concentrate on boundary conditions and interfaces, on rates of flow across boundaries—and not on the integrity of natural objects. 'Integrity' or 'sincerity' of the Western self gives way to decision procedures and expert systems. For example, control strategies applied to women's capacities to give birth to new human beings will be developed in the languages of population control and maximization of goal achievement for individual decision-makers. Control strategies will be formulated in terms of rates, costs of constraints, degrees of freedom. Human beings, like any other component or subsystem, must be localized in a system architecture whose basic modes of operation are probabilistic, statistical. No objects, spaces, or bodies are sacred in themselves; any component can be interfaced with any other if the proper standard, the proper code, can be constructed for processing signals in a common language. Exchange in this world transcends the universal translation effected by capitalist markets that Marx analysed so well. The privileged pathology affecting all kinds of components in this universe is stress—communications breakdown (Hogness, 1983). The cyborg is not subject to Foucault's biopolitics; the cyborg simulates politics, a much more potent field of operations.

This kind of analysis of scientific and cultural objects of knowledge which have appeared historically since the Second World War prepares us to notice some important inadequacies in feminist analysis which has proceeded as if the organic, hierarchical dualisms ordering discourse in 'the West' since Aristotle still ruled. They have been cannibalized, or as Zoe Sofia (Sofoulis) might put it, they have been 'techno-digested'. The dichotomies between mind and body, animal and human, organism and machine, public and private, nature and culture, men and women, primitive and civilized are all in question ideologically. The actual situation of women is their integration/exploitation into a world system of production/reproduction and communication called the informatics of domination. The home, workplace, market, public arena, the body itself—all can be dispersed and interfaced in nearly infinite, polymorphous ways, with large consequences for women and others—consequences that themselves are very different for different people and which make potent oppositional international movements difficult to imagine and essential for survival. One important route for reconstructing socialist-feminist politics is through theory and practice addressed to the social relations of science and technology, including crucially the systems of myth and meanings structuring our imaginations. The cyborg is a kind of disassembled and reassembled, postmodern collective and personal self. This is the self feminists must code.

Communications technologies and biotechnologies are the crucial tools recrafting our bodies. These tools embody and enforce new social relations for women worldwide. Technologies and scientific discourses can be partially understood as formalizations, i.e., as frozen moments, of the fluid social interactions constituting them, but they should also be viewed as instruments for enforcing meanings. The boundary is permeable between tool and myth, instrument and concept, historical systems of social relations and historical anatomies of possible bodies, including objects of knowledge. Indeed, myth and tool mutually constitute each other.

Furthermore, communications sciences and modern biologies are constructed by a common move—*the translation of the world into a problem of coding*, a search for a common language in which all resistance to instrumental control disappears and all heterogeneity can be submitted to disassembly, reassembly, investment, and exchange.

In communications sciences, the translation of the world into a problem in coding can be illustrated by looking at cybernetic (feedback-controlled) systems theories applied to telephone technology, computer design, weapons deployment, or data base construction and maintenance. In each case, solution to the key questions rests on theory of language and control; the key operation is determining the rates, directions, and probabilities of flow of a quantity called information. The world is subdivided by boundaries differentially permeable to information. Information is just that kind of quantifiable element (unit, basis of unity) which allows universal translation, and so unhindered instrumental power (called effective communication). The biggest threat to such power is interruption of communication. Any system breakdown is a function of stress. The fundamentals of this technology can be condensed into the metaphor C^3I, command-control-communication-intelligence, the military's symbol for its operations theory.

In modern biologies, the translation of the world into a problem in coding can be illustrated by molecular genetics, ecology, sociobiological evolutionary theory, and immunobiology. The organism has been translated into problems of genetic coding and read-out. Biotechnology, a writing technology, informs research broadly. In a sense, organisms have ceased to exist as objects of knowledge, giving way to biotic components, i.e., special kinds of information-processing devices. The analogous moves in ecology could be examined by probing the history and utility of the concept of the ecosystem. Immunobiology and associated medical practices are rich exemplars of the privilege of coding and recognition systems as objects of knowledge, as constructions of bodily reality for us. Biology here is kind of cryptography. Research is necessarily a kind of intelligence activity. Ironies abound. A stressed system goes awry, its communication processes break down; it fails to recognize the difference between self and other. Human babies with baboon hearts evoke national ethical perplexity—for animal rights activists at least as much as for the guardians of human purity. In the US gay men and intravenous drug users are the 'privileged' victims of an awful immune system disease that marks (inscribes on the body) confusion of boundaries and moral pollution (Triechler, 1987).

But these excursions into communications sciences and biology have been at a rarefied level; there is a mundane, largely economic reality to support my claim that these sciences and technologies indicate fundamental transformations in the structure of the world for us. Communications technologies depend on electronics. Modern states, multinational corporations, military power, welfare state apparatuses, satellite systems, political processes, fabrication of our imaginations, labour-control systems, medical constructions of our bodies, commercial pornography, the international division of labour, and religious evangelism depend intimately upon electronics. Microelectronics is the technical basis of simulacra; that is, of copies without originals.

Microelectronics mediates the translations of labour into robotics and word processing, sex into genetic engineering and reproductive technologies, and mind into artificial intelligence and decision procedures. The new biotechnologies concern more than human reproduction. Biology as a powerful engineering science for redesigning materials and processes has revolutionary implications for industry, perhaps most obvious today in areas of fermentation, agriculture, and energy. Communications sciences and biology are constructions of natural-technical objects of knowledge in which the difference between machine and organism is thoroughly blurred; mind, body, and tool are on very intimate terms. The 'multinational' material organization of the production and reproduction of daily life and the symbolic organization of the production and reproduction of culture and imagination seem equally implicated. The boundary-maintaining images of base and superstructure, public and private, or material and ideal never seemed more feeble.

I have used Rachel Grossman's (1980) image of women in the integrated circuit to name the situation of women in a world so intimately restructured through the social relations of science and technology. I used the odd circumlocution, 'the social relations of science and technology', to indicate that we are not dealing with a technological determinism, but with a historical system depending upon structured relations among people. But the phrase should also indicate that science and technology provide fresh sources of power, that we need fresh sources of analysis and political action (Latour, 1984). Some of the rearrangements of race, sex, and class rooted in high-tech-facilitated social relations can make socialist-feminism more relevant to effective progressive politics.

· · ·

WOMEN IN THE INTEGRATED CIRCUIT

Let me summarize the picture of women's historical locations in advanced industrial societies, as these positions have been restructured partly through the social relations of science and technology. If it was ever possible ideologically to characterize women's lives by the distinction of public and private domains—suggested by images of the division of working-class life into factory and home, of bourgeois life into market and home, and of gender existence into personal and political realms—it is now a totally misleading ideology, even to show how both terms of these dichotomies construct each other in practice and in theory. I prefer a network ideological image, suggesting the profusion of spaces and identities and the permeability of boundaries in the personal body and in the body politic. 'Networking' is both a feminist practice and a multinational corporate strategy—weaving is for oppositional cyborgs.

So let me return to the earlier image of the informatics of domination and trace one vision of women's 'place' in the integrated circuit, touching only a few idealized social locations seen primarily from the point of view of advanced capitalist societies: Home, Market, Paid Work Place, State, School, Clinic-Hospital, and Church. Each of these idealized spaces is logically and practically implied in every other locus, perhaps analogous to a holographic photograph. I want to suggest the impact of the social relations mediated and enforced by the new technologies in order to help formulate needed analysis and practical work. However, there is no 'place' for women in these networks, only geometrics of difference and contradiction crucial to women's cyborg identities. If we learn how to read these webs of power and social life, we might learn new couplings, new coalitions. There is no way to read the following list from a standpoint of 'identification', of a unitary self. The issue is dispersion. The task is to survive in the diaspora.

Home: Women-headed households, serial monogamy, flight of men, old women alone, technology of domestic work, paid homework, reemergence of home sweat-shops, home-based businesses and telecommuting, electronic cottage, urban homelessness, migration, module architecture, reinforced (simulated) nuclear family, intense domestic violence.

Market: Women's continuing consumption work, newly targeted to buy the profusion of new production from the new technologies (especially as the competitive race among industrialized and industrializing nations to avoid dangerous mass unemployment necessitates finding ever bigger new markets for ever less clearly needed commodities); bimodal buying power, coupled with advertising targeting of the numerous affluent groups and neglect of the previous mass markets; growing importance of informal markets in labour and commodities parallel to high-tech, affluent market structures; surveillance systems through electronic funds transfer; intensified market abstraction (commodification) of experience, resulting in ineffective utopian or equivalent cynical theories of community; extreme mobility (abstraction) of marketing/financing systems; interpretation of sexual and labour markets; intensified sexualization of abstracted and alienated consumption.

Paid Work Place: Continued intense sexual and racial division of labour, but considerable growth of membership in privileged occupational categories for many white women and people of colour; impact of new technologies on women's work in clerical, service, manufacturing (especially textiles), agriculture, electronics; international restructuring of the working classes; development of new time arrangements to facilitate the homework economy (flex-time, part time, over time, no time); homework and out work; increased pressures for two-tiered wage structures; significant numbers of people in cash-dependent populations worldwide with no experience or no further hope of stable employment; most labour 'marginal' or 'feminized'.

State: Continued erosion of the welfare state; decentralizations with increased surveillance and control; citizenship by telematics; imperialism and political power broadly in the form of information rich/information poor differentiation; increased high-tech militarization increasingly opposed by many social groups; reduction of civil service jobs as a result of the growing capital intensification of office work, with implications for occupational mobility for women of colour; growing privatization of material and ideological life and culture; close integration of privatization and militarization, the high-tech forms of bourgeois capitalist personal and public life; invisibility of different social groups to each other, linked to psychological mechanisms of belief in abstract enemies.

School: Deepening coupling of high-tech capital needs and public education at all levels; differentiated by race, class, and gender; managerial classes involved in educational reform and refunding at the cost of remaining progressive educational democratic structures for children and teachers; education for mass ignorance and repression in technocratic and militarized culture; growing anti-science mystery cults in dissenting and radical political movements; continued relative scientific illiteracy among white women and people of colour; growing industrial direction of education (especially higher education) by science-based multinationals (particularly in electronics- and biotechnology-dependent companies); highly educated, numerous élites in a progressively bimodal society.

Clinic-Hospital: Intensified machine–body relations; renegotiations of public metaphors which channel personal experience of the body, particularly in relation to reproduction, immune system functions, and 'stress' phenomena; intensification of reproductive politics in response to world historical implications of women's unrealized, potential control of their relation to reproduction; emergence of new, historically specific diseases; struggles over meanings and means of health in environments pervaded by high technology products and processes; continuing feminization of health work; intensified struggle over state responsibility for health; continued ideological role of popular health movements as a major form of American politics.

Church: Electronic fundamentalist 'super-saver' preachers solemnizing the union of electronic capital and automated fetish gods; intensified importance of churches in resisting the militarized state; central struggle over women's meanings and authority in religion; continued relevance of spirituality, intertwined with sex and health, in political struggle.

The only way to characterize the informatics of domination is as a massive intensification of insecurity and cultural impoverishment, with common failure of subsistence networks for the most vulnerable. Since much of this picture interweaves with the social relations of science and technology, the urgency of a socialist-feminist politics addressed to science and technology is plain. There is much now being done, and the grounds for political work are rich. For example, the efforts to develop forms of collective struggle for women in paid work, like SEIU's District 925 (Service Employees International Union's office workers' organization in the U.S.) should be a high priority for all of us. These efforts are profoundly tied to technical restructuring of labour processes and reformations of working classes. These efforts also are providing understanding of a more comprehensive kind of labour organization, involving community, sexuality, and family issues never privileged in the largely white male industrial unions.

The structural rearrangements related to the social relations of science and technology evoke strong ambivalence. But it is not necessary to be ultimately depressed by the implications of late twentieth-century women's relation to all aspects of work, culture, production of knowledge, sexuality, and reproduction. For excellent reasons, most Marxists see domination best and have trouble understanding what can only look like false consciousness and people's complicity in their own domination in late capitalism. It is crucial to remember that what is lost, perhaps especially from women's points of view, is often virulent forms of oppression, nostalgically naturalized in the face of current violation. Ambivalence towards the disrupted unities mediated by high-tech culture requires not sorting consciousness into categories of 'clear-sighted critique grounding a solid political epistemology' versus 'manipulated false consciousness', but subtle understanding of emerging pleasures, experiences, and powers with serious potential for changing the rules of the game.

There are grounds for hope in the emerging bases for new kinds of unity across race, gender, and class, as these elementary units of a socialist-feminist analysis themselves suffer protein transformations. Intensifications of hardship experienced world-wide in connection with the social relations of science and technology are severe. But what people are experiencing is not transparently clear, and we lack sufficiently subtle connections for collectively building effective theories of experience. Present efforts—Marxist, psychoanalytic, feminist, anthropological—to clarify even 'our' experience are rudimentary.

I am conscious of the odd perspective provided by my historical position—a PhD in biology for an Irish Catholic girl was made possible by Sputnik's impact on US national science-education policy. I have a body and mind as much constructed by the post-Second World War arms race and cold war as by the women's movements. There are more grounds for hope in focusing on the contradictory effects of politics designed to produce loyal American technocrats, which also produced large numbers of dissidents, than in focusing on the present defeats.

The permanent partiality of feminist points of view has consequences for our expectations of forms of political organization and participation. We do not need a totality in order to work well. The feminist dream of a common language, like all dreams for a perfectly true language, of perfectly faithful naming of experience, is a totalizing and imperialist one. In that sense, dialectics too is a dream language, longing to resolve contradiction. Perhaps, ironically, we can learn from our fusions with animals and machines how not to be Man, the embodiment of Western logos. From the point of view of pleasure in these potent and taboo fusions, made inevitable by the social relations of science and technology, there might indeed be a feminist science.

CYBORGS: A MYTH OF POLITICAL IDENTITY

· · ·

Writing is pre-eminently the technology of cyborgs, etched surfaces of the late twentieth century. Cyborg politics is the struggle for language and the struggle against perfect communication, against the one code that translates all meaning perfectly, the central dogma of phallogocentrism. That is why cyborg politics insist on noise and advocate pollution, rejoicing in the illegitimate fusions of animal and machine. These are the couplings which make Man and Woman so problematic, subverting the structure of desire, the force imagined to generate language and gender, and so subverting the structure and modes of reproduction of 'Western' identity, of nature and culture, of mirror and eye, slave and master, body and mind. 'We' did not originally choose to be cyborgs, but choice grounds a liberal politics and epistemology that imagines the reproduction of individuals before the wider replications of 'texts'.

From the perspective of cyborgs, freed of the need to ground politics in 'our' privileged position of the oppression that incorporates all other dominations, the innocence of the merely violated, the ground of those closer to nature, we can see powerful possibilities. Feminisms and Marxisms have run aground on Western epistemological imperatives to construct a revolutionary subject from the perspective of a hierarchy of oppressions and/or a latent position of moral superiority, innocence, and greater closeness to nature. With no available original dream of a common language or original symbiosis promising protection from hostile 'masculine' separation, but written into the play of a text that has no finally privileged reading or salvation history, to recognize 'oneself' as fully implicated in the world, frees us of the need to root politics in identification, vanguard parties, purity, and mothering. Stripped of identity, the bastard race teaches about the power of the margins and the importance of a mother like Malinche. Women of colour have transformed her from the evil mother of masculinist fear into the originally literate mother who teaches survival.

This is not just literary deconstruction, but liminal transformation. Every story that begins with original innocence and privileges the return to wholeness imagines the drama of life to be individuation, separation, the birth of the self, the tragedy of autonomy, the fall into writing, alienation; that is, war, tempered by imaginary respite in the bosom of the Other. These plots are ruled by a reproductive politics—rebirth without flaw, perfection, abstraction. In this plot women are imagined either better or worse off, but all agree they have less selfhood, weaker individuation, more fusion to the oral, to Mother, less at stake in masculine autonomy. But there is another route to having less at stake in masculine autonomy, a route that does not pass through Woman, Primitive, Zero, the Mirror Stage and its imaginary. It passes through women and other present-tense, illegitimate cyborgs, not of Woman born, who refuse the ideological resources of victimization so as to have a real life. These cyborgs are the people who refuse to disappear on cue, no matter how many times a 'Western' commentator remarks on the sad passing of another primitive, another organic group done in by 'Western' technology, by writing. These real-life cyborgs (for example, the Southeast Asian village women workers in Japanese and U.S. electronics firms described by Aihwa Ong) are actively rewriting the texts of their bod-

ies and societies. Survival is the stakes in this play of readings.

To recapitulate, certain dualisms have been persistent in Western traditions; they have all been systemic to the logics and practices of domination of women, people of colour, nature, workers, animals—in short, domination of all constituted as others, whose task is to mirror the self. Chief among these troubling dualisms are self/other, mind/body, culture/nature, male/female, civilized/primitive, reality/appearance, whole/part, agent/resource, maker/made, active/passive, right/wrong, truth/illusion, total/partial, God/man. The self is the One who is not dominated, who knows that by the service of the other, the other is the one who holds the future, who knows that by the experience of domination, which gives the lie to the autonomy of the self. To be One is to be autonomous, to be powerful, to be God; but to be One is to be an illusion, and so to be involved in a dialectic of apocalypse with the other. Yet to be other is to be multiple, without clear boundary, frayed, insubstantial. One is too few, but two are too many.

High-tech culture challenges these dualisms in intriguing ways. It is not clear who makes and who is made in the relation between human and machine. It is not clear what is mind and what body in machines that resolve into coding practices. In so far as we know ourselves in both formal discourse (for example, biology) and in daily practice (for example, the homework economy in the integrated circuit), we find ourselves to be cyborgs, hybrids, mosaics, chimeras. Biological organisms have become biotic systems, communications devices like others. There is no fundamental, ontological separation in our formal knowledge of machine and organism, of technical and organic. The replicant Rachel in the Ridley Scott film *Blade Runner* stands as the image of a cyborg culture's fear, love, and confusion.

One consequence is that our sense of connection to our tools is heightened. The trance state experienced by many computer users has become a staple of science-fiction film and cultural jokes. Perhaps paraplegics and other severely handicapped people can (and sometimes do) have the most intense experiences of complex hybridization with other communication devices. Anne McCaffrey's pre-feminist *The Ship Who Sang* (1969) explored the consciousness of a cyborg, hybrid of a girl's brain and complex machinery, formed after the birth of a severely handicapped child. Gender, sexuality, embodiment, skill: all were reconstituted in the story. Why should our bodies end at the skin, or include at best other beings encapsulated by skin? From the seventeenth century till now, machines could be animated—given ghostly souls to make them speak or move or to account for their orderly development and mental capacities. Or organisms could be mechanized—reduced to body understood as resource of mind. These machine/organism relationships are obsolete, unnecessary. For us, in imagination and in other practice, machines can be prosthetic devices, intimate components, friendly selves. We don't need organic holism to give impermeable wholeness, the total woman and her feminist variants (mutants?). Let me conclude this point by a very partial reading of the logic of the cyborg monsters of my second group of texts, feminist science fiction.

. . .

Monsters have always defined the limits of community in Western imaginations. The Centaurs and Amazons of ancient Greece established the limits of the centred polis of Greek male human by their disruption of marriage and boundary pollutions of the warrior with animality and woman. Unseparated twins and hermaphrodites were the confused human material in early modern France who grounded discourse on the natural and supernatural, medical and legal, portents and diseases—all crucial to establishing modern identity. The evolutionary and behavioural sciences of monkeys and apes have marked the multiple boundaries of late twentieth-century industrial identities. Cyborg monsters in feminist science fiction define quite different political possibilities and limits from those proposed by the mundane fiction of Man and Woman.

There are several consequences to taking seriously the imagery of cyborgs as other than our enemies. Our bodies, ourselves; bodies are maps of power and identity. Cyborgs are no exception. A cyborg body is not innocent; it was not born in a garden; it does not seek unitary identity and so generate antagonistic dualisms without end (or until the world ends); it takes irony for granted. One is too few, and two is only one possibility. Intense pleasure in skill, machine skill, ceases to be a sin,

but an aspect of embodiment. The machine is not an *it* to be animated, worshipped, and dominated. The machine is us, our processes, an aspect of our embodiment. We can be responsible for machines; *they* do not dominate or threaten us. We are responsible for boundaries; we are they. Up till now (once upon a time), female embodiment seemed to be given, organic, necessary; and female embodiment seemed to mean skill in mothering and its metaphoric extensions. Only by being out of place could we take intense pleasure in machines, and then with excuses that this was organic activity after all, appropriate to females. Cyborgs might consider more seriously the partial, fluid, sometimes aspect of sex and sexual embodiment. Gender might not be global identity after all, even if it has profound historical breadth and depth.

The ideologically charged question of what counts as daily activity, as experience, can be approached by exploiting the cyborg image. Feminists have recently claimed that women are given to dailiness, that women more than men somehow sustain daily life, and so have a privileged epistemological position potentially. There is a compelling aspect to this claim, one that makes visible unvalued female activity and names it as the ground of life. But *the* ground of life? What about all the ignorance of women, all the exclusions and failures of knowledge and skill? What about men's access to daily competence, to knowing how to build things, to take them apart, to play? What about other embodiments? Cyborg gender is a local possibility taking a global vengeance. Race, gender, and capital require a cyborg theory of wholes and parts. There is no drive in cyborgs to produce total theory, but there is an intimate experience of boundaries, their construction and deconstruction. There is a myth system waiting to become a political language to ground one way of looking at science and technology and challenging the informatics of domination—in order to act potently.

One last image: organisms and organismic, holistic politics depend on metaphors of rebirth and invariably call on the resources of reproductive sex. I would suggest that cyborgs have more to do with regeneration and are suspicious of the reproductive matrix and of most birthing. For salamanders, regeneration after injury, such as the loss of a limb, involves regrowth of structure and restoration of function with the constant possibility of twinning or other odd topographical productions at the site of former injury. The regrown limb can be monstrous, duplicated, potent. We have all been injured, profoundly. We require regeneration, not rebirth, and the possibilities for our reconstitution include the utopian dream of hope for a monstrous world without gender.

Cyborg imagery can help express two crucial arguments in this essay: first, the production of universal, totalizing theory is a major mistake that misses most of reality, probably always, but certainly now; and second, taking responsibility for the social relations of science and technology means refusing an anti-science metaphysics, a demonology of technology, and so means embracing the skilful task of reconstructing the boundaries of daily life, in partial connection with others, in communication with all of our parts. It is not just that science and technology are possible means of great human satisfaction, as well as a matrix of complex dominations. Cyborg imagery can suggest a way out of the maze of dualisms in which we have explained our bodies and our tools to ourselves. This is a dream not of a common language, but of a powerful infidel heteroglossia. It is an imagination of a feminist speaking in tongues to strike fear into the circuits of the super-savers of the new right. It means both building and destroying machines, identities, categories, relationships, space stories. Though both are bound in the spiral dance, I would rather be a cyborg than a goddess.

[1985]

REFERENCES

Grossman, Rachel (1980) 'Women's place in the integrated circuit', *Radical America* 14(1): 29–50.

Hogness, E. Rusten (1983) 'Why stress? A look at the making of stress, 1936–56', unpublished paper available from the author, 4437 Mill Creek Rd, Healdsburg, CA 95448.

Klein, Hilary (1984) 'Marxism, psychoanalysis, and mother nature', *Feminist Studies* 15(2): 255–278.

Latour, Bruno (1984) *Les microbes, guerre et paix, suivi des irréductions*. Paris: Métailié.

McCaffrey, Anne (1969) *The Ship Who Sang*. New York: Ballantine.

Marcuse, Herbert (1964) *One-Dimensional Man: Studies in the Ideology of Advanced Industrial Society*. Boston: Beacon.

Merchant, Carolyn (1980) *The Death of Nature: Women, Ecology, and the Scientific Revolution*. New York: Harper & Row.

Ong, Aihwa (1987) *Spirits of Resistance and Capitalist Discipline: Factory Workers in Malaysia*. Albany: State University of New York Press.

Sofia, Zoe (also Zoe Sofoulis) (1984) 'Exterminating fetuses: abortion, disarmament, and the sexo-semiotics of extra-terrestrialism', *Diacritics* 14(2): 47–59.

Sofoulis, Zoe (1987) 'Lacklein', University of California at Santa Cruz, unpublished essay.

Treichler, Paula (1987) 'AIDS, homophobia, and biomedical discourse: an epidemic of signification', *October* 43: 31–70.

 69

The Woman Question in Science to the Science Question in Feminism

SANDRA HARDING

SANDRA HARDING United States. 1935–   . Philosopher of Science. *Whose Science? Whose Knowledge? Thinking from Women's Lives* (1991), *The "Racial" Economy of Science: Toward a Democratic Future* (1993), *Is Science Multicultural?: Postcolonialisms, Feminisms, and Epistemologies* (1998), *Sciences from Below: Feminisms, Postcolonialisms, and Modernities* (2008).

Feminist scholars have studied women, men, and social relations between the genders within, across, and insistently against the conceptual frameworks of the disciplines. In each area we have come to understand that what we took to be humanly inclusive problematics, concepts, theories, objective methodologies, and transcendental truths are in fact far less than that. Instead, these products of thought bear the mark of their collective and individual creators, and the creators in turn have been distinctively marked as to gender, class, race, and culture.[1] We can now discern the effects of these cultural markings in the discrepancies between the methods of knowing and the interpretations of the world provided by the creators of modern Western culture and those characteristic of the rest of us. Western culture's favored beliefs mirror in sometimes clear and sometimes distorting ways not the world as it is or as we might want it to be, but the social projects of their historically identifiable creators.

The natural sciences are a comparatively recent subject of feminist scrutiny. The critiques excite immense anticipation—or fear—yet they remain far more fragmented and less clearly conceptualized than feminist analyses in other disciplines.

The anticipation and fear are based in the recognition that we are a scientific culture, that scientific rationality has permeated not only the modes of thinking and acting of our public institutions but even the ways we think about the most intimate details of our private lives. Widely read manuals and magazine articles on child rearing and sexual relations gain their authority and popularity by appealing to science. And during the last century, the social use of science has shifted: formerly an occasional assistant, it has become the direct generator of economic, political, and social accumulation and control. Now we can see that the hope to "dominate nature" for the betterment of the species has become the effort to gain unequal access to nature's resources for purposes of social domination. No longer is the scientist—if he ever was—an eccentric and socially marginal genius spending private funds and often private time on whatever purely intellectual pursuits happen to interest him. Only very rarely does his research have no foreseeable social uses. Instead, he (or, more recently, she) is part of a vast work force, is trained from elementary school on to enter academic, industrial, and governmental laboratories where 99+ percent of the research is expected to be immediately applicable to social projects. If these vast industrialized empires, devoted—whether intentionally or not—to material accumulation and social control, cannot be shown to serve the best interests of social progress by appeal to objective, dispassionate, impartial, rational knowledge-seeking, then in our culture they cannot be legitimated at all. Neither God nor tradition is privileged with the same credibility as scientific rationality in modern cultures.

Of course, feminists are not the first group to scrutinize modern science in this way. Struggles against racism, colonialism, capitalism, and homophobia, as well as the counter culture movement of the 1960s and the contemporary ecology and antimilitarism movements, have all produced pointed analyses of the uses and abuses of science. But the feminist criticisms appear to touch especially raw nerves. For one thing, at their best they incorporate the key insights of these other movements while challenging the low priority that specifically feminist concerns have been assigned in such agendas for social reform. For another, they question the division of labor by gender—a social aspect of the organization of human relations that has been deeply obscured by our perceptions of what is "natural" and what is social. Perhaps most disturbingly, they challenge our sense of personal identity at its most prerational level, at the core. They challenge the desirability of the gendered aspects of our personalities and the expression of gender in social practices, which for most men and women have provided deeply satisfying parts of self-identity.

Finally, as a symbol system, gender difference is the most ancient, most universal, and most powerful origin of many morally valued conceptualizations of everything else in the world around us. Cultures assign a gender to such nonhuman entities as hurricanes and mountains, ships and nations. As far back in history as we can see, we have organized our social and natural worlds in terms of gender meanings within which historically specific racial, class, and cultural institutions and meanings have been constructed. Once we begin to theorize gender—to define gender as an analytic category within which humans think about and organize their social activity rather than as a natural consequence of sex difference, or even merely as a social variable assigned to individual people in different ways from culture to culture—we can begin to appreciate the extent to which gender meanings have suffused our belief systems, institutions, and even such apparently gender-free phenomena as our architecture and urban planning. When feminist thinking about science is adequately theorized, we will have a clearer grasp of how scientific activity is and is not gendered in this sense.

Now it is certainly true that racism, classism, and cultural imperialism often more deeply restrict the life opportunities of individuals than does sexism. We can easily see this if we compare the different life opportunities available to women of the same race but in different classes, or of the same class but in different races, in the United States today or at any other time and place in history. Consequently, it is understandable why working-class people and victims of racism and imperialism often place feminist projects low on their political agendas. Furthermore, gender appears only in culturally specific forms. . . . [G]endered social life is produced through three distinct processes: it is the result of assigning dualistic gender metaphors to various perceived dichotomies that rarely have anything to do with sex differences; it is the consequence of appealing to these gender dualisms to organize social activity, of dividing necessary social activities between different groups of humans; it is a form of socially constructed individual identity only imperfectly correlated with either the "reality" or the perception of sex differences. I shall be referring to these three aspects of gender as *gender symbolism* (or, borrowing a term from anthropology, "gender totemism"), *gender structure* (or the division of labor by gender), and *individual gender*. The referents for all three meanings of masculinity and femininity differ from culture to culture, though within any culture the three forms of gender are related to each other. Probably few, if any, symbolic, institutional, or individual identity or behavioral expressions of masculinity and femininity can be observed in all cultures or at all times in history.

But the fact that there are class, race, and cultural differences between women and between men is not, as some have thought, a reason to find gender difference either theoretically unimportant or politically irrelevant. In virtually every culture, gender difference is a pivotal way in which humans identify themselves as persons, organize social relations, and symbolize meaningful natural and social events and processes. And in virtually all cultures, whatever is thought of as manly is more highly valued than what is thought of as womanly. Moreover, we need to recognize that in cultures stratified by both gender and race, gender is always also a racial category and race a gender category. That is, sexist public policies are different for people of the same gender but different race, and racist policies are different for women and men within the same race. One commentator has proposed that we think of these policies as, respectively, racist sexism and sexist racism.[2]

Finally, we shall later examine the important role to be played in emancipatory epistemologies and politics by open recognition of gender differences within racial groups and racial and cultural differences within gender groups. "Difference" can be a slippery and dangerous rallying point for inquiry projects and for politics, but each emancipatory struggle needs to recognize the agendas of other struggles as integral parts of its own in order to succeed. (After all, people of color come in at least two genders, and women are of many colors.) For each struggle, epistemologies and politics grounded in solidarities could replace the problematic ones that appeal to essentialized identities, which are, perhaps, spurious.

For all these reasons, feminist critiques claiming that science, too, is gendered appear deeply threatening to the social order, even in societies such as ours where racism, classism, and imperialism also direct all our lives. Obviously, the different forms of domination use one another as resources and support one another in complex ways. If we find it difficult to imagine the day-to-day details of living in a world no longer structured by racism and classism, most of us do not even know how to start imagining a world in which gender difference, in its equation of masculinity with authority and value, no longer constrains the ways we think, feel, and act. And the day-to-day world we live in is so permeated by scientific rationality as well as gender that to nonfeminists and perhaps even some feminists, the very idea of a feminist critique of scientific rationality appears closer to blasphemy than to social-criticism-as-usual.

Feminists in other fields of inquiry have begun to formulate clear and coherent challenges to the conceptual frameworks of their disciplines. By putting women's perspective on gender symbolism, gender structure, and individual gender at the center of their thinking, they have been able to reconceive the purposes of research programs in anthropology, history, literary criticism, and so forth.[3] They have begun to retheorize the proper subject matters of the understandings these disciplines could provide. But I think the proper subject matters and purposes of a feminist critique of science have, thus far, eluded the firm grip and the clear conceptualizations that are becoming evident in much of this other research. The voice of feminist science criticism alternates among five different kinds of projects, each with its own audience, subject matter, ideas of what science is and what gender is, and set of remedies for androcentrism. In certain respects, the assumptions guiding these analyses directly conflict. It is not at all clear how their authors conceive of the theoretical connections between them, nor, therefore, what a comprehensive strategy for eliminating androcentrism from science would look like. This is particularly troublesome because clarity about so fundamental a component of our culture can have powerful effects elsewhere in feminist struggles.

One problem may be that we have been so pre-occupied with responding to the sins of contemporary science in the same terms our culture uses to justify these sins that we have not yet given adequate attention to envisioning truly emancipatory knowledge-seeking. We have not yet found the space to step back and image up the whole picture of what science might be in the future. In our culture, reflecting on an appropriate model of rationality may well seem a luxury for the few, but it is a project with immense potential consequences: it could produce a politics of knowledge-seeking that would show us the conditions necessary to transfer control from the "haves" to the "have-nots."

What kind of understanding of science would we have if we began not with the categories we now use to grasp its inequities, misuses, falsities, and obscurities but with those of the biologist protagonist imagined by Marge Piercy in *Woman on the Edge of Time*, who can shift her/his sex at will and who lives in a culture that does not institutionalize (i.e., does not have) gender? or with the assumptions of a world where such categories as machine, human, and animal are no longer either distinct or of cultural interest, as in Anne McCaffrey's *The Ship Who Sang?*[4] Perhaps we should turn to our novelists and poets for a better intuitive grasp of the theory we need. Though often leaders in the political struggles for a more just and caring culture, they are professionally less conditioned than we to respond point by point to a culture's defenses of its ways of being in the world.

FIVE RESEARCH PROGRAMS

To draw attention to the lack of a developed feminist theory for the critique of the natural sciences is not to overlook the contributions these young but flourishing lines of inquiry have made. In a very short period of time, we have derived a far clearer picture of the extent to which science, too, is gendered. Now we can begin to understand the economic, political, and psychological mechanisms that

keep science sexist and that must be eliminated if the nature, uses, and valuations of knowledge-seeking are to become humanly inclusive ones. Each of these lines of inquiry raises intriguing political and conceptual issues, not only for the practices of science and the ways these practices are legitimated but also for each other. Details of these research programs are discussed in following chapters; I emphasize here the problems they raise primarily to indicate the undertheorization of the whole field.

First of all, equity studies have documented the massive historical resistance to women's getting the education, credentials, and jobs available to similarly talented men;[5] they have also identified the psychological and social mechanisms through which discrimination is informally maintained even when the formal barriers have been eliminated. Motivation studies have shown why boys and men more often want to excel at science, engineering, and math than do girls and women.[6] But should women want to become "just like men" in science, as many of these studies assume? That is, should feminism set such a low goal as mere equality with men? And to which men in science should women want to be equal—to underpaid and exploited lab technicians as well as Nobel Prize winners? Moreover, should women want to contribute to scientific projects that have sexist, racist, and classist problematics and outcomes? Should they want to be military researchers? Furthermore, what has been the effect of women's naiveté about the depth and extent of masculine resistance—that is, would women have struggled to enter science if they had understood how little equity would be produced by eliminating the formal barriers against women's participation?[7] Finally, does the increased presence of women in science have any effect at all on the nature of scientific problematics and outcomes?

Second, studies of the uses and abuses of biology, the social sciences, and their technologies have revealed the ways science is used in the service of sexist, racist, homophobic, and classist social projects. Oppressive reproductive policies; white men's management of all women's domestic labor; the stigmatization of, discrimination against, and medical "cure" of homosexuals; gender discrimination in workplaces—all these have been justified on the basis of sexist research and maintained through technologies, developed out of this research, that move control of women's lives from women to men of the dominant group.[8] Despite the importance of these studies, critics of the sexist uses of science often make two problematic assumptions: that there is a value-free, pure scientific research which can be distinguished from the social uses of science; and that there are proper uses of science with which we can contrast its improper uses. Can we really make these distinctions? Is it possible to isolate a value-neutral core from the uses of science and its technologies? And what distinguishes improper from proper uses? Furthermore, each misuse and abuse has been racist and classist as well as oppressive to women. This becomes clear when we note that there are different reproductive policies, forms of domestic labor, and forms of workplace discrimination mandated for women of different classes and races even within U.S. culture at any single moment in history. (Think, for instance, of the current attempt to restrict the availability of abortion and contraceptive information for some social groups at the same time that sterilization is forced on others. Think of the resuscitation of scientifically supported sentimental images of motherhood and nuclear forms of family life for some at the same time that social supports for mothers and nonnuclear families are systematically withdrawn for others.) Must not feminism take on as a central project of its own the struggle to eliminate class society and racism, homophobia and imperialism, in order to eliminate the sexist uses of science?

Third, in the critiques of biology and the social sciences, two kinds of challenges have been raised not just to the actual but to the possible existence of any pure science at all.[9] The selection and definition of problematics—deciding what phenomena in the world need explanation, and defining what is problematic about them—have clearly been skewed toward men's perception of what they find puzzling. Surely it is "bad science" to assume that men's problems are everyone's problems, thereby leaving unexplained many things that women find problematic, and to assume that men's explanations of what they find problematic are undistorted by their gender needs and desires. But is this merely—or, perhaps, even—an example of bad science? Will not the selection and definition of problems always bear the social fingerprints of the dominant groups in a culture? With these questions we glimpse the fundamental value-ladenness of knowledge-seeking and thus the impossibility of distinguishing between bad science and science-as-usual. Furthermore, the design and interpretation of research again and again has proceeded in masculine-biased ways. But if problems are necessarily value-laden, if theories are constructed to explain problems, if methodologies are always theory-laden, and if observations are methodology-laden, can there be value-neutral design and interpretation of research? This line of reasoning leads us to ask whether it is possible that some kinds of value-laden research are nevertheless maximally objective. For example, are overtly antisexist research designs inherently more objective than overtly sexist or, more important, "sex-blind" (i.e., gender-blind) ones? And are antisexist inquiries that are also self-consciously antiracist more objective than those that are not? There are precedents in the history of science for preferring the distinction between objectivity-increasing and objectivity-decreasing social values to the distinction between value-free and value-laden research. A different problem is raised by asking what implications these criticisms of biology and social science have for areas such as physics and chemistry, where the subject matter purportedly is physical nature rather than social beings ("purportedly" because, as we shall see, we must be skeptical about being able to make any clear distinctions between the physical and the nonphysical). What implications could these findings and this kind of reasoning about objectivity have for our understanding of the scientific world view more generally?

Fourth, the related techniques of literary criticism, historical interpretation, and psychoanalysis have been used to "read science as a text" in order to reveal the social meanings—the hidden symbolic and structural agendas—of purportedly value-neutral claims and practices.[10] In textual criticism, metaphors of gender politics in the writings of the fathers of modern science, as well as in the claims made by the defenders of the scientific world view today, are no longer read as individual idiosyncrasies or as irrelevant to the meanings science has for its enthusiasts. Furthermore, the concern to define and maintain a series of rigid dichotomies in science and epistemology no longer appears to be a reflection of the progressive character of scientific inquiry; rather, it is inextricably connected with specifically masculine—and perhaps uniquely Western and bourgeois—needs and desires. Objectivity vs. subjectivity, the scientist as knowing subject vs. the objects of his inquiry, reason vs. the emotions, mind vs. body—in each case the former has been associated with masculinity and the latter with femininity. In each case it has been claimed that human progress requires the former to achieve domination of the latter.[11]

Valuable as these textual criticisms have been, they raise many questions. What relevance do the writings of the fathers of modern science have to contemporary scientific practice? What theory would justify regarding these metaphors as fundamental components of scientific explanations? How can metaphors of gender politics continue to shape the cognitive form and content of scientific theories and practices even when they are no longer overtly expressed? And can we imagine what a scientific mode of knowledge-seeking would look like that was not concerned to distinguish between objectivity and subjectivity, reason and the emotions?

Fifth, a series of epistemological inquiries has laid the basis for an alternative understanding of how beliefs are grounded in social experiences, and of what kind of experience should ground the beliefs we honor as knowledge.[12] These feminist epistemologies imply a relation between knowing and being, between epistemology and metaphysics, that is an alternative to the dominant epistemologies developed to justify science's modes of knowledge-seeking and ways of being in the world. It is the conflicts between these epistemologies that generate the major themes of this study.

A GUIDE TO FEMINIST EPISTEMOLOGIES

The epistemological problem for feminism is to explain an apparently paradoxical situation. Feminism is a political movement for social change. But many claims, clearly motivated by feminist concerns, made by researchers and theorists in the social sciences, in biology, and in the social studies of the natural sciences appear more plausible—more likely to be confirmed by evidence—than the beliefs they

would replace. How can such politicized research be increasing the objectivity of inquiry? On what grounds should these feminist claims be justified?

We can usefully divide the main feminist responses to this apparent paradox into two relatively well-developed solutions and one agenda for a solution. I will refer to these three responses as *feminist empiricism*, the *feminist standpoint*, and *feminist postmodernism*.

Feminist empiricism argues that sexism and androcentrism are social biases correctable by stricter adherence to the existing methodological norms of scientific inquiry. Movements for social liberation "make it possible for people to see the world in an enlarged perspective because they remove the covers and blinders that obscure knowledge and observation."[13] The women's movement produces not only the opportunity for such an enlarged perspective but more women scientists, and they are more likely than men to notice androcentric bias.

This solution to the epistemological paradox is appealing for a number of reasons, not the least because it appears to leave unchallenged the existing methodological norms of science. It is easier to gain acceptance of feminist claims through this kind of argument, for it identifies only bad science as the problem, not science-as-usual.

Its considerable strategic advantage, however, often leads its defenders to overlook the fact that the feminist empiricist solution in fact deeply subverts empiricism. The social identity of the inquirer is supposed to be irrelevant to the "goodness" of the results of research. Scientific method is supposed to be capable of eliminating any biases due to the fact that individual researchers are white or black, Chinese or French, men or women. But feminist empiricism argues that women (or feminists, whether men or women) *as a group* are more likely to produce unbiased and objective results than are men (or nonfeminists) as a group.

Moreover, though empiricism holds that scientific method is sufficient to account for historical increases in the objectivity of the picture of the world that science presents, one can argue that history shows otherwise. It is movements for social liberation that have most increased the objectivity of science, not the norms of science as they have in fact been practiced, or as philosophers have rationally reconstructed them. Think, for instance, of the effects of the bourgeois revolution of the fifteenth to seventeenth centuries, which produced modern science itself; or of the effects of the proletarian revolution of the nineteenth and early twentieth centuries. Think of the effects on scientific objectivity of the twentieth-century deconstruction of colonialism.

We shall also see that a key origin of androcentric bias can be found in the selection of problems for inquiry, and in the definition of what is problematic about these phenomena. But empiricism insists that its methodological norms are meant to apply only to the "context of justification"—to the testing of hypotheses and interpretation of evidence—not to the "context of discovery" where problems are identified and defined. Thus a powerful source of social bias appears completely to escape the control of science's methodological norms. Finally, it appears that following the norms of inquiry is exactly what often results in androcentric results.

Thus, feminist attempts to reform what is perceived as bad science bring to our attention deep logical incoherences and what, paradoxically, we can call empirical inadequacies in empiricist epistemologies.

The feminist standpoint originates in Hegel's thinking about the relationship between the master and the slave and in the elaboration of this analysis in the writings of Marx, Engels, and the Hungarian Marxist theorist G. Lukacs. Briefly, this proposal argues that men's dominating position in social life results in partial and perverse understandings, whereas women's subjugated position provides the possibility of more complete and less perverse understandings. Feminism and the women's movement provide the theory and motivation for inquiry and political struggle that can transform the perspective of women into a "standpoint"—a morally and scientifically preferable grounding for our interpretations and explanations of nature and social life. The feminist critiques of social and natural science, whether expressed by women or by men, are grounded in the universal features of women's experience as understood from the perspective of feminism.[14]

While this attempted solution to the epistemological paradox avoids the problems that beset feminist empiricism, it generates its own tensions. First of all, those wedded to empiricism will be loath to commit themselves to the belief that the social identity of the observer can be an important variable in the potential objectivity of research results. Strategically, this is a less convincing explanation for the greater adequacy of feminist claims for all but the already convinced; it is particularly unlikely to appear plausible to natural scientists or natural science enthusiasts.

Considered on its own terms, the feminist standpoint response raises two further questions. Can there be *a* feminist standpoint if women's (or feminists') social experience is divided by class, race, and culture? Must there be Black and white, working-class and professional-class, American and Nigerian feminist standpoints? This kind of consideration leads to the postmodernist skepticism: "Perhaps 'reality' can have 'a' structure only from the falsely universalizing perspective of the master. That is, only to the extent that one person or group can dominate the whole, can 'reality' appear to be governed by one set of rules or be constituted by one privileged set of social relations."[15] Is the feminist standpoint project still too firmly grounded in the historically disastrous alliance between knowledge and power characteristic of the modern epoch? Is it too firmly rooted in a problematic politics of essentialized identities?

Before turning briefly to the feminist postmodernism from which this last criticism emerges, we should note that both of the preceding epistemological approaches appear to assert that objectivity never has been and could not be increased by value-neutrality. Instead, it is commitments to antiauthoritarian, antielitist, participatory, and emancipatory values and projects that increase the objectivity of science. Furthermore, the reader will need to avoid the temptation to leap to relativist understandings of feminist claims. In the first place, feminist inquirers are never saying that sexist and antisexist claims are equally plausible—that it is equally plausible to regard women's situation as primarily biological *and* as primarily social, or to regard "the human" both as identical *and* nonidentical with "the masculine." The *evidence* for feminist vs. nonfeminist claims may be inconclusive in some cases, and many feminist claims that today appear evidentially secure will no doubt be abandoned as additional evidence is gathered and better hypotheses and concepts are constructed. Indeed, there should be no doubt that these normal conditions of research hold for many feminist claims. But agnosticism and recognition of the hypothetical character of all scientific claims are quite different epistemological stances from relativism. Moreover, whether or not feminists take a relativist stance, it is hard to imagine a coherent defense of cognitive relativism when one thinks of the conflicting claims.

Feminist postmodernism challenges the assumptions upon which feminist empiricism and the feminist standpoint are based, although strains of postmodernist skepticism appear in the thought of these theorists, too. Along with such mainstream thinkers as Nietzsche, Derrida, Foucault, Lacan, Rorty, Cavell, Feyerabend, Gadamer, Wittgenstein, and Unger, and such intellectual movements as semiotics, deconstruction, psychoanalysis, structuralism, archeology/genealogy, and nihilism, feminists "share a profound skepticism regarding universal (or universalizing) claims about the existence, nature and powers of reason, progress, science, language and the 'subject/self.'"[16]

This approach requires embracing as a fruitful grounding for inquiry the fractured identities modern life creates: black-feminist, socialist-feminist, women-of-color, and so on. It requires seeking a solidarity in our oppositions to the dangerous fiction of the naturalized, essentialized, uniquely "human" (read "manly") and to the distortion and exploitation perpetrated on behalf of this fiction. It may require rejecting fantasized returns to the primal wholeness of infancy, preclass societies, or pregender "unitary" consciousnesses of the species—all of which have motivated standpoint epistemologies. From this perspective, feminist claims are more plausible and less distorting only insofar as they are grounded in a solidarity between these modern fractured identities and between the politics they create.

Feminist postmodernism creates its own tensions. In what ways does it, like the empiricist and standpoint epistemologies, reveal incoherences in its parental mainstream discourse? Can we afford to give up the necessity of trying to provide "one, true, feminist story of reality" in the face of the deep alliances between science and sexist, racist, classist, and imperialist social projects?

Clearly, there are contradictory tendencies among the feminist epistemological discourses, and each has its own set of problems. The contradictions and problems do not originate in the feminist discourses, however, but reflect the disarray in mainstream epistemologies and philosophies of science since the mid-1960s. They also reflect shifting configurations of gender, race, and class—both the analytic categories and the lived realities. New social groups—such as feminists who are seeking to bridge a gap between their own social experience and the available theoretical frameworks—are more likely to hone in on "subjugated knowledge" about the world than are groups whose experience more comfortably fits familiar conceptual schemes. Most likely, the feminist entrance into these disputes should be seen as making significant contributions to clarifying the nature and implications of paradoxical tendencies in contemporary intellectual and social life.

The feminist criticisms of science have produced an array of conceptual questions that threaten both our cultural identity as a democratic and socially progressive society and our core personal identities as gender-distinct individuals. I do not mean to overwhelm these illuminating lines of inquiry with criticisms so early in my study—to suggest that they are not really feminist or that they have not advanced our understanding. On the contrary, each has greatly enhanced our ability to grasp the extent of androcentrism in science. Collectively, they have made it possible for us to formulate new questions about science.

It is a virtue of these critiques that they quickly bring to our attention the socially damaging incoherences in all the nonfeminist discourses. Considered in the sequence described in this chapter, they move us from the Woman Question in science to the more radical Science Question in feminism. Where the first three kinds of criticism primarily ask how women can be more equitably treated within and by science, the last two ask how a science apparently so deeply involved in distinctively masculine projects can possibly be used for emancipatory ends. Where the Woman Question critiques still conceptualize the scientific enterprise we have as redeemable, as reformable, the Science Question critiques appear skeptical that we can locate anything morally and politically worth redeeming or reforming in the scientific world view, its underlying epistemology, or the practices these legitimate.

[1986]

NOTES

1. I make a sharp distinction between "sex" and "gender" (even though this is a dichotomy I shall later problematize); thus I refer to "gender roles" rather than "sex roles," etc., retaining only a few terms such as "sexism," where the substitution seems more distracting than useful. Otherwise (except in direct quotations), I use "sex" only when it is, indeed, biology that is at issue. There are two reasons for this policy. First, in spite of feminist insistence for decades, perhaps centuries, that women's and men's "natures" and activities are primarily shaped by social relations, not by immutable biological determinants, many people still do not grasp this point or are unwilling to commit themselves to its full implications (the current fascination with sociobiology is just one evidence of this problem). Second, the very thought of sex exerts its own fatal attraction for many otherwise well-intentioned people: such phrases as "sexual politics," "the battle between the sexes," and "male chauvinism" make the continuation of gender hostilities sound far more exciting than feminism should desire.

2. Boch (1983). See also Caulfield (1974); Davis (1971). (Works cited in my notes by author and year of publication receive full citation in the bibliography, which lists the sources I have found most useful for this study. Additional references appear in full in the footnotes.)

3. McIntosh (1983).

4. Marge Piercy, *Woman on the Edge of Time* (New York: Fawcett, 1981); Anne McCaffrey, *The Ship Who Sang* (New York: Ballantine, 1976). Donna Haraway (1985) discusses the potentialities that McCaffrey's kind of antidualism opens up for feminist theorizing.

5. See, e.g., Rossiter (1982b); Walsh (1977).

6. See Aldrich (1978).

7. Rossiter (1982b) makes this point.

8. See Tobach and Rosoff (1978; 1979; 1981; 1984); Brighton Women and Science Group (1980); Ehrenreich and English (1979); Rothschild (1983); Zimmerman (1983); Arditti, Duelli-Klein, and Minden (1984).

9. The literature here is immense. For examples of these criticisms, see Longino and Doell (1983); Hubbard, Henifin, and Fried (1982); Gross and Averill (1983); Tobach and Rosoff (1978; 1979; 1981; 1984); Millman and Kanter (1975); Andersen (1983); Westkott (1979).

10. Good examples are Keller (1984); Merchant (1980); Griffin (1978); Flax (1983); Jordanova (1980); Bloch and Bloch (1980); Harding (1980).

11. The key "object-relations" theorists among these textual critics are Dinnerstein (1976); Chodorow (1978); Flax (1983). See also Balbus (1982).

12. See Flax (1983); Rose (1983); Hartsock (1983); Smith (1974; 1977; 1979; 1981); Harding (1983); Fee (1981). Haraway (1985) proposes a somewhat different epistemology for feminism.

13. Millman and Kanter (1975, vii).

14. Flax (1983), Rose (1983), Hartsock (1983), and Smith (1974; 1977; 1979; 1981) all develop this standpoint approach.

15. Flax (1986, 17). Strains of postmodernism appear in all of the standpoint thinking. Of this group, Flax has most overtly articulated also the postmodernist epistemological issues.

16. Flax (1986, 3). This is Flax's list of the mainstream postmodernist thinkers and movements. See Haraway (1985), Marks and de Courtivron (1980), and *Signs* (1981) for discussion of the feminist postmodernist issues.

REFERENCES

Aldrich, Michele L. 1978. "Women in Science." *Signs: Journal of Women in Culture and Society* 4 (no. 1).

Andersen, Margaret. 1983. *Thinking about Women*. New York: Macmillan.

Arditti, Rita, Renate Duelli-Klein, and Shelly Minden, eds. 1984. *Test-Tube Women: What Future for Motherhood?* Boston: Pandora Press.

Balbus, Isaac. 1982. *Marxism and Domination*. Princeton, N.J.: Princeton University Press.

Bloch, Maurice, and Jean Bloch. 1980. "Women and the Dialectics of Nature in Eighteenth Century French Thought." In *Nature, Culture and Gender*, ed. C. MacCormack and M. Strathern. Cambridge: Cambridge University Press.

Boch, Gisela. 1983. "Racism and Sexism in Nazi Germany: Motherhood, Compulsory Sterilization, and the State." *Signs: Journal of Women in Culture and Society* 8(no. 3).

Brighton Women and Science Group. 1980. *Alice through the Microscope*. London: Virago Press.

Caulfield, Mina Davis. 1974. "Imperialism, the Family, and Cultures of Resistance." *Socialist Revolution* 4(no. 2).

Chodorow, Nancy. 1978. *The Reproduction of Mothering*. Berkeley: University of California Press.

Davis, Angela. 1971. "The Black Woman's Role in the Community of Slaves." *Black Scholar* 2.

Dinnerstein, Dorothy. 1976. *The Mermaid and the Minotaur: Sexual Arrangements and Human Malaise*. New York: Harper & Row.

Ehrenreich, Barbara, and Deirdre English. 1979. *For Her Own Good: 150 Years of Experts' Advice to Women*. New York: Doubleday.

Fee, Elizabeth. 1981. "Women's Nature and Scientific Objectivity." In *Woman's Nature: Rationalizations of Inequality*, eds. M. Lowe and R. Hubbard. New York: Pergamon Press. Originally appeared as "Is Feminism a Threat to Scientific Objectivity?" in *International Journal of Women's Studies* 4(no. 4)

Flax, Jane. 1983. "Political Philosophy and the Patriarchal Unconscious: A Psychoanalytic Perspective on Epistemology and Metaphysics." In *Discovering Reality: Feminist Perspectives on Epistemology, Metaphysics, Methodology and Philosophy of Science*, eds. S. Harding and M. Hintikka. Dordrecht: Reidel.

_____. 1986. "Gender as a Social Problem: In and For Feminist Theory." *American Studies/Amerika Studien*, journal of the German Association for American Studies.

Griffin, Susan. 1978. *Woman and Nature: The Roaring inside Her*. New York: Harper & Row.

Gross, Michael, and Mary Beth Averill. 1983. "Evolution and Patriarchal Myths of Scarcity and Competition." In *Discovering Reality: Feminist Perspectives on Epistemology, Metaphysics, Methodology and Philosophy of Science*, eds. S. Harding and M. Hintikka. Dordrecht: Reidel.

Haraway, Donna. 1985. "A Manifesto for Cyborgs: Science, Technology, and Socialist Feminism in the 1980's." *Socialist Review* 80.

Harding, Sandra. 1980. "The Norms of Social Inquiry and Masculine Experience." In *PSA 1980*, vol. 2, ed. P.D. Asquith and R.N. Giere. East Lansing, Mich.: Philosophy of Science Association.

____. 1983. "Why Has the Sex-Gender System Become Visible Only Now?" In *Discovering Reality: Feminist Perspectives on Epistemology, Metaphysics, Methodology and Philosophy of Science*, eds. S. Harding and M. Hintikka. Dordrecht: Reidel.

Hartsock, Nancy. 1983. "The Feminist Standpoint: Developing the Ground for a Specifically Feminist Historical Materialism." In *Discovering Reality: Feminist Perspectives on Epistemology, Metaphysics, Methodology and Philosophy of Science*, eds. S. Harding and M. Hintikka. Dordrecht: Reidel.

Hubbard, Ruth, M.S. Henifin, and Barbara Fried, eds. 1982. *Biological Woman: The Convenient Myth.* Cambridge, Mass.: Schenkman. Earlier version published 1979 under the title *Women Look at Biology Looking at Women.*

Jordanova, L.J. 1980. "Natural Facts: A Historical Perspective on Science and Sexuality." In *Nature, Culture and Gender*, eds. C. MacCormack and M. Strathern. New York: Cambridge University Press.

Keller, Evelyn Fox. 1984. *Reflections on Gender and Science.* New Haven, Conn.: Yale University Press.

Longino, Helen, and Ruth Doell. 1983. "Body, Bias, and Behavior: A Comparative Analysis of Reasoning in Two Areas of Biological Science." *Signs: Journal of Women in Culture and Society* 9(no. 2).

McIntosh, Peggy. 1983. "Interactive Phases of Curricular Revision: A Feminist Perspective." Working paper no. 124. Wellesley, Mass.: Wellesley College Center for Research on Women.

Marks, Elaine, and Isabelle de Courtivron, eds. 1980. *New French Feminisms.* Amherst: University of Massachusetts Press.

Merchant, Carolyn. 1980. *The Death of Nature: Women, Ecology and the Scientific Revolution.* New York: Harper & Row.

Millman, Marcia, and Rosabeth Moss Kanter, eds. 1975. *Another Voice: Feminist Perspectives on Social Life and Social Science.* New York: Anchor Books.

Rose, Hilary, and Steven Rose, eds. 1976. *Ideology of/in the Natural Sciences.* Cambridge, Mass.: Schenkman.

Rossiter, Margaret. 1982a. "Fair Enough?" *Isis* 72.

____. 1982b. *Women Scientists in America: Struggles and Strategies to 1940.* Baltimore, Md.: Johns Hopkins University Press.

Rothschild, Joan. 1983. *Machina ex Dea: Feminist Perspectives on Technology.* New York: Pergamon Press.

Signs: Journal of Women in Culture and Society. 1981. Special issue on French feminism, 7(no. 1).

Smith, Dorothy. 1974. "Women's Perspective as a Radical Critique of Sociology." *Sociological Inquiry* 44.

____. 1977. "Some Implications of a Sociology for Women." In *Woman in a Man-Made World: A Socioeconomic Handbook*, eds. N. Glazer and H. Waehrer. Chicago: Rand McNally.

____. 1979. "A Sociology For Women." In *The Prism of Sex: Essays in the Sociology of Knowledge*, eds. J. Sherman and E. T. Beck. Madison: University of Wisconsin Press.

____. 1981. "The Experienced World as Problematic: A Feminist Method." Sorokin Lecture no. 12 Saskatoon: University of Saskatchewan.

Tobach, Ethel, and Betty Rosoff, eds. 1978, 1979, 1981, 1984. *Genes and Gender*, vols. 1–4. New York: Gordian Press.

Westkott, Marcia. 1979. "Feminist Criticism of the Social Sciences." *Harvard Educational Review* 49.

Zimmerman, Jan, ed. 1983. *The Technological Woman: Interfacing with Tomorrow.* New York: Praeger.

 70

Jewish Memory from a Feminist Perspective

JUDITH PLASKOW

JUDITH PLASKOW United States. 1947–   . Feminist theologian. *Standing Again at Sinai: Judaism from a Feminist Perspective* (1990), *Weaving the Visions: New Patterns in Feminist Spirituality* (1989).

There is perhaps no verse in the Torah more disturbing to the feminist than Moses' warning to his people in Exodus 19:15, "Be ready for the third day; do not go near a woman." For here, at the very moment that the Jewish people stand at Mount Sinai ready to enter into the covenant—not now the covenant with the individual patriarchs but presumably with the people as a whole—Moses addresses the community only as men. The specific issue is ritual impurity: an emission of semen renders both a man and his female partner temporarily unfit to approach the sacred (Leviticus 15:16–18). But Moses does not say, "Men and women do not go near each other." At the central moment of Jewish history, women are invisible. It was not their experience that interested the chronicler or that informed and shaped the text.

This verse sets forth a pattern recapitulated again and again in Jewish sources. Women's invisibility at the moment of entry into the covenant is reflected in the content of the covenant which, in both grammar and substance, addresses the community as male heads of household. It is perpetuated by the later tradition that in its comments and codifications takes women as objects of concern or legislation but rarely sees them as shapers of tradition and actors in their own right.

It is not just a historical injustice that is at stake in this verse, however. There is another dimension to the problem of the Sinai passage essential for understanding the task of Jewish feminism today. Were this passage simply the record of a historical event long in the past, the exclusion of women at this critical juncture would be troubling, but also comprehensible for its time. The Torah is not just history, however, but also living memory. The Torah reading, as a central part of the Sabbath and holiday liturgy, calls to mind and recreates the past for succeeding generations. When the story of Sinai is recited as part of the annual cycle of Torah readings or as a special reading for Shavuot, women each time hear ourselves thrust aside anew, eavesdropping on a conversation among men and between man and God.[1]

Significant and disturbing as this passage is, however, equally significant is the tension between it and the reality of the Jewish woman who hears or reads it. The passage affronts because of the contradiction between the holes in the text and many women's felt experience. If Moses' words shock and anger, it is because women have always known or assumed our presence at Sinai; the passage is painful because it seems to deny what we have always taken for granted. On the one hand, of course we were there; on the other, how is it then that the text could imply we were not there?

This contradiction seems to me crucial, for construed a certain way, it is a potential bridge to a new relationship with the tradition. On the one hand, women can choose to accept our absence from Sinai, in which case we allow the male text to define us and our relationship to the tradition. On the other hand, we can stand on the ground of our experience, on the certainty of our membership in our own people. To do this, however, is to be forced to re-member and recreate its history. It is to move from anger at the tradition, through anger to empowerment. It is to begin the journey toward the creation of a feminist Judaism.

GIVE US OUR HISTORY

The notion that a feminist Judaism must reclaim Jewish history requires some explication, for it is by no means generally accepted. There are many Jewish feminists who feel that women can take on positions of authority, create new liturgy, and do what we need to do to create a community responsive to our needs in the present without dredging around in a history that can only cause us pain. What we need to do, according to this view, is to acknowledge and accept the patriarchal nature of the Jewish past and then get on with the issues of contemporary change.

But while the notion of accepting women's past subordination and attending to the present has some attractiveness, it strikes me as in the end untenable. If it is possible within any historical, textual tradition to create a present in dramatic discontinuity with the past—and I doubt that it is—it certainly seems impossible within Judaism. For as I have already suggested, the central events of the Jewish past are not simply history but living, active memory that continues to shape Jewish identity and self-understanding. In Judaism, memory is not simply a given but a religious obligation.[2] "We Jews are a community based on memory," says Martin Buber. "The spiritual life of the Jews is part and parcel of their memory."[3] It is in retelling the story of our past as Jews that we learn who we truly are in the present.

While the Passover Seder is perhaps the most vivid example of the importance of memory in Judaism, the rabbinic reconstruction of Jewish history after the destruction of the second Temple provides an example of remembrance that is also recreation. So deeply is the Jewish present rooted in Jewish history that after 70 C.E., when the rabbis profoundly transformed Jewish life, the changes they wrought in Jewish reality were also read back into the past so that they could be read out of the past as a foundation for the present. Again and again in rabbinic interpretations, we find contemporary practice projected back into earlier periods so that the chain of tradition can remain unbroken. In Genesis, for example, Abraham greets his three angelic visitors by killing a calf and serving it to them with milk (18:7–8), clearly a violation of the laws of kashrut which forbid eating milk and meat together. As later rabbinic sources read the passage, however, Abraham first served his visitors milk and only then meat, a practice permitted by rabbinic law.[4] The links between past and present were felt so passionately that any important change in the present had to entail a new understanding of history.

This is an important moral for Jewish feminists. We too cannot redefine Judaism in the present without redefining our past because our present grows out of our history. The Jewish need to reconstruct the past in light of the present converges with the feminist need to recover women's history within Judaism. Knowing that women are active members of the Jewish community in the present, we know that we were always part of the community, not simply as objects of male purposes but as subjects and shapers of tradition. To accept androcentric texts and contemporary androcentric histories as the whole of Jewish history is to enter into a secret collusion with those who would exclude us from full membership in the Jewish community. It is to accept the idea that men were the only significant agents in Jewish history when we would never accept this (still current) account of contemporary Jewish life. The Jewish community today is a community of women and men, and it has never been otherwise. It is time, therefore, to recover our history as the history of women and men, a task that will both restore our own history to women and provide a fuller Jewish history for the Jewish community as a whole.[5]

HISTORY, HISTORIOGRAPHY, AND TORAH

It is one thing to see the importance of recovering women's history, however, and another to accomplish this task in a meaningful way. First of all, as historian, the Jewish feminist faces all the same problems as any feminist historian trying to recover women's experience: both her sources and the historians who have gone before her record male activities and male deeds in accounts ordered by male values. What we know of women's past are those things men considered significant to remember, seen and interpreted through a value system that places men at the center.[6] But, as if this were not enough, the Jewish feminist faces additional problems raised by working with religious sources. The primary Jewish sources available to her for historical reconstruction are not simply collections of historical materials but also Torah. As Torah, as Jewish teaching, they are understood by the tradition to represent divine revelation, patterns of living adequate for all time. In seeking to restore the history of Jewish women, the Jewish feminist historian is not "simply" trying to revolutionize the writing of

history but is also implicitly or explicitly acting as theologian, claiming to amplify Torah, and thus questioning the finality of the Torah we have. It is important, therefore, in placing the recovery of women's history in the context of a feminist Judaism to confront the view of Torah that this implies.

I understand Torah, both in the narrow sense of the five books of Moses and in the broader sense of Jewish teaching, to be the partial record of the "Godwrestling" of part of the Jewish people.[7] Again and again in the course of its existence, the Jewish people has felt itself called by and held accountable to a power not of its own making, a power that seemed to direct its destiny and give meaning to its life. In both ordinary and extraordinary moments, it has found itself guided by a reality that both propelled and sustained it and to which gratitude and obedience seemed the only fitting response.

The term "Godwrestling" seems appropriate to me to describe the written residue of these experiences, for I do not imagine them à la Cecil B. DeMille as the booming of a clear (male) voice or the flashing of tongues of flame, publicly visible, publicly verifiable, needing only to be transcribed. Rather, they were moments of profound experience, sometimes of illumination but also of mystery, moments when some who had eyes to see understood the meaning of events that all had undergone. Such illumination might be hard-won, or sudden experiences of clarity or presence that come unexpected as precious gifts. But they would need to be interpreted and applied, struggled with and puzzled over, passed down and lived out before they came to us as the Torah of God.

I call this record partial, for moments of intense religious experience cannot be pinned down and reproduced; they can only be suggested and pointed to so that readers or listeners may, from time to time, catch for themselves the deeper reality vibrating behind the text. Moreover, while moments of revelation may lead to abandonment of important presuppositions and openness to ideas and experiences that are genuinely new, they can also occur within cultural frameworks that can never be escaped entirely, so that the more radical implications of a new understanding may not even be seen. I call Torah the record of part of the Jewish people because the experience and wrestling found there are for the most part those of men. The experience of being summoned and saved by a single power, the experience of human likeness to the creator God, the experiences of liberation and God's passion for justice were sustained within a patriarchal framework that the interpretation of divine revelation served to consolidate rather than shatter.[8]

There is a strand in the tradition that acknowledges this partiality of Torah and thus indirectly allows us to see what is at stake in the recovery of women's past. According to many ancient Jewish sources, the Torah pre-existed the creation of the world. It was the first of God's works, identified with divine wisdom in Proverbs 8. It was written with black fire on white fire and rested on the knee of God. It was the architectural plan God consulted in creating the universe.[9] For the Kabbalists, this pre-existent or primordial Torah is God's wisdom and essence; it expresses the immensity of God's being and power. The written Torah of ink and parchment is only the "outer garments," a limited interpretation of what lies hidden, a document that the initiate must penetrate more and more deeply to gain momentary glimpses of what lies behind. A later development of the idea of a secret Torah asserted that each of the 600,000 souls that stood at Sinai had its own special portion of Torah that only that soul could understand.[10] Obviously, no account of revelatory experience by men or women can describe or exhaust the depths of divine reality. But this image of the relation between hidden and manifest Torah reminds us that half the souls of Israel have not left for us the Torah they have seen. Insofar as we can begin to recover the God-wrestling of women, insofar as we can restore a part of their vision and experience, we have more of the primordial Torah, the divine fullness, of which the present Torah of Israel is only a fragment and a sign.

The recovery of primordial Torah is a large task, however, to ask "history" to perform. And in fact, in the foregoing discussion, I have been slipping back and forth between different meanings and levels of the term "history." The rabbinic reconstruction of history, which I used as an example of rewriting Jewish history, by no means involved "doing history" in our modern sense. On the contrary, it was anachronistic and ahistorical. Taking for granted the historical factuality of the momentous events at Sinai, the rabbis turned their attention to mining their eternal significance. Reshaping Jewish memory did not involve discovering what "really happened," but projecting later developments back onto the eternal present of Sinai.[11]

Recovering women's history through modern historiography, a second meaning of history that I have used implicitly, is not just different from rabbinic modes of thinking, it is in conflict with them. It assumes precisely that the original revelation, at least as we have it, is not sufficient, that there are enormous gaps both in tradition and in the scriptural record, that to recapture women's experiences we need to go behind our records and *add* to Torah, acknowledging that that is what we are doing.[12]

But while the tensions between feminist and traditional approaches to Jewish history are significant and real, there is one important thing they have in common. The feminist too is not simply interested in acquiring more knowledge about the past but in incorporating women's history as part of the living memory of the Jewish people. Information about women's past may be instructive and even stirring, but it is not transformative until it becomes part of the community's collective memory, part of what Jews call to mind in remembering Jewish history. While historiographical research may be crucial to recovering women's history, it is not sufficient to make that history live. The Jewish feminist reshaping of Jewish history must therefore proceed on several levels at once. Feminist historiography can open up new questions to be brought to the past and new perspectives to be gleaned from it. It must be combined, however, with feminist midrash, or storytelling, and feminist liturgy before it becomes part of a living feminist Judaism.

RESHAPING JEWISH MEMORY

Feminist historiography as a starting point for the feminist reconstruction of Jewish memory challenges the traditional androcentric view of Jewish history and opens up our understanding of the Jewish past. In the last two decades, feminist historians have demanded and effected a far-reaching reorientation of the presuppositions and methods of historical writing. Questioning the assumption that men have made history while women have stayed home and had babies, they have insisted that women and men have lived and shaped history together. Any account of a period or civilization that does not look at the roles of both women and men, their relation and interaction, is "men's history" rather than the universal history it generally claims to be.[13]

Any number of examples might show how the insights and methods of feminist historians have been applied to Jewish women's history. Archeologist Carol Meyers, for instance, has begun to reconstruct the roles of women in ancient Israel through a combination of biblical and archeological evidence. She asks important new questions about the changing roles of women in biblical society, questions that point to the social construction of gender in biblical culture. In the period of early settlement, she argues, when women's biological and agricultural contributions would have been crucial, their status was likely higher than in the different cultural context of the monarchy. Restrictions on women's roles that were initially practical only later became the basis for "ideologies of female inferiority and subordination."[14] New Testament scholar Bernadette Brooten, working on the inscriptional evidence for women's leadership in the ancient synagogue, shows that during the Roman and Byzantine periods, women took on important synagogue functions in a number of corners of the Jewish world.[15] Her research on the inscriptions, and also on Jewish women's exercise of the right to divorce,[16] sheds light on the wider social world in which the Mishnah (a second century code of Jewish law) emerged, clarifying and questioning the extent of its authority. Chava Weissler's work on the *tekhines*, the petitionary prayers of Eastern European Jewish women, provides us with sources that come in part from women's hands, giving us an intimate view of women's perceptions. While these sources have often been dismissed as "women's literature" or relegated to casual reading, they give us important glimpses of women's religious experiences. They also make us aware of the subtle interplay between the ways women have found to express themselves and the influence of patriarchal religion.[17]

While none of this women's history alters the fundamentally androcentric perspective of "normative" texts or proves that Judaism is really egalitarian, it does reveal another world around and underneath the textual tradition, a world in which women are historical agents struggling within and against a patriarchal culture. In the light of women's history, we cannot see the Tanakh (The Bible) or the Mishnah or any Jewish text simply as given, as having emerged organically from an eternal, unambiguous, uncontested religious vision. Indeed, feminist historians have come to recognize that religious, literary, and philosophical works setting forth women's nature or tasks are often prescriptive rather than descriptive of reality. So far from giving us the world "as it is," "normative" texts may reflect the tensions within patriarchal culture, seeking to maintain a particular view of the world over against social, political, or religious change.[18] "Normative" texts reflect the views of the historical winners, winners whose victories were often achieved at the expense of women and of religious forms that allowed women some power and scope.[19] Insofar as women's religious and social self-expression and empowerment are values we bring to these texts, the texts are relativized, their normative status shaken. We see them against the background of alternative religious possibilities, alternatives that must now be taken seriously because without them, we have only the Judaism of a male elite and not the Judaism of all Jews.

Recovering Jewish women's history, then, extends the realm of the potentially usable Jewish past. Women's experiences expand the domain of Jewish resources on which we can draw in recreating Judaism in the present. In writing women into Jewish history, we ground a contemporary Jewish community that can be a community of women and men. But historiography by itself cannot reshape Jewish memory. The gaps in the historical record alone would prompt us to seek other ways of remembering. However sensitively we read between the lines of mainstream texts seeking to recapture the reality of women's lives, however carefully we mine non-literary and non-Jewish materials using them to challenge "normative" sources, our constructions will remain speculations and many of our questions will go unanswered.

Moreover, even if it were not the case that the sources are sparse and unconcerned with our most urgent questions, feminist historiography would still provide only a fragile grounding for Jewish feminist memory. For historiography recalls events that memory does not recognize.[20] It challenges memory, tries to dethrone it; it calls it partial and distorted. History provides a more and more complex and nuanced picture of the past; memory is selective. How do we recover the parts of Jewish women's history that are forgotten, and how do we then ensure that they will be *remembered*—incorporated into our communal sense of self?

The answer to these questions is partly connected to the wider reconstruction of Jewish life. We turn to the past with new questions because of present commitments, but we also remember more deeply what a changed present requires us to know. Yet Jewish feminists are already entering into a new relationship with history based not simply on historiography but also on more traditional strategies for Jewish remembrance. The rabbinic reconstruction of Jewish history, after all, was not historiographical but midrashic. Assuming the infinite meaningfulness of biblical texts, the rabbis took passages that were sketchy or troubling and wrote them forward. They brought to the Bible their own questions and found answers that showed the eternal relevance of biblical truth. Why was Abraham chosen to be the father of a people? What was the status of the law before the Torah was given? Who was Adam's first wife? Why was Dinah raped? These were not questions for historical investigation but imaginative exegesis and literary amplification.

The open-ended process of writing midrash, simultaneously serious and playful, imaginative, metaphoric, has easily lent itself to feminist use. While feminist midrash—like all midrash—is a reflection of contemporary beliefs and experiences, its root conviction is utterly traditional. It stands on the rabbinic insistence that the Bible can be made to speak to the present day. If the Torah is our text, it can and must answer our questions and share our values; if we wrestle with it, it will yield meaning.

Together and individually then, orally and in writing, woman are exploring and telling stories that connect our history with present experience. Ellen Umansky, for example, retelling the story of the sacrifice of Isaac from Sarah's perspective, explores the dilemma of a women in patriarchal culture trying to hold onto her own sense of self. Isaac was God's gift to Sarah in her old age. She has no power to prevent Abraham's journey to Moriah; she can only wait wailing and trembling for him to return. But she is angry; she knows God does not require such sacrifices. Abraham cannot deprive her of her own religious understanding, whatever demands he may make upon her as his wife.[21]

While midrash can float entirely free from historiography, as it does in this example, the latter can also feed the former so that midrash plays with historical clues but extends them beyond the boundaries of the fragmentary evidence. In her midrash on the verse, "And Dinah . . . went out to see the daughters of the land" (Genesis 34:1), Lynn Gottlieb explores the possible relations between Dinah and Canaanite women based on the presumption of Israelite women's historical attachment to many gods and goddesses.[22] A group of my students once used the same historical theme to write their own midrash on the sacrifice of Isaac as experienced by Sarah. In their version, Sarah, finding Abraham and Isaac absent, calls to Yahweh all day without avail. Finally, almost in despair, she takes our her Asherah and prays to it, only to see her husband and son over the horizon wending their way home.

Moving from history into midrash, Jewish feminists cross a boundary to be both honored and ignored. Certainly, there is a difference between an ancient Aramaic divorce document written by a woman and a modern midrash on Miriam and Sarah. The former confronts and challenges; it invites us to find a framework for understanding the past broad enough to include data at odds with selective memory. The latter is more fully an expression of our own convictions, a creative imagining based on our own experience. Yet in the realm of Jewish religious expression, imagination is permitted and even encouraged. Midrash is not a violation of historical canons but an enactment of commitment to the fruitfulness and relevance of biblical texts. It is partly through midrash that the figurine or document, potentially integrable into memory but still on the periphery, is transformed into narrative the religious ear can hear. The discovery of women in our history can feed the impulse to create misrash; midrash can seize on history and make it religiously meaningful. Remembering and inventing together help recover the hidden half of Torah, reshaping Jewish memory to let women speak.

There is also a third mode of recovery: speaking/acting. Historically, the primary vehicle for transmission of Jewish memory has been prayer and ritual, the liturgical reenactment and celebration of formative events. Midrash can instruct, amuse, edify, but the cycles of the week and year have been the most potent reminders of central Jewish experience and values. The entry of the High Priest into the Holy of Holies on the Day of Atonement, the Exodus of Israel from Egypt every Passover: these are remembered not just verbally but through the body and thus doubly imprinted on Jewish consciousness.

Liturgy and ritual, therefore, have been particularly important areas for Jewish feminist inventiveness. Feminists have been writing liturgy and ritual that flow from and incorporate women's experience, in the process drawing on history and midrash but also allowing them to emerge from concrete forms. One of the earliest and most tenacious feminist rituals, for example, is the celebration of Rosh Hodesh, the new moon, as a woman's holiday. The numerous Rosh Hodesh groups that have sprung up around the country in the last decade have experimented with new spiritual forms within the framework of a traditional women's observance that had been largely forgotten. The association of women with the moon at the heart of the original ceremony provides a starting point for exploration of women's symbols within Judaism and cross-culturally. At the same time, the simplicity of the traditional ritual leaves ample space for invention.[23] Feminist haggadot, on the other hand, seek to inject a women's presence into an already established ritual, building on the theme of liberation to make women's experience and struggle an issue for the Seder. Drawing on history, poetry, and midrash, they seek to integrate women's experiences into the central Jewish story and central ritual enactment of the Jewish year.[24]

These two areas have provided basic structures around which a great deal of varied experimentation has taken place. But from reinterpretations of mikveh, to a major reworking of Sabbath blessings, to simple inclusion of the *imahot* (matriarchs) in daily and Sabbath liturgies—which, however minimally, says, "We too had a covenant; we too were there"—women are seeking to transform Jewish ritual so that it acknowledges our existence and experience.[25] In the ritual moment, women's history is made present.

We have then an interweaving of forms that borrow from and give life to each other. Women's history challenges us to confront the incompleteness of what has been called "Jewish history," to attend to the hidden and hitherto marginal, to attempt a true Jewish history which is a history of women and men. It restores to us some of women's voices in and out of the "normative" tradition, sometimes in accommodation and sometimes in struggle, but the voices of Jews defining their own Jewishness as they participate in the communal life. Midrash expands and burrows, invents the forgotten and prods the memory, takes from history and asks for more. It gives us the inner life history cannot follow, building links between the stories of our foremothers and our own joy and pain. Ritual asserts women's presence in the present. Borrowing from history and midrash, it transforms them into living memory. Creating new forms, it offers them to be remembered.

Thus, through diverse paths, we re-member ourselves. Moses' injunction at Sinai— "Do not go near a woman"—though no less painful, is only part of a story expanded and reinvigorated as women enter into the shaping of Torah. If in Jewish terms history provides a basis for identity, then out of our new sense of identity we are also claiming our past. Beginning with the conviction of our presence both at Sinai and now, we rediscover and invent ourselves in the Jewish communal past and present, continuing the age-old process of reshaping Jewish memory as we reshape the community today.

[1986]

NOTES

1. Rachel Adler, "'I've Had Nothing Yet So I Can't Take More,'" *Moment* 8 (Sept. 1983): 22–23.
2. Yosef Hayim Yerushalmi, *Zakhor: Jewish History and Jewish Memory* (Seattle, WA: University of Washington Press, 1982), 9.
3. Martin Buber, *Israel and the World: Essays in a Time of Crisis* (New York: Schocken Books, 1963), 146.
4. Louis Ginsberg, *The Legends of the Jews,* 7 vols. (Philadelphia: Jewish Publication Society, 1909), 5:235, n. 140.
5. Elisabeth Schüssler Fiorenza, *In Memory of Her: A Feminist Theological Reconstruction of Christian Origins* (New York: Crossroad, 1983), 14–20. I am indebted to Schüssler Fiorenza for this whole paragraph and,

indeed, much of my approach to the recovery of Jewish women's history.

6. Gerda Lerner, *The Majority Finds Its Past: Placing Women in History* (New York: Oxford University Press, 1979), 160, 168–169.

7. The term "Godwrestling" comes from Arthur Waskow, *Godwrestling* (New York: Schocken Books, 1978).

8. See Norman K. Gottwald, *The Tribes of Yahweh* (Maryknoll, NY: Orbis Books, 1979), 685.

9. Ginsberg, *The Legends of the Jews*, 1:3–4.

10. Gershom G. Scholem, *On the Kabbalah and Its Symbolism* (New York: Schocken Books, 1965), 37–65.

11. Gershom G. Scholem, "Tradition and Commentary as Religious Categories in Judaism," *Judaism* 15 (Winter 1966): 26.

12. See Yerushalmi, *Zakhor*, 94.

13. Lerner, *The Majority Finds Its Past*, chaps. 10–12, especially pp. 168, 180.

14. Carol Meyers, "The Roots of Restriction: Women in Early Israel," *Biblical Archeologist* 41 (Sept. 1978): 101. See the whole article (pp. 91–103) and also her "Procreation, Production, and Protection: Male-Female Balance in Early Israel," *Journal of the American Academy of Religion* 51 (December 1983): 569–593.

15. Bernadette J. Brooten, *Women Leaders in the Ancient Synagogue: Inscriptional Evidence and Background Issues* (Chico, CA: Scholars Press, 1982).

16. Bernadette J. Brooten, "Could Women Initiate Divorce in Ancient Judaism? The Implications for Mark 10:11–12 and I Corinthians 7:10–11" (The Earnest Cadman Colwell Lecture, School of Theology at Claremont, CA, April 14, 1981).

17. Chava Weissler, "Voices From the Heart: Women's Devotional Prayers," in *The Jewish Almanac*, ed. Richard Siegel and Carl Rheins (New York: Bantam Books, 1980), 541–545.

18. Lerner, *The Majority Finds Its Past*, 149. Schüssler Fiorenza makes this point repeatedly. See, for example, *In Memory of Her*, 60.

19. Sheila Collins, *A Different Heaven and Earth* (Valley Forge, PA: Judson Press), chap. 4; Carol P. Christ, "Heretics and Outsiders: The Struggle over Female Power in Western Religion," *Soundings* 61 (Fall 1978): 260–280.

20. Yerushalmi, *Zakhor*, 94.

21. Ellen M. Umansky, "Creating a Jewish Feminist Theology: Possibilities and Problems," *Anima* 10 (Spring Equinox 1984): 133–134.

22. Presentation at the First National Havurah Summer Institute, West Hartford, CT, 1980.

23. Arlene Agus, "This Month Is for You: Observing Rosh Hodesh as a Woman's Holiday," in *The Jewish Woman: New Perspectives*, ed. Elizabeth Koltun (New York: Schocken Books, 1976), 84–93; Penina Adelman, *Miriam's Well: Rituals for Jewish Women Around the Year* (Fresh Meadows, NY: Biblio Press, 1986).

24. See, for example, Esther Broner, "Honor and Ceremony in Women's Rituals," in *The Politics of Women's Spirituality: Essays on the Rise of Spiritual Power within the Feminist Movement*, ed. Charlene Spretnak (Garden City, NY: Doubleday, Anchor Press, 1982), 237–241; Aviva Cantor Zuckoff (now Cantor), "Jewish Women's Haggadah," in *The Jewish Women*, ed. Koltun, 94–102. There are numerous *haggadot* circulating privately.

25. Rachel Adler, "Tumah and Taharah; Ends and Beginnings," in *The Jewish Woman*, ed. Koltun, 63–71; Marcia Falk, "What About God?" *Moment* 10 (March 1985): 32–36, and her essay in *Weaving the Vision: New Patterns in Feminist Spirituality* (San Francisco: Harper, 1989).

 # 71

La Conciencia de la Mestiza: Towards a New Consciousness

GLORIA ANZALDÚA

GLORIA ANZALDÚA United States. 1942– . Writer of poetry, short stories, essays. Educator. *This Bridge Called My Back: Writings by Radical Women of Color* (1981), *Borderlands/La Frontera: The New Mestiza* (1987), *Making Face, Making Soul—Hacienda Caras: Creative and Critical Perspectives by Feminists of Color* (1990).

*Por la mujer de mi raza
hablará el espíritu.*[1]

Jose Vasconcelos, Mexican philosopher, envisaged *una raza mestiza, una mezcla de razas afines, una raza de color—la primera raza sintesis del globo*. He called it a cosmic race, *la raza cosmica*, a fifth race embracing the four major races of the world.[2] Opposite to the theory of the pure Aryan, and to the policy of racial purity that white America practices, his theory is one of inclusivity. At the confluence of two or more genetic streams, with chromosomes constantly "crossing over," this mixture of races, rather than resulting in an inferior being, provides hybrid progeny, a mutable, more malleable species with a rich gene pool. From this racial, ideological, cultural and biological cross-pollinization, an "alien" consciousness is presently in the making—a new *mestiza* consciousness, *una conciencia de mujer*. It is a consciousness of the Borderlands.

Una lucha de fronteras/ A Struggle of Borders

Because I, a *mestiza*,
continually walk out of one culture
and into another,

because I am in all cultures at the same time,
alma entre dos mundos, tres, cuatro,
me zumba la cabeza con lo contradictorio.
Estoy norteada por todas las voces que me hablan
simultáneamente.

The ambivalence from the clash of voices results in mental and emotional states of perplexity. Internal strife results in insecurity and indecisiveness. The *mestiza's* dual or multiple personality is plagued by psychic restlessness.

In a constant state of mental nepantilism, an Aztec word meaning torn between ways, *la mestiza* is a product of the transfer of the cultural and spiritual values of one group to another. Being tricultural, monolingual, bilingual or multilingual, speaking a patois, and in a state of perpetual transition, the *mestiza* faces the dilemma of the mixed breed: which collectivity does the daughter of a darkskinned mother listen to?

El choque de un alma atrapado entre el mundo del espíritu y el mundo de la ténica a veces la deja entullada. Cradled in one culture, sandwiched between two cultures, straddling all three cultures and their value systems, *la mestiza* undergoes a struggle of flesh, a struggle of borders, an inner war. Like all people, we perceive the version of reality that our culture communicates. Like others having or living in more than one culture, we get multiple, often opposing messages. The coming together of two self-consistent but habitually incompatible frames of reference[3] causes *un choque,* a cultural collision.

Within us and within *la cultura chicana,* commonly held beliefs of the white culture attack commonly held beliefs of the Mexican culture, and both attack commonly held beliefs of the indigenous culture. Subconsciously, we see an attack on ourselves and our beliefs as a threat and we attempt to block with a counterstance.

But it is not enough to stand on the opposite river bank, shouting questions, challenging patriarchal, white conventions. A counterstance locks one into a duel of oppressor and oppressed; locked in mortal combat, like the cop and the criminal, both are reduced to a common denominator of violence. The counterstance refutes the dominant culture's views and beliefs, and, for this, it is proudly defiant. All reaction is limited by, and dependent on, what it is reacting against. Because the counterstance stems from a problem with authority—outer as well as inner—it's a step towards liberation from cultural domination. But it is not a way of life. At some point, on our way to a new consciousness, we will have to leave the opposite bank, the split between the two mortal combatants somehow healed so that we are on both shores at once and, at once, see through serpent and eagle eyes. Or perhaps we will decide to disengage from the dominant culture, write it off altogether as a lost cause, and cross the border into a wholly new and separate territory. Or we might go another route. The possibilities are numerous once we decide to act and not react.

A TOLERANCE FOR AMBIGUITY

These numerous possibilities leave *la mestiza* floundering in uncharted seas. In perceiving conflicting information and points of view, she is subjected to a swamping of her psychological borders. She has discovered that she can't hold concepts or ideas in rigid boundaries. The borders and walls that are supposed to keep the undesirable ideas out are entrenched habits and patterns of behavior; these habits and patterns are the enemy within. Rigidity means death. Only by remaining flexible is she able to stretch the psyche horizontally and vertically. *La mestiza* constantly has to shift out of habitual formations; from convergent thinking, analytical reasoning that tends to use rationality to move toward a single goal (a Western mode), to divergent thinking,[4] characterized by movement away from set patterns and goals and toward a more whole perspective, one that includes rather than excludes.

The new *mestiza* copes by developing a tolerance for contradictions, a tolerance for ambiguity. She learns to be an Indian in Mexican culture, to be Mexican from an Anglo point of view. She learns to juggle cultures. She has a plural personality, she operates in a pluralistic mode—nothing is thrust out, the good, the bad and the ugly, nothing rejected, nothing abandoned. Not only does she sustain contradictions, she turns the ambivalence into something else.

She can be jarred out of ambivalence by an intense, and often painful, emotional event which inverts or resolves the ambivalence. I'm not sure exactly how. The work takes place underground—subconsciously. It is work that the soul performs.

That focal point or fulcrum, that juncture where the *mestiza* stands, is where phenomena tend to collide. It is where the possibility of uniting all that is separate occurs. This assembly is not one where severed or separated pieces merely come together. Nor is it a balancing of opposing powers. In attempting to work out a synthesis, the self has added a third element which is greater than the sum of its severed parts. That third element is a new consciousness—a *mestiza* consciousness—and though it is a source of intense pain, its energy comes from a continual creative motion that keeps breaking down the unitary aspect of each new paradigm.

En unas pocas centurias, the future will belong to the *mestiza.* Because the future depends on the breaking down of paradigms, it depends on the straddling of two or more cultures. By creating a new mythos—that is, a change in the way we perceive reality, the way we see ourselves and the ways we behave—*la mestiza* creates a new consciousness.

The work of *mestiza* consciousness is to break down the subject-object duality that keeps her a prisoner and to show in the flesh and through the images in her work how duality is transcended. The answer to the problem between the white race and the colored, between males and females, lies in healing the split that originates in the very foundation of our lives, our culture, our languages, our thoughts. A massive uprooting of dualistic thinking in the individual and collective consciousness is the beginning of a long struggle, but one that could, in our best hopes, bring us to the end of rape, of violence, of war.

La encrucijada/The Crossroads

A chicken is being sacrificed
   at a crossroads, a simple mound of earth
a mud shrine for *Eshu,*
   Yoruba god of indeterminacy,
who blesses her choice of path.
   She begins her journey.

Su cuerpo es una bocacalle. La mestiza has gone from being the sacrificial goat to becoming the officiating priestess at the crossroads.

As a *mestiza* I have no country, my homeland cast me out; yet all countries are mine because I am every woman's sister or potential lover. (As a lesbian I have no race, my own people disclaim me; but I am all races because there is the queer of me in all races.) I am cultureless because, as a feminist, I challenge the collective cultural/religious male-derived beliefs of Indo-Hispanics and Anglos; yet I am cultured because I am participating in the creation of yet another culture, a new story to explain the world and our participation in it, a new value system with images and symbols that connect us to each other and to the planet. *Soy un amasamiento,* I am an act of kneading, of uniting and joining that not only has produced both a creature of darkness and a creature of light, but also a creature that questions the definition of light and dark and gives them new meanings.

We are the people who leap in the dark, we are the people on the knees of the gods. In our flesh, (r)evolution works out the clash of cultures. It makes us crazy constantly, but if the center holds, we've made some kind of evolutionary step forward. *Nuestra alma el trabajo,* the opus, the great alchemical work; spiritual *mestizaje,* a "morphogenesis,"[5] an inevitable unfolding. We have become the quickening serpent movement.

· · ·

El camino de la mestiza/The *Mestiza* Way

Caught between the sudden contraction, the breath sucked in and the endless space, the brown woman stands still, looks at the sky. She decides to go down, digging her way along the roots of trees. Sifting through the bones, she shakes them to see if there is any marrow in them. Then, touching the dirt to her forehead, to her tongue, she takes a few bones, leaves the rest in their burial place.

She goes through her backpack, keeps her journal and address book, throws away the muni-bart metromaps. The coins are heavy and they go next, then the greenbacks flutter through the air. She keeps her knife, can opener and eyebrow pencil. She puts bones, pieces of bark, *hierbas,* eagle feather, snake-skin, tape recorder, the rattle and drum in her pack and she sets out to become the complete *tolteca.*

Her first step is to take inventory. *Despojando, desgranando, quitando paja.* Just what did she inherit from her ancestors? This weight on her back—which is the baggage from the Indian mother, which the baggage from the Spanish father, which the baggage from the Anglo?

Pero es difícil differentiating between *lo heredado, lo adquirido, lo impuesto.* She puts history through a sieve, winnows out the lies, looks at the forces that we as a race, as women, have been a part of. *Luego bota lo que no vale, los desmientos, los desencuentos, el embrutecimiento. Aguarda el juicio, hondo y enraizado, de la gente antigua.* This step is a conscious rupture with all oppressive traditions of all cultures and religions. She communicates that rupture, documents the struggle. She reinterprets history and, using new symbols, she shapes new myths. She adopts new perspectives toward the darkskinned, women and queers. She strengthens her tolerance (and intolerance) for ambiguity. She is willing to share, to make herself vulnerable to foreign ways of seeing and thinking. She surrenders all notions of safety, of the familiar. Deconstruct, construct. She becomes a *nahual,* able to transform herself into a tree, a coyote, into another person. She learns to transform the small "I" into the total Self. *Se hace moldeadora de su alma. Según la concepción que tiene de sí misma, así será.*

Que no se nos olvide los hombres

"Tú no sirves pa' nada—
you're good for nothing.
Eres pura vieja."

"You're nothing but a woman" means you are defective. Its opposite is to be *un macho.* The modern meaning of the word "machismo," as well as the concept, is actually an Anglo invention. For men like my father, being "macho" meant being strong enough to protect and support my mother and us, yet being able to show love. Today's macho has doubts about his ability to feed and protect his family. His "machismo" is an adaptation to oppression and poverty and low self-esteem. It is the result of hierarchical male dominance. The Anglo, feeling inadequate and inferior and powerless, displaces or transfers these feeling to the Chicano by shaming him. In the Gringo world, the Chicano suffers from excessive humility and self-effacement, shame of self and self-deprecation. Around Latinos he suffers from a sense of language inadequacy and its accompanying discomfort; with Native Americans he suffers from racial amnesia which ignores our common blood, and from guilt because the Spanish part of

him took their land and oppressed them. He has an excessive compensatory hubris when around Mexicans from the other side. It overlays a deep sense of racial shame.

The loss of a sense of dignity and respect in the macho breeds a false machismo which leads him to put down women and even to brutalize them. Co-existing with his sexist behavior is a love for the mother which takes precedence over that of all others. Devoted son, macho pig. To wash down the shame of his acts, of his very being, and to handle the brute in the mirror, he takes to the bottle, the snort, the needle and the fist.

Though we "understand" the root causes of male hatred and fear, and the subsequent wounding of women, we do not excuse, we do not condone and we will no longer put up with it. From the men of our race, we demand the admission/acknowledgment/disclosure/testimony that they wound us, violate us, are afraid of us and of our power. We need them to say they will begin to eliminate their hurtful put-down ways. But more than the words, we demand acts. We say to them: we will develop equal power with you and those who have shamed us.

It is imperative that *mestizas* support each other in changing the sexist elements in the Mexican-Indian culture. As long as woman is put down, the Indian and the Black in all of us is put down. The struggle of the *mestiza* is above all a feminist one. As long as *los hombres* think they have to *chingar mujeres* and each other to be men, as long as men are taught that they are superior and therefore culturally favored over *la mujer,* as long as to be a *vieja* is a thing of derision, there can be no real healing of our psyches. We're halfway there—we have such a love of the Mother, the good mother. The first step is to unlearn the *puta/virgen* dichotomy and to see *Coatlapopeuh—Coatlicue* in the Mother, *Guadalupe.*

Tenderness, a sign of vulnerability, is so feared that it is showered on women with verbal abuse and blows. Men, even more than women, are fettered to gender roles. Women at least have had the guts to break out of bondage. Only gay men have had the courage to expose themselves to the woman inside them and to challenge the current masculinity. I've encountered a few scattered and isolated gentle straight men, the beginnings of a new breed, but they are confused, and entangled with sexist behaviors that they have not been able to eradicate. We need a new masculinity and the new man needs a movement.

Lumping the males who deviate from the general norm with man, the oppressor, is a gross injustice. *Asombra pensar que nos hemos quedado en ese pozo oscuro donde el mundo encierra a las lesbianas. Asombra pensar que hemos, como femenistas y lesbianas, cerrado nuestros corazónes a los hombres, a nuestros hermanos, los jotos, desheredados y marginales como nosotros.* Being the supreme crossers of cultures, homosexuals have strong bonds with the queer white, Black, Asian, Native American, Latino and with the queer in Italy, Australia and the rest of the planet. We come from all colors, all classes, all races, all time periods. Our role is to link people with each other—the Blacks with Jews with Indians with Asians, with whites, with extraterrestrials. It is to transfer ideas and information from one culture to another. Colored homosexuals have more knowledge of other cultures; have always been at the forefront (although sometimes in the closet) of all liberation struggles in this country; have suffered more injustices and have survived them despite all odds. Chicanos need to acknowledge the political and artistic contributions of their queer. People, listen to what your *jotería* is saying.

The *mestizo* and the queer exist at this time and point on the evolutionary continuum for a purpose. We are a blending that proves that all blood is intricately woven together, and that we are spawned out of similar souls.

. . .

El día de la Chicana

I will not be shamed again
Nor will I shame myself.

I am possessed by a vision: that we as Chicanas and Chicanos have taken back or uncovered our true faces, our dignity and self-respect. It's a validation vision.

Seeing the Chicana anew in light of her history, I seek an exoneration, a seeing through the fictions of white supremacy, a seeing of ourselves in our true guises and not as the false racial personality that has been given to us and that we have given to ourselves. I seek our woman's face, our true features, the positive and the negative seen clearly, free of the tainted biases of male dominance. I seek new images of identity, new beliefs about ourselves, our humanity and worth no longer in question.

Estamos viviendo en la noche de la Raza, un tiempo cuando el trabajo se hace a lo quieto, en el oscuro. El día cuando aceptamos tal y como somos y para en donde vamos y porque—ese día será el día de la Raza. Yo tengo el conpromiso de expresar mi visión, mi sensibilidad, mi percepción de la revalidación de la gente mexicana, su mérito, estimación, honra, aprecio y validez.

On December 2nd when my sun goes into my first house, I celebrate *el día de la Chicana y el Chicano.* On that day I clean my altars, light my *Coatlalopeuh* candle, burn sage and copal, take *el baño para espantar basura*, sweep my house. On that day I bare my soul, make myself vulnerable to friends and family by expressing my feelings. On that day I affirm who we are.

On that day I look inside our conflicts and our basic introverted racial temperament. I identify our needs, voice them. I acknowledge that the self and the race have been wounded. I recognize the need to take care of our personhood, of our racial self. On that day I gather the splintered and disowned parts of *la gente mexicana* and hold them in my arms. *Todas las partes de nostros valen.*

On that day I say, "Yes, all you people wound us when you reject us. Rejection strips us of our self-worth; our vulnerability exposes us to shame. It is our innate identity you find wanting. We are ashamed that we need your good opinion, that we need your acceptance. We can no longer camouflage our needs, can no longer let defenses and fences sprout around us. We can no longer withdraw. To rage and look upon you with contempt is to rage and be contemptuous of ourselves. We can no longer blame you, nor disown the white parts, the male parts, the pathological parts, the queer parts, the vulnerable parts. Here we are weaponless with open arms, with only our magic. Let's try it our way, the *mestiza* way, the Chicana way, the woman way."

On that day, I search for our essential dignity as a people, a people with a sense of purpose—to belong and contribute to something greater than our *pueblo*. On that day I seek to recover and reshape my spiritual identity. *¡Anímate! Raza, a celebrar el día de la Chicana!*

El retorno

All movements are accomplished in six stages,
and the seventh brings return.   —I Ching[6]

Tanto tiempo sin verte casa mía,
mi cuna, mi hondo nido de la huerta.
                              —"Soledad"[7]

I stand at the river, watch the curving, twisting serpent, a serpent nailed to the fence where the mouth of the Rio Grande empties into the Gulf.

I have come back. *Tanto dolor me costó el alejamiento.* I shade my eyes and look up. The bone beak of a hawk slowly circling over me, checking me out as potential carrion. In its wake a little bird flickering its wings, swimming sporadically like a fish. In the distance the expressway and the slough of traffic like an irritated sow. The sudden pull in my gut, *la tierra, los aguaceros.* My land, *el viento soplando la arena, el lagartijo debajo de un nopalito. Me acuerdo como era antes. Una región desértica de vasta llanuras, costeras de baja altura, de escasa lluvia, de chaparrales formados por mesquites y huizaches.* If I look real hard I can almost see the Spanish fathers who were called "the cavalry of Christ" enter this valley riding their burros, see the clash of cultures commence.

Tierra natal. This is home, the small towns in the Valley, *los pueblitos* with chicken pens and goats picketed to mesquite shrubs. *En las colonias* on the other side of the tracks, junk cars line the front yards of hot pink and lavender-trimmed houses— Chicano architecture we call it, self-consciously. I have missed the TV shows where hosts speak in half and half, and where awards are given in the category of Tex-Mex music. I have missed the Mexican cemeteries blooming with artificial flowers, the fields of aloe vera and red pepper, rows of sugar cane, of corn hanging on the stalks, the cloud of *polvareda* in the dirt roads behind a speeding truck, *el sabor de tamales de rez y venado.* I have missed *la yegua colorada* gnawing the wooden gate of her stall, the smell of horse flesh from Carito's

corrals. *He hecho menos las noches calientes sin aire, noches de linternas y lechuzas* making holes in the night.

I still feel the old dispair when I look at the unpainted, dilapidated, scrap lumber houses consisting mostly of corrugated aluminum. Some of the poorest people in the U.S. live in the Lower Rio Grande Valley, an arid and semi-arid land of irrigated farming, intense sunlight and heat, citrus groves next to chaparral and cactus. I walk through the elementary school I attended so long ago, that remained segregated until recently. I remember how the white teachers used to punish us for being Mexican.

How I love this tragic valley of South Texas, as Ricardo Sánchez calls it; this borderland between the Nueces and the Rio Grande. This land has survived possession and ill-use by five countries: Spain, Mexico, The Republic of Texas, the Confederacy, and the U.S. again. It has survived Anglo-Mexican blood feuds, lynchings, burnings, rapes, pillage.

· · ·

I walk out to the back yard, stare at *los rosales de mamá.* She wants me to help her prune the rose bushes, dig out the carpet grass that is choking them. *Mamagrande Ramona también tenía rosales.* Here every Mexican grows flowers. If they don't have a piece of dirt, they use car tires, jars, cans, shoes boxes. Roses are the Mexican's favorite flower. I think, how symbolic—thorns and all.

Yes, the Chicano and Chicana have always taken care of growing things and the land. Again I see the four of us kids getting off the school bus, changing into our work clothes, walking out into the field with Papí and Mamí, all six of us bending to the ground. Below our feet, under the earth lie the watermelon seeds. We cover them with paper plates, putting *teremotes* on top of the plates to keep them from being blown away by the wind. The paper plates keep the freeze away. Next day or the next, we remove the plates, bare the tiny green shoots to the elements. They survive and grow, give fruit hundreds of times the size of the seed. We water them and hoe them. We harvest them. The vines dry, rot, are plowed under. Growth, death, decay, birth. The soil prepared again and again, impregnated, worked on. A constant changing of forms, *renacimientos de la tierra madre*.

This land was Mexican once
    was Indian always
        and is.
            And will be again.

[1987]

NOTES

1. This is my own "take-off" on Jose Vasconcelos' idea. Jose Vasconcelos, *La Raza Cósmica: Missión de la Raza Ibero-Americana* (México: Aguilar S.A. de Ediciones, 1961).
2. Vasconcelos.
3. Arthur Koestler termed this "bisociation." Albert Rothenberg, *The Creative Process in Art, Science, and Other Fields* (Chicago, IL: University of Chicago Press, 1979), 12.
4. In part, I derive my definitions for "convergent" and "divergent" thinking from Rothenberg, 12–13.
5. To borrow chemist Ilya Prigogine's theory of "dissipative structures." Prigogine discovered that substances interact not in predictable ways as it was taught in science, but in different and fluctuating ways to produce new and more complex structures, a kind of birth he called "morphogenesis," which created unpredictable innovations. See Harold Gilliam, "Searching for a New World View," *This World* (January, 1981), 23.
6. Richard Wilhelm, *The I Ching or Book of Changes*, trans. Cary F. Baynes (Princeton, NJ: Princeton University Press, 1950), 98.
7. "*Soledad*" is sung by the group Haciendo Punto en Otro Son.

 72

Cultural Feminism versus Post-Structuralism: The Identity Crisis in Feminist Theory

LINDA ALCOFF

LINDA ALCOFF ND. Philosopher. *Feminist Epistemologies* (1993), *Real-Knowing: New Versions of Coherence Epistemology* (1996), "The Politics of Postmodern Feminism, Revisited" (1997), *Thinking from the Underside of History* (2000), *Visible Identities: Race, Gender, and the Self* (2005).

For many contemporary feminist theorists, the concept of woman is a problem. It is a problem of primary significance because the concept of woman is the central concept for feminist theory and yet it is a concept that is impossible to formulate precisely for feminists. It is the central concept for feminists because the concept and category of woman is the necessary point of departure for any feminist theory and feminist politics, predicated as these are on the transformation of women's lived experience in contemporary culture and the reevaluation of social theory and practice from women's point of view. But as a concept it is radically problematic precisely for feminists because it is crowded with the overdeterminations of male supremacy, invoking in every formulation the limit, contrasting Other, or mediated self-reflection of a culture built on the control of females. In attempting to speak for women, feminism often seems to presuppose that it knows what women truly are, but such an assumption is foolhardy given that every source of knowledge about women has been contaminated with misogyny and sexism. No matter where we turn—to historical documents, philosophical constructions, social scientific statistics, introspection, or daily practices—the mediation of female bodies into constructions of woman is dominated by misogynist discourse. For feminists, who must transcend this discourse, it appears we have nowhere to turn.

Thus the dilemma facing feminist theorists today is that our very self-definition is grounded in a concept that we must deconstruct and de-essentialize in all of its aspects. Man has said that woman can be defined, delineated, captured—understood, explained, and diagnosed—to a level of determination never accorded to man himself, who is conceived as a rational animal with free will. Where man's behavior is undetermined, free to construct its own future along the course of its rational choice, woman's nature has overdetermined her behavior, the limits of her intellectual endeavors, and the inevitabilities of her emotional journey through life. Whether she is construed as essentially immoral and irrational (à la Schopenhauer) or essentially kind and benevolent (à la Kant), she is always construed as an essential *something* inevitably accessible to direct intuited apprehension by males. Despite the variety of ways in which man has construed her essential characteristics, she is always the Object, a conglomeration of attributes to be predicted and controlled along with other natural phenomena. The place of the free-willed subject who can transcend nature's mandates is reserved exclusively for men.

Feminist thinkers have articulated two major responses to this situation over the last ten years. The first response is to claim that feminists have the exclusive right to describe and evaluate woman. Thus cultural feminists argue that the problem of male supremacist culture is the problem of a process in which women are defined by men, that is, by a group who has a contrasting point of view and set of interests from women, not to mention a possible fear and hatred of women. The result of this has been a distortion and devaluation of feminine characteristics, which now can be corrected by a more accurate feminist description and appraisal. Thus the cultural feminist reappraisal construes woman's passivity as her peacefulness, her sentimentality as her proclivity to nurture, her subjectiveness as her advanced self-awareness, and so forth. Cultural feminists have not challenged the defining of woman but only that definition given by men.

The second major response has been to reject the possibility of defining woman as such at all. Feminists who take this tactic go about the business of deconstructing all concepts of woman and argue that both feminist and misogynist attempts to define woman are politically reactionary and ontologically mistaken. Replacing woman-as-housewife with woman-as-supermom (or earth mother or super professional) is no advance. Using French post-structuralist theory these feminists argue that such errors occur because we are in fundamental ways duplicating misogynist strategies when we try to define women, characterize women, or speak for women, even though allowing for a range of differences within the gender. The politics of gender or sexual difference must be replaced with a plurality of difference where gender loses its position of significance.

Briefly put, then, the cultural feminist response to Simone de Beauvoir's question, "Are there women?" is to answer yes and to define women by their activities and attributes in the present culture. The post-structuralist response is to answer no and attack the category and the concept of woman through problematizing subjectivity. Each response has serious

limitations, and it is becoming increasingly obvious that transcending these limitations while retaining the theoretical framework from which they emerge is impossible. As a result, a few brave souls are now rejecting these choices and attempting to map out a new course, a course that will avoid the major problems of the earlier responses. In this paper I will discuss some of the pioneer work being done to develop a new concept of woman and offer my own contribution toward it. But first, I must spell out more clearly the inadequacies of the first two responses to the problem of woman and explain why I believe these inadequacies are inherent.

CULTURAL FEMINISM

Cultural feminism is the ideology of a female nature or female essence reappropriated by feminists themselves in an effort to revalidate undervalued female attributes. For cultural feminists, the enemy of women is not merely a social system or economic institution or set of backward beliefs but masculinity itself and in some cases male biology. Cultural feminist politics revolve around creating and maintaining a healthy environment—free of masculinist values and all their offshoots such as pornography—for the female principle. Feminist theory, the explanation of sexism, and the justification of feminist demands can all be grounded securely and unambiguously on the concept of the essential female.

Mary Daly and Adrienne Rich have been influential proponents of this position. Breaking from the trend toward androgyny and the minimizing of gender differences that was popular among feminists in the early seventies, both Daly and Rich argue for a returned focus on femaleness.

For Daly, male barrenness leads to parasitism on female energy, which flows from our life-affirming, life-creating biological condition: "Since female energy is essentially biophilic, the female spirit/body is the primary target in this perpetual war of aggression against life. Gyn/Ecology is the reclaiming of life-loving female energy."[1] Despite Daly's warnings against biological reductionism,[2] her own analysis of sexism uses gender-specific biological traits to explain male hatred for women. The childless state of "all males" leads to a dependency on women, which in turn leads men to "deeply identify with 'unwanted fetal tissue.'"[3] Given their state of fear and insecurity it becomes almost understandable, then, that men would desire to dominate and control that which is so vitally necessary to them: the life-energy of women. Female energy, conceived by Daly as a natural essence, needs to be freed from its male parasites, released for creative expression and recharged through bonding with other women. In this free space women's "natural" attributes of love, creativity, and the ability to nurture can thrive.

Women's identification as female is their defining essence for Daly, their haecceity, overriding any other way in which they may be defined or may define themselves. Thus Daly states: "Women who accept false inclusion among the fathers and the sons are easily polarized against other women on the basis of ethnic, national, class, religious and other *male-defined differences,* applauding the defeat of 'enemy' women."[4] These differences are apparent rather than real, inessential rather than essential. The only real difference, the only difference that can change a person's ontological placement on Daly's dichotomous map is sex difference. Our essence is defined here, in our sex, from which flow all the facts about us: who are our potential allies, who is our enemy, what are our objective interests, what is our true nature. Thus, Daly defines women again and her definition is strongly linked to female biology.

Many of Rich's writings have exhibited surprising similarities to Daly's position described above, surprising given their difference in style and temperament. Rich defines a "female consciousness"[5] that has a great deal to deal with the female body.

> I have come to believe . . . that female biology—the diffuse, intense sensuality radiating out from clitoris, breasts, uterus, vagina; the lunar cycles of menstruation; the gestation and fruition of life which can take place in the female body—has far more radical implications than we have yet come to appreciate. Patriarchal thought has limited female biology to its own narrow specifications. The feminist vision has recoiled from female biology for these reasons; it will, I believe, come to view our physicality as a resource, rather than a destiny. . . . We must touch the unity and resonance of our physicality, our bond with the natural order, the corporeal ground for our intelligence.[6]

Thus Rich argues that we should not reject the importance of female biology simply because patriarchy has used it to subjugate us. Rich believes that "our biological grounding, the miracle and paradox of the female body and its spiritual and political meanings" holds the key to our rejuvenation and our reconnection with our specific female attributes, which she lists as "our great mental capacities . . . ; our highly developed tactile sense; our genius for close observation; our complicated, pain-enduring, multi-pleasured physicality."[7]

Rich further echoes Daly in her explanation of misogyny: "The ancient, continuing envy, awe and dread of the male for the female capacity to create life has repeatedly taken the form of hatred for every other female aspect of creativity."[8] Thus, Rich, like Daly, identifies a female essence, defines patriarchy as the subjugation and colonization of this essence out of male envy and need, and then promotes a solution that revolves around rediscovering our essence and bonding with other women. Neither Rich nor Daly espouses biological reductionism, but this is because they reject the oppositional dichotomy of mind and body that such a reductionism presupposes. The female essence for Daly and Rich is not simply spiritual or simply biological—it is both. Yet the key point remains that it is our specifically female anatomy that is the primary constituent of our identity and the source of our female essence. Rich prophesies that "the repossession by women of our bodies will bring far more essential change to human society than the seizing of the means of production by workers. . . . In such a world women will truly create new life, bringing forth not only children (if and as we choose) but the visions, and the thinking, necessary to sustain, console and alter human existence—a new relationship to the universe. Sexuality, politics, intelligence, power, motherhood, work, community, intimacy will develop new meanings; thinking itself will be transformed."[9]

. . .

Interestingly, I have not included any feminist writings from women of oppressed nationalities and races in the category of cultural feminism, nor does [Alice] Echols. I have heard it argued that the emphasis placed on cultural identity by such writers as Cherríe Moraga and Audre Lorde reveals a

above, that woman may represent the rupture in the functional discourse of what he calls logocentrism, an essentialist discourse that entails hierarchies of difference and a Kantian ontology. Because woman has in a sense been excluded from this discourse, it is possible to hope that she might provide a real source of resistance. But her resistance will not be at all effective if she continues to use the mechanism of logocentrism to redefine woman: she can be an effective resister only if she drifts and dodges all attempts to capture her. Then, Derrida hopes, the following futuristic picture will come true: "Out of the depths, endless and unfathomable, she engulfs and distorts all vestige of essentiality, of identity, of property. And the philosophical discourse, blinded, founders on these shoals and is hurled down these depths to its ruin."[14] For Derrida, women have always been defined as a subjugated difference within a binary opposition: man/woman, culture/nature, positive/negative, analytical/intuitive. To assert an essential gender difference as cultural feminists do is to reinvoke this oppositional structure. The only way to break out of this structure, and in fact to subvert the structure itself, is to assert total difference, to be that which cannot be pinned down or subjugated within a dichotomous hierarchy. Paradoxically, it is to be what is not. Thus feminists cannot demarcate a definitive category of "woman" without eliminating all possibility for the defeat of logocentrism and its oppressive power.

Foucault similarly rejects all constructions of oppositional subjects—whether the "proletariat," "woman," or "the oppressed,"—as mirror images that merely recreate and sustain the discourse of power. As Biddy Martin points out, "The point from which Foucault deconstructs is off-center, out of line, apparently unaligned. It is not the point of an imagined absolute otherness, but an 'alterity' which understands itself as an internal exclusion."[15]

Following Foucault and Derrida, an effective feminism could only be a wholly negative feminism, deconstructing everything and refusing to construct anything. This is the position Julia Kristeva adopts, herself an influential French post-structuralist. She says; "A woman cannot be; it is something which does not even belong in the order of being. *It follows that a feminist practice can only be*

negative, at odds with what already exists so that we may say 'that's not it' and 'that's still not it.'"[16] The problematic character of subjectivity does not mean, then, that there can be no political struggle, as one might surmise from the fact that post-structuralism deconstructs the position of the revolutionary in the same breath as it deconstructs the position of the reactionary. But the political struggle can have only a "negative function," rejecting "everything finite, definite, structured, loaded with meaning, in the existing state of society."[17]

The attraction of the post-structuralist critique of subjectivity for feminists is two-fold. First, it seems to hold out the promise of an increased freedom for women, the "free play" of a plurality of differences, unhampered by any predetermined gender identity as formulated by either patriarchy or cultural feminism. Second, it moves decisively beyond cultural feminism and liberal feminism in further theorizing what they leave untouched: the construction of subjectivity. We can learn a great deal here about the mechanisms of sexist oppression and the construction of specific gender categories by relating these to social discourse and by conceiving of the subject as a cultural product. Certainly, too, this analysis can help us understand right-wing women, the reproduction of ideology, and the mechanisms that block social progress. However, adopting nominalism creates significant problems for feminism. How can we seriously adopt Kristeva's plan for only negative struggle? As the Left should by now have learned, you cannot mobilize a movement that is only and always against: you must have a positive alternative, a vision of a better future that can motivate people to sacrifice their time and energy toward its realization. Moreover, a feminist adoption of nominalism will be confronted with the same problem theories of ideology have, that is, Why is right-wing woman's consciousness constructed via social discourse but a feminist's consciousness not? Post-structuralist critiques of subjectivity pertain to the construction of all subjects or they pertain to none. And here is precisely the dilemma for feminists: How can we ground a feminist politics that deconstructs the female subject? Nomination threatens to wipe out feminism itself.

. . .

A nominalist position on subjectivity has the deleterious effect of de-gendering our analysis, of in effect making gender invisible once again. Foucault's ontology includes only bodies and pleasures, and he is notorious for not including gender as a category of analysis. If gender is simply a social construct, the need and even the possibility of a feminist politics becomes immediately problematic. What can we demand in the name of women if "women" do not exist and demands in their name simply reinforce the myth that they do? How can we speak out against sexism as detrimental to the interests of women if the category is a fiction? How can we demand legal abortions, adequate child care, or wages based on comparable worth without invoking a concept of "women"?

Post-structuralism undercuts our ability to oppose the dominant trend (and, one might argue, the dominant danger) in mainstream Western intellectual thought, that is, the insistence on a universal, neutral, perspectiveless epistemology, metaphysics, and ethics. . . . For the post-structuralist, race, class, and gender are constructs and, therefore, incapable of decisively validating conceptions of justice and truth because underneath there lies no natural core to build on or liberate or maximize. Hence, once again, underneath we are all the same. It is, in fact, a desire to topple this commitment to the possibility of a worldview—purported in fact as the best of all possible worldviews—grounded in a generic human that motivates much of the cultural feminist glorification of femininity as a valid specificity legitimately grounding feminist theory.

The preceding characterizations of cultural feminism and post-structuralist feminism will anger many feminists by assuming too much homogeneity and by blithely pigeonholing large and complex theories. However, I believe the tendencies I have outlined toward essentialism and toward nominalism represent the main, current responses by feminist theory to the task of reconceptualizing "woman." Both responses have significant advantages and serious shortcomings. Cultural feminism has provided a useful corrective to the "generic human" thesis of classical liberalism and has promoted community and self-affirmation, but it cannot provide a long-range future course of action for feminist theory or practice, and it is founded on a

claim of essentialism that we are far from having the evidence to justify. The feminist appropriation of post-structuralism has provided suggestive insights on the construction of female and male subjectivity and has issued a crucial warning against creating a feminism that reinvokes the mechanisms of oppressive power. Nonetheless, it limits feminism to the negative tactics of reaction and deconstruction and endangers the attack against classical liberalism by discrediting the notion of an epistemologically significant, specific subjectivity. What's a feminist to do?

We cannot simply embrace the paradox. In order to avoid the serious disadvantages of cultural feminism and post-structuralism, feminism needs to transcend the dilemma by developing a third course, an alternative theory of the subject that avoids both essentialism and nominalism. This new alternative might share the post-structuralist insight that the category "woman" needs to be theorized through an exploration of the experience of subjectivity, as opposed to a description of current attributes, but it need not concede that such an exploration will necessarily result in a nominalist position on gender, or an erasure of it. Feminists need to explore the possibility of a theory of the gendered subject that does not slide into essentialism. In the following two sections I will discuss recent work★ that makes a contribution to the development of such a theory, or so I shall argue, and in the final section I will develop my own contribution in the form of a concept of gendered identity as positionality.

TERESA DE LAURETIS

Lauretis's influential book, *Alice Doesn't*, is a series of essays organized around an exploration of the problem of conceptualizing woman as a subject. This problem is formulated in her work as arising out of the conflict between "woman" as a "fictional construct" and "women" as "real historical beings."[18] She says: "The relation between women as historical subjects and the notion of woman as it is produced by hegemonic discourses is neither a direct relation of identity, a one-to-one

---

★[Editors' Note: In the discussion that follows Alcoff examines the work of both Teresa de Lauretis and Denise Riley. Only the first of these two discussions is included here.]

correspondence, nor a relation of simple implication. Like all other relations expressed in language, it is an arbitrary and symbolic one, that is to say, culturally set up. The manner and effects of that set-up are what the book intends to explore."[19] The strength of Lauretis's approach is that she never loses sight of the political imperative of feminist theory and, thus, never forgets that we must seek not only to describe this relation in which women's subjectivity is grounded but also to change it. And yet, given her view that we are constructed via a semiotic discourse, this political mandate becomes a crucial problem. As she puts it, "Paradoxically, the only way to position oneself outside of that discourse is to displace oneself within it—to refuse the question as formulated, or to answer deviously (though in its words), even to quote (but against the grain). The limit posed but not worked through in this book is thus the contradiction of feminist theory itself, at once excluded from discourse and imprisoned within it."[20] As with feminist theory, so, too, is the female subject "at once excluded from discourse and imprisoned within it." Constructing a theory of the subject that both concedes these truths and yet allows for the possibility of feminism is the problem Lauretis tackles throughout *Alice Doesn't*. To concede the construction of the subject via discourse entails that the feminist project cannot be simply "how to make visible the invisible" as if the essence of gender were out there waiting to be recognized by the dominant discourse. Yet Lauretis does not give up on the possibility of producing "the conditions of visibility for a different social subject."[21] In her view, a nominalist position on subjectivity can be avoided by linking subjectivity to a Peircean notion of practices and a further theorized notion of experience.[22] I shall look briefly at her discussion of this latter claim.

Lauretis's main thesis is that subjectivity, that is, what one "perceives and comprehends as subjective," is constructed through a continuous process, an ongoing constant renewal based on an interaction with the world, which she defines as experience: "And thus [subjectivity] is produced not by external ideas, values, or material causes, but by one's personal, subjective engagement in the practices, discourses, and institutions that lend significance (value, meaning, and affect) to the events of

the world."[23] . . . For all her insistence on a subjectivity constructed through practices, Lauretis is clear that *that* conception of subjectivity is not what she wishes to propose. A subjectivity that is fundamentally shaped by gender appears to lead irrevocably to essentialism, the posing of a male/female opposition as universal and ahistorical. A subjectivity that is not fundamentally shaped by gender appears to lead to the conception of a generic human subject, as if we could peel away our "cultural" layers and get to the real root of human nature, which turns out to be genderless. Are these really our only choices?

In *Alice Doesn't* Lauretis develops the beginnings of a new conception of subjectivity. She argues that subjectivity is neither (over)determined by biology nor by "free, rational, intentionality" but, rather, by experience, which she defines (via Lacan, Eco, and Peirce) as "a complex of habits resulting from the semiotic interaction of 'outer world' and 'inner world,' the continuous engagement of a self or subject in social reality."[24] Given this definition, the question obviously becomes, Can we ascertain a "female experience"? This is the question Lauretis prompts us to consider, more specifically, to analyze "that complex of habits, dispositions, associations and perceptions, which en-genders one as female."[25] Lauretis ends her book with an insightful observation that can serve as a critical starting point:

> This is where the specificity of a feminist theory may be sought: not in femininity as a privileged nearness to nature, the body, or the unconscious, an essence which inheres in women but to which males too now lay a claim; not in female tradition simply understood as private, marginal, and yet intact, outside of history but fully there to be discovered or recovered; not, finally, in the chinks and cracks of masculinity, the fissures of male identity or the repressed of phallic discourse; *but rather in that political, theoretical, self-analyzing practice* by which the relations of the subject in social reality can be rearticulated from the historical experience of women. Much, very much, is still to be done.[26]

Thus Lauretis asserts that the way out of the totalizing imprint of history and discourse is through our "political, theoretical self-analyzing practice." This should not be taken to imply that only intellectual articles in academic journals represent a free space or ground for maneuver but, rather, that all women can (and do) think about, criticize, and alter discourse and, thus, that subjectivity can be reconstructed through the process of reflective practice. The key component of Lauretis's formulation is the dynamic she poses at the heart of subjectivity: a fluid interaction in constant motion and open to alteration by self-analyzing practice.

Recently, Lauretis has taken off from this point and developed further her conception of subjectivity. In the introductory essay for her latest book, *Feminist Studies/Critical Studies,* Lauretis claims that an individual's identity is constituted with a historical process of consciousness, a process in which one's history "is interpreted or reconstructed by each of us within the horizon of meanings and knowledges available in the culture at given historical moments, a horizon that also includes modes of political commitment and struggle. . . . Consciousness, therefore, is never fixed, never attained once and for all because discursive boundaries change with historical conditions."[27] Here Lauretis guides our way out of the dilemma she articulated for us in *Alice Doesn't.* The agency of the subject is made possible through this process of political interpretation. And what emerges is multiple and shifting, neither "prefigured . . . in an unchangeable symbolic order" nor merely "fragmented, or intermittent."[28] Lauretis formulates a subjectivity that gives agency to the individual while at the same time placing her within "particular discursive configurations" and, moreover, conceives of the process of consciousness as a strategy. Subjectivity may thus become imbued with race, class, and gender without being subjected to an overdetermination that erases agency.

· · ·

A CONCEPT OF POSITIONALITY

· · ·

[I]t seems important to use Teresa de Lauretis's conception of experience as a way to begin to describe the features of human subjectivity. Lauretis starts with no given biological or psychological features and thus avoids assuming an essential characterization of subjectivity, but she also avoids the idealism that can follow from a rejection of materialist analyses by basing her conception on real practices and events. The importance of this focus on practices is, in part, Lauretis's shift away from the belief in the totalization of language or textuality to which most antiessentialist analyses become wedded. Lauretis wants to argue that language is not the sole source and locus of meaning, that habits and practices are crucial in the construction of meaning, and that through self-analyzing practices we can rearticulate female subjectivity. Gender is not a point to start from in the sense of being a given thing but is, instead, a posit or construct, formalizable in a nonarbitrary way through the matrix of habits, practices, and discourses. Further, it is an interpretation of our history within a particular discursive constellation, a history in which we are both subjects of and subjected to social construction.

The advantage of such an analysis is its ability to articulate a concept of gendered subjectivity without pinning it down one way or another for all time. Given this and given the danger that essentialist conceptions of the subject pose specifically for women, it seems both possible and desirable to construe a gendered subjectivity in relation to concrete habits, practices, and discourses while at the same time recognizing the fluidity of these.

As . . . Lacan . . . remind[s] us, we must continually emphasize within any account of subjectivity the historical dimension.[29] This will waylay the tendency to produce general, universal, or essential accounts by making all our conclusions contingent and revisable. Thus, through a conception of human subjectivity as an emergent property of a historicized experience, we can say "feminine subjectivity is construed here and now in such and such a way" without this ever entailing a universalizable maxim about the "feminine."

It seems to me equally important to add to this approach an "identity politics," a concept that developed from the Combahee River Collective's "A Black Feminist Statement."[30] The idea here is that one's identity is taken (and defined) as a political point of departure, as a motivation for action, and as a delineation of one's politics. Lauretis and the authors of *Yours in Struggle* are clear about the problematic nature of one's identity, one's subjectness, and yet argue that the concept of identity politics is useful because identity is a posit that is politically paramount. Their suggestion is to recognize one's identity as always a construction yet also a necessary point of departure.

· · ·

Identity politics provides a decisive rejoinder to the generic human thesis and the mainstream methodology of Western political theory. According to the latter, the approach to political theory must be through a "veil of ignorance" where the theorist's personal interests and needs are hypothetically set aside. The goal is a theory of universal scope to which all ideally rational, disinterested agents would acquiesce if given sufficient information. Stripped of their particularities, these rational agents are considered to be potentially equally persuadable. Identity politics provides a materialistic response to this and, in so doing, sides with Marxist class analysis. The best political theory will not be one ascertained through a veil of ignorance, a veil that is impossible to construct. Rather, political theory must base itself on the initial premise that all persons, including the theorist, have a fleshy, material identity that will influence and pass judgment on all political claims. Indeed, the best political theory for the theorist herself will be one that acknowledges this fact. As I see it, the concept of identity politics does not presuppose a prepackaged set of objective needs or political implications but problematizes the connection of identity and politics and introduces identity as a factor in any political analysis.

If we combine the concept of identity politics with a conception of the subject as positionality, we can conceive of the subject as nonessentialized and emergent from a historical experience and yet retain our political ability to take gender as an important point of departure. Thus we can say at one and the same time that gender is not natural, biological, universal, ahistorical, or essential and yet still claim that gender is relevant because we are taking gender as a position from which to act politically. What does position mean here?

When the concept "woman" is defined not by a particular set of attributes but by a particular position, the internal characteristics of the person thus identified are not denoted so much as the external context within which that person is situated. The external situation determines the person's relative position, just as the position of a pawn on a chessboard is considered safe or dangerous, powerful or weak, according to it relation to the other chess pieces. The essentialist definition of woman makes her identity independent of her external situation: since her nurturing and peaceful traits are innate they are ontologically autonomous of her position with respect to others or to the external historical and social conditions generally. The positional definition, on the other hand, makes her identity relative to a constantly shifting context, to a situation that includes a network of elements involving others, the objective economic conditions, cultural and political institutions and ideologies, and so on. If it is possible to identify women by their position within this network of relations, then it becomes possible to ground a feminist argument for women, not on a claim that their innate capacities are being stunted, but that their position within the network lacks power and mobility and requires radical change. The position of women is relative and not innate, and yet neither is it "undecidable." Through social critique and analysis we can identify women via their position relative to an existing cultural and social network.

It may sound all too familiar to say that the oppression of women involves their relative position within a society; but my claim goes further than this. I assert that the very subjectivity (or subjective experience of being a woman) and the very identity of women is constituted by women's position. However, this view should not imply that the concept of "woman" is determined solely by external elements and that the woman herself is merely a passive recipient of an identity created by these forces. Rather, she herself is part of the historicized, fluid movement, and she therefore actively contributes to the context within which her position can be delineated. I would include Lauretis's point here, that the identity of a woman is the product of her own interpretation and reconstruction of her history, as mediated through the cultural discursive context to which she has access.[31] Therefore, the concept of positionality includes two points: first, as already stated, that the concept of woman is a relational term identifiable only within a (constantly moving) context; but, second, that the position that women find themselves in can be actively utilized (rather than transcended) as a location for the construction of meaning, a place from where meaning is constructed, rather than simply the place where a meaning can be *discovered* (the meaning of femaleness). The concept of woman as positionality shows how women use their positional perspective as a place from which values are interpreted and constructed rather than as a locus of an already determined set of values. When women become feminists the crucial thing that has occurred is not that they have learned any new facts about the world but that they come to view those facts from a different position, from their own position as subjects. When colonial subjects begin to be critical of the formerly imitative attitude they had toward the colonists, what is happening is that they begin to identify with the colonized rather than the colonizers.[32] This difference in positional perspective does not necessitate a change in what are taken to be facts, although new facts may come into view from the new position, but it does necessitate a political change in perspective since the point of departure, the point from which all things are measured, has changed.

In this analysis, then, the concept of positionality allows for a determinate though fluid identity of woman that does not fall into essentialism: woman is a position from which a feminist politics can emerge rather than a set of attributes that are "objectively identifiable." Seen in this way, being a "woman" is to take up a position within a moving historical context and to be able to choose what we make of this position and how we alter this context. From the perspective of that fairly determinate though fluid and mutable position, women can themselves articulate a set of interests and ground a feminist politics.

· · ·

[1988]

NOTES

1. Mary Daly, *Gyn/Ecology* (Boston: Beacon, 1978), 355.
2. Ibid., 60.
3. Ibid., 59.
4. Ibid., 365 (my emphasis).
5. Adrienne Rich, *On Lies, Secrets, and Silence* (New York: Norton, 1979), 18.
6. Adrienne Rich, *Of Woman Born* (New York: Bantam, 1977), 21.
7. Ibid., 290.
8. Ibid., 21.
9. Ibid., 292.
10. Cherríe Moraga, "From a Long Line of Vendidas: Chicanas and Feminism," in *Feminist Studies/Critical Studies,* ed. Teresa de Lauretis (Bloomington: Indiana University Press, 1986), 180.
11. Michel Foucault, "Why Study Power: The Question of the Subject," in *Beyond Structuralism and Hermeneutics: Michel Foucault,* ed. Hubert L. Dreyfus and Paul Rabinow, 2nd ed. (Chicago: University of Chicago Press, 1983), 212.
12. Michel Foucault, "Nietzsche, Genealogy, History," in *The Foucault Reader,* ed. Paul Rabinow (New York: Pantheon, 1984), 83.
13. Jacques Derrida, *Spurs,* trans. Barbara Harlow (Chicago: University of Chicago Press, 1978), 49.
14. Ibid., 51.
15. Biddy Martin, "Feminism, Criticism, and Foucault," *New German Critique* 27 (1982): 11.
16. Julia Kristeva, "Woman Can Never Be Defined," in *New French Feminisms,* eds. Elaine Marks and Isabelle de Courtivron, (New York: Schocken, 1981), 137 (my italics).
17. Julia Kristeva, "Oscillation between Power and Denial," in Marks and Courtivron, eds., 166.
18. Teresa de Lauretis, *Alice Doesn't* (Bloomington: Indiana University Press, 1984), 5.
19. Ibid., 5–6.
20. Ibid., 7.
21. Ibid., 8–9.
22. Ibid., 11.
23. Ibid., 159.
24. Ibid., 182. The principal texts Lauretis relies on in her exposition of Lacan, Eco, and Peirce are Jacques Lacan, *Ecrits* (Paris: Seuil, 1966); Umberto Eco, *A Theory of Semiotics* (Bloomington: Indiana University Press, 1976), and *The Role of the Reader: Explorations in the Semiotic of Texts* (Bloomington: Indiana University Press, 1979); and Charles Sanders Peirce, *Collected Papers,* vols. 1–8 (Cambridge, Mass.: Harvard University Press, 1931–58).
25. Lauretis, *Alice Doesn't* (n. 18 above), 182.
26. Ibid., 186 (my italics).
27. Lauretis, ed. (n. 10 above), 8.
28. Ibid., 9.
29. See Juliet Mitchell, "Introduction I," in Mitchell and Rose, eds., 4–5.
30. This was suggested to me by Teresa de Lauretis in an informal talk she gave at the Pembroke Center, 1984–85.
31. See Teresa de Lauretis, "Feminist Studies/Critical Studies: Issues, Terms, Contexts," in Lauretis, ed. (n. 10 above), 8–9.
32. This point is brought out by Homi Bhabba in his "Of Mimicry and Man: The Ambivalence of Colonial Discourse," *October* 28 (1984): 125–33; and by Abdur Rahman in his *Intellectual Colonisation* (New Delhi: Vikas, 1983).

73

Does a Sex Have a History? from "Am I That Name?" Feminism and the Category of "Woman" in History

DENISE RILEY

DENISE RILEY England. 1948– . Poet. Theorist. *War in the Nursery: Theories of the Child and Mother (1983).*

Desdemona: Am I that name, Iago?
Iago: What name, fair lady?
Desdemona: Such as she says my lord did say I was.
(William Shakespeare, *Othello*,
Act IV, Scene II, 1622)

The black abolitionist and freed slave, Sojourner Truth, spoke out at the Akron convention in 1851, and named her own toughness in a famous peroration against the notion of woman's disqualifying frailty. She rested her case on her refrain 'Ain't I a woman?' It's my hope to persuade readers that a new Sojourner Truth might well—except for the catastrophic loss of grace in the wording—issue another plea: 'Ain't I a fluctuating identity?' For both a concentration on and a refusal of the identity of 'women' are essential to feminism. This its history makes plain.

The volatility of 'woman' has indeed been debated from the perspective of psychoanalytic theory; her fictive status has been proposed by some Lacanian work,[1] while it has been argued that, on the other hand, sexual identities are ultimately firmly secured by psychoanalysis.[2] From the side of deconstruction, Derrida among others has advanced what he calls the 'undecidability' of woman.[3] I want to sidestep these debates to move to the ground of historical construction, including the history of feminism itself, and suggest that not only 'woman' but also 'women' is troublesome—and that this extension of our suspicions is in the interest of feminism. That we can't bracket off either Woman, whose capital letter has long alerted

us to her dangers, or the more modest lower-case 'woman,' while leaving unexamined the ordinary, innocent-sounding 'women.'

This 'women' is not only an inert and sensible collective; the dominion of fictions has a wider sway than that. The extent of its reign can be partly revealed by looking at the crystallisations of 'women' as a category. To put it schematically: 'women' is historically, discursively constructed, and always relatively to other categories which themselves change; 'women' is a volatile collectivity in which female persons can be very differently positioned, so that the apparent continuity of the subject of 'women' isn't to be relied on; 'women' is both synchronically and diachronically erratic as a collectivity, while for the individual, 'being a woman' is also inconstant, and can't provide an ontological foundation. Yet it must be emphasised that these instabilities of the category are the *sine qua non* of feminism, which would otherwise be lost for an object, despoiled of a fight, and, in short, without much life.

But why should it be claimed that the constancy of 'women' can be undermined in the interests of feminism? If Woman is in blatant disgrace, and woman is transparently suspicious, why lose sleep over a straightforward descriptive noun, 'women?' Moreover, how could feminism gain if its founding category is also to be dragged into the shadows properly cast by Woman? And while, given the untidiness of word use, there will inevitably be some slippery margins between 'woman' and 'women,' this surely ought not to worry any level-headed speaker? If the seductive fraud of 'woman' is exposed, and the neutral collectivity is carefully substituted, then the ground is prepared for political fights to continue, armed with clarity. Not woman, but women—then we can get on with it.

It is true that socialist feminism has always tended to claim that women are socially produced in the sense of being 'conditioned' and that femininity is an effect. But 'conditioning' has its limits as an explanation, and the 'society' which enacts this process is a treacherously vague entity. Some variants of American and European cultural and radical feminism do retain a faith in the integrity of 'women' as a category. Some proffer versions of a female nature or independent system of values, which, ironically, a rather older feminism has always sought to shred to bits,[4] while many factions flourish in the shade cast by these powerful contemporary naturalisms about 'women.' Could it be argued that the only way of avoiding these constant historical loops which depart or return from the conviction of women's natural dispositions, to pacifism for example, would be to make a grander gesture—to stand back and announce that there *aren't any* 'women?' And then, hard on that defiant and initially absurd-sounding assertion, to be scrupulously careful to elaborate it—to plead that it means that all definitions of gender must be looked at with an eagle eye, wherever they emanate from and whoever pronounces them, and that such a scrutiny is a thoroughly feminist undertaking. The will to support this is not blandly social-democratic, for in no way does it aim to vault over the stubborn harshness of lived gender while it queries sexual categorisation. Nor does it aim at a glorious indifference to politics by placing itself under the banner of some renewed claim to androgyny, or to a more modern aspiration to a 'post-gendered subjectivity.' But, while it refuses to break with feminism by naming itself as a neutral deconstruction, at the same time it refuses to identify feminism with the camp of the lovers of 'real women.'

Here someone might retort that there are real, concrete women. That what Foucault did for the concept of 'the homosexual' as an invented classification just cannot be done for women, who indubitably existed long before the nineteenth century unfolded its tedious mania for fresh categorisations. That historical constructionism has run mad if it can believe otherwise. How can it be overlooked that women are a natural as well as a characterised category, and that their distinctive needs and sufferings are all too real? And how could a politics of women, feminism, exist in the company of such an apparent theoreticist disdain for reality, which it has mistakenly conflated with ideology as if the two were one?

A brief response would be that unmet needs and sufferings do not spring from a social reality of oppression, which has to be posed against what is said and written about women—but that they spring from the ways in which women are positioned, often

harshly or stupidly, *as* 'women.' This positioning occurs both in language, forms of description, and what gets carried out, so that it is misleading to set up a combat for superiority between the two. Nor, on the other hand, is any complete identification between them assumed.

It is true that appeals to 'women's' needs or capacities do not, on their own, guarantee their ultimately conservative effects any more than their progressivism; a social policy with innovative implications may be couched in a deeply familial language, as with state welfare provision at some periods. In general, which female persons under what circumstances will be heralded as 'women' often needs some effort of translation to follow; becoming or avoiding being named as a sexed creature is a restless business.

Feminism has intermittently been as vexed with the urgency of disengaging from the category 'women' as it has with laying claim to it; twentieth-century European feminism has been constitutionally torn between fighting against over-feminisation and against under-feminisation, especially where social policies have been at stake. Certainly the actions and the wants of women often need to be fished out of obscurity, rescued from the blanket dominance of 'man,' or 'to be made visible.' But that is not all. There are always too many invocations of 'women,' too much visibility, too many appellations which were better dissolved again—or are in need of some accurate and delimiting handling. So the precise specifying of 'women' for feminism might well mean occasionally forgetting them—or remembering them more accurately by refusing to enter into the terms of some public invocation. At times feminism might have nothing to say on the subject of 'women'—when their excessive identification would swallow any opposition, engulfing it hopelessly.

This isn't to imply that every address to 'women' is bad, or that feminism has some special access to a correct and tolerable level of feminisation. Both these points could generate much debate. What's suggested here is that the volatility of 'women' is so marked that it makes feminist alliances with other tendencies as difficult as they are inescapable. A political interest may descend to illuminate 'women' from almost anywhere in the rhetorical firmament, like lightning. This may happen against an older, slower backdrop of altering understandings as to what sexual characterisations are, and a politician's fitful concentration on 'women' may be merely superimposed on more massive alterations of thought. To understand all resonances of 'women,' feminist tactics would need to possess not only a great elasticity for dealing with its contemporary deployments, but an awareness of the long shapings of sexed classifications in their post-1790s upheavals.

This means that we needn't be tormented by a choice between political realism which will brook no nonsense about the uncertainties of 'women,' or deconstructionist moves which have no political allegiances. No one needs to believe in the solidity of 'women'; doubts on that score do not have to be confined to the giddy detachment of the academy, to the semiotics seminar rooms where politics do not tread. There are alternatives to those schools of thought which in saying that 'woman' is fictional are silent about 'women,' and those which, from an opposite perspective, proclaim that the reality of women is yet to come, but that this time, it's we, women, who will define her. Instead of veering between deconstruction and transcendence, we could try another train of speculations: that 'women' is indeed an unstable category, that this instability has a historical foundation, and that feminism is the site of the systematic fighting-out of that instability—which need not worry us.

It might be feared that to acknowledge any semantic shakiness inherent in 'women' would plunge one into a vague whirlpool of 'postgendered' being, abandoning the cutting edges of feminism for an ostensibly new but actually well-worked indifference to the real masteries of gender, and that the known dominants would only be strengthened in the process. This could follow, but need not. The move from questioning the presumed ahistoricity of sexed identities does not have to result in celebrating the carnival of diffuse and contingent sexualities. Yet this question isn't being proposed as if, on the other hand, it had the power to melt away sexual antagonism by bestowing a history upon it.

What then is the point of querying the constancy of 'men' or 'women?' Foucault has written, 'The purpose of history, guided by genealogy, is not to discover the roots of our identity but to commit itself to its dissipation.'[5] This is terrific—

but, someone continues to ask, whatever does feminism want with dissipated identities? Isn't it trying to consolidate a progressive new identity of women who are constantly mis-defined, half-visible in their real differences? Yet the history of feminism has also been a struggle against over-zealous identifications; and feminism must negotiate the quicksands of 'women' which will not allow it to settle on either identities or counter-identities, but which condemn it to an incessant striving for a brief foothold. The usefulness of Foucault's remark here is, I think, that it acts as a pointer to history. It's not that our identity is to be dissipated into airy indeterminacy, extinction; instead it is to be referred to the more substantial realms of discursive historical formation. Certainly the indeterminacy of sexual positionings can be demonstrated in other ways, most obviously perhaps by comparative anthropology with its berdache, androgynous and unsettling shamanistic figures. But such work is often relegated to exoticism, while psychoanalytic investigations reside in the confined heats of clinical studies. It is the misleading familiarity of 'history' which can break open the daily naturalism of what surrounds us.

★ ★ ★

There are differing temporalities of 'women,' and these substitute the possibility of being 'at times a woman' for eternal difference on the one hand, or undifferentiation on the other. This escapes that unappetising choice between 'real women' who are always solidly in the designation, regardless, or post-women, no-longer-women, who have seen it all, are tired of it, and prefer evanescence. These altering periodicities are not only played out moment by moment for the individual person, but they are also historical, for the characterisations of 'women' are established in a myriad of mobile formations.

Feminism has recognised this temporality in its preoccupation with the odd phenomenology of possessing a sex, with finding some unabashed way of recognising aloud that which is privately obvious—that any attention to the life of a woman, if traced out carefully, must admit the degree to which the effects of lived gender are at least sometimes unpredictable, and fleeting. The question of how far anyone can take on the identity of being a woman in a thoroughgoing manner recalls the fictive status accorded to sexual identities by some psychoanalytic thought. Can anyone fully inhabit a gender without a degree of horror? How could someone 'be a woman' through and through, make a final home in that classification without suffering claustrophobia? To lead a life soaked in the passionate consciousness of one's gender at every single moment, to will to be a sex with a vengeance—these are impossibilities, and far from the aims of feminism.

But if being a woman is more accurately conceived as a state which fluctuates for the individual, depending on what she and/or others consider to characterise it, then there are always different densities of sexed being in operation, and the historical aspects are in play here. So a full answer to the question 'At this instant am I a woman as distinct from a human being?' could bring into play three interrelated reflections. First, the female speaker's rejections of, adoptions of, or hesitations as to the rightness of the self description at that moment; second, the state of current understandings of 'women,' embedded in a vast web of description covering public policies, rhetorics, feminisms, forms of sexualisation or contempt; third, behind these, larger and slower subsidings of gendered categories, which in part will include the sedimented forms of previous characterisations, which once would have undergone their own rapid fluctuations.

Why is this suggestion about the consolidations of a classification any different from a history of ideas about women? Only because in it nothing is assumed about an underlying continuity of real women, above whose constant bodies changing aerial descriptions dance. If it's taken for granted that the category of women simply refers, over time, to a rather different content, a sort of Women Through the Ages approach, then the full historicity of what is at stake becomes lost. We would miss seeing the alterations in what 'women' are posed against, as well as established by—Nature, Class, Reason, Humanity and other concepts—which by no means form a passive backdrop to changing conceptions of gender. That air of a wearily continuous opposition of 'men' and 'women,' each always identically understood, is in part an effect of other petrifications.

To speculate about the history of sexual consolidations does not spring from a longing for lost innocence, as if 'once,' as John Donne wrote,[6]

Difference of sex no more wee knew
Than our Guardian Angells doe

Nor is it a claim made in the hope of an Edenic future; to suggest that the polarity of the engaged and struggling couple, men and women, isn't timeless, is not a gesture towards reconciliation, as if once the two were less mercilessly distinguished, and may be so again if we could stop insisting on divisive difference, and only love each other calmly enough. My supposition here—and despite my disclaimer, it may be fired by a conciliatory impulse—is rather that the arrangement of people under the banners of 'men' or 'women' are enmeshed with the histories of other concepts too, including those of 'the social' and 'the body.' And that this has profound repercussions for feminism.

It follows that both theories about the timelessness of the binary opposition of sexual antagonism and about the history of ideas of women could be modified by looking instead at the course of alignments into gendered categories. Some might object that the way to deal with the monotonous male/female opposition would be to substitute democratic differences for the one difference, and to let that be an end to it. But this route, while certainly economical, would also obliterate the feverish powers exercised by the air of eternal polarity, and their overwhelming effects. Nor does that pluralising move into 'differences' say anything about their origins and precipitations.

I've written about the chances for a history of alterations in the collectivity of 'women.' Why not 'men' too? It's true that the completion of the project outlined here would demand that, and would not be satisfied by studies of the emergence of patriarchs, eunuchs, or the cult of machismo, for example; more radical work could be done on the whole category of 'men' and its relations with Humanity. But nothing will be ventured here, because the genesis of these speculations is a concern with 'women' as a condition of and a trial to feminist history and politics. Nor will the term 'sexual difference' appear as an analytic instrument, since my point is neither to validate it nor to completely refuse it, but to look instead at how changing massifications of 'men' and 'women' have thrown up such terms within the armoury of contemporary feminist thought.

How might this be done? How could the peculiar temporality of 'women' be demonstrated? Most obviously, perhaps, by the changing relations of 'woman' and her variants to the concept of a general humanity. The emergence of new entities after the Enlightenment and their implicatedness with the collectivity of women—like the idea of 'the social.' The history of an increasing sexualisation, in which female persons become held to be virtually saturated with their sex which then invades their rational and spiritual faculties; this reached a pitch in eighteenth-century Europe. Behind this, the whole history of the idea of the person and the individual, including the extents to which the soul, the mind, and the body had been distinguished and rethought, and how the changing forms of their sexualisation have operated. For the nineteenth century, arguments as to how the concept of class was developed in a profoundly gendered manner, and how it in turn shaped modern notions of 'women'.[7] These suggestions could proliferate endlessly; in these pages I have only offered sketches of a couple of them.

What does it mean to say that the modern collectivity of women was established in the midst of other formations? Feminism's impulse is often, not surprisingly, to make a celebratory identification with a rush of Women onto the historical stage. But such 'emergences' have particular passages into life; they are the tips of an iceberg. The more engaging question for feminism is then what lies beneath. To decipher any collision which tosses up some novelty, you must know the nature of the various pasts that have led up to it, and allow to these their full density of otherness. Indeed there are no moments at which gender is utterly unvoiced. But the ways in which 'women' will have been articulated in advance of some prominent 'emergence' of the collectivity will differ, so what needs to be sensed is upon what previous layers the newer and more formalised outcropping has grown.

The grouping of 'women' as newly conceived political subjects is marked in the long suffrage debates and campaigns, which illustrate their volatile alignments of sexed meaning. Demands for the franchise often fluctuated between engagement with and disengagement from the broad category of Humanity—first as an abstraction to be exposed in its masculine bias and permeated, and then to be denounced for its continual and resolute adherence, after women had been enfranchised, to the same bias. An ostensibly unsexed Humanity, broken through political pressures of suffragist and antisuffragist forces into blocs of humans and women, men and women, closed and resealed at different points in different nations. In the history of European socialism, 'men' have often argued their way to universal manhood suffrage through a discourse of universal rights. But for women to ascend to being numbered among Humanity, a severe philosophical struggle to penetrate this category has not eliminated the tactical need to periodically break again into a separately gendered designation. The changing fate of the ideal of a non-sexed Humanity bears witness to its ambiguity.

★ ★ ★

Yet surely—it could be argued—some definitive upsurge of combative will among women must occur for the suffrage to be demanded in the first place? Must there not, then, be some unambiguously progressive identity of 'women' which the earliest pursuers of political rights had at their disposal? For, in order to contemplate joining yourself to unenfranchised men in their passion for emancipation, you would first have to take on that identity of being a woman among others *and* of being, as such, a suitable candidate too. But there is a difficulty; a dozen qualifications hedge around that simple 'woman,' as to whether she is married or not, a property-owner or not, and so forth. 'Women' *en masse* rarely present themselves, unqualified, before the thrones of power; their estates divide them as inequalities within their supposed unity.

Nevertheless, to point to sociological faults in the smoothness of 'women' does not answer the argument that there must be a progressive identity of women. How is it that they ever come to rank themselves together? What are the conditions for any joint consciousness of women, which is more than the mutual amity or commiseration of friends or relations? Perhaps it could be argued that in order for 'women' to speak as such, some formal consolidation of 'men against women' is the gloomy prerequisite. That it is sexual antagonism which shapes sexual solidarity; and that assaults and counter-assaults, with all their irritations, are what make for a rough kind of feminism.

★ ★ ★

Here there is plenty of ground. We could think of those fourteenth- and fifteenth-century treatises which began to work out a formal alignment of sex against sex. These included a genre of women's defences against their vilification. So Christine de Pisan wrote 'for women' in the *querelle des femmes.* The stage was set between a sexual cynicism which took marriage to be an outdated institution—Jean de Meung's stance in his popular *Roman de la Rose*—and a contrasted idealism which demanded that men profess loyalty to women, and adhere to marriage as a mark of respect for the female sex— Christine de Pisan's position in the *Débat sur le Roman de la Rose,* of about 1400 to 1402. This contest was waged again in her *Livre de la Cité des Dames* in 1405. As the narrator, she is visited by an allegorical triad; Reason, Rectitude and Justice. It is Reason who announces to her that her love of study has made her a fit choice of champion for her sex, as well as an apt architect to design an ideal city to be a sanctum for women of good repute. This city needs to be built, because men will vilify women. Their repeated slanders stem not only from their contempt for Eve, and her contribution to the Fall, but also from their secret convictions as to the superior capacities of all women. Chritine de Pisan's earlier *Épistre au Dieu d'Amours* is also couched in this protective vein.

To suffer slights in patience is the strategy recommended by this literature, which itself conspicuously does the opposite. Here submission can be a weapon, a brandished virtue secured against great odds. The more rigorous the trial, the higher the merits of the tenaciously submissive woman. Her *Épistre de la prison de vie humaine,* composed between 1416 and 1418, dedicated to Marie de Berry, was designed as a formal comfort to women for the deaths at Agincourt of their brothers, fathers, and husbands; now these were liberated from life's long pains. But this resignation in the face of death did not eclipse sexual triumph. Christine

de Pisan's last surviving work, the *Ditié de Jehann d'Arc,* was published in 1429, but written before Joan's execution; this was a song to celebrate her life as 'an honour for the female sex.'

Both the *querelles* and these other writings defend 'women' as unjustly slandered, champion heroines, and marry defiance with the advocacy of resignation, with the faith that earthly sufferings, if patiently endured, might be put to good account in the hereafter. Do these ingredients make a fifteenth-century feminism the start of a long chain ending in the demand for emancipation? Certainly there are some constant features of this literature which are echoed through the seventeenth-century writings. It argues in the name of 'women,' and in that it is unlike the earlier complicated typologies of the sexes of the works of the women mystics. The fourteenth- and fifteenth-century polemic proposes that noble women should withdraw to a place apart, a tower, a city, there to pursue their devotions untroubled by the scorn of men in the order of the world. In this, it is not far from some seventeenth-century suggestions, like those made by Mary Astell, that 'women' have no choice but to form an order apart if they want to win spiritual clarity.

Between the fifteenth- and seventeenth-century compositions, what remains constant is the formal defences of the sex, the many reiterations of 'Women are not, as you men so ignorantly and harshly claim, like that—but as we tell you now, we are really like this, and better than you.' This highly stylised counter-antagonism draws in 'all women' under its banner against 'all men.' Even though its references are to women of a high social standing and grace, nevertheless it is the collectivity which is being claimed and redeemed by debate. At times this literature abandons its claims to stoicism, fights clear of its surface resignation, and launches into unbridled counter-aggression. Thus 'Jane Anger,' who in 1589 published a broadside, *Jane Anger her Protection for Women, to defend them against the Scandalous Reports of a late Surfeiting Love. . . .* The writer, whether truly female or *agent provocateur,* burns on the page with wild rhetoric, the cry of sex against the attacking other sex, the mediaeval defences wound to the highest pitch:

Their slanderous tongues are so short, and all the time wherein they have lavished out their words freely has been so long, that they know we cannot catch hold of them to pull them out. And they think we will not write to reprove their lying lips, which conceits have already made them cocks.[8]

The retort to the surfeited lover's charges is to invert them, to mass all women against all men:

We are the grief of man, in that we take all the grief from man: we languish when they laugh, we sit sighing when they sit singing, and sit sobbing when they lie slugging and sleeping. *Mulier est hominis confusio* because her kind heart cannot so sharply reprove their frantic fits as these mad frenzies deserve.[9]

It is a litany of pure sexual outrage:

If our frowns be so terrible and our anger so deadly, men are too foolish in offering occasions of hatred, which shunned, a terrible death is prevented. There is a continual deadly hatred between the wild boar and tame hounds. I would there were the like between women and men, unless they amend their manners, for so strength should predominate, where now flattery and dissimulation have the upper hand. The lion rages when he is hungry, but man rails when he is glutted. The tiger is robbed of her young ones when she is ranging abroad, but men rob women of their honour undeservedly under their noses. The viper storms when his tail is trodden on, and may we not fret when all our body is a footstool to their vile lust?[10]

This furious lyricism is a late and high pitch of the long literature which heralded 'women' *en bloc* to redeem their reputations. Is this in any sense a precondition of feminism; a pre-feminism which is established, indeed raging, in Europe for centuries before the Enlightenment? Certainly seventeenth-century women writers were acutely conscious of the need to establish their claims to enter full humanity, and to do so by demonstrating their intellectual capacities. If women's right to any earthly democracy had to be earned, then their virtues did indeed have to be enunciated and defended; while traces of seemingly sex-specific vices were to be explained as effects of a thoughtless conditioning, an impoverished education—the path chosen by Poulain de la Barre in his *De l'Egalité des Deux Sexes* of 1673. When Mary

Wollstonecraft argued that 'the sexual should not destroy the human character'[11] in her *A Vindication of the Rights of Woman*, this encapsulated the seventeenth-century feminist analysis that women must somehow disengage from their growing endemic sexualisation.

It is this which makes it difficult to interpret the defences and proclamations of 'women' against 'men' as pre-feminism. To read the work of 'Jane Anger' and others as preconditions for eighteenth-century feminism elides too much, for it suggests that there is some clear continuity between defensive celebrations of 'women' and the beginning of the 1790s claims to rights for women, and their advancement as potential political subjects. But the more that the category of woman is asserted, whether as glowingly moral and unjustly accused, or as a sexual species fully apart, the more its apparent remoteness from 'humanity' is underwritten. It is a cruel irony, which returns at several watersheds in the history of feminism, that the need to insist on the moral rehabilitation of 'women' should have the effect of emphasising their distinctiveness, despite the fact that it may aim at preparing the way into the category of humanity. The transition, if indeed there is one, from passing consolidations of 'women' as candidates for virtue, to 'women' as candidates for the vote, is intricate and obscure.

★ ★ ★

When the name of feminism is plunged into disgrace—for example, in Britain immediately after the end of the First World War—then the mantle of a progressive democracy falls upon Humanity; though the resurgences of feminism in the 1920s tore this apart. But before even a limited suffrage is granted, it may have to be sought for a sex in the name of a sex-blind humanism, as an ethical demand. This may work for men, but not for women. Most interesting here are the intricate debates in Britain between socialist and feminist proponents of a universal adult suffrage, and feminists who supported a limited female suffrage instead as the best route to eventual democracy; these are discussed in detail below. But what has Humanity been conjugated against? Must it be endlessly undemocratic because 'gender-blind'—or 'race-blind'? Its democratic possibilities would depend on, for example, how thoroughly, at the time of any one articulation of the idea, the sex of the person was held to infuse and characterise her whole being, how much she was gender embodied. The question of race would demand analogous moves to establish the extent of the empire of racially suffused being over the general existence of the person. A history of several categories, then, would be demanded in order to glimpse the history of one.

★ ★ ★

If it is fair to speculate that 'women' as a category does undergo a broadly increasing degree of sexualisation between the late seventeenth and the nineteenth centuries, what would constitute the evidence? To put clear dates to the long march of the empires of gender over the entirety of the person would be difficult indeed. My suggestion isn't so much that after the seventeenth century a change in ideas about women and their nature develops; rather that 'women' itself comes to carry an altered weight, and that a re-ordered idea of Nature has a different intimacy of association with 'woman' who is accordingly refashioned. It is not only that concepts are forced into new proximities with one another—but they are so differently shot through with altering positions of gender that what has occurred is something more fundamental than a merely sequential innovation—that is, a reconceptualisation along sexed lines, in which the understandings of gender both re-order and are themselves re-ordered.

The nineteenth-century collective 'women' is evidently voiced in new ways by the developing human sciences of sociology, demography, economics, neurology, psychiatry, psychology, at the same time as a newly established realm of the social becomes both the exercising ground and the spasmodic vexation for feminism. The resulting modern 'women' is arguably the result of long processes of closure which have been hammered out, by infinite mutual references, from all sides of these classifying studies; closures which were then both underwritten and cross-examined by nineteenth- and twentieth-century feminisms, as they took up, or respecified, or dismissed these productions of 'women.'

'Women' became a modern social category when their place as newly re-mapped entities was distributed among the other collectivities established by these nineteenth-century sciences. 'Men' did not undergo any parallel re-alignments. But

society relied on 'man' too, but now as the opposite which secured its own balance. The couplet of man and society, and the ensuing riddle of their relationship, became the life-blood of anthropology, sociology, social psychology—the endless problem of how the individual stood *vis-à-vis* the world. This was utterly different from the ways in which the concept of the social realm both encapsulated and illuminated 'women.' When this effectively feminised social was then set over and against 'man,' then the alignments of the sexes in the social realm were conceptualised askew. It was not so much that women were omitted as that they were too thoroughly included in an asymmetrical manner. They were not the submerged opposite of man, and as such only in need of being fished up; they formed, rather, a kind of continuum of sociality against which the political was set.

'Man in society' did not undergo the same kind of immersion as did woman. He *faced* society, rather; a society already permeated by the feminine. This philosophical confrontation was the puzzle for those nineteenth-century socialist philosophies which contemplated historic and economic man. An intractable problem for marxist philosophy was how to engage with the question of individualisation; how was the individual himself historically formed? Marx tried, in 1857, to effect a new historicisation of 'man' across differing modes of production, because he wanted to save man as the political animal from mutation into a timeless extra-economic figure, the Robinson Crusoe advanced by some political economies.[12] But the stumbling-block for Marx's aim was its assumption of some prior, already fully constituted 'man' who was then dragged through the transformations of history; this 'man' was already locked into his distinctiveness from the social, so he was already a characterised and compromised creation.

As with man, so here—for once—with woman. No philosophical anthropology of woman can unfurl those mysteries it tries to solve, because that which is to be explicated, woman, stands innocently in advance of the task of 'discovering her.' To historicise woman across the means of production is also not enough. Nevertheless, another reference to Marx may be pressed into the service of sexual consolidations, and into the critique of the idea that sexual polarities are constant—his comment on the concept of Labour:

> The most general abstractions arise only in the midst of the richest possible concrete development, where one thing appears as common to many, to all . . . Labour shows strikingly how even the most abstract categories, despite their validity—precisely because of their abstractness—for all epochs are nevertheless, in the specific character of this abstraction, themselves likewise a product of historical relations, and possess their full validity only for and within those relations.[13]

★ ★ ★

The ideas of temporality which are suggested here need not, of course, be restricted to 'women.' The impermanence of collective identities in general is a pressing problem for any emancipating movement which launches itself on the appeal to solidarity, to the common cause of a new group being, or an ignored group identity. This will afflict racial, national, occupational, class, religious, and other consolidations. While you might choose to take on being a disabled person or lesbian, for instance, as a political position, you might not elect to make a politics out of other designations. As you do not live your life fully defined as a shop assistant, nor do you as a Greek Cypriot, for example, and you can always refute such identifications in the name of another description which, because it is more individuated, may ring more truthfully to you. Or, most commonly, you will skate across the several identities which will take your weight, relying on the most useful for your purposes of the moment; like Hanif Kureishi's suave character in the film *My Beautiful Laundrette,* who says impatiently, 'I'm a professional businessman, not a professional Pakistani.'

The troubles of 'women,' then, aren't unique But aren't they arguably peculiar in that 'women,' half the human population, do suffer from an extraordinary weight of characterisation? 'Mothers' also demonstrate this acutely, and interact with 'women' in the course of social policy invocations especially; in Britain after 1945 for instance, women were described as either over-feminised mothers, or as under-feminised workers, but the category of the working mother was not acknowledged.[14] So the general feminine description can be split in such

ways, and its elements played off against each other. But the overall effect is only to intensify the excessively described and attributed being of 'women.'

Feminism of late has emphasized that indeed 'women' are far from being racially or culturally homogeneous, and it may be thought that this corrective provides the proper answer to the hesitations I've advanced here about 'women.' But this is not the same preoccupation. Indeed there is a world of helpful difference between making claims in the name of an annoyingly generalised 'women' and doing so in the name of, say, 'elderly Cantonese women living in Soho.' Any study of sexual consolidations, of the differing metaphorical weightings of 'women,' would have to be alerted to the refinements of age, trade, ethnicity, exile, but it would not be satisfied by them. However the specifications of difference are elaborated, they still come to rest on 'women,' and it is the isolation of this last which is in question.

It's not that a new slogan for feminism is being proposed here—of feminism without 'women.' Rather, the suggestion is that 'women' is a simultaneous foundation of and an irritant to feminism, and that this is constitutionally so. It is true that the trade-off for the myriad namings of 'women' by politics, sociologies, policies and psychologies is that at this cost 'women' do, sometimes, become a force to be reckoned with. But the caveat remains: the risky elements to the processes of alignment in sexed ranks are never far away, and the very collectivity which distinguishes you may also be wielded, even unintentionally, against you. Not just against you as an individual, that is, but against you as a social being with needs and attributions. The dangerous intimacy between subjectification and subjection needs careful calibration. There is, as we have repeatedly learned, no fluent trajectory from feminism to a truly sexually democratic humanism; there is no easy passage from 'women' to 'humanity.' The study of the historical development and precipitations of these sexed abstractions will help to make sense of why not. That is how Desdemona's anguished question, 'Am I that name?', may be transposed into a more hopeful light.

[1988]

NOTES

1. See Jacqueline Rose, 'Introduction–II,' in J. Mitchell and J. Rose (eds.), *Feminine Sexuality, Jacques Lacan and the Ecole Freudienne,* London: Macmillan, 1982.
2. See Stephen Heath, 'Male Feminism,' *Dalhousie Review,* no. 64, 2 (1986).
3. Jacques Derrida, *Spurs; Nietzsche's Styles,* Chicago: University of Chicago Press, 1978, pp. 51, 55.
4. See arguments in Lynne Segal, *Is the Future Female? Troubled Thoughts on Contemporary Feminism,* London: Virago, 1987.
5. Michel Foucault, 'Nietzsche, Genealogy, History, in *Language, Counter-Memory, Practice: Selected Essays and Interviews,* Donald F. Bouchard and Sherry Simon (eds. and trans.), Ithaca: Cornell University Press, 1977, p. 162.
6. John Donne, 'The Relique', *Poems,* London, 1633.
7. See Joan Scott, 'L'Ouvrière! Mot Impie, Sordide . . .': Women Workers in the Discourse of French Political Economy (1840–1860)', in P. Joyce (ed.), *The Historical Meanings of Work,* Cambridge University Press, 1987.
8. Jane Anger, 'Jane Anger her Protection for Women . . . ,' London, 1589, in Joan Goulianos (ed.), *By a Woman Writt, Literature from Six Centuries By and About Women,* Baltimore, Maryland: Penguin Books Inc., 1974, p. 25.
9. Ibid, p. 27.
10. Ibid, p. 28.
11. Mary Wollstonecraft, *A Vindication of the Rights of Woman,* 1792, Harmondsworth: Penguin Books, 1982, p. 142.
12. Karl Marx, *Grundrisse,* Harmondsworth: Penguin Books, 1973, pp. 83, 496.
13. Ibid, pp. 104, 105.
14. Denise Riley, *War in the Nursery: Theories of the Child and Mother,* London: Virago, 1983, pp. 150–55, 195.

 74

Deconstructing Equality-versus-Difference: or, The Uses of Poststructuralist Theory for Feminism

JOAN W. SCOTT

JOAN W. SCOTT United States. 1941– . Historian. Key voice in shaping and theorizing the field of women's history. *Gender and the Politics of History* (1988), *Feminists Theorize the Political* (1992), *Only Paradoxes to Offer: French Feminists and the Rights of Man* (1996), *The Politics of the Veil* (2007), *Women's Studies on the Edge* (2008).

That feminism needs theory goes without saying (perhaps because it has been said so often). What is not always clear is what that theory will do, although there are certain common assumptions I think we can find in a wide range of feminist writings. We need theory that can analyze the workings of patriarchy in all its manifestations—ideological, institutional, organizational, subjective—accounting not only for continuities but also for change over time. We need theory that will let us think in terms of pluralities and diversities rather than of unities and universals. We need theory that will break the conceptual hold, at least, of those long traditions of (Western) philosophy that have systematically and repeatedly construed the world hierarchically in terms of masculine universals and feminine specificities. We need theory that will enable us to articulate alternative ways of thinking about (and thus acting upon) gender without either simply reversing the old hierarchies or confirming them. And we need theory that will be useful and relevant for political practice.

It seems to me that the body of theory referred to as poststructuralism best meets all these requirements. It is not by any means the only theory nor are its positions and formulations unique. In my own case, however, it was reading poststructuralist theory and arguing with literary scholars that provided the elements of clarification for which I was looking. I found a new way of analyzing constructions of meaning and relationships of power that called unitary, universal categories into question and historicized concepts otherwise treated as natural (such as man/woman) or absolute (such as equality or justice). In addition, what attracted me was the historical connection between the two movements. Poststructuralism and contemporary feminism are late-twentieth-century movements that share a certain self-conscious critical relationship to established philosophical and political traditions. It thus seemed worthwhile for feminist scholars to exploit that relationship for their own ends.[1]

This article will not discuss the history of these various "exploitations" or elaborate on all the reasons a historian might look to this theory to organize her inquiry.[2] What seems most useful here is to give a short list of some major theoretical points and then devote most of my effort to a specific illustration. The first part of this article is a brief discussion of concepts used by poststructuralists that are also useful for feminists. The second part applies some of these concepts to one of the hotly contested issues among contemporary (U.S.) feminists—the "equality-versus-difference" debate.

Among the useful terms feminists have appropriated from poststructuralism are language, discourse, difference, and deconstruction.

Language. Following the work of structuralist linguistics and anthropology, the term is used to mean not simply words or even a vocabulary and set of grammatical rules but, rather, a meaning-constituting system: that is, any system—strictly verbal or other—through which meaning is constructed and cultural practices organized and by which, accordingly, people represent and understand their world, including who they are and how they relate to others. "Language," so conceived, is a central focus of poststructuralist analysis.

Language is not assumed to be a representation of ideas that either cause material relations or from which such relations follow; indeed the idealist/materialist opposition is a false one to impose on this approach. Rather, the analysis of language provides a crucial point of entry, a starting point for understanding how social relations are conceived, and therefore—because understanding how they are conceived means understanding how they work—how institutions are organized, how relations of production are experienced, and how collective identity is established. Without attention to language and the processes by which meanings and categories are constituted, one only imposes oversimplified models on the world, models that perpetuate conventional understandings rather than open up new interpretive possibilities.

The point is to find ways to analyze specific "texts"—not only books and documents but also utterances of any kind and in any medium including cultural practices—in terms of specific historical and contextual meanings. Poststructuralists insist that words and texts have no fixed or intrinsic meanings, that there is no transparent or self-evident relationship between them and either ideas or things, no basic or ultimate correspondence between language and the world. The questions that must be answered in such an analysis, then, are

how, in what specific contexts, among which specific communities of people, and by what textual and social processes has meaning been acquired? More generally, the questions are: How do meanings change? How have some meanings emerged as normative and others been eclipsed or disappeared? What do these processes reveal about how power is constituted and operates?

Discourse. Some of the answers to these questions are offered in the concept of discourse, especially as it has been developed in the work of Michel Foucault. A discourse is not a language or a text but a historically, socially, and institutionally specific structure of statements, terms, categories, and beliefs. Foucault suggests that the elaboration of meaning involves conflict and power, that meanings are locally contested within discursive "fields of force," that (at least since the Enlightenment) the power to control a particular field resides in claims to (scientific) knowledge embodied not only in writing but also in disciplinary and professional organizations, in institutions (hospitals, prisons, schools, factories), and in social relationships (doctor/patient, teacher/student, employer/worker, parent/child, husband/wife). Discourse is thus contained or expressed in organizations and institutions as well as in words; all of these constitute texts or documents to be read.[3]

Discursive fields overlap, influence, and compete with one another; they appeal to one another's "truths" for authority and legitimation. These truths are assumed to be outside human invention, either already known and self-evident or discoverable through scientific inquiry. Precisely because they are assigned the status of objective knowledge, they seem to be beyond dispute and thus serve a powerful legitimating function. Darwinian theories of natural selection are one example of such legitimating truths; biological theories about sexual difference are another. The power of these "truths" comes from the way they function as givens or first premises for both sides in an argument, so that conflicts within discursive fields are framed to follow from rather than question them. The brilliance of so much of Foucault's work has been to illuminate the shared assumptions of what seemed to be sharply different arguments, thus exposing the limits of radical criticism and the extent of the power of dominant ideologies or epistemologies.

In addition, Foucault has shown how badly even challenges to fundamental assumptions often fared. They have been marginalized or silenced, forced to underplay their most radical claims in order to win a short term goal, or completely absorbed into an existing framework. Yet the fact of change is crucial to Foucault's notion of "archeology," to the way in which he uses contrasts from different historical periods to present his arguments. Exactly how the process happens is not spelled out to the satisfaction of many historians, some of whom want a more explicit causal model. But when causal theories are highly general, we are often drawn into the assumption of the very discourse we ought to question. (If we are to question those assumptions, it may be necessary to forgo existing standards of historical inquiry.) Although some have read Foucault as an argument about the futility of human agency in the struggle for social change, I think that he is more appropriately taken as warning against simple solutions to difficult problems, as advising human actors to think strategically and more self-consciously about the philosophical and political implications and meanings of the programs they endorse. From this perspective, Foucault's work provides an important way of thinking differently (and perhaps more creatively) about the politics of the contextual construction of social meanings, about such organizing principles for political action as "equality" and "difference."

Difference. An important dimension of post-structuralist analyses of language has to do with the concept of difference, the notion (following Ferdinand de Saussure's structuralist linguistics) that meaning is made through implicit or explicit contrast, that a positive definition rests on the negation or repression of something represented as antithetical to it. Thus, any unitary concept in fact contains repressed or negated material; it is established in explicit opposition to another term. Any analysis of meaning involves teasing out these negations and oppositions, figuring out how (and whether) they are operating in specific contexts. Oppositions rest on metaphors and cross-references, and often in patriarchal discourse, sexual difference (the contrast

masculine/feminine) serves to encode or establish meanings that are literally unrelated to gender or the body. In that way, the meanings of gender become tied to many kinds of cultural representations, and these in turn establish terms by which relations between women and men are organized and understood. The possibilities of this kind of analysis have, for obvious reasons, drawn the interest and attention of feminist scholars.

Fixed oppositions conceal the extent to which things presented as oppositional are, in fact, interdependent—that is, they derive their meaning from a particularly established contrast rather than from some inherent or pure antithesis. Furthermore, according to Jacques Derrida, the interdependence is hierarchical, with one term dominant or prior, the opposite term subordinate and secondary. The Western philosophical tradition, he argues, rests on binary oppositions: unity/diversity, identity/difference, presence/absence, and universality/specificity. The leading terms are accorded primacy; their partners are represented as weaker or derivative. Yet the first terms depend on and derive their meaning from the second to such an extent that the secondary terms can be seen as generative of the definition of the first terms. If binary oppositions provide insight into the way meaning is constructed, and if they operate as Derrida suggests, then analyses or meaning cannot take binary oppositions at face value but rather must "deconstruct" them for the processes they embody.

Deconstruction. Although this term is used loosely among scholars—often to refer to a dismantling or destructive enterprise—it also has a precise definition in the work of Derrida and his followers. Deconstruction involves analyzing the operations of difference in texts, the ways in which meanings are made to work. The method consists of two related steps: the reversal and displacement of binary oppositions. This double process reveals the interdependence of seemingly dichotomous terms and their meaning relative to a particular history. It shows them to be not natural but constructed oppositions, constructed for particular purposes in particular contexts. The literary critic Barbara Johnson describes deconstruction as crucially dependent on difference.

The starting point is often a binary difference that is subsequently shown to be an illusion created by the working of differences much harder to pin down. The differences *between* entities . . . are shown to be based on a repression of differences *within* entities, ways in which an entity differs from itself. . . . The "deconstruction" of a binary opposition is thus not an annihilation of all values or differences; it is an attempt to follow the subtle, powerful effects of differences already at work within the illusion of a binary opposition.[4]

Deconstruction is, then, an important exercise for it allows us to be critical of the way in which ideas we want to use are ordinarily expressed, exhibited in patterns of meaning that may undercut the ends we seek to attain. A case in point—of meaning expressed in a politically self-defeating way—is the "equality-versus-difference" debate among feminists. Here a binary opposition has been created to offer a choice to feminists, of either endorsing "equality" or its presumed antithesis "difference." In fact, the antithesis itself hides the interdependence of the two terms, for equality is not the elimination of difference, and difference does not preclude equality.

In the past few years, "equality-versus-difference" has been used as a shorthand to characterize conflicting feminist positions and political strategies.[5] Those who argue that sexual difference ought to be an irrelevant consideration in schools, employment, the courts, and the legislature are put in the equality category. Those who insist that appeals on behalf of women ought to be made in terms of the needs, interests, and characteristics common to women as a group are placed in the difference category. In the clashes over the superiority of one or another of these strategies, feminists have invoked history, philosophy, and morality and have devised new classificatory labels: cultural feminism, liberal feminism, feminist separatism, and so on. Most recently, the debate about equality and difference has been used to analyze the Sears case, the sex discrimination suit brought against the retailing giant by the Equal Employment Opportunities Commission (EEOC) in 1984, in which historians Alice Kessler-Harris and Rosalind Rosenberg testified on opposite sides.

There have been many articles written on the Sears case, among them a recent one by Ruth Milkman. Milkman insists that we attend to the political context of seemingly timeless principles: "We ignore the political dimensions of the equality-versus-difference debate at our peril, especially in a period of conservative resurgence like the present." She concludes:

As long as this is the political context in which we find ourselves, feminist scholars must be aware of the real danger that arguments about "difference" or "women's culture" will be put to uses other than those for which they were originally developed. That does not mean we must abandon these arguments or the intellectual terrain they have opened up; it does mean that we must be self-conscious in our formulations, keeping firmly in view the ways in which our work can be exploited politically.[6]

Milkman's carefully nuanced formulation implies that equality is our safest course, but she is also reluctant to reject difference entirely. She feels a need to choose a side, but which side is the problem. Milkman's ambivalence is an example of what the legal theorist Martha Minow has labeled in another context "the difference dilemma." Ignoring difference in the case of subordinated groups, Minow points out, "leaves in place a faulty neutrality," but focusing on difference can underscore the stigma of deviance. "Both focusing on and ignoring difference risk recreating it. This is the dilemma of difference."[7] What is required, Minow suggests, is a new way of thinking about difference, this involves rejecting the idea that equality-versus-difference constitutes an opposition. Instead of framing analyses and strategies as if such binary pairs were timeless and true, we need to ask how the dichotomous pairing of equality and difference itself works. Instead of remaining with the terms of existing political discourse, we need to subject those terms to critical examination. Until we understand how the concepts work to constrain and construct specific meanings, we cannot make them work for us.

A close look at the evidence in the Sears case suggests that equality-versus-difference may not accurately depict the opposing sides in the Sears case. During testimony, most of the arguments against equality and for difference were, in fact, made by the Sears lawyers or by Rosalind Rosenberg.

They constructed an opponent against whom they asserted that women and men differed, that "fundamental differences"—the result of culture on long-standing patterns of socialization—led to women's presumed lack of interest in commission sales jobs. In order to make their own claim that sexual difference and not discrimination could explain the hiring patterns at Sears, the Sears defense attributed to EEOC an assumption that no one had made in those terms—that women and men had identical interests. Alice Kessler-Harris did not argue that women were the same as men; instead she used a variety of strategies to challenge Rosenberg's assertions. First, she argued that historical evidence suggested far more variety in the jobs women actually took than Rosenberg assumed. Second, she maintained that economic considerations usually offset the effects of socialization in women's attitudes to employment. And, third, she pointed out that, historically, job segregation by sex was the consequence of employer preferences, not employee choices. The question of women's choices could not be resolved, Kessler-Harris maintained, when the hiring process itself predetermined the outcome, imposing generalized gendered criteria that were not necessarily relevant to the work at hand. The debate joined then not around equality-versus-difference but around the relevance of general ideas of sexual difference in a specific context.[8]

To make the case for employer discrimination, EEOC lawyers cited obviously biased job applicant questionnaires and statements by personnel officers, but they had no individuals to testify that they had experienced discrimination. Kessler-Harris referred to past patterns of sexual segregation in the job market as the product of employer choices, but mostly she invoked history to break down Rosenberg's contention that women as a group differed consistently in the details of their behavior from men, instead insisting that variety characterized female job choices (as it did male job choices), that it made no sense in this case to talk about women as a uniform group. She defined equality to mean a presumption that women and men might have an equal interest in sales commission jobs. She did not claim that women and men, by definition, had such an equal interest. Rather, Kessler-Harris

and the EEOC called into question the relevance for hiring decisions of generalizations about the necessarily antithetical behaviors of women and men. EEOC argued that Sears's hiring practices reflected inaccurate and inapplicable notions of sexual difference; Sears argued that "fundamental" differences between the sexes (and not its own actions) explained the gender imbalances in its labor force.

The Sears case was complicated by the fact that almost all the evidence offered was statistical. The testimony of the historians, therefore, could only be inferential, at best. Each of them sought to explain small statistical disparities by reference to gross generalizations about the entire history of working women; furthermore, neither historian had much information about what had actually happened at Sears. They were forced, instead, to swear to the truth or falsehood of interpretive generalizations developed for purposes other than legal contestation, and they were forced to treat their interpretive premises as matters of fact. Reading the cross-examination of Kessler-Harris is revealing in this respect. Each of her carefully nuanced explanations of women's work history was forced into a reductive assertion by the Sears lawyers' insistence that she answer questions only by saying yes or no. Similarly, Rosalind Rosenberg's rebuttal to Alice Kessler-Harris eschewed the historians subtle contextual reading of evidence and sought instead to impose a test of absolute consistency. She juxtaposed Kessler-Harris's testimony in the trial to her earlier published work (in which Kessler-Harris stressed differences between female and male workers in their approaches to work, arguing that women were more domestically oriented and less individualistic than men) in an effort to show that Kessler-Harris had misled the court.[9] Outside the courtroom, however, the disparities of the Kessler-Harris argument could also be explained in other ways. In relationship to a labor history that had typically excluded women, it might make sense to overgeneralize about women's experience, emphasizing difference in order to demonstrate that the universal term "worker" was really a male reference that could not account for all aspects of women's job experiences. In relationship to an employer who sought to justify discrimination by reference to sexual difference, it made more sense to deny the totalizing effects of difference by stressing instead the diversity and complexity of women's behavior and motivation. In the first case, difference served a positive function, unveiling the inequity hidden in a presumably neutral term; in the second case, difference served a negative purpose, justifying what Kessler-Harris believed to be unequal treatment. Although the inconsistency might have been avoided with a more self-conscious analysis of the "difference dilemma," Kessler-Harris's different positions were quite legitimately different emphases for different contexts; only in a courtroom could they be taken as proof of bad faith.[10]

The exacting demands of the courtroom for consistency and "truth" also point out the profound difficulties of arguing about difference. Although the testimony of the historians had to explain only a relatively small statistical disparity in the numbers of women and men hired for full-time commission sales jobs, the explanations that were preferred were totalizing and categorical.[11] In cross-examination, Kessler-Harris's multiple interpretations were found to be contradictory and confusing, although the judge praised Rosenberg for her coherence and lucidity.[12] In part, that was because Rosenberg held to a tight model that unproblematically linked socialization to individual choice; in part it was because her descriptions of gender differences accorded with prevailing normative views. In contrast, Kessler-Harris had trouble finding a simple model that would at once acknowledge difference *and* refuse it as an acceptable explanation for the employment pattern of Sears. So she fell into great difficulty maintaining her case in the face of hostile questioning. On the one hand, she was accused of assuming that economic opportunism equally affected women and men (and thus of believing that women and men were the same). How, then, could she explain the differences her own work had identified? On the other hand, she was tarred (by Rosenberg) with the brush of subversion, for implying that all employers might have some interest in sex typing the labor force, for deducing from her own (presumably Marxist) theory, a "conspiratorial" conclusion about the behavior of Sears.[13] If the patterns of discrimination that Kessler-Harris alluded to were real, after all, one of their effects might well be the kind of difference

Rosenberg pointed out. Caught within the framework of Rosenberg's use of historical evidence, Kessler-Harris and her lawyers relied on an essentially negative strategy, offering details designed to complicate and undercut Rosenberg's assertions. Kessler-Harris did not directly challenge the theoretical shortcomings of Rosenberg's socialization model, nor did she offer an alternative model of her own. That would have required, I think, either fully developing the case for employer discrimination or insisting more completely on the "differences" line of argument by exposing the "equality-versus-difference" formulation as an illusion.

In the end, the most nuanced arguments of Kessler-Harris were rejected as contradictory or inapplicable, and the judge decided in Sears's favor, repeating the defense argument that an assumption of equal interest was "unfounded" because of the differences between women and men.[14] Not only was EEOC's position rejected, but the hiring policies of Sears were implicitly endorsed. According to the judge, because difference was real and fundamental, it could explain statistical variations in Sears's hiring. Discrimination was redefined as simply the recognition of "natural" difference (however culturally or historically produced), fitting in nicely with the logic of Reagan conservatism. Difference was substituted for inequality, the appropriate antithesis of equality, becoming inequality's explanation and legitimation. The judges decision illustrates a process literary scholar Naomi Schor has described in another context: it essentializes difference and naturalizes social inequity."[15]

The Sears case offers a sobering lesson in the operation of a discursive, that is a political field. Analysis of language here provides insight not only into the manipulation of concepts and definitions but also into the implementation and justification of institutional and political power. References to categorical differences between women and men set the terms within which Sears defended its policies *and* EEOC challenged them. Equality-versus-difference was the intellectual trap within which historians argued not about tiny disparities in Sears's employment practices, but about the normative behaviors of women and men. Although we might conclude that the balance of power was against EEOC by the time the case was heard and that, therefore, its outcome was inevitable (part of the Reagan plan to reverse affirmative action programs of the 1970s), we still need to articulate a critique of what happened that can inform the next round of political encounter. How should that position be conceptualized?

When equality and difference are paired dichotomously, they structure an impossible choice. If one opts for equality, one is forced to accept the notion that difference in antithetical to it. If one opts for difference, one admits that equality is unattainable. That, in a sense, is the dilemma apparent in Milkman's conclusion cited above. Feminists cannot give up "difference"; it has been our most creative analytic tool. We cannot give up equality, at least as long as we want to speak to the principles and values of our political system. But it makes no sense for the feminist movement to let its arguments be forced into preexisting categories and its political disputes to be characterized by a dichotomy we did not invent. How then do we recognize and use notions of sexual difference and yet make arguments for equality? The only response is a double one: the unmasking of the power relationship constructed by posing equality as the antithesis of difference and the refusal of its consequent dichotomous construction of political choices.

Equality-versus-difference cannot structure choices for feminist politics; the oppositional pairing misrepresents the relationship of both terms. Equality, in the political theory of rights that lies behind the claims of excluded groups for justice, means the ignoring of differences between individuals for a particular purpose or in a particular context. Michael Walzer puts it this way: "The root meaning of equality is negative; egalitarianism in its origins is an abolitionist politics. It aims at eliminating not all differences, but a particular set of differences, and a different set in different times and places."[16] This presumes a social agreement to consider obviously different people as equivalent (not identical) for a stated purpose. In this usage, the opposite of equality is inequality or inequivalence, the noncommensurability of individuals or groups in certain circumstances, for certain purposes. Thus, for purposes of democratic citizenship, the measure of equivalence has been, at different times, independence or ownership of

property or race or sex. The political notion of equality thus includes, indeed depends on, an acknowledgment of the existence of difference. Demands for equality have rested on implicit and usually unrecognized arguments from difference; if individuals or groups were identical or the same there would be no need to ask for equality. Equality might well be defined as deliberate indifference to specified differences.

The antithesis of difference in most usages is sameness or identity. But even here the contrast and the context must be specified. There is nothing self-evident or transcendent about difference, even if the fact of difference—sexual difference, for example—seems apparent to the naked eye. The questions always ought to be, What qualities or aspects are being compared? What is the nature of the comparison? How is the meaning of difference being constructed? Yet in the Sears testimony and in some debates among feminists (sexual) difference is assumed to be an immutable fact, its meaning inherent in the categories female and male. The lawyers for Sears put it this way: "The reasonableness of the EEOC's *a priori* assumptions of male/female sameness with respect to preferences, interests, and qualifications is . . . the crux of the issue."[17] The point of the EEOC challenge, however, was never sameness but the irrelevance of categorical differences.

The opposition men/women, as Rosenberg employed it, asserted the incomparability of the sexes, and although history and socialization were the explanatory factors, these resonated with categorical distinctions inferred from the facts of bodily difference. When the opposition men/women is invoked, as it was in the Sears case, it refers a specific issue (the small statistical discrepancy between women and men hired for commission sales jobs) back to a general principle (the "fundamental" differences between women and men). The differences within each group that might apply to this particular situation—the fact, for example, that some women might choose "aggressive" or "risk-taking" jobs or that some women might prefer high- to low-paying positions—were excluded by definition in the antithesis between the groups. The irony is, of course, that the statistical case required only a small percentage of women's behaviors to be explained. Yet the historical testimony argued categorically about "women." It thus became impossible to argue (as EEOC and Kessler-Harris tried to) that within the female category, women typically exhibit and participate in all sorts of "male" behaviors, that socialization is a complex process that does not yield uniform choices. To make the argument would have required a direct attack on categorical thinking about gender. For the generalized opposition male/female serves to obscure the differences among women in behavior, character, desire, subjectivity, sexuality, gender identification, and historical experience. In the light of Rosenberg's insistence on the primacy of sexual difference, Kessler-Harris's insistence on the specificity (and historically variable aspect) of women's actions could be dismissed as an unreasonable and trivial claim.

The alternative to the binary construction of sexual difference is not sameness, identity, or androgyny. By subsuming women into a general "human" identity, we lose the specificity of female diversity and women's experiences; we are back, in other words, to the days when "Man's" story was supposed to be everyone's story, when women were "hidden from history," when the feminine served as the negative counterpoint, the "Other," for the construction of positive masculine identity. It is not sameness *or* identity between women and men that we want to claim but a more complicated historically variable diversity than is permitted by the opposition male/female, a diversity that is also differently expressed for different purposes in different contexts. In effect, the duality this opposition creates draws one line of difference, invests it with biological explanations, and then treats each side of the opposition as a unitary phenomenon. Everything in each category (male/female) is assumed to be the same; hence, differences within either category are suppressed. In contrast, our goal is to see not only differences between the sexes but also the way these work to repress differences within gender groups. The sameness constructed on each side of the binary opposition hides the multiple play of differences and maintains their irrelevance and invisibility.

Placing equality and difference in antithetical relationship has, then, a double effect. It denies the way in which difference has long figured in political notions of equality and it suggests that sameness is the only ground on which equality can be claimed.

It thus puts feminists in an impossible position, for as long as we argue within the terms of a discourse set up by this opposition we grant the current conservative premise that because women cannot be identical to men in all respects, we cannot expect to be equal to them. The only alternative, it seems to me, is to refuse to oppose equality to difference and insist continually on differences—differences as the condition of individual and collective identities, differences as the constant challenge to the fixing of those identities, history as the repeated illustration of the play of differences, differences as the very meaning of equality itself.

Alice Kessler-Harris's experience in the Sears case shows, however, that the assertion of differences in the face of gender categories is not a sufficient strategy. What is required in addition is an analysis of fixed gender categories as normative statements that organize cultural understandings of sexual difference. This means that we must open to scrutiny the terms women and men as they are used to define one another in particular contexts—workplaces, for example. The history of women's work needs to be retold from this perspective as part of the story of the creation of a gendered workforce. In the nineteenth century, for example, certain concepts of male skill rested on a contrast with female labor (by definition unskilled). The organization and reorganization of work processes was accomplished by reference to the gender attributes of workers, rather than to issues of training, education, or social class. And wage differentials between the sexes were attributed to fundamentally different family roles that preceded (rather than followed from) employment arrangements. In all these processes the meaning of "worker" was established through a contrast between the presumably natural qualities of women and men. If we write the history of women's work by gathering data that describes the activities, needs, interests, and culture of "women workers," we leave in place the naturalized contrast and reify a fixed categorical difference between women and men. We start the story, in other words, too late, by uncritically accepting a gendered category (the "woman worker") that itself needs investigation because its meaning is relative to its history.

If in our histories we relativize the categories woman and man, it means, of course, that we must also recognize the contingent and specific nature of our political claims. Political strategies then will rest on analyses of the utility of certain arguments in certain discursive contexts, without, however, invoking absolute qualities for women or men. There are moments when it makes sense for mothers to demand consideration for their social role, and contexts within which motherhood is irrelevant to women's behavior; but to maintain that womanhood is motherhood is to obscure the differences that make choice possible. There are moments when it makes sense to demand a reevaluation of the status of what has been socially constructed as women's work ("comparable worth" strategies are the current example) and contexts within which it makes much more sense to prepare women for entry into "nontraditional" jobs. But to maintain that femininity predisposes women to certain (nurturing) jobs or (collaborative) styles of work is to naturalize complex economic and social processes and, once again, to obscure the differences that have characterized women's occupational histories. An insistence on differences undercuts the tendency to absolutist, and in the case of sexual difference, essentialist categories. It does not deny the existence of gender difference, but it does suggest that its meanings are always relative to particular constructions in specified contexts. In contrast, absolutist categorizations of difference end up always enforcing normative rules.

It is surely not easy to formulate a "deconstructive" political strategy in the face of powerful tendencies that construct the world in binary terms. Yet there seems to me no other choice. Perhaps as we learn to think this way solutions will become more readily apparent. Perhaps the theoretical and historical work we do can prepare the ground. Certainly we can take heart from the history of feminism, which is full of illustrations of refusals of simple dichotomies and attempts instead to demonstrate that equality requires the recognition and inclusion of differences. Indeed, one way historians could contribute to a genuine rethinking of these concepts is to stop writing the history of feminisms as a story of oscillations between demands for equality and affirmations of difference. This approach inadvertently strengthens the hold of the binary construction, establishing it as inevitable by

giving it a long history. When looked at closely, in fact, the historical arguments of feminists do not usually fall into these neat compartments; they are instead attempts to reconcile theories of equal rights with cultural concepts of sexual difference, to question the validity of normative constructions of gender in the light of the existence of behaviors and qualities that contradict the rules, to point up rather than resolve conditions of contradiction, to articulate a political identity for women without conforming to existing stereotypes about them.

In histories of feminism and in feminist political strategies there needs to be at once attention to the operations of difference and an insistence on differences, but not a simple substitution of multiple for binary difference for it is not a happy pluralism we ought to invoke. The resolution of the "difference dilemma" comes neither from ignoring nor embracing difference as it is normatively constituted. Instead, it seems to me that the critical feminist position must always involve *two* moves. The first is the systematic criticism of the operations of categorical difference, the exposure of the kinds of exclusions and inclusions—the hierarchies—it constructs, and a refusal of their ultimate "truth." A refusal, however, not in the name of an equality that implies sameness or identity, but rather (and this is the second move) in the name of an equality that rests on differences—differences that confound, disrupt, and render ambiguous the meaning of any fixed binary opposition. To do anything else is to buy into the political argument that sameness is a requirement for equality, an untenable position for feminists (and historians) who know that power is constructed on and so must be challenged from the ground of difference.

[1988]

NOTES

1. On the problem of appropriating poststructuralism for feminism, see Biddy Martin, "Feminism, Criticism, Foucault," *New German Critique* 27 (Fall 1982): 3–30.
2. Joan W. Scott, "Gender: A Useful Category of Historical Analysis," *American Historical Review* 91 (December 1986); 1053–75; Donna Haraway, "A Manifesto for Cyborgs: Science, Technology, and Socialist Feminism in the 1980s," *Socialist Review* 15 (March/April 1985): 65–107.
3. Examples of Michel Foucault's work include *The Archeology of Knowledge* (New York: Harper & Row, 1976), *The History of Sexuality*, vol. 1, *An Introduction*

(New York: Vintage, 1980), and *Power/Knowledge: Selected Interviews and Other Writings, 1972–1977* (New York: Pantheon, 1980). See also Hubert L. Dreyfus and Paul Rabinow, *Michel Foucault: Beyond Structuralism and Hermeneutics* (Chicago: University of Chicago Press, 1983).

4. Barbara Johnson, *The Critical Difference: Essays in the Contemporary Rhetoric of Reading* (Baltimore: Johns Hopkins University Press, 1980): x–xi.

5. Most recently, attention has been focused on the issue of pregnancy benefits. See, for example, Lucina M. Finley, "Transcending Equality Theory: A Way Out of the Maternity and the Workplace Debate," *Columbia Law Review* 86 (October 1986): 1118–83. See Sylvia A. Law, "Rethinking Sex and the Constitution," *University of Pennsylvania Law Review* 132 (June 1984): 955–1040.

6. Ruth Milkman, "Women's History and the Sears Case," *Feminist Studies* 12 (Summer 1986): 394–95. In my discussion of the Sears case, I have drawn heavily on this careful and intelligent article, the best so far of the many that have been written on the subject.

7. Martha Minow, "Learning to Live with the Dilemma of Difference: Bilingual and Special Education," *Law and Contemporary Problems* 48, no. 2 (1984): 157–211; quotation is from p. 160; see also pp. 202–6.

8. Rosenberg's, "Offer of Proof" and Kessler-Harris's "Written Testimony" appeared in *Signs* 11 (Summer 1986): 757–79. The "Written Rebuttal Testimony of Dr. Rosalind Rosenberg" is part of the official transcript of the case. U.S. District Court for the Northern District of Illinois, Eastern Division, *EEOC vs. Sears,* Civil Action No. 79-C-4373. (I am grateful to Sanford Levinson for sharing the trial documents with me and for our many conversations about them.)

9. Appendix to the "Written Rebuttal Testimony of Dr. Rosalind Rosenberg," 1–12.

10. On the limits imposed by courtrooms and the pitfalls expert witnesses may encounter, see Nadine Taub, "Thinking about Testifying," *Perspectives* (American Historical Association Newsletter) 24 (November 1986): 10–11.

11. On this point, Taub asks a useful question: "Is there a danger in discrimination cases that historical or other expert testimony not grounded in the particular facts of the case will reinforce the idea that it is acceptable to make generalizations about particular groups?" (p.11).

12. See the cross-examination of Kessler-Harris, *EEOC vs Sears,* 16376–619.

13. The Rosenberg "Rebuttal" is particularly vehement on this question: "This assumption that all employers discriminate is prominent in her (Kessler-Harris's) work. . . . In a 1979 article, she wrote hopefully that women harbor values, attitudes, and behavior patterns potentially subversive to capitalism" (p. 11). "There are, of course, documented instances of employers limiting the opportunities of women. But the fact that some employers have discriminated does not prove that all do" (p. 19). The rebuttal raises another issue about the political and ideological limits of a courtroom or, perhaps it is better to say, about the way the courtroom reproduces dominant ideologies. The general notion that employers discriminate was unacceptable (but the general notion that women prefer certain jobs was not). This unacceptability was underscored by linking it to

subversion and Marxism, positions intolerable in U.S. political discourse. Rosenberg's innuendos attempted to discredit Kessler-Harris on two counts—first, by suggesting she was making a ridiculous generalization and second, by suggesting that only people outside acceptable politics could even entertain that generalization.

14. Milkman, 391.

15. Naomi Schor, "Reading Double: Sand's Difference," in *The Poetics of Gender,* ed. Nancy K. Miller (New York: Columbia University Press, 1986), 256.

16. Michael Walzer, *Spheres of Justice: A Defense of Pluralism and Equality* (New York: Basic Books, 1983), xii. See also Minow, 202–3.

17. Milkman, 384.

 75

Development, Ecology and Women

VANDANA SHIVA

VANDANA SHIVA. 1952– . India. Physicist. Environmental Activist. Author. *Ecofeminism* with Maria Meis (1993), *Close to Home: Women Reconnect Ecology, Health and Development Worldwide, Earth Democracy* (1994), *Water Wars: Pollution, Profits, and Privatization* (2001), *Justice, Sustainability, and Peace* (2005).

DEVELOPMENT AS A NEW PROJECT OF WESTERN PATRIARCHY

'Development' was to have been a post-colonial project, a choice for accepting a model of progress in which the entire world remade itself on the model of the colonising modern west, without having to undergo the subjugation and exploitation that colonialism entailed. The assumption was that western style progress was possible for all. Development, as the improved well-being of all, was thus equated with the westernisation of economic categories—of needs, of productivity, of growth. Concepts and categories about economic development and natural resource utilisation that had emerged in the specific context of industrialisation and capitalist growth in a centre of colonial power, were raised to the level of universal assumptions and applicability in the entirely different context of basic needs satisfaction for the people of the newly independent Third World countries. Yet, as Rosa Luxemburg has pointed out, early industrial development in western Europe necessitated the permanent occupation of the colonies by the colonial powers and the destruction of the local 'natural economy'.[1] According to her, colonialism is a constant necessary condition for capitalist growth: without colonies, capital accumulation would grind to a halt. 'Development' as capital accumulation and the commercialisation of the economy for the generation of 'surplus' and profits thus involved the reproduction not merely of a particular form of creation of wealth, but also of the associated creation of poverty and dispossession. A replication of economic development based on commercialisation of resource use for commodity production in the newly independent countries created the internal colonies. Development was thus reduced to a continuation of the process of colonisation; it became an extension of the project of wealth creation in modern western patriarchy's economic vision, which was based on the exploitation or exclusion of women (of the west and non-west), on the exploitation and degradation of nature, and on the exploitation and erosion of other cultures. 'Development' could not but entail destruction for women, nature and subjugated cultures, which is why, throughout the Third World, women, peasants and tribals are struggling for liberation from 'development' just as they earlier struggled for liberation from colonialism.

The UN Decade for Women was based on the assumption that the improvement of women's economic position would automatically flow from an expansion and diffusion of the development process. Yet, by the end of the Decade, it was becoming clear that development itself was the problem. Insufficient and inadequate 'participation' in 'development' was not the cause for women's increasing under-development; it was rather, their enforced but asymmetric participation in it, by which they bore the costs but were excluded from the benefits, that was responsible. Development exclusivity and dispossession aggravated and deepened the colonial processes of ecological degradation and the loss of political control over nature's sustenance base. Economic growth was a new colonialism, draining resources away from those who needed them most. The discontinuity lay in the fact that it was now new national elites, not colonial

powers, that masterminded the exploitation on grounds of 'national interest' and growing GNPs, and it was accomplished with more powerful technologies of appropriation and destruction.

Ester Boserup[2] has documented how women's impoverishment increased during colonial rule; those rulers who had spent a few centuries in subjugating and crippling their own women into de-skilled, de-intellectualised appendages, disfavoured the women of the colonies on matters of access to land, technology and employment. The economic and political processes of colonial underdevelopment bore the clear mark of modern western patriarchy, and while large numbers of women and men were impoverished by these processes, women tended to lose more. The privatisation of land for revenue generation displaced women more critically, eroding their traditional land use rights. The expansion of cash crops undermined food production, and women were often left with meagre resources to feed and care for children, the aged and the infirm, when men migrated or were conscripted into forced labour by the colonisers. As a collective document by women activists, organisers and researchers stated at the end of the UN Decade for Women, 'The almost uniform conclusion of the Decade's research is that with a few exceptions, women's relative access to economic resources, incomes and employment has worsened, their burden of work has increased, and their relative and even absolute health, nutritional and educational status has declined.'[3]

The displacement of women from productive activity by the expansion of development was rooted largely in the manner in which development projects appropriated or destroyed the natural resource base for the production of sustenance and survival. It destroyed women's productivity both by removing land, water and forests from their management and control, as well as through the ecological destruction of soil, water and vegetation systems so that nature's productivity and renewability were impaired. While gender subordination and patriarchy are the oldest of oppressions, they have taken on new and more violent forms through the project of development. Patriarchal categories which understand destruction as 'production' and regeneration of life as 'passivity' have generated a crisis of survival. Passivity, as an assumed category of the 'nature' of nature and of women, denies the activity of nature and life. Fragmentation and uniformity as assumed categories of progress and development destroy the living forces which arise from relationships within the 'web of life' and the diversity in the elements and patterns of these relationships.

. . .

The neglect of nature's work in renewing herself, and women's work in producing sustenance in the form of basic, vital needs is an essential part of the paradigm of maldevelopment, which sees all work that does not produce profits and capital as non or unproductive work. As Maria Mies[4] has pointed out, this concept of surplus has a patriarchal bias because, from the point of view of nature and women, it is not based on material surplus produced *over and above* the requirements of the community: it is stolen and appropriated through violent modes from nature (who needs a share of her produce to reproduce herself) and from women (who need a share of nature's produce to produce sustenance and ensure survival).

From the perspective of Third World women, productivity is a measure of producing life and sustenance; that this kind of productivity has been rendered invisible does not reduce its centrality to survival—it merely reflects the domination of modern patriarchal economic categories which see only profits, not life.

MALDEVELOPMENT AS THE DEATH OF THE FEMININE PRINCIPLE

In this analysis, maldevelopment becomes a new source of male-female inequality. 'Modernisation' has been associated with the introduction of new forms of dominance. Alice Schlegel[5] has shown that under conditions of subsistence, the interdependence and complementarity of the separate male and female domains of work is the characteristic mode, based on diversity, not inequality. Maldevelopment militates against this equality in diversity, and superimposes the ideologically constructed category of western technological man as a uniform measure of the worth of classes, cultures and genders. Dominant modes of perception based on reductionism, duality and linearity are unable to cope with equality in

diversity, with forms and activities that are significant and valid, even though different. The reductionist mind superimposes the roles and forms of power of western male-oriented concepts on women, all non-western peoples and even on nature, rendering all three 'deficient', and in need of 'development'. Diversity, and unity and harmony in diversity, become epistemologically unattainable in the context of maldevelopment, which then becomes synonymous with women's underdevelopment (increasing sexist domination), and nature's depletion (deepening, ecological crises). Commodities have grown, but nature has shrunk. The poverty crisis of the South arises from the growing scarcity of water, food, fodder and fuel, associated with increasing maldevelopment and ecological destruction, This poverty crisis touches women most severely, first because they are the poorest among the poor, and then because, with nature, they are the primary sustainers of society.

Maldevelopment is the violation of the integrity of organic, interconnected and interdependent systems, that sets in motion a process of exploitation, inequality, injustice and violence. It is blind to the fact that a recognition of nature's harmony and action to maintain it are preconditions for distributive justice. This is why Mahatma Gandhi said, 'There is enough in the world for everyone's need, but not for some people's greed.'

Maldevelopment is maldevelopment in thought and action. In practice, this fragmented, reductionist, dualist perspective violates the integrity and harmony of man in nature, and the harmony between men and women. It ruptures the co-operative unity of masculine and feminine, and places man, shorn of the feminine principle, above nature and women, and separated from both. The violence to nature as symptomatised by the ecological crisis, and the violence to women, as symptomatised by their subjugation and exploitation arise from this subjugation of the feminine principle. I want to argue that what is currently called development is essentially maldevelopment, based on the introduction or accentuation of the domination of man over nature and women. In it, both are viewed as the 'other', the passive non-self. Activity, productivity, creativity which were associated with the feminine principle are expropriated as qualities of nature and women, and transformed into the exclusive qualities of man. Nature and women are turned into passive objects, to be used and exploited for the uncontrolled and uncontrollable desires of alienated man. From being the creators and sustainers of life, nature and women are reduced to being 'resources' in the fragmented, anti-life model of maldevelopment.

TWO KINDS OF GROWTH, TWO KINDS OF PRODUCTIVITY

Maldevelopment is usually called 'economic growth', measured by the Gross National Product. Porritt, a leading ecologist has this to say of GNP:

> *Gross* National Product—for once a word is being used correctly. Even conventional economists admit that the hey-day of GNP is over, for the simple reason that as a measure of progress, it's more or less useless. GNP measures the lot, all the goods and services produced in the money economy. Many of these goods and services are not beneficial to people, but rather a measure of just how much is going wrong; increased spending on crime, on pollution, on the many human casualties of our society, increased spending because of waste or planned obsolescence, increased spending because of growing bureaucracies: it's all counted.[6]

The problem with GNP is that it measures some costs as benefits (e.g. pollution control) and fails to measure other costs completely. Among these hidden costs are the new burdens created by ecological devastation, costs that are invariably heavier for women, both in the North and South. It is hardly surprising, therefore, that as GNP rises, it does not necessarily mean that either wealth or welfare increase proportionately. I would argue that GNP is becoming, increasingly, a measure of how realwealth—the wealth of nature and that produced by women for sustaining life—is rapidly decreasing. When commodity production as the prime economic activity is introduced as development, it destroys the potential of nature and women to produce life and goods and services for basic needs. More commodities and more cash mean less life— in nature (through ecological destruction) and in society (through denial of basic needs). Women are devalued first, because their work cooperates with nature's processes, and second, because work which satisfies needs and ensures sustenance is devalued in general. Precisely because

more growth in maldevelopment has meant less sustenance of life and life-support systems, it is now imperative to recover the feminine principle as the basis for development which conserves and is ecological. Feminism as ecology, and ecology as the revival of Prakriti, the source of all life, become the decentred powers of political and economic transformation and restructuring.

This involves, first, a recognition that categories of 'productivity' and growth which have been taken to be positive, progressive and universal are, in reality, restricted patriarchal categories. When viewed from the point of view of nature's productivity and growth, and women's production of sustenance, they are found to be ecologically destructive and a source of gender inequality. It is no accident that the modern, efficient and productive technologies created within the context of growth in market economic terms are associated with heavy ecological costs, borne largely by women. The resource and energy intensive production processes they give rise to demand ever increasing resource withdrawals from the ecosystem. These withdrawals disrupt essential ecological processes and convert renewable resources into non-renewable ones. . . .

It is these resource and energy intensive processes of production which divert resources away from survival, and hence from women. What patriarchy sees as productive work, is, in ecological terms, highly destructive production. The second law of thermodynamics predicts that resource intensive and resource wasteful economic development must become a threat to the survival of the human species in the long run. Political struggles based on ecology in industrially advanced countries are rooted in this conflict between *long term survival options* and *short term over-production and over-consumption*. Political struggles of women, peasants and tribals based on ecology in countries like India are far more acute and urgent since they are rooted in the *immediate threat to the options for survival* for the vast majority of the people, *posed by resource intensive and resource wasteful economic growth* for the benefit of a minority.

In the market economy, the organising principle for natural resource use is the maximisation of profits and capital accumulation. Nature and human needs are managed through market mechanisms. Demands for natural resources are restricted to those demands registering on the market; the ideology of development is in large part based on a vision of bringing all natural resources into the market economy for commodity production. When these resources are already being used by nature to maintain her production of renewable resources and by women for sustenance and livelihood, their diversion to the market economy generates a scarcity condition for ecological stability and creates new forms of poverty for women.

· · ·

The economic system based on the patriarchal concept of productivity was created for the very specific historical and political phenomenon of colonialism. In it, the input for which efficiency of use had to be maximised in the production centres of Europe, was industrial labour. For colonial interest therefore, it was rational to improve the labour resource *even at the cost of wasteful use of nature's wealth*. This rationalisation has, however, been illegitimately universalised to all contexts and interest groups and, on the plea of increasing productivity, labour reducing technologies have been introduced in situations where labour is abundant and cheap, and resource demanding technologies have been introduced where resources are scarce and already fully utilised for the production of sustenance. Traditional economies with a stable ecology have shared with industrially advanced affluent economies the ability to use natural resources to satisfy basic vital needs. The former differ from the latter in two essential ways: first, the same needs are satisfied in industrial societies through longer technological chains requiring higher energy and resource inputs and excluding large numbers without purchasing power; and second, affluence generates new and artificial needs requiring the increased production of industrial goods and services. Traditional economies are not advanced in the matter of non-vital needs satisfaction, but as far as the satisfaction of basic and vital needs is concerned, they are often what Marshall Sahlins has called 'the original affluent society'. . . .

Thus are economies based on indigenous technologies viewed as 'backward' and 'unproductive'. Poverty, as the denial of basic needs, is not necessarily associated with the existence of traditional technologies, and its removal is not necessarily an outcome of the growth of modern ones. On the contrary, the destruction of ecologically sound traditional technologies, often created and used by women, along with the destruction of their material base is generally believed to be responsible for the 'feminisation' of poverty in societies which have had to bear the costs of resource destruction.

· · ·

The paradox and crisis of development arises from the mistaken identification of culturally perceived poverty with real material poverty, and the mistaken identification of the growth of commodity production as better satisfaction of basic needs. In actual fact, there is less water, less fertile soil, less genetic wealth as a result of the development process. Since these natural resources are the basis of nature's economy and women's survival economy, their scarcity is impoverishing women and marginalised peoples in an unprecedented manner. Their new impoverishment lies in the fact that resources which supported their survival were absorbed into the market economy while they themselves were excluded and displaced by it.

The old assumption that with the development process the availability of goods and services will automatically be increased and poverty will be removed, is now under serious challenge from women's ecology movements in the Third World, even while it continues to guide development thinking in centres of patriarchal power. Survival is based on the assumption of the sanctity of life; maldevelopment is based on the assumption of the sacredness of 'development'. Gustavo Esteva asserts that the sacredness of development has to be refuted because it threatens survival itself. 'My people are tired of development', he says, 'they just want to live.[7]

The recovery of the feminine principle allows a transcendance and transformation of these patriarchal foundations of maldevelopment. It allows a redefinition of growth and productivity as categories linked to the production, not the destruction, of life. It is thus simultaneously an ecological and a feminist political project which legitimises the way of knowing and being that creates wealth by enhancing life and diversity, and which deligitimises the knowledge and practise of a culture of death as the basis for capital accumulation.

[1989]

NOTES

1. Rosa Luxemberg, *The Accumulation of Capital*, London: Routledge and Kegan Paul, 1951.
2. Ester Boserup, *Women's Role in Economic Development*, London: Allen and Unwin, 1970.
3. DAWN, *Development Crisis and Alternative Visions: Third World Women's Perspectives*, Bergen: Christian Michelsen Institute, 1985, p. 21.
4. Maria Mies, *Patriarchy and Accumulation on a World Scale*, London: Zed Books, 1986.
5. Alice Schlegel (ed), *Sexual Stratification: A Cross-Cultural Study*, New York: Columbia University Press, 1977.
6. Jonathan Porritt, *Seeing Green*, Oxford: Blackwell, 1984.
7. G. Esteva, Remarks made at a Conference of the Society for International Development, Rome, 1985.

 76

Feminism: A Transformational Politic

bell hooks

bell hooks United States. 1952– . Feminist scholar. Writer. *Ain't I a Woman?* (1981), *Feminist Theory: From Margin to Center* (1984), *Talking Back: Thinking Feminist, Thinking Black* (1989), *Black Looks: Race and Representation* (1992), *Teaching to Transgress: Education as the Practice of Freedom* (1994), *Killing Rage: Ending Racism* (1995), *Bone Black: Memories of Girlhood* (1996), *Outlaw Culture: Resisting Representations* (2006).

We live in a world of crisis—a world governed by politics of domination, one in which the belief in a notion of superior and inferior, and its concomitant ideology—that the superior should rule over the inferior—affects the lives of all people everywhere, whether poor or privileged, literate or illiterate. Systematic dehumanization, worldwide famine, ecological devastation, industrial contamination, and the possibility of nuclear destruction are realities which remind us daily that we are in crisis. Contemporary feminist thinkers often cite sexual politics as the origin of this crisis. They point to the insistence on difference as that factor which becomes the occasion for separation and domination and suggest that differentiation of status

between females and males globally is an indication that patriarchal domination of the planet is the root of the problem. Such an assumption has fostered the notion that elimination of sexist oppression would necessarily lead to the eradication of all forms of domination. It is an argument that has led influential Western white women to feel that feminist movement should be *the* central political agenda for females globally. Ideologically, thinking in this direction enables Western women, especially privileged white women, to suggest that racism and class exploitation are merely the offspring of the parent system: patriarchy. Within feminist movement in the West, this has led to the assumption that resisting patriarchal domination is a more legitimate feminist action than resisting racism and other forms of domination. Such thinking prevails despite radical critiques made by black women and other women of color who question this proposition. To speculate that an oppositional division between men and women existed in early human communities is to impose on the past, on these non-white groups, a world view that fits all too neatly within contemporary feminist paradigms that name man as the enemy and woman as the victim.

Clearly, differentiation between strong and weak, powerful and powerless, has been a central defining aspect of gender globally, carrying with it the assumption that men should have greater authority than women, and should rule over them. As significant and important as this fact is, it should not obscure the reality that women can and do participate in politics of domination, as perpetrators as well as victims—that we dominate, that we are dominated. If focus on patriarchal domination masks this reality or becomes the means by which women deflect attention from the real conditions and circumstances of our lives, then women cooperate in suppressing and promoting false consciousness, inhibiting our capacity to assume responsibility for transforming ourselves and society.

Thinking speculatively about early human social arrangement, about women and men struggling to survive in small communities, it is likely that the parent-child relationship with its very real imposed survival structure of dependency, of strong and weak, of powerful and powerless, was a site for the construction of a paradigm of domination. While this circumstance of dependency is not necessarily one that leads to domination, it lends itself to the enactment of a social drama wherein domination could easily occur as a means of exercising and maintaining control. This speculation does not place women outside the practice of domination, in the exclusive role of victim. It centrally names women as agents of domination, as potential theoreticians, and creators of a paradigm for social relationships wherein those groups of individuals designated as "strong" exercise power both benevolently and coercively over those designated as "weak."

Emphasizing paradigms of domination that call attention to woman's capacity to dominate is one way to deconstruct and challenge the simplistic notion that man is the enemy, woman the victim; the notion that men have always been the oppressors. Such thinking enables us to examine our role as women in the perpetuation and maintenance of systems of domination. To understand domination, we must understand that our capacity as women and men to be either dominated or dominating is a point of connection, of commonality. Even though I speak from the particular experience of living as a black woman in the United States, a white-supremacist, capitalist, patriarchal society, where small numbers of white men (and honorary "white men") constitute ruling groups, I understand that in many places in the world oppressed and oppressor share the same color. I understand that right here in this room, oppressed and oppressor share the same gender. Right now as I speak, a man who is himself victimized, wounded, hurt by racism and class exploitation, is actively dominating a woman in his life—that even as I speak, women who are ourselves exploited, victimized, are dominating children. It is necessary for us to remember, as we think critically about domination, that we all have the capacity to act in ways that oppress, dominate, wound (whether or not that power is institutionalized). It is necessary to remember that it is first the potential oppressor within that we must resist—the potential victim within that we must rescue—otherwise we cannot hope for an end to domination, for liberation.

This knowledge seems especially important at this historical moment when black women and other women of color have worked to create awareness of the ways in which racism empowers white women to act as exploiters and oppressors. Increasingly this fact is considered a reason we should not support feminist struggle even though sexism and sexist oppression is a real issue in our lives as black women (see, for example, Vivian Gordon's *Black Women, Feminism, and Black Liberation: Which Way?*). It becomes necessary for us to speak continually about the convictions that inform our continued advocacy of feminist struggle. By calling attention to interlocking systems of domination—sex, race, and class—black women and many other groups of women acknowledge the diversity and complexity of female experience, of our relationship to power and domination. The intent is not to dissuade people of color from becoming engaged in feminist movement. Feminist struggle to end patriarchal domination should be of primary importance to women and men globally not because it is the foundation of all other oppressive structures but because it is that form of domination we are most likely to encounter in an ongoing way in everyday life.

Unlike other forms of domination, sexism directly shapes and determines relations of power in our private lives, in familiar social spaces, in that most intimate context—home—and in that most intimate sphere of relations—family. Usually, it is within the family that we witness coercive domination and learn to accept it, whether it be domination of parent over child, or male over female. Even though family relations may be, and most often are, informed by acceptance of a politic of domination, they are simultaneously relations of care and connection. It is this convergence of two contradictory impulses—the urge to promote growth and the urge to inhibit growth—that provides a practical setting for feminist critique, resistance, and transformation.

Growing up in a black, working-class, father-dominated household, I experienced coercive adult male authority as more immediately threatening, as more likely to cause immediate pain than racist oppression or class exploitation. It was equally clear that experiencing exploitation and oppression in the home made one feel all the more powerless when encountering dominating forces outside the home. This is true for many people. If we are unable to resist and end domination in relations where there is care, it seems totally unimaginable that we can resist and end it in other institutionalized relations of power. If we cannot convince the mothers and/or fathers who care not to humiliate and degrade us, how can we imagine convincing or resisting an employer, a lover, a stranger who systematically humiliates and degrades?

Feminist effort to end patriarchal domination should be of primary concern precisely because it insists on the eradication of exploitation and oppression in the family context and in all other intimate relationships. It is that political movement which most radically addresses the person—the personal—citing the need for transformation of self, of relationships, so that we might be better able to act in a revolutionary manner, challenging and resisting domination, transforming the world outside the self. Strategically, feminist movement should be a central component of all other liberation struggles because it challenges each of us to alter our person, our personal engagement (either as victims or perpetrators or both) in a system of domination.

Feminism, as liberation struggle, must exist apart from and as a part of the larger struggle to eradicate domination in all its forms. We must understand that patriarchal domination shares an ideological foundation with racism and other forms of group oppression, that there is no hope that it can be eradicated while these systems remain intact. This knowledge should consistently inform the direction of feminist theory and practice. Unfortunately, racism and class elitism among women have frequently led to the suppression and distortion of this connection so that it is now necessary for feminist thinkers to critique and revise much feminist theory and the direction of feminist movement. This effort at revision is perhaps most evident in the current widespread acknowledgement that sexism, racism, and class exploitation constitute interlocking systems of domination—that sex, race, and class, and not sex alone, determine the nature of any female's identity, status, and circumstance, the degree to which she will or will not be dominated, the extent to which she will have the power to dominate.

While acknowledgement of the complex nature of woman's status (which has been most impressed upon everyone's consciousness by radical women of color) is a significant corrective, it is only a starting point. It provides a frame of reference which must serve as the basis for thoroughly altering and revising feminist theory and practice. It challenges and calls us to re-think popular assumptions about the nature of feminism that have had the deepest impact on a large majority of women, on mass consciousness. It radically calls into question the notion of a fundamentally common female experience which has been seen as the prerequisite for our coming together, for political unity. Recognition of the interconnectedness of sex, race, and class highlights the diversity of experience, compelling redefinition of the terms for unity. If women do not share "common oppression," what then can serve as a basis for our coming together?

Unlike many feminist comrades, I believe women and men must share a common understanding—a basic knowledge of what feminism is—if it is ever to be a powerful mass-based political movement. In *Feminist Theory: from margin to center,* I suggest that defining feminism broadly as "a movement to end sexism and sexist oppression" would enable us to have a common political goal. We would then have a basis on which to build solidarity. Multiple and contradictory definitions of feminism create confusion and undermine the effort to construct feminist movement so that it addresses everyone. Sharing a common goal does not imply that women and men will not have radically divergent perspectives on how that goal might be reached. Because each individual starts the process of engagement in feminist struggle at a unique level of awareness, very real differences in experience, perspective, and knowledge make developing varied strategies for participation and transformation a necessary agenda.

Feminist thinkers engaged in radically revisioning central tenets of feminist thought must continually emphasize the importance of sex, race and class as factors which *together* determine the social construction of femaleness, as it has been so deeply ingrained in the consciousness of many women active in feminist movement that gender is the sole factor determining destiny. However, the work of education for critical consciousness (usually called consciousness-raising) cannot end there. Much feminist consciousness-raising has in the past focussed on identifying the particular ways men oppress and exploit women. Using the paradigm of sex, race, and class means that the focus does not begin with men and what they do to women, but rather with women working to identify both individually and collectively the specific character of our social identity.

Imagine a group of women from diverse backgrounds coming together to talk about feminism. First they concentrate on working out their status in terms of sex, race, and class, using this as the standpoint from which they begin discussing patriarchy or their particular relations with individual men. Within the old frame of reference, a discussion might consist solely of talk about their experiences as victims in relationship to male oppressors. Two women—one poor, the other quite wealthy—might describe the process by which they have suffered physical abuse by male partners and find certain commonalities which might serve as a basis for bonding. Yet if these same two women engaged in a discussion of class, not only would the social construction and expression of femaleness differ, so too would their ideas about how to confront and change their circumstances. Broadening the discussion to include an analysis of race and class would expose many additional differences even as commonalities emerged.

Clearly the process of bonding would be more complex, yet this broader discussion might enable the sharing of perspectives and strategies for change that would enrich rather than diminish our understanding of gender. While feminists have increasingly given "lip service" to the idea of diversity, we have not developed strategies of communication and inclusion that allow for the successful enactment of this feminist vision.

Small groups are no longer the central place for feminist consciousness-raising. Much feminist education for critical consciousness takes place in Women's Studies classes or at conferences which focus on gender. Books are a primary source of education, which means that already masses of people who do not read have no access. The separation of grassroots ways of sharing feminist thinking across kitchen tables from the spheres where much of that thinking is generated, the academy, undermines feminist movement. It would further feminist

movement if new feminist thinking could be once again shared in small group contexts, integrating critical analysis with discussion of personal experience. It would be useful to promote anew the small group setting as an arena for education for critical consciousness, so that women and men might come together in neighborhoods and communities to discuss feminist concerns.

Small groups remain an important place for education for critical consciousness for several reasons. An especially important aspect of the small group setting is the emphasis on communicating feminist thinking, feminist theory, in a manner that can be easily understood. In small groups, individuals do not need to be equally literate or literate at all because the information is primarily shared through conversation, in dialogue which is necessarily a liberatory expression. (Literacy should be a goal for feminists even as we ensure that it not become a requirement for participation in feminist education.) Reforming small groups would subvert the appropriation of feminist thinking by a select group of academic women and men, usually white, usually from privileged class backgrounds.

Small groups of people coming together to engage in feminist discussion, in dialectical struggle, make a space where the "personal is political" as a starting point for education for critical consciousness can be extended to include politicization of the self that focuses on creating understanding of the ways sex, race, and class together determine our individual lot and our collective experience. It would further feminist movement if many well known feminist thinkers would participate in small groups, critically re-examining ways their works might be changed by incorporating broader perspectives. All efforts at self-transformation challenge us to engage in ongoing, critical self-examination and reflection about feminist practice, about how we live in the world. This individual commitment, when coupled with engagement in collective discussion, provides a space for critical feedback which strengthens our efforts to change and make ourselves new. It is in this commitment to feminist principles in our words and deeds that the hope of feminist revolution lies.

Working collectively to confront difference, to expand our awareness of sex, race, and class as interlocking systems of domination, of the ways we reinforce and perpetuate these structures, is the context in which we learn the true meaning of solidarity. It is this work that must be the foundation of feminist movement. Without it, we cannot effectively resist patriarchal domination; without it, we remain estranged and alienated from one another. Fear of painful confrontation often leads women and men active in feminist movement to avoid rigorous critical encounter, yet if we cannot engage dialectically in a committed, rigorous, humanizing manner, we cannot hope to change the world. True politicization—coming to critical consciousness—is a difficult, "trying" process, one that demands that we give up set ways of thinking and being, that we shift our paradigms, that we open ourselves to the unknown, the unfamiliar. Undergoing this process, we learn what it means to struggle and in this effort we experience the dignity and integrity of being that comes with revolutionary change. If we do not change our consciousness, we cannot change our actions or demand change from others.

Our renewed commitment to a rigorous process of education for critical consciousness will determine the shape and direction of future feminist movement. Until new perspectives are created, we cannot be living symbols of the power of feminist thinking. Given the privileged lot of many leading feminist thinkers, both in terms of status, class, and race, it is harder these days to convince women of the primacy of this process of politicization. More and more, we seem to form select interest groups composed of individuals who share similar perspectives. This limits our capacity to engage in critical discussion. It is difficult to involve women in new processes of feminist politicization because so many of us think that identifying men as the enemy, resisting male domination, gaining equal access to power and privilege is the end of feminist movement. Not only is it not the end, it is not even the place we want revitalized feminist movement to begin. We want to begin as women seriously addressing ourselves, not solely in relation to men, but in relation to an entire structure of domination of which patriarchy is one part. While the struggle to eradicate sexism and sexist oppression is and should be the primary thrust of feminist movement, to prepare ourselves politically for this effort

we must first learn how to be in solidarity, how to struggle with one another.

Only when we confront the realities of sex, race, and class, the ways they divide us, make us different, stand us in opposition, and work to reconcile and resolve these issues will we be able to participate in the making of feminist revolution, in the transformation of the world. Feminism, as Charlotte Bunch emphasizes again and again in *Passionate Politics,* is a transformational politics, a struggle against domination wherein the effort is to change ourselves as well as structures. Speaking about the struggle to confront difference, Bunch asserts:

> A crucial point of the process is understanding that reality does not look the same from different people's perspective. It is not surprising that one way feminists have come to understand about differences has been through the love of a person from another culture or race. It takes persistence and motivation—which love often engenders—to get beyond one's ethnocentric assumptions and really learn about other perspectives. In this process and while seeking to eliminate oppression, we also discover new possibilities and insights that come from the experience and survival of other peoples.

Embedded in the commitment to feminist revolution is the challenge to love. Love can be and is an important source of empowerment when we struggle to confront issues of sex, race, and class. Working together to identify and face our differences—to face the ways we dominate and are dominated—to change our actions, we need a mediating force that can sustain us so that we are not broken in this process, so that we do not despair.

Not enough feminist work has focussed on documenting and sharing ways individuals confront differences constructively and successfully. Women and men need to know what is on the other side of the pain experienced in politicization. We need detailed accounts of the ways our lives are fuller and richer as we change and grow politically, as we learn to live each moment as committed feminists, as comrades working to end domination. In reconceptualizing and reformulating strategies for future feminist movement, we need to concentrate on the politicization of love, not just in the context of talking about victimization in intimate relationships, but in a critical discussion where love can be understood as a powerful force that challenges and resists domination. As we work to be loving, to create a culture that celebrates life, that makes love possible, we move against dehumanization, against domination. In *Pedagogy of the Oppressed*, Paulo Freire evokes this power of love, declaring:

> I am more and more convinced that true revolutionaries must perceive the revolution, because of its creative and liberating nature, as an act of love. For me, the revolution, which is not possible without a theory of revolution—and therefore science—is not irreconcilable with love. . . . The distortion imposed on the word "love" by the capitalist world cannot prevent the revolution from being essentially loving in character, nor can it prevent the revolutionaries from affirming their love of life.

That aspect of feminist revolution that calls women to love womanness, that calls men to resist dehumanizing concepts of masculinity, is an essential part of our struggle. It is the process by which we move from seeing ourselves as objects to acting as subjects. When women and men understand that working to eradicate patriarchal domination is a struggle rooted in the longing to make a world where everyone can live fully and freely, then we know our work to be a gesture of love. Let us draw upon that love to heighten our awareness, deepen our compassion, intensify our courage, and strengthen our commitment.

[1989]

REFERENCES

Bunch, Charlotte. *Passionate Politics,* New York: St. Martin's Press, 1987.

Freire, Paulo. *Pedagogy of the Oppressed,* New York: Herder and Herder, 1970.

Gordon, Vivian. *Black Women, Feminism and Black Liberation—Which Way?* Third World Press, 1991.

 77

The Ecology of Feminism and the Feminism of Ecology

YNESTRA KING

YNESTRA KING ND. *Rocking the Ship of State: Toward a Feminist Peace Politics* (1989), *Dangerous Intersections: Feminist Perspectives on Population, Environment, and Development* (1999).

> [Woman] became the embodiment of the biological function, the image of nature, the subjugation of which constituted that civilization's title to fame. For millennia men dreamed of acquiring absolute mastery over nature, of converting the cosmos into one immense hunting ground. It was to this that the idea of man was geared in a male-dominated society. This was the significance of reason, his proudest boast.
>
> —Horkheimer and Adorno, Dialectic of Enlightenment[1]

All human beings are natural beings. That may seem like an obvious fact, yet we live in a culture that is founded on the repudiation and domination of nature. This has a special significance for women because, in patriarchal thought, women are believed to be closer to nature than men. This gives women a particular stake in ending the domination of nature—in healing the alienation between human and nonhuman nature. This is also the ultimate goal of the ecology movement, but the ecology movement is not necessarily feminist.

For the most part, ecologists, with their concern for nonhuman nature, have yet to understand that they have a particular stake in ending the domination of women. They do not understand that a central reason for woman's oppression is her association with the despised nature they are so concerned about. The hatred of women and the hatred of nature are intimately connected and mutually reinforcing. Starting with this premise, this article explores why feminism and ecology need each other, and suggests the beginnings of a theory of ecological feminism: ecofeminism.

WHAT IS ECOLOGY?

Ecological science concerns itself with the interrelationships among all forms of life. It aims to harmonize nature, human and nonhuman. It is an integrative science in an age of fragmentation and specialization. It is also a critical science which grounds and necessitates a critique of our existing society. It is a reconstructive science in that it suggests directions for reconstructing human society in harmony with the natural environment.

Social ecologists are asking how we might survive on the planet and develop systems of food and energy production, architecture, and ways of life that will allow human beings to fulfill our material needs and live in harmony with nonhuman nature. This work has led to a social critique by biologists and to an exploration of biology and ecology by social thinkers. The perspective that self-consciously attempts to integrate both biological and social aspects of the relationship between human beings and their environment is known as *social ecology*. This perspective developed primarily by Murray Bookchin,[2] to whom I am indebted for my understanding of social ecology, has embodied the anarchist critique that links domination and hierarchy in human society to the despoliation of nonhuman nature. While this analysis is useful, social ecology without feminism is incomplete.

Feminism grounds this critique of domination by identifying the prototype of other forms of domination: that of man over woman. Potentially, feminism creates a concrete global community of interests among particularly life-oriented people of the world: women. Feminist analysis supplies the theory, program, and process without which the radical potential of social ecology remains blunted. Ecofeminism develops the connections between ecology and feminism that social ecology needs in order to reach its own avowed goal of creating a free and ecological way of life.

What are these connections? Social ecology challenges the dualistic belief that nature and culture are separate and opposed. Ecofeminism finds misogyny at the root of that opposition. Ecofeminist principles are based on the following beliefs:

1. The building of Western industrial civilization in opposition to nature interacts dialectically with and reinforces the subjugation of women, because women are believed to be closer to nature. Therefore, ecofeminists take on the life-struggles of all of nature as our own.

2. Life on earth is an interconnected web, not a hierarchy. There is no natural hierarchy; human hierarchy is projected onto nature and then used to justify social domination. Therefore, ecofeminist theory seeks to show the connections between all forms of domination, including the domination of nonhuman nature, and ecofeminist practice is necessarily antihierarchical.

3. A healthy, balanced ecosystem, including human and nonhuman inhabitants, must maintain diversity. Ecologically, environmental simplification is as significant a problem as environmental pollution. Biological simplification, i.e., the wiping out of whole species, corresponds to reducing human diversity into faceless workers, or to the homogenization of taste and culture through mass consumer markets. Social life and natural life are literally simplified to the inorganic for the convenience of market society. Therefore we need a decentralized global movement that is founded on common interests yet celebrates diversity and opposes all forms of domination and violence. Potentially, ecofeminism is such a movement.

4. The survival of the species necessitates a renewed understanding of our relationship to nature, of our own bodily nature, and of nonhuman nature around us; it necessitates a challenging of the nature-culture dualism and a corresponding radical restructuring of human society according to feminist and ecological principles. Adrienne Rich says, "When we speak of transformation we speak more accurately out of the vision of a process which will leave neither surfaces nor depths unchanged, which enters society at the most essential level of the subjugation of women and nature by men. . . ."[3]

The ecology movement, in theory and practice, attempts to speak for nature—the "other" that has no voice and is not conceived of subjectively in our civilization. Feminism represents the refusal of the original "other" in patriarchal human society to remain silent or to be the "other" any longer. Its challenge of social domination extends beyond sex to social domination of all kinds, because the domination of sex, race, and class and the domination of nature are mutually reinforcing. Women are the "others" in human society, who have been silent in public and who now speak through the feminist movement.

WOMEN, NATURE AND CULTURE: THE ECOFEMINIST POSITION

In the project of building Western industrial civilization, nature became something to be dominated, overcome, made to serve the needs of men. She was stripped of her magical powers and properties and was reduced to "natural resources" to be exploited by human beings to fulfill human needs and purposes which were defined in opposition to nature (see Merchant, who interprets the scientific revolution as the death of nature, and argues that it had a particularly detrimental effect on women.)[4] A dualistic Christianity had become ascendant with the earlier demise of old goddess religions, paganism, and animistic belief systems.[5] With the disenchantment of nature came the conditions for unchecked scientific exploration and technological exploitation.[6] We bear the consequences today of beliefs in unlimited control over nature and in science's ability to solve any problem, as nuclear power plants are built without provisions for waste disposal, and satellites are sent into space without provision for retrieval.

In this way, nature became "other," something essentially different from the dominant, to be objectified and subordinated. Women, who are identified with nature, have been similarly objectified and subordinated in patriarchal society. Women and nature, in this sense, are the original "others." Simone de Beauvoir has clarified this connection. For de Beauvoir, "transcendence" is the work of culture, it is the work of men. It is the process of overcoming immanence, a process of culture-building that is based on the increasing domination of nature. It is enterprise. "Immanence," symbolized by women, is that which calls men back, that which reminds man of what he wants to forget. It is his own link to nature that he must forget and overcome to achieve manhood and transcendence.

· · ·

And yet this transcendence over women and nature can never be total: thus the ambivalence, the lack of self without other, the dependence of the self on the other both materially and emotionally. Thus develops a love-hate fetishization of women's bodies, which finds its ultimate manifestation in the sadomasochistic, pornographic displays of women as objects to be subdued, humiliated, and raped—the visual enactment of these fears and desires. (See Griffin, *Pornography and Silence*, for a full development of the relationship between nature-hating, women-hating, and pornography.)[7]

An important contribution of de Beauvoir's work is to show that men seek to dominate women and nature for reasons that are not simply economic. They do so as well for psychological reasons that involve a denial of a part of themselves, as do other male culture-making activities. The process begins with beating the tenderness and empathy out of small boys and directing their natural human curiosity and joy in affecting the world around them into arrogant attitudes and destructive paths.

For men raised in woman-hating cultures, the fact that they are born of women and are dependent upon nonhuman nature for existence is frightening. The process of objectification, of the making of women and nature into "others" to be appropriated and dominated, is based on a profound forgetting by men. They forget that they were born of women, were dependent on women in their early helpless years, and are dependent on nonhuman nature all their lives, which allows first for objectification and then for domination. "The loss of memory is a transcendental condition for science. All objectification is a forgetting."[8]

But the denied part of men is never fully obliterated. The memory remains in the knowledge of mortality and the fear of women's power. A basic fragility of gender identity exists that surfaces when received truths about women and men are challenged and the sexes depart from their "natural" roles. Opposition to the not-very-radical Equal Rights Amendment can be partially explained on these grounds. More threatening are homosexuality and the gay liberation movement, because they name a more radical truth—that sexual orientation is not indelible, nor is it naturally heterosexual. Lesbianism, particularly, which suggests that women who possess this repudiated primordial power can be self-sufficient, reminds men that they may not be needed. Men are forced into remembering their own dependence on women to support and mediate the construction of their private reality and their public civilization. Again there is the need to repress memory and oppress women.

The recognition of the connections between women and nature and of women's bridge-like position between nature and culture poses three possible directions for feminism. One direction is the integration of women into the world of culture and production by severing the woman-nature connection. Writes anthropologist Sherry Ortner, "Ultimately, both men and women can and must be equally involved in projects of creativity and transcendence. Only then will women be seen as aligned with culture, in culture's ongoing dialectic with nature."[9] This position does not question nature-culture dualism itself, and it is the position taken by most socialist-feminists (see King, "Feminism and the Revolt of Nature")[10] and by de Beauvoir and Ortner, despite their insights into the connections between women and nature. They see the severance of the woman-nature connection as a condition of women's liberation.

Other feminists have reinforced the woman-nature connection: woman and nature, the spiritual and intuitive, versus man and the culture of patriarchal rationality.[11] This position also does not necessarily question nature-culture dualism or recognize that women's ecological sensitivity and life orientation is a socialized perspective that could be socialized right out of us depending on our day-to-day lives. There is no reason to believe that women placed in positions of patriarchal power will act any differently from men, or that we can bring about a feminist revolution without consciously understanding history and without confronting the existing economic and political power structures.

Ecofeminism suggests a third direction: a recognition that although the nature-culture dualism is a product of culture, we can nonetheless *consciously choose* not to sever the woman-nature connection by joining male culture. Rather, we can use it as a vantage point for creating a different kind of culture and politics that would integrate intuitive, spiritual, and rational forms of knowledge, embracing

both science and magic insofar as they enable us to transform the nature-culture distinction and to envision and create a free, ecological society.

ECOFEMINISM AND THE INTERSECTION OF FEMINISM AND ECOLOGY

The implications of a culture based on the devaluation of life-giving and the celebration of life-taking are profound for ecology and for women. This fact about our culture links the theories and politics of the ecology movement with those of the feminist movement. Adrienne Rich has written:

> We have been perceived for too many centuries as pure Nature, exploited and raped like the earth and the solar system; small wonder if we now long to become Culture: pure spirit, mind. Yet it is precisely this culture and its political institutions which have split us off from itself. In so doing it has also split itself off from life, becoming the death culture of quantification, abstraction, and the will to power which has reached its most refined destructiveness in this century. It is this culture and politics of abstraction which women are talking of changing, of bringing into accountability in human terms.[12]

The way to ground a feminist critique of "this culture and politics of abstraction" is with a self-conscious ecological perspective that we apply to all theories and strategies, in the way that we are learning to apply race and class factors to every phase of feminist analysis.

Similarly, ecology requires a feminist perspective. Without a thorough feminist analysis of social domination that reveals the interconnected roots of misogyny and hatred of nature, ecology remains an abstraction: it is incomplete. If male ecological scientists and social ecologists fail to deal with misogyny—the deepest manifestation of nature-hating in their own lives—they are not living the ecological lives or creating the ecological society they claim.

The goals of harmonizing humanity and nonhuman nature, at both the experiential and theoretical levels, cannot be attained without the radical vision and understanding available from feminism. The twin concerns of ecofeminism—human liberation and our relationship to nonhuman nature—open the way to developing a set of ethics required for decision-making about technology. Technology signifies the tools that human beings use to interact with nature, including everything from the digging stick to nuclear bombs.

Ecofeminism also contributes an understanding of the connections between the domination of persons and the domination of nonhuman nature. Ecological science tells us that there is no hierarchy in nature itself, but rather a hierarchy in human society that is projected onto nature. Ecofeminism draws on feminist theory, which asserts that the domination of woman was the original domination in human society, from which all other hierarchies—of rank, class, and political power—flow. Building on this unmasking of the ideology of a natural hierarchy of persons, ecofeminism uses its ecological perspective to develop the position that there is no hierarchy in nature: among persons, between persons and the rest of the natural world, or among the many forms of nonhuman nature. We live on the earth with millions of species, only one of which is the human species. Yet the human species in its patriarchal form is the only species which holds a conscious belief that it is entitled to dominion over the other species, and over the planet. Paradoxically, the human species is utterly dependent on nonhuman nature. We could not live without the rest of nature; it *could* live without us.

Ecofeminism draws on another basic principle of ecological science—unity in diversity—and develops it politically. Diversity in nature is necessary, and enriching. One of the major effects of industrial technology, capitalist or socialist, is environmental simplification. Many species are simply being wiped out, never to be seen on earth again. In human society, commodity capitalism is intentionally simplifying human community and culture so that the same products can be marketed anywhere to anyone. The prospect is for all of us to be alike, with identical needs and desires, around the globe: Coca-Cola in China, blue jeans in Russia, and American rock music virtually everywhere.

Few peoples of the earth have not had their lives touched and changed to some degree by the technology of industrialization. Ecofeminism as a social movement resists this social simplification through supporting the rich diversity of women the world over, and seeking a oneness in that diversity. Politically, ecofeminism opposes the ways that differences can separate women from each other, through the oppressions of class, privilege, sexuality, and race.

The special message of ecofeminism is that when women suffer through both social domination and the domination of nature, most of life on this planet suffers and is threatened as well. It is significant that feminism and ecology as social movements have emerged now, as nature's revolt against domination plays itself out in human history and in nonhuman nature at the same time. As we face slow environmental poisoning and the resulting environmental simplification, or the possible unleashing of our nuclear arsenals, we can hope that the prospect of the extinction of life on the planet will provide a universal impetus to social change. Ecofeminism supports utopian visions of harmonious, diverse, decentralized communities, using only those technologies based on ecological principles, as the only practical solution for the continuation of life on earth.

Visions and politics are joined as an ecofeminist culture and politics begin to emerge. Ecofeminists are taking direct action to effect changes that are immediate and personal as well as long-term and structural. Direct actions include learning holistic health and alternate ecological technologies, living in communities that explore old and new forms of spirituality which celebrate all life as diverse expressions of nature, considering the ecological consequences of our lifestyles and personal habits, and participating in creative public forms of resistance, including nonviolent civil disobedience.

TOWARD AN ECOFEMINIST PRAXIS: FEMINIST ANTIMILITARISM

Theory never converts simply or easily into practice: in fact, theory often lags behind practice, attempting to articulate the understanding behind things people are already doing. *Praxis* is the unity of thought and action, or theory and practice. Many of the women who founded the feminist antimilitarist movement in Europe and the United States share the ecofeminist perspective I have articulated. I believe that the movement as I will briefly describe it here grows out of such an understanding. For the last three years I have been personally involved in the ecofeminist antimilitarist movement, so the following is a firsthand account of one example of our praxis.

The connections between violence against women, a militarized culture, and the development and deployment of nuclear weapons have long been evident to pacifist feminists.[13] Ecofeminists like myself, whose concerns with all of life stem from an understanding of the connections between misogyny and the destruction of nature, began to see militarism and the death-courting weapons industry as the most immediate threat to continued life on the planet, while the ecological effects of other modern technologies pose a more long-term threat. In this manner militarism has become a central issue for most ecofeminists. Along with this development, many of us accepted the analysis of violence made by pacifist feminists and, therefore, began to see nonviolent direct action and resistance as the basis of our political practice.

The ecofeminist analysis of militarism is concerned with the militarization of culture and the economic priorities reflected by our enormous "defense" budgets and dwindling social services budgets. The level of weaponry and the militaristic economic priorities are products of patriarchal culture that speak violence at every level. Our freedom and our lives are threatened, even if there is no war and none of the nuclear weapons are ever used. We have tried to make clear the particular ways that women suffer from war-making—as spoils to victorious armies, as refugees, as disabled and older women and single mothers who are dependent on dwindling social services. We connect the fear of nuclear annihilation with women's fear of male violence in our everyday lives.

For ecofeminists, military technology reflects a pervasive cultural and political situation. It is connected with rape, genocide, and imperialism, with starvation and homelessness, with the poisoning of the environment, and with the fearful lives of the world's peoples—especially those of women. Military and state power hierarchies join and reinforce each other through military technology. Particularly as shaped by ecofeminism, the feminist anti-militarist movement in the United States and Europe is a movement against a monstrously destructive technology and set of power relationships embodied in militarism.

· · ·

While technocratic experts (including feminists) argue the merits and demerits of weapons systems,

ecofeminism approaches the disarmament issues on an intimate and moral level. Ecofeminism holds that a personalized, decentralized life-affirming culture and politics of direct action are crucially needed to stop the arms race and transform the world's priorities. Because such weaponry does not exist apart from a contempt for women and all of nature, the issue of disarmament and threat of nuclear war is a feminist issue. It is the ultimate human issue, and the ultimate ecological issue. And so ecology, feminism, and liberation for all of nature, including ourselves, are joined.

[1989]

NOTES

1. Max Horkheimer and Theodor W. Adorno, *Dialectic of Enlightenment*, Seabury Press, New York, 1972, p. 248.
2. Murray Bookchin, *The Ecology of Freedom: The Emergence and Dissolution of Hierarchy*, Cheshire Books, Palo Alto, 1982.
3. Adrienne Rich, *On Lies, Secrets, and Silence*, W. W. Norton, New York, 1979, p. 248.
4. Carolyn Merchant, *The Death of Nature: Women, Ecology, and the Scientific Revolution*, Harper & Row, New York, 1980.
5. Rosemary Radford Reuther, *New Woman/New Earth: Sexist Ideologies and Human Liberation*, Seabury Press, New York, 1975.
6. Merchant, *op. cit.*
7. Susan Griffin, *Pornography and Silence: "Culture's" Revenge against Nature*, Harper & Row, New York, 1981.
8. Horkheimer, *op. cit.*, p. 230.
9. Sherry B. Ortner, "Is Female to Male as Nature Is to Culture?" *Woman, Culture and Society*, Michele Zimbalist Rosaldo and Louise Lamphere, eds., Stanford University Press, Stanford, 1974, p. 87.
10. Ynestra King, "Feminism and the Revolt of Nature," *Heresies* 13: 12–16, 1981.
11. Many such feminists call themselves ecofeminists. Some of them cite Susan Griffin's, *Woman and Nature* (Harper & Row, San Francisco, 1978) as the source of their understanding of the deep connections between women and nature, and their politics. *Woman and Nature* is an inspirational poetic work with political implications. It explores the terrain of our deepest naturalness, but I do not read it as a delineation of a set of politics. To use Griffin's work in this way is to make it into something it was not intended to be. In personal conversation and in her more politically explicit works such as *Pornography and Silence* (1981), Griffin is anti-dualistic, struggling to bridge the false oppositions of nature and culture, passion and reason. Both science and poetry are deeply intuitive processes. Another work often cited by ecofeminists is Mary Daly's *Gyn/Ecology* (1978). Daly, a theologian/philosopher, is also an inspirational thinker, but she is a genuinely dualistic thinker, reversing the "truths" of patriarchal theology. While I have learned a great deal from Daly, my perspective differs from hers in that I believe that any truly ecological

politics, including ecological feminism, must be ultimately antidualistic.

12. Adrienne Rich, *Of Woman Born*, W. W. Norton, New York 1976, p. 285.
13. Barbara Deming, *We Cannot Live Without Our Lives*, Grossman, New York, 1974.

REFERENCES

Daly, Mary. *Gyn/Ecology: The Metaethics of Radical Feminism.* Boston: Beacon Press, 1978.
Griffin, Susan. *Woman and Nature.* New York: Harper & Row, 1978.
King, Ynestra. "All Is Connectedness: Scenes from the Women's Pentagon Action USA." In *Keeping the Peace: A Women's Peace Handbook*, Lynne Johnes, ed., London: The Women's Press, 1983.

 78

Sexuality from Toward a Feminist Theory of the State

CATHARINE A. MACKINNON

CATHARINE A. MACKINNON United States. 1946– . Lawyer. Writer. Activist involved in antipornography campaigns. Argued Supreme Court case that defined sexual harassment as sex discrimination. *Sexual Harassment of Working Women* (1979), *Feminism Unmodified: Discourses on Life and Law* (1987), *Toward a Feminist Theory of the State* (1989), *Only Words* (1993), *In Harm's Way: The Pornography Civil Rights Hearings* (1998).

then she says (and this is what I live through over
    and over)—she says: *I do not know*
        if sex is an illusion

I do not know
who I was when I did those things
or who I said I was
or whether I willed to feel
what I had read about
or who in fact was there with me
or whether I knew, even then
that there was doubt about these things
            —Adrienne Rich, "Dialogue"

I had always been fond of her in the most innocent,
asexual way. It was as if her body was always entirely

hidden behind her radiant mind, the modesty of her
behavior, and her taste in dress. She had never offered me
the slightest chink through which to view the glow of her
nakedness. And now suddenly the butcher knife of fear
had slit her open. She was as open to me as the carcass of
a heifer slit down the middle and hanging on a hook.
There we were . . . and suddenly I felt a violent desire to
make love to her. Or to be more exact, a violent desire to
rape her.
—Milan Kundera, *The Book of Laughter and Forgetting*

She had thought of something, something about the body,
about the passions which it was unfitting for her as a
woman to say. Men, her reason told her, would be
shocked. . . . Telling the truth about my own experiences
as a body, I do not think I solved. I doubt that any
woman had solved it yet. The obstacles against her are
still immensely powerful—and yet they are very difficult
to define.
—Virginia Woolf, "Professions for Women"

What is it about woman's experience that produces a distinctive perspective on social reality? How is an angle of vision and an interpretive hermeneutics of social life created in the group women? What happens to women to give them a particular interest in social arrangements, something to have a consciousness *of*? How are the qualities we know as male and female socially created and enforced on an everyday level? Sexual objectification of women—first in the world, then in the head, first in visual appropriation, then in forced sex, finally in sexual murder—provides answers.[1]

Male dominance is sexual. Meaning: men in particular, if not men alone, sexualize hierarchy; gender is one. As much a sexual theory of gender as a gendered theory of sex, this is the theory of sexuality that has grown out of consciousness raising in the women's movement. Recent feminist work, both interpretive and empirical—on rape, battery, sexual harassment, sexual abuse of children, prostitution, and pornography—supports it. These practices, taken together, express and actualize the distinctive power of men over women in society; their effective permissibility confirms and extends it. If one believes women's accounts of sexual use and abuse by men; if the pervasiveness of male sexual violence against women substantiated in these studies is not denied, minimized, or excepted as deviant[2] or episodic; if the fact that only 7.8 percent of women in the United States are not sexually assaulted or harassed in their lifetimes[3] is considered not ignorable or inconsequential; if the women to whom it happens are not considered expendable; if violation of women is understood as sexualized on some level—then sexuality itself can no longer be regarded as unimplicated. The meaning of practices of sexual violence cannot be categorized away as violence, not sex, either. The male sexual role, this work taken together suggests, centers on aggressive intrusion on those with less power. Such acts of dominance are experienced as sexually arousing, as sex itself.[4] They therefore are. The evidence on the sexual violation of women by men thus frames an inquiry into the place of sexuality in gender and of gender in sexuality.

A feminist theory of sexuality would locate sexuality within a theory of gender inequality, meaning the social hierarchy of men over women. To make a theory feminist, it is not enough that it be authored by a biological female. Nor that it describe female sexuality as different from (if equal to) male sexuality, or as if sexuality in women ineluctably exists in some realm beyond, beneath, above, behind—in any event, fundamentally untouched and unmoved by—an unequal social order. A theory of sexuality becomes feminist to the extent it treats sexuality as a social construct of male power: defined by men, forced on women, and constitutive in the meaning of gender. Such an approach centers feminism on the perspective of the subordination of women to men as it identifies sex—that is, the sexuality of dominance and submission—as crucial, as a fundamental, as on some level definitive, in that process. Feminist theory becomes a project of analyzing that situation in order to face it for what it is, in order to change it.

Focusing on gender inequality without a sexual account of its dynamics, as most work has, one could criticize the sexism of existing theories of sexuality and emerge knowing that men author scripts to their own advantage, women and men act them out; that men set conditions, women and men have their behavior conditioned; that men develop developmental categories through which men develop, and that women develop or not; that men are socially allowed selves hence identities with personalities into which sexuality is or is not well

integrated, women being that which is or is not integrated, that through the alterity of which a self experiences itself as having an identity; that men have object relations, women are objects of those relations, and so on. Following such critique, one could attempt to invert or correct the premises or applications of these theories to make them gender neutral, even if the reality to which they refer looks more like the theories—once their gender specificity is revealed—than it looks gender neutral. Or, one could attempt to enshrine a distinctive "women's reality" as if it really were permitted to exist as something more than one dimension of women's response to a condition of powerlessness. Such exercises would be revealing and instructive, even deconstructive, but to limit feminism to correcting sex bias by acting in theory as if male power did not exist in fact, including by valorizing in writing what women have had little choice but to be limited to becoming in life, is to limit feminist theory the way sexism limits women's lives: to a response to terms men set.

A distinctively feminist theory conceptualizes social reality, including sexual reality, on its own terms. The question is, What are they? If women have been substantially deprived not only of their own experience but of terms of their own in which to view it, then a feminist theory of sexuality that seeks to understand women's situation in order to change it must first identify and criticize the construct "sexuality" as a construct that has circumscribed and defined experience as well as theory. This requires capturing it *in the world*, in its situated social meanings, as it is being constructed in life on a daily basis. It must be studied in its experienced empirical existence, not just in the texts of history (as Foucault), in the social psyche (as Lacan) or in language (as Derrida). Sexual meaning is not made only, or even primarily, by words and in texts. In feminist terms, the fact that male power has power means that the interests of male sexuality construct what sexuality as such means in life, including the standard way it is allowed and recognized to be felt and expressed and experienced, in a way that determines women's biographies, including sexual ones. Existing theories, until they grasp this, will not only misattribute what they call female sexuality to women as such, as if it is not imposed on women daily, they will participate in enforcing the hegemony of the social construct "desire," hence its product, "sexuality," hence its construct "woman," on the world.

The gender issue thus becomes the issue of what is taken to be "sexuality": what sex means and what is meant by sex, when, how, and with whom and with what consequences to whom. Such questions are almost never systematically confronted, even in discourses that purport feminist awareness. What sex is—how it comes to be attached and attributed to what it is, embodied and practiced as it is, contextualized in the ways it is, signifying and referring to what it does—is taken as a baseline, a given, except when explaining what happened when it is thought to have gone wrong. It is as if "erotic," for example, can be taken as having an understood referent, although it is never defined. Except to imply that it is universal yet individual, ultimately variable and plastic. Essentially indefinable but overwhelmingly positive. "Desire," the vicissitudes of which are endlessly extolled and philosophized in culture high and low, is not seen as fundamentally problematic or calling for explanation on the concrete, interpersonal operative level, unless (again) it is supposed to be there and is not. To list and analyze what seem to be the essential elements for male sexual arousal, what has to be there for the penis to work, seems faintly blasphemous, like a pornographer doing market research. Sex is supposed both too individual and too universally transcendent for that. To suggest that the sexual might be continuous with something other than sex itself—something like politics—is seldom done, is treated as detumescent, even by feminists. It is as if sexuality comes from the stork.

Sexuality, in feminist light, is not a discrete sphere of interaction or feeling or sensation or behavior in which preexisting social divisions may or may not be played out. It is a pervasive dimension throughout the whole of social life, a dimension along which gender pervasively occurs and through which gender is socially constituted; in this culture, it is a dimension along which other social divisions, like race and class, partly play themselves out. Dominance eroticized defines the imperatives of its masculinity, submission eroticized defines its femininity. So many distinctive features of women's

status as second class—the restriction and constraint and contortion, the servility and the display, the self-mutilation and requisite presentation of self as a beautiful thing, the enforced passivity, the humiliation—are made into the content of sex for women. Being a thing for sexual use is fundamental to it. This identifies not just a sexuality that is shaped under conditions of gender inequality but this sexuality itself as the dynamic of the inequality of the sexes. It is to argue that the excitement at reduction of a person to a thing, to less than a human being, as socially defined, is its fundamental motive force. It is to argue sexual difference as a function of sexual dominance. It is to argue a sexual theory of the distribution of social power by gender, in which this sexuality that is sexuality is substantially what makes the gender division be what it is, which is male dominant, wherever it is, which is nearly everywhere.

Across cultures, from this perspective, sexuality is whatever a given culture defines it as. The next questions concern its relation to gender asymmetry and to gender as a division of power. Male dominance appears to exist cross-culturally, if in locally particular forms. Is whatever defines women as "different" the same as whatever defines women as "inferior" the same as whatever defines women's "sexuality"? Is that which defines gender inequality as merely the sex difference also the content of the erotic, cross-culturally? In this view, the feminist theory of sexuality is its theory of politics, its distinctive contribution to social and political explanation. To explain gender inequality in terms of "sexual politics"[5] is to advance not only a political theory of the sexual that defines gender but also a sexual theory of the political to which gender is fundamental.

In this approach, male power takes the social form of what men as a gender want sexually, which centers on power itself, as socially defined. Masculinity is having it; femininity is not having it. Masculinity precedes male as femininity precedes female and male sexual desire defines both. Specifically, "woman" is defined by what male desire requires for arousal and satisfaction and is socially tautologous with "female sexuality" and "the female sex." In the permissible ways a woman can be treated, the ways that are socially considered not violations but appropriate to her nature, one finds the particulars of male sexual interests and requirements. In the concomitant sexual paradigm, the ruling norms of sexual attraction and expressions are fused with gender identity formation and affirmation, such that sexuality equals heterosexuality equals the sexuality of (male) dominance and (female) submission.

Post-Lacan, actually post-Foucault,[6] it has become customary to affirm that sexuality is socially constructed. Seldom specified is what, socially, it is constructed of, far less who does the constructing or how, when, or where. When capitalism is the favored social construct, sexuality is shaped and controlled and exploited and repressed by capitalism; capitalism creates sexuality as we know it. When sexuality is a construct of discourses of power, gender is never one of them; force is central to its deployment but only through repressing it, not through constituting it; speech is not concretely investigated for its participation in this construction process. "Constructed" seems to mean influenced by, directed, channeled, like a highway constructs traffic patterns. Not: Why cars? Who's driving? Where's everybody going? What makes mobility matter? Who can own a car? Are all these accidents not very accidental? Although there are partial exceptions (but disclaimers notwithstanding), the typical model of sexuality that is tacitly accepted remains deeply Freudian and essentialist: sexuality is an innate primary natural prepolitical unconditioned drive divided along the biological gender line, centering on heterosexual intercourse, that is, penile intromission, full actualization of which is repressed by civilization. Even if the sublimation aspect of this theory is rejected, or the reasons for the repression are seen to vary (for the survival of civilization or to maintain fascist control or to keep capitalism moving), sexual expression is implicitly seen as the expression of something that is to a significant extent presocial and is socially denied its full force. Sexuality remains precultural and universally invariant to some extent, social only in that it needs society to take what are always to some extent socially specific forms. The impetus itself is a hunger, an appetite founded on a biological need; what it is specifically hungry for and how it is satisfied is then open to endless cultural and individual variance, like cuisine, like cooking.

Allowed/not-allowed are this sexuality's basic ideological axes. The fact that sexuality is ideologically bounded is known. That there are its axes, central to the way its "drive" is driven, and that this is fundamental to the gender difference, is not.[7] Its basic normative assumption is that whatever is considered sexuality should be allowed to be "expressed." Whatever is called sex is attributed a normatively positive valence, an affirmative valuation. This ex cathedra assumption, affirmation of which appears indispensable to one's credibility on any subject that gets near the sexual, means that sex as such (whatever it is) is good—natural, healthy, positive, appropriate, pleasurable, wholesome, fine, one's own, and to be approved and expressed. This, sometimes characterized as "sex-positive," is, rather, obviously, a value judgment.

· · ·

While intending the opposite, some feminists have encouraged and participated in this type of analysis by conceiving rape as violence not sex. While this approach gave needed emphasis to rape's previously effaced elements of power and dominance, it obscured its elements of sex. Aside from failing to answer the rather obvious question, if it's violence not sex why didn't he just hit her, this approach made it impossible to see that violence is sex when it is practiced as sex. This is obvious once what sexuality is, is understood as a matter of what it means, of how it is interpreted. To say rape is violence not sex preserves the "sex is good" norm by simply distinguishing forced sex as "not sex," whether it means sex to the perpetrator or even, later, to the victim, who has difficulty experiencing sex without reexperiencing the rape. Whatever is sex, cannot be violent; whatever is violent, cannot be sex. This analytic wish-fulfillment makes it possible for rape to be opposed by those who would save sexuality from the rapists while leaving the sexual fundamentals of male dominance intact.

While much prior work on rape has analyzed it as a problem of inequality between the sexes but not as a problem of unequal sexuality on the basis of gender,[8] other contemporary explorations of sexuality that purport to be feminist lack comprehension either of gender as a form of social power or of the realities of sexual violence. For instance, the editors of *Powers of Desire* take sex "as a central form of expression, one that defines identity and is seen as a primary source of energy and pleasure."[9] This may be how it "is seen" but it is also how they, operatively, see it. As if women choose sexuality as definitive of identity. As if it is as much a form of women's "expression" as it is men's. As if violation and abuse are not equally central to sexuality as women live it.

The *Diary* of the Barnard conference on sexuality pervasively equates sexuality with 'pleasure.' "Perhaps the overall question we need to ask is: How do women . . . negotiate sexual pleasure?"[10] As if women under male supremacy have power to. As if "negotiation" is a form of freedom. As if pleasure and how to get it, rather than dominance and how to end it, is the "overall" issue sexuality presents feminism. As if women do just need a good fuck. In these texts, taboos are treated as real restrictions—as things that really are not allowed—instead of as guises under which hierarchy is eroticized. The domain of the sexual is divided into "restriction, repression and danger" on the one hand and "exploration, pleasure and agency" on the other.[11] This division parallels the ideological forms through which dominance and submission are eroticized, variously socially coded as heterosexuality's male/female, lesbian culture's butch/femme, and sadomasochism's top/bottom.[12] Speaking in role terms, the one who pleasures in the illusion of freedom and security within the reality of danger is the "girl"; the one who pleasures in the reality of freedom and security, within the illusion of danger is the "boy." That is, the *Diary* uncritically adopts as an analytical tool the central dynamic of the phenomenon it purports to be analyzing. Presumably, one is to have a sexual experience of the text.

The terms of these discourses preclude or evade crucial feminist questions. What do sexuality and gender inequality have to do with each other? How do dominance and submission become sexualized, or, why is hierarchy sexy? How does it get attached to male and female? Why does sexuality center on intercourse, the reproductive act by physical design? Is masculinity the enjoyment of violation, femininity the enjoyment of being violated? Is that the central meaning of intercourse? Why do "men love death"?[13] What is the etiology of heterosexuality in women? Is its pleasure women's stake in subordination?

Taken together and taken seriously, feminist inquiries into the realities of rape, battery, sexual harassment, incest, child sexual abuse, prostitution, and pornography answer these questions by suggesting a theory of the sexual mechanism. Its script, learning, conditioning, developmental logos, imprinting of the microdot, its deus ex machina, whatever sexual process term defines sexual arousal itself, is force, power's expression. Force is sex, not just sexualized; force is the desire dynamic, not just a response to the desired object when desire's expression is frustrated. Pressure, gender socialization, withholding benefits, extending indulgences, the how-to books, the sex therapy are the soft end; the fuck, the fist, the street, the chains, the poverty are the hard end. Hostility and contempt, or arousal of master to slave, together with awe and vulnerability, or arousal of slave to master—these are the emotions of this sexuality's excitement. "Sadomasochism is to sex what war is to civil life: the magnificent experience," writes Susan Sontag.[14] It is hostility—the desire, overt or hidden, to harm another person—that generates and enhances sexual excitement," writes Robert Stoller.[15] Harriet Jacobs, a slave, speaking of her systematic rape by her master, writes, "It seems less demeaning to give one's self, than to submit to compulsion."[16] Looking at the data, the force in sex and the sex in force is a matter of simple empirical description—unless one accepts the force in sex is not force anymore, it is just sex; or, if whenever a woman is forced it is what she really wants or it or she does not matter; or, unless prior aversion or sentimentality substitutes what one wants sex to be, or will condone or countenance as sex, for what is actually happening.

To be clear: what is sexual is what gives a man an erection. Whatever it takes to make a penis shudder and stiffen with the experience of its potency is what sexuality means culturally. Whatever else does, fear does, hostility does, hatred does, the helplessness of a child or a student or an infantilized or restrained or vulnerable woman does, revulsion does, death does. Hierarchy, a constant creation of person/thing, top/bottom, dominance/subordination relations does. What is understood as violation, conventionally penetration and intercourse, defines the paradigmatic sexual encounter. The scenario of sexual abuse is: you do what I say. These textualities become sexuality. All this suggests that that which is called sexuality is the dynamic of control by which male dominance—in forms that range from intimate to institutional, from a look to a rape—eroticizes as man and woman, as identity and pleasure. It is also that which maintains and defines male supremacy as a political system. Male sexual desire is thereby simultaneously created and serviced, never satisfied once and for all, while male force is romanticized, even sacralized, potentiated, and naturalized, by being submerged into sex itself.

In contemporary philosophical terms, nothing is "indeterminate" in the poststructuralist sense here; it is all too determinate.[17] Nor does its reality provide just one perspective on a relativistic interpersonal world that could mean anything or its opposite.[18] The reality of pervasive sexual abuse and its eroticization does not shift relative to perspective, although whether or not one will see it or accord it significance may. Interpretation varies relative to place in sexual abuse, certainly; but the fact that women are sexually abused as women, in a social matrix of sexualized subordination does not go away because it is often ignored or authoritatively disbelieved or interpreted out of existence. Indeed, some ideological supports for its persistence rely precisely upon techniques of social indeterminacy: no language but the obscene to describe the unspeakable; denial by the powerful casting doubt on the facticity of the injuries; actually driving its victims insane. Indeterminacy is a neo-Cartesian mind game that undermines the actual social meaning of words by raising acontextualized interpretive possibilities that have no real social meaning or real possibility of any, dissolving the ability to criticize actual meanings without making space for new ones. The feminist point is simple. Men are women's material conditions. If it happens to women, it happens.

Women often find ways to resist male supremacy and to expand their spheres of action. But they are never free of it. Women also embrace the standards of women's place in this regime as "our own" to varying degrees and in varying voices—as affirmation of identity and right to pleasure, in order to be loved and approved and paid, in order just to make

it through another day. This, not inert passivity, is the meaning of being a victim. The term is not moral: who is to blame or to be pitied or condemned or held responsible. It is not prescriptive: what we should do next. It is not strategic: how to construe the situation so it can be changed. It is not emotional: what one feels better thinking. It is descriptive: who does what to whom and gets away with it?

. . .

Pornography is a means through which sexuality is socially constructed, a site of construction, a domain of exercise. It constructs women as things for sexual use and constructs its consumers to desperately want women to desperately want possession and cruelty and dehumanization. Inequality itself, subjection itself, hierarchy itself, objectification itself, with self-determination ecstatically relinquished, is the apparent content of women's sexual desire and desirability. "The major theme of pornography as a genre," writes Andrea Dworkin, "is male power."[19] Women are in pornography to be violated and taken, men to violate and take them, either on screen or by camera or pen, on behalf of the viewer. Not that sexuality in life or in media never expresses love and affection; only that love and affection are not what is sexualized in this society's actual sexual paradigm, as pornography testifies to it. Violation of the powerless, intrusion on women, is. The milder forms, possession and use, the mildest of which is visual objectification, are. The sexuality of observation, visual intrusion and access, of entertainment, makes sex largely a spectator sport for its participants.

If pornography has not become sex to and from the male point of view, it is hard to explain why the pornography industry makes a known ten billion dollars a year selling it as sex mostly to men; why it is used to teach sex to child prostitutes, recalcitrant wives and girlfriends and daughters, and to medical students, and to sex offenders; why it is nearly universally classified as a subdivision of "erotic literature"; why it is protected and defended as if it were sex itself.[20] And why a prominent sexologist fears that enforcing the views of feminists against pornography in society would make men "erotically inert wimps." No pornography, no male sexuality.

A feminist critique of sexuality in this sense is advanced in Andrea Dworkin's *Pornography: Men Possessing Women*. Building on her earlier identification of gender inequality as a system of social meaning,[21] an ideology lacking basis in anything other than the social reality its power constructs and maintains, she argues that sexuality is a construct of that power, given meaning by, through, and in pornography. In this perspective, pornography is not harmless fantasy or a corrupt and confused misrepresentation of otherwise natural healthy sex, nor is it fundamentally a distortion, reflection, projection, expression, representation, fantasy, or symbol of it.[22] Through pornography, among other practices, gender inequality becomes both sexual and socially real. Pornography "reveals that male pleasure is inextricably tied to victimizing, hurting, exploiting."[23] "Dominance in the male system is pleasure."[24] Rape is "the defining paradigm of sexuality,"[25] to avoid which boys choose manhood and homophobia.[26]

Women, who are not given a choice, are objectified, or, rather, "the object is allowed to desire, if she desires to be an object."[27] Psychology sets the proper bounds of this objectification by terming its improper excesses "fetishism,"[28] distinguishing the uses from the abuses of women. Dworkin shows how the process and content of women's definition as women, an underclass, are the process and content of their sexualization as objects for male sexual use. The mechanism is (again) force, imbued with meaning because it is the means to death[29] and death is the ultimate sexual act, the ultimate making of a person into a thing.

. . .

To be sexually objectified means having a social meaning imposed on your being that defines you as to be sexually used, according to your desired uses, and then using you that way. Doing this is sex in the male system. Pornography is a sexual practice of this because it exists in a social system in which sex in life is no less mediated than it is in representation. There is no irreducible essence, no "just sex." If sex is a social construct of sexism, men have sex with their image of a woman. Pornography creates an accessible sexual object, the possession and consumption of which is male sexuality, to be possessed and consumed as which is female sexuality.

This is not because pornography depicts objectified sex but because it creates the experience of a sexuality which is itself objectified. The appearance of choice or consent, with their attribution to inherent nature, are crucial in concealing the reality of force. Love of violation, variously termed female masochism and consent, comes to define female sexuality, legitimizing the political system by concealing the force on which it is based.

In this system, a victim, usually female, always feminized, is "never forced, only actualized."[30] Women whose attributes particularly fixate men—such as women with large breasts—are seen as full of sexual desire. Women men want, want men. Women fake vaginal orgasms, the only 'mature' sexuality, because men demand that they enjoy vaginal penetration.[31] Raped women are seen as asking for it: if a man wanted her, she must have wanted him. Men force women to become sexual objects, "that thing which causes erection, then hold themselves helpless and powerless when aroused by her."[32] Men who sexually harass, say women sexually harass them. They mean they are aroused by women who turn them down. This elaborate projective system of demand characteristics—taken to pinnacles like fantasizing a clitoris in women's throats so that men can enjoy forced fellatio in real life assured that women do too—is surely a delusional and projective structure deserving of serious psychological study. Instead, it is women who resist it that are studied, seen as in need of explanation and adjustment, stigmatized as inhibited and repressed and asexual. The assumption that, in matters sexual, women really want what men want from women makes male force against women in sex invisible. It makes rape sex. Women's sexual "reluctance, dislike, and frigidity," women's puritanism and prudery in the face of this sex, is the "silent rebellion of women against the force of the penis . . . an ineffective rebellion, but a rebellion nonetheless."[33]

Nor is homosexuality without stake in this gendered sexual system. Putting to one side the obviously gendered content of expressly adopted roles, clothing, and sexual mimicry, to the extent the gender of a sexual object is crucial to arousal, the structure of social power that stands behind and defines gender is hardly irrelevant, even if it is rearranged.

Some have argued that lesbian sexuality—meaning here simply women having sex with women not men—solves the problem of gender by eliminating men from women's voluntary sexual encounters.[34] Yet women's sexuality remains constructed under conditions of male supremacy; women remain socially defined as women in relation to men; the definition of women as men's inferiors remains sexual even if not heterosexual, whether men are present at the time or not. To the extent gay men choose men because they are men, the meaning of masculinity is affirmed as well as undermined. It may also be that sexuality is so gender marked that it carries dominance and submission with it, no matter the gender of its participants.

. . .

As pornography connects sexuality with gender in social reality, the feminist critique of pornography connects feminist work on violence against women with its inquiry into women's consciousness and gender roles. It is not only that women are the principal targets of rape, which by conservative definition happens to almost half of all women at least once in their lives. It is not only that over a third of all women are sexually molested by older trusted male family members or friends or authority figures as an early, perhaps initiatory, interpersonal sexual encounter. It is not only that at least the same percentage as adult women are battered in homes by male intimates. It is not only that about a fifth of American women have been or are known to be prostitutes, and most cannot get out of it. It is not only that 85 percent of working women will be sexually harassed on the job, many physically, at some point in their working lives.[35] All this documents the extent and terrain of abuse and the effectively unrestrained and systematic sexual aggression of one-half of the population against the other half. It suggests that it is basically allowed.

It does not by itself show that availability for this treatment defines the identity attributed to that other half of the population; or, that such treatment, all this torment and debasement, is socially considered not only rightful but enjoyable, and is in fact enjoyed by the dominant half; or, that the ability to engage in such behaviors defines the identity of that half. And not only of that half. Now consider the content of gender roles. All the social requirements for male sexual arousal and satisfaction are identical to the gender definition of "female." All the essentials of the male gender role are also the qualities sexualized as 'male' in male dominant sexuality. If gender is a social construct, and sexuality is a social construct, and the question is, of what is each constructed, the fact that their contents are identical—not to mention that the word 'sex' refers to both—might be more than a coincidence.

As to gender, what is sexual about pornography is what is unequal about social life. To say that pornography sexualizes gender and genders sexuality means that it provides a concrete social process through which gender and sexuality become functions of each other. Gender and sexuality, in this view, become two different shapes taken by the single social equation of male with dominance and female with submission. Being this as identity, acting it as role, inhabiting and presenting it as self, is the domain of gender. Enjoying it as the erotic, centering upon when it elicits genital arousal, is the domain of sexuality. Inequality is what is sexualized through pornography; it is what is sexual about it. The more unequal, the more sexual. The violence against women in pornography is an expression of gender hierarchy, the extremity of the hierarchy expressed and created through the extremity of the abuse, producing the extremity of the male sexual response. Pornography's multiple variations on and departures from the male dominant/female submissive sexual/gender theme are not exceptions to these gender regularities. They affirm them. The capacity of gender reversals (dominatrixes) and inversions (homosexuality) to stimulate sexual excitement is derived precisely from their mimicry or parody or negation or reversal of the standard arrangement. This affirms rather than undermines or qualifies the standard sexual arrangement as the standard sexual arrangement, the definition of sex, the standard from which all else is defined, that in which sexuality as such inheres.

Such formal data as exist on the relationship between pornography and male sexual arousal tend to substantiate this connection between gender hierarchy and male sexuality. 'Normal' men viewing pornography over time in laboratory settings become more aroused to scenes of rape than to scenes of explicit but not expressly violent sex, even if (especially if?) the woman is shown as hating it.[36] As sustained exposure perceptually inures subjects to the violent component in expressly violent sexual material, its sexual arousal value remains or increases. "On the first day, when they see women being raped and aggressed against, it bothers them. By day five, it does not bother them at all, in fact, they enjoy it."[37] Sexual material that is seen as nonviolent, by contrast, is less arousing to begin with, becomes even less arousing over time,[38] after which exposure to sexual violence is sexually arousing.[39] Viewing sexual material containing express aggression against women makes normal men more willing to aggress against women.[40] It also makes them see a woman rape victim as less human, more object-like, less worthy, less injured, and more to blame for the rape. Sexually explicit material that is not seen as expressly violent but presents women as hysterically responsive to male sexual demands, in which women are verbally abused, dominated and degraded, and treated as sexual things, makes men twice as likely to report willingness to sexually aggress against women than they were before exposure. So-called nonviolent materials like these make men see women as less than human, as good only for sex, as objects, as worthless and blameworthy when raped, and as really wanting to be raped and as unequal to men.[41] As to material showing violence only, it might be expected that rapists would be sexually aroused to scenes of violence against women, and they are.[42] But many normal male subjects, too, when seeing a woman being aggressed against by a man, perceive the interaction to be sexual even if no sex is shown.[43]

Male sexuality is apparently activated by violence against women and expresses itself in violence against women to a significant extent. If violence is seen as occupying the most fully achieved end of a dehumanization continuum on which objectification occupies the least express end, one question that is raised is whether some form of hierarchy—the dynamic of the continuum—is currently essential for male sexuality to experience itself. If so, and gender is understood to be a hierarchy, perhaps the sexes are unequal so that men can be sexually aroused. To put it another way, perhaps gender

must be maintained as a social hierarchy so that men will be able to get erections; or, part of the male interest in keeping women down lies in the fact that it gets men up. Maybe feminists are considered castrating because equality is not sexy.

Recent inquiries into rape support such suspicions. Men often rape women, it turns out, because they want to and enjoy it. The act, including the dominance, is sexually arousing, sexually affirming, and supportive of the perpetrator's masculinity. Many unreported rapists report an increase in self-esteem as a result of the rape.[44] Indications are that reported rapists perceive that getting caught accounts for most of the unpleasant effects of raping.[45] About a third of all men say they would rape a woman if they knew they wouldn't get caught.[46] That the low conviction rate[47] may give them confidence is supported by the prevalence rate.[48] Some convicted rapists see rape as an "exciting" form of interpersonal sex, a recreational activity or "adventure," or as a means of revenge or punishment on all women or some subgroup of women or an individual woman. Even some of those who did the act out of bad feelings make it clear that raping made them feel better. "Men rape because it is rewarding to do so."[49] If rapists experience rape as sex, does that mean there can be nothing wrong with it?

. . .

Compare victims' reports of rape with women's reports of sex. They look a lot alike.[50] Compare victims' reports of rape with what pornography says is sex. They look a lot alike.[51] In this light, the major distinction between intercourse (normal) and rape (abnormal) is that the normal happens so often that one cannot get anyone to see anything wrong with it. Which also means that anything sexual that happens often and one cannot get anyone to consider wrong is intercourse not rape, no matter what was done. The distinctions that purport to divide this territory look more like the ideological supports for normalizing the usual male use and abuse of women as "sexuality" through authoritatively pretending that whatever is exposed of it is deviant. This may have something to do with the conviction rate in rape cases (making all those unconvicted men into normal men, and all those acts into sex). It may have something to do with the fact that most convicted rapists, and many observers, find rape convictions incomprehensible.[52] And the fact that marital rape is considered by many to be a contradiction in terms. ("But if you can't rape your wife, who can you rape?")[53] And the fact that so many rape victims have trouble with sex afterward.[54]

What effect does the pervasive reality of sexual abuse of women by men have on what are deemed the more ordinary forms of sexual interaction? How do these material experiences create interest and point of view? Consider women. Recall that over a third of all girls experience sex, perhaps are sexually initiated, under conditions that even this society recognizes are forced or at least unequal. Perhaps they learn this process of sexualized dominance as sex. Top-down relations feel sexual. Is sexuality throughout life then ever not on some level a reenactment of, a response to, that backdrop? Rape, adding more women to the list, can produce similar resonance. Sexually abused women—most women—seem to become either sexually disinclined or compulsively promiscuous or both in series, trying to avoid the painful events, and/or repeating them over and over almost addictively, in an attempt to reacquire a sense of control or to make them come out right. Too, women widely experience sexuality as a means to male approval; male approval translates into nearly all social goods. Violation can be sustained, even sought out, to this end. Sex can, then, be a means of trying to feel alive by redoing what has made one feel dead, of expressing a denigrated self-image seeking its own reflection in self-action in order to feel fulfilled, or of keeping up one's stock with the powerful.

· · ·

If the existing social model and reality of sexuality centers on male force, and if that sex is socially learned and ideologically considered positive and is rewarded, what is surprising is that not all women eroticize dominance, not all love pornography, and many resent rape. As Valerie Heller has said of her experience with incest and use in pornography both as a child and as an adult, "I believed I existed only after I was turned on, like a light switch, by another person. When I needed to be nurtured I thought I wanted to be used. . . . Marks and bruises and being used was the way I measured my self worth. You must remember that I was taught that

because men were fucking my body and using it for their needs it meant I was loved."[55] Given the pervasiveness of such experiences, the truly interesting question becomes why and how sexuality in women is ever other than masochistic.

All women live in sexual objectification like fish live in water. Given the statistical realities, all women live all the time under the shadow of the threat of sexual abuse. The question is, what can life as a woman mean, what can sex mean to targeted survivors in a rape culture? Given the statistical realities, much of women's sexual lives will occur under post-traumatic stress. Being surrounded by pornography—which is not only socially ubiquitous but often directly used as part of sex[56]—makes this a relatively constant condition. Women cope with objectification through trying to meet the male standard, and measure their self-worth by the degree to which they succeed. Women seem to cope with sexual abuse principally through denial or fear. On the denial side, immense energy goes into defending sexuality as just fine and getting better all the time, and into trying to make sexuality feel all right, like it is supposed to feel. Women who are compromised, cajoled, pressured, tricked, blackmailed, or outright forced into sex (or pornography) often respond to the unspeakable humiliation, coupled with the sense of having lost some irreplaceable integrity, by claiming that sexuality as their own. Faced with no alternatives, the strategy to acquire self-respect and pride is: I chose it.

Consider the conditions under which this is done. This is a culture in which women are socially expected—and themselves necessarily expect and want—to be able to distinguish the socially, epistemologically, indistinguishable. Rape and intercourse are not authoritatively separated by any difference between the physical acts or amount of force involved but only legally, by a standard that revolves around the man's interpretation of the encounter. Thus, although raped women, that is, most women, are supposed to be able to feel every day and every night that they have some meaningful determining part in having their sex life—their life, period—not be a series of rapes, the most they provide is the raw data for the man to see as he sees it. And he has been seeing pornography. Similarly, "consent" is supposed the crucial line between rape and intercourse, but the legal standard for it is so passive, so acquiescent, that a woman can be dead and have consented under it. The mind fuck of all of this makes the complicitous collapse into "I chose it" feel like a strategy for sanity. It certainly makes a woman at one with the world.

. . .

So long as sexual inequality remains unequal and sexual, attempts to value sexuality as women's, possessive as if women possess it, will remain part of limiting women to it, to what women are now defined as being. Outside of truly rare and contrapuntal glimpses (which almost everyone thinks they live almost their entire sex life within), to seek an equal sexuality, to seek sexual equality, without political transformation is to seek equality under conditions of inequality. Rejecting this, and rejecting the glorification of settling for the best inequality has to offer or has stimulated the resourceful to invent, are what Ti-Grace Atkinson meant to reject when she said, "I do not know any feminist worthy of that name who, if forced to choose between freedom and sex, would choose sex. She'd choose freedom every time."[57]

[1989]

NOTES

1. See Jane Caputi, *The Age of Sex Crime* (Bowling Green, Ohio: Bowling Green State University Popular Press, 1987); Deborah Cameron and Elizabeth Frazer, *The Lust to Kill: A Feminist Investigation of Sexual Murder* (New York: New York University Press, 1987).
2. E. Schur, *Labeling Women Deviant: Gender, Stigma and Social Control* (New York: Random House, 1983) (a superb review urging a "continuum" rather than a "deviance" approach to issues of sex inequality).
3. Diana Russell produced this figure at my request from the random sample data base of 930 San Francisco households discussed in her *The Secret Trauma: Incest in the Lives of Girls and Women*, pp. 20–37, and *Rape in Marriage*, pp. 27–41. The figure includes all the forms of rape or other sexual abuse or harassment surveyed, noncontact as well as contact, from gang rape by strangers and marital rape to obscene phone calls, unwanted sexual advances on the street, unwelcome requests to pose for pornography, and subjection to peeping toms and sexual exhibitionists (flashers).
4. S. D. Smithyman, "The Undetected Rapist" (Ph.D. diss., Claremont Graduate School, 1978); N. Groth, *Men Who Rape: The Psychology of the Offender* (New York: St. Martin's, 1982); D. Scully and J. Marolla, "'Riding the Bull at Gilley's': Convicted Rapists Describe the Rewards of Rape," *Social Problems* 32 (1985): 251. (The manuscript version of this paper was subtitled "Convicted Rapists Describe the Pleasure of Raping.")

5. K. Millett, *Sexual Politics* (New York: Doubleday, 1970).
6. J. Lacan, *Feminine Sexuality*, trans. J. Rose (New York: Norton, 1982); M. Foucault, *The History of Sexuality*, vol. 1, *An Introduction* (New York: Random House, 1980), and *Power/Knowledge*, ed. C. Gordon (New York: Pantheon, 1980).
7. The contributions and limitations of Foucault in such an analysis are discussed illuminatingly in Frigga Haug, ed., *Female Sexualization*, trans. Erica Carter (London: Verso, 1987), pp. 190–98.
8. Brownmiller did analyze rape as something men do to women, hence as a problem of gender, even if her concept of gender is biologically based (see, e.g., her pp. 4, 6, and discussion in chap. 3). An exception is Clark and Lewis.
9. A. Snitow, C. Stansell, and S. Thompson, introduction to *Powers of Desire: The Politics of Sexuality*, eds. A. Snitow, C. Stansell, and S. Thompson (New York: Monthly Review Press, 1983), p. 9.
10. C. Vance, "Concept Paper: Toward a Politics of Sexuality," in H. Alderfer, B. Jaker, and M. Nelson, eds., *Diary of a Conference on Sexuality*, record of the planning committee of the Conference, The Scholar and the Feminist IX: Toward a Politics of Sexuality, April 24, 1982, p. 27: to address "women's sexual pleasure, choice, and autonomy, acknowledging that sexuality is simultaneously a domain of restriction, repression and danger as well as a domain of exploration, pleasure and agency." Parts of the *Diary*, with the conference papers, were later published. C. Vance, ed., *Pleasure and Danger: Exploring Female Sexuality* (London: Routledge & Kegan Paul, 1984).
11. Vance, "Concept Paper," p. 38.
12. For examples, see A. Hollibaugh and C. Moraga, "What We're Rolling around in Bed with: Sexual Silences in Feminism," in Snitow, Stansell, and Thompson, eds., pp. 394–405, esp. 398; Samois, *Coming to Power* (Berkeley, Calif.: Samois, 1983).
13. A. Dworkin, "Why So-called Radical Men Love and Need Pornography," in Lederer, ed., p. 48.
14. S. Sontag, "Fascinating Fascism," in her *Under the Sign of Saturn* (New York: Farrar, Straus & Giroux, 1975), p. 103.
15. R. Stoller, *Sexual Excitement: Dynamics of Erotic Life* (New York: Pantheon, 1979), p. 6.
16. Harriet Jacobs, quoted by Rennie Simson, "The Afro-American Female: The Historical Context of the Construction of Sexual Identity," in Snitow, Stansell, and Thompson, eds., p. 231. Jacobs subsequently resisted by hiding in an attic cubbyhole "almost deprived of light and air, and with no space to move my limbs, for nearly seven years" to avoid him.
17. A similar rejection of indeterminancy can be found in Linda Alcoff, "Cultural Feminism versus Post-Structuralism: The Identity Crisis in Feminist Theory," *Signs: Journal of Women in Culture and Society* 13 (1988): 419–20. The article otherwise misdiagnoses the division in feminism as that between so-called cultural feminists and post-structuralism, when the division is between those who take sexual misogyny seriously as a mainspring to gender hierarchy and those who wish, liberal-fashion, to affirm "differences" without seeing that sameness/difference is a dichotomy of exactly the sort post-structuralism purports to deconstruct.

18. See Sandra Harding, "Introduction: Is There a Feminist Methodology?" in *Feminism and Methodology,* ed. Sandra Harding (Bloomington: Indiana University Press, 1987).
19. Dworkin, *Pornography,* p. 24.
20. J. Cook, "The X-rated Economy," *Forbes* (1978), p. 18; Langelan (see Appendix), p. 5; *Public Hearings on Ordinances to Add Pornography as Discrimination against Women,* Minneapolis, Minnesota: December 12 and 13, 1983 (hereafter cited as *Public Hearings*); F. Schauer, "Response: Pornography and the First Amendment," *University of Pittsburgh Law Review* 40 (1979): 616.
21. A. Dworkin, "The Root Cause," in *Our Blood: Prophesies and Discourses on Sexual Politics* (New York: Harper & Row, 1976), pp. 96–111.
22. See MacKinnon, *Toward a Feminist Theory of the State* (Cambridge, Mass.: Harvard University Press, 1989), chap. 12 for further discussion.
23. Dworkin, *Pornography* (Appendix), p. 69.
24. Ibid., p. 136.
25. Ibid., p. 69.
26. Ibid., chap. 2, "Men and Boys."
27. Ibid., p. 109.
28. Ibid., pp. 113–28.
29. Ibid., p. 174.
30. Ibid., p. 146.
31. A. Koedt, "The Myth of the Vaginal Orgasm," *Notes from the Second Year: Women's Liberation,* vol. 2 (1970): Ti-Grace Atkinson, *Amazon Odyssey* (New York: Link Books, 1974); Phelps.
32. Dworkin, *Pornography,* p. 22.
33. Dworkin, "The Root Cause," p. 56.
34. A prominent if dated example is Jill Johnston, *Lesbian Nation* (New York: Simon & Schuster, 1974).
35. Kathleen Barry defines "female sexual slavery" as a condition of prostitution that one cannot get out of.
36. E. Donnerstein, testimony, *Public Hearings* (see n. 20 above), pp. 35–36. The relationship between consenting and nonconsenting depictions and sexual arousal among men with varying self-reported propensities to rape are examined in the following studies: N. Malamuth, "Rape Fantasies as a Function of Exposure to Violent-Sexual Stimuli," *Archives of Sexual Behavior* 6 (1977): 33–47; N. Malamuth and J. Check, "Penile Tumescence and Perceptual Responses to Rape as a Function of Victim's Perceived Reactions," *Journal of Applied Social Psychology* 10 (1980): 528–47; N. Malamuth, M. Heim, and S. Feshbach, "The Sexual Responsiveness of College Students to Rape Depictions: Inhibitory and Disinhibitory Effects," *Journal of Personality and Social Psychology* 38 (1980): 399–408; N. Malamuth and J. Check, "Sexual Arousal to Rape and Consenting Depictions: The Importance of the Woman's Arousal," *Journal of Abnormal Psychology* 39 (1980): 763–66; N. Malamuth, "Rape Proclivity among Males," *Journal of Social Issues* 37 (1981): 138–57; E. Donnerstein and L. Berkowitz, "Victim Reactions in Aggressive Erotic Films as a Factor in Violence against Women," *Journal of Personality and Social Psychology* 41 (1981): 710–24; J. Check and T. Guloien, "Reported Proclivity for Coercive Sex Following Repeated Exposure to Sexually Violent Pornography, Nonviolent Dehumanizing Pornography, and Erotica,"

in *Pornography: Recent Research, Interpretations, and Policy Considerations,* ed. D. Zillman and J. Bryant (Hillside, N.J.: Erlbaum, in press).
37. Donnerstein, testimony, *Public Hearings,* p. 36.
38. The soporific effects of explicit sex depicted without express violence are apparent in the *Report of the President's Commission on Obscenity and Pornography* (Washington, D.C.: Government Printing Office, 1971).
39. Donnerstein, testimony, *Public Hearings,* p. 36.
40. Donnerstein and Berkowitz (see n. 36 above): E. Donnerstein, "Pornography: Its Effect on Violence against Women," in Malamuth and Donnerstein, eds. (*Aggression: Theoretical and Empirical Reviews* [New York: Academic, 1985]). This conclusion is the cumulative result of years of experimental research showing that "if you can measure sexual arousal to sexual images and measure people's attitudes about rape you can predict aggressive behavior with women" (Donnerstein, testimony, *Public Hearings,* p. 29). Some of the more prominent supporting experimental work, in addition to citations previously referenced here, include E. Donnerstein and J. Hallam, "The Facilitating Effects of Erotica on Aggression toward Females," *Journal of Personality and Social Psychology* 36 (1978): 1270–77; R. G. Green, D. Stonner, and G. L. Shope, "The Facilitation of Aggression by Aggression: Evidence against the Catharsis Hypothesis," *Journal of Personality and Social Psychology* 31 (1975): 721–26; D. Zillman, J. Hoyt, and K. Day, "Strength and Duration of the Effects of Aggressive, Violent, and Erotic Communications on Subsequent Aggressive Behavior," *Communications Research* 1 (1974): 286–306; B. Sapolsky and D. Zillman, "The Effect of Soft-core and Hard-core Erotica on Provoked and Unprovoked Hostile Behavior," *Journal of Sex Research* 17 (1981): 319–43; D. L. Mosher, "Pornographic Films, Male Verbal Aggression against Women, and Guilt," in *Technical Report of the Commission on Obscenity and Pornography* (Washington, D.C.: Government Printing Office, 1971), vol. 8. See also E. Summers and J. Check, "An Empirical Investigation of the Role of Pornography in the Verbal and Physical Abuse of Women," *Violence and Victims* 2 (1987): 189–209; and P. Harmon, "The Role of Pornography in Women Abuse" (Ph.D. diss., York University, 1987). These experiments establish that the relationship between expressly violent sexual material and subsequent aggression against women is causal, not correlational.
41. Key research is summarized and reported in Check and Galoien (see n. 36 above); see also D. Zillman, "Effects of Repeated Exposure to Nonviolent Pornography," presented to U.S. Attorney General's Commission on Pornography, Houston, Texas (June 1986). Donnerstein's most recent experiments, as reported in *Public Hearings* and his book edited with Malamuth (see n. 40 above), clarify, culminate, and extend years of experimental research by many. See, e.g., D. Mosher, "Sex Callousness toward Women," in *Technical Report of the Commission on Obscenity and Pornography,* vol. 8; N. Malamuth and J. Check, "The Effects of Mass Media Exposure on Acceptance of Violence against Women: A Field Experiment," *Journal of Research in Personality* 15 (1981): 436–46. The studies are tending to confirm women's reports and feminist analyses of the

consequences of exposure to pornography on attitudes and behaviors toward women. See J. Check and N. Malamuth ("An Empirical Assessment of Some Feminist Hypotheses about Rape." *International Journal of Women's Studies* 8 (1985): 414–23.).

42. G. G. Abel, D. H. Barlow, E. Blanchard, and D. Guild, "The Components of Rapists' Sexual Arousal," *Archives of General Psychiatry* 34 (1977): 395–403; G. G. Abel, J. V. Becker, and I. J. Skinner, "Aggressive Behavior and Sex," *Psychiatric Clinics of North America* 3 (1980): 133–55; G. G. Abel, E. B. Blanchard, J. V. Becker, and A. Djenderedjian, "Differentiating Sexual Aggressiveness with Penile Measures," *Criminal Justice and Behavior* 2 (1978): 315–32.

43. Donnerstein, testimony, *Public Hearings,* p. 31.

44. Smithyman (n. 4 above).

45. Scully and Marolla (n. 4 above).

46. In addition to previous citations to Malamuth, "Rape Proclivity among Males" (see n. 36 above); and Malamuth and Check, "Sexual Arousal to Rape and Consenting Depictions" (see n. 36 above); see T. Tieger, "Self-Reported Likelihood of Raping and the Social Perception of Rape," *Journal of Research in Personality* 15 (1981):147–58; and N. Malamuth, S. Haber, and S. Feshbach, "Testing Hypotheses Regarding Rape: Exposure to Sexual Violence, Sex Differences, and the 'Normality' of Rape," *Journal of Research in Personality* 14 (1980): 121–37.

47. M. Burt and R. Albin, "Rape Myths, Rape Definitions and Probability of Conviction," *Journal of Applied Social Psychology,* vol. 11 (1981); G. D. LaFree, "The Effects of Sexual Stratification by Race on Official Reactions to Rape," *American Sociological Review* 4–5 (1984): 842–54, esp. 850; J. Galvin and K. Polk, "Attribution in Case Processing: Is Rape Unique?" *Journal of Research in Crime and Delinquency* 20 (1983):126–54. The latter work seems not to understand that rape can be institutionally treated in a way that is sex-specific even if comparable statistics are generated by crimes against the other sex. Further, this study assumes that 53 percent of rapes are reported, when the real figure is closer to 10 percent (Russell, *Sexual Exploitation*).

48. Russell, "The Prevalence and Incidence of Forcible Rape and Attempted Rape of Females," pp. 1–4.

49. Scully and Marolla, p. 2.

50. Compare, e.g., Hite (*The Hite Report: A Nationwide Survey of Female Sexuality* [New York: Macmillan, 1976]) with Russell, *The Politics of Rape* (New York: Stein & Day, 1975).

51. This is truly obvious from looking at the pornography. A fair amount of pornography actually calls the acts it celebrates "rape." Too, "In depictions of sexual behavior [in pornography] there is typically evidence of a difference

of power between the participants" (L. Baron and M. A. Straus, "Conceptual and Ethical Problems in Research on Pornography" [paper presented at the annual meeting of the Society for the Study of Social Problems, 1983], p. 6)." Given that this characterizes the reality, consider the content attributed to "sex itself" in the following methodologically liberal quotations on the subject: "Only if one thinks of *sex itself* as a degrading act can one believe that all pornography degrades and harms women" (P. Califia, "Among Us, against Us— The New Puritans," *Advocate* [April 17, 1980], p. 14 [emphasis added]). Given the realization that violence against women *is* sexual, consider the content of the "sexual" in the following criticism: "The only form in which a politics opposed to violence against women is being expressed is anti-sexual" (English, Hollibaugh, and Rubin, "Talking Sex: A Conversation on Sexuality and Feminism," *Socialist Review,* vol. 11 [1981], p. 51). And "the feminist anti-pornography movement has become deeply erotophobic and anti-sexual" (A. Hollibaugh, "The Erotophobic Voice of Women," *New York Native* [1983], p. 34).

52. J. Wolfe and V. Baker, "Characteristics of Imprisoned Rapists and Circumstances of the Rape," in *Rape and Sexual Assault*, ed. C. G. Warner (Germantown, Md.: Aspen Systems Co., 1980).

53. This statement was widely attributed to California State Senator Bob Wilson; see Joanne Schulman, "The Material Rape Exemption in the Criminal Law," *Clearinghouse Review*, vol. 14 [1980]) on the Rideout marital rape case. He has equally widely denied that the comment was seriously intended. I consider it by now apocryphal as well as stunningly revelatory, whether or not humorously intended, on the topic of the indistinguishability of rape from intercourse from the male point of view.

54. Carolyn Craven, "No More Victims: Carolyn Craven Talks about Rape, and What Women and Men Can Do to Stop It," ed. Alison Wells (Berkeley, Calif., 1978, mimeographed), p. 2; Russell, *The Politics of Rape* (New York: Stein & Day, 1975), pp. 84–85, 105, 114, 135, 147, 185, 196, and 205; P. Bart, "Rape Doesn't End with a Kiss," *Viva* 11 (1975): 39–41 and 100–101; J. Becker, L. Skinner, G. Abel, R. Axelrod, and J. Cichon, "Sexual Problems of Sexual Assault Survivors," *Women and Health* 9 (1984): 5–20.

55. March for Women's Dignity, New York City, May 1984.

56. *Public Hearings* (n. 20 above); M. Atwood, *Bodily Harm* (Toronto: McClelland & Stewart, 1983), pp. 207–12.

57. Ti-Grace Atkinson, "Why I'm against S/M Liberation," in *Against Sadomasochism: A Radical Feminist Analysis,* ed. R. Linden, D. Pagano, D. Russell, and S. Star (East Palo Alto, Calif.: Frog in the Well, 1982), p. 91.

79

The Theoretical Subject(s) of This Bridge Called My Back *and Anglo-American Feminism*

NORMA ALARCÓN

NORMA ALARCÓN Mexico. 1943– . Literary scholar. Writer. Editor. Lives and works in the United States. Founder of Third Woman Press. *The Sexuality of Latinas* (1993), *Listening to the Silences: New Essays in Feminist Criticism* (1994), *T(r)opographies of Hunger: Conjugating Subjects in a Transnational Frame* (1998).

This Bridge Called My Back: Writings by Radical Women of Color, edited by Chicana writers Cherríe Moraga and Gloria Anzaldúa,[1] was intended as a collection of essays, poems, tales and testimonials that would give voice to the contradictory experiences of "women of color." In fact, the editors state:

We are the colored in a white feminist movement.
We are the feminists among the people of our culture.
We are often the lesbians among the straight.[2]

By giving voice to such experiences, each according to her style, the editors and contributors believed they were developing a theory of subjectivity and culture that would demonstrate the considerable differences between them and Anglo-American women, as well as between them and Anglo-European men and men of their own culture. As speaking subjects of a new discursive formation, many of *Bridge*'s writers were aware of the displacement of their subjectivity across a multiplicity of discourses: feminist/lesbian, nationalist, racial, socio-economic, historical, etc. The peculiarity of their displacement implies a multiplicity of positions from which they are driven to grasp or understand themselves and their relations with the real, in the Althusserian sense of the word.[3] *Bridge* writers, in part, were aware that these positions are often incompatible or contradictory, and others did not have access to the maze of discourses competing for their body and voice. The self-conscious effort to reflect on their "flesh and blood experiences to concretize a vision that can begin to heal our 'wounded knee'"[4] led many *Bridge* speakers to take a position in conflict with multiple intercultural and intracultural discursive interpretations in an effort to come to grips with "the many-headed demon of oppression."[5]

Since its publication in 1981, *Bridge* has had a diverse impact on Anglo-American feminist writings in the United States. Teresa de Lauretis, for example, claims that *Bridge* has contributed to a "shift in feminist consciousness,"[6] yet her explanation fails to clarify what the shift consists of and for whom. There is little doubt, however, that *Bridge*, along with the 1980s writings by many women of color in the United States, has problematized many a version of Anglo-American feminism, and has helped open the way for alternate feminist discourses and theories. Presently, however, the impact among most Anglo-American theorists appears to be more cosmetic than not because, as Jane Flax has recently noted, "The modal 'person' in feminist theory still appears to be a self-sufficient individual adult."[7] This particular "modal person" corresponds to the female subject most admired in literature, which Gayatri Chakravorty Spivak had characterized as one who "articulates herself in shifting relationship to . . . the constitution and 'interpellation' of the subject not only as individual but as 'individualist'."[8] Consequently, the "native female" or "woman of color" can be excluded from the discourse of feminist theory. The "native female"—object of colonialism and racism—is excluded because, in Flax's terms, white feminists have not "explored how our understanding of gender relations, self, and theory are partially constituted in and through experiences of living in a culture in which asymmetric race relations are a central organizing principle of society."[9] Thus, the most popular subject of Anglo-American feminism is an autonomous, self-making, self-determining subject who first proceeds according to the *logic of identification* with regard to the subject of consciousness, a notion usually viewed as the purview of man, but now claimed for women.[10] Believing that in this respect she is the same as man, she now claims the right to pursue her own identity, to name herself, to pursue self-knowledge, and, in the words of Adrienne Rich, to effect "a change in the concept of sexual identity."[11]

Though feminism has problematized gender relations, indeed, as Flax observes, gender is "the single most important advance in feminist theory,"[12] it has not problematized the subject of knowledge and her complicity with the notion of consciousness as "synthetic unificatory power, the centre and active point of organization of representations determining their concatenation."[13] The subject (and object) of knowledge is now a woman, but the inherited view of consciousness has not been questioned at all. As a result, some Anglo-American feminist subjects of consciousness have tended to become a parody of the masculine subject of consciousness, thus revealing their ethnocentric liberal underpinnings. In 1982, Jean Bethke Elshtain had noted the "masculine cast" of radical feminist language, for example, noting the terms of "raw power, brute force, martial discipline, law and order with a feminist face—and voice."[14] Also in critiquing liberal feminism and its language, she notes that "no vision of the political community that might serve as the groundwork of a life in common is possible within a political life dominated by a self-interested, predatory individualism."[15] Althusser argues that this tradition "has privileged the category of the 'subject' as Origin, Essence and Cause, responsible in its internality for all determinations of the external object. In other words, this tradition has promoted Man, in his ideas and experience, as the source of knowledge, morals and history."[16] By identifying in this way with this tradition, standpoint epistemologists have substituted, ironically, woman for man. This 'logic of identification' as a first step in constructing the theoretical subject of feminism is often veiled from standpoint epistemologists because greater attention is given to naming female identity, and describing women's ways of knowing as being considerably different than men's.[17] By emphasizing 'sexual difference,' the second step takes place, often called oppositional thinking (counteridentifying). However, this gendered standpoint epistemology leads to feminism's bizarre position with regard to other liberation movements, working inherently against the interests of non-white women and no one else. For example, Sandra Harding argues that oppositional thinking (counteridentification) with white men should be retained even though "[t]here

are suggestions in the literature of Native Americans, Africans, and Asians that what feminists call feminine versus masculine personalities, ontologies, ethics, epistemologies, and world views may be what these other liberation movements call Non-Western versus Western personalities and world views. . . . I set aside the crucial and fatal complication for this way of thinking—the fact that one half of these people are women and that most women are not Western."[18] She further suggests that feminists respond by relinquishing the totalizing "master theory" character of our theory-making: "This response to the issue [will manage] to retain the categories of feminist theory . . . and simply set them alongside the categories of the theory making of other subjugated groups. . . . Of course, it leaves bifurcated (and perhaps even more finely divided) the identities of all except ruling-class white Western women. . . ."[19] The apperception of this situation is precisely what led to the choice of title for the book *All the Women Are White, All the Blacks Are Men, But Some of Us Are Brave*, edited by Gloria T. Hull, Patricia Bell Scott and Barbara Smith.[20]

Notwithstanding the power of *Bridge* to affect the personal lives of its readers, *Bridge*'s challenge to the Anglo-American subject of feminism has yet to effect a newer discourse. Women of color often recognize themselves in the pages of *Bridge*, and write to say, "The women writers seemed to be speaking to me, and they actually understood what I was going through. Many of you put into words feelings I have had that I had no way of expressing. . . . The writings justified some of my thoughts telling me I had a right to feel as I did."[21] On the other hand, Anglo feminist readers of *Bridge* tend to appropriate it, cite it as an instance of difference between women, and proceed to negate that difference by subsuming women of color into the unitary category of woman/women. The latter is often viewed as the "common denominator" in an oppositional (counteridentifying) discourse with some white men, that leaves us unable to explore relationships among women.

Bridge's writers did not see the so-called "common denominator" as the solution for the construction of the theoretical feminist subject. In the call for submissions the editors clearly stated: "We want to express to all women—especially to white middle class women—the experiences which divide us as feminists; we want to explore the causes, and sources of, and solutions to these divisions. We want to create a definition that expands what 'feminist' means to us."[22] Thus, the female subject of *Bridge* is highly complex. She is and has been constructed in a crisis of meaning situation which includes racial and cultural divisions and conflicts. The psychic and material violence that gives shape to that subjectivity cannot be underestimated nor passed over lightly. The fact that not all of this violence comes from men in general but also from women renders the notion of "common denominator" problematic.

It is clear, however, that even as *Bridge* becomes a resource for the Anglo-American feminist theory classroom and syllabus, there's a tendency to deny differences if those differences pose a threat to the "common denominator" category. That is, unity would be purchased with silence, putting aside the conflictive history of groups' interrelations and interdependence. In the words of Paula Treichler, "[h]ow do we address the issues and concerns raised by women of color, who may themselves be even more excluded from theoretical feminist discourse than from the women's studies curriculum? . . . Can we explore our 'common differences' without overemphasizing the division that currently seems to characterize the feminism of the United States and the world?"[23] Clearly, this exploration appears impossible without a reconfiguration of the subject of feminist theory, and her relational position to a multiplicity of others, not just white men.

Some recent critics of the "exclusionary practices in Women's Studies" have noted that its gender standpoint epistemology leads to a 'tacking on' of "material about minority women" without any note of its "significance for feminist knowledge."[24] The common approaches noted were the tendency to 1) treat race and class as secondary features in social organization (as well as representation) with primacy given to female subordination; 2) acknowledge that inequalities of race, class and gender generate different experiences and then set race and class inequalities aside on the grounds that information was lacking to allow incorporation into an analysis; 3) focus on descriptive aspects of the ways of life, values, customs and problems of women in

subordinate race and class categories with little attempt to explain their source or their broader meaning. In fact, it may be impossible for gender standpoint epistemology to ever do more than a "pretheoretical presentation of concrete problems."[25] Since the subject of feminist theory and its single theme—gender—go largely unquestioned, its point of view tends to suppress and repress voices that question its authority, and as Jane Flax remarks, "The suppression of these voices seems to be a necessary condition for the (apparent) authority, coherence, and universality of our own."[26] This may account for the inability to include the voices of "women of color" into feminist discourse, though they are not necessarily under-represented in the reading list.

For the standpoint epistemologists, the desire to construct a feminist theory based solely on gender, on the one hand, and the knowledge or implicit recognition that such an account might distort the representation of many women and/or correspond to that of some men, on the other, gives rise to anxiety and ambivalence with respect to the future of that feminism, especially in Anglo-America. At the core of that attitude is the often unstated recognition that if the pervasiveness of women's oppression is virtually 'universal' on some level, it is also highly diverse from group to group and that women themselves may become complicitous with that oppression. "Complicity arises," says Macdonell, "where through lack of a positive starting point either a practice is driven to make use of prevailing values or a critique becomes the basis for a new theory."[27] Standpoint epistemologists have made use of the now gendered and feminist notion of consciousness, without too much question. (This notion, of course, represents the highest value of European culture since the Enlightenment.) The inclusion of other analytical categories such as race and class becomes impossible for a subject whose consciousness refuses to acknowledge that "one becomes a woman" in ways that are much more complex than in a simple opposition to men. In cultures in which "asymmetric race and class relations are a central organizing principle of society," one may also "become a woman" in opposition to other women. In other words, the whole category of woman may also need to be problematized, a point that I shall take up later. In any case, one should not step into that category nor that of man that easily or simply.

Simone de Beauvoir and her key work *The Second Sex* have been most influential in the development of feminist standpoint epistemology. She may even be responsible for the creation of Anglo-American feminist theory's "episteme": a highly self-conscious ruling class white Western female subject locked in a struggle to the death with "Man." De Beauvoir has shaken the world of women, most especially with the ramification of her phrase, "One is not born, but rather becomes, a woman."[28] For over 400 pages of text after that statement, de Beauvoir demonstrates how a female is constituted as a "woman" by society as her freedom is curtailed from childhood. The curtailment of freedom incapacitates her from affirming "herself as a subject."[29] Very few women, indeed, can escape the cycle of indoctrination except perhaps the writer/intellectual because "[s]he knows that she is a conscious being, a subject."[30] This particular kind of woman can perhaps make of her gender a project and transform her sexual identity.[31] But what of those women who are not so privileged, who neither have the political freedom nor the education? Do they now, then, occupy the place of the Other (the 'Brave') while some women become subjects? Or do we have to make a subject of the whole world?

Regardless of our point of view in this matter, the way to becoming a female subject has been effected through consciousness-raising. In 1982, in a major theoretical essay, "Feminism, Method and the State: An Agenda for Theory," Catharine A. MacKinnon cited *Bridge* as a book that explored the relationship between sex and race and argued that "consciousness-raising" was *the* feminist method.[32] The reference to *Bridge* was brief. It served as an example, along with other texts, of the challenge that race and nationalism have posed for Marxism. According to her, Marxism has been unable to account for the appearance of these emancipatory discourses nor has it been able to assimilate them. Nevertheless, MacKinnon's major point was to demonstrate the epistemological challenge that feminism and its primary method, "consciousness-raising," posed for Marxism. Within Marxism, class as method of analysis has failed to

reckon with the historical force of sexism. Through "consciousness-raising" (from women's point of view), women are led to know the world in a different way. Women's experience of politics, of life as sex objects, gives rise to its own method of appropriating that reality: feminist method. It challenges the objectivity of the "empirical gaze" and "rejects the distinction between knowing subject and known object."[33] By having women be the subject of knowledge, the so-called "objectivity" of men is brought into question. Often, this leads to privileging women's way of knowing in opposition to men's way of knowing, thus sustaining the very binary opposition that feminism would like to change or transform. Admittedly, this is only one of the many paradoxical procedures in feminist thinking, as Nancy Cott confirms: "It acknowledges diversity among women while positing that women recognize their unity. It requires gender consciousness for its basis, yet calls for the elimination of prescribed gender roles."[34]

However, I suspect that these contradictions or paradoxes have more profound implications than is readily apparent. Part of the problem may be that as feminist practice and theory recuperate their sexual differential, through "consciousness-raising," women reinscribe such a differential as feminist epistemology or theory. With gender as the central concept in feminist thinking, epistemology is flattened out in such a way that we lose sight of the complex and multiple ways in which the subject and object of possible experience are constituted. The flattening effect is multiplied when one considers that gender is often solely related to white men. There's no inquiry into the knowing subject beyond the fact of being a "woman." But what is a "woman," or a "man" for that matter? If we refuse to define either term according to some "essence," then we are left with having to specify their conventional significance in time and space, which is liable to change as knowledge increases or interests change. The fact that Anglo-American feminism has appropriated the generic term for itself leaves many a woman in this country having to call herself otherwise, i.e., "woman of color," which is equally "meaningless" without further specification. It also gives rise to the tautology "Chicana women." Needless to say, the requirement of gender consciousness only in relationship to man leaves us in the dark about a good many things, including interracial and intercultural relations. It may be that the only purpose this type of differential has is as a political strategy. It does not help us envision a world beyond binary restrictions, nor does it help us to reconfigure feminist theory to include the "native female." It does, however, help us grasp the paradox that within this cultural context one cannot be a feminist without becoming a gendered subject of knowledge, which makes it very difficult to transcend gender at all and to imagine relations between women.

In *Feminist Politics and Human Nature*, Alison M. Jaggar, speaking as a socialist feminist, refers repeatedly to *Bridge* and other works by women of color. In that work, Jaggar states that subordinated women are unrepresented in feminist theory. Jaggar claims that socialist feminism is inspired by Marxist and radical feminist politics though the latter has failed to be scientific about its insights. *Bridge* is cited various times to counter the racist and classist position of radical feminists.[35] Jaggar charges that "[r]adical feminism has encouraged women to name their own experience but it has not recognized explicitly that this experience must be analyzed, explained and theoretically transcended."[36] In a sense, Jaggar's charge amounts to the notion that radical feminists were flattening out their knowledge by an inadequate methodology, i.e. gender consciousness-raising. Many of Jaggar's observations are a restatement of *Bridge*'s challenge to Anglo-American feminists of all persuasions, be it Liberal, Radical, Marxist, and Socialist, the types sketched out by Jaggar. For example, "[a] representation of reality from the standpoint of women must draw on the variety of all women's experience"[37] may be compared to Barbara Smith's view in *Bridge* that "Feminism is the political theory and practice to free *all* women: women of color, working-class women, poor women, physically challenged women, lesbians, old women, as well as white economically privileged heterosexual women."[38] Jaggar continues, "Since historically diverse groups of women, such as working-class women, women of color, and others have been excluded from intellectual work, they somehow must be enabled to participate as subjects as well as objects of feminist theorizing."[39]

Writers in *Bridge* did appear to think that "consciousness-raising" and the naming of one's experience would deliver some theory and yield a notion of "what 'feminist' means to us."[40] Except for Smith's statement, there is no overarching view that would guide us as to "what 'feminist' means to us." Though there is a tacit political identity—gender/class/race-encapsulated in the phrase "women of color" that connects the pieces—they tend to split apart into "vertical relations" between the culture of resistance and the culture resisted or from which excluded. Thus, the binary restrictions become as prevalent between race/ethnicity of oppressed versus oppressor as between the sexes. The problems inherent in Anglo-American feminism and race relations are so locked into the "Self/Other" theme that it is no surprise that *Bridge*'s co-editor Moraga would remark, "In the last three years I have learned that Third World feminism does not provide the kind of easy political framework that women of color are running to in droves. The *idea* of Third World feminism has proved to be much easier between the covers of a book than between real live women."[41] She refers to the United States, of course, because feminism is alive and well throughout the Third World largely within the purview of women's rights, or as a class struggle.[42]

The appropriation of *Bridge*'s observations in Jaggar's work differs slightly from the others in its view of linguistic use, implying to a limited extent that language is also reflective of material existence. The crucial question is how, indeed, can women of color be subjects as well as objects of feminist theorizing? Jaggar cites María Lugones' doubts: "We cannot talk to you in our language because you do not understand it. . . . The power of white Anglo women vis-à-vis Hispanas and Black women is in inverse proportion to their working knowledge of each other. . . . Because of their ignorance, white Anglo women who try to do theory with women of color inevitably disrupt the dialogue. Before they can contribute to collective dialogue, they need to 'know the text,' to have become familiar with an alternative way of viewing the world. . . . You need to learn to become unintrusive, unimportant, patient to the point of tears, while at the same time open to learning any possible lessons. You will have to come to terms with the sense of alienation, of not belonging, of having your world thoroughly disrupted, having it criticized and scrutinized from the point of view of those who have been harmed by it, having important concepts central to it dismissed, being viewed with mistrust. . . ."[43] One of *Bridge*'s breaks with prevailing conventions is linguistic. Lugones' advice to Anglo women to listen was post-*Bridge*. If prevailing conventions of speaking/writing had been observed, many a contributor would have been censored or silenced. So would have many a major document or writing of minorities. *Bridge* leads us to understand that the silence and silencing of people begins with the dominating enforcement of linguistic conventions, the resistance to relational dialogues, as well as the disenablement of peoples by outlawing their forms of speech. Anglo-American feminist theory assumes a speaking subject who is an autonomous, self-conscious individual woman. Such theory does not discuss the linguistic status of the person. It takes for granted the linguistic status which founds subjectivity. In this way it appropriates woman/women for itself, and turns its work into a theoretical project within which the rest of us are compelled to 'fit.' By 'forgetting' or refusing to take into account that we are culturally constituted in and through language in complex ways and not just engendered in a homogeneous situation, the Anglo-American subject of consciousness cannot come to terms with her (his) own class-biased ethnocentrism. She is blinded to her own construction not just as a woman but as an Anglo-American one. Such a subject creates a theoretical subject that could not possibly include all women just because we are women. It is against this feminist backdrop that many "women of color" have struggled to give voice to their subjectivity and which effected the publication of the writings collected in *Bridge*. However, the freedom of women of color to posit themselves as multiple-voiced subjects is constantly in peril of repression precisely at that point where our constituted contradictions put us at odds with women different from ourselves.

The pursuit of a "politics of unity" solely based on gender forecloses the "pursuit of solidarity" through different political formations and the exploration of alternative theories of the subject of consciousness. There is a tendency in more sophisticated and elaborate gender standpoint epistemologists to affirm "an identity made up of heterogeneous and heteronomous representations of gender, race, and class, and often indeed across languages and cultures"[44] with one breath, and with the next to refuse to explore how that identity may be theorized or analyzed, by reconfirming a unified subjectivity or "shared consciousness" through gender. The difference is handed over with one hand and taken away with the other. If it be true, as Teresa de Lauretis has observed, that "[s]elf and identity . . . are always grasped and understood within particular discursive configurations . . . ,"[45] it does not necessarily follow that one can easily and self-consciously decide "to reclaim [an identity] from a history of multiple assimilations,"[46] and still retain a "shared consciousness." Such a practice goes counter to the homogenizing tendency of the subject of consciousness in the United States. To be oppressed means to be disenabled not only from grasping an "identity," but also from reclaiming it. In this culture, to grasp or reclaim an identity means always already to have become a subject of consciousness. The theory of the subject of consciousness as a unitary and synthesizing agent of knowledge is always already a posture of domination. One only has to think of Gloria Anzaldúa's essay in *Bridge,* "Speaking in Tongues: A Letter to Third World Women Writers."[47] Though de Lauretis concedes that a racial "shared consciousness" may have prior claims than gender, she still insists on unity through gender: "the female subject is always constructed and defined in gender, starting from gender."[48] One is interested in having more than an account of gender, there are other relations to be accounted for. De Lauretis insists, in most of her work, that "the differences among women may be better understood as differences within women."[49] This position returns us all to our solitary, though different, consciousness, without noting that some differences are (have been) a result of relations of domination of women by women; that differences may be purposefully constituted for the purpose of domination or exclusion, especially in oppositional thinking. Difference, whether it be sexual, racial, social, has to be conceptualized within a political and ideological domain.[50] In *Bridge,* for example, Mirtha Quintanales points out that "in this country, in this world, racism is used *both* to create false differences among us *and* to mask very significant ones—cultural, economic, political."[51]

One of the most remarkable tendencies in the work reviewed is the implicit or explicit acknowledgement that women of color are excluded from feminist theory, on the one hand, and on the other the reminder that though excluded from theory, their books are read in the classroom and/or duly footnoted. It is clear that some of the writers in *Bridge* thought at some point in the seventies that feminism could be the ideal answer to their hope for liberation. Chrystos, for example, states her disillusionment as follows: "I no longer believe that feminism is a tool which can eliminate racism or even promote better understanding between different races and kinds of women."[52] The disillusionment is eloquently reformulated in the theme poem by Donna Kate Ruchin, "The Bridge Poem."[53] The dream of helping the people who surround her to reach an interconnectedness that would change society is given up in favor of self-translation into a "true self." In my view, the speaker's refusal to play "bridge," an enablement to others as well as self, is the acceptance of defeat at the hands of political groups whose self-definition follows the view of self as unitary, capable of being defined by a single "theme." The speaker's perception that the "self" is multiple ("I'm sick of mediating with your worst self/on behalf of your better selves,")[54] and its reduction harmful gives emphasis to the relationality between one's selves and those of others as an ongoing process of struggle, effort and tension. Indeed, in this poem the better "bridging self" of the speaker is defeated by the overriding notion of the unitary subject of knowledge and consciousness so prevalent in Anglo-American culture. Consciousness as a site of multiple voicings is the theoretical subject, par excellence, of *Bridge*. Concomitantly, these voicings (or thematic threads) are not viewed as necessarily originating with the subject, but as discourses that transverse consciousness and which the subject must struggle with constantly. Rosario Morales, for example, says "I want to be whole. I want to claim myself to be puertorican and U.S. American, working class and middle class, housewife and intellectual, feminist, Marxist

and anti-imperialist."[55] Gloria Anzaldúa observes, "What am I? *A third world lesbian feminist with Marxist and mystic leanings.* They would chop me up into little fragments and tag each piece with a label."[56] The need to assign multiple registers of existence is an effect of the belief that knowledge of one's subjectivity cannot be arrived at through a single discursive "theme." Indeed, the multiple-voiced subjectivity is lived in resistance to competing notions for one's allegiance or self-identification. It is a process of disidentification[57] with prevalent formulations of the most forcefully theoretical subject of feminism. The choice of one or many themes is both theoretical and a political decision. Like gender epistemologists and other emancipatory movements, the theoretical subject of *Bridge* gives credit to the subject of consciousness as the site of knowledge but problematizes it by representing it as a weave. In Anzaldúa's terms, the woman of color has a "plural personality." Speaking of the new mestiza in *Borderlands/La Frontera,* she says, "[s]he learns to juggle cultures. . . . [the] juncture where the mestiza stands is where phenomena tend to collide."[58] As an object of multiple indoctrinations that heretofore have collided upon her, their new recognition as products of the oppositional thinking of others can help her come to terms with the politics of varied discourses and their antagonistic relations.

Thus, current political practices in the United States make it almost impossible to go beyond an oppositional theory of the subject, which is the prevailing feminist strategy and that of others; however, it is not the theory that will help us grasp the subjectivity of women of color. Socially and historically, women of color have been now central, now outside antagonistic relations between races, classes, and gender(s); this struggle of multiple antagonisms, almost always in relation to culturally different groups and not just genders, gives configuration to the theoretical subject of *Bridge*. It must be noted, however, that each woman of color cited here, even in her positing of a "plurality of self," is already privileged enough to reach the moment of cognition of a situation for herself. This should suggest that to privilege the subject, even if multiple-voiced, is not enough.

[1990]

NOTES

1. Hereafter cited as *Bridge,* the book has two editions. I use the second edition published by Kitchen Table Press, 1983. The first edition was published by Persephone Press, 1981.
2. Moraga and Anzaldúa, 23.
3. Louis Althusser, *Lenin and Philosophy and Other Essays,* Ben Brewster, tr. (London: New Left Books, 1971).
4. Moraga and Anzaldúa, 23.
5. Moraga and Anzaldúa, 195.
6. Teresa de Lauretis, *Technologies of Gender* (Bloomington: Indiana University Press, 1987), 10.
7. Jane Flax, "Postmodernism and Gender Relations in Feminist Theory," *Signs* 12:4 (Summer 1987), 640.
8. Gayatri Chakravorty Spivak, "Three Women's Texts and a Critique of Imperialism," *Critical Inquiry* 12:1 (Autumn 1985), 243–44.
9. Flax, 640.
10. Julia Kristeva, "Women's Time," *Signs* 7:1 (Autumn 1981), 19.
11. Adrienne Rich, *On Lies, Secrets and Silence* (New York: W. W. Norton, 1979), 35.
12. Flax, 627.
13. Michel Pecheux, *Language, Semantics and Ideology* (New York: St. Martin's Press, 1982), 122.
14. Jean Bethke Elshtain, "Feminist Discourse and Its Discontents: Language, Power, and Meaning," *Signs* 7:3 (Spring 1982), 611.
15. Elshtain, 617.
16. Diane Macdonell, *Theories of Discourse: An Introduction* (New York: Basil Blackwell, 1986), 76.
17. For an intriguing demonstration of these operations, see Seyla Benhabib, "The Generalized and the Concrete Other: The Kohlberg-Gilligan Controversy and Feminist Theory" in Seyla Benhabib and Drucilla Cornell, *Feminism as Critique* (Minneapolis: University of Minnesota Press, 1987), 77–95.
18. Sandra Harding, "The Instability of the Analytical Categories of Feminist Theory," *Signs* 11:4 (Summer 1986), 659.
19. Harding, 660.
20. Gloria T. Hull, Patricia B. Scott and Barbara Smith, eds., *All the Women Are White, All the Blacks Are Men, But Some of Us Are Brave* (Westbury, N.Y.: Feminist Press, 1982).
21. Moraga and Anzaldúa, Foreword to the Second Edition, n.p.
22. Moraga and Anzaldúa, Introduction to the First Edition, xxiii.
23. Paula Treichler, "Teaching Feminist Theory," *Theory in the Classroom,* Cary Nelson, ed. (Urbana: University of Illinois Press, 1986), 79.
24. Maxine Baca Zinn, Lynn Weber Cannon, Elizabeth Higginbotham and Bonnie Thornton Dill, "The Cost of Exclusionary Practices in Women's Studies," *Signs* 11:4 (Summer 1986), 296.
25. Baca Zinn *et al.,* 296–97.
26. Flax, 633.
27. Macdonell, 62.
28. Simone de Beauvoir, *The Second Sex* (New York: Vintage Books, 1974), 301.
29. de Beauvoir, 316.
30. de Beauvoir, 761.
31. For a detailed discussion of this theme, see Judith Butler, "Variations on Sex and Gender: Beauvoir, Wittig, and Foucault" in Benhabib and Cornell, 128–42.
32. Catharine MacKinnon, "Feminism, Marxism, Method and the State: An Agenda for Theory," *Signs* 7:3 (Spring 1982), 536–38.
33. MacKinnon, 536.
34. Nancy F. Cott, "Feminist Theory and Feminist Movements: The Past before Us," *What Is Feminism? A Re-Examination,* Juliet Mitchell and Ann Oakley, eds. (New York: Pantheon Books, 1986), 49.
35. Alison M. Jaggar, *Feminist Politics and Human Nature* (Totowa, N.J.: Rowman & Allanheld, 1983), 249–50; 295–96.
36. Jaggar, 381.
37. Jaggar, 386.
38. Moraga and Anzaldúa, 61.
39. Jaggar, 386.
40. Moraga and Anzaldúa, Introduction, xxiii.
41. Moraga and Anzaldúa, Foreword to the Second Edition, n.p.
42. Miranda Davies, *Third World: Second Sex* (London: Zed Books, 1987).
43. Jaggar, 386.
44. Teresa de Lauretis, "Feminist Studies/Critical Studies: Issues, Terms, and Contexts," *Feminist Studies/Critical Studies,* Teresa de Lauretis, ed. (Bloomington: Indiana University Press, 1986), 9.
45. de Lauretis, *Feminist Studies,* 8.
46. de Lauretis, *Feminist Studies,* 9.
47. Moraga and Anzaldúa, 165–74.
48. de Lauretis, *Feminist Studies,* 14.
49. de Lauretis, *Feminist Studies,* 14.
50. Monique Wittig, cited in Elizabeth Meese, *Crossing the Double-Cross: The Practice of Feminist Criticism* (Chapel Hill: University of North Carolina Press, 1986), 74.
51. Moraga and Anzaldúa, 153.
52. Moraga and Anzaldúa, 69.
53. Moraga and Anzaldúa, xxi–xxii.
54. Moraga and Anzaldúa, xxii.
55. Moraga and Anzaldúa, 91.
56. Moraga and Anzaldúa, 205.
57. Pecheux, 158–59.
58. Gloria Anzaldúa, *Borderlands/La Frontera: The New Mestiza* (San Francisco: Spinsters/Aunt Lute, 1987), 79.

80

From Gender Trouble: Feminism and the Subversion of Identity

JUDITH BUTLER

JUDITH BUTLER United States. 1956– . Philosopher. Theorist. *Gender Trouble* is considered the founding text of queer theory. *Bodies That Matter: On the Discursive Limits of "Sex"* (1993), *Excitable Speech: A Politics of the Performative* (1997), *Antigone's Claim: Kinship between Life and Death* (2000), *Giving an Account of Oneself* (2005), *Who Sings the Nation-State?: Language, Politics and Belonging* with Gayatri Spivak (2007).

BODILY INSCRIPTIONS, PERFORMATIVE SUBVERSIONS

"Garbo 'got in drag' whenever she took some heavy glamour part, whenever she melted in or out of a man's arms, whenever she simply let that heavenly-flexed neck . . . bear the weight of her thrown-back head. . . . How resplendent seems the art of acting! It is all impersonation, whether the sex underneath is true or not."

—Parker Tyler, "The Garbo Image," quoted in Esther Newton, *Mother Camp*

Categories of true sex, discrete gender, and specific sexuality have constituted the stable point of reference for a great deal of feminist theory and politics. These constructs of identity serve as the points of epistemic departure from which theory emerges and politics itself is shaped. In the case of feminism, politics is ostensibly shaped to express the interests, the perspectives, of "women." But is there a political shape to "women," as it were, that precedes and prefigures the political elaboration of their interests and epistemic point of view? How is that identity shaped, and is it a political shaping that takes the very morphology and boundary of the sexed body as the ground, surface, or site of cultural inscription? What circumscribes that site as "the female body"? Is "the body" or "the sexed body" the firm foundation on which gender and systems of compulsory sexuality operate? Or is "the body" itself shaped by political forces with strategic interests in keeping that body bounded and constituted by the markers of sex?

The sex/gender distinction and the category of sex itself appear to presuppose a generalization of "the body" that preexists the acquisition of its sexed significance. This "body" often appears to be a passive medium that is signified by an inscription from a cultural source figured as "external" to that body. Any theory of the culturally constructed body, however, ought to question "the body" as a construct of suspect generality when it is figured as passive and prior to discourse. There are Christian and Cartesian precedents to such views which, prior to the emergence of vitalistic biologies in the nineteenth century, understand "the body" as so much inert matter, signifying nothing or, more specifically, signifying a profane void, the fallen state: deception, sin, the premonitional metaphorics of hell and the eternal feminine. There are many occasions in both Sartre's and Beauvoir's work where "the body" is figured as a mute facticity, anticipating some meaning that can be attributed only by a transcendent consciousness, understood in Cartesian terms as radically immaterial. But what establishes this dualism for us? What separates off "the body" as indifferent to signification, and signification itself as the act of a radically disembodied consciousness or, rather, the act that radically disembodies that consciousness? To what extent is that Cartesian dualism presupposed in phenomenology adapted to the structuralist frame in which mind/body is redescribed as culture/nature? With respect to gender discourse, to what extent do these problematic dualisms still operate within the very descriptions that are supposed to lead us out of that binarism and its implicit hierarchy? How are the contours of the body clearly marked as the taken-for-granted ground or surface upon which gender significations are inscribed, a mere facticity devoid of value, prior to significance?

Wittig suggests that a culturally specific epistemic *a priori* establishes the naturalness of "sex." But by what enigmatic means has "the body" been accepted as a *prima facie* given that admits of no genealogy? Even within Foucault's essay on the very theme of genealogy, the body is figured as a surface and the scene of a cultural inscription: "the body is the inscribed surface of events."[1] The task of genealogy, he claims, is "to expose a body totally imprinted by history." His sentence continues, however, by referring to the goal of "history"—here clearly understood on the model of Freud's "civilization"—as the "destruction of the body" (148). Forces and impulses with multiple directionalities are precisely that which history both destroys and preserves through the *entstehung* (historical event) of inscription. As "a volume in perpetual disintegration" (148), the body is always under siege, suffering destruction by the very terms of history. And history is the creation of values and meanings by a signifying practice that requires the subjection of the body. This corporeal destruction is necessary to produce the speaking subject and its significations. This is a body, described through the language of surface and force, weakened through a "single drama" of domination, inscription, and creation (150). This is not the *modus vivendi* of one kind of history rather than another, but is, for Foucault, "history" (148) in its essential and repressive gesture.

Although Foucault writes, "Nothing in man [*sic*]—not even his body—is sufficiently stable to serve as the basis for self-recognition or for understanding other men [*sic*]" (153), he nevertheless points to the constancy of cultural inscription as a "single drama" that acts on the body. If the creation of values, that historical mode of signification, requires the destruction of the body, much as the instrument of torture in Kafka's *In the Penal Colony* destroys the body on which it writes, then there must be a body prior to that inscription, stable and self-identical, subject to that sacrificial destruction. In a sense, for Foucault, as for Nietzsche, cultural values emerge as the result of an inscription on the body, understood as a medium, indeed, a blank page; in order for this inscription to signify, however, that medium must itself be destroyed—that is, fully transvaluated into a sublimated domain of values. Within the metaphorics of this notion of cultural values is the figure of history as a relentless writing instrument, and the body as the medium which must be destroyed and transfigured in order for "culture" to emerge.

By maintaining a body prior to its cultural inscription, Foucault appears to assume a materiality prior to signification and form. Because this distinction operates as essential to the task of genealogy as he defines it, the distinction itself is precluded as an object of genealogical investigation. Occasionally in his analysis of Herculine, Foucault subscribes to a prediscursive multiplicity of bodily forces that break through the surface of the body to disrupt the regulating practices of cultural coherence imposed upon that body by a power regime, understood as a vicissitude of "history." If the presumption of some kind of precategorical source of disruption is refused, is it still possible to give a genealogical account of the demarcation of the body as such as a signifying practice? This demarcation is not initiated by a reified history or by a subject. This marking is the result of a diffuse and active structuring of the social field. This signifying practice effects a social space for and of the body within certain regulatory grids of intelligibility.

Mary Douglas' *Purity and Danger* suggests that the very contours of "the body" are established through markings that seek to establish specific codes of cultural coherence. Any discourse that establishes the boundaries of the body serves the purpose of instating and naturalizing certain taboos regarding the appropriate limits, postures, and modes of exchange that define what it is that constitutes bodies:

> ideas about separating, purifying, demarcating and punishing transgressions have as their main function to impose system on an inherently untidy experience. It is only by exaggerating the difference between within and without, above and below, male and female, with and against, that a semblance of order is created.[2]

Although Douglas clearly subscribes to a structuralist distinction between an inherently unruly nature and an order imposed by cultural means, the "untidiness" to which she refers can be redescribed as a region of *cultural* unruliness and disorder. Assuming the inevitably binary structure of the nature/culture distinction, Douglas cannot point toward an alternative configuration of culture in which such distinctions become malleable or proliferate beyond the binary frame. Her analysis, however, provides a possible point of departure for understanding the relationship by which social taboos institute and maintain the boundaries of the body as such. Her analysis suggests that what constitutes the limit of the body is never merely material, but that the surface, the skin, is systemically signified by taboos and anticipated transgressions; indeed, the boundaries of the body become, within her analysis, the limits of the social *per se*. A poststructuralist appropriation of her view might well understand the boundaries of the body as the limits of the socially *hegemonic*. In a variety of cultures, she maintains, there are

> pollution powers which inhere in the structure of ideas itself and which punish a symbolic breaking of that which should be joined or joining of that which should be separate. It follows from this that pollution is a type of danger which is not likely to occur except where the lines of structure, cosmic or social, are clearly defined.

> A polluting person is always in the wrong. He [*sic*] has developed some wrong condition or simply crossed over some line which should not have been crossed and this displacement unleashes danger for someone.[3]

In a sense, Simon Watney has identified the contemporary construction of "the polluting person" as the person with AIDS in his *Policing Desire: AIDS, Pornography, and the Media*.[4] Not only is the illness figured as the "gay disease," but throughout the media's hysterical and homophobic response to the illness there is a tactical construction of a continuity between the polluted status of the homosexual by virtue of the boundary-trespass that *is* homosexuality and the disease as a specific modality of homosexual pollution. That the disease is transmitted through the exchange of bodily fluids suggests within the sensationalist graphics of homophobic signifying systems the dangers that permeable bodily boundaries present to the social order as such. Douglas remarks that "the body is a model that can stand for any bounded system. Its boundaries can represent any boundaries which are threatened or precarious."[5] And she asks a question which one might have expected to read in Foucault: "Why should bodily margins be thought to be specifically invested with power and danger?"[6]

Douglas suggests that all social systems are vulnerable at their margins, and that all margins are accordingly considered dangerous. If the body is synecdochal for the social system *per se* or a site in which open systems converge, then any kind of unregulated permeability constitutes a site of pollution and endangerment. Since anal and oral sex among men clearly establishes certain kinds of bodily permeabilities unsanctioned by the hegemonic order, male homosexuality would, within such a hegemonic point of view, constitute a site of danger and pollution, prior to and regardless of the cultural presence of AIDS. Similarly, the "polluted" status of lesbians, regardless of their low-risk status with respect to AIDS, brings into relief the dangers of their bodily exchanges. Significantly, being "outside" the hegemonic order does not signify being "in" a state of filthy and untidy nature. Paradoxically, homosexuality is almost always conceived within the homophobic signifying economy as *both* uncivilized and unnatural.

The construction of stable bodily contours relies upon fixed sites of corporeal permeability and impermeability. Those sexual practices in both homosexual and heterosexual contexts that open surfaces and orifices to erotic signification or close down others effectively reinscribe the boundaries of the body along new cultural lines. Anal sex among men is an example, as is the radical re-membering of the body in Wittig's *The Lesbian Body*. Douglas alludes to "a kind of sex pollution which expresses a desire to keep the body (physical and social) intact,"[7] suggesting that the naturalized notion of "the" body is itself a consequence of taboos that render that body discrete by virtue of its stable boundaries. Further, the rites of passage that govern various bodily orifices presuppose a heterosexual construction of gendered exchange, positions, and erotic possibilities. The deregulation of such exchanges accordingly disrupts the very boundaries that determine what it is to be a body at all. Indeed, the critical inquiry that traces the regulatory practices within which bodily contours are constructed constitutes precisely the genealogy of "the body" in its discreteness that might further radicalize Foucault's theory.[8]

Significantly, Kristeva's discussion of abjection in *The Powers of Horror* begins to suggest the uses of this structuralist notion of a boundary-constituting taboo for the purposes of constructing a discrete subject through exclusion.[9] The "abject" designates that which has been expelled from the body, discharged as excrement, literally rendered "Other." This appears as an expulsion of alien elements, but the alien is effectively established through this expulsion. The construction of the "not-me" as the abject establishes the boundaries of the body, which are also the first contours of the subject. Kristeva writes:

> *nausea* makes me balk at that milk cream, separates me from the mother and father who proffer it. "I" want none of that element, sign of their desire; "I" do not want to listen, "I" do not assimilate it, "I" expel it. But since the food is not an "other" for "me," who am only in their desire, I expel *myself,* I spit *myself* out, I abject *myself* within the same motion through which "I" claim to establish myself.[10]

The boundary of the body as well as the distinction between internal and external is established through the ejection and transvaluation of something originally part of identity into a defiling otherness. As Iris Young has suggested in her use of Kristeva to understand sexism, homophobia, and racism, the repudiation of bodies for their sex, sexuality, and/or color is an "expulsion" followed by a "repulsion" that founds and consolidates culturally hegemonic identities along sex/race/sexuality axes of differentiation.[11] Young's appropriation of Kristeva shows how the operation of repulsion can consolidate "identities" founded on the instituting of the "Other" or a set of Others through exclusion and domination. What constitutes through division the "inner" and "outer" worlds of the subject is a border and boundary tenuously maintained for the purposes of social regulation and control. The boundary between the inner and outer is confounded by those excremental passages in which the inner effectively becomes outer, and this excreting function becomes, as it were, the model by which other forms of identity-differentiation are accomplished. In effect, this is the mode by which Others become shit. For inner and outer worlds to remain utterly distinct, the entire surface of the body would have to achieve an impossible impermeability. This sealing of its surfaces would constitute the seamless boundary of the subject; but this enclosure would invariably be exploded by precisely that excremental filth that it fears.

Regardless of the compelling metaphors of the spatial distinctions of inner and outer, they remain linguistic terms that facilitate and articulate a set of fantasies, feared and desired. "Inner" and "outer" make sense only with reference to a mediating boundary that strives for stability. And this stability, this coherence, is determined in large part by cultural orders that sanction the subject and compel its differentiation from the abject. Hence, "inner" and "outer" constitute a binary distinction that stabilizes and consolidates the coherent subject. When that subject is challenged, the meaning and necessity of the terms are subject to displacement. If the "inner world" no longer designates a topos, then the internal fixity of the self and, indeed, the internal locale of gender identity, become similarly suspect. The critical question is not *how* did that identity become *internalized*? as if internalization were a process or a mechanism that might be descriptively reconstructed. Rather, the question is: From what strategic position in public discourse and for what reasons has the trope of interiority and the disjunctive binary of inner/outer taken hold? In what language is "inner space" figured? What kind of figuration is it, and through what figure of the body is it signified? How does a body figure on its surface the very invisibility of its hidden depth?

FROM INTERIORITY TO GENDER PERFORMATIVES

In *Discipline and Punish* Foucault challenges the language of internalization as it operates in the service of the disciplinary regime of the subjection and subjectivation of criminals.[12] Although Foucault objected to what he understood to be the psychoanalytic belief in the "inner" truth of sex in *The History of Sexuality,* he turns to a criticism of the doctrine of internalization for separate purposes in the context of his history of criminology. In a sense, *Discipline and Punish* can be read as Foucault's effort to rewrite Nietzsche's doctrine of internalization in *On the Genealogy of Morals* on the model of *inscription.* In the context of prisoners, Foucault writes, the strategy has been not to enforce a repression of their desires, but to compel their bodies to signify the prohibitive law as their very essence, style, and necessity. That law is not literally internalized, but incorporated, with the consequence that bodies are produced which signify that law on and through the body; there the law is manifest as the essence of their selves, the meaning of their soul, their conscience, the law of their desire. In effect, the law is at once fully manifest and fully latent, for it never appears as external to the bodies it subjects and subjectivates. Foucault writes:

> It would be wrong to say that the soul is an illusion, or an ideological effect. On the contrary, it exists, it has a reality, it is produced permanently *around, on, within,* the body by the functioning of a power that is exercised on those that are punished (my emphasis).[13]

The figure of the interior soul understood as "within" the body is signified through its inscription *on* the body, even though its primary mode of signification is through its very absence, its potent invisibility. The effect of a structuring inner space is produced through the signification of a body as a vital and sacred enclosure. The soul is precisely what the body lacks; hence, the body presents itself as a signifying lack. That lack which *is* the body signifies the soul as that which cannot show. In this sense, then, the soul is a surface signification that contests and displaces the inner/outer distinction itself, a figure of interior psychic space inscribed *on* the body as a social signification that perpetually renounces itself as such. In Foucault's terms, the soul is not imprisoned by or within the body, as some Christian imagery would suggest, but "the soul is the prison of the body."[14]

The redescription of intrapsychic processes in terms of the surface politics of the body implies a corollary redescription of gender as the disciplinary production of the figures of fantasy through the play of presence and absence on the body's surface, the construction of the gendered body through a series of exclusions and denials, signifying absences. But what determines the manifest and latent text of the body politic? What is the prohibitive law that generates the corporeal stylization of gender, the fantasied and fantastic figuration of the body? We have already considered the incest taboo and the prior taboo against homosexuality as the generative moments of gender identity, the prohibitions that produce identity along the culturally intelligible grids of an idealized and compulsory heterosexuality. That disciplinary production of gender effects a false stabilization of gender in the interests of the heterosexual construction and regulation of sexuality within the reproductive domain. The construction of coherence conceals the gender discontinuities that run rampant within heterosexual, bisexual, and gay and lesbian contexts in which gender does not necessarily follow from sex, and desire, or sexuality generally, does not seem to follow from gender—indeed, where none of these dimensions of significant corporeality express or reflect one another. When the disorganization and disaggregation of the field of bodies disrupt the regulatory fiction of heterosexual coherence, it seems that the expressive model loses its descriptive force. That regulatory ideal is then exposed as a norm and a fiction that disguises itself as a developmental law regulating the sexual field that it purports to describe.

According to the understanding of identification as an enacted fantasy or incorporation, however, it is clear that coherence is desired, wished for, idealized, and that this idealization is an effect of a corporeal signification. In other words, acts, gestures, and desire produce the effect of an internal core or substance, but produce this *on the surface* of the body, through the play of signifying absences that suggest, but never reveal, the organizing principle of identity as a cause. Such acts, gestures, enactments, generally construed, are *performative* in the sense that the essence or identity that they otherwise purport to express are *fabrications* manufactured and sustained through corporeal signs and other discursive means. That the gendered body is performative suggests that it has no ontological status apart from the various acts which constitute its reality. This also suggests that if that reality is fabricated as an interior essence, that very interiority is an effect and function of a decidedly public and social discourse, the public regulation of fantasy through the surface politics of the body, the gender border control that differentiates inner from outer, and so institutes the "integrity" of the subject. In other words, acts and gestures, articulated and enacted desires create the illusion of an interior and organizing gender core, an illusion discursively maintained for the purposes of the regulation of sexuality within the obligatory frame of reproductive heterosexuality. If the "cause" of desire, gesture, and act can be localized within the "self" of the actor, then the political regulations and disciplinary practices which produce that ostensibly coherent gender are effectively displaced from view. The displacement of a political and discursive origin of gender identity onto a psychological "core" precludes an analysis of the political constitution of the gendered subject and its fabricated notions about the ineffable interiority of its sex or of its true identity.

If the inner truth of gender is a fabrication and if a true gender is a fantasy instituted and inscribed on the surface of bodies, then it seems that genders can be neither true nor false, but are only produced as the truth effects of a discourse of primary and stable identity. In *Mother Camp: Female Impersonators in America,* anthropologist Esther Newton suggests that the structure of impersonation reveals one of the key fabricating mechanisms through which the social construction of gender takes place.[15] I would suggest as well that drag fully subverts the distinction between inner and outer psychic space and effectively mocks both the expressive model of gender and the notion of a true gender identity. Newton writes:

> At its most complex, [drag] is a double inversion that says, "appearance is an illusion." Drag says [Newton's curious personification] "my 'outside' appearance is feminine, but my essence 'inside' [the body] is masculine." At the same time it symbolizes the opposite inversion; "my appearance 'outside' [my body, my gender] is masculine but my essence 'inside' [myself] is feminine."[16]

Both claims to truth contradict one another and so displace the entire enactment of gender significations from the discourse of truth and falsity.

The notion of an original or primary gender identity is often parodied within the cultural practices of drag, cross-dressing, and the sexual stylization of butch/femme identities. Within feminist theory, such parodic identities have been understood to be either degrading to women, in the case of drag and cross-dressing, or an uncritical appropriation of sex-role stereotyping from within the practice of heterosexuality, especially in the case of butch/femme lesbian identities. But the relation between the "imitation"

and the "original" is, I think, more complicated than that critique generally allows. Moreover, it gives us a clue to the way in which the relationship between primary identification— that is, the original meanings accorded to gender—and subsequent gender experience might be reframed. The performance of drag plays upon the distinction between the anatomy of the performer and the gender that is being performed. But we are actually in the presence of three contingent dimensions of significant corporeality: anatomical sex, gender identity, and gender performance. If the anatomy of the performer is already distinct from the gender of the performer, and both of those are distinct from the gender of the performance, then the performance suggests a dissonance not only between sex and performance, but sex and gender, and gender and performance. As much as drag creates a unified picture of "woman" (what its critics often oppose), it also reveals the distinctness of those aspects of gendered experience which are falsely naturalized as a unity through the regulatory fiction of heterosexual coherence. *In imitating gender, drag implicitly reveals the imitative structure of gender itself—as well as its contingency.* Indeed, part of the pleasure, the giddiness of the performance is in the recognition of a radical contingency in the relation between sex and gender in the face of cultural configurations of causal unities that are regularly assumed to be natural and necessary. In the place of the law of heterosexual coherence, we see sex and gender denaturalized by means of a performance which avows their distinctness and dramatizes the cultural mechanism of their fabricated unity.

The notion of gender parody defended here does not assume that there is an original which such parodic identities imitate. Indeed, the parody is *of* the very notion of an original; just as the psychoanalytic notion of gender identification is constituted by a fantasy of a fantasy, the transfiguration of an Other who is always already a "figure" in that double sense, so gender parody reveals that the original identity after which gender fashions itself is an imitation without an origin. To be more precise, it is a production which, in effect—that is, in its effect—postures as an imitation. This perpetual displacement constitutes a fluidity of identities that suggests an openness to resignification and recontextualization; parodic proliferation deprives hegemonic culture and its critics of the claim to naturalized or essentialist gender identities. Although the gender meanings taken up in these parodic styles are clearly part of hegemonic, misogynist culture, they are nevertheless denaturalized and mobilized through their parodic recontextualization. As imitations which effectively displace the meaning of the original, they imitate the myth of originality itself. In the place of an original identification which serves as a determining cause, gender identity might be reconceived as a personal/cultural history of received meanings subject to a set of imitative practices which refer laterally to other imitations and which, jointly, construct the illusion of a primary and interior gendered self or parody the mechanism of that construction.

According to Fredric Jameson's "Postmodernism and Consumer Society," the imitation that mocks the notion of an original is characteristic of pastiche rather than parody:

> Pastiche is, like parody, the imitation of a peculiar or unique style, the wearing of a stylistic mask, speech in a dead language: but it is a neutral practice of mimicry, without parody's ulterior motive, without the satirical impulse, without laughter, without that still latent feeling that there exists something *normal* compared to which what is being imitated is rather comic. Pastiche is blank parody, parody that has lost its humor.[17]

The loss of the sense of "the normal," however, can be its own occasion for laughter, especially when "the normal," "the original" is revealed to be a copy, and an inevitably failed one, an ideal that no one *can* embody. In this sense, laughter emerges in the realization that all along the original was derived.

Parody by itself is not subversive, and there must be a way to understand what makes certain kinds of parodic repetitions effectively disruptive, truly troubling, and which repetitions become domesticated and recirculated as instruments of cultural hegemony. A typology of actions would clearly not suffice, for parodic displacement, indeed, parodic laughter, depends on a context and reception in which subversive confusions can be fostered. What performance where will invert the inner/outer distinction and compel a radical rethinking of the psychological presuppositions of gender identity and sexuality? What performance where will compel a reconsideration of the *place* and stability of the masculine and the feminine? And what kind of gender performance will enact and reveal the performativity of gender itself in a way that destabilizes the naturalized categories of identity and desire?

If the body is not a "being," but a variable boundary, a surface whose permeability is politically regulated, a signifying practice within a cultural field of gender hierarchy and compulsory heterosexuality, then what language is left for understanding this corporeal enactment, gender, that constitutes its "interior" signification on its surface? Sartre would perhaps have called this act "a style of being," Foucault, "a stylistics of existence." And in my earlier reading of Beauvoir, I suggest that gendered bodies are so many "styles of the flesh." These styles all never fully self-styled, for styles have a history, and those histories condition and limit the possibilities. Consider gender, for instance, as a *corporeal style*, an "act," as it were, which is both intentional and performative, where "*performative*" suggests a dramatic and contingent construction of meaning.

Wittig understands gender as the workings of "sex," where "sex" is an obligatory injunction for the body to become a cultural sign, to materialize itself in obedience to a historically delimited possibility, and to do this, not once or twice, but as a sustained and repeated corporeal project. The notion of a "project," however, suggests the originating force of a radical will, and because gender is a project which has cultural survival as its end, the term *strategy* better suggests the situation of duress under which gender performance always and variously occurs. Hence, as a strategy of survival within compulsory systems, gender is a performance with clearly punitive consequences. Discrete genders are part of what "humanizes" individuals within contemporary culture; indeed, we regularly punish those who fail to do their gender right. Because there is neither an "essence" that gender expresses or externalizes nor an objective ideal to which gender aspires, and because gender is not a fact, the various acts of gender create the idea of gender, and without those acts, there would be no gender at all. Gender is, thus, a construction that regularly conceals its genesis; the tacit collective agreement to perform, produce, and sustain discrete and polar genders as cultural fictions is obscured by the credibility of those productions—and the punishments that attend not agreeing to believe in them; the construction "compels" our belief in its necessity and naturalness. The historical possibilities materialized through various corporeal styles are nothing other than those punitively regulated cultural fictions alternately embodied and deflected under duress.

Consider that a sedimentation of gender norms produces the peculiar phenomenon of a "natural sex" or a "real woman" or any number of prevalent and compelling social fictions, and that this is a sedimentation that over time has produced a set of corporeal styles which, in reified form, appear as the natural configuration of bodies into sexes existing in a binary relation to one another. If these styles are enacted, and if they produce the coherent gendered subjects who pose as their originators, what kind of performance might reveal this ostensible "cause" to be an "effect"?

In what senses, then, is gender an act? As in other ritual social dramas, the action of gender requires a performance that is *repeated.* This repetition is at once a reenactment and reexperiencing of a set of meanings already socially established; and it is the mundane and ritualized form of their legitimation.[18] Although there are individual bodies that enact these significations by becoming stylized into gendered modes, this "action" is a public action. There are temporal and collective dimensions to these actions, and their public character is not inconsequential; indeed, the performance is effected with the strategic aim of maintaining gender within its binary frame—an aim that cannot be attributed to a subject, but, rather, must be understood to found and consolidate the subject.

Gender ought not to be construed as a stable identity or locus of agency from which various acts follow; rather, gender is an identity tenuously constituted in time, instituted in an exterior space through a *stylized repetition of acts.* The effect of gender is produced through the stylization of the body and, hence, must be understood as the mundane way in which bodily gestures, movements, and styles of various kinds constitute the illusion of an abiding gendered self. This formulation moves the conception of gender off the ground of a substantial model of identity to one that requires a conception of gender as a constituted *social temporality.* Significantly, if gender is instituted through acts which are internally discontinuous, then the *appearance of substance* is precisely that, a constructed identity, a performative accomplishment which the mundane social audience, including the actors themselves, come to believe and to perform in the mode of belief. Gender is also a norm that can never be fully internalized; "the internal" is a surface signification, and gender norms are finally phantasmatic, impossible to embody. If the ground of gender identity is the stylized repetition of acts through time and not a seemingly seamless identity, then the spatial metaphor of a "ground" will be displaced and revealed as a stylized configuration, indeed, a gendered corporealization of time. The abiding gendered self will then be shown to be structured by repeated acts that seek to approximate the ideal of a substantial ground of identity, but which, in their occasional *dis*continuity, reveal the temporal and contingent groundlessness of this "ground." The possibilities of gender transformation are to be found precisely in the arbitrary relation between such acts, in the possibility of a failure to repeat, a de-formity, or a parodic repetition that exposes the phantasmatic effect of abiding identity as a politically tenuous construction.

If gender attributes, however, are not expressive but performative, then these attributes effectively constitute the identity they are said to express or reveal. The distinction between expression and performativeness is crucial. If gender attributes and acts, the various ways in which a body shows or produces its cultural signification, are performative, then there is no preexisting identity by which an act or attribute might be measured; there would be no true or false, real or distorted acts of gender, and the postulation of a true gender identity would be revealed as a regulatory fiction. That gender reality is created through sustained social performances means that the very notions of an essential sex and a true or abiding masculinity or feminity are also constituted as part of the strategy that conceals gender's performative character and the performative possibilities for proliferating gender configurations outside the restricting frames of masculinist domination and compulsory heterosexuality.

Genders can be neither true nor false, neither real nor apparent, neither original nor derived. As credible bearers of those attributes, however, genders can also be rendered thoroughly and radically *incredible*.

[1990]

NOTES

1. Michel Foucault, "Nietzsche, Genealogy, History," in *Language, Counter-Memory, Practice: Selected Essays and Interviews by Michel Foucault*, trans. Donald F. Bouchard and Sherry Simon; ed. Donald F. Bouchard (Ithaca: Cornell University Press, 1977), p. 148. References in the text are to this essay.
2. Mary Douglas, *Purity and Danger* (London, Boston, and Henley: Routledge and Kegan Paul, 1969), p. 4.
3. Ibid., p. 113.
4. Simon Watney, *Policing Desire: AIDS, Pornography, and the Media* (Minneapolis: University of Minnesota Press, 1988).
5. Douglas, *Purity and Danger*, p. 115.
6. Ibid., p. 121.
7. Ibid., p. 140.
8. Foucault's essay, "A Preface to Transgression" (in *Language, Counter-Memory, Practice*) does provide an interesting juxtaposition with Douglas's notion of body boundaries constituted by incest taboos. Originally written in honor of Georges Bataille, this essay explores in part the metaphorical "dirt" of transgressive pleasures and the association of the forbidden orifice with the dirt-covered tomb. See pp. 46–48.
9. Kristeva discusses Mary Douglas's work in a short section of *The Powers of Horror: An Essay on Abjection*, trans. Leon Roudiez (New York: Columbia University Press, 1982), originally published as *Pouvoirs de l'horreur* (Paris: Éditions du Seuil, 1980). Assimilating Douglas's insights to her own reformulation of Lacan, Kristeva writes, "Defilement is what is jettisoned from the *symbolic system*. It is what escapes that social rationality, that logical order on which a social aggregate is based, which then becomes differentiated from a temporary agglomeration of individuals and, in short, constitutes a *classification system* or *a structure*" (p. 65).
10. Ibid., p. 3.
11. Iris Marion Young, "Abjection and Oppression: Unconscious Dynamics of Racism, Sexism, and Homophobia," paper presented at the Society of Phenomenology and Existential Philosophy Meetings, Northwestern University, 1988. The paper will be published in the proceedings of the 1988 meetings by the State University of New York Press. It will also be included as part of a larger chapter in her forthcoming *The Politics of Difference*.
12. Parts of the following discussion were published in two different contexts, in my "Gender Trouble, Feminist Theory, and Psychoanalytic Discourse," in *Feminism/Postmodernism*, ed. Linda J. Nicholson (New York: Routledge, 1989) and "Performative Acts and Gender Constitution: An Essay in Phenomenology and Feminist Theory," *Theatre Journal*, Vol. 20, No. 3, Winter 1988.
13. Michel Foucault, *Discipline and Punish: The Birth of the Prison*, trans. Alan Sheridan (New York: Vintage, 1979), p. 29.
14. Ibid., p. 30.
15. See the chapter "Role Models" in Esther Newton, *Mother Camp: Female Impersonators in America* (Chicago: University of Chicago Press, 1972).
16. Ibid., p. 103.
17. Fredric Jameson, "Postmodernism and Consumer Society," in *The Anti-Aesthetic: Essays on Postmodern Culture*, ed. Hal Foster (Port Townsend, WA: Bay Press, 1983), p. 114.
18. See Victor Turner, *Dramas, Fields and Metaphors* (Ithaca: Cornell University Press, 1974). See also Clifford Geertz, "Blurred Genres: The Refiguration of Thought," in *Local Knowledge, Further Essays in Interpretive Anthropology* (New York: Basic Books, 1983).

 81

From Black Feminist Thought

PATRICIA HILL COLLINS

PATRICIA HILL COLLINS. United States. 1948–   . Sociologist. African-American studies scholar. *Fighting Words: Black Women and the Search for Justice* (1998), *Black Sexual Politics: African-Americans, Gender and the New Racism* (2005), *From Black Power to Hip Hop: Racism, Nationalism and Feminism* (2006).

KNOWLEDGE CONSCIOUSNESS, AND THE POLITICS OF EMPOWERMENT

Black feminist thought demonstrates Black women's emerging power as agents of knowledge. By portraying African-American women as self-defined, self-reliant individuals confronting race, gender, and class oppression, Afrocentric feminist thought speaks to the importance that knowledge plays in empowering oppressed people. One distinguishing feature of Black feminist thought is its insistence that both the changed consciousness of individuals and the social transformation of political and economic institutions constitute essential ingredients for social change. New knowledge is important for both dimensions of change.

. . .

Epistemological Shifts: Dialogue, Empathy, and Truth

Black Women as Agents of Knowledge. Living life as an African-American woman is a necessary prerequisite for producing Black feminist thought because within Black women's communities thought is validated and produced with reference to a particular set of historical, material, and epistemological conditions. African-American women who adhere to the idea that claims about Black women must be substantiated by Black women's sense of our own experiences and who anchor our knowledge claims in an Afrocentric epistemology have produced a rich tradition of Black feminist thought.

Traditionally such women were blues singers, poets, autobiographers, storytellers, and orators validated by everyday Black women as experts on a Black women's standpoint. Only a few unusual African-American feminist scholars have been able to defy Eurocentric masculinist epistemologies and explicitly embrace an Afrocentric feminist epistemology. Consider Alice Walker's description of Zora Neale Hurston:

> In my mind, Zora Neale Hurston, Billie Holiday, and Bessie Smith form a sort of unholy trinity. Zora *belongs* in the tradition of black women singers, rather than among "the literati." . . . Like Billie and Bessie she followed her own road, believed in her own gods, pursued her own dreams, and refused to separate herself from "common" people. (Walker 1977, xvii–xviii)

Zora Neale Hurston is an exception for prior to 1950, few African-American women earned advanced degrees and most of those who did complied with Eurocentric masculinist epistemologies. Although these women worked on behalf of Black women, they did so within the confines of pervasive race and gender oppression. Black women scholars were in a position to see the exclusion of African-American women from scholarly discourse, and the thematic content of their work often reflected their interest in examining a Black women's standpoint. However, their tenuous status in academic institutions led them to adhere to Eurocentric masculinist epistemologies so that their work would be accepted as scholarly. As a result, while they produced Black feminist thought, those African-American women most likely to gain academic credentials were often least likely to produce Black feminist thought that used an Afrocentric feminist epistemology.

An ongoing tension exists for Black women as agents of knowledge, a tension rooted in the sometimes conflicting demands of Afrocentricity and feminism. Those Black women who are feminists are critical of how Black culture and many of its traditions oppress women. For example, the strong pronatal beliefs in African-American communities that foster early motherhood among adolescent girls, the lack of self-actualization that can accompany the double-day of paid employment and work in the home, and the emotional and physical abuse that many Black women experience from their fathers, lovers, and husbands all reflect practices opposed by African-American women who are feminists. But these same women may have a parallel desire as members of an oppressed racial group to affirm the value of that same culture and traditions (Narayan 1989). Thus strong Black mothers appear in Black women's literature, Black women's economic contributions to families are lauded, and a curious silence exists concerning domestic abuse.

As more African-American women earn advanced degrees, the range of Black feminist scholarship is expanding. Increasing numbers of African-American women scholars are explicitly choosing to ground their work in Black women's experiences, and, by doing so, they implicitly adhere to an Afrocentric feminist epistemology. Rather than being restrained by their both/and status of marginality, these women make creative use of their outsider-within status and produce innovative Afrocentric feminist thought. The difficulties these women face lie less in demonstrating that they have mastered white male epistemologies than in resisting the hegemonic nature of these patterns of thought in order to see, value, and use existing alternative Afrocentric feminist ways of knowing.

In establishing the legitimacy of their knowledge claims, Black women scholars who want to develop Afrocentric feminist thought may encounter the often conflicting standards of three key groups. First, Black feminist thought must be validated by ordinary African-American women who, in the words of Hannah Nelson, grow to womanhood "in a world where the saner you are, the madder you are made to appear" (Gwaltney 1980, 7). To be credible in the eyes of this group, scholars must be personal advocates for their material, be accountable for the consequences of their work, have lived or experienced their material in some fashion, and be willing to engage in dialogues about their findings with ordinary, everyday people. Second, Black feminist thought also must be accepted by the community of Black women scholars. These scholars place varying amounts of importance on rearticulating a Black women's standpoint using an Afrocentric feminist epistemology. Third, Afrocentric feminist thought within academia must be prepared to confront Eurocentric masculinist political and epistemological requirements.

The dilemma facing Black women scholars engaged in creating Black feminist thought is that a knowledge claim that meets the criteria of adequacy for one group and thus is judged to be an acceptable knowledge claim may not be translatable into the terms of a different group. Using the example of Black English, June Jordan illustrates the difficulty of moving among epistemologies:

> You cannot "translate" instances of Standard English preoccupied with abstraction or with nothing/nobody evidently alive into Black English. That would warp the language into uses antithetical to the guiding perspective of its community of users. Rather you must first change those Standard English sentences, themselves, into ideas consistent with the person-centered assumptions of Black English. (Jordan 1985, 130)

Although both worldviews share a common vocabulary, the ideas themselves defy direct translation.

For Black women who are agents of knowledge, the marginality that accompanies outsider-within status can be the source of both frustration and creativity. In an attempt to minimize the differences between the cultural context of African-American communities and the expectations of social institutions, some women dichotomize their behavior and become two different people. Over time, the strain of doing this can be enormous. Others reject their cultural context and work against their own best interests by enforcing the dominant group's specialized thought. Still others manage to inhabit both contexts but do so critically, using their outsider-within perspectives as a source of insights and

ideas. But while outsiders within can make substantial contributions as agents of knowledge, they rarely do so without substantial personal cost. "Eventually it comes to you," observes Lorraine Hansberry, "the thing that makes you exceptional, if you are at all, is inevitably that which must also make you lonely" (1969, 148).

Once Black feminist scholars face the notion that, on certain dimensions of a Black women's standpoint, it may be fruitless to try and translate ideas from an Afrocentric feminist epistemology into a Eurocentric masculinist framework, then other choices emerge. Rather than trying to uncover universal knowledge claims that can withstand the translation from one epistemology to another (initially, at least), Black women intellectuals might find efforts to rearticulate a Black women's standpoint especially fruitful. Rearticulating a Black women's standpoint refashions the concrete and reveals the more universal human dimensions of Black women's everyday lives. "I date all my work," notes Nikki Giovanni, "because I think poetry, or any writing, is but a reflection of the moment. The universal comes from the particular" (1988, 57). Bell Hooks maintains, "my goal as a feminist thinker and theorist is to take that abstraction and articulate it in a language that renders it accessible—not less complex or rigorous—but simply more accessible" (1989, 39). The complexity exists; interpreting it remains the unfulfilled challenge for Black women intellectuals.

Situated Knowledge, Subjugated Knowledge, and Partial Perspectives. "My life seems to be an increasing revelation of the intimate face of universal struggle," claims June Jordan:

> You begin with your family and the kids on the block, and next you open your eyes to what you call your people and that leads you into land reform into Black English into Angola leads you back to your own bed where you lie by yourself, wondering if you deserve to be peaceful, or trusted or desired or left to the freedom of your own unfaltering heart. And the scale shrinks to the size of a skull: your own interior cage. (Jordan 1981, xi)

Lorraine Hansberry expresses a similar idea: "I believe that one of the most sound ideas in dramatic writing is that in order to create the universal, you must pay very great attention to the specific. Universality, I think, emerges from the truthful identity of what is" (1969, 128). Jordan and Hansberry's insights that universal struggle and truth may wear a particularistic, intimate face suggest a new epistemological stance concerning how we negotiate competing knowledge claims and identify "truth."

The context in which African-American women's ideas are nurtured or suppressed matters. Understanding the content and epistemology of Black women's ideas as specialized knowledge requires attending to the context from which those ideas emerge. While produced by individuals, Black feminist thought as situated knowledge is embedded in the communities in which African-American women find ourselves (Haraway 1988).

A Black women's standpoint and those of other oppressed groups is not only embedded in a context but exists in a situation characterized by domination. Because Black women's ideas have been suppressed, this suppression has stimulated African-American women to create knowledge that empowers people to resist domination. Thus Afrocentric feminist thought represents a subjugated knowledge (Foucault 1980). A Black women's standpoint may provide a preferred stance from which to view the matrix of domination because, in principle, Black feminist thought as specialized thought is less likely than the specialized knowledge produced by dominant groups to deny the connection between ideas and the vested interests of their creators. However, Black feminist thought as subjugated knowledge is not exempt from critical analysis, because subjugation is not grounds for an epistemology (Haraway 1988).

Despite African-American women's potential power to reveal new insights about the matrix of domination, a Black women's standpoint is only one angle of vision. Thus Black feminist thought represents a partial perspective. The overarching matrix of domination houses multiple groups, each with varying experiences with penalty and privilege that produce corresponding partial perspectives, situated knowledges, and, for clearly identifiable subordinate groups, subjugated knowledges. No one group has a clear angle of vision. No one group possesses the theory or methodology that allows it to discover the absolute "truth" or, worse yet,

proclaim its theories and methodologies as the universal norm evaluating other groups' experiences. Given that groups are unequal in power in making themselves heard, dominant groups have a vested interest in suppressing the knowledge produced by subordinate groups. Given the existence of multiple and competing knowledge claims to "truth" produced by groups with partial perspectives, what epistemological approach offers the most promise?

Dialogue and Empathy.   Western social and political thought contains two alternative approaches to ascertaining "truth." The first, reflected in positivist science, has long claimed that absolute truths exist and that the task of scholarship is to develop objective, unbiased tools of science to measure these truths. But Afrocentric, feminist, and other bodies of critical theory have unmasked the concepts and epistemology of this version of science as representing the vested interests of elite white men and therefore as being less valid when applied to experiences of other groups and, more recently, to white male recounting of their own exploits. Earlier versions of standpoint theories, themselves rooted in a Marxist positivism, essentially reversed positivist science's assumptions concerning whose truth would prevail. These approaches suggest that the oppressed allegedly have a clearer view of "truth" than their oppressors because they lack the blinders created by the dominant group's ideology. But this version of standpoint theory basically duplicates the positivist belief in one "true" interpretation of reality and, like positivist science, comes with its own set of problems.

Relativism, the second approach, has been forwarded as the antithesis of and inevitable outcome of rejecting a positivist science. From a relativist perspective all groups produce specialized thought and each group's thought is equally valid. No group can claim to have a better interpretation of the "truth" than another. In a sense, relativism represents the opposite of scientific ideologies of objectivity. As epistemological stances, both positivist science and relativism minimize the importance of specific location in influencing a group's knowledge claims, the power inequities among groups that produce subjugated knowledges, and the strengths and limitations of partial perspective (Haraway 1988).

The existence of Black feminist thought suggests another alternative to the ostensibly objective norms of science and to relativism's claims that groups with competing knowledge claims are equal. In this volume I placed Black women's subjectivity in the center of analysis and examined the interdependence of the everyday, taken-for-granted knowledge shared by African-American women as a group, the more specialized knowledge produced by Black women intellectuals, and the social conditions shaping both types of thought. This approach allowed me to describe the creative tension linking how sociological conditions influenced a Black women's standpoint and how the power of the ideas themselves gave many African-American women the strength to shape those same sociological conditions. I approached Afrocentric feminist thought as situated in a context of domination and not as a system of ideas divorced from political and economic reality. Moreover, I presented Black feminist thought as subjugated knowledge in that African-American women have long struggled to find alternative locations and techniques for articulating our own standpoint. In brief, I examined the situated, subjugated standpoint of African-American women in order to understand Black feminist thought as a partial perspective on domination.

This approach to Afrocentric feminist thought allows African-American women to bring a Black women's standpoint to larger epistemological dialogues concerning the nature of the matrix of domination. Eventually such dialogues may get us to a point at which, claims Elsa Barkley Brown, "all people can learn to center in another experience, validate it, and judge it by its own standards without need of comparison or need to adopt that framework as their own" (1989, 922). In such dialogues, "one has no need to 'decenter' anyone in order to center someone else; one has only to constantly, appropriately, 'pivot the center'" (922).

Those ideas that are validated as true by African-American women, African-American men, Latina lesbians, Asian-American women, Puerto Rican men, and other groups with distinctive standpoints, with each group using the epistemological approaches growing from its unique standpoint, thus become the most "objective" truths. Each group speaks from its own standpoint and shares its own partial, situated knowledge. But because each group perceives its own truth as partial, its knowledge is unfinished. Each group becomes better able to consider other groups' standpoints without relinquishing the uniqueness of its own standpoint or suppressing other groups' partial perspectives. "What is always needed in the appreciation of art, or life," maintains Alice Walker, "is the larger perspective. Connections made, or at least attempted, where none existed before, the straining to encompass in one's glance at the varied world the common thread, the unifying theme through immense diversity" (1983, 5). Partiality and not universality is the condition of being heard; individuals and groups forwarding knowledge claims without owning their position are deemed less credible than those who do.

Dialogue is critical to the success of this epistemological approach, the type of dialogue long extant in the Afrocentric call-and-response tradition whereby power dynamics are fluid, everyone has a voice, but everyone must listen and respond to other voices in order to be allowed to remain in the community. Sharing a common cause fosters dialogue and encourages groups to transcend their differences.

Existing power inequities among groups must be addressed before an alternative epistemology such as that described by Elsa Barkley Brown or Alice Walker can be utilized. The presence of subjugated knowledges means that groups are not equal in making their standpoints known to themselves and others. "Decentering" the dominant group is essential, and relinquishing privilege of this magnitude is unlikely to occur without struggle. But still the vision exists, one encompassing "coming to believe in the possibility of a variety of experiences, a variety of ways of understanding the world, a variety of frameworks of operation, without imposing consciously or unconsciously a notion of the norm" (Brown 1989, 921).

· · ·

[1990]

REFERENCES

Brown, Elsa Barkley. 1986. *Hearing Our Mothers' Lives.* Atlanta: Fifteenth Anniversary of African-American and African Studies, Emory University. (unpublished)

———. 1989. "African-American Women's Quilting: A Framework for Conceptualizing and Teaching African-American Women's History." *Signs* 14(4): 921–29.

Foucault, Michel. 1980. *Power/Knowledge: Selected Interviews and Other Writings 1972–1977*, edited by Colin Gordon. New York: Pantheon.

Giovanni, Nikki. 1988. *Sacred Cows . . . and Other Edibles.* New York: Quill/William Morrow.

Gwaltney, John Langston. 1980. *Drylongso, A Self-Portrait of Black America.* New York: Vintage.

Hansberry, Lorraine. 1969. *To Be Young, Gifted and Black.* New York: Signet.

Haraway, Donna. 1988. "Situated Knowledges: The Science Question in Feminism and the Privilege of Partial Perspective." *Feminist Studies* 14(3): 575–99.

hooks, bell. 1989. *Talking Back: Thinking Feminist, Thinking Black.* Boston: South End Press.

Jordan, June. 1981. *Civil Wars.* Boston: Beacon.

———. 1985. *On Call.* Boston: South End Press.

Narayan, Uma. 1989. "The Project of Feminist Epistemology: Perspectives from a Nonwestern Feminist." In *Gender/Body/Knowledge: Feminist Reconstructions of Being and Knowing*, edited by Alison M. Jaggar and Susan R. Bordo, 256–69. New Brunswick, NJ: Rutgers University Press.

 82

Outcast Mothers and Surrogates: Racism and Reproductive Politics in the Nineties

ANGELA Y. DAVIS

ANGELA Y. DAVIS United States. 1944– . Philosopher. Activist. Writer. Active in the Black Power movement. Ran for vice president on the Communist Party ticket. *Women, Race and Class* (1982), *Violence against Women and the Ongoing Challenge to Racism* (1985), *Blues Legacies and Black Feminism: Gertrude "Ma" Rainey, Bessie Smith, and Billie Holiday* (1998).

The historical construction of women's reproductive role, which is largely synonymous with the historical failure to acknowledge the possibility of reproductive self-determination, has been informed by a peculiar constellation of racist and misogynist assumptions. These assumptions have undergone mutations even as they remain tethered to their historical origins. To explore the politics of reproduction in a contemporary context is to recognize the growing intervention of technology into the most intimate spaces of human life: from computerized

bombings in the Persian Gulf, that have taken life from thousands of children and adults as if they were nothing more than the abstract statistics of a video game, to the complex technologies awaiting women who wish to transcend biological, or socially induced infertility. I do not mean to suggest that technology is inherently oppressive. Rather, the socioeconomic conditions within which reproductive technologies are being developed, applied, and rendered accessible or inaccessible maneuver them in directions that most often maintain or deepen misogynist, anti-working class, and racist marginalization.

To the extent that fatherhood is denied as a socially significant moment in the process of biological reproduction, the politics of reproduction hinge on the social construction of motherhood. The new developments in reproductive technology have encouraged the contemporary emergence of popular attitudes—at least among the middle classes—that bear a remarkable resemblance to the nineteenth-century cult of motherhood, including the moral, legal, and political taboos it developed against abortion. While the rise of industrial capitalism led to the historical obsolescence of the domestic economy and the ideological imprisonment of (white and middle-class) women within a privatized home sphere, the late twentieth-century breakthroughs in reproductive technology are resuscitating that ideology in bizarre and contradictory ways. Women who can afford to take advantage of the new technology—who are often career women for whom motherhood is no longer a primary or exclusive vocation—now encounter a mystification of maternity emanating from the possibility of transcending biological (and socially defined) reproductive incapacity. It is as if the recognition of infertility is now a catalyst—among some groups of women—for a motherhood quest that has become more compulsive and more openly ideological than during the nineteenth century. Considering the anti-abortion campaign, it is not difficult to envision this contemporary ideological mystification of motherhood as central to the efforts to deny all women the legal rights that would help shift the politics of reproduction toward a recognition of our autonomy with respect to the biological functions of our bodies.

In the United States, the nineteenth-century cult of motherhood was complicated by a number of class- and race-based contradictions. Women who had recently immigrated from Europe were cast, like their male counterparts, into the industrial proletariat, and were therefore compelled to play economic roles that contradicted the increasing representation of women as wives/mothers. Moreover, in conflating slave motherhood and the reproduction of its labor force, the moribund slave economy effectively denied motherhood to vast numbers of African women. My female ancestors were not led to believe that, as women, their primary vocation was motherhood. Yet slave women were imprisoned within their reproductive role as well. The same socio-historical reasons for the ideological location of European women in an increasingly obsolete domestic economy as the producers, nurturers, and rearers of children caused slave women to be valuated in accordance with their role as breeders. Of course, both motherhood, as it was ideologically constructed, and breederhood, as it historically unfolded, were contingent upon the biological birth process. However, the one presumed to capture the moral essence of womaness, while the other denied, on the basis of racist presumptions and economic necessity, the very possibility of morality and thus also participation in this motherhood cult.

During the first half of the nineteenth century, when the industrial demand for cotton led to the obsessive expansion of slavery at a time when the importation of Africans was no longer legal, the "slaveocracy" demanded of African women that they bear as many children as they were biologically capable of bearing. Thus, many women had 14, 15, 16, 17, 18, 19, 20 children. My own grandmother, whose parents were slaves, was one of 13 children.

At the same time, therefore, that nineteenth-century white women were being ideologically incarcerated within their biological reproductive role, essentialized as mothers, African women were forced to bear children, not as evidence of their role as mothers, but for the purpose of expanding the human property held by the slave owners. The reproductive role imposed upon African slave women bore no relationship to a subjective project of motherhood. In fact, as Toni Morrison's novel,

Beloved, indicates—inspired as it is by an actual historical case of a woman killing her daughter—some slave women committed infanticide as a means of resisting the enslavement of their progeny.

Slave women were *birth mothers* or *genetic mothers*—to employ terms rendered possible by the new reproductive technologies—but they possessed no legal rights as mothers of any kind. Considering the commodification of their children—and indeed, of their own persons—their status was similar to that of the contemporary *surrogate mother.* I am suggesting that the term *surrogate mother* might be invoked as a retroactive description of their status because the economic appropriation of their reproductive capacity reflected the inability of the slave economy to produce and reproduce its own laborers—a limitation with respect to the forces of economic production that is being transformed in this era of advanced capitalism by the increasing computerization and robotization of the economy.

The children of slave mothers could be sold away by their owners for business reasons or as a result of a strategy of repression. They could also be forced to give birth to children fathered by their masters, knowing full well that the white fathers would never recognize their Black children as offspring. As a consequence of the socially constructed invisibility of the white father—a pretended invisibility strangely respected by the white and Black community alike—Black children would grow up in an intimate relation to their white half-brothers and sisters, except that their biological kinship, often revealed by a visible physical resemblance, would remain shrouded in silence. That feature of slave motherhood was something about which no one could speak. Slave women who had been compelled—or had, for their own reasons, agreed—to engage in sexual intercourse with their masters would be committing the equivalent of a crime if they publicly revealed the fathers of their children.[1] These women knew that it was quite likely that their children might also be sold or brutalized or beaten by their own fathers, brothers, uncles, or nephews.

If I have lingered over what I see as some of the salient reproductive issues in African-American women's history, it is because they seem to shed light on the ideological context of contemporary technological intervention in the realm of reproduction. Within the contemporary feminist discourse about the new reproductive technologies—in vitro fertilization, surrogacy, embryo transfer, etc.—concern has been expressed about what is sometimes described as the "deconstruction of motherhood"[2] as a unified biological process. While the new technological developments have rendered the fragmentation of maternity more obvious, the economic system of slavery fundamentally relied upon alienated and fragmented maternities, as women were forced to bear children, whom masters claimed as potentially profitable labor machines. Birth mothers could not therefore expect to be mothers in the legal sense. Legally these children were chattel and therefore motherless. Slave states passed laws to the effect that children of slave women no more belonged to their biological mothers than the young of animals belonged to the females that birthed them.[3]

At the same time, slave women and particularly those who were house slaves were expected to nurture and rear and mother the children of their owners. It was not uncommon for white children of the slave-owning class to have relationships of a far greater emotional intensity with the slave women who were their "mammies" than with their own white biological mothers. We might even question the meaning of this conception of "biological motherhood" in light of the fact that the Black nurturers of these white children were frequently "wet nurses" as well. They nourished the babies in their care with the milk produced by their own hormones. It seems, therefore, that Black women were not only treated as surrogates with respect to the reproduction of slave labor, they also served as surrogate mothers for the white children of the slave-owners.

. . .

The economic history of African-American women—from slavery to the present—like the economic history of immigrant women, both from European and colonized or formerly colonized nations, reveals the persisting theme of work as household servants. Mexican women and Irish women, West Indian women and Chinese women have been compelled, by virtue of their economic standing, to function as servants for the wealthy.

They have cleaned their houses and—our present concern—they have nurtured and reared their employers' babies. They have functioned as surrogate mothers. Considering this previous history, is it not possible to imagine the possibility that poor women—especially poor women of color—might be transformed into a special caste of hired pregnancy carriers? Certainly such fears are not simply the product of an itinerant imagination. In any event, whether or not such a caste of women baby-bearers eventually makes its way into history, these historical experiences constitute a socio-historical backdrop for the present debate around the new reproductive technologies. The very fact that the discussion over surrogacy tends to coincide, by virtue of corporate involvement and intervention in the new technologies, with the debate over surrogacy for profit, makes it necessary to acknowledge historical economic precedents for surrogate motherhood. Those patterns are more or less likely to persist under the impact of the technology in its market context. The commodification of reproductive technologies, and, in particular, the labor services of pregnant surrogate mothers, means that money is being made and that, therefore, someone is being exploited.

Once upon a time—and this is still the case outside the technologically advanced capitalist societies—a woman who discovered that she was infertile would have to reconcile herself to the impossibility of giving birth to her own biological offspring. She would therefore either try to create a life for herself that did not absolutely require the presence of children, or she chose to enter into a mothering relationship in other ways. There was the possibility of foster motherhood, adoptive motherhood, or play motherhood.[4] This last possibility is deeply rooted in the Black community tradition of extended families and relationships based both on biological kinship—though not necessarily biological motherhood—and on personal history, which is often as binding as biological kinship. But even within the biological network itself, relationships between, for example, an aunt and niece or nephew, in the African-American and other family traditions, might be as strong or stronger than those between a mother and daughter or son.

My own mother grew up in a family of foster parents with no siblings. Her best friend had no sisters and brothers either, so they invented a sister relation between them. Though many years passed before I became aware that they are not "really" sisters, this knowledge had no significant impact on me: I considered my Aunt Elizabeth no less my aunt later than during the earlier years of my childhood. Because she herself had no children, her relation to me, my sister, and two brothers was one of a second mother.

If she were alive and in her childbearing years today, I wonder whether she would bemoan the fact that she lacked the financial resources to employ all the various technological means available to women who wish to reverse their infertility. I wonder if she would feel a greater compulsion to fulfill a female vocation of motherhood. While working-class women are not often in the position to explore the new technology, infertile women—or the wives/partners of infertile men—who are financially able to do are increasingly expected to try everything. They are expected to try in vitro fertilization, embryo transplants, surrogacy. The availability of the technology further mythologizes motherhood as the true vocation of women. In fact, the new reproductive medicine sends out a message to those who are capable of receiving it: motherhood lies just beyond the next technology. The consequence is an ideological compulsion toward a palpable goal: a child one creates either via one's own reproductive activity or via someone else's.

Those who opt to employ a surrogate mother will participate in the economic as well as ideological exploitation of her services. And the woman who becomes a surrogate mother earns relatively low wages. A few years ago, the going rate was twenty thousand dollars. Considering the fact that pregnancy is a 24-hour-a-day job, what might seem like a substantial sum of money is actually not even a minimum wage. This commodification of motherhood is quite frightening in the sense that it comes forth as permission to allow women and their partners to participate in a program that is generative of life. However, it seems that what is really generated is sexism and profits.

The economic model evoked by the relationship between the surrogate mother and the woman [or man] who makes use of her services is the feudalistic bond between servant and her employer. Because domestic work has been primarily performed in the United States by women of color, native-born as well as recent immigrants (and immigrant women of European descent), elements of racism and class bias adhere to the concept of surrogate motherhood as potential historical features, even in the contemporary absence of large numbers of surrogate mothers of color.

If the emerging debate around the new reproductive technologies is presently anchored to the socioeconomic conditions of relatively affluent families, the reproductive issues most frequently associated with poor and working-class women of color revolve around the apparent proliferation of young single parents, especially in the African-American community. For the last decade or so, teenage pregnancy has been ideologically represented as one of the greatest obstacles to social progress in the most impoverished sectors of the Black community. In actuality, the *rate* of teenage pregnancy in the Black community—like that among white teenagers—has been waning for quite a number of years. According to a National Research Council study, fertility rates in 1960 were 156 births per 1,000 Black women aged 15 to 19, and 97 in 1985.[5] What distinguishes teenage pregnancy in the Black community today from its historical counterpart is the deceasing likelihood of teenage marriages. There is a constellation of reasons for the failure of young teenagers to consolidate traditional two-parent families. The most obvious one is that it rarely makes economic sense for an unemployed young woman to marry an unemployed young man. As a consequence of shop closures in industries previously accessible to young Black male workers—and the overarching deindustrialization of the economy—young men capable of contributing to the support of their children are becoming increasingly scarce. For a young woman whose pregnancy results from a relationship with an unemployed youth, it makes little sense to enter into a marriage that will probably bring in an extra adult as well as a child to be supported by her own mother/father/grandmother, etc.

The rise of single motherhood cannot be construed, however, as synonymous with the "fall" of the nuclear family within the Black community—

if only because it is an extremely questionable proposition that there was such an uncontested structure as the nuclear family to begin with. Historically, family relationships within the Black community have rarely coincided with the traditional nuclear model. The nuclear family, in fact, is a relatively recent configuration, integrally connected with the development of industrial capitalism. It is a family configuration that is rapidly losing its previous, if limited, historical viability: presently, the majority of U.S. families, regardless of membership in a particular cultural or ethnic group, cannot be characterized as "nuclear" in the traditional sense. Considering the gender-based division of labor at the core of the nuclear model, even those families that consist of the mother-father-children nucleus—often popularly referred to as "nuclear families"—do not, rigorously speaking, conform to the nuclear model. The increasingly widespread phenomenon of the "working mother," as opposed to the wife/mother whose economic responsibilities are confined to the household and the children, thoroughly contradicts and renders anachronistic the nuclear family model. Not too many mothers stay at home by choice anymore; not too many mothers can afford to stay at home, unless, of course, they benefit from the class privileges that accrue to the wealthy. In other words, even for those whose historical realities were the basis of the emergence of this nuclear family model, the model is rapidly losing its ability to contain and be responsive to contemporary social/economic/psychic realities.

It angers me that such a simplistic interpretation of the material and spiritual impoverishment of the African-American community as being largely rooted in teenage pregnancy is so widely accepted. This is not to imply that teenage pregnancy is unproblematic. It is extremely problematic, but I cannot assent to the representation of teenage pregnancy as "the problem." There are reasons why young Black women become pregnant and/or desire pregnancy. I do not think I am too far off-target when I point out that few young women who choose pregnancy are offered an alternative range of opportunities for self-expression and development. Are those Black teenage girls with the potential for higher education offered scholarships permitting them to study at colleges and universities like Le Moyne? Are teenagers who choose pregnancy offered even a vision of well-paying and creative jobs?

Is it really so hard to grasp why so many young women would choose motherhood? Isn't this path toward adulthood still thrust upon them by the old but persisting ideological constructions of femaleness? Doesn't motherhood still equal adult womanhood in the popular imagination? Don't the new reproductive technologies further develop this equation of womanhood and motherhood? I would venture to say that many young women make conscious decisions to bear children in order to convince themselves that they are alive and creative human beings. As a consequence of this choice, they are also characterized as immoral for not marrying the fathers of their children.

I have chosen to evoke the reproductive issues of single motherhood among teenagers in order to highlight the absurdity of locating motherhood in a transcendent space—as the anti-abortion theorists and activists do—in which involuntary motherhood is as sacred as voluntary motherhood. In this context, there is a glaring exception: motherhood among Black and Latina teens is constructed as a moral and social evil—but even so, they are denied accessible and affordable abortions. Moreover, teen mothers are ideologically assaulted because of their premature and impoverished entrance into the realm of motherhood while older, whiter, and wealthier women are coaxed to buy the technology to assist them in achieving an utterly commodified motherhood.

Further contradictions in the contemporary social compulsion toward motherhood—contradictions rooted in race and class—can be found in the persisting problem of sterilization abuse. While poor women in many states have effectively lost access to abortion, they may be sterilized with the full financial support of the government. While the "right" to opt for surgical sterilization is an important feature of women's control over the reproductive functions of their bodies, the imbalance between the difficulty of access to abortions and the ease of access to sterilization reveals the continued and tenacious insinuation of racism into the politics of reproduction. The astounding high—

and continually mounting—statistics regarding the sterilization of Puerto Rican women expose one of the most dramatic ways in which women's bodies bear the evidence of colonization. Likewise, the bodies of vast numbers of sterilized indigenous women within the presumed borders of the U.S. bear the traces of a 500-year-old tradition of genocide. While there is as yet no evidence of large-scale sterilization of African-American and Latina teenage girls, there is documented evidence of the federal government's promotion and funding of sterilization operations for young Black girls during the 1960s and 70s. This historical precedent convinces me that it is not inappropriate to speculate about such a future possibility of preventing teenage pregnancy. Or—to engage in further speculation—of recruiting healthy young poor women, a disproportionate number of whom would probably be Black, Latina, Native American, Asian, or from the Pacific Islands, to serve as pregnancy carriers for women who can afford to purchase these services.

· · ·

The process through which a significant portion of the population of young Black, Latina, Native American, Asian, and Pacific women are criminalized, along with the poor European women who, by their association with women of color, are deemed criminal, hinges on a manipulation of a certain ideological representation of motherhood. A poor teenage Black or Latina girl who is a single mother is suspected of criminality simply by virtue of the fact that she is poor and has had a child "out of wedlock." The process of criminalization affects the young men in a different way—not as fathers, but rather by virtue of a more all-embracing racialization. Any young Black man can be potentially labeled as criminal: a shabby appearance is equated with drug addiction, yet an elegant and expensive self-presentation is interpreted as drug dealing. While it may appear that this process of criminalization is unrelated to the construction of the politics of reproduction, there are significant implications here for the expansion of single motherhood in Black and Latino communities. The 25 percent of African-American men in jails and prisons,[6] for example, naturally find it difficult, even in a vicarious sense, to engage in any significant parenting projects.

In pursuing a few of the ways in which racism—and class bias—inform the contemporary politics of reproduction, I am suggesting that there are numerous unexplored vantage points from which we can reconceptualize reproductive issues. It is no longer acceptable to ground an analysis of the politics of reproduction in a conceptual construction of "woman" as a sex. It is not enough to assume that female beings whose bodies are distinguished by vaginas, ovarian tubes, uteri, and other biological features related to reproduction should be able to claim such "rights" to exercise control over the processes of these organs as the right to abortion. The social/economic/political circumstances that oppress and marginalize women of various racial, ethnic, and class backgrounds, and thus alter the impact of ideological conceptions of motherhood, cannot be ignored without affirming the same structures of domination that have led to such different—but related—politics of reproduction in the first place.

In conclusion, I will point to some of the strategic constellations that should be taken into consideration in reconceiving an agenda of reproductive rights. I do not present the following points as an exhaustive list of such goals, but rather I am trying to allude to a few of the contemporary issues requiring further theoretical examination and practical/political action. While the multiple arenas in which women's legal abortion rights are presently being assaulted and eroded can account for the foregrounding of this struggle, the failure to regard economic accessibility of birth control and abortion has equally important results in the inevitable marginalization of poor women's reproductive rights. With respect to a related issue, the "right" and access to sterilization is important, but again, it is equally important to look at those economic and ideological conditions that track some women toward sterilization, thus denying them the possibility of bearing and rearing children in numbers they themselves choose.

Although the new reproductive technologies cannot be construed as inherently affirmative or violative of women's reproductive rights, the anchoring of the technologies to the profit schemes of their producers and distributors results in a commodification of motherhood that complicates and deepens power relationships based on class and race. Yet, beneath this marriage of technology, profit, and the assertion of a historically obsolete bourgeois individualism lies the critical issue of the right to determine the character of one's family. The assault on this "right"—a term I have used throughout, which is not however, unproblematic—is implicated in the ideological offensive against single motherhood as well as in the homophobic refusal to recognize lesbian and gay family configurations—and especially in the persisting denial of custody (even though some changes have occurred) to lesbians with children from previous heterosexual marriages. This is one of the many ways in which the present-day ideological compulsion toward motherhood that I have attempted to weave into all of my arguments further resonates. Moreover, this ideology of motherhood is wedded to an obdurate denial of the very social services women require in order to make meaningful choices to bear or not to bear children. Such services include health care—from the prenatal period to old age—child care, housing, education, jobs, and all the basic services human beings require to lead decent lives. The privatization of family responsibilities—particularly during an era when so many new family configurations are being invented that the definition of family stretches beyond its own borders—takes on increasingly reactionary implications. This is why I want to close with a point of departure: the reconceptualization of family and of reproductive rights in terms that move from the private to the public, from the individual to the social.

[1991]

NOTES

1. See Harriet A. Jacobs. *Incidents in the Life of a Slave Girl.* Edited and Introduction by Jean Fagan Yellin. Cambridge, Mass.: Harvard University Press, p. 1087.
2. See Michelle Stanworth, ed. *Reproductive Technologies: Gender, Motherhood and Medicine.* Minneapolis: University of Minnesota Press, 1987.
3. See Paula Giddings. *When and Where I Enter: The Impact of Black Women on Race and Sex in America.* New York: William Morrow, 1984.
4. The tradition of Black women acting as "play mothers" is still a vital means of inventing kinship relations unrelated to biological origin.
5. Gerald David Jaynes and Robin M. Williams, Jr., eds. *A Common Destiny: Blacks and American Society,* Washington, D.C.: National Academy Press, 1989, p. 515.
6. See Marc Mauer, "Young Black Men and the Criminal Justice System: A Growing National Problem." A Report by the Sentencing Project, 918 F Street, N.W. Suite 501, Washington, D.C. 20004, February 1990.

 83

Making Gender Visible in the Pursuit of Nature's Secrets

EVELYN FOX KELLER

EVELYN FOX KELLER United States. 1936– . Historian. Philosopher of science. Trained as physicist and biologist. *A Feeling for the Organism: The Life and Work of Barbara McClintock* (1983). *Reflections on Gender and Science* (1985), *Secrets of Life, Secrets of Death: Essays on Language, Gender, Science* (1992), *Refiguring Life: Metaphors of 20th Century Biology* (1995).

In teaching us to see gender as a socially constructed and culturally transmitted organizer of our inner and outer worlds, in, as it were, making gender visible, feminist theory has provided us with an instrument of immense subversive power. And along with this provision comes a commitment: nothing less than the deconstruction and reconstitution of conventional knowledge. Necessarily, such a venture requires close textual reading of all attributions of gender, wherever they occur. My own work, for example, has focused on the implications for science and, accordingly, for all of us, of the uses of gender in modern constructions of mind, nature, and the relation between the two.[1] Ultimately, what we are most interested in is clarification of the space of alternative possibilities. If meaning depends on gender, we want to know what changes in meaning, in science as elsewhere, would accrue from shifting meanings or uses of gender—even from abandoning gender altogether—in our construction and de(con)struction of nature.

This method of feminist analysis is unquestionably powerful, but it is not always unproblematic. Two difficulties come to mind immediately: one arises from the obvious fact that images of male and female evoke different responses in different people, and the second arises from the fact that people are not necessarily consistent. Although labels of masculine and feminine are almost always used to designate polarities (or dichotomies), sometimes the two poles are distinguished in one way, sometimes in another. Consider, for example, discussions of brain lateralization: sometimes the right brain is said to be feminine, sometimes the left brain.[2] True, whichever is assumed to be better is sure to be seen as masculine. But my point is that however eager we seem to be to divide the world of personal attributes into categories of male and female, we are not always sure which is which.

So it is, as well, when we try to explore the function of gender in the world of archetypal myths and abstract categories. Sometimes the ambiguity of gender can itself be functional and indeed can be read as a map of another kind of structure. Nature, for instance, although almost always female in Western prescientific and scientific traditions, is not always so. As I have tried to show in examining the differences in imagery between Plato and Bacon, a great deal can be learned about the range of impulses and aims underlying the pursuit of scientific knowledge by exploring the differences of meaning that accrue as the gender of nature shifts.[3]

In this paper, I want to address—and even to take issue with—a reading of gender associations that has become familiar in recent feminist literary criticism. Christine Froula, for one, writes of "the archetypal association of maleness with invisibility, and of femaleness with visibility."[4] She cites Freud for rooting the evolution from immediate sense perception to abstract thinking (what Freud himself calls the "triumph of invisibility," "a victory of spirituality over the senses") in "the turning from the mother to the father." The basis for this presumed archetypal association, Freud tells us, is the fact that "maternity is proved by the senses whereas paternity is a surmise."[5]

For anyone who has thought about the psychology of gender, this claim must seem at least a little surprising, and to someone like myself, used to thinking about the function of gender metaphors in science, it is deeply startling. More reasonably, it might seem, the rise of modern science could be called the "triumph of the visible," its principal goal being clarity, elucidation, enlightenment, the elimination of opacity, and the vanquishing of darkness. The scientific text is, ideally, an open book, and the scientific society an open community—both constructed on a principled intolerance of secrets. Does that suggest that science should be seen as a

returning from the father to the mother? Clearly not. Rather, it reminds us of how necessary to our understanding of these archetypal associations it is that we ask: visibility of what, and to whom? An absence of which secrets, and from whom? Even a superficial inspection of scientific discourse, and indeed of much of ordinary language, suggests, at the very least, the need for a higher dimensional typology. At the very least, the link Froula (like Freud) intuits between masculinity and invisibility must, as I will try to show, be seen as mediated by a prior link between power and invisibility.

There is, in fact, a long historical tradition in which femaleness is most typically associated not with visibility but with obscurity: visible, to be sure, on the surface, but invisible in its (or her) interior, in her innermost and most vital parts. Prior to the advent of science, nature as female is dark, secretive, and opaque. In more immediate human experience, paternity may demand surmise from a father, but in principle, if not in practice, it can be clear enough to the mother: she remains the ultimate arbiter of doubt. Pregnancy, on the other hand, though visible to all the world in its outward signs, is—be it distressingly or miraculously—invisible in its internal dynamics. It is, in fact, the ultimate secret of life, knowable if not visible to the mother, but absolutely inaccessible to the father.

Well-kept secrets pose a predictable challenge to those who are not privy. Secrets function to articulate a boundary: an interior not visible to outsiders, the demarcation of a separate domain, a sphere of autonomous power. And indeed, the secrets of women, like the secrets of nature, are and have traditionally been seen by men as potentially threatening—or if not threatening, then alluring—in that they articulate a boundary that excludes them, and so invite exposure or require finding out. Nobel laureate Richard Feynman once said, perhaps by way of explaining the extraordinary facility for lock picking that had won him so much fame as a young physicist at Los Alamos: "One of my diseases, one of my things in life, is that anything that is secret, I try to undo."[6]

In Western culture, the threat of the allure presented by nature's secrets has met with a definitive response. Modern science has invented a strategy for dealing with this threat, for asserting power over nature's potentially autonomous sphere. That strategy is, of course, precisely a *method* for the "undoing" of nature's secrets; for the rendering of what was previously opaque, transparent, and of what was previously invisible, visible—to the mind's eye, if not to the physical eye. However, the representation of the book of nature as a transparent text is a move with consequences that are anything but transparent.

The ferreting out of nature's secrets, understood as the illumination of a female interior, or the tearing of nature's veil, may be seen as expressing one of the most unembarrassedly stereotypic impulses of the scientific project. In this interpretation, the task of scientific enlightenment—the illumination of the reality behind appearances—is an inversion of surface and interior, an interchange between visible and invisible, that effectively routs the last vestiges of archaic, subterranean female power. Like the deceptive solidity of Eddington's table, the visible surface dissolves into transparent unreality. Scientific enlightenment is in this sense a drama between visibility and invisibility, light and dark, a drama in need of constant reenactment at ever-receding recesses of nature's secrets.

In the remarks that follow, I want to give two examples, or rather one example and one counter example, which together serve to inform each other in their apparent contradiction. The example is a particularly vivid reenactment of that "drama" which can be seen in the story of the rise of molecular biology—a drama that was, in fact, quite explicitly cast in the language of "light and life,"[7] the quest for the secret of life, and then, once that secret was claimed to have been found, ended with the ultimate banishment of the very language of secrets, mystery, and darkness from biological discourse.

As it is usually told, in its classical format, the story of the rise of molecular biology is a drama between science and nature. It begins with the claim of a few physicists—most notably Erwin Schroedinger, Max Delbruck, and Leo Szilard—that the time was ripe to extend the promise of physics for clear and precise knowledge to the last frontier: the problem of life. Emboldened by their example, two especially brave young scientific adventurers, namely, James Watson and Francis Crick, took up the challenge and did, in fact, succeed in vanquishing nature's ultimate and definitive stronghold. As if in direct refutation of the earlier, more circumspect suggestion of Niels Bohr that what quantum mechanics taught us was that "the minimal freedom we must allow the organism will be just large enough to permit it, so to say, to hide its ultimate secrets from us,"[8] Watson and Crick succeeded in showing "that areas apparently too mysterious to be explained by physics and chemistry could in fact be so explained."[9] In short, they found the secret of life.

There is another story here, however, one that takes place in the realm of science itself—a drama not between science and nature but between competing motifs in science, indeed among competing visions of what a biological science should look like. When Watson and Crick embarked on a quest that they themselves described as a "calculated assault on the secret of life," they were employing a language that was, at the same time, not only grandiose and provocatively unfashionable but, as Donald Fleming has pointed out, "in total defiance of contemporary standards of good taste in biological discourse."[10] The story of real interest to historians of science, I suggest, is in the redefinition of what a scientific biology meant; the story of the transformation of biology from a science in which the language of mystery had a place not only legitimate but highly functional, to a science that tolerated no secrets, a science more like physics, predicated on the conviction that the mysteries of life were there to be unraveled. In this retelling, our focus inevitably shifts from the accomplishments of molecular biology to the representation of those accomplishments.

The subplot is in effect a story of cognitive politics. It is a story of the growing authority of physics, and physicists; of an authority that drew directly from the momentous achievements of quantum mechanics early in the century and indirectly from the very fresh acclaim accruing to physicists for their role in winning the Second World War. Told in this way, we can begin to make sense of the puzzle that has long plagued historians of contemporary biology. Despite initial claims and hopes, molecular biology gave no new laws of physics and revealed no paradoxes. What, then, did the physicists, described as having led the revolution of molecular biology, actually provide?

Leo Szilard said it quite clearly: it was "not any skills acquired in physics, but rather an attitude: the conviction which few biologists had at the time, that mysteries can be solved."[11] He went on to say, "If secrets exist, they must be explainable. You see, this is something which modern biologists brought into biology, something which the classical biologists did not have. . . . They lacked the faith that things are explainable—and it is this faith . . . which leads to major advances in biology."

And indeed, he was right. This attitude, this conviction that life's secrets could be found, this view of themselves (especially Watson and Crick) as conquistadors who could and would find it—a stance that drew directly and vigorously on the authority of physicists for its license—proved to be extraordinarily productive. It permitted the conviction, and just a few years later the sharing of that conviction, that life's secret *had* been found. As Max Delbruck said in his Nobel address in 1970:

> Molecular genetics has taught us to spell out the connectivity of life in such palpable detail that we may say in plain words, "The riddle of life has been solved."[12]

In shifting our focus from the successes of molecular biology to the representation of those successes, this retelling inevitably raises the question, What difference does such a representation make?

Much has been written about the race to the double helix—about why Rosalind Franklin, or even Erwin Chargaff, did not see it, about how long it would have taken Franklin if Watson and Crick had not beaten her to it, etc. And I've always thought that that was an essentially boring discussion. It was relevant, of course, to matters of credit, but it had no bearing, I thought, on the course of science. I now think differently. If Rosalind Franklin *had* found the structure of DNA, as she surely would have, she would also, almost equally surely, have seen in that structure a mechanism for genetic replication. *What she would not in all likelihood have seen in it was the secret of life.* Or, as Chargaff himself has written:

If Rosalind Franklin and I could have collaborated, we might have come up with something of the sort in one or two years. I doubt, however, that we could ever have elevated the double helix into "the mighty symbol that has replaced the cross as the signature of the biological alphabet."[13]

The representation of the mechanism of genetic replication as the secret of life was a move that neither Rosalind Franklin, nor Chargaff, nor any number of others could have made, for the simple reason that the traditions from which they came would not have permitted such a linguistic and ideological sweep. That Watson and Crick *were* able to make it was a direct consequence of the existence of a small but significant culture of like-minded "new thinkers" in biology that had grown up around them, in response to the same forces that had influenced them.

I also want to suggest that this description of the mechanism of genetic replication as the secret of life—or, conversely, this representation of the secret of life as the mechanism of genetic replication—had decisive consequences for the future course of biology. It permitted a more complete vindication of a set of beliefs than would otherwise have been possible: beliefs in the absolute adequacy of mechanism, in the incontrovertible value of simplicity, and in the decisive power of a particular conception of biology. No doubt the triumph of the double helix would have been major no matter how it had been described, but its particular representation allowed molecular biologists an assumption of scientific hegemony theretofore unfamiliar in biology. Having solved the problem of life "in principle if not in all details," as Jacques Monod put it,[14] there was no longer room for doubt, for uncertainty, for questions unanswerable within that framework, even for data that would not fit, or for another conception of biology. A science that had historically been characterized by diversity—perhaps like the life it presumed to study—became if not quite monolithic, then very close to it. Certainly in their own minds, molecular biology had become synonymous with scientific biology.

The representation of the secret of life as the mechanism of genetic replication led, once that mechanism had been illuminated, to the conclusion that life itself was not complex, as had been thought earlier, but simple; simple, indeed, beyond our wildest dreams. The only secret of nature was that there were no secrets, and now that secret was out. Henceforth, the very language of biological discourse was to be cleansed of any reference to mystery. Words such as *complexity* and *mystery,* words with a long-standing tradition in biology, soon became disreputable and manifestly unscientific.

Barbara McClintock, finally rewarded in 1983 with the Nobel prize, was for many years discounted, in part because of her blatant indifference to the new credo. If she continues to be described as "unscientific," it is for the same reason: mystery, for her, remained, and continues to remain, a positive value.[15] And if McClintock is revealed as a relic of a bygone era by her regard for mystery, Erwin Chargaff is revealed as not only old but also bitter and jealous. *Only* a bitter old man would say, in 1978, as he did,

> It would seem that man cannot live without mysteries. One could say, the great biologists worked in the very light of darkness. We have been deprived of this fertile light. . . . What will have to go next?[16]

Finally, it was not only language that changed. The very conception of what counted as a legitimate question also changed. Questions without clear and definitive answers not only were not worth asking, they were not asked. Similarly, the meaning of explanation was correspondingly circumscribed. Biological explanations were now limited to "how things worked." The proof of understanding was to be provided by a mechanism. That which mechanism failed to illuminate, rapidly fell from consciousness.

It is important to note, at this juncture, the great irony of the fact that in the end, it was the very pursuit of molecular mechanisms that ultimately created the conditions enabling the retelling of its own story. That is, the story of the representation of the successes of molecular biology can be told today precisely because of all the research that has emerged, from molecular biology itself, to challenge that representation.[17] Because of this work, we are granted *scientific* authority to look at the underside of the successes of molecular biology, to look at some of the costs that were incurred by embracing the metaphoric quest of nature as an open book or a transparent text harboring no secrets, having no interior, and science as a clear and apparent (although not transparent) reflection of that text. This quest is one in which both science and nature are collapsed into two-dimensional surfaces. Both are self-evident texts in which nothing is hidden; there is, apparently, nothing behind the text. But while it may or may not be true that nothing lies behind the book of nature, it is certainly the case that behind the scientific text lies its author—his invisibility and unassailability now secured by the very self-evidence of his text. Science thus becomes less of a mirror and more of a one-way glass, transparent to the scientist, but impenetrable to anyone or anything outside.

To return to my opening remarks, I think Freud was right when he argued that the invisibility of Moses' divine patriarch permitted believers "a much more grandiose idea of their God" (p. 143). But I suggest that Freud's crucial insight has more to do with the relationship between invisibility and power than with the relationship between invisibility and masculinity. That is to say, the invisibility of nature's interiority, like the invisibility of women's interiority, is threatening precisely because it threatens the balance of power between man and nature, and between men and women. To this problem, the culture of modern science has found a truly effective solution, indeed a far more effective solution than those that had gone before. Instead of banishing the Furies underground, out of sight, as did the Greeks, modern science has sought to expose female interiority, to bring it into the light, and thus to dissolve its threat entirely.

In a parallel assertion of power, the secrets of God are also put to the light: where the secrets of nature are *visible,* the laws of nature are *knowable,* that is to say, visible to the mind's eye. In this new ontology, invisibility is sanctioned in only one place: ideally, the scientific text has no signature. The author of the modern scientific text, or the authority of modern science, is simultaneously everywhere and nowhere; on the one hand, it is manifest, self-evident, the archenemy of secrets and secrecy, and on the other, anonymous, uninterpretable, and unidentifiable. There for all to see, eschewing all constraints, barriers, and walls, the scientific text denies the very possibility of decoding by its insistent visibility, and all the while remains, in its own interior, as invisible as Moses' patriarch.

That is the predominant mythology in its normal form. Powerful, formative, it shapes the very meaning of science. But before concluding, I want to put before you an apparent counterexample; in fact, an example illustrating what can happen to this mythic structure when its fundamental condition of openness is not met. As it happens, perhaps not accidentally, this example is drawn from the very events that served so conspicuously to bolster the authority of science in our own time, and, more specifically, to bolster the authority of physics at just the time when molecular biology was coming into existence.

Many people have written about the severe problems that the demands of military secrecy posed for the physicists of the Manhattan Project. The very nature of their enterprise, Oppenheimer claimed, demanded the free and open exchange of ideas and information—free and open amongst the physicists themselves, that is. Oppenheimer won enough concessions from General Groves to permit the physicists to proceed, but the larger demand for secrecy was, of course, never relaxed. The making of the bomb was perhaps the biggest and best-kept secret that science has ever harbored. It was a secret kept from the Germans and the Japanese, from the American public, and indeed from the wives of the very men who produced the bomb. Several of the Los Alamos wives have remarked that Alamogordo was the first they knew of what their husbands were doing, and indeed of what their entire community—a community fully dependent on intimacy and mutual dependency for its survival—was working toward.

The Manhattan Project was a project in which the most privileged secret belonged not to the women but to the men. It was a scientific venture predicated not on openness but on its opposite, on absolute secrecy. Hardly an open book that anyone could read, Los Alamos had an interior. And what was produced out of this interiority was (shall we say, with pregnant irony?) "Oppenheimer's baby." As Brian Easlea has amply documented, the metaphor of pregnancy and birth in fact became the prevailing metaphor surrounding the production and the testing of first the atomic bomb and

later the hydrogen bomb.[18] It was used not only as a precautionary code but as a mode of description that was fully embraced by the physicists at Los Alamos, by the government, and ultimately by the public at large.

As early as December 1942, physicists at Chicago received acknowledgment for their work on plutonium with a telegram from Ernest Lawrence that read, "Congratulations to the parents. Can hardly wait to see the new arrival."[19] In point of fact, they had to wait another two and a half years. Finally, in July 1945, Richard Feynman was summoned back to Los Alamos with a wire announcing the day on which the birth of the "baby" was expected. Robert Oppenheimer may have been the father of the A-bomb, but Kistiakowsky tells us that "the bomb, after all, was the baby of the Laboratory, and there was little the Security Office could do to dampen parental interests."[20]

Two days after the Alamogordo test, Secretary of War Henry Stimpson received a cable in Potsdam which read:

> Doctor has just returned most enthusiastic and confident that the little boy is as husky as his big brother. The light in his eyes discernible from here to Highhold and I could have heard his screams from here to my farm.[21]

And, as the whole world was to learn just three weeks later, the "little boy" was indeed as husky as his brother.

In this inversion of the traditional metaphor, this veritable backfiring, more monstrous in its reality than any fantasies of anal birth explored by psychoanalysts, nature's veil is rent, maternal procreativity is effectively coopted, but the secret of life has become the secret of death. When the bomb exploded, Oppenheimer was reminded of the lines from the Bhagavad-Gita: If the radiance of a thousand suns / were to burst into the sky, / that would be like / the splendor of the Mighty One. / But as the cloud rose up in the distance, he also recalled, I am become Death, the shatterer of worlds.[22]

It is perhaps not surprising if, after that, some physicists sought to retreat to the safer ground of biology. Here they could reassert a more traditional quest, now (merely!) the secret of life. But in this turn, or return, they brought with them a new authority, grounded in a vastly more terrible prowess.

[1993]

NOTES

1. Evelyn Fox Keller, "Feminism and Science," *Signs: Journal of Women in Culture and Society 7,* no. 3 (1982): 589–602; and *Reflections on Gender and Science* (New Haven: Yale University Press, 1985). For other work dedicated to the same venture, see Brian Easlea, *Science and Sexual Oppression* (London: Weidenfeld and Nicolson, 1981); Elizabeth Fee, "Is Feminism a Threat to Scientific Objectivity?" *International Journal of Women's Studies* 4 (1981): 378–92; Sandra Harding, "Is Gender a Variable in Conceptions of Rationality?" *Dialectica* 36, no. 2–3 (1982): 225–42; Carolyn Merchant, *The Death of Nature* (San Francisco: Harper & Row, 1980); Hilary Rose, "Hand, Brain, and Heart: A Feminist Epistemology for the Natural Sciences," *Signs* 9, no.1 (1983): 73–90.
2. For an excellent review of this subject, see Ruth Bleier, *Science and Gender* (New York: Pergamon, 1984).
3. See Keller, *Reflections,* chaps. 1, 2, and 3.
4. Christine Froula, "When Eve Reads Milton: Undoing the Canonical Economy," *Critical Inquiry* 10 (December 1983): 321–47.
5. Sigmund Freud, *Moses and Monotheism,* trans. Katherine Jones (New York, 1967), pp. 145–6, quoted by Froula, p. 133.
6. Richard Feynman, "Los Alamos from Below," *Engineering and Science* 39, no. 2 (1976):19.
7. See Niels Bohr, "Light and Life," in *Atomic Physics and Human Knowledge* (New York: John Wiley and Sons, 1958).
8. *Ibid.,* p.9.
9. Letter from Crick to Olby, in Robert Olby, "Francis Crick, DNA, and the Central Dogma," *Daedalus* (Fall 1970), pp. 938–87.
10. Donald Fleming, "Emigré Physicists and the Biological Revolution," *Perspectives in American History,* vol. 2 (Cambridge, Mass.: Harvard University Press, 1960), p. 155.
11. *Ibid.,* p. 161.
12. Max Delbruck, "A Physicist's Renewed Look at Biology: Twenty Years Later," *Science* 168 (1970): 1312.
13. Erwin Chargaff, *Heraclitean Fire* (New York: Rockefeller University Press, 1978), p. 103.
14. Quoted in Horace Freeland Judson, *The Eighth Day of Creation* (New York: Simon & Schuster, 1979), p. 216.
15. See Evelyn Fox Keller, *A Feeling for the Organism: The Life and Work of Barbara McClintock* (New York: W.H. Freeman, 1983).
16. *Chargaff, Heraclitean Fire,* p. 109.
17. See, e.g., Keller, A Feeling.
18. Brian Easlea, *Fathering the Unthinkable: Masculinity, Scientists, and the Nuclear Arms Race* (London: Pluto Press, 1983).
19. *Ibid.,* p. 107.
20. *Ibid.,* p. 203.
21. *Ibid.,* p. 90.
22. Robert Jungk, *Brighter Than a Thousand Suns* (New York: Grove Press, 1958), p. 201.

 84

The Body and the Reproduction of Femininity from Unbearable Weight: Feminism, Western Culture, and the Body

S U S A N   B O R D O

SUSAN BORDO. 1947–   . United States. Feminist philosopher and cultural theorist. One of the founding scholars of 'body studies.' *Gender/Body/Knowledge* with Allison Jagger (1989), *Twilight Zones: The Hidden Life of Cultural Images from Plato to O.J.* (1997), *The Male Body: A New Look at Men in Public and Private* (1999).

RECONSTRUCTING FEMINIST DISCOURSE ON THE BODY

The body—what we eat, how we dress, the daily rituals through which we attend to the body—is a medium of culture. The body, as anthropologist Mary Douglas has argued, is a powerful symbolic form, a surface on which the central rules, hierarchies, and even metaphysical commitments of a culture are inscribed and thus reinforced through the concrete language of the body.[1] The body may also operate as a metaphor for culture. From quarters as diverse as Plato and Hobbes to French feminist Luce Irigaray, an imagination of body morphology has provided a blueprint for diagnosis and/or vision of social and political life.

The body is not only a *text* of culture. It is also, as anthropologist Pierre Bourdieu and philosopher Michel Foucault (among others) have argued, a *practical,* direct locus of social control. Banally, through table manners and toilet habits, through seemingly trivial routines, rules, and practices, culture is "*made* body," as Bourdieu puts it—converted into automatic, habitual activity. As such it is put "beyond the grasp of consciousness . . . [untouchable] by voluntary, deliberate transformations."[2] Our conscious politics, social commitments, strivings for change may be undermined and betrayed by the life of our bodies—not the craving, instinctual body imagined by Plato, Augustine, and

Freud, but what Foucault calls the "docile body," regulated by the norms of cultural life.[3]

Throughout his later "genealogical" works (*Discipline and Punish, The History of Sexuality*), Foucault constantly reminds us of the primacy of practice over belief. Not chiefly through ideology, but through the organization and regulation of the time, space, and movements of our daily lives, our bodies are trained, shaped, and impressed with the stamp of prevailing historical forms of selfhood, desire, masculinity, femininity. Such an emphasis casts a dark and disquieting shadow across the contemporary scene. For women, as study after study shows, are spending more time on the management and discipline of our bodies than we have in a long, long time. In a decade marked by a reopening of the public arena to women, the intensification of such regimens appears diversionary and subverting. Through the pursuit of an ever-changing, homogenizing, elusive ideal of femininity—a pursuit without a terminus, requiring that women constantly attend to minute and often whimsical changes in fashion—female bodies become docile bodies—bodies whose forces and energies are habituated to external regulation, subjection, transformation, "improvement." Through the exacting and normalizing disciplines of diet, makeup, and dress—central organizing principles of time and space in the day of many women—we are rendered less socially oriented and more centripetally focused on self-modification. Through these disciplines, we continue to memorize on our bodies the feel and conviction of lack, of insufficiency, of never being good enough. At the farthest extremes, the practices of femininity may lead us to utter demoralization, debilitation, and death.

Viewed historically, the discipline and normalization of the female body—perhaps the only gender oppression that exercises itself, although to different degrees and in different forms, across age, race, class, and sexual orientation—has to be acknowledged as an amazingly durable and flexible strategy of social control. In our own era, it is difficult to avoid the recognition that the contemporary preoccupation with appearance, which still affects women far more powerfully than men, even in our narcissistic and visually oriented culture, may function as a backlash phenomenon, reasserting existing gender configurations against any attempts to shift or transform power relations. . . . In such an era we desperately need an effective political discourse about the female body, a discourse adequate to an analysis of the insidious, and often paradoxical, pathways of modern social control.

Developing such a discourse requires reconstructing the feminist paradigm of the late 1960s and early 1970s, with its political categories of oppressors and oppressed, villains and victims. Here I believe that a feminist appropriation of some of Foucault's later concepts can prove useful. Following Foucault, we must first abandon the idea of power as something possessed by one group and leveled against another; we must instead think of the network of practices, institutions, and technologies that sustain positions of dominance and subordination in a particular domain.

Second, we need an analytics adequate to describe a power whose central mechanisms are not repressive, but *constitutive*: "a power bent on generating forces, making them grow, and ordering them, rather than one dedicated to impeding them, making them submit, or destroying them." Particularly in the realm of femininity, where so much depends on the seemingly willing acceptance of various norms and practices, we need an analysis of power "from below," as Foucault puts it; for example, of the mechanisms that shape and proliferate—rather than repress—desire, generate and focus our energies, construct our conceptions of normalcy and deviance.[4]

And, third, we need a discourse that will enable us to account for the subversion of potential rebellion, a discourse that, while insisting on the necessity of objective analysis of power relations, social hierarchy, political backlash, and so forth, will nonetheless allow us to confront the mechanisms by which the subject at times becomes enmeshed in collusion with forces that sustain her own oppression.

This essay will not attempt to produce a general theory along these lines. Rather, my focus will be the analysis of one particular arena where the interplay of these dynamics is striking and perhaps exemplary. It is a limited and unusual arena, that of a group of gender-related and historically localized disorders: hysteria, agoraphobia, and anorexia nervosa.[5] I recognize that these disorders have also historically been class- and race-biased, largely (although not exclusively) occurring among white middle- and upper-middle-class women. Nonetheless, anorexia, hysteria, and agoraphobia may provide a paradigm of one way in which potential resistance is not merely undercut but *utilized* in the maintenance and reproduction of existing power relations.

The central mechanism I will describe involves a transformation (or, if you wish, duality) of meaning, through which conditions that are objectively (and, on one level, experientially) constraining, enslaving, and even murderous, come to be experienced as liberating, transforming, and life-giving. I offer this analysis, although limited to a specific domain, as an example of how various contemporary critical discourses may be joined to yield an understanding of the subtle and often unwitting role played by our bodies in the symbolization and reproduction of gender.

THE BODY AS A TEXT OF FEMININITY

The continuum between female disorder and "normal" feminine practice is sharply revealed through a close reading of those disorders to which women have been particularly vulnerable. These, of course, have varied historically: neurasthenia and hysteria in the second half of the nineteenth century; agoraphobia and, most dramatically, anorexia nervosa and bulimia in the second half of the twentieth century. This is not to say that anorectics did not exist in the nineteenth century—many cases were described, usually in the context of diagnoses of hysteria[6]—or that women no longer suffer from classical hysterical symptoms in the twentieth century. But the taking up of eating disorders on a mass scale is as unique to the culture of the 1980s as the epidemic of hysteria was to the Victorian era.[7]

The symptomatology of these disorders reveals itself as textuality. Loss of mobility, loss of voice, inability to leave the home, feeding others while starving oneself, taking up space, and whittling down the space one's body takes up—all have symbolic meaning, all have *political* meaning under the varying rules governing the historical construction of gender. Working within this framework, we see that whether we look at hysteria, agoraphobia, or anorexia, we find the body of the sufferer deeply inscribed with an ideological construction of femininity emblematic of the period in question. The construction, of course, is always homogenizing and normalizing, erasing racial, class, and other differences and insisting that all women aspire to a coercive, standardized ideal. Strikingly, in these disorders the construction of femininity is written in disturbingly concrete, hyperbolic terms: exaggerated, extremely literal, at times virtually caricatured presentations of the ruling feminine mystique. The bodies of disordered women in this way offer themselves as an aggressively graphic text for the interpreter—a text that insists, actually demands, that it be read as a cultural statement, a statement about gender.

Both nineteenth-century male physicians and twentieth-century feminist critics have seen, in the symptoms of neurasthenia and hysteria (syndromes that became increasingly less differentiated as the century wore on), an exaggeration of stereotypically feminine traits. The nineteenth-century "lady" was idealized in terms of delicacy and dreaminess, sexual passivity, and a charmingly labile and capricious emotionality.[8] Such notions were formalized and scientized in the work of male theorists from Acton and Krafft-Ebing to Freud, who described "normal," mature femininity in such terms.[9] In this context, the dissociations, the drifting and fogging of perception, the nervous tremors and faints, the anesthesias, and the extreme mutability of symptomatology associated with nineteenth-century female disorders can be seen to be concretizations of the feminine mystique of the period, produced according to rules that governed the prevailing construction of femininity. . . .

The hysteric's embodiment of the feminine mystique of her era, however, seems subtle and ineffable compared to the ingenious literalism of agoraphobia and anorexia. In the context of our culture this literalism makes sense. With the advent of movies and television, the rules for femininity have come to be culturally transmitted more and more through standardized visual images. As a result, femininity itself has come to be largely a matter of constructing, in the manner described by Erving Goffman, the appropriate surface presentation of the self.[10] We are no longer given verbal descriptions or exemplars of what a lady is or of what femininity consists. Rather, we learn the rules directly through bodily discourse: through images that tell us what clothes, body shape, facial expression, movements, and behavior are required.

In agoraphobia and, even more dramatically, in anorexia, the disorder presents itself as a virtual, though tragic, parody of twentieth-century constructions of femininity. The 1950s and early 1960s, when agoraphobia first began to escalate among women, was a period of reassertion of domesticity and dependency as the feminine ideal. *Career woman* became a dirty word, much more so than it had been during the war, when the economy depended on women's willingness to do "men's work." The reigning ideology of femininity, so well described by Betty Friedan and perfectly captured in the movies and television shows of the era, was childlike, nonassertive, helpless without a man, "content in a world of bedroom and kitchen, sex, babies and home."[11] The housebound agoraphobic lives this construction of femininity literally. "You want me in this home? You'll have me in this home—with a vengeance! . . ."

The emaciated body of the anorectic, of course, immediately presents itself as a caricature of the contemporary ideal of hyper-slenderness for women, an ideal that, despite the game resistance of racial and ethnic difference, has become the norm for women today. But slenderness is only the tip of the iceberg, for slenderness itself requires interpretation. . . . As such, the interpretation of slenderness yields multiple readings, some related to gender, some not. For the purposes of this essay I will offer an abbreviated, gender-focused reading. But I must stress that this reading illuminates only partially, and that many other currents not discussed here— economic, psychosocial, and historical, as well as ethnic and class dimensions—figure prominently.

We begin with the painfully literal inscription, on the anorectic's body, of the rules governing the construction of contemporary femininity. That construction is a double bind that legislates contradictory ideals and directives. On the one hand, our culture still widely advertises domestic conceptions of femininity, the ideological moorings for a rigorously dualistic sexual division of labor that casts woman as chief emotional and physical nurturer. The rules for this construction of femininity (and I speak here in a language both symbolic and literal)

require that women learn to feed others, not the self, and to construe any desires for self-nurturance and self-feeding as greedy and excessive. Thus, women must develop a totally other-oriented emotional economy. In this economy, the control of female appetite for food is merely the most concrete expression of the general rule governing the construction of femininity: that female hunger— for public power, for independence, for sexual gratification—be contained, and the public space that women be allowed to take up be circumscribed, limited. . . .

On the other hand, even as young women today continue to be taught traditionally "feminine" virtues, to the degree that the professional arena is open to them they must also learn to embody the "masculine" language and values of that arena— self-control, determination, cool, emotional discipline, mastery, and so on. Female bodies now speak symbolically of this necessity in their slender spare shape and the currently fashionable men's-wear look. . . . Our bodies, too, as we trudge to the gym every day and fiercely resist both our hungers and our desire to soothe ourselves, are becoming more and more practiced at the "male" virtues of control and self-mastery. . . .

PROTEST AND RETREAT IN THE SAME GESTURE

In hysteria, agoraphobia, and anorexia, then, the woman's body may be viewed as a surface on which conventional constructions of femininity are exposed starkly to view, through their inscription in extreme or hyperliteral form. They are written, of course, in languages of horrible suffering. It is as though these bodies are speaking to us of the pathology and violence that lurks just around the corner, waiting at the horizon of "normal" femininity. It is no wonder that a steady motif in the feminist literature on female disorder is that of pathology as embodied *protest*—unconscious, inchoate, and counterproductive protest without an effective language, voice, or politics, but protest nonetheless.

American and French feminists alike have heard the hysteric speaking a language of protest, even or perhaps especially when she was mute. . . .

A number of feminist writers, among whom Susie Orbach is the most articulate and forceful, have interpreted anorexia as a species of unconscious feminist protest. The anorectic is engaged in a "hunger strike," as Orbach calls it, stressing that this is a political discourse, in which the action of food refusal and dramatic transformation of body size "expresses with [the] body what [the anorectic] is unable to tell us with words"—her indictment of a culture that disdains and suppresses female hunger, makes women ashamed of their appetites and needs, and demands that women constantly work on the transformation of their body.[12]

The anorectic, of course, is unaware that she is making a political statement. She may, indeed, be hostile to feminism and any other critical perspectives that she views as disputing her own autonomy and control or questioning the cultural ideals around which her life is organized. Through embodied rather than deliberate demonstration she exposes and indicts those ideals, precisely by pursuing them to the point at which their destructive potential is revealed for all to see.

The same gesture that expresses protest, moreover, can also signal retreat; this, indeed, may be part of the symptom's attraction. Kim Chernin, for example, argues that the debilitating anorexic fixation, by halting or mitigating personal development, assuages this generation's guilt and separation anxiety over the prospect of surpassing our mothers, of living less circumscribed, freer lives.[13] Agoraphobia, too, which often develops shortly after marriage, clearly functions in many cases as a way to cement dependency and attachment in the face of unacceptable stirrings of dissatisfaction and restlessness.

Although we may talk meaningfully of protest, then, I want to emphasize the counterproductive, tragically self-defeating (indeed, self-deconstructing) nature of that protest. Functionally, the symptoms of these disorders isolate, weaken, and undermine the sufferers; at the same time they turn the life of the body into an all-absorbing fetish, beside which all other objects of attention pale into unreality. On the symbolic level, too, the protest collapses into its opposite and proclaims the utter capitulation of the subject to the contracted female world. The muteness of hysterics and their return to the level of pure, primary bodily expressivity have been interpreted, as we have seen, as rejecting the symbolic

order of the patriarchy and recovering a lost world of semiotic, maternal value. But *at the same time*, of course, muteness is the condition of the silent, uncomplaining woman—an ideal of patriarchal culture. Protesting the stifling of the female voice through one's own voicelessness—that is, employing the language of femininity to protest the conditions of the female world—will always involve ambiguities of this sort. . . .

COLLUSION, RESISTANCE, AND THE BODY

The pathologies of female protest function, paradoxically, as if in collusion with the cultural conditions that produce them, reproducing rather than transforming precisely that which is being protested. In this connection, the fact that hysteria and anorexia have peaked during historical periods of cultural backlash against attempts at reorganization and redefinition of male and female roles is significant. Female pathology reveals itself here as an extremely interesting social formation through which one source of potential for resistance and rebellion is pressed into the service of maintaining the established order.

In our attempt to explain this formation, objective accounts of power relations fail us. For whatever the objective social conditions are that create a pathology, the symptoms themselves must still be produced (however unconsciously or inadvertently) by the subject. That is, the individual must invest the body with meanings of various sorts. Only by examining this productive process on the part of the subject can we, as Mark Poster has put it, "illuminate the mechanisms of domination in the processes through which meaning is produced in everyday life"; that is, only then can we see how the desires and dreams of the subject become implicated in the matrix of power relations.[14]

Here, examining the context in which the anorexic syndrome is produced may be illuminating. Anorexia will erupt, typically, in the course of what begins as a fairly moderate diet regime, undertaken because someone, often the father, has made a casual critical remark. Anorexia *begins in*, emerges out of, what is, in our time, conventional feminine practice. In the course of that practice, for any number of individual reasons, the practice is pushed a little beyond the parameters of moderate dieting. The young woman discovers what it feels like to crave and want and need and yet, through the exercise of her own will, to triumph over that need. In the process, a new realm of meanings is discovered, a range of values and possibilities that Western culture has traditionally coded as "male" and rarely made available to women: an ethic and aesthetic of self-mastery and self-transcendence, expertise, and power over others through the example of superior will and control. The experience is intoxicating, habit-forming. . . .

Although the specific cultural practices and meanings are different, similar mechanisms, I suspect, are at work in hysteria and agoraphobia. In these cases too, the language of femininity, when pushed to excess—when shouted and asserted, when disruptive and demanding—deconstructs into its opposite and makes available to the woman an illusory experience of power previously forbidden to her by virtue of her gender. In the case of nineteenth-century femininity, the forbidden experience may have been the bursting of fetters—particularly moral and emotional fetters. John Conolly, the asylum reformer, recommended institutionalization for women who "want that restraint over the passions without which the female character is lost."[15] Hysterics often infuriated male doctors by their lack of precisely this quality. S. Weir Mitchell described these patients as "the despair of physicians," whose "despotic selfishness wrecks the constitution of nurses and devoted relatives, and in unconscious or half-conscious self-indulgence destroys the comfort of everyone around them."[16] It must have given the Victorian patient some illicit pleasure to be viewed as capable of such disruption of the staid nineteenth-century household. A similar form of power, I believe, is part of the experience of agoraphobia.

This does not mean that the primary reality of these disorders is not one of pain and entrapment. Anorexia, too, clearly contains a dimension of physical addiction to the biochemical effects of starvation. But whatever the physiology involved, the ways in which the subject understands and thematizes her experience cannot be reduced to a mechanical process. The anorectic's ability to live with minimal food intake allows her to feel powerful and worthy of admiration in a "world," as Susie

Orbach describes it, "from which at the most profound level [she] feels excluded" and unvalued.[17] The literature on both anorexia and hysteria is strewn with battles of will between the sufferer and those trying to "cure" her; the latter, as Orbach points out, very rarely understand that the psychic values she is fighting for are often more important to the woman than life itself.

TEXTUALITY, PRAXIS, AND THE BODY

The "solutions" offered by anorexia, hysteria, and agoraphobia, I have suggested, develop out of the practice of femininity itself, the pursuit of which is still presented as the chief route to acceptance and success for women in our culture. Too aggressively pursued, that practice leads to its own undoing, in one sense. For if femininity is, as Susan Brownmiller has said, at its core a "tradition of imposed limitations,"[18] then an unwillingness to limit oneself, even in the pursuit of femininity, breaks the rules. But, of course, in another sense the rules remain fully in place. The sufferer becomes wedded to an obsessive practice, unable to make any effective change in her life. She remains, as Toril Moi has put it, "gagged and chained to [the] feminine role," a reproducer of the docile body of femininity.[19]

This tension between the psychological meaning of a disorder, which may enact fantasies of rebellion and embody a language of protest, and the practical life of the disordered body, which may utterly defeat rebellion and subvert protest, may be obscured by too exclusive a focus on the symbolic dimension and insufficient attention to praxis. . . . The shift to the practical dimension is not a turn to biology or nature, but to another "register," as Foucault puts it, of the cultural body, the register of the "useful body" rather than the "intelligible body."[20] The distinction can prove useful, I believe, to feminist discourse.

The intelligible body includes our scientific, philosophic, and aesthetic representations of the body—our cultural *conceptions* of the body, norms of beauty, models of health, and so forth. But the same representations may also be seen as forming a set of *practical* rules and regulations through which the living body is "trained, shaped, obeys, responds," becoming, in short, a socially adapted and "useful body."[21] Consider this particularly clear and appropriate example: the nineteenth-century hourglass figure, emphasizing breasts and hips against a wasp waist, was an intelligible *symbolic* form, representing a domestic, sexualized ideal of femininity. The sharp cultural contrast between the female and the male form, made possible by the use of corsets and bustles, reflected, in symbolic terms, the dualistic division of social and economic life into clearly defined male and female spheres. At the same time, to achieve the specified look, a particular feminine *praxis* was required—straitlacing, minimal eating, reduced mobility—rendering the female body unfit to perform activities outside its designated sphere. This, in Foucauldian terms, would be the "useful body" corresponding to the aesthetic norm.

The intelligible body and the useful body are two arenas of the same discourse; they often mirror and support each other.... Another example can be found in the seventeenth-century philosophic conception of the body as a machine, mirroring an increasingly more automated productive machinery of labor. But the two bodies may also contradict and mock each other. A range of contemporary representations and images, as noted earlier, have coded the transcendence of female appetite and its public display in the slenderness ideal in terms of power, will, mastery, the possibilities of success in the professional arena. These associations are carried visually by the slender superwomen of prime-time television and popular movies and promoted explicitly in advertisements and articles appearing routinely in women's fashion magazines, diet books, and weight-training publications. Yet the thousands of slender girls and women who strive to embody these images and who in that service suffer from eating disorders, exercise compulsions, and continual self-scrutiny and self-castigation are anything *but* the "masters" of their lives.

Exposure and productive cultural analysis of such contradictory and mystifying relations between image and practice are possible only if the analysis includes attention to and interpretation of the "useful" or, as I prefer to call it, the practical body....

I view our bodies as a site of struggle, where we must *work* to keep our daily practices in the service of resistance to gender domination, not in the service of docility and gender normalization. This work requires, I believe, a determinedly skeptical attitude toward the routes of seeming liberation and pleasure offered by our culture. It also demands an awareness of the often contradictory relations between image and practice, between rhetoric and reality. Popular representations, as we have seen, may forcefully employ the rhetoric and symbolism of empowerment, personal freedom, "having it all." Yet female bodies, pursuing these ideals, may find themselves as distracted, depressed, and physically ill as female bodies in the nineteenth century were made when pursuing a feminine ideal of dependency, domesticity, and delicacy. The recognition and analysis of such contradictions, and of all the other collusions, subversions, and enticements through which culture enjoins the aid of our bodies in the reproduction of gender, require that we restore a concern for female praxis to its formerly central place in feminist politics.

[1993]

NOTES

1. Mary Douglas, *Natural Symbols* (New York: Pantheon, 1982), and *Purity and Danger* (London: Routledge and Kegan Paul, 1966).
2. Pierre Bourdieu, *Outline of a Theory of Practice* (Cambridge: Cambridge University Press, 1977), p. 94 (emphasis in original).
3. On docility, see Michel Foucault, *Discipline and Punish* (New York: Vintage, 1979), pp. 135–69. For a Foucauldian analysis of feminine practice, see Sandra Bartky, "Foucault, Femininity, and the Modernization of Patriarchal Power," in her *Femininity and Domination* (New York: Routledge, 1990); see also Susan Brownmiller, *Femininity* (New York: Ballantine, 1984).
4. Michel Foucault, *The History of Sexuality.* Vol. 1: *An Introduction* (New York: Vintage, 1980), pp.136, 94.
5. On the gendered and historical nature of these disorders: the number of female to male hysterics has been estimated at anywhere from 2:1 to 4:1, and as many as 80 percent of all agoraphobics are female (Annette Brodsky and Rachel Hare-Mustin, *Women and Psychotherapy* [New York: Guilford Press, 1980], pp. 116, 122). Although more cases of male eating disorders have been reported in the late eighties and early nineties, it is estimated that close to 90 percent of all anorectics are female (Paul Garfinkel and David Garner, *Anorexia Nervosa: A Multidimensional Perspective* [New York: Brunner/Mazel, 1982]. pp. 112–13.
6. Showalter, *The Female Malady*, pp. 128–29.
7. On the epidemic of hysteria and neurasthenia, see Showalter, *The Female Malady*; Carroll Smith-Rosenberg, "The Hysterical Woman: Sex Roles and Role Conflict in Nineteenth-Century America," in her

Disorderly Conduct:Visions of Gender in Victorian America (Oxford: Oxford University Press, 1985).

8. Martha Vicinus, "Introduction: The Perfect Victorian Lady," in Martha Vicinus, *Suffer and Be Still: Women in the Victorian Age* (Bloomington: Indiana University Press, 1972), pp. x–xi.

9. See Carol Nadelson and Malkah Notman, *The Female Patient* (New York: Plenum, 1982), p. 5; E. M. Sigsworth and T. J. Wyke, "A Study of Victorian Prostitution and Venereal Disease," in Vicinus, *Suffer and Be Still.*

10. Erving Goffman, *The Presentation of the Self in Everyday Life* (Garden City, N.J.: Anchor Doubleday, 1959).

11. Betty Friedan, *The Feminine Mystique* (New York: Dell, 1962), p. 36.

12. Orbach, *Hunger Strike,* p. 102.

13. Kim Chernin, *The Hungry Self:Women, Eating, and Identity* (New York: Harper and Row, 1985), esp. pp. 41–93.

14. Mark Poster, *Foucault, Marxism, and History* (Cambridge: Polity Press, 1984), p. 28.

15. Showalter, *The Female Malady,* p. 48.

16. Smith-Rosenberg, *Disorderly Conduct,* p. 207.

17. Orbach, *Hunger Strike,* p. 103.

18. Brownmiller, *Femininity,* p. 14.

19. Toril Moi, "Representations of Patriarchy: Sex and Epistemology in Freud's *Dora,*" in Charles Bernheimer and Claire Kahane, eds., *In Dora's Case: Freud—Hysteria—Feminism* (New York: Columbia University Press, 1985), p. 192.

20. Foucault, *Discipline and Punish,* p. 136.

21. Foucault, *Discipline and Punish,* p. 136.

 85

The Beijing Declaration and Platform for Action

BEIJING PLATFORM FOR ACTION Adopted at the Fourth U.N. World Conference on Women in Beijing in September 1995, the document was developed through a two-year consultation process in regional and national meetings worldwide. It is the outcome of a 20-year process that began at the 1975 conference in Mexico that opened the U.N. Decade of Women.

BEIJING DECLARATION

1. We, the Governments participating in the Fourth World Conference on Women,

2. Gathered here in Beijing in September 1995, the year of the fiftieth anniversary of the founding of the United Nations,

3. Determined to advance the goals of equality, development and peace for all women everywhere in the interest of all humanity,

4. Acknowledging the voices of all women everywhere and taking note of the diversity of women and their roles and circumstances, honouring the women who paved the way and inspired by the hope present in the world's youth,

5. Recognize that the status of women has advanced in some important respects in the past decade but that progress has been uneven, inequalities between women and men have persisted and major obstacles remain, with serious consequences for the well-being of all people,

6. Also recognize that this situation is exacerbated by the increasing poverty that is affecting the lives of the majority of the world's people, in particular women and children, with origins in both the national and international domains.

7. Dedicate ourselves unreservedly to addressing these constraints and obstacles and thus enhancing further the advancement and empowerment of women all over the world, and agree that this requires urgent action in the spirit of determination, hope, cooperation and solidarity, now and to carry us forward into the next century.

We reaffirm our commitment to:

8. The equal rights and inherent human dignity of women and men and other purposes and principles enshrined in the Charter of the United Nations, to the Universal Declaration of Human Rights and other international human rights instruments, in particular the Convention on the Elimination of All Forms of Discrimination against Women and the Convention on the Rights of the Child, as well as the Declaration on the Elimination of Violence against Women and the Declaration on the Right to Development;

9. Ensure the full implementation of the human rights of women and of the girl child as an inalienable, integral and indivisible part of all human rights and fundamental freedoms;

10. Build on consensus and progress made at previous United Nations conferences and summits—on women in Nairobi in 1985, on children in New York in 1990, on environment and development in Rio de Janeiro in 1992, on human rights in Vienna in 1993, on population and development in Cairo in 1994 and on social development in Copenhagen in 1995—with the objective of achieving equality, development and peace;

11. Achieve the full and effective implementation of the Nairobi Forward-looking Strategies for the Advancement of Women;

12. The empowerment and advancement of women, including the right to freedom of thought, conscience, religion and belief, thus contributing to the moral, ethical, spiritual and intellectual needs of women and men, individually or in community with others, and thereby guaranteeing them the possibility of realizing their full potential in society and shaping their lives in accordance with their own aspirations.

We are convinced that:

13. Women's empowerment and their full participation on the basis of equality in all spheres of society, including participation in the decision-making process and access to power, are fundamental for the achievement of equality, development and peace;

14. Women's rights are human rights;

15. Equal rights, opportunities and access to resources, equal sharing of responsibilities for the family by men and women, and a harmonious partnership between them are critical to their well-being and that of their families as well as to the consolidation of democracy;

16. Eradication of poverty based on sustained economic growth, social development, environmental protection and social justice requires the involvement of women in economic and social development, equal opportunities and the full and equal participation of women and men as agents and beneficiaries of people-centered sustainable development.

17. The explicit recognition and reaffirmation of the right of all women to control all aspects of their health, in particular their own fertility, is basic to their empowerment;

18. Local, national, regional and global peace is attainable and is inextricably linked with the advancement of women, who are a fundamental force for leadership, conflict resolution and the promotion of lasting peace at all levels;

19. It is essential to design, implement and monitor, with the full participation of women, effective, efficient and mutually reinforcing gender-sensitive policies and programmes, including development policies and programmes, at all levels that will foster the empowerment and advancement of women;

20. The participation and contribution of all actors of civil society, particularly women's groups and networks and other non-governmental organizations and community-based organizations, with full respect for their autonomy, in cooperation with Governments, are important to the effective implementation and follow-up of the Platform for Action;

21. The implementation of the Platform for Action requires commitment from Governments and the international community. By making national and international commitments for action, including those made at the Conference, Governments and the international community recognize the need to take priority action for the empowerment and advancement of women.

We are determined to:

22. Intensify efforts and actions to achieve the goals of the Nairobi Forward-looking Strategies for the Advancement of Women by the end of this century;

23. Ensure the full enjoyment by women and the girl child of all human rights and fundamental freedoms and take effective action against violations of these rights and freedoms;

24. Take all necessary measures to eliminate all forms of discrimination against women and the girl child and remove all obstacles to gender equality and the advancement and empowerment of women;

25. Encourage men to participate fully in all actions towards equality;

26. Promote women's economic independence, including employment, and eradicate the persistent and increasing burden of poverty on women by addressing the structural causes of poverty through changes in economic structures, ensuring equal access for all women, including those in rural areas, as vital development agents, to productive resources, opportunities and public services;

27. Promote people-centered sustainable development, including sustained economic growth, through the provision of basic education, lifelong education, literacy and training, and primary health care for girls and women;

28. Take positive steps to ensure peace for the advancement of women and, recognizing the leading role that women have played in the peace movement, work actively towards general and complete disarmament under strict and effective

international control, and support negotiations on the conclusion, without delay, of a universal and multi-laterally and effectively verifiable comprehensive nuclear-test-ban treaty which contributes to nuclear disarmament and the prevention of the proliferation of nuclear weapons in all its aspects;

29. Prevent and eliminate all forms of violence against women and girls;

30. Ensure equal access to and equal treatment of women and men in education and health care and enhance women's sexual and reproductive health as well as education;

31. Promote and protect all human rights of women and girls;

32. Intensify efforts to ensure equal enjoyment of all human rights and fundamental freedoms for all women and girls who face multiple barriers to their empowerment and advancement because of such factors as their race, age, language, ethnicity, culture, religion, or disability, or because they are indigenous people;

33. Ensure respect for international law, including humanitarian law, in order to protect women and girls in particular;

34. Develop the fullest potential of girls and women of all ages, ensure their full and equal participation in building a better world for all and enhance their role in the development process.

We are determined to:

35. Ensure women's equal access to economic resources, including land, credit, science and technology, vocational training, information, communication and markets, as a means to further the advancement and empowerment of women and girls, including through the enhancement of their capacities to enjoy the benefits of equal access to these resources, *inter alia,* by means of international cooperation;

36. Ensure the success of the Platform for Action, which will require a strong commitment on the part of Governments, international organizations and institutions at all levels. We are deeply convinced thateconomic development, social development and environmental protection are interdependent and mutually reinforcing components of sustainable development, which is the framework for our efforts to achieve a higher quality of life for all people. Equitable social development that recog-

nizes empowering the poor, particularly women living in poverty, to utilize environmental resources sustainably is a necessary foundation for sustainable development. We also recognize that broad-based and sustained economic growth in the context of sustainable development is necessary to sustain social development and social justice. The success of the Platform for Action will also require adequate mobilization of resources at the national and international levels as well as new and additional resources to the developing countries from all available funding mechanisms, including multilateral, bilateral and private sources for the advancement of women; financial resources to strengthen the capacity of national, subregional, regional and international institutions; a commitment to equal rights, equal responsibilities and equal opportunities and to the equal participation of women and men in all national, regional and international bodies and policy-making processes; and the establishment or strengthening of mechanisms at all levels for accountability to the world's women;

37. Ensure also the success of the Platform for Action in countries with economies in transition, which will require continued international cooperation and assistance;

38. We hereby adopt and commit ourselves as Governments to implement the following Platform for Action, ensuring that a gender perspective is reflected in all our policies and programmes. We urge the United Nations system, regional and international financial institutions, other relevant regional and international institutions and all women and men, as well as non-governmental organizations, with full respect for their autonomy, and all sectors of civil society, in cooperation with Governments, to fully commit themselves and contribute to the implementation of this Platform for Action.

. . .

Critical Areas of Concern

41. The advancement of women and the achievement of equality between women and men are a matter of human rights and a condition for social justice and should not be seen in isolation as a women's issue. They are the only way to build a sustainable, just and developed society. Empowerment of women and equality between women and men are prerequisites

for achieving political, social, economic, cultural and environmental security among all peoples.

42. Most of the goals set out in the Nairobi Forward-looking Strategies for the Advancement of Women have not been achieved. Barriers to women's empowerment remain, despite the efforts of Governments, as well as non-governmental organizations and women and men everywhere. Vast political, economic and ecological crises persist in many parts of the world. Among them are wars of aggression, armed conflicts, colonial or other forms of alien domination or foreign occupation, civil wars and terrorism. These situations, combined with systematic or de facto discrimination, violations of and failure to protect all human rights and fundamental freedoms of all women, and their civil, cultural, economic, political and social rights, including the right to development and ingrained prejudicial attitudes towards women and girls are but a few of the impediments encountered since the World Conference to Review and Appraise the Achievements of the United Nations Decade for Women: Equality, Development and Peace, in 1985.

43. A review of progress since the Nairobi Conference highlights special concerns—areas of particular urgency that stand out as priorities for action. All actors should focus action and resources on the strategic objectives relating to the critical areas of concern which are, necessarily, interrelated, interdependent and of high priority. There is a need for these actors to develop and implement mechanisms of accountability for all the areas of concern.

44. To this end, Governments, the international community and civil society, including non-governmental organizations and the private sector, are called upon to take strategic action in the following critical areas of concern:

- The persistent and increasing burden of poverty on women
- Inequalities and inadequacies in and unequal access to education and training
- Inequalities and inadequacies in and unequal access to health care and related services
- Violence against women
- The effects of armed or other kinds of conflict on women, including those living under foreign occupation

- Inequality in economic structures and policies, in all forms of productive activities and in access to resources
- Inequality between men and women in the sharing of power and decision-making at all levels
- Insufficient mechanisms at all levels to promote the advancement of women
- Lack of respect for an inadequate promotion and protection of the human rights of women
- Stereotyping of women and inequality in women's access to and participation in all communication systems, especially in the media
- Gender inequalities in the management of natural resources and in the safeguarding of the environment
- Persistent discrimination against and violation of the rights of the girl-child.

[1995]

 86

Mothers of Our Nations: Indigenous Women Address the World

WINONA LADUKE

WINONA LADUKE United States. 1959– . Human rights and Native American rights activist. Writer. Lecturer. Founder of White Earth Land Recovery Project, which works to recover lost tribal land. Ran for vice president on the Green Party ticket in 2000. *Last Standing Woman* (1997), *All Our Relations: Native Struggles for Land and Life* (1999).

Delivered at the NON-GOVERNMENTAL ORGANIZATION (NGO) FORUM, *Huairou, China, September 1995.*

It is a great honor as a young mother of two to be invited to speak to you sisters today, women who have great courage and commitment, women who are peers and leaders, and who like myself are the Mothers of Our Nations.

The Earth is our Mother. From her we get our life, and our ability to live. It is our responsibility to care for our Mother, and in caring for our Mother, we care for ourselves. Women, all females, are the manifestation of Mother Earth in human form. We are her daughters, and in my cultural instructions we are to care for her. I am taught to live in respect for Mother Earth. In indigenous societies, we are told that natural law is the highest law, higher than the laws made by nations, states, municipalities and the World Bank; that one would do well to live in accordance with natural law, with those of our Mother, and in respect for all our relations.

One hundred years ago, one of our great leaders, Chief Seattle, stated, "What befalls the Earth, befalls the people of the Earth." And that is the reality today, and the situation of the status of women, and the status of indigenous women and indigenous peoples.

While I am from one nation of indigenous peoples, there are an estimated 500 million indigenous peoples or some 5,000 nations of indigenous peoples worldwide. We are in the Cordilleras, East Timor, New Zealand, Australia, Tibet, New Caledonia, Hawaii, North America, South America, and beyond. We are not populations nor minority groups. We are peoples and nations of peoples. Under international law we meet the criteria of nation states with each having a common economic system, language, territory, history, culture, and governing institution—conditions which indicate nations of peoples. Despite this fact, indigenous nations are not allowed to participate in the United Nations.

Nations of indigenous peoples are not represented at the United Nations. Most decisions today are made by the 180 or so member states. Those states, by and large, have been in existence for only 200 years or less, while most indigenous nations, with few exceptions, have been in existence for thousands of years. Ironically, there would likely be little argument in this room, that most decisions made in the world today are actually made by some of the 47 transnational corporations and their international financiers whose annual income is larger than the gross national product for many countries of the world.

This is the centerpiece of the problem. Decision making is not made by those who are affected—people who live on the land—but the corporations with interests entirely different from that of the land and the people or the women of the land. This brings forth a fundamental question: What gives

corporations like Conoco, Shell, Exxon, Daishowa, ITT, Rio Tinto Zinc, and the World Bank the right which supersedes or is superior to my human right to live on my land, or that of my family, my community, my nation, our nations, and to us as women? What law gives that right to them? Not any law of the Creator or of Mother Earth. Is that right contained within their wealth? Is that right contained within their wealth, which was historically acquired immorally, unethically through colonialism and imperialism and paid for with the lives of millions of people, species of plants, and entire ecosystems? They should have no such right. And we clearly, as women and as indigenous peoples, demand and will recover that right—the right of self-determination, to determine our own destiny and that of our future generations.

The origins of this problem lie with the predator/prey relationship that industrial society has developed with the Earth and, subsequently, the people of the Earth. This same relationship exists vis-à-vis women. We collectively find that we are often in the role of the prey to a predator society whether through sexual discrimination, exploitation, sterilization, absence of control over our bodies, or being the subjects of repressive laws and legislation in which we have no voice. This occurs on an individual level, but equally and more significantly on a societal level. It is also critical to point out at this time most matrilineal societies, societies in which governance and decision making are largely controlled by women, have been obliterated from the face of the Earth by colonialism and industrialism. The only matrilineal societies that still exist in the world today are those of indigenous nations. Yet we also face obliteration.

On a worldwide scale and in North America, indigenous societies remain in a predator/prey relationship with industrial society. We are the peoples with the land—land and natural resources required for someone else's development program and amassing of wealth. The wealth of the United States, the nation that today determines much of world policy, was illegally expropriated from our lands. Similarly the wealth of indigenous peoples of South Africa, Central and South American countries, and Asia was taken for the industrial development of Europe and later for settler states which came to occupy those lands. The relationship between development and underdevelopment adversely affected the status of our indigenous societies and the status of indigenous women.

Eduardo Galeanos, the Latin American writer and scholar, writes: "In the colonial to neocolonial alchemy, gold changes to scrap metal and food to poison. We have become painfully aware of the mortality of wealth which nature bestows and imperialism appropriates."

Today, on a worldwide scale, we remain in the same situation as one hundred years ago, only with less land and fewer people. Fifty million indigenous peoples live in the world's rainforests. In the next decade, one million indigenous peoples are slated to be relocated because of dam projects (thanks to the Narmada Project in India, the Three Gorges Dam Project in China, and the James Bay Hydroelectric Project in northern Canada). Almost all atomic weapons which have been detonated in the world have been on lands or waters of indigenous peoples, most clearly evidenced here in China and in the Pacific with France's obscene proposal to detonate atomic weapons this upcoming month. This situation is mirrored in North America. Today, over 50 percent of our remaining lands are forested. Both Canada and the United States continue aggressive clear-cutting policies on our land. Over two thirds of the uranium resources and one third of all low-sulfur coal resources in the United States are on indigenous lands. We have huge oil reserves on our reservations. Over 650 atomic weapons have been detonated on the Western Shoshone Nation. We have two separate accelerated proposals to dump nuclear waste in our reservation lands, and similarly over 100 separate proposals for toxic waste dumps on our lands. We understand clearly the relationship between development for someone else and our own underdevelopment. We also understand clearly the relationship between the environmental impacts of types of development on our lands, and the environmental and subsequent health impacts on our bodies as women.

We also understand clearly that the analysis of North versus South is an erroneous analysis. There is, from our perspective, not a problem of the North dictating the economic policies of the South, and subsequently consuming the South. Instead, there is a problem of the Middle consuming both the North and the South. That is our situation. Let me explain.

The rate of deforestation in the Brazilian Amazon is one acre every nine seconds. Incidentally, the rate of extinction of indigenous peoples in the Amazon is one nation of indigenous peoples per year. The rate of deforestation of the boreal forest of Canada is one acre every twelve seconds. Siberia, thanks to American corporations like Weyerhauser, is not far behind. In all cases, indigenous peoples are endangered. And there is, frankly, no difference between the impact in the North and the South.

Uranium mining in northern Canada has left over 120 million tons of radioactive waste. Since 1975, hospitalizations for cancer, birth defects, and circulatory illnesses in that area have increased dramatically—between 123 percent and 600 percent. In other areas impacted by uranium mining, cancer and birth defects have in some cases increased to 8 times the national average. There is no distinction in this problem caused by radiation whether it is in the Dene of northern Canada, the Laguna Pueblo of New Mexico, or the people of Namibia.

The rapid increase in dioxins, organochlorides, and PCBs (polychlorinated biphenyls) in the world as a result of industrialization also has a devastating impact on indigenous peoples, indigenous women, and other women. Each year, according to Environmental Protection Agency statistics, the world's paper industry discharges from 600 to 3,200 grams of dioxin equivalents in water, sludge, and paper products. This quantity is equal to the amount that would cause 58,000 to 292,000 cases of cancer every year. According to a number of recent studies, this has significantly increased the risk of breast cancer in women. Similarly, heavy metals and PCB contamination of Inuit women of the Hudson Bay region of the Arctic indicates that they have the highest levels of breast milk contamination in the world—28 times higher than the average woman in Quebec and 10 times higher than that considered "safe" by the government. Consequently, it is clear to us that problems are also found in the South due to the export of chemicals and bio-accumulation of toxins. These are problems that emanate from industrial society's mistreatment and disrespect for our

Mother Earth, and are reflected in the devastation of the collective health and well-being of women.

In summary, I have presented these arguments to illustrate that these are very common issues for women, not only for indigenous women, but for all women. What befalls our Mother Earth, befalls her daughters—the women who are the mothers of our nations. Simply stated, if we can no longer nurse our children, if we can no longer bear children, and if our bodies are wracked with poisons, we will have accomplished little in the way of determining our destiny or improving our conditions. These problems, reflected in our health and well-being, are the result of historical processes and are inherently resulting in a decline of the status of women. We need to challenge these processes if we want to be ultimately in charge of our own destinies, our own self-determination, and the future of our Earth, our Mother.

I call on you to support the struggle of indigenous peoples of the world for recognition as peoples who have self-determination. I ask you to look into the Charter of the United Nations, which states that "all peoples have the right to self-determination. By virtue of that right, they may freely determine their political status and freely pursue their economic, social and political development." "All peoples" should be construed to mean that indigenous peoples have that right, too. Accord us the same rights as all other nations of peoples, and through that process, allow us to protect our ecosystems, their inherent biodiversity, human cultural diversity, and the last remaining matriarchal governments in the world.

Finally, while we are here in the commonness of this forum, speak of the common rights of all women and the fundamental human rights to self-determination. So long as the predator continues, so long as the Middle countries of the world continue to drive an increasing level of consumption, there will be no safety for the human rights of women, of indigenous peoples, and the basic protection of the Earth from which we get our life. Consumption causes the commodification of the sacred, the natural world, cultures, children, and women. And unless we speak and take meaningful action to address the high levels of consumption, we will never have any security for our individual human rights as women.

This is not a struggle for women of the dominant society in so-called "first world" countries to have equal pay and equal status if that pay and status continues to be based on a consumption model that is unsustainable. It is a struggle to recover our status as Daughters of the Earth. In that is our strength and security, not in the predator, but in the security of our Mother, for our future generations. In that, we can insure our security as the Mothers of Our Nations.

[1995]

PART VII

1995–2008

1995–2008: Introduction

This period, spanning the turn of a new century, brought feminist theory into dialogue with ideas and struggles that had been glimpsed in earlier decades but became
visible in this period in ways that none of us could have foreseen. In much of the
world, the late 1990s saw a time of increased prosperity. With their efforts informed
and supported by the coalitions and resolutions of the Beijing conference, women
across the globe emerged as agents of social change in struggles for economic, political, and personal freedoms. These struggles paralleled and at times intersected with
increasingly strong movements against global capital and its institutions—the World
Trade Organization, the World Bank, and the International Monetary Fund in
particular—and their depredations on the environment and Third World economies.
At the same time, the particular ways in which war affects the lives of women—the
ways in which women's lives are militarized—became all too apparent as ethnic conflicts tore apart countries (Yugoslavia, Côte d'Ivoire, Israel, Palestine, Afghanistan,
Iraq) on several continents, never without the intervention of the governments of
Europe and the United States.

Living the year 2000 moved many to reframe through a millennial lens changes
going on in many arenas, particularly those at the borders between the technological
and the social: the spread of global communications technologies, with their mixed
possibilities for communication, education, organizing, and surveillance; the transformation of family and kinship groups through reproductive technologies new (donor
insemination, in vitro fertilization) and old (open adoption, local and global). Questions of the relationship among sexuality, the body, and the law surfaced repeatedly
in debates about gay and lesbian unions and the 'defense' of marriage; reproductive
rights and sexual abuse; social welfare and health care; a continuing worldwide traffic
in women; and the fluidity or fixity of transgender and transsexual identities. Massive
demographic shifts challenged our conception of nations and borders: global migra-
tions from the rural to the urban on a scale not seen since European industrialization;
movements of refugee populations fleeing ethnic and gender violence as well as war,
drought, disease, and economic change; nations devastated by HIV/AIDS as the
disease's demographics shifted focus from gay men and intravenous drug users in
the cities to villages and towns in Africa and Asia. Simultaneously, discourses of race,
ethnicity, blood, tribe—the theological in struggle with the biological—were taking us
back to retooled questions of nature versus nurture.

During these years, gender studies has led the field of feminist theorizing even
as academic institutions have increasingly brought women's studies into the graduate curriculum with the establishment of close to twenty PhD programs and the
proliferation of MA programs. The shift in attention from women to gender as
a social and scientific subject of inquiry has not meant a turn away from the
conditions of women as subjects. Rather, it has made for more complex ways of

understanding what still makes for a world of wildly asymmetrical divisions of knowledge and power.

Feminist politics in this period was being reshaped by a discourse about generations: second wave and third wave. While the third wave seemed to be articulating its developing identity in online zines, music lyrics, and websites, the second wave was consolidating and reframing the last four decades of feminism through an outpouring of memoirs, document collections, and histories. For many, the continuities and connections between these waves seem stronger than the ruptures, even if the modes of action and expression differ, particularly in the face of the latest round of backlash against all forms of feminism and women's organizing and the continued local and global assaults on women's basic rights to health, education, reproductive freedom, and the fundamental means of survival.

The year 2008 sees us in a period of worldwide economic instability, environmental degradation, and growing inequality in which the resources of nations seem to be increasingly invested in technologies of war, terror, weapons of mass destruction, and "homeland security." The return of warrior cultures with the resources of these technologies keeps us mindful that we cannot think even briefly that some can enjoy their freedom when others fear for their lives as gendered subjects. This moment makes ever more apparent the need for a strong and multi-voiced feminist critique. Clearly, difficult dialogues and coalitions across differences are essential to the best feminist work as it continues its analyses of oppression, exploitation, and domination.

87

Riot Grrrl Philosophy

BIKINI KILL

BIKINI KILL A band from Olympia, Washington, closely associated with the Riot Grrrl movement, a community constituted through zines and elaborated online.

BECAUSE us girls crave records and books and fanzines that speak to US that WE feel included in and can understand in our own ways.

BECAUSE we wanna make it easier for girls to see/hear each other's work so that we can share strategies and criticize-applaud each other.

BECAUSE we must take over the means of production in order to create our own moanings.

BECAUSE viewing our work as being connected to our girlfriends-politics-real lives is essential if we are gonna figure out how [what] we are doing impacts, reflects, perpetuates, or DISRUPTS the status quo.

BECAUSE we recognize fantasies of Instant Macho Gun Revolution as impractical lies meant to keep us simply dreaming instead of becoming our dreams AND THUS seek to create revolution in our own lives every single day by envisioning and creating alternatives to the bullshit christian capitalist way of doing things.

BECAUSE we want and need to encourage and be encouraged in the face of all our own insecurities, in the face of beergutboyrock that tells us we can't play our instruments, in the face of "authorities" who say our bands/zines/etc. are the worst in the U.S. and

BECAUSE we don't wanna assimilate to someone else's (boy) standards of what is or isn't.

BECAUSE we are unwilling to falter under claims that we are reactionary "reverse sexists" AND NOT

THE TRUEPUNKROCKSOULCRUSADERS THAT WE KNOW we really are.

BECAUSE we know that life is much more than physical survival and are patently aware that the punk rock "you can do anything" idea is crucial to the coming angry grrrl rock revolution that seeks to save the psychic and cultural lives of girls and women everywhere, according to their own terms, not ours.

BECAUSE we are interested in creating non-hierarchical ways of being AND making music, friends, and scenes based on communication + understanding, instead of competition + good/bad categorizations.

BECAUSE doing/reading/seeing/hearing cool things that validate and challenge us can help us gain the strength and sense of community that we need in order to figure out how bullshit like racism, able-bodyism, ageism, speciesism, classism, thinism, sexism, anti-semitism and heterosexism figures in our own lives.

BECAUSE we see fostering and supporting girl scenes and girl artists of all kinds as integral to this process.

BECAUSE we hate capitalism in all its forms and see our main goal as sharing information and staying alive, instead of making profits or being cool according to traditional standards.

BECAUSE we are angry at a society that tells us Girl=Dumb, Girl=Bad, Girl=Weak.

BECAUSE we are unwilling to let our real and valid anger be diffused and/or turned against us via the internalization of sexism as witnessed in girl/girl jealousism and self-deafeating girltype behaviors.

BECAUSE I believe with my wholeheartmindbody that girls constitute a revolutionary soul force that can, and will, change the world for real.

[1995]

88

Femmenism

JEANNINE DELOMBARD

JEANNINE DELOMBARD. United States. ND. Scholar of American literature and culture. *Slavery on Trial: Law, Abolitionism, and Print Culture* (2007).

Waves—which, by definition, curve alternately in opposite directions—embody contradiction. For me femmenism is where the third wave of Western feminism and the third wave of American lesbianism intersect. Femmenism is the riptide that drags nature and nurture, essentialism and constructivism, and all other binary oppositions out to sea. Femmenism is nothing if not contradictory. Femmenism is looking like a straight woman and living like a dyke. Femmenism is being attracted to someone of the same sex who is very much your opposite. Femmenism is calling yourself a girly-girl and insisting that others call you a woman. Femmenism is playing up your femininity even when you know it can and will be used against you. Femmenism is using the master's tools to dismantle the master's house. Femmenism is political but not correct.

MEMOIRS OF AN OUT-OF-SYNC GIRLHOOD

I can still remember the day I learned what the word *lesbian* meant. I was in the third grade and had just kissed my best friend Erica on the lips. Suddenly everyone in my homeroom was screaming "Eeee-yew! Lezzies!" and making gagging noises. I didn't know what "lezzy" meant, but I could tell it wasn't good. When I discovered later that "lezzy" was short for "lesbian" and what *that* meant, I was more confused than ever. Despite the ugly way I learned it, I thought "lesbian" was the most beautiful word I had ever heard. Not even the image it conjured up, just the sound the vowels and the consonants made together. And when I did consider its meaning, I thought the word even more beautiful. For me, as a child, beautiful meant feminine, and what could be more feminine than two women making love?

The irony, of course, is that I was thinking all this in 1975, when the second wave of feminism was cresting, and many women (especially lesbians) were challenging traditional notions of femininity. Although she was no feminist activist, my mother considered herself a liberated woman and, looking back, I realize I must have driven her slightly crazy with my girliness. Not only did I embrace all things feminine, but I hated everything that I perceived as tainted with masculinity. I would only wear pants under duress and absolutely refused to wear jeans under any circumstances, although my mother and almost every other woman I knew wore them everyday. Needless to say, I hated boys, and I hated it even more when some friend of my parents would chuckle knowingly and say that *that* would change soon enough.

I clearly recall the battles my mother and I would have over "appropriate" clothing and toys. I wanted to wear pouffy pastel party dresses and Mary Janes every day of the week; she bought me corduroys and hiking boots. I routinely begged for—and was just as routinely denied—what I saw as the staples of girlhood: Barbies, a nurse kit, and Tinker Bell play makeup. Instead, I received entire clans of politically correct dolls (the Sunshine Family was white and the Happy Family was black, but their hair and facial features were the same). Even my literary heroes were wrong. I aspired to be just like clever, stylish Nancy Drew, whom my mother dismissed as prissy and dependent; she thought Laura Ingalls, the boisterous tomboy from the "Little House on the Prairie" TV series, a much better role model.

I grew up in a home where gender roles were anything but strict, and breaking out of them was strictly encouraged. Fresh out of the hospital, my mother, attempting to diaper a very small, squirmy baby with a very large, pointy diaper pin, passed out cold. My father, the oldest of seven children, finished the job neatly. I know this story not because it is a rare example of active parenting on my father's part, but because it illustrates how labor was divided in our household—on the basis of ability as much as gender. It was my father who stayed home with me (he was a student at the time) while my mother went off to work as a teacher in the local elementary school. (Later, when my father also began to work out of the home, a photograph of

Divine—in her trademark teal blue eyeshadow and body-hugging tulle dress—always hung above his desk.)

By a strange twist of sociocultural fate, my mother and I were in a similar situation: both of us would have gotten much of what we wanted as children if we only had been born boys. In the fifties, my mother's affinity for masculine clothing and activities was considered unnatural: in the seventies, my desire for ultra-feminine toys and accessories was perceived much the same way. Listening to "William Wants a Doll" on my Free to Be You and Me record, I understood that for a boy to plead for a baby doll was daring and original, while for a girl to do so would be old-fashioned and unimaginative. I have no doubt that, had I been born a boy, my parents would have tried to interest me in tea sets and Betty Crocker ovens in an effort to steer me away from G.I. Joes and Hot Wheels. Dominated by a new kind of double standard, my childhood taught me that avoiding gender roles can be every bit as frustrating, limiting, and ridiculous as adhering to them.

DROWNING IN THE SECOND WAVE

I came out in 1985, when I was a freshman at Vassar and political correctness was sweeping American campuses. Three years earlier at a Barnard women's studies conference, sex activists like Joan Nestle, Pat Califia, and Amber Hollibaugh had battled it out with hard-line feminists opposed to pornography, S/M, and butch-femme. These pivotal "lesbian sex wars" marked an end to old-style lesbian feminism with all its rigidity and uniformity, ushering in an era of sexual experimentation, diversity, and inclusiveness. Located just two hours up the Hudson from Barnard, Vassar's lesbian community remained blissfully unaware of these changes, thus avoiding the difficult challenges the conflict would have posed to our identities, our politics, and, last but most assuredly not least, our sex.

At Vassar and, I suspect, other college campuses of the time, the political often superseded the personal. For many of us, coming out didn't mean sleeping with a woman or even having a crush on one; it meant walking that longest mile every Thursday evening to the Gold Parlor, where LFL (the Lesbian Feminist League) met.

LFL is where I first heard about butch-femme—as an antiquated relic from the dark ages of lesbian herstory. While LFL's facilitator admitted that some poor misguided souls still engaged in such "role playing," the message was that butch-femme would soon be a thing of the past and not a minute too soon. When the topic came up again a couple years later, one woman, a histrionic British exchange student, told (complete with tears and supportive back-rubbing) of her traumatic experience as a femme—a cautionary tale for those of us tempted to enter into such an oppressive relationship.

Not that our own politically correct unions were particularly liberating. Like most other LFLers, I was in "a long-term, committed monogamous relationship" with a woman whom I resembled in thought, action, and dress. We shared our clothing (oversized men's shirts, bulky knee-length Greek fisherman's sweaters, and baggy Indonesian pants) and our politics (protesting the KKK in Philly, celebrating gay pride in New York, and marching for choice in D.C.). We even went to therapy together. Monogamy was no problem for me; having been date-raped at the age of fourteen by a man at least twice my age and cowed into sexual intercourse by numerous other males since, I approached *all* sex with more than a little trepidation. Our intimate, passionless relationship seemed to confirm the "Dear Abby" stereotype that women prefer snuggling to sex.

I had come to college with all my junior femme accessories in tow: trunks of kitschy 1950s prom dresses; countless fishnet stockings; black velvet pumps with four-inch heels; and, for everyday wear, skin-tight mini-skirts in a variety of colors. But after a year at Vassar, I was being chased out of women's rest rooms because with my buzzed hair, ripped jeans, leather jacket, clunky black shoes, and six-foot frame I looked like a man. By the time I graduated, I had not only entirely new political convictions (and a wardrobe to match); but a severe eating disorder and impenetrable (so to speak) sexual anxieties.

Looking back on all this now, I can't help but think that, for many of us, certain aspects of lesbian feminism were *enabling* (to use a term popular in the twelve-stepping eighties) rather that *empowering* (to use another). While even an ardent femmenist like myself is hesitant to add to the already considerable amount of time, energy, and paper that has been spent debating lesbians' sartorial preferences, I think it's worth pointing out that the standard dyke or lesbian feminist uniform—baggy, rumpled clothes, Birkenstocks, no makeup, unstyled hair—may have contributed to the negative body images many of us had (and may still have).

Studiously indifferent to our appearance, swaddled in loose, drab clothing, we were not androgynous, just asexual. For me, and, I suspect, for numerous others, the dyke aesthetic was economically as well as politically expedient: with a few minor adjustments, the same outfit could camouflage my body as it passed from anorexic scrawniness to bulimic bloat and back again.

Outwardly proud of our bravery and daring as lovers of women, we concealed our awkward bodies and unspoken anxieties under yards of fabric. Choosing not to wear makeup or "do" our hair not only articulated our rejection of patriarchal notions of femininity, but saved us from having to face ourselves in the mirror every day.

RENAISSANCE WOMAN

Two years after leaving college, in my second year of graduate school, I carried on a long-distance affair with a bartender I had met when I finally got up the nerve to go alone to Hepburn's, Philadelphia's only women's bar. Our relationship was a homecoming for me in many ways. This woman introduced me to a gay demimonde of drag queens, moving parties, leather bars, and after-hours clubs. In this new, glamorous, and sexually charged environment, I felt suddenly free—free to shed the formerly de rigueur, frumpy dyke uniform and don the slinky Spandex mini-dresses I'd been longing to wear. To my delight, this woman and her gay male friends not only refrained from doing an in-depth political analysis of my internalized heterosexism, but actually rewarded me by treating me like the prom queen I'd always dreamed of being. Finally, I felt like I had found the real me. I had come out years before as a lesbian, but I didn't really come to terms with my sexuality until I came out as a femme.

Apparently, I'm not alone. As Karen Everett and historian Lillian Faderman have pointed out, the lesbian community is in the throes of a butch-femme

renaissance. And as it turns out, I am a typical renaissance woman: a middle-class academic. But it's more than my class status and bookishness that set me apart from my pre-Stonewall predecessors, who were predominantly working-class bar dykes. On the one hand, I have benefited—often in ways I am not even aware of—from more than two decades of feminism and gay rights activism.

On the other hand, however, I feel a little like a freak in my own community, renaissance or not. During American lesbianism's first wave, young or newly out lesbians could count on being initiated into the mysteries of butch-femme courtship, dress, manners, and sex by a more experienced mentor. Today, although I know a lot of women I would describe as butch, and countless "lipstick lesbians," I know of only one self-identified butch-femme couple. (And the last time I saw them, the butch hit on me and the femme gave me laundry tips.) As a rule, my lesbian friends' response to butch-femme ranges from polite dismissal to scornful ridicule. To them, butch-femme is a label, it's role playing, and they want no part of it.

Not that I can blame them. Anyone who's had a pleasant walk with her lover spoiled by some jerk yelling, "Which one of you is the man?" knows the frustration of having one's lesbianism taken for a cheap imitation of heterosexuality. Likewise, anyone who's been called "sir," or worse yet, "little boy," simply because she has short hair, a flat chest, or unpierced ears knows how alienating *that* can be. But butch-femme is not about aping traditional notions of masculinity and femininity any more than it is about mimicking heterosexuality.

Nor has it ever been. From the late 1930s to the early 1960s, bar dykes implicitly understood butch and femme as two distinct lesbian-specific genders. Then, as now, you'll occasionally hear butch women jokingly call their evenings together "boys' night out." But unlike gay male culture, where drag queens and gay men often refer to each other as "she," both butches and femmes use the female pronoun when speaking of themselves and other lesbians.

I remember a conversation I had a couple of years ago with a friend who had just come back from a lesbian cruise. She said that you had to identify as either butch or femme to participate in the on-deck games. She refused to play at all and was angry because, as she put it, "I didn't pay $7,000 to have someone tell me I have to choose between butch and fuckin' femme." Although I am no more anxious than the next dyke to return to the days when butch and femme were the only options open to lesbians, I do wish that they could be accepted as two legitimate choices among many.

A year ago I expressed this wish in a review of Joan Nestle's groundbreaking anthology, *The Persistent Desire: A Femme-Butch Reader*. About a month later a woman wrote a letter to the editor of the alternative newspaper in which the review appeared, calling my article "dangerous" and accusing me of "proudly broadcasting restrictive, insulting, and oversimplified terms for behavior (Butch & Femme) without including some of the subtle intricacies, the complexities that truly make up a [lesbian] relationship." Ironically, the point I was trying to make in that essay is that butch-femme is nothing if not intricate, subtle, and highly complex, despite the fact that it is often oversimplified as a monolithic set of prescribed, restrictive behaviors by straight people and lesbians alike.

If lesbians see butch-femme as a capitulation to heterosexual norms, most of the straight world believes that butch-femme lurks at the core of *every* lesbian relationship, while the rest see it as a kinky, exotic sex game, better left in the bedroom closet along with the strap-on dildo, the handcuffs, and the edible underwear. Like pornography, everyone has an opinion about butch-femme, but no one seems very clear about what exactly it is.

My lover and I are no exception to the rule. Although we laughingly refer to *The Persistent Desire* as "the manual," we both have the sense that we are making up what it means to be butch and femme as we go along.

For me, being a femme means that I take pride in wearing just the right shade of lipstick, drawing the perfect black line above my eyelashes, keeping my legs smooth, and smelling good. Being a femmenist means knowing I am just as attractive when I don't wear makeup, shave, or put on perfume.

Being a femme also means that I want to be with a woman who appreciates it when I do these things—not silently, but openly and enthusiastically. A woman who sends me flowers; helps me out of cars; and knows how to take care of all the details,

like choosing the right wine, tipping the bartender, and calling a cab. Being a femmenist means both making sure that I know how to do all these things myself *and* getting an erotic charge of having them done for me.

Being a femme does *not* mean that I would rather be with a man, nor does it mean that I am attracted to masculine women. Unlike most of my friends, I prefer curvy, voluptuous women to buff, hard-bodied ones. But that doesn't mean I want to kiss a lipsticked mouth or caress a stockinged knee. Although I enjoy playing up my own femininity, I like to be with a woman who keeps hers under wraps, a gift for me alone to open and enjoy.

If butch women aren't masculine or even (in lesbian-feminist parlance) male-identified, what are they? To me a butch woman is one who exudes confidence, authority, independence, and a certain sexual cockiness. These may be considered masculine qualities, but I only find them attractive in women.

I remember one night my bartender girlfriend made a call from a pay phone at 3 A.M. Six feet tall, she was wearing heavy work shoes, black jeans, and a bomber jacket, her long blond hair hidden in her wool cap. As she was dialing, she tensed as a tough-looking young man approached, only to relax when he greeted her with, "Evening, officer." The man, making an assumption about her authority, not her gender, was responding to her butchness, not her "masculinity."

The same thing happens when my lover and I go out to dinner: no matter how we are dressed, invariably the server will take my order first, have my girlfriend taste the wine, and present her with the bill (even when I have requested it, credit card in hand).

According to the old dyke saying, there are more butches on the streets than between the sheets, which is just fine with me. What I love most about the woman I have been living with for the past two years is that underneath her crisp, starched shirts, behind her precise, controlled gestures is someone who is not only considerate, gentle, and patient, but beautifully, undeniably female. Far from simplifying our relationship, butch-femme layers it with a tantalizing intricacy and a highly erotic contradictoriness. If my girlfriend and I choose to split up our household chores fairly evenly, the division of labor in our bedroom is more complex. Suffice to say that when the sight of my lover's nude body makes me as hormonal as a thirteen-year-old boy, I feel perfectly free to act like one.

Life as a femme on the streets is seldom as pleasant or as safe as it is between the sheets. On the one hand, being a femme increases exponentially my much-publicized invisibility as a lesbian. Almost every day, and usually several times a day, all sorts of heterosexual men strike up conversations with me, comment on my appearance, or shout lewd remarks at me. Since to them I don't look like a dyke or even a liberated woman, they automatically assume that I look the way I do to provoke male attention and approval. For me, being a femme in public means constantly weighing my personal comfort against my personal safety. On the other hand, my lesbian invisibility is suddenly, dangerously, stripped away when I am with my lover. We found this out the hard way one night on vacation in France, when we were returning to our Left Bank hotel from a bar in the Marais, Paris, gay district. Conscious of the late hour, we resisted the temptation to stroll arm-in-arm or even touch hands. As we were walking in front of Notre Dame, a man passing in the opposite direction jammed his hand between my legs and roughly grabbed my crotch. Before I could get any words out, he was walking—not running—away, clearly unafraid of what my lover or myself might do to him.

I am convinced that the man attacked me because my girlfriend and I were so obviously lovers, not just because we were "unaccompanied" women. With that one gesture he challenged my lover's right to my body as much as he violated my right to myself. And it worked. For a few days, whenever my girlfriend touched me, all I could feel was that hand.

As a femme, I know that this kind of attack can and will happen again; as a femmenist, I am both willing to do everything I can to ensure that it doesn't and capable of understanding what's at stake when it does anyway.

RIDING THE THIRD WAVE

For years people gay and otherwise have tried to determine whether sexuality is a product of biology or environment. Like many gay men and lesbians,

I realize this is a moot point. Perhaps I would not have become a lesbian had I been born in a different era, culture, or even family, but I certainly would not be who I am without some very—shall we say—basic instincts.

Likewise, my femmenism. Although my early girly tendencies felt very instinctive to me, perhaps I would not have become a femme if my parents and the feminist movement had not pushed me so hard in the opposite direction. Perhaps being a femme is my way of rebelling against my parents; maybe it's just part of the current antifeminist backlash.

But I don't think so. I owe a lot to my first-wave foremothers: the turn of the century cultural feminists who based their politics on their femininity as well as the bar dykes of the forties and fifties who developed butch-femme into an art form. But I owe even more to my second-wave sisters: the feminists of the 1960s and '70s who separated gender from sex and sex from sexuality, and their lesbian counterparts who recognized in their homosexuality a source of pride, not shame.

This, it seems to me, is what femmenism is all about. Unlike my first- and second-wave predecessors, no one force-fed me femininity. Quite the contrary: I had to fight for it tooth and nail. I'm not claiming to have grown up in a vacuum: certainly, feminism or no feminism, there was still a lot of social pressure for me to get with the age-old restrictive feminine program. And I don't doubt that some of my femme identity comes from that pressure. But also unlike my lesbian/feminist predecessors, my female socialization was countered by feminism, a critical apparatus that enabled me, indeed forced me, to question every step I made along the long and winding road of gender-role identification. Having grown up in such an environment, I realize that my femmenism has not only been carefully nurtured, it is also perfectly natural.

This essay is dedicated in loving memory to Emily Polachek.

[1995]

89

Intersectionality and Identity Politics: Learning from Violence against Women of Color

KIMBERLÉ CRENSHAW

KIMBERLÉ CRENSHAW United States. 1959–   .
Law professor. International activist. Writer. One of
the founders of critical race theory. *Critical Race
Theory: The Key Writings That Formed the Movement*
(1995), *Words That Wound: Critical Race Theory,
Assaultive Speech, and the First Amendment* (1993).

INTRODUCTION

Over the past two decades, recognizing that the
political demands of many speak more powerfully
than the pleas of a few isolated voices, women have
organized against the almost routine violence that
shapes their lives. This politicization in turn has
transformed the way we understand violence
against women. For example, battering and rape,
once seen as private (family matters) and aberra-
tional (errant sexual aggression), are now largely
recognized as part of a broad-scale system of domination that affects women as a class.[1] This process
of recognizing as social and systemic what was formerly perceived as isolated and individual has also
characterized the development of what has been
called the "identity politics" of African Americans,
other people of color, and gays and lesbians, among
others. For those who engage in or advocate
identity-based politics, membership in a group—
defined by race, sex, class, sexual orientation or
other characteristics—both helps to explain the
nature of the oppression experienced by members
of that group and serves as a source of strength,
community, and intellectual development.

The problem with identity politics is that it frequently conflates or ignores intragroup differences.
In the context of violence against women, this elision of difference is problematic because the violence that many women experience is often shaped
by other dimensions of their identities, such as race,

class, and sexual orientation. Moreover, ignoring
difference *within* groups contributes to tension
among groups, another problem of identity politics
that bears on efforts to politicize violence against
women. Feminist efforts to politicize experiences
of women and anti-racist efforts to politicize experiences of people of color have frequently proceeded as though the issues and experiences they
each detail occur on mutually exclusive terrains.
Although racism and sexism readily intersect in the
lives of real people, they seldom do in feminist
and anti-racist theories and practices. And so, when
those theories and practices expound identity as
"woman" or "person of color" as an either/or proposition, they relegate the identity of women of color
to a location that resists telling.

My objective in this article is to advance the
telling of that location by exploring the race and
gender dimensions of violence against women of
color.[2] I consider how the experiences of women of
color are frequently the product of intersecting
patterns of racism and sexism, and how these experiences tend not to be represented within the discourses of either feminism or anti-racism, discourses
that are shaped to respond to one *or* the other, leaving women of color marginalized within both. I
do not mean to imply that the disempowerment of
women of color is singularly or even primarily
caused by feminist and anti-racist theorists or
activists. Rather, I hope to capture, at least in part,
how prevailing structures of domination shape various discourses of resistance. Although there are
significant political and conceptual obstacles to
moving against structures of domination with an
intersectional sensibility, I argue that the effort to
do so should be a central theoretical and political
objective of both anti-racism and feminism.

Although this article deals with violent assault
perpetrated by men against women, women are
also subject to violent assault by women. Violence
among lesbians is a hidden but significant problem.[3] Lesbian violence is often shrouded in secrecy
for similar reasons that have suppressed exposure
of heterosexual violence in communities of color—
fear of embarrassing other members of the community, which is already stereotyped as deviant, and
fear of being ostracized from the community. There
are nonetheless distinctions between heterosexual

violence against women and lesbian violence that warrant more analysis than is possible in this essay. I will therefore focus on the intersectionality of race and gender in the context of heterosexual violence.

In an earlier article, I used the concept of intersectionality to denote the various ways in which race and gender interact to shape the multiple dimensions of Black women's employment experiences.[4] My objective there was to illustrate that many of the experiences Black women face are not subsumed within the traditional boundaries of race or gender discrimination as these boundaries are currently understood, and that the intersection of racism and sexism factors into Black women's lives in ways that cannot be captured wholly by looking at the race or gender dimensions of those experiences separately. I build on those observations here by exploring the various ways in which race and gender intersect in shaping structural, political, and representational aspects of violence against women of color.

I end by addressing the implications of the intersectional approach within the broader scope of contemporary identity politics, and argue that we must recognize that the organized identity groups in which we and others find ourselves are in fact not monolithic but made up of members with different and perhaps competing identities as well. Rather than viewing this as a threat to group solidarity, we should view it as an opportunity for bridge building and coalition politics.

Intersectionality is not being offered here as some new, totalizing theory of identity. I consider intersectionality a provisional concept linking contemporary politics with postmodern theory. In mapping the intersections of race and gender, the concept does engage dominant assumptions that race and gender are essentially separate categories. By tracing the categories to their intersections, I hope to suggest a methodology that will ultimately disrupt the tendencies to see race and gender as exclusive or separable.[5] While the primary intersections that I explore here are between race and gender, the concept can and should be expanded by factoring in issues such as class, sexual orientation, age, and color. Indeed, factors I address only in part or not at all, such as class or sexual orientation, are often as critical in shaping the experiences of women of color. My focus on the intersections of race and gender only highlights the need to account for multiple grounds of identity when considering how the social world is constructed.

STRUCTURAL AND POLITICAL INTERSECTIONALITY AND BATTERING

I observed the dynamics of structural intersectionality during a brief field study of battered women's shelters located in minority communities in Los Angeles.[6] In most cases, the physical assault that leads women to these shelters is merely the most immediate manifestation of the subordination they experience. Many women who seek protection are unemployed or underemployed, and a good number of them are poor. Shelters serving these women cannot afford to address only the violence inflicted by the batterer; they must also confront the other multilayered and routinized forms of domination that often converge in these women's lives, hindering their ability to create alternatives to the abusive relationships that brought them to shelters in the first place. Many women of color, for example, are burdened by poverty, childcare responsibilities, and the lack of job skills. These burdens, largely the consequence of gender and class oppression, are then compounded by the racially discriminatory employment and housing practices women of color often face, as well as by the disproportionately high unemployment among people of color that makes battered women of color less able to depend on the support of friends and relatives for temporary shelter.

Where systems of race, gender, and class domination converge, as they do in the experiences of battered women of color, intervention strategies based solely on the experiences of women who do not share the same class or race backgrounds will be of limited help to women who face different obstacles. Such was the case in 1990 when Congress amended the marriage fraud provisions of the Immigration and Nationality Act to protect immigrant women who were battered or exposed to extreme cruelty by their spouses who were United States citizens or permanent residents. Under the marriage fraud provisions of the Act, a person who immigrated to the United States to marry a United States citizen or permanent resident had to remain "properly" married for two years before even applying for permanent resident status, at which time applications for the immigrant's permanent status were required of both spouses. Predictably, under these circumstances, many immigrant women were reluctant to leave even the most abusive of partners for fear of being deported. Reports of the tragic consequences of this double subordination put pressure on Congress to include in the Immigration Act of 1990 a provision amending the marriage fraud rules to allow for an explicit waiver for hardship caused by domestic violence.[7]

Yet many immigrant women, particularly immigrant women of color, have remained vulnerable to battering because they are unable to meet the conditions established for a waiver. The evidence required to support a waiver "can include, but is not limited to, reports and affidavits from police, medical personnel, psychologists, school officials, and social service agencies."[8] For many immigrant women, limited access to these resources can make it difficult for them to obtain the evidence needed for a waiver. And cultural barriers often further discourage immigrant women from reporting or escaping battering situations. Tina Shum, a family counselor at a social service agency, points out that "[t]his law sounds so easy to apply, but there are cultural complications in the Asian community that make even these requirements difficult. . . . Just to find the opportunity and courage to call us is an accomplishment for many." The typical immigrant spouse, she suggests, may live "[i]n an extended family where several generations live together, there may be no privacy on the telephone, no opportunity to leave the house and no understanding of public phones."[9] As a consequence, many immigrant women are wholly dependent on their husbands as their link to the world outside their homes.

Language barriers present another structural problem that often limits opportunities of non-English-speaking women to take advantage of existing support services. Such barriers not only limit access to information about shelters, but also limit access to the security shelters provide. Some shelters turn non-English-speaking women away for lack of bilingual personnel and resources. These examples illustrate how patterns of subordination intersect in women's experience of domestic violence. Intersectional subordination need not be

intentionally produced; in fact, it is frequently the consequence of the imposition of one burden that interacts with preexisting vulnerabilities to create yet another dimension of disempowerment. In the case of the marriage fraud provisions of the Immigration and Nationality Act, the imposition of a policy specifically designed to burden one class—immigrant spouses seeking permanent resident status—exacerbated the disempowerment of those already subordinated by other structures of domination. By failing to take into account the vulnerability of immigrant wives to their husbands' control, Congress positioned these women to absorb the simultaneous impact of its anti-immigration policy and their spouses' abuse.

The enactment of the domestic violence waiver of the marriage fraud provisions similarly illustrates how modest attempts to respond to certain problems can be ineffective when the intersectional location of women of color is not considered in fashioning the remedy. Cultural identity and class affect the likelihood that a battered spouse could take advantage of the waiver. Although the waiver is formally available to all women, the terms of the waiver make it inaccessible to some. Those immigrant women least able to take advantage of the waiver—women who are socially or economically the most marginal—are the ones most likely to be women of color.

The concept of political intersectionality highlights the fact that women of color are situated within at least two subordinated groups that frequently pursue conflicting political agendas. The need to split one's political energies between two sometimes opposing groups is a dimension of intersectional disempowerment that men of color and white women seldom confront. Indeed, their specific raced *and* gendered experiences, although intersectional, often define as well as confine the interests of the entire group. For example, racism as experienced by people of color who are of a particular gender—male—tends to determine the parameters of anti-racist strategies, just as sexism as experienced by women who are of a particular race—white—tends to ground the women's movement. The problem is not simply that both discourses fail women of color by not acknowledging the "additional" issue of race or of patriarchy but that the discourses are often inadequate even to the discrete tasks of articulating the full dimensions of racism and sexism. Because women of color experience racism in ways not always the same as those experienced by men of color and sexism in ways not always parallel to experiences of white women, anti-racism and feminism are limited, even on their own terms.

That the political interests of women of color are obscured and jeopardized by political strategies that ignore or suppress intersectional issues is illustrated by my experiences in gathering information for this essay. I attempted to review Los Angeles Police Department statistics reflecting the rate of domestic violence interventions by precinct because such statistics can provide a rough picture of arrests by racial group, given the degree of racial segregation in Los Angeles.[10] LAPD, however, would not release the statistics. A representative explained that one reason the statistics were not released was that domestic violence activists both within and outside the Department feared that statistics reflecting the extent of domestic violence in minority communities might be selectively interpreted and publicized so as to undermine long-term efforts to force the Department to address domestic violence as a serious problem. I was told that activists were worried that the statistics might permit opponents to dismiss domestic violence as a minority problem and, therefore, not deserving of aggressive action.

The informant also claimed that representatives from various minority communities opposed the release of these statistics. They were apparently concerned that the data would unfairly represent Black and Brown communities as unusually violent, potentially reinforcing stereotypes that might be used in attempts to justify oppressive police tactics and other discriminatory practices. These misgivings are based on the familiar and not unfounded premise that certain minority groups—especially Black men—have already been stereotyped as uncontrollably violent. Some worry that attempts to make domestic violence an object of political action may only serve to confirm such stereotypes and undermine efforts to combat negative beliefs about the Black community.

This account sharply illustrates how women of color can be erased by the strategic silences of anti-racism and feminism. The political priorities of both were defined in ways that suppressed information that could have facilitated attempts to confront the problem of domestic violence in communities of color.

DOMESTIC VIOLENCE AND ANTI-RACIST AND FEMINIST DISCOURSES AND POLITICS

Within communities of color, efforts to stem the politicization of domestic violence are often grounded in attempts to maintain the integrity of the community. Yet the violence that accompanies these attempts at unity is devastating, not only for the Black women who are victimized, but also for the entire Black community. The recourse to violence to resolve conflicts establishes a dangerous pattern for children raised in such environments. It has been estimated that nearly 40 percent of all homeless women and children have fled violence in the home, and an estimated 63 percent of young men between the ages of 11 and 20 who are imprisoned for homicide have killed their mothers' batterers. And yet, while gang violence, homicide, and other forms of Black-on-Black crime have increasingly been discussed within African-American politics, patriarchal ideas about gender and power preclude the recognition of domestic violence as yet another compelling incidence of Black-on-Black crime.

A common problem is that the political or cultural interests of the community are interpreted in a way that precludes full public recognition of the problem of domestic violence. While it would be misleading to suggest that white Americans have come to terms with the degree of violence in their own homes, race adds yet another dimension to why the problem of domestic violence is suppressed within non-white communities. People of color often must weigh their interests in avoiding issues that might reinforce distorted public perceptions against the need to acknowledge and address intracommunity problems. Yet the cost of suppression is seldom recognized, in part because the failure to discuss the issue shapes perceptions of how serious the problem is in the first place. Suppression of some of these issues in the name of anti-racism imposes real costs. Where information about violence in minority communities is not available, domestic violence is unlikely to be addressed as a serious issue.

The political imperatives of a narrowly focused anti-racist strategy support other practices that isolate women of color. For example, activists who have attempted to provide support services to Asian- and African-American women report intense resistance from those communities. At other times, cultural and social factors contribute to suppression. Nilda Rimonte, director of Everywoman's Shelter in Los Angeles, points out that in the Asian community, saving the honor of the family from shame is a priority.[11] Unfortunately, this priority tends to be interpreted as obliging women not to scream rather than obliging men not to hit.

Race and culture contribute to the suppression of domestic violence in other ways as well. Women of color are often reluctant to call the police, a hesitancy likely due to a general unwillingness among people of color to subject their private lives to the scrutiny and control of a police force that is frequently hostile. There is also a more generalized community ethic against public intervention, the product of a desire to create a private world free from the diverse assaults on the public lives of racially subordinated people. The home is not simply a man's castle in the patriarchal sense, but may also function as a safe haven from the indignities of life in a racist society. However, but for this "safe haven," in many cases, women of color victimized by violence might otherwise seek help.

There is also a general tendency within anti-racist discourse to regard the problem of violence against women of color as just another manifestation of racism. Gender domination within the community is reconfigured as a consequence of discrimination against men. Of course, it is probably true that racism contributes to the cycle of violence, given the stress that men of color experience in dominant society. It is therefore more than reasonable to explore the links between racism and domestic violence. But the chain of violence is more complex and extends beyond this single link. Racism is linked to patriarchy to the extent that racism denies men of color the power and privilege that dominant men enjoy. When violence is understood as an acting-out of being denied male power in other spheres, it seems

counterproductive to embrace constructs that implicitly link the solution to domestic violence to the acquisition of greater male power. The more promising political imperative is to challenge the legitimacy of such power expectations by exposing their dysfunctional and debilitating effect on families and communities of color. Moreover, while understanding links between racism and domestic violence is an important component of any effective intervention strategy, it is also clear that women of color need not await the ultimate triumph over racism before they can expect to live violence-free lives.

Not only do race-based priorities function to obscure the problem of violence suffered by women of color; feminist concerns often suppress minority experiences as well. Strategies for increasing awareness of domestic violence within the white community tend to begin by citing the commonly shared assumption that battering is a minority problem. The strategy then focuses on demolishing this strawman, stressing that spousal abuse also occurs in the white community. That battering occurs in families of all races and all classes seems to be an ever-present theme of anti-abuse campaigns.[12] Such disclaimers seem relevant only in the presence of an initial, widely held belief that domestic violence occurs primarily in minority or poor families. A few commentators have even transformed the message that battering is not *exclusively* a problem of the poor or minority communities into a claim that it *equally* affects all races and classes. I would suggest that assertions that the problem is the same across race and class are driven less by actual knowledge about the prevalence of domestic violence in different communities than by advocates' recognition that the image of domestic violence as an issue involving primarily the poor and minorities complicates efforts to mobilize against it. These comments seem less concerned with exploring domestic abuse within "stereotyped" communities than with removing the stereotype as an obstacle to exposing battering within white middle- and upper-class communities.

Women working in the field of domestic violence have sometimes reproduced the subordination and marginalization of women of color not only by speaking in universal terms about "batterers" and "victims" but also by adopting policies, priorities, or strategies of empowerment that either elide or wholly disregard the particular intersectional needs of women of color. While gender, race, and class intersect to create the particular context in which women of color experience violence, certain choices made by "allies" can reproduce intersectional subordination within the very resistance strategies designed to respond to the problem.

This problem is starkly illustrated by the inaccessibility of domestic violence support services to many non-English-speaking women. Diana Campos, Director of Human Services for Programas de Ocupaciones y Desarrollo Económico Real, Inc. (PODER), detailed the case of a Latina in crisis who was repeatedly denied accommodation at a shelter because she could not prove that she was English-proficient. The woman had fled her home with her teenage son, believing her husband's threats to kill them both. She called the domestic violence hotline administered by PODER seeking shelter for herself and her son. Because most shelters would not accommodate the woman with her son, they were forced to live on the streets for two days. The hotline counselor was finally able to find an agency that would take both the mother and the son, but when the counselor told the intake coordinator at the shelter that the woman spoke limited English, the coordinator told her that they could not take anyone who was not English-proficient. All of the women at the shelter are required to attend a support group and they would not be able to have her in the group if she could not communicate. The intake coordinator restated the shelter's policy of taking only English-speaking women, and stated further that the woman would have to call the shelter herself for screening.[13]

Despite this woman's desperate need, she was unable to receive the protection afforded English-speaking women, due to the shelter's rigid commitment to exclusionary policies. Perhaps even more troubling than the shelter's lack of bilingual resources was its refusal to allow a friend or relative to translate for the woman. This story illustrates the absurdity of a feminist approach that would make the ability to attend a support group without a translator a more significant consideration in the distribution of resources than the risk of physical harm on the street. The point is not that the

shelter's image of empowerment is empty, but rather that it was imposed without regard to the disempowering consequences for women who didn't match the kind of client the shelter's administrators imagined. And thus they failed to accomplish the basic priority of the shelter movement—to get the woman out of danger.

Here the woman in crisis was made to bear the burden of the shelter's refusal to anticipate and provide for the needs of non-English-speaking women. Said Campos, "It is unfair to impose more stress on victims by placing them in the position of having to demonstrate their proficiency in English in order to receive services that are readily available to other battered women."[14] The problem is not easily dismissed as one of well-intentioned ignorance. The specific issue of monolingualism and the monistic view of women's experience that set the stage for this tragedy were not new issues in New York. Indeed, several women of color reported that they had repeatedly struggled with the New York State Coalition Against Domestic Violence over language exclusion and other practices that marginalized the interests of women of color.[15] Yet despite repeated lobbying, the Coalition did not act to incorporate the specific needs of non-English-speaking women, many of whom are women of color, into their central organizing vision.

The struggle over which differences matter and which do not is neither an abstract nor an insignificant debate among women. Indeed, these conflicts are about more than difference as such; they raise critical issues of power. The problem is not simply that women who dominate the anti-violence movement are different from women of color but that they frequently have power to determine, either through material or rhetorical resources, whether the intersectional differences of women of color will be incorporated at all into the basic formulation of policy. Efforts to politicize the issue of violence against women challenge beliefs that violence occurs only in homes of "others." While it is unlikely that advocates and others intend to exclude or ignore the needs of poor and colored women, the underlying premise of this seemingly universalistic appeal is to keep the sensibilities of dominant social groups focused on the experiences of those groups. This strategy permits white women victims to come into focus, but does little to disrupt the patterns of neglect that permitted the problem to continue as long as it was imagined to be a minority problem. The experience of violence by minority women is ignored, except to the extent it gains white support for domestic violence programs in the white community. Unless policymakers ask why violence remained insignificant as long as it was understood as a minority problem, it is unlikely that women of color will share equally in the distribution of resources and concern. The struggle over incorporating these differences is not a petty or superficial conflict about who gets to sit at the head of the table. In the context of violence, it is sometimes a deadly serious matter of who will survive and who will not.

CONCLUSION

This essay has presented intersectionality as a way of framing the various interactions of race and gender in the context of violence against women of color. Yet intersectionality might be more broadly useful as a way of mediating the tension between assertions of multiple identity and the ongoing necessity of group politics. It is helpful in this regard to distinguish intersectionality from the closely related perspective of anti-essentialism, from which women of color have critically engaged white feminism for the absence of women of color on the one hand, and for speaking for women of color on the other.

One rendition of this anti-essentialist critique—that feminism essentializes the category woman—owes a great deal to the postmodernist idea that categories we consider natural or merely representational are actually socially constructed in a linguistic economy of difference.[16] While the descriptive project of postmodernism of questioning the ways in which meaning is socially constructed is generally sound, this critique sometimes misreads the meaning of social construction and distorts its political relevance.

One version of anti-essentialism, embodying what might be called the vulgarized social construction thesis, is that since all categories are socially constructed, there is no such thing as, say, Blacks or women, and thus it makes no sense to continue reproducing those categories by organizing around them. But to say that a category such as race or gender is socially constructed is not to say that the category has no significance in our world. On the contrary, a large and continuing project for subordinated people—and indeed, one of the projects for which postmodern theories have been very helpful—is thinking about the way power has clustered around certain categories and is exercised against others. This project attempts to unveil the processes of subordination and the various ways those processes are experienced by people who are subordinated and people who are privileged by them. It is, then, a project that presumes that categories have meaning and consequences. And this project's most pressing problem, in many if not most cases, is not the existence of the categories, but rather the particular values attached to them and the way those values foster and create social hierarchies.

This is not to deny that the process of categorization is itself an exercise of power, but the story is much more complicated and nuanced than that. First, the process of categorizing—or, in identity terms, naming—is not unilateral. Subordinated people can and do participate, sometimes even subverting the naming process in empowering ways. One need only think about the historical subversion of the category "Black" or the current transformation of "queer" to understand that categorization is not a one-way street. Clearly, there is unequal power, but there is nonetheless some degree of agency that people can and do exert in the politics of naming. And it is important to note that identity continues to be a site of resistance for members of different subordinated groups. At this point in history, a strong case can be made that the most critical resistance strategy for disempowered groups is to occupy and defend a politics of social location rather than to vacate and destroy it.

Vulgar constructionism thus distorts the possibilities for meaningful identity politics by conflating at least two separate but closely linked manifestations of power. One is the power exercised simply through the process of categorization; the other, the power to cause that categorization to have social and material consequences. While the former power facilitates the latter, the political implications of challenging one over the other matter greatly. We can look at debates over racial subordination throughout history and see that in each instance, there was a possibility of challenging either the construction of identity or the system of subordination based on that identity.

Consider, for example, the segregation system in *Plessy v. Ferguson*.[17] At issue were multiple dimensions of domination, including categorization, the sign of race, and the subordination of those so labeled. There were at least two targets for Plessy to challenge: the construction of identity ("What is a Black?"), and the system of subordination based on that identity ("Can Blacks and whites sit together on a train?"). Plessy actually made both arguments, one against the coherence of race as a category, the other against the subordination of those deemed to be Black. In his attack on the former, Plessy argued that the segregation statute's application to him, given his mixed race status, was inappropriate. The Court refused to see this as an attack on the coherence of the race system and instead responded in a way that simply reproduced the Black/white dichotomy that Plessy was challenging. As we know, Plessy's challenge to the segregation system was not successful either. In evaluating various resistance strategies today, it is useful to ask which of Plessy's challenges would have been best for him to have won—the challenge against the coherence of the racial categorization system or the challenge to the practice of segregation?

The same question can be posed for *Brown v. Board of Education*.[18] Which of two possible arguments was politically more empowering—that segregation was unconstitutional because the racial categorization system on which it was based was incoherent, or that segregation was unconstitutional because it was injurious to Black children and oppressive to their communities? While it might strike some as a difficult question, for the most part, the dimension of racial domination that has been most vexing to African Americans has not been the social categorization as such, but the myriad ways in which those of us so defined have been systematically subordinated. With particular regard to problems confronting women of color, when identity politics fails us, as it frequently does, it is not primarily because that politics takes as natural certain categories that are socially constructed but rather because the descriptive content of those categories

and the narratives on which they are based have privileged some experiences and excluded others.

Consider the Clarence Thomas/Anita Hill confrontation during the Senate hearings for the confirmation of Clarence Thomas to the Supreme Court. Anita Hill, in bringing allegations of sexual harassment against Thomas, was rhetorically disempowered in part because she fell between the dominant interpretations of feminism and anti-racism. Caught between the competing narrative tropes of rape (advanced by feminists) on the one hand and lynching (advanced by Thomas and his anti-racist supporters) on the other, the raced and gendered dimensions of her position could not be told. This dilemma could be described as the consequence of anti-racism's essentializing Blackness and feminism's essentializing womanhood. But recognizing as much does not take us far enough, for the problem is not simply linguistic or philosophical in nature. It is specifically political: the narratives of gender are based on the experience of white, middle-class women, and the narratives of race are based on the experience of Black men. The solution does not merely entail arguing for the multiplicity of identities or challenging essentialism generally. Instead, in Hill's case, for example, it would have been necessary to assert those crucial aspects of her location that were erased, even by many of her advocates—that is, to state what difference her difference made.

If, as this analysis asserts, history and context determine the utility of identity politics, how then do we understand identity politics today, especially in light of our recognition of multiple dimensions of identity? More specifically, what does it mean to argue that gendered identities have been obscured in anti-racist discourses, just as race identities have been obscured in feminist discourses? Does that mean we cannot talk about identity? Or instead, that any discourse about identity has to acknowledge how our identities are constructed through the intersection of multiple dimensions? A beginning response to these questions requires that we first recognize that the organized identity groups in which we find ourselves are in fact coalitions, or at least potential coalitions waiting to be formed.

In the context of anti-racism, recognizing the ways in which the intersectional experiences of women of color are marginalized in prevailing conceptions of identity politics does not require that we give up attempts to organize as communities of color. Rather, intersectionality provides a basis for reconceptualizing race as a coalition between men and women of color. For example, in the area of rape, intersectionality provides a way of explaining why women of color have to abandon the general argument that the interests of the community require the suppression of any confrontation around intraracial rape. Intersectionality may provide the means for dealing with other marginalizations as well. For example, race can also be a means to create a coalition of straight and gay people of color, and thus serve as a basis for critique of cultural institutions, including churches, that reproduce heterosexism.

With identity thus reconceptualized, it may be easier to understand the need and summon the courage to challenge groups that are after all, in one sense, "home" to us, in the name of the parts of us that are not made at home. This takes a great deal of energy and arouses intense anxiety. The most one could expect is that we will dare to speak against internal exclusions and marginalizations, that we might call attention to how the identity of "the group" has been centered on the intersectional identities of a few. Recognizing that identity politics takes place at the site where categories intersect thus seems more fruitful than challenging the possibility of talking about categories at all. Through an awareness of intersectionality, we can better acknowledge and ground the differences among us and negotiate the means by which these differences will find expression in constructing group politics.

[1997]

NOTES

1. See Susan Schechter, *Women and Male Violence: The Visions and Struggles of the Battered Women's Movement* (Boston: South End Press, 1982); R. Emerson Dobash and Russell Dobash, *Violence against Wives: A Case against the Patriarchy* (New York: Free Press, 1979); Lenore E. Walker, *Terrifying Love: Why Battered Women Kill and How Society Responds* (New York: Harper & Row, 1989).

2. For a body of legal scholarship that investigates the connections between race and gender, see, e.g., Regina Austin, "Sapphire Bound!", *Wisconsin Law Review* (1989), p. 539; Angela P. Harris, "Race and Essentialism in Feminist Legal Theory," *Stanford Law Review*, 42 (1990), p. 581; Marlee Kline, "Race, Racism and

Feminist Legal Theory," *Harvard Women's Law Journal*, 12 (1989), p. 115.

3. See Jane Garcia, "The Cost of Escaping Domestic Violence: Fear of Treatment in a Largely Homophobic Society May Keep Lesbian Abuse Victims from Calling for Help," *Los Angeles Times*, May 6, 1991, p. 2; see also Kerry Lobel, ed., *Naming the Violence: Speaking Out about Lesbian Battering* (Seattle: Seal Press, 1986); Ruthann Robson, "Lavender Bruises: Intralesbian Violence, Law and Lesbian Legal Theory," *Golden Gate University Law Review*, 20 (1990), p. 567.

4. Kimberlé Crenshaw, "Demarginalizing the Intersection of Race and Sex," *University of Chicago Legal Forum* (1989), p. 139.

5. Professor Mari Matsuda calls this inquiry "asking the other question." For example, we should look at an issue or condition traditionally regarded as a gender issue and ask, "Where's the racism in this?" Mari J. Matsuda, "Beside My Sister, Facing the Enemy: Legal Theory Out of Coalition," *Stanford Law Review*, 43 (1991).

6. During my research in Los Angeles, California, I visited Jenessee Battered Women's Shelter, the only shelter in the Western states primarily serving Black women, and Everywoman's Shelter, which primarily serves Asian women. I also visited Estelle Chueng at the Asian Pacific Law Foundation and I spoke with a representative of La Casa, a shelter in the predominantly Latino community of East Los Angeles.

7. Immigration Act of 1990, Pub. L. No. 101–649, 104 Stat. 4978. The Act, introduced by Representative Louise Slaughter (D-N.Y.), provides that a battered spouse who has conditional permanent resident status can be granted a waiver for failure to meet the requirements if she can show that "the marriage was entered into in good faith and that after the marriage the alien spouse was battered by or was subjected to extreme mental cruelty by the U.S. citizen or permanent resident spouse." H.R. Rep. No. 723(I), 101st Cong., 2d Sess. 78 (1990), reprinted in 1990 U.S.C.C.A.N. 6710, 6758.

8. H.R. Rep. No. 723(I) at 79, reprinted in 1990 U.S.C.C.A.N. 6710, 6759.

9. Ibid.

10. Most crime statistics are classified by sex or race but none are classified by sex *and* race. Because we know that most rape victims are women, the racial breakdown reveals, at best, rape rates for Black women. Yet, even given this head start, rates for other non-white women are difficult to collect. While there are some statistics for Latinas, statistics for Asian and Native American women are virtually non-existent. G. Chezia Carraway, "Violence against Women of Color," *Stanford Law Review*, 43 (1991).

11. Interview with Nilda Rimonte, Director of Everywoman Shelter, in Los Angeles, California (April 19, 1991). Also see Nilda Rimonte, "Cultural Sanction of Violence against Women in the Pacific-Asian Community," *Stanford Law Review*, 43 (1991).

12. Natalie Loder Clark, "Crime Begins at Home: Let's Stop Punishing Victims and Perpetuating Violence," *William and Mary Law Review*, 28 (1987), pp. 263, 282 n. 74 ("The problem of domestic violence cuts across all social lines and affects 'families regardless of their economic class, race, national origin, or educational background.'")

13. Letter of Diana M. Campos, Director of Human Services, PODER, to Joseph Semidei, Deputy Commissioner, New York State Department of Social Services (Mar. 26, 1992).

14. Ibid.

15. Roundtable Discussion on Racism and the Domestic Violence Movement (April 2, 1992) (transcript on file with the *Stanford Law Review*). The participants in the discussion—Diana Campos, Director, Bilingual Outreach Project of the New York State Coalition Against Domestic Violence; Elsa A. Rios, Project Director, Victim Intervention Project (a community-based project in East Harlem, New York, serving battered women); and Haydee Rosario, a social worker with the East Harlem Council for Human Services and a Victim Intervention Project volunteer—recounted conflicts relating to race and culture during their association with the New York State Coalition Against Domestic Violence, a state oversight group that distributed resources to battered women's shelters throughout the state and generally set policy priorities for the shelters that were part of the Coalition.

16. I follow the practice of others in linking anti-essentialism to postmodernism. See generally Linda Nicholson, *Feminism/Postmodernism* (New York: Routledge, 1990).

17. *Plessy v. Ferguson*, 163 U.S. 537 (1896).

18. *Brown v. Board of Education*, 347 U.S. (1954).

 90

Contesting Cultures: "Westernization," Respect for Cultures, and Third-World Feminists from Dislocating Cultures: Identities, Traditions, and Third World Feminisms

UMA NARAYAN

UMA NARAYAN India. ND. Philosopher. *Having and Raising Children: Unconventional Families, Hard Choices, and the Social Good* (1999), *Decentering the Center: Philosophy for a Multicultural, Postcolonial, and Feminist World* (2000).

INTRODUCTION

To try to define oneself intellectually and politically as a Third-World feminist is not an easy task. It is an unsettled and unsettling identity (as identities in general often are), but it is also an identity that often feels forced to give an account of itself. There is nothing inherently wrong about the project of giving an account of oneself—of one's specific location as speaker and thinker; of the complex experiences and perceptions and sense of life that fuel one's concerns; of the reasons, feelings, and anxieties that texture one's position on an issue; of the values that inform one's considered judgment of things.

Giving such an account of oneself has much to recommend it, for all of us. It enables one to see, with humility, and gratitude, and pain, how much one has been shaped by one's contexts, to sense both the extent and the boundaries of one's vision, to see how circumstances can circumscribe as well as inspire, and to become self-aware to some extent of one's perspectives on things. What is strange, I believe, for many Third-World feminists is the sense that, in our case, such an account is especially called for, *demanded* even, by the sense that others have that we occupy a suspect location, and that our perspectives are suspiciously tainted and problematic products of our "Westernization." Many Third-World feminists confront the attitude that our criticisms of our cultures are merely one more incarnation of a colonized consciousness, the views of "privileged native women in whiteface," seeking to attack their "non-Western culture" on the basis of "Western" values. This essay attempts to reveal some of the problems and paradoxes that are embedded in these charges of "Westernization" as well as to understand what provokes them.

I should admit at the outset the peculiarities of my own location. I have grown up and lived in a variety of places. I was born in India and lived in Bombay until I was eight, when I moved with my family to Uganda. I returned to India when I was fourteen and lived there until I was twenty-five. As is the case with many middle-class Indian children, my formal education was in the English language. For the last dozen years I have lived in the United States, which makes my currently calling myself a Third-World feminist problematic, in contrast, say, to feminists who live and function as feminists *entirely* within Third-World *national* contexts. Calling myself a "Third-World feminist" is problematic only if the term is understood narrowly, to refer exclusively to feminists living and functioning within Third-World countries, as it sometimes is. But, like many terms, "Third-World feminist" has a number of current usages. Some feminists from communities of color in Western contexts have also applied the term "Third World" to themselves, their communities, and their politics, to call political attention to similarities in the locations of, and problems faced by, their communities and communities in Third-World countries. As a feminist of color liv-ing in the United States, I continue to be a "Third-World feminist" in this broader sense of the term.

In writing this essay, I was caught in a struggle between my political desire to endorse this broader use of the term, and aspects of my project that seemed to indicate the narrower usage. For the most part, I have decided to use the term "Third-World feminist" more narrowly in this essay, to refer to feminists who acquired feminist views and engaged in feminist politics in Third-World countries, and those who continue to do so, since it is my project to argue that feminist perspectives are not "foreign" to these Third-World *national* contexts. Another reason for this choice is that the charge of being "Westernized" or having a "Westernized politics" that concerns me in this essay is more commonly leveled at feminists within Third-World national contexts. While feminists from *some* communities of color in Western contexts, such as feminists from Indian diasporic communities, are sometimes charged with "Westernization," the charges of "inauthenticity" leveled at many Black or Chicana feminists often take the form of asserting that they are embracing a "White" rather than a "Westernized" politics.[1] When confronted with such difficulties about terminology, perhaps the best one can do is to clarify one's use of the terms and give an account of the reasons for one's choices.

I wish to speak as a Third-World feminist in this essay for three important reasons. First, having lived the first quarter-century of my life in Third-World countries, and having come of age politically in such contexts, a significant part of my sensibilities and political horizons are indelibly shaped by Third World national realities. Second, this essay is an attempt to explicate the ways in which the concerns and analyses of Third-World feminists are rooted in and responsive to the problems women face within their national contexts, and to argue that they are not simpleminded emulations of Western feminist political concerns. I need to speak "as an insider" to make my point, even as I attempt to complicate the sense of what it is to inhabit a culture. Finally, though calling myself a Third-World feminist is subject to qualification and mediation, it is no more so than many labels one might attach to oneself—no more so than calling myself an Indian, a feminist, or a woman, for that matter, since all these identities are not simple givens but open to complex ways of being inhabited, and do not guarantee many specific experiences or concerns, even as they shape one's life in powerful ways.

I do not "locate myself" or specify who I am because I "*assume* . . . who I am *determines* what and how I know"[2] (italics mine), but rather to point to the complications of saying who I am, and of my assuming specific identities as a speaker. I do, however, wish to suggest some *linkages* between the complexities of who I am and what I claim to know. By "linkages," I wish to suggest *weaker* forms of influence or connection than is suggested by the term "determined." I do not simply *assume* such linkages, but attempt to give an account of them, a gesture that both "authorizes" my speech and opens the nature of this "authority" to evaluation and interrogation. To surrender the possibility of any connections between who I am and what I know is, for the purposes of this paper, to surrender my standing to speak as an "insider" to Third-World contexts, a standing that many Third-World feminists are often denied simply by virtue of their feminism.[3] This is a denial whose legitimacy is precisely what I wish to question.

· · ·

SPEECH AND SILENCE IN THE MOTHER TONGUE

Many feminists from Third-World contexts confront voices that are eager to convert any feminist criticism they make of their culture into a mere symptom of their "lack of respect for their culture," rooted in the "Westernization" that they seem to have caught like a disease. These voices emanate from disparate sources, from family members, and, ironically enough, from other intellectuals whose own political perspectives are indebted to political theories such as Marxism and liberalism that have

"Western" origins. This tendency to cast feminism as an aping of "Westernized" political agendas seems commonplace in a number of Third-World contexts.[4]. . . I shall try to reveal the problematic assumptions that underlie these rhetorical dismissals of Third-World feminist voices as rooted in elitist and "Westernized" views, and argue that, for many Third-World feminists, our feminist consciousness is not a hot-house bloom grown in the alien atmosphere of "foreign" ideas, but has its roots much closer to home.

My sense of entitlement to contest "my culture" is threaded through with both confidence and doubt. I grew up in a fairly traditional, middle-class, South Indian family, in the urban milieu of Bombay. Besides my parents, both my paternal grandparents also lived in the household, making us what in India is called a "joint family." As the eldest grandchild, and for several years the only child, I was raised with considerable indulgence. And I also remember the boundaries and limits to this indulgence. I remember my mother saying, "What sort of a girl are you to talk back like that to your father?" and my thinking, "But his reprimand was not deserved, and he will not listen to me, and she will not even let me speak."

I remember minding particularly that the injunction to be silent came from my mother, who told me so early, because she had no one else to tell, about her sufferings in her conjugal home. I remember my mother's anger and grief at my father's resort to a silencing "neutrality" that refused to "interfere" in the domestic tyrannies that his mother inflicted on my mother. The same mother who complained about her silencing enjoined me to silence, doing what she had to do, since my failures to conform would translate as her failures to rear me well.

I also remember my mother years later saying, "When I came to Bombay right after I was married, I was so innocent I did not know how to even begin to argue or protest when my mother-in-law harassed me," with a pride and satisfaction that were difficult for me to understand. That "innocence," that silence, indicated she was a good wife, a good daughter-in-law, well-brought up, a "good Indian woman," a matter of pride, even to her whose "innocence" had not prevented her from recognizing that what she was being subjected to was wrong, but which had prevented her from explicitly contesting it. And for once choosing to hold my tongue, I did not say, "But mother, you were not entirely silent. You laid it all on me. My earliest memory (you were the one who dated it after I described it to you, and were amazed that I remembered it) is of seeing you cry. I heard all your stories of your misery. The shape your 'silence' took is in part what has incited me to speech."

I am arguing that my eventual feminist contestations of my culture have something to do with the cultural dynamics of the family life that surrounded me as a child, something to do with my early sense of the "politics of home." My grandmother, whom I loved and who was indulgent to me in her own way, tormented my mother, whom I also loved, in several petty and some not so petty ways, using her inventiveness to add color and detail to the stock repertoire of domestic tyrannies available to Indian mothers-in-law. My father, clever and able and knowledgeable in so many other ways, would not "interfere." After all, "our" cultural traditions did not deem it appropriate for a son to reprimand his parents, providing a convenient cultural excuse for my father, despite his having had a "Westernized education" not very different from that which would later be blamed for the intransigence of his daughter! How could my loyalty and respect for "my culture" fail to be tainted by the fact that there was little justice or happiness for my mother in our house?

So it is strange, and perhaps not strange at all, that my mother adds her voice to so many others that blame my being "Westernized" for my feminist contestations of my culture. And I want to remind her, though I cannot bring myself to it, of her pain that surrounded me when I was young, a pain that was earlier than school and "Westernization," a call to rebellion that has a different and more primary root, that was not conceptual or English, but in the mother-tongue. One thing I want to say to all who would dismiss my feminist criticisms of my culture, using my "Westernization" as a lash, is that my mother's pain too has rustled among the pages of all those books I have read that partly constitute my "Westernization," and has crept into all the suitcases I have ever packed for my several exiles.

I would argue that, for many of us, women in different parts of the world, our relationships to our mothers resemble our relationships to the mother-lands of the cultures in which we were raised. . . .

It is not just that mothers and mother-cultures often raise their daughters with contradictory messages, but also that they often seem unaware of these contradictions. They give voice to the hardships and difficulties of being a woman that have marked their lives, teaching us the limitations and miseries of the routine fates that await us as women, while also resisting our attempts to deviate from these cultural scripts. And so they tend to regard their feminist daughters as symptoms of their failure to raise us with respect for "our" traditions, as daughters who have rejected the lessons they were taught by their mothers and mother-cultures. In seeing us in this mode, they fail to see how much what we are is precisely a response to the very things they have taught us, how much we have become the daughters they have shaped us into becoming.

. . .

Re-telling the story of a mother-culture in feminist terms is a *political* enterprise. It is an attempt to, publicly and in concert with others, challenge and revise an account that is neither the account of an individual nor an account "of the culture as a whole," but an account of *some* who have power within the culture. It is a political challenge to other political accounts that distort, misrepresent, and often intentionally fail to account for the problems and contributions of many inhabitants of the context. It is a political attempt to tell a counter-story that contests dominant narratives that would claim the entire edifice of "our Culture" and "our Nation" for themselves, converting them into a peculiar form of property, and excluding the voices, concerns, and contributions of many who are members of the national and political community.

Both mothers and mother-cultures often inspire the same sorts of complicated emotional responses from their feminist daughters—love and fear, the desire to repudiate and the desire to understand and be understood, a sense of deep connection and a desperate desire for distance. Acquiring one's own "take" or perspective on one's mother-culture seems no less vital and inevitable than developing one's own sense of one's mother, perspectives where love and loyalty often coexist, uneasily and painfully, with criticism. And no matter how far from them we move, we carry with us the shapes of their influence in much of what we do, even in our contestations and reworkings of the very lessons they taught us. Those who perceive our feminism as merely a symptom of our "Westernization," or accuse us of lack of "respect" for "our cultures," fail to see how complicated are an individual's relationships to powerful influences that shape both their conformities and their conflicts, fail to see the closeness between us and the contexts in which we have become both daughters and feminists.

I do not wish to suggest that there is any *necessary* connection between one's early experiences of oppressive gender roles within the family and one's subsequent feminist politics and perspectives. Some individuals might well acquire feminist political perspectives in ways less connected to familial experience; others might well experience oppressive gender roles without developing feminist perspectives on them. However, I also want to insist that, for many of us who do subsequently develop feminist perspectives, our early experiences of gender within the family do play a powerful part in our coming to see feminist perspectives as illuminating.

. . .

Feminist movements in various parts of the world develop when historical and political circumstances encourage public recognition that many of the norms, institutions, and traditions that structure women's personal and social lives, as well as the impact of new developments and social change, are detrimental to women's well-being, and enable political contestations in which the status quo is criticized and alternatives envisioned. Those in Third-World contexts who dismiss the politics of feminists in their midst as a symptom of "Westernization" not only fail to consider how these feminists' experiences within their Third-World contexts have shaped and informed their politics, but also fail to acknowledge that their feminist analyses are results of political organizing and political mobilization, initiated and sustained by women *within* these Third-World contexts.

. . .

SELECTIVE LABELING AND
THE MYTH OF "CONTINUITY"

In this section, I would like to shift to exploring some ways in which the sense of "cultural distinctiveness" from "Western culture" that developed in colonial contexts affects the ways in which the term "Westernization" is deployed in contemporary Third-World national contexts. I will argue that "Westernization" is often used to define "national culture" in ways that imagine more "cultural continuity" than is in fact the case. National cultures in many parts of the world seem susceptible to seeing themselves as *unchanging continuities* stretching back into a distant past. This picture tends to reinforce powerfully what I think of as the "Idea of Venerability," making people susceptible to the suggestion that practices and institutions are valuable *merely* by virtue of the fact that they are of long-standing. It is a picture of Nation and Culture that stresses continuities of tradition (often imagined continuities) over assimilation, adaptation, and change.

In some Third-World contexts, the past history of colonization seems to exacerbate this problem. For instance, many versions of Indian anticolonial nationalism relied greatly on appeals to a totalizing vision of "our ancient civilization," casting independence from colonialism as a recovery of this "ancient civilization" while simultaneously casting "Western civilization" as an uppity and adolescent newcomer to the stage of world history and civilization. Such discursive backgrounds often obscure the extent to which actual cultural practices, the significance of particular practices, as well as the material and social contexts of these practices, have undergone, and continue to undergo, substantial change. A frequent and noticeable peculiarity in these portrayals of unchanging "national culture, traditions, and values" in Third-World contexts is the degree to which there is an *extremely selective* rejection of "Westernization." What interests me is that while *some* incorporations of "Western" artifacts and practices are perceived and castigated as "Westernization," not all are, making some of these borrowings and changes contested and problematic in ways that other changes are not.

I believe that the term "Westernization" functions in colonial and postcolonial Third-World contexts

primarily as a sort of rhetorical term, and that the term is often deployed in inconsistent as well as problematic ways. Certain artifacts and not others are "picked out" and labeled "Western," and certain changes and perspectives are arbitrarily attributed to "Westernization" while others are not. This "selective labeling" of certain changes and not others as symptoms of "Westernization" reflects underlying political agendas. For instance, such "selective labeling" enables Hindu fundamentalists to characterize Indian feminist issues as symptoms of "Westernization" even while they skillfully use contemporary media such as television to propagate their ideological messages. Their commitment to "Indian traditions" seems unconcerned about whether the entry of television into Indian homes affects our "traditional way of life"! Feminist commitment to autonomy or equality for women can be portrayed as "Western values" by the same fundamentalists who discern no paradox, for instance, in appropriating the language of rights when it suits their interests.

Dismissing feminist criticisms as "Westernized" is, unfortunately, not unique to right-wing fundamentalists, but is a practice that can be found at various places in the political spectrum. Many Third-World intellectuals who are not fundamentalists also collaborate in depicting feminism as "Western" and a "foreign import" into Third-World contexts. Feminist political agendas are presumably deemed "tainted" by their alleged "origin" in the West. Many of these allegedly "Authentic Upholders of their Culture" seem to have few personal qualms, however, about using "Western" technology or buying "Western" consumer goods. Nor do they have political qualms about their Third-World nations spending their scarce monetary resources on the purchase of Western armaments.

This "selective labeling" of certain changes and not others as symptoms of "Westernization" enables the portrayal of unwelcome changes as unforgivable betrayals of deep-rooted and constitutive traditions, while welcome changes are seen as merely pragmatic adaptations that are utterly consonant with the "preservation of our culture and values." It has often struck me that many in Third-World contexts who condemn feminist criticism and contestations as "Westernization" would like to believe that there was a pristine and unchanging continuity in their "traditions and way of life," until we feminist daughters provided the first rude interruption.

Both my grandmothers were married at the age of thirteen. This was quite typical for the women of this particular community in that generation. I try not to think about what this meant to them, and above all what it could have meant to me if that particular "tradition" had continued. Like many other women of her generation and class and caste background, my mother was not married until she was twenty-one. How would my grandmothers have explained so significant a change in the space of one generation, a change that, however else it is to be explained, cannot be explained in terms of their daughters' rebellion against the practice of marriage following on the heels of the first indications of puberty?

It is not clear to me how illuminating or intelligible it is to attribute such a change to "Westernization," given *the complex interaction of local and colonial structures* that operated to produce this change. For instance, there were many more colleges for women by the time my mother was in her teens ("Westernization"?) than existed in my grandmothers' youths. A community that valued education as part of its particular caste-ethos (both my grandmothers had some schooling despite their early marriage, and were literate) was thus encouraged to educate its daughters longer, postponing the age of marriage. Indian nationalists (many of them men with "Westernized educations") whose attempts to "reform Hinduism" were linked to an attempt to create nationalist pride, and who criticized the practice of child-marriage, undoubtedly had some impact on this change.

It is not my intention to suggest that these startling changes with respect to women's education and the age of marriage happened without cultural notice or negotiation. Education for middle-class Indian women was clearly a contentious issue early in the nineteenth century, in part because it was initially predominantly organized by white Christian missionaries.[5] This raised the specters of both religious proselytization and the exposure of Indian women to the "harmful influences of Western culture." However, by the 1850s Indians opened their own schools for girls,[6] and before the end of the century, formal education "became not only acceptable,

but, in fact, a requirement for the new *bhadramahila* [respectable women]."[7] This process interestingly led to a few Indian women receiving university degrees "before most British Universities agreed to accept women on their examination rolls."[8]

There are difficulties in attempting to characterize changes such as education for Indian women as "Westernization." For one thing, education for *Western* women, especially college and professional education, was a deeply contested issue in the nineteenth century, and bitter struggles around higher education continued to be a part of Western feminist suffrage struggles of the early twentieth century.[9] Thus education for women could hardly be seen as an uncontroversial and longstanding aspect of "Western culture." For another, while Westerners, especially missionaries, were initially crucial causal components in setting up educational institutions for women, the success of these projects also depended on their being embraced and endorsed by segments of the Indian elites. Such endorsements were often couched in nationalist terms that specifically *resisted* seeing educating Indian women as "Westernization," seeing it variously as "making Indian women better wives and mothers," as helping to fulfill the urgent need for women doctors, and even as restoring to women the freedom, equality, and access to education they were believed to have enjoyed in the remote "golden age" of Hinduism. In many colonial and postcolonial contexts, it is difficult to clearly distinguish between the facts of change over time and "changes due to Western influence," since many of these changes involve complex "complicities and resistances" between aspects of "Western culture" and Third-World institutions, agents, and political agendas.

I wish to call attention to the fact that these undeniably significant changes in women's access to education and in the age of marriage were not, by my mother's lifetime, seen by my mother's family as a "surrender of our traditions" or as a problematic symptom of "Westernization." The traces of cultural conflict and negotiation that gave rise to them had vanished from view. For large segments of this particular Indian community, college education for its daughters and the correspondingly older age of marriage had, within a generation, become matter-of-fact elements of its "way of life."

It is far from my intention to suggest that the changes that led to my mother not being married at thirteen have affected the lives of *all* Indian women. Class, caste, religious, and ethnic differences pose problems for generalizations about women in Third-World contexts, in much the same way as differences among women pose problems for generalizations about women in Western contexts. Thirteen year olds continue to be married off in many poor and rural Indian communities. The forces of "modernization" that prevented my mother from being married at thirteen are, paradoxically, also responsible for the marriages of some contemporary thirteen year olds. Take the publicized recent case of Ameena, found sobbing in an Air India plane by an alert flight-attendant, in the company of a sixty-three-year-old Saudi man, who was taking her out of the country as his "wife." Today, there are businesses, paradigms of efficiency, organization, and modern entrepreneurial spirit, where skillful middle-men mediate, for a price, between poor Indian families anxious to marry off their barely teenage daughters and those with the foreign currency to purchase them as "wives": a complex interplay of "tradition" and "modernity," poverty and perversity, that has hundreds of Ameenas sobbing on their way to foreign fates that make my grandmothers' fates seem enviable.

I have been struck by the fact that it is not only religious fundamentalists who believe they are continuing "longstanding traditions" while ignoring the changes in which they have collaborated, but also women like my mother. My mother's vision manages to ignore the huge difference between her marriage at twenty-one and her mother's marriage at thirteen and sees both her life and her mother's as "upholding Indian traditions," while my life-choices are perceived to constitute a break with and rejection of tradition. My calling attention to the changes that mark the historical space between my mother's life and that of my grandmothers is an attempt to drive home the fact that it is not merely Third-World "intellectuals" or "Westernized feminists" who have been affected by profound changes in traditions, ways of life, and gender roles.

Third-World feminists, whose political agendas are constantly confronted with charges that they constitute betrayals of "our traditional ways of life,"

need to be particularly alert to how much relatively *uncontested change* in "ways of life" has taken place. We need to redescribe and challenge this picture of "unchanging traditions" that supposedly are only now in danger of "betrayal" as a result of feminist instigation. Some of these changes, while historically pretty recent, have become so "taken for granted" in our lifetimes that I am often amazed to confront the details and the extent of these changes.

. . .

I would argue that attempts to dismiss Third-World feminist views and politics as "Westernization" should be combatted, in part by calling attention to the selective and self-serving deployments of the term, and in part by insisting that our contestations are no less rooted in our experiences within "our cultures," no less "representative" of our complex and changing realities, than the views of our compatriots who do not share our perspectives. Third-World feminists urgently need to call attention to the facts of change within their contexts, so that our agendas are not delegitimized by appeals to "unchanging traditions." We need to point to how demands that we be deferential to "our" Culture, Traditions, and Nation have often amounted to demands that we continually defer the articulation of issues affecting women.

. . .

CONCLUSION

My intention has been to point to a number of assumptions that impede Third-World feminist criticisms of their cultures, and to challenge a number of assumptions about "Westernization" that are used to de-legitimize such criticisms. However, problematic pictures of "national identity" and "cultural authenticity" do not pose challenges exclusively for Third-World feminists. Dangerous visions of "Nation" and "national culture" seem ubiquitous across a range of nation-states in various parts of the world. I would like to end by examining the import of such views of "Nation" and "national culture" for feminist political contestations within Western as well as Third-World national contexts.

I am arguing that, instead of locating ourselves as "outsiders within" Third-World national contexts,

Third-World feminists need to challenge the notion that access to "Westernized educations," or our espousal of feminist perspectives, positions us "outside" of our national and cultural contexts. We need to problematize aspects of pictures of "our Culture and Traditions" that are deployed to de-legitimize our politics, and to insist that our views be accorded the privilege of substantive criticism rather than be subject to such dismissal. We need to insist that what divides us from those we oppose is not their "cultural authenticity" and our lack thereof, but differences of *ethical and political vision* about what sort of political entities our Nations should be and how they should treat their different members.

Given the interpenetration of "Western" values and institutions with the national political and cultural landscapes of "home," and the way that "Western" and "local" elements mesh in the geography of our lives, as well as in the lives of those in the Third World who do not share our cultural critiques, I believe many Third-World feminists would do better to insist that our voices are neither more or less "representative" of "our cultures" than the voices of many others who speak within our national contexts. In Third-World contexts, as elsewhere, feminist perspectives, like any political perspective, should not be considered valuable only if they accord with prevailing or dominant views and values. Political perspectives are often valuable precisely because they constitute new ways of seeing, fresh modes of reflection and assessment. New modes of assessment might well turn out to be as problematic as the older modes they critique, but that is a matter for sustained political discussion within a political community. What feminists everywhere need to insist on is not immunity from criticism but on the problematic nature of forms of dismissal that seek to undercut their very entry into such political dialogue.

We all need to recognize that critical postures do not necessarily render one an "outsider" to what one criticizes, and that it is often precisely one's status as "inside" the nation and culture one criticizes that gives one's criticisms their motivation and urgency. Third-World feminists are "insiders" in the sense that they are often both familiar with and affected by the practices, institutions, and policies they criticize. They are also active citizens within their respective national landscapes, whose political analyses and protests have been crucial to making issues affecting women into matters of national awareness and concern.

We need to move away from a picture of national and cultural contexts as sealed rooms, impervious to change, with a homogeneous space "inside" them, inhabited by "authentic insiders" who all share a uniform and consistent account of their institutions and values. Third-World national and cultural contexts are as pervaded by plurality, dissension, and change as are their "Western" counterparts. Both are often replete with unreflective and self-congratulatory views of their "culture" and "values" that disempower and marginalize the interests and concerns of many members of the national community, including women. We need to be wary about all ideals of "cultural authenticity" that portray "authenticity" as constituted by lack of criticism and lack of change. We need to insist that there are many ways to inhabit nations and cultures critically and creatively. Feminists everywhere confront the joint tasks of selectively appropriating and selectively rejecting various facets of their complex national, cultural, and political legacies, a critical engagement that can alone transform one's inheritances into a "culture" of one's own.

[1997]

NOTES

1. See, for instance, Barbara Smith, *Home Girls: A Black Feminist Anthology* (New York: Kitchen Table/Women of Color Press, 1983).
2. Christina Crosby further criticizes this assumption for being an assumption that "ontology is the ground of epistemology." "Dealing with Differences," in *Feminists Theorize the Political*, Judith Butler and Joan W. Scott, eds. (New York: Routledge, 1992), p. 137.
3. I have no desire to reify the category of "Third-World feminist" by implying that all feminists from Third-World backgrounds confront these dismissals. Nor do I wish to suggest that all Third-World women who engage in women-centered politics embrace the term "feminist." The term "feminism" has sometimes been questioned and sometimes been rejected by Third-World women because of its perceived limitations. See for instance, Madhu Kishwar, "Why I Do Not Call Myself a Feminist," *Manushi* 61 (Nov./Dec. 1990). Others refuse to surrender the term. See Cheryl Johnson-Odim's reasons for this position in "Common Themes, Different Contexts: Third World Women and Feminism," in C. Mohanty, A. Russo, and L. Torres, eds., *Third World Women and the Politics of Feminism* (Bloomington: Indiana University Press, 1991).

4. See the essays in *Identity Politics and Women: Cultural Reassertions and Feminisms in International Perspective*, Valentine M. Moghadam, ed. (Boulder, Colo.: Westview Press, 1994).

5. See Kumari Jayawardena's discussion of nineteenth-century missionary girls' schools in India and Sri Lanka in her chapter, "Christianity and the 'Westernized Oriental Gentlewomen'," in her *The White Women's Other Burden* (New York: Routledge, 1995).

6. Partha Chatterjee, "Colonialism, Nationalism and Colonized Women: The Contest in India," *American Ethnologist* (1989), p. 628.

7. Ibid.

8. Ibid.

9. Ibid., p. 624. Also see his *Nationalist Thought and the Colonial World: A Derivative Discourse?* (London: Zed Books, 1986.)

 91

About Canons and Culture Wars from Differencing the Canon: Feminist Desire and the Writing of Art's Histories

GRISELDA POLLOCK

GRISELDA POLLOCK. 1949– . South Africa. Lives and works in England. Art historian; feminist and cultural theorist. *Old Mistresses; Women, Art and Ideology* (1981), *Mary Cassatt Painter of Modern Women* (1998), *Vision and Difference: Feminism, Femininity and the Histories of Art* (2003), *Encounters in the Virtual Feminist Museum Time, Space and the Archive* (2007).

The term *canon* is derived from the Greek *kanon*, which means 'rule' or 'standard', evoking both social regulation and military organisation. Originally, the canon had religious overtones, being the officially accepted list of writings that forms the 'Scriptures'. The first canonisation exercise was the selection of the Hebrew Scriptures, made by an emergent priestly class around the seventh century BCE, of which the historian Ellis Rivkin has argued that the choice was 'not primarily the work of scribes, scholars or editors who sought out neglected traditions

about wilderness experience, but of a class struggling to gain power'.[1] Canons may be understood, therefore, as the retrospectively legitimating backbone of a cultural and political identity, a consolidated narrative of origin, conferring authority on the texts selected to naturalise this function. Canonicity refers to both the assumed quality of an included text and to the status a text acquires because it belongs within an authoritative collection. Religions confer sanctity upon their canonised texts, often implying, if not divine authorship, at least divine authority.

With the rise of academies and universities, canons have become secular, referring to bodies of literature or the pantheon of art. The canon signifies what academic institutions establish as the best, the most representative, and the most significant texts—or objects—in literature, art history or music. Repositories of transhistorical aesthetic value, the canons of various cultural practices establish what is unquestionably great, as well as what must be studied as a model by those aspiring to the practice. The canon comprehensively constitutes the patrimony of any person wanting to be considered 'educated'. As Dominick LaCapra comments, the canon reaffirms a 'displaced religious sense of the sacred text as the beacon of common culture for an educated elite'.[2]

Historically, there has never been just one, single canon. Art historically, there are competing canons. During the great era of art historical activity in the nineteenth century, many artists as well as schools and traditions were rediscovered and revalued. Rembrandt, for instance, was reclaimed in rhe nineteenth century as a great religious and spiritual artist instead of being dismissed, as he had been in the eighteenth, as a sloppy painter of low subjects, while Hals, long avoided as a minor Flemish genre painter of no great skill or distinction, became an inspiration to Manet and his generation of modernists in search of new techniques of painting 'life'.[3]

Always associated with canonicity as a structure, however, is the idea of naturally revealed, universal value and individual achievement that serves to justify the highly select and privileged membership of the canon that denies any selectivity. As the record of autonomous genius, the canon appears to arise spontaneously. In 'What is a Masterpiece?' the art historian Kenneth Clark acknowledged the fluctuations of taste according to social and historical vagaries that allowed Rembrandt to be disdained in the eighteenth century or artists that we no longer value to have been highly rated in the nineteenth. None the less, Clark insists that 'Although many meanings cluster around the word masterpiece, it is above all the work of an artist of genius who has been absorbed by the spirit of the time in a way that has made his individual experiences universal'.[4]

The canon is not just the product of the academy. It is also created by artists or writers. Canons are formed from the ancestral figures evoked in an artist/writer/composer's work through a process that Harold Bloom, author of the major defence of canonicity, *The Western Canon* (1994), identified as 'the anxiety of influence', and I, in another mode of argument, the avant-garde gambit of 'reference, deference, and difference'.[5] The canon thus not only determines what we read, look at, listen to, see at the art gallery and study in school or university. It is formed retrospectively by what artists themselves select as their legitimating or enabling predecessors. If, however, artists—because they are women or non-European—are both left out of the records and ignored as part of the cultural heritage, the canon becomes an increasingly impoverished and impoverishing filter for the totality of cultural possibilities generation after generation. Today, the canons are settled into well-known patterns because of the role of institutions such as museums, publishing houses and university curricula. We know these canons—Renaissance, modernist, etc. through what gets hung in art galleries, played in concerts, published and taught as literature or art history in universities and schools, gets put on the curriculum as the standard and necessary topics for study at all levels in the educating—acculturating, assimilating—process.

In recent years the culture wars have broken out as new social movements target canons as pillars of the established elites and supports of hegemonic social groups, classes and 'races'.[6] Canonicity has been subjected to a withering critique for the selectivity it disavows, for its racial and sexual exclusivity and for the ideological values which are enshrined not just in the choice of favoured texts but in the methods of their interpretation—celebratory affirmations of a world where, according to Henry Louis Gates Jnr., 'men were men and men were white, when scholar-critics were white men and when

women and people of colour were voiceless, faceless servants or laborers, pouring tea and filling brandy snifters in the boardrooms of old boys' clubs'.[7] Critique of the canon has been motivated by those who feel themselves voiceless and deprived of a recognised cultural history because the canon excludes the texts written, painted or composed and performed by their social, gender or cultural community. Without such recognition, these groups lack representations of themselves to contest the stereotyping, discriminating and oppressive ones which figure in that which has been canonised. Henry Louis Gates Jnr. explains the political implications of enlarged canons that accommodate the voice of the Other:

> To reform core curriculums, to account for the comparable eloquence of the African, the Asian, and the Middle Eastern traditions, is to begin to prepare our students for their roles as citizens of world cultures through a truly human notion of the 'humanities' rather than—as Mr. Bennett [Secretary for Education under Ronald Reagan] and Mr. [Harold] Bloom would have it—as guardians of the last frontier outpost of white male western culture, the keepers of the master's pieces.[8]

The 'discourse of the Other' must of necessity 'difference the canon'. Yet it reveals a new difficulty. However strategically necessary the new privileging of the Other certainly is in a world so radically imbalanced in favour of the 'privileged male of the white race', there is still a binary opposition in place which cannot ever relieve the Other of being *other* to a dominant norm.

Different kinds of moves have been necessary even to imagine a way beyond that trap. Toni Morrison has argued that American literature, whose canon so forcefully excludes African American voices, should, none the less, be read as structurally conditioned by 'a dark, abiding, signing Africanist presence'.[9] By identifying this structurally negative relationship to African culture and Africans within the American canon of white literature, notions of excluded others are transformed into questions about the formation of Eurocentric intellectual domination and the resultant impoverishment of what is read and studied. This argument can be compared with that Rozsika Parker and I first advanced in 1981 in opposition to an initial feminist attempt to put women into the canon of art history. We used the apparent exclusion of women as artists to reveal how, structurally, the discourse of phallocentric art history relied upon the category of a negated femininity in order to secure the supremacy of masculinity within the sphere of creativity.[10]

In the early 1990s, the issue of the total gender asymmetry in the canon, implicit in all feminist interrogations of art history, became an articulated platform through a panel organised by Linda Nochlin, *Firing the Canon*, in New York in 1990 and through the critical writing of Nanette Salomon on the canon from Vasari to Janson.[11] Feminist critics of the canons of Western culture could easily critique the all-male club represented by Ernst Gombrich's *Story of Art* and the original editions of H. W. Janson's *History of Art* that featured not one women artist.[12] Feminists have shown how canons actively create a patrilineal genealogy of father–son succession and replicate patriarchal mythologies of exclusively masculine creativity.[13] Susan Hardy Aiken, for instance, traces the parallels between the competitive modelling of academic practices, the Oedipal stories narrated by canons, the rivalries that serve as the unconscious motor of intellectual or cultural development, all of which produce the coincidence of the 'noble lineage of male textuality, the parallel formation of canons and the colonizing projects of western Europe organised rhetorically around the opposition civilisation and barbarism'. She concludes:

> These links between priestly authority, the implications of 'official' textuality, and the exclusionary and hegemonic motives within canon formation have obvious significance for the question of women and canonicity . . . Woman . . . becomes a profanation, a heretical voice from the wilderness that threatens the *patrius sermo*,—the orthodox, public, canonical Word—with the full force of another tongue—a mother tongue—the *lingua materna* that for those still within the confines of the old order must remain unspeakable.[14]

Is feminism to intervene to create a maternal genealogy to compete with the paternal lineage and to invoke the voice of the Mother to counter the text of the Father enshrined by existing canons? Susan Hardy Aiken warns: 'one might, by attacking, reify the power one opposes.'[15] Against the closed library, from which, in her famous feminist parable on the exclusivity of the canon, *A Room of One's Own* (1928), Virginia Woolf so eloquently showed women to be shut out, we might propose more than another bookroom. Instead we need a *polylogue*: 'the interplay of many voices, a kind of creative "barbarism" that would disrupt the monological, colonizing, centric drives of "civilisation" . . . Such a vision lives, as Adrienne Rich has taught us, in a re-vision: an eccentric re-reading, re-discovering what the canon's priestly mantle would conceal: the entanglements of all literature with the power dynamics of culture.'[16]

[1999]

NOTES

1. Ellis Rivkin, *The Shaping of Jewish History: A Radical New Interpretation* (New York: Scribner, 1971), p. 30.
2. Dominick Lacapra, 'Canons, Texts and Contexts', in *Representing the Holocaust: History, Theory, Trauma* (Ithaca: Cornell University Press, 1994), p. 19.
3. Théophile Thoré, 'Van der Meer of Delft', *Gazette des Beaux Arts*, 71 (1866), pp. 297–330, 458–70, 542–75; 'Frans Hals', *Gazette des Beaux Arts*, 24 (1868), pp. 219–30, 431–48; R. W. Scheller, 'Rembrandt's Reputatie Houbraken tot Scheltema', *Nederlands Kunsthistorische Jaarboek*, 12 (1961), pp. 81–118; S. Heiland and H. Lüdecke, *Rembrandt und die Nachwelt* (Leipzig, 1960); T. Reff, 'Manet and Blanc's *Histoire des Peintres*', *Burlington Magazine*, 107 (1970), pp. 456–8.
4. Kenneth Clark, 'What is a Masterpiece?', *Portfolio* (Feb./Mar. 1980), p. 53.
5. Harold Bloom, *The Anxiety of Influence* (Oxford: Oxford University Press, 1973); Griselda Pollock, *Avant-garde Gambits: Gender and the Colour of Art History* (London: Thames & Hudson, 1992).
6. Henry Louis Gates Jnr., *Loose Canons: Notes on the Culture Wars* (New York and Oxford: Oxford University Press, 1992).
7. Henry Louis Gates Jnr., 'Whose Canon Is It Anyway?', *New York Times Book Review* (26 February 1989), section 7, 3, reprinted in a revised version in *Loose Canons*, as 'The Master's Pieces: On Canon Formation and the African-American Tradition', pp. 17–42.
8. *Ibid.*, p. 4.
9. Toni Morrison, *Playing in the Dark: Whiteness and the Literary Imagination* (Cambridge, Mass. and London: Harvard University Press, 1992), p. 5.
10. Rozsika Parker and Griselda Pollock, *Old Mistresses: Women, Art & Ideology* (London: Pandora Books, 1981, new edn 1996; now London: Rivers Oram Press).
11. Jan Gorak, *The Making of the Modern Canon: Genesis and Crisis of a Literary Idea* (London: Athlone Press, 1991); Robert Von Hallberg, ed., *Canons* (Chicago: Chicago University Press, 1984); Paul Lauter, *Canons and Contexts* (New York: Oxford University Press, 1991) and a special issue of *Salmagundi*, 72 (1986). Nanette Salomon, 'The Art Historical Canon: Sins of Omission', in *(En)gendering Knowledge: Feminism in*

Academe, ed. Joan Hartmann and Ellen Messer-Davidow (Knoxville: University of Tennessee Press, 1991), pp. 222–36; Adrian Rifkin, 'Art's Histories', in *The New Art History*, ed. Al Rees and Frances Borzello (London: Camden Press, 1986), pp. 157–63. See 'Rethinking the Canon', a collection of essays, *Art Bulletin*, 78, 2 (June 1996), pp. 198–217.

12. H. W. Janson was challenged about this omission and he stated that there had never been a woman artist who had changed the direction of art history and thus none deserved inclusion in his work. Salomon, p. 225.

13. Susan Hardy Aiken, 'Women and the Question of Canonicity', *College English*, 48, 3 (March 1986), pp. 288–99.

14. *Ibid.*, p. 297.

15. *Ibid.*, p. 298.

16. *Ibid.*, p. 298.

 92

An Introduction to Female Masculinity from Female Masculinity

JUDITH HALBERSTAM

JUDITH HALBERSTAM United States. 1961– . Literary scholar. Also works in queer and gender studies. *Posthuman Bodies* (1995), *Skin Shows: Gothic Horror and the Technology of Monsters* (1995), *In a Queer Time and Place: Transgender Bodies, Subcultural Lives* (2005).

THE BATHROOM PROBLEM

If three decades of feminist theorizing about gender has thoroughly dislodged the notion that anatomy is destiny, that gender is natural, and that male and female are the only options, why do we still operate in a world that assumes that people who are not male are female, and people who are not female are male (and even that people who are not male are not people!). If gender has been so thoroughly defamiliarized, in other words, why do we not have multiple gender options, multiple gender categories, and real-life nonmale and nonfemale options for embodiment and identification? In a way, gender's very flexibility and seeming fluidity is precisely what allows dimorphic gender to hold sway. Because so few people actually match any given community standards for male or female, in

other words, gender can be imprecise and therefore multiply relayed through a solidly binary system. At the same time, because the definitional boundaries of male and female are so elastic, there are very few people in any given public space who are completely unreadable in terms of their gender.

Ambiguous gender, when and where it does appear, is inevitably transformed into deviance, thirdness, or a blurred version of either male or female. As an example, in public bathrooms for women, various bathroom users tend to fail to measure up to expectations of femininity, and those of us who present in some ambiguous way are routinely questioned and challenged about our presence in the "wrong" bathroom. For example, recently, on my way to give a talk in Minneapolis, I was making a connection at Chicago's O'Hare Airport. I strode purposefully into the women's bathroom. No sooner had I entered the stall than someone was knocking at the door: "Open up, security here!" I understood immediately what had happened. I had, once again, been mistaken for a man or a boy, and some woman had called security. As soon as I spoke, the two guards at the bathroom stall realized their error, mumbled apologies, and took off. On the way home from the same trip, in the Denver airport, the same sequence of events was repeated. Needless to say, the policing of gender within the bathroom is intensified in the space of the airport, where people are literally moving through space and time in ways that cause them to want to stabilize some boundaries (gender) even as they traverse others (national). However, having one's gender challenged in the women's rest room is a frequent occurrence in the lives of many androgynous or masculine women; indeed, it is so frequent that one wonders whether the category "woman," when used to designate public functions, is completely outmoded.

It is no accident, then, that travel hubs become zones of intense scrutiny and observation. But gender policing within airport bathrooms is merely an intensified version of a larger "bathroom problem." For some gender-ambiguous women, it is relatively easy to "prove" their right to use the women's bathroom—they can reveal some decisive gender trait (a high voice, breasts), and the challenger will generally back off. For others (possibly low-voiced or hairy or breastless people), it is quite difficult to justify their presence in the women's bathroom, and these people may tend to use the men's bathroom, where scrutiny is far less intense. Obviously, in these bathroom confrontations, the gender-ambiguous person first appears as not-woman ("You are in the wrong bathroom!"), but then the person appears as something actually even more scary, not-man ("No, I am not," spoken in a voice recognized as not-male). Not-man and not-woman, the gender-ambiguous bathroom user is also not androgynous or in-between; this person is gender deviant.

For many gender deviants, the notion of passing is singularly unhelpful. Passing as a narrative assumes that there is a self that masquerades as another kind of self and does so successfully; at various moments, the successful pass may cohere into something akin to identity. At such a moment, the passer has *become*. What of a biological female who presents as butch, passes as male in some circumstances and reads as butch in others, and considers herself not to be a woman but maintains distance from the category "man"? For such a subject, identity might best be described as process with multiple sites for becoming and being. To understand such a process, we would need to do more than map psychic and physical journeys between male and female and within queer and straight space; we would need, in fact, to think in fractal terms and about gender geometries. Furthermore . . ., when and where we discuss the sexualities at stake in certain gender definitions, very different identifications between sexuality, gender, and the body emerge. The stone butch, for example, in her self-definition as a non-feminine, sexually untouchable female, complicates the idea that lesbians share female sexual practices or women share female sexual desires or even that masculine women share a sense of what animates their particular masculinities.

I want to focus on what I am calling "the bathroom problem" because I believe it illustrates in remarkably clear ways the flourishing existence of gender binarism despite rumors of its demise. Furthermore, many normatively gendered women have no idea that a bathroom problem even exists and claim to be completely ignorant about the trials and tribulations that face the butch woman who needs to use a public bathroom. But queer literature is littered with references to the bathroom problem, and it would not be an exaggeration to call it a standard feature of the butch narrative. For example, Leslie Feinberg provides clear illustrations of the dimensions of the bathroom problem in *Stone Butch Blues*. In this narrative of the life of the he-she factory worker, Jess Goldberg, Jess recounts many occasions in which she has to make crucial decisions about whether she can afford to use the women's bathroom. On a shopping outing with some drag queens, Jess tells Peaches: "I gotta use the bathroom. God, I wish I could wait, but I can't." Jess takes a deep breath and enters the ladies' room:

> Two women were freshening their makeup in front of the mirror. One glanced at the other and finished applying her lipstick. "Is that a man or a woman?" She said to her friend as I passed them.
>
> The other woman turned to me. "This is the woman's bathroom," she informed me.
>
> I nodded. "I know."
>
> I locked the stall door behind me. Their laughter cut me to the bone. "You don't really know if that is a man or not," one woman said to the other. "We should call security to make sure."
>
> I flushed the toilet and fumbled with my zipper in fear. Maybe it was just an idle threat. Maybe they really would call security. I hurried out of the bathroom as soon as I heard both women leave.[1]

For Jess, the bathroom represents a limit to her ability to move around in the public sphere. Her body, with its needs and physical functions, imposes a limit on her attempts to function normally despite her variant gender presentation. The women in the rest room, furthermore, are depicted as spiteful, rather than fearful. They toy with Jess by calling into question her right to use the rest room and threatening to call the police. As Jess puts it: "They never would have made fun of a guy like that." In other words, if the women were truly anxious for their safety, they would not have toyed with the intruder, and they would not have hesitated to call the police. Their casualness about calling security indicates that they know Jess is a woman but want to punish her for her inappropriate self-presentation.

Another chronicle of butch life, *Throw It to the River*, by Nice Rodriguez, a Filipina-Canadian writer, also tells of the bathroom encounter. In a story called "Every Full Moon," Rodriguez tells a romantic tale about a butch bus conductor called Remedios who falls in love with a former nun called Julianita. Remedios is "muscular around the arms and shoulders," and her "toughness allows her to bully anyone who will not pay the fare."[2] She aggressively flirts with Julianita until Julianita agrees to go to a movie with Remedios. To prepare for her date, Remedios dresses herself up, carefully flattening out her chest with Band-Aids over the nipples: "She bought a white shirt in Divisoria just for this date. Now she worries that the cloth may be too thin and transparent, and that Julianita will be turned off when her nipples protrude out like dice" (33). With her "well-ironed jeans," her smooth chest, and even a man's manicure, Remedios heads out for her date. However, once out with Julianita, Remedios, now dressed in her butch best, has to be careful about public spaces. After the movie, Julianita rushes off to the washroom, but Remedios waits outside for her:

> She has a strange fear of ladies rooms. She wishes there was another washroom somewhere between the mens' and the ladies' for queers like her. Most of the time she holds her pee—sometimes as long as half a day—until she finds a washroom where the users are familiar with her. Strangers take to her unkindly, especially elder women who inspect her from head to toe. (40–41)

Another time, Remedios tells of being chased from a ladies' room and beaten by a bouncer. The bathroom problem for Remedios and for Jess severely limits their ability to circulate in public spaces and actually brings them into contact with physical violence as a result of having violated a cardinal rule of gender: one must be readable at a glance. After Remedios is beaten for having entered a ladies' room, her father tells her to be more careful, and Rodriguez notes: "She realized that being cautious means swaying her hips and parading her boobs when she enters any ladies room"(30).

If we use the paradigm of the bathroom as a limit of gender identification, we can measure the distance between binary gender schema and lived multiple gendered experiences. The accusation "you're in the wrong bathroom" really says two different things. First, it announces that your gender seems at odds with your sex (your apparent masculinity or androgyny is at odds with your

supposed femaleness); second, it suggests that single-gender bathrooms are only for those who fit clearly into one category (male) or the other (female). Either we need open-access bathrooms or multigendered bathrooms, or we need wider parameters for gender identification. The bathroom, as we know it, actually represents the crumbling edifice of gender in the twentieth century. The frequency with which gender-deviant "women" are mistaken for men in public bathrooms suggests that a large number of feminine women spend a large amount of time and energy policing masculine women. Something very different happens, of course, in the men's public toilet, where the space is more likely to become a sexual cruising zone than a site for gender repression. Lee Edelman, in an essay about the interpenetration of nationalism and sexuality, argues that "the institutional men's room constitutes a site at which the zones of public and private cross with a distinctive psychic charge."[3] The men's room, in other words, constitutes both an architecture of surveillance and an incitement to desire, a space of homosocial interaction and of homoerotic interaction.

So, whereas men's rest rooms tend to operate as a highly charged sexual space in which sexual interactions are both encouraged and punished, women's rest rooms tend to operate as an arena for the enforcement of gender conformity. Sex-segregated bathrooms continue to be necessary to protect women from male predations but also produce and extend a rather outdated notion of a public-private split between male and female society. The bathroom is a domestic space beyond the home that comes to represent domestic order, or a parody of it, out in the world. The women's bathroom accordingly becomes a sanctuary of enhanced femininity, a "little girl's room" to which one retreats to powder one's nose or fix one's hair. The men's bathroom signifies as the extension of the public nature of masculinity—it is precisely not domestic even though the names given to the sexual function of the bathroom—such as cottage or tearoom—suggest it is a parody of the domestic. The codes that dominate within the women's bathroom are primarily gender codes; in the men's room, they are sexual codes. Public sex versus private gender, openly sexual versus discreetly repressive, bathrooms beyond the home take on the proportions of a gender factory.

Marjorie Garber comments on the liminality of the bathroom in *Vested Interests* in a chapter on the perils and privileges of cross-dressing. She discusses the very different modes of passing and cross-dressing for cross-identified genetic males and females, and she observes that the restroom is a "potential waterloo" for both female-to-male (FTM) and male-to-female (MTF) cross-dressers and transsexuals.[4] For the FTM, the men's room represents the most severe test of his ability to pass, and advice frequently circulates within FTM communities about how to go unnoticed in male-only spaces. Garber notes: "The cultural paranoia of being caught in the ultimately wrong place, which may be inseparable from the pleasure of "passing" in that same place, depends in part on the same cultural binarism, the idea that gender categories are sufficiently uncomplicated to permit self-assortment into one of the two 'rooms' without deconstructive reading"(47). It is worth pointing out here (if only because Garber does not) that the perils for passing FTMS in the men's room are very different from the perils of passing MTFS in the women's room. On the one hand, the FTM in the men's room is likely to be less scrutinized because men are not quite as vigilant about intruders as women for obvious reasons. On the other hand, if caught, the FTM may face some version of gender panic from the man who discovers him, and it is quite reasonable to expect and fear violence in the wake of such a discovery. The MTF, by comparison, will be more scrutinized in the women's room but possibly less open to punishment if caught. Because the FTM ventures into male territory with the potential threat of violence hanging over his head, it is crucial to recognize that the bathroom problem is much more than a glitch in the machinery of gender segregation and is better described in terms of the violent enforcement of our current gender system.

Garber's reading of the perilous use of rest rooms by both FTMS and MTFS develops out of her introductory discussion of what Lacan calls "urinary segregation." Lacan used the term to describe the relations between identities and signifiers, and he ultimately used the simple diagram of the rest room signs "Ladies" and "Gentlemen" to

show that within the production of sexual difference, primacy is granted to the signifier over that which it signifies; in more simple terms, naming confers, rather than reflects, meaning.[5] In the same way, the system of urinary segregation creates the very functionality of the categories "men" and "women." Although restroom signs seem to serve and ratify distinctions that already exist, in actual fact these markers produce identifications within these constructed categories. Garber latches on to the notion of "urinary segregation" because it helps her to describe the processes of cultural binarism within the production of gender; for Garber, transvestites and transsexuals challenge this system by resisting the literal translation of the signs "Ladies" and Gentlemen." Garber uses the figures of the transvestite and the transsexual to show the obvious flaws and gaps in a binary gender system; the transvestite, as interloper, creates a third space of possibility within which all binaries become unstable. Unfortunately, as in all attempts to break a binary by producing a third term, Garber's third space tends to stabilize the other two. In "Tearooms and Sympathy," Lee Edelman also turns to Lacan's term "urinary segregation," but Edelman uses Lacan's diagram to mark heterosexual anxiety "about the potential inscriptions of homosexual desire and about the possibility of knowing or recognizing whatever might constitute 'homosexual difference'" (160). Whereas for Garber it is the transvestite who marks the instability of the markers "Ladies" and "Gentlemen," for Edelman it is not the passing transvestite but the passing homosexual.

Both Garber and Edelman, interestingly enough, seem to fix on the men's room as the site of these various destabilizing performances. As I am arguing here, however, focusing exclusively on the drama of the men's room avoids the much more complicated theater of the women's room. Garber writes of urinary segregation: "For transvestites and transsexuals, the 'men's room' problem is really a challenge to the way in which such cultural binarism is read" (14). She goes on to list some cinematic examples of the perils of urinary segregation and discusses scenes from *Tootsie* (1982), *Cabaret* (1972), and the *Female Impersonator Pageant* (1975). Garber's examples are odd illustrations of what she calls "the men's room problem" if only because at least one of her examples (*Tootsie*) demonstrates gender policing in the women's room. Also, Garber makes it sound as if vigorous gender policing happens in the men's room while the women's room is more of a benign zone for gender enforcement. She notes: "In fact, the urinal has appeared in a number of fairly recent films as a marker of the ultimate 'difference'—or studied indifference" (14). Obviously, Garber is drawing a parallel here between the conventions of gender attribution within which the penis marks the "ultimate difference"; however, by not moving beyond this remarkably predictable description of gender differentiation, Garber overlooks the main distinction between gender policing in the men's room and in the women's room. Namely, in the women's room, it is not only the MTF but *all* gender-ambiguous females who are scrutinized, whereas in the men's room, biological men are rarely deemed out of place. Garber's insistence that there is "a third space of possibility" occupied by the transvestite has closed down the possibility that there may be a fourth, fifth, sixth, or one hundredth space beyond the binary. The "women's room problem" (as opposed to the "men's room problem") indicates a multiplicity of gender displays even within the supposedly stable category of "woman."

So what gender are the hundreds of female-born people who are consistently not read as female in the women's room? And because so many women clearly fail the women's room test, why have we not begun to count and name the genders that are clearly emerging at this time? One could answer this question in two ways: On the one hand, we do not name and notice new genders because as a society we are committed to maintaining a binary gender system. On the other hand, we could also say that the failure of "male" and "female" to exhaust the field of gender variation actually ensures the continued dominance of these terms. Precisely because virtually nobody fits the definitions of male and female, the categories gain power and currency from their impossibility. In other words, the very flexibility and elasticity of the terms "man" and "woman" ensures their longevity. To test this proposition, look around any public space and notice how few people present formulaic versions of gender and yet how few are unreadable

or totally ambiguous. The "It's Pat" character on a *Saturday Night Live* skit dramatized the ways in which people insist on attributing gender in terms of male or female on even the most undecidable characters. The "It's Pat" character produced laughs by consistently sidestepping gender fixity—Pat's partner had a neutral name, and everything Pat did or said was designed to be read either way. Of course, the enigma that Pat represented could have been solved very easily; Pat's coworkers could simply have asked Pat what gender s/he was or preferred. This project on female masculinity is designed to produce more than two answers to that question and even to argue for a concept of "gender preference" as opposed to compulsory gender binarism. The human potential for incredibly precise classifications has been demonstrated in multiple arenas; why then do we settle for a paucity of classifications when it comes to gender? A system of gender preferences would allow for gender neutrality until such a time when the child or young adult announces his or her or its gender. Even if we could not let go of a binary gender system, there are still ways to make gender optional—people could come out as a gender in the way they come out as a sexuality. The point here is that there are many ways to depathologize gender variance and to account for the multiple genders that we already produce and sustain. Finally, as I suggested in relation to Garber's arguments about transvestism, "thirdness" merely balances the binary system and, furthermore, tends to homogenize many different gender variations under the banner of "other."

It is relatively easy in this society not to look like a woman. It is relatively difficult, by comparison, not to look like a man: the threats faced by men who do not gender conform are somewhat different than for women. Unless men are consciously trying to look like women, men are less likely than women to fail to pass in the rest room. So one question posed by the bathroom problem asks, what makes femininity so approximate and masculinity so precise? Or to pose the question with a different spin, why is femininity easily impersonated or performed while masculinity seems resilient to imitation? Of course, this formulation does not easily hold and indeed quickly collapses into the exact opposite: why is it, in the case of the masculine woman in the bathroom, for example, that one finds the limits of femininity so quickly, whereas the limits of masculinity in the men's room seem fairly expansive?

We might tackle these questions by thinking about the effects, social and cultural, of reversed gender typing. In other words, what are the implications of male femininity and female masculinity? One might imagine that even a hint of femininity sullies or lowers the social value of maleness while all masculine forms of femaleness should result in an elevation of status.[6] My bathroom example alone proves that this is far from true. Furthermore, if we think of popular examples of approved female masculinity like a buffed Linda Hamilton in *Terminator 2* (1991) or a lean and mean Sigourney Weaver in *Aliens*, it is not hard to see that what renders these performances of female masculinity quite tame is their resolute heterosexuality. Indeed, in *Alien Resurrection* (1997), Sigourney Weaver combines her hard body with some light flirtation with co-star Winona Ryder and her masculinity immediately becomes far more threatening and indeed "alien." In other words, when and where female masculinity conjoins with possibly queer identities, it is far less likely to meet with approval. Because female masculinity seems to be at its most threatening when coupled with lesbian desire, in this book I concentrate on queer female masculinity almost to the exclusion of heterosexual female masculinity. I have no doubt that heterosexual female masculinity menaces gender conformity in its own way, but all too often it represents an acceptable degree of female masculinity as compared to the excessive masculinity of the dyke. It is important when thinking about gender variations such as male femininity and female masculinity not simply to create another binary in which masculinity always signifies power; in alternative models of gender variation, female masculinity is not simply the opposite of female femininity, nor is it a female version of male masculinity. Rather, very often the unholy union of femaleness and masculinity can produce wildly unpredictable results. . . .

In this introduction, I have tried to chart the implications of the suppression of female masculinities in a variety of spheres: in relation to cultural studies discussions, the suppression of female masculinities allows for male masculinity to stand unchallenged as the bearer of gender stability and gender deviance. The tomboy, the masculine woman, and the racialized masculine subject, I argue, all contribute to a mounting cultural indifference to the masculinity of white males. Gender policing in public bathrooms, furthermore, and gender performances within public spaces produce radically reconfigured notions of proper gender and map new genders onto a utopian vision of radically different bodies and sexualities. By arguing for gender transitivity, for self-conscious forms of female masculinity, for indifference to dominant male masculinities, and for "nonce taxonomies," I do not wish to suggest that we can magically wish into being a new set of properly descriptive genders that would bear down on the outmoded categories "male" and "female." Nor do I mean to suggest that change is simple and that, for example, by simply creating the desegregation of public toilets we will change the function of dominant genders within heteropatriarchal cultures. However, it seems to me that there are some very obvious spaces in which gender difference simply does not work right now, and the breakdown of gender as a signifying system in these arenas can be exploited to hasten the proliferation of alternate gender regimes in other locations. From drag kings to spies with gadgets, from butch bodies to FTM bodies, gender and sexuality and their technologies are already excessively strange. It is simply a matter of keeping them that way.

NOTES

1. Leslie Feinberg, *Stone Butch Blues: A Novel* (Ithaca, N.Y.: Firebrand, 1993), 59.
2. Nice Rodriguez, *Throw It to the River* (Toronto, Canada: Women's Press, 1993), 25–26.
3. Lee Edelman, "Tearooms and Sympathy, or The Epistemology of the Water Closet," in *Homographesis: Essays in Gay Literary and Cultural Theory* (New York: Routledge, 1994), 158.
4. Marjorie Garber, *Vested Interests: Cross-Dressing and Cultural Anxiety* (New York: Routledge, 1992), 47.
5. See Jacques Lacan, "The Agency of the Letter in the Unconscious," in *Ecrits: A Selection*, trans. Alan Sheridan (New York: Norton, 1977), 151.
6. Susan Bordo argues this in "Reading the Male Body," *Michigan Quarterly Review* 32, no. 4 (fall 1993). She writes: "When masculinity gets 'undone' in this culture, the deconstruction nearly always lands us in the territory of the degraded; when femininity gets symbolically undone, the result is an immense elevation of status" (721).

93

When Soldiers Rape from Maneuvers: The International Politics of Militarizing Women's Lives

C Y N T H I A   E N L O E

CYNTHIA ENLOE United States. 1938– . Political Scientist. *Does Khaki Become You?: The Militarization of Women's Lives* (1988), *Bananas, Beaches and Bases: Making Feminist Sense of International Politics* (1989), *The Morning After: Sexual Politics at the End of the Cold War* (1993).

Prostitution seems routine.

Rape can be shocking.

Prostitution can seem comforting to some. They imagine it to be "the oldest profession." Around a military camp prostitutes connote tradition, not rupture; leisure, not horror; ordinariness, not mayhem. To many, militarized prostitution thus becomes *un*newsworthy.

Rape, by contrast, shocks. It shocks, but then it loses its distinctiveness. Typically, when rape happens in the midst of war, no individual soldier-rapists are identified by the victims, by their senior command, or by the media (if there). The women who suffer rape in wartime usually remain faceless as well. They merge with the pockmarked landscape; they are put on the list of war damage along with gutted houses and mangled rail lines. Rape evokes the nightmarishness of war, but it becomes just an indistinguishable part of a poisonous wartime stew called "lootpillageandrape."

Thus when we try to increase the visibility of particular rapes committed by particular men as soldiers, we are engaging in a political act.[1] It is an act that must be undertaken with self-consciousness, for there are two traps. The first: women must be listened to, but with an awareness that their stories are likely to be complex. Atina Grossman, a researcher who has begun the tricky task of uncovering the murky but explosive history of the widespread rapes of German women chiefly (though not solely) by Soviet troops in 1945 and 1946, offers a caveat.

To anyone who mistakenly imagines that it is a simple undertaking to reveal "the truth" about militarized rape, even brutal wartime rapes or mass-scale rapes, Atina Grossman warns: "Women's rape stories were framed in incredibly complicated ways, shaped by their audience and the motives behind their telling. Their experiences were ordered and given meaning within a complex grid of multiple images and discourses."[2]

The second trap: exposing militarized rapes does not automatically serve the cause of demilitarizing women's lives. Making visible those women raped by men as soldiers is usually a difficult task; but sometimes it is a task made dangerously easy. A woman outside the military who has been raped by someone else's soldiers can be *re*militarized if her ordeal is made visible chiefly for the purpose of mobilizing her male compatriots to take up arms to avenge her—and their—allegedly lost honor. Today, long after the perpetration of their wartime rapes, Indian and Bangladeshi women are still trying to make adequate non-patriarchal sense of those rapes in the ongoing evolution of domestic and international politics of nations and states.[3] The challenge, therefore, is to make visible women raped by men as soldiers *without* further militarizing those women in the process.

Militarized rape has gained visibility on the stage of international politics in recent years because of the incidence of mass rape that occurred in Bosnia during its 1992–1995 war and in Rwanda during its 1994 attempted genocide. Yet militarized rapes are far more diverse. Often, as in Haiti and Indonesia, action has been required through the organizing by women for women to uncover soldiers' systematic political uses of rape.[4] Rape perpetrated by men as soldiers has been experienced by women in a variety of forms:

> rape by a male soldier of a woman he thinks of as a "foreigner"[5]
>
> rape by an individual male soldier of a civilian woman of the same nationality while that soldier is "off duty"
>
> rape by a male soldier of a woman soldier in the same army, perhaps because he resents her presence in a previously all-male unit or because he is angry at her for her unwillingness to date him or flirt with him[6]

rapes of women held in military prisons by male soldiers serving as guards; rapes perpetrated by a soldier acting as an interrogator with the apparent purpose of forcing the woman victim to give information

rapes by a group of invading soldiers to force women of a different ethnicity or race to flee their home regions

rapes of captured women by soldiers of one communal or national group aimed principally at humiliating the men of an opposing group

rapes by men of one ethnicity, race, or nationality of men from the "enemy" group to make the latter feel humiliated because they have been, via rape, reduced to "mere women"[7]

rapes of women by men in accordance to male officers' system of morale-boosting rewards to their men after battle

rapes of women taking refuge in wartime refugee camps by men also taking refuge in those camps or by men who are assigned to protect women in those camps[8]

rapes of women by those men who are prostitution procurers, to "prepare" them for later service in a brothel organized for soldier clients

rapes of women in wartime by civilian men of their same ethnic or national community who are acting out a misogyny nurtured by and licensed by the militarized climate

rapes of women who publicly oppose militarization by men of their own supposed community who support militarization

This list may be exhausting, but it is not exhaustive.

There are as many different forms of militarized rape as there are subtle nuances in the relationships between militarized women and militarized men. Nonetheless, they share some important common features—features that will affect not only the rapist's sense of what he is doing and of what gives him license to do it but also the raped woman's responses to that assault. First, the male militarized rapist in some way imposes his understandings of "enemy," "soldiering," "victory," and "defeat" on both the woman to be raped and on the act of sexual assault. Second, consequently, the militarized rape is harder to privatize than nonmilitarized rape is, since it draws so much of its rationale from an imagining of societal conflict and/or the functions of a formal institution such as the state's national security or defense apparatus or an insurgency's military arm. Third, the woman who has endured militarized rape must devise her responses in the minutes, weeks, and years after that assault not only by weighing her relationships to the rapist and to her personal friends and relatives, to the prevailing norms of feminine respectability, and perhaps to the criminal justice system, but *in addition*, she must weigh her relationships to collective memory, collective notions of national destiny, and the very institutions of organized violence. . . .

"LOOTPILLAGEANDRAPE": WAR, RAPE, FEMINISM, AND NATIONALISM

Doctors without Frontiers (*Medecins sans Frontieres*), the international humanitarian group, sent Dr. Catherine Bonnet to Rwanda to assess the impact of the devastating 1994 civil war on women and children. She concluded that "the scope of rape in Rwanda defies imagination . . . It appears that every adult woman and every adolescent girl spared a massacre by militias was then raped."[9]

A majority of the Rwandan women chosen for rape were from families identified by the rapists as being Tutsi or as being of the Hutu intelligencia.[10] Many families in prewar Rwanda were formed by cross-ethnicity marriages; thus the rapists often made quite arbitrary choices. Most of the rapists were men who identified themselves as Hutu and who were members of paramilitary groups organized by the Hutu-dominated ruling party and trained by the government's regular military.[11]

The wartime rapes were carefully provoked during the prewar period. The regime used radio programs and newspapers to persuade Hutu Rwandan men and women that Tutsi women were both traitorous and seductive, both arrogant and sexually desirable. According to government propaganda, no genuinely patriotic Rwandan man—and certainly no Rwandan soldier—should choose a Tutsi woman for his wife because she would only use her wifely position to infiltrate and undermine the real nation. On the other hand, Tutsi women were portrayed as flaunting their physical attributes, tempting Hutu men to lust and Hutu women to resentment. In this politically ethnicized construction, Tutsi women were imagined by those Hutus in power to be women deserving of rape and worth raping.[12]

Yet few of the many news reports coming from Rwanda during the 1994 conflict evidenced a curiosity about the use of rape as an instrument of ethnically specific oppression or of generalized terror. This lack of attention was partly the consequence of the journalists' own insufficiently gendered political curiosity about the experiences of African women and partly the result of many women survivors choosing out of humiliation and fear not to tell strangers of their ordeals. Yet many Rwandan women, like thousands of Chinese, Jewish, German, Italian, and Bangladeshi women before them, did not want to allow to come to term pregnancies that originated in their rapes by soldiers. Consequently, they often overcame their fear and shame in order to tell anyone who might be able to provide them with abortions, abortions frequently made illegal by their own governments.[13] In Rwanda, Bonnet found that "disclosure occurs mainly to doctors and gynecologist-obstetricians because of: 1) visible genital infections, whose violent origins are disclosed in confidence; 2) attempted abortions after discovery of rape pregnancy (abortion is not legal in Rwanda); 3) request for therapeutic abortion at a late stage of pregnancy; 4) requests for 'advice' about the future of the child when the pregnancy is nearing term . . . Maternity clinics run by Tutsis are seeing a great deal more women pregnant by rape than Hutu-run clinics.[14]

Reporting particular sorts of violence is as much a gendered process as war waging itself. If the laws of society, such as those of prewar and postwar Rwanda, make women second-class citizens in realms such as marriage and ownership of land, then it is all the more dangerous for a woman to risk her respectability and family's support by telling of her experiences of sexual assault. Thus Shana Swiss and Joan Giller, each of whom has conducted scores of interviews with women in war zones, warn activists who are genuinely concerned about wartime rape not to let their own concern turn into the objectification of women as victims: "The very process of human rights documentation may conflict with the needs of the individual survivor. Recounting the details of a traumatic experience may trigger an intense reliving of the event

and, along with it, feelings of extreme vulnerability, humiliation, and despair.[15] Swiss tells of visiting one woman refugee who had previously been questioned by twelve other interviewers.[16]

One of the success stories of the second wave of the women's movement is indeed that so many women in so many cultures have come to feel empowered enough to report when they have been raped. Another success story of feminism's second wave is that so many people in authority are now compelled to take sexual assaults seriously and to record those reports. Reporting and recording— each is a political act. For her international atlas that graphically displays the conditions of women around the world, feminist geographer Joni Seager created a map on global rape. This double-page full-color map of the world documents the locations of widespread rapes during militarized conflicts of the early and mid-1990s: Rwanda, Georgia, Afghanistan, Angola, Mozambique, Cambodia, Peru, Djibouti, East Timor, Turkey, Sri Lanka, Burma, Kashmir (India), Kuwait, Liberia, Papua New Guinea, Somalia, Sudan, Bosnia, Haiti, Mexico.[17] To this list we can now add Kosovo. Different cultures, different religions, different political ideologies, different foreign allies, different modes of warfare, different military-civilian relationships—but in each situation the rapes of women were by men who thought of themselves as soldiers.

The sheer variety of wartime rape sites may lure us into reducing the cause of wartime rape to raw primal misogyny. And yet succumbing to this understandable analytical temptation carries with it several political risks: the risk that mere maleness will be accepted as the sufficient cause for wartime rape; the risk that the operation of particular military hierarchies will be deemed not worth examining; the risk that feminists will decide that they can do nothing to call individual rapists and their superiors to account or even, perhaps, to prevent rape in the next war.

Assuming that such a diffuse and elemental misogyny is the sufficient cause of wartime rapes carries with it yet another risk: paying dangerously little attention to the war-waging objectives to which rape is put by strategists and to the specific gender division of labor under-girding the definition of those objectives. For instance, *if* military strategists (and their civilian allies or superiors) imagine that women provide the backbone of the enemy's culture, *if* they define women chiefly as breeders, *if* they define women as men's property and as the symbols of men's honor, *if* they imagine that residential communities rely on women's work—*if* any or all these beliefs about society's proper gendered division of labor are held by war-waging policy makers—they will be tempted to devise an overall military operation that includes their male soldiers' sexual assault of women.

Rape was elevated to the status of a serious political issue (versus merely war's inevitable, natural side effect) during the 1991–1995 war in the former Yugoslavia. This elevation was caused by carefully garnered evidence suggesting that the rapes in this war were systematic.

For any string of occurrences to be "systematic" they must be found to be not random, not ad hoc. Occurrences that are systematic are those that fall into a pattern. That finding, in turn, suggests that those occurrences haven't been left to chance. They have been the subject of prior planning. Systematic rapes are *administered* rapes.

By contrast, the well-worn litany of "loot-pillage-and-rape" implies that male soldiers rape women the way a tornado inhales barns and tractors: anything that comes in the path of warfare, it is imagined analogously, is susceptible to warfare's random violence. Men caught up in the fury of battle cannot be expected to be subject to rules of conduct, much less the fine print of memos. Grabbing a stray chicken or a stray woman—it is simply what male soldiers do as they sweep across the landscape.

This portrait of battle breeds complacency. It blots out all intentionality.

The 1991–1995 war in the former Yugoslavia rattled this complacency. Many reporters, diplomats, and television viewers found themselves confronting rape directly for the first time. They became outraged. Perhaps more radically, they became curious. . . .

It was a combination of energetic journalism and organized pressure brought to bear by women in antiwar groups and human rights groups that eventually initiated serious and methodical international agency investigations of the scale of rape and its purposes in the Bosnian war. This two-pronged

campaign prompted justices of the International War Crimes Tribunal eventually to announce on June 27, 1996 the indictment of eight male Bosnian Serb military and police officers on charges of raping Bosnian Muslim women. It was a historic day in the *re*gendering of international organizations. The announcement marked the first time in history that rape was treated separately as a crime of war. In past international war crime trials, rape had been included but always as part of a string of charges; it was not given legal distinction. Christian Chartier, a spokesman for the court meeting in the Hague, described the change: "There is no precedent for this. It is of major legal significance because it illustrates the court's strategy to focus on gender-related crimes and give them their proper place in the prosecution of war crimes."[18]. . . .

The Hague International War Crimes Tribunal's first chief prosecutor, South Africa's anti-apartheid attorney Richard Goldstone, admitted to a journalist that "rape has never been the concern of the international community . . . [Now, however] we have to deal openly with these abuses."[19]

Once this new understanding of rape is articulated, how deeply entrenched will it be in the workings and consciousness of all the actors who try to shape the war crimes tribunal, itself still a fledgling institution? Any international institution—the World Trade Organization, European Union, UN Rapporteur on Violence against Women, International War Crimes Tribunal—should be closely monitored in its early years to determine how and why its internal culture and its formal doctrines become imbued with feminized or masculinized assumptions.

Thus, while many feminist human rights activists were gratified by the Tribunal's acknowledgment that rape is a distinct form of internationally condemned war crime, they were learning just how risky it was for any woman who had been raped in the Bosnian war to come forward and testify. Court procedures would have to be reassessed and reformed in ways that would make it safe for a woman to appear as a witness—and to then return home—without risking her already very precarious social standing or indeed her life. . . .

The wars in the former Yugoslavia, like all wars, have taken place at a particular point in the ongoing development of women's theorizing and organizing. Rapes in the American Revolution, rapes in the Boer War, rapes in World War II—each were conceptualized and responded to (or ignored) in large measure depending on how publicly self-conscious women were at the time about the gendered causes of militarized violence against women. By the 1990s, women legal activists, together with grassroots antiviolence activists, had developed a coherent feminist interpretation of human rights and a cross-national lobbying network with which to press for the adoption of this interpretation by heretofore masculinized international agencies. Rape in peacetime and rape in wartime were made explicit in this new feminist human rights discourse.

"Women's rights are human rights" was, nonetheless, a theoretical assertion (and a basis for organizing) still subjected to continuing debate even among feminists. Some feminists worried that so much preoccupation with rights would foster too individualistic a focus for feminist activism. It had been liberal feminism that had provided the most comfortable bridge connecting women's movements and international human rights politics. Liberal feminists, in turn, usually invested their energies in pursuing individual claims of equality. Those women's advocates who had come to their activism through socialist feminism, antiracist feminism, or anti-colonial feminism were made uneasy by such classic liberal unquestioning acceptance of individualism. Then, too, other feminists keeping track of the "women's rights are human rights" efforts expressed concern that the very inclusiveness of the language of human rights might blind its users to vital political, economic, and cultural differences among women. "Humanness" was real, but it was not adequate to express the diversity of women's conditions and aspirations—and the tough political work that was needed if women were to build alliances by confronting, not denying, this diversity and inequality. The gains that those activists employing a feminist interpretation of human rights made in a growing number of international political sites, consequently, were achieved in the midst of a lively and ever more broadly international feminist dialogue. How to think about what had happened to women in Bosnia became part of that lively dialouge.

Thus it was not mere happenstance that between 1992 and 1999, investigators from the UN Secretariat, the European Union, Human Rights Watch, Amnesty International, and the Organization for Security and Cooperation in Europe each were moved to launch investigations of wartime rape in the former Yugoslavia. These investigations were a critical part of the campaign that led to the Hague justices' subsequent change of consciousness toward rape as a separate war crime. By 1999, each of these international institutions had concluded that soldiers from all three militaries operating in Bosnia—Croat, Bosnian, and Serb—perpetrated rapes, but that the main perpetrators had been Bosnian Serb militiamen. Furthermore, the investigators concluded, the rapes of civilian women had been routinely used to terrorize people, forcing many to leave their hometowns. Because of the gendered dynamics that make it hard for many women of all cultures to speak about experiences of sexual assault, any numbers that were gathered were only estimates, but the European Union's investigators calculated that in 1992 alone, 20,000 Muslim Bosnian women and girls had been raped by Bosnian Serb male combatants.[20] By the time of the ceasefire in late 1995, the number of women from all communities who had endured wartime rape was estimated to be between 30,000 and 50,000.[21] The numerical uncertainty reflected the ongoing gendered politics of silence and denial. . . .

Just as militarized prostitution is usually the product of particular relationships between particular groups of people, so too sometimes, [a 1993] UN report reveals, is militarized wartime rape. [This] report implicated the following:

local Serbian policemen

local paramilitary militiamen

Serbian men from other militias

officers of the Serb-controlled, Belgrade-directed Yugoslav army, the JNA

local male politicians who took on military positions once war began

These different men's roles in the rapes of Bosnia's Muslim and Croat women were not identical. Yet these men appeared to have been known to one another, relied upon by one another; on occasion, they may even have coordinated their actions. Militarized rape rarely is a lonely or isolated act. It occurs within structured relationships. The woman who endures a militarized rape has more than one man to accuse. . . .

"Ethnic cleansing" became the phrase used to describe what appears to have been the overall objective of this intentional pattern of rapes conducted and permitted and relied upon by different groups of Bosnian Serb and Serb men. Cherif Bassiouni, director of a later UN investigation, offers this definition: "Considered in the context of the conflicts in the former Yugoslavia, 'ethnic cleansing' means rendering an area ethnically homogeneous by using force or intimidation to remove persons of given groups from the area. 'Ethnic cleansing' is contrary to international law."[22] . . .

For those militaristic nationalists who were intent upon breaking up the former Yugoslavia, militarized rape became a means for responding to their demographically frustrating lack of control of women that had been produced by intermarriage. According to Serbian feminist Stasa Zajovic, "seven million Yugoslavs had at least one cousin belonging to some other nation." She adds, tellingly, "Nationalistic propaganda, however, labeled these marriages as 'factories of bastards,' . . . [Thus] the female body as a spoil of war becomes, a territory whose borders spread through 'birth of enemy sons.'"[23]

"Serbian feminist" has been treated as a nonentity, even an oxymoron. Much of the mainstream media coverage, even that responsible for making visible the scale and pattern of rapes in the war, was so preoccupied with the Serb political officialdom in Belgrade or with the ethnic leadership of the Bosnian Serbs that journalists implied that Serbs were a monolithic community. Much of the media have portrayed all Serbs as having identical relationships to wartime rape. In actuality, among the most vocal groups criticizing Belgrade officials for their complicity in the Bosnian Serb militiamen's perpetration of rape were Serbian feminist groups in Belgrade, such as Women in Black and the SOS Hotline for Women and Children.[24]

Making visible and taking seriously the analyses of these Serbian feminist groups, many of which have roots going back more than a decade, helps us assess the intentionality behind the wartime rapes in Bosnia. First, these women's very existence as dissidents challenges the assumption that the wartime rapes are being done by "Serbs" rather than by *particular* Serbs for *particular* purposes. That recognition, in turn, prompts us to ask *which* Serbs, why *them*, why *then*. Second, these women's critical investigations, while pushed to the margins of Serb political life, suggest that rape in war has been part of a deliberate *policy*, not just ethnicity-run-wild. Third, Serb feminists' distinctive monitoring of daily life in wartime Serbia reveals how much the wartime operations being conducted across the border in Bosnia depended on the manipulation of Serbian women's senses of their femininity. Serbian women had to be persuaded to see themselves chiefly as feminine members of a national community.

Thus it was that Serbian feminists active in Women in Black (*Zene u Crnom*), for instance, denied Serbian President Milosevic the right to claim that his policy of supporting Serbian Bosnian militias was a policy supported by and in the interest of women of the Serb "nation." The feminists chose dramatic silence as their mode of political expression. Starting in 1991, a core group of twenty women, often joined by others, organized a silent protest vigil in downtown Belgrade every Wednesday. Senka Knezevic, a member of the group, explained: "We manifest our opposition by not allowing the regime to speak in our name. One of our most important messages to the regime . . . is 'Do not speak in our name—we will speak for ourselves!'"[25]

Paying close attention to Serbian feminists while trying to make sense of the Bosnian wartime rapes encourages us to be conscious of the specific relationship between the varieties of feminist and the accused soldier-rapist. To one feminist, the rapist-soldier may be her government's enemy; to another he is a minor character on a distant stage; while to still another feminist he may be a fellow citizen.

Feminists from many different countries and ethnic groups took actions in the years between 1992 and 1998 to ensure that the rapes of Bosnian women were made visible and treated as a distinct phenomenon with political import and to guarantee that those women who suffered rape by soldiers received effective and appropriate support. Serbian feminists, Croatian feminists, Bosnian feminists (of several ethnicities) all worked to make these things happen. So too did Spanish and Italian feminists, German, Canadian, American, and Algerian feminists. Together, they shared many concepts, explanations, and objectives. For instance, they commonly held that both militarism and nationalism were frequently informed by patriarchal values and that, consequently, both militarism and nationalism could deepen the privileging of men as a group and masculinity as an idea.

For all their diversity, those feminists from various countries who took up the issue of wartime rapes in Bosnia generally agreed that even the most patriarchal militarist and nationalist leaders needed to mobilize support among women for several reasons: to ensure that mothers urged their sons to enlist in the various militaries; to guarantee that household economies worked despite the scarcities imposed by war waging; to garner sufficient popular support for the war-waging regimes to claim that their leaders were legitimate; to "reproduce the race."[26]

Nevertheless, a Serb feminist, a Croatian feminist, and a Bosnian feminist faced quite dissimilar traps when each insisted that the mass rapes in the Bosnian conflict be acknowledged. When Serbian women launched a center in Belgrade to support women subjected to all forms of male violence, they believed it politically crucial to make clear that (1) they would welcome women subjected to all forms of violence, that is, not just violence perpetrated in the heat of war on the front lines, but also violence perpetrated by men in the living rooms and bedrooms on the allegedly safe national home front; and (2) that women of all ethnic groups and nationalities would be welcomed. Without these clarifying principles, they decided, even a women's rape crisis center could be militarized in 1990s Belgrade.[27] . . .

On the other hand, precisely because a majority of the rapes in Bosnia were the acts of men identified as Serbian, those Croatian and Bosnian women choosing to make such rapes a topic of organized concern risked being publicly embraced enthusiastically by their own Croatian or Bosnian war-waging governments. Some, like Dubravka Ugresic, soon left Croatia under pressure but continued from outside to write critical accounts of the new masculinized, militarized Croatian nationalism. For these women, "Yugoslav" remained an identity worth trying to hang on to. Others stayed in Croatia and organized support groups for women opposing their new country's gendered march toward militarism. These women kept a long arm's length away from the state. Some joined with those Bosnian women now forced to live in Croatia who had themselves experienced systematic rape in Serbian-run camps, such as the infamous Omarska, but who were trying to turn those experiences not into shame or revenge or silence, but into public testimony. The challenge was two-sided: first, to avoid becoming mere fodder for the story-hungry foreign media intent on using women's ordeals for the entertainment of their own home audiences; and second, to avoid becoming fodder for those Croat militarists who wanted to publicize the rapes of "their" women for the sake of postwar nationalist politics and perhaps future wars of communal revenge. Women working in Zagreb-based groups such as the Croatian Division of the International Association of Human Rights and the Association of Women of Bosnia-Herzegovina sought to devise ways of working with women that could lead to personal renewal and to internationally imposed nonmilitarized justice. Their mission proved very difficult. . . .

Feminists inside and outside the former Yugoslavia sent up warning signals when the Peace Accords were signed late in 1995 by the male leaders of the governments of Serbia (now Yugoslavia), Croatia, and Bosnia at the U.S. Air Force Base in Dayton, Ohio. Wars do not end so neatly. The women of Belgrade's Women in Black sent out an invitation to women from other countries to come join them in a conference to weigh the impacts on women of the peace accords. They began their invitation with a caution:

> The war in former Yugoslavia has allegedly ended. It no longer gets the top story in world news agencies and TV stations. The suffering of the civilian population is no longer "popular" and does not cause pity . . .
>
> Those of us who live in this region know that the war continues. The environment in which we live is permeated with the practice and logic of war and militarism. . . . This is carried out with the state's nationalistic-militaristic ideology and propaganda, so that women endure patriarchal violence in both the private and public spheres.[28] . . .

A year later, their analysis seemed to be confirmed. Serbian feminists were having to direct their meager resources to challenge the militarization of neighboring Kosovo. This Belgrade-controlled province had only a small ethnic Serb minority, but had long been imagined by Serb nationalists to be a landscape saturated with patriotic meaning. It had been on the plains of Kosovo that Serbs had fought the soldiers of the Ottoman Empire. By 1998, the Milosevic regime's heavy-handed authoritarian rule over the mainly Albanian population had created a radicalized resentment throughout Kosovo. For months the principal Kosovar ethnic Albanian leadership had mobilized nonviolent resistance to Belgrade's silencing and Serb-privileging policies. But as the oppressiveness increased in the form of police raids of local citizens, that approach and the leadership who proposed it began to lose its appeal, especially among the province's ethnic Albanian younger men. A new Albanian group, espousing full independence for Kosovo, now argued that peaceful resistance had run its course, that the time had arrived for Albanian men to take up arms, to use violent means to confront Belgrade's police, army, and paramilitary forces. Spring 1998 appeared to be a significant moment in the gendered political history of all Yugoslavia's ethnic communities. While the Serbian government's militarized actions seemed to be on the brink of provoking a dramatic increase in the militarization of Kosovar Albanian masculinity, Belgrade's nationalist regime was having to rely on police units to conduct its militarized Kosovar operations because growing numbers of Serbian men were becoming disenchanted with soldiering away from home for the sake of a Greater Serbia.[29]

While Serbian feminists tried to resist Belgrade's nationalist appeals to Serbian women and tried to provide support for small groups of Kosovo women activists, Kosovar Albanian men were choosing between nonviolent action and enlistment in the newly formed Kosovo Liberation Army (KLA). As more men chose guerrilla warfare in the KLA, a force whose leaders exhibited little desire to give up any of the privileges of patriarchy, more ethnic Albanian women were having to decide how they would relate to the two expressions of Albanian masculinity and how they would respond to the devastating militarization of Belgrade's ethnocentric rule.[30]

As women in late-twentieth-century Northern Ireland, Sri Lanka, Chechnya, Rwanda, and the Sudan could testify, such dual processes of gendered militarization radically shrink the spaces available for women to craft their own domestic, national, and international politics against rape and other forms of violence against women. In May 1998, a full year before most of the world was paying any attention to the escalating militarism in Kosovo, Belgrade's women activists published a warning that women activists elsewhere would find ominously familiar: if the militarization of masculinity is built upon the exclusion of others and the painting of feminist critics as national traitors, the outcome in today's world is not likely to be a merely local conflict; it is likely to be internationalized war. The Belgrade feminists began their multi-layered analytical caveat with this assertion: "We start from patriarchy.[31]

[2000]

NOTES

1. The writer who deserves credit for drawing feminists' attention early on to rape in war and to the feminist politics of addressing rape in war is Susan Brownmiller in her book *Against Our will: Men, Women, and Rape* (New York: Penguin Books, 1976).
2. Atina Grossman, "A Question of Silence: The Rape of German Women by Occupation Soldiers," *October Magazine*, no. 72 (spring 1995): 55.
3. See, for instance, Ritu Menon and Kamla Bhasin, *Borders and Boundaries: Women in India's Partition* (New Brunswick, N.J.: Rutgers University Press, 1998).
4. For a report on Haitian women health activists' gradual exposure of rape by soldiers to sustain the former military regime, see Sharon Lerner, "Haitian Women Demand Justice," *Ms. Magazine*, July/August 1998, 10–11. For the central role played by Indonesian feminist human rights groups in revealing soldiers' use of rape, see Seth Mydans, "In Jakarta, Reports of Numerous Rapes of Chinese in Riots," *New York Times*, 10 June 1998.
5. See Seth Mydans, "In Jakarta, Reports of Numerous Rapes of Chinese in Riots," *New York Times*, 10 June 1998; and Human Rights Watch, *Indonesia: The Damaging Debate on Rapes of Ethnic Chinese Women* (New York: Human Rights Watch, 1998).
6. For rapes by U.S. male soldiers of U.S. women soldiers during the 1990–91 Gulf War, see Cynthia Enloe, *The Morning After: Sexual Politics at the End of the Cold War* (Berkeley: University of California Press, 1992), 190–92. For rapes in Canadian armed forces, see Jane O'Hara, "Rape in the Military," *Maclean's*, 25 May 1998, 15–21; and Jane O'Hara, "Abuse of Power," *Maclean's*, 13 July 1998, 16–20.

7. See Richard Trexler, *Sex and Conquest: Gendered Violence, Political Order, and the European Conquest of the Americas* (Ithaca, New York: University Press, 1995).

8. See, for instance, Women's Rights Watch, "Widespread Rape of Somali Women Refugees" (New York: Human Rights Watch, October 1993); and United Nations High Commissioner for Refugees, "Sexual Violence against Refugees" (Geneva: UNHCR, 1995).

9. Catherine Bonnet, Doctors without Frontiers, New York, quoted by Melinda Lorenson, "No Woman Was Spared," *Ms. Magazine*, May/June 1996, 25.

10. Claire Duchen, "Summary of a Report from Rwanda, and a Call for Action, written by Dr. Catherine Bonnet on Behalf of Medecins sans Frontieres," *Women's Studies International Forum* 18, nos. 5–6 (September–December, 1995): ix.

11. Human Rights Watch Africa, *Genocide in Rwanda April–May 1994* (New York; Human Rights Watch, May 1994).

12. Women's Rights Watch, *Shattered Lives: Sexual Violence during the Rwandan Genocide and its Aftermath* (New York: Human Rights Watch, 1996), 18–19.

13. "Rape and Forced Pregnancy in War and Conflict Situations," Reproductive Freedom and Human Rights, 30 April 1996, I–II.

14. Duchen, "Report from Rwanda."

15. Shana Swiss and Joan E. Giller, "Rape as a Crime of War: A Medical Perspective," *Journal of the American Medical Association* 270 (4 August 1993): 614.

16. Conversation with the author, Cambridge, Mass., January 1996.

17. Joni Seager, *The State of Women in the World: An International Atlas* (New York: Penguin Books, 1997).

18. Quoted in: Marlise Simons, "For First Time, Court Defines Rape as War Crime," *New York Times*, 28 June 1996.

19. Simons, "Court Defines Rape as war Crime."

20. Ibid.

21. Klein, "War Crimes Prosecution," 22.

22. United Nations General Assembly, "Final Report of the Commission of Experts Established Pursuant to Security Council Resolution 780 (1992)," General Document S/1994/674, 27 May 1992, quoted directly by Allen, *Rape Warfare*, 43.

23. Stasa Zajovic, "About 'Cleansing,'" in *Women for Peace*, ed. Stasa Zajovic (Belgrade: Women in Black, 1994), 65.

24. Lepa Mladjenovic and Vera Litricin, "Belgrade Feminists 1992; Separation, Guilt, and Identity Crises," *Feminist Review*, no. 45 (autumn 1993): 113–19.

25. Quoted in the Women in Black's occasional newletter, Belgrade, June 1996, 3.

26. See, for instance, Zajovic, *Women for Peace*.

27. Ibid.

28. Women in Black newsletter, Belgrade, June 1996. The conference being announced was held in Novi Sad, 1–4 August 1996.

29. Jane Perlez, "Many Serbs Would Just Rather Not Fight to Keep Kosovo," *New York Times*, 12 March 1998.

30. Stasa Zajovic, "Report on the Current Situation at Kosovo, Serbia, and Montenegro," *Compilation of Information—Women Living under Muslim Laws* (winter 1998): 1–5; Women in Black, "Prevent War in Kosovo," *Compilation of Information—Women Living under Muslim Laws* (winter 1998): 18; Chris Hedges, "Kosovo: Yet Another Act in the Balkan Tragedy," *New York Times*, 30 April 1998.

31. Autonomous Women's Groups in Belgrade, Women in Black against War, Autonomous Women's Center against Sexual Violence, Femminist Publishers 94, Center for Women's Studies, Belgrade Women's Lobby, "War in Kosovo—The Logics of Patriarchy," in *Compilation of Information—Women Living under Muslim Laws* (spring-summer-fall 1998): 7–8.

 94

Should There Be Only Two Sexes? from Sexing the Body

ANNE FAUSTO-STERLING

ANNE FAUSTO-STERLING. 1944– . United States. Biologist. Gender Studies scholar. *Myths of Gender: Biological Theories About Men And Women* (1985, 1992), "How to Build a Man" (1995), "Gender, Race and Nation: the Comparative Anatomy of Hottentot Women in Europe I: 1815–1817" (1995).

HERMAPHRODITIC HERESIES

In 1993 I published a modest proposal suggesting that we replace our two-sex system with a five-sex one.[1] In addition to males and females, I argued, we should also accept the categories herms (named after "true" hermaphrodites), merms (named after male "pseudo-hermaphrodites"), and ferms (named after female "pseudo-hermaphrodites"). I'd intended to be provocative, but I had also been writing tongue in cheek, and so was surprised by the extent of the controversy the article unleashed. Right-wing Christians somehow connected my idea of five sexes to the United Nations–sponsored 4th World Conference on Women, to be held in Beijing two year later, apparently seeing some sort of global conspiracy at work. "It is maddening," says the text of a *New York Times* advertisement paid for by the Catholic League for Religious and Civil Rights, "to listen to discussions of 'five genders' when every sane person knows there are but two sexes, both of which are rooted in nature."[2]

John Money was also horrified by my article, although for different reasons. In a new edition of his guide for those who counsel intersexual children and their families, he wrote: "In the 1970's nurturists . . . became . . . 'social constructionists.' They align themselves against biology and medicine. . . . They consider all sex differences as artifacts of social construction. In cases of birth defects of the sex organs, they attack all medical and surgical interventions as unjustified meddling designed to force babies into fixed social molds of male and female. . . . One writer has gone even to the extreme of proposing that there are five sexes . . . (Fausto-Sterling)."[3] Meanwhile, those battling against the constraints of our sex/gender system were delighted by the article. The science fiction writer Melissa Scott wrote a novel entitled *Shadow Man*, which includes nine types of sexual preference and several genders, including terms (people with testes, XY chromosomes, and some aspects of female genitalia), herms (people with ovaries and testes), and mems (people with XX chromosomes and some aspects of male genitalia). Others used the idea of five sexes as a starting point for their own multi-gendered theories.[4]

Clearly I had struck a nerve. The fact that so many people could get riled up by my proposal to revamp our sex/gender system suggested that change (and resistance to it) might be in the offing. Indeed, a lot *has* changed since 1993, and I like to think that my article was one important stimulus. Intersexuals have materialized before our very eyes, like beings beamed up onto the Starship Enterprise. They have become political organizers lobbying physicians and politicians to change treatment practices. More generally, the debate over our cultural conceptions of gender has escalated, and the boundaries separating masculine and feminine seem harder than ever to define. Some find the changes under way deeply disturbing; others find them liberating.

I, of course, am committed to challenging ideas about the male/female divide. In chorus with a growing organization of adult intersexuals, a small group of scholars, and a small but growing cadre of medical practitioners; I argue that medical management of intersexual births needs to change. *First*, let there be no unnecessary infant surgery (by *necessary* I mean to save the infant's life or significantly improve h/her physical well-being). *Second*, let physicians assign a provisional sex (male or female) to the infant (based on existing knowledge of the probability of a particular gender identity formation—penis size be

damned!). *Third*, let the medical care team provide full information and long-term counseling to the parents and to the child. However well-intentioned, the methods for managing intersexuality, so entrenched since the 1950s, have done serious harm.

· · · ·

REVISITING THE FIVE SEXES

Those who defend current approaches to the management of intersexuality can, at best, offer a weak case for continuing the status quo. Many patients are scarred—both psychologically and physically—by a process heavy on surgical prowess and light on explanation, psychological support, and full disclosure. We stand now at a fork in the road. To the right we can walk toward reaffirmation of the naturalness of the number 2 and continue to develop new medical technology, including gene "therapy" and new prenatal interventions to ensure the birth of only two sexes. To the left, we can hike up the hill of natural and cultural variability. Traditionally, in European and American culture we have defined two genders, each with a range of permissible behaviors; but things have begun to change. There are househusbands and women fighter pilots. There are feminine lesbians and gay men both buff and butch. Male to female and female to male transsexuals render the sex/gender divide virtually unintelligible.

All of which brings me back to the five sexes. I imagine a future in which our knowledge of the body has led to resistance against medical surveillance, in which medical science has been placed at the service of gender variability, and genders have multiplied beyond currently fathomable limits. Suzanne Kessler suggests that "gender variability can . . . be seen . . . in a new way—as an expansion of what is meant by male and female."[5] Ultimately, perhaps, concepts of masculinity and femininity might overlap so completely as to render the very notion of gender difference irrelevant.

In the future, the hierarchical divisions between patient and doctor, parent and child, male and female, heterosexual and homosexual will dissolve. The critical voices of people discussed in this chapter all point to cracks in the monolith of current medical writings and practice. It is possible to envision a new ethic of medical treatment, one that permits ambiguity to thrive, rooted in a culture that has moved beyond gender hierarchies. In my utopia, an intersexual's major medical concerns would be the potentially life-threatening conditions that sometimes accompany intersex development, such as salt imbalance due to adrenal malfunction, higher frequencies of gonadal tumors, and hernias. Medical intervention aimed at synchronizing body image and gender identity would only rarely occur before the age of reason. Such technological intervention would be a cooperative venture among physician, patient, and gender advisers. As Kessler has noted, the unusual genitalia of intersexuals could be considered to be "intact" rather than "deformed"; surgery, seen now as a creative gesture (surgeons "create" a vagina), might be seen as destructive (tissue is destroyed and removed) and thus necessary only when life is at stake.[6]

Accepted treatment approaches damage both mind and body. And clearly, it is possible for healthy adults to emerge from a childhood in which genital anatomy does not completely match sex of rearing. But still, the good doctors are skeptical. So too are many parents and potential parents. It is impossible not to personalize the argument. What if you had an intersexual child? Could you and your child become pioneers in a new management strategy? Where, in addition to the new intersexual rights activists, might you look for advice and inspiration?

The history of transsexualism offers food for thought. In European and American culture we understand transsexuals to be individuals who have been born with "good" male or "good" female bodies. Psychologically, however, they envision themselves as members of the "opposite" sex. A transsexual's drive to have his/her body conform with his/her psyche is so strong that many seek medical aid to transform their bodies hormonally and ultimately surgically, by removal of their gonads and transformation of their external genitalia. The demands of self-identified transsexuals have contributed to changing medical practices, forcing recognition and naming of the phenomenon. Just as the idea that homosexuality is an inborn, stable trait did not emerge until the end of the nineteenth century, the transsexual did not fully emerge as a special type of person until the middle of the twentieth. Winning the right to surgical and legal sex changes, however, exacted a price: the reinforcement of a two-gender system. By requesting surgery to make

their bodies match their gender, transsexuals enacted the logical extreme of the medical profession's philosophy that within an individual's body, sex, and gender must conform. Indeed, transsexuals had little choice but to view themselves within this framework if they wanted to obtain surgical help. To avoid creating a "lesbian" marriage, physicians in gender clinics demanded that married transsexuals divorce before their surgery. Afterwards, they could legally change their birth certificates to reflect their new status.

Within the past ten to twenty years, however, the edifice of transsexual dualism has developed large cracks. Some transsexual organizations have begun to support the concept of *transgenderism*, which constitutes a more radical re-visioning of sex and gender. Whereas traditional transsexuals might describe a male transvestite—a man dressing in women's clothing—as a transsexual on the road to becoming a complete female, transgenderists accept "kinship among those with gender-variant identities. Transgenderism supplants the dichotomy of transsexual and transvestite with a concept of continuity." Earlier generations of transsexuals did not want to depart from gender norms, but rather to blend totally into their new gender role. Today, however, many argue that they need to come out as transsexuals, permanently assuming a transsexual identity that is neither male nor female in the traditional sense.[7]

Within the transgender community (which has its own political organizations and even its own electronic bulletin board on the Internet), gender variations abound. Some choose to become women while keeping their male genitals intact. Many who have undergone surgical transformation have taken up homosexual roles. For example, a male-to-female transsexual may come out as a lesbian (or a female-to-male as a gay male). Consider Jane, born a physiological male, now in her late thirties, living with her wife (whom she married when her name was still John). Jane takes hormones to feminize herself, but they have not yet interfered with her ability to have erections and intercourse as a man:

> From her perspective, Jane has a lesbian relationship with her wife (Mary). Yet she also uses her penis for pleasure. Mary does not identify herself as a lesbian, although she maintains love and attraction for Jane, whom she regards as the same person she fell in love

with although this person has changed physically. Mary regards herself as heterosexual . . . although she defines sexual intimacy with her spouse Jane as somewhere between lesbian and heterosexual.[8]

Does acceptance of gender variation mean the concept of gender would disappear entirely? Not necessarily. The transgender theorist Martine Rothblatt proposes a chromatic system of gender that would differentiate among hundreds of different personality types. The permutations of her suggested seven levels each of aggression, nurturance, and eroticism could lead to 343 ($7 \times 7 \times 7$) shades of gender. A person with a mauve gender, for example, would be "a low-intensity nurturing person with a fair amount of eroticism but not much aggressiveness."[9] Some might find Rothblatt's system silly or unnecessarily complex. But her point is serious and begins to suggest ways we might raise intersex children in a culture that recognizes gender variation.

Is it so unreasonable to ask that we focus more clearly on variability and pay less attention to gender conformity? The problem with gender, as we now have it, is the violence—both real and metaphorical—we do by generalizing. No woman or man fits the universal gender stereotype. "It might be more useful," writes the sociologist Judith Lorber, ". . . to group patterns of behavior and only then look for identifying markers of the people likely to enact such behaviors."[10]

Were we in Europe and America to move to a multiple sex and gender role system (as it seems we might be doing), we would not be cultural pioneers. Several Native American cultures, for example, define a third gender, which may include people whom we would label as homosexual, transsexual, or intersexual but also people we would label as male or female. Anthropologists have described other groups, such as the Hijras of India, that contain individuals whom we in the West would label intersexes, transsexuals, effeminate men, and eunuchs. As with the varied Native American categories, the Hijras vary in their origins and gender characteristics. Anthropologists debate about how to interpret Native American gender systems. What is important, however, is that the existence of other systems suggests that ours is not inevitable.

I do not mean to romanticize other gender systems; they provide no guarantee of social equality.

In several small villages in the Dominican Republic and among the Sambia, a people residing in the highlands of Papua, New Guinea, a genetic mutation causing a deficiency in the enzyme 5-α-reductase occurs with fairly high frequency. At birth, XY children with 5-α-reductase deficiency have a tiny penis or clitoris, undescended testes, and a divided scrotum. They can be mistaken for girls, or their ambiguity may be noticed. In adolescence, however, naturally produced testosterone causes the penises of XY teenagers deficient in 5-α-reductase to grow; their testes descend, their vaginal lips fuse to form a scrotum, their bodies become hairy, bearded, and musclebound.

And in both the Dominican Republic and New Guinea, DHT-deficient children—who in the United States are generally operated on immediately—are recognized as a third sex. The Dominicans call it *guevedoche*, or "penis at twelve," while the Sambians use the word *kwolu-aatmwol*, which suggests a person's transformation "into a male thing."[11] In both cultures, the DHT-deficient child experiences ambivalent sex-role socialization. And in adulthood s/he most commonly—but not necessarily with complete success—self-identifies as a male. The anthropologist Gil Herdt writes that, at puberty, "the transformation may be from female—possibly ambiguously reared—to male-aspiring third sex, who is, in certain social scenes, categorized with adult males."[12]

While these cultures know that sometimes a third type of child is born, they nevertheless recognize only two gender roles. Herdt argues that the strong preference in these cultures for maleness, and the positions of freedom and power that males hold, make it easy to understand why in adulthood the *kwolu-aatmwol* and the *guevedoche* most frequently chose the male over the female role. Although Herdt's work provides us with a perspective outside our own cultural framework, only further studies will clarify how members of a third sex manage in cultures that acknowledge three categories of body but offer only a two-gender system.

TOWARD THE END OF GENDER TYRANNY: GETTING THERE FROM HERE

Simply recognizing a third category does not assure a flexible gender system. Such flexibility requires political and social struggle. In discussing my "five sexes" proposal Suzanne Kessler drives home this point with great effect:

> The limitation with Fausto-Sterling's proposal is that legitimizing other sets of genitals . . . still gives genitals primary signifying status and ignores the fact that in the everyday world gender attributions are made without access to genital inspection . . . what has primacy in everyday life is the gender that is performed, regardless of the flesh's configuration under the clothes.

Kessler argues that it would be better for intersexuals and their supporters to turn everyone's focus away from genitals and to dispense with claims to a separate intersexual identity. Instead, she suggests, men and women would come in a wider assortment. Some women would have large clitorises or fused labia, while some men would have "small penises or misshapen scrota—phenotypes with no particular clinical or identity meaning."[13] I think Kessler is right, and this is why I am no longer advocating using discrete categories such as herm, merm, and ferm, even tongue in cheek.

The intersexual or transgender person who presents a social gender—what Kessler calls "cultural genitals"—that conflicts with h/her physical genitals often risks h/her life. In a recent court case, a mother charged that her son, a transvestite, died because paramedics stopped treating him after discovering his male genitals. The jury awarded her $2.9 million in damages. While it is heartening that a jury found such behavior unacceptable, the case underscores the high risk of gender transgression.[14] "Transgender warriors," as Leslie Feinberg calls them, will continue to be in danger until we succeed in moving them onto the "acceptable" side of the imaginary line separating "normal, natural, holy" gender from the "abnormal, unnatural, sick [and] sinful."[15]

A person with ovaries, breasts, and a vagina, but whose "cultural genitals" are male also faces difficulties. In applying for a license or passport, for instance, one must indicate "M" or "F" in the gender box. Suppose such a person checks "F" on his or her license and then later uses the license for identification. The 1998 murder in Wyoming of homosexual Matthew Shepherd makes clear the possible dangers. A masculine-presenting female is in danger of violent attack if she does not "pass" as male. Similarly, she can get into legal trouble if stopped for a traffic violation or passport control, as the legal authority can accuse her of deception—masquerading as a male for possibly illegal purposes. In the 1950s, when police raided lesbian bars, they demanded that women be wearing three items of women's clothing in order to avoid arrest.[16] As Feinberg notes, we have not moved very far beyond that moment.

Given the discrimination and violence faced by those whose cultural and physical genitals don't match, legal protections are needed during the transition to a gender-diverse utopia. It would help to eliminate the "gender" category from licenses, passports, and the like. The transgender activist Leslie Feinberg writes: "Sex categories should be removed from all basic identification papers—from driver's licenses to passports—and since the right of each person to define their own sex is so basic, it should be eliminated from birth certificates as well."[17] Indeed, why are physical genitals necessary for identification? Surely attributes both more visible (such as height, build, and eye color) and less visible (fingerprints and DNA profiles) would be of greater use.

Transgender activists have written "An International Bill of Gender Rights" that includes (among ten gender rights) "the right to define gender identity, the right to control and change one's own body, the right to sexual expression and the right to form committed, loving relationships and enter into marital contracts." The legal bases for such rights are being hammered out in the courts as I write, through the establishment of case law regarding sex discrimination and homosexual rights.

Intersexuality, as we have seen, has long been at the center of debates over the connections among sex, gender, and legal and social status. A few years ago the Cornell University historian Mary Beth Norton sent me the transcripts of legal proceedings from the General Court of the Virginia Colony. In 1629, one Thomas Hall appeared in court claiming to be both a man and a woman. Because civil courts expected one's dress to signify one's sex, the examiner declared Thomas was a woman and ordered her to wear women's clothing. Later, a second examiner overruled the first, declaring Hall a man who should, therefore, wear men's clothing. In fact,

Thomas Hall had been christened Thomasine and had worn women's clothing until age twenty-two, when he joined the army. Afterward s/he returned to women's clothing so that s/he could make a living sewing lace. The only references to Hall's anatomy say that he had a man's part as big as the top of his little finger, that he did not have the use of this part, and that—as Thomasine herself put it—she had "a peece of an hole." Finally, the Virginia Court, accepting Thomas(ine)'s gender duality, ordered that "it shall be published that the said Hall is a man *and* a woman, that all inhabitants around may take notice thereof and that he shall go clothed in man's apparel, only his head will be attired in a Coiffe with an apron before him."[18]

Today the legal status of operated intersexuals remains uncertain. Over the years the rights of royal succession, differential treatment by social security or insurance laws, gendered labor laws, and voting limitations would all have been at stake in declaring an intersex legally male or female. Despite the lessening of such concerns, the State remains deeply interested in regulating marriage and the family. Consider the Australian case of an XX intersex born with an ovary and fallopian tube on the right side, a small penis, and a left testicle. Reared as a male, he sought surgery in adulthood to masculinize his penis and deal with his developed breasts. The physicians in charge of his case agreed he should remain a male, since this was his psychosexual orientation. He later married, but the Australian courts annulled the union. The ruling held that in a legal system that requires a person to be either one or the other, for the purpose of marriage, he could be neither male nor female (hence the need for the right to marry in the Bill of Gender Rights).[19]

As usual, the debates over intersexuality are inextricable from those over homosexuality; we cannot consider the challenges one poses to our gender system without considering the parallel challenge posed by the other. In considering the potential marriage of an intersexual, the legal and medical rules often focus on the question of homosexual marriage. In the case of *Corbett v. Corbett 1970*, April Ashley, a British transsexual, married one Mr. Corbett, who later asked the court to annul the marriage because April was really a man. April argued that she was a social female and thus eligible for marriage. The

judge, however, ruled that the operation was pure artifact, imposed on a clearly male body. Not only had April Ashley been born a male, but her transforming surgery had not created a vagina large enough to permit penile penetration. Furthermore, sexual intercourse was "the institution on which the family is built, and in which the capacity for natural hetero-sexual intercourse is an essential element." "Marriage," the judge continued, "is a relationship which depends upon sex and not gender."[20]

An earlier British case had annulled a marriage between a man and a woman born without a vagina. The husband testified that he could not penetrate more than two inches into his wife's artificial vagina. Furthermore, he claimed even that channel was artificial, not the biological one due him as a true husband. The divorce commissioner agreed, citing a much earlier case in which the judge ruled, "I am of the opinion that no man ought to be reduced to this state of quasi-natural connexion."[21]

Both British judges declared marriage without the ability for vaginal-penile sex to be illegal, one even adding the criterion that two inches did not a penetration make. In other countries—and even in the several U.S. states that ban anal and oral contact between both same-sex and opposite-sex partners and those that restrict the ban to homosexual encounters[22]—engaging in certain types of sexual encounters can result in felony charges. Similarly, a Dutch physician discussed several cases of XX intersexuals, raised as males, who married females. Defining them as biological females (based on their two X chromosomes and ovaries), the physician called for a discussion of the legality of the marriages. Should they be dissolved "notwithstanding the fact that they are happy ones?" Should they "be recognized legally and ecclesiastically?"[23]

If cultural genitals counted for more than physical genitals, many of the dilemmas just described could be easily resolved. Since the mid-1960s the International Olympic Committee has demanded that all female athletes submit to a chromosome or DNA test, even though some scientists urge the elimination of sex testing. Whether we are deciding who may compete in the women's high jump or whether we should record sex on a newborn's birth certificate, the judgment derives primarily from social conventions. Legally, the interest of the state in maintaining a two-gender system focuses on questions of marriage, family structure, and sexual practices. But the time is drawing near when even these state concerns will seem arcane to us. Laws regulating consensual sexual behavior between adults had religious and moral origins. In the United States, at least, we are supposed to experience complete separation of church and state. As our legal system becomes further secularized (as I believe it will), it seems only a matter of time before the last laws regulating consensual bedroom behavior will become unconstitutional. At that moment the final legal barriers to the emergence of a wide range of gender expression will disappear.

The court of the Virginia Colony required Thomas/Thomasine to signal h/her physical genitals by wearing a dual set of cultural genitals. Now, as then, physical genitals form a poor basis for deciding the rights and privileges of citizenship. Not only are they confusing; they are not even publicly visible. Rather, it is social gender that we see and read. In the future, hearing a birth announced as "boy" or "girl" might enable new parents to envision for their child an expanded range of possibilities, especially if their baby were among the few with unusual genitals. Perhaps we will come to view such children as especially blessed or lucky. It is not so far-fetched to think that some can become the most desirable of all possible mates, able to pleasure their partners in a variety of ways. One study of men with unusually small penises, for example, found them to be "characterized by an experimental attitude to positions and methods." Many of these men attributed "partner sexual satisfaction and the stability of their relationships to their need to make extra effort including non-penetrating techniques."[23]

My vision is utopian, but I believe in its possibility. All of the elements needed to make it come true already exist, at least in embryonic form. Necessary legal reforms are in reach, spurred forward by what one might call the "gender lobby": political organizations that work for women's rights, gay rights, and the rights of transgendered people. Medical practice has begun to change as a result of pressure from intersexual patients and their supporters. Public discussion about gender and homosexuality

continues unabated with a general trend toward greater tolerance for gender multiplicity and ambiguity. The road will be bumpy, but the possibility of a more diverse and equitable future is ours if we choose to make it happen.

[2000]

NOTES

1. Fausto-Sterling 1993a. The piece was reprinted on the Op-Ed page of the, *New York Times* under the title "How Many Sexes Are There?" Fausto-Sterling 1994.
2. Rights 1995 Section 4, p. 11.
3. Money 1994.
4. See, for example, Rothblatt 1995; Burke 1996; and Diamond 1996.
5. Kessler, Suzannen. *Lessons from the Intersexed.* Rutgers UP, 1998, p. 131.
6. Ibid., p. 40
7. Bolin 1994, pp. 461, 473.
8. Ibid., p. 484.
9. Rothblatt 1995, p. 115.
10. Lorber 1993, p. 571.
11. Herdt and Davidson 1988; Herdt 1990b and 1994a, b.
12. Herdt 1994, p. 429.
13. Kessler 1998, p. 90.
14. Press 1998.
15. Rubin 1984, p. 282.
16. Kennedy and Davis 1993.
17. Feinberg 1996, p. 125.
18. In Norton 1996, pp. 187–88.
19. O'Donovan 1985.
20. O'Donovan 1985, p. 15.
21. Edwards 1959, p. 118.
22. Halley 1991.
23. Reilly and Woodhouse 1989, p. 571.

 95

Third Wave Manifesta from Manifesta

JENNIFER BAUMGARDNER AND
AMY RICHARDS

JENNIFER BAUMGARDNER United States. 1970– . Journalist. Organizer. Activist. *Sisterhood Interrupted: From Radical Woman to Grrls Gone Wild* with Deborah Siegel (2007), *Look Both Ways: Bisexual Politics* (2008). *Grassroots: A Field Guide for Feminist Activism* (with Amy Richards) (2004)

AMY RICHARDS United States. ND. Activist. Organizer. Founder of Third Wave Foundation. *Opting In: Having A Child without Losing Yourself*

(2008); *Grassroots: A Field Guide for Feminist Activism* (with Jennifer Baumgardner) (2004)

THIRD WAVE MANIFESTA: A THIRTEEN-POINT AGENDA

1. To out unacknowledged feminists, specifically those who are younger, so that Generation X can become a visible movement and, further, a voting block of eighteen- to forty-year-olds.

2. To safeguard a woman's right to bear or not to bear a child, regardless of circumstances, including women who are younger than eighteen or impoverished. To preserve this right throughout her life and support the choice to be childless.

3. To make explicit that the fight for reproductive rights must include birth control; the right for poor women and lesbians to have children; partner adoption for gay couples; subsidized fertility treatments for all women who choose them; and freedom from sterilization abuse. Furthermore, to support the idea that sex can be—and usually is—for pleasure, not procreation.

4. To bring down the double standard in sex and sexual health, and foster male responsibility and assertiveness in the following areas: achieving freedom from STDs; more fairly dividing the burden of family planning as well as responsibilities such as child care; and eliminating violence against women.

5. To tap into and raise awareness of our revolutionary history, and the fact that almost all movements began as youth movements. To have access to our intellectual feminist legacy and women's history; for the classics of radical feminism, womanism, *mujeristas*, women's liberation, and all our roots to remain in print; and to have women's history taught to men as well as women as a part of all curricula.

6. To support and increase the visibility and power of lesbians and bisexual women in the feminist movement, in high schools, colleges, and the workplace. To recognize that queer women have always been at the forefront of the feminist movement, and that there is nothing to be gained—and much to be lost—by downplaying their history, whether inadvertently or actively.

7. To practice "autokeonony" ("self in community"): to see activism not as a choice between self and community but as a link between them that creates balance.

8. To have equal access to health care, regardless of income, which includes coverage equivalent to men's and keeping in mind that women use the system more often than men do because of our reproductive capacity.

9. For women who so desire, to participate in all reaches of the military, including combat, and to enjoy all the benefits (loans, health care, pensions) offered to its members for as long as we continue to have an active military. The largest expenditure of our national budget goes toward maintaining this welfare system, and feminists have a duty to make sure women have access to every echelon.

10. To liberate adolescents from slut-bashing, listless educators, sexual harassment, and bullying at school, as well as violence in all walks of life, and the silence that hangs over adolescents' heads, often keeping them isolated, lonely, and indifferent to the world.

11. To make the workplace responsive to an individual's wants, needs, and talents. This includes valuing (monetarily) stay-at-home parents, aiding employees who want to spend more time with family and continue to work, equalizing pay for jobs of comparable worth, enacting a minimum wage that would bring a full-time worker with two children over the poverty line, and providing employee benefits for freelance and part-time workers.

12. To acknowledge that, although feminists may have disparate values, we share the same goal of equality, and of supporting one another in our efforts to gain the power to make our own choices.

13. To pass the Equal Rights Amendment so that we can have a constitutional foundation of righteousness and equality upon which future women's rights conventions will stand.

[2000]

96

Global Identities: Theorizing Transnational Studies of Sexuality

INDERPAL GREWAL AND
CAREN KAPLAN

INDERPAL GREWAL ND. Women's studies scholar focusing on transnational feminism. *Scattered Hegemonies: Postmodernity and Transnational Feminist Practices* (1994), *Home and Harem: Nation, Gender, Empire, and the Cultures of Travel* (1996), *Transnational America: Feminism, Diasporas, Neoliberalisms* (2005).

CAREN KAPLAN United States. 1955–   . Women's studies scholar focusing on transnational feminism. *Scattered Hegemonies: Postmodernity and Transnational Feminist Practices* (1994), *Questions of Travel: Postmodern Discourses of Displacement* (1996).

In modernity, identities inevitably become global. Indeed, few things remain local in the aftermath of the rise of capitalism. Just as goods and people come to circulate in new ways, so too identities emerge and come into specific relations of circulation and expansion. In this globalized framework of encounter and exchange, sexual identities are similar to other kinds of identities in that they are imbued with power relations. These power relations are connected to inequalities that result from earlier forms of globalization, but they have also generated new asymmetries. Our task is to examine both the specificities and the continuities within the globalization of sexual identities at the present juncture.

For the most part, throughout the twentieth century, what we might call politically "progressive" studies of sexuality emerged as a result of identity politics and social movements. Increasingly, with the rise of ethnic and postcolonial studies and the growing emphasis on diaspora in American studies, the scholarship on sexuality is globalized.[1] Yet thinking simply about global identities does not begin to get at the complex terrain of sexual politics that is at once national, regional, local, even "cross-cultural" and hybrid. In many works on globalization, the "global" is seen either as a homogenizing influence or as a neocolonial movement of ideas and capital from West to non-West. Debates on the nature of global identities have suggested the inadequacy of understanding globalization simply through political economy or through theories of "Western" cultural imperialism and have pushed us to probe further the relationship between globalization and culture. Yet how do we understand these emerging identities, given the divergent theories regarding the relationship between globalization and cultural formations? Can these identities be called "global identities," or is some other term more useful?

In light of the problems that some scholars have pointed out with the rhetoric of diversity and globality with respect to sexual identity, such that these discourses produce a "monumentalist gay identity" and elide "radical sexual difference," the term *transnational* seems to us more helpful in getting to the specifics of sexualities in postmodernity.[2] As we have argued elsewhere, the term *transnational* can address the asymmetries of the globalization process.[3] Yet it has become so ubiquitous in cultural, literary, and critical studies that much of its political valence seems to have become evacuated. Is this a function of globalization in its cultural aspects, of the ways in which it has become a truism that everyone and everything are always already displaced and hence "transnational"? Or is it a function of the modernist search for novelty and innovation leading to the adoption of a seemingly new term for a global world? Perhaps these two tendencies are intertwined, and this term works at this point because it has become "real" or "appropriate" in some way that it would do us good to examine. By thinking about the many ways in which the term is being rearticulated, we can understand the rhetorical imperative that underlies such uses. Since terms and critical practices are neither authentic nor pure, we do not wish to argue that one use is more correct than another. Rather, we need to examine the circulation of this term and its regulation through institutional sites, such as academic publishing, conference panels and papers, and academic personnel matters. By doing so, we can begin to understand how the study of sexuality remains bound by disciplinary constraints. A more interdisciplinary and transnational approach that addresses inequalities as well as new formations can begin more adequately to explore the nature of sexual identities in the current phase of globalization.

We can identify several primary ways in which the term *transnational* does a particular kind of work in the U.S. academy in general. First, it circulates widely as a more useful term to describe migration at the present time. This is the application that we find most often at work in anthropology, for example, in the work that theorizes migration as a transnational process.[4] In emphasizing labor migration, this approach leaves out other factors in the globalization of labor. We can also identify an application in the notion of "transnational flows," a concept that sometimes ignores inequities as well as those aspects of modernity that seem fixed or immobile.[5] Some Marxist commentators prefer the term *flexible* over the term *flow*, since it ties globalization to flexible accumulation in current capitalism.[6]

A second use of *transnational* is to signal the demise or irrelevance of the nation-state in the current phase of globalization.[7] A related "borderless world" argument suggests that cultures are more and more important or relevant than nations and that identities are linked to cultures more than to nations or to the institutions of the nation-state.[8] In this approach, the concept of transnational does not have to concern itself with the postcolonial state; that is, it erases political economy as well as new forms of governmentality. As Victoria Bernal has put it so powerfully, "Embracing globalization and transnationalism as forces that render the nation inconsequential may appeal to anthropologists and humanities scholars in part because it allows them to conveniently ignore the ambivalent and troubling postcolonial state in favor of more sympathetic social forms."[9] Thus, by eliminating the postcolonial nation-state, flows of people and shifts in culture appear to be almost inevitable and strangely ahistorical.

A third use of *transnational* that has become visible recently is as a synonym for *diasporic*. In this increasingly common usage, which follows on the current use of *transnational* as a term that describes cross-border migration, any reference to materials or evidence or texts from a region outside the United States is coded as "diasporic." And everyone in the United States is believed to be diasporic in some way. Often diasporics come to be figured as always in resistance to the nation-state in which they are located. In this formulation, diasporic groups can be best understood through the politics of cultural identity or cultural citizenship. Thus subcultures of immigration and migration are always already diasporas. Here we are not arguing that people are better understood simply through the politics of the local. Rather, we are pointing to the mystification and romanticization of displacement that often accompany this formulation.

A fourth use of *transnational* is to designate a form of neocolonialism. In this approach, *transnational* is a deeply problematic term, because it appears to be completely imbricated in the movements of transnational capital.[10] That is, the argument goes, globalization involves rapid movements of finance capital and thus facilitates a global economy in which transnational corporations have trampled on and destroyed local formations. In our view, this approach may inadvertently mystify what existed before the advent of late capitalism, whereas we would argue that earlier phases of globalization produced their own inequalities. Certainly, transnational capital is creating new forms of inequality and continuing older asymmetries. Consequently, a long historical viewpoint, indeed multiple views for many sites, is necessary.

A fifth use of *transnational* signals what has been called the NGOization of social movements.[11] In the wake of several decades of U.N. conferences on women, the emergence of global feminism as a policy and an activist arena, and the rise of human rights initiatives that enact new forms of governmentality, the term *transnational* has been adopted to stand for all of the above. Thus we find more and more references to "transnationalism from below" or to transnational women's movements (with *transnational* supplanting *global*).[12] Such a shift in usage is interesting and significant, since it signals an alternative to the problematic of the "global" and the "international" as it was articulated primarily by Western or Euro-American second-wave feminists as well as by multinational corporations, for which "becoming global" marks an expansion into new markets. Our response to this specific development is that we need to trace the histories of such movements through the modern period to understand how they have been tied to colonial processes and to imperialism. Thus such usage relied on a universal subject of feminism, while *transnational* could signal cultural and national difference. However, it is important to remain alert to these national and international histories, which are embedded in every so-called transnational social movement, regardless of the intention of committed individuals and organizations.

If we have pointed out some of the ways in which *transnational* is used so ubiquitously at the present moment, it is not to suggest that we should abandon the term on the grounds that it has been overused to the point of meaning nothing in particular. Since ignoring transnational formations has left studies of sexualities without the tools to address questions of globalization, race, political economy, immigration, migration, and geopolitics, it is important to bring questions of transnationalism into conversation with the feminist study of sexuality. The history of the way in which sexuality has been studied and described needs to be better understood. Many scholars working on sexuality have begun to identify how separate spheres of study have arisen as a result of the disciplinary divides in the U.S. academy. In this context, critical practices are at a bit of an impasse, relying heavily on conventional disciplinary approaches that are unable to address some key issues and problems.

What are these separate spheres? The first divide is the separation of sexuality from the study of race, class, nation, religion, and so on. If Western, Judeo-Christian culture has viewed sexuality as the other within each individual, the study of sexuality in the U.S. academy has been limited by the inability of the human sciences to address this feared aspect of human life. In general, in the social sciences sexuality has been discussed at length only as an attribute of "primitive" cultures—exerting a strong fascination and producing an enormous literature that continues to this day. As anthropologists begin to study their "own" cultures, we have begun to see some shifts in this dynamic. But the legacies of the rise of human sciences remain. And the Western body stands as the normative body in scholarly discourse and in public policy.

We have to turn to the rise of biomedicine and the emergence of eugenics, gynecology, endocrinology, genetics, and psychology to understand fully the social and political stakes in viewing sexuality as distinct from race, class, nation, and other factors in modernity. Gender and sexual difference have become understood as attributes of bodies unmarked in any other way, despite copious evidence that all of these modern identities are interconnected. The binary gender model is so pervasive and universalized that it has become naturalized. In most queer studies in the United States, destabilization of gender binarism seems to remain in the zone of gender permutation or diversity rather than including considerations of histories of political economies and forms of governmentality. For instance, if we can argue that historical analysis shows us that concepts of gender difference in medieval China were quite different from those in medieval Islamic cultures, we will begin to understand that the legacies of these traditions with attendant identities and practices produce new kinds of subjects in the present moment. Here we have to pause to note that we are not arguing that cultural specificity leads to complete difference. Rather, we want to add to this model of cultural difference a consideration of power, history, and analyses of contact and change.

In the study of sexuality in a transnational frame, we need a mapping of different medical traditions, conceptions of the body, scientific discourses, and, last but not least, political economies of the family. Such a mapping requires us to rethink the reliance on the family as a primary locus of difference and inequality. The family has been primarily treated as an entity that emerges in the context of a public-private split and as a result of divisions of labor. Internationalizing the public-private split and patriarchal divisions of labor has not changed the content of the scholarship much. Many of these approaches to the family produce representations of a heteronormative unit, a universal patriarchy, and, very often, a victimized and unified subject of feminism. If class comes to the fore in these analyses, sexuality remains in the realm of the exploitation and control of women via reproduction or trafficking. This emphasis on the family as a universal category of analysis also enables an allied mode of universalizing, that is, psychoanalytic criticism.

· · ·

The second instance of separated spheres that we wish to examine concerns the demarcation in the United States of international area studies from American studies. As Tani E. Barlow has argued, international area studies was implicated in the production of Cold War cultural and political knowledges about other cultures and nations.[13] American studies comes from a 1930s Marxist, popular-front effort to critique and oppose capitalism. During the conservative backlash of the Cold War, it was co-opted and became articulated as American exceptionalism. At that point, the whiteness of "American" studies became distinguishable from what was later called "ethnic studies." The emergence of ethnic studies has to be understood as a response to this conservative retrenching of an otherwise limited but more radical initial vision. So both international area studies and American studies as we know them today are Cold War productions generated to manage and negotiate the tensions that arose after the Second World War and during decolonization worldwide, that is, in distinction to the emergence of other nationalisms.

· · ·

How does the institutional divide between international area studies and American studies affect contemporary studies of sexuality? The academic study of sexuality that can be linked to the emergence of gay and lesbian politics of identity and new queer formations has focused on U.S. and European examples, with the primary emphasis on white, middle-class life. Thus the disciplinary divides that emerge out of other political arenas are played out on campus and off, that is, in academic as well as in "community-based" or activist locations. As a result, much of the experience-based literature rearticulates the divide between a sexuality-based lesbian or gay or queer culture or identity and one that is based on race or class or ethnicity. In recent years, both "articulation" theory and "intersectionality" approaches have attempted to resolve this problem by arguing for complex or hybrid subjects.[14] That is, the nationalist basis of these academic disciplinary formations has participated in

producing sexual subjects as nationalist subjects or as cultural-nationalist subjects. . . .

A third divide that we would like to bring up can be characterized as the tradition-modernity split. Following postcolonial studies, much has been said about this primary binary Western culture. What is noteworthy, however, is the reemergence of this split in the international study of sexuality. As we noted above, nationalist biases and geopolitics contribute to this binary formulation, in which the United States and Europe are figured as modern and thus as the sites of progressive social movements, while other parts of the world are presumed to be traditional, especially in regard to sexuality. If any countries or nations depart from this model, it is because they are interpellated by "primitivism." In general, the United States and Europe come to be seen as unified sites of "freedom" and "democratic choice" over and against locations characterized by oppression.

In our work on female sexual surgeries and the global and cultural feminist discourse of "female genital mutilation" (FGM), we have argued that the tradition-modernity binary is foundational and even modern in that sexual subjects are produced as traditional in order to create feminist modern subjects.[15] Thus the global feminist is one who has free choice over her body and a complete and intact rather than a fragmented or surgically altered body, while the traditional female subject of patriarchy is forcibly altered, fragmented, alienated from her innate sexuality, and deprived of choices or agency.

· · ·

Another example of the tradition-modernity divide at work in the study of sexuality can be found in the literature on migration and refugee asylum. In such work, the process of migration to the United States, Europe, and other metropolitan locations is figured as the movement from repression to freedom.[16] That is, "backward," often rural subjects flee their homes and/or patriarchal families or violent, abusive situations to come to the modern metropolis, where they can express their true nature and sexual identity in a state of freedom. This narrative is a hallowed one in domestic "coming-out" discourses as well as in a burgeoning international human rights arena. Refugee asylum in the United States, for instance, produces gay and lesbian subjects through a political and legal articulation of such narratives. Some recent research suggests that it is virtually impossible to stay in the country without deploying such a narrative, thereby questioning its "natural" origins.[17] Further inquiry into this international context of immigration and asylum would need to focus on the ways in which the state becomes involved in producing sexual identities in an era of globalization. This is why we are arguing that a cultural or psychoanalytic understanding of so-called global lesbian and gay movements is inadequate. Nation-states, economic formations, consumer cultures, and forms of governmentality all work together to produce and uphold subjectivities and communities.

· · ·

A fourth link in this chain of examples of separate spheres is the global-local divide. In the context of globalization and some kinds of transnational studies, the local is seen as working against or in resistance to the global. That is, local and global constitute two separate spheres that never contaminate each other. The global-local divide is a tempting device for many cultural critics, but, like all the other binaries we are discussing, this one obscures important aspects of postmodernity, not the least of which is that the local is often constituted through the global, and vice versa.[18] It is also a model that hails critics because of its liberatory and resistance qualities. In this formulation, the local serves as the space of oppositional consciousness and generates practices of resistance, and the global serves as an oppressive network of dominant power structures. In various critical engagements with this global-local binary, lesbian, gay, and queer theorists have argued that the site of the local destabilizes the homogenizing tendencies of global gay formations.[19] There is another formulation that advocates the globalizing of Euro-American identity politics of sexuality along the lines that we have discussed above, that is, to advance human rights and freedom of choice.

· · ·

In many ways we are addressing the problem of writing history, a problem foregrounded by many theorists and critics working in gay and lesbian and queer studies. That is, subjects are produced by the writing of history itself and thus may always be marked by a belated recognition or identification that is always already in the terms of the present. While we can see this problem at work in the representation of the past, we are not always as aware of the limits of representation in the present. This problem of the present is especially egregious when we look at other cultures near or far. That is, identity politics have structured our view so profoundly that we literally cannot see the link between representation and subject formation in the ways that we are calling for vis-à-vis a transnational framework. Actually, what we are really grappling with here is not just representation; it is also the emergence of new forms of governmentality with an entire repertoire of strategies, regulatory practices, and instrumentalities linking the state to bodies. Thus representation is always linked to production, consumption, and regulation.

· · ·

One of the best examples of the issues we are raising here is the production of HIV/AIDS discourses over the last two decades. In this field we can discern a massive shift from the separate spheres to which we have been referring to the new forms of global and transnational policy discussions that have been created in response to this emergency. We see also the interconnections among state policies, nationalist agendas, pharmaceutical corporate practices, biomedical institutions, and the varied sexual subjects, cultures, and practices that become visible and targeted in new ways. The discourse of the modern nation-state's heteronormative family and of sexuality as the purview of males has been disrupted by the circulation of discourses of viruses, consumer actions, treatment strategies, theories of origins, and new sexual subjects. This example enables us to see the limits of the separate spheres approach as well as the interconnections that transnational subjects engender.

In conclusion, we would like to return to the five points with which we began our discussion of the circulation of the term *transnational*. We pointed out the limits of current uses of the term and linked these uses to articulations of knowledge formations. These limits include the production of various kinds of separate spheres or binaries, which prevent an approach to the study of sexuality that would usefully enable us to examine some of the areas of study that we have mentioned. Although other such topics can be considered, we have raised a few here as a contribution to a discussion that can build a bridge between the fields of global and transnational studies and those of sexuality, gender, women's, ethnic, and cultural studies in the U.S. academy. Such interdisciplinary work will enable us to understand global identities at the present time and to examine complicities as well as resistances in order to create the possibility of critique and change.

[2000]

NOTES

1. See Jasbir Kaur Puar, "Global Circuits: Transitional Sexualities and Trinidad," *Signs* 26 (2001): 1039–65; Martin F. Manalansan IV, "Diasporic Deviants/Divas: How Filipino Gay Transmigrants 'Play with the World,'" in *Queer Diasporas*, eds. Cindy Patton and Benigno Sánchez-Eppler (Durham: Duke University Press, 2000), 183–203; Yukiko Hanawa, ed., "Circuits of Desire," special issue of *positions* 2, no. 1 (1994); Elizabeth A. Povinelli and George Chauncey, eds., "Thinking Sexuality Transnationally," special issue of *GLQ* 5, no. 4 (1999); Phillip Brian Harper et al., eds. "Queer Transexions of Race, Nation, and Gender," special issue of *Social Text*, nos. 52–53 (1997); and Engin F. Isin and Patricia K. Wood, *Citizenship and Identity* (London: Sage, 1999).

2. See Lisa Rofel, "Qualities of Desire: Imagining Gay Identities in China," *GLQ* 5 (1999): 451–74.

3. See Inderpal Grewal and Caren Kaplan, "Introduction: Transnational Feminist Practices and Questions of Postmodernity," in *Scattered Hegemonies: Postmodernity and Transnational Feminist Practices*, eds. Inderpal Grewal and Caren Kaplan (Minneapolis: University of Minnesota Press, 1994), 1–33.

4. See Linda Basch, Nina Glick Schiller, and Cristina Szanton Blanc, eds., *Nations Unbound: Transnational Projects, Postcolonial Predicaments, and Deterritorialized Nation-States* (Langhorne, Pa.: Gordon and Breach, 1994).

5. See Arjun Appadurai, *Modernity at Large: Cultural Dimensions of Globalization* (Minneapolis: University of Minnesota Press, 1999); Ulf Hannerz, *Transnational Connections* (London: Routledge, 1996); and Scott Lash and John Urry, *Economies of Signs and Space* (London: Sage, 1994).

6. See David Harvey, *The Condition of Postmodernity: An Enquiry into the Origins of Cultural Change* (Oxford: Blackwell, 1989).

7. See Appadurai, *Modernity at Large*.

8. See Hannerz, *Transnational Connections*.

9. Victoria Bernal, "The Nation and the World: Reflections on Nationalism in a Transnational Era," unpublished manuscript, 2001.

10. See Lisa Lowe and David Lloyd, eds., *The Politics of Culture in the Shadow of Capital* (Durham: Duke University Press, 1997).

11. We take this phrase from Sabine Lang, "The NGOization of Feminism," in *Transitions, Translations, Environments: Feminisms in International Politics*, ed. Joan W.

Scott, Cora Kaplan, and Debra Keates (New York: Routledge, 1997), 101–20.

12. See Teresa Carillo, "Cross-Border Talk: Transnational Perspectives on Labor, Race, and Sexuality," in *Talking Visions: Multicultural Feminism in a Transnational Age*, ed. Ella Shohat (New York: New Museum for Modern Art; Cambridge, Mass.: MIT Press, 1998), 391–412.

13. Tani E. Barlow, "Career in Postwar China Studies," *positions* 1, no. 1 (1993): 224–67.

14. For articulation theory see Lawrence Grossberg, ed., "On Postmodernism and Articulation: An Interview with Stuart Hall," *Journal of Communication Inquiry* 10, no. 2 (1986): 45–60. For intersectional theory see Kimberlé Crenshaw, "Mapping the Margins: Intersectionality, Identity Politics, and Violence against Women of Color," in *After Identity: A Reader in Law and Culture*, eds. Dan Danielson and Karen Engle (New York: Routledge, 1995), 332–54.

15. See Inderpal Grewal and Caren Kaplan, "Warrior Marks: Global Womanism's Neo-Colonial Discourse in a Multicultural Context," *Camera Obscura* 39 (1996): 5–33.

16. See Olivia Espin, *Women Crossing Boundaries: A Psychology of Immigration and Transformations of Sexuality* (New York: Routledge, 1999).

17. See Inderpal Grewal, *Transnational America: Gender, Nation, and Diaspora* (Durham: Duke University Press, forthcoming).

18. See Rob Wilson and Wimal Dissanayake, eds., *Global/Local: Cultural Production and the Transnational Imaginary* (Durham: Duke University Press, 1996).

19. Katie King, "Local and Global: AIDS Activism and Feminist Theory," *Camera Obscura* 28 (1992): 79–100.

 97

Integrating Disability, Transforming Feminist Theory

ROSEMARIE GARLAND-THOMSON

ROSEMARIE GARLAND-THOMSON United States. ND. Literary and disability studies scholar. *Freakery: Cultural Spectacles of the Extraordinary Body* (1998), *Extraordinary Bodies: Figuring Physical Disability in American Culture and Literature* (1999).

Over the last several years, disability studies has moved out of the applied fields of medicine, social work, and rehabilitation to become a vibrant new field of inquiry within the critical genre of identity studies. Charged with the residual fervor of the Civil Rights Movement, Women's Studies and race studies established a model in the academy for identity-based critical enterprises that followed, such as gender studies, queer studies, disability studies, and a proliferation of ethnic studies, all of which have enriched and complicated our understandings of social justice, subject formation, subjugated knowledges, and collective action.

Even though disability studies is now flourishing in disciplines such as history, literature, religion, theater, and philosophy in precisely the same way feminist studies did twenty-five years ago, many of its practitioners do not recognize that disability studies is part of this larger undertaking that can be called identity studies. Indeed, I must wearily conclude that much of current disability studies does a great deal of wheel reinventing. This is largely because many disability studies scholars simply do not know either feminist theory or the institutional history of Women's Studies. All too often, the pronouncements in disability studies of what we need to start addressing are precisely issues that feminist theory has been grappling with for years. This is not to say that feminist theory can be transferred wholly and intact over to the study of disability studies, but it is to suggest that feminist theory can offer profound insights, methods, and perspectives that would deepen disability studies.

Conversely, feminist theories all too often do not recognize disability in their litanies of identities that inflect the category of woman. Repeatedly, feminist issues that are intricately entangled with disability—such as reproductive technology, the place of bodily differences, the particularities of oppression, the ethics of care, the construction of the subject—are discussed without any reference to disability. Like disability studies practitioners who are unaware of feminism, feminist scholars are often simply unacquainted with disability studies' perspectives. The most sophisticated and nuanced analyses of disability, in my view, come from scholars conversant with feminist theory. And the most compelling and complex analyses of gender intersectionality take into consideration what I call the ability/disability system—along with race, ethnicity, sexuality, and class.

I want to give the omissions I am describing here the most generous interpretation I can. The archive, Foucault has shown us, determines what we can know. There has been no archive, no template for understanding disability as a category of analysis and knowledge, as a cultural trope, and an historical community. So just as the now widely recognized centrality of gender and race analyses to all knowledge was unthinkable thirty years ago, disability is still not an icon on many critical desktops. I think, however, that feminist theory's omission of disability differs from disability studies' ignorance of feminist theory. I find feminist theory and those familiar with it quick to grasp the broad outlines of disability theory and eager to consider its implications. This, of course, is because feminist theory itself has undertaken internal critiques and proved to be porous and flexible. Disability studies is news, but feminist theory is not. Nevertheless, feminist theory is still resisted for exactly the same reasons that scholars might resist disability studies: the assumption that it is narrow, particular, and has little to do with the mainstream of academic practice and knowledge (or with themselves). This reductive notion that identity studies are intellectual ghettos limited to a narrow constituency demanding special pleading is the persistent obstacle that both feminist theory and disability studies must surmount.

Disability studies can benefit from feminist theory and feminist theory can benefit from disability studies. Both feminism and disability studies are comparative and concurrent academic enterprises. Just as feminism has expanded the lexicon of what we imagine as womanly, has sought to understand and destigmatize what we call the subject position of woman, so has disability studies examined the identity *disabled* in the service of integrating people with disabilities more fully into our society. As such, both are insurgencies that are becoming institutionalized, underpinning inquiries outside and inside the academy. A feminist disability theory builds on the strengths of both.

FEMINIST DISABILITY THEORY

· · ·

This essay aims to amplify feminist theory by articulating and fostering feminist disability theory. In naming feminist disability studies here as an academic field of inquiry, I am sometimes describing work that is already underway, some of which explicitly addresses disability and some of which gestures implicitly to the topic. At other times, I am calling for study that needs to be done to better illuminate feminist thought. In other words, this essay, in part, sets an agenda for future work in feminist disability theory. Most fundamentally, though, the goal of feminist disability studies, as I lay it out in this essay, is to augment the terms and confront the limits of the ways we understand human diversity, the materiality of the body, multiculturalism, and the social formations that interpret bodily differences. The fundamental point I will make here is that integrating disability as a category of analysis and a system of representation deepens, expands, and challenges feminist theory.

Academic feminism is a complex and contradictory matrix of theories, strategies, pedagogies, and practices. One way to think about feminist theory is to say that it investigates how culture saturates the particularities of bodies with meanings and probes the consequences of those meanings. Feminist theory is a collaborative, interdisciplinary inquiry and a self-conscious cultural critique that interrogates how subjects are multiply interpellated: in other words, how the representational systems of gender, race, ethnicity, ability, sexuality, and class mutually construct, inflect, and contradict one another. These systems intersect to produce and sustain ascribed, achieved, and acquired identities—both those that claim us and those that we claim for ourselves. A feminist disability theory introduces the ability/disability system as a category of analysis into this diverse and diffuse enterprise. It aims to extend current notions of cultural diversity and to more fully integrate the academy and the larger world it helps shape.

A feminist disability approach fosters complex understandings of the cultural history of the body. By considering the ability/disability system, feminist disability theory goes beyond explicit disability topics such as illness, health, beauty, genetics, eugenics, aging, reproductive technologies, prosthetics, and access issues. Feminist disability theory addresses such broad feminist concerns as the unity of the category *woman,* the status of the lived body, the politics of appearance, the medicalization of the body, the privilege of normalcy, multiculturalism, sexuality, the social construction of identity, and the commitment to integration. To borrow Toni Morrison's notion that blackness is an idea that permeates

American culture, disability too is a pervasive, often unarticulated, ideology informing our cultural notions of self and other (1992). Disability—like gender—is a concept that pervades all aspects of culture: its structuring institutions, social identities, cultural practices, political positions, historical communities, and the shared human experience of embodiment. . . .

Integrating disability does not obscure our critical focus on the registers of race, sexuality, ethnicity, or gender, nor is it additive. Rather, considering disability shifts the conceptual framework to strengthen our understanding of how these multiple systems intertwine, redefine, and mutually constitute one another. Integrating disability clarifies how this aggregate of systems operates together, yet distinctly, to support an imaginary norm and structure the relations that grant power, privilege, and status to that norm. Indeed, the cultural function of the disabled figure is to act as a synecdoche for all forms that culture deems non-normative.

We need to study disability in a feminist context to direct our highly honed critical skills toward the dual scholarly tasks of unmasking and re-imagining disability, not only for people with disabilities, but for everyone. As Simi Linton puts it, studying disability is "a prism through which one can gain a broader understanding of society and human experience" (1998, 118). It deepens our understanding of gender and sexuality, individualism and equality, minority group definitions, autonomy, wholeness, independence, dependence, health, physical appearance, aesthetics, the integrity of the body, community, and ideas of progress and perfection in every aspect of cultures. A feminist disability theory introduces what Eve Sedgwick has called a "universalizing view" of disability that will replace an often persisting "minoritizing view." Such a view will cast disability as "an issue of continuing, determinative importance in the lives of people across the spectrum" (1990, 1). In other words, understanding how disability operates as an identity category and cultural concept will enhance how we understand what it is to be human, our relationships with one another, and the experience of embodiment. The constituency for feminist disability studies is all of us, not only women with disabilities: disability is the most human of experiences, touching every family and—if we live long enough—touching us all.

THE ABILITY/DISABILITY SYSTEM

Feminist disability theory's radical critique hinges on a broad understanding of disability as a pervasive cultural system that stigmatizes certain kinds of bodily variations. At the same time, this system has the potential to incite a critical politics. The informing premise of feminist disability theory is that disability, like femaleness, is not a natural state of corporeal inferiority, inadequacy, excess, or a stroke of misfortune. Rather, disability is a culturally fabricated narrative of the body, similar to what we understand as the fictions of race and gender. The disability/ability system produces subjects by differentiating and marking bodies. Although this comparison of bodies is ideological rather than biological, it nevertheless penetrates into the formation of culture, legitimating an unequal distribution of resources, status, and power within a biased social and architectural environment. As such, disability has four aspects: first, it is a system for interpreting and disciplining bodily variations; second, it is a relationship between bodies and their environments; third, it is a set of practices that produce both the able-bodied and the disabled; fourth, it is a way of describing the inherent instability of the embodied self. The disability system excludes the kinds of bodily forms, functions, impairments, changes, or ambiguities that call into question our cultural fantasy of the body as a neutral, compliant instrument of some transcendent will. Moreover, disability is a broad term within which cluster ideological categories as varied as sick, deformed, crazy, ugly, old, maimed, afflicted, mad, abnormal, or debilitated—all of which disadvantage people by devaluing bodies that do not conform to cultural standards. Thus, the disability system functions to preserve and validate such privileged designations as beautiful, healthy, normal, fit, competent, intelligent—all of which provide cultural capital to those who can claim such statuses, who can reside within these subject positions. It is, then, the various interactions between bodies and world that materialize disability from the stuff of human variation and precariousness.

A feminist disability theory denaturalizes disability by unseating the dominant assumption that disability is something that is wrong with someone. By this I mean, of course, that it mobilizes feminism's highly developed and complex critique of gender, class, race, ethnicity, and sexuality as exclusionary and oppressive systems rather than as the natural and appropriate order of things. To do this, feminist disability theory engages several of the fundamental premises of critical theory: 1) that representation structures reality, 2) that the margins define the center, 3) that gender (or disability) is a way of signifying relationships of power, 4) that human identity is multiple and unstable, 5) that all analysis and evaluation have political implications.

In order to elaborate on these premises, I discuss here four fundamental and interpenetrating domains of feminist theory and suggest some of the kinds of critical inquiries that considering disability can generate within these theoretical arenas. These domains are: 1) representation, 2) the body, 3) identity, and 4) activism. While I have disentangled these domains here for the purposes of setting up a schematic organization for my analysis, these domains are, of course, not discrete in either concept or practice, but rather tend to be synchronic.

REPRESENTATION

The first domain of feminist theory that can be deepened by a disability analysis is representation. Western thought has long conflated female-ness and disability, understanding both as defective departures from a valued standard. Aristotle, for example, defined women as "mutilated males." Women, for Aristotle, have "improper form"; we are "monstrosit[ies]" (1944, 27–8, 8–9). As what Nancy Tuana calls "misbegotten men," women thus become the primal freaks in Western history, envisioned as what we might now call congenitally deformed as a result of what we might now term genetic disability (1993, 18). More recently, feminist theorists have argued that female embodiment is a disabling condition in sexist culture. Iris Marion Young, for instance, examines how enforced feminine comportment delimits women's sense of embodied agency, restricting them to "throwing like a girl" (1990, 141). Young concludes that, "Women in a sexist society are physically handicapped" (1990,

153). Even the general American public associates femininity with disability. A recent study on stereotyping showed that housewives, disabled people, blind people, so-called retarded people, and the elderly were all judged as being similarly incompetent. Such a study suggests that intensely normatively feminine positions—such as a housewife—are aligned with negative attitudes about people with disabilities (Fiske, Cuddy, and Glick 2001).[1]

Recognizing how the concept of disability has been used to cast the form and functioning of female bodies as non-normative can extend feminist critiques. Take, for example, the exploitation of Saartje Bartmann, the African woman exhibited as a freak in nineteenth-century Europe (Fausto-Sterling 1995; Gilman 1985). Known as the Hottentot Venus, Bartmann's treatment has come to represent the most egregious form of racial and gendered degradation. What goes unremarked in studies of Bartmann's display, however, are the ways that the language and assumptions of the ability/disability system were implemented to pathologize and exoticize Bartmann. Her display invoked disability by presenting as deformities or abnormalities the characteristics that marked her as raced and gendered. I am not suggesting that Bartmann was disabled, but rather that the concepts of disability discourse framed her presentation to the Western eye. Using disability as a category of analysis allows us to see that what was normative embodiment in her native context became abnormal to the Western mind. More important, rather than simply supposing that being labeled as a freak is a slander, a disability analysis presses our critique further by challenging the premise that unusual embodiment is inherently inferior. The feminist interrogation of gender since Simone de Beauvoir (1974) has revealed how women are assigned a cluster of ascriptions, like Aristotle's, that mark us as Other. What is less widely recognized, however, is that this collection of interrelated characterizations is precisely the same set of supposed attributes affixed to people with disabilities.

The gender, race, and ability systems intertwine further in representing subjugated people as being pure body, unredeemed by mind or spirit. This sense of embodiment is conceived of as either a lack or an excess. Women, for example, are considered castrated, or to use Marge Piercy's wonderful term, "penis-poor" (1969). They are thought to be hysterical or have overactive hormones. Women have been cast as alternately having insatiable appetites in some eras and as pathologically self-denying in other times. Similarly, disabled people have supposedly extra chromosomes or limb deficiencies. The differences of disability are cast as atrophy, meaning degeneration, or hypertrophy, meaning enlargement. People with disabilities are described as having aplasia, meaning absence or failure of formation, or hypoplasia, meaning underdevelopment. All these terms police variation and reference a hidden norm from which the bodies of people with disabilities and women are imagined to depart. . . .

Subjugated bodies are pictured as either deficient or profligate. For instance, what Susan Bordo describes as the too-muchness of women also haunts disability and racial discourses, marking subjugated bodies as ungovernable, intemperate, or threatening (1993). The historical figure of the monster, as well, invokes disability, often to serve racism and sexism. Although the term has expanded to encompass all forms of social and corporeal aberration, *monster* originally described people with congenital impairments. As departures from the normatively human, monsters were seen as category violations or grotesque hybrids. The semantics of monstrosity are recruited to explain gender violations such as Julia Pastrana, for example, the Mexican Indian "bearded woman," whose body was displayed in nineteenth-century freak shows both during her lifetime and after her death. Pastrana's live and later her embalmed body spectacularly confused and transgressed established cultural categories. Race, gender, disability, and sexuality augmented one another in Pastrana's display to produce a spectacle of embodied otherness that is simultaneously sensational, sentimental, and pathological (Thomson 1999). Furthermore, much current feminist work theorizes figures of hybridity and excess such as monsters, grotesques, and cyborgs to suggest their transgressive potential for a feminist politics (Haraway 1991; Braidotti 1994; Russo 1994). However, this metaphorical invocation seldom acknowledges that these figures often refer to the actual bodies of people with disabilities. Erasing real disabled bodies from the history of these terms compromises the very critique they intend to launch and misses an opportunity to use disability as a feminist critical category.

Such representations ultimately portray subjugated bodies not only as inadequate or unrestrained but at the same time as redundant and expendable. Bodies marked and selected by such systems are targeted for elimination by varying historical and cross-cultural practices. Women, people with disabilities or appearance impairments, ethnic Others, gays and lesbians, and people of color are variously the objects of infanticide, selective abortion, eugenic programs, hate crimes, mercy killing, assisted suicide, lynching, bride burning, honor killings, forced conversion, coercive rehabilitation, domestic violence, genocide, normalizing surgical procedures, racial profiling, and neglect. All these discriminatory practices are legitimated by systems of representation, by collective cultural stories that shape the material world, underwrite exclusionary attitudes, inform human relations, and mold our senses of who we are. Understanding how disability functions along with other systems of representation clarifies how all the systems intersect and mutually constitute one another.

THE BODY

. . .

Feminist disability theory offers a particularly trenchant analysis of the ways that the female body has been medicalized in modernity. As I have already suggested, both women and the disabled have been imagined as medically abnormal—as the quintessential sick ones. Sickness is gendered feminine. This gendering of illness has entailed distinct consequences in everything from epidemiology and diagnosis to prophylaxis and therapeutics.

Perhaps feminist disability theory's most incisive critique is revealing the intersections between the politics of appearance and the medicalization of subjugated bodies. Appearance norms have a long history in Western culture. . . . The classical ideal was to be worshiped rather than imitated, but increasingly, in modernity the ideal has migrated to become the paradigm that is to be attained. As many feminist critics have pointed out, the beauty system's mandated standard of the female body has become a goal to be achieved through self-

regulation and consumerism (Wolf 1991; Haiken 1997). Feminist disability theory suggests that appearance and health norms often have similar disciplinary goals. For example, the body braces developed in the 1930s to ostensibly correct scoliosis discipline the body to conform to dictates of both the gender and the ability systems by enforcing standardized female form similarly to the nineteenth-century corset, which, ironically, often disabled female bodies. Although both devices normalize bodies, the brace is part of medical discourse while the corset is cast as a fashion practice.

Similarly, a feminist disability theory calls into question the separation of reconstructive and cosmetic surgery, recognizing their essentially normalizing function as what Sander L. Gilman calls "aesthetic surgery" (1998). Cosmetic surgery, driven by gender ideology and market demand, now enforces feminine body ideals and standardizes female bodies toward what I have called the "normate"—the corporeal incarnation of culture's collective, unmarked, normative characteristics (1997, 8). Cosmetic surgery's twin, reconstructive surgery, eliminates disability and enforces the ideals of what might be thought of as the normalcy system. Both cosmetic and reconstructive procedures commodify the body and parade mutilations as enhancements that correct flaws to improve the psychological well-being of the patient. The conception of the body as what Susan Bordo terms "cultural plastic" (1993, 246) through surgical and medical interventions increasingly pressures people with disabilities or appearance impairments to become what Michel Foucault calls "docile bodies" (1979, 135). The twin ideologies of normalcy and beauty posit female and disabled bodies, particularly, as not only spectacles to be looked at, but as pliable bodies to be shaped infinitely so as to conform to a set of standards called *normal* and *beautiful*.

. . .

A feminist disability theory should illuminate and explain, not become ideological policing or set orthodoxy. The kinds of critical analyses I am discussing offer a counterlogic to the overdetermined cultural mandates to comply with normal and beautiful at any cost. The medical commitment to healing, when coupled with modernity's faith in technology and interventions that control outcomes, has increasingly shifted toward an aggressive intent to fix, regulate, or eradicate ostensibly deviant bodies. Such a program of elimination has often been at the expense of creating a more accessible environment or providing better support services for people with disabilities. The privileging of medical technology over less ambitious programs such as rehabilitation has encouraged the cultural conviction that disability can be extirpated; inviting the belief that life with a disability is intolerable. As charity campaigns and telethons repeatedly affirm, cure rather than adjustment or accommodation is the overdetermined cultural response to disability (Longmore 1997). For instance, a 1949 March of Dimes poster shows an appealing little girl stepping out of her wheelchair into the supposed redemption of walking: "Look, I Can Walk Again!" the text proclaims, while at once charging the viewers with the responsibility of assuring her future ambulation. Nowhere do we find posters suggesting that life as a wheelchair user might be full and satisfying, as many people who actually use them find their lives to be. This ideology of cure is not isolated in medical texts or charity campaigns, but in fact permeates the entire cultural conversation about disability and illness. . . .

The ideology of cure directed at disabled people focuses on changing bodies imagined as abnormal and dysfunctional rather on changing exclusionary attitudinal, environmental, and economic barriers. The emphasis on cure reduces the cultural tolerance for human variation and vulnerability by locating disability in bodies imagined as flawed rather than social systems in need of fixing. A feminist disability studies would draw an important distinction between prevention and elimination. Preventing illness, suffering, and injury is a humane social objective. Eliminating the range of unacceptable and devalued bodily forms and functions the dominant order calls disability is, on the other hand, a eugenic undertaking. The ostensibly progressive socio-medical project of eradicating disability all too often is enacted as a program to eliminate people with disabilities through such practices as forced sterilization, so-called physician-assisted suicide and mercy killing, selective abortion, institutionalization, and segregation policies.

A feminist disability theory extends its critique of the normalization of bodies and the medicalization of

appearance to challenge some widely-held assumptions about reproductive issues as well. The cultural mandate to eliminate the variations in form and function that we think of as disabilities has undergirded the reproductive practices of genetic testing and selective abortion (Saxton 1998; Parens and Asch 2000; Rapp 1999). Some disability activists argue that the "choice" to abort fetuses with disabilities is a coercive form genocide against the disabled (Hubbard 1990). A more nuanced argument against selective abortion comes from Adrienne Asch and Gail Geller, who wish to preserve a woman's right to choose whether to bear a child, but who at the same time object to the ethics of selectively aborting a wanted fetus because it will become a person with a disability (1996). Asch and Geller counter the quality-of-life and prevention-of-suffering arguments so readily invoked to justify selective abortion, as well as physician-assisted suicide, by pointing out that we cannot predict, or more precisely, control in advance such equivocal human states as happiness, suffering, or success. Neither is any amount of prenatal engineering going to produce the life that any of us desires and values. Indeed, both hubris and a lack of imagination characterize the prejudicial and reductive assumption that having a disability ruins lives. A vague notion of suffering and its potential deterrence drives much of the logic of elimination that rationalizes selective abortion (Kittay 2000). Life chances and quality are simply far too contingent to justify prenatal prediction.

Similarly, genetic testing and applications of the Human Genome Project as the key to expunging disability are often critiqued as enactments of eugenic ideology, what the feminist biologist Evelyn Fox Keller calls a "eugenics of normalcy" (1992). The popular utopian belief that all forms of disability can be eliminated through prophylactic manipulation of genetics will only serve to intensify the prejudice against those who inevitably will acquire disabilities through aging and encounters with the environment. In the popular celebrations of the Human Genome Project as the quixotic pinnacle of technological progress, seldom do we hear a cautionary logic about the eugenic implications of this drive toward what Priscilla Wald calls "future perfect" (2000, 1). Disability scholars have entered the debate over so-called physician-assisted suicide as well, by arguing that oppressive attitudes toward disability distort the possibility of unbiased free choice (Battin, Rhodes, and Silvers 1998). The practices of genetic and prenatal testing as well as physician-administered euthanasia, then, become potentially eugenic practices within the context of a culture deeply intolerant of disability. Both the rhetoric and the enactment of this kind of disability discrimination create a hostile and exclusionary environment for people with disabilities that perhaps exceeds the less virulent architectural barriers that keep them out of the workforce and the public sphere.

· · ·

A disability perspective nuances feminist theory's consideration of the ethics of care by examining the power relations between the givers and receivers of care. Anita Silvers has argued strongly that being the object of care precludes the equality that a liberal democracy depends upon and undermines the claim to justice as equality that undergirds a civil rights approach used to counter discrimination (1995). Eva Kittay, on the other hand, formulates a "dependency critique of equality," which asserts that the ideal of equality under liberalism repudiates the fact of human dependency, the need for mutual care, and the asymmetries of care relations (1999, 4). Similarly, Barbara Hillyer has called attention to dependency in order to critique a liberal tendency in the rhetoric of disability rights (1993). Disability itself demands that human interdependence and the universal need for assistance be figured into our dialogues about rights and subjectivity.

IDENTITY

· · ·

Disabled women are, of course, a marked and excluded—albeit quite varied—group within the larger social class of women. The relative privileges of normative femininity are often denied to disabled women (Fine and Asch 1988). Cultural stereotypes imagine disabled women as asexual, unfit to reproduce, overly dependent, unattractive—as generally removed from the sphere of true womanhood and feminine beauty. Women with disabilities often must struggle to have their sexuality and rights to bear children recognized (Finger 1990). Disability thus both intensifies and attenuates the

cultural scripts of femininity. Aging is a form of disablement that disqualifies older women from the limited power allotted females who are young and meet the criteria for attracting men. Depression, anorexia, and agoraphobia are female-dominant, psychophysical disabilities that exaggerate normative gender roles. Feminine cultural practices such as footbinding, clitorectomies, and corseting—as well as their less hyperbolic costuming rituals such as stiletto high heels, girdles, and chastity belts—impair women's bodies and restrict their physical agency, imposing disability on them.

Banishment from femininity can be both a liability and a benefit. Let me offer—with some irony—an instructive example from popular culture. Barbie, that cultural icon of femininity, offers a disability analysis that clarifies both how multiple identity and diversity are commodified and how the commercial realm might offer politically useful feminist counter images. Perhaps the measure of the group's arrival into the mainstream of multiculturalism is to be represented in the Barbie pantheon. While Barbie herself still identifies as able-bodied—despite her severely deformed body—we now have several incarnations of Barbie's "friend," Share-A-Smile Becky. One Becky uses a cool hot pink wheelchair; another is Paralympic Champion Becky, brought out for the 2000 Sydney Olympics in a chic red-white-and-blue warm-up suit with matching chair. Most interesting however is Becky, the school photographer, clad in a preppy outfit, complete with camera and red high-top sneakers. As she perkily gazes at an alluring Barbie in her camera's viewfinder, this Becky may be the incarnation of what Erica Rand has called "Barbie's queer accessories" (1995).

A disabled, queer Becky is certainly a provocative and subversive fusion of stigmatized identities, but more important is that Becky challenges notions of normalcy in feminist ways. The disabled Becky, for example, wears comfortable clothes: pants with elastic waists, sensible shoes, and roomy shirts. Becky is also one of the few dolls with flat feet and legs that bend at the knee. The disabled Becky is dressed and poised for agency, action, and creative engagement with the world. In contrast, the prototypical Barbie performs excessive femininity in her restrictive sequined gowns, crowns, and push-up bras. So while Becky implies, on the one hand, that disabled girls are purged from the feminine economy, on the other hand, Becky also suggests that disabled girls might be liberated from those oppressive and debilitating scripts. The last word on Barbies comes from a disability activist who quipped that he would like to outfit a disabled doll with a power wheelchair and a briefcase to make her a civil rights lawyer who enforces the *Americans with Disabilities Act* (1990). He wants to call her "Sue-Your-Ass-Becky."[2] I think she would make a very good role model.

The paradox of Barbie and Becky, of course, is that the ultra-feminized Barbie is a target for sexual appropriation both by men and beauty practices while the disabled Becky escapes such sexual objectification at the potential cost of losing her sense of identity and power as a feminine sexual being. Some disabled women negotiate this possible identity crisis by developing alternate sexualities, such as lesbianism (Brownworth and Raffo 1999).

· · ·

Another aspect of subject formation that disability confirms is that identity is always in transition. Disability reminds us that the body is, as Denise Riley asserts, "an unsteady mark, scarred in its long decay" (1999, 224). As Caroline Walker Bynum's intriguing work on werewolf narratives suggests, the body is in a perpetual state of transformation (1999). Caring for her father for over twenty years of Alzheimer's disease prompted Bynum to investigate how we can understand individual identity as continuous even though both body and mind can and do change dramatically, certainly over a lifetime and sometimes quite suddenly. Disability invites us to query what the continuity of the self might depend upon if the body perpetually metamorphoses. We envision our racial, gender, or ethnic identities as tethered to bodily traits that are relatively secure. Disability and sexual identity, however, seem more porous, although sexual mutability is imagined as elective where disability is seldom conceived of as a choice. . . .

Our collective cultural consciousness emphatically denies the knowledge of vulnerability, contingency, and mortality. Disability insists otherwise, contradicting such phallic ideology. I would argue that disability is perhaps the essential characteristic

of being human. The body is dynamic, constantly interactive with history and environment. We evolve into disability. Our bodies need care; we all need assistance to live. An equality model of feminist theory sometimes prizes individualistic autonomy as the key to women's liberation. A feminist disability theory, however, suggests that we are better off learning to individually and collectively accommodate bodily limits and evolutions than trying to eliminate or deny them. . . .

A feminist disability theory can also highlight intersections and convergences with other identity-based critical perspectives such as queer and ethnic studies. Disability coming-out stories, for example, borrow from gay and lesbian identity narratives to expose what previously was hidden, privatized, and medicalized in order to enter into a political community. The politicized sphere into which many scholars come out is feminist disability studies, which enables critique, claims disability identity, and creates affirming counternarratives. Disability coming-out narratives raise questions about the body's role in identity by asking how markers so conspicuous as crutches, wheelchairs, hearing aids, guide dogs, white canes, or empty sleeves be closeted.

Passing as nondisabled complicates ethnic and queer studies' analyses of how this seductive but psychically estranging access to privilege operates. Some of my friends, for example, have measured their regard for me by saying, "But I don't think of you as disabled." What they point to in such a compliment is the contradiction they find between their perception of me as valuable, capable, lovable person and the cultural figure of the disabled person whom they take to be precisely my opposite: worthless, incapable, and unlovable. People with disabilities routinely announce that they do not consider themselves as disabled. Although they are often repudiating the literal meaning of the word *disabled*, their words nevertheless serve to disassociate them from the identity group of the disabled. Our culture offers profound disincentives and few rewards to identifying as disabled. The trouble with such statements is that they leave intact, without challenge, the oppressive stereotypes that permit, among other things, the unexamined use of disability terms such as *crippled, lame, dumb, idiot, moron* as verbal gestures of derision. The refusal to claim disability identity is in part due to a lack of ways to understand or talk about disability that are not oppressive. People with disabilities and those who care are about them flee from the language of *crippled* or *deformed* and have no other alternatives. Yet, the Civil Rights Movement and the accompanying black-is-beautiful identity politics have generally shown white culture what is problematic with saying to black friends, "I don't think of you as black." Nonetheless, by disavowing disability identity, many of us learned to save ourselves from devaluation by a complicity that perpetuates oppressive notions about ostensibly real disabled people. Thus, together we help make the alternately menacing and pathetic cultural figures who rattle tin cups or rave on street corners, ones we with impairments often flee from more surely than those who imagine themselves as nondisabled.

ACTIVISM

The final domain of feminist theory that a disability analysis expands is activism. . . . I want to suggest here two unlikely, even quirky, cultural practices that function in activist ways but are seldom considered as potentially transformative. One practice is disabled fashion modeling and the other is academic tolerance. Both are different genres of activism from the more traditional marching-on-Washington or chaining-yourself-to-a-bus modes. Both are less theatrical, but perhaps fresher and more interestingly controversial ways to change the social landscape and to promote equality, which I take to be the goal of activism. . . .

Images of disabled fashion models in the media can shake up established categories and expectations. Because commercial visual media are the most widespread and commanding sources of images in modern, image-saturated culture, they have great potential for shaping public consciousness—as feminist cultural critics are well aware. Fashion imagery is the visual distillation of the normative, gilded with the chic and the luxurious to render it desirable. The commercial sphere is completely amoral, driven as it is by the single logic of the bottom line. As we know, it sweeps through culture seizing with alarming neutrality anything it senses will sell. This value-free aspect of advertising produces a

kind of pliable potency that sometimes can yield unexpected results.

Take, for example, a shot from the monthly fashion feature in *WE Magazine,* a *Cosmopolitan* knock-off targeted toward the disabled consumer market. In this conventional, stylized, high fashion shot, a typical female model—slender, white, blond, clad in a black evening gown—is accompanied by her service dog. My argument is that public images such as this are radical because they fuse two previously antithetical visual discourses, the chic high fashion shot and the earnest charity campaign. Public representations of disability have traditionally been contained within the conventions of sentimental charity images, exotic freak show portraits, medical illustrations, or sensational and forbidden pictures. Indeed, people with disabilities have been excluded most fully from the dominant, public world of the marketplace. Before the civil rights initiatives of the mid-twentieth century began to transform the public architectural and institutional environment, disabled people were segregated to the private and the medical spheres. Until recently, the only available public image of a woman with a service dog that shaped the public imagination was a street-corner beggar or a charity poster. By juxtaposing the elite body of a visually normative fashion model with the mark of disability, this image shakes up our assumptions about the normal and the abnormal, the public and the private, the chic and the desolate, the compelling and the repelling. Introducing a service dog—a standard prop of indigents and poster children—into the conventional composition of an upscale fashion photo forces the viewer to reconfigure assumptions about what constitutes the attractive and the desirable.

I am arguing that the emergence of disabled fashion models is inadvertent activism without any legitimate agent for positive social change. Their appearance is simply a result of market forces. This both troubling and empowering form of entry into democratic capitalism produces a kind of instrumental form of equality: the freedom to be appropriated by consumer culture. In a democracy, to reject this paradoxical liberty is one thing; not to be granted it is another. . . .

Such images, then, are at once liberatory and oppressive. They do the cultural work of integrating a previously excluded group into the dominant order—for better or worse—much like the inclusion of women in the military.

This form of popular resymbolization produces counterimages that have activist potential. A clearer example of disability activism might be Aimee Mullins, who is a fashion model, celebrity, champion runner, Georgetown University student, and double amputee. Mullins was also one of *People* magazine's 50 Most Beautiful People of 1999. An icon of disability pride and equality, Mullins exposes—in fact calls attention to—the mark of her disability in most photos, refusing to normalize or hide her disability in order to pass for nondisabled. Indeed, the public version of her career is that her disability has been a benefit: she has several sets of legs, both cosmetic and functional, and so is able to choose how tall she wants to be. Photographed in her functional prosthetic legs, she embodies the sexualized jock look that demands women be both slender and fit. In her cosmetic legs, she captures the look of the high fashion beauty in the controversial shoot by Nick Knight called *Accessible*, showcasing outfits created by designers such as Alexander McQueen. But this is high fashion with a difference. In the jock shot, her functional legs are brazenly displayed, and even in the voguishly costumed shot, the knee joints of her artificial legs are exposed. Never is there an attempt to disguise her prosthetic legs; rather all of the photos thematically echo her prostheses and render the whole image chic. Mullins's prosthetic legs—whether cosmetic or functional—parody, indeed proudly mock, the fantasy of the perfect body that is the mark of fashion, even while the rest of her body conforms precisely to fashion's impossible standards. So rather than concealing, normalizing, or erasing disability, these photos use the hyperbole and stigmata traditionally associated with disability to quench postmodernity's perpetual search for the new and arresting image. Such a narrative of advantage works against oppressive narratives and practices usually invoked about disabilities. First, Mullins counters the insistent narrative that one must overcome an impairment rather than incorporating it into one's life and self, even perhaps as a benefit. Second, Mullins counters the practice of passing for nondisabled that people with disabilities are often obliged to enact in the public sphere. Mullins uses her conformity with beauty standards to assert her disability's violation of those very standards. As legless and beautiful, she is an embodied paradox, invoking an inherently disruptive potential. . . .

The concluding version of activism I offer is less controversial and subtler than glitzy fashion spreads. It is what I call academic activism, the activism of integrating education, in the very broadest sense of that term. The academy is no ivory tower but rather it is the grassroots of the educational enterprise. Scholars and teachers shape the communal knowledge and the pedagogical archive that is disseminated from kindergarten to the university. Academic activism is most self-consciously vibrant in the aggregate of interdisciplinary identity studies—of which Women's Studies is exemplary—that strive to expose the workings of oppression, examine subject formation, and offer counternarratives for subjugated groups. Their cultural work is building an archive through historical and textual retrieval, canon reformation, role modeling, mentoring, curricular reform, and course and program development.

A specific form of feminist academic activism can be deepened through the complication of a disability analysis. I call this academic activism the methodology of intellectual tolerance. By this I do not mean tolerance in the more usual sense of tolerating each other—although that would be useful as well. What I mean is the intellectual position of tolerating what has been thought of as incoherence. As feminism has embraced the paradoxes that have emerged from its challenge to the gender system, it has not collapsed into chaos, but rather it has developed a methodology that tolerates internal conflict and contradiction. This method asks difficult questions, but accepts provisional answers. This method recognizes the power of identity, at the same time that it reveals identity as a fiction. This method both seeks equality and claims difference. This method allows us to teach with authority at the same time that we reject notions of pedagogical mastery. This method establishes institutional presences even while it acknowledges the limitations of institutions. This method validates the personal but implements disinterested inquiry. This method both writes new stories and recovers traditional ones. Considering disability as a vector of identity that intersects gender is one more internal challenge that threatens the coherence of woman, of course. But feminism can accommodate such complication and the contradictions it cultivates. Indeed the intellectual tolerance I am arguing for espouses the partial, the provisional, the particular. Such an intellectual habit can be informed by disability experience and acceptance. To embrace the supposedly flawed body of disability is to critique the normalizing phallic fantasies of wholeness, unity, coherence, and completeness. The disabled body is contradiction, ambiguity, and partiality incarnate.

[2001]

NOTES

1. Interestingly, in Fiske's study, feminists, businesswomen, Asians, Northerners, and black professionals were stereotyped as highly competent, thus envied. In addition to having very low competence, housewives, disabled people, blind people, so-called retarded people, and the elderly were rated as warm, thus pitied.

2. Personal conversation with Paul Longmore, San Francisco, California, June 2000.

REFERENCES

Americans with Disabilities Act of 1990. Retrieved 15 August 2002, from http://www.usdoj.gov/crt/ada/pubs/ada.txt.

Aristotle. 1944. *Generation of Animals.* Trans. A. L. Peck. Cambridge, MA: Harvard University Press.

Battin, Margaret P., Rosamond Rhodes, and Anita Silvers, eds. 1998. *Physician Assisted Suicide: Expanding the Debate.* New York: Routledge.

Bordo, Susan. 1993. *Unbearable Weight: Feminism, Western Culture and the Body.* Berkeley: University of California Press.

Braidotti, Rosi. 1994. *Nomadic Subjects: Embodiment and Sexual Difference in Contemporary Feminist Thought.* New York: Columbia University Press.

Brownworth, Victoria A., and Susan Raffo, eds. 1999. *Restricted Access: Lesbians on Disability.* Seattle, WA: Seal Press.

Bynum, Caroline Walker. 1999. "Shape and Story: Metamorphosis in the Western Tradition." Paper presented at NEH Jefferson Lecture. 22 March, at Washington, DC.

de Beauvoir, Simone. (1952) 1974. *The Second Sex.* Trans. H.M. Parshley. New York: Vintage Press.

Fausto-Sterling, Anne. 2000. *Sexing the Body: Gender Politics and the Construction of Sexuality.* New York: Basic Books.

_____.1995. "Gender, Race, and Nation: The Comparative Anatomy of Hottentot Women in Europe 1815–1817." In *Deviant Bodies: Cultural Perspectives in Science and Popular Culture,* eds. Jennifer Terry and Jacqueline Urla, 19–48. Bloomington: Indiana University Press.

Fine, Michelle, and Adrienne Asch, eds. 1988. *Women with Disabilities: Essays in Psychology, Culture, and Politics.* Philadelphia: Temple University Press.

Finger, Anne. 1990. *Past Due: A Story of Disability, Pregnancy, and Birth.* Seattle, WA: Seal Press.

Fiske, Susan T., Amy J. C. Cuddy, and Peter Glick. 2001. "A Model of (Often Mixed) Stereotype Content: Competence and Warmth Respectively Follow from Perceived Status and Competition." Unpublished study.

Foucault, Michel. 1979. *Discipline and Punish: The Birth of the Prison.* Trans. Alan M. Sheridan-Smith. New York: Vintage Books.

Gilman, Sander. 1998. *Creating Beauty to Cure the Soul.* Durham, NC: Duke University Press.

_____.1985. *Difference and Pathology: Stereotypes of Sexuality, Race, and Madness.* Ithaca, NY: Cornell University Press.

Haiken, Elizabeth. 1997. *Venus Envy: A History of Cosmetic Surgery.* Baltimore, MD: Johns Hopkins University Press.

Haraway, Donna. 1991. *Simians, Cyborgs, and Women.* New York: Routledge.

Hillyer, Barbara. 1993. *Feminism and Disability.* Norman: University of Oklahoma Press.

Keller, Evelyn Fox. 1992. "Nature, Nurture and the Human Genome Project." In *The Code of Codes: Scientific and Social Issues in the Human Genome Project,* eds. Daniel J. Kevles and Leroy Hood, 281–99. Cambridge, MA: Harvard University Press.

Kittay, Eva, with Leo Kittay. 2000. "On the Expressivity and Ethics of Selective Abortion for Disability: Conversations with My Son." In *Prenatal Testing and Disability Rights,* eds. Erik Parens and Adrienne Asch, 165–95. Georgetown, MD: Georgetown University Press.

Linton, Simi. 1998. *Claiming Disability: Knowledge and Identity.* New York: New York University Press.

Longmore, Paul K. 1997. "Conspicuous Contribution and American Cultural Dilemmas: Telethon Rituals of Cleansing and Renewal." In *The Body and Physical Difference: Discourses of Disabiity,* eds. David Mitchell and Sharon Snyder, 134–58. Ann Arbor: University of Michigan Press.

Morrison, Toni. 1992. *Playing in the Dark: Whiteness and the Literary Imagination.* Cambridge, MA: Harvard University Press.

Parens, Erik, and Adrienne Asch. 2000. *Prenatal Testing and Disability Rights,* Georgetown, MD: Georgetown University Press.

Piercy, Marge. 1969. "Unlearning Not to Speak." In her *Circles on Water,* 97. New York: Doubleday.

Rand, Erica. 1995. *Barbies's Queer Accessories.* Durham, NC: Duke University Press.

Rapp, Rayna. 1999. *Testing Women, Testing the Fetus: The Social Impact of Amniocentesis in America.* New York: Routledge.

Riley, Denise. 1999. "Bodies, Identities, Feminisms." In *Feminist Theory and the Body: A Reader,* eds. Janet Price and Margrit Shildrick, 220–6. Edinburgh, Scotland: Edinburgh University Press.

Russo, Mary. 1994. *The Female Grotesque: Risk, Excess, and Modernity.* New York: Routledge.

Saxton, Marsha. 1998. "Disability Rights and Selective Abortion." In *Abortion Wars: A Half Century of Struggle (1950–2000),* ed. Ricky Solinger, 374–93. Berkeley: University of California Press.

Sedgwick, Eve Kosofsky. 1990. *Epistemology of the Closet.* Berkeley: University of California Press.

Silvers, Anita. 1995. "Reconciling Equality to Difference: Caring (f)or Justice for People with Disabilities." *Hypatia* 10(1): 30–55.

Thomson, Rosemarie Garland. 1999. "Narratives of Deviance and Delight: Staring at Julia Pastrana, 'The Extraordinary

Lady." In *Beyond the Binary*, ed. Timothy Powell, 81–106. New Brunswick, NJ: Rutgers University Press.

———. 1997. *Extraordinary Bodies: Figuring Physical Disability in American Culture and Literature*. New York: Columbia University Press.

Tuana, Nancy. 1993. *The Less Noble Sex: Scientific, Religious and Philosophical Conceptions of Woman's Nature*. Bloomington: Indiana University Press.

Wald, Priscilla. 2000. "Future Perfect: Grammar, Genes, and Geography." *New Literary History* 31(4):681–708.

Williams, John M. 1999. "And Here's the Pitch: Madison Avenue Discovers the 'Invisible Consumer.'" *WE Magazine*, July/August:28–31.

Wolf, Naomi. 1991. *The Beauty Myth: How Images of Beauty Are Used against Women*. New York: William Morrow and Co.

Young, Iris Marion. 1990. "Throwing Like a Girl." In her *Throwing Like a Girl and Other Essays in Feminist Philosophy and Social Theory*, 141–59. Bloomington: Indiana University Press.

 98

Looking for Warrior Woman (Beyond Pocahontas)

JOANNE BARKER

JOANNE BARKER. Lenape. ND. Scholar. Professor of Native American Studies. *Sovereignty Matters: Locations of Contestation and Possibility in Indigenous Struggles for Self-Determination* (editor), (2005) "The Human Genome Diversity Project: 'Peoples', 'Populations', and the Cultural Politics of Identification" (2004).

In June 1998 while reading through my monthly subscriptions to *News from Indian Country* and *Indian Country Today* I came across an ad soliciting job applications for the U.S. Secret Service.[1] I am going to call this ad Warrior Woman. Centered at the top, in bold-faced print, the ad seeks "*a new kind of* WARRIOR." Below, an American Indian woman stands direct in a black suit and white buttoned-up dress shirt. Behind her left arm a detail of the Secret Service's badge shadows her in gray outline. In her right hand, she holds a spear garnered with feathers and wrapped in cloth (you almost forget to notice her polished nails, matching lipstick, and silver ring). Around her left ear; dangling into the inside of her jacket's lapel, is an almost transparent ear-piece.

On her lapel, there is a small silver pin in the shape and colors of the U.S. flag. The first button on her jacket is large and silver, bearing a design of four arrows pointing out. Framing the bottom of the ad is the main text, overlaid another U.S. flag. The badge centers the "Secret Service." Below appears the following text: "Everyday the U.S. Secret Service battles to protect our nation's leaders and financial systems. We are looking for young Americans with diverse skills and backgrounds who are interested in a challenging career in federal law enforcement. To find out more, give us a call (202) 435–5800 www.treas.gov/treasury/bureaus/usss."

It is a stunning ad. The image is bold; the textures and lines are sharp; the woman is proud and powerful. For one quick moment, you actually consider a career in federal law enforcement. And for any woman of indigenous citizenship, that is one very long, richly complex moment.

. . .

A "*new kind of* WARRIOR" Woman?

There are as many versions of the story of Pocahontas as there are representations of her in U.S. popular culture. It would be impossible to sort through all these images and the ensuing questions about their factuality and significance here. Were she and John Smith in love? Did she save Smith from her father? Why did Smith only write of the scene in his draft of the *Generall Historie of Virginie* (1624) after Pocahontas had gained notoriety in England as the famed "Indian Princess"? Why did Pocahontas spend all of her time at the fort? Why did she marry John Rolfe, convert to Christianity, change her name to Rebecca, leave for England? Why was she returning home? (And why did Thomas Rolfe later lead U.S. troops against his mother's people?)

I do not mean to minimize these compelling questions' importance. Several scholars have pointed out the necessity of understanding the historical and cultural context from which Pocahontas came, for it informed the political agenda of her father, Powhatan, concerning their respective relations with Smith and the colony. Indian women have cared very deeply about what Pocahontas's story tells us about the history of Indian women's roles generally and Pocahontas's role as a Powhatan woman specifically. Was the famed salvation scene actually an enactment of a Powhatan adoption ceremony that would have brought Smith under Powhatan's authority? Is it possible that Pocahontas spent so much time at the fort because estranged from her own community following an alleged rape? Was she spying for her father, carrying out an elaborate scheme to obtain intelligence on the colonists and their plans?

My efforts are not to recover "the facts." Rather, I want to try to understand how the narrative works. It is a different strategy that cares about the way "facts" are put to use rather than, say, deconstructing the plausibility of particular fact-claims in understanding what histories still need to get told.

In "The Pocahontas Perplex" Cherokee scholar Rayna Green suggests that the persistence of Pocahontas's story has been its utility within U.S. nationalism's mythic structures, particularly in (re)enacting the inferiority of Pocahontas's culture and the dominion of Smith's in what was to be figured as America. Pocahontas's alleged defiance of her father, her choice to save Smith, her attention to Smith and the other colonists' survival, her marriage and conversion, her Christian renaming, and her move to England are made evidence that she knew that her own culture lacked the qualities valued by Smith's and the New World (Berkhofer). Stripped of any vestiges of her own political agenda and her own cultural affiliation and identity, Pocahontas is made to speak to that new world, to that America, as heroine and ancestor.[2]

These interpretative practices transfiguring Pocahontas into a quintessential American hero are insidious: such inventions render her insignificant outside her heterosexualized relationships to men and erase her affiliation as a Powhatan. Dispossessing Pocahontas of her sovereign identity, culture, and history—and thus political concerns and agendas other than those serving U.S. colonial men and interests—makes it impossible to consider that she might have spoken for or to other issues, such as those addressing her father's powerful position, her people's autonomy and survival, and the colonists' treatment of Indians. Instead, Pocahontas becomes merely everybody's great-great-grandmother, resolving conflicted problems of dispossession and genocide that characterized her and her nation's history with an all too easy and hypocritical "affirmation of relationship" (Green, 20).

Warrior Woman is more than coincidentally (in)formed by the representational practices of Indian women as icons of U.S. nationalism. These practices are registered in the very moment Warrior Woman is dispossessed from her own history, culture, and identity and invites Indian people to identify with and emulate that dispossession. The ad's call for recruits is juxtaposed with the text soliciting "*a new kind of* WARRIOR." But what exactly does it mean by "new"? . . .

That the Indian Warrior is a woman is central to how the ad carries out its signifying chain from the old to the new to the old again. The Warrior Woman wants us to believe that what would be "new" is neither the idea of Indians in the Service nor the relevancy of their "skills and backgrounds" to the Secret Service but rather the very notion that the Warrior would be a woman. The "*new kind of* WARRIOR" *is a Woman* is the jingle that I believe the ad invites its audiences to sing. The Secret Service wants to foreground its acknowledgment of "diversity" by extending it from Indian to woman—from race to gender—in one sweeping Affirmative Action gesture. It wants us to believe that the Secret Service counters the often hyper-masculinized and racist notions of U.S. patriotism, particularly those associated with the growing incidence of Euro-American militia activities in the United States, with the very radical idea that the Secret Service already recognizes and reveres Indian women's heroic loyalty. In circuitry, of course, that quality is an invention of the very U.S. nationalism on which the Secret Service stands.

The "new" erases a multitude of historical and cultural sins from the pages of U.S. history. The fact that Indians continually transformed their "skills and backgrounds" in order to defend themselves against U.S. military, economic, and cultural aggression; that anywhere from 60 to 95 percent of the Indian population in the U.S. died by disease and armed conflict in the 1800s alone (Stiffarm with Lane); that Indian people have been systematically removed from their lands, communities, beliefs, and languages in efforts to eradicate Indians from everything Indian; and that U.S. national leaders and economic systems have had an instrumental hand in directing and implementing these policies in practice are all shaken from the ad's apparent affirmations of anti-racism and anti-sexism as if Indian-U.S. history were an Etch-A-Sketch drawing that could be turned upside down and started anew when the lines got too messy.

The Warrior Woman suggests that what is "new" about herself is that a woman could be a warrior (like there weren't ever any Indian women warriors!) or that the service of Indian women as a whole in the Secret Service has been unnoticed until now. But I believe that she is fooling herself. That the Warrior is a Woman is as much a precondition of the erasure of the history of the role of U.S. national leaders and economic systems in carrying out U.S. imperialism as it is a reconfiguration of it. The Warrior Woman simultaneously constructs an Indian woman removed from her own histories and cultures, as a detribalized Indian generically adorned, as a deterritorialized warrior without a nation of her own "to protect and to serve," as she constructs those erasures to be lived within. The cost of her ability to serve the secret intents of federal and economic policy is displaced from the very scene that celebrates the possibility of that service.

ENOUGH IS ENOUGH

In "Thoughts on Indian Feminism," Assiniboine (Nakota, Fort Peck Reservation) scholar Kathryn Shanley argues that American Indian women have too often been made into "tokens" for a "white feminist movement" that has ignored the historical and cultural specificities of their own particular struggles and beliefs (213–15). Shanley posits that the concerns characteristic of the "white women's movement" over the economic and social oppression of the mainstream workforce and "nuclear family" have little translation into contemporary Indian women's lives and concerns. For Shanley, sovereignty and cultural tradition are the basis for any reformulation or understanding of Indian women's epistemologies and politics, informing the range of their activism concerning environmental, resource, and land rights, domestic violence, language retention, education, health care, and a myriad of other issues.

In "Relocations upon Relocations" Chicana/Nez Perce scholar Inés Hernández-Ávila argues that Native American women's writings are situated within their commitments to their unique *home(lands)* and shared histories of (re)location, within their own communities' struggles for political and cultural sovereignty. She also maintains that Native women's epistemologies are informed by an emphasis on homelands; while *home* generally refers to a domestic sphere of familial relation and responsibility, *homelands* refers to the historical forces that have very publicly relocated Native peoples from their territories, cultures, and identities. In this way, Hernández-Ávila demonstrates that Native women's writings pivot on an axis of political sovereignty and cultural autonomy.

Drawing from Shanley and Hernández-Ávila, I suggest that an oppositional reading strategy for the Warrior Woman ad could start from an understanding that Indian women are first and foremost situated within and concerned about the struggles of their own unique nations for sovereignty and cultural autonomy as well as that of all indigenous people in the Americas—North and South. This methodological perspective takes sovereignty and cultural autonomy as the primary frames of reference for understanding the politics of representation for/of/about/by American Indian women. This is not to suggest that all Indian women have experienced histories of relocation, dispossession, and genocide in the same way, nor that their ideas and goals about how to accomplish the repatriation of their histories, cultures, and identities are the same. Rather, by insisting on sovereignty and autonomy as the primary frames of reference for a hermeneutics of Indian women's representations, the strategy emphasizes the embeddedness of Indian histories, cultures, and identities in meaning systems that are discrete *and* related. National and cultural survivance, concepts of membership and belonging, and socially defined roles and political agendas provide the context from which to interpret representational practices of/by Indian women (Kauanui). . . .

What happens when we read the Warrior Woman, insisting on sovereignty and autonomy as the frames of reference? Unlike Pocahontas, Warrior Woman is not a historical figure per se. Believing that agency is something you do and not something you are or are not given, I suggest that Warrior Woman's political and cultural agency is located within her self-determining history, culture, and identity. The challenge, of course, is that the image does not identify her Indian national affiliation; the codes provided by the term *warrior* and the emblematic spear are far too tribally generic to be helpful. So I'll have to look elsewhere to enact the reading.

In "Rosebuds of the Plateau," Rayna Green suggests a story for the two Indian women lounging on Japanese-American photographer Frank Matsura's fainting couch (*Two Girls on Couch*, 1910). Though I would never presume to speak for Warrior Woman, I would like to take my cue from Green and make up a story that might fill in her confused dress, proud stance, and role in the Secret Service. Because at some level I can not quite explain away, I like her. I am transfixed by her. I am deeply troubled by her. . . .

So I've decided that the story I like best for her is that she is a double agent. . . .

From the seemingly endless reserve of data banks, filing cabinets, and musty ill-numbered boxes in Pentagon basements and Nebraska warehouses, Warrior Woman is passing to her people information that she has finally been made privy to after years of loyal and quiet service. So loyal and quiet, in fact, that she is almost unnoticed. Almost invisible: Even now. And who could doubt the likelihood of that scenario? A woman too dark, too smart, too competent to be seen by the hyperheterosexualized patriarchal structures in which she works; appearing in conference rooms and department meetings only on year-end personnel review and employment statistic forms filed before they're really read; seen only as a satisfaction of a quotient for "race" and "gender" diversity, as if that's what Affirmative Action was about.

So she decides to take advantage of her invisibility. Unbeknownst to any of her colleagues in one of the world's most infamous intelligence agencies, the dust-ridden secrets hidden away in encryption codes and storehouses are brought out of their hiding places and passed on to those who can decipher their significance, break their codes, and unseal their overdue warnings for "confidentiality" and "national security" to assist them in their struggles for sovereignty.

On the day this picture was taken, Warrior Woman had scheduled a rendezvous with one of her contacts. She has discovered a password for *www.treas.gov/treasury/bureaus/usss* that allows the user to enter all *usss* files at will and she is anxious to pass it on.

She has been well placed at the front of the president's caravan in a parade for some misconstrued national holiday down New York City's main street—the perfect Kodak moment. She resisted carrying the spear, arguing that it would get in the way if there were trouble, but her superior had had it specially dug out of a box of supplies in the oldest part of a Nebraska warehouse. Marching through the heat, stopping occasionally to pose for pictures, she imagines the spear's history.

She has decided that the spear was used in the special "citizenship ceremonies" developed by Secretary of the Interior Franklin Lane in 1916. Lane made the delivery of land patents and the commensurate status of U.S. citizenship under the provisions of the General Allotment Act of 1887 a ceremonial event, probably because he thought he knew how important rituals were to Indian people. . . . At the ceremony's closing, they were presented with an American flag directed to repeat the following phrase: "Forasmuch as the President has said that I am worthy to be a citizen of the United States, I now promise this flag that I will give my hands, my head, and my heart to the doing of all that will make me a true American citizen" (McDonnell, 95). To conclude the ceremony, the presiding official pinned a badge decorated with an American eagle and the national colors on the recipient to remind the Indian to act in a way that would honor the flag and the privileges of U.S. citizenship that had been afforded to him/her that day. (These ceremonies were first performed on the Yankton reservation in South Dakota in 1916, and were conducted by Lane himself [McDonnell, 95–96]).

As Warrior Woman carried the spear down Main Street, she wondered about those who participated in the citizenship ceremonies. She is sure that many of them went through the ceremony half-heartedly, even mockingly, but that probably many more were *interpolated* into the life it enacted. Participation didn't have to mean compliance, but it would be hard for a spectator to tell the difference. Those watching her march down Main Street like an emblem of the president's Affirmative Action prowess, a symbol of Secret Service loyalty and patriotism, would probably believe her a modern-day Pocahontas—a hero, a traitor, depending. They wouldn't know that she had switched the frequency of her radio over to a station playing Buffy St. Marie's "The Universal Soldier." That she had flipped over the pin on her lapel so that the flag was upside down. That she was waiting for her contact to bump into her through the crowds so that she could pass on the small notepad hidden in her left coat pocket. But that's all okay, she thought. She knew.

WHEN ALL THINGS OLD ARE NEW AGAIN . . .

American Indian women, while sharing experiences with other "women of color" in the context of ongoing histories of U.S. nationalism, are not another "ethnicity" in the rainbow of American cultural difference. Identifying as Indian is not quite the same thing as identifying, for instance, as "Black" or "Chinese American" or "Chicana." To identify or mark indigeneity is to claim oneself as a member of a people—a "collective nonstate entity" (Wilmer, 164) with internationally recognized legal rights to political and cultural sovereignty and autonomy. This is why so many Indian people insist on their national or tribal identities in opposition to being identified as Indian. In fact, the very processes of racialization as *Indians* has been integral to the political processes that have sought to undermine Indian sovereignty and autonomy. To the extent that Indians have been counted as "minorities," "under-represented," and/or as making up an "ethnic group" within the larger U.S. polity, the notion that they are citizens of their own unique nations has been undermined, displaced. This has important and immediate consequences to self-government, land and resource rights, juridical autonomy, and cultural survivance. In other words, the *ethnicization* of Indians and the representational practices that employ it have been extremely useful in the systematic negation of Indian people's sovereignty and autonomy (Barker).

Of course, issues of dual citizenship and the more slippery concepts of membership and belonging for mixed-race and mixed-tribal Indians complicate matters even further. There are Indians, for instance, who want to be recognized as U.S. citizens and consider themselves patriots; there are those who have not recognized themselves as citizens of Indian nations at all; and there are those who

believe themselves to be citizens of two countries. Further, the identities and memberships of "mixed-bloods"—those of mixed racial and/or mixed tribal descent—make it impossible to render a simple notion of what it means to identify or be identified as Indian within the context of representational practices. I do not mean to dismiss these complexities but rather to suggest that for Indian people in the United States the erasure of the sovereign from the Indian has been a particularly strategic goal of dispossession, genocide, and assimilation. This goal is encapsulated by the Warrior Woman: denationalized, detribalized, an emblem of diversity within the "our" of U.S. politics and economics.

The issues Warrior Woman embodies are foregrounded by the way the ad sets up a tension between U.S. nationalism's hegemonic knowledge practices and American Indian women's oppositional strategies. It is not a natural tension. It is very much a construction of the kinds of power imagined within colonialism, capitalism, and patriarchalism. Pocahontas as a historical figure is enigmatic of these troubles, her dispossession and death the precondition of her usefulness in maintaining the mythic structures of U.S. nationalist discourses. Warrior Woman indicates that these troubles have been carried forward in the continued possibilities for making Indians speak to/for the very political and economic agendas that have undermined their struggles for sovereignty and autonomy. It follows that the precondition of her service is the erasure of their own unique and diverse histories, cultures, and identities. I have tried to show how it might be otherwise.

[2002]

NOTES

1. See inserts, *News from Indian Country* (June 11, 1998, 9A) and *Indian Country Today* (June 8–15, 1998, B8).
2. As Green shows in "The Pocahontas Perplex," the Pocahontas image is troubled further by her twin, the squaw/whore, who shares her one-dimensional referentiality to colonial men and colonial processes.

99

Beside Oneself: On the Limits of Sexual Autonomy from Undoing Gender

JUDITH BUTLER

What makes for a livable world is no idle question. It is not merely a question for philosophers. It is posed in various idioms all the time by people in various walks of life. If that makes them all philosophers, then that is a conclusion I am happy to embrace. It becomes a question for ethics, I think, not only when we ask the personal question, what makes my own life bearable, but when we ask, from a position of power, and from the point of view of distributive justice, what makes, or ought to make, the lives of others bearable? Somewhere in the answer we find ourselves not only committed to a certain view of what life is, and what it should be, but also of what constitutes the human, the distinctively human life, and what does not. There is always a risk of anthropocentrism here if one assumes that the distinctively human life is valuable—or most valuable—or is the only way to think the problem of value. But perhaps to counter that tendency it is necessary to ask both the question of life and the question of the human, and not to let them fully collapse into one another.

I would like to start, and to end, with the question of the human, of who counts as the human, and the related question of whose lives count as lives, and with a question that has preoccupied many of us for years: what makes for a grievable life? I believe that whatever differences exist within the international gay and lesbian community, and there are many, we all have some notion of what it is to have lost somebody. And if we've lost, then it seems to follow that we have had, that we have desired and loved, and struggled to find the conditions for our desire. We have all lost someone in recent decades from AIDS, but there are other losses that inflict us, other diseases; moreover, we are, as a community, subjected to violence, even if some of us individually have not been. And this means that we are constituted politically in part

by virtue of the social vulnerability of our bodies; we are constituted as fields of desire and physical vulnerability, at once publicly assertive and vulnerable. . . .

Let's face it. We're undone by each other. And if we're not, we're missing something. If this seems so clearly the case with grief, it is only because it was already the case with desire. One does not always stay intact. It may be that one wants to, or does, but it may also be that despite one's best efforts, one is undone, in the face of the other, by the touch, by the scent, by the feel, by the prospect of the touch, by the memory of the feel. And so when we speak about *my* sexuality or *my* gender, as we do (and as we must) we mean something complicated by it. Neither of these is precisely a possession, but both are to be understood as *modes of being dispossessed*, ways of being for another or, indeed, by virtue of another. It does not suffice to say that I am promoting a relational view of the self over an autonomous one, or trying to redescribe autonomy in terms of relationality. The term "relationality" sutures the rupture in the relation we seek to describe, a rupture that is constitutive of identity itself. This means that we will have to approach the problem of conceptualizing dispossession with circumspection. One way of doing this is through the notion of ecstasy.

We tend to narrate the history of the broader movement for sexual freedom in such a way that ecstasy figures in the 60s and 70s and persists midway through the 80s. But maybe ecstasy is more historically persistent than that, maybe it is with us all along. To be ec-static means, literally, to be outside oneself, and this can have several meanings: to be transported beyond oneself by a passion, but also to be *beside oneself* with rage or grief. I think that if I can still speak to a "we," and include myself within its terms, I am speaking to those of us who are living in certain ways *beside ourselves*, whether it is in sexual passion, or emotional grief, or political rage. In a sense, the predicament is to understand what kind of community is composed of those who are beside themselves.

We have an interesting political predicament, since most of the time when we hear about "rights," we understand them as pertaining to individuals, or when we argue for protection against discrimination, we argue as a group or a class. And in that language and in that context, we have to present ourselves as bounded beings, distinct, recognizable, delineated, subjects before the law, a community defined by sameness. Indeed, we had better be able to use that language to secure legal protections and entitlements. But perhaps we make a mistake if we take the definitions of who we are, legally, to be adequate descriptions of what we are about. Although this language might well establish our legitimacy within a legal framework ensconced in liberal versions of human ontology, it fails to do justice to passion and grief and rage, all of which tear us from ourselves, bind us to others, transport us, undo us, and implicate us in lives that are not are own, sometimes fatally, irreversibly. . . .

It is not easy to understand how a political community is wrought from such ties. One speaks, and one speaks for another, to another, and yet there is no way to collapse the distinction between the other and myself. When we say "we" we do nothing more than designate this as very problematic. We do not solve it. And perhaps it is, and ought to be, insoluble. We ask that the state, for instance, keep its laws off our bodies, and we call for principles of bodily self-defense and bodily integrity to be accepted as political goods. Yet, it is through the body that gender and sexuality become exposed to others, implicated in social processes, inscribed by cultural norms, and apprehended in their social meanings. In a sense, to be a body is to be given over to others even as a body is, emphatically, "one's own," that over which we must claim rights of autonomy. This is as true for the claims made by lesbians, gays, and bisexuals in favor of sexual freedom as it is for transsexual and transgender claims to self-determination; as it is for intersex claims to be free of coerced medical, surgical, and psychiatric interventions; as it is for all claims to be free from racist attacks, physical and verbal; and as it is for feminism's claim to reproductive freedom. It is difficult, if not impossible, to make these claims without recourse to autonomy and, specifically, a sense of bodily autonomy. Bodily autonomy, however, is a lively paradox. I am not suggesting, though, that we cease to make these claims. We have to, we must. And I'm not saying that we have to make these claims reluctantly or strategically. They are part of the normative aspiration of any movement that

seeks to maximize the protection and the freedoms of sexual and gender minorities, of women, defined with the broadest possible compass, of racial and ethnic minorities, especially as they cut across all the other categories. But is there another normative aspiration that we must also seek to articulate and to defend? Is there a way in which the place of the body in all of these struggles opens up a different conception of politics?

The body implies mortality, vulnerability, agency: the skin and the flesh expose us to the gaze of others but also to touch and to violence. The body can be the agency and instrument of all these as well, or the site where "doing" and "being done to" become equivocal. Although we struggle for rights over our own bodies, the very bodies for which we struggle are not quite ever only our own. The body has its invariably public dimension; constituted as a social phenomenon in the public sphere, my body is and is not mine. Given over from the start to the world of others, bearing their imprint, formed within the crucible of social life, the body is only later, and with some uncertainty, that to which I lay claim as my own. Indeed, if I seek to deny the fact that my body relates me—against my will and from the start—to others I do not choose to have in proximity to myself (the subway or the tube are excellent examples of this dimension of sociality), and if I build a notion of "autonomy" on the basis of the denial of this sphere or a primary and unwilled physical proximity with others, then do I precisely deny the social and political conditions of my embodiment in the name of autonomy? If I am struggling *for* autonomy, do I not need to be struggling for something else as well, a conception of myself as invariably in community, impressed upon by others, impressing them as well and in ways that are not always clearly delineable, in forms that are not fully predictable?

Is there a way that we might struggle for autonomy in many spheres but also consider the demands that are imposed upon us by living in a world of beings who are, by definition, physically dependent on one another, physically vulnerable to one another. Is this not another way of imagining community in such a way that it becomes incumbent upon us to consider very carefully when and where we engage violence, for violence is, always, an exploitation of that primary tie, that primary way in which we are, as bodies, outside ourselves, for one another.

If we might then return to the problem of grief, to the moments in which one undergoes something outside of one's control and finds that one is beside oneself, not at one with oneself, we can say grief contains within it the possibility of apprehending the fundamental sociality of embodied life, the ways in which we are from the start, and by virtue of being a bodily being, already given over, beyond ourselves, implicated in lives that are not our own. Can this situation, one that is so dramatic for sexual minorities, one that estabiishes a very specific political perspective for anyone who works in the field of sexual and gender politics, supply a perspective with which to begin to apprehend the contemporary global situation? . . .

There is a more general conception of the human at work here, one in which we are, from the start, given over to the other, one in which we are, from the start, even prior to individuation itself, and by virtue of our embodiment, given over to an other: this makes us vulnerable to violence, but also to another range of touch, a range that includes the eradication of our being at the one end, and the physical support for our lives, at the other.

We cannot endeavor to "rectify" this situation. And we cannot recover the source of this vulnerability, for it precedes the formation of "I." This condition of being laid bare from the start, dependent on those we do not know is, one with which we cannot precisely argue. We come into the world unknowing and dependent, and, to a certain degree, we remain that way. We can try, from the point of view of autonomy, to argue with this situation, but we are perhaps foolish, if not dangerous, when we do. Of course, we can say that for some this primary scene is extraordinary, loving, and receptive, a warm tissue of relations that support and nurture life in its infancy. For others, this is, however, a scene of abandonment or violence or starvation; they are bodies given over to nothing, or to brutality, or to no sustenance. No matter what the valence of that scene is, however, the fact remains that infancy constitutes a necessary dependency, one that we never fully leave behind. Bodies still must

be apprehended as given over. Part of understanding the oppression of lives is precisely to understand that there is no way to argue away this condition of a primary vulnerability, of being given over to the touch of the other, even if, or precisely when, there is no other there, and no support for our lives. To counter oppression requires that one understand that lives are supported and maintained differentially, that there are radically different ways in which human physical vulnerability is distributed across the globe. Certain lives will be highly protected, and the abrogation of their claims to sanctity will be sufficient to mobilize the forces of war. And other lives will not find such fast and furious support and will not even qualify as "grievable."

What are the cultural contours of the notion of the human at work here? And how do the contours that we accept as the cultural frame for the human limit the extent to which we can avow loss as loss? This is surely a question that lesbian, gay, and bistudies has asked in relation to violence against sexual minorities, and that transgendered people have asked as they have been singled out for harassment and sometimes murder, and that intersexed people have asked, whose formative years have so often been marked by an unwanted violence against their bodies in the name of a normative notion of human morphology. This is no doubt as well the basis of a profound affinity between movements centered on gender and sexuality with efforts to counter the normative human morphologies and capacities that condemn or efface those who are physically challenged. It must, as well, also be part of the affinity with antiracist struggles, given the racial differential that undergirds the culturally viable notions of the human—ones that we see acted out in dramatic and terrifying ways in the global arena at the present time. . . .

I began this chapter with a suggestion that perhaps the interrelated movements and modes of inquiry that collect here might need to consider autonomy as one dimension of their normative aspirations, one value to realize when we ask ourselves, in what direction ought we to proceed, and what kinds of values ought we to be realizing? I suggested as well that the way in which the body figures in gender and sexuality studies, and in the struggles for a less oppressive social world for the otherwise gendered and for sexual minorities of all kinds, is precisely to underscore the value of being beside oneself, of being a porous boundary, given over to others, finding oneself in a trajectory of desire in which one is taken out of oneself, and resituated irreversibly in a field of others in which one is not the presumptive center. The particular sociality that belongs to bodily life, to sexual life, and to becoming gendered (which is always, to a certain extent, becoming gendered *for others*) establishes a field of ethical enmeshment with others and a sense of disorientation for the first-person, that is, the perspective of the ego. As bodies, we are always for something more than, and other than, ourselves. To articulate this as an entitlement is not always easy, but perhaps not impossible. It suggests, for instance, that "association" is not a luxury, but one of the very conditions and prerogatives of freedom. Indeed, the kinds of associations we maintain importantly take many forms. It will not do to extol the marriage norm as the new ideal for this movement, as the Human Rights Campaign has erroneously done.[1] No doubt, marriage and same-sex domestic partnerships should certainly be available as options, but to install either as a model for sexual legitimacy is precisely to constrain the sociality of the body in acceptable ways. In light of seriously damaging judicial decisions against second parent adoptions in recent years, it is crucial to expand our notions of kinship beyond the heterosexual frame. It would be a mistake, however, to reduce kinship to family, or to assume that all sustaining community and friendship ties are extrapolation of kin relations. . . .

In recent years, the new gender politics has offered numerous challenges from transgendered and transsexual peoples to established feminist and lesbian/gay frameworks, and the intersex movement has rendered more complex the concerns and demands of sexual rights advocates. If some on the Left thought that these concerns were not properly or substantively political, they have been under pressure to rethink the political sphere in terms of its gendered and sexual presuppositions. The suggestion that butch, femme, and transgendered lives are not essential referents for a refashioning of political life, and for a more just and equitable society, fails to acknowledge the violence that the otherwise gendered suffer in the public world and

fails as well to recognize that embodiment denotes a contested set of norms governing who will count as a viable subject within the sphere of politics. Indeed, if we consider that human bodies are not experienced without recourse to some ideality, some frame for experience itself, and that this is as true for the experience of one's own body as it is for experiencing another, and if we accept that that ideality and frame are socially articulated, we can see how it is that embodiment is not thinkable without a relation to a norm, or a set of norms. The struggle to rework the norms by which bodies are experienced is thus crucial not only to disability politics, but to the intersex and transgendered movements as they contest forcibly imposed ideals of what bodies ought to be like. The embodied relation to the norm exercises a transformative potential. To posit possibilities beyond the norm or, indeed, a different future for the norm itself, is part of the work of fantasy when we understand fantasy as taking the body as a point of departure for an articulation that is not always constrained by the body as it is. If we accept that altering these norms that decide normative human morphology give differential "reality" to different kinds of humans as a result, then we are compelled to affirm that transgendered lives have a potential and actual impact on political life at its most fundamental level, that is, who counts as a human, and what norms govern the appearance of "real" humanness.

Moreover, fantasy is part of the articulation of the possible; it moves us beyond what is merely actual and present into a realm of possibility, the not yet actualized or the not actualizable. The struggle to survive is not really separable from the cultural life of fantasy, and the foreclosure of fantasy—through censorship, degradation, or other means—is one strategy for providing for the social death of persons. Fantasy is not the opposite of reality; it is what reality forecloses, and, as a result, it defines the limits of reality, constituting it as its constitutive outside. The critical promise of fantasy, when and where it exists, is to challenge the contingent limits of what will and will not be called reality. Fantasy is what allows us to imagine ourselves and others otherwise; it establishes the possible in excess of the real; it points elsewhere, and when it is embodied, it brings the elsewhere home.

How do drag, butch, femme, transgender, trans-sexual persons enter into the political field? They make us not only question what is real, and what "must" be, but they also show us how the norms that govern contemporary notions of reality can be questioned and how new modes of reality can become instituted. These practices of instituting new modes of reality take place in part through the scene of embodiment, where the body is not understood as a static and accomplished fact, but as an aging process, a mode of becoming that, in becoming otherwise, exceeds the norm, reworks the norm, and makes us see how realities to which we thought we were confined are not written in stone. Some people have asked me what is the use of increasing possibilities for gender. I tend to answer: Possibility is not a luxury; it is as crucial as bread. I think we should not underestimate what the thought of the possible does for those for whom the very issue of survival is most urgent. If the answer to the question, is life possible, is yes, that is surely something significant. It cannot, however, be taken for granted as the answer. That is a question whose answer is sometimes "no," or one that has no ready answer, or one that bespeaks an ongoing agony. For many who can and do answer the question in the affirmative, that answer is hard won, if won at all, an accomplishment that is fundamentally conditioned by reality being structured or restructured in such a way that the affirmation becomes possible. . . .

What place does the thinking of the possible have within political theorizing? Is the problem that we have no norm to distinguish among kinds of possibility, or does that only appear to be a problem if we fail to comprehend "possibility" itself as a norm? Possibility is an aspiration, something we might hope will be equitably distributed, something that might be socially secured, something that cannot be taken for granted, especially if it is apprehended phenomenologically. The point is not to prescribe new gender norms, as if one were under an obligation to supply a measure, gauge, or norm for the adjudication of competing gender presentations. The normative aspiration at work here has to do with the ability to live and breathe and move and would no doubt belong somewhere in what is called a philosophy of freedom. The thought of a possible life is only an indulgence for those who already

know themselves to be possible. For those who are still looking to become possible, possibility is a necessity. . . .

To assert sexual rights, then, takes on a specific meaning against this background. It means, for instance, that when we struggle for rights, we are not simply struggling for rights that attach to my person, but we are struggling *to be conceived as persons*. And there is a difference between the former and the latter. If we are struggling for rights that attach, or should attach, to my personhood, then we assume that personhood as already constituted. But if we are struggling not only to be conceived as persons, but to create a social transformation of the very meaning of personhood, then the assertion of rights becomes a way of intervening into the social and political process by which the human is articulated. International human rights is always in the process of subjecting the human to redefinition and renegotiation. It mobilizes the human in the service of rights, but also rewrites the human and rearticulates the human when it comes up against the cultural limits of its working conception of the human, as it does and must. . . .

I have tried here to argue that our very sense of personhood is linked to the desire for recognition, and that desire places us outside ourselves, in a realm of social norms that we do not fully choose, but that provides the horizon and the resource for any sense of choice that we have. *This means that the ec-static character of our existence is essential to the possibility of persisting as human.* In this sense, we can see how sexual rights brings together two related domains of ec-stasy, two connected ways of being outside of ourselves. As sexual, we are dependent on a world of others, vulnerable to need, violence, betrayal, compulsion, fantasy; we project desire, and we have it projected onto us. To be part of a sexual minority means, most emphatically, that we are also dependent on the protection of public and private spaces, on legal sanctions that protect us from violence, on safeguards of various institutional kinds against unwanted aggression imposed upon us, and the violent actions they sometimes instigate. In this sense, our very lives, and the persistence of our desire, depend on there being norms of recognition that produce and sustain our viability as human. Thus, when we speak about sexual rights, we are not merely talking about rights that pertain to our individual desires but to the norms on which our very individuality depends. That means that the discourse of rights avows our dependency, the mode of our being in the hands of others, a mode of being with and for others without which we cannot be. . . .

That we cannot predict or control what permutations of the human might arise does not mean that we must value all possible permutations of the human; it does not mean that we cannot struggle for the realization of certain values, democratic and nonviolent, international and antiracist. The point is only that to struggle for those values is precisely to avow that one's own position is not sufficient to elaborate the spectrum of the human, that one must enter into a collective work in which one's own status as a subject must, for democratic reasons, become disoriented, exposed to what it does not know.

The point is not to apply social norms to lived social instances, to order and define them (as Foucault has criticized), nor is it to find justificatory mechanisms for the grounding of social norms that are extra-social (even as they operate under the name of the social). There are times when both of these activities do and must take place: we level judgments against criminals for illegal acts, and so subject them to a normalizing procedure; we consider our grounds for action in collective contexts and try to find modes of deliberation and reflection about which we can agree. But neither of these is all we do with norms. Through recourse to norms, the sphere of the humanly intelligible is circumscribed, and this circumscription is consequential for any ethics and any conception of social transformation. We might try to claim that we must *first* know the fundamentals of the human in order to preserve and promote human life as we know it. But what if the very categories of the human have excluded those who should be described and sheltered within its terms? What if those who ought to belong to the human do not operate within the modes of reasoning and justifying validity claims that have been proffered by western forms of rationalism? Have we ever yet known the human? And what might it take to approach that knowing? Should we be wary of knowing it too soon or of any final or definitive

knowing? If we take the field of the human for granted, then we fail to think critically and ethically about the consequential ways that the human is being produced, reproduced, and deproduced. This latter inquiry does not exhaust the field of ethics, but I cannot imagine a responsible, ethics or theory of social transformation operating without it. . . .

A reductive relativism would say that we cannot speak of the human or of international human rights, since there are only and always local and provisional understandings of these terms, and that the generalizations themselves do violence to the specificity of the meanings in question. This is not my view. I'm not ready to rest there. Indeed, I think we are compelled to speak of the human, and of the international, and to find out in particular how human rights do and do not work, for example, in favor of women, of what women are, and what they are not. But to speak in this way, and to call for social transformations in the name of women, we must also be part of a critical democratic project. Moreover, the category of women has been used differentially and with exclusionary aims, and not all women have been included within its terms; women have not been fully incorporated into the human. Both categories are still in process, underway, unfulfilled, thus we do not yet know and cannot ever definitively know in what the human finally consists. This means that we must follow a double path in politics: we must use this language to assert an entitlement to conditions of life in ways that affirm the constitutive role of sexuality and gender in political life, and we must also subject our very categories to critical scrutiny. We must find out the limits of their inclusivity and translatability, the presuppositions they include, the ways in which they must be expanded, destroyed, or reworked both to encompass and open up what it is to be human and gendered. When the United Nations conference at Beijing met a few years ago, there was a discourse on "women's human rights" (or when we hear of the International Gay and Lesbian Human Rights Commission), which strikes many people as a paradox. Women's human rights? Lesbian and gay human rights? But think about what this coupling actually does. It performs the human as contingent, a category that has in the past, and continues in the present, to define a variable and restricted population, which may or may not include lesbians and gays, may or may not include women, which has several racial and ethnic differentials at work in its operation. It says that such groups have their own set of human rights, that what human may mean when we think about the humanness of women is perhaps different from what human has meant when it has functioned as presumptively male. It also says that these terms are defined, variably, in relation to one another. And we could certainly make a similar argument about race. Which populations have qualified as the human and which have not? What is the history of this category? Where are we in its history at this time?

I would suggest that in this last process, we can only rearticulate or resignify the basic categories of ontology, of being human, of being gendered, of being recognizably sexual, to the extent that we submit ourselves to a process of cultural translation. The point is not to assimilate foreign or unfamiliar notions of gender or humanness into our own as if it is simply a matter of incorporating alienness into an established lexicon. Cultural translation is also a process of yielding our most fundamental categories, that is, seeing how and why they break up, require resignification when they encounter the limits of an available episteme: what is unknown or not yet known. It is crucial to recognize that the notion of the human will only be built over time in and by the process of cultural translation, where it is not a translation between two languages that stay enclosed, distinct, unified. But rather, *translation will compel each language to change in order to apprehend the other*, and this apprehension, at the limit of what is familiar, parochial, and already known, will be the occasion for both an ethical and social transformation. It will constitute a loss, a disorientation, but one in which the human stands a chance of coming into being anew.

When we ask what makes a life livable, we are asking about certain normative conditions that must be fulfilled for life to become life. And so there are at least two senses of life, the one that refers to the minimum biological form of living, and another that intervenes at the start, which establishes minimum conditions for a livable life with regard to human life.[2] And this does not imply

that we can disregard the merely living in favor of the livable life, but that we must ask, as we asked about gender violence, what humans require in order to maintain and reproduce the conditions of their own livability. And what are our politics such that we are, in whatever way is possible, both conceptualizing the possibility of the livable life, and arranging for its institutional support? There will always be disagreement about what this means, and those who claim that a single political direction is necessitated by virtue of this commitment will be mistaken. But this is only because to live is to live a life politically, in relation to power, in relation to others, in the act of assuming responsibility for a collective future. To assume responsibility for a future, however, is not to know its direction fully in advance, since the future, especially the future with and for others, requires a certain openness and unknowingness; it implies becoming part of a process the outcome of which no one subject can surely predict. It also implies that a certain agonism and contestation over the course of direction will and must be in play. Contestation must be in play for politics to become democratic. Democracy does not speak in unison; its tunes are dissonant, and necessarily so. It is not a predictable process; it must be undergone, like a passion must be undergone. It may also be that life itself becomes foreclosed when the right way is decided in advance, when we impose what is right for everyone and without finding a way to enter into community, and to discover there the "right" in the midst of cultural translation. It may be that what is right and what is good consist in staying open to the tensions that beset the most fundamental categories we require, in knowing unknowingness at the core of what we know, and what we need, and in recognizing the sign of life in what we undergo without certainty about what will come.

[2004]

NOTES

1. The Human Rights Campaign is the main lobbying organization for lesbian and gay rights in the United States. Situated in Washington, D.C. it has maintained that gay marriage is the number one priority of lesbian and gay politics in the U.S. See www.hrc.org.
2. See Giorgio Agamben, *Homo Sacer: Sovereign Power and Bare Life*, 1–12.

100

The Subject of Freedom from The Politics of Piety

SABA MAHMOOD

SABA MAHMOOD. Pakistan. 1962–   .
Anthropologist. "Feminism, the Taliban, and Politics
of Counter-Insurgency" with Charles Hirschkind
(2002), "Feminist Theory, Embodiment, and the
Docile Agent: Some Reflections on the Egyptian
Islamic Revival" (2001).

Over the last two decades, a key question has occupied many feminist theorists: how should issues of
historical and cultural specificity inform both the
analytics and the politics of any feminist project?
While this question has led to serious attempts
at integrating issues of sexual, racial, class, and
national difference within feminist theory, questions
regarding religious difference have remained relatively unexplored. The vexing relationship between
feminism and religion is perhaps most manifest in
discussions of Islam. This is due in part to the historically contentious relationship that Islamic societies have had with what has come to be called "the
West," but also due to the challenges that contemporary Islamist movements pose to secular-liberal
politics of which feminism has been an integral (if
critical) part. The suspicion with which many feminists tended to view Islamist movements only intensified in the aftermath of the September 11, 2001,
attacks launched against the United States, and the
immense groundswell of anti-Islamic sentiment that
has followed since. If supporters of the Islamist
movement were disliked before for their social conservatism and their rejection of liberal values (key
among them "women's freedom"), their now almost
taken-for-granted association with terrorism has
served to further reaffirm their status as agents of a
dangerous irrationality.

Women's participation in, and support for, the
Islamist movement provokes strong responses from
feminists across a broad range of the political spectrum. One of the most common reactions is the
supposition that women Islamist supporters are
pawns in a grand patriarchal plan, who, if freed

from their bondage, would naturally express their
instinctual abhorrence for the traditional Islamic
mores used to enchain them. Even those analysts
who are skeptical of the false-consciousness thesis
underpinning this approach nonetheless continue
to frame the issue in terms of a fundamental
contradiction: why would such a large number of
women across the Muslim world actively support a
movement that seems inimical to their "own interests and agendas," especially at a historical moment
when these women appear to have more emancipatory possibilities available to them. Despite important differences between these two reactions, both
share the assumption that there is something intrinsic to women that *should* predispose them to
oppose the practices, values, and injunctions that
the Islamist movement embodies. Yet, one may ask,
is such an assumption valid? What is the history by
which we have come to assume its truth? What kind
of a political imagination would lead one to think in
this manner? More importantly, if we discard such
an assumption, what other analytical tools might be
available to ask a different set of questions about
women's participation in the Islamist movement?

. . . I will explore some of the conceptual challenges that women's involvement in the Islamist
movement poses to feminist theory in particular,
and to secular-liberal thought in general, through
an ethnographic account of an urban women's
mosque movement that is part of the larger Islamic
Revival in Cairo, Egypt. . . .

The women's mosque movement, as part of the
Islamic Revival, emerged twenty-five or thirty years
ago when women started to organize weekly religious lessons—first at their homes and then within
mosques—to read the Quran, the *hadith* (the
authoritative record of the Prophet's exemplary
speech and actions), and associated exegetical and
edificatory literature. By the time I began my fieldwork in 1995, this movement had become so popular that there were hardly any neighborhoods in this
city of eleven million inhabitants that did not offer
some form of religious lessons for women. . . .

My goal, however, is not just to provide an
ethnographic account of the Islamic Revival. It is
also to make this material speak back to the normative liberal assumptions about human nature against
which such a movement is held accountable—such

as the belief that all human beings have an innate desire for freedom, that we all somehow seek to assert our autonomy when allowed to do so, that human agency primarily consists of acts that challenge social norms and not those that uphold them, and so on. Thus, my ethnographic tracings will sustain a running argument with and against key analytical concepts in liberal thought, as these concepts have come to inform various strains of feminist theory through which movements such as the one I am interested in are analyzed. As will be evident, many of the concepts I discuss under the register of feminist theory in fact enjoy common currency across a wide range of disciplines, in part because liberal assumptions about what constitutes human nature and agency have become integral to our humanist intellectual traditions.

AGENCY AND RESISTANCE

As I suggested at the outset, women's active support for socioreligious movements that sustain principles of female subordination poses a dilemma for feminist analysts. On the one hand, women are seen to assert their presence in previously male-defined spheres while, on the other hand, the very idioms they use to enter these arenas are grounded in discourses that have historically secured their subordination to male authority. In other words, women's subordination to feminine virtues, such as shyness, modesty, and humility, appears to be the necessary condition for their enhanced public role in religious and political life. While it would not have been unusual in the 1960s to account for women's participation in such movements in terms of false consciousness or the internalization of patriarchal norms through socialization, there has been an increasing discomfort with explanations of this kind. Drawing on work in the humanities and the social sciences since the 1970s that has focused on the operations of human agency within structures of subordination, feminists have sought to understand how women resist the dominant male order by subverting the hegemonic meanings of cultural practices and redeploying them for their "own interests and agendas." A central question explored within this scholarship has been: how do women contribute to reproducing their own domination, and how do they resist or subvert it?

Scholars working within this framework have thus tended to analyze religious traditions in terms of the conceptual and practical resources they offer to women, and the possibilities for redirecting and recoding these resources in accord with women's "own interests and agendas"—a recoding that stands as the site of women's agency.[1]

When the focus on locating women's agency first emerged, it played a crucial role in complicating and expanding debates about gender in non-Western societies beyond the simplistic registers of submission and patriarchy. In particular, the focus on women's agency provided a crucial corrective to scholarship on the Middle East that for decades had portrayed Arab and Muslim women as passive and submissive beings shackled by structures of male authority.[2] Feminist scholarship performed the worthy task of restoring the absent voice of women to analyses of Middle Eastern societies, portraying women as active agents whose lives are far richer and more complex than past narratives had suggested (Abu-Lughod 1986; Altorki 1986; Atiya 1982; S. Davis 1983; Dwyer 1978; Early 1993; Fernea 1985; Wikan 1991). This emphasis on women's agency within gender studies paralleled, to a certain extent, discussions of the peasantry in New Left scholarship, a body of work that also sought to restore a humanist agency (often expressed metonymically as a "voice") to the peasant in the historiography of agrarian societies—a project articulated against classical Marxist formulations that had assigned the peasantry a non-place in the making of modern history (Hobsbawm 1980; James Scott 1985). The Subaltern Studies Project is the most recent example of this scholarship (see, for example, Guha and Spivak 1988).

The ongoing importance of feminist scholarship on women's agency cannot be emphasized enough, especially when one remembers that Western popular media continues to portray Muslim women as incomparably bound by the unbreakable chains of religious and patriarchal oppression. This acknowledgment notwithstanding, it is critical to examine the assumptions and elisions that attend this focus on agency, especially the ways in which these assumptions constitute a barrier to the exploration of movements such as the one I am dealing with here. In what follows, I will explore how the notion of human agency most often invoked by feminist scholars—one that locates agency in the political and moral autonomy of the subject—has been brought to bear upon the study of women involved in patriarchal religious traditions such as Islam. Later, in the second half of this chapter, I will suggest alternative ways of thinking about agency, especially as it relates to embodied capacities and means of subject formation.

Janice Boddy's work is an eloquent and intelligent example of the anthropological turn to an analysis of subaltern gendered agency. Boddy conducted fieldwork in a village in an Arabic-speaking region of northern Sudan on a women's *zār* cult—a widely practiced healing cult that uses Islamic idioms and spirit mediums and whose membership is largely female (1989). Through a rich ethnography of women's cultic practices, Boddy proposes that in a society where the "official ideology" of Islam is dominated and controlled by men, the zār practice might be understood as a space of subordinate discourse—as "a medium for the cultivation of women's consciousness" (1989, 345). She argues that zār possession serves as "a kind of counterhegemonic process . . . : *a feminine response to hegemonic praxis*, and the privileging of men that this ideologically entails, which ultimately escapes neither its categories nor its constraints" (1989, 7; emphasis added). She concludes by asserting that the women she studied "use perhaps unconsciously, perhaps strategically, what we in the West might prefer to consider *instruments of their oppression* as means to assert their value both collectively, through the ceremonies they organize and stage, and individually, in the context of their marriages, so insisting on their dynamic complementarity with men. *This in itself is a means of resisting and setting limits to domination. . . .*" (1989, 345; emphasis added).

The ethnographic richness of this study notwithstanding, what is most relevant for the purposes of my argument is the degree to which the female agent in Boddy's work seems to stand in for a sometimes repressed, sometimes active feminist consciousness, articulated against the hegemonic male cultural norms of Arab Muslim societies. As Boddy's study reveals, even in instances when an explicit *feminist* agency is difficult to locate, there is a tendency among scholars to look for expressions and moments of resistance that may suggest a challenge to male domination. When women's actions seem to reinscribe what appear to be "instruments of their own oppression," the social analyst can point to moments of disruption of, and articulation of points of opposition to, male authority—moments that are located either in the interstices of a woman's consciousness (often read as a nascent feminist consciousness), or in the objective effects of women's actions, however unintended these may be. Agency, in this form of analysis, is understood as the capacity to realize one's own interests against the weight of custom, tradition, transcendental will, or other obstacles (whether individual or collective). Thus the humanist desire for autonomy and self-expression constitutes the substrate, the slumbering ember that can spark to flame in the form of an act of resistance when conditions permit.

Lila Abu-Lughod, one of the leading figures among those scholars who helped reshape the study of gender in the Middle East, has criticized some of the assumptions informing feminist scholarship, including those found in her own previous work (Abu-Lughod 1990, 1993). In one of her earlier works, Abu-Lughod had analyzed women's poetry among the Bedouin tribe of Awlād 'Ali as a socially legitimate, semipublic practice that was an expression of women's resistance and protest against the strict norms of male domination in which Bedouin women live (Abu-Lughod 1986). Later, in a reflective essay on this work, Abu-Lughod asks the provocative question: how might we recognize instances of women's resistance without "misattributing to them forms of consciousness or politics that are not part of their experience—something like a feminist consciousness or feminist politics?" (Abu-Lughod 1990, 47), In exploring this question, Abu-Lughod criticizes herself and others for being too preoccupied with "explaining resistance and finding resisters" at the expense of understanding the workings of power (1990, 43). She argues:

> In some of my earlier work, as in that of others, there is perhaps a tendency to *romanticize resistance*, to read all forms of resistance as signs of ineffectiveness of systems of power and of *the resilience and creativity of the human spirit in its refusal to be dominated.* By reading resistance in this way, we

collapse distinctions between forms of resistance and foreclose certain questions about the workings of power. (1990, 42; emphasis added)

As a corrective, Abu-Lughod recommends that resistance be used as a "diagnostic of power" (1990, 42), to locate the shifts in social relations of power that influence the resisters as well as those who dominate. To illustrate her point, Abu-Lughod gives the example of young Bedouin women who wear sexy lingerie to challenge parental authority and dominant social mores. She suggests that instead of simply reading such acts as moments of opposition to, and escape from, dominant relations of power, they should also be understood as reinscribing alternative forms of power that are rooted in practices of capitalist consumerism and urban bourgeois values and aesthetics (1990, 50).

Abu-Lughod concludes her provocative essay with the following observation:

My argument . . . has been that we should learn to read in various local and everyday resistances the existence of a range of specific strategies and structures of power. Attention to *the forms of resistance in particular societies* can help us become critical of partial or reductionist theories of power. The problem has been that those of us who have sensed that there is something admirable about resistance have tended to look to it for hopeful confirmations of the failure—or partial failure—-of systems of oppression. Yet it seems to me that *we respect everyday resistance* not just by arguing for the dignity or heroism of the resisters but by letting their practices teach us about complex interworkings of historically changing structures of power. (1990, 53; emphasis added)

While Abu-Lughod's attention to understanding resistance as a diagnostic of differential forms of power marks an important analytical step that allows us to move beyond the simple binary of resistance/subordination, she nevertheless implies that the task of identifying an act as one of "resistance" is a fairly unproblematic enterprise. She revises her earlier analysis by suggesting that in order to describe the specific forms that acts of resistance take, they need to be located within fields of power rather than outside of them. Thus, even though Abu-Lughod starts her essay by questioning the ascription of a "feminist consciousness" to those for whom this is not a meaningful category (1990, 47), this does not lead her to

challenge the use of the term "resistance" to describe a whole range of human actions, including those which may be socially, ethically, or politically indifferent to the goal of opposing hegemonic norms. I believe it is critical that we ask whether it is even possible to identify a universal category of acts—such as those of resistance—outside of the ethical and political conditions within which such acts acquire their particular meaning. Equally important is the question that follows: does the category of resistance impose a teleology of progressive politics on the analytics of power—a teleology that makes it hard for us to see and understand forms of being and action that are not necessarily encapsulated by the narrative of subversion and reinscription of norms?

What perceptive studies such as these by Boddy and Abu-Lughod fail to problematize is the universality of the desire—central for liberal and progressive thought, and presupposed by the concept of resistance it authorizes—to be free from relations of subordination and, for women, from structures of male domination. This positing of women's agency as consubstantial with resistance to relations of domination, and the concomitant naturalization of freedom as a social ideal, are not simply analytical oversights on the part of feminist authors. Rather, I would argue that their assumptions reflect a deeper tension within feminism attributable to its dual character as both an *analytical* and a *politically prescriptive* project.[3] Despite the many strands and differences within feminism, what accords the feminist tradition an analytical and political coherence is the premise that where society is structured to serve male interests, the result will be either neglect, or direct suppression, of women's concerns. Feminism, therefore, offers both a *diagnosis* of women's status across cultures and a *prescription* for changing the situation of women who are understood to be marginalized, subordinated, or oppressed (see Strathern 1988; 26–28). Thus the articulation of conditions of relative freedom that enable women both to formulate and to enact self-determined goals and interests remains the object of feminist politics and theorizing. Freedom is normative to feminism, as it is to liberalism, and critical scrutiny is applied to those who want to limit women's freedom rather than those who want to extend it.[4]

. . .

FEMINISM AND FREEDOM

My intention here is not to question the profound transformation that the liberal discourse of freedom and individual autonomy has enabled in women's lives around the world, but rather to draw attention to the ways in which these liberal presuppositions have become naturalized in the scholarship on gender. It is quite clear that both positive and negative notions of freedom have been used productively to expand the horizon of what constitutes the domain of legitimate feminist practice and debate. For example, in the 1970s, in response to the call by white middle-class feminists to dismantle the institution of the nuclear family, which they believed to be a key source of women's oppression, Native- and African American feminists argued that freedom, for them, consisted in being able to form families, since the long history of slavery, genocide, and racism had operated precisely by breaking up their communities and social networks (see, for example, Brant 1984; Collins 1991; A. Davis 1983; Lorde 1984).[5] Such arguments successfully expanded feminist understandings of "self-realization/self-fulfillment" by making considerations of class, race, and ethnicity central, thereby forcing feminists to rethink the concept of individual autonomy in light of other issues.

Since then a number of feminist theorists have launched trenchant critiques of the liberal notion of autonomy from a variety of perspectives. While earlier critics had drawn attention to the masculinist assumptions underpinning the ideal of autonomy (Chodorow 1978; Gilligan 1982), later scholars faulted this ideal for its emphasis on the atomistic, individualized, and bounded characteristics of the self at the expense of its relational qualities formed through social interactions within forms of human community (Benhabib 1992; Young 1990). Consequently, there have been various attempts to redefine autonomy so as to capture the emotional, embodied, and socially embedded character of people, particularly of women (Friedman 1997, 2003; Joseph 1999; Nedelsky 1989). A more radical strain of poststructuralist theory has situated its critique of autonomy within a larger challenge posed to the *illusory* character of the rationalist, self-authorizing, transcendental subject presupposed by Enlightenment thought in general, and the liberal tradition

in particular. Rational thought, these critics argue, secures its universal scope and authority by performing a necessary exclusion of all that is bodily, feminine, emotional, nonrational, and intersubjective (Butler 1999; Gatens 1996; Grosz 1994). This exclusion cannot be substantively or conceptually recuperated, however, through recourse to an unproblematic feminine experience, body, or imaginary (*pace* Beauvoir and Irigaray), but must be thought through the very terms of the discourse of metaphysical transcendence that enacts these exclusions.

In what follows, I would like to push further in the direction opened by these poststructuralist debates. In particular, my argument for uncoupling the notion of self-realization from that of the autonomous will is indebted to poststructuralist critiques of the transcendental subject, voluntarism, and repressive models of power. Yet, as will become clear, my analysis also departs from these frameworks insomuch as I question the overwhelming tendency within poststructuralist feminist scholarship to conceptualize agency in terms of subversion or resignification of social norms, to locate agency within those operations that resist the dominating and subjectivating modes of power. In other words, I will argue that the normative political subject of poststructuralist feminist theory often remains a liberatory one, whose agency is conceptualized on the binary model of subordination and subversion. In doing so, this scholarship elides dimensions of human action whose ethical and political status does not map onto the logic of repression and resistance. In order to grasp these modes of action indebted to other reasons and histories, I will suggest that it is crucial to detach the notion of agency from the goals of progressive politics.

It is quite clear that the idea of freedom and liberty as *the* political ideal is relatively new in modern history. Many societies, including Western ones, have flourished with aspirations other than this. Nor, for that matter, does the narrative of individual and collective liberty exhaust the desires with which people live in liberal societies. If we recognize that the desire for freedom from, or subversion of, norms is not an innate desire that motivates all beings at all times, but is also profoundly mediated by cultural and historical conditions, then the question arises: how do we analyze operations of power that construct different kinds of bodies, knowledges, and subjectivities whose trajectories do not follow the entelechy of liberatory politics?

. . .

It is important to note that there are several points on which [Judith] Butler [in defining her theory of the subject] departs from the notions of agency and resistance that I criticized earlier. To begin with, Butler questions what she calls an "emancipatory model of agency," one that presumes that all humans qua humans are "endowed with a will, a freedom, and an intentionality" whose workings are "thwarted by relations of power that are considered external to the subject" (Benhabib et al. 1995, 136). In its place, Butler locates the possibility of agency within structures of power (rather than outside of it) and, more importantly, suggests that the reiterative structure of norms serves not only to *consolidate* a particular regime of discourse/power but also provides the means for its *destabilization*.[6] In other words, there is no possibility of "undoing" social norms that is independent of the "doing" of norms; agency resides, therefore, within this productive reiterability. Butler also resists the impetus to tether the meaning of agency to a predefined teleology of emancipatory politics. As a result, the logic of subversion and resigntfication cannot be predetermined in Butler's framework because acts of resignification/subversion are, she argues, contingent and fragile, appearing in unpredictable places and behaving in ways that confound our expectations.

I find Butler's critique of humanist conceptions of agency and subject very compelling, and, indeed, my arguments in this book are manifestly informed by it. I have, however, found it productive to argue with certain tensions that characterize Butler's work in order to expand her analytics to a somewhat different, if related, set of problematics. One key tension in Butler's work owes to the fact that while she emphasizes the ineluctable relationship between the consolidation and destabilization of norms, her discussion of agency tends to focus on those operations of power that resignify and subvert norms. Thus even though Butler insists time and again that all acts of subversion are a product of the terms of violence that they seek to oppose, her analysis of agency often privileges those moments that "open possibilities

for resignifying the terms of violation against their violating aims" (1993, 122), or that provide an occasion "for a radical rearticulation" of the dominant symbolic horizon (1993, 23). In other words, the concept of agency in Butler's work is developed primarily in contexts where norms are thrown into question or are subject to resignification.

. . .

THE SUBJECT OF NORMS

. . . . I would like to expand Butler's insight that norms are not simply a social imposition on the subject but constitute the very substance of here intimate, valorized inferiority. . . .

Consider, for example, the Islamic virtue of female modesty (*al-ihtishām, alhayā'*) that many Egyptian Muslims uphold and value. Despite a consensus about its importance, there is considerable debate about how this virtue should be lived, and particularly about whether its realization requires the donning of the veil. A majority of the participants in the mosque movement (and the larger piety movement of which the mosque movement is an integral part) argue that the veil is a necessary component of the virtue of modesty because the veil both expresses "true modesty" and is the means through which modesty is acquired. They draw, therefore, an ineluctable relationship between the norm (modesty) and the bodily form it takes (the veil) such that the veiled body becomes the necessary means through which the virtue of modesty is both created *and* expressed. In contrast to this understanding is a position (associated with prominent secularist writers) that argues that the virtue of modesty is no different than any other human attribute—such as moderation or humility: it is a facet of character but does not commit one to any particular expressive repertoire such as donning the veil. Notably, these authors oppose the veil but not the virtue of modesty, which they continue to regard as appropriate to feminine conduct. The veil, in their view, has been invested with an importance that is unwarranted when it comes to judgments about female modesty.

. . .

Some of the questions that follow from this observation are: How do we analyze the work that the body performs in there different conceptualizations of the norm? Is performative behavior differently understood in each of these views and, if so, how? How is the self differently tied to the authority the norm commands in these two imaginaries? Furthermore, what sorts of ethical and political subjects are presupposed by these two imaginaries, and what forms of ethico-political life do they enable or foreclose? The questions cannot be answered as long as we remain in the binary logic of doing and undoing norms. They require, instead, that we explode the category of norms into its constituent elements—to examine the immanent form that norms take, and to inquire into the attachment their particular morphology generates within the topography of the self.

MODES OF SUBJECTIVATION AND THE MOSQUE MOVEMENT

· · ·

In comparison with other currents within the Islamic Revival, the mosque movement is unique in the extraordinary degree of pedagogical emphasis it places on outward markers of religiosity—ritual practices, styles of comporting oneself, dress, and so on. The participants in the mosque movement regard these practices as the necessary and ineluctable means for realizing the form of religiosity they are cultivating. For the mosque participants, it is the various movements of the body that comprise the material substance of the ethical domain. There exists an elaborate system of techniques by which the body's actions and capacities can be examined and worked upon, both individually and collectively. The mosque lessons are one important space where training in this kind of ascetic practice is acquired. . . . [W]omen learn to analyze the movements of the body and soul in order to establish coordination between inner states (intentions, movements of desire and thought, etc.) and outer conduct (gestures, actions, speech, etc.). Indeed, this distinction between inner and outer aspects of the self provides a central axis around which the panoply of ascetic practices is organized. . . .

The women I worked with did not regard trying to emulate authorized models of behavior as an external social imposition that constrained individual freedom. Rather, they treated socially authorized forms of performance as the potentialities—

the ground if you will—through which the self is realized. As a result, one of the questions this book raises is: How do we conceive of individual freedom in a context where the distinction between the subject's own desires and socially prescribed performances cannot be easily presumed, and where submission to certain forms of (external) authority is a condition for achieving the subject's potentiality? In other words, how does one make the question of politics integral to the analysis of the architecture of the self?

· · ·

ETHICS AND AGENCY

How does this intertwining of the ethical and the political impact my critique of regnant notions of agency within liberal-progressive accounts? First of all, as I hope I have made clear, I am not interested in offering *a* theory of agency, but rather I insist that the meaning of agency must be explored within the grammar of concepts within which it resides. My argument in brief is that we should keep the meaning of agency open and allow it to emerge from "within semantic and institutional networks that define and make possible particular ways of relating to people, things, and oneself" (T. Asad 2003, 78). This is why I have maintained that the concept of agency should be delinked from the goals of progressive politics, a tethering that has often led to the incarceration of the notion of agency within the trope of resistance against oppressive and dominating operations of power. This does not mean that agency never manifests itself in this manner; indeed it sometimes does. But the questions that follow from this relatively simple observation are complicated and may be productively explored, I would suggest, through the nexus of ethics and politics.

Consider, for example, the fact that the practices of the mosque participants often pose a challenge to hegemonic norms of secular-liberal sociability as well as aspects of secular-liberal governance. . . . These challenges, however, have impacted conditions of secularity in a manner that has far exceeded both the intentionality of the pietists and the expectations of their most severe retractors. For example, . . . the pietists' interpretation of Islamic rituals and observances has proved to be enormously unsettling to the state-oriented Islamists as much as their secular critics because of the implicit challenge this interpretation poses to key assumptions about the role ascribed to the body within the nationalist imaginary. As a result, the supposedly apolitical practices of the mosque movement have been met, on the one hand, with the disciplinary mechanisms of the state and, on the other hand, with a robust critique of this form of religiosity from secular-liberal Muslims and Islamist political parties who share a certain nationalist-identitarian worldview. One might say that the political agency of the mosque movement (the "resistance" it poses to secularization) is a contingent and unanticipated consequence of the effects its ethical practices have produced in the social field.

What I want to emphasize here are two interrelated points: first, that it is impossible to understand the political agency of the movement without a proper grasp of its ethical agency; and second, that to read the activities of the mosque movement primarily in terms of the resistance it has posed to the logic of secular-liberal governance and its concomitant modes of sociability ignores an entire dimension of politics that remains poorly understood and undertheorized within the literature on politics and agency.

. . . .

ETHICS AND CRITIQUE

. . .

I believe that one needs to unpack all that remains congealed under the admission that it is the "social conservatism" of movements like the piety movement that makes liberals and progressives uncomfortable, and to examine the constitutive elements and sensibilities that comprise this discomfort. This task takes on a particular urgency since the events of September 11, 2001, wherein a rather heterogeneous collection of images and descriptions associated with "Islamic social conservatism" (key among them, women's subordinate status in Muslim societies) are made to stand in for all that liberals and leftists are supposed to find threatening to their entire edifice of beliefs, values, and political system (see Hirschkind and Mahmood 2002). In many ways, this book is an exploration of, to evoke

Connolly again, the "visceral modes of appraisal" that produce such a reaction among many fellow liberal-left intellectuals and feminists, as much as it is an exploration of the sensibilities that animate such movements. The aim of this book, therefore, is more than ethnographic: its goal is to parochialize those assumptions—about the constitutive relationship between action and embodiment, resistance and agency, self and authority—that inform our judgments about nonliberal movements such as the women's mosque movement.

It is in the course of this encounter between the texture of my own repugnance and the textures of the lives of the women I worked with that the political and the ethical have converged for me again in a personal sense. In the course of conducting fieldwork and writing this book, I have come to recognize that a politically responsible scholarship entails not simply being faithful to the desires and aspirations of "my informants" and urging my audience to "understand and respect" the diversity of desires that characterizes our world today (cf. Mahmood 2001a). Nor is it enough to reveal the assumptions of my own or my fellow scholars' biases and (in)tolerances. As someone who has come to believe, along with a number of other feminists, that the political project of feminism is not predetermined but needs to be continually negotiated within specific contexts, the questions I have come to ask myself again and again are: What do we mean when we as feminists say that gender equality is the central principle of our analysis and politics? How does my enmeshment within the thick texture of my informants' lives affect my openness to this question? Are we willing to countenance the sometimes violent task of remaking sensibilities, life worlds, and attachments so that women of the kind I worked with may be taught to value the principle of "freedom"? Furthermore, does a commitment to the ideal of equality in our own lives endow us with the capacity to know that this ideal captures what is or should be fulfilling for everyone else? If it does not, as is surely the case, then I think we need to rethink, with far more humility than we are accustomed to, what feminist politics really means. (Here I want to be clear that my comments are not directed at "Western feminists" alone, but also include "Third World" feminists and all those who are located somewhere within this polarized terrain, since these questions implicate all of us given the liberatory impetus of the feminist tradition.)

The fact that I pose these questions does not mean that I am advocating that we abandon our critical stance toward what we consider to be unjust practices in the situated contexts of our lives, or that we uncritically embrace and promote the pious lifestyles of the women I worked with. To do so would be only to mirror the teleological certainty that characterizes some of the versions of progressive liberalism that I criticized earlier. Rather, my suggestion is that we might leave open the possibility that our political and analytical certainties might be transformed in the process of exploring nonliberal movements of the kind I studied, that the lives of the women I worked with might have something to teach us beyond what we can learn form the circumscribed social-scientific exercise of "understanding and translation."

· · ·

[2005]

NOTES

1. Examples from the Muslim context include Boddy 1989; Hale 1987; Hegland 1998; MacLeod 1991; Torab 1996. For a similar argument made in the context of Christian evangelical movements, see Brusco 1995; Stacey 1991.
2. For a review of this scholarship on the Middle East, see Abu-Lughod 1990a.
3. As a number of feminist scholars have noted, these two dimensions of the feminist project often stand in a productive tension against each other. See W. Brown 2001; Butler 1999; Mohanty 1991; Rosaldo 1983; Strathern 1987, 1988.
4. John Stuart Mill, a figure central to liberal and feminist thought, argues: "the burden of proof is supposed to be with those who are against liberty; who contend for any restriction or prohibition. . . . The *a priori* presumption is in favour of freedom. . . ." (Mill 1991, 472).
5. Similarly "A Black Feminist Statement" by the Combahee River Collective rejected the appeal for lesbian separatism made by white feminists on the grounds that the history of racial oppression required black women to make alliances with male members of their communities in order to continue fighting against institutionalized racism (Hull, Bell-Scott, and Smith 1982).
6. Echoing Foucault, Butler argues, "The paradox of subjectivation (*assujetissement*) is precisely that the subject who would resist such norms is itself enabled, if not produced, by such norms. Although this constitutive constraint does not foreclose the possibility of agency, it does locate agency as a reiterative or rearticulatory practice, immanent to power, and not a relation of external opposition to power" (1993, 15).

REFERENCES

Abu-Laghod, Lila. 1986. *Veiled Sentiments: Honors and Poetry in Bedouin Society.* Berkeley and LA: University of California Press.

_____. 1990. "The romance of Resistance: Tracing Transformations of Power through Bedouin Women." *American Ethnologist* 17 (1): 41–55.

_____. 1993. *Writing Women's Worlds: Bedouin Stories.* Berkeley and LA: University of California Press.

Altorki, Saroya. 1986. *Women in Saudi Arabia: Ideology and Behavior among the Elite.* New York: Columbia University Press.

Asad, Talal. 2003. *Formations of the Secular: Christianity, Islam, and Modernity.* Standord, CA: Stanford University Press.

Atiya, Nayra. 1982. *Khul-Khaal: Five Egyptian Women Tell Their Stories.* Syracuse, NY: Syracuse University Press.

Benhabib, Seyla. 1992. *Situating the Self: Gender, Community, and Postmodernism in Contemporary Ethics.* New York: Routledge.

_____, et. al. 1995. *Feminist Contentions: A Philosophical Exchange.* New York: Routledge.

Boddy, Janice. 1989. *Wombs and Alien Spirits: Women, Men, and the Zãr Cult in Northern Sudan.* Madison, University of Wisconsin Press.

Brant, Beth, ed. 1984. *A Gathering of Spirits: Writing and Art by North American Indian Women.* Rockland, ME: Sinister Wisdom.

Butler, Judith. 1993. *Bodies That Matter: On the Discursive Limits of 'Sex.'* New York: Routledge.

_____. 1999. *Gender Trouble: Feminism and the Subversion of Identity.* New York: Routledge.

Chodorow, Nancy. 1978. *The Reproduction of Mothering: Psychoanalysis and the Sociology of Gender.* Berkeley and LA: University of California Press.

Collins, Patricia Hill. 1991. *Black Feminist Thought: Knowledge, Consciousness, and the Politics of Empowerment.* New York: Routledge.

Davis, Angela. 1983. *Women, Race and Class.* New York, Vintage Books.

Davis, Susan. Patience and Power: *Explorations in Cosmology in Turkish Village Society.* Berkeley and LA: University of California Press.

Dwyer, Daisy. 1978. *Images and Self-Images: Male and Female in Morocco.* New York: Columbia University Press.

Early, Evelynn. 1993. *Baladi Women of Cairo: Playing with and Egg and a Stone.* Boulder, CO: Lynne Reinner.

Fernea, Elizabeth, ed. 1985. *Women and Family in the Middle-East.* Austin: University of Texas Press.

Freidman, Marilyn. 1997. "Autonomy and Social Relationships: Rethinking the Feminist Critique." In *Feminist Rethink the Self,* ed. D. T. Myers et. Al. New York: New Press.

_____. 2003. *Autonomy, Gender and Politics.* New York: Oxford University Press.

Gatens, Moira. 1996. *Imaginary Bodies: Ethics, Power and Corporeality.* London: Routledge.

Gilligan, Carol. 1982. *In a Different Voice: Psychological Theory and Women's Development.* Cambridge: Harvard University Press.

Grosz, Elizabeth. 1994. *Volatile Bodies: Toward a Corporeal Feminism.* Bloomington: Indiana University Press.

Guha, Ranajit and Gayatri Spivak, eds. 1988. *Selected subaltern Studies.* Delhi: Oxford University Press.

Hobsbawm, Eric, ed. 1980. *Peasants in History: Essays in Honors of David Thorner.* Calcutta: Oxford University Press.

Joseph, Suad, ed. 1999. *Intimate Selving in Arab Families: Gender, Self and Identity.* Syracuse: Syracuse University Press.

Lorde, Audre. 1984. *Sister Outsider: Essays and Speeches.* Trumansburg, NY: Crossings Press.

Nedelsky, Jennifer. 1989. "Reconceiving Autonomy: Sources, Thoughts and Possibility." *Yale Journal of Law and Feminism* 1 (1): 7–36.

Scott, James. 1985. *Weapons of the Weak: Everyday Forms of Peasant Resistance.* New Haven, CT: Yale University Press.

Strathern, Marilyn. 1988. *The Gender of the Gift: Problems with Women and Problems in Society in Melanesia.* Berkeley and LA: University of California Press.

Wikan, Unni. 1991. *Behind the Veil in Arabia: Women in Oman.* Chicago: University of Chicago Press.

Young, Iris. 1990. *Justice and the Politics of Difference.* Princeton, NJ: Princeton University Press.

Bibliography

1792–1920

Addams, Jane. (1910). *Twenty Years at Hull House*. New York: Macmillan.

Bebel, August. (1910). *Woman and Socialism* (Meta Stem, Trans.). New York: Socialist Literature. (Originally published 1885.)

Butler, Josephine. (1868). *The Education and Employment of Women*. London: Macmillan.

_____. (1869). *Woman's Work and Woman's Culture: A Series of Essays*. London: Macmillan.

Caird, Mona. (1897). *The Morality of Marriage and Other Essays on the Status and Destiny of Woman*. London: G. Redway.

Catt, Carrie Chapman. (1897). *The Ballot and the Bullet*. Philadelphia: A. J. Ferris.

Cobbe, Frances Power. (1881). *The Duties of Women: A Course of Lectures*. London: Williams and Norgate.

_____. (1863). *Essays on the Pursuits of Women*. London: E. Faithful.

Fawcett, Millicent Garrett. (1871). *Electoral Disabilities of Women*. London: Tavistock.

_____. (1891). "The Emancipation of Women." *Fortnightly Review*, NS 50, 672–685.

_____. (1868). "The Uses of Higher Education for Women." *The Fortnightly Review*, 4, 554–557.

Freud, Sigmund. (1963). "Dora: An Analysis of a Case of Hysteria." *Collected Papers of Sigmund Freud*. New York: Collier.

Fuller, Margaret. (1845). *Woman in the Nineteenth Century*. London: Clarke.

Gage, Matilda Joslyn. (1893). *Woman, Church, and State: The Original Exposé of Male Collaboration against the Female Sex*. Chicago: C. H. Kem.

Jacobs, Harriet Brent. (1973). *Incidents in the Life of a Slave Girl*. New York: Harcourt Brace. (Originally published 1861.)

Key, Ellen. (1976). *The Woman Movement*. (Mamah Bouton Borthwick, Trans.). Westport, CT: Hyperion. (Originally published 1912.)

Martineau, Harriet. (1832). *Illustrations of Political Economy*. London: Charles Fox.

Pankhurst, Cristabel. (1913). *The Great Scourge and How to End It*. London: E. Pankhurst.

Pankhurst, Emmeline. (1914). *My Own Story*. London: John Day.

Schreiner, Olive. (1987). *An Olive Schreiner Reader: Writings on Women and South Africa*. London: Pandora.

_____. (1911.) *Women and Labor*. London: Frederick A. Stokes.

Simcox, E. J. (1877). *Natural Law, An Essay in Ethics*. London: Trubner.

Stewart, Maria W. (1987). *America's First Black Woman Political Writer: Essays and Speeches*. [1820s and 30s]. Bloomington, IN: Indiana University Press.

Stopes, Marie. (1918). *Married Love: A New Contribution to the Solution of Sex Difficulties*. London: Putnam.

Wright, Frances. (1821). *Views on Society and Manners in America*. New York: Bliss and White.

1920–1963

Addams, Jane. (1922). *Peace and Bread in Time of War*. New York: Macmillan.

Beard, Mary Ritter. (1931). *On Understanding Women*. New York: Longmans.

_____. (1946). *Woman as a Force in History*. New York: Persea Books.

Beauvoir, Simone de. (1959). *Memoirs of a Dutiful Daughter*. Cleveland, OH: World.

Catt, Carrie Chapman, and Nettie Rogers Shuler. (1923). *Woman Suffrage and Politics: The Inner Story of the Suffrage Movement.* New York: Scribner.

Deutsch, Helene. (1944). *Psychology of Women: A Psychoanalytic Interpretation.* New York: Grune and Stratton.

Diner, Helen. (1965). *Mothers and Amazons: The First Feminine History of Culture.* (John Philip Lundin, Trans.). New York: Julian Press.

Foster, Jeannette. (1956). *Sex Variant Women in Literature.* New York: Vantage Press.

Freud, Sigmund. (1933). *Femininity,* Standard Edition. London: Hogarth Press.

Klein, Melanie. (1949). *The Psychoanalysis of Children.* (Alix Strachey, Trans.). London: Hogarth Press.

Klein, Viola. (1946). *The Feminine Character. History of an Ideology.* London: K. Paul, Trench & Trubner.

Koedt, Anne and Shulamith Firestone. (1970). *Notes from the First Year: Women's Liberation, Major Writing of the Radical Feminists.* New York, N.Y.

Komarovsky, Mirra. (1953). *Women in the Modern World: Their Education and Dilemmas.* Boston: Little, Brown.

Lafollette, Suzanne. (1926). *Concerning Women.* New York: A. C. Boni.

Roosevelt, Eleanor. (1995). *What I Hope to Leave Behind: The Essential Essays of Eleanor Roosevelt.* Allida Black (Ed.). New York: Carlson.

Russell, Dora. (1983). *The Dora Russell Reader: 57 Years of Writing and Journalism, 1925–1982.* London: Routledge.

Sand, George. (1929). *The Intimate Journals of George Sand.* (Marie Howe, Trans.). New York: John Day.

Webb, Beatrice. (1926). *My Apprenticeship.* London: Longmans.

———— with Sidney Webb. (1923). *The Decay of Capitalist Civilization.* New York: Harcourt Brace.

Winnicott, D. W (1958). *Collected Papers: Through Pediatrics to Psychoanalysis.* London: Tavistock.

Zetkin, Clara. (1984). *Selected Writings.* Philip Foner (Ed.). New York: International.

1963–1975

Bernard, Jessie. (1972). *The Future of Marriage.* New York: World Publishing.

————. (1974). *The Future of Motherhood.* New York: Penguin.

Bird, Caroline. (1968). *Born Female: The High Cost of Keeping Women Down.* New York: D. McKay.

Boserup, Esther. (1970). *Women and Economic Development.* New York: St. Martin's.

Bunch, Charlotte, and Nancy Myron. (1975). *Lesbianism and the Women's Movement.* Baltimore, MD: Diana Press.

Daly, Mary. (1968). *The Church and the Second Sex.* New York: Harper & Row.

————. (1973). *Beyond God the Father.* Boston: Beacon Press.

Douglas, Mary. (1975). *Implicit Meanings: Essays in Anthropology.* London: Routledge.

Dworkin, Andrea. (1974). *Woman Hating.* New York: Dutton.

Ellman, Mary. (1968). *Thinking about Women.* New York: Harcourt Brace.

Figes, Eva. (1970). *Patriarchal Attitudes.* New York: Stein and Day.

Gornick, Vivian, and Barbara Moran (Eds.). (1971). *Women in Sexist Society.* New York: Basic Books.

Greer, Germaine. (1970). *The Female Eunuch.* London: McGibbon Kaye.

Kristeva, Julia. (1977). *About Chinese Women.* (Anita Barrows, Trans.). London: Boyars.

Lacan, Jacques. (1977). "The Signification of the Phallus." In *Ecrits: A Selection.* (Alan Sheridan, Trans.). New York: W. W. Norton. (Originally published 1966.)

Lerner, Gerda (Ed.). (1972). *Black Women in White America.* New York: Pantheon.

————. (1973). *Woman's Estate.* Harmondsworth, U.K.: Penguin.

Morgan, Robin. (1970). *Sisterhood Is Powerful.* New York: Vintage.

Nochlin, Linda. (1971). "Why Have There Been No Great Women Artists?" In Vivian Gornick and Barbara Moran (Eds.). *Women in Sexist Society.* New York: Basic Books.

Oakley, Ann. (1974). *Women's Work: The Housewife Past and Present.* Totowa, NJ: Roman and Allenheld.

Reed, Evelyn. (1975). *Women's Evolution: From Matriarchal Clan to Patriarchal Family.* New York: Pathfinder.

Reuther, Rosemary. (1970). *Religion and Sexism.* New York: Simon & Schuster.

Rosaldo, Michelle, and Louise Lamphere (Eds.). (1974). *Woman, Culture and Society.* Stanford, CA: Stanford University Press.

Rossi, Alice. (1970). *The Feminist Papers: From Adams to de Beauvoir.* New York: Bantam.

Rowbotham, Sheila. (1973). *Women's Consciousness, Man's World.* Harmondsworth, U.K.: Penguin.

1975–1985

Beck, Evelyn Torten. (1984). *Nice Jewish Girls: A Lesbian Anthology.* Trumansburg, NY: Crossing Press.

Bleier, Ruth. (1984). *Science and Gender: A Critique of Biology and Its Theories on Women.* New York: Pergamon.

Bowles, Gloria, and Renate Duelli Klein (Eds.). (1983). *Theories of Women's Studies.* London: Routledge.

Brownmiller, Susan. (1975). *Against Our Will: Men, Women and Rape.* New York: Simon & Schuster.

_____. (1984). *Femininity.* New York: Simon & Schuster.

Bulkin, Ellie, et al. (1984). *Yours in Struggle: Three Feminist Perspectives on Anti-Semitism and Racism.* New York: Longhaul.

Bunch, Charlotte. (1987). "Lesbians in Revolt." In *Passionate Politics: Feminist Theory in Action.* New York: St. Martin's. (Originally published 1972.)

Christ, Carol, and Judith Plaskow (Eds.). (1979). *Womanspirit Rising.* San Francisco, CA: Harper & Row.

Cixous, Hélène. (1986). *The Newly Born Woman.* (Betsy Wing, Trans.). Minneapolis, MN: University of Minnesota Press. (Originally published 1975.)

Corea, Gena. (1977). *The Hidden Malpractice: How American Medicine Treats Women as Patients and Professionals.* New York: Morrow.

Cott, Nancy. (1977). *The Bonds of Womanhood: Woman's Sphere in New England 1780–1835.* New Haven, CT: Yale University Press.

Cruikshank, Margaret. (1982). *Lesbian Studies: Present and Future.* Old Westbury, NY: Feminist Press.

Coward, Rosalind. (1983). *Patriarchal Precedents: Sexuality and Social Relations.* London: Routledge.

Culley, Margo, and Catherine Portugues. (1985). *Gendered Subjects.* London: Routledge.

Davis, Angela. (1980). *Women, Race and Class.* New York: Random House.

de Lauretis, Teresa. (1984). *Alice Doesn't: Sexuality, Semiotics, Cinema.* Bloomington, IN: Indiana University Press.

Dreifus, Claudia (Ed.). (1977). *Seizing Our Bodies: The Politics of Women's Health.* New York: Vintage.

Dworkin, Andrea. (1983). *Right-Wing Women.* New York: Putnam.

Ehrenreich, Barbara and Deirdre English. (1978). *For Her Own Good: 150 Years of the Experts' Advice to Women.* New York: Anchor.

Eisenstein, Hester, and Alice Jardine, (Eds.). (1980). *The Future of Difference.* Boston: G. K. Hall.

_____. (1981). *The Radical Future of Liberal Feminism.* Boston: G. K. Hall.

Faderman, Lillian. (1981). *Surpassing the Love of Men: Romantic Friendship and Love between Women from the Renaissance to the Present*. New York: Morrow.

Flax, Jane. (1990). *Thinking Fragments: Psychoanalysis, Feminism, and Postmodernism in the Contemporary West*. Berkeley: University of California Press.

Freedman, Estelle. (1985). *The Lesbian Issue: Essays from* Signs. Chicago: University of Chicago Press.

French, Marilyn. (1983). *Beyond Power: On Women, Men and Morals*. London: Cape.

Gilbert, Sandra, and Susan Gubar. (1977). *The Madwoman in the Attic: The Woman Writer and the Nineteenth-Century Literary Imagination*. New Haven, CT: Yale University Press.

Griffin, Susan. (1981). *Pornography and Silence: Culture's Revenge against Nature*. New York: Harper.

Howe, Florence. (1984). *Myths of Coeducation: Selected Essays, 1963–84*. Bloomington, IN: Indiana University Press.

Hubbard, Ruth, and Marion Lowe. (1983). *Woman's Nature: Rationalizations of Inequality*. New York: Pergamon.

Jacobus, Mary, Evelyn Fox Keller, and Sally Shuttleworth, (Eds.). (1990). *Body/Politics: Women and the Discourses of Science*. New York: Routledge.

Jaggar, Alison. (1983). *Feminist Politics and Human Nature*. Totowa, NJ: Roman and Allenheld.

Jardine, Alice. (1985). *Gynesis: Configurations of Women and Modernity*. Ithaca, NY: Cornell University Press.

Jehlen, Myra. (1981). "Archimedes and the Paradox of Feminist Criticism." *Signs*, 6(4), 575–601.

Johnson-Reagon, Bernice. (1984). "Coalition Politics: Turning the Century." *Homegirls: A Black Feminist Anthology*. New York: Kitchen Table Press.

Joseph, Gloria, and Jill Lewis. (1981). *Common Differences: Conflicts in Black and White Feminist Perspectives*. Garden City, NY: Anchor.

Kaplan, Cora. (1983). *Sea Changes: Culture and Feminism*. London: Verso.

Kaplan, E. Ann. (1983). *Women and Film: Both Sides of the Camera*. New York: Routledge.

Keller, Evelyn Fox. (1978). "Gender and Science." *Psychoanalysis and Contemporary Thought*, 6, 409–433.

Kelly-Gadol, Joan. (1984). *Women, History and Theory*. Chicago: University of Chicago Press.

King, Ynestra. (1981). "Feminism and the Revolt against Nature." *Heresies*, no. 13.

Kristeva, Julia. (1980). *Desire in Language: A Semiotic Approach to Literature and Art. 1969/1977*. Leon S. Roudiez (Ed.). (Thomas Gets, Alice Jardine, and Leon S. Roudiez, Trans.). New York: Columbia University Press. (Originally published 1969, 1977.)

_____. (1981). "Woman's Time." (Alice Jardine and Harry Blake, Trans.) *Signs*, 7, 13–35.

Lerner, Gerda. (1986). *The Creation of Patriarchy*. Oxford: Oxford University Press.

Lloyd, Genevieve. (1984). *The Man of Reason: "Male" and "Female" in Western Philosophy*. Minneapolis, MN: University of Minnesota Press.

Marks, Elaine, and Isabel de Courtivron. (1980). *New French Feminisms*. New York: Schocken.

Merchant, Carolyn. (1980). *The Death of Nature: Women, Ecology and the Scientific Revolution*. San Francisco, CA: Harper & Row.

Moi, Toril. *Sexual/Textual Politics*. London: Methuen.

Radway, Janice. (1984). *Reading the Romance: Women, Patriarchy and Popular Literature*. Chapel Hill, NC: University of North Carolina Press.

_____. (1979). *On Lies, Secrets, and Silence: Selected Prose, 1966–1978*. New York: W. W. Norton.

Ruddick, Sara. (1989). *Maternal Thinking: Toward a Politics of Peace*. Boston: Beacon Press.

Showalter, Elaine. (1979). "Towards a Feminist Poetics." In *Women Writing and Writing about Women*. Mary Jacobus (Ed.). London: Croom Helm.

Smith, Barbara. (1977). "Toward a Black Feminist Criticism," *All the Women Are White, All the Blacks Are Men, But Some of Us Are Brave: Black Women's Studies*. Old Westbury, NY: Feminist Press.

Smith-Rosenberg, Carroll, (1986). *Disorderly Conduct: Visions of Gender in Victorian America.* New York: Knopf.

Snitow, Ann, Christine Stansell, and Sharon Thompson. (1983). *Powers of Desire: The Politics of Sexuality.* New York: Monthly Review Press.

Spender, Dale. (1980). *Man-Made Language.* New York: Pergamon.

Stanley, Liz, and Sue Wise. (1983). *Breaking Out: Feminist Consciousness and Feminist Research.* London: Routledge.

Trebilcot, Joyce. (1983). *Mothering: Essays in Feminist Theory.* Totowa, NJ: Roman and Allenheld.

1985–1995

Alcoff, Linda and Elizabeth Potter (Eds.). (1993). *Feminist Epistemologies.* New York: Routledge.

Allen, Jeffner (Ed.). (1990). *Lesbian Philosophies and Cultures.* Albany, NY: SUNY Press.

Allen, Paula Gunn. (1986). *The Sacred Hoop: Recovering the Feminine in American Indian Traditions.* Boston: Beacon.

Benhabib, Seyla, and Drucilla Cornell. (1987). *Feminism as Critique: Essays on the Politics of Gender in Late-Capitalist Societies.* Cambridge, U.K.: Polity.

Braidotti, Rosi. (1994). *Nomadic Subjects: Embodiment and Sexual Difference in Contemporary Feminist Theory.* New York: Columbia University Press.

Chapkis, Wendy. (1997). *Live Sex Acts: Women Performing Erotic Labor.* New York: Routledge.

Chodorow, Nancy. (1994). *Femininities, Masculinities, Sexualities: Freud and Beyond.* Lexington, KY: University Press of Kentucky.

Christian, Barbara. (1989). "The Race for Theory." In Linda Kauffman (Ed.). *Gender and Theory: Dialogues in Feminist Criticism.* Oxford: Blackwell.

Corea, Gena, et al. (Eds.). (1985). *Man-Made Woman: How New Reproductive Technologies Affect Women.* London: Hutchinson.

Cott, Nancy. (1987). *The Grounding of Modern Feminism.* New Haven: Yale University Press.

Davies Miranda. (1987). *Third World: Second Sex.* London: Zed Books.

Delmar, Rosalyn. (1986). "What Is Feminism?" In Juliet Mitchell and Ann Oakley (Eds.). *What Is Feminism?* Oxford: Blackwell.

Echols, Alice. (1989). *Daring to Be Bad: Radical Feminism in America 1967–1975.* Minneapolis, MN: University of Minnesota Press.

Flax, Jane. (1993). *Disputed Subjects: Essays on Psychoanalysis, Politics and Philosophy.* New York: Routledge.

Fraser, Nancy. (1989). *Unruly Practices: Power, Discourse and Gender in Contemporary Social Thought.* Minneapolis, MN: University of Minnesota Press.

Frye, Marilyn. (1992). *Willful Virgin: Essays in Feminism.* Trumansburg, NY: Crossing Press.

Fuss, Diana. (1989). *Essentially Speaking: Feminism, Nature and Difference.* New York: Routledge.

_____ (1991). *Inside/Out: Lesbian Theories, Gay Theories.* New York: Routledge.

Grant, Judith. (1993). *Fundamental Feminisms: Contesting the Core Concepts of Feminist Theory.* New York: Routledge.

Heilbrun, Caroline. (1989). *Writing a Woman's Life.* New York: W. W. Norton.

Hirsch, Marianne, and Evelyn Fox Keller (Eds.). (1992). *Conflicts in Feminism.* New York: Routledge.

James, Stanlie, and Abenia Busia. (1993). *Theorizing Black Feminisms.* New York: Routledge.

Jardine, Alice, and Paul Smith. (1987). *Men in Feminism.* London: Methuen.

Kaplan, E. Ann. (1992). *Motherhood and Representation: The Mother in Popular Culture and Melodrama.* New York: Routledge.

King, Katie. (1994). *Theory in Its Feminist Travels.* Bloomington, IN: Indiana University Press.

Lauretis, Teresa de. (1994). *The Practice of Love: Lesbian Sexuality and Perverse Desire.* Bloomington, IN: Indiana Books.

Lazreg, Marnia. (1994). *The Eloquence of Silence: Algerian Women in Question*. New York: Routledge.

Lorber, Judith. (1995). *Paradoxes of Gender*. New Haven, CT: Yale University Press.

Mies, Maria, and Vandana Shiva. (1993). *Ecofeminism*. London: Zed Books.

Modleski, Tanya. (1991). *Feminism without Women: Culture and Criticism in a "Postfeminist" Age*. New York: Routledge.

Morrison, Toni. (1992). *Playing in the Dark: Whiteness and the Literary Imagination*. New York: Vintage.

Nicholson, Linda. (1990). *Feminism/Postmodernism*. New York: Routledge.

Petchesky, Rosalind. (1986). *Abortion and Woman's Choice*. London: Verso.

Phelan, Shane. (1991). *Identity Politics: Lesbian Feminism and the Limits of Community*. Philadelphia, PA: Temple University Press.

Roof, Judith. (1991). *A Lure of Knowledge: Lesbian Sexuality and Theory*. New York: Columbia.

Sayers, Janet, et al. (Eds.). (1987). *Engels Revisited: New Feminist Essays*. London: Tavistock.

1995–2008

Ahmed, Sara (Ed.) (2000). *Thinking through Feminism*. New York: Routledge.

Antony, Louise M., and Charlotte Witt. (Eds.). (2002). *A Mind of One's Own: Feminist Essays on Reason and Objectivity*. Boulder, CO: Westview.

Armstrong, Elisabeth. (2002). *The Retreat from Organization: U.S. Feminism Reconceptualized*. Albany, NY: SUNY Press.

Barrett, Michèle. (1999). *Imagination in Theory: Culture, Writing, Words, and Things*. New York: NYU Press.

Bartky, Sandra Lee. (2002). *"Sympathy and Solidarity" and Other Essays*. Lanham, MD; Oxford: Rowman & Littlefield.

Bell, Vikki. (1999). *Feminist Imagination: Genealogies in Feminist Theory*. London: Sage.

Benhabib, Seyla. (2002). *The Claims of Culture: Equality and Diversity in a Child Era*. Princeton: Princeton University Press.

Benlont, Louren. (2008). *The Female Complaint: The Unfinished Business of Sentimelality in American Culture*. Durham, NC: Duke University Press.

Bhavnani, Kum-Kum (Ed.). (2001). *Feminism and "Race."* Oxford: Oxford University Press.

Bondi, Liz (Ed.). (2002). *Subjectivities, Knowledges, and Feminist Geographies: The Subjects and Ethics of Social Research*. Lanham, MD; Oxford: Rowman & Littlefield Publishers, Inc.

Braig, Marianne, and Sonja Wölt (Eds.). (2002). *Common Ground or Mutual Exclusion? Women's Movements and International Relations*. London: Zed Books.

Brewer, Mary (Ed.). (2002). *Exclusions in Feminist Thought: Challenging the Boundaries of Womanhood*. Portland, OR: Sussex Academic Press.

Bronfen, Elisabeth, and Misha Kavka, (Eds.). (2001). *Feminist Consequences: Theory for the New Century*. New York: Columbia.

Brown, Wendy. (2001). *Politics out of History*. Princeton, NJ: Princeton University Press.

———— (2008). *Regulating Aversion: Tolerance in the Age of Identity and Empire*. Princeton: Princeton University Press.

Conboy. Katie. Nadia Medina, and Sarah Stanbury (Eds.). (1997). *Writing on the Body: Female Embodiment and Feminist Theory*. New York: Columbia University Press.

Cornell, Drucilla. (1999). *Beyond Accommodation: Ethical Feminism, Deconstruction, and the Law*. Lanham, MD; Oxford: Rowman & Littlefield.

Cuomo, Chris J. (2003). *The Philosopher Queen: Feminist Essays on War, Love, and Knowledge*. Lanham, MD; Oxford: Rowman & Littlefield.

Currie, Gail, and Celia Rothenberg (Eds.). (2001). *Feminist (Re)visions of the Subject: Landscapes, Ethnoscapes, and Theoryscapes*. Lanham, MD; Oxford: Lexington Books.

Davis, Kathy. (1995). *Reshaping the Female Body: The Dilemma of Cosmetic Surgery*. New York: Routledge.

Dean, Jodi. (1996). *Solidarity of Strangers: Feminism after Identity Politics*. Berkeley: University of California Press.

DeKoven, Marianne (Ed.). (2001). *Feminist Locations: Global and Local, Theory and Practice*. New Brunswick NJ: Rutgers University Press.

Dhruvarajan, Vanaja, and Jill Vickers (Eds.). (2002). *Gender, Race, and Nation: A Global Perspective*. Toronto: University of Toronto Press.

Dicker, Rory, and Alison Piepmeier (Eds.). (2003). *Catching a Wave: Reclaiming Feminism for the 21st Century*. Boston, MA: Northeastern University Press.

Duran, Jane. (2001). *Worlds of Knowing: Global Feminist Epistemologies*. New York: Routledge.

Eschle, Catherine. (2001). *Global Democracy, Social Movements, and Feminism*. Boulder, CO: Westview.

Felski, Rita. (2000). *Doing Time: Feminist Theory and Postmodern Culture*. New York: New York University Press.

Fenstermaker, Sarah, and Candace West (Eds.). (2002). *Doing Gender, Doing Difference: Inequality, Power, and Institutional Change*. New York: Routledge.

Fiore, Robin N., and Hilde Lindemann Nelson (Eds.). (2003). *Recognition, Responsibility, and Rights: Feminist Ethics and Social Theory*. Lanham, MD; Oxford: Rowman & Littlefield.

Franklin, Sarah, Celia Lury, and Jackie Stacey (Eds.). (2000). *Global Nature, Global Culture*. London: Sage.

Friedman, Marilyn. (2003). *Autonomy, Gender, Politics*. Oxford: Oxford University Press.

Friedman, Susan Stanford. (1998). *Mappings: Feminism and the Cultural Geographies of Encounter*. Princeton, NJ: Princeton University Press.

Garcia, Alma M. (Ed.). (1997). *Chicana Feminist Thought: The Basic Historical Writings*. New York: Routledge.

Gardiner, Judith Kegan (Ed.). (2002). *Masculinity Studies & Feminist Theory: New Directions*. New York: Columbia University Press.

Garland-Thompson, Rosemarie (1999). *Extraordinary Bodies: Figuring Physical Disability in American Culture and Literature*. New York: Columbia University Press.

Groenhout, Ruth E. and Marya Bower (Eds.). (2003). *Philosophy, Feminism, and Faith*. Bloomington: Indiana University Press.

Grosz, E. A. (1995). *Space, Time, and Perversion: Essays on the Politics of Bodies*. New York: Routledge.

Gubar, Susan. (2000). *Critical Condition: Feminism at the Turn of the Century*. New York: Columbia University Press.

Harding, Sandra. (2008). *Sciences from Below: Feminisms, Postcolonialities, and Modernities*. Durham, NC: Duke University Press.

Haukesworth, Mary. (2006). *Feminist Inquiry: From Political Conviction to Methodological Innovation*. New Brunswick, Rutgers University Press.

Hawthorne, Susan, and Renate Klein (Eds.). (1999). *Cyberfeminism: Connectivity, Critique and Creativity*. North Melbourne: Spinifex Press.

Henry, Astrid. (2004). *Not My Mother's Sister: Generational Conflict and Third-Wave Feminism*. Bloomington: Indiana Unviersity Press.

Hernandez, Daisy, et al. (2002). *Colonize This! Young Women of Color on Today's Feminism*. Berkeley: Seal Press.

Heywood, Leslie, and Jennifer Drake (Eds.). (1997). *Third Wave Agenda: Being Feminist, Doing Feminism*. Minneapolis: University of Minnesota Press.

Hirschmann, Nancy J. (2003). *The Subject of Liberty: Toward a Feminist Theory of Freedom*. Princeton, NJ: Princeton University Press.

Holmstrom, Nancy (Ed.). (2002). *The Socialist Feminist Project: A Contemporary Reader in Theory and Politics*. New York: Monthly Review Press.

Hong, Grace Kyungwon. (2006). *The Ruptures of American Capital: Women of Color, Feminism, and the Culture of Immigrant Labor*. Minneapolis: University of Minnesota Press.

Howard, Judith A., and Carolyn Allen. (Eds.). (2000). *Feminisms at a Millennium*. Chicago: University of Chicago Press.

Jackson, Sandra, and Ann Russo. (Eds.). (2002). *Talking Back and Acting Out: Women Negotiating the Media across Culture*. New York: Peter Lang.

Jakobsen, Janet R. (1998). *Working Alliances and the Politics of Difference: Diversity and Feminist Ethics*. Bloomington: Indiana University Press.

James, Stanlie M., and Claire C. Robertson. (Eds.) (2002). *Genital Cutting and Transnational Sisterhood: Disputing U.S. Polemics*. Urbana: University of Illinois Press.

Keaton, Trica Danielle. (2006). *Muslim Girls and the Other France: Race, Identity Politics, & Social Exclusion*. Bloomington: Indiana University Press.

Kruks, Sonia. (2001). *Retrieving Experience: Subjectivity and Recognition in Feminist Politics*. Ithaca, NY: Cornell University Press.

Landes, Joan B. (Ed.). (1998). *Feminism, the Public and the Private*. Oxford: Oxford University Press.

Lay, Mary M., Janice Monk, and Deborah S. Rosenfelt (Eds.). (2002). *Encompassing Gender: Integrating International Studies and Women's Studies*. New York: Feminist Press at the City University of New York.

Levine-Rasky, Cynthia. (Ed.). (2002). *Working through Whiteness: International Perspectives*. Albany, NY: SUNY Press.

Lloyd, Genevieve. (Ed.). (2002). *Feminism and History of Philosophy*. Oxford: Oxford University Press.

Macrobbie, Angela. (2008). *Displacement Feminism*. Sage.

McLaren, Margaret A. (2002). *Feminism, Foucault, and Embodied Subjectivity*. Albany, NY: SUNY Press.

Maglin, Nan Bauer, and Donna Perry (Eds.) (1996). *"Bad Girls"/"Good Girls": Women, Sex, and Power in the Nineties*. New Brunswick, NJ: Rutgers University Press.

Martinez, Jacqueline M. (2000). *Phenomenology of Chicana Experience and Identity: Communication and Transformation in Praxis*. Lanham, MD; Oxford : Rowman & Littlefield Publishers.

Messer-Davidow, Ellen. (2000). *Disciplining Feminism: From Social Activism to Academic Discourse*. Durham, NC: Duke University Press.

Morgan, Lynn M., and Meredith W. Michaels (Eds.). (1999). *Fetal Subjects, Feminist Positions*. Philadelphia: University of Pennsylvania Press.

Mortensen, Ellen. (2002). *Touching Thought: Ontology and Sexual Difference*. Lanham, MD; Oxford: Lexington Books.

Moscovici, Claudia. (1996). *From Sex Objects to Sexual Subjects*. New York: Routledge.

Naples, Nancy. *Feminism and Method: Ethnography, Discourse Analysis, and Activist Research*. New York: Routledge, 2003.

Newman, Louise Michelle. (1999). *White Women's Rights: The Racial Origins of Feminism in the US*. Oxford: Oxford University Press.

Ngan-ling Chow, Esther. Doris Wilkinson, and Maxine Baca Zinn (Eds.). (1996). *Race, Class, & Gender: Common Bonds, Different Voices*. London: Sage.

Parati, Graziella, and Rebecca West (Eds.). (2002). *Italian Feminist Theory and Practice: Equality and Sexual Difference*. Madison, NJ: Fairleigh Dickinson University Press; London: Associated University Presses.

Pough, Gwendolyn, et al., (Eds.). (2007). *Home Girls Make Some Noise: A Hip Hop Feminist Anthology*. Parker Publishing.

Reger, Jo (Ed.). (2005). *Different Wavelengths: Studies of the Contemporary Women's Movement*. New York: Taylor and Francis.

Robinson, Hilary (Ed.). (2001). *Feminism-Art-Theory: An Anthology, 1968–2000*. Oxford: Blackwell.

Rosser, Sue Vilhauer. (2000). *Women, Science, and Society: The Crucial Union*. New York: Teachers College Press.

Rowe, Aimee Carrillo. (2008). *Power Lines: On the Subject of Feminist Alliances.* Durham, NC: Duke University Press.

Saunders, Kriemild (Ed.). (2002). *Feminist Post-Development Thought: Rethinking Modernity, Post-Colonialism & Representation.* London: Zed Books Ltd, Hampshire, U.K.: Palgrave Macmillan.

Schiebinger, Londa (Ed.). (2000). *Feminism and the Body.* Oxford: Oxford University Press.

Scott-Dixon, Krista (Ed.). (2006). *Trans/Forming Feminisms: Transfeminist Voices Speak Out.* Toronto: Sumach Press.

Segal, Lynne. (1999). *Why Feminism? Gender, Psychology, Politics.* New York: Columbia University Press.

Shildrick, Margrit. (1997). *Leaky Bodies and Boundaries: Feminism, Postmodernism and (Bio)Ethics.* New York: Routledge.

The Social Justice Group at The Center for Advanced Feminist Studies (Ed.). (2000). *Is Academic Feminism, Dead? Theory in Practice.* University of Minnesota, New York: NYU Press.

Strum, Shirley C., and Linda M. Fedigan. (Eds.). (2000). *Primate Encounters: Models of Science, Gender, and Society.* Chicago: University of Chicago Press.

Sudbury, Julia. (2004). *Global Lockdown: Race, Gender, and the Prison-Industrial Complex.* New York: Routledge.

Tuana, Nancy and Sandra Morgen (Eds.). (2001). *Engendering Rationalities.* Albany: SUNY Press.

Twine, France Winddance, and Kathleen M. Blee (Eds.). (2001). *Feminism and Antiracism: International Struggles for Justice.* New York: NYU Press.

Voet, Maria Christine Bernadetta. (1998). *Feminism and Citizenship.* London: Sage.

Walker, Rebecea (Ed.). (1995). *To Be Real: Telling the Truth and Changing the Face of Feminism.* New York: Anchor Books.

Weed, Elizabeth and Naomi Schor (Eds.). (1997). *Feminism Meets Queer Theory.* Bloomington: Indiana University Press.

Weedon, Chris. (1999). *Feminism, Theory, and the Politics of Difference.* Oxford: Blackwell.

Young, Iris Marion. (1997). *Intersecting Voices: Dilemmas of Gender, Political Philosophy, and Policy.* Princeton, NJ: Princeton University Press.

Credits

ALARCÓN, NORMA. "The Theoretical Subject(s) of *This Bridge Called My Back* and Anglo-American Feminism" from *Making Face, Making Soul*. Copyright © 1990 by Norma Alarcón. Reprinted by permission of Aunt Lute Books, www.auntlute.com.

ALCOFF, LINDA. "Cultural Feminism versus Post-Structuralism: The Identity Crisis in Feminist Theory" excerpted from *Signs* 13:3 (1988) pp. 405–36. Reprinted by permission of The University of Chicago Press and the author.

ANTHONY, SUSAN B. Speech given on the occasion of her trial for voting illegally, along with 15 other women, in the 1872 presidential election. Reprinted as Document 13 in *The Elizabeth Cady Stanton–Susan B. Anthony Reader: Correspondence, Writing, Speeches*, eds. E. DuBois & G. Lerner, Northeastern University Press (1992).

ANZALDÚA, GLORIA. "La Conciencia de la Mestiza: Towards a New Consciousness." From *Borderlands/La Frontera: The New Mestiza*. Copyright © 1987, 1999 by Gloria Anzaldúa. Reprinted by permission of Aunt Lute Books, www.auntlute.com.

BAMBARA, TONI CADE. "Foreword" to the first edition of "*This Bridge Called My Back: Writings by Radical Women of Color*," Cherrie Morega & Gloria Anzaldúa, eds. Copyright © 1981, 1983 by Cherrie Morega and Gloria Anzaldúa.

BARKER, JOANNE. "Looking for Warrior Woman (Beyond Pocahontas)" from *This Bridge We Call Home: Radical Visions for Transformation* by Joanne Barker. Copyright © 2002 by Taylor & Francis Group LLC-Books. Reproduced with permission of Taylor & Francis Group LLC-Books in the format Textbook via Copyright Clearance Center.

BAUMGARDNER, JENNIFER & AMY RICHARDS. "Third Wave Manifesta" from *Manifesta: Young Women, Feminism, and the Future* by Jennifer Baumgardner & Amy Richards. Copyright © 2000 by Jennifer Baumgardner and Amy Richards. Reprinted by permission of Farrar, Straus, and Giroux, LLC.

BEAUVOIR, SIMONE DE. From *The Second Sex* by Simone de Beauvoir, translated by H.M. Parshley, copyright 1925 and renewed 1980 by Alfred A. Knopf, a division of Random House, Inc. Used by permission of Alfred A. Knopf, a division of Random House, Inc.

BEIJING DECLARATION AND PLATFORM FOR ACTION. From the Fourth World Conference on Women Platform for Action. Reprinted by permission of the United Nations Publications Board.

BIKINI KILL. Excerpt from "Riot Grrrl: Revolutions from Within" by Jessica Rosenberg and Gitano Garofalo, *Signs* 23 (1998), no. 3:812–13. Reprinted by permission of The University of Chicago Press and the authors.

BORDO, SUSAN. "The Body and the Reproduction of Feminity" from *Unbearable Weight: Feminism, Western Culture, and the Body* by Susan Bordo. Copyright © 1995 by University of California Press-Books. Reproduced with permission of University of California Press-Books in the format Textbook via Copyright Clearance Center.

BROWNE, STELLA. "Studies in Feminine Inversion." *Journal of Sexology and Psychoanalysis*, (1923): 51–58.

BUNCH, CHARLOTTE. "Not by Degrees" from *Learning Our Way: Essays in Feminist Education* by Charlotte Bunch and Sandra Pollack. Copyright © 1983. Published by The Crossing Press, a division of Ten Speed Press. Reprinted with permission from the author.

BUNCH, CHARLOTTE. "Not for Lesbians Only" from *Passionate Politics* by Charlotte Bunch. Copyright © 1987 by Charlotte Bunch. Reprinted with permission from the author.

BUNCH, CHARLOTTE. "Not by Degrees" from *Learning Our Way: Essays in Feminist Education* by Charlotte Bunch and Sandra Pollack. Copyright © 1983. Published by The Crossing Press, a division of Ten Speed Press. Reprinted with permission from the author.

BUTLER, JOSEPHINE. "Letter to My Countrywomen, Dwelling in the Farmsteads and Cottages of England," 1871. Reprinted in *The Sexuality Debates*, ed. Sheila Jeffreys, Routledge (1991).

BUTLER, JUDITH. "Bodily Inscriptions, Performative Subversions." From *Gender Trouble: Feminism and the Subversion of Identity* by Judith Butler. Copyright 1990 by Taylor & Francis LLC-Books.

LUGONES, MARIA C. and ELIZABETH V. SPELMAN. Reprinted from *Women's Studies International Forum*, 6:6, Lugones & Spelman, "Have We Got a Theory for You: Feminist Theory, Cultural Imperialism and the Demand for the Woman's Voice," 573–581, 1983, with permission from Elsevier.

MACKINNON, CATHARINE. "Sexuality" from *Toward a Feminist Theory of the State*, by Catharine MacKinnon, Harvard University Press, 1989. © 1989, 1991 Catharine MacKinnon. Reprinted by permission of the author.

MAHMOOD, SABA. "The Subject of Freedom" from *Politics of Piety*. Copyright © 2005 by Princeton University Press. Reprinted by permission of Princeton University Press.

MEAD, MARGARET. "Sex and Temperament" from *Sex and Temperament in Three Primitive Societies* by Margaret Mead. Copyright © 1935, 1950, 1963 by Margaret Mead. Reprinted by permission of HarperCollins Publishers. William Morrow.

MERNISSI, FATIMA. "Conclusion: Women's Liberation in Muslim Countries" from *Beyond the Veil, Revised Edition: Male-Female Dynamics in Modern Muslim Society Revised Edition. pp. 165–177.* © 1987 by Indiana University Press. Reprinted with permission of Indiana University Press.

MILL, JOHN STUART. "The Subjection of Women." Originally published as an essay (1869). Reprinted London: Longmans (1869).

MILLETT, KATE. *Sexual Politics* by Kate Millet. Copyright © 1969, 1970, 1990, 2000 by Kate Millett. Reprinted by premission of Georges Borchardt, Inc., on behalf of the author.

MOHANTY, CHANDRA TALPADE. "Under Western Eyes: Feminist Scholarship and Colonial Discourses" from *Third World Women and the Politics of Feminism* by Chandra Talpade Mohanty, Ann Russo, & Lourdes Torres. Indiana University Press, 1991. Reprinted by permission of the author.

MURRAY, PAULI. "The Liberation of Black Women" from *Voice of the New Feminism*. Copyright © 1970 by Pauli Murray. Reprinted by permission of The Charlotte Sheedy Literary Agency, Inc.

NARAYAN, UMA. From *Dislocating Cultures (Hard)* by Uma Narayan. Copyright 1997 by Taylor & Francis Group LLC-Books. Reproduced with permission of Taylor & Francis Group LLC-Books in the format Textbook via Copyright Clearance Center.

NATIONAL ORGANIZATION FOR WOMEN, INC. Reprinted by permission of the National Organization for Women. This is a historical document (1996) and does not reflect the current language or priorities of the organization.

NAVAJO ORIGIN MYTH (Anonymous, N.D.) "The Changing Woman" from *The Third Woman: Minority Women Writers of the United States,* Dexter Fisher, ed. (Boston: Houghton Mifflin, 1980), p. 44.

NIETOGOMEZ, ANNA. "Chicana Feminism." Copyright © 1972 by Anna Nieto Gomez. Reprinted by permission of the author.

OLDER WOMEN'S LEAGUE. "Why OWL (Older Women's Liberation)?" by the Older Women's League from *Voices from Women's Liberation*, L. Tanner, ed. © 1970 Signet. Reprinted by permisson of the Older Women's League.

ORTNER, SHERRY B. "Is Female to Male as Nature Is to Culture?" from *Woman, Culture, and Society*, Rosaldo, Michelle Zimbalist, and Louise Lamphere, eds. Copyright © 1974 by the Board of Trustees of the Leland Stanford Junior University. All rights reserved. Used with permission of Stanford University Press, www.sup.org.

PAGELS, ELAINE H. "What Became of God the Mother? Conflicting Images of God in Early Christianity" excerpted from *Signs 2:2* (1976) pp. 273–303. Reprinted by permission of The University of Chicago Press and the author.

PLASKOW, JUDITH. "Standing Again at Sinai: Jewish Memory From a Feminist Perspective." Reprinted with permission from *Tikkun:* A Bimonthly Interfaith Critique of Politics, Culture, & Society.

POLLOCK, GRISELDA. "About Canons and Culture Wars" from *Differencing the Canon: Feminist Desire and the Writing of Art History* by Griselda Pollock. Copyright © 1999 Routledge. Reproduced by permission of Taylor & Francis Books UK.

RADICALESBIANS. "The Woman-Identified Woman" from *Second Wave: A Reader in Feminist Theory* by Radicalesbians. Copyright 1997 by Taylor & Francis Group LLC-Books. Reproduced with permission of Taylor & Francis Group LLC-Books in the format Textbook via Copyright Clearance Center.

REDSTOCKINGS MANIFESTO. The Redstockings Manifesto was issued in New York City on July 7, 1969. It appeared as a mimeographed flier, designed for distribution at women's liberation events. A catalog containing ordering information for this and other documents from the 1960's rebirth years of feminism is available from the Redstockings Women's Liberation Archives for Action Distribution Project, P.O. Box 2625, Gainesville, FL 32602-2625.

RICH, ADRIENNE. Excerpts from "Compulsory Heterosexuality and Lesbian Existence," from *Blood, Bread, and Poetry:* Selected Prose 1979–1985 by Adrienne Rich. Copyright © 1986 by Adrienne Rich. Used by permission of the author and W. W. Norton & Company, Inc.

RILEY, DENISE. "Does a Sex Have a History?" in *"Am I That Name?" Feminism and the Category of "Woman" in History.* Copyright © 1988 by Denise Riley. Reprinted by permission of University of Minnesota Press.

RIVIÉRE, JOAN. "Womanliness as a Masquerade" from *The International Journal of Psychoanalysis.* 44 (1929) no. 9: 303–313. Copyright © International Journal of Psychoanalysis. Reprinted by permission of Wiley-Blackwell Publishing.

RUBIN, GAYLE. "The Traffic in Women Notes on the 'Political Economy' of Sex" by Gayle Rubin from *Toward an Anthropology of Women,* Rayna Reiter, ed. Copyright © 1975 by Reiter. Reprinted by permission of Monthly Review Foundation.

SANGER, MARGARET. "Birth Control—A Parents' Problem or Woman's?" from *Woman and the New Race,* New York: Brentano's (1920).

SCOTT, JOAN W. "Deconstructing Equality-versus-Difference: Or, The Uses of Poststructuralist Theory for Feminism," was originally published in *Feminist Studies,* 14:1 (Spring 1988): 33–50, by permission of the publisher, *Feminist Studies,* Inc.

SHIVA, VANDANA. "Development, Ecology and Women" from *Staying Alive.* Copyright © 1989 Vandana Shiva. Reprinted by permission of Zed Books, Ltd.

SOLANAS, VICTORIA. From *SCUM Manifesto* by Victoria Solanas, published by AK Press. Copyright © 1996 AK Press and Freddie Baer. Reprinted with permission of AK Press.

STANTON, ELIZABETH CADY. "Solitude of Self." Stanton's resignation speech from NAWSA. Reprinted as Document 20 in *The Elizabeth Cady Stanton–Susan B. Anthony Reader: Correspondence, Writing, Speeches,* eds. E. DuBois & G. Lerner, Northeastern University Press (1992).

STANTON, ELIZABETH CADY (Seneca Falls). "Declaration of Sentiments" from *The History of Women's Suffrage,* eds. Stanton, Anthony, Gage. Rochester, NY (1881).

TAYLOR, HARRIET. "Enfranchisement of Women." *Westminster and Foreign Quarterly Review,* July 1851.

TERRELL, MARY CHURCH. "The Progress of Colored Women" from *Voice of the Negro* (July 1904): 291–94. Reprinted *A Colored Woman in a White World.* Washington, D.C.: Ransdell Inc. (1940).

TREICHLER, PAULA & CHERIS KRAMARAE. From *The Feminist Dictionary.* 1985. Reprinted with permission from the authors.

TRUTH, SOJOURNER. "Ain't I a Woman?" Speech delivered at the Women's Rights Convention in Akron, OH, 1851.

TRUTH, SOJOURNER. "Keeping the Thing Going While Things Are Stirring." Address to the American Equal Rights Association, New York City, 9 May 1867.

VANCE, CAROLE S. "Pleasure and Danger: Toward a Politics of Sexuality" from *Pleasure and Danger: Exploring Female Sexuality,* C. Vance, ed. Copyright © 1984 Carole S. Vance. Reprinted with permission of the author.

WALKER, ALICE. "Womanist" from *In Search of Our Mothers' Gardens: Womanist Prose,* copyright © 1983 by Alice Walker, reprinted by permission of Houghton Mifflin Harcourt Publishing Co.

WEATHERS, MARY ANN. "An Argument for Black Women's Liberation as a Revolutionary Force" from *No More Fun and Games: A Journal of Female Liberation,* Cambridge, MA, by *Cell 16* 1, no. 2 (Feb. 1969). Reprinted courtesy of Dana Densmore, co-founder of Cell 16.

WELLS-BARNETT, IDA B. "Lynching and the Excuse for It," originally published in *The Independent,* a progressive periodical, 16 May, 1901.

WITTIG, MONIQUE "The Straight Mind" from *The Straight Mind* by Monique Wittig. Copyright © 1992 by Monique Wittig. Reprinted by permission of Beacon Press, Boston.

WOLLSTONECRAFT, MARY. "A Vindication of the Rights of a Woman." London: J. Johnson (1792).

WOODHULL, VICTORIA. "The Elixir of Life: or, Why Do We Die?" Oration delivered before the tenth annual convention of the American Association of Spiritualists at Grow's Opera House, Chicago, Ill. Published in New York (1873) in the paper edited with her sister. (Woodhull & Claflin.)

WOOLF, VIRGINIA. Excerpts from *A Room of One's Own* by Virginia Woolf, copyright 1929 by Houghton Mifflin Harcourt Publishing Company and renewed 1957 by Leonard Woolf, reprinted by permission of the publisher.

YAMADA, MITSUYE. "Asian Pacific American Women and Feminism" by Mitsuye Yamada from *This Bridge Called My Back,* C. Moraga & G. Anzaldúa, ed. © 1984 Kitchen Table: Women of Color Press. Reprinted by permission of the author.

Index